A HISTORY OF
WORLD
SOCIETIES

A HISTORY OF
WORLD
SOCIETIES

**THIRD
EDITION**

**VOLUME I
TO 1715**

John P. McKay

UNIVERSITY OF ILLINOIS AT URBANA-CHAMPAIGN

Bennett D. Hill

GEORGETOWN UNIVERSITY

John Buckler

UNIVERSITY OF ILLINOIS AT URBANA-CHAMPAIGN

HOUGHTON MIFFLIN COMPANY BOSTON TORONTO

DALLAS GENEVA, ILLINOIS

PALO ALTO PRINCETON, NEW JERSEY

Sponsoring Editor: John Weingartner
Senior Development Editor: Lance Wickens
Project Editor: Christina Horn
Electronic Production Specialist: Karla K. Grinnell
Production Coordinator: Frances Sharperson
Manufacturing Coordinator: Priscilla Bailey
Marketing Manager: Diane Gifford

Chapter Opener Credits   appear on page C-1.

Cover Credit   Attributed to the painter Bijapur, "Sultan Ibrahim Adil Shah II Playing the Tambur," ca 1595–1600. 14 × 14.8 cm. Courtesy of the Naprstek Museum, Prague. Photography by Pavel Sust.

Printed in the U.S.A.

Library of Congress Catalog Card Number: 91–71974

ISBN: 0–395–60795–7

ABCDEFGHIJ—VH—987654321

Text Credits   Figures 1.1 and 13.1: from John P. McKay, Bennett D. Hill, and John Buckler, *A History of Western Society,* Fourth Edition. Copyright © 1991 by Houghton Mifflin Company. Used with permission. Page 20: Figure based on information from *The Sumerians: Their History, Culture and Character* by S. N. Kramer, pp. 302–306. Copyright © 1964 by The University of Chicago Press. Used with permission. Pages 20, 22, and 25: excerpts from *The Sumerians: Their History, Culture and Character* by S. N. Kramer, pp. 150, 238, and 251. Copyright © 1964 by The University of Chicago Press. Used with permission. Page 96: excerpts from *Lao Tzu* by Tao Te Ching, translated with an introduction by D. C. Lau (Penguin Classics, 1963), copyright © D. C. Lau, 1963. Reprinted with permission of Penguin Books Ltd. Pages 230, 234, 235–236, and 238–239: excerpts from *The Jerusalem Bible,* copyright © 1966 by Darton, Longman & Todd, Ltd., and Doubleday, a division of Bantam Doubleday Dell Publishing Group, Inc. Reprinted with permission of the publisher. Pages 237–238: excerpt from J. T. McNeil and H. Gamer, translators, *Medieval Handbooks of Penance,* Octagon Books, New York, 1965. Reprinted by permission of Columbia University Press. Pages 303 and 304: excerpts from *The Wonder That Was India,* translated by A. L. Basham (Grove, 1954), pp. 161, 459–460. Reprinted with permission of Sidgwick & Jackson, London. Page 318: excerpts from *Translations from the Chinese,* translated by Arthur Waley. Copyright © 1919. Reprinted with permission of HarperCollins Publishers. Pages 406 and 418: excerpts from *English Historical Documents,* Vol. 2, edited by D. C. Douglas and G. E. Greenaway (London: Eyre & Spottiswoode, 1961), pp. 853, 969–970. Reprinted with permission of Methuen, an imprint of Octopus Publishing Group.

About the Authors

John P. McKay Born in St. Louis, Missouri, John P. McKay received his B.A. from Wesleyan University (1961), his M.A. from the Fletcher School of Law and Diplomacy (1962), and his Ph.D. from the University of California, Berkeley (1968). He began teaching history at the University of Illinois in 1966 and became a professor there in 1976. John won the Herbert Baxter Adams Prize for his book *Pioneers for Profit: Foreign Entrepreneurship and Russian Industrialization, 1885–1913* (1970). He has also written *Tramways and Trolleys: The Rise of Urban Mass Transport in Europe* (1976) and has translated Jules Michelet's *The People* (1973). His research has been supported by fellowships from the Ford Foundation, the Guggenheim Foundation, the National Endowment for the Humanities, and IREX. His articles and reviews have appeared in numerous journals, including *The American Historical Review, Business History Review, The Journal of Economic History,* and *Slavic Review.* He edits *Industrial Development and the Social Fabric: An International Series of Historical Monographs.*

Bennett D. Hill A native of Philadelphia, Bennett D. Hill earned an A.B. at Princeton (1956) and advanced degrees from Harvard (A.M., 1958) and Princeton (Ph.D., 1963). He taught history at the University of Illinois at Urbana, where he was department chairman from 1978 to 1981. He has published *English Cistercian Monasteries and Their Patrons in the Twelfth Century* (1968) and *Church and State in the Middle Ages* (1970); and articles in *Analecta Cisterciensia, The New Catholic Encyclopaedia, The American Benedictine Review,* and *The Dictionary of the Middle Ages.* His reviews have appeared in *The American Historical Review, Speculum, The Historian, The Catholic Historical Review,* and *Library Journal.* He has been a fellow of the American Council of Learned Societies and has served on committees for the National Endowment for the Humanities. Now a Benedictine monk of St. Anselm's Abbey, Washington, D.C., he is also a Visiting Professor at Georgetown University.

John Buckler Born in Louisville, Kentucky, John Buckler received his B.A. from the University of Louisville in 1967. Harvard University awarded him the Ph.D. in 1973. From 1984 to 1986 he was the Alexander von Humboldt Fellow at Institut für Alte Geschichte, University of Munich. He is currently a professor at the University of Illinois. In 1980 Harvard University Press published his *The Theban Hegemony, 371–362 B.C.* He has also published *Philip II and the Sacred War* (Leiden 1989), and co-edited *BOIOTIKA: Vorträge vom 5. International Böotien-Kolloquium* (Munich 1989). His articles have appeared in journals both here and abroad, like the *American Journal of Ancient History, Classical Philology, Rheinisches Museum für Philologie, Classical Quarterly, Wiener Studien,* and *Symbolae Osloenses.*

Contents in Brief

Contents

15

AFRICA BEFORE EUROPEAN INTRUSION, CA 400–1500 461

16

THE AMERICAS BEFORE EUROPEAN INTRUSION, CA 400–1500 485

17

EUROPEAN SOCIETY IN THE AGE OF THE RENAISSANCE AND REFORMATION 507

18

THE AGE OF EUROPEAN EXPANSION AND RELIGIOUS WARS

19

ABSOLUTISM AND CONSTITUTIONALISM IN EUROPE, CA 1589–1725

Free Copy
Not to Be Sold

Maps

Timelines/Genealogies

Note: *Italics* indicate comparative tables.

Preface

A HISTORY OF WORLD SOCIETIES grew out of the authors' desire to infuse new life into the study of world civilizations. We knew full well that historians were using imaginative questions and innovative research to open up vast new areas of historical interest and knowledge. We also recognized that these advances had dramatically affected the subject of economic, intellectual, and, especially, social history, while new research and fresh interpretations were also revitalizing the study of the traditional mainstream of political, diplomatic, and religious development. Despite history's vitality as a discipline, however, it seemed to us that both the broad public and the intelligentsia were generally losing interest in the past. The mathematical economist of our acquaintance who smugly quipped "What's new in history?"— confident that the answer was nothing and that historians were as dead as the events they examine—was not alone.

It was our conviction, based on considerable experience introducing large numbers of students to the broad sweep of civilization, that a book reflecting current trends could excite readers and inspire a renewed interest in history and the human experience. Our strategy was twofold. First, we made social history the core element of our work. Not only did we incorporate recent research by social historians, but also we sought to re-create the life of ordinary people in appealing human terms. A strong social element seemed to us especially appropriate in a world history, for identification with ordinary people of the past allows today's reader to reach an empathetic understanding of different cultures and civilizations. At the same time we were determined to give great economic, political, intellectual, and cultural developments the attention they unquestionably deserve. We wanted to give individual readers and instructors a balanced, integrated perspective, so that they could pursue on their own or in the classroom those themes and questions that they found particularly exciting and significant.

Second, we made a determined effort to strike an effective global balance. We were acutely aware of the great drama of our times—the passing of the European era and the simultaneous rise of Asian and African peoples in world affairs. Increasingly, the whole world interacts, and to understand that interaction and what it means for today's citizens we must study the whole world's history. Thus we adopted a comprehensive yet realistic global perspective. We studied all geographical areas and the world's main civilizations, conscious of their separate identities and unique contributions. Yet we also stressed the links between civilizations, for these links eventually transformed multicentered world history into a complex interactive process of different continents, peoples, and civilizations in recent times. Finally, it was our place neither to praise nor to vilify our own civilization's major role in the growth of global integration, accepting it rather as part of our world heritage and seeking to understand it and the consequences for all concerned. Four years ago, in an effort to realize fully the potential of our fresh yet balanced perspective, we made many changes, large and small, in the second edition.

Changes in the New Edition

In preparing the third edition we have worked hard to keep our book up-to-date and to make it still more effective. First, we have carefully examined the entire book and each of its sections for organization, clarity, and balance. Above all, the treatment of non-European societies has been expanded and enriched, while the history of European developments has been tightened and condensed. In the new edition, therefore, the history of Africa from 400 to 1500 receives a full chapter-length treatment in Chapter 15, permitting a more extensive analysis of early African kingdoms, and an expanded discussion of Mesoamerican civilizations is included in Chapter 16, the Americas before European intrusion. Similarly, in order to do justice to the complex developments occurring in Africa and western Asia in the early modern period, Africa is discussed in Chapter 22 of the new edition and the Middle East and India are the subject of Chapter 23.

As for Europe, Chapter 14 now brings together the history of the high and later Middle Ages in a single chapter. The emergence of royal absolutism and constitutionalism in western and eastern Europe in the early modern period is similarly combined in a reorganized and more sharply focused Chapter 19. For greater clarity, recent social developments in the West have been integrated into the larger, fully up-dated discussion of recovery and crisis in Europe after 1945 in Chapter 36. This chapter covers the transforming events in eastern Europe of recent years, including the revolutions of 1989.

Other major changes include a new section on the study of history and the meaning of civilization in Chapter 1. Islam and Islamic societies receive expanded and reworked coverage throughout the book. Chapter 34 contains a revised discussion of twentieth-century intellectual trends that emphasizes the connection between these movements and subsequent political developments, and Chapter 35 provides a unified account of the Second World War. With these changes and with numerous modifications highlighting cross-cultural linkages, we feel we have improved the geographical and cultural balance of our text and written a more integrated and effective world history.

Second, every chapter has been carefully revised to incorporate recent scholarship. Many of our revisions relate to the ongoing explosion in social history, and once again important findings on such subjects as class relations, population, and the family have been integrated into the text. We have made a special effort to keep up with the rapidly growing and increasingly sophisticated scholarship being done in women's history, adding or revising sections on women in early Jewish society and in the Crusades, as well as in the Renaissance, the Reformation, and the Industrial Revolution. The roots of modern feminism have been explored. The revised discussion of the origins and early development of Islam reflects recent scholarship, as does the extended reconsideration of the Ottomans and their cultural and intellectual achievements. Japanese feudalism is also reconsidered in the light of current scholarly thinking.

A major effort has also been made to improve the treatment of economic development and accompanying social changes in the light of new research and fresh concepts. We are proud of the resulting changes, which include a consideration of early Islamic capitalism and agricultural innovation in Chapter 10, a new discussion of early modern crises in Chapter 19, a reexamination of the social and demographic effects of the slave trade in Africa in Chapter 22, and a fundamental rethinking of European industrialization in Chapter 26 and its global significance in Chapter 30. Other subjects not mentioned above that incorporate new scholarship in this edition include early human evolution, Germanic tribes, the Inquisition, industrial progress in early modern China, French industrialization and utopian socialism, and the development of modern Arab nationalism. New topics designed to keep the work fresh and appealing include *I-Ching* thinking in ancient China, Greek federalism, Sufism in the Islamic world, the early European reaction to knowledge of China and Japan, the settlement and the emergence of Australia, reform and revolution in the Soviet Union and eastern Europe in the 1980s, and the recent breakthrough in the struggle for racial equality in South Africa.

Third, the addition of more problems of historical interpretation in the second edition was well received, and we have continued in that direction in this edition. We believe that the problematic element helps the reader develop the critical-thinking skills that are among the most precious benefits of studying history. New examples of this more open-ended, more interpretive approach include the significance of Chinese economic development in the eighteenth century (Chapter 24), the social costs of English enclosure and the impact of industrialization on women and the standard of living (Chapter 26), and the impact of slavery on the black family in the United States (Chapter 31).

Finally, the illustrative component of our work has been completely revised. There are many new illustrations, including nearly two hundred color reproductions that let both great art and important events come alive. As in earlier editions, all illustrations have been carefully selected to complement the text, and all carry captions that enhance their value. Artwork remains an integral part of our book, for the past can speak in pictures as well as in words.

The use of full color throughout this edition also serves to clarify the maps and graphs and to enrich the textual material. Again for improved clarity, maps from the second edition have been completely redesigned to provide easily read and distinguished labels and prominent boundaries and topographical relief. We have also added new maps that illustrate social as well as political developments, including maps on Europe at 1715, the Safavid Empire, the ethnic and political boundaries of the Soviet republics, the reform movements of 1989 in eastern Europe, the world drug trade, and the Persian Gulf War.

In addition to the many maps that support text discussion, we offer a new, full-color map essay at the beginning of each volume. Our purpose is twofold. First, by reproducing and describing such cartographic landmarks as the Babylonian world map, the Islamic al-Idrisi map, the medieval Ebstorf map, the twelfth-century map of China, maps of the Americas and Africa based on Ptolemy and Mercator, the Japanese world map of 1645, and contemporary global projections and satellite images, we hope to demonstrate for students the evolution of cartography and to guide them toward an understanding of the varied functions and uses of maps. Second, the map essay is intended to show depictions of the world from different cultural perspectives and to reveal the changing concepts of our world and its interrelated parts from antiquity to the present. In a real sense, the map essay may serve as an introduction to the course as well as to cartography.

Distinctive Features

Distinctive features from earlier editions remain in the third. To help guide the reader toward historical understanding we have posed specific historical questions at the beginning of each chapter. These questions are then answered in the course of the chapter, each of which concludes with a concise summary of the chapter's findings. The timelines have proved useful, and the double-page comparative timelines, which allow students to compare simultaneous developments within different world areas, have been revised and updated.

We have also tried to suggest how historians actually work and think. We have quoted extensively from a wide variety of primary sources and have demonstrated in our use of these quotations how historians sift and weigh evidence. We want the reader to think critically and to realize that history is neither a list of cut-and-dried facts nor a sense-less jumble of conflicting opinions. It is our further hope that the primary quotations, so carefully fitted into their historical context, will give the reader a sense that even in the earliest and most remote periods of human experience, history has been shaped by individual men and women, some of them great aristocrats, others ordinary folk.

Each chapter concludes with carefully selected suggestions for further reading. These suggestions are briefly described to help readers know where to turn to continue thinking and learning about the world. The chapter bibliographies have been revised and expanded to keep them current with the vast and complex new work being done in many fields.

World civilization courses differ widely in chronological structure from one campus to another. To accommodate the various divisions of historical time into intervals that fit a two-quarter, three-quarter, or two-semester period, *A History of World Societies* is published in three versions, each set embracing the complete work:

One-volume hardcover edition, A HISTORY OF WORLD SOCIETIES; a two-volume paperback, A HISTORY OF WORLD SOCIETIES *Volume I: To 1715* (Chapters 1–19), *Volume II: Since 1500* (Chapters 18–39); and a three-volume paperback, A HISTORY OF WORLD SOCIETIES *Volume A: From Antiquity Through the Middle Ages* (Chapters 1–16), *Volume B: From 1100 Through the French Revolution* (Chapters 14–25), *Volume C: From the French Revolution to the Present* (Chapters 25–39).

Note that overlapping chapters in the two- and three-volume sets permit still wider flexibility in matching the appropriate volume with the opening and closing dates of a course term.

Ancillaries

Learning and teaching ancillaries, including a *Study Guide, MicroStudy Plus* (a computerized version of the *Study Guide*), *Instructor's Resource Manual, Test Items, MicroTest* (a computerized version of the *Test Items*), and *Map Transparencies,* also contribute to the usefulness of the text. The excellent *Study Guide* has been thoroughly revised by Professor James Schmiechen of Central Michigan University. Professor Schmiechen has been a tower of strength ever since he critiqued our initial prospectus, and he has continued to give us many valuable suggestions and his warmly appreciated support. His *Study Guide* contains chapter summaries, chapter outlines, review questions, extensive multiple-choice exercises, self-check lists of important concepts and events, and a variety of study aids and suggestions. New to the third edition are study-review exercises on the interpretation of visual sources and major political ideas as well as suggested issues for discussion and essay and chronology reviews. Another major addition is the section, Understanding the Past Through Primary Sources. Seven primary source documents widely used by historians are included, each preceded by a description of the author and source and followed by questions for analysis. The *Study Guide* also retains the very successful sections on studying effectively. These sections take the student by ostensive example through reading and studying activities like underlining, summarizing, identifying main points, classifying information according to sequence, and making historical comparisons. To enable both students and instructors to use the *Study Guide* with the greatest possible flexibility, the guide is available in two volumes, with considerable overlapping of chapters. Instructors and students who use only Volumes A and B of the text have all the pertinent study materials in a single volume, *Study Guide, Volume 1* (Chapters 1–25); likewise, those who use only Volumes B and C of the text also have all the necessary materials in one volume, *Study Guide, Volume 2* (Chapters 14–39).

The multiple-choice sections of the *Study Guide* are also available as *MicroStudy Plus,* a computerized, tutorial version that tells students not only which response is correct but also why each of the other choices is wrong and provides the page numbers of the text where each question is discussed. *MicroStudy Plus* is available for both IBM and Macintosh computers.

The *Instructor's Resource Manual,* prepared by Professor John Marshall Carter of Oglethorpe University, contains learning objectives, chapter synopses, suggestions for lectures and discussion, paper and class activity topics, and lists of audiovisual resources. Professor Carter also offers suggestions for the instructor who is teaching world history for the first time. The accompanying *Test Items,* by Professor Charles Crouch of St. John's University in Collegeville, Minnesota, offer identification, multiple-choice, and essay questions for a total of approximately two thousand test items. These test items are available to adopters in both IBM and Macintosh versions, both of which include editing capabilities. In addition, a set of full-color *Map Transparencies* of all the maps in the text is available on adoption.

JOHN P. MCKAY

BENNETT D. HILL

JOHN BUCKLER

Acknowledgments

It is a pleasure to thank the many instructors who have read and critiqued the manuscript through its development:

Martin Berger
Youngstown State University

Elton Daniel
University of Hawaii, Manoa

Ronald Davis
Western Michigan University

Joseph Dorinson
Long Island University

Surjit Dulai
Michigan State University

Bruce Garver
University of Nebraska, Omaha

Robert Gowen
East Carolina University

Bruce Haight
Western Michigan University

Hines Hall
Auburn University

Deanna Haney
Lansing Community College

Eugene Huck
Kennesaw State College

Margaret Hutton
Jackson State University

Jim Jackson
Point Loma Nazarene College

Gregory Kozlowski
DePaul University

Glenn Nichols
Sul Ross State University

William Ochsenwald
Virginia Polytechnic Institute and State University

Donathan Olliff
Auburn University

Oliver Pollak
University of Nebraska, Omaha

Donald Reid
Georgia State University

John Ruedy
Georgetown University

Lowell Satre
Youngstown State University

Martin Seedorf
Eastern Washington University

Anita Shelton
Eastern Illinois University

Sara Sohmer
University of Hawaii, Manoa

Alexander Sydorenko
Arkansas State University

Joanne Van Horne
Fairmont State College

James Weland
Bentley College

Many colleagues at the University of Illinois provided information and stimulation for our book, often without even knowing it. N. Frederick Nash, Rare Book Librarian, gave freely of his time and made many helpful suggestions for illustrations. The World Heritage Museum at the University continued to allow us complete access to its sizable holdings. James Dengate kindly supplied information on objects from the museum's collection. Caroline Buckler took many excellent photographs of the museum's objects and generously helped us at crucial moments in production. We greatly appreciate such wide-ranging expertise. Bennett Hill wishes to express his sincere appreciation to Ramón de la Fuente of Washington, D.C., for his support, encouragement, and research assistance in the preparation of this third edition.

Each of us has benefited from the generous criticism of his co-authors, although each of us assumes responsibility for what he has written. John Buckler has written Chapters 1–8 and 11; Bennett Hill has continued the narrative in Chapters 9–10, 12–18, part of 19, 23–24, and 31; and John McKay has written part of 19 and Chapters 20–21, 25–30, and 32–39. Finally, we continue to welcome from our readers comments and suggestions for improvements, for they have helped us greatly in this ongoing endeavor.

Expanding Horizons: Mapmaking in the World

Today cartography, the art of making maps, is as widespread as typography, the process of printing. Maps are so much a part of daily life that people take them for granted. But people are not born with maps in their heads, as they are with fingers on their hands. The very concept of a map is a human invention of vast intellectual and practical importance. Like writing itself, cartography depends on people's use of visual and symbolic means to portray reality. Earth is not a flat table. Instead it is marked by features such as mountains, valleys, rivers, and oceans and by the distances that separate them all. Knowledge of these physical features and the accurate mapping of them allow people to understand their relationship to the planet on which they live.

Cartographers contribute something singular to the understanding of peoples. Human beings, no matter where they live, have a natural curiosity about their world and find joy in discovering new parts of it or in learning more about regions not well known. The Roman statesman and orator Cicero once asked, "Ubinam gentium sumus?" ("Where in the world are we?") Although he used this question as a figure of speech, many people have been quite serious about finding an accurate answer to it. Such curiosity and desire have led people to examine not only the earth but its relation to the cosmos of which it is a part. Early cartographers learned to use the stars as fixed points for the measurement of place and distance. Even today American nuclear submarines depend on

MAP 1 Babylonian world map, ca 600 B.C. *(Source: Courtesy of the Trustees of the British Museum)*

celestial navigation, transmitted by satellite, to determine their course and position. Once people looked to the stars, they began to wonder about the shape, nature, and content of the universe itself. Mapping of the earth was no longer enough; people began to chart the cosmos. The Hubble space satellite, launched in May 1990, is a sign that the quest continues today.

For ordinary purposes cartography fills a host of practical needs. Maps were first used to describe people's immediate environment—to illustrate the shape of villages and the boundaries of fields. As knowledge of the earth grew, maps became indispensable for travel, both on land and at sea. It was necessary for people to know where their destination lay, how to reach it, and what to expect along the way. Mariners used the geographical knowledge provided by maps to sail from one port to another.

Other uses of early maps were economic. As people came into contact with one another, they saw new opportunities for barter and trade. It was no longer enough to know how to travel to different locations. Merchants needed to understand the geography of their markets and to know what foreign lands produced and what trading partners wanted in return for their goods. In short, economic contact itself increased knowledge of the face of the land, and that knowledge could be preserved on maps by symbols to indicate the natural resources and products of various lands.

Another important function of early maps was military. Rulers and generals needed information about distances and the terrain through which their armies would move and fight. This need spurred interest in *topography,* the detailed description and representation of the natural and artificial features of a landscape, and led to greater accuracy of maps and better definition of the physical environment.

The demands of empire were not only military but also administrative. An area cannot be governed effectively unless the ruler knows where each part of it is located and what its importance is. Rulers need precise maps to enforce their authority, dispatch commands, collect taxes, and maintain order. Thus the value to historians of some maps lies in their illustration of people's knowledge of the world in relation to the needs of government and the exercise of authority over broad distances.

Those are only a few of the uses of cartography. But what of the maps themselves? How do cartographers visually and accurately depict large sections of land or the entire face of the globe? The ways are numerous and some more exact than others.

The earliest maps are pictures of towns showing spatial relationships within a very limited area. A more accurate way of making a map was derived from land surveys. Beginning about 1500 B.C., surveyors trained in geometry and trigonometry began to study the land in question and to divide its physical features into a series of measured angles and elevations. Cartographers then placed this information on a grid so that they could represent visually, according to a consistent and logical system, relations among areas. Although the method sounds simple, it presented a daunting problem, one that still exists. Mapmakers must represent on a two-dimensional surface the face of a three-dimensional globe. To complicate matters even further, the earth is not a perfect sphere. How cartographers have grappled with these problems can be seen from the maps reproduced here.

Since maps are basically visual, it is best to trace their evolution in their own context. People of all cultures have mapped their lands, and in many cases their approaches have been strikingly similar. The earliest known representation of the world is a Babylonian world map that dates to about 600 B.C. (Map 1). It is not a map of the entire globe, for the Babylonians were ignorant of the existence of many people beyond their immediate frontiers. Instead, Babylon, with its neighbors around it, lies at the center of the world. Surrounding the land is the ocean, depicted as a circle. The triangles beyond the ocean indicate that the Babylonians knew something of the peoples beyond the ocean. Here for the first time is evidence of a people who attempted to put themselves geographically into the context of their larger world.

The greatest geographer of the Greco-Roman period was Claudius Ptolemaeus, better known as Ptolemy, who lived in Alexandria in the second century A.D. He advanced far beyond the schematic Babylonian world map to produce a scientific atlas based on data. He knew from previous scholars that the world was spherical, so he devised a way of using conic lines of *longitude,* angular distances east and west, and *latitude,* angular distances north and south, to plot the positions and distances of the earth's features. Despite its distortions, Ptolemy's *Geographia* became the standard Western work on geography until Europeans sailed out to explore the broader world around them (ca 1450–1650). The best illustration of Ptolemy's brilliant vision actually dates much later than its first representation. It dates to a manuscript produced in the German city of Ulm in 1482 (Map 2). Ptolemy put cartography on a scientific basis.

Some of the fruits of Ptolemy's labor can be seen in the series of maps known as the Peutinger Table, which probably dates to ca A.D. 500. The Table is a good example of how cartography served the Roman Empire. The section shown here is typical of the entire series: it indicates roads, rivers, mountains, cities, and towns in Greece (Map 3). In that respect it is an ancient road map, for its purpose was not to define the known world, as Ptolemy had done, but to inform the emperor and his bureaucracy how they could most easily administer and communicate with the provinces. Although alien to modern notions of the shape of Europe, the Peutinger Table is a remarkably accurate atlas of routes and distances and thus displays vividly and beautifully one of the most practical functions of cartography. The table received its name from Konrad Peutinger of Augsburg, an owner of the maps in the sixteenth century.

Islamic cartographers also drew heavily on Ptolemy's research, but they relied on exploration as well. The most famous of them as al-Idrisi, who lived in the twelfth century. His atlas depicted the entire known world and was accompanied by a

MAP 2 Map from Ptolemy's *Geographica (Source: Michael Holford)*

MAP 3 Section of the Peutinger Table illustrating Greece, ca A.D. 500 *(Source: Oster-reichische Nationalbibliothek)*

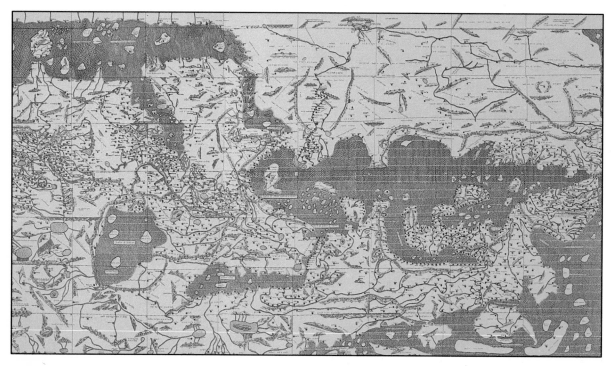

MAP 4 Portion of the map of al-Idrisi, thirteenth century *(Source: Reproduced by permission of Norman J. W. Thrower, Department of Geography, UCLA)*

MAP 5 Ebstorf Map, thirteenth century *(Source: Niedersächsische Landesbibliothek Hannover)*

written commentary about the places illustrated. The portion shown here represents the eastern Mediterranean and the Middle East (Map 4). As in the Peutinger Table, physical features such as rivers and mountains are stylized, but al-Idrisi made a serious effort to delineate the general features of the landmass. His map looks different from modern maps because he used south as his basic point of orientation, not north as do modern cartographers. As a result, the atlas appears upside down to our eyes, with south being at the top of the map.

Europeans in the Middle Ages, like their predecessors, drew maps of the world, but religion became an ingredient of cartography. Ptolemy's concepts of geography remained in force, but maps also served another and different purpose for society. The Ebstorf Map, drawn during the thirteenth century, shows the world surrounded by the ocean, a conception dating to antiquity (Map 5). Yet the map has several novel features. In its background is the crucified Jesus. His head, portrayed at the top, signifies the east. His outstretched arms point north and south. His feet, at the bottom, signify the west. Jerusalem occupies the center of the map to represent the place of Jesus's death as the center of the Christian world. The Ebstorf Map, unlike the practical maps of the Peutinger Table, was intended to convey a religious message, a declaration of faith.

Like the Romans, the Chinese early found it necessary to draw maps to administer efficiently the vast tracts of land under their control. The Chinese so successfully mastered the problem of reducing a huge amount of territory into a visually manageable scale that in the twelfth century they produced the Yü Chi Thu Map (Map of the Tracks of Yü the Great) (Map 6). Although the name of the geographer is unknown, his achievement is monumental. He used a system of uniform square grids to locate features of the land in exact and measured relationship to one another. The outline of the coast and the courses of the rivers are remarkably accurate. As in the case of early European maps of Africa (see Map 10), knowledge of the interior was somewhat scanty. Nonetheless, the geographer devised a reliable system in which new discoveries could be easily fitted into what was already known.

In the Americas, maps were sometimes put to a novel use. The pre-Columbian picture map (Map 7) at first sight does not look like a map at all. Dating from sometime before the sixteenth century, it portrays the history of the Mixtec people of Mexico, who can be traced from about 800. Geographical features are incidental to the historical narrative. Nevertheless, the map amply demonstrates the originality of the pre-Columbian Americans in the art of mapmaking.

Meanwhile, the people of the European Middle Ages continued to draw maps along the lines set out by Ptolemy, yet they made improvements on the work of the master. Indeed, they explored the concept of triangulation to survey the land and to navigate the seas. Cartographers chose several major points to serve as hubs of a series of lines extended to other major points. The face of the globe was thereby cut up into a pattern of triangles, rectangles, and occasionally squares. Al-

Map 6 After the Yü Chi Thu Map, twelfth century *(Source: Pei Lin Museum, Sian, China)*

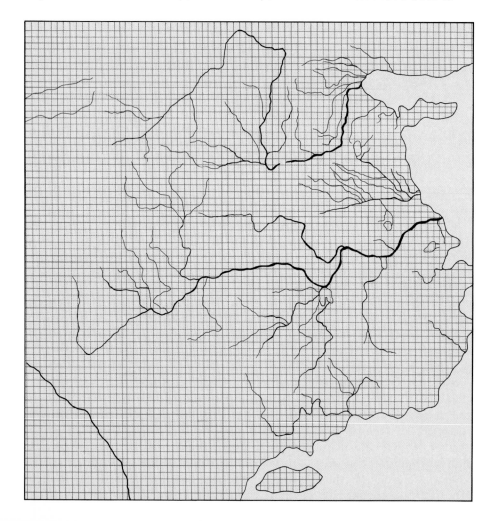

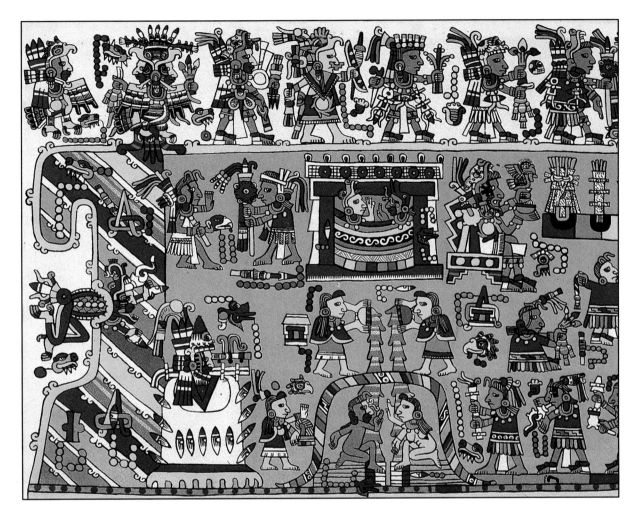

MAP 7 The Dominions of Quetzalcoatl 9 Wind, *Lord of the Toltecs. From the Codex Zouche-Nuttall (Source: Courtesy of the Trustees of the British Museum (Museum of Mankind))*

though this system proved complicated and unwieldy, triangulation did improve the utility of maps for explorers. An excellent example of a triangulated map comes from the Catalan Atlas of 1375 (Map 8). The atlas is more functional than other early maps because the cartographer indicated orientation, so that users could locate their position according to the points of a compass.

Only when the Europeans began to explore the broader world around them did they make significant advances over Ptolemy's view of the world. Sailors and navigators who voyaged to find new lands or to learn more about familiar places had to be able to calculate where they were. They knew that the world was curved, and they used the stars as fixed points to guide them. It is thus ironic that one of the most important advances in geographic knowledge came by mistake. In 1492 Christopher Columbus, looking for a sea passage to India, discovered the New World by sailing westward from Europe. Although Columbus himself did not immediately recognize the full significance of his achievement, his discovery revolutionized geographical thinking: there was more to the world than Ptolemy had known; and the basic features of the earth had to be explored, relationships rethought, and a new way of looking at the globe found.

Perhaps nothing better indicates the fluid state of geography and cartography at the end of the fifteenth century than Juan de la Cosa's map of Columbus's second voyage to the Americas (Map 9). A navigator and an explorer, de la Cosa charted the newly found coast of Central America using the points of the compass to orient the fall of the land and triangulation to project his findings inland. Although he could depict the coastline accurately because of direct observation, he could reveal little about the land beyond.

The discoveries of the European explorers opened a new era in the West and throughout the rest of the world, both in how people thought of the world and in how mapmakers depicted the new findings. These pioneers were also on the threshold of uniting European, American, and Asian traditions of cartography. The real breakthrough came with Geradus Mercator (1512–1594). Mercator improved Ptolemy's system of latitude and longitude by substituting straight lines for Ptolemy's curved lines. In that respect, Mercator's cartographic organization was similar to that used by the Chinese geographer of the Yü Chi Thu Map, but Mercator's plan applied over the face of the globe. Mercator used this grid to incorporate the discoveries in a completely new atlas. Admittedly, his method distorts the actual physical relations of the landmasses over broad spaces. Areas in the polar regions appear larger than lands near the equator. For instance, Greenland on his grid is larger than South America. More important, however, Mercator showed that every portion of the world may be portrayed as possessing four right angles to orient users of any one of his maps to any portion of his other maps. Mercator's grid, in one form or another, endures as a cartographic staple to this day.

The cumulative effects of the advance of knowledge in geography and cartography can best be

MAP 8 Catalan Atlas of 1375 *(Source: Bibliothèque Nationale, Paris/Photo Hubert Josse)*

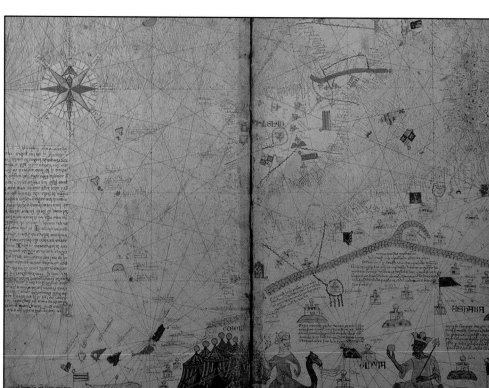

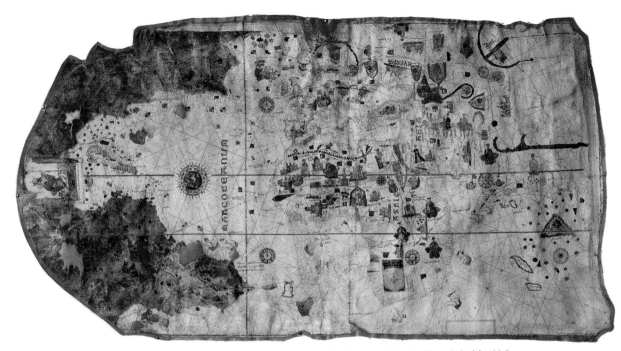

MAP 9 Juan de la Cosa's map of Columbus's discoveries, 1493 *(Source: Museo Naval de Madrid)*

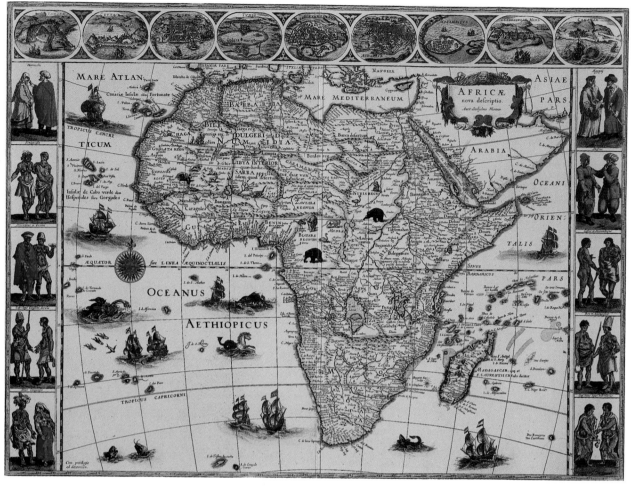

MAP 10 Blaeu's map of Africa, from *Grooten Atlas*, 1648–65 *(Source: The British Library, Department of Maps)*

seen in two maps that demonstrate increasing familiarity with Africa. The map of Dutch cartographer Willem Blaeu, dating to the early seventeenth century, brings together the concepts of scale maps and picture maps (Map 10). Explorers had an accurate idea only of the shape of the continent. The inland was *terra incognita,* unknown territory where dwelt fabulous beasts and peoples. The amazing progress of human knowledge of the land and how to map it can be seen by comparing Blaeu's map of Africa with the one of French cartographer Jean-Baptiste d'Anville published in 1747 (Map 11). D'Anville made excellent use of Mercator's system to produce a profile of Africa that could find its place in any modern atlas. Yet

d'Anville was intellectually honest enough to leave the interior of Africa largely blank. D'Anville's map is not so visually delightful as Blaeu's, but in terms of cartography it is far more important. It showed its users what was yet to be discovered and how to proceed with finding it.

European penetration of Asia excited another desire for maps. In 1822 the Frenchman J. B. J. Gentil published a map of India (Map 12) that bears some slight similarity to Blaeu's earlier map of Africa. The map, which dates from 1770, is actually a drawing by an Indian of Chadjeanabad province. Like Blaeu's map, it contains drawings of animals, fruits, and costumes of the local natives. It is also similar to the pre-Columbian map of the

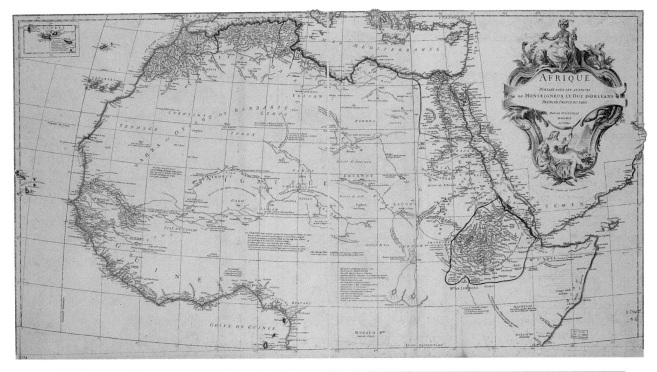

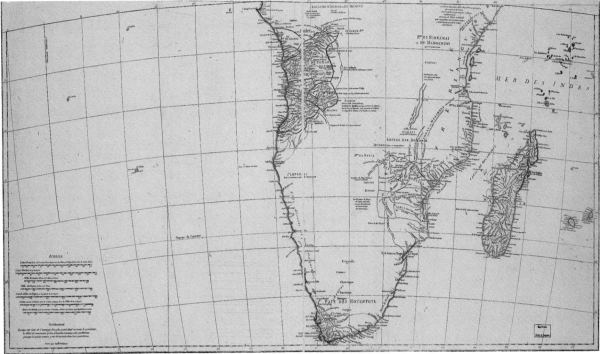

MAP 11 D'Anville's map of Africa, 1747 *(Source: Library of Congress, Department of Maps)*

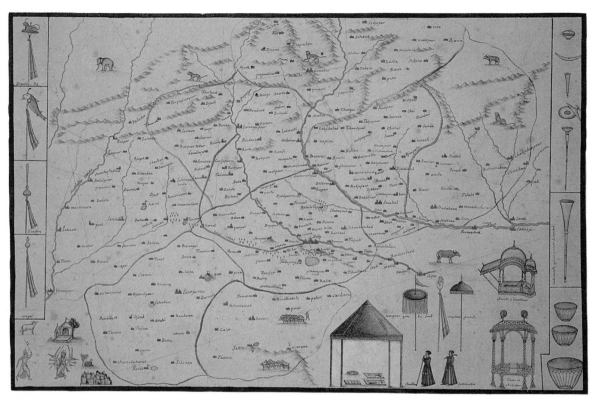

MAP 12 Map of Chadjeanabad province, India, 1770 *(Source: The British Library, Oriental and India Office Collections)*

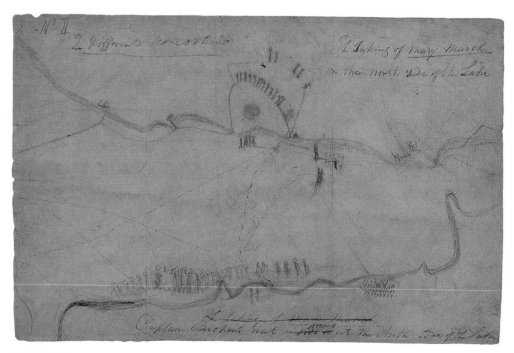

MAP 13 Shanawdithit's map of central Newfoundland, 1829 *(Source: Newfoundland Museum)*

MAP 14 Kiangsi province in southeast China, eighteenth century *(Source: The British Library, Department of Maps)*

dominions of Quetzalcoatl (see Map 7) in that it possesses little geographical significance. Yet it portrays many of the salient human, zoological, and botanical features of the region.

An excellent example of the combination of pictorial and geographical features of a landscape comes from a map drawn in 1829 by Shanawdithit, a woman who was the last of the Beothuk Indians of Newfoundland (Map 13). This historico-pictorial map depicts the trek of her tribe crossing an ice-covered lake along the Exploits River in central Newfoundland. It tells the story of the journey while giving an impression of the geographical features of the land through which she and her people passed.

A beautiful early-eighteenth-century Chinese map of Kiangsi province (Map 14) shows a single prefecture, at the center of which is a walled town. The mapmaker carefully depicted the features of Kiangsi, to the point of showing individual buildings in their geographical setting. Thus the nature of the landscape, both rivers and mountains, is pictorially displayed, not as on a map but rather as a view seen from above. Although this is a picture-map, unlike the more technical map by al-Idrisi (see Map 4), it gives the user a vivid sense of the landscape.

Interesting by contrast is the Bankoku Sozu (or World Map) drawn in Japan in 1645, a half-century earlier than the Chinese map of Kiangsi.

MAP 15 Bankoku Sozu, Map of the World, 1645 *(Source: Kobe City Museum)*

This map (Map 15) resembles Ptolemy's map of the world in its definition of landmasses, their configurations, and their major features. Like d'Anville (see Map 11), the Japanese cartographer indicated candidly—in the legends at the top and bottom of the map—that geographical knowledge of these regions was hazy because few people had explored them. Yet in its basics the concept behind this map is Ptolemy's. Both were more interested in portraying the nature of the landmass and the physical relation of one place to another than in drawing a picture of the landscape.

Mapmakers still grapple with the problem of accurately depicting landmasses—their shapes and their spatial relationships—on an earth that is not a perfect sphere. No matter what projection they use, some geographical areas are distorted. In struggling with this problem, cartographers have used circles, ovals, and rectangles to display regions of the earth on a flat surface. The orthographic projection (the circular maps at the four corners of Map 16) uses circles and is one of the oldest projections. Because it shows only one hemisphere at a time, distortion is minimized, especially at the center of the map, where attention is focused. It allows a realistic view of the globe, but it makes possible the display of only one hemisphere at a time. One way to minimize distortion while showing more than one hemisphere is to represent the tops of the poles as lines rather than as points, as shown in the Robinson projection (the center image of Map 16). There is still some distortion (note how large Antarctica is), but cutting off the poles diminishes it. The Robinson projection is a compromise because it sacrifices some accuracy in area to achieve less distortion in shape.

Modern attempts to depict visually the nearly spherical earth on flat maps remind people that the problems first perceived by early cartographers remain to be solved. Yet contemporary cartographers enjoy the use of a new and unusual tool for

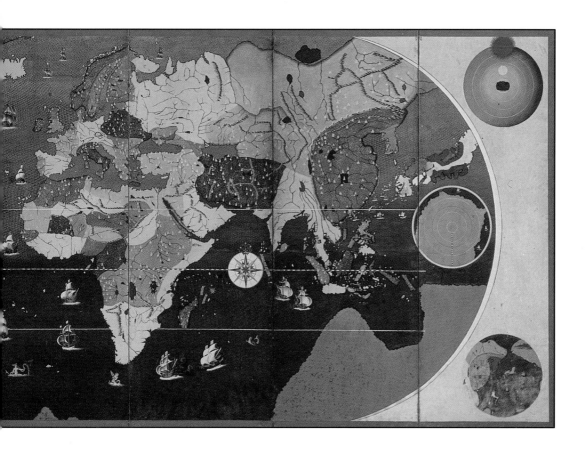

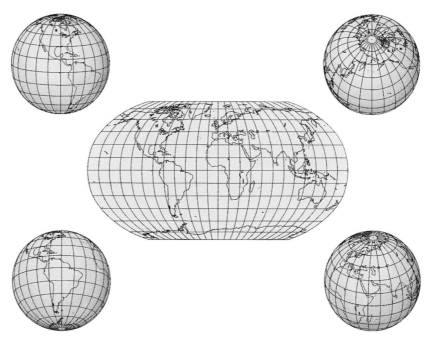

MAP 16 The Robinson projection *(Source: Reproduced with permission from WHICH MAP IS BEST?* © *1988, by the American Congress on Surveying and Mapping)*

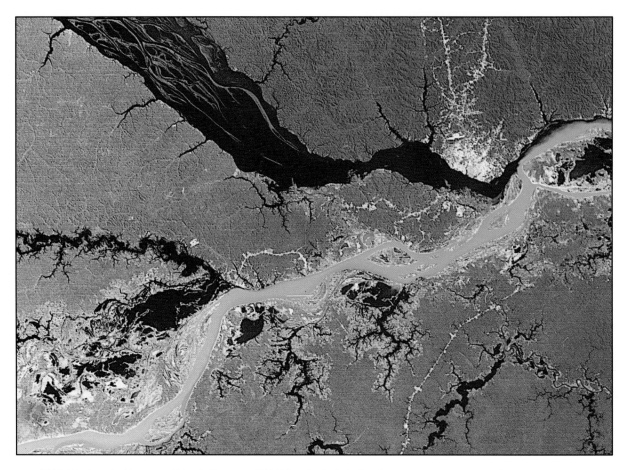

MAP 17   Landsat image of Brazil *(Source: GEOPIC*™, Earth Satellite Corporation)

mapping the globe and exploring the universe: the orbiting satellite. Technology has become so precise within the past ten years that the parts of the earth difficult to enter or too remote and forbidding to explore can be examined with minute accuracy from space. The Landsat satellite image of Brazil (Map 17) gives an excellent idea of how much more there is to learn about the earth.

JOHN BUCKLER

SUGGESTED READING

Bagrow, Leo. *History of Cartography.* 2d ed. Chicago: Precedent Publishing, 1985. Brown, Lloyd A. *The Story of Maps.* New York: Dover, 1979. Dilke, O. A. W. *Greek and Roman Maps.* Ithaca: Cornell University Press, 1985. Harley, J. B., and D. Woodward, eds. *The History of Cartography,* Vol. 1: *Cartography in Prehistoric, Ancient and Medieval Europe and the Mediterranean.* Chicago: University of Chicago Press, 1967. Harvey, Paul D. A. *The History of Topographical Maps.* London: Thames & Hudson, 1980. Hodgkiss, Alan G. *Understanding Maps: A Systematic History of Their Use and Development.* Folkestone, England: Dawson, 1981. Skelton, Raleigh A. *Decorative Printed Maps of the Fifteenth to Eighteenth Centuries.* London: Staples Press, 1952, reprinted by Spring Books, 1970. Skelton, Raleigh A. *Explorers' Maps: Chapters in the Cartographic Record of Geographical Discovery.* London: Routledge and Kegan Paul, 1958, reprinted by Spring Books, 1970. Thrower, Norman J. W. *Maps & Man: An Examination of Cartography in Relation to Culture and Civilization.* Englewood Cliffs, N.J.: Prentice-Hall, 1978, Tooley, R. V., Cand Bricker, and G. R. Crone. *A History of Cartography: 2500 Years of Maps and Mapmakers.* London: Thames & Hudson, 1969.

1

Origins

Peace panel from the Royal Standard of Ur

Before the dawn of history, bands of people across the earth gradually developed numerous cultures, each unique in some ways while at the same time having features in common. Especially important to the history of the world are events that took place in the ancient Near East (Mesopotamia, Anatolia, and Egypt), India, and China, where human beings abandoned the life of roaming and hunting to settle in stable agricultural communities. From these communities grew cities and civilizations, societies that invented concepts and techniques now integral to contemporary life. Fundamental is the independent development of writing by the Sumerians in Mesopotamia and by the Chinese, an invention that enabled knowledge to be preserved and facilitated the spread and accumulation of learning, lore, literature, and science. Mathematics, astronomy, and architecture were all innovations of ancient civilizations. So, too, were the first law codes and religious concepts, which still permeate daily life across the globe.

- How did nomadic hunters become urban dwellers?
- What geographical factors influenced this change?
- How do geographical factors explain both the elements common to different cultures and the features that differentiate them?

These questions serve as themes for the first four chapters. Chapters 1 and 2 look at how ancient Near Eastern civilizations helped to shape modern Western society. Chapters 3 and 4 explore the response of the peoples of ancient India and China to these same questions.

WHAT IS HISTORY AND WHY?

History is an effort to reconstruct the past to discover what people thought and did and how their beliefs and actions continue to influence human life. In order to appreciate the past fully, we must put it into perspective so that we can understand the factors that have helped to shape us as individuals, the society in which we live, and the nature of other peoples' societies. Why else should we study periods so separated from ours through

time, distance, and culture as classical Greece, medieval India, early Japan, and modern Russia and Africa? Although most of the people involved in these epochs are long dead, what they did has touched everyone alive today.

The matter of perspective is more important than simple. In a perfect world all human experience would be equally valuable for its own sake, even if it had little or no impact on the mainstream of history. Yet the evidence on which historians depend for their understanding of the past is far from perfect. Some peoples have left so few traces of themselves that they cannot be understood even in their own right, much less in connection with others. Excellent examples of this problem are the Tocharians, an Indo-European-speaking people who lived in central Asia during the first millennium A.D. What they were doing there in the first place and how they related to their neighbors are complete mysteries. Such peoples for the moment remain historical enigmas, best left to specialists while other historians examine the principal currents of human development. Historical perspective demands that most attention be devoted to peoples who are best known in their own context and to how they have contributed to history.

Historians begin to reconstruct the past by posing questions about it. How and why, for example, did cities emerge? How did the political system of a particular society evolve? How did people create an economic system to sustain a complex society? What were a society's religious beliefs, and how did they influence daily life? Historians ask these kinds of questions to guide their research and focus their approach to the past.

To answer such questions, historians examine *primary sources,* the firsthand accounts of people who lived through the events—men and women who were in the best position to know what happened. Thus historians most commonly rely on the written record of human experience because, no matter how extensive the physical remains of a civilization may be, much of its history remains a mystery if it has not left records that we can read. Until we are able to decipher the written texts left by the ancient civilization of Minoan Crete, for example, we can draw only vague conclusions about its history. Nonetheless, the historian's responsibility is to examine all of the evidence, including visual evidence. Examined properly, visual sources provide a glimpse of the world as contemporaries saw it. Especially in conjunction with written documents, art can be a valuable and striking means of understanding the past. Similarly, archeology has proved a valuable avenue to the past, whether an excavation uncovers an ancient Greek city, a medieval temple, or a modern factory building. Things as dissimilar as beautiful paintings and ordinary machines tell historians much about the ways in which people have lived and worked.

In the fifth century B.C., a Greek named Herodotus wrote the first truly historical account of people and events in an effort to understand a great conflict between the Persians and the Greeks. Herodotus, now considered the "father of history," wrote that he was publishing an "inquiry" into the past. The Greek word that he used for "inquiry" was *historia,* from which we derive the word *history.* The two concepts of inquiry and history, first joined by Herodotus, became inseparable, and their connection is as valid today as when Herodotus wrote.

When studying sources—the most basic activity in research—historians assess the validity and perspective of each account. They try to determine whether sources are honest and accurate, generally by comparing and contrasting the testimony of several different observers. They criticize sources externally, to attempt to uncover forgeries and errors; and they criticize sources internally, to find an author's motives for writing, inconsistencies within a document, biases, and even cases of outright lying. Some contemporary written accounts, especially from ancient and medieval periods, have been lost; they are known to posterity only because people who read the originals later incorporated the information into their own writings. Historians analyze the viewpoints and accuracy of such *secondary sources* very carefully; these derivative writings have preserved much history that otherwise would have been lost. For the modern period historians have a vast supply of contemporary accounts of events, memoirs, personal letters, economic statistics, and government reports, all of them useful for an understanding of the past.

Once historians have pieced together what happened and have determined the facts, they interpret what they have found. Understanding the past does not necessarily come easily. Because no two historical events are precisely alike, history, unlike the exact physical sciences, cannot reproduce experiments under controlled conditions. A historian cannot put people into test tubes. Men, women, and children—the most complex organisms on this planet—are not as predictable as atoms or hydrocarbons.

To complicate matters, for many epochs only the broad outlines are known, so interpretation is especially difficult. For example, historians know that the Hittite Empire collapsed at the height of its power, but interpretations of the causes of the collapse are still speculative. On the other end of the spectrum, some developments are so vast and complex that historians must master mountains of data before they can even begin to venture an interpretation. Events as diverse as the end of the Roman Empire, the causes of the French Revolution, and the rise of communism in China are very complicated because so many people brought so many different forces to bear for so many different reasons. For such developments, one simple explanation will never satisfy everyone, and this fact itself testifies to the complexity of life.

Still another matter stands in the way of an accurate understanding of the past. The attempt to understand history is a uniquely human endeavor. Interpretations of the past sometimes change because people's points of view change. The values and attitudes of one generation are not necessarily shared by another. Despite such differences in interpretation, the effort to examine and understand the past can give historians a perspective that is valuable in the present. By analyzing and interpreting evidence, historians come to understand not only the past but the relationship of the past to life today.

Social history itself, an important subject of this book, is an example of historians' reappraisal of the meaning of the past. For centuries historians took the basic facts, details, and activities of life for granted. Obviously, people lived in certain types of houses, ate certain foods that they either raised or bought, and reared families. These matters seemed so ordinary that few serious historians gave them much thought. Yet within this generation a growing number of scholars have demonstrated that the ways in which people have lived over the years deserve as much study as the reigns of monarchs, the careers of great political figures, and the outcomes of big battles.

The topics of history and human societies lead to this question: What is civilization? *Civilization* is easier to describe than to define. The word comes from the Latin adjective *civilis,* which refers to a citizen. Citizens willingly and mutually bind themselves in political, economic, and social organizations in which individuals merge themselves, their energies, and their interests in a larger community. In the course of time, *civilization* has come to embrace not only a people's social and political organization but also its particular shared way of thinking and believing, its art, and other facets of its culture—the complex whole that sets one people apart from other peoples who have different shared values and practices. One way to understand this idea is to observe the origins and development of major civilizations, analyzing similarities and differences among them. At the fundamental level, the similarities are greater than the differences. Almost all peoples in the world share some values, even though they may live far apart, speak different languages, and have different religions and political and social systems. By studying these shared cultural values, which stretch through time and across distance, we can see how the various events of the past have left their impression on the present and even how the present may influence the future.

A further word about culture is in order. *Culture* is often defined as a particular type or stage of the intellectual, moral, artistic, and communal practices of a civilization. All people on this planet confront elemental challenges such as how to feed and shelter themselves (the economic aspect of culture) and how to govern their lives in harmony with others (the political and social aspects of culture). These basic economic, political, and social aspects of culture are inseparable from other aspects. All cultures have felt the need to transmit what they have learned to future generations. Sometimes the content of the transmission is intellectual—for example, the preservation of astronomical information. Sometimes it is religious—for example, beliefs about the gods and their relation to humanity. The artistic appreciation of life and the surrounding world has led all peoples to create their own forms of art and music. Historians note not only the common themes to be found among various peoples but also various peoples' unique response to the realities they face. Historians also study the differences among peoples. In short, the study of history is the examination of how various peoples confronted and responded to the circumstances of their lives, what their responses had in common with the responses of others, and how they remained individual over the space of time and across the planet earth.

THE FIRST HUMAN BEINGS

On December 27, 1831, young Charles Darwin stepped aboard the H.M.S. *Beagle* to begin a voyage to South America and the Pacific Ocean. In the course of that five-year voyage, he became convinced that species of animals and human beings had evolved from lower forms. At first Darwin was reluctant to publicize his theories because they ran counter to the biblical account of creation, which claimed that God had made Adam in one day. Finally, however, in 1859 he published *On the Origin of Species.* In 1871 he followed it with *The Descent of Man,* in which he argued that human beings and apes are descended from a common ancestor. Even before Darwin had proclaimed his theories, evidence to support them had come to light. In 1856 the fossilized bones of an early form of human were discovered in the Neander Valley of Germany. Called "Neanderthal man" after the place of his discovery, he was physically more primitive than modern man (*Homo sapiens,* or thinking man). But he was clearly a human being and not an ape. Neanderthal man offered proof of Darwin's theory that *Homo sapiens* had evolved from less developed forms.

The theories of Darwin, supported by the evidence of fossilized remains, ushered in a new scientific era in which scientists and scholars have re-examined the very nature of human beings and their history. Men and women of the twentieth century have made many discoveries, solved some old problems, but raised many new ones. Although the fossil remains of primitive unicellular organisms can be dated back roughly two and a half billion years, the fossil record is far from complete. Thus the whole story of evolution cannot yet be known.

Ideas of human evolution have changed dramatically, particularly in the past few years. Generations of paleoanthropologists—better remembered as fossil-hunters—have sought the "missing link." Ever since Darwin published his theories of evolution, scholars have tried to find the one fossil that would establish the point from which human beings and apes went their own different evolutionary ways. In 1974 an American team of scholars working in Africa discovered extensive remains of a skeleton that they named "Lucy." Lucy was an ape that had walked upright some three million years ago and had displayed human characteristics. Had the missing link finally been found? No. Lucy was an intriguing step along the road of development between human beings and apes, but she was only a step, not the missing link.

Since the discovery of Lucy, many other less spectacular but nonetheless instructive finds have caused scholars to question the very concept of the missing link and its implications. Fossil remains in China and Southeast Asia suggest that evolution was more complicated than paleoanthropologists previously thought and even that human beings may not have originated in Africa. It is not simply that paleoanthropologists, like historians, must interpret their data; they must rethink everything that they have discovered in the light of their latest findings.

Many contemporary paleoanthropologists working in widely separated parts of the world have proposed some startling ideas. Some suggest that the search for a missing link is itself a blind alley. They point out that the fossil record, extensive but incomplete, suggests that thousands of missing links may have existed, no one of them more important than any other. Given the small numbers of these primates and the extent of the globe, there is an almost infinitesimal chance of finding a skeleton that can be considered the missing link between other primates and human beings. Instead, contemporary scholars stress the need to study all of these fossil remains to open new vistas for the understanding of evolution. That conclusion should not be surprising. A number of years ago Loren Eiseley, a noted American anthropologist, offered the wisest and humblest observation: "The human interminglings of hundreds of thousands of years of prehistory are not to be clarified by a single generation of archeologists."[1]

Despite the enormous uncertainty surrounding human development, a reasonably clear picture can be drawn of two important early periods: the Paleolithic, or Old Stone Age; and the Neolithic, or New Stone Age. The immensely long Paleolithic Age, which lasted from about 400,000 to 7000 B.C. takes its name from the crude stone tools that the earliest hunters chipped from flint and obsidian, a black volcanic rock. During the much shorter Neolithic Age, which lasted from about 7000 to 3000 B.C., human beings began using new types of stone tools and, more important, pursuing agriculture.

Paleolithic Cave Painting   All Paleolithic peoples relied primarily on hunting for their survival. This scene, painted on the wall of a cave in southern France, depicts the animals that this group normally hunted. Paleolithic peoples may have hoped that by drawing these animals they gained a magical power over them. *(Source: Douglas Mazonowicz/ Gallery of Prehistoric Art)*

THE PALEOLITHIC AGE

Life in the Paleolithic Age was perilous and uncertain at best. Survival depended on success of the hunt, but the hunt often brought sudden and violent death. Paleolithic peoples hunted in a variety of ways, depending on the climate and environment. Many hunters stationed themselves at river fords and waterholes and waited for prey to come to them. Paleolithic hunters were thoroughly familiar with the habits of the animals on which they relied and paid close attention to migratory habits. Other hunters trapped their quarry, and those who lived in open areas stalked and pursued game. Paleolithic peoples hunted a huge variety of animals, ranging from elephants in Spain to deer in China.

Success in the hunt was likely to depend more on the quality and effectiveness of the hunters' social organization than on bravery. Paleolithic hunters were organized—they hunted in groups. They used their knowledge of the animal world and their power of thinking to plan how to down their prey. The ability to think and act as an organized social group meant that Paleolithic hunters could successfully feed on animals that were bigger, faster, and stronger than themselves.

Paleolithic peoples also nourished themselves by gathering nuts, berries, and seeds. Just as they knew the habits of animals, so they had vast knowledge of the plant kingdom. Some Paleolithic peoples even knew how to plant wild seeds to supplement their food supply. Thus they relied on every part of the environment for survival.

Home for Paleolithic folk also varied according to the environment. Particularly in cold regions, they sought refuge in caves from the weather, predatory animals, and other people. In warmer climates and in open country they built shelters, some no more elaborate than temporary huts or sunscreens.

The basic social unit of Paleolithic societies was probably the family, but family bonds were no doubt stronger and more extensive than those of families in modern urban and industrialized societies. It is likely that the bonds of kinship were strong not just within the nuclear family of father, mother, and children but throughout the extended family of uncles, aunts, cousins, nephews, and nieces. People in nomadic societies typically depend on the extended family for cooperative work and mutual protection. The ties of kinship probably also extended beyond the family to the tribe. A *tribe* was a group of families, led by a *patriarch*, a dominant male who governed the group. Tribe members considered themselves descendants of a common ancestor. Most tribes probably consisted of thirty to fifty people.

As in the hunt, so too in other aspects of life—group members had to cooperate to survive. The adult males normally hunted and between hunts made stone weapons. The women's realm was probably the camp. There they made utensils and—the likely inventors of weaving—fashioned skins into clothing, tents, and footwear. They left the camp to gather nuts, grains, and fruits to supplement the group's diet. The women's primary responsibility was the bearing of children, who were essential to the continuation of the group. Women also had to care for the children, especially the infants. Part of women's work was tending the fire, which served for warmth, cooking, and protection against wild animals. Paleolithic peoples were also world travelers. Before the dawn of history, bands of *Homo sapiens* flourished in Europe, Africa, and Asia and had crossed into the continents of North and South America and Australia. By the end of the Paleolithic Age, there were very few "undiscovered" areas left in the world.

Some of the most striking accomplishments of Paleolithic peoples were intellectual. The development of the human brain made abstract concepts possible. Unlike animals, whose lives are conditioned by instinct and learned behavior, Paleolithic peoples used reason to govern their actions. Thought and language permitted the lore and experience of the old to be passed on to the young. An invisible world also opened up to *Homo sapiens*. The Neanderthalers developed the custom of burying their dead and leaving offerings with the body, perhaps in the belief that somehow life continued after death.

Paleolithic peoples produced the first art. They decorated cave walls with paintings of animals and scenes of the hunt. They also began to fashion clay models of pregnant women and of animals. Many of the surviving paintings, such as those at Altamira in Spain and at Lascaux in France, are located deep in caves, in areas not easily accessible. These areas were probably places of ritual and initiation, where young men were taken when they joined the ranks of the hunters. They were also places of magic. The animals depicted on the walls were those either hunted for food or feared as predators. Many are shown wounded by spears or arrows; others are pregnant. The early artists may have been expressing the hope that the hunt would be successful and game plentiful. By portraying the animals as realistically as possible, the artist-hunters may have hoped to gain power over them. The statuettes of pregnant women seem to express a wish for fertile women to have babies and thus ensure the group's survival. The wall paintings and clay statuettes represent the earliest yearnings of human beings to control their environment.

Despite their many achievements, Paleolithic peoples were sometimes their own worst enemies. At times they fought one another for control of hunting grounds, and some early hunters wiped out less aggressive peoples. On rare occasions Paleolithic peoples seem to have preyed on one another, probably under the threat of starvation. One of the grimmest indications that Neanderthal man was at times cannibalistic comes from a cave in Yugoslavia, where investigators found human bones burned and split open. Nevertheless, the overriding struggle of the Paleolithic Age was with an unforgiving environment.

THE NEOLITHIC AGE

Hunting is at best a precarious way of life, even when the diet is supplemented with seeds and fruits. If the climate changes even slightly, the all-important herds might move to new areas. As recently as the late 1950s the Caribou Eskimos of the Canadian Northwest Territories suffered a severe famine when the caribou herds, their only source of food and bone for weapons, changed their migration route. Paleolithic tribes either moved with the herds and adapted themselves to new circumstances or, like the Caribou Eskimos, perished. Several long ice ages—periods when huge glaciers covered vast parts of Europe and North America—subjected small bands of Paleolithic hunters to extreme hardship.

Not long after the last ice age, around 7000 B.C. some hunters and gatherers began to rely chiefly on agriculture for their sustenance. This development has traditionally been called the "Agricultural Revolution." Yet contemporary scholars point out that ancient peoples had long practiced

agriculture. The real transformation of human life occurred when hunters and gatherers gave up their nomadic way of life to depend primarily on the grain they grew and the animals they domesticated. Agriculture enabled a more stable and secure life. Neolithic peoples thus flourished, fashioning an energetic, creative era.

They were responsible for many fundamental inventions and innovations that the modern world takes for granted. First, obviously, is systematic agriculture. Neolithic peoples relied on agriculture as their primary, not merely subsidiary, source of food. Thus they developed the primary economic activity of the entire ancient world and the basis of all modern life. From the settled routine of Neolithic farmers came the evolution of towns and eventually cities. Neolithic farmers usually raised more food than they could consume, and their surpluses permitted larger, healthier populations. Population growth in turn created an even greater reliance on settled farming, as only systematic agriculture could sustain the increased numbers of people. Since surpluses of food could also be bartered for other commodities, the Neolithic era witnessed the beginnings of large-scale trade. In time the increasing complexity of Neolithic societies led to the development of writing, prompted by the need to keep records and later by the urge to chronicle experiences, learning, and beliefs.

The transition to settled life also had a profound impact on the family. The shared needs and pressures that encourage extended family ties in nomadic societies are less prominent in settled societies. Bonds to the extended family weakened. In towns and cities the nuclear family was more dependent on its immediate neighbors than on kinfolk.

Meanwhile the nomadic way of life and the family relationships it nurtured continued to flourish alongside settled agriculture. But nomadic life did change. Neolithic nomads traveled with flocks of domesticated animals, their main source of wealth and food. Often farmers and nomads bartered peaceably with each other, one group trading its surpluses for those of the other. Still, although nomadic peoples existed throughout the Neolithic period and exist in modern times, the future belonged to the Neolithic farmers and their descendants. The development of systematic agriculture may not have been revolutionary, but the changes that it ushered in certainly were.

Until recently, scholars thought that agriculture originated in the ancient Near East and gradually spread elsewhere. Contemporary work, however, points to a more complex pattern of development. For unknown reasons people in various parts of the world all seem to have begun domesticating plants and animals at roughly the same time, around 7000 B.C. Four main points of origin have been identified. In the Near East, people in places as far apart as Tepe Yahya in modern Iran, Jarmo in modern Iraq, Jericho in Palestine, and Hacilar in modern Turkey (Map 1.1) raised wheat, barley, peas, and lentils. They also kept herds of sheep, pigs, and possibly goats. In western Africa, Neolithic farmers domesticated many plants, including millet, sorghum, and yams. In northeastern China, peoples of the Yangshao culture developed techniques of field agriculture, animal husbandry, potterymaking, and bronze metallurgy. Innovations in Central and South America were equally striking: Indians domesticated a host of plants, among them corn, beans, and squash. From these wide-ranging areas, knowledge of farming techniques spread to other regions.

The deliberate planting of crops led to changes in plants' genetic structure. The plants and animals cultivated by Neolithic farmers gradually evolved to the point where most of them could no longer survive in the wild. Thus human beings and the plants and animals they domesticated depended on one another for survival. Contemporary work on the origins of farming has led to a chilling revelation: the genetic base of most modern domesticated plants, such as wheat and corn, is so narrow that a new pest or plant disease could destroy many of them. The result would be widespread famine. Human society depends on a precarious food base.

Once people began to rely on farming for their livelihood, they settled in permanent villages and built houses. The location of the village was crucial. Early farmers chose places where the water supply was constant and adequate for their crops and flocks. At first, villages were small, consisting of a few households. As the population expanded and prospered, villages usually developed into towns. Between 8000 and 7000 B.C. the community at Jericho grew to at least two thousand people. Jericho's inhabitants lived in mud-brick houses built on stone foundations, and they surrounded their town with a massive fortification wall. The Neolithic site of Çatal Hüyük in Anatolia (modern Turkey) covered thirty-two acres. The outer houses of the settlement formed a solid wall of mud brick, which served as a bulwark against attack. At Tepe Yahya as well, the Neolithic farmers surrounded their town with a wall.

Walls offered protection and permitted a more secure, stable way of life than that of the nomad. They also prove that towns grew in size, population, and wealth, for these fortifications were so large that they could have been raised only by a large labor force. They also indicate that towns were developing social and political organization. The fortifications, the work of the whole community, would have been impossible without central planning.

One of the major effects of the advent of agriculture and settled life was a dramatic increase in population. No census figures exist for this period, but the number and size of the towns prove that Neolithic society was expanding. Early farmers found that agriculture provided a larger, much more dependable food supply than did hunting and gathering. No longer did the long winter months mean the threat of starvation. Farmers raised more food than they could consume and learned to store the surplus for the winter. Because the farming community was better fed than ever before, it was also more resistant to diseases that kill people suffering from malnutrition. Thus Neolithic farmers were healthier and lived longer than their predecessors. All these factors explain the growth of towns like Jericho and Jarmo.

The surplus of food had two other momentous consequences. First, grain became an article of commerce. The farming community traded surplus grain for items it could not produce itself. The community thus obtained raw materials such as precious gems and metals. In Mesopotamia the early towns imported copper from the north, and eventually copper replaced stone for tools and weapons. Trade also brought Neolithic communities into touch with one another, making possible the spread of ideas and techniques.

Second, agricultural surplus made possible the division of labor. It freed some members of the community from the necessity of raising food. Artisans and craftsmen devoted their attention to making the new stone tools that farming demanded—hoes and sickles for working in the fields and mortars and pestles for grinding grain. Other artisans began to shape clay into pottery vessels, which were used to store grain, wine, and

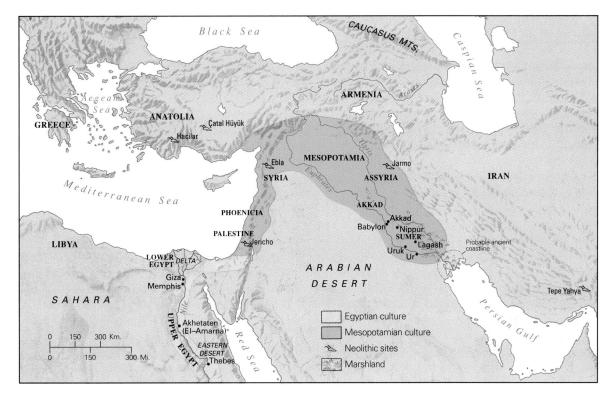

MAP 1.1 Spread of Cultures in the Ancient Near East   This map illustrates the spread of Mesopotamian and Egyptian culture through a semicircular stretch of land often called the "Fertile Crescent." From this area knowledge and use of agriculture spread throughout the western part of Asia Minor.

oil and served as kitchen utensils. Still others wove baskets and cloth. People who could specialize in particular crafts produced more and better goods than any single farmer could.

Until recently it was impossible to say much about these goods. But in April 1985 archeologists announced the discovery near the Dead Sea in modern Israel of a unique deposit of Neolithic artifacts. Buried in a cave were fragments of the earliest cloth yet found, the oldest painted mask, remains of woven baskets and boxes, and jewelry. The textiles are surprisingly elaborate, some woven in eleven intricate designs. These artifacts give eloquent testimony to the sophistication and artistry of Neolithic craftsmanship.

Prosperity and stable conditions nurtured other innovations and discoveries. Neolithic farmers improved their tools and agricultural techniques. They domesticated bigger, stronger animals, such as the bull and the horse, to work for them. To harness the power of these animals, they invented tools such as the plow, which came into use by 3000 B.C. The first plows had wooden shares and could break only light soils, but they were far more efficient than stone hoes. By 3000 B.C., the wheel had been invented, and farmers devised ways of hitching bulls and horses to wagons. These developments enabled Neolithic farmers to raise more food more efficiently and easily than ever before, simply because animals and machines were doing a greater proportion of the work.

In arid regions such as Mesopotamia and Egypt, farmers learned to irrigate their land and later to drain it to prevent the build-up of salt in the soil. By diverting water from rivers, they were able to open new land to cultivation. River waters flooding the fields deposited layers of rich mud, which increased the fertility of the soil. Thus the rivers, together with the manure of domesticated animals, kept replenishing the land. One result was a further increase in population and wealth. Irrigation, especially on a large scale, demanded group effort. The entire community had to plan which land to irrigate and how to lay out the canals.

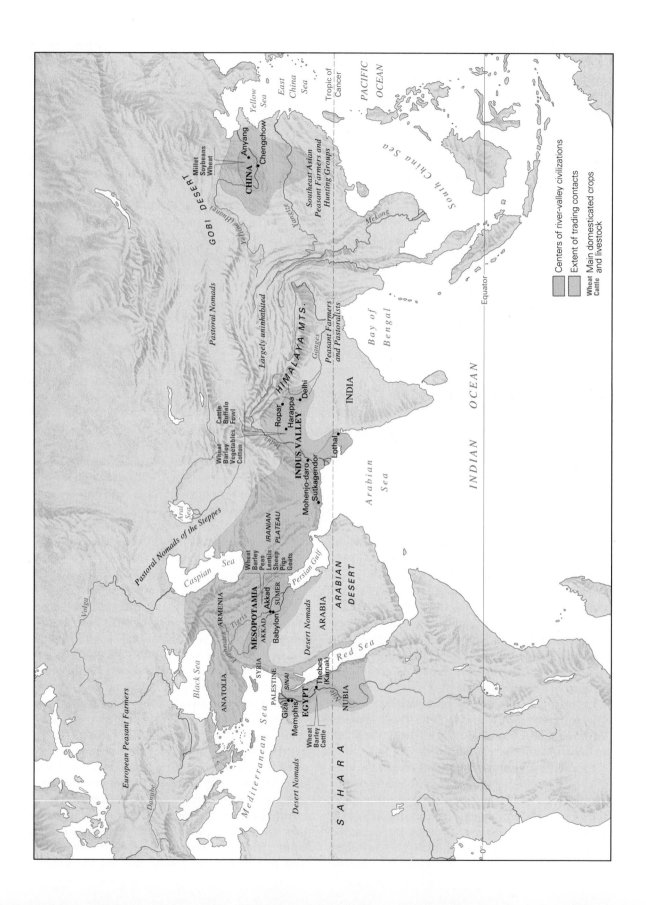

PACIFIC
OCEAN

East
China
Sea

Yellow
Sea

South China Sea

Tropic of Cancer

CHINA
Anyang
Chengchow

Millet
Soybeans
Wheat

GOBI DESERT

Yellow (Hwang)

Yangtze

Mekong

Southeast Asian
Peasant Farmers and
Hunting Groups

Pastoral Nomads

Largely uninhabited

HIMALAYA MTS.

Peasant Farmers
and Pastoralists

Cattle
Buffalo
Fowl

Ropar
Harappa
Delhi

Ganges

Bay of
Bengal

INDIA

INDUS VALLEY

Wheat
Barley
Vegetables
Cotton

Indus

Mohenjo-daro
Sutkagendor
Lothal

Pastoral Nomads of the Steppes

Aral
Sea

IRANIAN
PLATEAU

Arabian
Sea

INDIAN OCEAN

Caspian Sea

Wheat
Barley
Peas
Lentils
Sheep
Pigs
Goats

Volga

Persian Gulf

Equator

ARMENIA

MESOPOTAMIA

Tigris

Euphrates

AKKAD
Akkad
SUMER
Babylon

Desert Nomads

ARABIA

ARABIAN
DESERT

Black Sea

ANATOLIA

SYRIA

PALESTINE
SINAI

Mediterranean Sea

European Peasant Farmers

Danube

Red Sea

Giza
Memphis
EGYPT
Thebes
(Karnak)

NUBIA

Wheat
Barley
Cattle

S A H A R A

Desert Nomads

Centers of river-valley civilizations

Extent of trading contacts

Wheat Main domesticated crops
Cattle and livestock

Then everyone had to help dig the canals. The demands of irrigation underscored the need for strong central authority within the community. Successful irrigation projects in turn strengthened such central authority by proving it effective and beneficial. Thus corporate spirit and governments to which individuals were subordinate—the makings of urban life—began to evolve.

The development of systematic agriculture was a fundamental turning point in the history of civilization. Farming gave rise to stable, settled societies, which enjoyed considerable prosperity. It made possible an enormous increase in population. Some inhabitants of the budding towns turned their attention to the production of goods that made life more comfortable. Settled circumstances and a certain amount of leisure made the accumulation and spread of knowledge easier. Finally, sustained farming prepared the way for urban life.

RIVERS, RESOURCES, AND CIVILIZATIONS

The development of systematic agriculture made possible a huge leap in human development, a leap that took place in several different parts of the world at roughly the same time (Map 1.2). In the ancient Near East, India, and China, Neolithic farmers created the conditions that permitted the evolution of urban civilization.

Certain geographical features were common to these early civilizations. The most important were the mighty river valleys in which they developed. The Egyptians relied on the Nile, which flows some 4,000 miles before reaching the Mediterranean Sea. To the east the Euphrates, roughly 1,675 miles in length, and the Tigris, a mere 600 miles long, created Mesopotamia, the Greek name for the land between them. The Indus River, flowing about 1,980 miles before reaching the ocean, nourished ancient Indian civilization; and the

MAP 1.2 River-Valley Civilizations Although systematic agriculture developed in four great river valleys, variations in geography and climate meant that different crops were grown and societies emerged in distinct but similar ways.

great Yellow River, some 2,700 miles long, made the birth of Chinese civilization possible. Thus all four ancient civilizations could depend on a steady source of water, which also brought nutrients to the soil and fish as a source of food. Except for the violent Tigris and Yellow, the rivers also served as an easy means of communication. It was safer and simpler to use the Nile as a highway than to travel across the deserts surrounding Egypt. Likewise the Indus offered the fastest, most convenient path through the jungle. The rivers enabled people throughout a large area to keep in touch with one another, and easy communications facilitated the exchange of ideas while breaking down the barriers of isolation. The size and fertility of the broad valleys made possible a vast increase in the land that could be cultivated, which in turn meant a vast increase in wealth and population, necessary ingredients to the development of large sophisticated social structures.

Although great rivers were a common feature of these civilizations, soil and climate differed, and these differences left a significant imprint on human development. The rich African mud carried by the Nile allowed abundant crops of wheat, and the dry desert air made it simple to preserve surpluses of grain. The Indus flows through rich subtropical land well suited to growing a large variety of crops, but the humid climate quickly brought rot. Different climates meant that the rivers nurtured different crops and required different methods of agriculture. Geography and the means by which people turned it to their uses, then, influenced the way in which societies evolved.

The rivers themselves are different. The Nile is gentle and predictable, the source of Egyptian life; the Tigris and Yellow rivers are violent and unpredictable, at times bringing floods and destruction. The nature of the rivers demanded differences in the ways they were used. In Egypt and China, the peoples employed irrigation to bring water to arid land, enabling them to cultivate more fields. That was true in Mesopotamia too, but the farmers there also relied on irrigation to drain land to reclaim it for cultivation. In India farmers protected themselves against the flood waters of the Indus while taking advantage of the rich alluvium that the river deposited. Whatever the differences, the rivers challenged early peoples to work together to make the best use of their geographical gifts, whether to divert water to new soil, to draw water from uncultivated fields, or to prevent water from destroying land already being farmed.

The effort needed to make the rivers useful to human life had several by-products. First, and most important, the more land brought under cultivation, the larger the population grew and the richer in material goods it became. As the river-valley societies in the ancient Near East, India, and China outgrew their Neolithic past, they were forced to diversify their activities and abilities. New, centrally organized forms of government were required on a regular, permanent basis, to coordinate massive irrigation projects, to administer the land, to govern the people, and to defend them in time of war. Specialization in government and defense was part of a larger division of labor. Some members of society abandoned the plow to master the technology of metalworking, while others devoted themselves to the study of mathematics and architecture to meet the building needs of society. In the firm belief that they belonged to a world inhabited by gods, some people tried to explain the origin and workings of these higher beings, both to honor them and to teach their mysteries to others so that the divine and human could live in harmony. In the process they preserved traditions not only about their beliefs but also about their own lives—traditions that linked them to the past and helped them shape the future.

Knowledge had become too valuable to lose and too complicated to be mastered easily. Whatever their specialization, people increasingly found it necessary to preserve knowledge and experience in a permanent form. To meet this need, they invented writing, which enabled them not only to record their accumulated wisdom but also to pass essential information about the past and the present to future generations. They extended the experience of humanity beyond the individual's lifetime and created the foundations of an intellectual continuity that defied both time and death.

North and South America, Europe, sub-Saharan Africa, and Southeast Asia can all boast of many rivers. Yet only the peoples of Mesoamerica and the Incas of Peru in South America established civilizations comparable to those in the Near East, India, and China, and even they came many centuries after the rise of the river-valley civilizations. Factors other than rivers were obviously essential to the development of civilization. Cli-

mate may be a limiting factor in places such as equatorial Africa and Southeast Asia. But why did nothing similar to Egyptian, Mesopotamian, Indian, and Chinese advances occur in areas of North America and Europe where the climate is relatively mild?

North America and sub-Saharan Africa are rich in raw materials, but often those raw materials were inaccessible. Early peoples lacked the tools and the technology to mine the coal in Kentucky or the diamonds in South Africa. Tools were primitive and totally inadequate. Instead of plowing the soil, early farmers not living in the river valleys of the Near East, India, or China mainly used hoes and digging-sticks, and they lacked the work animals necessary to haul burdens, pull plows, and grind grain. They relied on their own labor, not on animal power, to sow, harvest, and process grain. They worked hard to get crop yields that were so small that they could not expect sizable surpluses. That in turn made it hard for them to develop specialization of labor, to expand population, to build cities, and to accumulate knowledge in a durable form. Furthermore, areas such as parts of sub-Saharan Africa and the Caribbean are so naturally rich in readily available natural food resources that people did not have to toil for a living. Seldom did peoples in such areas develop sophisticated urban cultures.

Thus, something more than geography, natural resources, climate, sustained agriculture, and population is needed to constitute a civilization. Though important in themselves, together they permit people to live in villages, towns, and cities. The significance of urban life to the growth of civilization cannot be overestimated. By banding together and observing common laws and values of life, people could pool their resources. While some people were farmers or craftsmen, others magistrates or priests, all cooperated to sustain the community and to protect it. The invention of writing enabled them to hand on knowledge of values, law, religion, and history to later generations. Urban life provided the wealth, security, and stability to create civilization in its many forms.

Among the river-valley societies, nowhere can these abstractions be better seen than in the urban culture that flowered in the demanding environment of Mesopotamia, the first of the four societies to attain a level of development that can reasonably be called a civilization.

Map of Nippur   The oldest map in the world, dating to ca 1500 B.C., shows the layout of the Mesopotamian city of Nippur. Inscribed on a clay tablet, the map has enabled archeologists to locate ruined buildings: (A) the ziggurat, (B) canal, (C) enclosure and gardens, (D) city gates, and (E) the Euphrates River. *(Source: The University Museum, University of Pennsylvania)*

MESOPOTAMIAN CIVILIZATION

Mesopotamia, an area roughly equivalent to modern Iraq, drew its life from the Euphrates and Tigris rivers. Both rivers have their headwaters in the mountains of Armenia in modern Turkey. Both are fed by numerous tributaries, and the entire river system drains a vast mountainous region. Overland routes in Mesopotamia usually followed the Euphrates because the banks of the Tigris are frequently steep and difficult. North of the ancient city of Babylon the land levels out into a barren expanse. The desert continues south of Babylon and still farther south gives way to a 6,000-square-mile region of marshes, lagoons, mud flats, and reed banks. At last, in the extreme south, the Euphrates and the Tigris unite and empty into the Persian Gulf.

This area became the home of many folk and the land of the first cities. The region around Akkad, near modern Baghdad, was occupied by bands of Semitic nomads, people related to one another by their language, Semitic, a family of languages that includes Hebrew and Arabic. Into the south came the Sumerians, farmers and city builders who probably migrated from the east. By 3000 B.C. they had established a number of cities in the southernmost part of Mesopotamia, which became known as Sumer. As the Sumerians pushed north, they came into contact with the Semites, who readily adopted Sumerian culture and turned to urban life. The Sumerians soon changed the face of the land and made Mesopotamia the source of values and techniques that fundamentally influenced the societies of their immediate neighbors, both in the West and the East (see Map 1.2).

In the context of world history, the capitalized terms "Western" and "Eastern" and "West" and "East" are *Eurocentric,* which means that they describe events and culture from the viewpoint of European experience and values. The concept behind these terms goes back to the ancient Greeks, who contrasted their life with the lives of their non-Greek neighbors in Africa and western Asia. Peoples in Asia and Africa would probably have dismissed the notion, and no one today uses the categories "West" and "East" to indicate the superiority of one set of historical developments to the other. Despite their flaws, however, the terms have come into general use as a useful, but artificial way to distinguish historical developments in Europe and the Americas from those in Asia.

Another term already used in these pages, "the ancient Near East" also requires some explanation. It refers to a specific area of western Asia and northeastern Africa. In the north the ancient Near East included the western part of modern Turkey, extending south through the area now called the "Middle East" to Egypt in Africa. The major justification for this term is historical, not geographical. Although various peoples in this area developed their own civilizations to some extent independently, they did not develop in complete isolation but formed a well-defined unit.

Environment and Mesopotamian Culture

From the outset, geography had a profound effect on the evolution of Mesopotamian civilization. In this region agriculture is possible only with irrigation and good drainage. Consequently, the Sumerians and later the Akkadians built cities along the Tigris and Euphrates and their branches. Major cities such as Ur and Uruk took root on tributaries of the Euphrates, while others, notably Lagash, were built on tributaries of the Tigris (see Map 1.1). The rivers supplied fish, a major element of the city dwellers' diet. The rivers also provided reeds and clay for building materials. Since this entire area lacks stone, mud brick became the primary building block of Mesopotamian architecture.

The rivers sustained life, and simultaneously they acted as a powerful restraining force, particularly on Sumerian political development. They made Sumer a geographical maze. Between the rivers, streams, and irrigation canals stretched open desert or swamp where nomadic tribes roamed. Communication between the isolated cities was difficult and at times dangerous. Thus each Sumerian city became a state, independent of the others and protective of its independence. Any city that tried to unify the country was resisted by the other cities. As a result, the political history of Sumer is one of almost constant warfare. The experience of the city of Nippur (see Map 1.1) is an example of how bad conditions could become. At one point in its history Nippur was conquered eighteen times in twenty-four years. Although Sumer was eventually unified, unification came late and was always tenuous.

The harsh environment fostered a grim, even pessimistic, spirit among the Mesopotamians. They especially feared the ravages of flood. The Tigris can bring quick devastation, as it did to Baghdad in 1831, when flood waters destroyed seven thousand homes in a single night. The same tragedy occurred often in antiquity. Vulnerability to natural disaster deeply influenced Mesopotamian religious beliefs.

Sumerian Society

The Sumerians sought to please and calm the gods, especially the patron deity of the city. Encouraged and directed by a traditional priesthood long dedicated to understanding the ways of the gods, people erected shrines in the center of each city and then built their houses around them. The best way to honor a god was to make the shrine grand and impressive, for a god who had a splendid temple might think twice about sending floods to destroy the city.

The temple had to be worthy of the god, a symbol of his power, and it had to last. Special skills and materials were needed to build it. Only stone was suitable for its foundations, and only precious metals and colorful glazed tiles were fit for its decoration. Since the Mesopotamians had to import both stone and metals, temple construction encouraged trade. Architects, engineers, craftsmen, and workers had to devote a great deal of thought, effort, and time to build the temple. By 2000 B.C. the result was Mesopotamia's first monumental architecture—the *ziggurat,* a massive stepped tower that dominated the city.

Once the ziggurat was built, the traditional priesthood assumed the additional duty of running it and performing the god's rituals. The people of the city met the expenses of building the temple and maintaining both the temple and its priests by setting aside extensive tracts of land. The priests took charge of the produce of the temple lands and the sacred flocks. Part of the yield fed and clothed them and the temple staff. Part was used as offerings to the gods, and part was sold or bartered to obtain goods, such as precious metals and stone, needed for construction, maintenance, and ritual.

Until recently, the dominant position and wealth of the temple had led historians to consider the Sumerian city-state an absolute *theocracy,* or government by an established priesthood. According to this view, the temple and its priests owned the city's land and controlled its economy. Newly discovered documents and recent work, however, have resulted in new ideas about the Sumerian city. It is now known that the temple owned a large fraction, but not all, of the city's territory and did not govern the city. A king *(lugal)* or local governor *(ensi)* exercised political power, and most of the city's land was the property of individual citizens.

Sumerian society was based on a complex arrangement of freedom and dependence. It was divided into four categories: nobles, free clients of the nobility, commoners, and slaves. The nobility consisted of the king and his family, the chief priests, and high palace officials. Generally the king rose to power as a war leader, elected by the citizenry. He established a regular army, trained it, and led it into battle. The might of the king and the frequency of warfare in Mesopotamia quickly made the king the supreme figure in the city, and

Aerial View of Ur This photograph gives a good idea of the size and complexity of Ur, one of the most powerful cities in Mesopotamia. In the lower right-hand corner stands the massive ziggurat of Urnammu. *(Source: Georg Gerster/Comstock)*

kingship soon became hereditary. The symbol of his status was the palace, which rivaled the temple in grandeur.

The king and the lesser nobility held extensive tracts of land that, like the estates of the temple, were worked by clients and slaves. Clients were free men and women who were dependent on the nobility. In return for their labor the clients received small plots of land to work for themselves. Although this arrangement assured the clients of a livelihood, the land they worked remained the possession of the nobility or the temple. Thus, not only did the nobility control most—and probably the best—land, they also commanded the obedience of a huge segment of society. They were the dominant force in Mesopotamian society.

Commoners were free citizens. They were independent of the nobility; however, they could not rival the nobility in social status and political power. Commoners belonged to large patriarchal families who owned land in their own right. Commoners could sell their land, if the family approved, but even the king could not legally take their land without their approval. Commoners had a voice in the political affairs of the city and full protection under the law.

Slavery has been a fact of life throughout history, until comparatively recent times. Some Sumerian slaves were foreigners and prisoners of war. Some were criminals who had lost their freedom as punishment for their crimes. Still others served as slaves to repay their debts. They were more fortunate than the others because the law required that they be freed after three years. But all slaves were subject to whatever treatment their owners might mete out. Although they could be beaten and even branded, they were not considered dumb beasts. Slaves engaged in trade and made profits. Indeed, many slaves bought their freedom. They could borrow money and received at least some legal protection.

THE SPREAD OF MESOPOTAMIAN CULTURE

The Sumerians established the basic social, economic, and intellectual patterns of Mesopotamia, but the Semites played a large part in spreading Sumerian culture far beyond the boundaries of Mesopotamia. Despite the cultural ascendancy of the Sumerians, continual wars wasted their strength. In 2331 B.C. the Semitic chieftain Sargon conquered Sumer and created a new empire. The symbol of his triumph was a new capital, the city of Akkad. Sargon, the first "world conqueror," led his armies to the Mediterranean Sea. Although his empire lasted only a few generations, it spread Mesopotamian culture throughout the Fertile Crescent, the belt of rich farmland that extends from Mesopotamia in the east up through Syria in the north and down to Egypt in the west (see Map 1.1).

Sargon's impact and the extent of Mesopotamian influence even at this early period have been dramatically revealed at Ebla in modern Syria. In 1964 archeologists there unearthed a once-flourishing Semitic civilization that had assimilated political, intellectual, and artistic aspects of Mesopotamian culture. In 1975 the excavators uncovered thousands of clay tablets, which proved that the people of Ebla had learned the art of writing from the Mesopotamians. Eblaite artists borrowed heavily from Mesopotamian art but developed their own style, which in turn influenced Mesopotamian artists. The Eblaites transmitted the heritage of Mesopotamia to other Semitic centers in Syria. In the process, a universal culture developed in the ancient Near East, a culture basically Mesopotamian but fertilized by the traditions, genius, and ways of many other peoples.

When the clay tablets of Ebla were discovered, many scholars confidently predicted that they would shed fresh light on the Bible. Some even claimed to recognize in them biblical names like Jerusalem and the "Five Cities of the Plain," which included Sodom and Gomorrah. Careful study since then suggests that these claims were more often optimistic than accurate. So far the Ebla tablets have added very little to biblical scholarship, yet they are a gold mine of data on the ancient history of northern Syria. They confirm the existence and importance of direct contact between Mesopotamia and Syria as early as the third millennium B.C. Moreover, they demonstrate the early influence of Mesopotamian civilization far beyond its own borders.

The Triumph of Babylon

Although the empire of Sargon was extensive, it was short-lived. The Semites, too, failed to solve the problems posed by Mesopotamia's geography and population pattern. It was left to the Babylonians to unite Mesopotamia politically and culturally. The Babylonians were Amorites, a Semitic people who had migrated from Arabia and settled on the site of Babylon, along the middle Euphrates. Babylon enjoyed an excellent geographical position and was ideally suited to be the capital of Mesopotamia. It dominated trade on the Tigris and Euphrates rivers: all commerce to and from Sumer and Akkad had to pass by its walls. It also looked beyond Mesopotamia. Babylonian merchants followed the Tigris north to Assyria and Armenia. The Euphrates led merchants to Syria, Palestine, and the Mediterranean. The city grew great because of its commercial importance and soundly based power (see Map 1.1).

Babylon was also fortunate in its farseeing and able king Hammurabi (1792–1750 B.C.). Hammurabi set out to do three things: make Babylon secure, unify Mesopotamia, and win for the Babylonians a place in Mesopotamian civilization. The first two he accomplished by conquering Assyria and Akkad in the north and Sumer in the south. Then he turned to his third goal.

Politically, Hammurabi joined in his kingship the Semitic concept of the tribal chieftain and the Sumerian idea of urban kingship. Culturally, he encouraged the spread of myths that explained how Marduk, the god of Babylon, had been elected king of the gods by the other Mesopotamian deities. Hammurabi's success in making Marduk the god of all Mesopotamians made Babylon the religious center of Mesopotamia. Through Hammurabi's genius the Babylonians made their own contribution to Mesopotamian culture—a culture vibrant enough to maintain its identity while assimilating new influences. Hammurabi's conquests and the activity of Babylonian merchants spread this enriched culture north to Anatolia and west to Syria and Palestine.

The Invention of Writing and the First Schools

Mesopotamian culture spread as rapidly as it did because of the invention and evolution of writing. Until recently, scholars have credited the Sumerians with the invention of writing in the Western world. Recent work, however, suggests that the Sumerian achievement, a form of writing called

Stele of Naramsin Naramsin, the grandson of Sargon, was one of the greatest of the Akkadian kings. The topmost figure on this stele, or commemorative tablet, he displays his power by defeating his enemies in battle. Naramsin's horned crown suggests that he considered himself divine. *(Source: Louvre/Cliché des Musées Nationaux, Paris)*

cuneiform—from the Latin term for "wedge-shaped" (used to describe the strokes of the stylus) may have been a comparatively late stage in the development of writing. The origins of writing probably go back thousands of years earlier than previously thought. As early as the ninth millennium

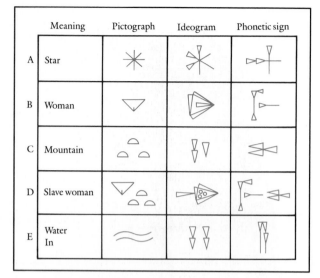

	Meaning	Pictograph	Ideogram	Phonetic sign
A	Star			
B	Woman			
C	Mountain			
D	Slave woman			
E	Water In			

Figure 1.1 Sumerian Writing *(Source: Excerpted from S. N. Kramer,* The Sumerians: Their History, Culture and Character, *University of Chicago Press, Chicago, 1963, pp. 302–306)*

B.C., Near Eastern peoples used clay tokens as record-keeping counters. By the fourth millennium B.C., people had realized that drawing pictures of the tokens on clay was simpler than making tokens. This breakthrough in turn suggested that more information could be conveyed by adding pictures of still other objects. The result was a complex system of *pictographs,* in which each sign pictured an object. Pictographs were the forerunners of cuneiform writing.

How did this pictographic system work and how did it evolve into cuneiform writing? At first, if a scribe wanted to indicate "star," he simply drew a picture of a star on a wet clay tablet (see line A of Figure 1.1), which became rock hard when baked. Anyone looking at the picture would know what it meant and would think of the word for "star." This complicated and laborious system had serious limitations. It could not represent abstract ideas or combinations of ideas. For instance, how could it depict a slave woman?

The solution appeared when the scribe discovered that he could combine signs to express meaning. To refer to a slave woman, he used the sign for "woman" (line B) and the sign for "mountain" (line C)—literally, "mountain woman" (line D). Since the Sumerians regularly obtained their slave women from the mountains, this combination of signs was easily understandable.

The next step was to simplify the system. Instead of drawing pictures, the scribe made conventionalized signs. Thus the signs became *ideograms:* they symbolized ideas. The sign for "star" could also be used to indicate "heaven," "sky," or even "god."

The real breakthrough came when the scribe learned to use signs to represent sounds. For instance, the scribe drew two parallel wavy lines to indicate the word "a" or "water" (line E). The word "a" in Sumerian also meant "in" (as well as "water"). The word "in" expresses a relationship that is very difficult to represent pictorially. Instead of trying to invent a sign to mean "in," some clever scribe used the sign for "water" because the two words sounded alike. This phonetic use of signs made possible the combining of signs to convey abstract ideas.

The Sumerian system of writing was so complicated that only professional scribes mastered it, and even they had to study it for many years. By 2500 B.C. scribal schools flourished throughout Sumer. Most students came from wealthy families and were male. Each school had a master, teachers, and monitors. Discipline was strict, and students were caned for sloppy work and misbehavior. One graduate of a scribal school had few fond memories of the joy of learning:

My headmaster read my tablet, said:
"There is something missing," caned me.

. . .

The fellow in charge of silence said:
"Why did you talk without permission," caned me.
The fellow in charge of the assembly said:
"Why did you stand at ease without permission,"
caned me.[2]

The Sumerian system of schooling set the educational standards for Mesopotamian culture, and the Akkadians and Babylonians adopted its practices and techniques. Students began by learning how to prepare clay tablets and make signs. They studied grammar and word lists and solved simple mathematical problems. Mesopotamian education always had a practical side because of the economic and administrative importance of scribes. Most scribes took administrative positions in the temple or palace, where they kept records of business transactions, accounts, and inventories. But scribal schools did not limit their curriculum to business affairs. They were also centers of culture and learning. Topics of study included mathematics, botany, and linguistics. Advanced students copied and studied the classics of Mesopotamian literature. Talented students and learned scribes wrote compositions of their own. As a result, many literary, mathematical, and religious texts survive today, giving a surprisingly full picture of Mesopotamian intellectual and spiritual life.

Mesopotamian Thought and Religion

The Mesopotamians made significant and sophisticated advances in mathematics using a numerical system based on units of sixty. For practical purposes they also used factors of ten and six. They developed the concept of *place value*—that the value of a number depends on where it stands in relation to other numbers. Mesopotamian mathematical texts are of two kinds: tables and problems. Scribes compiled tables of squares and square roots, cubes and cube roots, and reciprocals. They wrote texts of problems that dealt not only with equations and pure mathematics but also with practical problems such as how to plan irrigation ditches. The Mesopotamians did not consider mathematics a purely theoretical science. The building of cities, palaces, temples, and canals demanded practical knowledge of geometry and trigonometry. In not turning their knowledge into theories, the Mesopotamians were different from the Greeks, who enjoyed theorizing.

Mesopotamian medicine was a combination of magic, prescriptions, and surgery. Mesopotamians believed that demons and evil spirits caused sickness and that magic spells could drive them out. Or, they believed, a physician could force a demon out by giving the patient a foul-tasting prescription. As medical knowledge grew, some prescriptions were found to work and thus were true medicines. The physician relied heavily on plants, animals, and minerals for recipes, often mixing them with beer to cover their unpleasant taste. Surgeons practiced a dangerous occupation, and the penalties for failure were severe. One section of Hammurabi's law code (see page 23) decreed: "If a physician performed a major operation on a seignior with a bronze lancet and has caused the seignior's death, or he opened up the eye-socket . . . and has destroyed the . . . eye, they shall cut off his hand."[3] No wonder that one medical text warned physicians to avoid a dying person.

Sumerian Clay Tablet This Sumerian clay tablet dating from about 3000 B.C. shows Sumerian writing in transition. The scribe has begun to use pictures of things to represent abstractions, which is an advance from pictographs to ideograms (see Figure 1.1). *(Source: Courtesy of the Trustees of the British Museum)*

Mesopotamian thought had its profoundest impact on theology and religion. The Sumerians originated many beliefs, and the Akkadians and Babylonians added to them. Although the Mesopotamians thought that many gods ran the world, they did not consider all gods and goddesses equal. Some deities had very important jobs, taking care of music, law, sex, and victory, while others had lesser tasks, overseeing leatherworking and basket weaving. The god in charge of metalworking was hardly the equal of the god of wisdom.

Divine society was a hierarchy. According to the Sumerians the air-god Enlil was the king of the gods and laid down the rules by which the universe was run. Enki, the god of wisdom, put Enlil's plans into effect. The Babylonians believed that the gods elected Marduk as their king and that he assigned the lesser gods various duties. Once the gods received their tasks, they carried them out forever.

Mesopotamian gods lived their lives much as human beings lived theirs. The gods were *anthropomorphic,* or human in form. Unlike men and women, they were powerful and immortal and could make themselves invisible; otherwise, they were very human. They celebrated with food and drink, and they raised families. They enjoyed their own "Garden of Eden," a green and fertile place.

They could be irritable, and they were not always holy. Even Enlil was punished by other gods because he had once raped the goddess Ninlil.

The Mesopotamians considered natural catastrophes to be the work of the gods. At times the Sumerians described their chief god, Enlil, as "the raging flood which has no rival." The gods, they believed, even used nature to punish the Mesopotamians. According to the myth of the Deluge, which gave rise to the biblical story of Noah, the god Enki warned Ziusudra, the Sumerian Noah:

A flood will sweep over the cult-centers;
To destroy the seed of mankind . . .
Is the decision, the word of the assembly of the
  gods.[4]

The Mesopotamians did not worship their deities because the gods were holy. Human beings were too insignificant to pass judgment on the conduct of the gods, and the gods were too superior to honor human morals. Rather, the Mesopotamians worshiped the gods because they were mighty. Likewise, it was not the place of men and women to understand the gods. The Sumerian equivalent to the biblical Job once complained to his god:

The man of deceit has conspired against me,
And you, my god, do not thwart him,
You carry off my understanding.[5]

The motives of the gods were not always clear. In times of affliction one could only pray and offer sacrifices to appease them.

The Mesopotamians had many myths to account for the creation of the universe. According to one Sumerian myth (echoed in Genesis, the first book of the Old Testament), only the primeval sea existed at first. The sea produced heaven and earth, which were united. Heaven and earth gave birth to Enlil, who separated them and made possible the creation of the other gods.

These myths are the earliest known attempts to answer the question "How did it all begin?" The Mesopotamians obviously thought about these matters, as about the gods, in human terms. They never organized their beliefs into a philosophy, but their myths offered understandable explanations of natural phenomena. They were emotionally satisfying, and that was their greatest appeal.

Mesopotamian myths also explained the origin of human beings. In one myth the gods decided to make their lives easier by creating servants, whom they wanted made in their own image. Nammu, the goddess of the watery deep, brought the matter to Enki. After some thought, Enki instructed Nammu and the others:

Mix the heart of the clay that is over the abyss.
The good and princely fashioners will thicken the
  clay.
You, do you bring the limbs into existence.[6]

In Mesopotamian myth, as in Genesis, men and women were made in the divine image. However, human beings lacked godlike powers. The myth "The Creation of the Pickax" gives an idea of their insignificance. According to this myth, Enlil drove his pickax into the ground, and out of the hole crawled the Sumerians, the first people. As Enlil stood looking at them, some of his fellow gods approached him. They were so pleased with Enlil's work that they asked him to give them some people to serve them. Consequently, the Mesopotamians believed it their duty to supply the gods with sacrifices of food and drink and to house them in fine temples. In return, they hoped that the gods would be kind.

In addition to myths, the Sumerians produced the first epic poem, the *Epic of Gilgamesh*. The epic recounts the wanderings of Gilgamesh—the semihistorical king of Uruk—and his companion Enkidu, their fatal meeting with the goddess Ishtar in which Enkidu is killed, and Gilgamesh's subsequent search for eternal life. Although Gilgamesh finds a miraculous plant that gives immortality to anyone who eats it, a great snake steals it from him. Despite this loss, Gilgamesh visits the lower world to bring Enkidu back to life, thereby learning of life after death. The *Epic of Gilgamesh* is not only an excellent piece of literature but also an intellectual triumph. It shows the Sumerians grappling with such enduring questions as life and death, mankind and deity, and immortality. Despite its great antiquity, it addresses questions of importance to men and women today.

These ideas about the creation of the universe and of human beings are part of the Mesopotamian legacy to modern civilization. They spread throughout the ancient Near East and found a home among the Hebrews, who adopted much of

Mesopotamian religious thought and made it part of their own beliefs. Biblical parallels to Mesopotamian literary and religious themes are many. Such stories as the creation of Adam, the Garden of Eden, the Deluge, and the trials of Job can be traced back to Mesopotamian originals. Through the Bible, Mesopotamian as well as Jewish religious concepts influenced Christianity and Islam. Thus these first attempts by women and men to understand themselves and their world are still alive today.

DAILY LIFE IN MESOPOTAMIA

The law code of King Hammurabi offers a wealth of information about daily life in Mesopotamia. Hammurabi's was not the first law code in Mesopotamia; indeed the earliest goes back to ca 2100 B.C. Yet, like earlier lawgivers, Hammurabi proclaimed that he issued his laws on divine authority to "establish law and justice in the language of the land, thereby promoting the welfare of the people." His code may seem harsh, but it was no harsher than the Mosaic law of the Hebrews, which it heavily influenced. Hammurabi's code inflicted such penalties as mutilation, whipping, and burning. Today in parts of the Islamic world these punishments are still in use. Despite its severity, a spirit of justice and a sense of responsibility pervade the code. Hammurabi genuinely felt that his duty was to govern the Mesopotamians as righteously as possible. He tried to regulate the relations of his people so that they could live together in harmony.

Hammurabi's code has two striking characteristics. First, the law differed according to the social status of the offender. Aristocrats were not punished as harshly as commoners, nor commoners as harshly as slaves. Even slaves had rights, however, and received some protection under the law. Second, the code demanded that the punishment fit the crime. Like the Mosaic law of the Hebrews, it called for "an eye for an eye, and a tooth for a tooth," at least among equals. However, an aristocrat who destroyed the eye of a commoner or slave could pay a fine instead of losing his own eye. Otherwise, as long as criminal and victim shared the same social status, the victim could demand exact vengeance.

Gilgamesh   The epic hero Gilgamesh here holds two bulls with human faces. Gilgamesh is not being an animal lover. The scene probably depicts his epic battle with these monstrous and powerful enemies. *(Source: The University Museum, University of Pennsylvania)*

Hammurabi's code began with legal procedure. There were no public prosecutors or district attorneys, so individuals brought their own complaints before the court. Each side had to produce written documents or witnesses to support its case. In cases of murder, the accuser had to prove the defendant guilty; any accuser who failed to do so was put to death. This strict law was designed to prevent people from lodging groundless charges. The Mesopotamians were very worried about witchcraft and sorcery. Anyone accused of witchcraft, even if the charges were not proved, underwent an ordeal by water. The gods themselves would decide the case. The defendant was thrown into the Euphrates, which was considered the instrument of the gods. A defendant who sank was guilty; a defendant who floated was innocent. (In medieval Europe and colonial America, accused witches also underwent ordeals by water, but they were considered innocent only if they sank.) Another procedural regulation covered the conduct of judges. Once a judge had rendered a verdict, he could not change it. Any judge who did so was fined heavily and deposed. In short, the code tried to guarantee a fair trial and a just verdict.

Consumer protection is not a modern idea; it goes back to Hammurabi's day. Merchants and

Law Code of Hammurabi Hammurabi ordered his code to be inscribed on a stone pillar and set up in public. At the top of the pillar Hammurabi is depicted receiving the scepter of authority from the god Shamash. *(Source: Louvre/Cliché des Musées Nationaux, Paris)*

businessmen had to guarantee the quality of their goods and services. A boatbuilder who did sloppy work had to repair the boat at his own expense. A boatman who lost the owner's boat or sank someone else's boat replaced it and its cargo. Housebuilders guaranteed their work with their lives. Careless work could result in the collapse of a house and the death of its inhabitants. If that happened, the builder himself was put to death. A merchant who tried to increase the interest rate on a loan forfeited the entire amount. Hammurabi's laws tried to ensure that consumers got what they paid for and paid a just price.

Crime was a feature of Mesopotamian urban life just as it is in modern cities. Burglary was a serious problem, hard to control. Because houses were built of mud brick, it was easy for an intruder to dig through the walls. Hammurabi's punishment for burglary matched the crime. A burglar caught in the act was put to death on the spot, and his body was walled into the breach that he had made. The penalty for looting was also grim: anyone caught looting a burning house was thrown into the fire.

Mesopotamian cities had breeding places of crime. Taverns were notorious haunts of criminals, who often met at taverns to make their plans. Tavernkeepers were expected to keep order and arrest anyone overheard planning a crime. Taverns were normally run by women, and they also served as houses of prostitution. Prostitution was disreputable but neither illegal nor regulated by law. Despite their social stigma, taverns were popular places, for Mesopotamians were fond of beer and wine. Tavernkeepers made a nice profit, but if they were caught increasing their profits by watering drinks, they were drowned.

Because farming was essential to Mesopotamian life, Hammurabi's code dealt greatly with agriculture. Tenant farming was widespread, and tenants rented land on a yearly basis, paying a proportion of their crops as rent. Unless the land was carefully cultivated, it quickly reverted to wasteland. Thus tenants faced severe penalties for neglecting the land or not working it at all. Since irrigation was essential to grow crops, tenants had to keep the canals and ditches in good repair. Otherwise the land would be subject to floods and farmers to crippling losses. Anyone whose neglect of the canals resulted in damaged crops had to bear all the expense of the lost crops. A tenant who could not pay the costs was sold into slavery.

The oxen that farmers used for plowing and threshing grain were ordinarily allowed to roam the streets. If an ox gored a passer-by, its owner had to pad its horns, tie it up, or bear the responsibility for future damages. Sheep raising was very lucrative because textile production was a major Mesopotamian industry. (Mesopotamian cloth was famous throughout the Near East.) The shepherd was a hired man with considerable responsibility. He was expected to protect the flock from wild animals, which were a standing problem, and to keep the sheep out of the crops. This strict regulation of agriculture paid rich dividends. The Mesopotamians often enjoyed bumper crops of grain, which fostered a large and thriving population.

Hammurabi gave careful attention to marriage and the family. As elsewhere in the Near East, marriage had aspects of a business agreement. The prospective groom and the father of the future bride arranged everything. The man offered the father a bridal gift, usually money. If the man and his bridal gift were acceptable, the father provided his daughter with a dowry. After marriage the dowry belonged to the woman (although the husband normally administered it) and was a means of protecting her rights and status. Once the two men agreed on financial matters, they drew up a contract; no marriage was considered legal without one. Either party could break off the marriage, but not without paying a stiff penalty. Fathers often contracted marriages while their children were still young. The girl either continued to live in her father's house until she reached maturity or went to live in the house of her father-in-law. During this time she was legally considered a wife. Once she and her husband came of age, they set up their own house.

The wife was expected to be rigorously faithful. The penalty for adultery was death. According to Hammurabi's code: "If the wife of a man has been caught while lying with another man, they shall bind them and throw them into the water."[7] The husband had the power to spare his wife by obtaining a pardon for her from the king. He could, however, accuse his wife of adultery even if he had not caught her in the act. In such a case she could try to clear herself before the city council, which investigated the charge. If she was found innocent, she could take her dowry and leave her husband. If a woman decided to take the direct approach and kill her husband, she was impaled.

The husband had virtually absolute power over his household. He could even sell his wife and children into slavery to pay debts. Sons did not lightly oppose their fathers, and any son who struck his father could have his hand cut off. A father was free to adopt children and include them in his will. Artisans sometimes adopted children to teach them the family trade. Although the father's power was great, he could not disinherit a son without just cause. Cases of disinheritance became matters for the city to decide, and the code ordered the courts to forgive a son for his first offense. Only if a son wronged his father a second time could he be disinherited.

Hammurabi's law code centered on social problems; it provides a bleak view of things. Other Mesopotamian documents give a happier glimpse of life. Although the code dealt with marriage shekel by shekel, a Mesopotamian poem tells of two people meeting secretly in the city. Their parting is delightfully modern:

Come now, set me free, I must go home,
Kuli-Enlil . . . set me free, I must go home.
What can I say to deceive my mother?[8]

Countless wills and testaments show that husbands habitually left their estates to their wives, who in turn willed the property to their children. All this suggests happy family life. Hammurabi's code restricted married women from commercial pursuits, but financial documents prove that many women engaged in business without hindrance. Some carried on the family business; others became wealthy landowners in their own right. Mesopotamians found their lives lightened by holidays and religious festivals. Traveling merchants brought news of the outside world and swapped marvelous tales. Despite their pessimism the Mesopotamians enjoyed a vibrant and creative culture, a culture that left its mark on the entire Near East.

EGYPT, THE LAND OF THE PHARAOHS (3100–1200 B.C.)

The Greek historian and traveler Herodotus in the fifth century B.C. called Egypt the "gift of the Nile." No other single geographical factor had such a fundamental, profound impact on the shap-

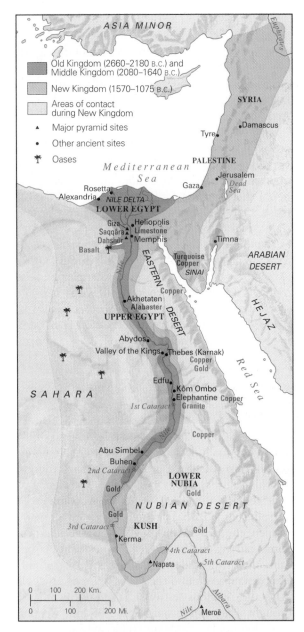

MAP 1.3 Ancient Egypt Geography and natural resources provided Egypt with centuries of peace and abundance.

areas, the Nile served to unify Egypt. The river was the principal highway and promoted easy communication throughout the valley. As individual bands of settlers moved into the Nile Valley, they created stable agricultural communities. By about 3100 B.C. there were some forty of these communities in constant contact with one another. This contact, encouraged and facilitated by the Nile, virtually ensured the early political unification of Egypt.

Egypt was fortunate in that it was nearly self-sufficient. Besides the fertility of its soil, Egypt possessed enormous quantities of stone, which served as the raw material of architecture and sculpture. Abundant clay was available for pottery, as was gold for jewelry and ornaments. The raw materials that Egypt lacked were close at hand. The Egyptians could obtain copper from Sinai and timber from Lebanon. They had little cause to look to the outside world for their essential needs, which helps to explain the insular quality of Egyptian life.

Geography further encouraged isolation by closing Egypt off from the outside world. To the east and west of the Nile Valley stretch grim deserts. The Nubian Desert and the cataracts of the Nile discourage penetration from the south. Only in the north does the Mediterranean Sea leave Egypt exposed. Thus geography shielded Egypt from invasion and from extensive immigration. Unlike the Mesopotamians, the Egyptians enjoyed centuries of peace and tranquillity during which they could devote most of their resources to the development of their distinctive civilization.

Yet Egypt was not completely sealed off. As early as 3250 B.C. Mesopotamian influences, notably architectural techniques and materials and perhaps even writing, made themselves felt in Egyptian life. Still later, from 1680 to 1580 B.C., northern Egypt was ruled by foreign invaders, the Hyksos. Infrequent though they were, such periods of foreign influence fertilized Egyptian culture without changing it in any fundamental way.

The God-King of Egypt

The geographical unity of Egypt quickly gave rise to political unification of the country under the authority of a king whom the Egyptians called "pharaoh." The details of this process have been lost. The Egyptians themselves told of a great

ing of Egyptian life, society, and history as the Nile (Map 1.3). Unlike the Tigris in Mesopotamia, it rarely brought death and destruction. The river was primarily a creative force. The Egyptians never feared the relatively tame Nile in the way the Mesopotamians feared the Tigris.

Whereas the Tigris and Euphrates and their tributaries carved up Mesopotamia into isolated

king, Menes, who united Egypt into a single kingdom around 3100 B.C. Thereafter the Egyptians divided their history into dynasties, or families of kings. For modern historical purposes, however, it is more useful to divide Egyptian history into periods (see page 31). The political unification of Egypt ushered in the period known as the "Old Kingdom," an era remarkable for prosperity, artistic flowering, and the evolution of religious beliefs.

In religion, the Egyptians developed complex, often contradictory ideas about an afterlife. These beliefs were all rooted in the environment itself. The climate of Egypt is so stable that change is cyclical and dependable: though the heat of summer bakes the land, the Nile always floods and replenishes it. The dry air preserves much that would decay in other climates. Thus there was an air of permanence about Egypt; the past was never far from the present.

This cyclical rhythm permeated Egyptian religious beliefs. According to the Egyptians, Osiris, a fertility god associated with the Nile, dies each year, and each year his wife Isis brings him back to life. Osiris eventually became king of the dead, weighing human beings' hearts to determine whether they had lived justly enough to deserve everlasting life. Osiris's care of the dead was shared by Anubis, the jackal-headed god who annually helped Isis resuscitate Osiris. Anubis was the god of mummification, so essential to Egyptian funerary rites.

The focal point of religious and political life in the Old Kingdom was the pharaoh, who commanded the wealth, resources, and people of all Egypt. The pharaoh's power was such that the

Narmer Palette   This ceremonial object celebrates the deeds of Narmer, but it also illustrates several of the attributes of the pharaoh in general. On left at top, the conquering pharaoh views the decapitated corpse of an unknown enemy, showing his duty to defend Egypt by defeating its enemies. This same theme recurs on the right where the pharaoh—also represented by the falcon, symbol of Horus—is about to kill a captive. *(Source: Jean Vertut)*

Egyptians considered him to be the falcon-god Horus in human form. The link between the pharaoh and the god Horus was doubly important. In Egyptian religion Horus was the son of Osiris (king of the dead), which meant that the pharaoh, a living god on earth, became one with Osiris after death. The pharaoh was not simply the mediator between the gods and the Egyptian people. He was the power that achieved the integration between gods and humans, between nature and society, that ensured peace and prosperity for the land of the Nile. The pharaoh was thus a guarantee to his people, a pledge that the gods of Egypt (unlike those of Mesopotamia) cared for their people.

The king's surroundings had to be worthy of a god. Only a magnificent palace was suitable for his home; in fact, the word *pharaoh* means "great house." The king's tomb also had to reflect his might and exalted status. To this day the great pyramids at Giza near Cairo bear silent but magnificent testimony to the god-kings of Egypt. The pharaoh's ability to command the resources and labor necessary to build a huge pyramid amply demonstrates that the god-king was an absolute ruler.

The religious significance of the pyramid is as awesome as the political. The pharaoh as a god was the earthly sun, and the pyramid, which towered to the sky, helped him ascend to the heavens after death. The pyramid provided the dead king with everything that he would need in the afterlife. His body had to be preserved from decay if his *ka,* an invisible counterpart of the body, was to survive. So the Egyptians developed an elaborate process of embalming the dead pharaoh and wrapping his corpse in cloth. As an added precaution, they carved his statue out of hard stone; if anything happened to the fragile mummy, the pharaoh's statue would help keep his ka alive. The need for an authentic likeness accounts for the naturalism of Egyptian portraiture. Artistic renderings of the pharaohs combine accuracy and the abstract in an effort to capture the essence of the living person. This approach produced the haunting quality of Egyptian sculpture—portraits of lifelike people imbued with a solemn, ageless, serene spirit.

To survive in the spirit world, the ka required everything that the pharaoh needed in life: food and drink, servants and armed retainers, costly ornaments, and animal herds. In Egypt's prehistoric period, the king's servants and herdsmen and their flocks were slaughtered at the tomb to provide for the ka. By the time of the Old Kingdom, artists had substituted statues of scribes, officials, soldiers, and servants for their living counterparts. To remind the ka of daily life, artists covered the walls of the tomb with scenes ranging from agricultural routines to banquets and religious festivities, from hunting parties to gardens and ponds. Designed to give joy to the ka, these paintings, models of furniture, and statuettes today provide an intimate glimpse of Egyptian life 4,500 years ago.

The Pharaoh's People

Because the common folk stood at the bottom of the social and economic scale, they were always at the mercy of grasping officials. The arrival of the tax collector was never a happy occasion. One Egyptian scribe described the worst consequences of such a visit:

And now the scribe lands on the river-bank and is about to register the harvest-tax. The janitors carry staves and the Nubians rods of palm, and they say, Hand over the corn, though there is none. The cultivator is beaten all over, he is bound and thrown into a well, soused and dipped head downwards. His wife has been bound in his presence and his children are in fetters.[9]

That was an extreme situation. Nonetheless, taxes might amount to 20 percent of the harvest, and tax collection could be brutal.

On the other hand, everyone, no matter how lowly, had the right of appeal, and the account of one such appeal, "The Tale of the Eloquent Peasant," was a favorite Egyptian story. The hero of the tale, Khunanup, was robbed by the servant of the high steward, and Khunanup had to bring his case before the steward himself. When the steward delayed his decision, Khunanup openly accused him of neglecting his duty, saying, "The arbitrator is a spoiler; the peace-maker is a creator of sorrow; the smoother over of differences is a creator of soreness."[10] The pharaoh himself ordered the steward to give Khunanup justice, and the case was decided in the peasant's favor.

Egyptian society seems to have been a curious mixture of freedom and constraint. Slavery did not become widespread until the New Kingdom. There was neither a caste system nor a color bar, and humble people could rise to the highest posi-

The Pyramids at Giza   Giza was the burial place of the pharaohs of the Old Kingdom and of their aristocracy, whose rectangular tombs are visible behind the middle pyramid. The small pyramids at the foot of the foremost pyramid probably belong to the pharaohs' wives. *(Source: Geoffrey Clifford/Woodfin Camp)*

tions if they possessed talent. The most famous example of social mobility (which, however, dates to the New Kingdom) is the biblical story of Joseph, who came to Egypt as a slave and rose to be second only to the pharaoh. Most ordinary folk, however, were probably little more than serfs who could not easily leave the land of their own free will. Peasants were also subject to forced labor, including work on the pyramids and canals. Young men were drafted into the pharaoh's army, which served both as a fighting force and as a labor corps.

The Egyptian view of life and society is alien to those raised on the concepts of individual freedom and human rights. To ancient Egyptians the pharaoh embodied justice and order—harmony among humans, nature, and the divine. If the pharaoh was weak or allowed anyone to challenge his unique position, he opened the way to chaos. Twice in Egyptian history the pharaoh failed to maintain rigid centralization. During these two eras, known as the "First and Second Intermediate periods," Egypt was exposed to civil war and invasion. Yet even in the darkest times the monarchy survived,

and in each period a strong pharaoh arose to crush the rebels or expel the invaders and restore order.

The Hyksos in Egypt (1640–1570 B.C.)

While Egyptian civilization flourished behind its bulwark of sand and sea, momentous changes were taking place in the ancient Near East, changes that would leave their mark even on rich, insular Egypt. These changes involved enormous and remarkable movements, especially of peoples who spoke Semitic tongues.

The original home of the Semites was probably the Arabian peninsula. Some tribes moved into northern Mesopotamia, others into Syria and Palestine, and still others into Egypt. By 1640 B.C., people whom the Egyptians called *Hyksos*, which means "Rulers of the Uplands," began to settle in the Nile Delta. Egyptian tradition, as later recorded by the priest Manetho in the third century B.C., depicted the coming of the Hyksos as a brutal invasion:

Although the Egyptians portrayed the Hyksos as a conquering horde, they were probably no more than nomads looking for good land. Their entry into the delta was probably gradual and generally peaceful. The Hyksos "invasion" was one of the fertilizing periods of Egyptian history; it introduced new ideas and techniques into Egyptian life. The Hyksos brought with them the method of making bronze and casting it into tools and weapons that became standard in Egypt. They thereby brought Egypt fully into the Bronze Age culture of the Mediterranean world, a culture in which the production and use of bronze implements became basic to society. Bronze tools made farming more efficient than ever before because they were sharper and more durable than the copper tools they replaced. The Hyksos' use of bronze armor and weapons as well as horse-drawn chariots and the composite bow, made of laminated wood and horn and far more powerful than the simple wooden bow, revolutionized Egyptian warfare. However much the Egyptians learned from the Hyksos, Egyptian culture eventually absorbed the newcomers. The Hyksos came to worship Egyptian gods and modeled their monarchy on the pharaoh's.

The New Kingdom: Revival and Empire (1570–1200 B.C.)

Politically, Egypt was only in eclipse. The Egyptian sun shone again when a remarkable line of kings, the pharaohs of the Eighteenth Dynasty, arose to challenge the Hyksos. The pharaoh Ahmose (1558–1533 B.C.) pushed the Hyksos out of the delta. Thutmose I (1512–1500 B.C.) subdued Nubia in the south, and Thutmose III (1490–1436 B.C.) conquered Palestine and Syria and fought inconclusively with the Hurrians, who had migrated into the upper Euphrates from the north and created there the kingdom of Mitanni. These warrior-pharaohs inaugurated the New Kingdom—a period in Egyptian history characterized by enormous wealth and conscious imperialism. During this period, probably for the first time, widespread slavery became a feature of Egyptian life. The pharaoh's armies returned home leading hordes of slaves, who constituted a new labor force for imperial building projects. The Hebrews, who according to the Old Testament migrated into Egypt during this period to escape a

Hippopotamus Hunt   This wall painting depicts the success of two men in a small boat who have killed a hippopotamus, seen in the lower right-hand corner. Behind the hippopotamus swims a crocodile hoping for a snack. *(Source: Egyptian Museum SMPK, Berlin/Bildarchiv Preussischer Kulturbesitz)*

In the reign of Toutimaios—I do not know why—the wind of god blew against us. Unexpectedly from the regions of the east men of obscure race, looking forward confidently to victory, invaded our land, and without a battle easily seized it all by sheer force. Having subdued those in authority in the land, they then barbarously burned our cities and razed to the ground the temples of the gods. They fell upon all the natives in an entirely hateful fashion, slaughtering them and leading both their children and wives into slavery. At last they made one of their people king, whose name was Salitis. This man resided at Memphis, leaving in Upper and Lower Egypt tax collectors and garrisons in strategic places.[11]

PERIODS OF EGYPTIAN HISTORY

Period	Dates	Significant Events
Archaic	3100–2660 B.C.	Unification of Egypt
Old Kingdom	2660–2180 B.C.	Construction of the pyramids
First Intermediate	2180–2080 B.C.	Political chaos
Middle Kingdom	2080–1640 B.C.	Recovery and political stability
Second Intermediate	1640–1570 B.C.	Hyksos "invasion"
New Kingdom	1570–1075 B.C.	Creation of an Egyptian empire
		Akhenaten's religious policy

drought, were soon enslaved and put to work on imperial construction projects.

The kings of the Eighteenth Dynasty created the first Egyptian empire. They ruled Palestine and Syria through their officers and incorporated the African region of Nubia. Egyptian religion and customs flourished in Nubia, making a huge impact on African culture there and in neighboring areas. The warrior-kings celebrated their success with monuments on a scale unparalleled since the pharaohs of the Old Kingdom had built the pyramids. Even today the colossal granite statues of these pharaohs and the rich tomb objects of Tutankhamen ("King Tut") testify to the might and splendor of the New Kingdom.

Akhenaten and Monotheism

One of the most extraordinary of this unusual line of kings was Akhenaten (1367–1350 B.C.), a pharaoh concerned more with religion than with conquest. Nefertiti, his wife and queen, encouraged his religious bent. The precise nature of Akhenaten's religious beliefs remains debatable. During his own lifetime his religion was often unpopular among the people and the traditional priesthood, and its practice declined in the later years of his reign. After his death, it was condemned and denounced; consequently, not much is known about it. Most historians, however, agree that Akhenaten and Nefertiti were *monotheists*—that is, they believed that the sun-god Aton, whom they worshiped, was universal, the only god. They consid-

ered all other Egyptian gods and goddesses frauds and disregarded their worship.

The religious notions and actions of Akhenaten and Nefertiti were in direct opposition to traditional Egyptian beliefs. The Egyptians had long worshiped a host of gods, chief among whom was Amon-Re. Originally Amon and Re had been two distinct sun-gods, but the Egyptians merged them and worshiped Amon-Re as the king of the gods. Besides Amon-Re, the Egyptians honored such other deities as Osiris, Osiris's wife Isis, and his son Horus. Egyptian religion had room for many gods and an easy tolerance for new gods.

To these genuine religious sentiments were added the motives of the traditional priesthood. Although many priests were genuinely scandalized by Akhenaten's monotheism, many others were concerned more about their own welfare. What were the priests of the outlawed gods to do? Akhenaten had destroyed their livelihood and their reason for existence. On grounds of pure self-interest, the established priesthood opposed the pharaoh. Opposition in turn drove Akhenaten to intolerance and persecution. With a vengeance he tried to root out the old gods and their rituals.

Akhenaten celebrated his break with the past by building a new capital, Akhetaten, the modern El-Amarna (see Map 1.3). There Aton was honored with an immense temple and proper worship. Worship of Aton focused on truth (as Akhenaten defined it) and a desire for the natural. The pharaoh and his queen demanded that the truth be carried over into art. Unlike Old Kingdom painting and sculpture, which blended the actual and the abstract, the art of this period became relentlessly realistic. Sculptors molded exact likenesses of Akhenaten, despite his ugly features and misshapen body. Artists portrayed the pharaoh in intimate family scenes, playing with his infant daughter or expressing affection to members of his family. On one relief Akhenaten appears gnawing a cutlet of meat; on another he lolls in a chair. Akhenaten was being portrayed as a mortal man, not as the dignified pharaoh of Egypt.

Akhenaten's monotheism was imposed from above and failed to find a place among the people. The prime reason for Akhenaten's failure is that his god had no connection with the past of the Egyptian people, who trusted the old gods and felt comfortable praying to them. Average Egyptians were no doubt distressed and disheartened when their familiar gods were outlawed, for they were the heavenly powers that had made Egypt powerful and unique. The fanaticism and persecution that accompanied the new monotheism were in complete defiance of the Egyptian tradition of tolerant *polytheism,* or worship of several gods. Thus, when Akhenaten died, his religion died with him.

THE HITTITE EMPIRE

At about the time the Hyksos entered the Nile Delta, other parts of the Near East were also troubled by the arrival of newcomers. Two new groups of peoples, the Hurrians and Kassites, carved out kingdoms for themselves. Meanwhile the Hittites, who had long been settled in Anatolia (modern Turkey), became a major power in that region and began to expand eastward (Map 1.4). Around 1595 B.C. a century and a half after Hammurabi's death, the Hittites and the Kassites brought down the Babylonian kingdom and established Kassite rule there. The Hurrians created the kingdom of Mitanni on the upper reaches of the Euphrates and Tigris.

The Hittites were an Indo-European people. The term *Indo-European* refers to a large family of languages that includes English, most of the languages of modern Europe, Greek, Latin, Persian, and Sanskrit, the sacred tongue of ancient India. During the eighteenth and nineteenth centuries, European scholars learned that peoples who spoke related languages had spread as far west as Ireland and as far east as central Asia. In the twentieth century, linguists deciphered the language of the Hittites and the Linear B script of Mycenaean Greece. When both languages proved to be Indo-European, scholars were able to form a clearer picture of these vast movements. Archeologists were able to date the migrations roughly and put them into their historical context.

Despite the efforts of many scholars, the original home of the Indo-Europeans remains to be identified. Judging primarily from the spread of the languages, linguists have suggested that the migrations started from the steppes region north of the Black and Caspian seas. Although two great waves began around 2000 B.C. and 1200 B.C., these

The Goddess Selket Selket appears in this statuette dressed as a queen. The goddess was originally a water scorpion who later assumed human form. She was the goddess who healed stings and bites. *(Source: Egyptian Museum, Cairo/Lee Boltin)*

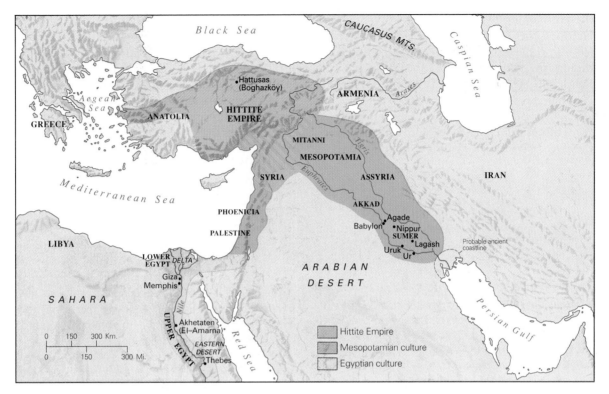

MAP 1.4 Balance of Power in the Near East   This map shows the regions controlled by the Hittites and Egyptians at the height of their power. The striped area represents the part of Mesopotamia conquered by the Hittites during their expansion eastward.

migrations on the whole followed a sporadic and gradual progression. The Celtic-speaking Gauls, for example, did not move into the area of present-day France, Belgium, and Germany until the seventh century B.C., long after most Indo-Europeans had found new homes.

Around 2000 B.C. Indo-Europeans were on the move on a massive scale. Peoples speaking the ancestor of Latin pushed into Italy, and Greek-speaking Mycenaeans settled in Greece. The Hittites came into prominence in Anatolia (modern Turkey), and other folk thrust into Iran, India, and central Asia. At first the waves of Indo-Europeans and other peoples disrupted already existing states, but in time the newcomers settled down.

The Rise of the Hittites

Until recently, scholars thought that as part of these vast movements the Hittites entered Anatolia only around 1800 B.C. Current archeological work and new documents, however, prove that the Hittites had settled there at least as early as 2700

B.C. Nor did they overrun the country in a sweeping invasion, burning, looting, and destroying. Their arrival and diffusion seem to have been rather peaceful, accompanied by intermarriage and alliance with the natives. So well did the Hittites integrate themselves into the local culture of central Anatolia that they even adopted the worship of several native deities.

Their mastery of iron technology set the Hittites apart. Although it is not yet known whether the Hittites were first to discover the possibilities of iron and the ways to use it, they mastered iron technology before anyone else in the Near East. Their knowledge permitted them to craft weapons and tools far superior to those of their neighbors, which gave them a decided advantage in both war and commerce.

Although much uncertainty still surrounds the earliest history of the Hittites, their rise to prominence in Anatolia is well documented. During the nineteenth century B.C. the native kingdoms in the area engaged in warfare that left most of Anatolia's once-flourishing towns in ashes and rubble. Taking advantage of this climate of exhaustion, the Hittite king Hattusilis I built a hill citadel at Hattusas, the modern Boghazköy, from which he led his people against neighboring kingdoms. Although the Hittites extended their arms as far as Babylon, where they snuffed out the dynasty of Hammurabi, they were themselves vulnerable to attack by vigilant and tenacious enemies. Yet once the Hittites were united behind a strong king, they were a power with which to be reckoned.

Hittite Society

The geography of central Anatolia encouraged the rise of self-contained agricultural communities. Each group was probably originally ruled by a

The Hittite God Atarluhas This statue of the god Atarluhas, with two lions at his feet, was set up near the gateway of the Hittite city of Carchemish. A bird-headed demon holds the lions. In 1920 this statue was destroyed during a war between Turkey and Syria. *(Source: Courtesy of the Trustees of the British Museum)*

petty king, but under the Hittites local officials known as "Elders" handled community affairs. Besides the farming population, a well-defined group of artisans fashioned the pottery, cloth, leather goods, and metal tools needed by society. Documents also report that traveling merchants peddled goods and gossip, reminding individual communities that they were part of a larger world. As in many other societies, ancient and modern, the Hittites held slaves, who nonetheless enjoyed certain rights under the law.

At the head of Hittite society stood the king and queen. The king was supreme commander of the army, chief judge, and supreme priest. He carried on all diplomatic dealings with foreign powers and in times of war personally led the Hittite army into the field. The queen, who was highly regarded, held a strong, independent position. She had important religious duties to perform, and some queens even engaged in diplomatic correspondence with foreign queens.

Below the king and queen was the aristocracy, among whom the relatives of the king constituted a privileged group. The king's relations were a mighty and often unruly group who served as the chief royal administrators. The royal family was often a threat to the king, for some members readily resorted to murder as a method of seizing power. Hittite nobles often revolted against the king, thereby weakening central authority and leaving Hittite society open to outside attack. At the base of society stood the warriors, who had the right to meet in their own assembly, the *pankus*. The pankus met to hear the will of the king but could not vote on policy. It was, however, a court of law, with the authority to punish criminals.

The Hittites, like many newcomers to the ancient Near East, readily assimilated the cultures that they found, such as Anatolia's. Soon they fell under the powerful spell of the superior Mesopotamian culture. The Hittites adopted the cuneiform script for their own language. Hittite kings published law codes, just as Hammurabi had done. Royal correspondence followed Mesopotamian form. The Hittites delighted in Mesopotamian myths, legends, and epics. Of Hittite art, one scholar has observed that "there is hardly a single Hittite monument which somewhere does not show traces of Mesopotamian influence."[12] To the credit of the Hittites, they used these Mesopotamian borrowings to create something of their own.

The Era of Hittite Greatness
(ca 1475–ca 1200 B.C.)

The Hittites, like the Egyptians of the New Kingdom, eventually produced an energetic and capable line of kings who restored order and rebuilt Hittite power. Once Telepinus (1525–1500 B.C.) had brought the aristocracy under control, Suppiluliumas I (1380–1346 B.C.) secured central Anatolia, and Mursilis II (1345–1315 B.C.) regained Syria. Around 1300 B.C. Mursilis's son stopped the Egyptian army of Rameses II at the battle of Kadesh in Syria. Having fought each other to a standstill, the Hittites and Egyptians first made peace, then an alliance. Alliance was followed by friendship; friendship, by active cooperation. The two greatest powers of the early Near East tried to make war between themselves impossible.

The Hittites exercised remarkable political wisdom and flexibility in the organization and administration of their empire. Some states they turned into vassal-kingdoms, ruled by the sons of the Hittite king; the king and his sons promised each other mutual support in times of crisis. Still other kingdoms were turned into protectorates, where native kings were allowed to rule with considerable freedom. The native kings swore obedience to the Hittite king and had to contribute military contingents to the Hittite army. Although they also sent tribute to the Hittites, the financial burden was moderate. The common people probably felt Hittite overlordship little if at all.

Although the Hittites were often at war, owing to the sheer number of enemies surrounding them, they did seek diplomatic and political solutions to their problems. They were realistic enough to recognize the limits of their power and far-sighted enough to appreciate the value of peace and alliance with Egypt. Together the two kingdoms provided much of the ancient Near East with a precious interlude of peace. Unfortunately, however, both were seriously weakened in the process.

THE FALL OF EMPIRES (1200 B.C.)

This stable and generally peaceful situation endured until the cataclysm of the thirteenth century B.C., when both the Hittite and the Egyptian empires were destroyed by invaders. The most famous

Temple of Rameses II These colossal statues of Rameses II, carved literally out of the side of a hill, guard the entrance of a temple itself created by tunneling through rock. The statues of the last great pharaoh measure about 40 feet in height. *(Source: Geoffrey Clifford/Woodfin Camp)*

of these marauders, called the "Sea Peoples" by the Egyptians, remains one of the puzzles of ancient history. Despite much new work, modern archeology is still unable to identify the Sea Peoples satisfactorily. It is known, however, that they were part of a larger movement of peoples. Although there is serious doubt about whether the Sea Peoples alone overthrew the Hittites, they did deal both the Hittites and the Egyptians a hard blow, making the Hittites vulnerable to overland invasion from the north and driving the Egyptians back to the Nile Delta. The Hittites fell under the external blows, but the Egyptians, shaken and battered, retreated to the delta and held on.

In 1200 B.C. as earlier, both Indo-European and Semitic-speaking peoples were on the move. They brought down the old centers of power and won new homes for themselves. In Mesopotamia the Assyrians destroyed the kingdom of Mitanni and struggled with the Kassites; the Hebrews moved into Palestine; and another wave of Indo-Europeans penetrated Anatolia. But once again these victories were political and military, not cultural. The old cultures—especially that of Mesopotamia—impressed their ideas, values, and ideals on the newcomers. Although the chaos of the thirteenth century B.C. caused a serious material decline throughout the ancient Near East, the old cultures lived on through a dark age.

Although the societies of the Near East suffered stunning blows in the thirteenth century B.C., more persisted than perished. The great achievements of Mesopotamia and Egypt survived to enhance the lives of those who came after.

NOTES

1. L. Eiseley, *The Unexpected Universe* (New York: Harcourt Brace Jovanovich, 1969), p. 102.
2. Quoted in S. N. Kramer, *The Sumerians* (Chicago: University of Chicago Press, 1964), p. 238.
3. J. B. Pritchard, ed., *Ancient Near Eastern Texts,* 3d ed. (Princeton: Princeton University Press, 1969), p. 175. Hereafter called *ANET.*
4. *ANET,* p. 44.
5. *ANET,* p. 590.
6. Kramer, *The Sumerians,* p. 150.
7. *ANET,* p. 171.
8. Kramer, *The Sumerians,* p. 251.
9. Quoted in A. H. Gardiner, "Ramesside Texts Relating to the Taxation and Transport of Corn," *Journal of Egyptian Archaeology* 27 (1941): 19–20.
10. A. H. Gardiner, "The Eloquent Peasant," *Journal of Egyptian Archaeology* 9 (1923): 17.
11. Manetho, *History of Egypt,* frag. 42.75–77.
12. M. Vieyra, *Hittite Art 2300–750 B.C.* (London: Alec Tiranti, 1955), p. 12.

SUMMARY

During the long span of years covered by this chapter, human beings made astonishing strides, advancing from primitive hunters to become builders of sophisticated civilizations. Four great rivers provided the natural conditions necessary to sustain settled life. Yet because the rivers presented different problems to different peoples, developments across the globe were not identical. By mastering the plant and animal worlds, human beings prospered dramatically. With their basic bodily needs more than satisfied, they realized even greater achievements, including more complex social groupings, metal technology, and long-distance trade. The intellectual achievements of these centuries were equally impressive. Ancient Near Eastern peoples created advanced mathematics, monumental architecture, and engaging literature.

SUGGESTED READING

Those interested in the tangled and incomplete story of human evolution will be rewarded by a good deal of new work, much of it difficult. C. E. Oxnard, *Fossils, Teeth and Sex* (1987), uses current information to conclude that the very search for the "missing link" is the wrong approach. R. Singer and J. K. Lundy, *Variation, Culture and Evolution in African Populations* (1986)—especially chap. 16—discusses recent developments in Africa. C. Gamble, *The Palaeolithic Settlement of Europe* (1986), covers both methodology and recent finds to offer a new interpretation of how early peoples spread through Europe. I. Rouse, *Migrations in Prehistory* (1989), uses information from cultural remains to study population movements. A much broader book is T. C. Champion et al., *Prehistoric Europe* (1984). See also G. Lerner, *The Creation of Patriarchy* (1986), for recent findings of anthropologists. F. Dahlberg, *Woman the Gatherer* (1981), demonstrates the importance for primitive societies of women's role in gathering. A broader and newer study is M. Ehrenberg, *Women in Prehistory* (1989). A study of how primitive peoples depended on both hunting and gathering for survival is provided by T. D. Price and J. A. Brown, *Prehistoric Hunter-Gatherers* (1985), which also studies how hunting and gathering led to a more complex culture.

The origins of agriculture and the Neolithic Age have recently received a great deal of attention. J. R. Harlan's conclusions are set out in a series of works including "Agricultural Origins: Centers and Noncenters," *Science* 174 (1971): 468–474; *Crops and Man* (1975); and "The Plants and Animals That Nourish Man," *Scientific American* 235 (September 1976): 89; F. Wendorf and R. Schild, "The Earliest Food Producers," *Archaeology* 34 (September–October 1981): 30–36.

G. Barker, *Prehistoric Farming in Europe* (1984), and P. S. Wells, *Farms, Villages and Cities* (1984), treat the problem of commerce and urban origins in late prehistoric Europe. A very readable study, A. Ferrill, *The Origins of War* (1985), treats the topic of warfare from the Neolithic Age to Alexander the Great. Ferrill makes the interesting suggestion that more organized methods of warfare influenced the trend toward urbanization.

For the societies of Mesopotamia, see A. Leo Oppenheim, *Ancient Mesopotamia,* rev. ed. (1977); M. E. L. Mallowan, *Early Mesopotamia and Iran* (1965); and H. W. F. Saggs, *The Greatness That Was Babylon* (1962). H. W. F. Saggs, *Everyday Life in Babylonia and Assyria* (1965), offers a delightful glimpse of Mesopotamian life. S. Dalley, ed., *Myths from Mesopotamia* (1989), is a good translation of such prevailing myths as the Creation, the Flood, Gilgamesh, and many others. The best recent synthesis of the finds at Ebla can be found in G. Pettinato, *Ebla* (1991); the author has been a participant in the excavations since their beginnings.

C. B. Kemp, *Ancient Egypt: Anatomy of a Civilization* (1988), is a comprehensive reassessment of Egyptian society. D. B. Redford, *Akhenaten: The Heretic King* (1984), puts Akhenaten into his historical context, both political and religious. B. S. Lesko, *The Remarkable Women of Ancient Egypt,* 2d ed. (1987), a brief survey of aristocratic and ordinary women, concludes that Egyptian women led freer lives than the women of the Greco-Roman period. The title of L. Manniche, *Sexual Life in Ancient Egypt* (1987), aptly describes the book's subject. J. M. White, *Everyday Life in Ancient Egypt* (1963), provides a broad survey of Egyptian society. M. Lichtheim, *Ancient Egyptian Literature,* 3 vols. (1975–1980), is a selection of readings covering the most important periods of Egyptian history. D. B. Red-

ford, *Akhenaton* (1987), with illustrations, offers the most recent assessment of this complex pharaoh.

Introductions to problems and developments shared by several Near Eastern societies can be found in the studies edited by T. A. Wertime and J. D. Muhly, *The Coming of the Age of Iron* (1980), as well as in J. B. Pritchard, *The Ancient Near East,* 2 vols. (1958, 1976). The latter work is a fine synthesis by one of the world's leading Near Eastern specialists. A sweeping survey is C. Burney, *The Ancient Near East* (1977). Pioneering new work on the origins of writing appears in a series of pieces by D. Schmandt-Besserat, notably "An Archaic Recording System and the Origin of Writing," *Syro-Mesopotamian Studies* 1–2 (1977): 1–32, and "Reckoning Before Writing," *Archaeology* 32 (May–June 1979): 23–31.

O. R. Gurney, *The Hittites,* 2d ed. (1954), is still a fine introduction by an eminent scholar. Good also is J. G. MacQueen, *The Hittites and Their Contemporaries in Asia Minor,* 2d ed. (1986). J. P. Mallory, *In Search of the Indo-Europeans* (1989), uses language, archeology, and myth to study the Indo-Europeans. The 1960s were prolific years for archeology in Turkey. A brief survey by one of the masters of the field is J. Mellaart, *The Archaeology of Modern Turkey* (1978), which also tests a great number of widely held historical interpretations. The Sea Peoples have been the subject of two recent studies: A. Nibbi, *The Sea Peoples and Egypt* (1975), and N. K. Sandars, *The Sea Peoples* (1978).

A truly excellent study of ancient religions, from those of Sumer to those of the late Roman Empire, is M. Eliade, ed., *Religions of Antiquity* (1989), which treats concisely but amply all of the religions mentioned in Chapters 1 through 6. For Near Eastern religion and mythology, good introductions are E. O. James, *The Ancient Gods: The History and Diffusion of Religion in the Ancient Near East and the Eastern Mediterranean* (1960), and J. Gray, *Near Eastern Mythology* (1969). A survey of Mesopotamian religion by one of the foremost scholars in the field is T. Jacobsen, *The Treasures of Darkness: A History of Mesopotamian Religion* (1976).

Surveys of Near Eastern art include R. D. Barnett and D. J. Wiseman, *Fifty Masterpieces of Ancient Near Eastern Art* (1969); and J. B. Pritchard, *The Ancient Near East in Pictures,* 2d ed. (1969). For literature, see S. Fiore, *Voices from the Clay: The Development of Assyro-Babylonian Literature* (1965); W. K. Simpson, ed., *The Literature of Ancient Egypt* (1973); and, above all, J. B. Pritchard, ed., *Ancient Near Eastern Texts,* 3d ed. (1969).

2

Small Kingdoms and Mighty Empires in the Near East

Audience hall of King Darius, Persepolis

The migratory invasions that brought down the Hittites and stunned the Egyptians in the late thirteenth century B.C. ushered in an era of confusion and weakness. Although much was lost in the chaos, the old cultures of the ancient Near East survived to nurture new societies. In the absence of powerful empires, the Phoenicians, Syrians, Hebrews, and many other peoples carved out small independent kingdoms. During this period Hebrew culture and religion evolved under the influence of urbanism, kings, and prophets.

In the ninth century B.C. this jumble of small states gave way to an empire that for the first time embraced the entire Near East. Yet the ferocity of the Assyrian Empire led to its downfall only two hundred years later. In 550 B.C. the Persians and Medes, who had migrated into Iran, created a vast empire stretching from Anatolia in the west to the Indus Valley in the east. For over two hundred years the Persians gave the ancient Near East peace and stability.

- How did Egypt, its political greatness behind it, pass on its cultural heritage to its African neighbors?

- How did the Hebrew state evolve, and what was daily life like in Hebrew society?

- What forces helped to shape Hebrew religious thought, still powerfully influential in today's world?

- What enabled the Assyrians to overrun their neighbors, and how did their cruelty finally cause their undoing?

- How did Iranian nomads create the Persian Empire?

In this chapter we seek answers to these questions.

MIGRATIONS

The migrations of peoples on a huge scale during this period were merely a single aspect of a larger picture of human movement that has continued over the course of history, from the Paleolithic Age to the present day. Just as Indo-European and Semitic-speaking peoples sought new land around 1200 B.C., so in the nineteenth and twentieth centuries peoples from Europe and Asia came to North America seeking new opportunities for a more prosperous life. In antiquity, however, the picture is especially complex and the reasons for movement are varied and unclear. The Hyksos moved into Egypt looking for new land (see pages 29–30). The later onslaught of the Sea Peoples on Egypt seems more like random raids than migrations, even though many of the Sea Peoples established permanent homes elsewhere in the Mediterranean (pages 35–36). The Hebrews left Egypt to escape a harsh government (pages 43–44). In short, one major reason for migrations is poverty of the environment, sometimes combined with overpopulation, which forces people to seek better land. Another is the reaction to such vast movements. Weaker folk were pushed ahead of the newcomers and sought new homes elsewhere. In the process, they created for others the same problems and challenges that they themselves confronted. Still other migrants simply tried to escape cruel or oppressive governments to find a place of their own. In many instances several or all of these factors lay behind the migrations. Each case must be studied individually.

The effects of migrations are as varied as the reasons for them. In these instances, the various peoples involved assimilated aspects of the others' culture. Some newcomers, like the Hyksos and the Hittites, who came peaceably, drew important lessons from the established peoples whom they encountered and contributed something of their own to the cultural environment. In the process, both the new arrivals and the native inhabitants found their cultures mutually but differently enriched. Other migrations resulted in the obliteration of the native population so that some peoples are known today only by name. No one has yet studied this vast historical phenomenon on its own massive scale, but it can be safely said that many of these migrations were a combination of destruction and fertilization. Intellectually and socially enriched cultures often grew out of them.

EGYPT, A SHATTERED KINGDOM

An example of the complexities involved in large movements of peoples comes from the invasions that ended the Hittite Empire and from the Sea Peoples' onslaught on Egypt. The invasions of the Sea Peoples brought the great days of Egyptian power to an end. One scribe left behind a somber portrait of Egypt stunned and leaderless:

The land of Egypt was abandoned and every man was a law to himself. During many years there was no leader who could speak for others. Central government lapsed, small officials and headmen took over the whole land. Any man, great or small, might kill his neighbor. In the distress and vacuum that followed . . . men banded together to plunder one another. They treated the gods no better than men, and cut off the temple revenues.[1]

No longer able to dream of foreign conquests, Egypt looked to its own security from foreign invasion. Egyptians suffered a four-hundred-year period of political fragmentation, a new dark age known to Egyptian specialists as the Third Intermediate Period (eleventh to seventh centuries B.C.).

The decline of Egypt was especially sharp in foreign affairs. Whereas the pharaohs of the Eighteenth Dynasty had held sway as far abroad as Syria, their weak successors found it unsafe to venture far from home. In the wake of the Sea Peoples, numerous small kingdoms sprang up in the Near East, each fiercely protective of its own independence. To them Egypt was a memory, and foreign princes often greeted Egyptian officials with suspicion or even contempt. In the days of Egypt's greatness, petty kings would never have dared to treat Egyptian officials in such a humiliating fashion.

Disrupted at home and powerless abroad, Egypt fell prey to invasion by its African neighbors. Libyans from North Africa filtered into the Nile Delta, where they established independent dynasties. Indeed, from 950 to 730 B.C. northern Egypt was ruled by Libyan pharaohs. The Libyans built cities, and for the first time a sturdy urban life grew up in the delta. Although the coming of the Libyans changed the face of the delta, the Libyans genuinely admired Egyptian culture and eagerly adopted Egypt's religion and way of life.

In southern Egypt, meanwhile, the pharaoh's decline opened the way to the energetic Africans of Nubia, who extended their authority northward throughout the Nile Valley. Nubian influence in these years, though pervasive, was not destructive. Since the imperial days of the Eighteenth Dynasty (see pages 30–32), the Nubians, too, had adopted many features of Egyptian culture. Now Nubian kings and aristocrats embraced Egyptian culture wholesale. The thought of destroying the heritage of the pharaohs would have struck them as stupid and barbaric. Thus the Nubians and the Libyans repeated an old phenomenon: new peoples conquered old centers of political and military power but were nevertheless assimilated into the older culture.

The reunification of Egypt occurred late and unexpectedly. With Egypt distracted and disorganized by foreign invasions, an independent African state, the Kingdom of Kush, grew up in modern Sudan with its capital at Nepata. These Africans, too, worshiped Egyptian gods and used Egyptian hieroglyphs. In the eighth century B.C. their king Piankhy swept through the entire Nile Valley from Nepata in the south to the delta in the north. United once again, Egypt enjoyed a brief period of peace during which Egyptians continued to assimilate their conquerors. In the Kingdom of Kush, Egyptian methods of administration and bookkeeping, arts and crafts, and economic practices became common, especially among the aristocracy. Nonetheless, reunification of the realm did not lead to a new Egyptian empire. In the centuries between the fall of the New Kingdom and the recovery of Egypt, several small but vigorous kingdoms had taken root and grown to maturity in the ancient Near East. By 700 B.C. Egypt was once again a strong kingdom but no longer a mighty empire.

Yet Egypt's legacy to its African neighbors remained vibrant and rich. By trading and exploring southward along the coast of the Red Sea, the Egyptians introduced their goods and ideas as far south as the land of Punt, probably a region on the Somali coast. As early as the New Kingdom, Egyptian pharaohs had exchanged gifts with the monarchs of Punt, and contact between the two areas persisted. Egypt was the primary civilizing force in Nubia, which became another version of the pharaoh's realm, complete with royal pyramids and Egyptian deities. Egyptian religion penetrated as far south as Ethiopia. Just as Mesopotamian culture enjoyed wide appeal throughout the Near East, so Egyptian culture had a massive impact on northeastern Africa.

THE CHILDREN OF ISRAEL AND THEIR NEIGHBORS

The fall of the Hittite Empire and Egypt's collapse created a vacuum of power in the Near East that allowed for the rise of numerous small states. No longer crushed between the Hittites in the north and the Egyptians in the south, various peoples—some of them newcomers—created homes and petty kingdoms in Syria, Phoenicia, and Palestine. After the Sea Peoples had raided Egypt, a branch of them, known in the Bible as Philistines, settled along the coast of modern Israel (Map 2.1). Establishing themselves in five cities somewhat inland from the sea, the Philistines set about farming and raising flocks.

MAP 2.1 Small Kingdoms in the Near East   This map illustrates the political fragmentation of the Near East after the great wave of invasions that occurred during the thirteenth century B.C.

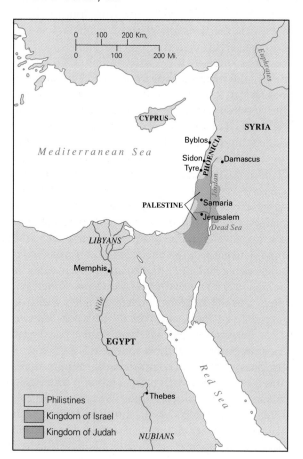

Another sturdy new culture was that of the Phoenicians, a Semitic-speaking people who had long inhabited several cities along the coast of modern Lebanon. They had lived under the shadow of the Hittites and Egyptians, but in this period the Phoenicians enjoyed full independence. Unlike the Philistine newcomers, who turned from seafaring to farming, the Phoenicians took to the sea and became outstanding merchants and explorers. In trading ventures they sailed as far west as modern Tunisia, where in 813 B.C. they founded the city of Carthage, which would one day struggle with Rome for domination of the western Mediterranean. Phoenician culture was urban, based on the prosperous commercial centers of Tyre, Sidon, and Byblos. The Phoenicians' overwhelming cultural achievement was the development of an alphabet: they, unlike other literate peoples, used one letter to designate one sound and vastly simplified writing and reading. This streamlined alphabet was handed on to the Greeks in the late eighth century B.C. to apply to their own language.

The Phoenicians made another significant contribution by spreading the technical knowledge of ironworking. The Hittites were the first people in the Near East to smelt iron, but the Phoenicians passed the complex technique west to the Greeks and south to the Africans. Once in Africa, the technology spread farther south, though gradually. Most of West Africa had acquired the process by 250 B.C., and sub-Saharan Africa produced steel by A.D. 500.

South of Phoenicia arose the kingdom of the Hebrews or ancient Jews. Although smaller, poorer, less important, and less powerful than neighboring kingdoms, the realm of the Hebrews was to nourish religious ideas that underlie much of world civilization. Who were these people, and what brought them to this new land? Early Mesopotamian and Egyptian sources refer to people called "Habiru" or "Hapiru," which seems to mean a class of homeless, independent nomads. One such group of Habiru were the biblical Hebrews. Their original homeland was probably northern Mesopotamia, and the most crucial event in their historical development was enslavement in Egypt. According to the Old Testament, the Hebrews followed their patriarch Abraham out of Mesopotamia into Canaan, in modern Israel, where they became identified as the "Children of

Phoenician Cargo Vessels   An Assyrian artist has captured all of the energy and vivacity of the seafaring Phoenicians. The sea is filled with Phoenician cargo ships, which ranged the entire Mediterranean. These ships are transporting cedar from Lebanon, some of it stowed on board, while other logs float in their wake. *(Source: Louvre/Giraudon/Art Resource)*

Israel" after the patriarch Jacob, who was also called "Israel."

The Old Testament, the first part of the Bible, is the major literary source for many events involving the early Hebrews. A mere reading of the Bible proves that the Old Testament was composed in various stages. Modern scholars have demonstrated that the origins of the earliest books go back to a time between 950 and 800 B.C. In this period literate people collected oral traditions of the Hebrew past, which included legends, myths, songs, proverbs, and laws, and wove them into a narrative account. Later prophets, priests, and historians added to the narrative until the Old Testament took its final form. Archeologists can help to clarify biblical events by trying to ascertain what happened around the time of the Hebrew exodus from Egypt. The archeological record indicates that the thirteenth century B.C. was a time of warfare, disruption, and destruction and seems to confirm the biblical portrayal of the exodus as a long period of turmoil. It also shows that the situation in Palestine was far more complicated than the Bible suggests.

Many different peoples rubbed shoulders in Palestine in the thirteenth century B.C. Amorites, distant relatives of Hammurabi's Babylonians, had entered the area around 1800 B.C. There they found a Semitic-speaking people, the Canaanites, with whom they freely mingled. Hebrew tribes also arrived, an event about which there is great uncertainty as to time and detail. During the Eighteenth Dynasty of Egypt, some Hebrews were either taken to Egypt or migrated there voluntarily. Meanwhile, other Hebrews remained behind in Palestine. In Egypt the Hebrews were enslaved and forced to labor on building projects. During the thirteenth century B.C. Moses, who may be a mythical figure, led a group of Hebrews from Egypt. According to the biblical book of Exodus, this group consisted of twelve tribes, believed to be descended from the twelve great-grandsons of Abraham. Their wanderings took them to Palestine, where in a series of vicious wars and savage slaughters they slowly won a place (see Map 2.1). Success was not automatic, and the Hebrews suffered defeats and setbacks; but gradually they spread their power northward. Some assimilated

Nomadic Semitic Tribe   This Egyptian fresco captures the essentials of nomadic life. These Semites have captured a gazelle and an ibex. The four men behind the leaders are portrayed with their weapons, a bow and spears, which were used for both hunting and defense. Bringing up the rear is a domesticated burro. *(Source: Erich Lessing Culture and Fine Arts Archive)*

themselves to the culture of the natives, even going so far as to worship Baal, an ancient Semitic fertility god. Striking confirmation of this came in July 1990 from an American excavation in Israel. The excavators found in a temple a statuette of a calf, which lends physical support to the notion that the Hebrews derived some of their religious practices from the Canaanites. In other instances, the Hebrews carved out little strongholds and enslaved the natives. Even after the conquest, nearly constant fighting was required to consolidate their position.

The greatest danger to the Hebrews came from the Philistines, whose superior technology and military organization at first made them invincible. In Saul (ca 1000 B.C.), a farmer of the tribe of Benjamin, the Hebrews found a champion and a spirited leader. In the biblical account Saul carried the war to the Philistines, often without success, yet in the meantime he established a monarchy over the twelve Hebrew tribes. Thus, under the peril of the Philistines, the Hebrew tribes evolved from scattered independent units into a centralized political organization in which the king directed the energies of the people. Saul's work was carried on by David of Bethlehem, who repulsed the Hebrews' enemies and established his capital at Jerusalem. His work in consolidating the mon-

archy and enlarging the kingdom paved the way for his son Solomon (ca 965–925 B.C.), who applied his energies to creating a nation out of a collection of tribes. Solomon built and dedicated a great temple in Jerusalem that was to be the religious heart of the kingdom and the symbol of Hebrew unity. At Solomon's death, the Hebrews broke into political halves (see Map 2.1). The northern part of the kingdom of David and Solomon became Israel, with its capital at Samaria. The southern half was Judah, and Solomon's city of Jerusalem remained its center. This political division mirrored a religious one. In Israel, the northern kingdom, the people worshiped Yahweh and other gods; in Judah, the southern kingdom, they worshiped only Yahweh. Within two centuries Israel was wiped out by the Assyrians, but Judah survived through several more centuries of war and unrest. The people of Judah came to be known as "Jews" and gave their name to *Judaism,* the worship of Yahweh.

The Evolution of Jewish Religion

While evolving politically from fierce nomads to urban dwellers, the Hebrews were also evolving spiritual ideas that still permeate contemporary societies. Their chief literary product, the Old Testament, has fundamentally influenced both Christianity and Islam and still exerts a compelling force on the modern world.

Fundamental to an understanding of Jewish religion is the concept of the *Covenant,* a formal agreement between Yahweh and the Hebrew people. According to the Bible, the god Yahweh, later often called "Jehovah," appeared to Moses on Mount Sinai. There Yahweh made a covenant with the Hebrews that was in fact a contract: if the Hebrews worshiped Yahweh as their only god, he would consider them his chosen people and protect them from their enemies. The Hebrews believed that Yahweh had led them out of bondage in Egypt and had helped them conquer their new land, the promised land. In return, the Hebrews worshiped Yahweh and Yahweh alone. They also obeyed Yahweh's Ten Commandments, an ethical code of conduct revealed to them by Moses.

Yahweh was unique because he was a lone god. Unlike the gods of Mesopotamia and Egypt, Yahweh was not the son of another god, nor did he have a divine wife or family. Initially anthropomorphic, Yahweh gradually lost human form and became totally spiritual. Although Yahweh could assume human form, he was not to be depicted in any form. Thus the Hebrews considered graven images—statues and other physical representations—idolatrous.

At first Yahweh was probably viewed as no more than the god of the Hebrews, who sometimes faced competition from Baal and other gods in Palestine. Enlil, Marduk, Amon-Re, and the others sufficed for foreigners. In time, however, the Hebrews came to regard Yahweh as the only god. This was the beginning of true monotheism.

Yahweh was considered the creator of all things; his name means "he causes to be." He governed the cosmic forces of nature, including the movements of the sun, moon, and stars. His presence filled the universe. At the same time Yahweh was a personal god. Despite his awesome power, he was neither too mighty nor too aloof to care for the individual. The Hebrews even believed that Yahweh intervened in human affairs.

Unlike Akhenaten's monotheism, Hebrew monotheism was not an unpopular religion imposed from above. It was the religion of a whole people, deeply felt and cherished. Some might fall away from Yahweh's worship, and various holy men had to exhort the Hebrews to honor the Cov-

The Silver Calf The worship of calves was common among many of the peoples of Palestine, including the Hebrews sometimes. In August 1990 American archeologists from Harvard University discovered this small figurine of a calf in the ancient city of Ashkelon in modern Israel. It provides evidence for the cult practice before the biblical Exodus. *(Source: Ashkelon Excavations: Leon Levy Expedition. Carl Andrews, photographer)*

enant, but on the whole the people clung to Yahweh. Yet the Hebrews did not consider it their duty to spread the belief in the one god. The Hebrews rarely proselytized, as later the Christians did. As the chosen people, their chief duty was to maintain the worship of Yahweh as he demanded. That worship was embodied in the Ten Commandments, which forbade the Hebrews to steal, murder, lie, or commit adultery.

From the Ten Commandments evolved Hebrew law, a code of law and custom originating with Moses and built on by priests and prophets. The earliest part of this code, the Torah or Mosaic law, was often as harsh as Hammurabi's code, which had a powerful impact on it. Later tradition, largely the work of prophets who lived from the eleventh to the fifth centuries B.C., was more humanitarian.

The evolution of Hebrew monotheism resulted in one of the world's greatest religions, which deeply influenced the development of two others. Many parts of the Old Testament show obvious debts to Mesopotamian culture. Nonetheless, to the Hebrews goes the credit for developing a religion so emotionally satisfying and ethically grand that it has not only flourished but also profoundly influenced Christianity and Islam. Without Moses there could not have been Jesus or Muhammad. The religious standards of the modern world are deeply rooted in Judaism.

Daily Life in Israel

Historians generally know far more about the daily life of the aristocracy and the wealthy in ancient societies than about the conditions of the common people. Jewish society is an exception be-

cause the Old Testament, which lays down laws for all Jews, has much to say about peasants and princes alike. Comparisons with the social conditions of Israel's ancient neighbors and modern anthropological work among Palestinian Arabs shed additional light on biblical practices. Thus the life of the common people in ancient Israel is better known, for instance, than is that of ordinary Romans or ancient Chinese.

Initially life centered around the tribe, numerous families who thought of themselves as related to one another. At first good farmland, pasture, and water sources were held in common by the tribe. Common use of land was—and still is—typical of nomadic peoples. Typically each family or group of families in the tribe drew lots every year to determine who worked which fields. But as formerly nomadic peoples turned increasingly to settled agriculture, communal use of land gave way to family ownership. In this respect the experi-

Aerial View of Hazor Hazor was a Jewish citadel built in the ninth century B.C. Organized on a rectangular plan, Hazor commanded the surrounding countryside and was well fortified. Nonetheless, the Assyrians destroyed the citadel in 732 B.C. *(Source: From HAZOR II, Y. Yadin, Pl. XIII.)*

ence of the ancient Hebrews seems typical of that of many early peoples. Slowly but surely the shift from nomad to farmer affected far more than just how people fed themselves. Family relationships reflected evolving circumstances. The extended family, organized in tribes, is even today typical of nomads. With the transition to settled agriculture, the tribe gradually becomes less important than the extended family. With the advent of village life and finally full-blown urban life, the extended family in turn gives way to the nuclear family.

The family—people related to one another, all living in the same place—was the primary social institution among the Jews. At its head stood the father, who, like the Mesopotamian father, held great powers. The father was the master of his wife and children, with power of life and death over his family. By the eighth century B.C. the advent of full-blown urban life began to change the shape of family life again. The father's power and the overall strength of family ties relaxed. Much of the father's power, especially the power of life and death over his children, passed to the elders of the town. One result was the liberation of the individual from the tight control of the family.

Marriage was one of the most important and joyous events in Hebrew family life. When the Hebrews were still nomads, a man could have only one lawful wife but any number of concubines. Settled life changed marriage customs, and later Jewish law allowed men to be polygamous. Not only did kings David and Solomon have harems, but rich men also could have several wives. The chief reason for this custom, as in Mesopotamia, was the desire for children. Given the absence of medical knowledge and the rough conditions of life, women faced barrenness, high infant mortality, and rapid aging. The presence of several women in the family led to some quarrelsome households; the first wife, if she were barren, could be scorned and ridiculed by her husband's other wives.

Betrothal and marriage were serious matters in ancient Israel. As in Mesopotamia, they were left largely in parents' hands. Many boys and girls were married when they were little more than children, and the parents naturally made the arrangements. Rarely were the prospective bride and groom consulted. Marriages were often contracted within the extended family, commonly among first cousins—a custom still found among Palestinian Arabs today. Although early Jewish custom permitted marriage with foreigners, the fear of alien religions soon led to restrictions against mixed marriages.

The father of the groom offered a bridal gift to the bride's father. This custom, the marriage price, also existed among the Mesopotamians and survives among modern Palestinian Arabs. The gift was ordinarily money, the amount depending on the social status and wealth of the two families. In other instances, the groom could work off the marriage price by performing manual labor. At the time of the wedding the man gave his bride and her family wedding presents; unlike Mesopotamian custom, the bride's father did not provide her with a dowry.

As in Mesopotamia, marriage was a legal contract, not a religious ceremony. At marriage a woman left her own family and joined the family and clan of her husband. The occasion when the bride joined her husband's household was festive. The groom wore a crown and his best clothes. Accompanied by his friends, also dressed in their finest and carrying musical instruments, the bridegroom walked to the bride's house, where she awaited him in her richest clothes, jewels, and a veil, which she removed only later when the couple was alone. The bride's friends joined the group, and together they all marched in procession to the groom's house, their way marked by music and songs honoring the newlyweds. Though the wedding feast might last for days, the couple consummated their marriage on the first night. The next day the bloody linen was displayed to prove the bride's virginity.

Divorce was available only to the husband; the right to initiate a divorce was denied the wife. Even adultery by the husband was not necessarily grounds for divorce. Jewish law, like the Code of Hammurabi, punished a wife's adultery with death. Jewish custom generally frowned on divorce, and the typical couple entered into marriage fully expecting to spend the rest of their lives together.

The newly married couple was expected to begin a family at once. Children, according to the Book of Psalms, "are an heritage of the lord: and the fruit of the womb is his reward."[2] The desire for children to perpetuate the family was so strong that if a man died before he could sire a son, his brother was legally obliged to marry the widow. The son born of the brother was thereafter considered the offspring and heir of the dead man. If the brother refused, the widow had her revenge by denouncing him to the elders in public:

Then shall his brother's wife come unto him in the presence of the elders, and loose his shoe from off his foot, and spit in his face, and shall answer and say, So shall it be done unto that man that will not build up his brother's house.[3]

Sons were especially desired because they maintained the family bloodline and kept the ancestral property within the family. The first-born son had special rights, honor, and responsibilities. At his father's death he became the head of the household and received a larger inheritance than did his younger brothers. Daughters were less highly valued because they would eventually marry and leave the family. Yet in Jewish society, unlike other cultures, infanticide was illegal; Yahweh had forbidden it.

The Old Testament often speaks of the pain of childbirth. Professional midwives frequently helped during deliveries. The newborn infant was washed, rubbed with salt, and wrapped in swaddling clothes—bands of cloth that were wrapped around the baby. Normally the mother nursed the baby herself and weaned the infant at about the age of three. The mother customarily named the baby immediately after birth, but children were free to change names after they grew up. Eight days after the birth of a son, the ceremony of *circumcision*—removal of the foreskin of the penis—took place. Circumcision signified that the boy belonged to the Jewish community and, according to Genesis, was the symbol of Yahweh's covenant with Abraham.

As in most other societies, in ancient Israel the early education of children was in the mother's hands. She taught her children right from wrong and gave them their first instruction in the moral values of society. As boys grew older, they received more education from their fathers. Fathers instructed their sons in religion and the history of their people. Many children were taught to read and write, and the head of each family was probably able to write. Fathers also taught sons the family craft or trade. Boys soon learned that inattention could be painful, for Jewish custom advised fathers to be strict: "He that spareth his rod hateth his son: but he that loveth him chasteneth him betimes."[4]

Once children grew to adulthood, they entered fully into economic and social life. For most that meant farm life, for which demands and rhythm changed little over time. Young people began with light tasks. Girls traditionally tended flocks of sheep and drew water from the well for household use. At the well, which was a popular meeting spot, girls could meet other young people and travelers passing through the country with camel caravans. After the harvest, young girls followed behind the reapers to glean the fields. Even this work was governed by law and custom. Once the girls had gone through the fields, they were not to return, for Yahweh had declared that anything left behind belonged to the needy.

Boys also tended flocks, especially in wild areas. Like the young David, they practiced marksmanship with slings and entertained themselves with music. They shared light work such as harvesting grapes and beating the limbs of olive trees to shake the fruit loose. Only when they grew to full strength did they perform the hard work of harrowing, plowing, and harvesting.

With the success of the first Hebrew kings, the future of many family farms was endangered. With peace, more settled conditions, and increasing prosperity, some Jews began to amass larger holdings by buying out poor and struggling farmers. Far from discouraging this development, the kings created their own huge estates. In many cases slaves, both Jewish and foreign, worked these large farms and estates shoulder to shoulder with paid free men.

In still later times, rich landowners rented plots of land to poor free families; the landowners provided the renters with seed and livestock and normally took half the yield as rent. Although many Old Testament prophets denounced the destruction of the family farm, the trend continued toward large estates that were worked by slaves and hired free men.

The development of urban life among the Jews created new economic opportunities, especially in crafts and trades. People specialized in occupations such as milling flour, baking bread, making pottery, weaving, and carpentry. All these crafts were family trades. Sons worked with their father, daughters with their mother. If the business prospered, the family might be assisted by a few paid workers or slaves. The practitioners of a craft usually lived in a particular street or section of the town, a custom still prevalent in the Middle East. By the sixth century B.C. craftsmen had joined together in associations known as "guilds," intended like European guilds in the Middle Ages (see page 419) to protect and aid their members. By banding together, craftsmen gained corporate status within the community.

Commerce and trade developed later than crafts. In the time of Solomon, foreign trade was the king's domain. Aided by the Phoenicians, who ranked among the leading merchants of the Near East, Solomon built a fleet to trade with Red Sea ports. Solomon also participated in the overland caravan trade. Otherwise, trade with neighboring countries was handled by foreigners, usually Phoenicians. Jews dealt mainly in local trade, and in most instances craftsmen and farmers sold directly to their customers. Many of Israel's wise men disapproved of commerce and, like the ancient Chinese, considered it unseemly and immoral to profit from the work of others.

Between the eclipse of the Hittites and Egyptians and the rise of the Assyrians, the Hebrews moved from nomadism to urban life and full participation in the mainstream of ancient Near East-ern culture. Keeping their unique religion and customs, they drew from the practices of other peoples and influenced the lives of their neighbors.

ASSYRIA, THE MILITARY MONARCHY

Small kingdoms like those of the Phoenicians and the Hebrews could exist only in the absence of a major power. The beginning of the ninth century B.C. saw the rise of such a power: the Assyrians of northern Mesopotamia, whose chief capital was at Nineveh on the Tigris River. The Assyrians were a Semitic-speaking people, heavily influenced, like so many peoples of the Near East, by the Mesopotamian culture of Babylonia to the south. They were also one of history's most warlike peoples.

The Rise of Assyrian Power

For over two centuries the Assyrians labored to dominate the Near East. Year after relentless year, their armies hammered at the peoples of the west,

Siege of a City Art here serves to glorify horror. The Assyrian king Tiglath-pileser III launches an assault on a fortified city. The impaled bodies shown at center demonstrate the cruelty of Assyrian warfare. Also noticeable are the various weapons and means of attack used against the city. *(Source: Courtesy of the Trustees of the British Museum)*

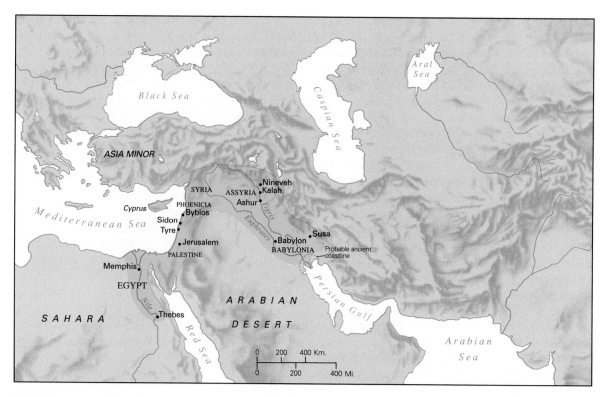

MAP 2.2 The Assyrian Empire The Assyrian Empire at its height included almost all of the old centers of power in the ancient Near East. As comparison with Map 2.3 shows, however, its size was far smaller than that of the later Persian Empire.

to overcome the constant efforts of Syria and the two Jewish kingdoms to maintain or recover their independence. Eventually the Assyrians conquered both Babylonia and northern Egypt. By means of almost constant warfare, they carved out an empire that stretched from east and north of the Tigris River to central Egypt (Map 2.2).

Although empire certainly was an objective of the Assyrian people, their preoccupation with war was in large part a response to the threat of incursion by their neighbors. Living in an open, exposed land, the Assyrians experienced frequent devastating attacks at the hands both of the wild war-loving tribes to the north and east and of the Babylonians to the south. These constant threats promoted political cohesion and military might among the Assyrians. That cohesion was critical to their survival, as evidenced by the immediate stirrings of freedom throughout the Near East in the occasional periods of Assyrian political instability.

An empire forged with so much blood and effort was vulnerable to revolt, and revolt provoked brutal retaliation. Though atrocity and terrorism

struck unspeakable fear into Assyria's subjects, Assyria's success was actually due to sophisticated, far-sighted, and effective military organization. By 716 B.C. the Assyrians had invented the mightiest military machine the ancient Near East had ever seen. The mainstay of the Assyrian army, the soldier who ordinarily decided the outcome of battles, was the infantryman armed with spear and sword and protected by helmet and armor. The Assyrian army also featured archers, some on foot, others on horseback, still others in chariots—the last ready to wield lances once they had expended their supply of arrows. Some infantry archers wore heavy armor, strikingly similar to the armor worn much later by William the Conqueror's Normans. These soldiers served as a primitive field artillery, whose job was to sweep the enemy's walls of defenders so that others could storm the defenses. Slingers also served as artillery in pitched battles. For mobility on the battlefield, the Assyrians organized a corps of chariots.

Assyrian military genius was remarkable for the development of a wide variety of siege machinery and techniques, including excavation to undermine city walls and battering-rams to knock down walls and gates. Never before in the Near East had anyone applied such technical knowledge to warfare. The Assyrians even invented the concept of a corps of engineers, who bridged rivers with pontoons or provided soldiers with inflatable skins for swimming. Furthermore, the Assyrians knew how to coordinate their efforts, both in open battle and in siege warfare. They were too powerful and well organized and far too tenacious to let themselves be defeated by isolated strongholds, no matter how well situated or defended.

Assyrian Rule

Not only did the Assyrians know how to win battles, they also knew how to use their victories.

As early as the reign of Tiglath-pileser III (774–727 B.C.), Assyrian kings began to organize their conquered territories into an empire. The lands closest to Assyria became provinces governed by Assyrian officials. Kingdoms beyond the provinces were not annexed but became dependent states that followed Assyria's lead. Assyrian kings chose their rulers either by regulating the succession of native kings or by supporting native kings who appealed to them. Against more distant states the kings waged frequent war in order to conquer them outright or make their dependent status secure.

Royal roads linked the Assyrian Empire, and Assyrian records describe how swift, mounted royal messengers brought the king immediate word of unrest or rebellion within the empire. Because of good communications, Assyrian kings could generally move against rebels at a moment's notice.

Royal Lion Hunt This relief from the palace of Ashurbanipal at Nineveh, which shows the king fighting two lions, is a typical representation of the energy and artistic brilliance of Assyrian sculptors. The lion hunt, portrayed in a series of episodes, was a favorite theme of Assyrian palace reliefs. *(Source: Courtesy of the Trustees of the British Museum)*

Thus, though rebellion was common in the Assyrian Empire, it rarely got the opportunity to grow serious before meeting with harsh retaliation from the king.

In the seventh century B.C. Assyrian power seemed secure. From their capitals at Nineveh, Kalah, and Ashur on the Tigris River, the Assyrians ruled a vast empire. An efficient army, calculated terrorism, and good communications easily kept down the conquered populations. With grim efficiency the Assyrians sacked rebellious cities, leaving forests of impaled prisoners or piles of severed heads to signal their victory. In other cases they deported whole populations, wrenching them from their homelands and resettling them in strange territories. The Assyrians introduced systematic terror tactics into warfare. Their ferocity horrified their subjects and bred a vast hatred.

Yet the downfall of Assyria was swift and complete. The burden of Assyrian taxation and the terror of Assyrian oppression at last prompted an alliance between the Medes, a new Indo-European-speaking folk from Iran, and the Babylonians for the primary purpose of destroying Assyrian rule. Together the allies conquered the Assyrian Empire in 612 B.C., paving the way for the rise of the Persians. The Hebrew prophet Nahum spoke for many when he proclaimed: "Nineveh is laid waste: who will bemoan her?"[5] Their cities destroyed and their power shattered, the Assyrians disappeared from history, remembered only as a cruel people of the Old Testament who oppressed the Hebrews. Two hundred years later, when the Greek adventurer and historian Xenophon passed by the ruins of Nineveh, he marveled at their extent but knew nothing of the Assyrians. The glory of their empire was forgotten.

THE EMPIRE OF THE PERSIAN KINGS

Like the Hittites before them, the Iranians were Indo-Europeans from the steppes north of the Black and Caspian seas who migrated into a land inhabited by more primitive peoples. Once settled in the area between the Caspian Sea and the Persian Gulf, the Iranians, like the Hittites, fell under the spell of the more sophisticated cultures of their Mesopotamian neighbors. Yet the Iranians went on to create one of the greatest empires of antiquity, an empire that encompassed scores of peoples and cultures. The Persians, the most important of the Iranian peoples, had a far-sighted conception of empire. Though as conquerors they willingly used force to accomplish their ends, they normally preferred to depend on diplomacy. They usually respected their subjects and allowed them to practice their native customs and religions. Thus the Persians gave the Near East both political unity and cultural diversity. Never before had a conquering people viewed empire in such intelligent and humane terms.

The Land of Mountains and Plateau

Persia—the modern country of Iran—is a land of towering mountains and flaming deserts, with a broad central plateau in the heart of the country (Map 2.3). Iran stretches from the Caspian Sea in the north to the Persian Gulf in the south. Between the Tigris-Euphrates Valley in the west and the Indus Valley in the east rises an immense plateau, surrounded on all sides by lofty mountains that cut off the interior from the sea.

The central plateau is very high, a landscape of broad plains, scattered oases, and two vast deserts. The high mountains, which catch the moisture coming from the sea, generate ample rainfall for the plain. This semitropical area is fertile, in marked contrast to the aridity of most of Iran. The mountains surrounding the central plateau are dotted with numerous oases, often very fertile, which have from time immemorial served as havens for small groups of people.

At the center of the plateau lies an enormous depression—a region devoid of water and vegetation, so glowing hot in summer that it is virtually impossible to cross. This depression forms two distinct grim and burning salt deserts, perhaps the most desolate spots on earth. These two deserts form a barrier between East and West.

Iran's geographical position and topography explain its traditional role as the highway between East and West. Throughout history nomadic peoples migrating from the broad steppes of Russia and central Asia have streamed into Iran. Confronting the uncrossable salt deserts, most have turned either eastward or westward, moving on until they reached the advanced and wealthy urban centers of Mesopotamia and India. When cities emerged along the natural lines of East-West communication, Iran became the area where no-

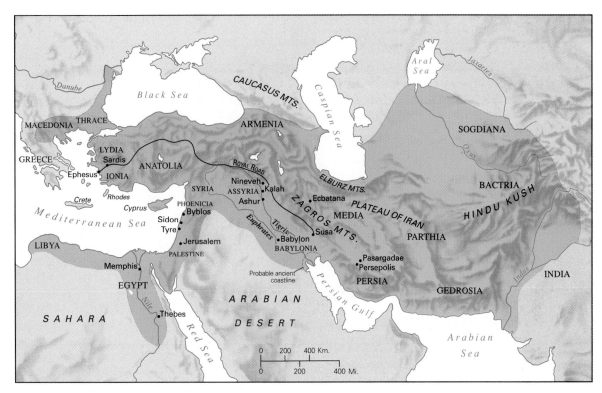

MAP 2.3 The Persian Empire   The Persian Empire not only included more of the ancient Near East than had the Assyrian Empire, but it also extended as far east as western India. With the rise of the empire, the balance of power in the Near East shifted east of Mesopotamia for the first time.

mads met urban dwellers, a meeting ground of unique significance for the civilizations of both East and West.

The Coming of the Medes and Persians

The history of human habitation in Iran is long and rich: traces of prehistoric peoples date back as far as 15,000 to 10,000 B.C. About the prehistoric period historians and archeologists still have much to learn. The Iranians entered this land around 1000 B.C. The most historically important of them were the Medes and the Persians, related peoples who settled in different areas. Both groups were part of the vast movement of Indo-European-speaking peoples whose wanderings led them in many successive waves into Europe, the Near East, and India. These Iranians were nomads who migrated with their flocks and herds. Like their kinsmen the Aryans, who moved into India, they were horse breeders, and the horse gave them a decisive

military advantage over the prehistoric peoples of Iran. The Iranians rode into battle in horse-drawn chariots or on horseback and easily swept the natives before them. Yet, because the influx of Iranians went on for centuries, cultural interchange between victorious newcomers and conquered natives proved constant.

Excavations at Siyalk, some 125 miles south of present-day Tehran, provide a valuable glimpse of the encounter of Iranian and native. The village of Siyalk had been inhabited since prehistoric times before falling to the Iranians. The new lords fought all comers: natives, rival Iranians, even the Assyrians, who often raided far east of the Tigris. Under the newly arrived Iranians, Siyalk became a fortified town with a palace and perhaps a temple, all enclosed by a wall that was strengthened by towers and ramparts. The town was surrounded by fields and farms because agriculture was the foundation of this evolving society.

The Iranians initially created a patchwork of tiny kingdoms, of which Siyalk was one. The chief-

Jug of Siyalk   Though later the Persians derived their art primarily from their neighbors, this jug, which dates to ca 1000 B.C., demonstrates that the early settlers possessed a vigorous sense of art themselves. While some features of this jug were borrowed from neighboring artistic traditions, others are solely Persian. This jug was probably used to pour wine. *(Source: The Ancient Art and Architecture Collection)*

tain or petty king was basically a warlord who depended on fellow warriors for aid and support. This band of noble warriors, like the Greek heroes of the *Iliad,* formed the fighting strength of the army. The king owned estates that supported him and his nobles; for additional income the king levied taxes, which were paid in kind and not in cash. He also demanded labor services from the peasants. Below the king and his warrior nobles were free people who held land and others who owned nothing. Artisans produced the various goods needed to keep society running. At the bottom of the social scale were slaves—probably both natives and newcomers—to whom fell the drudgery of hard labor and household service to king and nobles.

This early period saw some significant economic developments. The use of iron increased. By the seventh century B.C. iron farm implements had become widespread, leading to increased productivity, greater overall prosperity, and higher standards of living. At the same time Iranian agriculture saw the development of the small estate. Farmers worked small plots of land, and the general pros-

perity of the period bred a sturdy peasantry, who enjoyed greater freedom than their peers in Egypt and Mesopotamia.

Iran had considerable mineral wealth, and its iron, copper, and lapis lazuli attracted Assyrian raiding parties. Even more important, mineral wealth and Iranian horse breeding stimulated brisk trade with the outside world. Kings found that merchants, who were not usually Iranians, produced large profits to help fill the king's coffers. Overland trade also put the Iranians in direct contact with their neighbors.

Gradually two groups of Iranians began coalescing into larger units. The Persians had settled in Persis, the modern region of Fars, in southern Iran. Their kinsmen the Medes occupied Media, the modern area of Hamadan in the north, with their capital at Ecbatana. The Medes were exposed to attack by nomads from the north, but their greatest threat was the frequent raids of the Assyrian army. Even though distracted by grave pressures from their neighbors, the Medes united under one king around 710 B.C. and extended their control over the Persians in the south. In 612 B.C.

the Medes were strong enough to join the Babylonians in overthrowing the Assyrian Empire. With the rise of the Medes, the balance of power in the area for the first time shifted east of Mesopotamia.

The Creation of the Persian Empire

In 550 B.C. Cyrus the Great (559–530 B.C.), king of the Persians and one of the most remarkable statesmen of antiquity, threw off the yoke of the Medes by conquering them and turning their country into his first *satrapy,* or province. In the space of a single lifetime, Cyrus created one of the greatest empires of antiquity. Two characteristics lifted Cyrus above the common level of warrior-kings. First, he thought of Iran, not just Persia and Media, as a state. His concept has survived a long, complex, often turbulent history to play its part in the contemporary world.

Second, Cyrus held an enlightened view of empire. Many of the civilizations and cultures that fell to his armies were, he realized, far older, more advanced, and more sophisticated than his. Free of the narrow-minded snobbery of the Egyptians, the religious exclusiveness of the Hebrews, and the calculated cruelty of the Assyrians, Cyrus gave his subject peoples and their cultures his respect, toleration, and protection. Conquered peoples continued to enjoy their institutions, religion, language, and way of life under the Persians. The Persian Empire, which Cyrus created, became a political organization sheltering many different civilizations. To rule such a vast area and so many diverse peoples demanded talent, intelligence, sensitivity, and a cosmopolitan view of the world. These qualities Cyrus and many of his successors possessed in abundance. Though the Persians were sometimes harsh, especially with those who rebelled against them, they were for the most part

Tomb of Cyrus For all of his greatness Cyrus retained a sense of perspective. His tomb, though monumental in size, is rather simple and unostentatious. Greek writers reported that it bore the following epitaph: "O man, I am Cyrus the son of Cambyses. I established the Persian Empire and was king of Asia. Do not begrudge me my memorial." *(Source: The Oriental Institute, University of Chicago)*

enlightened rulers. Consequently, the Persians gave the ancient Near East over two hundred years of peace, prosperity, and security.

With Iran united, Cyrus looked at the broader world. He set out to achieve two goals: first, to win control of the west and thus of the terminal ports of the great trade routes that crossed Iran and Anatolia. Second, Cyrus strove to secure eastern Iran from the pressure of nomadic invaders. In

Funeral Pyre of Croesus This scene, an excellent example of the precision and charm of ancient Greek vase painting, depicts the Lydian king Croesus on his funeral pyre. He pours a libation to the gods while his slave lights the fire. Herodotus has a happier ending when he says that Cyrus the Great set fire to the pyre but that Apollo sent rain to put it out. *(Source: Louvre Cliché des Musées Nationaux, Paris)*

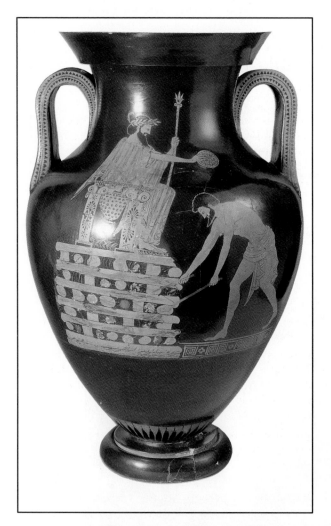

550 B.C. neither goal was easy. To the northwest was the young kingdom of Lydia in Anatolia, whose king Croesus was proverbial for his wealth. To the west was Babylonia, enjoying a new period of power now that the Assyrian Empire had been crushed. To the southwest was Egypt, still weak but sheltered behind its bulwark of sand and sea. To the east ranged tough, mobile nomads, capable of massive and destructive incursions deep into Iranian territory.

Cyrus turned first to Croesus' Lydian kingdom, which fell to him around 546 B.C., along with the Greek cities on the coast of Anatolia. For the first time the Persians came into direct contact with the Greeks, a people with whom their later history was to be intimately connected. Then Cyrus turned eastward to Parthia, Bactria, and even the most westerly part of India. Finally, in 540 B.C., Cyrus moved against Babylonia, now isolated from outside help. The Persian king treated all of these conquered peoples with magnanimity. He respected their religions, which he often subsidized, and their cultures, which he nurtured. Seldom have conquerors been as wise, sensitive, and far-sighted as Cyrus and his Persians.

Thus Spake Zarathustra

Iranian religion was originally simple and primitive. Ahuramazda, the chief god, was the creator and benefactor of all living creatures. Yet, unlike Yahweh, he was not a lone god. The Iranians were polytheistic. Mithra, the sun-god, whose cult would later spread throughout the Roman Empire (page 206), saw to justice and redemption. Other Iranian deities personified the natural elements: moon, earth, water, and wind. As in ancient India, the god of fire was particularly important. The sacred fire consumed the blood sacrifices that the early Iranians offered to all of their deities.

Early Iranian religion was close to nature and unencumbered by ponderous theological beliefs. A priestly class, the Magi, developed among the Medes to officiate at sacrifices, chant prayers to the gods, and tend the sacred flame. A description of this early worship comes from the great German historian Eduard Meyer:

Iranian religion knew neither divine images nor temples. On a hilltop one called upon god and his man-

ANCIENT NEAR EAST

ca 1700 B.C.	Covenant formed between Yahweh and the Hebrews; emergence of Hebrew monotheism
ca 1570–ca 1075 B.C.	New Kingdom in Egypt
ca 1475–ca 1200 B.C.	Rise and fall of the Hittite Empire
13th century B.C.	Moses leads Exodus of the Hebrews from Egypt into Palestine
ca 1100–700 B.C.	Founding of numerous small kingdoms, including those of the Phoenicians, Syrians, Philistines, and Hebrews
ca 1000 B.C.	Saul establishes monarchy over Hebrew tribes, under threat of Philistines
	Persians and Medes enter central plateau of Persia
10th century B.C.	David captures Jerusalem, which becomes religious and political center of Judah; Solomon inherits the throne and further unites Hebrew kingdom
925 B.C.	Solomon dies; Hebrew kingdom is divided politically into Israel and Judah
ca 900–612 B.C.	Rise and fall of the Assyrian Empire
813 B.C.	Phoenicians found Carthage
774–705 B.C.	Assyrian kings Tiglath-pileser III and Sargon II conquer Palestine, Syria, Anatolia, Israel, Judah, and Egypt
ca 710 B.C.	Medes unite under one king and conquer Persians
626 B.C.	Babylonia wins independence from Assyria
612 B.C.	Babylonians and Medes destroy Assyrian capital of Nineveh
ca 600 B.C.	Zoroaster revitalizes Persian religion
550 B.C.	Persian king Cyrus the Great conquers Medes, founds Persian Empire
546 B.C.	Cyrus defeats Croesus, wins Lydia
540 B.C.	Persian soldiers under Cyrus enter Babylon
525 B.C.	Cambyses, Cyrus's heir to the throne, conquers Egypt
521–464 B.C.	Kings Darius I and Xerxes complete Persian conquest of ancient Near East, an area stretching from Anatolia in the west to the Indus Valley in the east; Persian attempts to invade Greece unsuccessful

ifestations—sun and moon, earth and fire, water and wind—and erected altars with their eternal fire. But in other appropriate places one could, without further preparation, pray to the deity and bring him his offerings, with the assistance of the Magi.[6]

In time the Iranians built fire temples for these sacrifices. As late as the nineteenth century, fire was still worshiped in Baku, a major city on the Russian-Iranian border.

Around 600 B.C. the prophet Zarathustra— or Zoroaster, as he is more generally known— breathed new meaning into Iranian religion. So little is known of Zoroaster that even the date of his birth is unknown, but it cannot be earlier than around 1000 B.C. Whatever the exact dates of his life, his work endured long afterward.

The most reliable information about Zoroaster comes from the Zend Avesta, a collection of hymns and poems, the earliest part of which treats Zoroaster and primitive Persian religion. Like Moses, Zoroaster preached a novel concept of divinity and human life. Life, he taught, is a constant battleground for two opposing forces, good and evil. Ahuramazda embodied good and truth but was opposed by Ahriman, a hateful spirit who stood for evil and falsehood. Ahuramazda and Ahriman were locked together in a cosmic battle for the human race, a battle that stretched over thousands of years. But, according to Zoroaster, people

Darius and Xerxes This relief from the Persian capital of Persepolis shows King Darius and Crown Prince Xerxes in state. Behind them the royal bodyguard stands at attention, as the royal pair receives the guard's commander. *(Source: The Oriental Institute, University of Chicago)*

were not mere pawns in this struggle. Each person had to choose which side to join—whether to lead a life of good behavior and truthful dealings with others or of wickedness and lies.

Zoroaster emphasized the individual's responsibility in this decision. He taught that people possessed the free will to decide between Ahuramazda and Ahriman and that they must rely on their own consciences to guide them through life. Their decisions were crucial, Zoroaster warned, for there would be a time of reckoning. He promised that Ahuramazda would eventually triumph over evil and lies and that at death each person would stand before the tribunal of good. Ahuramazda, like the Egyptian god Osiris, would judge whether the dead had lived righteously and would weigh their lives in the balance. Then good and truth would conquer evil and lies. In short, Zoroaster taught the concept of a Last Judgment at which Ahuramazda would decide each person's eternal fate on the basis of that person's deeds in life.

In Zoroaster's thought the Last Judgment was linked to the notion of a divine kingdom after death for those who had lived according to good and truth. They would accompany Ahuramazda to a life of eternal truth in what Zoroaster called the "House of Song" and the "Abode of Good Thought." There they would dwell with Ahuramazda forever. Liars and the wicked, denied this

blessed immortality, would be condemned to eternal pain, darkness, and punishment. Thus Zoroaster preached a Last Judgment that led to a heaven or a hell.

Though tradition has it that Zoroaster met with opposition and coldness, his thought converted Darius (521–486 B.C.), one of the most energetic men ever to sit on the Persian throne. The Persian royal family adopted Zoroastrianism but did not try to impose it on others. Under the protection of the Persian kings, Zoroastrianism swept through Iran, winning converts and sinking roots that sustained healthy growth for centuries. Zoroastrianism survived the fall of the Persian Empire to influence religious thought in the age of Jesus and to make a vital contribution to Manicheanism, a theology that was to spread through the Byzantine Empire and pose a significant challenge to Christianity. A handful of the faithful still follow the teachings of Zoroaster, whose vision of divinity and human life has transcended the centuries.

Persia's World Empire

Cyrus's successors rounded out the Persian conquest of the ancient Near East. In 525 B.C. Cyrus's son Cambyses (530–522 B.C.) subdued Egypt. Darius (521–486 B.C.) and his son Xerxes (486–464

B.C.) invaded Greece but were fought to a standstill and forced to retreat (see pages 128–129); the Persians never won a permanent foothold in Europe. Yet Darius carried Persian arms into India. Around 513 B.C. western India became the Persian satrapy of Hindu Kush, which included the valley of the Indus River. Thus within thirty-seven years the Persians transformed themselves from a subject people to the rulers of an empire that included Anatolia, Egypt, Mesopotamia, Iran, and western India. They created an empire encompassing all of the oldest, most honored kingdoms and peoples of the ancient Near East, which never before had been united in one such vast political organization (see Map 2.3).

The Persians knew how to use the peace they had won on the battlefield. The sheer size of the empire made it impossible for one man to rule it effectively. Consequently they divided the empire into some twenty huge satrapies measuring hundreds of square miles, many of them kingdoms in themselves. Each satrapy had a governor, drawn from the Median and Persian nobility and often a relative of the king; the governor or *satrap* was directly responsible to the king. An army officer, also responsible to the king, commanded the mili-

The Royal Palace at Persepolis King Darius began and King Xerxes finished building a grand palace worthy of the glory of the Persian Empire. Pictured here is the monumental audience hall, where the king dealt with ministers of state and foreign envoys. *(Source: George Holton/Photo Researchers)*

tary forces stationed in the satrapy. Still another official collected the taxes. Moreover, the king sent out royal inspectors to watch the satraps and other officials.

Effective rule of the empire demanded good communications. To meet this need the Persians established a network of roads. The main highway, known as the "Royal Road," spanned some 1,677 miles from the Greek city of Ephesus on the coast of western Asia to Susa in western Iran (see Map 2.3). The distance was broken into 111 post stations, each equipped with fresh horses for the king's messengers. Other roads branched out to link all parts of the empire from the coast of the Mediterranean to the valley of the Indus River. This system of communications enabled the Persian king to keep in touch with his subjects and officials. He was able to rule efficiently, keep his ministers in line, and protect the rights of the peoples under his control.

Conquered peoples, left free to enjoy their traditional ways of life, found in the Persian king a capable protector. No wonder that many Near Eastern peoples were, like the Jews, grateful for the long period of peace they enjoyed as subjects of the Persian Empire.

Meanwhile, farther east the Indians and Chinese were confronting many of the same problems that the peoples farther west were solving. The direction of developments in India and China differed from that in the Near East, largely, but not entirely, because of geography. The results, however, were essentially the same: sophisticated civilizations based on systematic agriculture, complex social structures, cultures, and religions.

NOTES

1. J. H. Breasted, *Ancient Records of Egypt,* vol. 4, (Chicago: University of Chicago Press, 1907), para. 398.
2. Psalms 128:3.
3. Deuteronomy 25:9.
4. Proverbs 13:24.
5. Nahum 3:7.
6. E. Meyer, *Geschichte des Altertums*, 7th ed., vol. 4, part 1 (Darmstadt: Wissenschaftliche Buchgesellschaft, 1975), pp. 114–115. Unless otherwise credited, all quotations from a foreign language in this chapter are translated by John Buckler.

SUMMARY

Between around 1200 and 500 B.C. the Near East passed from fragmentation to political unification under the Persian Empire. On the road from chaos to order, from widespread warfare to general peace, peoples in many areas wrought vast and enduring achievements. The homeless Hebrews laboriously built a state and entered the broader world of their neighbors. Simultaneously they evolved religious and ethical beliefs that permeate the modern world.

Although the Assyrians made the Near East tremble in terror of their armies, they too contributed to the heritage of these long years. Their military and, particularly, political abilities gave the Persians the tools they needed to govern a host of different peoples. Those tools were to be well used. For over two hundred years Persian kings offered their subjects enlightened rule. The Persians gave the ancient Near East a period of peace and stability in which peoples enjoyed their native traditions and lived in concord with their neighbors.

SUGGESTED READING

Although late Egyptian history is still largely a specialist's field, K. A. Kitchen, *The Third International Period in Egypt* (1973), is a good synthesis of the period from 1100 to 650 B.C. Valuable, too, is M. L. Bierbrier's monograph, *Late New Kingdom in Egypt, c. 1300–664 B.C.* (1975). More general is R. David, *The Egyptian Kingdoms* (1975). A. H. Gardiner, ed., *Late Egyptian Stories* (1973), contains other pieces of late Egyptian literature.

G. Herm, *The Phoenicians: The Purple Empire of the Ancient World* (1975), treats Phoenician seafaring and commercial enterprises. A more general treatment of the entire area is R. Fedden, *Syria and Lebanon,* 3d ed. (1965).

The Jews have been one of the best studied peoples in the ancient world; the reader can easily find many good treatments of Jewish history and society. A readable and balanced book is J. Bright, *A History of Israel,* 2d ed. (1972). Other useful general books include G. W. Anderson, *The History and Religion of Israel* (1966), a solid, scholarly treatment of the subject. The archeological exploration of ancient Israel is so fast paced that nearly any book is quickly outdated. Nonetheless, A. Negev, *Ar-*

chaeological Encyclopedia of the Holy Land (1973), which is illustrated, is still a good place to start.

M. R. de Vaux, *Ancient Israel, Its Life and Institutions,* 2d ed. (1965), which ranges across all eras of early Jewish history, is especially recommended because of its solid base in the ancient sources. The period of Jewish kingship has elicited a good deal of attention. B. Halpern, *The Constitution of the Monarchy in Israel* (1981), makes the significant point that the Jews are the only ancient Near Eastern people to have recorded the decision to adopt monarchy as a form of government. For an excellent discussion of the evolution of the Old Testament, see M. Smith, *Palestinian Parties and Politics That Shaped the Old Testament,* 2d ed. (1987). G. W. Ahlstrom, *Royal Administration and National Religion in Ancient Palestine* (1982), treats secular and religious aspects of Hebrew history. Last, W. D. Davis et al., *The Cambridge History of Judaism,* vol. 1 (1984), begins an important new synthesis with work on Judaism in the Persian period. R. Hachlili, *Ancient Jewish Art and Archaeology in the Land of Israel* (1988), attempts to trace the development and meaning of Jewish art in its archeological context.

The Assyrians, despite their achievements, have not attracted the scholarly attention that the ancient Jews and other Near Eastern peoples have. Even though outdated, A. T. Olmstead, *History of Assyria* (1928), has the merit of being soundly based in the original sources. More recent and more difficult is J. A. Brinkman, *A Political History of Post-Kassite Babylonia, 1158–722 B.C.* (1968), which treats the Babylonian response to the rise of Assyria. M. Cogan, *Imperialism and Religion: Assyria, Judah and Israel in the Eighth and Seventh Centuries B.C.*

(1973), traces the various effects of Assyrian expansion on the two Jewish kingdoms.

A new edition of an earlier work, H. W. F. Skaggs, *Everyday Life in Babylonia and Assyria,* rev. ed. (1987), offers a general and well-illustrated survey of Mesopotamian history from 3000 to 300 B.C. Those who appreciate the vitality of Assyrian art should start with the masterful work of R. D. Barnett and W. Forman, *Assyrian Palace Reliefs,* 2d ed. (1970), an exemplary combination of fine photographs and learned, but not difficult, discussion.

Several new general works on ancient Iran have lately appeared. A comprehensive survey of Persian history is given by one of the leading scholars in the field, R. N. Frye, *History of Ancient Iran* (1984). I. Gershevitch, ed., *The Cambridge History of Iran,* vol. 2 (1985), offers a full account of ancient Persian history, but many of the chapters are already out of date. E. E. Herzfeld, *Iran in the Ancient East* (1987), puts Persian history in a broad context, as does M. A. Dandamaev, *A Political History of the Achaemenid Empire* (1989).

J. H. Moulton, *Early Zoroastrianism: The Origins, the Prophet, and the Magi* (1972), is a sound treatment of the beginnings and early spread of Zoroastrianism. R. C. Zaehner, *The Dawn and Twilight of Zoroastrianism* (1961), discusses the whole course of Zoroastrianism's history. Zaehner also provides a good introduction to the basic teachings of Zoroastrianism in his *Teachings of the Magi: A Compendium of Zoroastrian Beliefs* (1975). Finally, M. Boyce, a leading scholar in the field, offers a sound and readable treatment in her *Zoroastrianism* (1979).

3

Ancient India to
ca A.D. 200

King Vidudabha visiting the Buddha, from the Bharhut Stupa

While the peoples of the ancient Near East were spreading their cultures and grappling with the demands of political administration of large tracts of land, people in India were wrestling with similar problems—taming the land, improving agricultural techniques, building cities and urban cultures, and asking basic questions about social organization and the nature of human life.

The earliest Indian civilization, like those of Mesopotamia and Egypt, centered on a great river, in this case the Indus. The people of ancient India also were confronted with challenging climate and topography. They suffered monsoons; they faced jungle in some areas and desert in others. The fertile but undeveloped and underpopulated territory offered Neolithic pioneers and their descendants either prosperity or extinction, depending on how well they met the varied demands of the land. As in the ancient Near East, so too in India agricultural exploitation of the land promoted an increase in population, and the needs of metal technology encouraged wider contacts.

- How did the ancient Indians respond to the problems that ancient Near Eastern peoples were confronting?

- How did they meet the challenge of the land itself?

- What kind of social and political organization developed in India?

- What intellectual and religious values did this society generate?

These questions are the central concern of this chapter.

THE LAND AND ITS FIRST TAMERS
(CA 2500–1500 B.C.)

Ancient India—which encompassed modern Pakistan, Nepal, and part of Afghanistan as well as the modern state of India—was a geographically protected and relatively self-contained land. The subcontinent of India, a land mass as large as western Europe, juts southward into the warm waters of the Indian Ocean. India is a land of contrasts.

Some regions are among the wettest on earth; others are dry and even arid desert and scrub land. High mountain ranges in the north drop off to the low river valleys of the Indus and Ganges. These geographical variations greatly influenced the pattern of human development within India.

Three regions of India are of overriding geographical significance: (1) the ring of mountains in the north that separates India from its neighbors, (2) the great river valleys of the Indus and Ganges and their tributaries, and (3) the southern peninsula, especially the narrow coastal plains and the large Deccan Plateau (Map 3.1). The lower reaches of the Himalaya Mountains—the northern geographical boundary of the subcontinent—are covered by some of India's densest forests, sustained by heavy rainfall. Immediately to the south the land drops away to the fertile river valleys of the Indus and Ganges. These lowland plains, which stretch all the way across the subcontinent, are the most fertile parts of India. Here Indian agriculture has traditionally flourished. Furthermore, the flat terrain enabled invaders to sweep across and beyond the northern Indian plain, once they passed the area of Delhi. South of these valleys rise the Vindhya Mountains and the dry, hilly Deccan Plateau. Only along the coasts do the hills give way to narrow plains. In short, geography sets India off from its neighbors and simultaneously divides the country into many subregions, some of them huge, fertile, and capable of sustaining large and vigorous populations.

The Himalayas, which in many places exceed 25,000 feet in height, protected ancient India from wandering peoples in search of new lands to settle. The Indian Ocean, later a busy avenue to the outside world, served throughout much of antiquity as an immense moat, keeping out invaders while fostering maritime trade with both the Near East and China. Only in the northwest—the area between modern Afghanistan and Pakistan—was India accessible to outsiders. This region, penetrated by the famous Khyber Pass, has traditionally been the highway of invaders—a highway whose other terminus was the flourishing cultures of the ancient Near East. Thus geography segregated India, but it also made possible contact with the ideas, practices, and technology of the earliest civilizations.

The Himalayas shield the subcontinent from the northern cold. They also hold in the monsoon

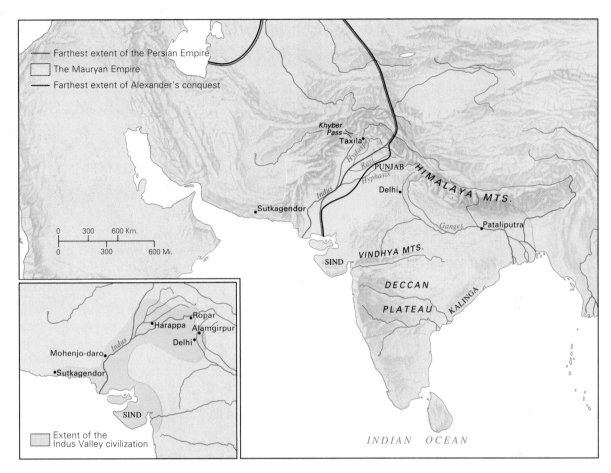

MAP 3.1 The Development of India, ca 2500–ca 250 B.C. This map shows the development of India from the days of the Indus Valley civilization to the reign of Ashoka. Although northwestern India might fall to foreign conquerors like the Persians or Alexander the Great, most of India was unscathed by these incursions. Ashoka created the first real Indian empire.

rains that sweep northward from the Indian Ocean each summer. The monsoons in the south and the melting snows of the Himalayas in the north provide India with most of its water. In some areas the resulting moistness and humidity created vast tracts of jungle and swamp; the Ganges was a particularly forbidding region, and only gradually did settlers move there from the tamer west. Much of India, however, is not blessed with abundant water: instead of jungle, the environment is subtropical and dry. In general, the monsoon area of southeastern India experiences the heaviest rainfall, while the driest region is the northwest. Geography and climate, and especially good water resources, combined to make the Pun-

jab and the valley of the Indus River—now in Pakistan—the most attractive regions for India's first settlers.

The story of the first civilization in India, known as the Indus civilization, is one of the most dramatic in the entire ancient world. In 1921 archeologists discovered astonishing evidence of a thriving and sophisticated urban culture dating to about 2500 B.C. Until that time India had been the home of primitive tribes of hunters and food gatherers; then some newcomers began to develop a truly revolutionary way of life. About the tantalizing problem of the origin of the Indus civilization, the eminent English archeologist Sir Mortimer Wheeler has commented:

Figurine from Mohenjo-daro Part of the heritage of the Indus civilization was its artistic creations, such as this figurine of a bearded man. The composition is at once bold and sophisticated. Yet even such glimpses as this give little clue to the origins of the creators of the Indus civilization. *(Source: National Museum, Karachi)*

By the middle of the 3rd millennium, something very important was happening in the Indus valley, and happening probably at great speed. Then or rather earlier, certain of the little communities in the Baluch foothills of modern Pakistan were emboldened to experiment. Who the first leaders were who led their people, however hesitantly, down to the wide and jungle-ridden plain we shall never know, nor why they ventured; but they were bold men, pioneers in the fullest sense, no mere ejects from the highland zone. Some, perhaps many of them, led forlorn hopes and perished. . . . Seemingly the attempted colonization of the valley continued intermittently, failure succeeding failure, until at last a leader, more determined and far-sighted and fortunate than the rest, won through.[1]

These hardy adventurers created an urban culture based on large-scale agriculture. Like the Mesopotamian city, the Indian city was surrounded by extensive farmland, which fed its inhabitants. These pioneers also developed a script, which is still undeciphered. Contact was early and frequent between the Indus civilization and the great cultures of Mesopotamia. As early as the reign of Sargon of Akkad in the third millennium B.C. (see page 18), trade between India and Mesopotamia carried goods and ideas between the two cultures, probably by way of the Persian Gulf.

The Indus civilization extended over fully 1.25 million square kilometers in the Indus Valley, an area that exceeded the boundaries of modern Pakistan. Its two best-known cities were Mohenjo-daro in southern Pakistan and Harappa some four hundred miles to the north in the Punjab. Other sites have since been found in southern Pakistan, at Sutkagendor in the west, as far east as Alamgirpur near modern Delhi, and as far north as Ropar (see Map 3.1). Numerous sites are still being excavated, and a full portrait of this vast civilization will have to await archeologists' findings. It is already clear, however, that the Indus civilization was marked by a striking uniformity of culture and, simultaneously, by regional variation.

Some important new linguistic work suggests that other peoples were also filtering into India from western Asia while the Indus civilization was flourishing. The ancestors of the Dravidians, who are usually considered natives of central and southern India, probably moved through the Indus Valley at about this time. In short, the movement of ancient peoples into India was a far more complex process than anyone imagined even a few years ago. Only future work in a variety of fields can clarify this immense phenomenon.

Mohenjo-daro and Harappa are currently the best-understood keys to the Indus civilization. Both cities were huge, over three miles in circumference, and housed large populations. Built of fired mud brick, Mohenjo-daro and Harappa were largely unfortified, although both were defended by great citadels that towered 40 or 50 feet above the surrounding plain. Both cities were logically planned from the outset, not merely villages that grew and sprawled haphazardly. In both, blocks of houses were laid out on a grid plan, centuries be-

Mohenjo-daro The architectural vision and engineering expertise of the Indus civilization are obvious in this view of Mohenjo-daro. The central planning and huge scale of the city reflect a flourishing community. *(Source: Josephine Powell, Rome)*

fore the Greeks used this method of urban design. Streets were straight and wide, varying from 9 to 34 feet. The houses of both cities were substantial, many two stories tall, some perhaps three. The focal point of the Indus houses was a central open courtyard, onto which the rooms opened. The houses' brick exteriors were bland and blank, and the city streets must have presented a monotonous face to pedestrians.

Perhaps the most surprising aspect of the elaborate planning of these cities is their complex system of drainage, well preserved at Mohenjo-daro. Each house had a bathroom with a drain connected to municipal drains located under the major streets. These brick-built channels, which carried off refuse, had openings to allow the clearing of blockages. This system not only demonstrates a sophisticated appreciation of hygiene but also attests to the existence of a strong central authority capable of urban planning.

Centralized government is also apparent in both cities' numerous large structures, which excavators think were public buildings. One of the most important is the state granary, a large storehouse for the community's grain. Moreover, a set of tene-

ment buildings next to a series of round working-floors near the granary at Harappa suggests that the central government dominated the storage and processing of the city's cereal crops. The citadel at Mohenjo-daro further testifies to the power of the city's rulers: here stood monumental buildings, including a marketplace or place of assembly, a palace, and a huge bath featuring a pool some 39 feet by 23 feet and 8 feet deep. The Great Bath, like later Roman baths, was an intricate structure with spacious dressing rooms for the bathers. Because the Great Bath at Mohenjo-daro resembles the ritual purification pools of later Indian society, some scholars have speculated that power was in the hands of a priest-king. They also suggest that the Great Bath played a role in the religious rituals of the city; if so, the dressing rooms may have served the priests who performed the rituals. But little is yet known about the religious life of Mohenjo-daro and Harappa or about their government. Lacking readable written records, archeology cannot answer these questions. Nonetheless, the power and authority of the government, whether secular or religious, are apparent in the intelligent central planning of these cities.

The prosperity of the Indus civilization depended on constant and intensive cultivation of the rich river valley. The Indus, like the Nile, provided farmers with fertile alluvial soil enriched by annual floods. Farmers built earth embankments to hold the flood waters. The results of this labor were abundant crops of wheat, barley, vegetables, and cotton. The Indus people also domesticated cattle, buffalo, fowl, and possibly pigs and asses. Their efforts led to a high standard of living and to the surpluses that they traded with Mesopotamia. They were also in contact with neighbors closer to home, trading with the peoples of southern India for gold and with the ancient Afghans for silver.

Despite tantalizing glimpses of a serene and stable society, the intellectual and religious life of the Indus people is largely unknown. Fertility was a major concern to them, as it is to most agricultural people: they apparently worshiped a mother-goddess who looked after the welfare of the community. Some later Indian religious beliefs may have originated in this period. One of the most engaging of the early Indian deities—who is depicted at Mohenjo-daro with his customary three faces, surrounded by wild animals—closely resembles Siva, a major Hindu god. The Indus people's great fondness for animals is apparent in the popularity of terra-cotta animal figurines. Their attitude prefigures the deep respect for the animal world that Indians have traditionally felt. Indeed they give the impression of having been a people in tune with the world around them, a world they understood and enjoyed. The Indus people maintained their equilibrium with nature for hundreds of years, spreading their culture throughout the valley and enjoying a tranquil development.

Yet this civilization, which appeared in history so suddenly, perished just as mysteriously. After years of prosperity, Mohenjo-daro and Harappa suffered a long decline, perhaps as a result of deforestation, a change in climate, and their huge demands on the land. The first excavators of Mohenjo-daro concluded that the city met a violent end: they found some skeletons of men, women, and children, many with ax or sword wounds, scattered across the ground. Contemporary archeologists, however, have reinterpreted these findings. Some point out that too few skeletons at Mohenjo-daro showed signs of violence to indicate wholesale slaughter. Others suggest that the population may have fallen prey to diseases such as malaria. Thus the reasons for the disappearance of this intriguing civilization are obscure and disputed. It is known, however, that many of the Indus people lived on, though disrupted and scattered. With them they carried the accomplishments and values of their culture, which became an important element in the development of later Indian civilization.

Toy Ram The people of Mohenjo-daro not only respected animals, but they also enjoyed them. Here is a terra cotta ram on wheels that a child could pull around on a string. *(Source: Jehangir Gazdar/Woodfin Camp & Associates)*

THE ASCENDANCY OF THE ARYANS (CA 1500–500 B.C.)

Many scholars think that the Indus civilization fell at the hands of the Aryans, an Indo-European people who entered India from the northwest. There is, however, no sound evidence to support this view. In fact, the Aryans may not have reached India until many years after the fall of the Indus civilization. Nevertheless, the Aryans, like the Hittites and later the Greeks, formed part of the widespread migrations that transformed the face of much of the ancient world. In any case, the arrival of the Aryans was a turning point in Indian history, an event that forever changed the face of India. The Aryans were part of the enormous movement of Indo-Europeans described in Chapter 1 (see page 4). Nomadic wanderers, they came in search of land; the Indus Valley, with its rich plains and predictable climate, lured them on.

Most knowledge of the early Aryans comes from the Rigveda, the oldest and most sacred of the Hindu "scriptures." The Rigveda is not a history but a collection of hymns in praise of the Aryan gods. Even so, the hymns contain some historical information that sheds light on the Aryans and on native Indians. The Rigveda and the other Vedas, which were also sacred writings, are crucial to understanding the social evolution of India during this period, sometimes called the "Dark Ages of India."

The Rigveda portrays the Aryans as a group of battle-loving pastoral tribes, at war with one another and with the native population of India. In that respect, they can be seen as conquerors of the local peoples. Their use of horses and bronze weapons in warfare gave them superiority over the natives. At the head of the Aryan tribe was its chief, or *raja,* who led his followers in battle and ruled them in peacetime. Next to the chief was the priest, entrusted with sacrifices to the gods and the knowledge of sacred rituals. In time, as Aryan, also called "Vedic," society laid increasing emphasis on proper performance of the religious rituals, priests evolved into a distinct class possessing precise knowledge of the complex rituals and of the invocations and formulas that accompanied them. The warrior nobility rode to battle in chariots and perhaps on horseback and expressed their will in assemblies. The commoners supported society by tending herds and, increasingly as conditions settled, working the land. To the non-Aryan slaves fell the drudgery of menial tasks. Women held a more favorable position in this period than in later times: they were not yet given in child marriage, and widows had the right to remarry. In brief, the Rigveda portrays the early Aryans, with their pride of conquest and delight in battle, as a heroic folk.

Gradually the Aryans pushed farther eastward into the valley of the Ganges River, a land of thick jungle populated by tribes. The jungle was as stubborn an enemy as its inhabitants, and clearing it presented a tremendous challenge. For the next six hundred years, the Aryans migrated eastward, finally founding the important city of Delhi. During this time the Aryans and their Indian predecessors blended their cultures, each influencing the other. If the Aryans brought new customs, they themselves adopted traditional ones. The re-sulting synthesis constituted an entirely new Indian society.

The Shaping of Indian Society

Because the push into the jungle demanded a larger and more tightly organized political entity than before, tribes merged under strong rulers whose power grew increasingly absolute. As rulers claimed sovereignty over specific territory, political rule shifted from tribal chieftainship to kingship. The priests, or *Brahmans,* supported the growth of royal power in return for royal confirmation of their own religious rights, power, and status; the Brahmans also served a political function as advisers to the kings. In the face of this royal-priestly alliance, the old tribal assemblies of warriors withered away.

Development of the newly won territory led to further changes in Aryan society and its political structure. Once conquered and cleared, the land was ready for cultivation. However, constant work was needed to keep the land from reverting to jungle. The typical response to this challenge was the village. In this period India evolved into the land of villages it still is today. Even the later growth of cities did not eclipse the village as the hallmark of Indian society. Yet villages did not conform to a single social pattern. In the south the typical village consisted of groups of families who considered themselves related to one another. Each family was a large patriarchal joint or extended family composed of several nuclear families who lived and worked together. In the north, by contrast, marriage outside the village was common, and families' kinship ties extended over wider areas than in the south. What all Indian villages had in common was a tradition of mutual cooperation born of common interests and obligations. The close-knit society of the village has consistently been a stabilizing element in Indian history.

Sustained agriculture and settled conditions promoted prosperity and population growth, which in turn gave rise to the growth of towns and eventually cities. Thus the Aryans gradually transformed themselves from a tribal organization into an urban, as well as a village, society. Prosperity further enhanced royal power. Another feature of this process was frequent warfare among territorial states, the smaller and weaker of which were con-

Bronze Sword   A striking example of the quality of Aryan arms is this bronze sword, with its rib in the middle of the blade for strength. Native Indians lacked comparable weapons. *(Source: Courtesy of the Trustees of the British Museum)*

tem." A *caste* is a hereditary class of social equals who share the same religion, pursue a specific trade or occupation, and avoid extensive social intercourse with members of other castes. Initially this system had two goals: to distinguish Aryans from non-Aryans and to mark birth or descent. The caste system was fluid at first and allowed for a surprising amount of social mobility. Even in the early days of conquest the Aryans mixed with the conquered population, and that slow mingling eventually resulted in the Indian society that emerged into the full light of history. The blending was intellectual and religious as well as social. Only as conditions stabilized over the years did the system become strict and the number of castes grow.

By about 500 B.C. four main groups of Indian society—the priests *(Brahman),* the warriors *(Kshatriya),* the peasants *(Vaishya),* and the serfs *(Shudra)*—were steadily evolving. Indians themselves ascribed this stratification to the gods, as the Rig-veda testifies:

*When they divided the [primeval] Man
    into how many parts did they divide him?
What was his mouth, what were his arms,
    what were his thighs and his feet called?
The Brahman was his mouth, of his
    arms was made the warrior.
His thighs became the Vaishya, of
    his feet the Shudra was born.*[2]

According to this division of duties, the priests conducted religious sacrifices and treasured the religious lore. The warriors defended society on the battlefield, and the peasants grew the food and paid the taxes. The serfs, who were originally the property of the tribe, served the others by performing hard labor. Those without places in this tidy social division—that is, those who entered it later than the others or who had lost their caste status through violations of ritual—were *outcastes.* These people probably earned their livings by performing such undesirable jobs as slaughtering animals and dressing skins. Although their work was economically valuable, it was considered unworthy and socially polluting. These "impure" people were the *untouchables.*

This convenient summary of the caste system fails to do full justice to its complexity. For example, in southern India there were only two orders of caste, Brahman and Shudra; and throughout

quered and absorbed, giving rise to a number of large kingdoms. By about 500 B.C. the Aryans had created a new political map of India characterized by larger kingdoms, village life, and islands of urban culture.

As the Aryans struggled to dominate the land of India, they increasingly had to contend with its people. Social contact between Aryans and natives led to the development of the complicated system of social organization known as the "caste sys-

the subcontinent variations of the system were common. Yet in one aspect the caste system was uniform: it severely limited social mobility, not only among individuals but also among groups of people.

Slavery was also a feature of social life, as it was elsewhere in antiquity. The scanty evidence available suggests that slavery in Aryan society resembled Mesopotamian slavery. In India there was no caste of slaves, although in practice most slaves would have come from the lower castes, which were economically disadvantaged. In the Vedic period, slaves were often people captured in battle, but these captives could be ransomed by their families. Still later, slavery was less connected with warfare; it was more of an economic and social institution. Slave children automatically at birth became the slaves of their parents' masters. Indian slaves could be bought, used as collateral, or even given away. As in ancient Mesopotamia, a free man might sell himself and his family into slavery because he could not pay his debts. And, as in Hammurabi's Mesopotamia, he could, if clever, hard working, or fortunate, buy his and his family's way out of debt.

Slaves in India performed tasks similar to those of slaves in other societies. Like Joseph in ancient Egypt, a man might serve as a royal counselor, having more actual authority than many a free man. Otherwise slaves served in their masters' fields, mines, or houses. Whatever their economic function, socially they were members of their master's household. Indian masters were legally responsible for the last rites of their slaves and were obliged to perform the customary duties necessary for the welfare of the soul of a deceased slave. Indian law forbade a master from abandoning slaves in their old age; it also recommended manumission of slaves as an act of piety. Nonetheless, in Indian literature there is ample evidence of the abuse of slaves; and as in other societies—both ancient and modern—it is sometimes impossible to determine to what extent laws and social injunctions were actually put into practice.

Early Indian Religion

In religion and intellectual life, a momentous revolution was occurring in Indian society. The Aryan gods represented natural phenomena. Some of them were great brawling figures, like Agni, the god of fire; Indra, wielder of the thunderbolt and god of war; and Rudra, the divine archer who spread disaster and disease by firing his arrows at people. Others were shadowy figures, like Dyaus, the father of the gods, who appears in Greek as Zeus and in Latin as Jupiter. Varuna, the god of order in the universe, was a hard god, quick to punish those who sinned and thus upset the balance of nature. Ushas, the goddess of dawn, was a refreshingly gentle deity, who welcomed the birds, gave delight to human beings, and kept off evil spirits. Although the Aryan gods had their duties, they differed from the Greek deities and Mesopotamian gods in that they rarely had distinctive personalities or extensive mythologies. All the Aryan gods enjoyed sacrifices, however, and ritual was an essential ingredient in early Aryan religion. Gradually, under the priestly monopoly of the Brahmans, correct sacrifice and proper ritual became so important that most Brahmans believed a properly performed ritual would force a god to grant a worshiper's wish. These beliefs became known as "Brahmanism." Religion became sterile and unsatisfying to many, even among the priestly class.

In search of a faith richer and more mystical, some Brahmans retreated to the forests to seek a personal road to the gods. Through *asceticism*—severe self-discipline and self-denial—and meditation on the traditional teachings of the Vedas, these pioneers breathed new life into the old rituals. They concluded that disciplined meditation on the ritual sacrifice could produce the same results as the physical ritual itself. Thus they reinterpreted the ritual sacrifices as symbolic gestures with mystical meanings. Slowly Indian religion was changing from primitive worship to a way of thought that nourished human needs and eased human fears. Two cardinal doctrines prevailed: *samsara,* the transmigration of souls by a continual process of rebirth, and *karma,* the tally of good and bad deeds that determined the status of an individual's next life. Karma was more than a concept of retribution for people's acts in life; it also embraced the human and animal worlds. Good deeds led to better future lives, but evil, to worse, even to reincarnation as an animal. The concept of samsara, when joined with that of karma, provided the Hindus with two methods of escape from continual reincarnation: extreme asceticism and yoga, or intense meditation. Either method, if pursued successfully, allowed the individual to be absorbed into a timeless and changeless state. Thus gradually arose the concept of a wheel of life that in- cluded human beings, animals, and even gods.

To most people, especially those on the low end of the economic and social scale, these concepts were attractive. All existence, no matter how harsh and bitter, could be progress to better things. By living righteously and doing good deeds, people could improve their lot in the next life. Yet there was another side to these ideas: the wheel of life could be seen as a treadmill, giving rise to a yearning for release from the relentless cycle of birth and death. Hence the new concepts created tension in religious thought.

The solution to this baffling problem appears in the Upanishads, a collection of sacred texts created by ascetics who opened up new vistas in religious speculation. The authors of the Upanishads fostered the concept of *moksha,* or release from the wheel of life. All people, they taught, have in themselves an eternal truth and reality called *atman,* which corresponds to a greater all-encompassing reality called *Brahma.* The truth in each person and the universal truth are eternal and identical. These mystics and ascetics claimed that life in the world is actually an illusion, and the only way to escape it and the wheel of life is to realize that reality is unchanging. By studying the Vedas, by penance, and by meditation, one could join one's individual self with the universal reality. This profound and subtle teaching they summed up in one sentence: "Thou art That." What does this sentence mean? The Chandogya Upanishad tells the story of a father explaining it to his son:

"Believe me, my son, an invisible and subtle essence is the Spirit of the whole universe. That is Reality. That is Atman. THOU ART THAT."

"Explain more to me, father," said Svetaketu.

A Brahman and the Vedas   Here a Brahman reads from a manuscript of the holy book of the Vedas. For centuries, however, knowledge of these poems was preserved only by oral tradition. *(Source: Francis Watson)*

"So be it, my son.

"Place this salt in water and come to me tomorrow morning."

Svetaketu did as he was commanded, and in the morning his father said to him: "Bring me the salt you put into the water last night."

Svetaketu looked into the water, but could not find it, for it had dissolved.

His father then said: "Taste the water from this side. How is it?"

"It is salt."

"Taste it from the middle. How is it?"

"It is salt."

"Taste it from that side. How is it?"

"It is salt."

"Look for the salt again and come again to me."

The son did so, saying: "I cannot see the salt. I only see water."

His father then said: "In the same way, O my son, you cannot see the Spirit. But in truth he is here.

"An invisible and subtle essence is the Spirit of the whole universe. That is Reality. That is Truth. THOU ART THAT." [3]

These great religious thinkers gave society a transcendent means to escape the problems presented by the wheel of life. These revolutionary ideas appealed to those who were dissatisfied with the old Brahman religion of sacrifice, and they even won the support of the Brahmans and kings. The thought of the Upanishads gave Brahmans a high status to which the poor and lowly could aspire in future life; consequently the Brahmans greeted these concepts, and those who taught them, with tolerance and understanding. They made a place for them in traditional religious practice. The rulers of Indian society had excellent practical reasons to encourage the new trends. The doctrines of samsara and karma encouraged the poor and oppressed to labor peacefully and dutifully. The revolutionary new doctrines actually promoted stability in social and political life.

By about 500 B.C., all these trends—political, social, and religious—had led to a society, shaped by conqueror and conquered, in which all had a place. Urban life flourished alongside a vigorous village life, both sustained by agriculture. Gone were the warrior chieftains, their place taken by hereditary kings who ruled large territorial states with the support of a hereditary priestly class. Many of India's basic values already had taken shape at this early date.

INDIA'S SPIRITUAL FLOWERING

India's spiritual growth came into full bloom in the sixth and fifth centuries B.C., a period of stunning moral and philosophical thought that gave rise to three of the world's greatest religions: Hinduism, Jainism, and Buddhism. The evolution of these sects is complex and somewhat obscure. Hinduism is the most direct descendant of the old Vedic religion. Jainism and Buddhism shared that heritage but reacted against it and against Hinduism. Jainism and Buddhism originated as schools of moral philosophy, preoccupied with the nature of ultimate reality and with ethical conduct.

Hinduism

Hinduism may be the world's oldest flourishing religion. It is certainly one of the world's largest faiths, with millions of adherents in India and other Asian countries, the West Indies, and South Africa; it is also a complex of social customs, doctrines, and beliefs.

Although influenced by Jainism and Buddhism, Hinduism was most firmly rooted in traditional Indian religion. The bedrock of Hinduism is the belief that the Vedas are sacred revelations and that a specific caste system is implicitly prescribed in them. Thus Hinduism is both a collection of religious beliefs and a sacred division of society with each part having its own moral law. Religiously and philosophically, Hinduism is diverse. It assumes that there are innumerable legitimate ways of worshiping the supreme principle of life. Consequently it readily incorporates new sects, doctrines, beliefs, rites, and deities. The numerous Hindu gods are all considered aspects of Brahma, the supreme and undefinable principle of life. According to Hinduism, Brahma suffuses all things and at the same time transcends all things. The various deities are considered specific manifestations of Brahma, each of whom helps people to reach Brahma by means of rituals.

Hinduism is a guide to life, whose goal is to reach Brahma. There are four steps in this search, progressing from study of the Vedas in youth to complete asceticism in old age. In their quest for Brahma, people are to observe *dharma*, a moral law nearly as complex as Hinduism itself. Dharma stipulates the legitimate pursuits of Hindus: material

Siva   One of the three most important Vedic gods, Siva represented both destruction and procreation. Here Siva, mounted on a bull and carrying a spear, attacks the demon Andhaka. Siva is seen as a fierce and bloodthirsty warrior. *(Source: C. M. Dixon/Photo Resources)*

gain, so long as it is honestly and honorably achieved; pleasure and love, for the perpetuation of the family; and moksha, release from the wheel of life and unity with Brahma. The society that a scrupulous observance of dharma could create is depicted in the Mahabharata, a long epic poem in which the law is personified as King Dharma, the bull of the Bharatas:

All the people, relying on King Dharma, lived happily like souls that rely on their own bodies that are favored with auspicious marks and deeds. The bull of the Bharatas cultivated Law, Profit, and Pleasure alike, like a family man honoring three kinsmen alike to himself. To Law, Profit, and Pleasure, now incarnated on earth in equal proportions, the king himself appeared as the fourth. In this overlord of men the Ve-

das found a superb student, the great sacrifices a performer, the four classes a pure guardian. Luck had found her place, wisdom its apex, all Law its kinsman with this lord of the earth.[4]

In short, Hinduism spells out the goals of life and how to attain them.

After the third century B.C., Hinduism began to emphasize the roles and personalities of powerful gods—especially Siva, the cosmic dancer who both creates and destroys, and Vishnu, the preserver and sustainer of creation. Since these gods are personal manifestations of Brahma, Brahma can be known through them. Thus people could reach Brahma by devotion to personal gods. From this emphasis on a god-force in all life came a tradition of nonviolence to all living creatures.

India's best-loved sacred hymn, the Bhagavad Gita, is a spiritual guide to the most serious problem facing a Hindu—how to live in the world and yet honor dharma and thus achieve release. The heart of the Bhagavad Gita is the spiritual conflict confronting Arjuna, a human hero about to ride into battle against his own kinsmen. As he surveys the battlefield, struggling with the grim notion of killing his relatives, Arjuna voices his doubts to his charioteer, none other than the god Krishna himself. When at last Arjuna refuses to spill his family's blood, Krishna—who is a manifestation of the great god Vishnu—instructs him, as he has instructed generations of Hindus, on the true meaning of Hinduism:

Interwoven in his creation, the Spirit Brahma is beyond destruction. No one can bring to an end the Spirit which is everlasting. For beyond time he dwells in these bodies, though these bodies have an end in their time; but he remains immeasurable, immortal. Therefore, great warrior, carry on thy fight. If any man thinks he slays, and if another thinks he is slain, neither knows the ways of truth. The Eternal in man cannot kill; the Eternal in man cannot die. He is never born, and he never dies. He is in Eternity: he is for evermore. Never born and eternal, beyond times gone or to come, he does not die when the body dies. When a man knows him as never-born, everlasting, never-changing, beyond all destruction, how can that man kill a man, or cause another to kill?[5]

Krishna then clarifies the relation between human reality and the eternal spirit. He explains compassionately to Arjuna the duty to act—to live

Kali Ma was the consort of Siva. Like him, she represented both destructive and procreative powers. Here she assumes her role as the mother goddess, but the necklace of skulls reminds the viewer of her ferocity. *(Source: C. M. Dixon/Photo Resources)*

in the world and carry out his duties as a warrior. Indeed, the Bhagavad Gita urges the necessity of action, which is essential for the welfare of the world.

The intimate relation between Hindu religion and the social structure of Indian life merits special attention. They are inseparable parts of a unity that forms the core of Indian civilization. The caste system on the social and economic side forms one part of the equation, and Hinduism on the religious side forms the other. Religion justifies the caste system, and that social system in turn stands as visible proof of the validity of religious teaching. The stability of the village is proof of the strength of this social and religious bond, which allows each village to be almost a complete universe in itself. The village, and not higher forms of social and political organization, was absolutely basic to Indian civilization.

Early in India's history Hinduism provided a complex and sophisticated philosophy of life and a religion of enormous emotional appeal. Hinduism also inspired and preserved, in Sanskrit and the major regional languages of India, the vast literature that is India's priceless literary heritage.

Jainism

The founder and most influential thinker of Jainism, Vardhamana Mahavira (ca 540–468 B.C.), the son of an aristocrat, accepted the doctrines of karma and rebirth but developed the animistic philosophy that human beings, animals, plants, and even inanimate objects and natural phenomena all have living souls. Mahavira taught that the universe and everything in it are composed of souls, usually mixed with matter. These souls, though infinite in number, are finite in nature, having definite limits. Souls float or sink, according to Mahavira, depending on the amount of matter with which they are mixed. The only way for any soul to reach eternal happiness is to rid itself of all matter so that it can float to the top of the universe.

Mahavira's followers, known as Jains, believed that people could achieve eternal bliss only by living lives of asceticism and avoiding evil thoughts and actions. The Jains considered all life too sacred to be destroyed. Yet if everything in the world possesses a soul, how can one live without destroying other life? The rigorously logical answer is that one cannot. Strictly speaking, the Jains could adhere to their beliefs only by starving to death. Instead of going to this extreme, the Jains created a hierarchy of life, with human beings at the apex, followed by animals, plants, and inanimate objects. A Jain who wished to do the least possible violence to life became a vegetarian. Nonviolence became a cardinal principle of Jainism and soon took root throughout Indian society. Although Jainism never took hold as widely as Hinduism and Buddhism, it has been an influential strand in Indian thought, and numbers several million adherents in India today.

Siddhartha Gautama and Buddhism

Siddhartha Gautama (ca 563–483 B.C.), better known as the Buddha, meaning the "Enlightened One," lived at the time when Jainism and Hinduism were evolving. The Buddha, like Mahavira, the founder of Jainism, was a Kshatriya, from a class likely to resent Brahman privilege. They both became dissatisfied with settled life and abandoned it for a wandering ascetic existence. The Buddha was so distressed by human suffering that he abandoned his family's Hindu beliefs in a quest for a more universal, ultimate enlightenment. He tried techniques of extreme asceticism, including fasting, but found that they led nowhere. Only through meditation did he achieve the universal enlightenment in which he comprehended everything, including how the world of samsara actually worked. His followers later believed that the Buddha taught them only what was necessary, but that he had seen much more. In this view, what he considered necessary were the "Four Noble Truths" contained in his first sermon. The message of the Four Noble Truths is that pain and suffering, frustration, and anxiety are ugly but inescapable parts of human life; that suffering and anxiety are caused by the human weaknesses of greed, selfishness, and egoism; that people can understand these weaknesses and triumph over them; and that this triumph is made possible by following a simple code of conduct, which the Buddha called the "Eightfold Path."

First, Buddha explained, people have to understand the evils they are suffering. Ultimate release can be achieved only if one has a clear view of the pain and misery of one's life. Next, one has to decide firmly to free oneself from suffering. This one can do by means of what Buddha called "right conduct" and "right speech," a way of living in which one practices the virtues of love and compassion, joy, and serenity in daily life. The fifth step on the Eightfold Path is to choose "right livelihood," a means of earning a living that does not interfere with the attainment of ultimate enlightenment. The sixth step is "right endeavor," the conscious effort to eliminate distracting and harmful desires. People can most readily see the worthlessness of desires, according to Buddha, by recognizing that everything and everyone in the world will pass away. Nothing is permanent. The seventh step is "right awareness," constant contemplation of one's deeds and words, giving full

The Great Buddha   This figure of Buddha sits grandly and serenely in a cave in Jung-Kang. Here Buddha is typical of Theravada Buddhism, in which individuals sought their salvation alone through asceticism, meditation, and monasticism. *(Source: Werner Forman Archive)*

thought to their importance and whether or not they lead to enlightenment. "Right contemplation" is the last step expected of travelers on the Eightfold Path. This step entails deep meditation on the impermanence of everything in the world. With the attainment of the eighth step, the traveler achieves *nirvana,* a state of happiness gained by the extinction of self and desires and the release from the effects of karma. Thus Buddha propounded his own version of karma and how it worked. Though rooted in Hinduism, Buddhism set off on a road of its own, a road that eventually led out of India, into Ceylon and parts of Southeast Asia, through central Asia, into China, Korea, Japan, and Vietnam.

Buddha also taught that if people understand that everything changes with time, they will neither cling to their egos nor worry about what they believe to be their eternal souls. To Buddhists a human being is a collection of parts, physical and mental. As long as the parts remain combined, that combination can be called "I." When that combination changes, as at death, the various parts remain in existence, ready to become the building blocks of different combinations. According to Buddhist teaching, life is passed from person to person as a flame is passed from candle to candle.

Buddhism placed little emphasis on gods. The gods might help people out of difficulties like illness, but they could never help people achieve enlightenment. In Buddhist teachings, the gods are not judges who monitor human life and reign beyond the grave. Like human beings, the gods are subject to the laws of change. Nevertheless, Buddha was not strictly an atheist. He conceived of a divine power that was infinite and immortal. As he told his followers: "There is an unborn, an uno-riginated, an unmade, an uncompounded; were there not . . . there would be no escape from the world of the born, the originated, the made and the compounded."[6] This unborn and unmade power had nothing to do with the journey to nir-vana. That was entirely up to the individual.

The success of Buddhism largely resulted from Buddha's teaching that everyone, noble and peas-ant, educated and ignorant, could follow the Eightfold Path. Moreover, Buddha was extraordi-narily undogmatic. Convinced that each person must achieve enlightenment alone, he emphasized that the Path was important only because it led the traveler to enlightenment, not for its own sake. He compared it to a raft, essential to cross a river but useless once on the far shore. Buddha warned his followers not to let dogma stand in the way of the journey. Buddhism differed from Hinduism by its willingness to accept anyone who wished to join, and in effect it tacitly rejected the caste system.

Buddha welcomed everyone, regardless of social status or sex, to join him in his exalted journey. He also formed a circle of disciples, the *Sangha*—an order of Buddhist monks. Buddha continually re-minded his followers that each must reach ulti-mate fulfillment by individual effort, but he also recognized the value of a group of people striving for the same goal.

After Buddha's death, the Sangha met to decide exactly what Buddhist doctrine was and to smooth out differences of interpretation. The result was the split of Buddhism into two great branches: the Theravada (or Hinayana, School of the Elders, or Lesser Vehicle) and the Mahayana (or Larger Ve-hicle). The Theravada branch, which found its greatest popularity in Southeast Asia, from Ceylon to Kampuchea (modern Cambodia), asserted that its tenets rested on the authentic teachings of Buddha—in short, that it represented the oldest and purest form of Buddhism. By ca 20 B.C. the monks of the Theravada branch met to write down what they considered the authentic teachings of Buddha and Buddhist tradition. Theravada Bud-dhism is called the "Lesser Vehicle" because of its conservative and strict doctrines. Followers be-lieved that the individual is saved only through a rigorous monastic life; because monasticism was the way for both men and women to follow Bud-dha's injunction to seek their own salvation, Ther-avada Buddhism created codes of monastic con-duct for communal life.

Mahayana Buddhism, far more liberal than the Theravada branch, believed that Buddhism was a vast system capable of saving many living things. It also held that the teachings of Buddha were fluid and would evolve over time according to different cultures and climates. Mahayana doctrine differed from Theravada teachings by maintaining that not all of Buddha's message was included in the canon of sacred teachings. Mahayana Buddhism empha-sized the compassionate side of Buddha's message. It was known as the "Larger Vehicle" because it maintained that there were many ways to salva-tion. Mahayana Buddhism stressed the possibility of other buddhas yet to come and taught that all buddhas follow a path open to everyone in the world. Mahayana held that Buddha in his previ-ous lives had been a *bodhisattva*—a wise being, a buddha-in-becoming. Bodhisattvas have achieved enlightenment but decline the reward of nirvana to help others. Later Mahayana Buddhism created a huge pantheon of heavenly buddhas and bodhi-sattvas to whom people could pray for help toward enlightenment. Mahayana Buddhism eventually won the hearts and minds of the Chinese, Japa-nese, Koreans, and Vietnamese. Yet not until the dramatic conversion of the Indian king Ashoka, some two centuries after the death of the Buddha, did Buddhist teachings spread much beyond India.

INDIA AND THE WEST (CA 513–298 B.C.)

Between the arrival of the Aryans and the rise of Hinduism, India enjoyed freedom from outside in-terference. In the late sixth century B.C., however, western India was swept up in events that were changing the face of the ancient Near East. Dur-ing this period the Persians were creating an em-pire that stretched from the western coast of Ana-tolia to the Indus River (see page 59). India became involved in these events when the Persian emperor Darius conquered the Indus Valley about 513 B.C.

Persian control did not reach eastward beyond the banks of the Indus. Even so, as part of the Per-sian Empire, western India enjoyed immediate contact not only with the old cultures of Egypt

INDIA TO CA A.D. 200

ca 2500–1500 B.C.	Indus civilization
ca 1500–500 B.C.	Arrival of the Aryans and development of Vedic society
6th–5th centuries B.C.	Development of Hinduism, Janism, and Buddhism
ca 513 B.C.	Persian conquest of northwestern India and the Indus Valley
326 B.C.	Alexander the Great conquers northwestern India and the Indus Valley
322–298 B.C.	Reign of Chandragupta
ca 269–232 B.C.	Reign of Ashoka
ca 261 B.C.	Ashoka conquers Kalinga, leading to spread of Buddhism in India
ca 183–145 B.C.	Greek invasion of India
ca 140 B.C.	First Chinese ambassadors to India
1st century A.D.	Shaka and Kushan invasions of India
A.D. 25–3rd century	Kushan rule in northwestern India
ca A.D. 78	Kushan emperor Kanishka promotes Buddhism

and Mesopotamia but also with the young and vital culture of the Greeks. What effects did contact with Persia and the lands farther west have on India?

Culturally the Persian conquest resembled the Hyksos period in Egypt (see page 29) in that it was a fertilizing event, introducing new ideas, techniques, and materials into India. In fact, the period of Persian rule was one of thoroughgoing innovation. As members of the vast Persian Empire, Indians learned the administrative techniques of ruling large tracts of land and huge numbers of people. The adoption of coined money for economic transactions was a far-reaching innovation. From the Persians the Indians learned the technique of minting silver coins, and they adopted the Persian standard to facilitate trade with other parts of the empire. Even states in the Ganges Valley, which were never part of the empire, adopted the use of coinage. Another innovation was the introduction of the Aramaic language and script, the official language of the Persian Empire. Indians adapted the Aramaic script to their needs and their languages—enabling them to keep records and publish proclamations just as the Persians did.

Likewise, India participated in the larger economic world created by the Persians. Trade increased dramatically with other regions under Persian rule. Once again hardy merchants took the sea route to the West, as had their predecessors of the Indus civilization. Caravan cities grew in number and wealth, as overland trade thrived in the peace brought about by Persian rule. New prosperity and new techniques also gave rise to rough-stone architecture, notably at the important city of Taxila in the northern Indus Valley (see Map 3.1). In short, the arrival of the Persians drew India into the mainstream of sophisticated urban, commercial, and political life in the ancient world.

Into this world stormed Alexander the Great, who led his Macedonian and Greek troops through the Khyber Pass into the Indus Valley in 326 B.C. (see pages 148–150). What he found in India is most readily apparent in Taxila, a major center of trade in the Punjab. The Greeks described Taxila as "a city great and prosperous, the biggest of those between the Indus River and the Hydaspes the modern [Jhelum River]—a region not inferior to Egypt in size, with especially good pastures and rich in fine fruits."[7] Modern archeology has shed light on Indian urban life in this period and in the process has proved the Greeks' praise excessive: despite its prosperity and importance as a seat of Hindu learning, Taxila was an unassuming town, a poor town when compared with the cities of the Near East.

From Taxila, Alexander marched to the mouth of the Indus River before turning west and leaving India forever. A riot of bloodshed and destruction, Alexander's invasion facilitated the rise of the first kingdom to embrace all of India.

THE MAURYAN EMPIRE
(CA 322–232 B.C.)

Alexander disrupted the political map of western India and died without organizing his conquests, leaving the area in confusion. Chandragupta, the ruler of a small state in the Ganges Valley, took advantage of this situation by defeating his enemies

Lion Capital of Ashoka   This lion capital from a column of Ashoka handsomely represents the emperor's political power. It also illustrates significant Near Eastern and Greek influences on the Indian art of this period. *(Source: Raghubir Singh)*

piecemeal until, by 322 B.C., he had made himself sole master of India. He justified his position as king of India in 304 B.C. by defeating the forces of Seleucus, a general of Alexander the Great who founded the Seleucid monarchy. In the wake of this battle, Seleucus surrendered the easternmost provinces of his monarchy and concluded a treaty of alliance with Chandragupta. Hence Chandragupta not only defeated one of the mightiest of Alexander's lieutenants, he also entered the world of Hellenistic politics (see Chapter 5).

The real heir to Alexander's conquest, Chandragupta created the great Mauryan Empire, which stretched from the Punjab and Himalayas in the north almost to the tip of the subcontinent, from modern Afghanistan in the west to Bengal in the east. In the administration of his empire, Chandragupta adopted the Persian practice of dividing the area into provinces. Each province was assigned a governor, most of whom were drawn from Chandragupta's own family. The smallest unit in this system was typically the village, the mainstay of Indian life. From his capital at Pataliputra, in the valley of the Ganges, the king sent agents to the provinces to oversee the workings of government and to keep him informed of conditions in his realm. Chandragupta also enjoyed the able assistance of his great minister Kautilya, who wrote a practical treatise on statecraft. For the first time in Indian history, one man governed most of the subcontinent, exercising control through delegated power.

Chandragupta applied the lessons learned from Persian rule with stunning effectiveness. He established a complex bureaucracy to see to the operation of the state and a bureaucratic taxation system that financed public services. Chandragupta also built a regular army, complete with departments for everything from naval matters to the collection of supplies. He exercised tight control, to some degree repressing the people in order to retain power.

Megasthenes, a Greek ambassador of King Seleucus, left a lively description of life at Chandragupta's court. Like many other monarchs, Chandragupta feared treachery, especially assassination, but nonetheless refused to leave government to others. Therefore he took elaborate precautions against intrigue. According to Megasthenes:

Attendance on the king's person is the duty of women, who indeed are bought from their fathers. Outside the gates of the palace stand the bodyguards and the rest of the soldiers. . . . Nor does the king sleep during the day, and at night he is forced at various hours to change his bed because of those plotting against him. Of his non-military departures from the palace one is to the courts, in which he passes the day hearing cases to the end, even if the hour arrives for attendance on his person. . . . When he leaves to hunt, he is thickly surrounded by a circle of women, and on the outside by spear-carrying bodyguards. The road is fenced off with ropes, and to anyone who passes within the ropes as far as the women death is the penalty.[8]

These measures worked: after resigning the king-ship, Chandragupta died the peaceful death of a Jain ascetic in 298 B.C.

Chandragupta left behind a kingdom organized to maintain order and defend India from invasion. India enjoyed economic prosperity and communi-cations with its neighbors. At a time when many of the major cultures of the world were in direct touch with one another, the Indians, who had created much from their own experience and had learned much from others, could proudly make their own contributions in both cultural and ma-terial spheres.

The Reign of Ashoka (ca 269–232 B.C.)

The years after Chandragupta's death in 298 B.C. were an epoch of political greatness, thanks largely to Ashoka, one of India's most remarkable figures. The grandson of Chandragupta, Ashoka extended the Mauryan Empire to its farthest limits. The era of Ashoka was enormously important in the relig-ious and intellectual history of the world. A man in search of spiritual solace, Ashoka embraced Buddhism and helped to establish it as an impor-tant religion. Buddhism would take deep and last-ing root throughout much of the East, but not in India itself.

As a young prince, Ashoka served as governor of two important provinces, both seats of Bud-dhism—at this time still solely an Indian relig-ion—and both commercially wealthy. While gov-ernor, Ashoka met and married Devi, a lady of the merchant class who would later end her life spread-ing Buddhism to Ceylon. The young prince spent his leisure hours hunting, horseback riding, and enjoying lavish feasts. Yet he was a sensitive and perceptive young man, known for his fondness for

and study of birds. In religion Ashoka was deeply influenced by Brahmanism and Jainism, which pointed him toward a broad religious outlook.

At the death of his father about 274 B.C., Ashoka rebelled against his older brother, the rightful king, and after four years of fighting succeeded in his bloody bid for the throne. Crowned king of In-dia, he extended Mauryan conquests, initiated or renewed friendly relations with neighboring pow-ers, and reorganized his empire. Ashoka ruled in-telligently and energetically. He was equally seri-ous about his pleasures, especially those of the banquet hall and harem. In short, Ashoka in the early years of his reign was an efficient and con-tented king whose days were divided between business and pleasure.

The change that occurred in the ninth year of his reign affected not just Ashoka and his subjects but the subsequent history of India and the world. In that year Ashoka conquered Kalinga, the mod-ern state of Orissa on the east coast of India; in a grim and savage campaign, Ashoka reduced Ka-linga by wholesale slaughter. As Ashoka himself admitted, "In that (conquest) one hundred and fifty thousand were killed (or maimed) and many times that number died."[9]

Yet instead of exulting like a conqueror, Ashoka was consumed with remorse and revulsion at the horror of war. On the battlefield of Kalinga, the conquering hero looked for a new meaning in life; the carnage of Kalinga gave birth to a new Ashoka. The king embraced Buddhism and used the ma-chinery of his empire to spread Buddhist teachings throughout India. Ashoka's remarkable crisis of conscience has been the subject of considerable de-bate, much like the later conversion to Christianity of the Roman emperor Constantine. No one will ever know the content of Ashoka's mind, but the practical results of his conversion led to a more hu-mane governance of India.

Ashoka emphasized compassion, nonviolence, and adherence to dharma. He may have perceived dharma as a kind of civic virtue, a universal ethical model capable of uniting the diverse peoples of his extensive empire. Ashoka erected inscriptions to inform the people of his policy. In one edict, he spoke to his people like a father:

Whatever good I have done has indeed been accom-plished for the progress and welfare of the world. By these shall grow virtues namely: proper support of mother and father, regard for preceptors and elders,

Sanchi Topa This great monument of Mauryan architecture is the north gate of a stupa, or large mound built to house Buddhist relics. Standing eighteen feet high, the gateway is richly carved and decorated with Buddhist motifs. *(Source: BBC Hulton/The Bettmann Archive)*

proper treatment of Brahmans and ascetics, of the poor and the destitute, slaves and servants.[10]

Ashoka's new outlook can be seen as a form of *paternalism,* well-meaning government that provides for the people's welfare without granting them much responsibility or freedom. He appointed new officials to oversee the moral welfare of the realm and made sure that local officials administered humanely.

Ashoka felt the need to protect his new religion and keep it pure. Warning Buddhist monks that he would not tolerate schism—divisions based on differences of opinion about doctrine or ritual—he threw his support to religious orthodoxy. At the same time, Ashoka honored India's other religions. Hinduism and Jainism were revered and respected, and the emperor even built shrines for their worshipers. Buddhism, though royally favored, competed peacefully with Hinduism and Jainism for the hearts and minds of the Indian people.

Despite his devotion to Buddhism, Ashoka never neglected his duties as emperor. He tightened the central government of the empire and kept a close check on local officials. He also built roads and rest spots to improve communications within the realm. Ashoka himself described this work:

On the highways Banyan trees have been planted so that they may afford shade to men and animals; mango-groves have been planted; wells have been dug at an interval of every half a kos, approximately every two miles; resting places have been set up; watering-places have been established for the benefit of animals and men.[11]

These measures also facilitated the march of armies and the armed enforcement of Ashoka's authority. Ashoka's efforts were eminently successful: never before his reign and not again until the modern period did so much of India enjoy peace, prosperity, and humane rule.

India and Its Invaders
(ca 250 B.C.–A.D. 200)

Ashoka's reign was the high point of ancient India's political history. Ashoka's successors remained on the throne until about 185 B.C.; there-

after India was subject to repeated foreign invasions, confined principally to the northwest, that constantly changed the political map of the country. For many years the history of India was a tale of relentless war between invaders and Indians and among native Indian kings as well. The energy consumed by these internal wars prevented the Indians from driving out the invaders, from bringing peace and prosperity to the land. Still, even though each wave of newcomers left its mark on the cultural heritage of India, Indian civilization triumphed, changing the invaders as well as being fertilized by them.

The Kushans, whose authority in India lasted until the third century A.D., were particularly significant because their empire encompassed much of central Asia as well as northwestern India. The Kushans put India in closer contact with its eastern neighbors. The Kushan invaders were assimilated into Indian society as Kshatriyas, of higher status than native Vaisya, Shudra, outcastes, and untouchables, and once again a backward nomadic people fell under the spell of a more sophisticated civilization.

The political map of India after Ashoka was fragmented: the Kushans and earlier invaders held northwestern India, and petty Indian kings ruled small realms in the rest of India. For many years the political history of India was a tale of relentless war among local Indian kings. The energy these wars consumed did nothing for India's capacity to resist foreign invaders.

Although the Kushans were the final nail in the coffin of Ashoka's political efforts to unite India, they played a valuable role by giving northwest India a long period in which to absorb the newcomers and adapt the cultural innovations introduced by the various invaders. The Kushans were receptive to external influence and were subject to many of the influences that acted on the Indians. Kushans and Indians alike absorbed Greek ideas. Greek culture made its greatest impression on Indian art. Greek artists and sculptors working in India adorned Buddhist shrines, modeling the earliest representation of Buddha on Hellenistic statues of Apollo, and were the leading force behind the Gandhara school of art in India. Only the form, however, was Greek; the content was purely Buddhist. In short, India owes a modest cultural debt to Hellenism. Just as Ashoka's Buddhist missionaries made no impression on the Greek world, so Hellenism gave India some fresh ideas but had no lasting impact on the essence of Indian life. Only Buddhism, which addressed itself to all human beings rather than to any particular culture, was at all significant as a meeting-ground for the Greeks, Indians, and Kushans. Otherwise, the outlooks and values of Greek and Indian cultures were too different and too tenacious for one to assimilate the essence of the other.

The most significant and lasting gift of these years was the spread of Buddhism to China. India's invaders embraced Buddhism enthusiastically and protected the Buddhist order. They preferred the teachings of the Mahayana sect, more compassionate and flexible than its rival Theravada branch. In the course of their commercial dealings, they carried Mahayana Buddhism across inner Asia to China, transforming it from a purely Indian sect into an international religion.

SUMMARY

By roughly 250 B.C. India had developed a highly accomplished urban civilization sustained by systematic agriculture. Many of the fundamental ideals, beliefs, customs, and religious practices that would leave their mark on succeeding generations had already taken shape. These early years of Indian history were especially rich in religion. Not only did the Indians form several different views of the nature of life and visions of an afterlife, but they also made a fundamental impact on life in China by the spread of Buddhism. Hinduism, both religious and social in nature, was for the Indians themselves perhaps the most important development of this period, an ancient heritage that is still a vital factor in Indian life.

NOTES

1. M. Wheeler, *Early India and Pakistan to Ashoka* (London: Thames and Hudson, 1959), pp. 106–107.
2. Rigveda 10.90, translated by A. L. Basham, in *The Wonder That Was India* (New York: Grove Press, 1959), p. 241.
3. J. Mascaro, trans., *The Upanishads* (London: Penguin Books, 1965), pp. 117–118.

4. J. A. B. van Buitenen, trans., *The Mahabharata,* vol. 1, *The Book of the Beginning* (Chicago: University of Chicago Press, 1973), 214.1–7.
5. J. Mascaro, trans., *The Bhagavad Gita* (London: Penguin Books, 1962), 2.17–21.
6. Quoted in N. W. Ross, *Three Ways of Asian Wisdom* (New York: Simon and Schuster, 1966), p. 94.
7. Arrian, *Anabasis* 5.8.2; Plutarch, *Alexander* 59.1. Translation by John Buckler.
8. Strabo 15.1.55. Translation by John Buckler.
9. Quoted in B. G. Gokhale, *Asoka Maurya* (New York: Twayne Publishers, 1966), p. 157.
10. Pillar Edict 7, quoted ibid., p. 169.
11. Quoted ibid., pp. 168–169.

SUGGESTED READING

Much splendid work has been done on the geographical background of ancient Indian society. Two fine works are O. H. K. Spate and A. T. A. Learmouth, *India and Pakistan: A General and Regional Geography,* 3d ed. (1967); and B. L. C. Johnson, *South Asia: Selective Studies of the Essential Geography of India, Pakistan, and Ceylon* (1969). A masterpiece in its own right is J. Schwartzberg, ed., *An Historical Atlas of South Asia* (1978), the epitome of what a historical atlas should be. Its contents range well into contemporary times.

General histories of India are too numerous to list, with the exception of A. L. Basham, *The Wonder That Was India* (1959), one of the monuments of the field and a good introduction to nearly every aspect of ancient Indian history. Solid too are R. Thapar's two books, *History of India,* vol. I (1966), and *Ancient Indian Social History* (1978). Both are highly recommended. Especially rewarding are Z. Liu, *Ancient India and Ancient China* (1988); S. F. Mahmud, *A Concise History of Indo-Pakistan,* 2d ed. (1988); and H. Scharff, *The State in Indian Tradition* (1989), which covers the period from the Vedic to the Muslims.

Work on the Indus civilization continues at a rapid pace. A good recent survey is D. P. Agrawal, *The Archaeology of India* (1982), which is marked by good sense and sound judgment. Equally recent is G. L. Possehl, ed., *Harappan Civilization: A Contemporary Perspective* (1982), which combines excavation reports and analysis of material. His *Ancient Cities of the Indus* (1979) reprints articles by a number of scholars, thus providing a variety of perspectives on early Indus developments. Trade between the Indus and Mesopotamian civilizations is treated in E. C. L. During Caspers, "Sumer, Coastal Arabia and the Indus Valley in Protoliterate and Early Dynastic Eras," *Journal of Economic and Social History of the Orient* 22 (1979): 121–135. See also G. L. Possehl and M. H. Ravel, *Harappan Civilization and*

Rojdi (1989), which uses the newest archeological findings to explore the Harappan civilization.

For the arrival of the Aryans and subsequent developments, N. R. Banerjee, *The Iron Age in India* (1965), and C. Chakraborty, *Common Life in the Rigveda and Atharvaveda* (1977), treat the period from different points of view. More difficult but rewarding is F. Southworth, "Lexical Evidence for Early Contacts Between Indo-Aryan and Dravidian," in M. M. Deshpande and P. E. Hook, eds., *Aryan and Non-Aryan in India* (1979), pp. 191–234; the book contains a number of stimulating articles on the period.

Early Indian religion is a complex subject, but a series of books provides a good introduction to the topic. Old but still a classic is A. B. Keith, *Religion and Philosophy of the Vedas and Upanishads*, 2 vols. (1925). P. S. Jaini, *The Jaina Path of Purification* (1979), and T. Hopkins, *Hindu Religious Tradition* (1971), cover two of the major religions, to which should be added K. K. Klostermaier, *A Survey of Hinduism* (1989), and K. H. Potter, *Guide to Indian Philosophy* (1988).

Buddhism is such a popular topic that the bibliography is virtually endless. A valuable introduction by a leading scholar is E. Zurcher, *Buddhism: Its Origins and Spread in Words, Maps, and Pictures* (1962). A shorter and more spiritual approach is E. Conze, *A Short History of Buddhism* (1980). Also enlightening is W. Rahula, *What the Buddha Taught* (1971), which sheds light on the Theravada tradition, and R. Robinson and W. Johnson, *The Buddhist Religion*, 3d ed. (1982), which is more comprehensive. Still unsurpassed for its discussion of the relations between Buddhism and Hinduism is the grand work of C. N. Eliot, *Hinduism and Buddhism*, 3 vols. (reprinted 1954), which traces the evolution of theistic ideas in both religions. C. Humphreys has written extensively about Buddhism. The student may wish to consult *Buddhism* (1962), *Exploring Buddhism* (1975), or *The Wisdom of Buddhism* (new ed., 1979).

More recent is D. Fox, *The Heart of Buddhist Wisdom* (1985).

A stimulating and far-reaching discussion of intellectual developments in India is R. Thapar, "Ethics, Religion, and Social Protest in the First Millennium B.C. in North India," *Daedalus* 104 (Spring 1975): 119–132. Good translations of Indian literature discussed in the chapter are listed in the Notes.

Among the numerous works describing India's relations with the Persian Empire and Alexander the Great are several titles cited in Suggested Reading for Chapters 2 and 6. P. H. L. Eggermont, *Alexander's Campaigns in Sind and Baluchistan* (1975), focuses solely on Alexander's activities in India, as does E. Badian in I. Gershevitch, ed., *The Cambridge History of Iran* (1985). A. J. Dani, *The Historic City of Taxila* (1988), uses anthropological and historic evidence to study this important city and its influence.

Chandragupta's reign is treated in R. K. Mookerji, *Chandragupta Maurya and His Times*, rev. ed. (1966). J. C. Heesterman, "Kautilya and the Ancient Indian State," *Wiener Zeitschrift* 15 (1971): 5–22, analyzes the work and thought of Chandragupta's great minister of state.

The kingdom of Ashoka has attracted much attention. In addition to Gokhale's book cited in the Notes, R. Thapar's excellent *Asoka and the Decline of the Mauryas* (1961) is still an indispensable work on the subject.

For the Greek invasions, see W. W. Tarn, *The Greeks in Bactria and India* (1951), a difficult book but still valuable. A. K. Narain's more recent treatment, *The Indo-Greeks* (1967), is equally valuable and a bit more readable. For contact between the Hellenistic world and India, see J. W. Sedlar, *India and the Greek World* (1980), which approaches the problem of cultural transmission between the two civilizations. C. Drekmeier, *Kingship and Community in Early India* (1968), takes a broader approach to early developments.

4

The Rise and Growth of China to ca A.D. 200

Clay Warriors from the tomb of the First Emperor

ncient China provides another example of an early people confronting a formidable geographical challenge in order first to survive and then to build a complex and sophisticated civilization. The Chinese had inhabited this region of eastern Asia from the beginning of human existence. Like the Egyptians, they prospered along a great river. But the Yellow River was hardly the gentle Nile. It needed to be tamed before it would sustain life, and taming it called for group effort on a massive scale. The success of the Chinese in meeting this awesome challenge is reflected in the flowering of Chinese culture, in the overall political stability of the area and the prosperity of its people. As in Mesopotamia, Egypt, and India, so in China there were wars, and dynasty followed dynasty, but political disruption never crippled Chinese cultural evolution. Moreover, the Chinese were remarkably successful in governing a huge population settled over a vast area. Their success resulted in political and social stability seldom, if ever, found elsewhere in the ancient world.

- How did the early Chinese confront the geographical factors of climate, soil, and land?

- What did their response share with the solutions of ancient Near Eastern and Indian peoples to these same problems, and how did it differ?

- What form did Chinese success take in the shaping of society?

These are the questions addressed in this chapter.

THE LAND AND ITS CHALLENGE

While geography had left India an opening to the northwest and thus to the civilizations of the ancient Near East, terrain and distance made China's links to the broader world tenuous (Map 4.1). Between India and China towered the ice-clad and forbidding peaks of the Himalayas and the Pamirs, and beyond lay the vast expanses of Tibet and Chinese Turkestan. Geography isolated China in other directions as well. To the north stretched the Gobi Desert, some 500,000 square miles of desolate waste, and the Mongolian Plateau. To the south

rose mountains covered with forests and tracts of jungle. Beyond the shores of China lay Japan, inhabited at this early period by primitive peoples; the islands of the South China Sea; and the huge and then-uncharted expanse of the Pacific Ocean. China's main avenue to the major civilizations of the outside world was a threadlike corridor to the northwest, through the vastness of central Asia, past India, and ultimately to Mesopotamia. Though isolated, China was not sealed off completely. Like India, it enjoyed a link to other seats of civilization.

China encompasses two immense river basins: those of the Yellow River in the north and the Yangtze in the south. Both rivers rise in the mountains of Tibet and flow eastward across China (see Map 4.1). The Yellow River carries tons of loess, a fine light-colored dust whose color gives the river its name. Loess is exceptionally fertile and easy to cultivate, and this basin was the site of China's earliest agricultural civilization in the Neolithic Age (see page 13). Yet like the Tigris in Mesopotamia, the Yellow River can be a rampaging torrent, bringing disastrous floods and changing course unpredictably. Frequently called "China's Sorrow," the Yellow River had to be tamed with dikes. The taming of the river allowed China's great northern plain to be farmed, eventually nurturing a huge population.

The basins of the Yellow and Yangtze rivers are separated in the west by mountains, which give way to hills and finally disappear altogether in the flat country near the coast. The two basins are quite distinct, however, when it comes to farming. Dry farming of wheat and millet characterizes the Yellow River basin in the north; irrigated rice agriculture predominates in the warmer and wetter basin of the Yangtze. In the extreme south is the valley of the Hsi, or West, River, an area of mild climate and fertile soil that would later form the southern boundary of China. Within this enormous expanse of land the climate varies greatly from north to south and from east to west, with milder and wetter conditions prevailing in the south. Except for the river valleys, China is largely mountainous or semidesert land, which meant that people could thrive only in certain areas. Geography thus helped to ensure that human development in China would cling to the mighty river systems.

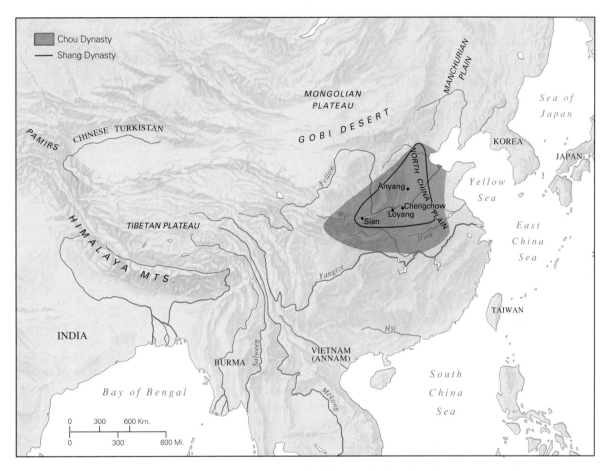

MAP 4.1 China Under the Shang and Chou Dynasties, 1523–221 B.C. The heartland of Chinese development is illustrated by this map, which shows the importance of the Yellow River in early Chinese life. Under the Chou, Chinese authority reached the Yangtze.

THE SHANG DYNASTY (CA 1523–1027 B.C.)

At about the time the Aryans were transforming Indian life, the kings of the Shang Dynasty rose to power in northern China. Unlike the Aryans, the Shang were natives, very closely linked to indigenous Neolithic peoples. Chinese Neolithic farmers had long ago settled into a life of sustained agriculture and animal domestication. Asian scholars dispute the nature and degree of outside influence on early Chinese development, but most agree that ancient Chinese culture was largely a native

growth. China did not suffer massive foreign invasion. To this relatively self-contained society, the Shang gave a long period of political rule. Once considered legendary rather than historical, the Shang Dynasty has been verified from its own written records and the work of modern archeologists.

Social Organization

The excavations at the modern cities of Anyang, the Shang capital, and Chengchou, perhaps the oldest city in China, have shed surprisingly bright

Shang House The ordinary farming family of Shang lived in a house very much like its Neolithic ancestors. The house was dark, close, and cramped, but the central hearth provided warmth and light. *(From John Hay,* Ancient China, *London: The Bodley Head, 1973, p. 41)*

light on the Shang kings and the society they ruled. Social divisions among the Shang were apparently simple but sharp: a ruling class of aristocrats, headed by a king and an incipient bureaucracy, directed the work and lives of everyone else. Warfare was a constant feature of Shang life, and the nobles were the warriors of Shang, those who enforced Shang rule. The Shang kings ruled northern China as a kind of family patrimony. The kings and the aristocracy owned slaves, many of whom had been captured in war. They also controlled the peasants, who served as semifree serfs.

The common people—serfs and slaves—performed all the economic functions of society. Most were farmers, whose way of life was basically Neolithic. Even in this remote period, however, Shang farmers knew how to cultivate the silkworm. Silken threads were woven into fine cloth, and under later emperors silk became China's prime export. Nonetheless, Shang farmers worked their fields with Neolithic tools and methods. Their homes too were Neolithic in construction. Each family dug in the ground a pit that served as the living area. Often they dug an entrance passage with a small platform inside the pit to keep water from running down the passage into the house. The central feature of the house was the hearth, which was dug out of the floor of the pit. Beside the hearth were wooden roof supports, against

which the roof timbers sloped. The family thatched the roof with reeds and clay, making a conical hutlike house. Although they helped create the wealth of Shang, peasant farmers enjoyed little of it themselves.

Other commoners were artisans. Dependent on the nobles, they manufactured the weapons, ritual vessels, jewelry, and other items demanded by the aristocracy. Shang craftsmen worked in stone, bone, and bronze but are best known for their bronze work. These early Chinese artists created some of the world's most splendid bronze pieces. Among the Shang, bronze was considered a noble metal, fit for weapons and ceremonial vessels but much too precious to be made into tools.

At the top of Shang society lived the king and his nobles, mighty figures elevated far above the common people. They lived in palatial houses built on huge platforms of pounded earth. The architecture of these houses set a pattern for house building that has flourished into modern times. The king and nobles enjoyed the magnificent bronze work of the artisans and carried bronze weapons into battle. Even after death, the king and his relatives had crucial social roles to play. The living worshiped and entreated them to intercede with the great gods, especially Shang-ti, the supreme god, to protect the lives and future hopes of their descendants. At first only the king and his family were worthy of such honors, but this custom was the forerunner of Chinese ancestor worship, an abiding element of Chinese religious belief.

Origins of Chinese Writing

The origins of Chinese writing appear to be deeply rooted in Shang religion. The kings of Shang were also high priests and frequently wanted to ask questions of the gods. Their medium was oracle bones, generally the shoulder bones of oxen or the bottom shells of tortoises. On one side of the bone or shell the king or priest wrote his message; on the other side he drilled a small hole, to which he applied a heated point. When the bone or shell split, the priest interpreted the cracks in relation to the writing.

Writing developed considerably later in China than in Sumer or India, but the Shang system was already highly developed and sophisticated. Originally pictographic, the signs used by the Shang contained phonetic values. Even so, the Shang and their successors created thousands of signs, resulting in a very complex system. Yet despite this complexity, like Sumerian cuneiform, mastery of even a few signs enabled people to keep records. Fluent literacy, however, demanded dedication, time, leisure, and thus wealth.

This system of writing proved popular and enduring. Later, when the script was simplified and standardized, it could be written and understood readily by literate Chinese who spoke different dialects. This accessibility was important, since many Chinese dialects were mutually unintelligible. The standardization of the written language, once achieved, proved to be indispensable for political, social, and cultural stability for centuries to come. The script spread throughout China and eventually to Korea and Japan, where it was adapted to local needs. The Koreans adopted the entire Chinese written language, including an approximation of the Chinese pronunciation of the signs. The Japanese went further than the Koreans, evolving a system in which the Chinese characters served as ideographs that had wholly Japanese pronunciations. In addition, they fashioned two other purely phonetic systems.

Literary mastery required such an effort that those who achieved it were a learned elite. Literacy

Shang Oracle Bone On one side of the bone the Shang diviner wrote his questions to the gods, and on the other side he applied a hot point. When the cracks in the bone led to the writing, the interpreter read the gods' message. Most questions dealt with the harvest, weather, travel, and hunting. *(Source: The Peabody Museum, Harvard University)*

was so politically important and socially valuable that education and scholarship were revered; the literate elite was essential to the king and deeply respected by the peasants. Literacy made possible a bureaucracy capable of keeping records and conducting correspondence with commanders and governors far from the palace. Hence literacy became the ally of royal rule, facilitating communication with and effective control over the realm. Literacy also preserved the learning, lore, and experience of early Chinese society, a precious historical heritage for future ages.

THE TRIUMPH OF THE CHOU
(CA 1027–221 B.C.)

Some Shang oracle bones mention the king of Chou, a small realm in the basin of the Wei River, a tributary of the Yellow River on the western frontier of the Shang domains. The Chou were an agricultural people who had emigrated into the region, perhaps from the northwest. They were also culturally sophisticated masters of bronze and of horse-drawn chariots. In the eleventh century B.C. the Chou king, a dependent of the Shang, became increasingly rebellious and ultimately overturned the Shang Dynasty.

The Rule of the Chou

When the Chou overthrew the Shang, they led China into the historical period. They extended Chinese rule beyond the boundaries of the Shang, and they grappled with the problems of governing the newly won territory. Because their contact with the Shang resulted in their adoption of much of Shang culture, the political victory of the Chou caused no cultural break. Nevertheless, the Chou made significant social and cultural strides. They succeeded in giving China a long period in which to consolidate these advances.

To justify their conquest ideologically, the Chou founders declared that the last Shang king had forfeited his right to rule because of his excesses and incompetence. They asserted that Heaven itself had transferred its mandate to rule China from the Shang house to its worthier rivals, the Chou. The justification belief of the Chou later served as the basis of the broader concept of the Mandate of Heaven (see page 104).

The victorious Chou confronted the formidable challenge of governing enormous areas of land. Communication within the realm was poor, and one king could not administer it all effectively. Moreover, the original Chou capital was near Sian in western China, too remote for efficient rule of the new domain. The Chou solved these problems by building a second capital at Loyang in the North China Plain (see Map 4.1) and by creating something resembling a loosely governed state.

The king of the Chou gave huge tracts of land to members of the royal family and to others who had demonstrated their talent and loyalty. At the outset, the newly appointed lords received their authority from the king. In a formal ceremony the king handed the new lord a lump of earth, symbolizing the king's gift of land to the lord. The lord pledged loyalty to the king and usually promised to send the king military forces if he requested them. A written record was made of the grant and the new lord's obligations and rights—an unprecedented secular use of writing. In effect, the Chou king was the political overlord of the land. He was also the supreme religious leader, who interceded with the gods for the welfare of Chinese society.

At first the Chou kings exercised strong control over their political dependencies. Gradually, however, the lords tried to strengthen their own positions, even at the expense of the king. Furthermore, the power of the lords grew with the prosperity of their holdings. The dependencies of the Chou were actually small islands of settlement scattered all over northern China, separated by wide tracts of undeveloped land. Over several centuries the growing populations of these settlements cleared new land, and eventually permanent cities arose. Once small and vulnerable, these settlements began to coalesce into compact regional states and then to fight among themselves over borders and territories. In this conflict the states in the interior of China were eclipsed by those on the borders, which took advantage of their geographical position to expand. The expansion spread Chinese culture ever wider. While conquering new territory, the lords of the border states were also wringing the most they could from their traditional seats of power. They became absolute rulers in their own right. Around them developed a hereditary class of aristocratic ministers of state, warriors, administrators, and tax collectors. China was gradually becoming a land of numerous independent kingdoms.

Along with the growing independence of the lords went a decline in the power and stature of the Chou kings. The lords used their troops to realize their own ambitions and stopped sending forces to the kings, disregarding their political obligations. In 771 B.C. a Chou king was defeated and killed by rebel lords. After that the Chou abandoned their western capital and made Loyang, the eastern capital, their permanent seat.

During the period known as the "Era of the Warring States" (402–221 B.C.), the entire political organization of the Chou Dynasty disintegrated. The Chou kings were little more than figureheads. The dreary cycle of warfare finally ended in 221 B.C., when the ruler of Ch'in, who had forced the abdication of the last Chou king in 256 B.C., conquered all the other states.

Social Change and Cultural Advancement in the Chou Period

The political events of the Chou period were to have a lasting impact on Chinese society. As the older interior states declined in stature, the aristocracies of these states lost their wealth. Educated, literate, and talented people were forced to seek their fortunes far from home. And the border states, dependent as they were on military and administrative efficiency, needed capable people to keep the wheels of government turning. The upshot was that impoverished aristocrats gravitated to the border states, where their much-needed talents opened the door to careers as ministers and officials. Merit, not birth, made the difference. This period saw the origins of a trained and able civil service, a group who saw to the daily workings of government and, later, gave a warm reception to the great philosophies of the Chou period. The rise of Chinese philosophy was largely a response to the political turmoil and warfare that wracked the country, which helps to explain its secular orientation.

Despite the long years of warfare and slaughter, the Chou period could boast of some remarkable cultural achievements. Cities grew up around the walled garrisons that the Chou established to hold down the Shang people. They evolved from army camps into genuine cities, some with huge populations. The roads and canals built to import food and goods to the city dwellers stimulated trade and agriculture. Trade was also stimulated and made easier by the invention of coined money.

A surge in technology during the Chou period permanently altered warfare, agriculture, and ultimately urban life. Under the Chou, craftsmen and artisans discovered the use of iron and rapidly developed its uses. Chou metalsmiths produced both wrought and cast iron—a remarkable achievement not matched in Europe until the fourteenth century. Chou craftsmen turned out an imposing number of weapons, especially dagger-axes and

Ritual Vessel This Shang bronze vessel excellently demonstrates the sophistication and technical mastery of early Chinese artists. The usual interpretation of the piece is that the tiger is protecting the man who is the head of his clan. Or the tiger may be having breakfast. *(Source: Michael Holford)*

swords (a mute commentary about life in the period). Use of the chariot in warfare led to improved harnesses for horses. The Shang had harnessed horses with bands around their girths and throats—a primitive arrangement that choked the horse when the harness was pulled hard. The Chinese did not perfect the harness until a later era, but they did so centuries before the medieval Europeans.

In agriculture the Chinese under the Chou Dynasty progressed from Neolithic farming methods to a metal technology. In place of the stone and bone tools of the Shang, Chou farmers used iron. Plows with iron shares broke the ground easily. Iron sickles, knives, and spades made the raising

Chou Ritual Vessel This bronze vessel is ample proof that Chou bronzesmiths could rival their Shang predecessors. Although not as richly decorated as the vessel on page 93, the bronzeworking is complicated and the fanciful animal shape delightful. *(Source: Robert Harding)*

and harvesting of crops easier and far more efficient than ever before. By increasing productivity, metal technology gave Chou farmers the tools to support a thriving urban culture.

THE BIRTH OF CHINESE PHILOSOPHY

The Chou period was an era of intellectual creativity. Many thoughtful and literate people turned their minds to the basic question of how people could live the happiest and most productive lives in the most efficiently run society. Chinese thinkers were more secular than religious in their outlook. While Indian mystics were creating a complex socioreligious system, the Chinese were

exploring philosophies of political development. Fascinated by political, social, and economic problems, they sought universal rules for human conduct. This period gave rise to three branches of thought—Confucianism, Taoism, and Legalism—and the popular belief represented by *I Ching* that left an indelible stamp on the history of China.

CONFUCIANISM

Of the three schools of thought, Confucianism has had the most profound impact on China. The historical K'ung Fu-tzu (551–479 B.C.)—better known in the West as Confucius—was primarily a teacher and did not put his thoughts into writing. His fame comes largely from his students, who collected his sayings in a book called the *Analects*.

Confucius's family was aristocratic but poor, and the young man had few immediate prospects of success. His family had him educated so that he could take his place in the civil service, yet he achieved fame as a teacher, not as a minister of state, an irony that failed to satisfy him. Confucius taught the sons of nobles but yearned to advise lords. Setting out with a small band of students, he sought employment from the lords of the emerging regional states in northeastern China. He served intermittently as a minor official and continued to spread his ideas. At last Confucius returned home to die among his students, considering himself a failure because he had never held high office.

Confucius's thought centered on the duties and proper behavior of the individual within society. He was far more interested in orderly and stable human relationships than in theology or religious matters. For all his fame, Confucius was not so much an original thinker as a brilliant synthesizer of old ideas. He taught that there is a universal law that even the sun, moon, and stars follow and that human beings too should live according to this law. Confucius considered the family the basic unit of society. Within the family, male was superior to female, age to youth. Thus husband was obeyed by wife, father by son, elder brother by younger. The eldest male was the head of the family. This order was to be respected even when those in authority were wrong:

The Master said, In serving his father and mother a man may gently remonstrate with them. But if he sees that he has failed to change their opinion, he should resume an attitude of deference and not thwart them; he may feel discouraged, but not resentful.[1]

Order in the family was the essential building block of order in society at large.

A man of moderation, Confucius was an earnest advocate of gentlemanly conduct. Only such conduct, which involved a virtuous and ethical life, could bring about peaceful social relations and well-run government. The Confucian gentleman was a man of integrity, education, and culture, a man schooled in proper etiquette. Asked to evaluate Tzu-ch'an, a minister of the Cheng state, Confucius discussed the virtues of a "gentleman":

In him were to be found four of the virtues that belong to the Way of the true gentleman. In his private conduct he was courteous, in serving his master he was punctilious, in providing for the needs of the people he gave them even more than their due; in exacting service from the people, he was just.[2]

The way in which a gentleman disciplined himself is apparent in the conduct of Master Tseng, the most important of Confucius's followers:

Master Tseng said, Every day I examine myself on these three points: in acting on behalf of others, have I always been loyal to their interests? In intercourse with my friends, have I always been true to my word? Have I failed to repeat the precepts that have been handed down to me?[3]

Confucius pointed out that aristocratic birth did not automatically make a man a gentleman. Even men of humble birth could reach this exalted level through education and self-discipline. Confucius did not advocate social equality, but his teachings minimized the importance of class distinctions and opened the way for intelligent and talented people to rise in the social scale. The Confucian gentleman was made, not born.

This gentleman found his calling as a civil servant: he advised the ruler wisely, administered the kingdom intelligently, and dealt with the people humanely. Confucianism urged good government, emphasizing the duty of a good ruler to rule his people wisely and with compassion. Confucius commented on the qualities of a good ruler:

A country of a thousand war-chariots cannot be administered unless the ruler attends strictly to business, punctually observes his promises, is economical in expenditure, shows affection towards his subjects in general, and uses the labour of the peasantry only at the proper times of year.[4]

Confucianism was a vital ingredient in the evolution of an effective civil service. As a social movement, Confucianism was a distinct and specially recruited community, whose membership was ideally restricted to learned and talented people who embraced high standards of ethical awareness and conduct. Confucianism offered those in authority a body of expertise on the creation and consolidation of a well-ordered, sound, and powerful state. That expertise, like medical knowledge, demanded to be taken on its own innate merits and was thus offered in the form of advice and persuasion; it could not legitimately be imposed by violence. Neither revolutionaries nor toadies, Confucian scholar-bureaucrats opposed bad government by upholding in nonviolent ways the best ideals of statecraft. The Confucian ideal proved so powerful that it continued to shape Chinese society nearly to the present day.

Taoism

The later Chou period was a time of philosophical ferment. Many others besides Confucius were grappling with the problems of humanity, society, and the universal. Especially significant were the Taoists, followers of a school of thought traditionally ascribed to Lao-tzu. Little is known about Lao-tzu's life; he is supposed to have lived in the sixth century B.C., but his very existence has been questioned. The book attributed to him, *Tao Te Ching (Book of the Way and Its Power)*, is probably the work of several people and dates only from the fourth century B.C.

Where Confucian political thought was practical and humanistic, Taoism argued that political authority cannot bestow peace and order if it restricts itself to the rules and customs of society. The only effective social control stems, according to Lao-tzu, from adherence to the ultimate nature of reality. The Taoist sage points the way to that nature, and without his mystic vision of nature effective rule is impossible. The only way to achieve this end, Lao-tzu taught, is to follow Tao, or the Way of Nature. *Tao Te Ching* portrays the Way as the creative force of nature:

There is a thing confusedly formed,
Born before heaven and earth.
Silent and void
It stands alone and does not change,
Goes round and does not weary.
It is capable of being the mother of the world.
I know not its name
So I style it "the way."[5]

According to Taoists, people could be happy only if they abandoned the world and reverted to nature, living simply and alone. Those who followed the Way had no further need of human society. If the philosophy of Taoism had ever been carried to its logical extreme, Taoism would have created a world of hermits.

Taoism treated the problems of government in a dramatically different way from Confucianism. In essence, the Taoists were convinced that government could do most for people by doing as little as possible. *Tao Te Ching* boldly declares that people are better-off left to themselves:

Exterminate the sage, discard the wise,
And the people will benefit a hundredfold;
Exterminate benevolence, discard rectitude,
And the people will again be filial;
Exterminate ingenuity, discard profit,
And there will be no more thieves and bandits.[6]

Lao-tzu argued that public works and services, from road building to law courts, led to higher taxes, which in turn led to unhappiness and even popular resistance. The fewer laws and rules, the better, Taoists urged. The Taoists also spelled out how, if there had to be a government at all, the people should be ruled:

Therefore in governing the people, the sage
empties their minds but fills their bellies,
weakens their wills but strengthens their
bones. He always keeps them innocent of
knowledge and free from desire, and ensures
that the clever never dare to act.[7]

The people are to be well treated, according to the Taoists, but they will be happiest if they remain uneducated and materially satisfied.

Taoism was most popular among the rulers and ministers who actually governed Chinese society. It gave them a safety valve in a rough-and-tumble world, a way of coping with the extreme pressures they faced. If a ruler suffered defeat or a minister fell out of favor, he could always resign himself to his misfortune by attributing it to the chaos of the world. In this respect Taoism became a philosophy of consolation—but only for a chosen few. The elite often adopted Taoism for consolation and Confucianism for serious everyday affairs.

Legalism

More pragmatic than Confucianism was Legalism, the collective name later given to a number of distinct but related schools of practical political theory that flourished during the late Chou period. Among the founders of Legalism were Han Fei-tzu (d. 233 B.C.) and Li Ssu (d. 208 B.C.), both former Confucians who had been heavily influenced by Taoism. Both were pragmatic realists who thought that the state should possess as much power as possible and extend it relentlessly. Their ideal state was authoritarian: the sensible ruler, in their view, should root out all intellectual dissent or resistance and all competing political ideas. Since human nature is evil, according to the Legalists, the ruler must keep the people disciplined and even suppressed if they are rebellious. The people should be well treated but need not be educated. The ruler should appropriate their labor to feed his armies and their wealth to fill his coffers. No frivolity is to be tolerated: people are to work and produce; they should not waste their time on the

A Meeting of the Minds   The three figures here—representing a Confucian, a Buddhist, and a Taoist—discuss their philosophies in an atmosphere of peace and harmony. *(Source: China Classic Publishing Company)*

study of history, philosophy, and other unproductive pursuits. Legalism was ruthless in its approach to the problems of government. Rather than refute Confucian political ideas, it repressed or dismissed them, as many twentieth-century ideologies have done to conflicting ideas. Nonetheless, Legalism was realistic and offered Chinese rulers practical solutions to the problems of governing large populations over great distances.

Legalism was at first influential in practical affairs. Both Han Fei-tzu and Li Ssu were high officials, in a position to put Legalist theories into practice. Though Legalism offered an effective, if harsh, solution to the problems confronting Chou society, it was ultimately too narrow to compete successfully as an independent school with Confucianism and Taoism.

I Ching and Yin and Yang

Chinese thought was not entirely tied to philosophical schools or outlooks. It remained greatly influenced, especially at the popular level, by a belief that individuals were integral parts of a cosmic whole that they could understand. One aspect of this attitude was the belief that people could learn profound truths and receive dependable guidance to successful lives through interpretations of oracles. The Shang had much earlier used oracle bones to learn the will of the gods. At this period in the Han Dynasty, *I Ching (The Book of Changes)* fulfilled a similar purpose. *I Ching* directs readers in how to lead an ethical life and how to live in harmony with the universe. It is thus more ethical than philosophical, yet its philosophical content and importance should not be denied.

The *I Ching* is essentially a book of oracles, and readers used its contents by reading the result of randomly tossed coins. When people wanted answers to questions troubling them, they read the results of the throw of the coins and consulted the appropriate oracle. For instance, for those seeking to understand the continuous flow of life, the appropriate oracle was the following:

Creativity is a constant—flowing through our lives and our world; the very essence of all things. It is one moment built upon its predecessor, the continuous flow of existence. From this, the cosmic example, one must model his inner self, aspiring to consistency in his moments of cosmic unity. It is in this construct of

persistent contact and identification with the ceaseless power of heaven that the goal is realized.[8]

For those who wanted to be in harmony with this flow, the best oracle was this:

If one is to be in touch with the cosmic flow, he must develop a consciousness that will permit communication. Through the wide gate of his spirit's awareness, the sage receives the earth-intended force and humbly puts it to use for all men. Through this attitude of serving, he builds cooperation so that men may learn to work together in the shaping of their destinies.[9]

These two examples are enough to demonstrate that the *I Ching* uses ethics, philosophy, and plain common sense to enable people to live a happy, moral life. The *I Ching* did not demand acceptance of any particular philosophical or political doctrine; it simply provided sound advice.

Another attempt to understand the relationship between cosmic forces and human life led to the concept of Yin and Yang. Han thinkers developed the idea that these two elementary powers were a constant cosmic process, with Yang representing the strong, radiant, dry, and manly, while Yin was weak, dark, moist, and womanly; yet they constantly work together to bring about a changing but predictable relation of power in the world, a power that is related to the four seasons. Yang becomes strong in spring and comes to fullest strength in summer, only to decline in autumn and still further in winter. Yin reigns supreme in autumn and winter. Together they represent the powers and natural rhythms of the year, those of birth, growth, and death. Both are essential to the process of life, for they are in essence dual. Yin and Yang are not opponents like good and evil. Rather they are complementary. Neither can exist alone.

The concept of Yin and Yang attempted to put the observable facts of human life into an intelligible form. It accounts for the changes in the seasons, their natures, their fruits, the climates of each, and the place of human beings in this natural and eternal cycle. Unlike Hindu religion, which held out the opportunity to escape from the burdens of life, Yin and Yang helped people to think of themselves as a legitimate part of a natural order, and not necessarily as an alien or unfortunate part. They belonged just as much as did spring or winter and the fruits of the earth. Both *I Ching* and Yin and Yang gave people a simple and unsophisticated way of orienting themselves in the world, and the very simplicity of the two contributed to their popularity in ways that the more learned philosophies could not.

THE AGE OF EMPIRE

The leader of the state of Ch'in deposed the last Chou king in 256 B.C. Within thirty-five years he had made himself sole ruler of China, taking the title Ch'in Shih Huang Ti, or First Emperor. Thus began the Ch'in Dynasty. Although the Ch'in Dynasty lasted only some fifteen years, the work of its emperors endured for centuries. Indeed, the Western name for China is derived from the Ch'in. The First Emperor unified China under a central government, and the Han Dynasty, which replaced the Ch'in, maintained this unity for centuries. Under the emperors of the Ch'in and Han, China flourished economically, culturally, and socially.

The Ch'in and Unification of China

The ancient Chinese historian Ssu-ma Ch'ien left this vivid description of the victory of the First Emperor:

With its superior strength Ch'in pressed the crumbling forces of its rivals, pursued those who had fled in defeat, and overwhelmed and slaughtered the army of a million until their shields floated upon a river of blood. Following up the advantages of its victory, Ch'in gained mastery over the empire and divided up its mountains and rivers. The powerful states begged to submit to its sovereignty and the weaker ones paid homage at its court. [10]

The Ch'in extended their sway as far south as modern Hong Kong and the South China Sea, introducing Chinese influence into vast new areas. Ch'in armies even penetrated as far as northern Vietnam. With this hard-won victory came political unity, which the First Emperor was determined to maintain.

The First Emperor considered a highly centralized state necessary to ensure a united China. He and his prime minister, Li Ssu, a founder of Legalism, embarked on an imaginative, sweeping, and rigorous program of centralization that touched the lives of nearly everyone in China. At the head of the state stood the emperor, an autocrat possessing absolute power. His first act was to cripple the nobility. As Louis XIV of France was to do many centuries later, the First Emperor ordered the nobles to leave their lands and appear at his court. Aristocratic families all across China were torn from their estates and transported to Hsienyang, the capital of Ch'in, where they built new homes around the court. The emperor took over their estates and organized China into a system of large provinces subdivided into smaller units.

The emperor controlled the provinces by appointing governors and lesser administrators, as well as other officials to keep watch on them. These officers were not drawn from the old aristocracy; they owed their power and position entirely to the favor of the emperor. Unlike the old aristocracy, they could not claim hereditary rights to their positions. The governors kept order in the provinces, enforcing laws and collecting taxes. One of their most important and least popular duties was to draft men for the army and for work on huge building projects.

In the interest of harnessing the enormous human resources of his people, the First Emperor ordered a census of the entire population. This information helped the imperial bureaucracy to plan its activities, estimating the costs of public works and the tax revenues needed to pay for them. The census also enabled the emperor to calculate the labor force available for military service and building projects.

A highly centralized empire needs good communications. Yet communication over an area as vast as China presented huge challenges, which the emperor met in several ways. First there was the problem of language itself. During the Chou period, states often spoke their own distinct dialects, which frequently borrowed words from other dialects. Written language also varied from dialect to dialect, with some people using signs that were unintelligible to others. These variations in language made central administration difficult. However literate, a governor might find himself transferred to a province whose dialect and script were unfamiliar; in such a case, he would be handicapped in carrying out his duties. The First Emperor and his ministers solved this problem by standardizing the written script.

Next the First Emperor standardized the weights, measures, and coinage of the realm. The

The Great Wall of China   The size and sheer awesomeness of the Great Wall comes through strikingly in this print. Over hill and through valley the Great Wall spanned some 3,000 miles of northern China. *(From D. Mennie and P. Weale,* The Pageant of Peking, *1922)*

old coinage was abolished in favor of new round coins with square holes in the center. The new coinage and system of weights and measures made it much easier for the central government to collect taxes. The emperor also standardized the axle lengths of carts. Most Chinese roads at the time were nothing more than deep tracks cut by the wheels of carts. Uniform axle lengths meant that all carts could use the same ruts, improving communications, strengthening imperial control, and making travel quicker and more convenient.

The First Emperor initiated land reforms that gave peasant farmers greater rights. He furthered irrigation projects and encouraged land reclamation to bring more soil under cultivation. These efforts, together with the widespread use of iron tools, increased agricultural production and fostered prosperity. The emperor also promoted the weaving of textiles, especially silk, which remained the aristocrat of Chinese fabrics. Thanks to the new road system, goods moved more easily than ever before and trade increased. Merchants became important figures, although their social status remained low; the First Emperor looked down on them as distinctly less than gentlemen. The growth of trade stimulated the growth of towns. Ch'in reforms and centralization helped to broaden the economy and thus enlarged the tax base for the government.

Foreign Danger and Internal Unrest

While the First Emperor was working to bring China unity and prosperity, he faced constant peril

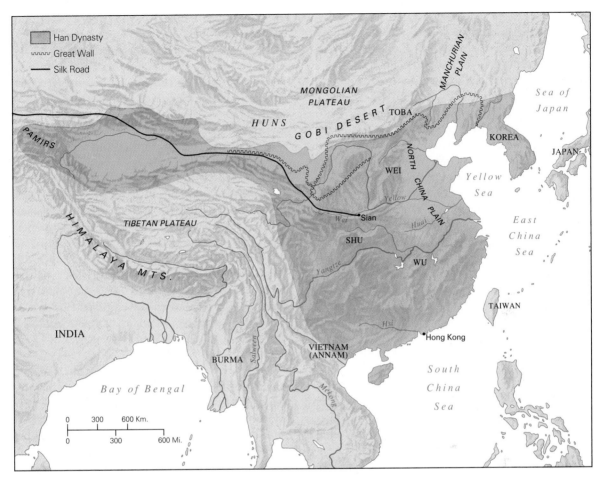

MAP 4.2 China Under the Han Dynasty, 206 B.C.–A.D. 220   The glory of the Han Dynasty is evident from this map. Unlike China under the Chou, frontiers have been pushed far into central and southeastern Asia. The Han ruled over far more territory than any previous dynasty.

on the northern border. For years the Chinese had pushed northward, driving out the nomads and taking over their grassy pasture lands. These nomads were the Huns, who in later centuries would carry death, destruction, and terror to the decaying Roman Empire. Chinese encroachment endangered the very survival of the Huns, each of their scattered tribes led by its own chieftain. In retaliation the Huns, on horseback and armed with swords and bows, struck back at the Chinese. In quick and repeated raids, they plundered prosperous towns and farms and disappeared into the vastness of the north.

Since Chinese expansion in the north had all along met stiff opposition, the northern states had built long walls for self-protection as early as the fourth century B.C. The First Emperor ordered

these various stretches of wall to be linked together in one great wall, extending from the sea some 1,400 miles to the west (see Map 4.2). The number of laborers who worked on the wall and the sheer amount of construction material needed are stunning tribute to the First Emperor's power. The Great Wall of China is probably humanity's most immense ancient creation. The Great Wall and the huge numbers of troops guarding the frontier gave the north a period of peace.

Despite their innovations and achievements and the peace they brought to the north, the Ch'in were unpopular rulers. The First Emperor was no altruist. Primarily interested in his own wealth and power, he was determined to reap the profits of his work. Nor was he a man to tolerate opposition: as a Legalist, he distrusted Confucian scholars, some

460 of whom he reportedly had buried alive. He tried without success to destroy Confucian literature and China's ancient literary heritage by a massive campaign of book burning. He enforced the tenets of Legalism vigorously and ruthlessly in an effort to wipe out any system of thought that might challenge his autocratic position. The Ch'in demanded obedience, not intelligence.

The common people fared no better than the Confucian scholars. The Ch'in took advantage of the new prosperity to levy heavy taxes, especially on the peasants. Taxation and forced labor on the Great Wall and on other projects mercilessly ground down the peasantry. Forced labor and military service disrupted many peasant households; while the men were away, their families worked long, dreary hours to feed themselves and meet the staggering burden of taxes.

The oppressiveness of the Ch'in bred fierce hatred among the people, one of whom described the First Emperor as a monster who "had the heart of a tiger and a wolf. He killed men as though he thought he could never finish, he punished men as though he were afraid he would never get around to them all."[11] The death of the First Emperor in 210 B.C. sparked massive revolts. Huge bands of peasants took up arms against the new emperor. In the ensuing struggle for power, Liu Pang, a peasant and petty official of the Ch'in, defeated his opponents and in 206 B.C. established the Han Dynasty.

The Glory of the Han Dynasty
(206 B.C.–A.D. 220)

The Han Dynasty marked the beginning of China's early imperial age. The dynasty also gave the Chinese their own name: they have traditionally called themselves "men of Han." Liu Pang, the victorious rebel, was no revolutionary. Because he, as a former Ch'in official, retained the main features of Ch'in administration and made no social reforms, there was no serious break in politics or culture between the two dynasties. The extreme political centralization of the Ch'in was relaxed, but the Han did not revive the feudalism of the Chou emperors. At least in theory, the Han Empire had an autocratic emperor aided by an educated but nonaristocratic bureaucracy. The basis of the empire, as always, was China's vigorous and hard-working peasants.

Under capable emperors like Liu Pang (206–195 B.C.) and his immediate successors, China recovered from the oppression and turmoil of the Ch'in period. Unable to conquer the Huns, who were renewing their threats on the northern border, the Chinese first tried to buy them off with lavish presents and stirred up internal trouble among Hun chieftains. In 133 B.C., however, Emperor Han Wu Ti changed this policy and went on the attack. In fourteen years of fighting, the Han drove the Huns still farther north. Chinese armies advanced into western Turkestan, where they opened up direct relations with the subcontinent of India. Equally impressive were the Han emperors' gains in the east. Chinese armies conquered western Korea, where they took over trade with Japan. The Han also extended their rule to modern-day Canton and the southeastern coast of China. By 111 B.C. when the emperor Han Wu Ti conquered northern Vietnam, Chinese rule had spread far beyond the natural boundaries of China (Map 4.2).

Han military conquests brought the Chinese into closer contact with distant peoples, which resulted in a dramatic increase in trade with the outside world. After Wu Ti conquered northern Vietnam, Chinese and foreign merchants moved in and set up trading stations under the supervision of Chinese officials. Southern China and northern Vietnam became meeting grounds for different cultures. The people of northern Vietnam accepted Chinese culture, and regions not far to the south were falling under the influence of Indian culture carried there by Indian merchants. Indeed, an independent state, called Funan by the Chinese, arose in modern southern Vietnam and Kampuchea among Malayan people who adopted many aspects of Indian culture.

Chinese rule in the south stimulated trade, and under the Han emperors Chinese merchants opened a new route from southwestern China via the rivers of Vietnam and Burma to ports on the Bay of Bengal. At first the Chinese were content to leave maritime trade in the hands of foreigners, but a later Han emperor sent an ambassador direct to the West (see page 216). Trade between China and its neighbors, together with the political and social stability of Han rule, gave China an unparalleled time of peace and prosperity. The Han historian Ssu-ma Ch'ien left a glowing report of Han administration as it existed around the year 136 B.C.:

The nation had met with no major disturbances so that, except in times of flood or drought, every person was well supplied and every family had enough to get along on. The granaries in the cities and the countryside were full and the government treasuries were running over with wealth. In the capital the strings of cash had stacked up by the hundreds of millions until the cords that bound them had rotted away and they could no longer be counted. In the central granary of the government, new grain was heaped on top of the old until the building was full and the grain overflowed and piled up outside, where it spoiled and became unfit to eat. . . . Even the keepers of the community gates ate fine grain and meat.[12]

By excelling in the art of government, the Han emperors ruled a huge expanse of territory and improved vastly the quality of life for their subjects.

Han Confucianism and Intellectual Revolt

Confucianism made a comeback during the Han Dynasty, but it was a changed Confucianism. Many Confucian texts had fed the First Emperor's bonfires, never to be recovered. Some dedicated scholars had hidden their books, and others had memorized whole books: one ninety-year-old man

The Army of the First Emperor   When the grave of the First Emperor was recently discovered, an army of ceramic soldiers came to light. Six thousand statues, armed with spears, swords, bows, and crossbows, were found intact in a huge pit, here seen still in excavation. The statues give a vivid idea of the army that unified China. *(Source: Xinhua News Agency)*

was able to recite two books virtually in their entirety. These heroic efforts saved much of China's ancient literature and Confucian thought from the Ch'in holocaust. Yet there was extensive corruption of traditional Confucian texts, and non-Confucian elements were introduced into them.

While trying to reconstruct the past, the new Confucianism was influenced by other schools of thought, even by the hated Legalism. Strengthened by these influences, Confucianism again took hold—a hold so strong that Confucianism endured as the intellectual and cultural basis in China until the twentieth century.

During the Han era Confucian scholars pondering China's past put into systematic form a concept that went back to the Chou. They elaborated the related theories of the *dynastic cycle* and the *Mandate of Heaven*. The link between the cycle and the mandate was divine approval of the performance of a dynasty. Rule of China was the gift of Heaven, which was considered a deity. With Heaven's blessing the duty of the emperor and his successors was to expand the borders, if possible, or at least to foster prosperity and maintain order for noble and peasant alike. Once emperors failed in their duty, whether through weakness or corruption, conditions deteriorated, and the empire was left prey to foreign invasion and internal unrest. At that point, Confucian scholars argued, the dynastic cycle came full circle. By failing to maintain the Mandate of Heaven, the last emperor of the dynasty lost his authority to the first man who could restore order and prosperity. That man succeeded because Heaven transferred the mandate to him. Dynasties waxed and waned according to how well they served the requirements of Heaven; thus the Confucians accounted for the rise and fall of dynasties.

According to Han Confucianism, the emperor was the intermediary between his subjects and Heaven. He served this function by performing all the sacred rites to the deities correctly and scrupulously and by watching for signs that Heaven was displeased. He was also responsible for protecting the empire from outside threats and invasions and for maintaining order with as little interference as possible in the lives of the people. If the emperor failed in these tasks, he lost the Mandate of Heaven and risked losing his throne to a worthier claimant. Confucianism explained history by looking to the virtues and vices of individuals, especially emperors and dynasties. Confucian historians saw history not as progressive but as cyclical, as repetitions of the same kinds of events.

In this climate of thought, the study of history flourished. Generations of Chinese scholars devoted their efforts to studying particular dynasties and events and individual rulers, ministers, and generals. The Chinese, like the Greeks, conceived of history as broader and more complex than the mere chronicling of events. Indeed, during the Han Dynasty China produced one of its finest historians, Ssu-ma Ch'ien (ca 145–86 B.C.), who can be seen as the Chinese equivalent of the Greek Thucydides. Like Thucydides, he believed fervently in visiting the sites where history was made, examining artifacts, and questioning people about events. Ssu-ma was also interested in China's geographical variations, local customs, and local history. As an official of the emperor, he had access to important people and documents and to the imperial library. Having decided to write a history of China down to his own time, Ssu-ma set about interviewing eyewitnesses and those who had shaped events. He also reviewed official documents and written records. The result, ten years in the making, was his classic *Records of the Grand Historian,* a massive work of literary and historical genius.

Nor did Ssu-ma's work die with him. The Pan, a remarkably creative family, took up his study of the Han. Among the most eminent of them was Pan Chao, China's first woman historian and scholar. Pan Chao also wrote poems and essays, notably *Lessons for Women* on the education of women. Taking up Ssu-ma Ch'ien's history, the Pan family wrote the first history of a Chinese dynasty. Thereafter, official court historians wrote the history of every dynasty. Like their Greco-Roman counterparts, Chinese historians considered recent and current history important in their investigations.

Han intellectual pursuits were not limited to history. In medicine, the Han period produced its own Hippocrates, Ching Chi, a practicing physician whose *Treatise on Fevers* became a standard work in Chinese medicine. Chinese surgeons grappled with the problem of reducing the pain of surgery, and the Han physician Hua To developed a drug that, mixed with wine, would render a patient unconscious.

The career of Chang Heng (A.D. 78–139), the great mathematician, was strikingly similar to that of the Hellenistic philosopher Eratosthenes. Both delved deeply into astronomy and concluded that

Village Life   These tomb figures depict an ordinary scene of village life in Han China. The two mounted figures represent wealthy men, for most villagers were too poor to keep horses. *(Source: The St. Louis Art Museum, Gift of the heirs of Berenice Ballard)*

the world is round, not flat as many of their contemporaries assumed. Chang Heng was not content to speculate; he also built models to test his theories. He even designed a seismograph capable of discerning the direction in which an earthquake was taking place, though not its severity. The brilliance of Han intellectual activity shone in its breadth and achievements.

Daily Life During the Han Dynasty

Because the people who chronicled events in Han China were an elite writing for other elites, more is known about the upper levels of society than about the lower levels. The lives of the common people were taken for granted or considered too vulgar to write about. Yet, though a complete portrayal is beyond reach, it is possible to sketch the outlines of daily life in Han China.

The peasant farmer was the backbone of Han society. Agriculture was considered an important and honorable human activity that distinguished the civilized Chinese from their barbaric and nomadic neighbors. Small households of farmers worked the land and generated most of the revenue of the empire. The Chinese peasant family was probably small, four or five people, frequently including a grandparent. Women were significant economic assets to poor farmers: both husband and wife performed hard manual labor in the fields. Men were typically required to spend time each year in the service of the emperor; and while they were away, their wives ran the farm. Farmers' existence was tenuous, for floods, drought, and unduly harsh taxes could wipe them out completely. Especially injurious was harsh, inefficient and sometimes corrupt government. When severely oppressed, the peasants revolted, turned to a life of begging or banditry, or they put themselves under the protection of powerful landlords. Thus it is easy to understand why the Han emperors were so proud of the peace and security of their reigns, which spared Chinese farmers the worst evils.

The staple grain under cultivation varied with the soil and climate. In the warm and wet south, rice was the traditional crop; in the north, farmers raised millet and wheat wherever possible. In northwestern China, peasants raised barley, which thrived on land too poor for wheat. Farmers also grew hemp, which was woven into coarse clothing for the common people. Some fortunate farmers had groves of timber or bamboo to supplement their crops. Most fortunate of all were those who grew mulberry trees, the leaves of which nourish silkworms, or groves of lac trees, which produced decorative lacquer. Wherever possible, farmers grew fruit and nut trees; farmers near cities found ready profit growing vegetables and ginger and other spices for city folk. Tea and sugar cane were raised in southern China but were still luxury items during the Han period.

Land use became systematic and effective under the Han, probably as a result of experience and of innovations recommended by Chao Kuo, a Han minister. Chao Kuo introduced a systematic ridge-and-furrow system of planting, with seeds planted in lines along the furrows. This method yielded fairly regular harvests and facilitated crop rotation because the position of the ridges and furrows would change annually. To maintain the fertility of the soil farmers treated their land with manure and crushed bones. The intensive character of Chinese agriculture meant that very little land was available for pasturage. Unlike his Indian counterpart, the Chinese farmer seldom raised cattle, horses, or donkeys. Dogs, pigs, and chickens were the typical domestic farm animals. The lack of draft animals meant that most farm work was done by hand and foot.

Farmers used a variety of tools, but the most important was the plow. The earliest wooden plow was a simple tool, more often pulled by humans than by animals. The new and more effective plow introduced during the Han period was fitted with two plowshares and guided by a pair of handles. This plow too could be pulled by manpower, but was typically pulled by a pair of oxen. The Chinese also developed an elaborate system using long hammers to mill grain and pound earth. At first the hammers were driven by people working pedals; later they were operated by animals and waterpower. Farmers used fans to blow the chaff from kernels of grain, and they used either mortar and pestle or hand mills to grind grain into flour. Irrigation water was pumped into the fields with devices ranging from a simple pole with attached

bucket and counterweight to a sophisticated machine worked by foot.

The agricultural year began in mid-February with the breaking up of heavy soil and manuring of the fields. February was also the beginning of the new year, a time of celebration and an important religious festival. This was the time to sow gourds, onions, melons, and garlic and to transplant oak, pine, and bamboo trees. Besides grain, farmers sowed beans and hemp and a variety of herbs. During the second and third months of the year, farmers practiced their archery to defend themselves against the bandits who infested the countryside; as a further precaution, they repaired the gates and locks of their houses. The fifth month was the time to cut the hay; the sixth, to hoe the fields. Meanwhile the women of the family were hard at work nurturing silkworms and making silk cloth, which they would later dye. Women also worked the hemp into coarse cloth. With the harvest, processing, and storage of the crop, farmers were ready for winter and the coming year.

City life was varied and hectic compared with the regularity of farming. The wealthiest urbanites lived in splendid houses of two or more stories, surrounded by walls and containing at least one courtyard. These palatial homes had such features as storage rooms and rooms for animals in the courtyard. The rooms or outhouses used for grain storage were built on stilts to protect against rats and moisture, which could cause rot or mildew.

The house itself was usually four-sided, with the door in one wall. The floors of the poor were covered with animal skins and mats of woven grass; those of the rich, with finely embroidered cushions and wool rugs. The bedrooms of wealthy homes were furnished with wooden beds, embroidered draperies, and beautiful screens for privacy. Fine furniture of expensive wood and beautifully lacquered bowls graced the houses of the wealthy.

Wealthy urban dwellers loved costly clothes, and everyone who could afford to bought fine and brightly colored silks. The wealthy also spent money on furs, usually fox and squirrel and sometimes badger. Expensive shoes lined with silk and decorated with leather became extremely popular. Wealthy women wore jewelry of jade and other precious and semiprecious stones, as well as gold earrings and finger rings. The urban poor probably had easier and somewhat cheaper access to silk garments than their rural neighbors, but their clothing was primarily made of coarse hemp cloth.

The diet of city folk, like their clothing, could be rich and varied. Owing to general prosperity, people during the Han period began to eat meat more frequently. Demand increased dramatically for wild game and young animals and fish, which were seasoned with leeks, ginger, and herbs. No longer was rice wine, like meat, a luxury for festival days. It began to be consumed avidly, and wealthy Chinese began to age vintages for twenty to thirty years. The Chinese were especially fond of pork, and roast pig was one of the most popular gourmet dishes. Other favorites were minced fish prepared in herbs and spices and fowl served in orange sauce, together with pickles and a variety of relishes. The Chinese also enjoyed liver and dog meat. Wood and pottery utensils were standard features of common households, but rich people relegated wood and pottery to the kitchen and dined on dishes decorated with gold and silver.

People with money and taste patronized music, and the rich often maintained private musical troupes consisting of small choirs, bells, drums, and pipes. Flutes and stringed instruments were also popular. People of more common taste flocked to puppet shows and performances of jugglers and acrobats. Magic shows dazzled the impressionable, and cockfighting appealed to bloody tastes. Gambling was popular but considered decidedly vulgar. Archeologists have found several board games.

As gangs of bandits infested the countryside, so crime plagued the cities. Officials were open to corruption and sometimes connived with criminals and gangs of thugs who had the support of wealthy and powerful families. At times the situation got so far out of hand that private armies roamed the streets, wearing armor and carrying knives and preying on the weak and helpless. Poor people who lacked influence suffered outrages and violence with no hope of justice or retribution.

Silk was in great demand all over the known world during the Han period, and strings of caravans transported bales of it westward. Another distinctive Chinese product was lacquered ware. Parts of China nourish the lac tree, which secretes a resinous fluid refinable to a hard and durable varnish. Han craftsmen developed lacquer work to a fine art. Because lacquer creates a hard surface that withstands wear, it was ideal for cups, dishes,

toilet articles, and even parts of carriages. Lacquered boxes and other articles were often decorated with ornamental writing or inlaid with precious metals. Such works of art were only for the rich; poor people contented themselves with plain lacquered ware at best. Some of the most splendid examples of lacquer work are elaborately carved; Chinese craftsmen loved geometric designs, and some of their work is so accurate that it suggests that they used mechanical tools.

Perhaps the most momentous product of Han imagination was the invention of paper, which the Chinese traditionally date to A.D. 105. Scribes had previously written on strips of bamboo and wood. Fine books like those in the royal library were written on silk rolls, but only the wealthiest could afford such luxury. Ts'ai Lun, to whom the Chinese attribute the invention of paper, worked the fibers of rags, hemp, bark, and other scraps into sheets of paper. Though far less durable than wood, paper was far cheaper than silk. As knowledge of papermaking spread, paper became a cheap and convenient means of conveying the written word. By the fifth century, paper was in common use, preparing the way for the invention of printing.

Han craftsmen continued the Chinese tradition of excellent metallurgy. By the beginning of the first century A.D., China had about fifty state-run ironworking factories. These factories smelted iron ore, processed it with chemicals, and fashioned the metal into ingots before turning it over to the craftsmen who worked it into tools and other articles. The products of these factories demonstrate a sophisticated knowledge of metals. Han workmen turned out iron plowshares, agricultural tools with wooden handles, and such weapons as swords, spears, armor, and arrowheads. Han metalsmiths were mass-producing superb crossbows long before the crossbow was dreamed of in Europe.

Iron was replacing bronze in tools, but bronzeworkers still turned out a host of goods. Bronze was prized for jewelry, dishes, and spoons. It was the preferred metal for crossbow triggers and ornate mirrors. Bronze was also used for minting coins and for precision tools such as carpenters' rules and adjustable wrenches. Bronze and wood were used for wagon and carriage wheels; Han wheels were made either convex or concave to give a smooth ride. Surviving bronze gear-and-cog wheels bear eloquent testimony to the sophistication of Han machinery.

Distribution of the products of Han craftsmen was in the hands of merchants, whom Chinese aristocrats, like ancient Hebrew wise men, considered necessary but lowly. In the Chinese scale of values, agriculture was honorable because farmers worked to win the gifts that nature bestowed. Merchants, however, thrived on the toil of others, and the art of winning profits was considered ungentlemanly and not quite legitimate. The first Han emperor took action to put merchants in their place, as the great historian Ssu-ma relates:

After peace had been restored to the empire, Kao-tsu [Liu Pang's posthumous name as emperor] issued an order forbidding merchants to wear silk or ride in carriages, and increased the taxes that they were obliged to pay in order to hamper and humiliate them.[13]

Yet the emperors and ministers of Han China realized that merchants had become indispensable. One outcome of this ambiguity was the conclusion that merchants ought to be regulated. Another was an early form of limited socialism—state monopolies on essential commodities like iron and salt, which made for price stability.

Retail merchants set up shop in stalls in the markets, grouped together according to their wares. All the butchers, for example, congregated in one part of the market, each trying to outsell the others. Nearly everything could be found in the markets, from food to horses and cattle, from ox carts and metal hardware to fine silks. The markets were also the haunts of entertainers and fortunetellers. The imperial government stationed officials in the markets to police the selling of goods and to levy taxes on the merchants. The imperial government also chose markets for the public execution of criminals: the rolling of heads served as an example and a warning to would-be criminals and political agitators in the crowd.

The transportation of goods in bulk was still difficult and expensive. Roads were primitive, but the Han developed several sturdy and effective types of carts and wagons, and a new harness for horses came into widespread use. Where earlier harnesses had fitted around the horse's neck, choking the animal when it pulled a load, the new harness fitted around the horse's chest and over its back, enabling it to pull heavier loads with less effort. This efficient horse collar finally reached medieval Europe in the eighth century A.D., a product of Asian technology that vastly influenced the history of the West.

Because of the difficulty of overland travel, the Chinese relied heavily on water transport. Since the major rivers of China run from east to west, canals were cut between the rivers to make north-south traffic possible. Bulk foodstuffs and goods could be transported fairly cheaply and swiftly on river boats, which also provided reasonably comfortable living quarters for crew and passengers. Maintenance of canals and dikes was expensive and made huge demands on the labor force, but these waterways allowed China to establish a flexible and effective network of communications.

Jade Burial Suit   Made from thousands of jade pieces connected by gold thread, this suit totally clothed the body of Lady Tou, the wife of Liu Sheng, a Han prince. Jade was especially esteemed because the Chinese believed that it preserved the corpse. In fact, the contents of the suit consisted of only a few teeth. *(Source: Robert Harding Picture Library)*

CHINA TO CA A.D. 400

ca 1523–ca 1027 B.C.	Shang Dynasty and invention of writing
ca 1027–221 B.C.	Chou Dynasty
551–479 B.C.	Confucius and rise of Confucianism
4th century B.C.	Lao-tzu and development of Taoism
ca 250–208 B.C.	Han Fei-tzu and Li Ssu and development of Legalism
221–210 B.C.	Establishment of the Ch'in Dynasty and unification of China
	Construction of the Great Wall
	Destruction of Confucian literature
202 B.C.–A.D. 220	Establishment of the Han Dynasty
111 B.C.	Chinese expansion to the South China Sea and Vietnam
A.D. 221–280	Three Kingdoms Era
4th–5th centuries	Barbarian invasions

The Fall of Han China

The Han Empire was an imposing political edifice. Eventually, however, wars on the frontiers and the emperors' enormous building projects put an intolerable strain on society. The emperors drew so heavily on the peasants as soldiers and workers that agricultural production declined severely. Great landlords saw their chance to expand their holdings and to shift the burden of taxation onto the already hard-pressed peasantry. Ground down by ambitious emperors and unscrupulous landowners, many peasants lost their land and sold their children, farm animals, and tools to the landowners, ending as tenants, hired laborers—or outlaws.

The emperor Wang Mang (A.D. 9–23), who was a usurper, attempted to reverse these trends. He tried to re-establish a state monopoly on grain so that private speculators could not exploit famines and shortages to make huge profits. He set about redistributing land to the peasants and wanted to abolish slavery. Unfortunately, Wang Mang's commendable efforts did little to improve conditions, and he was killed in a peasant uprising. Han Kuang Wu in turn defeated the rebels and established the later Han Empire in A.D. 25.

After a century of peace, the later Han emperors found themselves facing the same problems that Wang Mang had tried to solve. Once again, excessive demands were made on the peasants. Great landlords took over peasants' land and burdened them with heavy taxes. Disorder, intrigue, and assassination at court distracted the government, making intelligent leadership nearly impossible. A murderous rivalry developed between the old scholar-officials, who had traditionally administered political affairs, and the palace eunuchs, men usually of lowly origin who wielded huge influence from their lair among the women of the imperial harem. Turmoil and palace revolt meant that the great landlords were left unhindered. Once again the peasants staged massive uprisings. When the imperial armies were dispatched to put down the unrest, the victorious generals used their forces to carve out petty kingdoms for themselves. The palace eunuchs revolted against the emperor and his scholar-officials, and the Han Empire collapsed in general turmoil.

In the years that followed, known as the "Three Kingdoms Era" (A.D. 221–280), the empire was broken into three separate kingdoms. These kingdoms conformed to the natural geographical divisions of the land: the kingdom of Wei held the north; Shu, the upper Yangtze River Valley; and Wu, the lower Yangtze River Valley (see Map 4.2). Throughout this period, China experienced further disorder and barbarian trouble.

The difficulties with barbarians increased in later years, with catastrophic invasions from the north. Most significant were the conquests by the nomadic Toba from Mongolia, who created their own northern dynasty. Early in the fifth century the Toba assumed control of northern China,

Trieu Au Although Chinese armies were mighty, the Vietnamese held out against them. Trieu Au, seen here riding into combat on an elephant, played her part in the war against China in the third century. Having suffered defeat in battle, she committed suicide, but she is still revered today in Vietnam. *(Source: Yale University)*

making the Great Wall their northern boundary. They extended their sway into central Asia and stopped further barbarian invasions of China. Southern China, which remained under Chinese rule, actually benefited from these invasions: thousands of Chinese, among them many scholar-officials, fled to the south, where they devoted their energies and talents to developing southern China economically and culturally.

Barbarian invasions caused China distress and disruption, but the Toba and other nomads quickly came under the spell of Chinese culture linguistically, politically, and economically. The Toba emperor ordered the Toba nobility to speak Chinese at his court and to dress and act like the Chinese elite. The Toba adopted Chinese agricultural techniques and the bureaucratic method of administering the empire. Chinese culture withstood the impact of invasion so well that it remained vital and essentially unshaken. China's political system was so excellently suited to the land and its people that no barbarian invader could have done without it. That system encompassed not just a bureaucracy fully dependent on the Chinese language, but the culture, religion, and outlook of Chinese society. In that respect, China absorbed its invaders more successfully than had India.

SUMMARY

Chinese mastery of the land led to the harnessing of China's resources. A vital aspect of this triumph was the development of a systematic method of agriculture capable of sustaining a huge population. Prosperity and growth in population allowed the Chinese to shape their lives as never before. One result was a vibrant and sophisticated intellectual life. Whereas Indian society was largely permeated by religion, Chinese thought was for the most part secular in orientation. Although China sometimes experienced internal disorder and the threat of invasion, political upheaval never destroyed China's cultural heritage. By the end of the Han Dynasty, writing, Confucianism, and complex political organization of a huge region had left an enduring mark on the Chinese people.

NOTES

1. A. Waley, trans., *The Analects of Confucius* (London: George Allen and Unwin, 1938), 4.18.
2. Ibid., 5.15.
3. Ibid., 1.4.
4. Ibid., 1.5.
5. D. C. Lau, trans., *Lao Tzu, Tao Te Ching* (London: Penguin Books, 1963), 1.25.56.
6. Ibid., 1.19.43.
7. Ibid., 1.3.9.
8. Anonymous, *Change* (Virginia Beach: A.R.E. Press, 1971), p. 1.
9. Ibid., p. 2.
10. B. Watson, trans., *Records of the Grand Historian of China Translated from the Shih chi of Ssu-ma Ch'ien*

(New York: Columbia University Press, 1961), 1.31.
11. Ibid., 1.53.
12. Ibid., 2.81.
13. Ibid., 2.79.

SUGGESTED READING

The Shang Dynasty, once considered legendary, is now the subject of considerable attention. The best place to start is K. C. Chang, *Shang Civilization* (1981). D. Keightley, "The Religious Commitment: Shang Theology and the Genesis of Chinese Political Culture," *History of Religions* 17 (1978): 211–223, studies the development of Shang royal bureaucracy. Early Chinese agriculture is a hotly debated topic. Scholars like Ho Ping-ti, "Loess and the Origins of Chinese Agriculture," *American Historical Review* 75 (1969): 1–36, argue that Chinese technological and agricultural methods occurred without any significant outside influence; others, like W. Watson, *Cultural Frontiers in Ancient East Asia* (1971), maintain that the Chinese imported techniques from the West. See also Z. Liu, *Ancient India and Ancient China* (1988). Other solid general treatments of East Asia include C. Schirokauer, *A Brief History of Chinese and Japanese Civilizations,* 2d ed. (1989), and A. Craig, *East Asia, Tradition and Transformation,* rev. ed. (1989).

For the development of the Chinese language, B. Karlgren, *The Chinese Language* (1949), is a clear discussion, although it ignores the Shang. Newer and more comprehensive in its discussion of earlier writing is Ho Ping-ti, *The Cradle of the East* (1975). A lively and readable account of early life and the origins of writing, told primarily from an archeological standpoint, is J. Hay, *Ancient China* (1973). More technical are K. C. Chang, *The Archaeology of Ancient China,* 3d ed. (1977), and *Food in Chinese Culture* (1977), an edited volume containing historical and anthropological material. A somewhat dated but still useful survey of the early periods is provided by T. Cheng, *Archaeology in China,* 3 vols. (1957–1963), which treats the prehistoric, Shang, and Chou periods. H. G. Creel, one of the foremost scholars of early Chinese thought, in *The Origins of Statecraft in China* (1970), argues forcefully that early Chou emperors maintained firm control over their political dependencies in the first centuries of their dynasty.

A fascinating starting point for the study of early Chinese thought is B. I. Schwartz, "Transcendence in Ancient China," *Daedalus* 104 (Spring 1975): 57–68, which argues that the emphasis in ancient China was on social and political rather than religious themes. So much has been written on Confucius and the Confucian tradition that only a few works can be singled out for mention. A. Waley's translation of the *Analects of Confucius* (1938) is an eminently readable version of the work attributed to Confucius. H. G. Creel, *Confucius and the Chinese Way* (1960), deals with both the historical and the mythological Confucius.

The complexities of Taoism are lucidly set out by H. G. Creel, *What Is Taoism?* (1970), which discusses the differences between purposive and contemplative Taoism. One of the most significant of the contemplative Taoists was Chuang-tzu, whose career is studied by A. C. Graham, *Chuang-tzu: The Seven Inner Chapters* (1981). D. C. Lau's *Lao-Tzu, Tao Te Ching* (1963) is a vigorous translation of Lao-tzu's classic. H. G. Creel provides a sound introduction to Legalism in *Shen Pu-hai* (1974), which demonstrates that, far from being monolithic, Legalism consisted of a number of schools of practical political theory. On the careers of Han Fei-tzu and Li Ssu, see D. Bodde, *China's First Unifier* (1938).

The political and military success of the Ch'in is the subject of D. Bodde, *China's First Unifier: A Study of the Ch'in Dynasty as Seen in the Life of Li Ssu (280?–208 B.C.)* (1958). P. Nancarrow, *Early China and the Wall* (1978), discusses the importance of the Great Wall of China to early Chinese society. A good account of Ch'in road building is J. Needham, *Science and Civilization in China,* vol. 4, part 3 (1970).

The Han Dynasty has been amply treated by a master scholar, H. H. Dubs, whose *History of the Former Han Dynasty,* 3 vols. (1938–1955), is comprehensive. The turmoil of Confucianism in this period is ably treated in a series of studies, among them E. Balazs, *Chinese Civilization and Bureaucracy* (1964); H. Welch and A. Seidel, eds., *Facets of Taoism* (1979), which ranges more broadly than its title might suggest; and especially C. Chang, *The Development of Neo-Confucian Thought* (1957), a solid discussion of Han Confucianism. B. Watson has provided two good studies of Ssu-ma Ch'ien and his historical work: *Records of the Grand Historian of China* (1961) and *Ssu-ma Ch'ien: Grand Historian of China* (1958). China's most important woman scholar is the subject of N. L. Swann, *Pan Chao: Foremost Woman Scholar of China* (1950). K. Frifelt and P. Sorensen, eds., *South Asian Archaeology* (1988), contains a number of papers devoted to South Asia and its broader connections.

M. Loewe, *Everyday Life in Early Imperial China* (1968), paints a vibrant picture of ordinary life during the Han period, a portrayal that attempts to include all segments of Han society. Last, W. Zhongshu, *Han Civilization* (1982), excellently treats many aspects of material life under the Han, including architecture, agriculture, manufacture, and burial.

PERIOD (CA 10,000–CA 500 B.C.)	AFRICA AND THE MIDDLE EAST	THE AMERICAS
10,000 B.C.	New Stone Age culture, ca 10,000–3500	Migration into Americas begins, ca 11,000
5000 B.C.	"Agricultural Revolution" originates in Tigris-Euphrates and Nile river valleys, ca 6000 First writing in Sumeria; Sumerian city-states emerge, ca 3500 Egypt unified under Narmer, 3100–2660 Metal-working in Caucasuses, 3000	Maize domesticated in Mexico, ca 5000
2500 B.C.	Old Kingdom in Egypt; construction of the pyramids, 2660–2180 Akkadian Empire, 2370–2150 Middle Kingdom in Egypt, 2080–1640 Hyksos "invade" Egypt, 1640–1570 Hammurabi, 1792–1750 Hebrew monotheism, ca 1700	First pottery in Americas, Ecuador, ca 3000 First metal-working in Peru, ca 2000
1500 B.C.	Hittite Empire, ca 1450–1200 Akhenaten institutes worship of Aton, ca 1360 New Kingdom in Egypt; creation of Egyptian empire, 1570–1075 Moses leads Hebrews out of Egypt, ca 1300–1200	Olmec civilization, Mexico, ca 1500 B.C.–A.D. 300
1000 B.C.	Political fragmentation of Egypt; rise of small kingdoms, ca 1100–700 United Hebrew kingdom, 1020–922: Saul, David, Solomon Iron-working spreads throughout Africa, ca 1000 B.C.–A.D. 300 Divided Hebrew kingdom: Israel (922–721), Judah (922–586) Assyrian Empire, 745–612 Zoroaster, ca 600	Olmec center at San Lorenzo destroyed, ca 900; power passes to La Venta in Tabasco Chavin civilization in Andes, ca 1000–200 B.C.
500 B.C.	Babylonian captivity of the Hebrews, 586–539 Cyrus the Great founds Persian Empire, 550 Persians conquer Egypt, 525	

EAST ASIA	INDIA AND SOUTHEAST ASIA	EUROPE
"Agricultural Revolution" originates in Yellow River Valley, ca 4000		
Horse domesticated in China, ca 2500	Indus River Valley civilization, ca 2500–1500; capitals at Mohenjo-Daro and Harappa	Greek Bronze Age, 2000–1100 Arrival of Greeks in peninsular Greece
Shang Dynasty, first writing in China, ca 1523–ca 1027	Aryans arrive in India; Early Vedic Age, ca 1500–1000 *Vedas,* oldest Sanskrit literature	Height of Minoan culture, 1700–1450 Mycenaeans conquer Minoan Crete, ca 1450 Mycenaean Age, 1450–1200
Chou Dynasty, promulgation of the Mandate of Heaven, ca 1027–221	Later Vedic Age; solidification of caste system, ca 1000–500 *Upanishads;* foundation of Hinduism, 800–600	Trojan War, ca 1180 Fall of the Mycenaean Kingdom, 1100 Greek Dark Age, ca 1100–800 Greek Lyric Age; rise of Sparta and Athens, 800–500
Confucius, 551–479 First written reference to iron, ca 521	Siddhartha Gautama (Buddha), 563– 483	Roman Republic founded, 509 Origin of Greek *polis,* ca 500 Persian wars, 499–479 Growth of Athenian Empire; flowering of Greek drama, philosophy, history, fifth century Peloponnesian War, 431–404 Plato, 426–347

5

The Legacy of Greece

The Erechtheum, Parthenon

The rocky peninsula of Greece was the home of the civilization that fundamentally shaped the civilization of Europe and later the rest of the world. The Greeks were the first to explore most of the questions that continue to concern thinkers to this day. Going beyond myth making and religion, the Greeks strove to understand, in logical, rational terms, both the universe and the position of people in it. The result was the birth of philosophy and science in Europe—subjects that were far more important to most Greek thinkers than religion. The Greeks speculated on human beings and society and created the very concept of politics.

The history of the Greeks is divided into two broad periods. The Hellenic (the subject of this chapter) spanned roughly the time between the arrival of the Greeks (approximately 2000 B.C.) and the victory over Greece in 338 B.C. of Philip of Macedon. The Hellenistic (the subject of Chapter 6) began with the remarkable reign of Philip's son Alexander the Great (336–323 B.C.) and ended with the Roman conquest of the Hellenistic East (200–148 B.C.).

- What geographical factors helped to mold the evolution of the city-state and to shape the course of the Greek experience?

- What was the nature of the early Greek experience, the impact of the Minoans and Mycenaeans, which led to the concept of a heroic past?

- How did the Greeks develop basic political forms—forms as different as democracy and tyranny—that have influenced all of later Western and much of modern Asian history?

- What did the Greek intellectual triumph entail, and what were its effects?

- How and why did the Greeks eventually fail?

These profound questions, which can never be fully answered, are explored in this chapter.

HELLAS: THE LAND

Hellas, as the ancient and modern Greeks called their land, encompassed the Aegean Sea and its islands as well as the Greek peninsula (Map 5.1).

The Greek peninsula itself is an extension of the Balkan system of mountains stretching in the direction of Egypt and the Near East. Greece is mountainous; its rivers are never more than creeks, and most of them go dry in the summer. It is, however, a land blessed with good harbors, the most important of which look to the east. The islands of the Aegean continue to sweep to the east and serve as steppingstones between the peninsula and Asia Minor (Anatolia). As early as 1000 B.C., Greeks from the peninsula had settled along the coastline of Asia Minor; the heartland of these eastern Greeks was in Ionia. Thus geography encouraged the Greeks to turn their attention to the old civilizations of Asia Minor and Egypt.

Despite the poverty of its soil, Greece is strikingly beautiful, as the eminent German historian K. J. Beloch has written:

Greece is an alpine land, which rises from the waters of the Mediterranean sea, scenically probably the most beautiful region in southern Europe. The noble contours of the mountains, the bare, rocky slopes, the dusty green of the conifer forests, the white cover of snow which envelops the higher summits for the greatest part of the year, added to which is the profound blue surface of the sea below, and above everything the diffused brightness of the southern sun; this gives a total picture, the charm of which impresses itself unforgettably on the soul of the observer.[1]

The Greeks gloried in their land, and its beauty was one of the factors that elicited their loyalty to the soil of this hard peninsula. The climate of Greece is mild; though hot in summer, the air is dry and stirred by breezes. In winter snow may blanket the mountain slopes but rarely covers the lowlands.

Simultaneously, geography acted as an enormously divisive force in Greek life. The mountains of Greece dominate the landscape, cutting the land into many small pockets and isolating areas of inhabitation. Innumerable peninsulas open to the sea, which is dotted with islands, most of them small and many uninhabitable. The geographical

MAP 5.1 Ancient Greece In antiquity the home of the Greeks included the islands of the Aegean and the western shore of Asia Minor as well as the Greek peninsula itself.

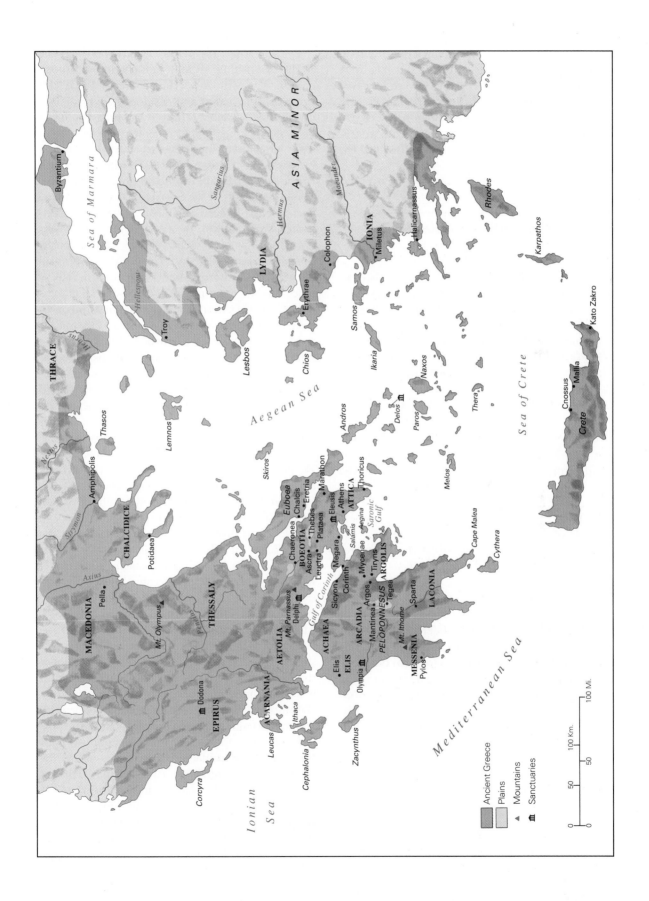

THRACE

Sea of Marmara

Byzantium

ASIA MINOR

Hellespont

Sangarius

Hermus

Maeander

LYDIA

Colophon

IONIA

Miletus

Halicarnassus

Rhodes

Karpathos

Troy

Erythrae

Lesbos

Chios

Samos

Ikaria

Naxos

Paros

Thera

Sea of Crete

Cnossus

Mallia

Kato Zakro

Crete

Amphipolis

Strymon

Mestos

Axius

CHALCIDICE

Potidaea

Thasos

Lemnos

Skiros

Aegean Sea

Andros

Delos

Melos

Cape Malea

Cythera

Mediterranean Sea

MACEDONIA

Pella

Mt. Olympus

Peneus

THESSALY

Euboea

Chalcis

Eretria

Marathon

Chaeronea

Thebes

Athens

ATTICA

Ascra

Plataea

Eleusis

Thoricus

BOEOTIA

Leuctra

Megara

Salamis

Aegina

Saronic

Gulf

Mt. Parnassus

Delphi

Gulf of Corinth

Sicyon

Corinth

Mycenae

Tiryns

ARGOLIS

Argos

AETOLIA

ACHAEA

Mantinea

Tegea

Sparta

LACONIA

ACARNANIA

Ithaca

ARCADIA

PELOPONNESUS

Mt. Ithome

Elis

ELIS

Olympia

MESSENIA

Pylos

EPIRUS

Dodona

Leucas

Cephalonia

Zacynthus

Corcyra

Ionian
Sea

Ancient Greece

Plains

Mountains

Sanctuaries

100 Km.

50

100 Mi.

50

fragmentation of Greece encouraged political fragmentation. Furthermore, communications were extraordinarily poor. Rocky tracks were far more common than roads, and the few roads were unpaved. Usually they were nothing more than a pair of ruts cut into the rock to accommodate wheels. The small physical units of Greece discouraged the growth of great empires.

THE MINOANS AND MYCENAEANS (CA 1650–CA 1100 B.C.)

Neither historians, archeologists, nor linguists can confidently establish when Greek-speaking peoples made the Balkan peninsula of Greece their homeland. Yet it can safely be said that they, like the Hittites, Persians, and Aryans, were still another wave of Indo-Europeans who were expanding throughout many parts of Europe and Asia during much of antiquity. By ca 1650 B.C. Greeks had established themselves at the great city of Mycenae in the Peloponnesus and elsewhere in Greece. Before then the area from Thessaly in the north to Messenia in the south was inhabited by small farming communities. Quite probably the Greeks merged with these natives and from that union emerged the society that modern scholars call "Mycenaean," after Mycenae, the most important site of this new Greek-speaking culture.

Of this epoch the ancient Greeks themselves remembered almost nothing. The *Iliad* and the *Odyssey,* the magnificent epic poems of Homer (eighth century B.C.), retain some dim memory of this period but very little that is authentic. One of the sterling achievements of modern archeology is the discovery of this lost past. In the nineteenth century Heinrich Schliemann, a German businessman, fell in love with the *Iliad* and decided to find the sites it mentioned. He excavated Troy in modern Turkey, Mycenae, and sites in Greece to discover the lost past of the Greek people. At the turn of this century the English archeologist Sir Arthur Evans uncovered the remains of an entirely unknown civilization at Cnossus in Crete, to which he gave the name "Minoan" after the mythical Cretan king Minos. Scholars since then have further illuminated this long-lost era, and despite many uncertainties a reasonably clear picture of the Minoans and Mycenaeans is possible.

By ca 1650 B.C. the island of Crete was the home of the flourishing, vibrant, and charming Minoan culture. The Minoans occupied Crete from at least the Neolithic period and developed a written language, now called "Linear A," which has never been deciphered. Only archeology and art offer clues to Minoan life, but they cannot provide a history of it. The symbol of Minoan culture was the palace. The palace was the political and economic center of Minoan society, which, like many ancient Near Eastern societies, was rigorously controlled from above. By ca 1650 B.C. Crete was dotted with palaces, such as those at Mallia on the northern coast and Kato Zakro on the eastern tip of the island. Towering above all others in importance was the main palace at Cnossus.

Nothing very definite can be said of Minoan society except that at its head stood a king and his nobles, who governed the lives and toil of Crete's farmers, sailors, shepherds, and artisans. The implements of the Minoans, like those of the Mycenaeans, were bronze, so archeologists have named this period the "Bronze Age." Minoan society was wealthy and, to judge from the absence of fortifications on Crete, peaceful. The Minoans were enthusiastic sailors and merchants who traded with Egypt and the cities of the Levant, the general area of the eastern Mediterranean. Their ships also penetrated the Aegean Sea, throughout which they established trading posts. Their voyages in this direction brought them into contact with the Mycenaeans on the Greek peninsula.

By ca 1650 B.C. Greek speakers were firmly settled at Mycenae, which became a major city and trading center. Later other Mycenaean palaces and cities grew at Thebes, Athens, Tiryns, and Pylos. The political unit of the Mycenaeans was also the kingdom. The king and his warrior-aristocracy stood at the top of society. The seat and symbol of the king's power and wealth was his palace, which was also the economic center of the kingdom. Within its walls royal craftsmen fashioned jewelry and rich ornaments, made and decorated fine pottery, forged weapons, prepared hides and wool for clothing, and manufactured the goods needed by the king and his retainers. Palace scribes kept records in Greek with a script known as "Linear B," which was derived from Minoan Linear A. The scribes kept account of taxes and drew up inventories of the king's possessions. From the palace, as at Cnossus, the Mycenaean king directed the lives

Minoan Naval Scene This fresco, newly discovered at Thera, probably depicts the homecoming of a Minoan fleet of warships. Though later Greeks thought that the Minoans had ruled the sea, fleets such as the one pictured here probably protected Minoan maritime interests and suppressed piracy. Despite its military nature, the scene displays a general air of festivity, characteristic of Minoan art. *(Source: National Archaeological Museum, Athens/Ekdotike Athenon)*

of his subjects. Little is known of the king's subjects except that they were artisans, tradesmen, and farmers. The Mycenaean economy was marked by an extensive division of labor, all tightly controlled from the palace. At the bottom of the social scale were the slaves; normally owned by the king and aristocrats, they also worked for ordinary craftsmen.

Contacts between the Minoans and Mycenaeans were originally peaceful, and Minoan culture flooded the Greek mainland. The two peoples at first engaged in peaceful commercial rivalry, but around 1450 B.C. the Mycenaeans attacked Crete, destroying many Minoan palaces and taking possession of the grand palace at Cnossus. For about the next fifty years the Mycenaeans ruled much of the island until a further wave of violence left Cnossus in ashes. These events are more disputed than understood, and the fate of Cnossus in particular has sparked fiery controversy.

There is no question, however, that the Mycenaean kingdoms in Greece benefited from the fall

of Cnossus and the collapse of Minoan trade. Mycenaean commerce quickly expanded throughout the Aegean, reaching as far abroad as Asia Minor, Cyprus, and Egypt. Throughout central and southern Greece Mycenaean culture flourished. Palaces became grander, and citadels were often protected by mammoth stone walls. Prosperity, however, did not bring peace, and between 1300 and 1000 B.C. kingdom after kingdom suffered attack and destruction. Later Greeks accused the Dorians, who spoke a dialect of Greek, of overthrowing the Mycenaean kingdoms. Yet some modern linguists argue that the Dorians dwelt in Greece during the Mycenaean period. Archeologists generally conclude that the Dorians, if not already present, could have entered Greece only long after the era of destruction. Furthermore, not one alien artifact has been found on any of these sites; there is no indication that any alien invader was responsible for the damage. Instead legends preserved by later Greeks told of grim wars between Mycenaean kingdoms and of the fall of great royal families. Apparently Mycenaean Greece destroyed itself in a long series of internecine wars, a pattern that later Greeks would repeat.

The fall of the Mycenaean kingdoms ushered in a period of such poverty, disruption, and backwardness that historians usually call it the "Dark Age" of Greece (1100–800 B.C.). Even literacy was a casualty of the chaos. Still, this period was important to the development of Greek civilization. It was a time of widespread movements of Greek-speaking peoples. Some sailed to Crete, where they established new communities. A great wave of Greeks spread eastward through the Aegean to the coast of Asia Minor. These immigrations turned the Aegean into a Greek lake. The people who stayed behind on the mainland gradually rebuilt Greek society. They thus provided an element of continuity, a link between the Mycenaean period and the Greek culture that emerged from the Dark Age.

Funeral Games   At the end of the *Iliad* Homer describes the funeral games given in honor of Patroclus, the companion of Achilles. The main event was the chariot race. Here the race has begun, and the painter states in the Greek inscription that one of the chariots seen here belonged to Achilles. *(Source: National Archaeological Museum, Athens/Ekdotike Athenon)*

HOMER AND THE HEROIC PAST (1100–800 B.C.)

The Greeks, unlike the Hebrews, had no sacred book that chronicled their past. Instead they had the *Iliad* and the *Odyssey,* which described a time when gods still walked the earth. For all his importance to Greek thought and literature, Homer was a shadowy figure. Later Greeks knew little about him and were not even certain when he had lived. This uncertainty underscores the fact that the Greeks remembered very little of their own past, especially the time before they entered Greece. They had also forgotten a great deal about the Bronze and Dark ages.

Instead of authentic history the poems of Homer offered the Greeks an ideal past, a largely legendary heroic age. In terms of pure history these poems contain scraps of information about the Bronze Age, much about the early Dark Age, and some about the poet's own era. Chronologically, then, the heroic age falls mainly in the period between the collapse of the Mycenaean world and the rebirth of literacy. Yet it is a mistake to treat the *Iliad* and the *Odyssey* as history; they are magnificent blendings of legends, myth, and a little authentic tradition.

The *Iliad* recounts an expedition of Mycenaeans, whom Homer called "Achaeans," to besiege the city of Troy in Asia Minor. The heart of the *Iliad,* however, is the quarrel between Agamemnon, the king of Mycenae, and Achilles, the tragic hero of the poem, and how their quarrel brought suffering to the Achaeans. Only when Achilles put away his anger and pride did he consent to come forward, face, and kill the Trojan hero Hector. The *Odyssey,* probably composed later than the *Iliad,* narrates the adventures of Odysseus, one of the Achaean heroes who fought at Troy, during his voyage home from the fighting.

The splendor of these poems does not lie in their plots, though the *Odyssey* is a marvelous adventure story. Rather, both poems portray engaging but often flawed characters who are larger than life and yet typically human. Achilles, the hero of the *Iliad,* is capable of mastering Trojan warriors but can barely control his own anger. Agamemnon commands kings yet is a man beset by worries. Hector, the hero of the Trojans, is a formidable, noble, and likable foe. Odysseus, the

The Shape of the Athenian Polis   This print of the Athenian acropolis shows clearly the geographical requirements of the polis. Early Greeks desired an elevated spot, or acropolis, for refuge; later it became the seat of the polis' temples. At the foot of the citadel spread the agora, public buildings, and private homes. *(Source: Caroline Buckler)*

hero of the *Odyssey,* trusts more to his wisdom and good sense than to his strength. Odysseus's wife Penelope faithfully endures the long years of war and separation, patiently waiting for her beloved husband to return from Troy.

Homer was strikingly successful in depicting the deeds of the great gods, who sit on Mount Olympus and watch the fighting at Troy as if they were spectators at a baseball game. Sometimes they even participate in the action. Homer's deities are reminiscent of Mesopotamian gods and goddesses. Hardly a decorous lot, the Olympians are raucous, petty, deceitful, and splendid. In short, they are human.

THE POLIS

After the upheavals that ended the Mycenaean period and the slow recovery of prosperity during the Dark Age, the Greeks developed their basic political and institutional unit, the *polis,* or city-state. The details of this development are largely lost, but by the end of the Dark Age the polis was common throughout Greece. Rarely did there occur the combination of extensive territory and political unity that allowed one polis to rise above others. Only three city-states were able to muster the resources of an entire region behind them (see Map 5.1): Sparta, which dominated the regions of Laconia and Messenia; Athens, which united the large peninsula of Attica under its rule; and Thebes, which in several periods marshaled the resources of the fertile region of Boeotia. Otherwise, the political pattern of ancient Greece was one of many small city-states, few of which were much stronger or richer than their neighbors.

Physically the term *polis* designated a city or town and its surrounding countryside. The typical polis consisted of people living in a compact group of houses within the city. The city's water supply came from public fountains and cisterns. By the fifth century B.C. the city was generally surrounded by a wall. The city contained a point, usually elevated, called the "acropolis," and a public square or marketplace *(agora).* On the acropolis, which in the early period was a place of refuge, stood the temples, altars, public monuments, and various dedications to the gods of the polis. The agora was originally the place where the warrior assembly met, but it became the political center of the polis. In the agora were porticoes, shops, and public buildings and courts.

The unsettled territory of the polis was typically its source of wealth. This territory consisted of arable land, pasture land, and wasteland. Farmers left the city each morning to work their fields or tend their flocks of sheep and goats, and they returned at night. On the wasteland men often quarried stone, mined for precious metals, or at certain times of the year obtained small amounts of fodder. Thus the polis encompassed a combination of urban and agrarian life.

Regardless of its size or wealth, the polis was fundamental to Greek life. Aristotle, who lived in the fourth century B.C. and was perhaps Greece's greatest thinker, could not envisage civilized life apart from the polis. "The polis," he wrote, "exists by nature, and man is by nature a being of the polis."[2] Aristotle was summing up the Greek view that the life of men and women in the polis was the only way to live according to nature. The polis was far more than a political institution. Above all it was a community of citizens, and the affairs of the community were the concern of all citizens. The intimacy of the polis was an important factor, one hard for modern city dwellers to imagine.

The mild climate of Greece meant that much of Greek life was spent outdoors. In a polis, as in a modern Greek village, a person might easily see most other citizens in the course of a day. Simi-

larly, the citizen would normally see the public buildings and the temples of the polis daily. The monuments of past victories, the tombs of dead warriors, all would be personal and familiar. In short, life in the polis was very public. The smallness of the polis enabled Greeks to see how the individual fitted into the overall system—how the human parts made up the social whole. These simple facts go far to explain why the Greek polis was fundamentally different from the great empires of Persia and China. The Greeks knew their leaders and elected them to limited terms of office. They were unlike the subjects of the Mauryan Empire or the Han Dynasty, who might spend their entire lives without ever seeing their emperors. One result of these factors is the absence in Greek politics of a divine emperor. Another is the lack of an extensive imperial bureaucracy and a standing army. The Classical Greeks were their own magistrates, administrators, and soldiers.

The customs of the community were at the same time the laws of the polis. Rome later created a single magnificent body of law, but the Greeks had as many law codes as they had city-states. Though the laws of one polis might be roughly similar to those of another, the law of any given polis was unique simply because the customs and the experience of each polis were unique.

The government of a polis could take any of several forms. It could be a *monarchy,* a term derived from the Greek for "the rule of one man." In a monarchy, a king represented the community, reigning according to law and respecting the rights of the citizens. In an *aristocracy,* the nobility governed the state. In an *oligarchy,* which literally means "the rule of a few," the running of the polis was the duty and prerogative of a small group of wealthy citizens, regardless of their status at birth. In a *democracy,* which means "the rule of the people," all citizens, without respect to birth or wealth, administered the workings of government. How a polis was governed depended on who had the upper hand. When the wealthy held power, they usually instituted oligarchies. When the people could break the hold of the rich, they established democracies. In any case, no polis ever had an iron-clad, unchangeable constitution.

Still another form of Greek government was *tyranny.* Under tyranny the polis was ruled by a *tyrant,* a man who had seized power by unconstitutional means. The Greeks did not in theory consider tyranny a legitimate form of government, but in practice it flourished from the seventh century B.C. to the end of the Classical period (338 B.C.). By the Classical Age, however, the Greeks considered tyranny a political perversion.

Ironically, the very integration of the polis proved to be one of its weaknesses. Because the bonds that held the polis together were so intimate, Greeks were extremely reluctant to allow foreigners to share fully in its life. An alien, even someone Greek by birth, could almost never expect to be made a citizen. Nor could women play an active political role. Women participated in the civic cults and served as priestesses, but the polis had no room for them in state affairs. Thus the exclusiveness of the polis doomed it to a limited horizon.

The individualism of the polis proved to be another serious weakness. The citizens of each polis were determined to remain free and autonomous. Rarely were the Greeks willing to unite in larger political bodies. When they did, they preferred leagues or confederations in which each polis insisted on its autonomy. The political result in Greece, as in Sumer, was almost constant warfare. The polis could dominate, but unlike Rome it could not incorporate.

THE LYRIC AGE (800–500 B.C.)

The maturation of the polis coincided with one of the most vibrant periods of Greek history, an era of extraordinary expansion geographically, artistically, and politically. Greeks ventured as far east as the Black Sea and as far west as Spain (Map 5.2). Politically these were the years when Sparta and Athens—the two poles of the Greek experience—rose to prominence.

Overseas Expansion

During the years 1100 to 800 B.C., the Greeks not only recovered from the breakdown of the Mycenaean world but also grew in wealth and numbers.

MAP 5.2 Colonization of the Mediterranean Though both the Greeks and the Phoenicians colonized the Mediterranean basin at roughly the same time, the Greeks spread over a far greater area.

Mosaic Portrait of Sappho The Greek letters in the upper left corner identify this idealized portrait as that of Sappho. The mosaic, which was found at Sparta, dates to the late Roman Empire and testifies to Sappho's popularity in antiquity. *(Source: Caroline Buckler)*

This new prosperity brought new problems. Greece is a small and not especially fertile country. The increase in population meant that many men and their families had very little land or none at all. Land hunger and the resulting social and political tensions drove many Greeks to seek new homes outside of Greece. Other factors—the desire for a new start, a love of excitement and adventure, and natural curiosity about what lay beyond the horizon—played their part as well.

The Mediterranean offered the Greeks an escape valve, for they were always a seafaring people. To them the sea was a highway, not a barrier. Through their commercial ventures they had long been familiar with the rich areas of the western Mediterranean. Moreover, the geography of the Mediterranean basin favored colonization. The land and climate of the Mediterranean region are remarkably uniform. Greeks could travel to new areas, whether to Cyprus in the east or to Malta in the west, and establish the kind of settlement they had had in Greece. They could also raise the same crops they had raised in Greece. The move to a new region was not a move into totally unknown conditions. Once the colonists had established themselves in new homes, they continued life essentially as in Greece.

From about 750 to 550 B.C., Greeks from the mainland and from Asia Minor poured onto the coasts of the northern Aegean, the Ionian Sea, and the Black Sea, and into North Africa, Sicily, southern Italy, southern Gaul, and Spain (see Map 5.2). Just as the migrations of the Dark Age had turned the Aegean into a Greek lake, this later wave of colonization spread the Greeks and their culture throughout the Mediterranean. Colonization on this scale had a profound impact on the course of world civilization. It meant that the prevailing culture of the Mediterranean basin would be Greek, the heritage to which Rome would later fall heir.

Lyric Poets

Two individuals can in many ways stand as symbols of the vital and robust era of colonization. Surprisingly, they were both poets: Archilochus, who had himself been a colonist, and Sappho, who seldom left her native island of Lesbos. What made them symbolic was their individualism. For the first time in Western civilization, men and women like Archilochus and Sappho began to write of their own experiences, and in so doing they set a new tone in Greek literature. To them poetry did not belong solely to the gods or the great heroes on the plain of Troy. In effect, they helped to liberate the individual emotionally, just as colonization opened new physical vistas to the Greeks. In their poetry they reveal two sides of Greek life in this period. Archilochus exemplifies the energy and adventure of the age, while Sappho expresses the intensely personal side of life. The link connecting the two poets is their individualism, their faith in themselves, and their desire to reach out to others to share their experiences, thoughts, and wisdom.

The Growth of Sparta

During the Lyric Age the Spartans expanded the boundaries of their polis and made it the leading power in Greece. Like other Greeks, the Spartans faced the problems of overpopulation and land hunger. Unlike other Greeks, the Spartans solved these problems by conquest, not by colonization.

The Hoplite Phalanx When the Greeks adopted heavy armor, weapons, and shields, their lack of mobility forced them to fight in several dense lines, each behind the other. Cohesion and order became as valuable as courage. To help the hoplites maintain their pace during the attack, a flute player here plays a marching tune. *(Source: Villa Giulia Museum/Gabinetto Fotografico Nazionale)*

To gain more land the Spartans set out in about 735 B.C. to conquer Messenia, a rich, fertile region in the southwestern Peloponnesus. This conflict, the First Messenian War, lasted for twenty years and ended in a Spartan triumph. The Spartans appropriated Messenian land and turned the Messenians into *helots,* or state serfs.

In about 650 B.C., Spartan exploitation and oppression of the Messenian helots led to a helot revolt so massive and stubborn that it became known as the Second Messenian War. The Spartan poet Tyrtaeus, a contemporary of these events, vividly portrayed the ferocity of the fighting:

For it is a shameful thing indeed
  When with the foremost fighters
An elder falling in front of the young men
  Lies outstretched,
Having white hair and grey beard,
Breathing forth his stout soul in the dust,
Holding in his hands his genitals
  Stained with blood.[3]

Confronted with such horrors, Spartan enthusiasm for the war waned. Finally, after some thirty years of fighting, the Spartans put down the revolt. Nevertheless, the political and social strain it caused led to a transformation of the Spartan polis.

It took the full might of the Spartan people, aristocrat and commoner alike, to win the Second Messenian War. After the victory the non-nobles, who had done much of the fighting, demanded rights equal to those of the nobility. These men were called "hoplites" because of their heavy armor, or *hopla.* Unlike modern soldiers who receive their equipment from the state, the Greek hoplite provided his own weapons. For this he needed a certain amount of wealth. He took his place in the battle line next to his aristocratic neighbors but lacked the social prestige and political rights of his noble companions. The agitation of the hoplites disrupted society until the aristocrats agreed to remodel the state. Nor were the Spartans alone in these developments. In other Greek city-states where hoplites came to the fore, they sought greater political rights and a larger role in society.

Although the Spartans later claimed that the changes brought about by this compromise were the work of Lycurgus, a legendary, semidivine lawgiver, they were really the work of the entire Spartan people. The "Lycurgan regimen," as these reforms were called, was a new political, economic, and social system. Political distinctions among the Spartans were officially eliminated, and all citizens became legally equal. In effect the Lycurgan regimen abolished the aristocracy and made the government an oligarchy. Actual governance of the polis was in the hands of two kings, who were primarily military leaders. The kings and twenty-eight elders made up a council that deliberated on foreign and domestic matters and prepared legislation for the assembly, which consisted of all Spartan citizens. The real executive power of the polis was in the hands of five *ephors,* or overseers, elected from and by all the people.

To provide for their economic needs the Spartans divided the land of Messenia among all citizens. Helots worked the land, raised the crops, provided the Spartans with their living, and occasionally served in the army. The Spartans kept the helots in line by means of systematic terrorism, hoping to beat them down and keep them quiet. Spartan citizens were supposed to devote their time exclusively to military training.

In the Lycurgan system every citizen owed primary allegiance to Sparta. Suppression of the individual together with emphasis on military prowess led to a barracks state. Family life was sacrificed to the polis. If an infant was deformed or handicapped at birth, the polis could demand that it be put out to die. In this respect the Spartans were no better or worse than other Greeks. Infanticide was common in ancient Greece and Rome; many people resorted to it as a way of keeping population down. In other Greek states, however, the decision to kill a child belonged to the parents, not to the polis.

Once a Spartan boy reached the age of seven, he lived in barracks with other boys his age. Spartan youth all underwent rugged physical and military training until they reached age twenty-four, when they became front-line soldiers. For the rest of their lives, Spartan men kept themselves prepared for combat. Their military training never ceased, and older men were expected to be models of endurance, frugality, and sturdiness to the younger

men. In battle Spartans were supposed to stand and die rather than retreat. An anecdote about one Spartan mother sums up Spartan military values. As her son was setting off to battle, the mother handed him his shield and advised him to come back either victorious, carrying the shield, or dead, being carried on it. In short, in the Lycurgan regimen Spartans were expected to train vigorously, disdain luxury and wealth, do with little, and like it.

Yet it is too easy to see the Spartans as merely a military people. The Lycurgan regimen instilled the civic virtues of dedication to the state and provided a code of moral conduct. These aspects of the Spartan system were generally admired throughout the Greek world.

The Evolution of Athens

Like Sparta, Athens faced pressing social and economic problems during the Lyric Age, but the Athenian response was far different from that of the Spartans. Instead of creating an oligarchy, the Athenians extended to all citizens the right and duty of governing the polis. Indeed, the Athenian democracy was one of the most thoroughgoing in Greece.

In the seventh century B.C., however, the aristocracy still governed Athens oppressively. The aristocrats owned the best land, met in an assembly to govern the polis, and interpreted the law. Noble landowners were forcing small farmers into economic dependence. Many families were sold into slavery; others were exiled and their land was pledged to the rich. Poor farmers who borrowed from their wealthy neighbors put up their land as collateral. If a farmer was unable to repay the loan, his creditor put a stone on the borrower's field to signify his indebtedness and thereafter took one-sixth of the annual yield until the debt was paid. If the farmer had to borrow again, he pledged himself and at times his family. If he was again unable to repay the loan, he became the slave of his creditor. Because the harvests of the poor farmer were generally small, he normally raised enough to live on but not enough to repay his loan.

The peasants, however, were strong in numbers and demanded reforms. They wanted the law to be published so that everyone would know its contents. Under pressure, the aristocrats relented and turned to Draco, a fellow aristocrat, to codify the law. In 621 B.C. Draco published the first law code of the Athenian polis. His code was thought harsh, but it nonetheless embodied the ideal that the law belonged to all citizens. The aristocrats hoped in vain that Draco's law code would satisfy the peasants. Many of the poor began demanding redistribution of the land, and it was obvious that broader reform was needed. Unrest among the peasants continued.

In many other city-states conditions such as those in Athens led to the rise of tyrants. The word *tyrant* brings to mind a cruel and bloody dictator, but the Greeks seem at first to have used the word only to denote a leader who seized power without legal right. Many of the first tyrants, though personally ambitious, were men who kept the welfare of the polis in mind. They usually enjoyed the support of the peasants because they reduced the power of the aristocrats. Later tyrants were often harsh and arbitrary; when they were, peasants and aristocrats alike suffered—the Greeks then began to use the word in the modern sense.

Only one person in Athens had the respect of both aristocrats and peasants: Solon (ca 638–ca 559 B.C.), himself an aristocrat and poet, but a man opposed to tyrants. Solon used his poetry to condemn the aristocrats for their greed and dishonesty. He recited his poems in the Athenian agora, where everyone could hear his relentless call for justice and fairness. The aristocrats realized that Solon was no revolutionary, and the common people trusted him. Around 594 B.C. the aristocrats elected him *archon,* chief magistrate of the Athenian polis, and gave him extraordinary power to reform the state.

Solon immediately freed all people enslaved for debt, recalled all exiles, canceled all debts on land, and made enslavement for debt illegal. He also divided society into four legal groups on the basis of wealth. In the most influential group were the wealthiest citizens, but even the poorest and least powerful group enjoyed certain rights. Solon allowed them into the old aristocratic assembly, where they could take part in the election of magistrates. In all his work Solon gave thought to the rights of the poor as well as the rich. He gave the commoners a place in government and a voice in the political affairs of Athens. His work done, Solon insisted that all swear to uphold his reforms. Then, since many were clamoring for him to become tyrant, he left Athens.

Although Solon's reforms solved some immediate problems, they did not bring peace to Athens. Some aristocrats attempted to make themselves tyrants, while others banded together to oppose them. In 546 B.C. Pisistratus, an exiled aristocrat, returned to Athens, defeated his opponents, and became tyrant. Pisistratus reduced the power of the aristocracy while supporting the common people. Under his rule Athens prospered, and his building program began to transform it into one of the splendors of Greece. His reign as tyrant promoted the growth of democratic ideas by arousing in the Athenians rudimentary feelings of equality.

Athenian acceptance of tyranny did not long outlive Pisistratus, for his son Hippias ruled harshly, and his excesses led to his overthrow. After a brief period of turmoil between factions of the nobility, Cleisthenes, a wealthy and prominent aristocrat, emerged triumphant in 508 B.C., largely because he won the support of the people. Cleisthenes created the Athenian democracy with the full knowledge and approval of the Athenian people. He reorganized the state completely but presented every innovation to the assembly for discussion and ratification. All Athenian citizens had a voice in Cleisthenes' work.

Cleisthenes used the *deme,* a local unit, to serve as the basis of his political system. Citizenship was tightly linked to the deme, for each deme kept the roll of those within its jurisdiction who were admitted to citizenship. Cleisthenes also created ten new tribes as administrative units. All the demes were grouped in tribes, which thus formed the link between the demes and the central government. The central government included an assembly of all citizens and a new council of five hundred members. The council prepared legislation for the assembly to consider, and it handled diplomatic affairs. Cleisthenes is often credited with the institution of *ostracism,* the banishment by means of a vote of the Athenian people of a citizen considered dangerous to the polis. The man receiving the most votes went into exile. The goal of ostracism was to rid the state peacefully of a difficult or potentially dangerous politician. The result of Cleisthenes' work was to make Athens a democracy with a government efficient enough to permit effective popular rule.

Athenian democracy was to prove an inspiring ideal in civilization. It demonstrated that a large group of people, not just a few, could efficiently run the affairs of state. By heeding the opinions, suggestions, and wisdom of all its citizens, the state enjoyed the maximum amount of good counsel. Since all citizens could speak their minds, they did not have to resort to rebellion or conspiracy to express their desires.

Athenian democracy, however, must not be thought of in modern terms. In Athens democracy was a form of government in which poor men as well as rich enjoyed political power and responsibility. In practice, though, most important offices were held by aristocrats. Furthermore, Athenian democracy denied political rights to many people, including women and slaves. Foreigners were seldom admitted to citizenship. Unlike modern democracies, Athenian democracy did not empower citizens to vote for others who then ran the state. Instead, every citizen was expected to be able to perform the duties of most magistrates. In Athens citizens voted and served. The people were the government. They enjoyed equal rights under the law, and the voice of the majority determined law. This union of the individual and the state—the view that the state exists for the good of the citizen, whose duty is to serve the state well—has made Athenian democracy so compelling an ideal.

THE CLASSICAL PERIOD (500–338 B.C.)

In the years 500 to 338 B.C., Greek civilization reached its peak in politics, art, and thought. In this period the Greeks beat back the armies of the Persian Empire. Then, turning their spears against one another, they destroyed their own political system in a century of warfare. Some thoughtful Greeks recorded and analyzed these momentous events; the result was the creation of history in Europe. This era also saw the flowering of philosophy, as thinkers in Ionia and on the Greek mainland began to ponder the nature and meaning of the universe and human experience. Not content to ask *why,* they used their intellects to explain the world around them and to determine humanity's place in it. The Greeks invented drama, and the Athenian tragedians Aeschylus, Sophocles, and Euripides explored themes that inspire audiences today. Greek architects created buildings whose very ruins still inspire awe. Because Greek intellectual and artistic efforts attained their fullest and finest expression in these years, this age is called

the "Classical Period." Few periods in the history of the world can match it in dynamism and achievement.

The Deadly Conflicts (499–404 B.C.)

One of the hallmarks of the Classical Period was warfare. In 499 B.C. the Ionian Greeks, with the feeble help of Athens, rebelled against the Persian Empire. In 490 B.C. the Persians struck back at Athens but were beaten off at the Battle of Marathon, fought on a small plain in Attica. This failure only prompted the Persians to try again. In 480 B.C. the Persian king Xerxes led a mighty invasion force into Greece. In the face of this emergency the Greeks united and pooled their resources to resist the invaders. The Spartans provided the overall leadership and commanded the Greek armies. The Athenians, led by the wily Themistocles, provided the heart of the naval forces.

The first confrontation between the Persians and the Greeks occurred at the pass of Thermopylae and in the waters off Cape Artemisium in northern Greece (see Map 5.1). At Thermopylae the Greek hoplites—the heavily armed troops—showed their mettle. Before the fighting began, a report came in that when the Persian archers shot their bows the arrows darkened the sky. One gruff Spartan merely replied, "Fine, then we'll fight in the shade." The Greeks at Thermopylae fought to the last man, but the Persians took the position. In their next two battles, the Greeks fared better. In 480 B.C. the Greek fleet smashed the Persian navy at Salamis, an island south of Athens. The following year, the Greek army destroyed the Persian forces at Plataea, a small polis at Boeotia.

The significance of these Greek victories is nearly incalculable. By defeating the Persians, the Greeks ensured that a Near Eastern monarchy would not stifle the Greek achievement. The Greeks were thus able to develop their particular genius in freedom. The decisive victories at Salamis and Plataea meant that Greek political forms and intellectual concepts would be the heritage of the West.

After turning back the invasion, the Greeks took the fight to the Persian Empire. In 478 B.C. the Greeks decided to continue hostilities until they had liberated the Ionians from Persian rule. To achieve that goal a strong navy was essential. The Greeks turned to Athens, the leading naval power in the Aegean, for leadership. Athens and other states, especially those in the Aegean, responded by establishing the Delian League. Athens controlled the Delian League, providing most of the warships for operations and determining how much money each member should contribute to the league's treasury.

Over the next twenty years Athens drove the Persians out of the Aegean and turned the members of the Delian League into an Athenian empire. Athenian rule became severe, and the Athenian polis became openly imperialistic. Although all members of the Delian League were supposed to be free and independent states, Athens reduced them to the status of subjects. A sense of the harshness of Athenian rule can be gained from the regulations the Athenians imposed on their subject allies. After the Athenians had suppressed a revolt in Euboea, they imposed an oath on the people:

I will not revolt from the people of Athens either by any means or devices whatsoever or by word or deed, nor will I be persuaded by anyone who does revolt. And I will pay the tribute to the Athenians that I can persuade the Athenians to levy. I will be to them the best and truest ally possible. I will help and defend the people of Athens if anyone wrongs them, and I will obey the people of Athens.[4]

The Athenians dictated to the people of Erythrae, a polis on the coast of Asia Minor, their form of government:

There will be a council of 120 men chosen by lot. . . . The Athenian overseers and garrison commander will choose the current council by lot and establish it in office. Henceforth the council and the Athenian garrison commander will do these things thirty days before the council goes out of office.[5]

The Athenians were willing to enforce their demands by armed might, and they were ready both to punish violations and to suppress discontent.

The expansion of Athenian power and the aggressiveness of Athenian rule alarmed Sparta and its allies. While relations between Athens and Sparta cooled, Pericles (ca 494–429 B.C.) became the leading statesman in Athens. An aristocrat of solid intellectual ability, he turned Athens into the wonder of Greece. But like the democracy he led, Pericles was aggressive and imperialistic. He made

Greek Family in Mourning   This funeral relief commemorates the death of a young girl. She stands on the right as though still living, bidding farewell to her mother, who is seated. Her father stands in the background. The scene is subdued but serene. Any Greek who saw this relief would know that parents and daughter were saying "XAIPE," which in Greek means "hello" as well as "good-bye." *(Source: Caroline Buckler)*

no effort to allay Spartan fear and instead continued Athenian expansion. At last, in 459 B.C. Sparta and Athens went to war over conflicts between Athens and some of Sparta's allies. The war ended fourteen years later with no serious damage to either side and nothing settled. But this war had divided the Greek world between two great powers.

Athens continued its severe policies toward its subject allies and came into conflict with Corinth, one of Sparta's leading allies (Map 5.3). Once again Athens and Sparta were drifting toward war. In 432 B.C. the Spartans convened a meeting of their allies, who complained of Athenian aggression and demanded that Athens be stopped. With

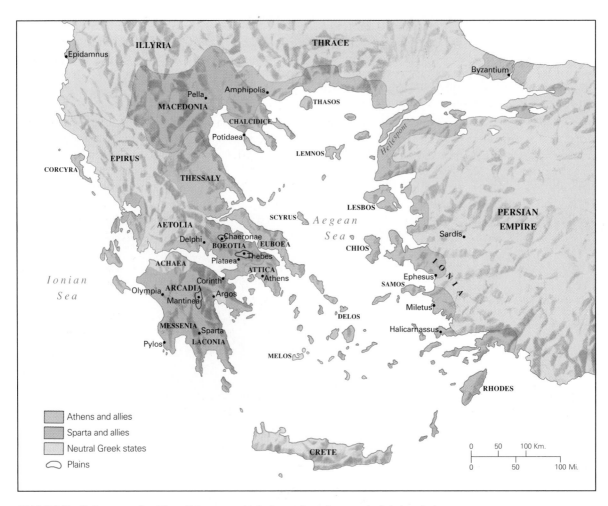

MAP 5.3 The Peloponnesian War   This map, which shows the alignment of states during the Peloponnesian War, vividly illustrates the large scale of the war and its divisive impact.

a show of reluctance, the Spartans agreed to declare war. The real reason for war, according to Thucydides, the Athenian historian who also fought as a general in the war, was simple: "The truest explanation, though the one least mentioned, was the great growth of Athenian power and the fear it caused the Lakedaimonians [Spartans] which drove them to war."[6]

At the outbreak of this, the Peloponnesian War, a Spartan ambassador warned the Athenians: "This day will be the beginning of great evils for the Greeks." Few have ever spoken more prophetically. The Peloponnesian War lasted a generation (431–404 B.C.) and brought in its wake fearful plagues, famine, civil wars, widespread destruction, and huge loss of life. Thucydides described its cataclysmic effects:

For never had so many cities been captured and destroyed, whether by the barbarians or by the Greeks who were fighting each other. . . . Never had so many men been exiled or slaughtered, whether in the war or because of civil conflicts.[7]

As the war dragged on for years, older leaders like Pericles died and were replaced by men of the war generation. In Athens the most prominent of this new breed of politicians was Alcibiades (ca 450–404 B.C.), who was an aristocrat, a kinsman of Pericles, and a student of the philosopher Socrates. Alcibiades was brilliant, handsome, charming, and popular with the people. He was also self-seeking and egotistical; a shameless opportunist, his first thoughts were always for himself.

Alcibiades' schemes helped bring Athens down to defeat. Having planned an invasion of Sicily that ended in disaster, he deserted to the Spartans and plotted with the Persians, who had sided with Sparta, against his homeland. In the end, all of Alcibiades' intrigues failed. The Spartans defeated the Athenian fleet in the Aegean and blockaded Athens by land and sea. Finally, in 404 B.C. the Athenians surrendered and watched helplessly while the Spartans and their allies destroyed the walls of Athens to the music of flute girls. The Peloponnesian War lasted twenty-seven years, and it dealt Greek civilization a serious blow.

Athenian Arts in the Age of Pericles

In the last half of the fifth century B.C., Pericles turned Athens into the showplace of Greece. He appropriated Delian League funds to pay for a huge building program, planning temples and other buildings to honor Athena, the patron goddess of the city, and to display to all Greeks the glory of the Athenian polis. Pericles also pointed out that his program would employ a great many Athenians and bring economic prosperity to the city.

Thus began the undertaking that turned the Athenian acropolis into a monument for all time. Construction of the Parthenon began in 447 B.C., followed by the Propylaea, the temple of Athena Nike (Athena the Victorious), and the Erechtheion (Map 5.4). Even today in their ruined state they still evoke awe. Plutarch, a Greek writer who lived in the first century A.D., observed:

In beauty each of them was from the outset antique, and even now in its prime fresh and newly made. Thus each of them is always in bloom, maintaining its appearance as though untouched by time, as though an ever-green breath and undecaying spirit had been mixed in its construction.[8]

Mosaic Portrait of Alcibiades The artist has caught all the craftiness, intelligence, and quickness of Alcibiades, who became a romantic figure in antiquity. Besides the artistic merit of the portrait, the mosaic is interesting because Alcibiades' name in the upper right corner is misspelled. *(Source: Caroline Buckler)*

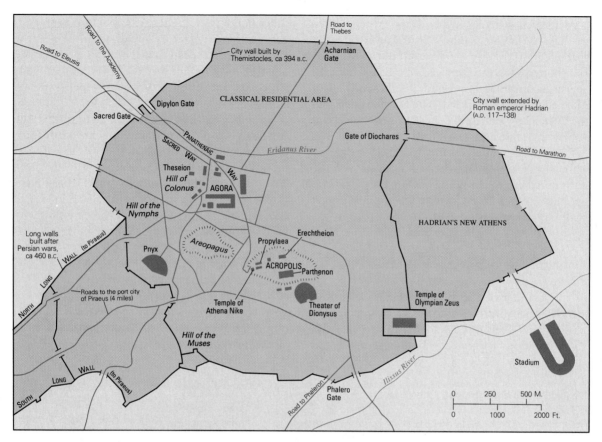

MAP 5.4 Ancient Athens By modern standards the city of Athens was hardly more than a town, not much larger in size than one square mile. Yet this small area reflects the concentration of ancient Greek life in the polis.

Even the pollution of modern Athens, although it is destroying the ancient buildings, cannot rob them of their splendor and charm.

The planning of the architects and the skill of the workers who erected these buildings were very sophisticated. Visitors approaching the Acropolis first saw the Propylaea, the ceremonial gateway, a building of complicated layout and grand design whose Doric columns seem to hold up the sky. On the right was the small temple of Athena Nike, whose dimensions harmonize with those of the Propylaea. The temple was built to commemorate the victory over the Persians, and the Ionic frieze above its columns depicted the battle of the Greeks and the Persians. Here for all the world to see was a tribute to Athenian and Greek valor— and a reminder of Athens' part in the victory.

Ahead of the visitors as they stood in the Propylaea was the huge statue of Athena Promachus (the Frontline Fighter), so gigantic that the crest of Athena's helmet and the point of her spear could be seen by sailors entering the harbor of Athens. This statue celebrated the Athenian victory at the Battle of Marathon and was paid for by the spoils taken from the Persians. To the left stood the Erechtheion, an Ionic temple that housed several ancient shrines. On its southern side is the famous Portico of the Caryatids, a porch whose roof is supported by statues of Athenian maidens. The graceful Ionic columns of the Erechtheion provide a delicate relief from the prevailing Doric order of the massive Propylaea and Parthenon.

As visitors walked on they obtained a full view of the Parthenon, thought by many to be the perfect Doric temple. The Parthenon was the chief monument to Athena and her city. The sculptures that adorned the temple portrayed the greatness of Athens and its goddess. The figures on the eastern pediment depicted Athena's birth; those on the west, the victory of Athena over the god Poseidon for the possession of Attica. Inside the Parthenon stood a huge statue of Athena, the masterpiece of Phidias, one of the greatest sculptors of all time.

In many ways the Athenian acropolis is the epitome of Greek art and its spirit, which exhibits the rational side of Greek art. There is no violent emotion in this art, but instead a quiet intensity. Likewise, there is nothing excessive, for "nothing too much" was the canon of artist and philosopher alike. Greek artists portrayed action in a balanced, restrained, and sometimes even serene fashion, capturing the noblest aspects of human beings: their reason, dignity, and promise.

Other aspects of Athenian cultural life were as rooted in the life of the polis as were the architecture and sculpture of the Acropolis. The development of drama was tied to the religious festivals of the city. The polis sponsored the production of plays and required that wealthy citizens pay the expenses of their production. At the beginning of the year dramatists submitted their plays to the archon. He chose those he considered best and assigned a theatrical troupe to each playwright. Although most Athenian drama has perished, enough has survived to prove that the archons had superb taste. Many plays were highly controversial, but the archons neither suppressed nor censored them.

The Athenian dramatists were the first artists in Western society to examine such basic questions as the rights of the individual, the demands of society on the individual, and the nature of good and

Sectional View of the Parthenon   This figure both indicates what the Parthenon looked like in antiquity and explains the complex nature of Greek temple-building. As the illustration shows, the Parthenon's apparently simple façade is a work of great architectural sophistication. (*Source: Guide to Sculptures of the Parthenon, a British Museum publication*)

evil. Conflict is a constant element in Athenian drama. The dramatists used their art to portray, understand, and resolve life's basic conflicts.

Aeschylus (525–456 B.C.), the first of the great Athenian dramatists, was the first to express the agony of the individual caught in conflict. In his trilogy of plays, *The Oresteia,* Aeschylus deals with the themes of betrayal, murder, and reconciliation. Sophocles (496–406 B.C.), too, dealt with matters personal and political. In *Antigone* he examined the relationship between the individual and the state by exploring a conflict between the ties of kinship and the demands of the polis. As the play progresses, Antigone comes to stand for the precedence of divine law over human defects. Sophocles touches on the need for recognition of, and adherence to, the law as prerequisites for a tranquil state. Sophocles' masterpieces have become classics of literature, and his themes have inspired generations of playwrights. In his famous plays *Oedipus the King* and *Oedipus at Colonus*

Sophocles seems to be saying that human beings should do the will of the gods, even without fully understanding it, for the gods stand for justice and order.

Euripides (ca 480–406 B.C.), the last of the three great Greek dramatists, also explored the theme of personal conflict within the polis and sounded the depths of the individual. With Euripides drama entered a new, in many ways more personal, phase. To him the gods were far less important than human beings. Euripides viewed the human soul as a place where opposing forces struggle, where strong passions such as hatred and jealousy conflict with reason. The essence of Euripides' tragedy is flawed character—men and women who bring disaster on themselves and their loved ones because their passions overwhelm reason. Although Euripides' plays were less popular in his lifetime than those of Aeschylus and Sophocles, Euripides was a dramatist of genius whose work later had a significant impact on Roman drama.

The Parthenon Stately and graceful, the Parthenon symbolizes the logic, order, and sense of beauty of Greek architecture. The Parthenon was also the centerpiece of Pericles' plan to make Athens the artistic showcase of the Greek world. *(Source: Caroline Buckler)*

Writers of comedy treated the affairs of the polis bawdily and often coarsely. Even so, their plays, too, were performed at religious festivals. The comic playwrights dealt primarily with the political affairs of the polis and the conduct of its leading politicians. Best known is Aristophanes (ca 445–386 B.C.), an ardent lover of his city and a merciless critic of cranks and quacks. It is a tribute to the Athenians that such devastating attacks could openly and freely be made on the city's leaders and foreign policy. Even at the height of the Peloponnesian War, Aristophanes proclaimed that peace was preferable to the ravages of war. Like Aeschylus, Sophocles, and Euripides, Aristophanes used his art to dramatize his ideas on the right conduct of the citizen and the value of the polis.

Perhaps never were art and political life so intimately and congenially bound together as at Athens. Athenian art was the product of deep and genuine love of the polis. It aimed at bettering the lives of the citizens and the quality of life in the state.

Daily Life in Periclean Athens

In sharp contrast with the rich intellectual and cultural life of Periclean Athens was the simplicity of its material life. The Athenians—and in this respect they were typical of Greeks in general—lived very happily with comparatively few material possessions. There were few material goods to own. The thousands of machines, tools, and gadgets considered essential for modern life had no counterparts in Athenian life. The inventory of Alcibiades' goods, which the Athenians confiscated after his desertion, is enlightening. His household possessions consisted of chests, beds, couches, tables, screens, stools, baskets, and mats. Other necessities of the Greek home included pottery, metal utensils for cooking, tools, luxury goods such as jewelry, and a few other things. These items the Athenians had to buy from craftsmen. Whatever else they needed, such as clothes and blankets, they produced at home.

The Athenian house was rather simple. Whether large or small, the typical house consisted of a series of rooms built around a central courtyard, with doors opening onto the courtyard. Many houses had bedrooms on an upper floor. Artisans and craftsmen often set aside a room to use as a shop or work area. The two principal rooms were

A Greek God Few pieces of Greek art better illustrate the conception of the gods as greatly superior forms of human beings than this magnificent statue, over six feet, ten inches in height. Here, the god, who may be either Poseidon or Zeus, is portrayed as powerful and perfect but basically human in form. *(Source: National Archaeological Museum, Athens)*

the men's dining room and the room where the women worked wool. Other rooms included the kitchen and bathroom. By modern standards there was not much furniture. In the men's dining room were couches, a sideboard, and small tables. Cups and other pottery often hung on the wall from pegs.

In the courtyard were a well, a small altar, and a washbasin. If the family lived in the country, the stalls of the animals faced the courtyard. Country-folk kept oxen for plowing, pigs for slaughtering, sheep for wool, goats for cheese, and mules and donkeys for transportation. Even in the city, chickens and perhaps a goat or two roamed the courtyard together with dogs and cats.

Theater of Delphi This scene admirably illustrates the religious quality of Greek drama. The theater, in which the great plays of Aeschylus, Sophocles, and Euripides were performed, overlooks the rest of the sanctuary of Apollo of which it is a significant part. The theater stands as a monument to the importance of drama to Greek cultural life. *(Source: Ekdotike Athenon)*

Cooking, done over a hearth in the house, provided welcome warmth in the winter. Baking and roasting were done in ovens. Food consisted of various grains, especially wheat and barley, as well as lentils, olives, figs, and grapes. Garlic and onion were popular garnishes, and wine was always on hand. These foods were stored at home in large jars; with them the Greek family ate fish, chicken, and vegetables. Women ground wheat into flour, baked it into bread, and on special occasions made honey or sesame cakes. The Greeks used olive oil for cooking, as families still do in modern Greece; they also used it as an unguent and as lamp fuel.

On special occasions, such as important religious festivals, the family ate the animal sacrificed to the god and gave the god the exquisite delicacy of the thighbone wrapped in fat. The only Greeks who consistently ate meat were the Spartan warriors. They received a small portion of meat each day, together with the infamous Spartan black broth, a ghastly concoction of pork cooked in blood, vinegar, and salt. One Greek, after tasting the broth, commented that he could easily understand why the Spartans were so willing to die.

In the city a man might support himself as a craftsman—a potter, bronzesmith, sail maker, or tanner—or he could contract with the polis to work on public buildings, such as the Parthenon and Erechtheion. Men without skills worked as paid laborers but competed with slaves for work. Slaves—usually foreigners, barbarian as well as Greek—were paid the same amount for their employment as were free men.

Slavery was commonplace in Greece, as it was throughout the ancient world. In its essentials Greek slavery resembled Mesopotamian slavery. Slaves received some protection under the law and could buy their freedom. On the other hand, masters could mistreat or neglect their slaves short of killing them, which was illegal. The worst-treated slaves were those of the silver mines at Laurium, who lived, worked, and died in wretchedness. Yet slavery elsewhere was not generally brutal. One crusty aristocrat complained that in Athens one could not tell the slaves from the free. Most slaves in Athens served as domestics and performed light labor around the house. Nurses for children, teachers of reading and writing, and guardians for young men were often slaves, whose lives were much like those of their owners. Other slaves were skilled workers, who could be found working on public buildings or in small workshops.

The importance of slavery in Athens must not be exaggerated. Apart from those who leased from Athens the right to operate the Laurium mines, Athenians did not own huge gangs of slaves as did Roman owners of large estates. Slave labor competed with free labor and kept wages down, but it never replaced free labor, which was the mainstay of the Athenian economy.

Most Athenians supported themselves by agriculture, but unless a family was fortunate enough to possess holdings in a plain more fertile than most of the land, reaping a good crop from the soil was difficult. Wealthy landowners sold their excess produce in the urban marketplace, but many people must have consumed nearly everything they raised. The plow, though wooden, sometimes had an iron share and was pulled by oxen. Attic farmers were free men. Though hardly prosperous, they were by no means destitute. Greek farmers could usually expect yields of five bushels of wheat and ten of barley per acre for every bushel of grain sown. A bad harvest meant a lean year. In many places farmers grew more barley than wheat because of the soil. Wherever possible farmers also cultivated vines and olive trees. In Greece arable land was much smaller in extent and less fertile than in Egypt, Mesopotamia, India, and China. Thus Greece could not provide sustenance for a population nearly so large as its Eastern neighbors. The economic basis for an empire resembling that of the Mauryan Empire or the Chou Dynasty did not exist for the Greeks. Although the Greeks also looked to the sea for their livelihood, even this economic resource was limited. Geography placed its own physical limits on Greek growth.

For sport both countryman and city dweller often hunted for rabbits, deer, or wild boar. A suc-cessful hunt supplemented the family's regular diet. Wealthy men hunted on horseback; most others hunted on foot with their dogs. Hunting also allowed a man to display to his fellows his bravery and prowess in the chase. If wild boar were the prey, the sport could be dangerous, as Odysseus discovered when a charging boar slashed open his foot.

The social condition of Athenian women has been the subject of much debate and little agreement. One thing is certain: the status of a free woman of the citizen class was strictly protected by law. Only her children, not those of foreigners or slaves, could be citizens. Only she was in charge of the household and the family's possessions. Yet the law protected her primarily to protect her husband's interests. Raping a free woman was a lesser crime than seducing her because seduction involved the winning of her affections. This law was concerned not with the husband's feelings but with ensuring that he need not doubt the legitimacy of his children.

Ideally, respectable women lived a secluded life in which the only men they saw were relatives. How far this ideal was actually put into practice is impossible to say. Athenian women seem to have enjoyed a social circle of other women of their own class. They also attended public festivals, sacrifices, and funerals. Nonetheless, prosperous and respectable women probably spent much of their time in the house. A white complexion—a sign that a woman did not have to spend her days in the fields —was valued highly.

Courtesans lived the freest lives of all Athenian women. Although some courtesans were simply prostitutes, others added intellectual accomplishments to physical beauty. In constant demand, cultured courtesans moved freely in male society. Their artistic talents and intellectual abilities appealed to men who wanted more than sex. The most famous of all courtesans was Aspasia, mistress of Pericles and supposedly friend of Socrates. Under Pericles' roof, she participated in intellectual discussions equally with some of the most stimulating thinkers of the day. Yet her position, like that of most other courtesans, was precarious. After Pericles' death, Aspasia fended for herself, ending her days as the madam of a house of prostitution.

A woman's main functions were to raise the children, oversee the domestic slaves and hired labor, and together with her maids work wool into cloth. The women washed the wool in the courtyard and then brought it into the women's room, where the loom stood. They spun the wool into thread and wove the thread into cloth. They also dyed wool at home and decorated the cloth by weaving in colors and designs. The woman of the household either did the cooking herself or directed her maids. In a sense, poor women lived freer lives than did wealthier women. They performed manual labor in the fields or sold goods in the agora, going about their affairs much as men did.

A distinctive feature of Athenian life and of Greek life in general was acceptance of homosexuality. No one has satisfactorily explained how the

Women Working The scene on this vase represents the women of the household at work. It shows how they produced woolen cloth, from the spinning of yarn to the completion of the cloth itself, here held by two women. *(Source: The Metropolitan Museum of Art, Fletcher Fund, 1931)*

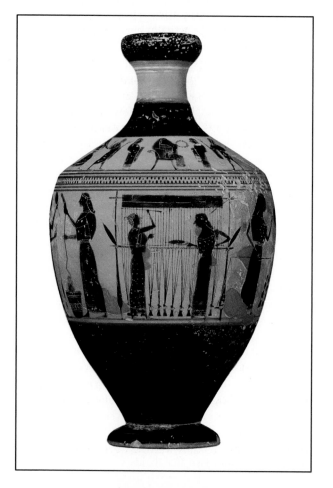

Greek attitude toward homosexual love developed or determined how common homosexual behavior was. Homosexuality was probably far more common among the aristocracy than among the lower classes. It is impossible to be sure, simply because most of what the modern world knows of ancient Greece and Rome comes from the writings of aristocrats. Since aristocratic boys and girls were often brought up separately, the likelihood of homosexual relationships was very great. This style of life was impossible for the common folk because every member of the family—husband and wife, son and daughter—got out and worked. Among the poorer classes the sexes mingled freely.

Despite some modern speculation to the contrary, relations between Athenian husbands and wives were probably close. The presence of female slaves in the home could be a source of trouble; men were always free to resort to prostitutes; and some men and women engaged in homosexual love affairs. But basically husbands and wives depended on each other for mutual love and support. The wife's position and status in the household were guaranteed by her dowry, which came from her father and remained her property throughout her married life. If the wife felt that her marriage was intolerable, she could divorce her husband far more easily than could a Mesopotamian wife.

One particularly important aspect of social life in Athens and elsewhere in Greece was religion. Yet Greek religion is extremely difficult for modern people to understand, largely because of the great differences between Greek and modern cultures. In the first place, it is not even easy to talk about "Greek religion," since the Greeks had no uniform faith or creed. Although the Greeks usually worshiped the same deities—Zeus, Hera, Apollo, Athena, and others—the cults of these gods and goddesses varied from polis to polis. The Greeks had no sacred books, such as the Bible, and Greek religion was often a matter more of ritual than of belief. Nor did cults impose an ethical code of conduct. Greeks did not have to follow any particular rule of life, practice certain virtues, or even live decent lives in order to participate. Unlike the Egyptians, Hebrews, and Indians, the Greeks lacked a priesthood as the modern world understands the term. In Greece priests and priestesses cared for temples and sacred property and conducted the proper rituals but did not make religious rules or doctrines, much less enforce them.

In short, there existed in Greece no central ecclesiastical authority and no organized creed.

Although temples to the gods were common, they were unlike modern churches, temples, or synagogues in that they were not normally places where a congregation met to worship as a spiritual community. Instead the individual Greek either visited the temple occasionally on matters of private concern or walked in a procession to a particular temple to celebrate a particular festival. In Greek religion the altar was important; when the Greeks sought the favor of the gods, they offered them sacrifices. Greek religious observances were generally cheerful. Festivals and sacrifices were frequently times for people to meet socially, times of high spirits and conviviality rather than pious gloom. By offering the gods parts of the sacrifice while consuming the rest themselves, worshipers forged a bond with the gods.

Besides the Olympian gods, each polis had its own minor deities, each with his or her own local cult. In many instances Greek religion involved the official gods and goddesses of the polis and their cults. The polis administered the cults and festivals, and all were expected to participate in this civic religion, regardless of whether they believed in the deities being worshiped. Participating unbelievers, who seem to have been a small minority, were not considered hypocrites. Rather they were seen as patriotic, loyal citizens who in honoring the gods also honored the polis. If this attitude seems contradictory, an analogy may help. Before baseball games Americans stand at the playing of the national anthem, whether they are Democrats, Republicans, or neither, and whether they agree or disagree with the policies of the administration in authority. They honor their nation as represented by its flag. In somewhat the same way ancient Greeks honored their polis and demonstrated their solidarity with it by participating in the state cults.

Though Greek religion in general was individual or related to the polis, the Greeks also shared some pan-Hellenic festivals, the chief of which were held at Olympia in honor of Zeus and at Delphi in honor of Apollo. The festivities at Olympia included the famous games, athletic contests that have inspired the modern Olympic games. Held every four years, these games were for the glory of Zeus. They attracted visitors from all over the Greek world and lasted well into Christian times. The Pythian games at Delphi were also held every four years, but these contests differed from the Olympic games by including musical and literary contests. Both the Olympic and the Pythian games were a unifying factor in Greek life, bringing Greek citizens together culturally as well as religiously. Finally, there were some mystery cults, like that of Eleusis in Attica, which were open only to Greeks, who first had to master a body of arcane and secret ritual and who then purified themselves for initiation into the cult. Once admitted, they were not permitted to reveal any details of the cult. Though few in Classical Greece, other and new mystery cults grew up and became common in the Hellenistic period.

The Flowering of Philosophy

The myths and epics of the Mesopotamians and Indians are ample testimony that speculation about the origin of the universe and of humankind did not begin with the Greeks. The signal achievement of the Greeks was willingness to treat these questions in rational rather than mythological terms. Although Greek philosophy did not fully flower until the Classical Period, Ionian thinkers had already begun in the Lyric Age to ask what the universe was made of. These men are called the "Pre-Socratics," for their work preceded the philosophical revolution begun by the Athenian Socrates. Though they were born observers, the Pre-Socratics rarely undertook deliberate experimentation. Instead they took individual facts and wove them into general theories. Despite appearances, they believed, the universe was actually simple and subject to natural laws. Drawing on their observations, they speculated about the basic building blocks of the universe.

The first of the Pre-Socratics, Thales (ca 640–546 B.C.), learned mathematics and astronomy from the Babylonians and geometry from the Egyptians. Yet there was an immense and fundamental difference between Near Eastern thought and the philosophy of Thales. The Near Eastern peoples considered such events as eclipses as evil omens. Thales viewed them as natural phenomena that could be explained in natural terms. In short, he asked *why* things happened. He believed the basic element of the universe to be water. Although he was wrong, the way in which he asked the question was momentous: it was the beginning of the scientific method.

Thales' follower Anaximander continued his work. Anaximander was the first of the Pre-Socratics to use general concepts, which are essential to abstract thought. One of the most brilliant of the Pre-Socratics, a man of striking originality, Anaximander theorized that the basic element of the universe is the "boundless" or "endless"—something infinite and indestructible. In his view, the earth floats in a void, held in balance by its distance from everything else in the universe.

Anaximander even concluded that humankind had evolved naturally from lower organisms: "In water the first animal arose covered with spiny skin, and with the lapse of time some crawled onto dry land and breaking off their skins in a short time they survived."[9] This remarkable speculation corresponds crudely to Darwin's theory of the evolution of species, which it predated by two and a half millennia.

Another Ionian, Heraclitus (ca 500 B.C.), declared the primal element to be fire. He also declared that the world had neither beginning nor end: "This world, the world of all things, neither any god nor man made, but it always was and it is and it will be: an everlasting fire, measures kindling and measures going out."[10] Although the universe was eternal, according to Heraclitus, it changed constantly. An outgrowth of this line of speculation was the theory of Democritus that the universe is made of invisible, indestructible atoms. The culmination of Pre-Socratic thought was the theory that four simple substances make up the universe: fire, air, earth, and water.

With this impressive heritage behind them, the philosophers of the Classical Period ventured into new areas of speculation. This development was partly due to the work of Hippocrates (ca 460–ca 377 B.C.), a pioneer in the science of medicine.

Like Thales, Hippocrates sought natural explanations for natural phenomena. Basing his opinions on empirical knowledge, not on religion or magic, he taught that natural means could be employed to fight disease. In his treatise *On Airs, Waters, and Places,* he noted the influence of climate and environment on health. Hippocrates and his followers put forth a theory that was to prevail in European medical circles until the eighteenth century. The human body, they declared, contains four *humors,* or fluids: blood, phlegm, black bile, and yellow bile. In a healthy body the four humors are in perfect balance; too much or too little of any particular humor causes illness. Hippocrates and his pupils shared the Ionian belief that they were dealing with phenomena that could be explained purely in natural terms. But Hippocrates broke away from the mainstream of Ionian speculation by declaring that medicine was a separate craft—just as ironworking was—that had its own principles.

Socrates According to tradition, Socrates was homely at best. Yet this Roman copy of a fourth-century Greek statue has captured the simplicity and the thoughtfulness of the man. It also gives a sense of his intellectual exploration of basic human values. *(Source: Courtesy of the Trustees of the British Museum)*

The distinction between natural science and philosophy, on which Hippocrates insisted, was also promoted by the Sophists, who traveled the Greek world teaching young men. Despite differences of opinion on philosophical matters, the Sophists all agreed that human beings were the proper subject of study. They also believed that excellence could be taught, and they used philosophy and rhetoric to prepare young men for life in the polis. The Sophists laid great emphasis on logic and the meanings of words. They criticized traditional beliefs, religion, rituals, and myth and even questioned the laws of the polis. In essence they argued that nothing is absolute, that everything—even the customs and constitution of the state—is relative. Hence many Greeks of more traditional inclination considered them wanton and harmful, men who were interested in "making the worse seem the better cause."

One of those whose contemporaries thought him a Sophist was Socrates (ca 470–399 B.C.), who sprang from the class of small artisans. Socrates spent his life in investigation and definition. Not strictly speaking a Sophist because he never formally taught or collected fees from anyone, Socrates shared the Sophists' belief that human beings and their environment are the essential subjects of philosophical inquiry. Like the Sophists, Socrates thought that excellence could be learned and passed on to others. His approach when posing ethical questions and defining concepts was to start with a general topic or problem and to narrow the matter to its essentials. He did so by continuous questioning, a running dialogue. Never did he lecture. Socrates thought that by constantly pursuing excellence, an essential part of which was knowledge, human beings could approach the supreme good and thus find true happiness. Yet in 399 B.C. Socrates was brought to trial, convicted, and executed on charges of corrupting the youth of the city and introducing new gods.

Socrates' student Plato (427–347 B.C.) carried on his master's search for truth. Unlike Socrates, Plato wrote down his thoughts and theories and founded a philosophical school, the Academy. Plato developed the theory that all visible, tangible things are unreal and temporary, copies of "forms" or "ideas" that are constant and indestructible. Only the mind, not the senses, can perceive eternal forms. In Plato's view the highest form is the idea of good.

In *The Republic* Plato applied his theory of forms to politics in an effort to describe the ideal polis. His perfect polis is utopian; it aims at providing the greatest good and happiness to all its members. Plato thought that the ideal polis could exist only if its rulers were philosophers. He divided society into rulers, guardians of the polis, and workers. The role of people in each category is decided by the education, wisdom, and ability of the individual. In Plato's republic men and women are equal to one another, and women can become rulers. The utopian polis is a balance, with each individual doing what he or she can to support the state and with each receiving from the state his or her just due.

In a later work, *The Laws,* Plato discarded the ideal polis of *The Republic* in favor of a second-best state. The polis of *The Laws* grimly presages the modern dictatorship. At its head is a young tyrant who is just and good. He meets with a council that sits only at night, and together they maintain the spirit of the laws. Nearly everything about this state is coercive; the free will of the citizens counts for little. The laws speak to every aspect of life; their sole purpose is to make people happy.

Aristotle (384–322 B.C.) carried on the philosophical tradition of Socrates and Plato. A student of Plato, Aristotle went far beyond him in striving to understand the universe. The range of Aristotle's thought is staggering. Everything in human experience was fit subject for his inquiry. In *The Politics* Aristotle followed Plato's lead by writing about the ideal polis. Yet Aristotle approached the question more realistically than Plato had done and criticized *The Republic* and *The Laws* on many points. In *The Politics* and elsewhere, Aristotle stressed moderation, concluding that the balance of his ideal state depended on people of talent and education who could avoid extremes.

Not content to examine old questions, Aristotle opened up whole new fields of inquiry. He tried to understand the changes of nature—what caused them and where they led. In *Physics* and *Metaphysics* he evolved a theory of nature that developed the notions of matter, form, and motion. He attempted to bridge the gap between abstract truth and concrete perception that Plato had created.

In *On the Heaven,* Aristotle took up the thread of Ionian speculation. His theory of cosmology added ether to air, fire, water, and earth as building blocks of the universe. He concluded that the universe revolves and that it is spherical and eter-

PERIODS OF GREEK HISTORY

Period	Significant Events	Major Writers
Bronze Age 2000–1100 B.C.	Arrival of the Greeks in Greece Rise and fall of the Mycenaean kingdoms	
Dark Age 1100–800 B.C.	Greek migrations within the Aegean basin Social and political recovery Evolution of the polis Rebirth of literacy	Homer Hesiod
Lyric Age 800–500 B.C.	Rise of Sparta and Athens Colonization of the Mediterranean basin Flowering of lyric poetry Development of philosophy and science in Ionia	Archilochus Sappho Tyrtaeus Solon Anaximander Heraclitus
Classical Age 500–338 B.C.	Persian Wars Growth of the Athenian Empire Peloponnesian War Rise of drama and historical writing Flowering of Greek philosophy Spartan and Theban hegemonies Conquest of Greece by Philip of Macedon	Herodotus Thucydides Aeschylus Sophocles Euripides Aristophanes Plato Aristotle

nal. He wrongly thought that the earth is the center of the universe, with the stars and planets revolving around it. The Hellenistic scientist Aristarchus of Samos later realized that the earth revolves around the sun, but Aristotle's view was accepted until the time of the fifteenth-century Polish astronomer Nicolaus Copernicus.

Aristotle's scientific interests also included zoology. In several works he describes various animals and makes observations on animal habits, anatomy, and movement. He also explored the process of reproduction. Intending to examine the entire animal kingdom, he assigned the world of plants to his follower Theophrastus (see page 165).

Aristotle possessed one of the keenest and most curious philosophical minds of civilization. While rethinking the old topics explored by the Pre-

Socratics, he also created whole new areas of study. In short, he tried to learn everything possible about the universe and everything in it. He did so in the belief that all knowledge could be synthesized to produce a simple explanation of the universe and of humanity.

The Final Act (403–338 B.C.)

Immediately after the Peloponnesian War, with Athens humbled, Sparta began striving for empire over the Greeks. The arrogance and imperialism of the Spartans turned their former allies against them. Even with Persian help Sparta could not maintain its hold on Greece. In 371 B.C. the Spartans met their match on the plain of Leuctra in Boeotia. A Theban army under the command of

Epaminondas, one of Greece's most brilliant generals, destroyed the flower of the Spartan army on a single summer day. The victory at Leuctra left Thebes the most powerful state in Greece. Under Epaminondas the Thebans destroyed Sparta as a first-rank power and checked the ambitions of Athens, but they were unable to bring peace to Greece. In 362 B.C. Epaminondas was killed in battle, and a period of stalemate set in. The Greek states were virtually exhausted.

The man who turned the situation to his advantage was Philip II, king of Macedonia (359–336 B.C.). Throughout most of Greek history Macedonia, which bordered Greece in the north (in modern Greece and Yugoslavia), had been a backward, disunited kingdom, but Philip's genius, courage, and drive turned it into a major power. One of the ablest statesmen of antiquity, Philip united his powerful kingdom, built a redoubtable army, and pursued his ambition with drive and determination. His horizon was not limited to Macedonia, for he realized that he could turn the rivalry and exhaustion of the Greek states to his own purposes. By clever use of his wealth and superb army Philip won control of the northern Aegean and awakened fear in Athens, which had vital interests there. Demosthenes, an Athenian patriot and a fine orator, warned his fellow citizens against Philip. Others, too, saw Philip as a threat. A comic playwright depicted one of Philip's ambassadors warning the Athenians:

Do you know that your battle will be with men
Who dine on sharpened swords,
And gulp burning firebrands for wine?
Then immediately after dinner the slave
Brings us dessert—Cretan arrows
Or pieces of broken spears.
We have shields and breastplates for
Cushions and at our feet slings and arrows,
And we are crowned with catapults.[11]

Finally the Athenians joined forces with Thebes, which also appreciated the Macedonian threat, to stop Philip. In 338 B.C. the combined Theban-Athenian army met Philip's veterans at the Boeotian city of Chaeronea. Philip's army won a hard-fought victory. Philip conquered Greece and put an end to Greek freedom. Because the Greeks could not put aside their quarrels, they fell to an invader.

The Lion of Chaeronea This stylized lion marks the mass grave of nearly 300 elite Theban soldiers who valiantly died fighting the Macedonians at the Battle of Chaeronea. After the battle, Philip said: "May those who suppose that these men did or suffered anything dishonorable perish wretchedly." *(Source: Caroline Buckler)*

SUMMARY

In a comparatively brief span of time the Greeks progressed from a primitive folk, backward and rude compared with their Near Eastern neighbors, to one of the most influential peoples of history. These originators of science and philosophy asked penetrating questions about the nature of life and society and came up with deathless responses to many of their own questions. Greek achievements range from the development of sophisticated political institutions to the creation of a stunningly rich literature. Brilliant but quarrelsome, they were their own worst enemies. As the Roman historian Pompeius Trogus later said of their fall:

The states of Greece, while each one wished to rule alone, all squandered sovereignty. Indeed, hastening without moderation to destroy one another in mutual ruin, they did not realize, until they were all crushed, that every one of them lost in the end.[12]

Nonetheless, their achievements outlived their political squabbles to become the cornerstone of all later Western development.

NOTES

1. K. J. Beloch, *Griechische Geschichte*, vol. I, pt. I (Strassburg: K. J. Trubner, 1912), p. 49. Unless otherwise credited, all quotations from a foreign language in this chapter are translated by John Buckler.
2. Aristotle, *Politics* 1253a3–4.
3. J. M. Edmonds, *Greek Elegy and Iambus* (Cambridge, Mass.: Harvard University Press, 1931), 1.70, frag. 10.
4. R. Meiggs and D. Lewis, *A Selection of Greek Historical Inspirations* (Oxford: Clarendon Press, 1969), 52. 21–32.
5. Ibid., 40. 9–11.
6. Thucydides, *History of the Peloponnesian War* 1.23.
7. Ibid.
8. Plutarch, *Life of Pericles* 13.5.
9. E. Diels and W. Krantz, *Fragmente der Vorsokratiker*, 8th ed. (Berlin: Weidmannsche Verlagsbuchhandlung, 1960), Anaximander frag. A30.
10. Ibid. Heraclitus frag. B30.
11. J. M. Edmonds, *The Fragments of Attic Comedy* (Leiden: E. J. Brill, 1971), 2.366–369, Mnesimachos frag. 7.
12. Justin, 8.1.1–2.

SUGGESTED READING

Translations of the most important writings of the Greeks and Romans can be found in the volumes of the Loeb Classical Library published by Harvard University Press. Paperback editions of the major Greek and Latin authors are available in the Penguin Classics. Recent translations of documents include two volumes of *Translated Documents of Greece and Rome:* volume 1, by C. Fornara, *Archaic Times to the End of the Peloponnesian War* (1977); and volume 2, by P. Harding, *From the End of the Peloponnesian War to the Battle of Ipsus* (1985).

Among the many general treatments of Greek history is that of H. Bengtson, *Griechische Geschichte,* 4th ed. (1969), which is now available in an English translation by E. F. Bloedow under the title *History of Greece* (1988); the translation is additionally valuable because of the added bibliography. Another sound general treatment is J. Fine, *The Ancient Greeks* (1984).

A number of books on early Greece are available in addition to those cited in the Notes. A good, careful, and learned synthesis can be found in Lord W. Taylour, *The Mycenaeans,* rev. ed. (1983). More recent and wider in coverage is R. Drews, *The Coming of the Greeks* (1988), which puts the movements of the Greeks in the broader context of Indo-European migrations. M. Mueller, *The Iliad* (1984), discusses both the historical and the heroic aspects of one of the world's great poems. No finer introduction to the Lyric Age can be found than A. R. Burn, *The Lyric Age* (1960). Its sequel, *Persia and the Greeks,* 2d ed. (1984), which is also unsurpassed, carries the history of Greece to the defeat of the Persians in 479 B.C. More recent is J. Boardman et al., *The Cambridge Ancient History,* 2d ed., vol. 4 (1988), which is profusely illustrated. C. Roebuck, *Economy and Society in the Early Greek World* (1984), treats several aspects of early Greek developments. A. J. Graham, *Colony and Mother City in Ancient Greece,* rev. ed. (1984), gives a good account of Greek colonization.

A good survey of work on Sparta is P. Cartledge, *Sparta and Lakonia* (1979), which can be warmly recommended. J. F. Lazenby, *The Spartan Army* (1985), studies the evolution and performance of the Spartan army somewhat apart from its social setting. The Athenian democracy and the society that produced it continue to attract scholarly attention. Interesting and important are two studies by R. Osborne. His *Demos* (1985) deals with many political and social aspects of early Athenian history. His *Classical Landscape with Figures* (1987) takes a new look at the relation of the polis to its surrounding territory, part of a growing trend in ancient history to blend archeological and literary evidence to understand ancient society. A series of new studies re-evaluates aspects of the Athenian democracy: M. Ostwald, *From Popular Sovereignty to the Sovereignty of Law* (1986); M. H. Hanson, *The Athenian Assembly* (1987); and J. Ober, *Mass and Elite in Democratic Athens* (1989); and P. B. Manyville, *The Origins of Citizenship in Ancient Athens* (1990).

The Athenian Empire and the outbreak of the Peloponnesian War are covered by R. Meiggs, *The Athenian Empire* (1972), and M. McGregor, *The Athenians and Their Empire* (1987). The best account of the outbreak of the Peloponnesian War, despite its defects, is G. E. M. de Ste. Croix, *The Origins of the Peloponnesian War* (1972). A concise treatment of the Peloponnesian War from a military point of view can be found in A. Ferrill, *The Origins of War* (1985), chap. 4. A. Forde, *The Ambition to Rule* (1989), places Thucydides' treatment of Alcibiades in the context of politics and imperialism.

The fourth century has been one of the most fertile fields of recent research. G. Proietti, *Xenophon's Sparta* (1987), and P. Cartledge, *Agesilaos and the Crisis of Sparta* (1987), both treat Spartan government and society in its period of greatness and collapse. J. Buckler, *The Theban Hegemony, 371–362 B.C.* (1980), treats the period of Theban ascendancy, and Buckler, *Philip II and the Sacred War* (1989), studies the ways in which Philip of Macedonia used Greek politics to his own ends. J. Cargill, *The Second Athenian League* (1981), a significant study, traces Athenian policy during the fourth century. J. R. Ellis, *Philip II and Macedonian Imperialism* (1976), and G. Cawkwell, *Philip of Macedon* (1978), analyze the career of the great conqueror.

Greek social life has recently received a great deal of attention. R. Just, *Women in Athenian Law and Life* (1988), explores such topics as daily life, the family, and women's role in society. W. K. Lacey, *The Family in Classical Greece* (1984), is the place to start for those who wish to learn more about ordinary family relations, and B. Zimmermann, *Greek Tragedy* (1990). D. Sansone, *Greek Athletics and the Genesis of Sport* (1988), well illustrated, provides a good and far-ranging treatment of what athletics meant to the classical Greek world. The topic of ancient Greek slavery is one of frequent interest, and two books address it in different but interesting ways: Y. Garlan, *Slavery in Ancient Greece* (1988), is sound; more adventurous is E. M. Wood, *Peasant-Citizen and Slave* (1988), which links the two groups to the founding of the Athenian democracy.

For Greek literature, culture, and science, see A. Lesky, *History of Greek Literature* (English translation, 1963); M. Golden, *Children and Childhood in Classical Athens* (1990); J. Burnet, *Early Greek Philosophy*, 4th ed. (1930); M. Clagett, *Greek Science in Antiquity* (1971); and E. R. Dodds, *The Greeks and the Irrational* (1951).

The classic treatment of Greek architecture is W. B. Dinsmoor, *The Architecture of the Ancient Greeks*, 3d ed. (1950). More recent (and perhaps more readable) is A. W. Lawrence, *Greek Architecture*, 3d ed. (1973). J. Boardman, *Greek Art*, rev. ed. (1973), is both perceptive and sound, as is J. J. Pollitt, *Art and Experience in Classical Greece* (1972). D. Haynes, *Greek Art and the Idea of Freedom* (1981), traces the evolving freedom of the human personality in Greek art.

J. Pinsent, *Greek Mythology* (1969), is a handy introduction. G. S. Kirk, *The Nature of Greek Myths* (1974), examines Greek religion and myth in the contemporary context. Newer treatments of Greek religion include E. Simon, *Festivals of Athens* (1983), which describes Athenian religious festivals in their archeological context; and W. Burkert, *Greek Religion* (1987), which gives a masterful survey of ancient religious beliefs.

6

Hellenistic Diffusion

Detail from the Alexander Sarcophagus at Sidon, Phoenicia

wo years after his conquest of Greece, Philip of Macedon fell victim to an assassin's dagger. Philip's twenty-year-old son, historically known as "Alexander the Great" (336–323 B.C.), assumed the Macedonian throne. This young man, one of the most remarkable personalities in history, was to have a profound impact on history. By overthrowing the Persian Empire and by spreading *Hellenism*—Greek culture, language, thought, and the Greek way of life—as far as India, Alexander was instrumental in creating a new era, traditionally called "Hellenistic" to distinguish it from the Hellenic. As a result of Alexander's exploits, the individualistic and energetic culture of the Greeks came into intimate contact with the venerable older cultures of Africa and Asia.

The impact of Philip and Alexander was so enormous that the great German historian Hermann Bengtson has recently commented:

Philip and his son Alexander were the ones who opened the door of the world to the Macedonians and Greeks. With Macedonian imperialism was joined the diffusion of the Greek spirit, which permeated the entire ancient world. Without the achievement of these two kings neither the Roman Empire nor the diffusion of Christianity would have been conceivable.[1]

- Is Bengtson's estimation correct or is it mere rhetoric?
- What did the spread of Hellenism mean to the Greeks and the peoples of Asia?
- What did the meeting of West and East hold for the development of economics, religion, philosophy, women's concerns, science, and medicine?

These questions are explored in this chapter.

ALEXANDER AND THE GREAT CRUSADE

In 336 B.C. Alexander inherited not only Philip's crown but also his policies. After his victory at Chaeronea, Philip had organized the states of Greece into a huge league under his leadership and announced to the Greeks his plan to lead them and his Macedonians against the Persian Empire. Fully intending to carry out Philip's designs, Alexander proclaimed to the Greek world that the invasion of Persia was to be a great crusade, a mighty act of revenge for the Persian invasion of Greece in 480 B.C. Despite his youth, Alexander was well prepared to lead the attack. In 334 B.C. he led an army of Macedonians and Greeks into western Asia. In the next three years he won three major battles—at the Granicus River, at Issus, and at Gaugamela—victories that stand almost as road signs marking his march to the east (Map 6.1). Having overthrown the Persian Empire, he crossed the Indus River in 326 B.C. and entered India, where he saw hard fighting. Finally, at the Hyphasis River his troops refused to go farther. Still eager to explore the limits of the world, Alexander turned south to the Indian Ocean and then turned west. In 324

Bust of Alexander This Roman portrait of Alexander the Great is a copy of a Greek original. Alexander's youth and self-confidence are immediately apparent. Yet the style is surprisingly simple for a bust of someone who had conquered the Persian Empire. The Greek inscription is equally simple: "Alexander, the son of Philip, Macedonian." *(Source: Louvre/Giraudon/Art Resource)*

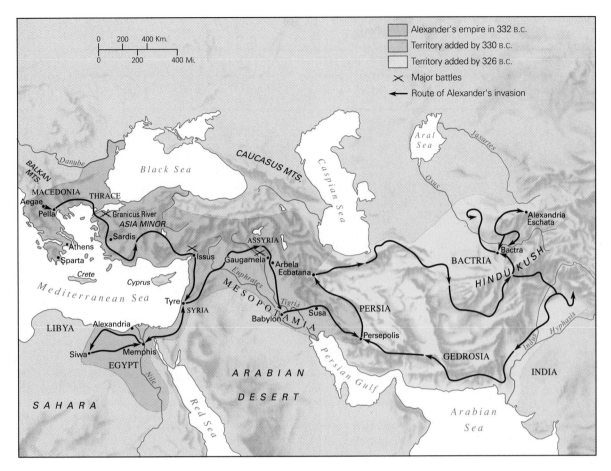

MAP 6.1 Alexander's Conquests This map shows the course of Alexander's invasion of the Persian Empire and the speed of his progress. More important than the success of his military campaigns was his founding of Hellenistic cities in the East.

B.C. a long, hard march brought him back to his camp at Susa. The great crusade was over, and Alexander himself died the next year in Babylon.

The political result of Alexander's premature death was chaos. Since several of the chief Macedonian officers aspired to Alexander's position as emperor and others opposed these ambitions, civil war lasting forty-three years tore Alexander's empire apart. By the end of this conflict, the most successful generals had carved out their own small and more or less stable monarchies.

Ptolemy immediately seized Egypt and transformed the native system of administration by appointing Greeks and Macedonians to the chief bureaucratic positions. Meanwhile, Seleucus won the bulk of Alexander's empire; his monarchy extended from western Asia to India. In the third

century B.C., however, the eastern parts of Seleucus's monarchy gained their independence, with the Parthians coming to power in Iran and the Greeks creating a monarchy of their own in Bactria. Antigonus maintained control of the Macedonian monarchy in Europe. Until the arrival of the Romans in the eastern Mediterranean in the second century B.C., these great monarchies were often at war with one another, but without winning any significant political or military advantage. In that respect, the Hellenistic monarchy was no improvement on the Greek polis.

Despite the disintegration of his empire, Alexander was instrumental in changing the face of politics in the eastern Mediterranean. His campaign swept away the Persian Empire, which had ruled the East for over two hundred years. In its

Alexander at the Battle of Issus   At left, Alexander the Great, bareheaded and wearing a breastplate, charges King Darius, who is standing in a chariot. The moment marks the turning point of the battle, as Darius turns to flee from the attack. *(Source: National Museum, Naples/Alinari/Scala/Art Resource)*

place he established a Macedonian monarchy. More important in the long run was his founding of new cities and military colonies, which scattered Greeks and Macedonians throughout the East. Thus the practical result of Alexander's campaign was to open the East to the tide of Hellenism.

THE SPREAD OF HELLENISM

When the Greeks and Macedonians entered Asia Minor and Egypt, they encountered civilizations older than their own. In some ways the Eastern cultures were more advanced than the Greek, in others less so. Thus this third great tide of Greek migration differed from preceding waves (see pages 119 and 124), which had spread over land that was uninhabited or inhabited by less developed peoples.

What did the Hellenistic monarchies offer Greek immigrants politically and materially? More broadly, how did Hellenism and the cultures of the East affect one another? What did the meeting of West and East entail for the history of the world?

Cities and Kingdoms

Although Alexander's generals created huge kingdoms, the concept of monarchy never completely replaced the ideal of the polis. Consequently the monarchies never won the deep emotional loyalty that Greeks had once felt for the polis. Hellenistic kings needed large numbers of Greeks to run their kingdoms. Otherwise royal business would grind to a halt, and the conquerors would soon be swallowed up by the far more numerous conquered population. Obviously, then, the kings had to encourage Greeks to immigrate and build new homes. To these Greeks monarchy was something out of the heroic past, something found in Homer's *Iliad,* not in daily life. The Hellenistic kings thus confronted the problem of making life in the new monarchies resemble the traditional Greek way of life. Since Greek civilization was urban, the kings continued Alexander's policy of establishing cities throughout their kingdoms in order to entice Greeks to immigrate. Yet the creation of these cities posed a serious political problem that the Hellenistic kings failed to solve.

To the Greeks civilized life was unthinkable without the polis, which was far more than a mere city. The Greek polis was by definition *sovereign*— it was an independent, autonomous state run by its citizens and free of any outside power or restraint. Hellenistic kings, however, refused to grant sovereignty to their cities. In effect these kings willingly built cities but refused to build a polis. Instead they attempted a compromise that ultimately failed.

Hellenistic monarchs gave their cities all the external trappings of a polis. Each had an assembly of citizens, a council to prepare legislation, and a board of magistrates to conduct the city's political business. Yet, however similar to the Greek city-state they appeared, these cities could not engage in diplomatic dealings, make treaties, pursue their own foreign policies, or wage their own wars. None could govern its own affairs without interference from the king, who, even if he stood in the background, was the real sovereign. In the eyes of the king the cities were important parts of the kingdom, but the welfare of the whole kingdom came first. The cities had to obey royal orders, and the king often placed his own officials in the cities to see that his decrees were followed.

A new Hellenistic city differed from a Greek polis in other ways as well. A Greek polis had enjoyed political and social unity even though it was normally composed of citizens, slaves, and resident aliens. A polis had one body of law and one set of customs. In a Hellenistic city, Greeks represented an elite class of citizens. Natives and non-Greek foreigners who lived in Hellenistic cities usually possessed rights inferior to those of the Greeks and often had their own laws. In some instances the disparity spurred natives to assimilate Greek culture in order to rise politically and socially. Other peoples, including many Jews, firmly resisted the essence of Hellenism. A Hellenistic city was not homogeneous and could not spark the intensity of feeling inspired by a polis.

In many respects a Hellenistic city resembled a modern city. It was a cultural center with theaters, temples, and libraries. It was a seat of learning, home of poets, writers, teachers, and artists. It was a place where people could find amusement. A Hellenistic city was also an economic center that provided a ready market for grain and produce raised in the surrounding countryside. The city was an emporium, scene of trade and manufacturing. In short, a Hellenistic city offered cultural and economic opportunities but did not foster a sense of united, integrated enterprise.

There were no constitutional links between city and king. A city was simply his possession. Its citizens had no voice in how the kingdom was run. A city had no rights except for those the king granted, and even those he could summarily take away. Ambassadors from a city could entreat the king for favors and petition him on such matters as taxes, boundary disputes, and legal cases. But a city had no right to advise the king on royal policy and enjoyed no political function in the kingdom.

Hellenistic kings tried to make the kingdom the political focus of citizens' allegiance. If the king could secure the frontiers of his kingdom, he could give it a geographical identity. He could then hope that his subjects would direct their primary loyalty to the kingdom rather than to a particular city. However, the kings' efforts to fix their borders led only to sustained warfare. Boundaries were determined by military power, and rule by force became the chief political principle of the Hellenistic world (Map 6.2).

Border wars were frequent and exhausting. The Seleucids and Ptolemies, for instance, waged five wars for the possession of southern Syria. Other kings refused to acknowledge boundaries at all. They followed Alexander's example and waged wars to reunify his empire under their own authority. By the third century B.C., a weary balance of power was reached, but only as the result of stalemate. It was not maintained by any political principle.

Though Hellenistic kings never built a true polis, that does not mean that their urban policy failed. Rather, the Hellenistic city was to remain the basic social and political unit in the Hellenistic East until the sixth century A.D. Cities were the chief agents of Hellenization, and their influence spread far beyond their walls. These cities formed a broad cultural network in which Greek language, customs, and values flourished. Roman rule in the Hellenistic East would later be based on this urban culture, which facilitated the rise and spread of Christianity. In broad terms Hellenistic cities were remarkably influential and successful.

The Greeks and the Opening of Asia and Africa

If the Hellenistic kings failed to satisfy the Greeks' political yearnings, they nonetheless succeeded in giving the Greeks unequaled economic and social opportunities. The ruling dynasties of the Hellenistic world were Macedonian, and Greeks filled all important political, military, and diplomatic positions. Macedonians and Greeks constituted an upper class that sustained Hellenism in the East. Besides building Greek cities, Hellenistic kings offered Greeks land and money as lures to further immigration.

The opening of the East offered ambitious Greeks opportunities for well-paying jobs and economic success. The Hellenistic monarchy, unlike the Greek polis, did not depend solely on its citizens to fulfill its political needs. Talented Greeks could expect to rise quickly in the government bureaucracy. Appointed by the king, these administrators did not have to stand for election each year, as had many officials of a Greek polis. Since they held their jobs year after year, they had ample time to evolve new administrative techniques. Naturally they became more efficient than the amateur officials common in Hellenic Greek city-states. The

MAP 6.2 The Hellenistic World After Alexander's death, no single commander could hold his vast conquests together, and his empire broke up into several kingdoms and leagues.

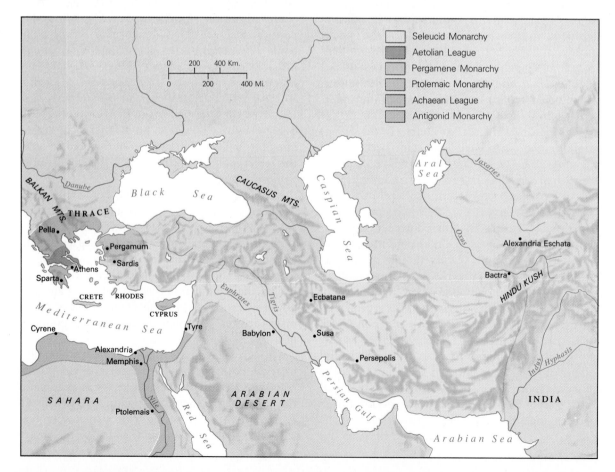

Priene The city of Priene in Asia Minor is an excellent example of the new Greek cities that sprang to life during the Hellenistic period. Greek architects designed the city of Priene to fit the slope of a hill that dominated the plain below. From the theater the spectator can see much of the city and the surrounding countryside. *(Source: Robert Harding)*

needs of the Hellenistic monarchy and the opportunities it offered thus gave rise to a professional corps of Greek administrators.

Greeks and Macedonians also found ready employment in the armies and navies of the Hellenistic monarchies. Alexander had proved the Greco-Macedonian style of warfare to be far superior to that of the Easterners, and Alexander's successors, themselves experienced officers, realized the importance of trained Greek and Macedonian soldiers. Moreover, Hellenistic kings were extremely reluctant to arm the native population or to allow them to serve in the army, fearing military rebellions among their conquered subjects. The result was the emergence of professional armies and navies comprising only Greeks and Macedonians.

Greeks were able to dominate other professions as well. In order to be truly philhellenic, the king-

doms and cities recruited Greek writers and artists to create Greek literature, art, and culture on Asian and African soil. Architects, engineers, and skilled craftsmen found their services in great demand because of the building policies of the Hellenistic monarchs. If Hellenistic kingdoms were to have Greek cities, those cities needed Greek buildings—temples, porticoes, gymnasia, theaters, fountains, and houses. Architects and engineers were sometimes commissioned to design and build whole cities, which they laid out in checkerboard fashion and filled with typical Greek buildings. An enormous wave of construction took place during the Hellenistic period.

Despite the opportunities they offered, the Hellenistic monarchies were hampered by their artificial origins. Their failure to win the political loyalty of their Greek subjects and their policy of wooing Greeks with lucrative positions encouraged a feeling of uprootedness and self-serving individualism among Greek immigrants. Once a Greek had left home to take service with, for instance, the army or the bureaucracy of the Ptolemies, he had no incentive beyond his pay and the comforts of life in Egypt to keep him there. If the Seleucid king offered him more money or a promotion, he might well accept it and take his talents to Asia Minor. Why not? In the realm of the Seleucids he, a Greek, would find the same sort of life and environment that the kingdom of the Ptolemies had provided him. Thus professional Greek soldiers and administrators were very mobile and apt to look to their own interests, not their kingdom's.

As long as Greeks continued to replenish their professional ranks, the kingdoms remained strong. In the process they drew an immense amount of talent from the Greek peninsula, draining the vitality of the Greek homeland. However, the Hellenistic monarchies could not keep recruiting Greeks forever, in spite of their wealth and willingness to spend lavishly to attract and keep the Greeks coming. In time the huge surge of immigration slowed greatly. Even then the Hellenistic monarchs were reluctant to recruit Easterners to fill posts normally held by Greeks. The result was at first the stagnation of the Hellenistic world and finally, after 202 B.C., collapse in the face of the young and vigorous Roman Republic.

Greeks and Easterners

The Greeks in Asia and Africa were a minority, and Hellenistic cities were islands of Greek culture in an Eastern sea. But Hellenistic monarchies were remarkably successful in at least partially Hellenizing Easterners and spreading a uniform culture throughout the East, a culture to which Rome eventually fell heir. The prevailing institutions, laws, and language of the East became Greek. Indeed, the Near East had seen nothing comparable since the days when Mesopotamian culture had spread throughout the area.

Yet the spread of Greek culture was wider than it was deep. At best it was a veneer, thicker in some places than in others. Hellenistic kingdoms were never entirely unified in language, customs, and thought. Greek culture took firmest hold along the shores of the Mediterranean, but in central Asia, in Persia and Bactria, it eventually gave way to Eastern cultures.

The Ptolemies in Egypt made no effort to spread Greek culture, and unlike other Hellenistic kings, they were not city builders. Indeed, they founded only the city of Ptolemais near Thebes (see Map 6.2). At first the native Egyptian population, the descendants of the pharaoh's people, retained their traditional language, outlook, religion, and way of life. Initially untouched by Hellenism, the natives continued to be the foundation of the state: they fed it by their labor in the fields and financed its operations with their taxes.

Throughout the third century B.C., the Greek upper class had little to do with the native population. Many Greek bureaucrats established homes in Alexandria and Ptolemais, where they managed finances, served as magistrates, and administered the law. Other Greeks settled in military colonies and supplied the monarchy with fighting men.

In the second century B.C. Greeks and native Egyptians began to intermarry and mingle their cultures. The language of the native population influenced Greek, and many Greeks adopted Egyptian religion and ways of life. Simultaneously natives adopted Greek customs and language and began to play a role in the administration of the kingdom and even to serve in the army. Although many Greeks and Egyptians remained aloof from one another, the overall result was the evolution of a widespread Greco-Egyptian culture.

Meanwhile, in order to nurture a vigorous and large Greek population, the Seleucid kings established many cities and military colonies in western Asia and along the banks of the Tigris and Euphrates rivers. Especially important to the Seleucids were the military colonies, for they depended on Greeks to defend the kingdom. The Seleucids had no elaborate plan for Hellenizing the native population, but the arrival of so many Greeks was bound to have an impact. Seleucid military colonies were generally founded near native villages, thus exposing Easterners to all aspects of Greek life. Many Easterners found Greek political and cultural forms attractive and imitated them. In western Asia and Syria, for instance, numerous native villages and towns developed along Greek lines, and some of them became Hellenized cities. Farther east the Greek kings who replaced the Seleucids in the third century B.C. spread Greek culture to their neighbors, even into the Indian subcontinent.

For Easterners the prime advantage of Greek culture was its pervasiveness. The Greek language became the common speech of the East. A common dialect called *koine* even influenced the speech of peninsular Greece itself. Greek became the speech of the royal court, bureaucracy, and armed forces. It was also the speech of commerce: any Easterner who wanted to compete in business had to learn it. As early as the third century B.C., some Greek cities were giving citizenship to Hellenized natives.

The vast majority of Hellenized Easterners, however, took only the externals of Greek culture while retaining the essentials of their own way of life. Though Greeks and Easterners adapted to each other's ways, there was never a true fusion of cultures. Nonetheless, each found useful things in the civilization of the other, and the two fertilized each other. This fertilization, this mingling of Greek and Eastern elements, is what makes Hellenistic culture unique and distinctive.

THE ECONOMIC SCOPE OF THE HELLENISTIC WORLD

Alexander's conquest of the Persian Empire not only changed the political face of the ancient world, it also brought the East fully into the sphere of Greek economics. Yet the Hellenistic period did not see a revolution in the way people lived and worked. The material demands of Hellenistic society remained as simple as those of Athenian society in the fifth century B.C. Clothes and furniture were essentially unchanged, as were household goods, tools, and jewelry. The real achievement of Alexander and his successors was linking East and West in a broad commercial network. The spread of Greeks throughout the East created new markets and stimulated trade. The economic unity of the Hellenistic world, like its cultural bonds, would later prove valuable to the Romans.

Commerce

Alexander's conquest of the Persian Empire had immediate effects on trade. In the Persian capitals Alexander found vast sums of gold, silver, and other treasure. This wealth financed the creation of new cities, the building of roads, and the development of harbors. Most of the great monarchies coined their money on the Attic standard. Thus much of the money used in Hellenistic kingdoms had the same value, and traders were less in need of moneychangers than in the days when each major power coined money on a different standard. As a result of Alexander's conquests, geographical knowledge of the East increased dramatically, making the East far better known to the Greeks than previously. The Greeks spread their law and methods of transacting business throughout the East. Whole new fields lay open to Greek merchants, who eagerly took advantage of the new opportunities. Commerce itself was a leading area where Greeks and Easterners met on grounds of common interest. In bazaars, ports, and trading centers Greeks learned of Eastern customs and traditions while spreading knowledge of their own culture.

The Seleucid and Ptolemaic dynasties traded as far afield as India, Arabia, and Africa. Overland trade with India and Arabia was conducted by caravan and was largely in the hands of Easterners. The caravan trade never dealt in bulk items or essential commodities; only luxury goods were transported in this very expensive fashion. Once the goods reached the Hellenistic monarchies, Greek merchants took a hand in the trade.

In the early Hellenistic period the Seleucids and Ptolemies ensured that the caravan trade was efficient. Later in the period—a time of increased war and confusion—they left the caravans unprotected. Taking advantage of this situation, Palmyra in the Syrian desert and Nabataean Petra in Arabia arose as caravan states. Such states protected the caravans from bandits and marauders and served as dispersal areas of caravan goods.

The Ptolemies discovered how to use monsoon winds to establish direct contact with India. One hardy merchant, who sailed from Egypt, left a firsthand account of sailing this important maritime link:

Hippalos, the pilot, observing the position of the ports and the conditions of the sea, first discovered how to sail across the ocean. Concerning the winds of the ocean in this region, when with us the Etesian winds begin, in India a wind between southwest and south, named for Hippalos, sets in from the open sea. From then until now some mariners set forth from Kanes and some from the Cape of Spices. Those sailing to

Harbor and Warehouses at Delos During the Hellenistic period Delos became a thriving trading center. Shown here is the row of warehouses at water's edge. From Delos cargoes were shipped to virtually every part of the Mediterranean. *(Source: Adam Woolfitt/Woodfin Camp)*

Dimurikes in southern India throw the bow of the ship farther out to sea. Those bound for Barygaza and the realm of the Sakas in northern India hold to the land no more than three days; and if the wind remains favorable, they hold the same course through the outer sea, and they sail along past the previously mentioned gulfs.[2]

Although this sea route never replaced overland caravan traffic, it kept direct relations with Europe alive, stimulating the exchange of ideas as well as goods.

More economically important than exotic trade were commercial dealings in essential commodities like raw materials, grain, and industrial products. The Hellenistic monarchies usually raised enough grain for their own needs as well as a surplus for export. For the cities of Greece and the Aegean this trade in grain was essential because many could not grow enough. Fortunately for them, abundant wheat supplies were available nearby in Egypt and in the Crimea in southern Russia.

The large-scale wars of the Hellenistic period often interrupted both the production and the distribution of grain. This was especially true when Alexander's successors were trying to carve out kingdoms. In addition natural calamities, such as excessive rain or drought, frequently damaged harvests. Throughout the Hellenistic period famine or severe food shortage remained a grim possibility.

Most trade in bulk commodities was seaborne, and the Hellenistic merchant ship was the workhorse of the day. Maritime trade gave rise to other industries and trades: sailors, shipbuilders, dock workers, merchants, accountants, teamsters, and pirates. Piracy was always a factor in the Hellenistic world and remained so until Rome extended its naval power throughout the eastern Mediterranean.

Slaves were a staple of Hellenistic trade. The wars provided prisoners for the slave market; to a lesser extent so did kidnapping and capture by pirates. The number of slaves involved cannot be estimated, but there is no doubt that slavery flourished. Both old Greek states and new Hellenistic kingdoms were ready slave markets, as was Rome when it emerged triumphant from the Second Punic War (see page 181). The war took a huge toll on Italian manpower, and Rome bought slaves in vast numbers to replace fieldworkers.

Throughout the Mediterranean world, slaves were almost always in demand. Only the Ptolemies discouraged both the trade and slavery itself, and they did so only for economic reasons. Their system had no room for slaves, who would only have competed with free labor. Otherwise, slave labor was to be found in the cities and temples of the Hellenistic world, in the factories and fields, and in the homes of wealthy people. In Italy and some parts of the East, slaves performed manual labor for large estates and worked the mines. They constituted a vital part of the Hellenistic economy.

Industry

Although demand for goods increased during the Hellenistic period, no new techniques of production appear to have developed. The discoveries of Hellenistic mathematicians and thinkers failed to produce any significant corresponding technological development. Manual labor, not machinery, continued to turn out the raw materials and few manufactured goods used by the Hellenistic world. Human labor was so cheap and so abundant that kings had no incentive to encourage the invention and manufacture of labor-saving machinery.

Pottery remained an important commodity, and most of it was made locally. The pottery used in the kitchen, the coarse ware, did not change at all. Indeed, it is impossible to tell whether specimens of this type of pottery are Hellenic or Hellenistic. Fancier pots and bowls decorated with a shiny black glaze came into use during the Hellenistic period. This ware originated in Athens, but potters in other places began to imitate its style, heavily cutting into the Athenian market. In the second century B.C., a red-glazed ware, often called "Samian," burst on the market and soon dominated it. Athens still held its own, however, in the production of fine pottery. Despite the change in pottery styles, the method of production of all pottery, whether plain or fine, remained essentially unchanged.

Although new techniques of production and wider use of machinery in industry did not occur, the volume of goods produced increased in the Hellenistic period. Small manufacturing establishments existed in nearly all parts of the Hellenistic world.

Agriculture

Hellenistic kings paid special attention to agriculture. Much of their revenue was derived from the produce of royal land, rents paid by the tenants of royal land, and taxation of agricultural land. Some Hellenistic kings even sought out and supported agricultural experts. The Ptolemies, for instance, sponsored experiments on seed grain, selecting seeds that seemed hardy and productive and trying to improve their characteristics. Hellenistic authors wrote handbooks discussing how farms and large estates could most profitably be run. These handbooks described soil types, covered the proper times for planting and reaping, and discussed care of farm animals. Whether these efforts had any impact on the average farmer, however, is difficult to determine.

The Ptolemies made the greatest strides in agriculture, but their success was largely political. Egypt had a strong tradition of central authority dating back to the pharaohs. The Ptolemies inherited this tradition and tightened the centralization. They could decree what crops Egyptian farmers would plant and what animals would be raised, and they had the power to carry out their commands. The Ptolemies recognized the need for well-planned and constant irrigation, and much native labor went into the digging and maintenance of canals and ditches. The Ptolemies also reclaimed a great deal of land from the desert, including the Fayum, a dry lake bed near the Nile.

The centralized authority of the Ptolemies accounts for the occurrence of agricultural advances

Scene from Daily Life Art in the Hellenistic period often pursued two themes: increased realism and scenes from daily life. This statuette illustrates both. Here a peasant follows his donkey, which has fallen, to sell his grapes in the city. The peasant saves his grapes with one hand while trying to pull the donkey to its feet with the other. *(Source: National Archaeological Museum, Athens)*

at the local level in Egypt. But such progress was not possible in any other Hellenistic monarchy. Despite royal interest in agriculture and a studied approach to it in the Hellenistic period, there is no evidence that agricultural productivity increased. Whether Hellenistic agricultural methods had any influence on Eastern practices is unknown.

RELIGION IN THE HELLENISTIC WORLD

In religion Hellenism gave Easterners far less than the East gave the Greeks. At first the Hellenistic period saw the spread of Greek religious cults throughout the East. When Hellenistic kings founded cities, they also built temples and established new cults and priesthoods for the old Olympian gods. The new cults enjoyed the prestige of being the religion of the conquerors, and they were supported by public money. The most attractive aspects of the Greek cults were their rituals and festivities. Greek cults sponsored literary, musical, and athletic contests, which were staged in beautiful surroundings among impressive Greek buildings. In short, the cults offered bright and lively entertainment, both intellectual and physical. They fostered Greek culture and traditional sports and thus were a splendid means of displaying Greek civilization in the East.

Despite various advantages, Greek cults suffered from some severe shortcomings. They were primarily concerned with ritual. Participation in the civic cults did not even require belief (see page 139). On the whole, the civic cults neither appealed to religious emotions nor embraced matters such as sin and redemption. Greek mystery religions helped fill this gap, but the centers of these religions were in old Greece. Although the new civic cults were lavish in pomp and display, they could not satisfy deep religious feelings or spiritual yearnings.

Even though the Greeks participated in the new cults for cultural reasons, they felt little genuine religious attachment to them. In comparison with the emotional and sometimes passionate religions of the East, the Greek cults seemed sterile. Greeks increasingly sought solace from other sources. Educated and thoughtful people turned to philosophy as a guide to life; others turned to superstition, magic, or astrology. Still others might shrug

and speak of *Tyche,* which meant "Fate" or "Chance," "Doom," or "Fortune"—a capricious and sometimes malevolent force.

In view of the spiritual decline of Greek religion, it is surprising that Eastern religions did not make more immediate headway among the Greeks, but at first they did not. Although Hellenistic Greeks clung to their own cults as expressions of their Greekness rather than for any ethical principles, they did not rush to embrace native religions. Only in the second century B.C., after a century of exposure to Eastern religions, did Greeks begin to adopt them.

Nor did Hellenistic kings make any effort to spread Greek religion among their Eastern subjects. The Greeks always considered religion a matter best left to the individual. Greek cults were attractive only to those socially aspiring Easterners who adopted Greek culture for personal advancement. Otherwise Easterners were little affected by Greek religion. Nor did native religions suffer from the arrival of the Greeks. Some Hellenistic kings limited the power of native priesthoods, but they also subsidized some Eastern cults with public money. Alexander the Great actually reinstated several Eastern cults that the Persians had suppressed.

The only significant junction of Greek and Eastern religious traditions was the growth and spread of new "mystery religions," so called because they featured a body of ritual not to be divulged to anyone not initiated into the cult. The new mystery cults incorporated aspects of both Greek and Eastern religions and had broad appeal for both Greeks and Easterners who yearned for personal immortality. Since the Greeks were already familiar with old mystery cults, such as the Eleusinian mysteries in Attica, the new cults did not strike them as alien or barbarian. Familiar, too, was the concept of preparation for an initiation. Devotees of the Eleusinian mysteries and other such cults had to prepare themselves mentally and physically before entering the gods' presence. Thus the mystery cults fitted well with Greek usage.

The new religions enjoyed one tremendous advantage over the old Greek mystery cults. Whereas old Greek mysteries were tied to particular places, such as Eleusis, the new religions spread throughout the Hellenistic world. People did not have to undertake long and expensive pilgrimages just to become members of the religion. In that sense the new mystery religions came to the people, for temples of the new deities sprang up wherever Greeks lived.

The mystery religions all claimed to save their adherents from the worst that fate could do and promised life for the soul after death. They all had a single concept in common: the belief that by the rites of initiation devotees became united with the god, who had died and risen from the dead. The sacrifice of the god and his or her victory over death saved the devotee from eternal death. Similarly, all mystery religions demanded a period of preparation in which the convert strove to become holy—that is, to live by the religion's precepts. Once aspirants had prepared themselves, they went through an initiation in which they learned the secrets of the religion. The initiation was usually a ritual of great emotional intensity, baptism into a new life.

The Eastern mystery religions that took the Hellenistic world by storm were the Egyptian cults of Serapis and Isis. Serapis, who was invented by King Ptolemy, combined elements of the Egyptian god Osiris with aspects of the Greek gods Zeus, Pluto (the prince of the underworld), and Asclepius (god of medicine). Serapis was believed to be the judge of souls, who rewarded virtuous and righteous people with eternal life. Like Asclepius, he was a god of healing. Serapis became an international god, and many Hellenistic Greeks thought of him as Zeus. Associated with Isis and Serapis was Anubis, the old Egyptian god who, like Charon in the Greek pantheon, guided the souls of initiates to the realm of eternal life.

The cult of Isis enjoyed even wider appeal than that of Serapis. Isis, wife of Osiris, claimed to have conquered Tyche and promised to save any mortal who came to her. She became the most important goddess of the Hellenistic world, and her worship was very popular among women. Her priests claimed that she bestowed on humanity the gift of civilization and founded law and literature. She was the goddess of marriage, conception, and childbirth—like Serapis, a deity who promised to save the souls of her believers.

There was neither conflict between Greek and Eastern religions nor wholesale acceptance of one or the other. Nonetheless, Greeks and Easterners noticed similarities among one another's deities and assumed that they were worshiping the same gods in different garb. These tendencies toward religious universalism and the desire for personal immortality would prove significant when the Hellenistic world came under the sway of Rome, for Hellenistic developments paved the way for the spread of Christianity.

PHILOSOPHY AND THE COMMON MAN

Philosophy during the Hellenic period was the exclusive province of the wealthy, for only they had leisure enough to pursue philosophical studies. During the Hellenistic period, however, philosophy reached out to touch the lives of more men and women than ever before. The reasons for this development were several. Since the ideal of the polis had declined, politics no longer offered people a satisfying intellectual outlet. Moreover, much of Hellenistic life, especially in the new cities of the East, seemed unstable and without venerable traditions. Greeks were far more mobile than they had ever been before, but their very mobility left them feeling uprooted. Many people in search of something permanent, something unchanging in a changing world, turned to philosophy. Another reason for the increased influence of philosophy was the decline of traditional religion and a growing belief in Tyche. To protect against the worst that Tyche could do, many Greeks looked to philosophy, particularly to the Cynics, Epicureans, and Stoics.

Cynics

Undoubtedly the most unusual of the new philosophers were the Cynics, who urged a return to nature. They advised men and women to discard traditional customs and conventions (which were in decline anyway) and live simply. The Cynics believed that by rejecting material things people become free and that nature will provide all necessities.

The founder of the Cynics was Antisthenes (b. ca 440 B.C.), but it was Diogenes of Sinope (ca 412–323 B.C.), one of the most colorful men of the period, who spread the philosophy. Diogenes came to Athens to study philosophy and soon evolved his own ideas on the ideal life. He hit on the notion that happiness was possible only by liv-

Tyche This statue depicts Tyche as the city-goddess of Antioch, a new Hellenistic foundation of the Seleucid king Antiochus. Some Hellenistic Greeks worshiped Tyche in the hope that she would be kind to them. Philosophers tried to free people from her whimsies. Antiochus tried to win her favor by honoring her. *(Source: Photo Vatican Museums)*

the streets and marketplaces. They more than any other philosophical group tried to reach the common people. As part of their return to nature they often did without warm clothing, sufficient food, or adequate housing, which they considered unnecessary. The Cynics also tried to break down political barriers by declaring that people owed no allegiance to any city or monarchy. Rather, they said, all people are cosmopolitan—that is, citizens of the world. The Cynics reached across political boundaries to create a community of people, sharing the common traits of all humanity and living as close to nature as humanly possible. The Cynics set a striking example of how people could turn away from materialism. Although comparatively few men and women could follow such rigorous precepts, the Cynics influenced all the other major schools of philosophy.

Epicureans

Epicurus (340–270 B.C.), who founded his own school of philosophy at Athens, based his view of life on scientific theories. Accepting Democritus's theory that the universe is composed of indestructible particles, Epicurus put forth a naturalistic theory of the universe. Although he did not deny the existence of the gods, he taught that they had no effect on human life. The essence of Epicurus's belief was that the principal good of human life is pleasure, which he defined as the absence of pain. Epicurus did not advocate drunken revels or sensual dissipation, which he thought actually cause pain. Instead, he warned that any violent emotion is undesirable. Drawing on the teachings of the Cynics, he advocated mild self-discipline. Even poverty he considered good, as long as people have enough food, clothing, and shelter. Epicurus also taught that individuals can most easily attain peace and serenity by ignoring the outside world and looking inward, to their personal feelings and reactions. Thus Epicureanism led to quietism.

Epicureanism taught its followers to ignore politics and issues, for politics led to tumult, which would disturb the soul. Although the Epicureans thought that the state originated through a social contract among individuals, they did not care about the political structure of the state. Content to live in a democracy, oligarchy, monarchy, or whatever, they never speculated about the ideal state. Their ideals stood outside all political forms.

ing according to nature and forgoing luxuries. He attacked social conventions because he considered them contrary to nature. Throughout Greece he gained fame for the rigorous way in which he put his beliefs into practice.

Diogenes did not establish a philosophical school in the manner of Plato and Aristotle. Instead he and his followers took their teaching to

Stoics

Opposed to the passivity of the Epicureans, Zeno (335–262 B.C.), a philosopher from Citium in Cyprus, advanced a different concept of human beings and the universe. When Zeno first came to Athens, he listened avidly to the Cynics. Concluding, however, that the Cynics were extreme, he stayed in Athens to form his own school, the Stoa, named after the building where he preferred to teach.

Stoicism became the most popular Hellenistic philosophy and the one that later captured the mind of Rome. Zeno and his followers considered nature an expression of divine will; in their view people could be happy only when living in accordance with nature. They stressed the unity of man and the universe, stating that all men were brothers and obliged to help one another. Stoicism's science was derived from Heraclitus, but its broad and warm humanity was the work of Zeno and his followers.

Unlike the Epicureans, the Stoics taught that people should participate in politics and worldly affairs. Yet this idea never led to the belief that individuals ought to try to change the order of things. Time and again the Stoics used the image of an actor in a play: the Stoic plays an assigned part and never tries to change the play. To the Stoics the important question was not whether they achieved anything, but whether they lived virtuous lives. Through virtuous living they could triumph over Tyche, for Tyche could destroy achievements but not the nobility of their lives.

Although the Stoics developed the concept of a world order, they thought of it strictly in terms of the individual. Like the Epicureans, they were indifferent to specific political forms. They believed that people should do their duty to the state in which they found themselves. The universal state they preached about was ethical, not political. The Stoics' most significant practical achievement was the creation of the concept of natural law. The Stoics concluded that since all men were brothers, partook of divine reason, and were in harmony with the universe, one law—a part of the natural order of life—governed them all.

The Stoic concept of a universal state governed by natural law is one of the finest heirlooms that the Hellenistic world passed on to Rome. The Stoic concept of natural law, of one law for all people, became a valuable tool when the Romans began to deal with many different peoples with different laws. The ideal of the universal state gave the Romans a rationale for extending their empire to the farthest reaches of the world. The duty of individuals to their fellows served the citizens of the Roman Empire as the philosophical justification for doing their duty. In this respect, too, the real fruit of Hellenism was to ripen only under the cultivation of Rome.

HELLENISTIC WOMEN

With the growth of monarchy in the Hellenistic period came a major new development: the importance of royal women, many of whom played an active part in political and diplomatic life. In the Hellenic period the polis had replaced kingship, except at Sparta, and queens were virtually unknown apart from myth and legend. Even in Sparta queens did not participate in politics. Hellenistic queens, however, did exercise political power, either in their own right or by manipulating their husbands. Many Hellenistic queens were depicted as willful or ruthless, especially in power struggles over the throne, and in some cases those charges are accurate. Other Hellenistic royal women, however, set an example of courage and nobility.

The example of the queens had a profound effect on Hellenistic attitudes toward women in general. In fact, the Hellenistic period saw a great expansion in social and economic opportunities for women. More women than ever before received educations that enabled them to enter medicine and other professions. Literacy among women increased dramatically, and their options expanded accordingly. Some won fame as poets, while others studied with philosophers and contributed to the intellectual life of the age. These developments, however, touched only wealthy women. Poor women—and probably the majority of women—were barely literate, if literate at all.

Women began to participate in politics on a limited basis. Often they served as priestesses, as they had in the Hellenic period, but they also began to serve in civil capacities. For their services to the state they received public acknowledgment. Women sometimes received honorary citizenship from foreign cities because of aid given in times of crisis. Few women achieved these honors, however, and those who did were from the upper classes.

This major development was not due to male enlightenment. Although Hellenistic philosophy addressed itself to many new questions, the position of women was not one of them. The Stoics, in spite of their theory of the brotherhood of man, thought of women as men's inferiors. Only the Cynics, who waged war on all accepted customs, treated women as men's equals. The Cynics were interested in women as individuals, not as members of a family or as citizens of the state. Their view did not make much headway. Like other aspects of Cynic philosophy, this attitude was more admired than followed.

The new prominence of women was largely due to their increased participation in economic affairs. During the Hellenistic period some women took part in commercial transactions. Nonetheless, they still lived under legal handicaps. In Egypt, for example, a Greek woman needed a male guardian to buy, sell, or lease land, to borrow money, and to represent her in other transactions. Yet often such a guardian was present only to fulfill the letter of the law. The woman was the real agent and handled the business being transacted. In Hellenistic Sparta, women accumulated large fortunes and vast amounts of land. As early as the beginning of the Hellenistic period women owned two-fifths of the land of Laconia. Spartan women, however, were exceptional. In most other areas, even women who were wealthy in their own right were formally under the protection of a male relative.

These changes do not amount to a social revolution. Women had begun to participate in business, politics, and legal activities. Yet such women were rare and labored under handicaps unknown to men. Even so, it was a start.

HELLENISTIC SCIENCE

The area in which Hellenistic culture achieved its greatest triumphs was science. Here, too, the ancient Near East made contributions to Greek thought. The patient observations of the Babylonians, who for generations had scanned the skies, had provided the raw materials for Thales' speculations, which were the foundation of Hellenistic astronomy. The most notable of the Hellenistic as-

Old Shepherdess Daily life for the poor and elderly was as hard in the Hellenistic period as in other times. Here a tough, old, scantily clothed shepherdess brings a sheep to market. Such scenes were common during the period; but art, not written sources, has preserved them for posterity. (*Source: Alinari/Art Resource*)

tronomers was Aristarchus of Samos (ca 310–230 B.C.), who was educated in Aristotle's school. Aristarchus concluded that the sun is far larger than the earth and that the stars are enormously distant from the earth. He argued against Aristotle's view that the earth is the center of the universe. Instead Aristarchus propounded the *heliocentric theory*—that the earth and planets revolve around the sun. His work is all the more impressive because he lacked even a rudimentary telescope. Aristarchus had only the human eye and brain, but they were more than enough.

Aristarchus's theories, however, did not persuade the ancient world. In the second century A.D., Claudius Ptolemy, a mathematician and astronomer in Alexandria, accepted Aristotle's theory of the earth as the center of the universe, and that view prevailed for 1,400 years. Moreover, Ptolemy based his conclusions on extensive observations of the stars and planets, which formed the scientific basis of his work. Aristarchus's heliocentric theory lay dormant until resurrected by the brilliant Polish astronomer Nicolaus Copernicus (1473–1543).

In geometry Hellenistic thinkers discovered little that was new, but Euclid (ca 300 B.C.), a mathematician who lived in Alexandria, compiled a valuable textbook of existing knowledge. His book *The Elements of Geometry* has exerted immense influence on European civilization, for it rapidly became the standard introduction to geometry. Generations of students, from the Hellenistic period to the present, have learned the essentials of geometry from it.

The greatest thinker of the Hellenistic period was Archimedes (ca 287–212 B.C.), who was a clever inventor as well. He lived in Syracuse in Sicily and watched Rome emerge as a power in the Mediterranean. When the Romans laid siege to Syracuse in the Second Punic War (see page 181), Archimedes invented a number of machines to thwart the Roman army. His catapults threw rocks large enough to sink ships and disrupt battle lines. His grappling devices lifted warships out of the water. In the Hellenistic period the practical applications of principles of mechanics were primarily military, for the building of artillery and siege engines. In a more peaceful vein, Archimedes invented the Archimedean screw and the compound pulley. Plutarch described Archimedes' dramatic demonstration of how easily his pulley could move huge weights with little effort:

A three-masted merchant ship of the royal fleet had been hauled on land by hard work and many hands. Archimedes put aboard her many men and the usual freight. He sat far away from her; without haste, but gently working a compound pulley with his hand, he drew her towards him smoothly and without faltering, just as though she were running on the surface of the sea.[3]

Archimedes was far more interested in pure mathematics than in practical inventions. His mathematical research, covering many fields, was his greatest contribution to thought. In his book *On Plane Equilibriums* Archimedes dealt for the first time with the basic principles of mechanics, including the principle of the lever. He once said that if he were given a lever and a suitable place to stand, he could move the world. In his treatise *Sand-Counter* Archimedes devised a system to express large numbers, a difficult matter considering the deficiencies of Greek numerical notation. *Sand-Counter* also discussed the heliocentric theory of Aristarchus. With his treatise *On Floating Bodies* Archimedes founded the science of hydrostatics. He concluded that whenever a solid floats in a liquid, the weight of the solid is equal to the volume of liquid displaced. The way he made his discovery has become famous:

When he was devoting his attention to this problem, he happened to go to a public bath. When he climbed down into the bathtub there, he noticed that water in the tub equal to the bulk of his body flowed out. Thus, when he observed this method of solving the problem, he did not wait. Instead, moved with joy, he sprang out of the tub, and rushing home naked he kept indicating in a loud voice that he had indeed discovered what he was seeking. For while running he was shouting repeatedly in Greek, "eureka, eureka" ("I have found it, I have found it").[4]

Archimedes was willing to share his work with others, among them Eratosthenes (285–ca 204 B.C.), a man of almost universal interests. From his native Cyrene in North Africa, Eratosthenes traveled to Athens, where he studied philosophy and mathematics. He refused to join any of the philosophical schools, for he was interested in too many things to follow any particular dogma. Hence his thought was eclectic, taking doctrines from many schools of thought. Around 245 B.C. King Ptolemy invited Eratosthenes to Alexandria. The Ptolemies

The Celestial Globe In Greek mythology the god Atlas held the world on his strong shoulders, thereby preventing it from falling. Hellenistic scientists formed a very accurate idea of the shape and dimension of the earth. Here Atlas holds the globe, which rests on its axis and displays the skies, with figures representing constellations, as well as the equator, tropics, and polar circles. *(Source: National Museum, Naples/Alinari/Art Resource)*

had done much to make Alexandria an intellectual, cultural, and scientific center. They had established a lavish library and museum, undoubtedly the greatest seat of learning in the Hellenistic world. At the crown's expense, the Ptolemies maintained a number of distinguished scholars and poets. Eratosthenes came to Alexandria to become librarian of the royal library, a position of great prestige. While there he continued his mathematical work and by letter struck up a friendship with Archimedes.

Unlike his friend Archimedes, Eratosthenes did not devote his life entirely to mathematics, although he never lost interest in it. He used mathematics to further the geographical studies for which he is most famous. He calculated the circumference of the earth geometrically, estimating it as about 24,675 miles. He was not wrong by much: the earth is actually 24,860 miles in circumference. Eratosthenes also concluded that the earth is a spherical globe, that the land mass is roughly four-sided, and that the land is surrounded by ocean. He discussed the shapes and sizes of land and ocean and the irregularities of the earth's surface. He drew a map of the earth and used his own system of explaining the divisions of the earth's land mass.

Using geographical information gained by Alexander the Great's scientists, Eratosthenes tried to fit the East into Greek geographical knowledge. Although for some reason he ignored the western Mediterranean and Europe, he declared that a ship could sail from Spain either around Africa to India or directly westward to India. Not until the great days of Western exploration did sailors such as Vasco da Gama and Magellan actually prove Eratosthenes' theories. Like Eratosthenes, Greek geographers also turned their attention southward to Africa. During this period the people of the Mediterranean learned of the climate and customs of Ethiopia and gleaned some scant information about equatorial Africa.

In his life and work Eratosthenes exemplifies the range and vitality of Hellenistic science. His varied interests included the cultural and humanistic as well as the purely scientific. Although his chief interest was in the realm of speculative thought, he did not ignore the practical. He was quite willing to deal with old problems and to break new ground.

In the Hellenistic period the scientific study of botany had its origin. Aristotle's pupil Theophras-

SPREAD OF HELLENISM

338 B.C.	Battle of Chaeronea: Philip II of Macedon conquers Greece
336 B.C.	Assassination of Philip II; Alexander III (the Great) inherits Macedonian crown
334–330 B.C.	Alexander overthrows the Persian Empire
334 B.C.	Battle of Granicus River
333 B.C.	Battle of Issus: Alexander conquers Asia Minor
331 B.C.	Battle of Gaugamela: Alexander conquers Mesopotamia
330 B.C.	Fall of Persepolis, principal Persian capital
	Fall of Ecbatana, last Persian capital
330–326 B.C.	Alexander conquers Bactria
326 B.C.	Alexander enters India; mutiny of his troops at the Hyphasis River
323 B.C.	Alexander dies in Babylon at the age of 32
323–275 B.C.	Empire divided into three monarchies; new dynasties founded by Ptolemy I (Egypt), Antigonus Gonatar (Macedonia, Asia Minor), and Seleucus I (Mesopotamia)
3d century B.C.	Development of the Hellenistic city
ca 300 B.C.	Euclid, *The Elements of Geometry*
ca 300–250 B.C.	Diffusion of philosophy; new schools founded by Epicurus (Epicureans) and Zeno (Stoics)
	Medical advances by Herophilus, Erasistratus, Philinus, and Serapion
263 B.C.	Eumenes of Pergamum wins independence from the Seleucids, establishes the Pergamene monarchy
ca 250–200 B.C.	Scientific advances by Archimedes, Eratosthenes, and Aristarchus of Samos

tus (ca 372–288 B.C.), who became head of the Lyceum, the school established by Aristotle, studied the botanical information made available by Alexander's penetration of the East. Aristotle had devoted a good deal of his attention to zoology, and Theophrastus extended his work to plants. He wrote two books on the subject, *History of Plants* and *Causes of Plants*. He carefully observed phenomena and based his conclusions on what he had actually seen. Theophrastus classified plants and accurately described their parts. He detected the process of germination and realized the importance of climate and soil to plants. Some of Theophrastus's work found its way into agricultural handbooks, but for the most part Hellenistic science did not carry the study of botany any further.

Despite its undeniable brilliance, Hellenistic science suffered from a remarkable weakness almost impossible for practical-minded Americans to understand. Although scientists of this period invented such machines as the air gun, the water organ, and even the steam engine, they never used their discoveries as labor-saving devices. No one has satisfactorily explained why these scientists were so impractical, but one answer is quite possible: they and the rest of society saw no real need for machines. Slave labor, which was abundant, made the use of labor-saving machinery superfluous. Science was applied only to war. Principles of physics were used to build catapults and other siege machinery. Even though Hellenistic science did not lead the ancient world to an industrial revolution, later Hellenistic thinkers preserved the knowledge of these machines and the principles behind them. In so doing, they saved the discoveries of Hellenistic science for the modern age.

HELLENISTIC MEDICINE

The study of medicine flourished during the Hellenistic period, and Hellenistic physicians carried the work of Hippocrates into new areas. Herophilus, who lived in the first half of the third century

B.C., worked at Alexandria and studied the writings of Hippocrates. He accepted Hippocrates' theory of the four humors and approached the study of medicine in a systematic, scientific fashion. He dissected corpses and measured what he observed. He discovered the nervous system and concluded that two types of nerves, motor and sensory, exist. Herophilus also studied the brain, which he considered the center of intelligence, and discerned the cerebrum and cerebellum. His other work dealt with the liver, lungs, and uterus. His younger contemporary, Erasistratus, also conducted research on the brain and nervous system and improved on Herophilus's work. He, too, followed in the tradition of Hippocrates and preferred to let the body heal itself by means of diet and air.

Tower of the Four Winds This remarkable building, which still stands in Athens, was built by an astronomer to serve as a sundial, water-clock, and weather vane. It is one of the few examples of the application of Hellenistic science to daily life. *(Source: Ekdotike Athenon)*

Both Herophilus and Erasistratus were members of the Dogmatic school of medicine at Alexandria. In this school speculation played an important part in research. So, too, did the study of anatomy. To learn more about human anatomy Herophilus and Erasistratus not only dissected corpses but even vivisected criminals whom King Ptolemy contributed for the purpose. *Vivisection*—cutting into the body of a living animal or person—was seen as a necessary cruelty. The Dogmatists argued that the knowledge gained from the suffering of a few evil men benefited many others. Nonetheless, the practice of vivisection seems to have been short-lived, although dissection continued. Better knowledge of anatomy led to improvements in surgery. These advances enabled the Dogmatists to invent new surgical instruments and techniques.

In about 280 B.C. Philinus and Serapion, pupils of Herophilus, led a reaction to the Dogmatists. Believing that the Dogmatists had become too speculative, they founded the Empiric school of medicine at Alexandria. Claiming that the Dogmatists' emphasis on anatomy and physiology was misplaced, they concentrated instead on the observation and cure of illnesses. They also laid heavier stress on the use of drugs and medicine to treat illnesses. Heraclides of Tarentum (perhaps first century B.C.) carried on the Empirical tradition and dedicated himself to observation and the use of medicines. He discovered the benefits of opium and worked with other drugs that relieved pain. He also steadfastly rejected magic as pertinent to the application of drugs and medicines.

Hellenistic medicine had its dark side, for many physicians were money grubbers, fools, and quacks. One of the angriest complaints comes from the days of the Roman Empire:

Of all men only a physician can kill a man with total impunity. Oh no, on the contrary, censure goes to him who dies and he *is guilty of excess, and furthermore* he *is blamed. . . . Let me not accuse their [physicians'] avarice, their greedy deals with those whose fate hangs in the balance, their setting a price on pain, and their demands for down payment in case of death, and their secret doctrines.*[5]

Abuses already existed in the Hellenistic period. As is true today, many Hellenistic physicians did not take the Hippocratic oath very seriously.

Hellenistic Medicine During the Hellenistic period, the practice of medicine expanded greatly, and medical research made huge strides. Despite much harm done by quacks and dishonorable physicians, Hellenistic medicine made substantial progress in healing. In this relief, the physician at left treats a patient while other patients wait to the right. The invention of the waiting room also belongs to classical antiquity. *(Source: National Archaeological Museum, Athens)*

The Hellenistic world was also plagued by people who claimed to cure illnesses through incantations and magic. Their potions included such concoctions as blood from the ear of an ass mixed with water to cure fever, or the liver of a cat killed when the moon was waning, and preserved in salt. Broken bones could be cured by applying the ashes of a pig's jawbone to the break. The dung of a goat mixed with old wine would heal broken ribs. One charlatan claimed that he could cure epilepsy by making the patient drink, from the skull of a man who had been killed but not cremated, water drawn from a spring at night. These quacks even claimed that they could cure mental illness. The treatment for a person suffering from melancholy was calf dung boiled in wine. No doubt the patient became too sick to be depressed.

Quacks who prescribed such treatments were very popular but did untold harm to the sick and injured. They and greedy physicians also damaged the reputation of dedicated doctors who honestly and intelligently tried to heal and alleviate pain. The medical abuses that arose in the Hellenistic period were so flagrant that the Romans who later entered the Hellenistic world developed an intense contempt for physicians. The Romans considered the study of Hellenistic medicine beneath the dignity of a Roman, and even as late as the Roman Empire few Romans undertook the study of Greek medicine. Nonetheless the work of men like Herophilus and Serapion made valuable contributions to the knowledge of medicine, and the fruits of their work were preserved and handed on to the world.

SUMMARY

It can safely be said that Philip and Alexander broadened Greek and Macedonian horizons, but not in ways that they had intended. Although Alexander established Macedonian and Greek colonies across western and central Asia for military reasons, they resulted in the spread of Hellenism as a side effect. In the Aegean and Near East the fusion of Greek and Eastern cultures laid the social, intellectual, and cultural foundations on which the Romans would later build. In the heart of the old Persian Empire, Hellenism was only another new influence that was absorbed by older ways of thought and life. Yet overall, in the exchange of ideas and the opportunity for different cultures to learn about one another, a new cosmopolitan society evolved. That society in turn made possible such diverse advances as broadened trade and agriculture, the creation of religious and philosophical ideas that paved the way for Christianity, and greater freedom for women. People of the Hellenistic period also made remarkable advances in science and medicine. They not only built on the achievements of their predecessors, but they also produced one of the most creative intellectual eras of classical antiquity.

NOTES

1. H. Bengtson, *Philipp und Alexander der Grosse* (Munich: Callwey, 1985), p. 7. Unless otherwise credited, all quotations from a foreign language in this chapter are translated by John Buckler.
2. *Periplous of the Erythraian Sea* 57.
3. Ibid., 14.13.
4. Vitruvius, *On Architecture* 9. Pref. 10.
5. Pliny the Elder, *Natural History* 29.8.18, 21.

SUGGESTED READING

General treatments of Hellenistic political, social, and economic history can be found in F. W. Walbank et al., *The Cambridge Ancient History,* 2d ed., vol. 7, pt. 1 (1984). Shorter is F. W. Walbank, *The Hellenistic World* (1981), a fresh appraisal by one of the foremost scholars in the field. The undisputed classic in this area is M. Rostovtzeff, *The Social and Economic History of the Hellenistic World,* 3 vols. (1941). A leading American scholar, E. S. Gruen, has recently chronicled the Roman expansion into the Hellenistic East in *The Hellenistic World and the Coming of Rome,* 2 vols. (1984). Good selections of primary sources in accurate and readable translation can be found in M. M. Austin, *The Hellenistic World from Alexander to the Roman Conquest* (1981), and S. M. Burstein, *The Hellenistic Age from the Battle of Ipsos to the Death of Kleopatra III* (1985).

Each year brings a new crop of biographies of Alexander the Great. Still the best, however, is J. R. Hamilton, *Alexander the Great* (1973). Old but still useful is U. Wilcken, *Alexander the Great* (English translation, 1967), which has had a considerable impact on scholars and students alike. Although many historians have idealized Alexander the Great, recent scholarship has provided a more realistic and unflattering view of him. The foremost expert on Alexander is E. Badian, who has reinterpreted Alexander's career in a variety of journal articles: *Historia* 7 (1958): 425–444; *Classical Quarterly* 52 (1958): 144–157; *Journal of Hellenic Studies* 81 (1961): 16–43; and *Greece and Rome* 12 (1965): 166–182. Badian's analysis of Alexander also appears in *The Cambridge History of Iran,* vol. 2 (1985), chap. 8. Recent political studies of the Hellenistic period include A. B. Bosworth, *Conquest and Empire* (1988), which sets Alexander's career in a broad context, and F. L. Holt, *Alexander the Great and Bactria* (1988), which discusses the formation of a Greco-Macedonian frontier in central Asia. A. K. Bowman, *Egypt After the Pharaohs* (1986), is a readable account of the impact of the Greeks and Macedonians on Egyptian society. The same topic is treated by N. Lewis, a major scholar in the field, in his *Greeks in Ptolemaic Egypt* (1986); and a brief, new study comes from the pen of another major scholar, A. E. Samuel, *The Shifting Sands of History: Interpretations of Ptolemaic Egypt* (1989), which deals with history and historiography. E. V. Hansen, *The Attalids of Pergamon,* 2d ed. (1971), though dated, is still the best treatment of that kingdom. B. Bar-Kochva, *Judas Maccabaeus* (1988), treats the Jewish struggle against the Seleucids and Hellenistic influences. A good portrait of one of the busiest ports in the Hellenistic world can be found in R. Garland, *The Piraeus* (1987).

Much new work has focused on the spread of Hellenism throughout the Near East. Very extensive is A. Kuhrt and S. Sherwin-White, eds., *Hellenism in the East* (1988), which touches on a broad range of topics, including biblical studies, Christianity, and Islam. A. E. Samuels, *The Promise of the West* (1988), studies the connections among Greek, Roman, and Jewish culture and thought and their significance for Western history. P. McKechnie, *Outsiders in the Greek Cities of the Fourth*

Century (1989), provides an interesting study of the social dislocation of the Greeks in the time of Philip II and Alexander the Great.

No specific treatment of women in the Hellenistic world yet exists, but two recent studies shed light on certain aspects of the topic. The first, an illustrated collection of essays covering the whole of the ancient world, is I. van Sertima, ed., *Black Women in Antiquity*, 2d ed. (1985). S. B. Pomeroy, *Women in Hellenistic Egypt* (1984), studies women in the kingdom from which the most ancient evidence has survived.

Two general studies of religion in the Hellenistic world are F. Grant, *Hellenistic Religion: The Age of Syncretism* (1953), and H. J. Rose, *Religion in Greece and Rome* (1959). For the effects of Hellenistic religious developments on Christianity, see A. D. Nock, *Early Gentile Christianity and Its Hellenistic Background* (1964). R. van den Broek et al., eds., *Knowledge of God in the Graeco-Roman World* (1988), is a difficult but rewarding collection of essays that points out how similarly pagans, Hellenistic Jews, and Christians thought about human attempts to know god. R. E. Witt, *Isis in the Graeco-Roman World* (1971), an illustrated volume, studies the origins and growth of the Isis cult; and more specifically, S. K. Heyob, *The Cult of Isis Among Women in the Graeco-Roman World* (1975), explores its popularity among women. The cult of Isis's consort Osiris is the subject of J. G. Griffiths, *The Origins of Osiris and His Cult* (1980); and for the mystery cults in general, see W. Burkert, *Ancient Mystery Cults* (1987), written by one of the finest scholars in the field.

Hellenistic philosophy and science have attracted the attention of a number of scholars, and the various philosophical schools are especially well covered. A new general treatment can be recommended because it deals with the broader question of the role of the intellectual in the Classical and Hellenistic worlds: F. L. Vatai, *Intellectuals in Politics in the Greek World from Early Times to the Hellenistic Age* (1984). Broader is S. Blundell, *The Origin of Civilization in Greek and Roman Thought* (1986), a survey of classical political and social theories through a period of ten centuries, from Aristotle to the Stoics and their Roman successors. A convenient survey of Hellenistic philosophy is A. A. Long, *Hellenistic Philosophy* (1974). F. Sayre, *The Greek Cynics* (1948), focuses on Diogenes' thought and manners; and C. Bailey, *Epicureans* (1926), though decidedly dated, is still a useful study of the origins and nature of Epicureanism. Three treatments of Stoicism are J. Rist, *Stoic Philosophy* (1969); F. H. Sandbach, *The Stoics* (1975); and M. L. Colish, *The Stoic Tradition from Antiquity to the Early Middle Ages*, 2 vols. (1985), which devotes a great deal of attention to the impact of Stoicism on Christianity. A good survey of Hellenistic science is G. E. R. Lloyd, *Greek Science After Aristotle* (1963). Specific studies of major figures can be found in T. L. Heath, *Aristarchos of Samos* (1920), still unsurpassed, and E. J. Dijksterhuis, *Archimedes*, rev. ed. (1987).

7

The Rise of Rome

The Pont du Gard, Roman aqueduct at Nîmes in southern France

*W*ho is so thoughtless and lazy that he does not want to know in what way and with what kind of government the Romans in less than 53 years conquered nearly the entire inhabited world and brought it under their rule—an achievement previously unheard of?"[1] This question was first asked by Polybius, a Greek historian who lived in the second century B.C. With keen awareness Polybius realized that the Romans were achieving something unique in world history.

What was that achievement? Was it simply the creation of a huge empire? Hardly. The Persians had done the same thing. For that matter, Alexander the Great had conquered vast territories in a shorter time. Was it the creation of a superior culture? Even the Romans admitted that in matters of art, literature, philosophy, and culture they learned from the Greeks. Rome's achievement lay in the ability of the Romans not only to conquer peoples but to incorporate them into the Roman system. In other words, Rome succeeded where the Greek polis had failed. Unlike the Greeks, who refused to share citizenship, the Romans extended their citizenship first to the Italians and later to the peoples of the provinces. With that citizenship went Roman government and law. Rome created a single state that embraced the entire Mediterranean area.

Nor was Rome's achievement limited to antiquity. Rome's law, language, and administrative practices were a precious heritage to medieval and modern Europe. London, Paris, Vienna, and many other modern European cities began as Roman colonies or military camps. When the founding fathers of the United States created the American Republic, they looked to Rome as a model. On the dark side, Napoleon and Mussolini paid their own tribute to Rome by aping its forms. Whether founding fathers or modern autocrats, all were acknowledging admiration for the breadth of Roman achievement.

Roman history is usually divided into two periods: the Republic, the age in which Rome grew from a small city-state to ruler of an empire, and the Empire, the period when the republican constitution gave way to constitutional monarchy.

■ How did Rome rise to greatness?

■ What effects did the conquest of the Mediterranean have on the Romans themselves?

■ Why did the republic collapse?

These questions are addressed in this chapter.

THE LAND AND THE SEA

To the west of Greece the boot-shaped peninsula of Italy, with Sicily at its toe, occupies the center of the Mediterranean basin. As Map 7.1 shows, Italy and Sicily thrust southward toward Africa. The distance between southwestern Sicily and the northern African coast is at one point only about a hundred miles. Italy and Sicily literally divide the Mediterranean in two and form the focal point between the halves.

Like Greece and other Mediterranean lands, Italy enjoys a genial, almost subtropical climate. The winters are rainy, but the summer months are dry. Because of the climate, the rivers of Italy usually carry little water during the summer, and some go entirely dry. Clearly these small rivers were unsuitable for regular, large-scale shipping. Italian rivers never became major thoroughfares for commerce and communications.

Geography encouraged Italy to look to the western Mediterranean. In the north Italy is protected by the Apennine Mountains, which break off from the Alps and form a natural barrier. The Apennines retarded but did not prevent peoples from penetrating Italy from the north. Throughout history, in modern times as well as ancient, various invaders have entered Italy by this route. North of the Apennines lies the Po Valley, an important part of modern Italy. In antiquity this valley did not become Roman territory until late in the history of the Republic. From the north the Apennines run southward the entire length of the Italian boot. They virtually cut off access to the Adriatic Sea and further induced Italy to look west to Spain and Carthage rather than east to Greece.

MAP 7.1 Italy and the City of Rome The geographical configuration of the Italian peninsula shows how Rome stood astride north-south communications and how the state that united Italy stood poised to move into Sicily and northern Africa.

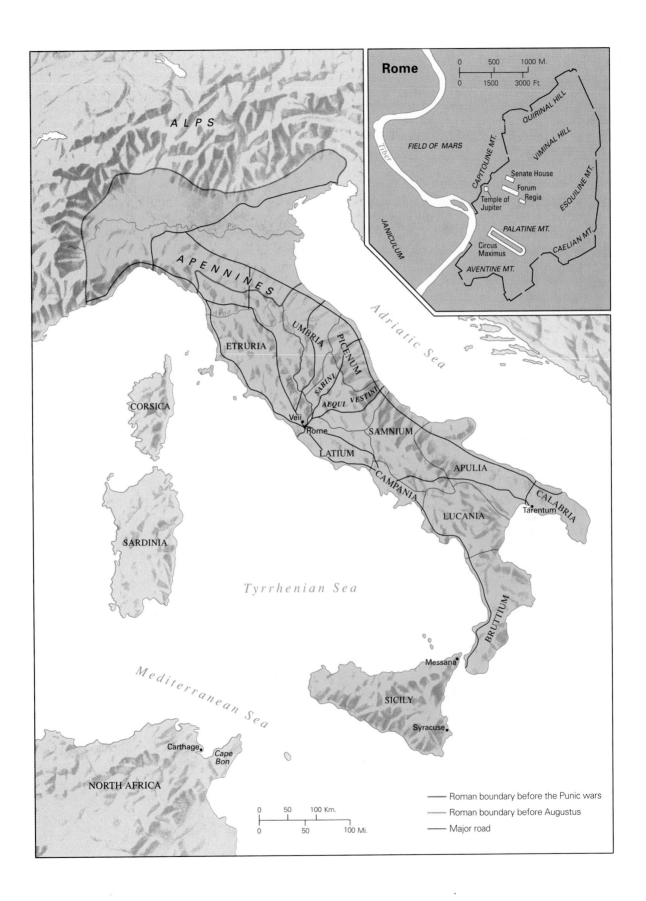

ALPS

APENNINES

Po

Arno

UMBRIA

ETRURIA

PICENUM

SABINI

AEQUI VESTINI

Veii

Rome

SAMNIUM

LATIUM

APULIA

CAMPANIA

CALABRIA

LUCANIA

Tarentum

CORSICA

Adriatic Sea

SARDINIA

Tyrrhenian Sea

BRUTTIUM

Messana

SICILY

Syracuse

Mediterranean Sea

Carthage

Cape Bon

NORTH AFRICA

0   50   100 Km.

0   50   100 Mi.

Roman boundary before the Punic wars

Roman boundary before Augustus

Major road

Rome

0   500   1000 M.

0   1500   3000 Ft.

Tiber

FIELD OF MARS

QUIRINAL HILL

VIMINAL HILL

CAPITOLINE MT.

Senate House

Forum

Regia

ESQUILINE MT.

Temple of Jupiter

JANICULUM

PALATINE MT.

CAELIAN MT.

Circus Maximus

AVENTINE MT.

Even though most of the land is mountainous, the hill country is not as inhospitable as are the Greek highlands. In antiquity the general fertility of the soil and its extent provided the basis for a large population. Nor did the mountains of Italy so carve up the land as to prevent the development of political unity. Geography proved kinder to Italy than to Greece.

In their southward course the Apennines leave two broad and fertile plains, those of Latium and Campania. These plains attracted settlers and invaders from the time when peoples began to move into Italy. Among these peoples were the Romans, who established their city on the Tiber River in Latium. This site enjoyed several advantages. The Tiber provided Rome with a constant source of water. Located at an easy crossing point on the Tiber, Rome thus stood astride the main avenue of inland communications between northern and southern Italy. The famous seven hills of Rome were defensible and safe from the floods of the Tiber. Rome was in an excellent position to develop the resources of Latium and maintain contact with the rest of Italy.

THE ETRUSCANS AND ROME (753–509 B.C.)

In recent years archeologists have found traces of numerous early peoples in Italy. The origins of these cultures and their precise relations with one another are not yet well understood. In fact, no clear account of the prehistory of Italy is yet possible. In the period between 1200 and 753 B.C., before the appearance of the Etruscans, one fundamental fact is indisputable: peoples speaking Indo-European languages were moving into Italy from the north, probably in small groups. They were part of the awesome but imperfectly understood movement of peoples who spread the Indo-European family of languages from Spain to India (see page 32). Only with the coming of the Greeks does Italy enter the light of history. A great wave of Greek immigration swept into southern Italy and Sicily during the eighth century B.C. (see pages 123–124). The Greeks brought urban life to these regions, spreading cultural influence far beyond their city-states.

In the north the Greeks encountered the Etruscans, one of the truly mysterious peoples of antiqu-

ity. Who the Etruscans were, where they came from, and what language they spoke are unknown. Nonetheless, this fascinating people was to leave an indelible mark on the Romans. Skillful metalworkers, the Etruscans amassed extensive wealth by trading their manufactured goods in Italy and beyond. The strength of their political and military institutions enabled them to form a loosely organized league of cities whose dominion extended as far north as the Po Valley and as far south as Latium and Campania (see Map 7.1). In Latium they founded cities and took over control of Rome. Like the Greeks, the Etruscans promoted urban life, and one of the places that benefited from Etruscan influence was Rome.

The Etruscans found the Romans settled on three of Rome's seven hills. The site of the future Forum Romanum, the famous public square and center of political life, was originally the cemetery of the small community. According to Roman legend, Romulus and Remus founded Rome in 753 B.C. During the years 753 to 509 B.C. the Romans embraced many Etruscan customs. They adopted the Etruscan alphabet, which the Etruscans had adopted from the Greeks. The Romans later handed on this alphabet to medieval Europe and thence to the modern Western world. Indeed, the great and deep influences of the Etruscans on the Romans have provided historians with particular and perhaps insoluble problems. No one can now determine whether the social, political, and military systems found later in the early Republic were indigenous to the Romans, an Etruscan creation imposed on the Romans, or a combination of the two. Most authentic Roman documents were destroyed in the Gallic raid of 390 B.C., and the first true history of the earliest periods was written some seven hundred years after the event. Thus there is very little authentic information about the origins of Rome.

Etruscan power and influence at Rome were so strong that Roman traditions preserved the memory of Etruscan kings who ruled the city. Under the Etruscans Rome enjoyed contacts with the larger Mediterranean world, and the city began to grow. In the years 575 to 550 B.C. temples and public buildings began to grace the city. The Capitoline Hill became the religious center of the city when the temple of Jupiter Optimus Maximus (Jupiter the Best and Greatest) was built there. The Forum ceased to be a cemetery and began its history as a public meeting place, a development parallel to that of the Greek agora. Trade in metal-work became common, and the wealthiest Roman classes began to import large numbers of fine Greek vases. The Etruscans had found Rome a collection of villages and made it a city.

THE ROMAN CONQUEST OF ITALY (509–290 B.C.)

Early Roman history is an uneven mixture of fact and legend. Roman traditions often contain an important kernel of truth, but that does not make them history. In many cases they are significant because they illustrate the ethics, morals, and ideals valued by Roman society. According to Roman tradition, the Romans expelled the Etruscan king Tarquin the Proud from Rome in 509 B.C. and founded the Republic. They did so in reaction to the harshness of Etruscan rule. In the years that followed, the Romans fought numerous wars with their neighbors on the Italian peninsula. They became soldiers, and the grim fighting bred tenacity, a prominent Roman trait. War also involved diplomacy, at which the Romans became masters. At an early date they learned the value of alliances and how to provide leadership for their allies. Alliances with the Latin towns around them provided them with a large reservoir of manpower. Their alliances involved the Romans in still other wars and took them farther afield in the Italian peninsula.

The growth of Roman power was slow but steady. Not until roughly a century after the founding of the Republic did the Romans try to drive the Etruscans entirely out of Latium. In 405 B.C. they laid siege to Veii, the last neighboring Etruscan city. After its destruction, they overshadowed their Latin allies and enemies alike. Yet about 390 B.C. they suffered a major setback when a new people, the Celts—or "Gauls," as the Romans called them—swept aside a Roman army and sacked Rome. More intent on loot than on land, the Gauls agreed to abandon Rome in return for a thousand pounds of gold.

During the century from 390 to 290 B.C., Romans rebuilt their city and recouped their losses. They also reorganized their army to create the mobile legion, a flexible unit capable of fighting on either broken or open terrain. The Romans finally brought Latium and their Latin allies fully under their control and conquered Etruria. In 343 B.C.

Etruscan Apollo A masterpiece of Etruscan art, this statue of Apollo testifies both to the artistic and the religious influence of the early Greeks. Yet Etruscan sculptors were not mere imitators, and they adapted Greek art to serve their own tastes. *(Source: Villa Giulia Museum, Rome/Art Resource)*

they grappled with the Samnites in a series of bitter wars for the possession of Campania and southern Italy. The Samnites were a formidable enemy and inflicted serious losses on the Romans. But the superior organization, institutions, and manpower of the Romans won out in the end. Although Rome had yet to subdue the whole peninsula, for the first time in history the city stood unchallenged in Italy.

Rome's success in diplomacy and politics was as important as its military victories. Unlike the Greeks, the Romans did not simply conquer and dominate. Instead, they shared with other Italians both political power and degrees of Roman citizenship. With many of their oldest allies, such as the Italian cities, they shared full Roman citizenship. In other instances they granted citizenship without the franchise (*civitas sine suffragio*). Allies who held this status enjoyed all the rights of Roman citizenship but could not vote or hold Roman offices. They were subject to Roman taxes and calls for military service but ran their own local affairs. The Latin allies were able to acquire full Roman citizenship by moving to Rome.

By their willingness to extend their citizenship, the Romans took Italy into partnership. Here the political genius of Rome triumphed where Greece had failed. Rome proved itself superior to the Greek polis because it both conquered and shared the fruits of victory with the conquered. The unwillingness of the Greek polis to share its citizenship condemned it to a limited horizon. Not so with Rome. The extension of Roman citizenship strengthened the state, gave it additional manpower and wealth, and laid the foundation of the Roman Empire.

THE ROMAN STATE

The Romans summed up their political existence in a single phrase: *senatus populusque Romanus,* "the Roman senate and the people." The real genius of the Romans lay in politics and law. Unlike the Greeks, they did not often speculate on the ideal state or on political forms. Instead they realistically met actual challenges and created institutions, magistracies, and legal concepts to deal with practical problems. Change was consequently commonplace in Roman political life, and the constitution of 509 B.C. was far simpler than that

of 27 B.C. Nonetheless, the political framework of the state can be sketched.

In the early Republic, social divisions determined the shape of politics. Political power was in the hands of the aristocracy—the *patricians,* who were wealthy landowners. Patrician families formed clans, as did aristocrats in early Greece. They dominated the affairs of state, provided military leadership in time of war, and monopolized knowledge of law and legal procedure. The common people of Rome, the *plebeians,* had few of the patricians' advantages. Some plebeians formed their own clans and rivaled the patricians in wealth. Many plebeian merchants increased their wealth in the course of Roman expansion, but most plebeians were poor. They were the artisans, small farmers, and landless urban dwellers. The plebeians, rich and poor alike, were free citizens with a voice in politics. Nonetheless, they were overshadowed by the patricians.

Perhaps the greatest institution of the Republic was the senate, which had originated under the Etruscans as a council of noble elders who advised the king. During the Republic the senate advised the consuls and other magistrates. Because the senate sat year after year, while magistrates changed annually, it provided stability and continuity. It also served as a reservoir of experience and knowledge. Technically the senate could not pass legislation; it could only offer its advice. But increasingly, because of the senate's prestige, its advice came to have the force of law.

The Romans created several assemblies through which the people elected magistrates and passed legislation. The earliest was the *comitia curiata,* which had religious, political, and military functions. According to Roman tradition, King Servius Tullius (578–535 B.C.), who reorganized the state into 193 *centuries* (military and political units) for military purposes, created the *comitia centuriata,* which served as a political body to decide Roman policy. Since the patricians shouldered most of the burden of defense, they dominated the comitia centuriata and could easily outvote the plebeians. In 471 B.C. the plebeians won the right to meet in an assembly of their own, the *concilium plebis,* and to pass ordinances. In 287 B.C. the bills passed in the concilium plebis were recognized as binding on the entire population.

The chief magistrates of the Republic were two *consuls,* elected for one-year terms. At first the consulship was open only to patricians. The consuls commanded the army in battle, administered state business, convened the comitia centuriata, and supervised financial affairs. In effect, they and the senate ran the state. The consuls appointed *quaestors* to assist them in their duties, and in 421 B.C. the quaestorship became an elective office open to plebeians. The quaestors took charge of the public treasury and prosecuted criminals in the popular courts.

In 366 B.C. the Romans created a new office, that of *praetor,* and in 227 B.C. the number of praetors was increased to four. When the consuls were away from Rome, the praetors could act in their place, primarily dealing with the administration of justice. When he took office, a praetor issued a proclamation declaring the principles by which he would interpret the law. These proclamations became important because they usually covered areas where the law was vague and thus helped clarify the law.

Other officials included the powerful *censors,* created in 443 B.C. They had many responsibilities, the most important being supervision of public morals, the power to determine who lawfully could sit in the senate, the registration of citizens, and the leasing of public contracts. Later officials were the *aediles,* four in number, who supervised the streets and markets and presided over public festivals.

After the age of overseas conquest (see pages 179–182), the Romans divided the Mediterranean area into provinces governed by ex-consuls and ex-praetors. Because of their experience in Roman politics, these officials were well suited to administer the affairs of the provincials and to fit Roman law and custom into new contexts.

The Roman Forum   The forum was the center of Roman political life. From simple beginnings it developed into the very symbol of Rome's imperial majesty. *(Source: Josephine Powell, Rome)*

One of the most splendid achievements of the Romans was their development of law. Roman law began as a set of rules that regulated the lives and relations of citizens. This civil law, or *ius civile,* consisted of statutes, customs, and forms of procedure. Roman assemblies added to the body of law, and praetors interpreted it. The spirit of the law aimed at protecting the property, lives, and reputations of citizens, redressing wrongs, and giving satisfaction to victims of injustice.

As the Romans came into more frequent contact with foreigners, they had to devise laws to deal with disputes between Romans and foreigners and between foreigners under Roman jurisdiction. In these instances, where there was no precedent to guide the Romans, the legal decisions of the praetors proved of immense importance. The praetors adopted aspects of other legal systems and resorted to the law of equity—what they thought was right and just to all parties. Free in effect to determine law, the praetors enjoyed a great deal of flexibility. By addressing specific, actual circumstances, the praetors developed a body of law, the *ius gentium,* "the law of peoples," that applied to Romans and foreigners and that laid the foundation for a universal conception of law. By the time of the late Republic, Roman jurists were reaching decisions on the basis of the Stoic concept of *ius naturale,* "natural law," a universal law that could be applied to all societies.

SOCIAL CONFLICT IN ROME

War was not the only aspect of Rome's early history. In Rome itself a great social conflict, usually known as the "Struggle of the Orders," developed between patricians and plebeians. What the plebeians wanted was real political representation and safeguards against patrician domination. The plebeians' efforts to obtain recognition of their rights are the crux of the Struggle of the Orders.

Rome's early wars gave the plebeians the leverage they needed: Rome's survival depended on the army, and the army needed the plebeians. The first confrontation between plebeians and patricians came, according to tradition, in 494 B.C. To force the patricians to grant concessions, the plebeians seceded from the state; they literally walked out of Rome and refused to serve in the army. The plebeians' general strike worked, and because of it the patricians made important concessions. One of the first was social. In 445 B.C. the patricians passed a law, the *lex Canuleia,* which for the first time allowed patricians and plebeians to marry one another. Furthermore, the patricians recognized the right of plebeians to elect their own officials, the *tribunes.* The tribunes in turn had the right to protect the plebeians from the arbitrary conduct of patrician magistrates. The tribunes brought plebeian complaints and grievances to the senate for resolution. In 471 B.C., when the plebeians won the right to hold their own assembly, the *concilium plebis,* and enact ordinances that concerned only themselves, the plebeians became a state within a state. This situation could have led to chaos, but Rome was not a house divided against itself. The plebeians were not bent on undermining the state. Rather they used their gains only to win full equality under the law.

The law itself was the plebeians' next target. Only the patricians knew what the law was, and only they could argue cases in court. All too often they had used the law for their own benefit. The plebeians wanted the law codified and published. The result of their agitation was the "Law of the Twelve Tables," so called because the laws, which covered civil and criminal matters, were inscribed on large bronze plaques. The plebeians had broken the patricians' legal monopoly and henceforth enjoyed full protection under the law.

The decisive plebeian victory came with the passage of the Licinian-Sextian rogations (or laws) in 367 B.C. Licinius and Sextus were plebeian tribunes who led a ten-year fight for further reform. Rich plebeians, like Licinius and Sextus themselves, joined the poor to mount a sweeping assault on patrician privilege. Wealthy plebeians wanted the opportunity to provide political leadership for the state. They demanded that the patricians allow them access to all the magistracies of the state. If they could hold the consulship, they could also sit in the senate and advise the senate on policy. The senate did pass a law that stipulated that one of the two consuls, elected annually, must be a plebeian. Though decisive, the Licinian-Sextian rogations did not automatically end the Struggle of the Orders. That happened only in 287 B.C. with the passage of a *lex Hortensia,* a law that gave the resolutions of the concilium plebis the force of law for patricians and plebeians alike.

The Struggle of the Orders resulted in a Rome stronger and more tightly united than before. It

The Town of Terracina The Romans founded numerous colonies, first in Italy and later throughout the Mediterranean. Roman colonies, which often grew into cities, were intended to be self-sufficient. This ancient drawing shows the colonia Axurnas, now Terracina, with its walls and towers for protection of the population sitting astride the Appian Way, the famous road to Rome. The lines to the left show how Roman surveyors had marked out the land for cultivation. *(Source: Bibliotheca Apostolica Vaticana)*

could have led to anarchy, but again certain Roman traits triumphed. The values fostered by their social structure predisposed the Romans to compromise, especially in the face of common danger. Resistance and confrontation in Rome never exploded into class warfare. Instead, both sides resorted to compromises to hammer out a realistic solution. Important, too, were Roman patience, tenacity, and a healthy sense of the practical. These qualities enabled both sides to keep working until they had resolved the crisis. The Struggle of the Orders ended with a new concept of Roman citizenship. All citizens shared equally under the law. Theoretically, all could aspire to the highest political offices. Patrician or plebeian, rich or poor, Roman citizenship was equal for all.

THE AGE OF OVERSEAS CONQUEST (282–146 B.C.)

In 282 B.C. Rome embarked on a series of wars that left it the ruler of the Mediterranean world. There was nothing ideological about these wars. Unlike Napoleon or Hitler, the Romans did not map out grandiose strategies for world conquest. They had no idea of what lay before them. If they could have looked into the future, they would have stood amazed. In many instances the Romans did not even initiate action; they simply responded to situations as they arose. Nineteenth-century Englishmen were fond of saying, "We got our empire in a fit of absence of mind." The Romans could not go quite that far. Although they sometimes declared war reluctantly, they nonetheless felt the need to dominate, to eliminate any state that could threaten them.

Rome was imperialistic, and its imperialism took two forms. In barbarian western Europe, the home of fierce tribes, Rome resorted to bald aggression to conquer new territory. In areas such as Spain and later Gaul, the fighting was fierce and savage, and gains came slowly. In civilized eastern Europe and western Asia, the world of Hellenistic states, Rome tried to avoid annexing territory. The east was already heavily populated, and those people would have become Rome's responsibility. New responsibilities meant new problems, and such headaches the Romans shunned. In the east the Romans preferred to be patrons rather than masters. Only when that loose policy failed did

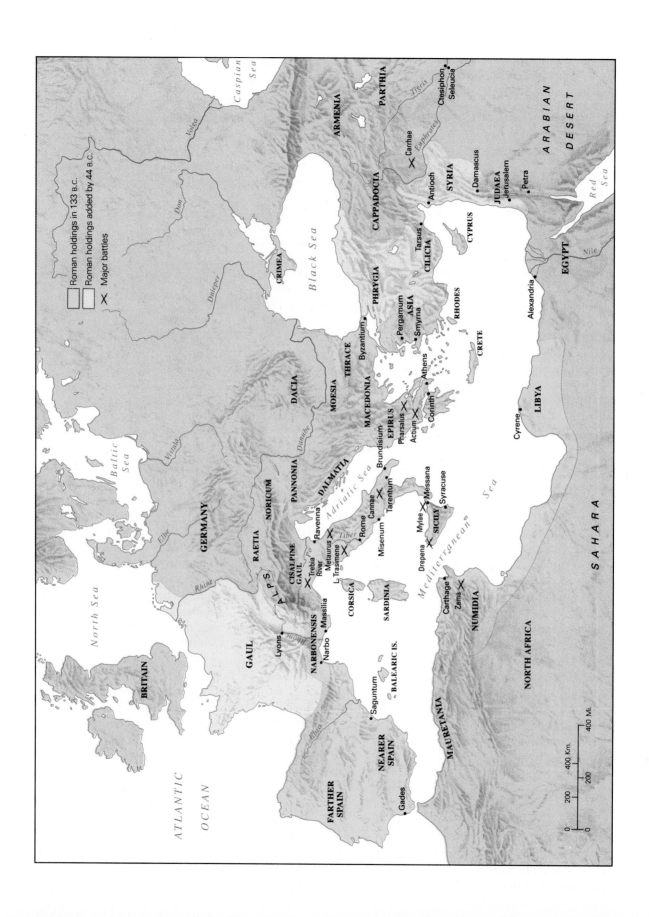

Roman holdings in 133 B.C.
Roman holdings added by 44 B.C.
✕ Major battles

ATLANTIC OCEAN

North Sea

Baltic Sea

BRITAIN

GERMANY

GAUL

Lyons

Rhine

Elbe

Vistula

Don

Volga

Caspian Sea

Dnieper

Danube

DACIA

CRIMEA

Black Sea

ARMENIA

PARTHIA

Tigris

Ctesiphon
Seleucia

Carrhae ✕

Euphrates

CAPPADOCIA

ARABIAN DESERT

SYRIA
Antioch
Damascus

JUDAEA
Jerusalem
Petra

Red Sea

CILICIA
Tarsus

CYPRUS

EGYPT

Nile

Alexandria

PHRYGIA
Pergamum
Smyrna
ASIA

RHODES

CRETE

Athens
Corinth ✕
Actium ✕
Pharsalus ✕
EPIRUS

MACEDONIA
THRACE
Byzantium
MOESIA

PANNONIA
NORICUM
RAETIA
ALPS
CISALPINE GAUL
Ravenna
Trebia ✕
River
Metaurus ✕
L. Trasimene ✕

DALMATIA
Adriatic Sea
Brundisium

Tarentum
Cannae ✕
Rome
Tiber
Misenum

CORSICA

SARDINIA

Mylae ✕
Messana
SICILY
Drepena ✕
Syracuse

Mediterranean Sea

LIBYA
Cyrene

NARBONENSIS
Massilia
Narbo

BALEARIC IS.

Saguntum

NEARER SPAIN

FARTHER SPAIN

Gades

Ebro

MAURETANIA

NORTH AFRICA

Carthage
Zama ✕
NUMIDIA

SAHARA

0   200   400 Mi.
0   200   400 Km.

they directly annex land. But in 282 B.C. all this lay in the future.

The Samnite wars had drawn the Romans into the political world of southern Italy. In 282 B.C., alarmed by the powerful newcomer, the Greek city of Tarentum in southern Italy called for help from Pyrrhus, king of Epirus in western Greece. A relative of Alexander the Great and an excellent general, Pyrrhus won two furious battles but suffered heavy casualties—thus the phrase "Pyrrhic victory" for a victory involving severe losses. Against Pyrrhus's army the Romans threw new legions, and in the end manpower proved decisive. In 275 B.C. the Romans drove Pyrrhus from Italy and extended their sway over southern Italy. Once they did, the island of Sicily became key for them.

The Phoenician city of Carthage, in North Africa (Map 7.2), had for centuries dominated the western Mediterranean. Sicily had long been a Carthaginian target. Since Sicily is the stepping-stone to Italy, the Romans could not let it fall to an enemy. In 264 B.C. Carthage and Rome came to blows over the city of Messana, which commanded the straits between Sicily and Italy. This conflict, the First Punic War (the word "Punic" refers to the Carthaginians), lasted for twenty-three years (264–241 B.C.). The Romans quickly learned that they could not conquer Sicily unless they controlled the sea. Yet they lacked a fleet and hated the sea as fervently as cats hate water. Nevertheless, with grim resolution the Romans built a navy and challenged the Carthaginians at sea. The Romans fought seven major naval battles with the Carthaginians and won six. Twice their fleet went down in gales. But finally the Romans wore down the Carthaginians. In 241 B.C., the Romans defeated them and took possession of Sicily, which became their first real province. Once again Rome's resources, manpower, and determination proved decisive.

The First Punic War was a beginning, not an end. Carthage was still a formidable enemy. After the First Punic War the Carthaginians expanded their power to Spain and turned the Iberian Pen-

insula into a rich field of operations. By 219 B.C. Carthage had found its avenger—Hannibal (ca 247–183 B.C.). In Spain, Hannibal learned how to lead armies and to wage war on a large scale. A brilliant general, he realized the advantages of swift mobile forces, and he was an innovator in tactics.

In 219 B.C. Hannibal defied the Romans by laying siege to the small city of Saguntum in Spain. When the Romans declared war the following year, he gathered his forces and led them on one of the most spectacular marches in ancient history. Hannibal carried the Second Punic War to the very gates of Rome. Starting in Spain, he led his troops—infantry, cavalry, and elephants—over the Alps and into Italy on a march of more than a thousand miles. Once in Italy, he defeated one Roman army at the Battle of Trebia (218 B.C.) and another at the Battle of Lake Trasimene (217 B.C.). At the Battle of Cannae in 216 B.C. Hannibal inflicted some forty thousand casualties on the Romans. He spread devastation throughout Italy but failed to crush Rome's iron circle of Latium, Etruria, and Samnium. The wisdom of Rome's political policy of extending rights and citizenship to its allies showed itself in these dark hours. Italy stood solidly with Rome against the invader. And Rome fought back.

The Roman general Scipio Africanus (ca 236–ca 183 B.C.) copied Hannibal's methods of mobile warfare. Scipio gave his new army combat experience in Spain, which he wrested from the Carthaginians. Meanwhile the Roman fleet dominated the western Mediterranean and interfered with Carthaginian attempts to reinforce Hannibal. In 204 B.C. the Roman fleet landed Scipio in Africa, prompting the Carthaginians to recall Hannibal from Italy to defend the homeland.

In 202 B.C. near the town of Zama (see Map 7.2), Scipio Africanus defeated Hannibal in one of the world's truly decisive battles. Scipio's victory meant that the world of the western Mediterranean would henceforth be Roman. Roman language, law, and culture, fertilized by Greek influences, would in time permeate this entire region. The victory at Zama meant that Rome's heritage—not Carthage's—would be passed on to the Western world. The Second Punic War contained the seeds of still other wars. Scipio Aemilianus, grandson of Scipio Africanus, completed the conquest of North Africa and Spain by 133 B.C.

MAP 7.2 Roman Expansion During the Republic The main spurt of Roman expansion occurred between 264 and 133 B.C., when most of the Mediterranean fell to Rome, followed by the conquest of Gaul and the eastern Mediterranean by 44 B.C.

Coin of Hannibal   This Carthaginian coin bears one of the few profiles of Hannibal. The style of the profile is Roman, but the artist has captured the actual likeness of the arch-enemy of Rome. *(Source: Courtesy of the Trustees of the British Museum)*

When the Romans intervened in the Hellenistic East, they went from triumph to triumph. The Romans dealt with the Greeks in a relatively civilized fashion. There were hard-fought battles in the east, but the bloodletting and carnage that marked the battles in the west were not generally repeated in the more cultured east. Nevertheless, the consequences were essentially the same. The kingdom of Macedonia fell to the Roman legions, as did Greece and the Seleucid monarchy. By 146 B.C., the Romans stood unchallenged in the eastern Mediterranean, and they had turned many states and kingdoms into provinces. In 133 B.C., the king of Pergamum, which was in Asia Minor, left his kingdom to the Romans in his will. The Ptolemies of Egypt meekly obeyed Roman wishes. By 146 B.C., however, the work of conquest was largely done. The Romans had turned the entire Mediterranean basin into *mare nostrum*, "our sea."

OLD VALUES AND GREEK CULTURE

Rome had conquered the Mediterranean world, but some Romans considered that victory a misfortune. The historian Sallust (86–34 B.C.), writing from hindsight, complained that the acquisition of an empire was the beginning of Rome's troubles:

But when through labor and justice our Republic grew powerful, great kings defeated in war, fierce nations and mighty peoples subdued by force, when Carthage the rival of the Roman people was wiped out root and branch, and the seas and lands lay open, then fortune began to be harsh and to throw everything into confusion. The Romans had easily borne labor, danger, uncertainty, and hardship. To them leisure, riches—otherwise desirable—proved to be burdens and torments. So at first money, then desire for power grew great. These things were a sort of cause of all evils.[2]

Sallust was not alone in his feelings. At the time, some senators had opposed the destruction of Carthage on the grounds that fear of their old rival would keep the Romans in check. Yet in the second century B.C., Romans learned that they could not return to what they fondly considered a simple life. They were rulers of the Medierranean world. The responsibilities they faced were complex and awesome. They had to change their institutions, social patterns, and way of thinking to meet the new era. They were in fact building the foundations of a great imperial system. It was an awesome challenge, and there were failures along the way. Roman generals and politicians would destroy one another. Even the republican constitution would eventually be discarded. But in the end Rome triumphed here just as it had on the battlefield, for out of the turmoil would come the *pax Romana,* "Roman peace."

How did the Romans of the day meet these challenges? How did they lead their lives and cope with these momentous changes? Obviously there are as many answers to these questions as there were Romans. Yet two men of different generations represent the major trends of the second century B.C. Cato the Elder shared the mentality of those who longed for the good old days and idealized the traditional agrarian way of life. Scipio Aemilianus led those who embraced the new urban life, with its eager acceptance of Greek culture. Forty-nine years older than Scipio, Cato was the product of an earlier generation, one that confronted a rapidly changing world. Cato and Scipio were both aristocrats and neither of them was typical, even of the aristocracy. But they do exemplify the opposing sets of attitudes that marked Roman society and politics in the age of conquest.

Battle Between the Romans and Barbarians   All of the brutality and fury of Rome's wars with the barbarians of western Europe come to life in this decoration for a horse's harness. Even the bravery and strength of the barbarians were no match for the steadiness and discipline of the Roman legions. *(Source: Museo Archeologico, Aosta/Scala Art Resource)*

Cato and the Traditional Ideal

Marcus Cato (234–149 B.C.) was born a plebeian, but his talent and energy carried him to Rome's highest offices. He cherished the old virtues and consistently imitated the old ways. In Roman society ties within the family were very strong. In this sense Cato and his family were typical. Cato was *paterfamilias,* a term that meant far more than merely "father." The paterfamilias was the oldest dominant male of the family. He held nearly absolute power over the lives of his wife and children as long as he lived. He could legally kill his wife for adultery or divorce her at will. He could kill his children or sell them into slavery. He could force them to marry against their will. Until the paterfamilias died, his sons could not legally own property. At his death, his wife and children inherited his property.

Despite his immense power, the paterfamilias did not necessarily act alone or arbitrarily. To deal with important family matters, he usually called a council of the adult males. In this way the leading members of the family aired their views. They had the opportunity to give their support to the paterfamilias or to dissuade him from harsh decisions. In these councils the women of the family had no formal part, but it can be safely assumed that they played an important role behind the scenes. Although the possibility of serious conflicts between a paterfamilias and his grown sons is obvious, no one in ancient Rome ever complained about the institution. Perhaps in practice the paterfamilias preferred to be lenient rather than absolute.

Like most Romans, Cato and his family began the day early in the morning. The Romans divided the period of daylight into twelve hours and the darkness into another twelve. The day might begin as early as half past four in summer, as late as half past seven in winter. Because Mediterranean summers are invariably hot, the farmer and his wife liked to take every advantage of the cool mornings. Cato and his family, like modern Italians, ordinarily started the morning with a light breakfast, usually nothing more than some bread and cheese. After breakfast the family went about its work.

Cato's wife also followed the old ways, and she ran the household. She spent the morning spinning and weaving wool for the clothes they wore. She supervised the domestic slaves, planned the meals, and devoted a good deal of attention to her son. In wealthy homes during this period the matron had begun to employ a slave as a wet nurse. Cato's wife refused to delegate maternal duties. Like most ordinary Roman women, she nursed her son herself and bathed and swaddled him daily. Later the boy was allowed to play with toys and terra-cotta dolls. Roman children, like children everywhere, kept pets. Dogs were especially popular and valuable as house guards. Children played all sorts of games, and games of chance were very popular. Until the age of seven the child was under the matron's care. During this time the mother began to educate her daughter in the management of the household. After the age of seven, the son—and in many wealthy households the daughter, too—began to undertake formal education.

In the country, Romans like Cato continued to take their main meal at midday. This meal included either coarse bread made from the entire husk of wheat or porridge made with milk or water; it also included turnips, cabbage, olives, and beans. When Romans ate meat, they preferred pork. Unless they lived by the sea, the average farm family did not eat fish, an expensive delicacy. Cato once complained that Rome was a place where a fish could cost more than a cow. With the midday meal the family drank ordinary wine mixed with water. Afterward, any Roman who could took a nap. This was especially true in the summer, when the Mediterranean heat can be fierce. Slaves, artisans, and hired laborers, however, continued their work. In the evening, Romans ate a light meal and went to bed at nightfall.

The agricultural year followed the sun and the stars—the farmer's calendar. Spring was the season for plowing. Roman farmers plowed their land at least twice and preferably three times. The third plowing was to cover the sown seed in ridges and to use the furrows to drain off excess water. The Romans used a variety of plows. Some had detachable shares. Some were heavy for thick soil, others light for thin, crumbly soil. Farmers used oxen and donkeys to pull the plow, collecting the dung of the animals for fertilizer. Besides spreading manure, some farmers fertilized their fields by planting lupines and beans; when they began to pod, farmers plowed them under. The main money crops, at least for rich soils, were wheat and flax. Forage crops included clover, vetch, and alfalfa. Prosperous farmers like Cato raised olive trees chiefly for the oil. They also raised grapevines for the production of wine. Cato and his neighbors harvested their cereal crops in summer and their grapes in autumn. Harvests varied depending on the soil, but farmers could usually expect yields of 5,112 bushels of wheat or 10,112 bushels of barley per acre. Roman farmers were much more fortunate than their Greek counterparts in that they generally enjoyed more fertile land and larger tracts of it.

An influx of slaves resulted from Rome's wars and conquests. Prisoners from Spain, Africa, and the Hellenistic East and even some blacks from Hannibal's army came to Rome as the spoils of war. The Roman attitude toward slaves and slavery had little in common with modern views. To the Romans slavery was a misfortune that befell some people, but it did not entail any racial theories. Races were not enslaved because the Romans thought them inferior. The black African slave was treated no worse—and no better—than the Spaniard. Indeed, some slaves were valued because of their physical distinctiveness: black Africans and blond Germans were particular favorites. For the talented slave, the Romans always held out the hope of eventual freedom. *Manumission*—the freeing of individual slaves by their masters—became so common that it had to be limited by law. Not even Christians questioned the institution of slavery. It was just a fact of life.

Slaves were entirely their master's property and might be treated with great cruelty. Many Romans were practical enough to realize that they got more out of their slaves by kindness than by severity. Yet in Sicily slave owners treated their slaves viciously. They bought slaves in huge numbers, branded them for identification, put them in irons, and often made them go without food and clothing. In 135 B.C. these conditions gave rise to a major slave revolt, during which many of the most brutal masters died at their slaves' hands. Italy, too, had trouble with slave unrest, but conditions there were generally better than in Sicily.

For Cato and most other Romans, religion played an important part in life. Originally the Romans thought of the gods as invisible, shapeless natural forces. Only through Etruscan and Greek influence did Roman deities take on human form. Jupiter, the sky god, and his wife, Juno, became equivalent to the Greek Zeus and Hera. Mars was the god of war but also guaranteed the fertility of the farm and protected it from danger. The gods of the Romans were not loving and personal. They were stern, powerful, and aloof. But as long as the

Manumission of Slaves During the Republic some Roman masters began to free slaves in public ceremonies. Here two slaves come before their master or a magistrate, who is in the process of freeing the kneeling slave by touching him with a manumission-rod. The other slave shows his gratitude and his good faith with a handshake. *(Source: Collection Waroque, Mariemont, Belgium, © A.C.L. Brussels)*

Romans honored the cults of their gods, they could expect divine favor.

Along with the great gods the Romans believed in spirits who haunted fields, forests, crossroads, and even the home itself. Some of these deities were hostile; only magic could ward them off. The spirits of the dead, like ghosts in modern horror films, frequented places where they had lived. They, too, had to be placated but were ordinarily benign. As the poet Ovid (43 B.C.–A.D. 17) put it:

The spirits of the dead ask for little.
They are more grateful for piety than for an expen-
   sive gift.
Not greedy are the gods who haunt the Styx below.
A rooftile covered with a sacrificial crown,
Scattered kernels, a few grains of salt,
Bread dipped in wine, and loose violets—
These are enough.
Put them in a potsherd and leave them in the middle
   of the road.[3]

A good deal of Roman religion consisted of rituals such as those Ovid describes. These practices lived on long after the Romans had lost interest in the great gods. Even Christianity could not entirely wipe them out. Instead Christianity was to incorporate many of these rituals into its own style of worship.

Scipio: Greek Culture and Urban Life

The old-fashioned ideals that Cato represented came into conflict with a new spirit of wealth and leisure. The conquest of the Mediterranean world and the spoils of war made Rome a great city. Roman life, especially in the cities, was changing and becoming less austere. The spoils of war went to build baths, theaters, and other places of amusement. Romans and Italian townsmen began to spend more of their time in the pursuit of leisure. But simultaneously the new responsibilities of governing the Mediterranean world produced in Rome a sophisticated society. Romans developed new tastes and a liking for Greek culture and literature. They began to learn the Greek language. It became common for an educated Roman to speak both Latin and Greek. Hellenism dominated the cultural life of Rome. Even diehards like Cato found a knowledge of Greek essential for political and diplomatic affairs. The poet Horace (64–8 B.C.) summed it up well: "Captive Greece captured her rough conqueror and introduced the arts into rustic Latium."[4]

One of the most avid devotees of Hellenism and the new was Scipio Aemilianus (185–129 B.C.), the destroyer of Carthage. Scipio realized that broad and worldly views had to replace the old Roman narrowness. The new situation called for new ways. Rome was no longer a small city on the Tiber; it was the capital of the Mediterranean world, and Romans had to adapt themselves to

that fact. Scipio was ready to become an innovator in both politics and culture. He broke with the past in the conduct of his political career. He embraced Hellenism wholeheartedly. Perhaps more than anyone else of his day, Scipio represented the new Roman: imperial, cultured, and independent.

In his education and interests, too, Scipio broke with the past. As a boy he had received the traditional patrician training, learning to read and write Latin and becoming acquainted with the law. He mastered the fundamentals of rhetoric and learned how to throw the javelin, fight in armor, and ride a horse. But later Scipio also learned Greek and became a fervent Hellenist. As a young man he formed a lasting friendship with Polybius, who actively encouraged him in his study of Greek culture and in his intellectual pursuits. The new Hellenism profoundly stimulated the growth and development of Roman art and literature. The Roman conquest of the Hellenistic East resulted in wholesale confiscation of Greek paintings and sculpture to grace Roman temples, public buildings, and private homes. Roman artists copied many aspects of Greek art, but their emphasis on realistic portraiture carried on a native tradition.

Fabius Pictor (second half of the third century B.C.), a senator, wrote the first *History of Rome* in Greek. Other Romans translated Greek classics into Latin. Still others, such as the poet Ennius (239–169 B.C.), the father of Latin poetry, studied Greek philosophy, wrote comedies in Latin, and adapted many of Euripides' tragedies for the Roman stage. Ennius also wrote a history of Rome in Latin verse. Plautus (ca 254–184 B.C.) specialized in rough humor. He, too, decked out Greek plays in Roman dress but was no mere imitator. The Roman dramatist Terence (ca 195–159 B.C.) wrote comedies of refinement and grace that owed their essentials to Greek models, but his plays lacked the energy and the slapstick of Plautus's rowdy plays. All of early Roman literature was derived from the Greeks, but it managed in time to speak in its own voice and to flourish because it had something of its own to say.

The conquest of the Mediterranean world brought the Romans leisure, and Hellenism influenced how they spent their free time. During the second century B.C., the Greek custom of bathing became a Roman passion and an important part of the day. In the early Republic Romans had bathed infrequently, especially in the winter. Now large buildings containing pools and exercise rooms went up in great numbers, and the baths became an essential part of the Roman city. Architects built intricate systems of aqueducts to supply the bathing establishments with water. The baths included gymnasia, where men exercised and played ball. Women had places of their own to bathe, generally sections of the same baths used by men; for some reason, women's facilities lacked gymnasia. The baths contained hot-air rooms to induce a good sweat and pools of hot and cold water to finish the actual bathing. They also contained snack bars and halls where people chatted and read. The baths were socially important places where men and women went to see and be seen. Social climbers tried to talk to "the right people" and wangle invitations to dinner; politicians took advantage of the occasion to discuss the affairs of the day.

This period also saw a change in the eating habits of urban dwellers. The main meal of the day shifted from midday to evening. Dinner became a more elaborate meal and dinner parties became fashionable. Although Scipio Aemilianus detested fat people, more and more Romans began to eat excessively. Rich men and women displayed their wealth by serving exotic dishes and gourmet foods. After a course of vegetables and olives came the main course of meat, fish, or fowl. Pig was a favorite dish, and a whole suckling pig might be stuffed with sausage. A lucky guest might even dine on peacock and ostrich, each served with rich sauces. Dessert, as in Italy today, usually consisted of fruit. With the meal the Romans served wine, and in this era vintage wines became popular.

Although the wealthy gorged themselves whenever they could, poor artisans and workers could rarely afford rich meals. Their dinners resembled Cato's. Yet they, too, occasionally spent generously on food, especially during major festivals. The Roman calendar was crowded with religious festivals, occasions not of dreary piety but of cheerful celebration.

Did Hellenism and new social customs corrupt the Romans? Perhaps the best answer is this: the Roman state and the empire it ruled continued to exist for six more centuries. Rome did not collapse; the state continued to prosper. The golden age of literature was still before it. The high tide of Rome's prosperity still lay in the future. The Romans did not like change but took it in stride. That was part of their practical turn of mind and their strength.

Roman Baths Once introduced into the Roman world, social bathing became a passion. These baths, which date to the Roman Empire, are located in Bath, England, to which they gave their name. A triumph of sophisticated engineering, they also demonstrate how Roman culture and institutions influenced life even on the perimeters of the Roman Empire. *(Source: Michael Holford)*

THE LATE REPUBLIC (133–27 B.C.)

The wars of conquest created serious problems for the Romans, some of the most pressing of which were political. The republican constitution had suited the needs of a simple city-state but was inadequate to meet the requirements of Rome's new position in international affairs (see Map 7.2). Sweeping changes and reforms were necessary to make it serve the demands of empire. A system of provincial administration had to be established. Officials had to be appointed to govern the provinces and administer the law. These officials and administrative organs had to find places in the constitution. Armies had to be provided to defend the provinces, and a system of tax collection had to be created.

Roman Table Manners This mosaic is a floor that can never be swept clean. It whimsically suggests what a dining room floor looked like after a lavish dinner and also tells something about the menu: a chicken head, a wishbone, remains of various seafood, vegetables, and fruit are easily recognizable. *(Source: Museo Gregoria-Profano/Scala/Art Resource)*

Other political problems were equally serious. During the wars Roman generals commanded huge numbers of troops for long periods of time. Men such as Scipio Aemilianus were on the point of becoming too mighty for the state to control. Although Rome's Italian allies had borne much of the burden of the fighting, they received fewer rewards than did Roman officers and soldiers. Italians began to agitate for full Roman citizenship and a voice in politics.

There were also serious economic problems. Hannibal's operations and the warfare in Italy had

left the countryside a shambles. The movements of numerous armies had disrupted agriculture. The prolonged fighting had also drawn untold numbers of Roman and Italian men away from their farms for long periods. The families of these soldiers could not keep the land under full cultivation. The people who defended Rome and conquered the Mediterranean world for Rome became impoverished for having done their duty.

These problems, complex and explosive, largely account for the turmoil of the closing years of the Republic. The late Republic was one of the most dramatic eras in Roman history. It produced some of Rome's most famous figures: the Gracchi, Marius, Sulla, Cicero, Pompey, and Julius Caesar, among others. In one way or another each man attempted to solve Rome's problems. Yet they were also striving for the glory and honor that were the supreme goals of the senatorial aristocracy. Personal ambition often clashed with patriotism to create political tension throughout the period.

When the legionaries returned to their farms in Italy, they encountered an appalling situation. All too often their farms looked like the farms of people they had conquered. Two courses of action were open to them. They could rebuild as their ancestors had done. Or they could take advantage of an alternative not open to their ancestors and sell their holdings. The wars of conquest had made some men astoundingly rich. These men wanted to invest their wealth in land. They bought up small farms to create huge estates, which the Romans called *latifundia*.

Most veterans migrated to the cities, especially to Rome. Although some found work, most did not. Industry and small manufacturing were generally in the hands of slaves. Even when there was work, slave labor kept the wages of free men low. Instead of a new start, veterans and their families encountered slum conditions that matched those of modern American cities.

This trend held ominous consequences for the strength of Rome's armies. The Romans had always believed that only landowners should serve in the army, for only they had something to fight for. Landless men, even if they were Romans and lived in Rome, could not be conscripted into the army. A large pool of experienced manpower was going to waste. The landless former legionaries wanted a new start, and they were willing to support any leader who would provide it.

THE ROMAN REPUBLIC

509 B.C.	Expulsion of the Etruscan king and founding of the Roman republic
471 B.C.	Plebeians win official recognition of their assembly, the *concilium plebis*
ca 450 B.C.	Law of the Twelve Tables
390 B.C.	The Gauls sack Rome
390–290 B.C.	Rebuilding of Rome; reorganization of the army; Roman expansion in Italy
367 B.C.	Licinian-Sextian rogations
287 B.C.	Legislation of the *concilium plebis* made binding on entire population
282–146 B.C.	The era of overseas conquest
264–241 B.C.	First Punic War: Rome builds a navy, defeats Carthage, acquires Sicily
218–202 B.C.	Second Punic War: Scipio defeats Hannibal; Rome dominates the western Mediterranean
200–148 B.C.	Rome conquers the Hellenistic east
149–146 B.C.	Third Punic War: savage destruction of Carthage
133–121 B.C.	The Gracchi introduce land reform; murder of the Gracchi by some senators
107 B.C.	Marius becomes consul and begins the professionalization of the army
91–88 B.C.	War with Rome's Italian allies
88 B.C.	Sulla marches on Rome and seizes dictatorship
79 B.C.	Sulla abdicates
78–27 B.C.	Era of civil war
60–49 B.C.	First Triumvirate: Pompey, Crassus, Julius Caesar
45 B.C.	Julius Caesar defeats Pompey's forces and becomes dictator
44 B.C.	Assassination of Julius Caesar
43–36 B.C.	Second Triumvirate: Marc Antony, Lepidus, Augustus
31 B.C.	Augustus defeats Antony and Cleopatra at Actium

One man who recognized the plight of Rome's peasant farmers and urban poor was an aristocrat, Tiberius Gracchus (163–133 B.C.). Appalled by what he saw, Tiberius warned his countrymen that the legionaries were losing their land while fighting Rome's wars:

The wild beasts that roam over Italy have every one of them a cave or lair to lurk in. But the men who fight and die for Italy enjoy the common air and light, indeed, but nothing else. Houseless and homeless they wander about with their wives and children. And it is with lying lips that their generals exhort the soldiers in their battles to defend sepulchres and shrines from the enemy, for not a man of them has an hereditary altar, not one of all these many Romans an ancestral tomb, but they fight and die to support others in luxury, and though they are styled masters of the world, they have not a single clod of earth that is their own.[5]

Until his death Tiberius Gracchus sought a solution to the problems of the veterans and the urban poor.

After his election as tribune of the people, Tiberius in 133 B.C. proposed that public land be given to the poor in small lots. His was an easy and sensible plan, but it angered many wealthy and noble people who had usurped large tracts of public land for their own use. They had no desire to give any of it back, and they bitterly resisted Tiberius's efforts. Violence broke out in Rome when a large body of senators killed Tiberius in cold blood. It was a grim day in Roman history. The very people who directed the affairs of state and administered the law had taken the law into their own hands. The death of Tiberius was the beginning of an era of political violence. In the end that violence would bring down the republic.

Although Tiberius was dead, his land bill became law. Furthermore, Tiberius's brother Gaius

(153–121 B.C.) took up the cause of reform. Gaius was a veteran soldier with an enviable record, but this fiery orator also made his mark in the political arena. Gaius too became tribune, and demanded even more extensive reform than his brother. To help the urban poor Gaius pushed legislation to provide them with cheap grain for bread. He defended his brother's land law and suggested other measures for helping the landless. He proposed that Rome send many of its poor and propertyless people out to form colonies in southern Italy. The poor would have a new start and lead productive lives. The city of Rome would immediately benefit because excess and nonproductive families would leave for new opportunities abroad. Rome would be less crowded, sordid, and dangerous.

Gaius went a step further and urged that all Italians be granted full rights of Roman citizenship.

Roman Legionary   The backbone of the Roman army was the legionary, shown here in battle. His basic equipment—shield, sword, spear, and armor—is simple and allowed great flexibility of movement. *(Source: Laurie Platt Winfrey, Inc.)*

This measure provoked a storm of opposition, and it was not passed in Gaius's lifetime. Yet in the long run he proved wiser than his opponents. In 91 B.C., many Italians revolted against Rome over the issue of full citizenship. After a brief but hard-fought war the senate gave Roman citizenship to all Italians. Had the senate listened to Gaius earlier, it could have prevented a great deal of needless bloodshed. Instead, reactionary senators rose against Gaius and murdered him and three thousand of his supporters. Once again the cause of reform had met with violence. Once again it was Rome's leading citizens who flouted the law.

More trouble for Rome came from an unexpected source. In 112 B.C. war broke out in North Africa, when a Numidian king named Jugurtha rebelled against Rome. The Roman legions made little headway against him until 107 B.C., when Gaius Marius, an Italian "new man" (a politician not from the traditional Roman aristocracy), became consul. A man of fierce vigor and courage, Marius saw the army as the tool of his ambition. To prepare for the war with Jugurtha, Marius reformed the Roman army. He took the unusual, but not wholly unprecedented, step of recruiting an army by permitting the landless to serve in the legions. Marius thus tapped Rome's vast reservoir of idle manpower. His volunteer army was a professional force, not a body of draftees, and in 106 B.C. it handily defeated Jugurtha.

There was, however, a disturbing side to Marius's reforms, one that later would haunt the Republic. To encourage enlistments, Marius promised land to his volunteers after the war. Poor and landless veterans flocked to him, but when Marius proposed a bill to grant land to his veterans, the senate refused to act, in effect turning its back on the soldiers of Rome. This was a disastrous mistake. Henceforth, the legionaries expected their commanders—not the senate or the state—to protect their interests. By failing to reward the loyalty of Rome's troops, the senate set the stage for military rebellion and political anarchy.

Trouble was not long in coming. The senate's refusal to honor Marius's promises to his soldiers and a brief but bitter war between the Romans and their Italian allies (91–88 B.C.) set off serious political disturbances in Rome. In 88 B.C. the Roman general and conqueror Sulla (138–78 B.C.) marched on Rome with his army to put an end to the turmoil. Sulla made himself dictator, put his enemies to death, and confiscated their land. The constitution thus disrupted never was put back together effectively.

In 79 B.C. Sulla voluntarily abdicated as dictator and permitted the republican constitution to function once again. Yet his dictatorship cast a long shadow over the late Republic. Sulla the political reformer proved far less influential than Sulla the successful general and dictator. Civil war was to be the constant lot of Rome for the next fifty years, until the republican constitution gave way to the empire of Augustus in 27 B.C. The history of the late Republic is the story of the power struggles of some of Rome's most famous figures: Julius Caesar and Pompey, Augustus and Marc Antony. One figure who stands apart is Cicero (106–43 B.C.), a practical politician whose greatest legacy to the Roman world and to civilization is his mass of political and oratorical writings.

Pompous, vain, and sometimes silly, Cicero was nonetheless one of the few men of the period to urge peace and public order. As consul in 63 B.C. he put down a conspiracy against the Republic but refused to use force to win political power. Instead he developed the idea of "concord of the orders," an idealistic, probably unattainable, balance among the elements that constituted the Roman state. Yet Cicero commanded no legions, and only legions commanded respect.

In the late Republic the Romans were grappling with the simple and inescapable fact that their old city-state constitution was unequal to the demands of overseas possessions and the problems of governing provinces. Once the senate and the other institutions of the Roman state had failed to come to grips with the needs of empire, once the authorities had lost control of their own generals and soldiers, and once the armies put their faith in their commanders instead of in Rome, the Republic was doomed.

Sulla's real political heirs were Pompey and Julius Caesar, who realized that the days of the old republican constitution were numbered. Pompey (106–48 B.C.), a man of boundless ambition, began his career as one of Sulla's lieutenants. After his army put down a rebellion in Spain, he himself threatened to rebel unless the senate allowed him to run for consul. He and another ambitious politician, Crassus (ca 115–53 B.C.), pooled their political resources and both won the consulship. They dominated Roman politics until the rise of Julius Caesar, who became consul in 59 B.C. Together the

Julius Caesar Both the majesty of empire and the way in which it was won shine forth from this statue of Julius Caesar. The famous conqueror wears the armor of the Roman legionary. His pose, however, is derived from that common among representations of Hellenistic kings. *(Source: Giraudon/Art Resource)*

three concluded an unofficial political alliance, the First Triumvirate, in which they agreed to advance one another's interests.

The man who cast the longest shadow over these troubled years was Julius Caesar (100–44 B.C.). More than a mere soldier, Caesar was a cultivated man. Born of a noble family, he received an excellent education, which he furthered by studying in Greece with some of the most eminent teachers of the day. He was also a shrewd politician of unbridled ambition, to which he added a successful military career.

In 58 B.C., Caesar became governor of Gaul, the region of modern France (see Map 7.2), a huge area that he had conquered in the name of Rome. Caesar's account of his operations, his *Commentaries* on the Gallic wars, became a classic in Western literature and most schoolchildren's introduction to Latin. By 49 B.C. the First Triumvirate had fallen apart. Crassus had died in battle, and Caesar and Pompey, each suspecting the other of treachery, came to blows. The result was a long and bloody civil war, which raged from Spain across northern Africa to Egypt. Although Pompey enjoyed the official support of the government, Caesar finally defeated Pompey's forces in 45 B.C. He had overthrown the Republic and made himself dictator.

Julius Caesar was not merely another victorious general. Politically brilliant, he was determined to make basic reforms, even at the expense of the old constitution. He took the first long step to break down the barriers between Italy and the provinces, extending citizenship to many of the provincials who had supported him. Caesar also took measures to cope with Rome's burgeoning population. By Caesar's day perhaps 750,000 people lived in Rome. Caesar drew up plans to send his veterans and some 80,000 of the poor and unemployed to colonies throughout the Mediterranean. He founded at least twenty colonies, most of which were located in Gaul, Spain, and North Africa. These colonies were important agents in spreading Roman culture in the western Mediterranean. Caesar's work would eventually lead to a Roman empire composed of citizens, not subjects.

In 44 B.C. a group of conspirators assassinated Caesar and set off another round of civil war. Caesar had named his eighteen-year-old grandnephew, Octavian—or Augustus, as he is better known to historians—as his heir. Augustus joined forces with two of Caesar's lieutenants, Marc Antony and Lepidus, in a pact known as the Second Triumvirate, and together they hunted down and defeated Caesar's murderers. In the process, however, Augustus and Antony came into conflict. Antony, "boastful, arrogant, and full of empty exultation and capricious ambition," proved to be the major threat to Augustus's designs.[6] In 33 B.C. Augustus

branded Antony a traitor and a rebel. He painted lurid pictures of Antony lingering in the eastern Mediterranean, a romantic and foolish captive of the seductive Cleopatra, queen of Egypt and bitter enemy of Rome. In 31 B.C., with the might of Rome at his back, Augustus met and defeated the army and navy of Antony and Cleopatra at the Battle of Actium in Greece (see Map 7.2). Augustus's victory put an end to an age of civil war that had lasted since the days of Sulla.

SUMMARY

The final days of the Republic, though filled with war and chaos, should not obscure the fact that much of the Roman achievement survived the march of armies. The Romans had conquered the Mediterranean world only to find that conquest required them to change their way of life. Socially, they imbibed Greek culture and adjusted themselves to the superior civilization of the Hellenistic East. Politically, their city-state constitution broke down and expired in the wars of the Republic. Even so, men like Caesar and later Augustus sought new solutions to the problems confronting Rome. The result, as Chapter 8 describes, was a system of government capable of administering an empire with justice and fairness. Out of the failure of the Republic arose the pax Romana of the empire.

NOTES

1. Polybius, *The Histories* 1.1.5. Unless otherwise credited, all quotations from a foreign language in this chapter are translated by John Buckler.
2. Sallust, *War with Catiline* 10.1–3.
3. Ovid, *Fasti* 2.535–539.
4. Horace, *Letters* 2.1.156.
5. Plutarch, *Life of Tiberius Gracchus* 9.5–6.
6. Plutarch, *Life of Antony* 2.8.

SUGGESTED READING

H. H. Scullard covers much of Roman history in a series of books: *The Etruscan Cities and Rome* (1967), *A History of the Roman World, 753–146 B.C.*, 3d ed. (1961), and

From the Gracchi to Nero, 5th ed. (1982). R. T. Ridley, *The History of Rome* (1989), is a new, undogmatic history of Rome, firmly based in the sources. A. E. Astin, ed., *The Cambridge Ancient History,* 2d ed., vol. 7 (1988), discusses the rise of Rome and its relations with other Mediterranean powers. The Etruscans have inspired a great deal of work, most notably R. M. Ogilvie, *Early Rome and the Etruscans* (1976), an excellent account of Rome's early relations with those people from the north; and G. Dennis, *Cities and Cemeteries of Etruria,* rev. ed. (1985). K. Christ, *The Romans* (English translation, 1984), is a general treatment by one of Germany's finest historians. A very broad study, J. Ch. Meyer, *Pre-Republican Rome* (1983), treats the cultural relations of early Rome chronologically between 1000 and 500 B.C.

E. T. Salmon, *The Making of Roman Italy* (1982), analyzes Roman expansion and its implications for Italy. Roman expansion is also the subject of R. M. Errington, *The Dawn of Empire* (1971); and W. V. Harris, *War and Imperialism in Republican Rome 327–70 B.C.* (1979). J. F. Lazenby, *Hannibal's War: A Military History of the Second Punic War* (1978), is a detailed treatment of one of Rome's greatest struggles. One of the best studies of Rome's political evolution is the classic by A. N. Sherwin-White, *The Roman Citizenship,* 2d ed. (1973), a work of enduring value. S. L. Dyson, *The Creation of the Roman Frontier* (1985), deals with the process by which the Romans established their frontiers. Two other works concentrate on Rome's penetration of the Hellenistic East: A. N. Sherwin-White, *Roman Foreign Policy in the Near East* (1984), and the far better but longer book by E. S. Gruen, *The Hellenistic World and the Coming of Rome,* 2 vols. (1984). A. Keaveney, *Rome and the Unification of Italy* (1988), treats the way in which the Romans put down the revolt of their Italian allies and then integrated them into the Roman political system.

The great figures and events of the late Republic have been the object of much new work. E. S. Gruen, *The Last Generation of the Roman Republic* (1974), treats the period as a whole. Very important are the studies of E. Badian, *Roman Imperialism in the Late Republic* (1968), and *Publicans and Sinners* (1972). R. Syme, *The Roman Revolution,* rev. ed. (1952), is a classic. Valuable also are P. A. Brunt, *Social Conflicts in the Roman Republic*

(1971); A. J. Toynbee, *Hannibal's Legacy,* 2 vols. (1965); and A. W. Lintott, *Violence in the Roman Republic* (1968).

Many new works deal with individual Romans who left their mark on this period. H. C. Boren, *The Gracchi* (1968), treats the work of the two brothers, and A. M. Eckstein, *Senate and Generals* (1987), discusses how the decisions of individual generals affected both the senate and Roman foreign relations. A. Keaveney, *Sulla: The Last Republican* (1983), is a new study of a man who thought of himself as a reformer. A. E. Astin has produced two works that are far more extensive than their titles indicate: *Scipio Aemilianus* (1967) and *Cato the Censor* (1978). J. Leach, *Pompey the Great* (1978), surveys the career of this politician, and C. Habicht, *Cicero the Politician* (1989), offers a sensible view of Cicero, one that emphasizes both his laudable patriotism as well as his political weaknesses. M. Gelzer, *Caesar, Politician and Statesman* (English translation, 1968), is easily the best study of one of history's most significant figures. E. G. Huzar, *Marc Antony* (1987), offers a new assessment of the career of the man who challenged Augustus for control of the Roman world. Caesar's one-time colleague Marcus Crassus is studied in A. Ward, *Marcus Crassus and the Late Roman Republic* (1977).

K. D. White, *Roman Farming* (1970), deals with agriculture, and J. P. V. D. Balsdon covers social life in the Republic and the Empire in two works: *Life and Leisure in Ancient Rome* (1969) and *Roman Women,* rev. ed. (1974). Greek cultural influence on Roman life is the subject of A. Wardman, *Rome's Debt to Greece* (1976). F. Schulz, *Classical Roman Law* (1951), is a useful introduction to an important topic. H. H. Scullard, *Festivals and Ceremonies of the Roman Republic* (1981), gives a fresh look at religious practices. Work on Roman social history has advanced in several areas. G. Alfoeldy, a major scholar, has written *The Social History of Rome* (1985), an ambitious undertaking. R. M. Ogilvie, *Roman Literature and Society* (1980), uses literature to examine the development and achievements of Roman society. Work on Roman women, with emphasis on the aristocracy, includes J. P. Hallett, *Fathers and Daughters in Roman Society* (1984). S. Dixon, *The Roman Mother* (1988), focuses specifically on women's role as mothers within the Roman family.

8

The Pax Romana

Hadrian's Wall, Cuddy's Crag, Northumberland

*H*ad the Romans conquered the entire Mediterranean world only to turn it into their battlefield? Would they, like the Greeks before them, become their own worst enemies, destroying one another and wasting their strength until they perished? At Julius Caesar's death in 44 B.C. it must have seemed so to many. Yet finally, in 31 B.C. Augustus (63 B.C.–A.D. 14), restored peace to a tortured world, and with peace came prosperity, new hope, and a new vision of Rome's destiny. The Roman poet Virgil expressed this vision most nobly:

You, Roman, remember—these are your arts:
To rule nations, and to impose the ways of peace,
To spare the humble and to war down the proud.[1]

In place of the Republic, Augustus established what can be called a constitutional monarchy. He attempted to achieve lasting cooperation in government and balance among the people, magistrates, senate, and army. His efforts were not always successful. His settlement of Roman affairs did not permanently end civil war. Yet he carried on Julius Caesar's work. It was Augustus who created the structure that the modern world calls the "Roman Empire." He did his work so well and his successors so capably added to it that Rome realized Virgil's hope. For the first and second centuries A.D. the lot of the Mediterranean world was peace—the pax Romana, a period of security, order, harmony, flourishing culture, and expanding economy. It was a period that saw the wilds of Gaul, Spain, Germany, and eastern Europe introduced to Greco-Roman culture. By the third century A.D., when the empire began to give way to the Western medieval world, the greatness of Rome and the blessings of Roman culture had left an indelible mark on the ages to come.

- How did the Roman emperors govern the empire, and how did they spread Roman influence into northern Europe?

- What were the fruits of the pax Romana?

- Why did Christianity, originally a minor local religion, sweep across the Roman world to change it fundamentally?

- How did the Roman Empire meet the grim challenge of barbarian invasion and subsequent economic decline?

This chapter focuses on the answers to these questions.

AUGUSTUS'S SETTLEMENT (31 B.C.–A.D. 14)

When Augustus put an end to the civil wars that had raged since 88 B.C., he faced monumental problems of reconstruction. He could easily have declared himself dictator, as Julius Caesar had done, but the thought was repugnant to him. Augustus was neither an autocrat nor a revolutionary. His solution, as he put it, was to restore the Republic. But was that possible? Years of anarchy and civil war had shattered the republican constitution. It could not be rebuilt in a day. Augustus recognized these problems but did not let them stop him. From 29 to 23 B.C., he toiled to heal Rome's wounds. The first problem facing him was to rebuild the constitution and the organs of government. Next he had to demobilize the army and care for the welfare of the provinces. Then he had to face the danger of barbarians at Rome's European frontiers. Augustus successfully met these challenges. His gift of peace to a war-torn world sowed the seeds of a literary flowering that produced some of the finest fruits of the Roman mind.

The Principate and the Restored Republic

Augustus claimed that in restoring constitutional government he was also restoring the Republic. One of the biggest challenges in that effort was creating for himself an official place in the new government. Typically Roman, he preferred not to create anything new; he intended instead to modify republican forms and offices to meet new circumstances. Augustus planned for the senate to take on a serious burden of duty and responsibility. He expected it to administer some of the provinces, continue to be the chief deliberative body of the state, and act as a court of law. Yet he did not give the senate enough power to become his partner in government. As a result, the senate could not live up to the responsibilities that Augustus assigned, and many of its prerogatives shifted by default to Augustus and his successors.

Augustus's own position in the restored Republic was something of an anomaly. He could not simply surrender the reins of power, for someone else would seize them. But how was he to fit into a republican constitution? Again Augustus had his own answer. He became *princeps civitatis,* the "first citizen of the state." This prestigious title carried no power; it indicated only that Augustus was the most distinguished of all Roman citizens. In effect it designated Augustus as the first among equals and a little more equal than anyone else. His real power resided in the magistracies he held, the powers granted him by the senate, and above all his control of the army, which he turned into a permanent, standing organization. Clearly, much of the *principate,* as the position of First Citizen is known, was a legal fiction. Yet that need not imply that Augustus, like a modern dictator, tried to clothe himself with constitutional legitimacy. In an inscription known as *Res Gestae (The Deeds of Augustus),* Augustus described his constitutional position:

In my sixth and seventh consulships [28–27 B.C.], I had ended the civil war, having obtained through universal consent total control of affairs. I transferred the Republic from my power to the authority of the Roman people and the senate. . . . After that time I stood before all in rank, but I had power no greater than those who were my colleagues in any magistracy.[2]

Augustus was not exactly being a hypocrite, but he carefully kept his real military power in the background. As consul he had no more constitutional and legal power than his fellow consul. Yet in addition to the consulship Augustus held many other magistracies, which his fellow consul did not. Constitutionally, his ascendancy within the state stemmed from the number of magistracies he held and the power granted him by the senate. At first he held the consulship annually; then the senate voted him proconsular power on a regular basis. The senate also voted him *tribunicia potestas*—the "full power of the tribunes." Tribunician power gave Augustus the right to call the senate into session, present legislation to the people, and defend their rights. He held either high office or the powers of chief magistrate year in and year out. No other magistrate could do the same. In 12 B.C. he became *pontifex maximus,* "chief priest of the state." By assuming this position of great honor, Augustus became chief religious official in the state. Without specifically saying so, he had created the office of emperor, which included

Augustus   This statue portrays Augustus as the Pontifex Maximus, "chief priest of the state." The emperor thereby emphasized his peaceful role and his position as the intermediary between the Roman people and the gods. *(Source: Alinari/Art Resource)*

many traditional powers separated from their traditional offices.

The main source of Augustus's power was his position as commander of the Roman army. His title *imperator,* with which Rome customarily honored a general after a major victory, came to mean "emperor" in the modern sense of the term. Augustus governed the provinces where troops were needed for defense. The frontiers were his special concern. There Roman legionaries held the German barbarians at arm's length. The frontiers were also areas where fighting could be expected to break out. Augustus made sure that Rome went to war only at his command. He controlled deployment of the Roman army and paid its wages. He granted bonuses and gave veterans retirement benefits. Thus he avoided the problems with the army that the old senate had created for itself. Augustus never shared control of the army, and no Roman found it easy to defy him militarily.

The size of the army was a special problem for Augustus. Rome's legions numbered thousands of men, far more than were necessary to maintain peace. What was Augustus to do with so many soldiers? This problem had constantly plagued the late Republic, whose leaders never found a solution. Augustus gave his own answer in the *Res*

Roma et Augustus The nature of the cult of *Roma et Augustus* is immediately obvious from this cameo. Seated to the left is Augustus, who holds a scepter, which symbolizes his right to reign. He speaks with Roma, who personified Rome and who holds in her lap a shield, a symbol of her protection of the city of Rome and its empire. *(Source: Kunsthistorisches Museum, Vienna)*

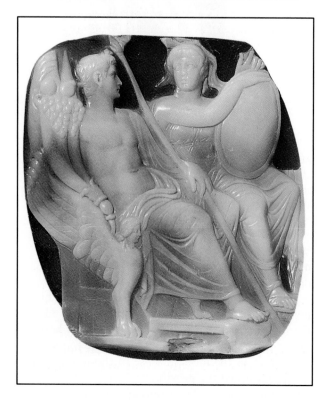

Gestae: "I founded colonies of soldiers in Africa, Sicily, Macedonia, Spain, Achaea, Gaul, and Pisidia. Moreover, Italy has 28 colonies under my auspices."[3] At least forty new colonies arose, most of them in the western Mediterranean. Augustus's veterans took abroad with them their Roman language and culture. His colonies, like Julius Caesar's, were a significant tool in the further spread of Roman culture throughout the West.

What is to be made of Augustus's constitutional settlement? Despite his claims to the contrary, Augustus had not restored the Republic. In fact, he would probably have agreed with the words of John Stuart Mill, the nineteenth-century English philosopher: "When society requires to be rebuilt, there is no use in attempting to rebuild it on the old plan." Augustus had created a constitutional monarchy, something completely new in Roman history. The title *princeps,* "first citizen," came to mean in Rome, as it does today, "prince" in the sense of a sovereign ruler.

Augustus also failed to solve a momentous problem. He never found a way to institutionalize his position with the army. The ties between the princeps and the army were always personal. The army was loyal to the princeps but not necessarily to the state. The Augustan principate worked well at first, but by the third century A.D. the army would make and break emperors at will. Nonetheless, it is a measure of Augustus's success that his settlement survived as long and as well as it did.

Augustus's Administration of the Provinces

To gain an accurate idea of the total population of the empire, Augustus ordered a census to be taken in 28 B.C. In Augustus's day the population of the Roman Empire was between 70 and 100 million people, fully 75 percent of whom lived in the provinces. In the areas under his immediate jurisdiction, Augustus put provincial administration on an ordered basis and improved its functioning. Believing that the cities of the empire should look after their own affairs, he encouraged local self-government and urbanism. Augustus respected local customs and told his governors to do the same.

To create a spiritual bond between the provinces and Rome, Augustus encouraged the cult of Roma, goddess and guardian of the state. In the Hellenistic East, where king-worship was an established custom, the cult of *Roma et Augustus,* "Roma and Augustus," grew and spread rapidly. Augustus then introduced the concept of the cult in the West. By the time of his death in A.D. 14, nearly every province in the empire could boast an altar or shrine to *Roma et Augustus.* In the West it was not the person of the emperor who was worshiped but his *genius*—his guardian spirit. In praying for the good health and welfare of the emperor, Romans and provincials were praying for the empire itself. The cult became a symbol of Roman unity.

Roman Expansion into Northern and Western Europe

For the history of Western civilization a momentous aspect of Augustus's reign was Roman expansion into the wilderness of northern and western Europe (Map 8.1). In this Augustus was following in Julius Caesar's footsteps. Between 58 and 51 B.C., Caesar had subdued Gaul and unsuccessfully attacked Britain. Carrying on his work, Augustus pushed Rome's frontier into the region of modern Germany. The Germanic tribes were tough opponents, and the Roman legions saw much bitter fighting against them in the north.

Augustus began his work in the north by completing the conquest of Spain. In Gaul, apart from minor campaigns, most of his work was peaceful. He founded twelve new towns. The Roman road system linked new settlements with one another and with Italy. But the German frontier, along the Rhine River, was the scene of hard fighting. In 12 B.C. Augustus ordered a major invasion of Germany beyond the Rhine. Roman legions advanced to the Elbe River, and a Roman fleet explored the North Sea and Jutland. The area north of the Main River and west of the Elbe was on the point of becoming Roman. But in A.D. 9 Augustus's general Varus lost some twenty thousand troops at the Battle of the Teutoburger Forest. Thereafter the Rhine remained the Roman frontier.

Meanwhile, more successful generals extended the Roman standards as far as the Danube. Roman legions penetrated the area of modern Austria and western Hungary. The regions of modern Serbia, Bulgaria, and Romania fell. Within this area the legionaries built fortified camps. Roads linked these camps with one another, and settlements grew up around the camps. Traders began to frequent the frontier and to traffic with the barbarians. Thus Roman culture—the rough-and-ready kind found in military camps—gradually spread into the northern wilderness.

The achievements of Augustus in the north were monumental. For the first time in history, Greco-Roman culture spread beyond the sunny Mediterranean into the heart of Europe. Amid the vast expanse of forests, Roman towns, trade, language, and law began to exert a civilizing influence on the barbarians. The Roman way of life attracted the barbarians, who soon recognized the benefits of assimilating Roman culture. Many military camps became towns, and many modern European cities owe their origins to the forts of the Roman army. For the first time, the barbarian north came into direct, immediate, and continuous contact with Mediterranean culture.

Literary Flowering

The Augustan settlement's gift of peace inspired a literary flowering unparalleled in Roman history. With good reason this period is known as the "golden age" of Latin literature. Augustus and many of his friends actively encouraged poets and writers. The poet Horace summed up Augustus and his era:

With Caesar Augustus the guardian of the state
Not civil rage nor violence shall drive out peace,
  Nor wrath which forges swords
  And turns unhappy cities against each other[4]

These lines are not empty flattery, despite Augustus's support of many contemporary Latin writers. To a generation that had known only vicious civil war, Augustus's settlement was a blessing.

The tone and ideal of Roman literature, like that of the Greeks, was humanistic and worldly. Roman poets and prose writers celebrated the dignity of humanity and the range of its accomplishments. They stressed the physical and emotional joys of a comfortable, peaceful life. Their works were highly polished, elegant in style, and intellectual in conception. Roman poets referred to the gods frequently and treated mythological themes, but always the core of their work was human, not divine.

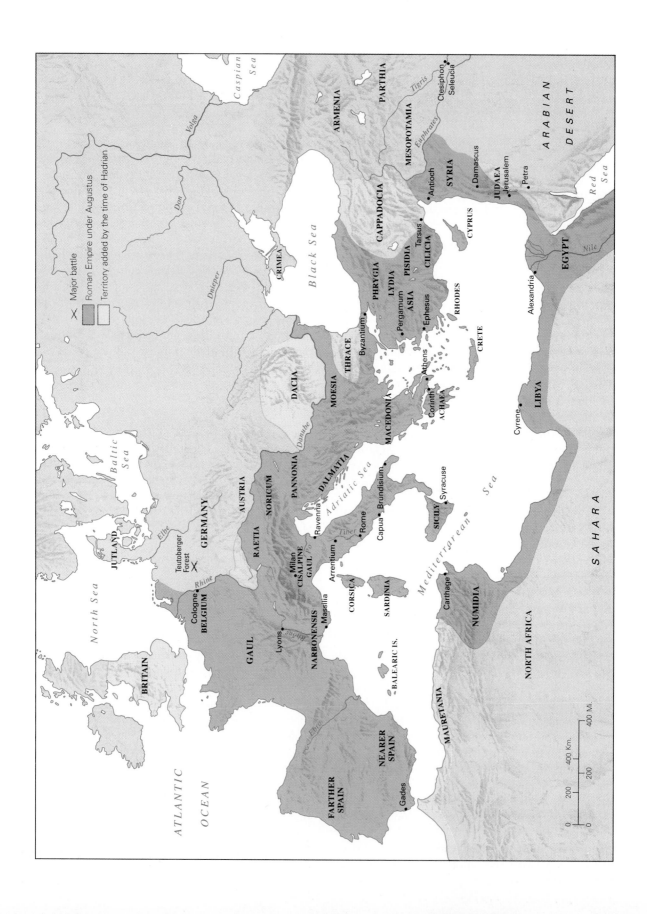

Virgil (70–19 B.C.) celebrated the new age in the *Georgics,* a long poetic work on agriculture. Virgil delighted in his own farm, and his poems sing of the pleasures of peaceful farm life. The poet also tells how to keep bees, grow grapes and olives, plow, and manage a farm. Throughout the *Georgics* Virgil wrote about things he himself had seen, rather than drawing his theme from the writings of others. Virgil's poetry is robust yet graceful. A sensitive man who delighted in simple things, Virgil left in his *Georgics* a charming picture of life in the Italian countryside during a period of peace.

Virgil's masterpiece is the *Aeneid,* an epic poem that is the Latin equivalent of the Greek *Iliad* and *Odyssey.* In the *Aeneid* Virgil expressed his admiration for Augustus's work by celebrating the shining ideal of a world blessed by the pax Romana. Virgil's account of the founding of Rome and the early years of the city gave final form to the legend of Aeneas, the Trojan hero who escaped to Italy at the fall of Troy. The principal Roman tradition held that Romulus was the founder of Rome, but the legend of Aeneas was also very old; it was known by the Etruscans as early as the fifth century B.C. Although Rome could not have had two founders, Virgil linked the legends of Aeneas and Romulus and kept them both. In so doing, he also connected Rome with Greece's heroic past. Recounting the story of Aeneas and Dido, the queen of Carthage, Virgil made their ill-fated love affair the cause of the Punic wars. But above all, the *Aeneid* is the expression of Virgil's passionate belief in Rome's greatness. It is a vision of Rome as the protector of the good and noble against the forces of darkness and disruption.

In its own way Livy's history of Rome, entitled simply *Ab Urbe Condita (From the Founding of the City),* is the prose counterpart of the *Aeneid.* Livy (59 B.C.–A.D. 17) received training in Greek and Latin literature, rhetoric, and philosophy. He even urged the future emperor Claudius to write history. Livy loved and admired the heroes and great deeds of the Republic, but he was also a friend of

Augustus and a supporter of the principate. He especially approved of Augustus's efforts to restore republican virtues.

The poet Horace (65–8 B.C.) rose from humble beginnings to friendship with Augustus. The son of a former slave and tax collector, Horace nonetheless received an excellent education. He loved Greek literature and finished his education in Athens. After Augustus's victory he returned to Rome and became Virgil's friend. Horace acquired a small farm north of Rome, which delighted him. He was as content as Virgil on his farm and expressed his joy in a few lines:

Strive to add nothing to the myrtle plant!
The myrtle befits both you, the servant,
And me, the master, as I drink under the
Thick-leaved vine.[5]

Horace happily turned his pen to celebrating Rome's newly won peace and prosperity. One of

Virgil and *The Aeneid*   Virgil's great epic poem, *The Aeneid,* became a literary classic immediately on its appearance and has lost none of its power since. The Roman world honored Virgil for his poetic genius not only by treasuring his work but also by portraying him in art. Here two muses, who inspired artists, flank the poet while he writes his epic poem. *(Source: C. M. Dixon)*

MAP 8.1 Roman Expansion Under the Empire   Following Roman expansion during the Republic, Augustus added vast tracts of Europe to the Roman Empire, which the emperor Hadrian later enlarged by assuming control over parts of central Europe, the Near East, and North Africa.

Ara Pacis Augustae This scene from the Ara Pacis Augustae, the Altar of Augustan Peace, celebrates Augustus's restoration of peace and the fruits of peace. Here Mother Earth is depicted with her children. The cow and the sheep under the goddess represent the prosperity brought by peace, especially the agricultural prosperity so highly cherished by Virgil. *(Source: Bildarchiv Foto Marburg/Art Resource)*

his finest odes commemorates Augustus's victory over Cleopatra at Actium in 31 B.C. Cleopatra is depicted as a frenzied queen, drunk with desire to destroy Rome. Horace saw in Augustus's victory the triumph of West over East, of simplicity over Oriental excess. One of the truly moving aspects of Horace's poetry, like Virgil's, is his deep and abiding gratitude for the pax Romana.

For Rome, Augustus's age was one of hope and new beginnings. Augustus had put the empire on a new foundation. Constitutional monarchy was firmly established, and government was to all appearances a partnership between princeps and senate. The Augustan settlement was a delicate structure, and parts of it would in time be discarded. Nevertheless it worked, and by building on it later emperors would carry on Augustus's work. The solidity of Augustus's work became obvious at his death in A.D. 14. Since the principate was not tech-

nically an office, Augustus could not legally hand it to a successor. Augustus had recognized this problem and long before his death had found a way to solve it. He shared his consular and tribunician powers with his adopted son, Tiberius, thus grooming him for the principate. In his will Augustus left most of his vast fortune to Tiberius, and the senate formally requested Tiberius to assume the burdens of the principate. All the formalities apart, Augustus had succeeded in creating a dynasty.

THE COMING OF CHRISTIANITY

During the reign of the emperor Tiberius (A.D. 14–37), perhaps in A.D. 29, Pontius Pilate, prefect of Judaea, the Roman province created out of the

Jewish kingdom of Judah, condemned Jesus of Nazareth to death. At the time a minor event, this has become one of the best-known moments in history. How did these two men come to their historic meeting? The question is not idle, for Rome was as important as Judaea to Christianity. Jesus was born in a troubled time, when Roman rule aroused hatred and unrest among the Jews. This climate of hostility affected the lives of all who lived in Judaea, Roman and Jew alike. It forms the backdrop of Jesus's life, and it had a fundamental impact on his ministry. Without an understanding of this age of anxiety in Judaea, Jesus and his followers cannot fully be appreciated.

The entry of Rome into Jewish affairs was anything but peaceful. The civil wars that destroyed the Republic wasted the prosperity of Judaea and the entire eastern Mediterranean world. Jewish leaders took sides in the fighting, and Judaea suffered its share of ravages and military confiscations. Peace brought little satisfaction to the Jews. Although Augustus treated Judaea generously, the Romans won no popularity by making Herod king of Judaea. King Herod gave Judaea prosperity and security, but the Jews hated his acceptance of Greek culture. He was also a bloodthirsty prince, who murdered his own wife and sons. Upon his death, the Jews broke out in revolt. For the next ten years Herod's successor waged almost constant war against the rebels. Added to the horrors of civil war were years of crop failure, which caused famine and plague. Men calling themselves "prophets" proclaimed the end of the world and the coming of the Messiah, the savior of Israel.

At length the Romans intervened to restore order. Augustus put Judaea under the charge of a prefect answerable directly to the emperor. Religious matters and local affairs became the responsibility of the *Sanhedrin,* the highest Jewish judicial body. Although many prefects tried to perform their duties scrupulously and conscientiously, many others were rapacious and indifferent to Jewish culture. Often acting from fear rather than cruelty, some prefects fiercely stamped out any signs of popular discontent. Pontius Pilate, prefect from A.D. 26 to 36, is typical of such incompetent officials. Although eventually relieved of his duties in disgrace, Pilate brutally put down even innocent demonstrations. Especially hated were the Roman tax collectors, called "publicans," many of whom pitilessly gouged the Jews. *Publicans* and *sinners*— the words became synonymous. Clashes between Roman troops and Jewish guerrillas inflamed the anger of both sides.

Among the Jews two movements spread. First was the rise of the Zealots, extremists who worked and fought to rid Judaea of the Romans. Resolute in their worship of Yahweh, they refused to pay any tax other than the tax levied by the Jewish temple. Their battles with the Roman legionaries were marked by savagery on both sides. As usual, the innocent caught in the middle suffered grievously. As Roman policy grew tougher, even moderate Jews began to hate the conquerors. Judaea came more and more to resemble a tinderbox, ready to burst into flames at a single spark.

The second movement was the growth of militant apocalyptic sentiment—the belief that the coming of the Messiah was near. This belief was an old one among the Jews. But by the first century A.D. it had become more widespread and fervent than ever before. Typical was the Apocalypse of Baruch, which foretold the destruction of the Roman Empire. First would come a period of great tribulation, misery, and injustice. At the worst of the suffering, the Messiah would appear. The Messiah would destroy the Roman legions and all the kingdoms that had ruled Israel. Then the Messiah would inaugurate a period of happiness and plenty.

This was no abstract notion among the Jews. As the ravages of war became more widespread and conditions worsened, more and more people prophesied the imminent coming of the Messiah. One such was John the Baptist, "The voice of one crying in the wilderness, Prepare ye the way of the lord."[6] Many Jews did just that. The sect described in the Dead Sea Scrolls readied itself for the end of the world. Its members were probably Essenes, and their social organization closely resembled that of early Christians. Members of this group shared possessions, precisely as John the Baptist urged people to do. Yet this sect, unlike the Christians later, also made military preparations for the day of the Messiah.

Jewish religious aspirations were only one part of the story. What can be said of the pagan world of Rome and its empire into which Christianity was shortly to be born? To answer that question, one must first explore the spiritual environment of the pagans, many of whom would soon be caught up in the new Christian religion. Paganism at the time of Jesus's birth can be broadly divided into three spheres: the official state religion of Rome, the traditional Roman cults of hearth and countryside, and the new mystery religions that flowed from the Hellenistic East. The official state religion and its cults honored the traditional deities: Jupiter, Juno, Mars, and such newcomers as Isis (see page 159). This very formal religion was conducted on an official level by socially prominent state priests. It was above all a religion of ritual and grand spectacle, but it provided little emotional or spiritual comfort. The state cults were a bond between the gods and the people, a religious contract to ensure the well-being of Rome. Most Romans felt that the official cults must be maintained, despite their lack of spiritual content, simply to ensure the welfare of the state. After all, observance of the traditional official religion had brought Rome victory, empire, security, and wealth.

For emotional and spiritual satisfaction, many Romans observed the old cults of home and countryside, the same cults that had earlier delighted Cato the Elder (see page 185). These traditional cults brought the Romans back in touch with nature and with something elemental to Roman life. Particularly popular were rustic shrines—often a small building or a sacred tree in an enclosure—to honor the native spirit of the locality. Though familiar and simple, even this traditional religion was not enough for many. They wanted something more personal and immediate. Many common people believed in a supernatural world seen dimly through dreams, magic, miracles, and spells. They wanted some sort of revelation about this supernatural world and security in it during the hereafter. Some people turned to astrology in the belief that they could read their destiny in the stars. But that was cold comfort, since they could not change what the stars foretold.

Many people in the Roman Empire found the answer to their need for emotionally satisfying religion and spiritual security in the various Hellenistic mystery cults. Such cults generally provided their adherents with an emotional outlet. For example, the cult of Bacchus was marked by its wine drinking and often drunken frenzy. Although the cult of the Great Mother, Cybele, was celebrated with emotional and even overwrought processions, it offered its worshipers the promise of immortality. The appeal of the mystery religions was not simply that they provided emotional release. They gave their adherents what neither the traditional cults nor philosophy could—above all, security. Yet at the same time, the mystery religions

were by nature exclusive, and none was truly international, open to everyone.

Into this climate of Roman religious yearning and political severity, fanatical zealotry, and messianic hope came Jesus of Nazareth (ca 5 B.C.–A.D. 29). Raised in Galilee, stronghold of the Zealots, Jesus himself was a man of peace. Jesus urged his listeners to love God as their father and one another as God's children. The kingdom that he proclaimed was no earthly one, but one of eternal happiness in a life after death. Jesus's teachings are strikingly similar to those of Hillel (30 B.C.–A.D. 9), a great rabbi and interpreter of the Scriptures. Hillel taught the Jews to love one another as they loved God. He taught them to treat others as they themselves wished to be treated. Jesus's preaching was in this same serene tradition.

Jesus's teachings were Jewish. He declared that he would change not one jot of the Jewish law. His orthodoxy enabled him to preach in synagogues and the temple. His only deviation from orthodoxy was his insistence that he taught in his own name, not in the name of Yahweh. Was he then the Messiah? A small band of followers thought so, and Jesus revealed himself to them as the Messiah. Yet Jesus had his own conception of the Messiah. Unlike the Messiah of the Apocalypse of Baruch, Jesus would not destroy the Roman Empire. He told his disciples flatly that they were to "render unto Caesar the things that are Caesar's." Jesus would establish a spiritual kingdom, not an earthly one. Repeatedly he told his disciples that his kingdom was "not of this world."

Of Jesus's life and teachings the prefect Pontius Pilate knew little and cared even less. All that concerned him was the maintenance of peace and order. The crowds following Jesus at the time of Passover, a highly emotional time in the Jewish year, alarmed Pilate. Some Jews believed that Jesus was the long-awaited Messiah. Others were disappointed because he refused to preach rebellion against Rome. Still others hated and feared Jesus and wanted to be rid of him. The last thing Pilate wanted was a riot.

Christian tradition has made much of Pontius Pilate. In the medieval West he was considered a monster. In the Ethiopian church he is considered a saint. Neither monster nor saint, Pilate was simply a hard-bitten Roman official. He did his duty, at times harshly. In Judaea his duty was to enforce the law and keep the peace. These were the problems on his mind when Jesus stood before him. Je-

Pontius Pilate and Jesus   This Byzantine mosaic from Ravenna illustrates a dramatic moment in Jesus' trial and crucifixion. Jesus stands accused before Pilate, but Pilate symbolically washes his hands of the whole affair. *(Source: Scala/Art Resource)*

sus as king of the Jews did not worry him. The popular agitation surrounding Jesus did. To avert riot and bloodshed, Pilate condemned Jesus to death. It is a bitter historical irony that such a gentle man died such a cruel death. After being scourged, he was hung from a cross until he died in the sight of family, friends, enemies, and the merely curious.

Once Pilate's soldiers had carried out the sentence, the entire matter seemed to be closed. Yet on the third day after Jesus's crucifixion, an odd rumor began to circulate in Jerusalem. Some of Jesus's followers were saying he had risen from the dead, while others accused the Christians of having stolen his body. For these earliest Christians and for generations to come, the resurrection of Jesus became a central element of faith and, more than that, a promise: Jesus had triumphed over

death, and his resurrection promised all Christians immortality. In Jerusalem the tumult subsided. Jesus's followers lived quietly and peacefully, unmolested by Roman or Jew. Pilate had no quarrel with them, and Judaism already had many minor sects. Peter (d. A.D. 67?), the first of Jesus's followers, became the head of the sect, which continued to observe Jewish law and religious customs. A man of traditional Jewish beliefs, Peter felt that Jesus's teachings were meant exclusively for the Jews. Only in their practices of baptism and the sacrament of the *Eucharist,* the communal celebration of the Lord's Supper, did the sect differ from normal Jewish custom. Meanwhile, they awaited the return of Jesus.

Christianity might have remained a purely Jewish sect had it not been for Paul of Tarsus (A.D. 5?–67?). The conversion of Hellenized Jews and of

Gentiles (non-Jews) to Christianity caused the sect grave problems. Were the Gentiles subject to the law of Moses? If not, was Christianity to have two sets of laws? The answer to these questions was Paul's momentous contribution to Christianity. Paul was unlike Jesus or Peter. Born in a thriving, busy city filled with Romans, Greeks, Jews, Syrians, and others, he was at home in the world of Greco-Roman culture. After his conversion to Christianity, he taught that his native Judaism was the preparation for the Messiah and that Jesus by his death and resurrection had fulfilled the prophecy of Judaism and initiated a new age. Paul taught that Jesus was the son of God, the beginning of a new law, and he preached that Jesus's teachings were to be proclaimed to all, whether Jew or Gentile. Paul thus made a significant break with Judaism, Christianity's parent religion, for Judaism was exclusive and did not seek converts.

Paul's influence was far greater than that of any other early Christian. He traveled the length and breadth of the eastern Roman world, spreading his doctrine and preaching of Jesus. To little assemblies of believers in cities as distant as Rome and Corinth he taught that Jesus had died to save all people. Paul's vision of Christianity won out over Peter's traditionalism. Christianity broke with Judaism and embarked on its own course.

What was Christianity's appeal to the Roman world? What did this obscure sect give people that other religions did not? Christianity possessed many different attractions. One of its appeals was its willingness to embrace both men and women, slaves and nobles. Many of the Eastern mystery religions with which Christianity competed were exclusive in one way or another. Mithraism, a mystery religion descended from Zoroastrianism, spread throughout the entire empire. Mithras, the sun-god, embodied good and warred against evil. Like Christianity, Mithraism offered elaborate and moving rituals including a form of baptism, a code of moral conduct, and the promise of life after death. Unlike Christianity, however, Mithraism permitted only men to become devotees. Much the same was true of the ancient Eleusinian mysteries of Greece, which were open only to Greeks and Romans.

Indeed, Christianity shared many of the features of mystery religions. It possessed a set of beliefs, such as the divinity of Jesus, and a literary history. Paul's *epistles,* or letters, to various Christian communities were the earliest pieces of literature dealing with Christian beliefs and conduct. Shortly thereafter some of the disciples wrote *gospels,* or accounts of Jesus's life and teachings. Once people had prepared themselves for conversion by learning of Jesus's message and committing themselves to live by it, they were baptized. Like initiates in mystery religions, they entered the community of believers. The Christian community of believers was strengthened by the sacrament of the Eucharist. Christianity also had more than a priesthood to officiate at rituals; it had an ecclesiastical administration that helped to ensure continuity within the new church.

Christianity appealed to common people and to the poor. Its communal celebration of the Lord's Supper gave men and women a sense of belonging. Christianity also offered its adherents the promise of salvation. Christians believed that Jesus on the cross had defeated evil and that he would reward his followers with eternal life after death. Christianity also offered the possibility of forgiveness. Human nature was weak, and even the best Christians would fall into sin. But Jesus loved sinners and forgave those who repented. In its doctrines of salvation and forgiveness alone, Christianity had a powerful ability to give solace and strength to believers.

Christianity was attractive to many because it gave the Roman world a cause. Hellenistic philosophy had attempted to make men and women self-sufficient: people who became indifferent to the outside world could no longer be hurt by it. That goal alone ruled out any cause except the attainment of serenity. The Romans, never innovators in philosophy, merely elaborated this lonely and austere message. Instead of passivity Christianity stressed the ideal of striving for a goal. Each and every Christian, no matter how poor or humble, supposedly worked to realize the triumph of Christianity on earth. This was God's will, a sacred duty for every Christian. By spreading the word of Jesus, Christians played their part in God's plan. No matter how small, the part each Christian played was important. Since this duty was God's will, Christians believed that the goal would be achieved. The Christian was not discouraged by temporary setbacks, believing Christianity to be invincible.

Christianity gave its devotees a sense of community. No Christian was alone. All members of the

Christian community strove toward the same goal of fulfilling God's plan. Each individual community was in turn a member of a greater community. And that community, the Church General, was indestructible. After all, Jesus himself had promised, "Thou art Peter, and upon this rock I will build my church; and the gates of hell shall not prevail against it."[7]

Christianity's attractions, therefore, were many, from forgiveness of sin to an exalted purpose for each individual. Its insistence on the individual's importance gave solace and encouragement, particularly to the poor and meek. Its claim to divine protection encouraged hope in the eventual success of the Christian community. Christianity thus made participation in the universal possible for everyone. The ultimate reward promised by Christianity was eternal bliss after death.

THE JULIO-CLAUDIANS AND THE FLAVIANS (27 B.C.–A.D. 96)

For fifty years after Augustus's death the dynasty that he established—known as the Julio-Claudians because all members were of the Julian and Claudian clans—provided the emperors of Rome. Some of the Julio-Claudians, such as Tiberius and Claudius, were sound rulers and able administrators. Others, Caligula and Nero, were weak and frivolous men who exercised their power stupidly and brought misery to the empire. Yet even their occasional weaknesses cannot obscure the fact that Julio-Claudians were responsible for some notable achievements, among them the conquest of Britain in A.D. 43, and that during their reigns the empire prospered.

One of the most momentous achievements of the Julio-Claudians was Claudius's creation of an imperial bureaucracy composed of professional administrators. Even the most energetic emperor could not run the empire alone. Numerous duties and immense responsibilities prompted Claudius to delegate power. He began by giving the freedmen of his household official duties, especially in finances. It was a simple, workable system. Claudius knew his former slaves well and could discipline them at will. The effect of Claudius's innovations was to enable the emperor to rule the empire more easily and efficiently.

One of the worst defects of Augustus's settlement—the army's ability to interfere in politics—became obvious during the Julio-Claudian period. Augustus had created a special standing force, the Praetorian Guard, as an imperial bodyguard. In A.D. 41 one of the praetorians murdered Caligula while others hailed Claudius as the emperor. Under the threat of violence, the senate ratified the praetorians' choice. It was a bloody story repeated all too frequently. During the first three centuries of the empire the Praetorian Guard all too often murdered emperors they were supposed to protect and saluted emperors of their own choosing.

In A.D. 68 Nero's inept rule led to military rebellion and his death, thus opening the way to widespread disruption. In A.D. 69, known as the "Year of the Four Emperors," four men claimed the position of emperor. Roman armies in Gaul, on the Rhine, and in the east marched on Rome to make their commanders emperor. The man who emerged triumphant was Vespasian, commander of the eastern armies, who entered Rome in 70 and restored order. Nonetheless, the Year of the Four Emperors proved the Augustan settlement had failed to end civil war.

Not a brilliant politician, Vespasian did not institute sweeping reforms, as had Augustus, or solve the problem of the army in politics. To prevent usurpers from claiming the throne, Vespasian designated his sons Titus and Domitian as his successors. By establishing the Flavian (the name of Vespasian's clan) dynasty, Vespasian turned the principate into an open and admitted monarchy. He also expanded the emperor's power by increasing the size of the budding bureaucracy created by Claudius.

The Flavians carried on Augustus's work on the frontiers. Domitian, the last of the Flavians, won additional territory in Germany and consolidated it in two new provinces. He defeated barbarian tribes on the Danube frontier and strengthened that area as well. Nonetheless, Domitian was one of the most hated of Roman emperors because of his cruelty, and he fell victim to an assassin's dagger. Still, the Flavians gave the Roman world peace and kept the legions in line. Their work paved the way for the era of the "five good emperors," the golden age of the empire.

Triumph of Titus After Titus, the son of Vespasian and later himself emperor, conquered Jerusalem, he ordered his soldiers to carry off as spoils of war the sacred objects of the rebellious Jews, most notably in this scene the seven-branched candlestick. *(Source: Art Resource)*

THE AGE OF THE "FIVE GOOD EMPERORS" (A.D. 96–180)

In the second century A.D. a line of emperors, usually called the "five good emperors," gave the Roman Empire its last burst of summer before an autumn of failure and a winter of barbarism. It was a period of almost unparalleled prosperity and victorious wars generally confined to the frontiers.

The Antonine Monarchy

The age of the Antonines was the age of full-blown monarchy. Augustus had claimed that his influence arose from the collection of offices the senate had bestowed on him. However, there was in law no such office as emperor. Augustus was merely the First Citizen. Under the Flavians the principate became a full-blown monarchy, and by the time of the Antonines the principate was an office with definite rights, powers, and prerogatives. In the years between Augustus and the

Antonines, the emperor had become an indispensable part of the imperial machinery. In short, without the emperor the empire would quickly have fallen to pieces. Augustus had been monarch in fact but not in theory; during their reigns, the Antonines were monarchs in both.

The Antonines were not power-hungry autocrats. The concentration of power was the result of empire. The easiest and most efficient way to run the Roman Empire was to invest the emperor with vast powers. Furthermore, Roman emperors on the whole proved to be effective rulers and administrators. As capable and efficient emperors assumed new tasks and functions, the emperor's hand was felt in more areas of life and government. Increasingly the emperors became the source of all authority and guidance in the empire. The five good emperors were benevolent and exercised their power intelligently, but they were absolute kings all the same. Lesser men would later throw off the facade of constitutionality and use this same power in a despotic fashion.

Typical of the five good emperors is the career of Hadrian, who became emperor in A.D. 117. He was born in Spain, a fact that illustrates the importance of the provinces in Roman politics. Hadrian received his education at Rome and became an ardent admirer of Greek culture. He caught the attention of his elder cousin Trajan, the future emperor, who started him on a military career. At age nineteen Hadrian served on the Danube frontier, where he learned the details of how the Roman army lived and fought and saw for himself the problems of defending the frontiers. When Trajan became emperor in A.D. 98, Hadrian was given important positions in which he learned how to defend and run the empire. At Trajan's death in 117, Hadrian assumed power.

Roman government had changed since Augustus's day. One of the most significant changes was the enormous growth of the imperial bureaucracy created by Claudius. Hadrian reformed this system by putting the bureaucracy on an organized, official basis. He established imperial administrative departments to handle the work formerly done by imperial freedmen. Hadrian also separated civil service from military service. Men with little talent or taste for the army could instead serve the state as administrators. Hadrian's bureaucracy demanded professionalism from its members. Administrators made a career of the civil service. These innovations made for a more efficiently run empire and increased the authority of the emperor—the ruling power of the bureaucracy.

Changes in the Army

The Roman army had also changed since Augustus's time. The Roman legion had once been a mobile unit, but its duties under the empire no longer called for mobility. The successors of Augustus generally called a halt to further conquests. The army was expected to defend what had already been won. Under the Flavian emperors (A.D. 69–96), the frontiers became firmly fixed. Forts and watch stations guarded the borders. Behind the forts the Romans built a system of roads that

Scene from Trajan's Column   From 101 to 107 Trajan fought the barbarian tribes along the Danube. This scene depicts Roman soldiers unloading supplies at a frontier city. Such walled cities serve as Roman strong points, as well as centers of Roman civilization, with shops, homes, temples, and amphitheaters. (*Source: Alinari/Art Resource*)

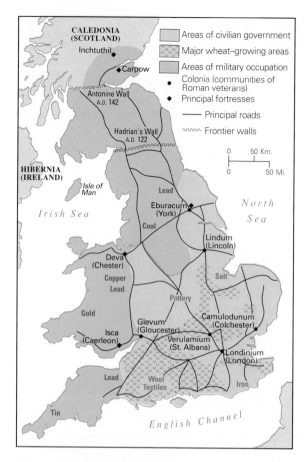

MAP 8.2 Roman Britain Although the modern state of Great Britain stands squarely in the center of current international affairs, Britain was a peripheral part of the Roman Empire, a valuable area but nonetheless on the frontier.

allowed the forts to be quickly supplied and reinforced in times of trouble. The army had evolved into a garrison force, with legions guarding specific areas for long periods.

The personnel of the legions was changing, too. Italy could no longer supply all the recruits needed for the army. Increasingly, only the officers came from Italy and from the most Romanized provinces. The legionaries were mostly drawn from the less civilized provinces, especially the ones closest to the frontiers. A major trend was already obvious in Hadrian's day: fewer and fewer Roman soldiers were really Roman. In the third century A.D., the barbarization of the army would result in an army indifferent to Rome and its traditions. In the age of the Antonines, however, the army was still a source of economic stability and a Romanizing agent (Map 8.2). Men from the provinces and even barbarians joined the army to learn a trade and to gain Roman citizenship. Even so, the signs were ominous. Veterans from Julius Caesar's wars would hardly have recognized Hadrian's troops as Roman legionaries.

LIFE IN THE "GOLDEN AGE"

If a man were called to fix the period in the history of the world during which the condition of the human race was most happy and prosperous, he would without hesitation name that which elapsed from the death of Domitian to the accession of Commodus.[8]

Thus, according to Edward Gibbon, the age of the five good emperors was a golden age in human history. How does Edward Gibbon's picture correspond to the popular image of Rome as a city of bread, brothels, and gladiatorial games? If the Romans were degenerates who spent their time carousing, who kept Rome and the empire running? Can life in Rome be taken as representative of life in other parts of the empire?

Truth and exaggeration are mixed in Gibbon's view and in the popular image of Rome. Rome and the provinces must be treated separately. Rome no more resembled a provincial city like Cologne than New York resembles Keokuk, Iowa. Rome was unique and must be seen as such. Only then can one turn to the provinces to obtain a full and reasonable picture of the empire under the Antonines.

Imperial Rome

Rome was truly an extraordinary city, especially by ancient standards. It was also enormous, with a population somewhere between 500,000 and 750,000. Although it could boast of stately palaces, noble buildings, and beautiful residential areas, most people lived in jerrybuilt apartment houses. Fire and crime were perennial problems, even after Augustus created fire and urban police forces. Streets were narrow and drainage was inadequate. Under the empire this situation improved. By comparison with medieval and early modern

European cities, Rome was a healthy enough place to live.

Rome was such a huge city that the surrounding countryside could not feed it. Because of the danger of starvation, the emperor, following republican practice, provided the citizen population with free grain for bread and, later, oil and wine. By feeding the citizenry, the emperor prevented bread riots caused by shortages and high prices. For the rest of the urban population who did not enjoy the rights of citizenship, the emperor provided grain at low prices. This measure was designed to prevent speculators from forcing up grain prices in times of crisis. By maintaining the grain supply, the emperor kept the favor of the people and ensured that Rome's poor and idle did not starve.

The emperor also entertained the Roman populace, often at vast expense. The most popular forms of public entertainment were gladiatorial contests and chariot racing. Gladiatorial fighting was originally an Etruscan funerary custom, a blood sacrifice for the dead. Many gladiators were criminals; some were the slaves of gladiatorial trainers; others were prisoners of war. Still others were free men who volunteered for the arena. Even women at times engaged in gladiatorial combat. Although some Romans protested gladiatorial fighting, most delighted in it. Not until the fifth century did Christianity put a stop to it.

The Romans were even more addicted to chariot racing than to gladiatorial shows. Under the empire, four permanent teams competed against one another. Each had its own color—red, white, green, or blue. Some Romans claimed that people cared more about their favorite team than about the race itself. Two-horse and four-horse chariots ran a course of seven laps, about five miles. A successful driver could be the hero of the hour. One

Apartment Houses at Ostia At heavily populated places such as Rome and Ostia, which was the port of Rome, apartment buildings housed urban dwellers. The brick construction of this building is a good example of solid Roman work. In Rome some apartment buildings were notoriously shoddy and unsafe. *(Source: Art Resource)*

charioteer, Gaius Appuleius Diocles, raced for twenty-four years. During that time he drove 4,257 starts and won 1,462 of them. His admirers honored him with an inscription that proclaimed him champion of all charioteers.

But people like the charioteer Diocles were no more typical of the common Roman than Babe Ruth is of the average American. Ordinary Romans were proud of their work and accomplishments. They dealt with everyday problems and rejoiced over small pleasures. Ordinary Romans left their mark in the inscriptions that grace their graves. The funerary inscription of Paprius Vitalis to his wife is particularly engaging:

If there is anything good in the lower regions—I, however, finish a poor life without you—be happy there too, sweetest Thalassia . . . married to me for 40 years.[9]

As moving is the final tribute of a patron to his former slave:

To Grania Clara, freedwoman of Aulus, a temperate freedwoman. She lived 23 years. She was never vexatious to me except when she died.[10]

Most Romans went about their lives as people have always done. Though fond of brutal spectacles, they also had their loves and dreams.

The Provinces

In the provinces and even on the frontiers, many men and women would have agreed with Gibbon's opinion of the second century. The age of the Antonines was one of extensive prosperity, especially in western Europe. The Roman army had beaten back the barbarians and exposed them to the civilizing effects of Roman traders. The resulting peace and security opened Britain, Gaul, Germany, and the lands of the Danube to immigration. Agriculture flourished as large tracts of land came under cultivation. Most of this land was in the hands of free tenant farmers. From the time of Augustus, slavery had declined in the empire as had the growth of latifundia (see page 188). Augustus and his successors encouraged the rise of free farmers. Under the Antonines this trend continued, and the holders of small parcels of land

throve as never before. The Antonines provided loans on easy terms to farmers. These loans enabled them to rent land previously worked by slaves. It also permitted them to cultivate the new lands that were being opened up. Consequently the small tenant farmer was becoming the backbone of Roman agriculture.

Since the time of Augustus, towns had gradually grown up around the camps and forts. The roads that linked the frontier with the rearward areas served as commercial lifelines for the new towns and villages. Part Roman, part barbarian, these towns were truly outposts of civilization, much like the raw towns of the American West. In the course of time, many of them grew to be Romanized cities, and emperors gave them the status of full Roman municipalities, with charters and constitutions. This development was pronounced along the Rhine and Danube frontiers. Thus, while defending the borders, the army also spread Roman culture. This process would go so far that in A.D. 212 the emperor Caracalla would grant Roman citizenship to every free man within the empire.

The eastern part of the empire also participated in the boom. The Roman navy had swept the sea of pirates, and eastern Mediterranean merchants traded throughout the sea. The flow of goods and produce in the East matched that of the West. Venerable cities like Corinth, Antioch, and Ephesus flourished as rarely before. The cities of the East built extensively, bedecking themselves with new amphitheaters, temples, fountains, and public buildings. For the East, the age of the Antonines was the heyday of the city. Life there grew ever richer and more comfortable.

Trade among the provinces increased dramatically. Britain and Belgium became prime grain producers, much of their harvests going to the armies of the Rhine. Britain's famous wool industry probably got its start under the Romans. Italy and southern Gaul produced wine in huge quantities. The wines of Italy went principally to Rome and

MAP 8.3 The Economic Aspect of the Pax Romana   The Roman Empire was not merely a political and military organization but also an intricate economic network through which goods from Armenia and Syria were traded for Western products from as far away as Spain and Britain.

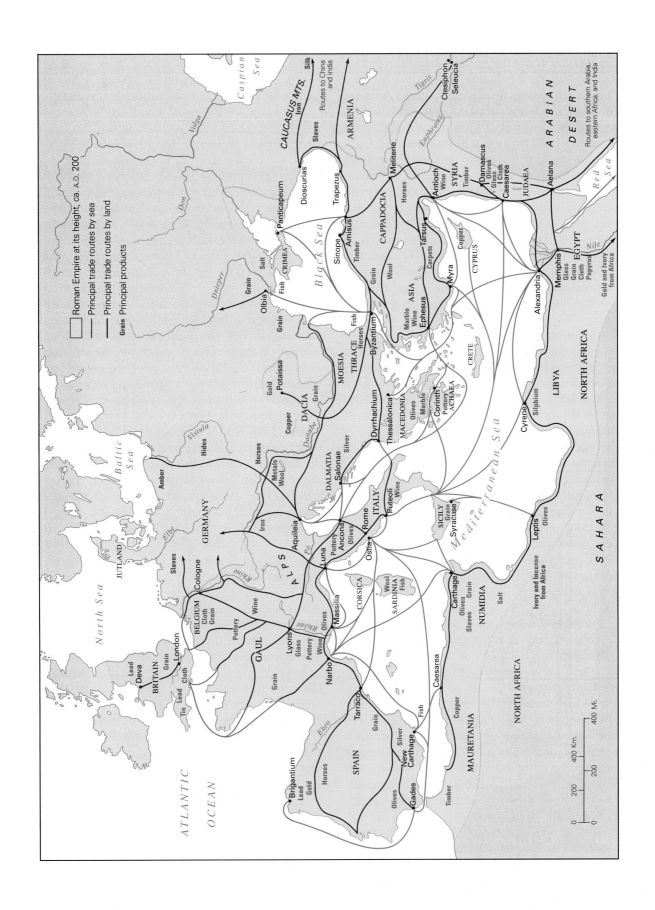

Legend:

Roman Empire at its height, ca. A.D. 200

Principal trade routes by sea

Principal trade routes by land

Grain Principal products

Map labels (by region):

ATLANTIC OCEAN

North Sea

JUTLAND

Baltic Sea

Caspian Sea

CAUCASUS MTS. — Iron — Silk — Routes to China and India

ARMENIA

BRITAIN — Lead, Deva, Tin, Lead, Cloth, London, Grain

Brigantium — Lead, Gold

SPAIN — Horses, New Carthage, Silver, Gades, Olives, Tarraco, Grain, Ebro

Caesarea, Fish, Copper, Timber

MAURETANIA

NUMIDIA — Olives, Slaves, Grain, Salt

NORTH AFRICA

GAUL — Grain, Wine, Pottery, Lyons, Glass, Pottery, Narbo, Massilia, Olives, Rhône

BELGIUM — Cloth, Grain, Cologne, Slaves

GERMANY — Hides, Amber, Horses, Iron, Metals, Wool, Elbe, Rhine

Vistula

DACIA — Gold, Potaissa, Copper, Grain, Danube

MOESIA

THRACE — Fish, Horses, Byzantium

DALMATIA — Salonae, Silver

ALPS — Aquileia, Luna, Po, Ancona, Pottery, Olives

ITALY — Rome, Ostia, Puteoli, Wine

CORSICA

SARDINIA — Wool, Fish

SICILY — Grain, Syracuse

Carthage — Olives, Grain

Leptis — Olives

LIBYA

Cyrene — Silphium

SAHARA

Ivory and Incense from Africa

MACEDONIA — Olives, Marble, Thessalonica, Dyrrhachium

ACHAEA — Corinth, Pottery, Marble

CRETE

Mediterranean Sea

ASIA — Marble, Wine, Ephesus, Wool, Myra

CAPPADOCIA — Horses, Carpets, Tarsus, Copper, Amisus, Timber, Sinope, Grain, Melitene

CYPRUS

Black Sea

CRIMEA — Salt, Fish, Panticapeum, Grain

Olbia — Grain, Fish

Dioscurias, Trapezus — Slaves

Dnieper, Don, Volga

SYRIA — Antioch, Wine, Damascus, Olives, Glass, Cloth, Caesarea, Timber

JUDAEA — Aelana

Ctesiphon, Seleucia, Tigris, Euphrates

ARABIAN DESERT

Routes to southern Arabia, eastern Africa, and India

EGYPT — Memphis, Glass, Grain, Cloth, Papyrus, Nile

Alexandria

Gold and Ivory from Africa

Red Sea

Scale:

400 Mi.

0   200   400 Km.
0   200   400 Mi.

the Danube; Gallic wines were shipped to Britain and the Rhineland. Roman colonists had introduced the olive to southern Spain and northern Africa, an experiment so successful that these regions produced most of the oil consumed in the western empire. In the East, Syrian farmers continued to cultivate the olive, and oil production reached an all-time high. Egypt was the prime grain producer of the East, and tons of Egyptian wheat went to feed the Roman populace. The Roman army in Mesopotamia consumed a high percentage of the raw materials and manufactured products of Syria and Asia Minor. The spread of trade meant the end of isolated and self-contained economies. By the time of the Antonines, the empire had become an economic as well as a political reality (Map 8.3).

One of the most striking features of this period was the growth of industry in the provinces. Cities in Gaul and Germany eclipsed the old Mediterranean manufacturing centers. Italian cities were particularly hard hit by this development. Cities like Arretium and Capua had dominated the production of glass, pottery, and bronze ware. Yet in the second century A.D., Gaul and Germany took over the pottery market. Lyons in Gaul became the new center of the glassmaking industry. The technique of glass blowing spread to Britain and Germany, and later in the second century, Cologne replaced Lyons in glass production. The cities of Gaul were nearly unrivaled in the manufacture of bronze and brass. Gallic craftsmen invented a new technique of tin-plating and decorated their work with Celtic designs. Their wares soon drove Italian products out of the northern European market. For the first time in history, northern Europe was able to rival the Mediterranean world as a producer of manufactured goods. Europe had entered fully into the economic and cultural life of the Mediterranean world.

The age of the Antonines was generally one of peace, progress, and prosperity. The work of the Romans in northern and western Europe was a permanent contribution to the history of Western society. The cities that grew up in Britain, Belgium, Gaul, Germany, Austria, and elsewhere survived the civil wars that racked the empire in the third century A.D. Likewise, they survived the barbarian invasions that destroyed the western empire and handed on a precious cultural and material heritage to the medieval world. The period of the Antonine monarchy was also one of consolidation.

Roads and secure sea lanes linked the empire in one vast web. The empire had become a commonwealth of cities, and urban life was its hallmark.

ROME AND THE EAST

Their march to empire and their growing interest in foreign peoples brought the Romans into contact with a world much larger than Europe and the Mediterranean. As early as the late Republic, Roman commanders in the East encountered peoples who created order out of the chaos left by Alexander the Great and his Hellenistic successors. This meeting of West and East had two immediate effects. The first was a long military confrontation between the Romans and their Iranian neighbors. Second, Roman military expansion to the east coincided with Chinese expansion to the west, and the surprising result was a period when the major ancient civilizations of the world were in touch with one another. For the first time in history, peoples from the Greco-Roman civilization of the Mediterranean and peoples from central Asia, India, and China met one another and observed one another's cultures at first hand. This was an era of human exploration, and key figures in the process were the peoples of cental Asia, especially the Parthians and Sassanids of Iran.

Romans Versus Iranians

When Roman armies moved into Mesopotamia in 92 B.C., they encountered the Parthians, a people who had entered the Iranian plateau from central Asia in the time of the Persian kings. The disintegration of Alexander's eastern holdings enabled them to reap the harvest of his victory. They created an empire that once stretched from Armenia and Babylonia in the west to the Hellenistic kingdom of Bactria in the east (Map 8.4). They divided their realm into large provinces, or satrapies, and created a flexible political organization to administer their holdings. Unlike China, however, Parthia never had a sophisticated bureaucracy. Nonetheless, the loose provincial organization enabled the Parthians to govern the many different peoples who inhabited their realm. The Romans marveled at Parthia's success, as the Greek geographer Strabo (ca 65 B.C.–A.D. 19) attests:

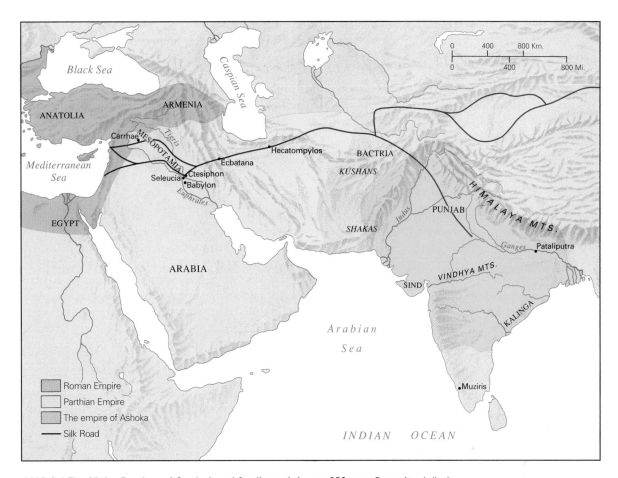

MAP 8.4 The Major Empires of Central and Southern Asia, ca 250 B.C. From Anatolia in the west to the Himalayas in the east, three great empires ruled western, central, and southern Asia. During these years, frontiers fluctuated, but the Silk Road served as a thread connecting them all.

Now at first he [the Parthian king] Arsaces was weak, carrying the war to those whose land he had taken, both he and his successors. In this way the Parthians subsequently became mighty, taking neighboring territory through success in wars, so that accomplishing these feats, they established themselves as lords within the entire area east of the Euphrates. They also took part of Bactria . . . and now they rule so much territory and so many people that they have become in a way rivals of the Romans in the greatness of their empire.[11]

In the process the Parthians won their place in history as the heirs of the Persian Empire.

Although Augustus sought peace with the Parthians, later Roman emperors, beginning with Nero in A.D. 58, struggled to wrest Armenia and Mesopotamia from them. The great military emperors Trajan, in 114 and 115, and Septimius Severus, between 197 and 199, threw the Parthians eastward beyond the Tigris River, but their victories were short-lived. Until their downfall in 226, the Parthians met the Roman advance to the east with iron and courage.

The Romans found nothing to celebrate in the eclipse of the Parthians, for their place was immediately taken by the Sassanids, a people indigenous to southern Iran, who overthrew them. As early as 230 the Sassanids launched a campaign to the west, which the Romans blunted. The setback was only temporary, for in 256 the great Persian king Shapur overran Mesopotamia and the Roman province of Syria. Four years later Shapur defeated the legions of the emperor Valerian, whom he took prisoner. Thereafter, the Romans and Sassanids fought long, bitter, and destructive wars in western Asia as the Romans battled to save their eastern provinces. Not until the reign of Diocletian did the Romans solidly anchor their eastern frontier on the Euphrates. Constantine followed up Diocletian's victory, and again Roman rule was firmly established in western Asia.

Trade and Contact

Although warfare between Roman emperors and Iranian kings disrupted western Asia, it did not prevent the major empires of the ancient world from coming and staying in direct contact with one another. Essential to the process was the geographical position of Iran as a link between East and West, a position that facilitated communications between the Roman and Chinese empires, the two wealthiest and most commercially active realms in the ancient world. The overland lines of communication stretched from China across the vast lands under Parthian control to the eastern provinces of the Roman Empire. Maritime routes linked the Romans to India and even to China. As the middlemen in this trade, the Parthians cleverly tried to keep the Chinese and Romans from making direct contact—and thus from learning how large a cut the Parthians took in commercial transactions.

An elaborate network of roads linked Parthia to China in the east, India in the south, and the Roman Empire in the west. The many branch roads even included routes to southern Russia. The most important of the overland routes was the famous Silk Road, named for the shipments of silk that passed from China through Parthia to the Roman Empire. Many other luxury items also passed along this route: the Parthians exported exotic fruits, rare birds, ostrich eggs, and other dainties to China in return for iron and delicacies like apricots. Other easily portable luxury goods included gems, gold, silver, spices, and perfumes. From the Roman Empire came glassware, statuettes, and slaves trained as jugglers and acrobats.

Rarely did a merchant travel the entire distance from China to Mesopotamia. Chinese merchants typically sold their wares to Parthians at the Stone Tower, located at modern Tashkurghan in Afghanistan. From there Parthian traders carried goods across the Iranian plateau to Mesopotamia or

Egypt. This overland trade fostered urban life in Parthia as cities arose and prospered along the caravan routes. In the process, the Parthians themselves became important consumers of goods, contributing to the volume of trade and reinforcing the commercial ties between East and West.

More than goods passed along these windswept roads. Ideas, religious lore, and artistic inspiration also traveled the entire route. A fine example of how ideas and artistic influences spread across long distances is a Parthian coin that caught the fancy of an artist in China. The coin bore an inscription—a practice the Parthians had adopted from the Greeks—and although the artist could not read it, he used the lettering as a motif on a bronze vessel. Similarly, thoughts, ideas, and literary works found ready audiences; Greek plays were performed at the court of the Parthian king. At a time when communication was difficult and often dangerous, trade routes were important avenues for the spread of knowledge about other societies.

This was also an era of exciting maritime exploration. Roman ships sailed from Egyptian ports to the mouth of the Indus River, where they traded local merchandise and wares imported by the Parthians. Merchants who made the voyage had to contend with wind, shoal waters, and pirates, as the Roman writer Pliny the Elder recounts:

For those bound for India the most advantageous sailing is from Ocelis [a city in Arabia]. From there with the wind Hippalos blowing, the voyage is forty days to Muziris, the first port in India. It is not a desirable spot because of neighboring pirates, who occupy a place by the name of Nitrias. Nor is there an abundance of merchandise there. Besides, the anchorage for ships is a far distance from land. Cargoes are brought in and carried out by lighters [barges].[12]

Despite such dangers and discomforts, hardy mariners pushed into the Indian Ocean and beyond, reaching Malaya, Sumatra, and Java.

Direct maritime trade between China and the West began in the second century A.D. The period of this contact coincided with the era of Han greatness in China. It was the Han emperor Wu Ti who took the momentous step of opening the Silk Road to the Parthian Empire. Indeed, a later Han emperor sent an ambassador directly to the Roman Empire by sea. The ambassador, Kan Ying, sailed to the Roman province of Syria, where during the reign of the Roman emperor Nerva

(96–98) he became the first Chinese official to have a firsthand look at the Greco-Roman world. Kan Ying enjoyed himself thoroughly, and in A.D. 97 delivered a fascinating report of his travels to his emperor:

The inhabitants of that country are tall and well-proportioned, somewhat like the Chinese, whence they are called Ta-ts'in. *The country contains much gold, silver, and rare precious stones . . . corals, amber, glass . . . gold embroidered rugs and thin silk-cloth and asbestos cloth. All the rare gems of other foreign countries come from there. They make coins of gold and silver. Ten units of silver are worth one of gold. They traffic by sea with An-hsi (Parthia) and T'ien-chu (India), the profit of which trade is ten-fold. They are honest in their transactions and there are no double prices. Cereals are always cheap. . . . Their kings always desired to send embassies to China, but the An-hsi (Parthians) wished to carry on trade with them in Chinese silks, and it is for this reason that they were cut off from communication.*[13]

The sea route and to a lesser extent the Silk Road included India in this long web of communications that, once established, was never entirely broken.

CIVIL WARS AND INVASION IN THE THIRD CENTURY

The age of the Antonines gave way to a period of chaos and stress. During the third century A.D., the empire was stunned by civil wars and barbarian invasions. By the time peace was restored, the economy was shattered, cities had shrunk in size, and agriculture was becoming manorial. In the disruption of the third century and the reconstruction of the fourth, the European medieval world had its origins.

After the death of Marcus Aurelius, the last of the five good emperors, his son Commodus, a man totally unsuited to govern the empire, came to the throne. Misrule led to Commodus's murder and a renewal of civil war. After a brief but intense spasm of fighting, the African general Septimius Severus defeated other rival commanders and established the Severan dynasty (A.D. 193–235). Although Septimius Severus was able to stabilize the empire, his successors proved incapable of disciplining the legions. When the last of the Severi was killed by one of his own soldiers, the empire plunged into still another grim, destructive, and this time prolonged round of civil war.

Over twenty different emperors ascended the throne in the forty-nine years between 235 and 284, and many rebels died in the attempt to seize power. At various times, parts of the empire were lost to rebel generals, one of whom, Postumus, set up his own empire in Gaul for about ten years (A.D. 259–269). Yet other men like the iron-willed Aurelian (A.D. 270–275) dedicated their energies to restoring order. So many military commanders seized rule that the middle of the third century has become known as the age of the "barracks emperors." The Augustan principate had become a military monarchy, and that monarchy was nakedly autocratic.

The disruption caused by civil war opened the way for widespread barbarian invasions. Throughout the empire, barbarian invasions and civil war devastated towns, villages, and farms and caused a catastrophic economic depression. Indeed, the Roman Empire seemed on the point of collapse.

The first and most disastrous result of the civil wars was trouble on the frontiers. It was Rome's misfortune that this era of anarchy coincided with immense movements of barbarian peoples, still another example of the effects of mass migrations in ancient history, this time against one of the best organized empires of antiquity. Historians still dispute the precise reason for these migrations, though their immediate cause was pressure from tribes moving westward across Asia. In the sixth century A.D., Jordanes, a Christianized Goth, preserved the memory of innumerable wars among the barbarians in his *History of the Goths*. Goths fought Vandals, Huns fought Goths. Steadily the defeated and displaced tribes moved toward the Roman frontiers. Finally, like "a swarm of bees"—to use Jordanes's image—the Goths burst into Europe in A.D. 258.

When the barbarians reached the Rhine and Danube frontiers, they often found huge gaps in the Roman defenses. Through much of the third century A.D., bands of Goths devastated the Balkans as far south as Greece. They even penetrated Asia Minor. The Alamanni, a German people, swept across the Danube. At one point they entered Italy and reached Milan before they were beaten back. Meanwhile the Franks, still another German folk, hit the Rhine frontier. The Franks then invaded eastern and central Gaul and north-eastern Spain. Saxons from Scandinavia entered the English Channel in search of loot. In the east the Sassanids, of Persian stock, overran Mesopotamia. If the army had been guarding the borders instead of creating and destroying emperors, none of these invasions would have been possible. The barracks emperors should be credited with one accomplishment, however: they fought barbarians when they were not fighting one another. Only that kept the empire from total ruin.

Diocletian's Tetrarchy The emperor Diocletian's attempt to reform the Roman Empire by dividing rule among four men is represented in this piece of sculpture, which in many features illustrates the transition from ancient to medieval art. Here the four tetrarchs demonstrate their solidarity by clasping one another on the shoulder. Nonetheless each man has his other hand on his sword—a gesture that proved prophetic when Diocletian's reign ended and another struggle for power began. (*Source: Alinari/Art Resource*)

RECONSTRUCTION UNDER DIOCLETIAN AND CONSTANTINE (A.D. 284–337)

At the close of the third century A.D., the emperor Diocletian (284–305) put an end to the period of turmoil. Repairing the damage done in the third century was the major work of the emperor Constantine (306–337) in the fourth. But the price was high.

Under Diocletian, Augustus's polite fiction of the emperor as first among equals gave way to the emperor as absolute autocrat. The princeps became *dominus,* "lord." The emperor claimed that he was "the elect of God"—that he ruled because of God's favor. Constantine even claimed to be the equal of Jesus's first twelve followers. No mere soldier but rather an adroit administrator, Diocletian gave serious thought to the empire's ailments. He recognized that the empire and its difficulties had become too great for one man to handle. He also realized that during the third century provincial governors had frequently used their positions to foment or participate in rebellions. To solve the first of these problems Diocletian divided the empire into a western and an eastern half (Map 8.5). Diocletian assumed direct control of the eastern part; he gave the rule of the western part to a colleague, along with the title *augustus,* which had become synonymous with "emperor." Diocletian and his fellow augustus further delegated power by appointing two men to assist them. Each man was given the title of *caesar* to indicate his exalted rank. Although this system is known as the *Tetrarchy* because four men ruled the empire, Diocletian was clearly senior partner and final source of authority.

Each half of the empire was further split into two prefectures, each governed by a prefect responsible to an augustus. Diocletian organized the prefectures into small administrative units called "dioceses," which were in turn subdivided into small provinces. He reduced the power of the old provincial governors by dividing provinces into

MAP 8.5 The Roman World Divided Under Diocletian, the Roman Empire was first divided into a western and an eastern half, a development that foreshadowed the medieval division between the Latin West and the Byzantine East.

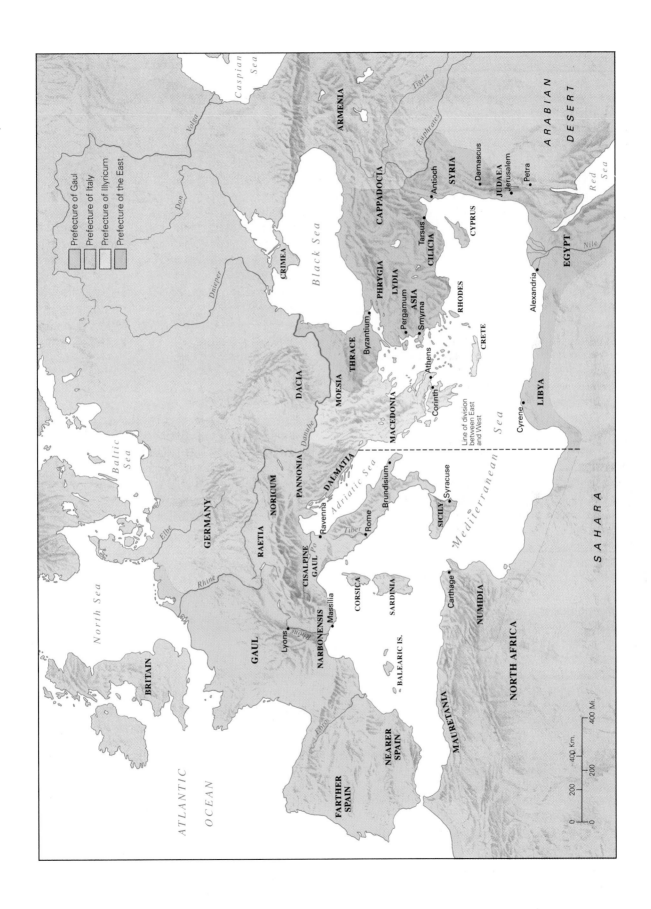

Prefecture of Gaul
Prefecture of Italy
Prefecture of Illyricum
Prefecture of the East

ATLANTIC OCEAN

North Sea

Baltic Sea

Caspian Sea

Black Sea

Red Sea

Mediterranean Sea

Adriatic Sea

BRITAIN

GERMANY

GAUL

Lyons

NARBONENSIS

Massilia

RAETIA

NORICUM

CISALPINE GAUL

Ravenna

Rome

Brundisium

PANNONIA

DALMATIA

DACIA

MOESIA

THRACE

MACEDONIA

Corinth

Athens

Byzantium

CRIMEA

ARMENIA

CAPPADOCIA

PHRYGIA

LYDIA

ASIA

Pergamum

Smyrna

CILICIA

Tarsus

Antioch

SYRIA

Damascus

JUDAEA

Jerusalem

Petra

CYPRUS

RHODES

CRETE

EGYPT

Alexandria

LIBYA

Cyrene

ARABIAN DESERT

SAHARA

NORTH AFRICA

NUMIDIA

Carthage

MAURETANIA

NEARER SPAIN

FARTHER SPAIN

SARDINIA

CORSICA

BALEARIC IS.

SICILY

Syracuse

Line of division between East and West

FARTHER SPAIN

Volga

Don

Dnieper

Danube

Elbe

Rhine

Rhône

Po

Tiber

Ebro

Tigris

Euphrates

Nile

0   200   400 Mi.
0   200   400 Km.

A Large Roman Villa   During the third and fourth centuries, when the Roman Empire was breaking up, large villas such as this one in Carthage became the focus of daily life. The villa was at once a fortress, as the towers at the corners of the building indicate, and the economic and social center of the neighborhood. *(Source: Courtesy, German Archaeological Institute)*

smaller units. Provincial governors were also deprived of their military power and were left with only civil and administrative duties.

Diocletian's political reforms were a momentous step. The Tetrarchy soon failed, but Diocletian's division of the empire into two parts became permanent. Constantine and later emperors tried hard to keep the empire together, but without success. Throughout the fourth century A.D., the east and the west drifted apart. In later centuries the western part witnessed the fall of Roman government and the rise of barbarian kingdoms, while

the eastern empire evolved into the majestic Byzantine Empire.

The most serious immediate matters confronting Diocletian and Constantine were economic, social, and religious. They needed additional revenues to support the army and the imperial court. Yet the wars and the barbarian invasions had caused widespread destruction and poverty. The fighting had struck a serious blow to Roman agriculture, which the emperors tried to revive. Christianity had become too strong either to ignore or to crush. How Diocletian, Constantine, and their successors dealt with those problems helped to create the economic and social patterns inherited by medieval Europe.

Inflation and Taxes

The barracks emperors had dealt with economic hardship by depreciating the currency, cutting the silver content of coins until money was virtually worthless. As a result the entire monetary system fell into ruin. The immediate result was crippling inflation throughout the empire.

The empire was less capable of recovery than in earlier times. Wars and invasions had disrupted normal commerce and the means of production. Mines were exhausted in the attempt to supply much-needed ores, especially gold and silver. War and invasion had hit the cities especially hard. Markets were disrupted, and travel became dangerous. Craftsmen, artisans, and traders rapidly left devastated regions. The prosperous industry and commerce of Gaul and the Rhineland declined markedly. Those who owed their prosperity to commerce and the needs of urban life likewise suffered. Cities were no longer places where trade and industry thrived. The devastation of the countryside increased the difficulty of feeding and supplying the cities. The destruction was so extensive that many wondered whether the ravages could be repaired at all.

The response of Diocletian and Constantine to these problems was marked by compulsion, rigidity, and loss of individual freedom. Diocletian's attempt to curb inflation illustrates the methods of absolute monarchy. In a move unprecedented in Roman history, he issued an edict that fixed maximum prices and wages throughout the empire. The measure proved a failure because it was unrealistic as well as unenforceable.

The emperors dealt with the tax system just as strictly and inflexibly. As in the past, local officials bore the responsibility of collecting imperial taxes. Constantine made these officials into a hereditary class; son followed father whether he wanted to or not. In this period of severe depression, many localities could not pay their taxes. In such cases these local officials had to make up the difference from their own funds. This system soon wiped out a whole class of moderately wealthy people.

With the monetary system in ruins, most imperial taxes became payable in kind—that is, in goods or produce instead of money. The major drawback of payment in kind is its demands on transportation. Goods have to be moved from where they are grown or manufactured to where they are needed. Accordingly, the emperors locked into their occupations all those involved in the growing, preparation, and transportation of food and essential commodities. A baker or shipper could not go into any other business, and his son took up the trade at his death. The late empire had a place for everyone, and everyone had a place.

The Legalization of Christianity

In religious affairs Constantine took the decisive step of recognizing Christianity as a legitimate religion. No longer would Christians suffer persecution for their beliefs. Constantine himself died a Christian in 337. Constantine has been depicted both as a devout convert to Christianity and as a realistic opportunist who used the young religion to his own imperial ends. Certainly Constantine was realistic enough to recognize and appreciate Christianity's spread and hold on his subjects. He correctly gauged the strength of the Christian ecclesiastical organization and realized that the new church could serve as a friend of his empire. Yet there is no solid reason to doubt the sincerity of his conversion to the Christian religion. In short, Constantine was a man personally inclined toward Christianity and an emperor who could bestow on it a legal and legitimate place within the Roman Empire.

Why had the pagans—those who believed in the Greco-Roman gods—persecuted Christians in the first place? Polytheism is by nature tolerant of new gods and accommodating in religious matters. Why was Christianity singled out for violence? These questions are still matters of scholarly debate, but some broad answers can be given.

Even so educated and cultured a man as the historian Tacitus opposed Christianity. He believed that Christians hated the whole human race. As a rule early Christians, like the Jews, kept to themselves. Romans distrusted and feared their exclusiveness, which seemed unsociable and even subversive. Most pagans genuinely misunderstood Christian practices. They thought that the Lord's Supper, at which Christians said they ate and drank the body and blood of Jesus, was an act of cannibalism. Pagans thought that Christians

ROMAN HISTORY AFTER AUGUSTUS

Period	Important Emperors	Significant Events
Julio-Claudians 27 B.C.–A.D. **68**	Augustus 27 B.C.–A.D. 14 Tiberius, 14–37 Caligula, 37–41 Claudius, 41–54 Nero, 54–68	Augustan settlement Beginning of the principate Birth and death of Jesus Expansion into northern and western Europe Creation of the imperial bureaucracy
Year of the Four Emperors **68–69**	Nero Galba Otho Vitellius	Civil War Major breakdown of the concept of the principate
Flavians **69–96**	Vespasian, 69–79 Titus, 79–81 Domitian, 81–96	Growing trend toward the concept of monarchy Defense and further consolidation of the European frontiers
Antonines **96–192**	Nerva, 96–98 Trajan, 98–117 Hadrian, 117–138 Antoninus Pius, 138–161 Marcus Aurelius, 161–180 Commodus, 180–192	The "golden age"—the era of the "five good emperors" Economic prosperity Trade and growth of cities in northern Europe Beginning of barbarian menace on the frontiers
Severi **193–235**	Septimius Severus, 193–211 Caracalla, 211–217 Elagabalus, 218–222 Severus Alexander, 222–235	Military monarchy All free men within the empire given Roman citizenship
"Barracks Emperors" **235–284**	Twenty-two emperors in forty-nine years	Civil war Breakdown of the empire Barbarian invasions Severe economic decline
Tetrarchy **284–337**	Diocletian, 284–305 Constantine, 306–337	Political recovery Autocracy Legalization of Christianity Transition to the Middle Ages in the west Birth of the Byzantine Empire in the east

indulged in immoral and indecent rituals. They considered Christianity one of the worst of the Oriental mystery cults, for one of the hallmarks of many of those cults was disgusting rituals.

Even these feelings of distrust and revulsion do not entirely account for persecution. The main reason seems to have been sincere religious convic-

tion on the part of the pagans. Time and again they accused Christians of atheism. Indeed, Christians either denied the existence of pagan gods or called them evil spirits. For this same reason many Romans hated the Jews. Tacitus no doubt expressed the common view when he said that Jews despised the gods. Christians went even further than Jews: they said that no one should worship pagan gods.

At first some pagans were repelled by the fanaticism of these monotheists. No good could come from scorning the gods. The whole community might end up paying for the wickedness and blasphemy of the Christians. Besides—and this is important—pagans did not demand that Christians believe in pagan gods. Greek and Roman religion was never a matter of belief or ethics. It was purely a religion of ritual. One of the clearest statements of pagan theological attitudes comes from the Roman senator Symmachus in the later fourth century A.D.:

We watch the same stars; heaven is the same for us all; the same universe envelops us: what importance is it in what way anyone looks for truth? It is impossible to arrive by one route at such a great secret.[14]

Yet Roman religion was inseparable from the state. An attack on one was an attack on the other.

The Romans were being no more fanatical or intolerant than an eighteenth-century English judge who declared the Christian religion part of the law of the land. All the pagans expected was performance of the ritual act, a small token sacrifice. Any Christian who sacrificed went free, no matter what he or she personally believed. The earliest persecutions of the Christians were minor and limited. Even Nero's famous persecution was temporary and limited to Rome. Subsequent persecutions were sporadic and local.

The stress of the third century, however, seemed to some emperors the punishment of the gods. What else could account for such anarchy? With the empire threatened on every side, a few emperors thought that one way to appease the gods was by offering them the proper sacrifices. Such sacrifices would be a sign of loyalty to the empire, a show of Roman solidarity. Consequently, a new wave of persecutions began. Yet even they were never very widespread or long-lived; by the late third century, pagans had become used to Chris-

The Arch of Constantine To celebrate the victory that made him emperor, Constantine built this triumphal arch in Rome. Rather than decorate the arch with the inferior work of his own day, Constantine plundered other Roman monuments, including those of Trajan and Marcus Aurelius. *(Source: C. M. Dixon)*

tianity. Although a few emperors, including Diocletian, vigorously persecuted Christians, most pagans left them alone. Nor were they very sympathetic to the new round of persecutions. Pagan and Christian alike must have been relieved when Constantine legalized Christianity.

In time the Christian triumph would be complete. In 380 the emperor Theodosius made Christianity the official religion of the Roman Empire. At that point Christians began to persecute the pagans for their beliefs. History had come full circle.

The Construction of Constantinople

The triumph of Christianity was not the only event that made Constantine's reign a turning point in Roman history. Constantine took the bold step of building a new capital for the empire. Constantinople, the New Rome, was constructed on the site of Byzantium, an old Greek city on the Bosporus. Throughout the third century, emperors had found Rome and the West hard to defend. The eastern part of the empire was more easily defensible and escaped the worst of the barbarian devastation. It was wealthy and its urban life still vibrant. Moreover, Christianity was more widespread in the East, and the city of Constantinople was intended to be a Christian center.

SUMMARY

The Roman Empire created by Augustus nearly collapsed before being restored by Diocletian and Constantine. Much was lost along the way but much was at the same time gained. Constantine's legalization and patronage of Christianity and his shift of the capital from Rome to Constantinople marked a new epoch in Western history as the ancient world gave way to the medieval. In the process the Roman Empire came into direct contact with its Asian neighbors, sometimes in anger but more often in peace. Never before in Western history and not again until modern times did one state govern so much territory for so long a time.

The true heritage of Rome is its long tradition of law and freedom. Under Roman law and government, the empire enjoyed relative peace and security for extensive periods of time. Through Rome the best of ancient thought and culture was preserved to make its contribution to modern life. Perhaps no better epitaph for Rome can be found than the words of Virgil:

While rivers shall run to the sea,
While shadows shall move across the valleys of
* mountains,*
While the heavens shall nourish the stars,
Always shall your honor and your name and your
* fame endure.*[15]

NOTES

1. Virgil, *Aeneid* 6.851–853. Unless otherwise credited, all quotations from a foreign language in this chapter are translated by John Buckler.
2. Augustus, *Res Gestae* 6.34.
3. Ibid., 5.28.
4. Horace, *Odes* 4.15.
5. Ibid., 1.38.
6. Matthew 3:3.
7. Ibid., 16:18.
8. E. Gibbon, *The History of the Decline and Fall of the Roman Empire* (New York: Modern Library, n.d.), 1.70.
9. *Corpus Inscriptionum Latinarum,* vol. 6 (Berlin: G. Reimer, 1882), no. 9792.
10. Ibid., vol. 10, no. 8192.
11. Strabo, 11.9.2.
12. Pliny, *Natural History* 6.26
13. Quoted in W. H. Schoff, *The Periplus of the Erythraean Sea* (London: Longmans, Green, 1912), p. 276.
14. Symmachus, *Relations* 3.10.
15. Virgil, *Aeneid* 1.607–609.

SUGGESTED READING

Some good general treatments of the empire include B. Levick, *The Government of the Roman Empire: A Source Book* (1984), a convenient collection of sources illustrating the workings of Roman imperial government; P. Garnsey and R. Saller, *The Roman Empire* (1987); and J. Wacher, ed., *The Roman World,* 2 vols. (1987), which attempts a comprehensive survey of the world of the Roman Empire. The role of the emperor is superbly treated by F. Millar, *The Emperor in the Roman World* (1977), and the defense of the empire is studied by E. N. Luttwak, *The Grand Strategy of the Roman Empire* (1976). The army that carried out that strategy is the subject of G. Webster, *The Roman Imperial Army* (1969).

G. W. Bowersock, *Augustus and the Greek World* (1965), is excellent intellectual history. C. M. Wells, *The German Policy of Augustus* (1972), uses archeological findings to illustrate Roman expansion into northern Europe. H. Schutz, *The Romans in Central Europe* (1985), treats Roman expansion, its problems, and its successes in a vital area of the empire. In *The Augustan Aristocracy* (1985), one of the great Roman historians of this century, R. Syme, studies the new order that Augustus created to help him administer the empire. Rather than study the Augustan poets individually, one can now turn to D. A. West and A. J. Woodman, *Poetry and Politics in the Age of Augustus* (1984). J. B. Campbell, *The Emperor and the Roman Army, 31 B.C.–A.D. 235* (1984), stresses the reliance of the Roman emperor on the army throughout the empire's history. Recent work on the Roman army includes M. Speidel, *Roman Army Studies*, vol. 1 (1984), and L. Keppie, *The Making of the Roman Army from Republic to Empire* (1984). Even though Augustus himself still remains an enigma, F. Millar and E. Segal, eds., *Caesar Augustus: Seven Aspects* (1984), is an interesting volume of essays that attempts, not always successfully, to penetrate the official facade of the emperor. N. Hannestad, *Roman Art and Imperial Policy* (1988), examines the way in which the emperors used art as a means of furthering imperial policy. M. Hammond, *The Antonine Monarchy* (1959), is a classic study of the evolution of the monarchy under the Antonines.

The commercial life of the empire is the subject of an interesting book by K. Greene, *The Archaeology of the Roman Economy* (1986), which offers an intriguing way in which to picture the Roman economy through physical remains. The classic treatment, which ranges across the empire, is M. Rostovtzeff, *The Economic and Social History of the Roman Empire* (1957). P. W. de Neeve, *Colonies: Private Farm-Tenancy in Roman Italy* (1983), covers agriculture and the styles of landholding from the Republic to the early years of the empire.

Social aspects of the empire are the subject of R. Auguet, *Cruelty and Civilization: The Roman Games* (English translation, 1972); P. Garnsey, *Social Status and Legal Privilege in the Roman Empire* (1970); and A. N. Sherwin-White, *Racial Prejudice in Imperial Rome* (1967). A general treatment is R. MacMullen, *Roman Social Relations, 50 A.D. to A.D. 284* (1981), and a recent contribution is L. A. Thompson, *Romans and Blacks* (1989). N. Kampen, *Image and Status: Roman Working Women in Ostia* (1981), is distinctive for its treatment of ordinary Roman women. An important feature of Roman history is treated by R. P. Saller, *Personal Patronage Under the Early Empire* (1982). J. Humphrey, *Roman Circuses and Chariot Racing* (1985), treats a topic very dear to the hearts of ancient Romans. K. R. Bradley, *Slaves and Masters in the Roman Empire* (1988), discusses social controls in a slave-holding society. Lastly, B. Cunliffe, *Greeks, Romans and Barbarians* (1988), uses archeological and literary evidence to discuss the introduction of Greco-Roman culture into western Europe.

Christianity, paganism, Judaism, and the ways in which they all met have received lively recent attention. K. Wengst, *Pax Romana and the Peace of Jesus Christ* (English translation, 1987), is an interesting study of the social atmosphere of the lower classes at the time when Christianity was spreading. More recent is A. Chester, *The Social Context of Early Christianity* (1989). J. Liebeschuetz, *Continuity and Change in Roman Religion* (1979), emphasizes the evolution of Roman religion from the late Republic to the late Empire. M. P. Speidel, *Mithras-Orion, Greek Hero and Roman Army God* (1980), studies the cult of Mithras, a mystery religion that was an early competitor with Christianity. The evolution of Christianity in its Hellenistic background, both pagan and Jewish, can be traced through a series of recent books: R. H. Nash, *Christianity and the Hellenistic World* (1984); T. Barnes, *Early Christianity and the Roman Empire* (1984); S. Benko, *Pagan Rome and Early Christians* (1985); and R. L. Wilken, *The Christians as the Romans Saw Them* (1984). Last, R. MacMullen, *Christianizing the Roman Empire* (1984), treats the growth of the Christian church as seen from a pagan perspective.

Convenient surveys of Roman literature are J. W. Duff, *Literary History of Rome from the Origins to the Close of the Golden Age* (1953), and Duff, *Literary History of Rome in the Silver Age*, 3d ed. (1964).

Ever since Gibbon's *Decline and Fall of the Roman Empire,* one of the masterpieces of English literature, the decline of the empire has been a fertile field of investigation. S. Perowne, *Hadrian* (1987), is a new assessment of the emperor who attempted to limit Roman expansion. Broader are A. M. H. Jones, *The Decline of the Ancient World* (1966); F. W. Walbank, *The Awful Revolution* (1969); and R. MacMullen's two books: *Soldier and Civilian in the Later Roman Empire* (1963) and *Enemies of the Roman Order: Treason, Unrest, and Alienation in the Empire* (1966). S. N. C. Lieu and M. Dodgeon, *Rome's Eastern Frontier, A.D. 226–363* (1988), relies primarily on documents to trace Rome's policy in the East during this difficult period. Two studies analyze the attempts at recovery from the breakdown of the barracks emperors: T. D. Barnes, *The New Empire of Diocletian and Constantine* (1982), which, as its title indicates, concerns itself with the necessary innovations made by the two emperors; and, more narrowly, S. Williams, *Diocletian and the Roman Recovery* (1985). A. Ferrill, *The Fall of the Roman Empire* (1986), with plans and illustrations, offers a military explanation for the "fall" of the Roman Empire. R. MacMullen, *Constantine* (1988), written by a leading scholar, provides a broad and lucid interpretation of Constantine and the significance of his reign.

PERIOD (CA 500 B.C.–A.D. 200)	AFRICA AND THE MIDDLE EAST	THE AMERICAS
500 B.C.	Babylonian captivity of the Hebrews, 586–539 Cyrus the Great founds Persian Empire, 550 Persians conquer Egypt, 525 Darius and Xerxes complete Persian conquest of Middle East, 521–464	Olmec civilization, ca 1500 B.C.–A.D. 300 Fall of La Venta; Tres Zapotes becomes leading Olmec site
300 B.C.	Alexander the Great extends empire, 334–331 Death of Alexander (323): Ptolemy conquers Egypt, Seleucus rules Asia	
200 B.C.	Scipio Africanus defeats Hannibal at Zama, 202	
100 B.C.	Dead Sea Scrolls Pompey conquers Syria and Palestine, 63	
A.D. 100	Jesus Christ, ca 4 B.C.–A.D. 30 Paul, d. ca 65 Bantu migrations begin Jews revolt from Rome, Romans destroy Hebrew temple in Jerusalem: end of the ancient Hebrew state, 70	
A.D. 200	Camel first used for trans-Saharan transport	Classic age of the Maya, ca 300–900

EAST ASIA	INDIA AND SOUTHEAST ASIA	EUROPE
Confucius, 551–479 First written reference to iron, ca 521	Siddhartha Gautama (Buddha), 563–483	Roman Republic founded, 509 Origin of Greek polis, ca 500 Growth of Athenian Empire; flowering of Greek drama, philosophy, history, fifth century
Lao–tzu and development of Taoism, fourth century Han Fei-tzu and Li Ssu and development of Legalism, ca 250–208	Alexander invades India, 327–326 Chandragupta founds Mauryan Dynasty, 322–ca 185 Ashoka, 273–232 King Arsaces of Parthia defeats Seleucid monarchy and begins conquest of Persia, ca 250–137	Peloponnesian War, 431–404 Plato, 426–347 Gauls sack Rome, ca 390 Roman expansion, 390–146 Conquests of Alexander the Great, 334–323 Punic wars, destruction of Carthage, 264–146
Ch'in Dynasty and unification of China; construction of the Great Wall, destruction of Confucian literature, 221–210 Han Dynasty, 202 B.C.–A.D. 220	Greeks invade India, ca 183–145 Mithridates creates Parthian Empire, ca 171–131	Late Roman Republic, 133–27
Chinese expansion to South China Sea and Vietnam ca 111 Silk Road opens to Parthian and Roman empires; Buddhism enters China, ca 104	First Chinese ambassadors to India and Parthia, ca 140 *Badhavadgita,* ca 100 B.C.–A.D. 100	Formation of First Triumvirate (Caesar, Crassus, Pompey), 60 Julius Caesar killed, 44 Formation of Second Triumvirate, (Octavian, Antony, Lepidus), 43 Octavian seizes power, 31
First written reference (Chinese) to Japan, A.D. 57 Chinese invent paper, 105 Emperor Wu, 140–186	Shakas and Kushans invade eastern Parthia and India, first century A.D. Roman attacks on Parthian Empire, 115–211	Octavian rules imperial Rome as Augustus, 27 B.C.–A.D. 14 Roman Empire at greatest extent, 117
Three Kingdoms era, 221–280	Fall of Parthian Empire; rise of the Sassanids	End of the *Pax Romana;* civil wars, economic decline, invasion, 180–285 Reforms by Diocletian, 285–305

9

The Making of Europe

Apse mosaic of S. Apollinare in Classe, Ravenna

The centuries between approximately 400 and 1000 present a paradox. They witnessed the disintegration of the Roman Empire, which had been one of humanity's great political and cultural achievements. But they were also a creative and important period, during which Europeans laid the foundations for medieval and modern Europe. Thus, this period saw the making of Europe.

The basic ingredients that went into the making of a distinctly European civilization were the cultural legacy of Greece and Rome, the customs and traditions of the Germanic peoples, and the Christian faith. The most important of these was Christianity, because it absorbed and assimilated the other two. It reinterpreted the classics in a Christian sense. It instructed the Germanic peoples and gave them new ideals of living and social behavior. Christianity became the cement that held European society together.

During this period the Byzantine Empire, centered at Constantinople, served as a protective buffer between Europe and regions to the east. The Greeks and the Muslims (see Chapter 10) preserved the philosophical and scientific texts of the ancient world—texts that later formed the basis for study in science and medicine and produced the Justinian Code, a great synthesis of Roman law. In urbane and sophisticated Constantinople, the Greeks set a standard far above the primitive existence of the West.

European civilization resulted from the fusion of the Greco-Roman heritage, Germanic traditions, and the Christian faith.

- How did these components act on one another?
- How did they cause the making of Europe?
- What influence did the Byzantine culture have on the making of European civilization?

This chapter will focus on these questions.

THE GROWTH OF THE CHRISTIAN CHURCH

While many elements of the Roman Empire disintegrated, the Christian church survived and grew. What is the church? According to scriptural schol-

ars, the earliest use of the word *church* (in Greek, *ekklesia*) in the New Testament appears in Saint Paul's First Letter to the Christians of Thessalonica in northern Greece, written about A.D. 51. By *ekklesia* Paul meant the local community of Christian believers. In Paul's later letters, the term *church* refers to the entire Mediterranean-wide assembly of Jesus's followers. After the legalization of Christianity by the emperor Constantine (see page 221) and the growth of institutional offices and officials, the word *church* was sometimes applied to those officials—much as the terms *the college* or *the university* are used to refer to academic administrators. The bishop of Rome—known as "pope" from the Latin word *papa,* meaning "father"—claimed to speak and act for all Christians. The popes claimed to be the successors of Saint Peter and heirs to his authority as chief of the apostles—Christ's first twelve followers. Their claim was based on Jesus's words to Peter:

You are Peter, and on this rock I will build my church, and the jaws of death shall not prevail against it. I will entrust to you the keys of the kingdom of heaven. Whatever you declare bound on earth shall be bound in heaven; whatever you declare loosed on earth shall be loosed in heaven.[1]

Roman bishops used that text, which is known as the "Petrine Doctrine," to support their assertions of authority over other bishops in the church. The popes maintained that they represented "the church." The word *church,* therefore, has several connotations. Modern Catholic theology frequently defines the church as "the people of God" and identifies the church with local and international Christian communities. In the Middle Ages, the institutional and monarchial interpretations of the word tended to be stressed.

The church possessed able administrators and leaders and highly literate and creative thinkers. Having gained the support of the fourth-century emperors, the church gradually adapted the Roman system of organization to church purposes. Christianity, moreover, had a dynamic missionary policy, and the church slowly succeeded in *assimilating*—that is, adapting—pagan peoples, both Germans and Romans, to Christian teaching. These factors help to explain the survival and growth of the Christian church in the face of repeated Germanic invasions.

The Church and the Roman Emperors

The church benefited considerably from the emperors' support. In return, the emperors expected the support of the Christian church in maintaining order and unity. Constantine had legalized the practice of Christianity within the empire in 312. Although he was not baptized until he was on his deathbed, Constantine encouraged Christianity throughout his reign. He freed the clergy from imperial taxation. At the churchmen's request, he helped settle theological disputes and thus preserved doctrinal unity within the church. Constantine generously endowed the building of Christian churches, and one of his gifts—the Lateran Palace in Rome—remained the official residence of the popes until the fourteenth century. Constantine also declared Sunday a public holiday, a day of rest for the service of God. As the result of its favored position in the empire, Christianity slowly became the leading religion.

In 380 the emperor Theodosius (r. 379–395) went further than Constantine and made Christianity the official religion of the empire. Theodosius stripped Roman pagan temples of statues, made the practice of the old Roman state religion a treasonable offense, and persecuted Christians who dissented from orthodox doctrine. Most significant, he allowed the church to establish its own courts. Church courts began to develop their own body of law—*canon law*. These courts, not the Roman government, had jurisdiction over the clergy and ecclesiastical disputes. At the death of Theodosius, the Christian church was considerably independent of the authority of the Roman state. The foundation for the power of the medieval church had been laid.

What was to be the church's relationship to secular powers? How was the Christian to render unto Caesar the things that were Caesar's while returning to God God's due? This problem had troubled the earliest disciples of Christ. The toleration of Christianity and the coming to power of Christian emperors in the fourth century did not make it any easier. Striking a balance between responsibility to secular rulers and loyalty to spiritual duties was difficult.

In the fourth century, theological disputes frequently and sharply divided the Christian community. Some disagreements had to do with the nature of Jesus Christ. For example, Arianism, which originated with Arius (ca 250–336), a priest

The Council of Nicaea (A.D. 325) In this ninth-century pen-and-ink drawing, sixty-six bishops and theologians sit around the presiding bishop while scribes record the proceedings. The Council produced the Nicene Creed, drawn up to defend the orthodox faith against the Arians. *(Source: Bibliotheek der Rijksuniversitet, Utrecht)*

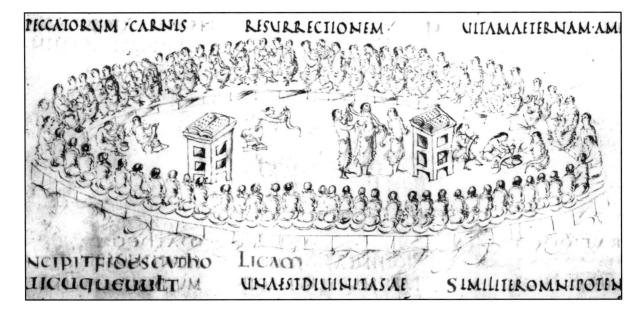

of Alexandria, denied two tenets of orthodox Christian belief: that Christ was divine and that he had always existed with God the Father. Arius held that God was by definition uncreated and unchangeable and that he had created Christ as his instrument for the redemption of humankind. Because Christ was created, Arius reasoned, he could not have been co-eternal with the Father. Orthodox Christians branded Arianism a *heresy*—the denial of a doctrine of faith. Nevertheless, Arianism enjoyed such popularity and provoked such controversy that Constantine, to whom religious disagreement meant civil disorder, interceded. In 325 he summoned a council of church leaders to Nicaea in Asia Minor and presided over it personally. The council produced the Nicene Creed, which defined the orthodox position that Christ is "eternally begotten of the Father" and of the same substance as the Father. Arius and those who refused to accept the creed were banished (this was the first case of civil punishment for heresy). The participation of Emperor Constantine in a theological dispute within the church paved the way for later emperors to claim that they could do the same.

So active was the emperor Theodosius's participation in church matters that he eventually came to loggerheads with Bishop Ambrose of Milan (339–397). Theodosius ordered Ambrose to hand over his cathedral church to the emperor. Ambrose's response had important consequences for the future:

At length came the command, "Deliver up the Basilica"; I reply, "It is not lawful for us to deliver it up, nor for your Majesty to receive it. By no law can you violate the house of a private man, and do you think that the house of God may be taken away? It is asserted that all things are lawful to the Emperor, that all things are his. But do not burden your conscience with the thought that you have any right as Emperor over sacred things. Exalt not yourself, but if you would reign the longer, be subject to God. It is written, God's to God and Caesar's to Caesar. The palace is the Emperor's, the Churches are the Bishop's. To you is committed jurisdiction over public, not over sacred buildings." [2]

Ambrose's statement was to serve as the cornerstone of the ecclesiastical theory of state-church relations throughout the Middle Ages. Ambrose insisted that the church was independent of the state's jurisdiction. He insisted that, in matters relating to the faith or to the church, the bishops were to be the judges of emperors, not the other way around. In a Christian society, harmony and peace depended on agreement between the bishop and the secular ruler. But if disagreement developed, the church was ultimately the superior power because the church was responsible for the salvation of all (including the emperor). Theodosius accepted Ambrose's argument and bowed to the church. In later centuries, theologians, canonists, and propagandists repeatedly cited Ambrose's position as the basis of relations between the two powers.

Inspired Leadership

The early Christian church benefited from the brilliant administrative abilities of some church leaders and from identification of the authority and dignity of the bishop of Rome with the grand imperial traditions of the city. Some highly able Roman citizens accepted baptism and applied their intellectual powers and administrative skills to the service of the church rather than the empire. With the empire in decay, educated people joined and worked for the church in the belief that it was the one institution able to provide leadership. Bishop Ambrose, for example, was the son of the Roman prefect of Gaul, a trained lawyer and governor of a province. He is typical of those Roman aristocrats who held high public office, were converted to Christianity, and subsequently became bishops. Such men later provided social continuity from Roman to Germanic rule. As bishop of Milan, Ambrose himself exercised considerable responsibility in the temporal as well as the ecclesiastical affairs of northern Italy.

During the reign of Diocletian (r. 284–305), the Roman Empire had been divided for administrative purposes into geographical units called "dioceses." Gradually the church made use of this organizational structure. Christian *bishops*—the leaders of early Christian communities, popularly elected by the Christian people—established their headquarters, or *sees*, in the urban centers of the old Roman dioceses. A bishop's jurisdiction extended throughout all parts of a diocese. The center of a bishop's authority was his cathedral (the word derives from the Latin *cathedra,* meaning "chair"). Thus church leaders capitalized on the

Roman imperial method of organization and adapted it to ecclesiastical purposes.

After the removal of the capital and the emperor to Constantinople (page 224), the bishop of Rome exercised vast influence in the West because he had no real competitor there. Successive bishops of Rome began to identify their religious offices with the imperial traditions of the city. They stressed that Rome had been the capital of a worldwide empire and emphasized the special importance of Rome in the framework of that empire. Successive bishops of Rome reminded Christians in other parts of the world that Rome was the burial place of Saint Peter and Saint Paul. Moreover, according to tradition, Saint Peter, the chief of Christ's apostles, had lived and been executed in Rome. No other city in the world could make such claims.

In the fifth century, the bishops of Rome began to stress Rome's supremacy over other Christian communities and to urge other churches to appeal to Rome for the resolution of complicated doctrinal issues. Thus Pope Innocent I (r. 401–417) wrote to the bishops of Africa:

[We approve your action in following the principle] that nothing which was done even in the most remote and distant provinces should be taken as finally settled unless it came to the notice of this See, that any just pronouncement might be confirmed by all the authority of this See, and that the other churches might from thence gather what they should teach.[3]

The prestige of Rome and of the church as a whole was also enhanced by the courage and leadership of the Roman bishops. According to tradition, Pope Leo I (r. 440–461) met the advancing army of Attila the Hun in 452 and, through his power of persuasion, saved Rome from destruction. Three years later Leo persuaded the Vandal leader Gaiseric not to burn the city, though the pope could not prevent a terrible sacking.

By the time Gregory I (r. 590–604) became pope, there was no civic authority left to handle the problems pressing the city. Flood, famine, plague, and invasion by the Lombards made for an almost disastrous situation. Pope Gregory concluded a peace with the Lombards, organized relief services that provided water and food for the citizens, and established hospitals for the sick and dying. The fact that it was Christian leaders, rather than imperial administrators, who responded to

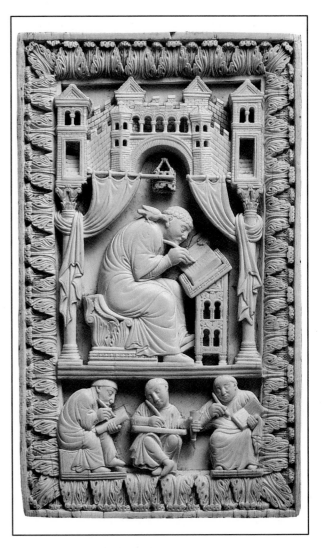

Pope Gregory I (590–604) and Scribes One of the four "Doctors" (or Learned Fathers) of the Latin Church, Gregory is shown in this tenth-century ivory book cover writing at his desk while the Holy Spirit in the form of a dove whispers in his ear. Below, scribes copy Gregory's works. *(Source: Kunsthistorisches Museum, Vienna)*

the city's dire needs could not help but increase the prestige and influence of the church.

Missionary Activity

The word *catholic* derives from a Greek word meaning "general," "universal," or "worldwide." Christ had said that his teaching was for all peoples, and Christians sought to make their faith

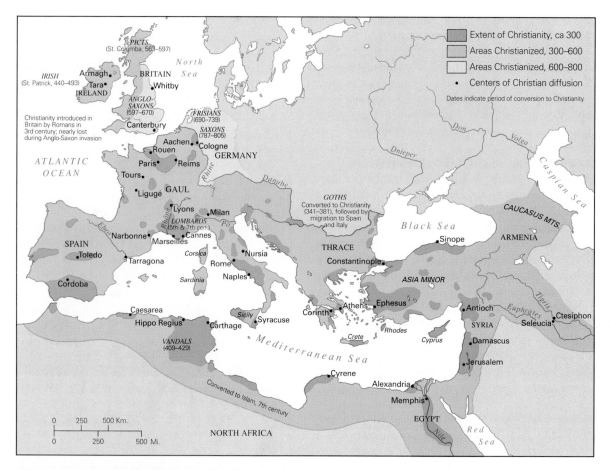

MAP 9.1 The Spread of Christianity   Originating in Judaea, the southern part of modern
Israel and Jordan, Christianity spread throughout the Roman world. Roman sea lanes
and Roman roads facilitated the expansion.

catholic—that is, believed everywhere. This goal
could be accomplished only through missionary
activity. As Saint Paul had written to the Christian
community at Colossae in Asia Minor:

*You have stripped off your old behavior with your old
self, and you have put on a new self which will progress towards true knowledge the more it is renewed in
the image of its creator; and in that image there is no
room for distinction between Greek and Jew, between
the circumcised or the uncircumcised, or between barbarian or Scythian, slave and free man. There is only
Christ; he is everything and he is in everything.*[4]

Paul urged Christians to bring the "good news" of
Christ to all peoples. The Mediterranean served as
the highway over which Christianity spread to the
cities of the empire (Map 9.1).

During the Roman occupation, communities
were scattered throughout Gaul and Britain. The
effective beginnings of Christianity in Gaul were
due to Saint Martin of Tours (ca 316–397), a Roman soldier who, after giving half of his cloak to a
naked beggar, had a vision of Christ and was baptized. Martin founded the monastery of Ligugé,
the first in Gaul, which became a center for the
evangelization of the surrounding country districts. In 372 he became bishop of Tours and introduced a rudimentary parish system. A parish is
a subdivision of a diocese, under the jurisdiction of
a priest who is responsible for the spiritual welfare
of the Christians living in the area.

Tradition strongly identifies the conversion of
Ireland with Saint Patrick (ca 385–461), one of
the most effective missionaries in history. Born in
western England to a Christian family of Roman

citizenship, Patrick was captured and enslaved by Irish raiders and taken to Ireland. He worked there for six years as a herdsman then escaped and returned to England, where a vision urged him to Christianize Ireland. In preparation, Patrick studied in Gaul and in 432 was consecrated a bishop. He landed in Ireland, and at Tara in present-day County Meath—seat of the high kings of Ireland—he made his first converts. From Tara, Patrick first baptized the king and then converted the Irish, tribe by tribe. In 445 with the approval of Pope Leo I, Patrick established his see in Armagh.

The ecclesiastical organization that Patrick set up differed in a fundamental way from church structure on the Continent: Armagh was a monastery, and the monastery, rather than the diocese, served as the center of ecclesiastical organization. Local tribes and the monastery were interdependent. The tribes supported the monastery economically, and the monastery provided religious and educational services for the tribes. Patrick introduced the Roman alphabet and supported the codification of traditional Irish laws. By the time of his death, the majority of the Irish people had received Christian baptism.

A strong missionary fervor characterized Irish Christianity. Perhaps the best representative of Irish-Celtic zeal was Saint Columba (ca 521–597), who established the monastery of Iona on an island in the Inner Hebrides off the west coast of Scotland. Iona served as a base for converting the pagan Picts of Scotland. Columba's proselytizing efforts won him the title "Apostle of Scotland," and his disciples carried the Christian Gospel to the European continent.

The Christianization of the English really began in 597, when Pope Gregory I sent a delegation of monks under the Roman Augustine (d. 604?) to Britain to convert the Angles and Saxons. Augustine's approach, like Patrick's, was to concentrate on converting the king. When he succeeded in converting Ethelbert, king of Kent, the baptism of Ethelbert's people took place as a matter of course. Augustine established his headquarters, or cathedral seat, at Canterbury, the capital of Kent. Kings who converted, such as Ethelbert and the Frankish chieftain Clovis (see page 247), sometimes had Christian wives. Besides being a sign of the personal influence that a Christian wife exerted on her husband, conversion may have indicated that barbarian kings wanted to enjoy the cultural advantages that Christianity brought, such as literate assistants and an ideological basis for their rule.

In the course of the seventh century, two Christian forces competed for the conversion of the pagan Anglo-Saxons: Roman-oriented missionaries traveling north from Canterbury and Celtic monks from Ireland and northwestern Britain. Monasteries were established at Iona, Lindisfarne, Jarrow, and Whitby (see Maps 9.1 and 9.3).

The Roman and Celtic traditions differed completely in their forms of church organization, types of monastic life, and methods of arriving at the date of Easter, the central feast of the Christian calendar. At the Synod (ecclesiastical council) of Whitby in 664, the Roman tradition was completely victorious. The conversion of the English and the close attachment of the English church to Rome had far-reaching consequences because Britain later served as a base for the Christianization of the Continent. Between the fifth and tenth centuries, the great majority of peoples living on the European continent and the nearby islands accepted the Christian religion—that is, they received baptism, though baptism in itself did not automatically transform people into Christians.

Religion influenced all aspects of tribal life. All members of a tribe participated in religious observances because doing so was a social duty. Religion was not a private or individual matter; the religion of a chieftain or king determined the religion of the people. Thus missionaries concentrated their initial efforts not on the people but on kings or tribal chieftains. According to custom, tribal chiefs negotiated with all foreign powers, including the gods. Because the Christian missionaries represented a "foreign" power (the Christian god), the king dealt with them. If a ruler accepted Christian baptism, his people also did so. The result was mass baptism.

Once a ruler had marched his people to the waters of baptism, the work of Christianization had only begun. Baptism meant either sprinkling water on the head or immersing the body in water. Conversion, however, meant mental and heartfelt acceptance of the beliefs of Christianity. What does it mean to be a Christian? This question has troubled sincere people from the time of Saint Paul to the present. The problem rests in part in the basic teaching of Jesus in the Gospel:

Then fixing his eyes on his disciples he said: "How happy are you who are poor: yours is the kingdom of

God. Happy you who are hungry now: you shall be satisfied. Happy you who weep now: you shall laugh."

"Happy are you when people hate you, drive you out, abuse you, denounce your name as criminal, on account of the Son of Man. Rejoice when that day comes and dance for joy, then your reward will be great in heaven. This was the way their ancestors treated the prophets."

The Curses
"But alas for you who are rich: you are having your consolation now. Also for you who have your fill now: you shall go hungry. Alas for you who laugh now: you shall mourn and weep."

Love of Enemies
"But I say this to you who are listening: Love your enemies, do good to those who hate you, bless those who curse you, pray for those who treat you badly. To the man who slaps you on one cheek, present the other cheek too; to the man who takes your cloak from you, do not refuse your tunic. Give to everyone who asks you, and do not ask of your property back from the man who robs you. Treat others as you would like them to treat you."[5]

These ideas are among the most radical and revolutionary that the world has heard.

The German peoples were warriors who idealized the military virtues of physical strength, ferocity in battle, and loyalty to the leader. Victors in battle enjoyed the spoils of success and plundered the vanquished. Thus the Germanic tribes found the Christian notions of sin and repentance virtually incomprehensible. In Christian thought, sin meant disobedience to the will of God as revealed in the Ten Commandments and the teachings of Christ. To the barbarians, good or "moral" behavior meant the observance of tribal customs and practices, and dishonorable behavior led to social ostracism. The inculcation of Christian ideals took a very long time.

Conversion and Assimilation

In Christian theology, conversion involves a turning toward God—that is, a conscious effort to live according to the Gospel message. How did missionaries and priests get masses of pagan and illiterate peoples to understand and live by Christian ideals and teachings? Through preaching, through assimilation, and through the penitential system. Preaching aimed at instruction and edification. Instruction presented the basic teachings of Christianity. Edification was intended to strengthen the newly baptized in their faith through stories about the lives of Christ and the saints. Deeply ingrained pagan customs and practices could not be stamped out by words alone or even by imperial edicts. Christian missionaries often pursued a policy of assimilation, easing the conversion of pagan men and women by stressing similarities between their customs and beliefs and those of Christianity. A letter that Pope Gregory I wrote to Augustine of Canterbury beautifully illustrates this policy. Sent to Augustine in Britain in 601, it expresses the pope's intention that pagan buildings and practices be given a Christian significance:

To our well beloved son Abbot Mellitus: Gregory servant of the servants of God. . . . Therefore, when . . . you reach our most reverent brother, Bishop Augustine, we wish you to inform him that we . . . have come to the conclusion that the temples of the idols among that people should on no account be destroyed. The idols are to be destroyed, but the temples themselves are to be aspersed with holy water, altars set up in them, and relics deposited there. For if these temples are well-built, they must be purified from the worship of demons and dedicated to the service of the true God. In this way . . . the people, seeing that their temples are not destroyed, may abandon their error and, flocking more readily to their accustomed resorts, may come to know and adore the true God.[6]

How assimilation works is perhaps best appreciated through the example of a festival familiar to all Americans, Saint Valentine's Day. There were two Romans named Valentine. Both were Christian priests, and both were martyred for their beliefs around the middle of February in the third century. Since about 150 B.C. the Romans had celebrated the festival of Lupercalia, at which they asked the gods for fertility for themselves, their fields, and their flocks. This celebration occurred in mid-February, shortly before the Roman New Year and the arrival of spring. Thus the early church "converted" the old festival of Lupercalia into Saint Valentine's Day. (Nothing in the lives of the two Christian martyrs connects them with lovers or with the exchange of messages and gifts.

The Pantheon (Interior)   Originally a temple for the gods, the Pantheon later served as a Christian church. As such, it symbolizes the adaptation of pagan elements to Christian purposes. *(Source: Alinari/Art Resource)*

That practice began in the later Middle Ages.) The fourteenth of February was still celebrated as a festival, but it had taken on Christian meaning.

Probably more immediate in its impact on the unconverted masses was the penitential system. *Penitentials* were manuals for the examination of conscience. Irish priests wrote the earliest ones, which English missionaries then carried to the Continent. An illiterate penitent knelt beside a priest, who questioned the penitent about sins he or she might have committed. The recommended penance was then imposed. Penance usually meant fasting for three days each week on bread and water, which served as a "medicine" for the soul. Here is a section of the penitential prepared by Archbishop Theodore of Canterbury (r. 668–690), which circulated widely at the time:

If anyone commits fornication with a virgin he shall do penance for one year. If with a married woman, he shall do penance for four years, two of these entire, and in the other two during the three forty-day periods and three days a week.

A male who commits fornication with a male shall do penance for three years.

If a woman practices vice with a woman, she shall do penance for three years.

Whoever has often committed theft, seven years is his penance, or such a sentence as his priest shall determine, that is, according to what can be arranged with those whom he has wronged. . . .

If a layman slays another with malice aforethought, if he will not lay aside his arms, he shall do penance for seven years; without flesh and wine, three years. . . .

Women who commit abortion before the fetus has life, shall do penance for one year or for the three forty-day periods or for forty days, according to the nature of the offense; and if later, that is, more than forty days after conception, they shall do penance as murderesses, that is, for three years on Wednesdays and Fridays and in the three forty-day periods. This according to the canons is judged punishable by ten years. . . .

If a poor woman slays her child, she shall do penance for seven years. In the canon it is said that if it is a case of homicide, she shall do penance for ten years.[7]

As this sample suggests, writers of penitentials were preoccupied with sexual transgressions. Penitentials are much more akin to the Jewish law of the Old Testament than to the spirit of the New Testament. They provide an enormous amount of information about the ascetic ideals of early Christianity and about the crime-ridden realities of Celtic and Germanic societies. Penitentials also reveal the ecclesiastical foundations of some modern attitudes toward sex, birth control, and abortion. Most important, the penitential system contributed to the growth of a different attitude toward religion: formerly public, corporate, and social, religious observances became private, personal, and individual.[8]

CHRISTIAN ATTITUDES TOWARD CLASSICAL CULTURE

Probably the major dilemma faced by the early Christian church concerned Greco-Roman culture. The Roman Empire as a social, political, and economic force gradually disintegrated. Its culture, however, survived. In Greek philosophy, art, and architecture, in Roman law, literature, education, and engineering, the legacy of a great civilization continued. The Christian religion had begun and spread within this intellectual and psychological milieu. What was to be the attitude of Christians to the Greco-Roman world of ideas?

Hostility

Christians in the first and second centuries believed that the end of the world was near. Christ had promised to return, and Christians expected to witness that return. Thus they considered knowledge useless and learning a waste of time. The important duty of the Christian was to prepare for the Second Coming of the Lord.

Early Christians harbored a strong hatred of pagan Roman culture—in fact, of all Roman civilization. Had not the Romans crucified Christ? Had not the Romans persecuted Christians and subjected them to the most horrible tortures? Did not the Book of Revelation in the New Testament call Rome the great whore of the world, filled with corruption, sin, and every kind of evil? Roman culture was sexual, sensual, and materialistic. The sensual poetry of Ovid, the political poetry of Virgil, even the rhetorical brilliance of Cicero represented a threat, in the eyes of serious Christians, to the spiritual aims and ideals of Christianity. Good Christians who sought the Kingdom of Heaven through the imitation of Christ believed they had to disassociate themselves from the "filth" that Roman culture embodied.

As Saint Paul wrote, "The wisdom of the world is foolishness, we preach Christ crucified." Tertullian (ca 160–220), an influential African Christian writer, condemned all secular literature as foolishness in the eyes of God. "What has Athens to do with Jerusalem," he demanded, "the Academy with the Church? We have no need for curiosity since Jesus Christ, nor for inquiry since the gospel." Tertullian insisted that Christians would find in the Bible all the wisdom they needed.

Compromise and Adjustment

At the same time, Christianity encouraged adjustment to the ideas and institutions of the Roman world. Some biblical texts clearly urged Christians to accept the existing social, economic, and political establishment. Specifically addressing Christians living among non-Christians in the hostile environment of Rome, the author of the First Letter of Saint Peter had written about the obligations of Christians:

Toward Pagans
Always behave honourably among pagans, so that they can see your good works for themselves and, when the day of reckoning comes, give thanks to God for the things which now make them denounce you as criminals.

Toward Civil Authority

For the sake of the Lord, accept the authority of every social institution: the emperor, as the supreme authority, and the governors as commissioned by him to punish criminals and praise good citizenship. God wants you to be good citizens. . . . Have respect for everyone and love for your community; fear God and honour the emperor.[9]

Christians really had little choice. Greco-Roman culture was the only culture they knew. Only men received a formal education, and they went through the traditional curriculum of grammar and rhetoric. They learned to be effective speakers in the forum or law courts. No other system of education existed. Many early Christians had grown up as pagans, been educated as pagans, and been converted only as adults. Toward homosexuality, for example, according to a recent controversial study, Christians of the first three or four centuries simply imbibed the attitude of the world in which they lived. Many Romans indulged in homosexual activity, and contemporaries did not consider such behavior (or inclinations to it) immoral, bizarre, or harmful. Several emperors were openly homosexual, and homosexuals participated freely in all aspects of Roman life and culture. Early Christians, too, considered homosexuality a conventional expression of physical desire and were no more susceptible to antihomosexual prejudices than pagans were. Some prominent Christians experienced loving same-gender relationships that probably had a sexual element. What eventually led to a change in public and Christian attitudes toward sexual behavior was the shift from the sophisticated urban culture of the Greco-Roman world to the rural culture of medieval Europe.[10]

Even if early Christians had wanted to give up classical ideas and patterns of thought, they would have had great difficulty doing so. Therefore, they had to adapt their Roman education to their Christian beliefs. Saint Paul himself believed there was a good deal of truth in pagan thought, as long as it was correctly interpreted and understood.

The result was a compromise. Christians gradually came to terms with Greco-Roman culture. Saint Jerome (340–419), a distinguished theologian and linguist, remains famous for his translation of the Old and New Testaments from Hebrew and Greek into vernacular Latin. Called the "Vulgate," his edition of the Bible served as the official translation until the sixteenth century; even today, scholars rely on it. Saint Jerome was also familiar with the writings of such classical authors as Cicero, Virgil, and Terence. He believed that Christians should study the best of ancient thought because it would direct their minds to God. Jerome maintained that the best ancient literature should be interpreted in light of the Christian faith.

Synthesis: Saint Augustine

The finest representative of the blending of classical and Christian ideas, and indeed one of the most brilliant thinkers in the history of the Western world, was Saint Augustine of Hippo (354–430). Aside from the scriptural writers, no

The Antioch Chalice This earliest surviving Christian chalice, which dates from the fourth century A.D., combines the typical Roman shape with Christian motifs. The chalice is decorated with figures of Christ and the apostles, leaves, and grapes, which represent the sacrament of the Eucharist. *(Source: The Metropolitan Museum of Art; The Cloisters Collection. Purchase, 1950 (50.4))*

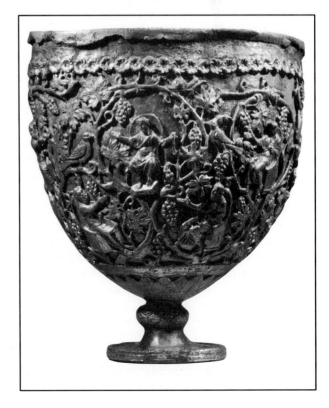

one else has had a greater impact on Christian thought in succeeding centuries. Saint Augustine was born into an urban family in what is now Algeria in North Africa. His father was a pagan, his mother a devout Christian. Because his family was poor—his father was a minor civil servant—the only avenue to success in a highly competitive world was a classical education.

Augustine's mother believed that a good classical education, though pagan, would make her son a better Christian, so Augustine's father scraped together the money to educate him. The child received his basic education in the local school. By modern and even medieval standards, that education was extremely narrow: textual study of the writings of the poet Virgil, the orator-politician Cicero, the historian Sallust, and the playwright Terence. At that time, learning meant memorization. Education in the late Roman world aimed at appreciation of words, particularly those of renowned and eloquent orators.

At the age of seventeen, Augustine went to nearby Carthage to continue his education. There he took a mistress with whom he lived for fifteen years. At Carthage, Augustine entered a difficult psychological phase and began an intellectual and spiritual pilgrimage that led him through experiments with several philosophies and heretical Christian sects. In 383 he traveled to Rome, where he endured illness and disappointment in his teaching: his students fled when their bills were due.

Finally, in Milan in 387, through the insights he gained from reading Saint Paul's *Letter to the Romans*, Augustine received Christian baptism. He later became bishop of the seacoast city of Hippo Regius in his native North Africa (see Map 9.1). He was a renowned preacher to Christians there, a vigorous defender of orthodox Christianity, and the author of over ninety-three books and treatises.

Augustine's autobiography, *The Confessions*, is a literary masterpiece and one of the most influential books in the history of Europe. Written in the form of a prayer, its language is often incredibly beautiful:

Too late have I loved thee, O beauty ever ancient and ever new, too late have I loved thee! And behold! Thou wert within and I without, and it was without that I sought thee. Thou wert with me, and I was not with

thee. Those creatures held me far from thee which, were they not in thee, were not at all. Thou didst call, thou didst cry, thou didst break in upon my deafness; thou didst gleam forth, thou didst shine out, thou didst banish my blindness; thou didst send forth thy fragrance, and I drew breath and yearned for thee; I tasted and still hunger and thirst; thou didst touch me, and I was on flame to find thy peace.[11]

The Confessions describes Augustine's moral struggle, the conflict between his spiritual and intellectual aspirations and his sensual and material self. *The Confessions* reveals the change and development of a human mind and personality steeped in the philosophy and culture of the ancient world.

Many Greek and Roman philosophers had taught that knowledge and virtue are the same: a person who really knows what is right will do what is right. Augustine rejected this idea. He believed that a person may know what is right but fail to act righteously because of the innate weakness of the human will. People do not always act on the basis of rational knowledge. Here Augustine made a profound contribution to the understanding of human nature: he demonstrated that a learned person can also be corrupt and evil. *The Confessions*, written in the rhetorical style and language of late Roman antiquity, marks the synthesis of Greco-Roman forms and Christian thought.

Augustine also contributed to the discussion on the nature of the church that arose around the Donatist heretical movement. Promoted by Donatus, the North African bishop of Carthage, Donatism denied the value of sacraments administered by priests or bishops who had denied their faith under persecution or had committed grave sin. For the Donatists, the holiness of the minister was as important as the sacred rites he performed. Donatists viewed themselves as a separate "chosen people" who had preserved their purity and identity in a corrupt world. Thus they viewed the church as a small spiritual elite that was an alternative to society. Augustine responded to Donatism with extensive preaching and the treatise *On Baptism and Against the Donatists* (A.D. 400), written in the best classical Latin. He argued that, through the working of God's action, the rites of the church have an objective and permanent validity, regardless of a priest's spiritual condition. Being a Christian and a member of the church, Augustine maintained, meant striving for holiness, and rather than seeing oneself as apart from society, the Christian must live in and transform society. The notion of the church as a special spiritual elite, distinct from and superior to the rest of society, recurred many times in the Middle Ages. Each time it was branded a heresy, and Augustine's arguments were marshaled against it.

When the Visigothic chieftain Alaric conquered Rome in 410, horrified pagans blamed the disaster on the Christians. In response, Augustine wrote *City of God*. This profoundly original work contrasts Christianity with the secular society in which it existed. *City of God* presents a moral interpretation of the Roman government—in fact, of all history. Written in Latin and filled with references to ancient history and mythology, it remained for centuries the standard statement of the Christian philosophy of history.

According to Augustine, history is the account of God acting in time. Human history reveals that there are two kinds of people: those who live according to the flesh in the city of Babylon and those who live according to the spirit in the City of God. The former will endure eternal hellfire, the latter eternal bliss.

Augustine maintained that states came into existence as the result of Adam's fall and people's inclination to sin. The state is a necessary evil, responsible only for providing the peace and order that Christians need in order to pursue their pilgrimage to the City of God. The particular form of government—whether monarchy, aristocracy, or democracy—is basically irrelevant. Any civil government that fails to provide justice is no more than a band of gangsters.

Since the state results from moral lapse, from sin, it follows that the church, which is concerned with salvation, is responsible for everyone, including Christian rulers. Churchmen in the Middle Ages used Augustine's theory to defend their belief in the ultimate superiority of the spiritual power over the temporal. This remained the dominant political theory until the late thirteenth century.

Augustine had no objection to drawing on pagan knowledge to support Christian thought. Augustine used Roman history as evidence to defend Christian theology. In doing so, he assimilated Roman history, and indeed all of classical culture, into Christian teaching.

MONASTICISM AND THE RULE OF SAINT BENEDICT

Christianity began and spread as a city religion. Since the first century, however, some especially pious Christians had felt that the only alternative to the decadence of urban life was complete separation from the world. All-consuming pursuit of material things, gross sexual promiscuity, and general political corruption disgusted them. They believed that the Christian life as set forth in the Gospel could not be lived in the midst of such immorality. They rejected the established values of Roman society and were the first real nonconformists in the church.

Beginnings

Intellectual currents widespread in Syria, Egypt, and Palestine in the first and second centuries influenced the development of monasticism. One such current was *gnosticism,* a religious and philosophical movement that combined astrology, magic, elements of the Jewish tradition, Persian mysticism, and the Platonic dualism of mind and spirit (see page 141). The term *gnosis* means "knowledge," and some Christian gnostic sects claimed to possess a secret tradition that Jesus had taught the apostles in private. Gnostics believed in a dualism of spirit and matter, of mind and body; they stressed that all matter was evil and that the soul must strive through knowledge *(gnosis)* to free itself from family ties, material possessions and worldly obligations, and sexual desires. Gnostics held to a fierce determinism or predestinarianism. They believed that the vast majority of people were earthly clods damned to destruction but the few gnostics were the elect, their souls containing elements of the divine. Orthodox Christian teaching condemned these ideas, but they permeated monastic thought as it evolved in the West and later Sufi mysticism as that movement grew in Islam (see page 284).

The fourth century witnessed a significant change in the relationship of Christianity and the broader society. Until Constantinople's legalization of Christianity, Christians were a persecuted minority. The persecutions of Decius in 250 and Diocletian in 304 were especially severe. Christians greatly revered the men and women who suffered and died for their faith, the *martyrs*. They, like Jesus, made the ultimate sacrifice. The martyrs were the great heroes of the early Church. When Christianity was legalized and the persecutions ended, a new problem arose. Where Christians had been a suffering minority, now they came to be identified with the state: non-Christians could not advance in the imperial service. And if Christianity had triumphed, so had "the world," since secular attitudes and values pervaded the church. The church of martyrs no longer existed. Some scholars believe that the monasteries provided a way of life for those Christians who wanted to make a total response to Christ's teachings, people who wanted more than a lukewarm Christianity. The monks became the new martyrs. Saint Anthony of Egypt (d. 356), the first monk for whom there is concrete evidence and the father of monasticism, went to Alexandria during the last persecution in the hope of gaining martyrdom. Christians believed that monks, like the martyrs before them, could speak for God and that their prayers had special influence with God.

At first individuals and small groups left the cities and went to live in caves or rude shelters in the desert or mountains. These people were called "hermits," from the Greek word *eremos*, meaning "desert." There is no way of knowing how many hermits there were in the fourth and fifth centuries, partly because their conscious aim was a secret, hidden life known only to God.

In western Europe, several factors worked against the eremitical variety of monasticism. The cold, snow, ice, and fog that covered much of Europe for many months of the year discouraged isolated living. Dense forests filled with wild animals and wandering barbaric German tribes presented obvious dangers. Furthermore, church leaders did not really approve of eremitical life. Hermits sometimes claimed to have mystical experiences, direct communications with God. No one could verify these experiences. If hermits could communicate directly with the Lord, what need had they for the priest and the institutional church? The church hierarchy, or leaders, encouraged *coenobitic monasticism*—that is, communal living in monasteries. Communal living provided an environment for training the aspirant in the virtues of charity, poverty, and freedom from self-deception. The Egyptian ascetic Pachomius (290–346/7) organized the first successful coenobitic community at Tabennisi on the Upper Nile. It drew thousands of recruits.

In the fifth and sixth centuries, many experiments in communal monasticism were made in Gaul, Italy, Spain, Anglo-Saxon England, and Ireland. After studying both eremitical and coenobitic monasticism in Egypt and Syria, John Cassian established two monasteries near Marseilles in Gaul around 415. One of Cassian's books, *Conferences,* based on conversations he had had with holy men in the East, discussed the dangers of the isolated hermit's life. The abbey or monastery of Lérins on the Mediterranean Sea near Cannes (ca 410) also had significant contacts with monastic centers in the Middle East and North Africa. Lérins encouraged the severely penitential and extremely ascetic behavior common in the East, such as long hours of prayer, fasting, and self-flagellation. It was this tradition of harsh self-mortification that the Roman-British monk Saint Patrick carried from Lérins to Ireland in the fifth century. Church organization in Ireland became closely associated with the monasteries, and Irish monastic life followed the ascetic Eastern form.

Around 540 the Roman senator Cassiodorus retired from public service and established a monastery, the Vivarium, on his estate in Italy. Cassiodorus wanted the Vivarium to become an educational and cultural center and enlisted highly educated and sophisticated men for it. He set the monks to copying both sacred and secular manuscripts, intending this task to be their sole occupation. Cassiodorus started the association of monasticism with scholarship and learning. This association developed into a great tradition in the medieval and modern worlds. But Cassiodorus's experiment did not become the most influential form of monasticism in European society. The fifth and sixth centuries witnessed the appearance of many other monastic lifestyles.

The Rule of Saint Benedict

In 529 Benedict of Nursia (480–543), who had experimented with both the eremitical and the communal forms of monastic life, wrote a brief set of regulations for the monks who had gathered around him at Monte Cassino between Rome and Naples. Recent research has shown that Benedict's *Rule* derives from a longer, more detailed and anonymously written document known as *The Rule*

St. Benedict   Holding his *Rule* in his left hand, the seated and cowled Patriarch of Western Monasticism blesses the abbot of Monte Cassino with his right hand. The monastery is in the background. *(Source: Biblioteca Apostolica Vaticana)*

of the Master, which was actually suitable only for the place for which it was written. Benedict's guide for monastic life proved more adaptable and slowly replaced all others. *The Rule of Saint Benedict* has influenced all forms of organized religious life in the Roman church.

Saint Benedict conceived of his *Rule* as a simple code for ordinary men. It outlined a monastic life of regularity, discipline, and moderation. Each monk had ample food and adequate sleep. Self-destructive acts of mortification were forbidden. In an atmosphere of silence, a monk spent part of the day in formal prayer, which Benedict called the "Work of God." This consisted of chanting psalms and other prayers from the Bible in the part of the monastery church called the "choir." The rest of the day was passed in study and manual labor. After a year of probation, a monk made three vows. First the monk vowed stability: he promised to live his entire life in the monastery of his profession.

The vow of stability was Saint Benedict's major contribution to Western monasticism; his object was to prevent the wandering so common in his day. Second, the monk vowed conversion of manners—that is, to strive to improve himself and to come closer to God. Third, he promised obedience, the most difficult vow because it meant the complete surrender of his will to the *abbot,* or head of the monastery.

The Rule of Saint Benedict expresses the assimilation of the Roman spirit into Western monasticism. It reveals the logical mind of its creator and the Roman concern for order, organization, and respect for law. Its spirit of moderation and flexibility is reflected in the patience, wisdom, and understanding with which the abbot is to govern and, indeed, with which life is to be led. The *Rule* could be used in vastly different physical and geographical circumstances, in damp and cold Germany as well as in warm and sunny Italy. The *Rule* was quickly adapted for women, and many convents of nuns were established in the early Middle Ages.

Saint Benedict's *Rule* implies that a person who wants to become a monk or nun need have no previous ascetic experience or even a particularly strong bent toward the religious life. Thus it allowed for the admission of newcomers with different backgrounds and personalities. From Chapter 59, "The Offering of Sons by Nobles or by the Poor," and from Benedict's advice to the abbot in Chapter 2—"The abbot should avoid all favoritism in the monastery. . . . A man born free is not to be given higher rank than a slave who becomes a monk"—it is clear that men of different social classes belonged to his monastery. This flexibility helps to explain the attractiveness of Benedictine monasticism throughout the centuries. *The Rule of Saint Benedict* is a superior example of the way in which the Greco-Roman heritage and Roman patterns of thought were preserved.

At the same time, the *Rule* no more provides a picture of actual life in a Benedictine abbey of the seventh or eighth (or twentieth) century than the American Constitution of 1789 describes living conditions in the United States today. A code of laws cannot do that. *The Rule of Saint Benedict* had one fundamental purpose: to draw the individual slowly but steadily away from attachment to the world and love of self and toward the love of God.

The Success of Benedictine Monasticism

Why was the Benedictine form of monasticism so successful? Why did it eventually replace other forms of Western monasticism? The answer lies partly in its spirit of flexibility and moderation and partly in the balanced life that it provided. Early Benedictine monks and nuns spent part of the day in prayer, part in study or in some other form of intellectual activity, and part in manual labor. The monastic life as conceived by Saint Benedict did not lean too heavily in any one direction; it struck a balance between asceticism and idleness. It thus provided opportunities for persons of entirely different abilities and talents—from mechanics to gardeners to literary scholars. Benedict's *Rule* contrasts sharply with Cassiodorus's narrow concept of the monastery as a place for aristocratic scholars and bibliophiles.

Benedictine monasticism also suited the social circumstances of early medieval society. The German invasions had fragmented European life: the self-sufficient rural estate replaced the city as the basic unit of civilization. A monastery, too, had to be economically self-sufficient. It was supposed to produce from its lands and properties all that was needed for food, clothing, shelter, and liturgical service of the altar. The monastery fitted in—indeed, represented—the trend toward localism.

Benedictine monasticism also succeeded partly because it was so materially successful. In the seventh and eighth centuries, monasteries pushed back forest and wasteland, drained swamps, and experimented with crop rotation. For example, the abbey of Saint Wandrille, founded in 645 near Rouen in northwestern Gaul, sent squads of monks to clear the forests that surrounded it. Within seventy-five years, the abbey was immensely wealthy. The abbey of Jumièges, also in the diocese of Rouen, followed much the same pattern. Such Benedictine houses made a significant contribution to the agricultural development of Europe. The communal nature of their organization, whereby property was held in common and profits pooled and reinvested, made this contribution possible.

Finally, monasteries conducted schools for local young people. Some learned about prescriptions and herbal remedies and went on to provide medical treatment for their localities. A few copied manuscripts and wrote books. This training did not go unappreciated in a society desperately in need of it. Local and royal governments drew on the services of the literate men and able administrators produced by the monasteries. This was not what Saint Benedict had intended, but the effectiveness of the institution that he designed made it perhaps inevitable.

THE MIGRATION OF THE GERMANIC PEOPLES

The migration of peoples from one area to another has been a dominant and continuing feature of European history. Mass movements of Europeans occurred in the fourth through sixth centuries, in the ninth and tenth centuries, and in the twelfth and thirteenth centuries. From the sixteenth century to the present, such movements have been almost continuous, involving not just the European continent but the entire world. The causes have varied and are not thoroughly understood by scholars. But there is no question that migration profoundly affects both the regions to which peoples move and the ones they leave behind.

The *Völkerwanderungen,* or migrations of the Germanic peoples, were important in the decline of the Roman Empire. Many twentieth-century historians and sociologists have tried to explain who the Germans were and why they migrated, but scholars have not had much success at answering these questions. The surviving evidence is primarily archeological, scanty, and not yet adequately explored. As an authority on the Ostrogoths recently wrote, "Despite a century of keen historical investigation and archaeological excavation, the cause and nature of the *Völkerwanderung* challenge the inquirer as much as ever." Perhaps overpopulation and the resulting food shortages caused migration. Perhaps victorious tribes forced the vanquished to move southward. Probably the "primary stimulus for this gradual migration was the Roman frontier, which increasingly offered service in the army and work for pay around the camps."[12]

The answers that do exist rest on archeological evidence—bone fossils, cooking utensils, jewelry, instruments of war, and other artifacts—found later inside the borders of the Roman Empire. Like the Vikings, who first terrorized and then settled in many sections of Europe in the ninth and tenth centuries, the Germans inhabited the regions of present-day northern Germany, southern Sweden and Denmark, and the shores of the Baltic. At the time of their migrations, they had little ethnic solidarity.

Since about 150, Germanic tribes had pressed along the Rhine-Danube frontier of the Roman Empire. Depending on their closeness to that border, these tribes differed considerably from one another in level of civilization. Some tribes, such as the Visigoths and Ostrogoths, led a settled existence, engaged in agriculture and trade, and accepted Arian Christianity. Tribes such as the Anglo-Saxons and the Huns, who lived far from the Roman frontiers, were not affected by the civilizing influences of Rome. They remained nomadic, even barbaric, peoples.

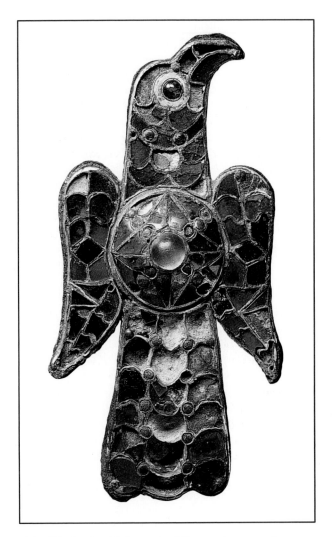

Visigothic Eagle (Sixth century) The eagle was a standard symbol of nobility and power among the Germanic peoples. A fine example of Visigothic craftsmanship, this richly jewelled eagle—worn as a cloak clasp or as a brooch—could be afforded only by the wealthiest and most powerful members of the nobility. *(Source: Walters Art Gallery, Baltimore)*

Historians do not know exactly when the Mongolian tribe called the Huns began to move westward from China, but about 370 they pressured the Goths living along the Rhine-Danube frontier. The Huns easily defeated the Ostrogoths, and the frightened Visigoths petitioned the emperor to be allowed to settle within the empire. Once inside, however, they revolted. In 378 a Visigothic army decisively defeated the emperor's army. This date

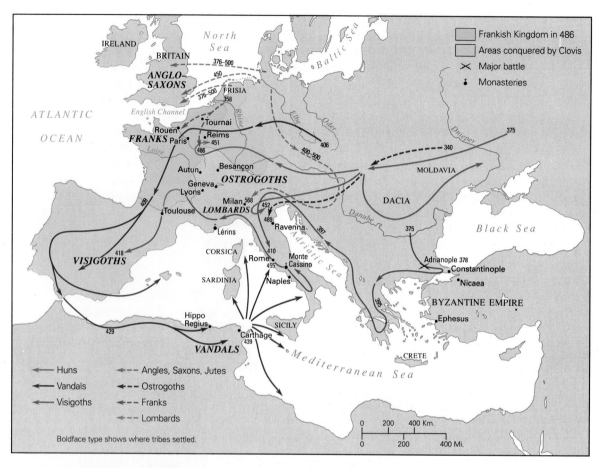

MAP 9.2 The Germanic Migrations The Germanic tribes infiltrated and settled in all parts of western Europe. The Huns, who were not German ethnically, originated in central Asia. The Huns' victory over the Ostrogoths led the emperor to allow the Visigoths to settle within the empire, a decision that proved disastrous for Rome.

marks the beginning of massive Germanic invasions into the empire (Map 9.2).

Some tribes that settled within the borders of the Roman Empire numbered perhaps no more than ten thousand individuals. Others, such as the Ostrogoths and Visigoths, were about twenty or thirty times larger. Because they settled near and quickly intermingled with Romans and Romanized peoples, it is impossible to specify numbers of original migrators. Dense forests, poor soil, and inadequate equipment probably kept food production low. This meant that the Germans could not increase very rapidly in their new locations.

Except for the Lombards, whose conquests of Italy persisted into the mid-eighth century, the movements of Germanic peoples on the Continent ended about 600. Between 450 and 565, the Germans established a number of kingdoms, but none except the Frankish kingdom lasted very long. Since the German kingdoms were not states with definite geographical boundaries, their locations are approximate. The Visigoths overran much of southwestern Gaul. Establishing their headquarters at Toulouse, they exercised a weak domination over Spain until a great Muslim victory at Guadalete in 711 ended Visigothic rule. The Vandals, whose destructive ways are commemorated in the word *vandal,* settled in North Africa. In northern and western Europe in the sixth century, the Burgundians established rule over lands roughly circumscribed by the old Roman army camps at Lyon, Besançon, Geneva, and Autun.

In northern Italy, the Ostrogothic king Theodoric (r. 474–526) pursued a policy of assimilation between Germans and Romans. He maintained close relations with the Roman emperor at Constantinople and drew Roman scholars and diplomats into the royal civil service. He was a crude German, however, whose reign was disliked by pagan Roman aristocrats. Moreover, he was an Arian Christian, so Roman Catholics disliked him as heretical. His royal administration fell apart during Justinian's sixth-century reconquest of Italy. War and plague then made northern Italy ripe for Lombard conquest in the seventh century.

The most enduring Germanic kingdom was established by the Frankish chieftain Clovis (r. 481–511). Originally only a petty chieftain with headquarters in the region of Tournai in northwestern Gaul (modern Belgium), Clovis began to expand his territories in 486. His defeat of the Gallo-Roman general Syagrius extended his jurisdiction to the Loire River. Clovis's conversion to orthodox Christianity in 496 won him the crucial support of the papacy and the bishops of Gaul. As the defender of Roman Catholicism against heretical German tribes, he went on to conquer the Visigoths, extending his domain as far as the Pyrenees and making Paris his headquarters. Because he was descended from the half-legendary chieftain Merovech, the dynasty founded by Clovis has been called "Merovingian." Clovis's sons subjugated the Burgundians in eastern Gaul and the Ostrogothic tribes living north of the Alps.

Baptism of Clovis (A.D. 496) In this ninth-century ivory carving, St. Remi, bishop of Reims, baptizes the Frankish chieftain by immersing him in a pool of water. Legend holds that on this occasion a dove brought a vial of holy oil from heaven, later used in the coronations of French kings. *(Source: Musée Condé. Chantilly/Laurie Platt Winfrey, Inc.)*

GERMANIC SOCIETY

The Germans replaced the Romans as rulers of most of the European continent, and German customs and traditions formed the basis of European society for centuries. What patterns of social, political, and economic life characterized the Germans?

Scholars are hampered in answering this question because the Germans could not write and thus kept no records before their conversion to Christianity. The earliest information about them comes from moralistic accounts by such Romans as the historian Tacitus, who was acquainted only with the tribes living closest to the borders of the empire. Furthermore, Tacitus wrote his *Germania* at the end of the first century A.D., and by the fifth century German practices differed from those of Tacitus's time. Current knowledge of the Germans depends largely on records written in the sixth and seventh centuries and projected backward.

Kinship, Custom, and Class

The Germans had no notion of the *state* as the term is used in the twentieth century; they thought in social, not political terms. The basic Germanic social unit was the *folk*, or tribe. Members of the folk believed that they were all descended from a common ancestor. Blood united them. Kinship protected them. Law was custom—unwritten, preserved in the minds of the elders of the tribe, and handed down by word of mouth from generation to generation. Custom regulated everything. Every tribe had its customs, and every member of the tribe knew what they were. Members were subject to their tribe's customary law wherever they went, and friendly tribes respected one another's laws.

Germanic tribes were led by kings or tribal chieftains. The chief was that member of the folk recognized as the strongest and bravest in battle, elected from among the male members of the strongest family. He led the tribe in war, settled disputes among its members, conducted negotiations with outside powers, and offered sacrifices to the gods. The period of migrations and conquests of the western Roman Empire witnessed the strengthening of kingship among the Germanic tribes. Tribes that did not migrate did not develop kings.

Closely associated with the king in some southern tribes was the *comitatus*, or war band. Writing at the end of the first century, Tacitus described the war band as the bravest young men in the tribe. They swore loyalty to the chief, fought with him in battle, and were not supposed to leave the battlefield without him; to do so implied cowardice and disloyalty and brought social disgrace. Social egalitarianism existed among members of the war band.

During the *Völkerwanderungen* of the fourth century, however, and as a result of constant warfare, the war band was transformed into a system of stratified ranks. For example, among the Ostrogoths a warrior nobility and several other nobilities evolved. Contact with the Romans, who produced armbands for trade with the barbarians, stimulated demand for armbands. Ostrogothic warriors wanted armbands because of the status and distinctiveness that they conferred. Thus armbands, especially the gold ones reserved for the "royal families," promoted the development of hierarchical ranks within war bands. During the Ostrogothic conquest of Italy under Theodoric, warrior-nobles also sought to acquire land, both as a mark of prestige and as a means to power. As land and wealth came into the hands of a small elite class, social inequalities emerged and were gradually strengthened.[13] These inequalities help to explain the origins of the European noble class (see page 334).

Law

As long as custom determined all behavior, the early Germans had no need for written law. Beginning in the late sixth century, however, German tribal chieftains began to collect, write, and publish lists of their customs. Why then? The Christian missionaries who were slowly converting the Germans to Christianity wanted to know the tribal customs, and they encouraged German rulers to set down their customs in written form. Churchmen wanted to read about German ways in order to assimilate the tribes to Christianity. Augustine of Canterbury, for example, persuaded King Ethelbert of Kent to have his folk laws written down: these *Dooms of Ethelbert* date from 601 to 604, roughly five years after Augustine's arrival in Britain. Moreover, by the sixth century the German kings needed rules and regulations for the

Romans living under their jurisdiction as well as for their own people.

Today if a person holds up a bank, American law maintains that the robber attacks both the bank and the state in which it exists—a sophisticated notion involving the abstract idea of the state. In early German law, all crimes were regarded as crimes against a person.

According to the code of the Salian Franks, every person had a particular monetary value to the tribe. This value was called the *wergeld,* which literally means "man-money" or "money to buy off the spear." Men of fighting age had the highest wergeld, then women of child-bearing age, then children, and finally the aged. Everyone's value reflected his or her potential military worthiness. If a person accused of a crime agreed to pay the wergeld and if the victim and his or her family accepted the payment, there was peace (hence the expression "money to buy off the spear"). If the accused refused to pay the wergeld or if the victim's family refused to accept it, a blood feud ensued. Individuals depended on their kin for protection, and kinship served as a force of social control.

Historians and sociologists have difficulty applying the early law codes, partly because they are patchwork affairs studded with additions made in later centuries. For example, the Salic Law—the law code of the Salian Franks issued by Clovis—offers a general picture of Germanic life and problems in the early Middle Ages and is typical of the law codes of other tribes, such as the Visigoths, Burgundians, Lombards, and Anglo-Saxons.

The Salic Law lists the money fines to be paid to the victim or the family for such injuries as theft, rape, assault, arson, and murder:

If any person strike another on the head so that the brain appears, and the three bones which lie above the brain shall project, he shall be sentenced to 1200 denars, which make 300 shillings. . . .

If any one have hit a free woman who is pregnant, and she dies, he shall be sentenced to 2800 denars, which make 700 shillings.

If any one have killed a free woman after she has begun bearing children, he shall be sentenced to 2400 denars, which make 600 shillings.

If any one shall have drawn a harrow through another's harvest after it has sprouted, or shall have gone through it with a wagon where there was no

road, he shall be sentenced to 120 denars, which make 30 shillings.[14]

This is really not a code of law at all but a list of tariffs or fines for particular offenses. German law aimed at the prevention or reduction of violence. It was not concerned with abstract justice.

At first, Romans had been subject to Roman law and Germans to Germanic custom. As German kings accepted Christianity and as Romans and Germans increasingly intermarried, the distinction between the two laws blurred and, in the course of the seventh and eighth centuries, disappeared. The result was a new feudal law, to which Romans and Germans were subject alike.

German Life

How did the Germans live? The dark, dense forests that dotted the continent of Europe were the most important physical and psychological factor in the lives of the Germanic peoples who were not quickly Romanized. Forests separated one tribe from another. The pagan Germans believed that gods and spirits inhabited the forests. Trees were holy, and to cut them down was an act of grave sacrilege. Thus the Germans cut no trees. They also feared building a mill or a bridge on a river, lest the river spirit be offended. This attitude prevented the clearing of land for farming and tended to keep the Germans isolated.

In the course of the sixth through eighth centuries, the Germans slowly adapted to Greco-Roman and Christian attitudes and patterns of behavior. Acceptance of Christianity and the end of animistic beliefs that spiritual forces live in natural objects had profound consequences. In fact, the decline of animistic beliefs marks a turning point in the economic and intellectual progress of the West. A more settled, less nomadic way of life developed as people no longer feared to make use of natural resources such as rivers and forests. Once animistic beliefs were dispelled, the forests were opened to use, and all members of the community had common rights in them. Trees provided wood for building and for fuel; the forests served as the perfect place for grazing animals. The steady reduction of forest land between the sixth and thirteenth centuries was a major step in the agricultural development of Europe.

Vandal Landowner   The adoption of Roman dress—short tunic, cloak, and sandals—reflects the way the Germanic tribes accepted Roman lifestyles. Likewise both the mosaic art form and the man's stylized appearance show the Germans' assimilation of Roman influences. (Notice that the rider has a saddle but not stirrups.) *(Source: Courtesy of the Trustees of the British Museum)*

Migrating Germans clustered in small settlements of a few families each. For example, the groups of Ostrogoths who settled in Moldavia in present-day central Romania lived in small, one-room huts in widely scattered villages near rivers. The huts were constructed of mud, wood, or *wattle* (poles intertwined with twigs or reeds) and were scattered over small clearings without alignment or evidence of town planning.

The closer they settled to sites of Roman civilization, such as Roman towns or army camps, the more quickly the Germans were Romanized. Most Germans were farmers, and all members of the community assisted in cultivation. They grew oats and rye for bread and hops for beer. Tribes such as the Ostrogoths also raised sheep, horses, pigs, and chickens. Archeological evidence dating from the

fifth century, from areas of Roman Dacia where the Goths frequently came in contact with Roman outposts and towns, reveals the steady acculturation of the Germans to Roman practices. Dietary habits shifted toward Roman tastes, as the Germans increasingly grew to prefer wheat bread and wine. German dress, especially among the warrior elite, copied Roman military garb. German nobles imitated the Roman fashion of multiple neck chains, though they clung to the traditional cloisonné *fibula,* or clasps, that fastened a cloak to the shoulders. Along the Rhine-Danube frontiers of the Roman Empire, Goths and other German peoples lived in sight of or within Roman army camps and towns. Many Germans found employment in the Roman army. As the Germans were Romanized, the Roman army was Germanized. Army officers gave their orders in military Latin, but talk and jokes around the evening campfires were in Germanic tongues.[15]

Anglo-Saxon England

The island of Britain, conquered by Rome during the reign of Claudius (r. A.D. 41–54), shared fully in the life of the Roman Empire during the first four centuries of the Christian era. A military aristocracy governed, and the official religion was the cult of the emperor. Towns were planned in the Roman fashion, with temples, public baths, theaters, and amphitheaters. In the countryside, large manors controlled the surrounding lands. Roman merchants brought Eastern luxury goods and Eastern religions—including Christianity—into Britain. The native Britons, a gentle Celtic people, had become thoroughly Romanized. Their language was Latin. Their lifestyle was Roman. Then an event in the distant eastern province of Thrace changed all this.

In 378 the Visigoths inflicted a severe defeat on the Roman emperor Valens at Adrianople. Even Britain felt the consequences. Rome was forced to retrench, and in 407 Roman troops were withdrawn from the island, leaving it unprotected. The savage Picts from Scotland harassed the north. Teutonic tribes from Scandinavia and modern-day Belgium—the Angles, Saxons, and Jutes—stepped up their assaults, attacking in a hit-and-run fashion. Their goal was plunder, and at first their invasions led to no permanent settlements.

As more Germans arrived in Britain, however, they took over the best lands and humbled the Britons. Increasingly the natives fled to the west and settled in Wales. Sporadic raids continued for over a century and led to Germanic control of most of Britain. Historians have labeled the period from 500 to 1066 "Anglo-Saxon." Except for the Jutes, who probably came from Frisia (modern Belgium), the Teutonic tribes came from the least Romanized and least civilized parts of Europe. They destroyed Roman culture in Britain. Tribal custom superseded Roman law.

The beginnings of the Germanic kingdoms in Britain are very obscure, but scholars suspect they came into being in the seventh and eighth centuries. Writing in the eighth century, the scholar Bede (see pages 341–342) described seven kingdoms: the Jutish kingdom of Kent; the Saxon

kingdoms of the East Saxons (Essex), South Saxons (Sussex), and West Saxons (Wessex); and the kingdoms of the Angles, Mercians, and Northumbrians (Map 9.3). The names imply that these peoples thought of themselves in tribal rather than geographical terms. They referred to the "kingdom of the West Saxons," for example, rather than simply to "Wessex." Because of Bede's categorization, scholars call the seven kingdoms the "Heptarchy" of Anglo-Saxon Britain. The suggestion of total Anglo-Saxon domination, however, is not entirely accurate. Germanic tribes never subdued Scotland, where the Picts remained strong, or Wales, where the Celts and native Britons continued to put up stubborn resistance.

Thus Anglo-Saxon England was divided along racial and political lines. The Teutonic kingdoms

MAP 9.3 Anglo-Saxon England The seven kingdoms of the Heptarchy—Northumbria, Mercia, East Anglia, Essex, Kent, Sussex, and Wessex—dominated but did not subsume Britain. Scotland remained a Pict stronghold, and the Celts resisted invasion of their native Wales by Germanic tribes.

in the south, east, and center were opposed by the native Britons in the west, who wanted to get rid of the invaders. The Anglo-Saxon kingdoms also fought among themselves, causing boundaries to shift constantly. Finally in the ninth century, under pressure of the Danish, or Viking, invasions, the Britons and the Germanic peoples were molded together under the leadership of King Alfred of Wessex (r. 871–899).

THE BYZANTINE EAST (CA 400–1000)

Constantine (r. 306–337) had tried to maintain the unity of the Roman Empire, but during the fifth and sixth centuries the western and eastern halves drifted apart. Later emperors worked to hold the empire together. Justinian (r. 527–565) waged long and hard-fought wars against the Ostrogoths and temporarily regained Italy and North Africa, but his conquests had disastrous consequences. Justinian's wars exhausted the resources of the Byzantine state, destroyed Italy's economy, and killed a large part of its population. The wars paved the way for the easy conquest of Italy by another Germanic tribe, the Lombards, shortly after Justinian's death. In the late sixth century, the territory of the western Roman Empire came under Germanic sway, while in the East the Byzantine Empire continued the traditions and institutions of the caesars.

Latin Christian culture was only one legacy that the Roman Empire bequeathed to the Western world. The Byzantine culture centered at Constantinople—Constantine's New Rome—was another. The Byzantine Empire maintained a high standard of living, and for centuries the Greeks were the most civilized people in the Western world. The Byzantine Empire held at bay, or at least hindered, barbarian peoples who could otherwise have wreaked additional devastation on western Europe, retarding its development. Most important, however, is the role of the Byzantines, together with the Muslims (see pages 289–292), as preservers of the wisdom of the ancient world. Throughout the long years when barbarians in western Europe trampled down the old and then painfully built something new, Byzantium protected and then handed on to the West the intellectual heritage of Greco-Roman civilization.

The Separation of Byzantine East and Germanic West

As imperial authority disintegrated in the West during the fifth century, civic functions were performed first by church leaders and then by German chieftains. Meanwhile in the East, the Byzantines preserved the forms and traditions of the old Roman Empire and even called themselves "Romans." Byzantine emperors traced their lines back past Constantine to Augustus. The senate that sat in Constantinople carried on the traditions and preserved the glory of the old Roman senate. The army that defended the empire was the direct descendant of the old Roman legions. Even the chariot factions of the Roman Empire lived on under the Byzantines, who cheered their favorites as enthusiastically as had the Romans of Hadrian's day.

The position of the church differed considerably in the Byzantine East and the Germanic West. The fourth-century emperors Constantine and Theodosius had wanted the church to act as a unifying force within the empire, but the Germanic invasions made that impossible. The bishops of Rome repeatedly called on the emperors at Constantinople for military support against the invaders, but rarely could the emperors send it. The church in the West steadily grew away from the empire and became involved in the social and political affairs of the West. Nevertheless, until the eighth century, the popes, who were often selected by the clergy of Rome, continued to send announcements of their elections to the emperors at Constantinople—a sign that the Roman popes long thought of themselves as bishops of the Roman Empire.

The popes were preoccupied with conversion of the Germans, the Christian attitude toward classical culture, and relations with German rulers. Because the Western church concentrated on its missionary function, it took centuries for the clergy to be organized. Most church theology in the West came from the East, and the overwhelming majority of popes were of Eastern origin.

Tensions occasionally developed between church officials and secular authorities in the West. The dispute between Bishop Ambrose of Milan and Emperor Theodosius (see page 232) is a good example. A century later, Pope Gelasius I (r. 492–496) insisted that bishops, not civil authorities, were responsible for the administration

Justinian and His Court   The Emperor Justinian (center) with ecclesiastical and court officials personifies the unity of the Byzantine state and the orthodox church in the person of the emperor. Just as the emperor was both king and priest, so all his Greek subjects belonged to the orthodox church. *(Source: Scala/Art Resource)*

of the church. Gelasius maintained that two powers governed the world: the sacred authority of popes and the royal power of kings. Moreover, because priests have to answer to God even for the actions of kings, the sacred power was the greater.

Such an assertion was virtually unheard of in the East, where the emperor's jurisdiction over the church was fully acknowledged. The emperor in Constantinople nominated the *patriarch,* as the highest prelate of the Eastern church was called. The emperor looked on religion as a branch of the state. Religion was such a vital aspect of the social life of the people that the emperor devoted considerable attention to it. He considered it his duty to protect the faith, not only against heathen enemies but also against heretics within the empire. In case of doctrinal disputes, the emperor, following Constantine's example at Nicaea, summoned councils of bishops and theologians to settle problems.

The steady separation of the Byzantine East and the Germanic West rests partly on the ways Christianity and classical culture were received in the two parts of the Roman Empire. In the West, Christians initially constituted a small, alien minority within the broad Roman culture; they kept apart from the rest of society. They condemned, avoided, and demystified Roman society and classical culture—as Saint Augustine's *City of God* shows. In Byzantium, by contrast, most Greeks were Christian. *Apologists,* or defenders, of Christianity insisted on harmony between Christianity and classical culture: they used Greek philosophy to buttress Christian tenets. Politically, emperors beginning with Constantine worked for unanimity between church and state.

Distinctive attitudes toward holy persons illustrate the differences between the two societies. A *holy person* was a kind of hero whose life and character embodied the spiritual ideals of the group. *Confessors* publicly manifested their faith in Christ. *Martyrs* held to their Christian faith, even suffering death for it and revealing unique courage and fortitude. *Virgins* displayed outstanding qualities of earthly and sexual renunciation. Christians believed that spiritual ideals existed in the physical body of the holy person. The dead body of the holy person, or *saint,* as he or she came to be recognized, became an object of veneration. Saints were *ministers,* who carried people's prayers and petitions to God and interceded with God on behalf of the living. Completely contrary to pagan and Jewish attitudes toward holy persons, the dead saints, because of their intercessory powers, played an extremely important role in Christian worship.

In the Germanic West, many saints had been socially prominent persons, such as nobles or bishops, and had exercised real power during their lifetimes. The locus of the supernatural power associated with a Western saint was fixed with precision. People knew exactly where a saint's body was buried because that place was the source of his or her holiness and intercessory influence. Relatively few such sites existed in the Germanic West.

In the Byzantine East, by contrast, the saints during their lifetimes had usually shunned human contact and avoided society and those who exercised power; they had fulfilled no social function. Eastern saints drew their spiritual power and influence from outside of society—from a retreat in the desert and from the ability to speak directly to God. In the East, Christians accepted many people as bearers or agents of the holy, and the locus of spiritual power was more ambiguous than in the West; holiness often touched socially marginal persons such as monks, prostitutes, and soldiers. In the West, holiness was vested in those who had known how to rule, and their posthumous holiness tended to be concentrated in cathedral, monastery, or shrine.[16] Holiness in the West, therefore, could be utilized for political or economic purposes. In the East the socially marginal role of the holy person made it very difficult to use his or her reputation for political purposes.

External Threats and Internal Conflicts

The wars of Justinian's reign left the Byzantine Empire economically and demographically weakened. Over the next two centuries, two additional troubles threatened its very survival: foreign invasion and internal theological disputes.

Beginning around 560, the Avars, a mounted Asiatic nomad group, and the Slavs, an Indo-European people probably originating in Galicia (southeastern Poland and the western Ukraine), burst into the Balkan peninsula. In the meantime, the Sassanid Persians threatened the eastern provinces. By 602 both the northern and the eastern frontiers of the Byzantine Empire had collapsed. In 626 a combined force of Persians and Avars attacked Constantinople itself. Only Byzantine control of the sea and the superhuman exertions of the emperor Heraclius (r. 610–641) saved the empire. But this effort so thoroughly exhausted both the Persians and the Greeks that they proved no match for the Arabs, who overran the eastern provinces of the empire between 632 and 640 (see pages 268–269).

Arab armies pushed into Asia Minor while Arab navies seized the Greek islands of Cyprus, Rhodes, and Chios and attacked the coastal cities of the empire. Again Constantinople faced sieges between 674 and 678 and from 717 to 718. Again Byzantine naval supremacy and the use of "Greek fire" (see page 258) saved the day. The Balkans, however, were lost to the Slavs; the eastern provinces, to the Arabs.

From all of these military disruptions certain benefits did result. First, the territories lost to the empire contained peoples of very diverse ethnic origins, languages, and religions. The territories that continued under imperial authority gradually achieved a strong cultural unity. They were Greek in culture and administration, orthodox in religion.

Second, foreign invasions created the need for internal reorganization. Since the third century, the imperial administration had been based on Diocletian's separation of civil and military authority (see pages 218, 220). In times of crisis, such as during the Arab invasions, this structure had led to paralysis. Heraclius and his successors militarized the administration. The empire was divided into *themes,* or military districts, governed by *strategoi,* or generals, who held both civil and military authority. The strategoi were responsible directly to the emperor. This reorganization brought into being a new peasant army. Foreign invasion had broken up the great landed estates of the empire, and the estate land was distributed to peasant soldiers, who equipped and supported

THE ORIGINS OF EUROPE

312	Constantine legalizes Christianity
ca 315	Constantine removes capital of the Roman Empire to Constantinople
325	Nicene Creed
ca 370	Huns defeat the Ostrogoths
380	Theodosius recognizes Christianity as the official imperial religion
	Bishop Ambrose refuses to yield cathedral church of Milan to Theodosius, thereby asserting church's independence from state
ca 390	Publication of *The Confessions* of Saint Augustine
ca 400	Donatist heretical movement reaches its height
5th century	Germanic raids of western Europe
476	Death of Roman emperor Romulus Augustus signals end of empire in the West
ca 490	Clovis issues Salic Law of the Franks
496	Clovis adopts Roman Christianity
529	Publication of the *Rule* of Saint Benedict
	Publication of the *Law Code* of Justinian
ca 560–720	Foreign invasion of the Byzantine Empire
597	Pope Gregory I sends missionaries to convert the Britons
7th century	Monasteries established throughout Anglo-Saxon England
ca 602	Publication of the *Dooms of Ethelbert*
664	Roman Christianity upheld over Celtic tradition at Synod of Whitby
730	Leo III orders destruction of icons throughout the Byzantine Empire, thereby initiating the iconoclastic controversy
843	Byzantine icons restored; civil wars cease

themselves from the profits of the land. Formerly the Byzantine state had relied on foreign mercenaries. Now each theme had an army of native soldiers with a permanent (landed) interest in the preservation of the empire. The government saved the costs of hiring troops and was assured the loyalty of native soldiers. The elevation of peasants to military status revitalized the social structure.

Third, some scholars maintain that the military disasters of the period led to an increase in popular piety and devotion to icons. An *icon* is an image or representation in painting, bas-relief, or mosaic of God the Father, Jesus, the Virgin, or the saints, which is venerated (revered) in religious devotion. Since the third century, the church had allowed people to venerate icons. Although all prayer had to be directed to God the Father, Christian teaching held that icons representing the saints fostered reverence and that Jesus and the saints could most effectively plead a cause to God the Father.

Iconoclasts, those who favored the destruction of icons, argued that people were worshiping the image itself, rather than what it signified. This, they claimed, constituted *idolatry,* a violation of the Mosaic prohibition of graven images in the Ten Commandments. Moreover, said iconoclasts, people's belief that certain icons had spiritual and magical powers was gross superstition.

The result of the controversy over icons was a terrible theological conflict that split the Byzantine world for a century. In 730 the emperor Leo III (r. 717–741) ordered the destruction of the images. The removal of icons from Byzantine churches provoked a violent reaction: entire provinces revolted, and the empire and Roman papacy severed relations. Since Eastern monasteries were the fiercest defenders of icons, Leo's son Constantine V (r. 741–775), nicknamed "Copronymous" ("Dung-name") by his enemies, took the war to the monasteries. Constantine seized their properties, executed some of the monks, and forced others into the army. Theological disputes and civil disorder over the icons continued intermittently until 843, when the icons were restored.

The implications of the iconoclastic controversy extended far beyond strictly theological issues. Iconoclasm raised the question of the right of the emperor to intervene in religious disputes, a central problem in the relations of church and state. Iconoclasm antagonized the pope and served to encourage him in his quest for an alliance with the Frankish monarchy (see page 336); iconoclasm thus contributed to the end of Byzantine political influence in central Italy. Arab control of the Mediterranean in the seventh and eighth centuries furthered the separation of the Roman and Byzantine churches by dividing the two parts of Christendom. Separation bred isolation. Isolation, combined with prejudice on both sides, bred hostility. In 1054 a theological disagreement led the bishop of Rome and the patriarch of Constantinople to excommunicate each other. The outcome was a continuing *schism,* or split, between the Roman Catholic and the Greek Orthodox churches. The bitterness generated by iconoclasm contributed to that schism. Finally, the acceptance of icons profoundly influenced subsequent religious art. That art rejected the Judaic and Islamic prohibition of figural representation and continued in the Greco-Roman tradition of human representation.

In spite of wars and internal theological disputes, the empire recovered with new vitality. Turning from conflict to peace, the Byzantines set about converting the Slavs. In antiquity the Slavs had lived as a single people in central Europe. With the start of the mass migrations of the late Roman Empire, the Slavs moved in different directions and split into several groups. Between the fifth and ninth centuries, the eastern Slavs, from whom the Ukrainians, the Russians, and the White Russians descend, moved into the vast and practically uninhabited area of present-day European Russia and the Ukraine (see Map 19.4). This enormous area consisted of an immense virgin forest to the north, where most of the eastern Slavs settled, and an endless prairie grassland to the south. Probably organized as tribal communities, the eastern Slavs, like many North American pioneers much later, lived off the great abundance of wild game and a crude "slash and burn" agriculture. After clearing a piece of the forest to build log cabins, they burned the stumps and brush. The ashes left a rich deposit of potash and lime, and the land gave several good crops before it was exhausted. The people then moved on to another untouched area and repeated the process.

In the ninth century, the Vikings (see pages 350–352) appeared in the lands of the eastern Slavs. Called "Varangians" in the old Russian chronicles, the Vikings were interested primarily in international trade, and the opportunities were good because the Muslim conquests of the eighth century had greatly reduced Christian trade in the Mediterranean (see page 269). Moving up and down the rivers, the Vikings soon linked Scandinavia and northern Europe with the Black Sea and with the Byzantine Empire, whose capital was at Constantinople. They built a few strategic forts along the rivers, from which they raided the neighboring Slavic tribes and collected tribute. Slaves were the most important article of tribute, and *Slavs* even became the word for "slave" in several European languages.

In order to increase and protect their international commerce, the Vikings declared themselves the rulers of the eastern Slavs. According to tradition, the semilegendary chieftain Ruirik founded the princely dynasty about 860. In any event, the Varangian ruler Oleg (r. 878–912) established his residence at Kiev. He and his successors ruled over a loosely united confederation of Slavic territories—the Kievan state—until 1054. The Viking prince and his clansmen quickly became assimilated into the Slavic population, taking local wives and emerging as the noble class.

Byzantine missionaries preached Christianity to the Vikings and local Slavs and in the process speeded up the assimilation of the two peoples. The missionary Cyril invented a Slavic alphabet using Greek characters, and this script (the Cyrillic alphabet) is still used. Cyrillic script made possible the birth of Russian literature. Similarly, Byzantine art and architecture became the basis and inspiration of Russian forms. In the realm of government, the Byzantines, in converting the Slavified Vikings, contributed to the unity of early Russia. So powerful was the Byzantine impact on Russia that the Russians claimed to be successors of the Byzantine Empire. For a time, Moscow was even known as the "Third Rome" (the second Rome being Constantinople).

The Law Code of Justinian

One of the most splendid achievements of the Byzantine emperors was the preservation of Roman law for the medieval and modern worlds. Roman law had developed from many sources—decisions by judges, edicts of the emperors, legislation passed by the senate, and the opinions of jurists expert in the theory and practice of law. By the fourth century, Roman law had become a huge, bewildering mass. Its sheer bulk made it almost unusable. Some laws had become outdated; some repeated or contradicted others. Faced with this vast, complex, and confusing hodgepodge, the emperor Theodosius decided to clarify and codify the law. He explained why:

When we consider the enormous multitude of books, the diverse modes of process and the difficulty of legal cases, and further the huge mass of imperial constitutions, which hidden as it were under a rampart of gross mist and darkness precludes men's intellects from gaining a knowledge of them, we feel that we have met a real need of our age, and dispelling the darkness have given light to the laws by a short compendium.[17]

Theodosius's work was only a beginning. He left centuries of Roman law untouched.

A far more sweeping and systematic codification took place under the emperor Justinian. Justinian intended to simplify the law and make it known to everyone. He appointed a committee of eminent jurists to sort through and organize the laws. The result, published in 529, was the *Code*, which distilled the legal genius of the Romans into a coherent whole, eliminated outmoded laws and contradictions, and clarified the law itself. Not content with the *Code*, Justinian set about bringing order to the equally huge body of Roman *jurisprudence*, the science or philosophy of law.

During the second and third centuries, the foremost Roman jurists, at the request of the emperors, had expressed learned opinions on complex legal problems, but often these opinions differed from one another. To harmonize this body of knowledge, Justinian directed his jurists to clear up disputed points and to issue definitive rulings. Accordingly, in 533 his lawyers published the *Digest*, which codified Roman legal thought. Finally, Justinian's lawyers compiled a handbook of civil law, the *Institutes*.

These three works—the *Code, Digest,* and *Institutes*—are the backbone of the *corpus juris civilis*, the "body of civil law," which is the foundation of law for nearly every modern European nation. The work of Justinian and his dedicated band of jurists

still affects the modern world nearly fifteen hundred years later.

Intellectual Life

Among the Byzantines, education was highly prized, and because of them many masterpieces of ancient Greek literature survived to fertilize the intellectual life of the modern world. The literature of the Byzantine Empire was predominantly Greek, although Latin was long spoken among top politicians, scholars, and lawyers. Indeed, Justinian's *Code* was first written in Latin. Among the large reading public, history was a favorite subject. Generations of Byzantines read the historical works of Thucydides and others. Some Byzantine historians abbreviated long histories, such as those of Polybius, while others wrote detailed narratives of their own days.

The most remarkable Byzantine historian was Procopius (ca 500–ca 562), who left a rousing account of Justinian's reconquest of North Africa and Italy. Proof that the wit and venom of Aristophanes and other ancient writers lived on in the Byzantine era can be found in Procopius's *Secret History*, a vicious and uproarious attack on Justinian and his wife, the empress Theodora. The Byzantines are often depicted as dull and lifeless, but such opinions are hard to defend in the face of Procopius's descriptions of Justinian's character:

For he was at once villainous and amenable; as people say colloquially, a moron. He was never truthful with anyone, but always guileful in what he said and did, yet easily hoodwinked by any who wanted to deceive him. His nature was an unnatural mixture of folly and wickedness.[18]

The *Secret History* may not be great history, but it is robust literature.

Later Byzantine historians chronicled the victories of their emperors and the progress of their barbarian foes. They were curious about foreigners and left striking descriptions of the Turks, who eventually overwhelmed Byzantium. They sometimes painted unflattering pictures of the uncouth and grasping princes of France and England, whom they encountered on the Crusades.

In mathematics and geometry the Byzantines discovered nothing new. Yet they were exceptionally important as catalysts, for they passed

siege machinery. Just as Archimedes had devised machines to stop the Romans (see page 163), so did Byzantine scientists improve and modify devices for defending their empire.

The Byzantines devoted a great deal of attention to medicine, and the general level of medical competence was far higher in the Byzantine Empire than it was in the medieval West. The Byzantines assimilated the discoveries of Hellenic and Hellenistic medicine but added very few of their own. The basis of their medical theory was Hippocrates' concept of the four humors (see page 140). Byzantine physicians emphasized the importance of diet and rest and relied heavily on herbal drugs. Perhaps their chief weakness was excessive use of bleeding and burning, which often succeeded only in further weakening an already feeble patient. Hospitals were a prominent feature of Byzantine life, and the army, too, had a medical corps.

Private Life

In the tenth century Constantinople was the greatest city in the Christian world. The seat of the imperial court and administration, a large population center, and the pivot of an extensive volume of international trade, Constantinople held Christian supremacy. As a natural geographical entrepôt between East and West, the city's markets offered goods from many parts of the world. About 1060 the Spanish Jew, Benjamin of Tudela, reported that Constantinople had merchant communities from Babylon, Canaan, Egypt, Hungary, Persia, Russia, Sennar (in the Sudan), and Spain, plus two thousand Jews.

Not that Constantinople enjoyed constant political stability. Between the accession of Heraclius in 610 and the fall of the city to Western Crusaders in 1204 (see page 365), four separate dynasties ruled at Constantinople. Imperial government involved such intricate court intrigue, assassinations, and military revolts that the word *byzantine* is sometimes used in English to mean extremely entangled and complicated politics. For example, in 963 the emperor Nicephorus I Phocas married Theophano, the widow of the emperor Romanus II. In 969 Nicephorus was murdered and replaced by his nephew John I Tzimisces, Theophano's lover and an exceptionally able general.

In commerce, Jewish, Muslim (see pages 286–288), and Italian merchants controlled most

Woman Carrying Pitcher   This detail from a floor mosaic in the Great Palace at Constantinople shows a buxom peasant woman balancing a huge water ewer on her shoulder. Notice the large earrings. *(Source: Scala/Art Resource)*

Greco-Roman learning on to the Arabs, who assimilated it and made remarkable advances with it. The Byzantines were equally uncreative in astronomy and natural science, but at least they faithfully learned what the ancients had to teach.

Only when science could be put to military use did the Byzantines make advances. The best-known Byzantine scientific discovery was chemical—"Greek fire," a combustible liquid that was the medieval equivalent of the flame thrower. In mechanics the Byzantines continued the work of Hellenistic and Roman inventors of artillery and

foreign trade. Beginning in the eleventh century, the Venetians acquired important commercial concessions in Byzantium, thereby laying the foundations for future Venetian prosperity (see pages 508, 510). Among the Greeks, commerce faced ancient prejudices, and aristocrats and monasteries usually invested their wealth in real estate, which involved little risk but brought little gain. As in the medieval West and early modern China, rural ideals permeated Byzantine society. The landed aristocracy always held the dominant social position in the empire. Greek merchants and craftsmen, even when they acquired considerable wealth, never won social prominence.

The monasteries represented one of the most important elements in the social structure of the Byzantine Empire. Deriving from the ascetic ideals of the ancient hermits (see page 242), monasticism spread rapidly in the Byzantine world during the third and fourth centuries and again in the eighth and ninth centuries. Many of the bishops in the Greek church and most of the patriarchs of Constantinople came from the monasteries. The people respected the monks, and the emperors consulted them and sought their blessings before important undertakings. Everyone believed that the monks' prayers constituted a spiritual force on which the security of the state depended. The monasteries, consequently, possessed great influence and acquired considerable wealth.

Behind the public life of the imperial court with its assassinations and proverbially complicated politics, beyond the noise and bustle of the marketplaces thronged with Venetian and Eastern merchants, and behind the monastery walls enclosing the sophisticated theological debates of the monks, what do we know of the private life of the Constantinopolitan Greeks? Recent research has revealed a fair amount about the Byzantine *oikos*, or household. The Greek household included family members and servants, some of whom were slaves. Artisans lived and worked in their shops. Clerks, civil servants, minor officials, business people—those who today would be called "middle class"—commonly dwelled in multistory buildings perhaps comparable to the apartment complexes of modern American cities. Wealthy aristocrats resided in freestanding mansions that frequently included interior courts, galleries, large reception halls, small sleeping rooms, reading and writing rooms, baths, and *oratories,* chapels where all members of the household met for religious services. A complicated system of locks protected most houses from intrusion.

In the homes of the upper classes, the segregation of women seems to have been the first principle of interior design. Private houses contained a *gynaikonitis,* or women's apartment, where women were kept strictly separated from the outside world. (The Muslim harem, discussed on page 284, probably derives from this Greek institution.) The fundamental reason for this segregation was the family's honor: "An unchaste daughter is guilty of harming not only herself but also her parents and relatives. That is why you should keep your daughters under lock and key, as if proven guilty or imprudent, in order to avoid venomous bites," as an eleventh-century Byzantine writer put it.[19] Women did not receive outside guests, at least in theory. Although they were allowed at family banquets, they could not attend if wine was served or questionable entertainment was given. To do so gave a husband grounds for divorce.

Marriage served as part of a family's strategy for social advancement. The family and the entire kinship group participated in the selection of brides and grooms. Wealth and social connections were the chief qualities sought in potential candidates. Weddings could take place at home, in the oratory of the bride's house, or in the local church.

Scholars know a great deal about the sleeping arrangements of the imperial couples. The emperor Romanus III (r. 1028–1034), for example, shared the bed of his wife, the empress Zoe; she shared the bed of her lover, later the emperor Michael IV (r. 1034–1041). The domestic arrangements of Byzantine rulers, however, were hardly typical, and little is known about the sleeping and sexual practices of lesser mortals. The church prescribed periods of abstinence, especially during Lent (the forty days before Easter) and on Saturday and Sunday. How closely practice conformed to precept is not known. The availability of relatively good medical attention suggests that those who could afford a physician secured his services. Women delivered children seated or standing up.

SUMMARY

Saint Augustine died in 430 as the Vandals approached the coastal city of Hippo. Scholars have sometimes described Augustine as standing with one foot in the ancient world and one in the Middle Ages. Indeed, Augustine represents the end of ancient culture and the birth of what has been called the Middle Ages. A new and different kind of society was gestating in the mid-fifth century.

The world of the Middle Ages combined Germanic practices and institutions, classical ideas and patterns of thought, Christianity, and a significant dash of Islam (see Chapter 10). Christianity, because it creatively and energetically fashioned the Germanic and classical legacies, was the most powerful agent in the making of Europe. Saint Augustine of Hippo, dogmatic thinker and Christian bishop, embodied the coming world view. In the Byzantine Empire a vigorous intellectual life, which preserved Greek scientific and medical knowledge and Roman law, flourished.

NOTES

1. Matthew 16:18–19 *(Jerusalem Bible).*
2. Quoted in R. C. Petry, ed., *A History of Christianity: Readings in the History of Early and Medieval Christianity* (Englewood Cliffs, N.J.: Prentice-Hall, 1962), p. 70.
3. Quoted in H. Bettenson, ed., *Documents of the Christian Church* (Oxford: Oxford University Press, 1947), p. 113.
4. Colossians 3:9–11 *(Jerusalem Bible).*
5. Luke 6:20–32 *(Jerusalem Bible).*
6. Quoted in L. Sherley-Price, trans., *Bede: A History of the English Church and People* (Baltimore: Penguin Books, 1962), pp. 86–87.
7. J. T. McNeill and H. Gamer, trans., *Medieval Handbooks of Penance* (New York: Octagon Books, 1965), pp. 184–197.
8. L. White, "The Life of the Silent Majority," in *Life and Thought in the Early Middle Ages,* ed. R. S. Hoyt (Minneapolis: University of Minnesota Press, 1967), p. 100.
9. I Peter 2:11–20 *(Jerusalem Bible).*
10. See J. Boswell, *Christianity, Social Tolerance, and Homosexuality: Gay People in Western Europe from the Beginning of the Christian Era to the Fourteenth Century* (Chicago: University of Chicago Press, 1980), chaps. 3 and 5, esp. pp. 87, 127–131.
11. F. J. Sheed, trans., *The Confessions of St. Augustine* (New York: Sheed & Ward, 1953), 1, 3.
12. T. Burns, *A History of the Ostrogoths* (Bloomington, Ind.: Indiana University Press, 1984), pp. 18, 21.
13. Ibid., pp. 108–112.
14. Quoted in E. F. Henderson, ed., *Select Historical Documents of the Middle Ages* (London: G. Bell & Sons, 1912), pp. 176–189.
15. Burns, pp. 113–119.
16. P. Brown, *Society and the Holy in Late Antiquity* (Berkeley: University of California Press, 1982), pp. 166–195.
17. Quoted in J. B. Bury, *History of the Later Roman Empire,* vol. 1 (New York: Dover, 1958), pp. 233–234.
18. R. Atwater, trans., *Procopius: The Secret History* (Ann Arbor: University of Michigan Press, 1963), 8.
19. Quoted in E. Patlagean, "Byzantium in the Tenth and Eleventh Centuries," in *A History of Private Life,* ed. P. Aries and G. Duby, vol. 1, *From Pagan Rome to Byzantium,* ed. P. Veyne (Cambridge, Mass.: Harvard University Press, 1987), p. 573. This section leans on Patlagean's article.

SUGGESTED READING

In addition to the studies listed in the Notes, students may consult the following works for a more detailed treatment of the early Middle Ages. Both M. Grant, *The Dawn of the Middle Ages* (1981), which emphasizes innovation and development, and P. Brown, *The World of Late Antiquity, A.D. 150–750* (1971), which stresses social and cultural change, are lavishly illustrated and lucidly written introductions to the entire period. Grant has especially valuable material on the Germanic kingdoms, Byzantium, and eastern Europe. B. Lyon, *The Origins of the Middle Ages: Pirenne's Challenge to Gibbon* (1972), is an excellent bibliographical essay with extensive references.

There is a rich literature on the Christian church and its role in the transition from ancient to medieval civilization. F. Oakley, *The Medieval Experience: Foundations of Western Cultural Singularity* (1974), emphasizes the Christian roots of Western cultural uniqueness. W. Meeks, *The First Urban Christians: The Social World of the Apostle Paul* (1983), provides fascinating material on the early Christians and shows that they came from all social classes. J. Richards, *Consul of God: The Life and Times of Gregory the Great* (1980), is the first major study in seventy years of this watershed pontificate. History, archeology, and language are critically examined in C. Thomas, *Christianity in Roman Britain to A.D. 500* (1981), a very learned study emphasizing the continuity in Britain's Christian history. P. Brown, *The Cult of the Saints: Its Rise and Function in Latin Christianity* (1982), describes the significance of the saints in popular religion. Students seeking a thorough treatment of Christianity through the sixth century should consult W. H. C. Frend, *The Rise of Christianity* (1984), an almost exhaustive treatment by a leading scholar-theologian.

For the synthesis of classical and Christian cultures, see C. N. Cochrane, *Christianity and Classical Culture* (1957), a deeply learned monograph. T. E. Mommsen, "Saint Augustine and the Christian Idea of Progress," *Journal of the History of Ideas* 12 (1951): 346–374, and G. B. Ladner, *The Idea of Reform* (1959), examine ideas of history and progress among the early church fathers. The best biography of Saint Augustine is P. Brown, *Augustine of Hippo* (1967), which treats him as a symbol of change.

The phenomenon of monasticism has attracted interest throughout the centuries. L. Doyle, trans., *St. Benedict's Rule for Monasteries* (1957), presents the monastic guide in an accessible, pocket-size form; a more learned edition is J. McCann, ed. and trans., *The Rule of Saint Benedict* (1952). The best modern edition of the document is T. Fry et al., eds., *RB 1980: The Rule of St. Benedict in Latin and English with Notes* (1981), which contains a history of Western monasticism and a scholarly commentary on the *Rule*. L. Eberle, trans., *The Rule of the Master* (1977), offers the text of and a commentary on Benedict's major source. Especially useful for students is O. Chadwick, *The Making of the Benedictine Ideal* (1981), a short but profound essay that emphasizes the personality of Saint Benedict in the development of the Benedictine ideal. G. Constable, *Medieval Monasticism: A Select Bibliography* (1976), is a useful research tool. Two beautifully illustrated syntheses by leading authorities are D. Knowles, *Christian Monasticism* (1969), which sketches monastic history through the middle of the twentieth century, and G. Zarnecki, *The Monastic Achievement* (1972), which focuses on the medieval centuries. L. J. Daly, *Benedictine Monasticism* (1965), stresses day-to-day living, and H. W. Workman, *The Evolution of the Monastic Ideal* (1962), shows the impact of the monastic ideal on later religious orders. For women in monastic life, see S. F. Wemple, *Women in Frankish Society: Marriage and the Cloister, 500–900* (1981), an important book with a good bibliography.

For the Germans, see, in addition to Burns's work cited in the Notes, J. M. Wallace-Hadrill, *The Barbarian West: The Early Middle Ages* A.D. *400–1000* (1962), and A. Lewis, *Emerging Europe,* A.D. *400–1000* (1967), both of which describe German customs and society and the Germanic impact on the Roman Empire. F. Lot, *The End of the Ancient World* (1965), emphasizes the economic and social causes of Rome's decline. On Rome itself and the Germans' impact on it, C. Hibbert, *Rome: The Biography of a City* (1985), contains instructive and entertaining material. G. Le Bras, "The Sociology of the Church in the Early Middle Ages," in S. L. Thrupp, ed., *Early Medieval Society* (1967), discusses the Christianization of the barbarians.

For Byzantium, the best starting point is probably the articles by Peter Charanis, "Byzantine Economy and Society," and T. E. Gregory, "Byzantine History (330–1025)," in J. R. Strayer, ed., *Dictionary of the Middle Ages,* vol. 2 (1983), pp. 475–491. G. Ostrogorsky, *History of the Byzantine State,* rev. ed. (1969), is probably the most useful one-volume introduction, but see also A. A. Vasiliev, *History of the Byzantine Empire* (1968); J. Hussey, *The Byzantine World* (1961); and S. Runciman, *Byzantine Civilization* (1956). For the reign of Justinian, see R. Browning, *Justinian and Theodora* (1971), and A. Bridge, *Theodora: Portrait in a Byzantine Landscape* (1984), a romantic and amusing biography of the courtesan who became empress. The best studies of the difficulties of the eighth and ninth centuries are probably A. Bryer and J. Herrin, eds., *Iconoclasm* (1977), and S. Gero, *Byzantine Iconoclasm During the Reign of Leo III* (1973). For the conversion of the Slavs, see F. Dvornik, *Byzantine Missions Among the Slavs* (1970).

10

The Islamic World, ca 600–1400

Alhambra Palace, Granada

Around 610, in the important commercial city of Mecca in what is now Saudi Arabia, a merchant called Muhammad began to have religious visions. By the time he died in 632, most of Arabia had accepted his creed. A century later, his followers controlled Syria, Palestine, Egypt, Iraq, Persia (present-day Iran), northern India, North Africa, Spain, and part of France. Within another century Muhammad's beliefs had been carried across central Asia to the borders of China. In the ninth, tenth, and eleventh centuries the Muslims created a brilliant civilization centered at Baghdad in Iraq, a culture that profoundly influenced the development of both Eastern and Western civilizations.

- Who were the Arabs?
- What are the main tenets of the Muslim faith?
- What factors account for the remarkable spread of Islam?
- How did the Muslims govern the vast territories they conquered?
- Why did the Shi'ite Muslim tradition arise, and how did the Shi'ite/Sunni split affect the course of Islam?
- What position did women hold in Muslim society?
- What features characterized the societies of the great Muslim cities of Baghdad and Cordoba?
- How did the Muslims view Western society and culture?

This chapter explores those questions.

THE ARABS BEFORE ISLAM

The Arabian peninsula, perhaps a third of the size of Europe or the United States, covers about a million square miles. Ancient Greek geographers named the peninsula *Arabian* after the Bedouin Arabs, nomads who grazed their animals in the sparse patches of grass that dotted the vast, semi-arid land. Thus *Arab* originally meant a native of Arabia. After Islam spread and peoples of various ethnic backgrounds attached themselves to or intermarried with the Arabs, they assumed an Arab identity. Today, the term *Arab* refers to an

ethnic identity; *Arabic* means a linguistic and cultural heritage.

In the sixth century A.D. most Arabs were not nomads; most led a settled existence. In the southwestern mountain valleys of the Arabian peninsula, plentiful rainfall and sophisticated irrigation techniques resulted in highly productive agriculture that supported fairly dense population settlements. In other areas scattered throughout the peninsula, the presence of underground water prompted the digging of wells. Oasis towns based on the cultivation of date palms grew up around the wells. Some oasis towns sustained sizable populations including artisans, merchants, and religious leaders. Some, such as Mecca, served as important trading outposts. The presence of the Ka'ba, a temple containing a black stone thought to be a god's dwelling place, attracted pilgrims and enabled Mecca to become the metropolis of western Arabia. Mecca combined economic and religious/cultic functions.

Thinly spread over the entire peninsula, the nomadic Bedouins migrated from place to place, grazing their sheep, goats and camels. Although Bedouins were always small in number, they were the most important political and military force in the region because of their toughness, solidarity, fighting traditions, and ability to control trade and lines of communication. Between the peoples settled in oasis towns and the Bedouin nomads were semi-nomads who, as the agricultural conditions around them fluctuated, practiced either settled agriculture or nomadic pastoralism.

For all Arabs the basic social unit was the tribe—a group of blood relations that descended in the male line. The tribe provided protection and support and in turn received members' total loyalty. Like the Germanic peoples in the age of their migrations (see pages 244–247), Arab tribes were not static entities but continually evolving groups. A particular tribe might include both nomadic and sedentary members.

Strong economic links joined all Arab peoples. Nomads, seminomads, and settled peoples were economically interdependent. Nomads and seminomads depended on the agriculturally productive communities for food they could not produce, cloth, metal products, and weapons. Nomads paid for these goods with the livestock, milk and milk products, hides, and hair wanted by oasis towns. Nomads acquired income by serving as desert guides and as guards for caravans. Plundering caravans or extorting "protection money" also yielded funds.

In northern and central Arabia, tribal confederations dominated by a warrior aristocracy characterized Arab political organization. The warrior aristocrats possessed several assets that help to explain their power. They had tremendous physical toughness. They possessed a few horses, which though difficult to maintain in desert conditions gave them great speed and mobility. Warriors paid tribute to no one and claimed blood descent from some great chief. Within a confederation, tribes competed for pre-eminence.

In the southern parts of the peninsula in the early seventh century, religious aristocracies tended to hold political power. Many oasis or market towns contained *harams,* sacred enclaves controlled or dominated by one holy family. Members of the holy family claimed to be servants or priests of the deity who resided in the town, and they served as guardians of the deity's shrine. The family imposed rules for behavior at the shrine. Murder was forbidden at the shrine, and a tribesman knew that even his bitterest enemy would not attack him there. At the haram, a *mansib,* or cultic leader, adjudicated disputes and tried to get agreements among warrior tribes. All Arabs respected the harams because they feared retribution if the gods' shrines were desecrated and because the harams served as neutral places for arbitration among warring tribes.

The power of the northern warrior aristocracy rested on its fighting skills. The southern religious aristocracy, by contrast, depended on its cultic and economic power. Located in agricultural areas that were also commercial centers, the religious aristocracy had a stronger economic base than the warrior aristocrats. Moreover, recent scholarship has shown that the arbitrator role of the mansib marks a step toward a society governed by law.[1] The political genius of Muhammad was to bind together these different tribal groups into a strong unified state.

MUHAMMAD AND THE FAITH OF ISLAM

A fair amount is known about Jesus after he began his public ministry at about age thirty, but little is known about his early life. Similarly, a good deal is known about Muhammad after his "call" as God's messenger at age forty, but little is known about him before then. Except for a few vague remarks in the Qur'an, the sacred book of Islam, no contemporary account of Muhammad's life (ca 570–632) survives. Arabic tradition accepts as historically true some of the sacred legends that developed about him, but those legends were not written down until about a century after his death. (Similarly, the earliest accounts of the life of Jesus, the Christian Gospels, were not written down until forty or fifty years after his death.)

Orphaned at the age of six, Muhammad was brought up by his paternal uncle. As a young man he became a merchant in the caravan trade. Later he entered the service of a wealthy widow, Khadija, and their subsequent marriage brought him financial security while she lived. Muhammad apparently was an extremely pious man, self-disciplined, and devoted to contemplation. At about forty, in a cave in the hills near Mecca where he was accustomed to pray, Muhammad had a profound religious experience. In a vision an angelic being (whom Muhammad later interpreted to be Gabriel, God's messenger) commanded him to preach the revelations that God would be sending him. Muhammad began to preach to the people of Mecca, urging them to give up their idols and submit to the one indivisible God. During his lifetime Muhammad's followers jotted down his revelations haphazardly. After his death scribes organized the revelations into chapters. In 651 they published the version of them that Muslims consider authoritative, the *Qur'an* (from an Arabic word meaning "reading" or "recitation"). Muslims revere the Qur'an for its sacred message and for the beauty of its Arabic language.

Islam, the strict monotheistic faith that is based on the teachings of Muhammad, rests on the principle of the absolute unity and omnipotence of Allah, God. The word *Islam* means "submission to God," and *Muslim* means "a person who submits." Thus the community of Muslims consists of people who have submitted to God by accepting his teachings as revealed by Muhammad. Muhammad, the Prophet, preached God's word and carried his message. Muslims believe that Muhammad was the last of the prophets, completing the work begun by Abraham, Moses, and Jesus. Muslims believe that they worship the same God as Jews and Christians. Islam's uncompromising monotheism—the oneness of God—spelled the end of paganism everywhere that Islam was accepted.

Page from the Qur'an. Kufic Script, 9th Century   The Arabic text of the Qur'an was always written with a slant-cut reed pen in a calligraphy intended not only to convey the message of Allah but also, through its beauty, to reflect the glory of God. The Kufic script, developed in the seventh century, stressed horizontal and vertical strokes and used loops sparingly. *(Source: Courtesy of the Freer Gallery of Art, Smithsonian Institution)*

Western writers have tended to place the origins of Islam in seventh-century Arabia. Recent research stresses that this view is historically inaccurate and from a Muslim perspective theologically wrong. Monotheism flourished in Middle Eastern Semitic and Persian cultures for centuries before Muhammad. "Muhammad was not the founder of Islam; he did not start a new religion." Like the Old Testament prophets, Muhammad came as a reformer. In Jewish, Christian, and Muslim theology, a prophet is not someone who predicts the future; a prophet speaks the word of God. Muhammad insisted that he was not preaching a new message; rather, he was calling people back to the one, true God, urging his contemporaries to reform their lives, to return to the faith of Abraham, the first monotheist.[2]

Likewise, Western secular scholars have distinguished between Muhammad's religious and his sociopolitical ideas. For a Muslim, this distinction is nonsensical because Muhammad's social and political views are inseparable from his religious ideas. Muhammad displayed genius as both political strategist and religious teacher. He gave Arabs the idea of a unique and unified *umma,* or community, which consisted of all those whose primary identity and bond was a common religious faith and commitment, not a tribal tie. The *umma* was to be religious and political community led by Muhammad for the achievement of God's will on earth.

In the early seventh century southern Arab society was characterized by tribal confederations centered around sacred enclaves. These confederations lacked cohesiveness and unity and were constantly warring; they recognized no single higher authority. Muhammad's goal was a Muslim community that rejected all paganism, a universal community of Muslim believers. The Islamic notion of an absolute higher authority fostered the political consolidation of the tribal confederations. Islam teaches that God is not only all-powerful and all-knowing but has set forth a law against which *all* human actions are measured. The *umma* regulated the behavior of community members by means of rules that transcended the boundaries of individual tribal units. Within the *umma*, authority was centralized in Muhammad. The fundamental tenet of Islam, to which any believer must subscribe, is "There is no God but God and Muhammad is his Prophet." If one accepts the idea of God's oneness and Muhammad's claim to be his Prophet, then it follows that all authority comes from God *through Muhammad.* Within the *umma*, the law of God was discerned and applied through Muhammad. Thus, in the seventh century, Islam centralized authority, both political and religious, in Muhammad's hands.[3]

The Qur'an is much holier to Muslims than the Torah and the Gospels are to Jews and Christians. The Qur'an prescribes a strict code of moral behavior. A Muslim must recite a profession of faith in God and in Muhammad as his prophet: "There is no God but God and Muhammad is his Prophet." A believer must also pray five times a day, fast and pray during the sacred month of Ramadan, make a pilgrimage to the holy city of Mecca once during his or her lifetime, and give alms to the Muslim poor. The Qur'an forbids alcoholic beverages and gambling. It condemns *usury* in business—that is, lending money at interest rates—and taking advantage of market demand for products by charging high prices. Some foods, such as pork, are forbidden, a dietary regulation perhaps adopted from the Mosaic law of the Hebrews.

By earlier Arab standards, the Qur'an sets forth an austere sexual code. Muslim jurisprudence condemned licentious behavior by both men and women, and the status of women improved. About marriage, illicit intercourse, and inheritance, the Qur'an states:

Of . . . women who seem good in your eyes, marry but two, three, or four; and if ye still fear that ye shall not act equitably, then only one. . . .

The whore and the fornicator: whip each of them a hundred times. . . .

The fornicator shall not marry other than a whore; and the whore shall not marry other than a fornicator. . . .

They who defame virtuous women, and fail to bring four witnesses to swear that they did not, are to be whipped eighty times. . . .

Men who die and leave wives behind shall bequeath to them a year's maintenance. . . . And your wives shall have a fourth part of what you leave, if you have no issue; but if you have issue, then they shall have an eighth part.

With regard to your children, God commands you to give the male the portion of two females; and if there be more than two females, then they shall have two-thirds of what their father leaves; but if there be one daughter only, she shall have the half.[4]

By contrast, Western law has tended to punish prostitutes, not their clients.

With respect to matters of property in the seventh and eighth centuries, Muslim women were more emancipated than Western women. Islamic law gave a woman control of all the property she brought to her marriage, except for the dowry. Half of the dowry went to the husband; the other half remained hers in case the marriage failed. A Muslim woman could dispose of her property in any way she wished. A Western woman had no such power.

Islam warns about the Last Judgment and the importance of the life to come. The Islamic Last Judgment bears striking resemblance to the Christian one: on that day God will separate the saved and the damned. The Qur'an describes in detail the frightful tortures with which God will punish the damned: scourgings, beatings with iron clubs, burnings, and forced drinking of boiling water. Muhammad's account of the heavenly rewards of the saved and the blessed are equally graphic but are different in kind from those of Christian theology. The Muslim vision of heaven features lush green gardens surrounded by refreshing streams. There, the saved, clothed in rich silks, lounge on brocaded couches, nibbling ripe fruits, sipping delicious beverages, and enjoying the companionship of physically attractive people.

How did the Muslim faithful merit the rewards of heaven? Salvation is by God's grace and choice alone. Because God is all-powerful, he knows from the moment of conception whether a person will be saved. Nevertheless, predestination should not take from the believer the will and courage to try to achieve heaven. Muslims who suffered and died for the faith in battle were ensured the rewards of heaven. For others, the Qur'anic precepts were the path to salvation.

THE EXPANSION OF ISLAM

Muhammad's preaching at first did not appeal to many people. Legend has it that for the first three years he attracted only fourteen believers. Because he preached a revelation that attacked the undue accumulation of wealth and social stratification, a revelation that held all men as brothers within a social order ordained by God, Muhammad's teaching constituted social revolution. The bankers and merchants of Mecca fought him. Moreover, he urged the destruction of the idols in the Ka'ba at Mecca, a site that drew thousands of devout Arabs annually and thus brought important revenue to the city. The townspeople turned against him, and he and his followers were forced to flee to Medina. This *hijra,* or emigration, occurred in 622, and Muslims later dated the beginning of their era from that event. At Medina, Muhammad attracted increasing numbers of believers, and his teachings began to have an impact.

Expansion to the West

By the time Muhammad died in 632, he had welded together all the Bedouin tribes. The crescent of Islam, the Muslim symbol, controlled most of the Arabian peninsula. In the next hundred

Jonah and the Whale The story of Jonah in the Old Testament describes a prophet who tried to avoid his responsibilities and is swallowed up by a whale; it is a parable of divine mercy, urging people to repent and seek forgiveness. The Chinese artist who executed this superb painting had never seen a whale but he possessed imagination, delicacy, and mastery of movement. *(Source: Edinburgh University Library)*

years, one rich province of the old Roman Empire after another came under Muslim domination—first Syria, then Egypt, then all of North Africa (Map 10.1).

In 711 a Muslim force crossed the Strait of Gibraltar and at the Guadalete River easily defeated the weak Visigothic kingdom in Spain. A few Christian princes supported by the Frankish rulers held out in the Pyrenees Mountains, but the Muslims controlled most of Spain until the twelfth century. The political history of Christian Spain in the Middle Ages is the history of the *reconquista*, the Christian reconquest of that country.

In 719 the Muslims pushed beyond the Pyrenees into the kingdom of the Franks. At the Battle of Tours in 733, the Frankish chieftain Charles Martel defeated the Arabs and halted their northern expansion. The Muslims had greatly overextended their forces. Ultimately, Charlemagne expelled them from France.

Expansion to the East

Between 632 and 640, the Arabs surged to the east into the Sassanid kingdom of Persia (see page 254). Between 635 and 651, one city after another fell to them. When they defeated the Persians at Nihawand in 651, Muslim control of the Persian Empire was completed. The wealth seized at the Persian capital, Ctesiphon, astounded the victorious, uneducated Bedouin tribesmen, who according to one modern scholar did not understand what they had won:

Some of the warriors, unfamiliar with gold pieces, were willing to exchange them for silver ones. Others, who had never seen camphor before, took it for salt and used it in cooking. When blamed at Hira for selling an aristocratic woman who had fallen as his share of booty for only a thousand silver pieces, an Arabian replied that he never thought there was a number higher than ten hundred.[5]

The government headquarters of the vast new empire was transferred from Medina to Damascus in Syria. A contemporary proverb speaks of the Mediterranean as a Muslim lake.

The Muslims continued their drive eastward. In the mid-seventh century, they occupied the province of Khorasan, where the city of Merv became

The Hijra from Mecca to Medina Muhammad's career gave rise to a rich body of legends that became a permanent part of Islamic lore and culture. This Turkish illustration of the hijra shows the Prophet and his friend Abu Bakr having been pursued and found by a man from Mecca. When the Meccan tried to approach, he was thrown from his horse (at right). Muhammad has granted the repentant Meccan a written pardon, which he receives from Abu Bakr (foreground). *(Source: The New York Public Library, The Spenser Collection)*

the center of Muslim control over eastern Persia (Map 10.2) and the base for campaigns farther east. By 700 the Muslims had crossed the Oxus River and swept toward Kabul, today the capital of Afghanistan. From the city of Balkh, they launched raids into Transoxiana as far as the Jaxartes River. Crossing that river, they penetrated Kazakhstan and then seized Tashkent, one of the oldest cities in central Asia. The clash of Muslim horsemen with a Chinese army at the Talas River in 751 seems to mark the farthest Islamic penetration into central Asia.

From Makran in southern Persia a Muslim force marched into the Indus Valley in northern India and in 713 founded an Islamic community at Multan. This settlement became isolated from the rest of the Islamic world and did not expand. Beginning in the eleventh century, however, Muslim dynasties from Ghazni in Afghanistan carried Islam

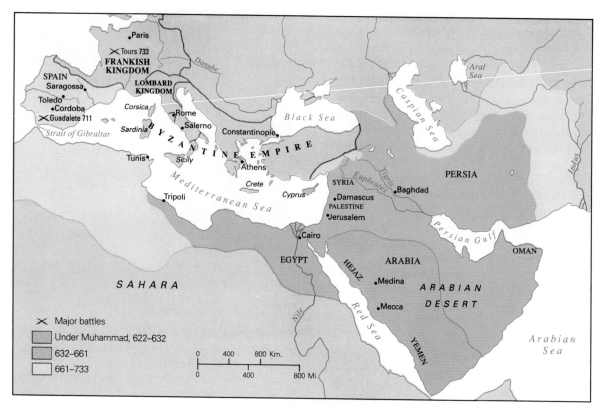

MAP 10.1 The Expansion of Islam to 733 Political weaknesses in the territories they conquered, as well as superior fighting skills, help explain the speed with which the Muslims expanded.

deeper into the Indian subcontinent (see pages 307–309).

Reasons for the Spread of Islam

By the beginning of the eleventh century the crescent of Islam flew from the Iberian heartlands to northern India. How can this rapid and remarkable expansion be explained? Muslim historians attribute Islamic victories to God's support for the Muslim faith. True, the Arabs won their military successes because they possessed a religious fervor and loyalty that their enemies could not equal. They were convinced of the necessity of the *jihad*, or holy war. The Qur'an does not explicitly mention this subject, but because the Qur'an does suggest that God sent the Prophet to establish justice on earth, it follows that justice will take effect only where Islam triumphs. Just as Christians have the missionary obligation of spreading their faith, so Muslims have the obligation, as individuals and as a community, to strive to lead a virtuous life and to

extend the Islamic community. *Jihad* also came to mean the struggle for the defense of Islam. Those who waged it were assured happiness in the world to come.

The Muslim outburst from Arabia and subsequent successes had strong economic, political, and military, as well as religious, causes. The Arab surge reflects the economic needs of a tough people squeezed into a semibarren, overpopulated area and the desire to share in the rich life of the Fertile Crescent. Arab expansion in the seventh and eighth centuries was another phase of the infiltration that had taken the ancient Hebrews to the other end of the Fertile Crescent (see Map 1.1). Also, recent conflicts between the Byzantine and Sassanid empires had left both weak and divided. Byzantine and Sassanid armies, composed of many diverse peoples scattered over vast territories, could not be easily assembled at a threatened place.

In the Byzantine provinces of Egypt and Syria, moreover, theological squabbles and factional divisions helped the Muslim advance. Groups alien-

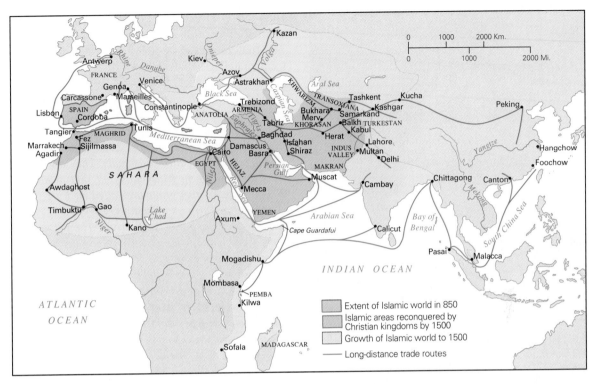

MAP 10.2 Islamic Expansion to 1500   Islam spread along the commercial arteries that extended from the eastern Mediterranean all the way to China, Southeast Asia, and Malaysia.

ated from Byzantine rule expressed their dissatisfaction by quickly capitulating to the Arabs in return for promises of religious freedom and the protection of their property. In the period between 642 and 643, an Arab army officer recorded his pledges to the people of Qum, in Persia:

In the name of God, the Merciful and the Compassionate. This is what Suwayd ibn Muqarrin gave to the inhabitants of Qumis and those who are dependent on them, concerning safe-conduct for themselves, their religions and their property, on condition that they pay the jizya [a poll tax] from the hand of every adult male, according to his capacity, that they show goodwill and do not deceive, that they guide the Muslim traveler, and that they accommodate Muslims who make a halt with them for a day and a night with their average food. If they change this or make light of their obligations, the pact [dhimma] with them is void.[6]

The Muslim conquest of Syria provides an example of the combination of motives—economic,

religious, and political—that propelled early Muslim expansion. Situated to the north of the Arabian peninsula, Syria had been under Byzantine-Christian (or Roman) rule for centuries. Arab caravans knew the market towns of southern Syria and the rich commercial centers of the north, such as Edessa, Aleppo, and Damascus. Syria's economic prosperity attracted the Muslims, and perhaps Muhammad saw the lands as a potential means of support for the poor who flooded Medina. Syria also contained sites important to the Muslim faith: Jerusalem, where Jesus and other prophets mentioned in the Qur'an had lived and preached; and Hebron, the traditional burial place of Abraham, the father of monotheism. Finally, a practical political reason encouraged expansion. Muhammad and the ruling elite insisted that all Arab tribes accept Muslim leadership. The centralization of the Islamic state depended on the control of the nomadic tribes of the Arabian and Syrian deserts. In the 630s the Byzantine state, barely recovering from a long war with the Sassanid empire of Persia over Syria, was trying

Muezzin Calling People to Prayer A mosque is usually surrounded by an open courtyard containing a fountain for ritual ablutions and a *minaret,* or lofty tower surrounded by projecting balconies from which an official, the muezzin, summons the faithful to prayer. *(Source: Ian Graham)*

to forge alliances with the nomadic tribes. From the Muslim perspective, the Islamic state had to win over these peoples before the Byzantines did so. Expansion in Syria, therefore, was absolutely essential.[7]

Military organization also helps account for the Muslims' rapid success. The leadership maintained a cohesive hold on the troops, and internal conflicts did not arise initially to slow their advances. The military elite solved the problem of recruitment for the army. Fixed salaries, regular pay, and the lure of battlefield booty attracted the rugged tribesmen. In the later campaigns to the east, many recruits were recent converts to Islam from Christian, Persian, and Berber backgrounds. The assurance of army wages secured the loyalty of

these very diverse men. Here is an eleventh-century description of the Egyptian army (remember that medieval numbers were always greatly exaggerated):

Each corps has its own name and designation. One group are called Kitamis [a Berber tribe]. These came from Qayrawan in the service of al-Mu'izz li-Din Allah. They are said to number 20,000 horsemen. . . . Another group is called Masmudis. They are blacks from the land of the Masmudis and said to number 20,000 men. Another group are called the Easterners, consisting of Turks and Persians. They are so-called because they are not of Arab origin. Though most of them were born in Egypt, their name derives from their origin. They are said to number 10,000 power-fully built men. Another group are called the slaves by purchase. . . . They are slaves bought for money and are said to number 30,000 men. Another group are called Bedouin. They are from the Hijaz [Hejaz] and are all armed with spears. They are said to number 50,000 horsemen. Another group are called Ustads. These are servants [?eunuchs], black and white, bought for service. They number 30,000 horsemen.[8]

In classical Islam, concepts of nation, country, and political sovereignty played a very small role. Before the nineteenth century, Islamic peoples rarely defined political power and authority in territorial or ethnic terms. For Muslims, religion was the core of identity. They divided the world into two fundamental sections: the House of Islam, which consisted of all those regions where the law of Islam prevailed, and the House of War, which was the rest of the world. "As there is one God in heaven, so there can be only one ruler on earth." By the logic of Islamic law, no political entity outside of Islam can exist permanently. Every Muslim, accordingly, has the religious duty of the *jihad*—carrying out the war of conversion. Consequently, a state of war exists permanently between the House of Islam and the House of War. With the conversion or conquest of all humankind, the war will end.

In practice, of course, Muslims did recognize divisions among unbelievers. The most basic distinction was between those who possessed revealed religions—Jews and Christians, whose faiths are based on the revelations in the Scriptures—and those who did not. Jews and Christians who submitted to Islam enjoyed the protection of the state because they were people of the book. They were known as *dhimmis,* or "protected people" (see page 292). Theoretically, Islam offered atheistic and polytheistic peoples the choice of conversion or death. In practice, Islam also accommodated Zoroastrians, Hindus, Buddhists, and other polytheists. Muslims' policy was far more liberal and tolerant than the policy of medieval Europeans toward Muslims. Europeans regarded Muslims as "heretics" or "infidels" who when conquered had to choose between conversion and death.[9] There were, of course, many exceptions, but in general the Christian attitude toward Islam was far more bigoted than was the attitude of Islam toward Christianity (see page 292).

Finally, the Muslim practice of establishing camp cities in newly conquered territories facilitated expansion. New military towns, such as Al-Fustat in Egypt and Basra in Iraq, became sites from which future conquests were planned and directed. They safeguarded Muslim identity and prevented the Muslim conquerors, at first a small minority, from being assimilated into the larger indigenous population. As the subject peoples became Muslim, the army towns became major centers for the spread of Islamic culture.

CONSOLIDATION OF THE ISLAMIC STATE

Although centered in towns, Islam arose within a tribal society that lacked stable governing institutions. When Muhammad died in 632, he left a large Muslim *umma,* but this community stood in danger of disintegrating into separate tribal groups. Some tribespeople even attempted to elect new chiefs. What provisions did Muhammad make for the religious and political organization of his followers? How was the vast and hastily acquired empire that came into existence within one hundred years of his death to be governed?

The Caliphate

Muhammad fulfilled his prophetic mission, but his religious work remained. The Muslim *umma* had to be maintained and Islam carried to the rest of the world. In order to achieve these goals, political and military power had to be exercised. But nei-

ther the Qur'an nor the *Sunna,* the account of the Prophet's sayings and conduct in particular situations, offered guidance for the succession (see page 274).

In this crisis, a group of Muhammad's ablest followers elected Abu Bakr (573–634), a close supporter of the Prophet, and hailed him as *khalifa,* or caliph, an Arabic term combining the ideas of leader, successor, and deputy (of the Prophet). This election marked the decisive victory of the concept of a universal community of Muslim believers. The selection of Abu Bakr showed that Muslims agreed that the faith revealed to Muhammad should continue as a unifying religious system that would reshape society. The goals of the Muslim *umma* were to promote the faith set down in the Qur'an and to make those revelations the cornerstone of Muslim law, government, and personal behavior.

When Muhammad died, Muslim "law" was still very primitive. It consisted of the tribal customs of Medina as corrected or altered by Qur'anic revelation and the decisions of the Prophet. Because the law of the Qur'an was to guide the community, there had to be an authority to enforce the law. Muslim teaching held that the law was paramount. According to Islam, God is the sole source of the law, and the ruler is bound to obey the law; the law is independent of the ruler and the ruler's will. Government exists not to make law but to enforce it. Muslim teaching also maintained that there is no distinction between the temporal and spiritual domains: social law is a basic strand in the fabric of comprehensive religious law. Thus religious belief and political power are inextricably intertwined: the first sanctifies the second, and the second sustains the first.[10] The creation of Islamic law in an institutional sense took three or four centuries and is one of the great achievements of medieval Islam.

In the two years of his rule (632–634), Abu Bakr governed on the basis of his personal prestige within the Muslim *umma.* He sent out military expeditions, collected taxes, dealt with tribes on behalf of the entire community, and led the community in prayer. His small group of advisers and scribes did not constitute an administrative structure, nor did his office become an institution.

Gradually, under Abu Bakr's first three successors, Umar (r. 634–644), Uthman (r. 644–656), and Ali (r. 656–661), the caliphate did emerge as an institution. The three continued Abu Bakr's policies and expanded on them. Umar succeeded in exerting his authority over the Bedouin tribes involved in ongoing conquests. Uthman asserted the right of the caliph to protect the economic interests of the entire *umma*. Uthman's publication of the definitive text of the Qur'an showed his concern for the unity of the *umma*. But Uthman's enemies accused him of nepotism—of using his position to put his family in powerful and lucrative jobs—and of unnecessary cruelty. Opposition coalesced around Ali, and when Uthman was assassinated in 656, Ali was chosen to succeed him.

The issue of responsibility for Uthman's murder troubled Ali's reign: it raised the question of whether Ali's accession was legitimate. Uthman's cousin Mu'awiya, a member of the Umayyad family, who had built a power base as governor of Syria, refused to recognize Ali as caliph. In the ensuing civil war, Ali was assassinated, and Mu'awiya (r. 661–680) assumed the caliphate. The Umayyads were the wealthiest and most powerful family of Mecca; they had bitterly fought Muhammad's ministry. Mu'awiya's victory and assumption of the caliphate, therefore, constituted social and political counterrevolution. The political and economic forces that had initially opposed Muhammad had now won. Mu'awiya founded the Umayyad dynasty and shifted the capital of the Islamic state from Medina to Damascus in Syria. From 661 to 750 Damascus served as the center of Muslim governmental bureaucracy.

The first four caliphs were elected by their peers, and the theory of an elected caliphate remained the Islamic legal ideal. Three of the four "patriarchs," as they were called, were murdered, however, and civil war ended the elective caliphate. Beginning with Mu'awiya, the office of caliph was in fact, but never in theory, dynastic. Two successive dynasties, the Umayyad (661–750) and the Abbasid (750–1258), held the caliphate.

From its inception with Abu Bakr, the caliphate rested on the principle that Muslim political and religious unity transcended tribalism. Mu'awiya, a consummate diplomat, bided his time. He always took care to confer periodically with the sheiks, or tribal leaders. He also, at least initially, behaved with them only as a *sayyid,* or first among equals. Mu'awiya sought to enhance the power of the caliphate by making the tribal leaders dependent on him for concessions and special benefits. At the same time, his control of a loyal and well-disci-

plined army enabled him to develop the caliphate in an authoritarian direction. Through intimidation he forced the tribal leaders to accept his son Yazid as his heir—thereby establishing the dynastic principle of succession. By distancing himself from a simple life within the *umma* and withdrawing into the palace that he built at Damascus, and by surrounding himself with symbols and ceremony, Mu'awiya laid the foundations for an elaborate caliphal court. Many of Mu'awiya's innovations were designed to protect him from assassination. A new official, the *hajib,* or chamberlain, restricted access to the caliph, who received visitors seated on a throne surrounded by bodyguards. Beginning with Mu'awiya, the Umayyad caliphs developed court ritual into a grand spectacle.

The assassination of Ali and the assumption of the caliphate by Mu'awiya had another profound consequence. It gave rise to a fundamental division in the *umma* and in Muslim theology. Ali had claimed the caliphate on the basis of family ties—he was Muhammad's cousin and son-in-law. When Ali was murdered, his followers argued—partly because of the blood tie, partly because Muhammad had designated Ali *imam,* or leader in community prayer—that Ali had been the Prophet's designated successor. These supporters of Ali were called *Shi'ites,* or *Shi'at Ali,* or simply *Shi'a,* Arabic terms all meaning "supporters" or "partisans" of Ali. In succeeding generations, opponents of the Umayyad dynasty emphasized their blood descent from Ali and claimed to possess divine knowledge that Muhammad had given them as his heirs.

Other Muslims adhered to the practice and beliefs of the *umma,* based on the precedents of the Prophet. They were called *Sunnis,* a term derived from the Arabic word *Sunna.* When a situation arose for which the Qur'an offered no solution, Sunnite scholars searched for a precedent in the Sunna, which gained an authority comparable to the Qur'an itself.

What basically distinguished Sunni and Shi'ite Muslims was the Shi'ite doctrine of the *imamate.* According to the Sunnites, the caliph, the elected successor of the Prophet, possessed political and military leadership but not Muhammad's religious authority. In contrast, according to the Shi'ites, the *imam* (leader) is directly descended from the Prophet and is the sinless, divinely inspired political leader and religious guide of the community. Put another way, both Sunnites and Shi'ites main-

THE ISLAMIC WORLD, CA 600–1258

610	Muhammad preaches reform, monotheism
610–733	Spread of Islam across Arabia, southern Europe, Africa, and Asia as far as India
622	The hijra—Muhammad and his followers are forced to leave Mecca and emigrate to Medina
632	Muhammad dies
632–661	Caliphate emerges as an institution
642	Muslims' victory at Nehawand signals their control of the Persian Empire
651	Publication of the Qur'an, the sacred book of Islam
661–750	The Umayyad dynasty
661	Umayyads move Muslim capital from Medina to Damascus
713	Spread of Islam to India, with the founding of a Muslim community at Multan
733	Charles Martel defeats Arabs at Battle of Tours, halting spread of Islam in northwestern Europe
750–1258	The Abbasid dynasty
751	Battle at Talas River ends Islamic penetration of central Asia
762	Abbasids move Muslim capital from Damascus to Baghdad
945	Buyids occupy Baghdad
946	Blinding of Caliph al-Muslakfi signals the practical end of the Abbasid dynasty
1055	Baghdad falls to the Seljuk Turks
1258	Mongols destroy Baghdad and kill the last of the Abbasid caliphs

tain that authority within Islam lies first in the Qur'an and then in the Sunna. Who interprets these sources? Shi'ites claim that the *imam* does, for he is invested with divine grace and insight. Sunnites insist that interpretation comes from the consensus of the *ulema,* a group of religous scholars.

The Umayyad caliphs were Sunnis, and the Shi'ites constituted a major source of discontent throughout the Umayyad period. Shi'ite rebellions expressed religious opposition in political terms. The Shi'ites condemned the Umayyads as worldly and sensual rulers, in contrast to the pious and true "successors" of Muhammad.

The Abbasid clan, which based its claim to the caliphate on the descent of Abbas, Muhammad's uncle, exploited the situation. The Abbasids agitated the Shi'ites, encouraged dissension among tribal factions, and contrasted Abbasid piety with the pleasure-loving style of the Umayyads. Finally, through open rebellion in 747, the Abbasids overthrew the Umayyads. In 750 the Abbasids won recognition as caliphs and later set up their capital at Baghdad in Iraq. The Abbasid dynasty lasted until 1258, but its real power began to disintegrate in the mid-ninth century.

Scholars agree that the Abbasid revolution established a basis for rule and citizenship more cosmopolitan and *Islamic* than the narrow, elitist, and Arab basis that had characterized Umayyad government. Abbasid rule had a strong impact on the Islamizing of the entire Middle East. Moreover, under the Umayyads the Muslim state had been governed by one ruler; during the Abbasid caliphate, steady disintegration occurred as provincial governors gradually won independent power. Although at first Muslims represented only a small minority of the conquered peoples, Abbasid rule provided the political and religious milieu in which Islam gained, over the centuries, the allegiance of the vast majority of the population from Spain to Afghanistan.

Administration of the Islamic State

The Islamic conquests brought into being a new imperial system that dominated southwestern Asia and North Africa. The Muslims adopted the patterns of administration used by the Byzantines in Egypt and Syria and by the Sassanids in Persia. Arab *emirs,* or governors, were appointed and given overall responsibility for good order, the maintenance of the armed forces, and tax collecting. Below them, experienced native officials—Greeks, Syrians, Copts (Egyptian Christians)—remained in office. Thus there was continuity with previous administrations.

The Arab conquerors developed devices to meet the changing needs of their empire. Tradition holds that the second caliph, Umar, established the *diwan,* or financial bureau. This agency recorded the names of soldiers, together with their salaries from state revenues. The *diwan* converted payments in kind to monetary equivalents and dispersed sums to tribal chieftains for distribution to their followers. All later departments of Muslim administration derive from this core.

The Umayyad caliphate witnessed the further development of the imperial administration. At the head stood the caliph, who led the holy war against unbelievers. Theoretically, he had the ultimate responsibility for the interpretation of the sacred law. In practice, the *ulema,* a group of scholars outstanding in learning and piety, interpreted the law as revealed in the Qur'an and in the Sunna. In the course of time the *ulema's* interpretations constituted a rich body of law, the *shari'a,* which covered social, criminal, political, commercial, and ritualistic matters. The *ulema* enjoyed great prestige in the Muslim community and was consulted by the caliph on difficult legal and spiritual matters. The *qadis,* or judges, who were well versed in the sacred law, carried out the judicial functions of the state. Nevertheless, Muslim law prescribed that all people had access to the caliph, and he set aside special times for hearing petitions and for the direct redress of grievances.

The central administrative organ was the *diwan al-kharaj,* which collected the two basic taxes on which the state depended. All persons paid the *kharaj,* a tax on land and movables. "Protected people"—Jews, Christians, and Zoroastrians—also paid the *jizya,* a poll tax. Revenues from these sources paid soldiers' salaries and financed charitable and public works that the caliph undertook, such as aid to the poor (as the Qur'an prescribed) and construction of mosques, irrigation works, and public baths.

As Arab conquests extended into Spain, central Asia, and Afghanistan, lines of communication had to be kept open. Emirs and other officials, remote from the capital at Damascus and later Baghdad, might revolt. Thus a relay network known as the *barid* was established to convey letters and intelligence reports between the capital and the various outposts. The *barid* employed a special technical vocabulary, as had similar networks used by the Byzantine and Sassanid empires.

The early Abbasid period witnessed considerable economic expansion and population growth, and the work of government became more complicated. New and specialized departments emerged, each with a hierarchy of officials. The most important new official was the *vizier,* a position that the Abbasids adopted from the Persians.

Initially, the vizier was the caliph's chief assistant—advising the caliph on matters of general policy, supervising the bureaucratic administration, and, under the caliph, superintending the army, the provincial governors, and relations with foreign governments. As the caliphs withdrew from leading Friday prayers and other routine functions, the viziers gradually assumed power. Khalid ibn-Barmak, vizier during the caliphate of Harun al-Rashid (r. 786–809), tried to make the office hereditary, as did some other viziers. But the authority and power of the vizier usually depended on the caliph's personality and direct involvement in state affairs. Many viziers used their offices for personal gain and wealth. Although some careers ended with the vizier's execution, there were always candidates seeking the job.

The vizier al-Fustat (d. 924) set down some of his reflections on government. They sound more like cynical aphorisms than serious policy principles:

The basis of government is trickery; if it succeeds and endures, it becomes policy.

It is better to keep the affairs of government moving on the wrong path than to stand still on the right one.

If you have business with the vizier and can settle it with the archivist of the diwan *or with the privy secretary, do so and do not bring it to the vizier himself.*[11]

In theory, the caliph and his central administration governed the whole empire. In practice, the many parts of the empire enjoyed considerable local independence; and as long as public order was maintained and taxes were forwarded to the *diwan al-kharaj,* the central government rarely interfered.

In theory, Muslim towns did not possess the chartered self-governing status of the towns and cities of medieval Europe (see pages 418–420). In practice, although a capable governor kept a careful eye on municipal activities, wealthy merchants and property owners had broad local autonomy.

DECENTRALIZATION OF THE ISLAMIC STATE

The Umayyad state virtually coincided with all Islamic states. Under the Abbasids, decentralization began nearly from the start of the dynasty. In 755 a Umayyad prince who had escaped death at the hands of the triumphant Abbasids and fled to Spain set up an independent regime at Cordoba (see Map 10.2). In 800, the emir in Tunisia in North Africa set himself up as an independent ruler and refused to place the caliph's name on the local coinage. In 820, Tahir, the son of a slave who had supported the caliphate, was rewarded with the governorship of Khorasan. Once there, Tahir ruled independently of Baghdad, not even mentioning the caliph's name in the traditional Friday prayers in recognition of caliphal authority.

This sort of decentralization occurred all over the Muslim world. The enormous distance separating many provinces from the imperial capital enabled the provinces to throw off the caliph's jurisdiction. Particularism and ethnic or tribal tendencies, combined with strength and fierce ambition, led to the creation of local dynasties. Incompetent or immature caliphs at Baghdad were unable to enforce their authority over distant and strong local rulers. This pattern led to the decline of the Abbasids and invasion by foreign powers.

Decline of the Abbasids

To check the power of the provincial governors, the caliph al-Mu'tasin (r. 833–842) expanded his military guard with a large corps of Turkish slaves loyal to him alone. The Turkish guard soon realized the degree of the caliph's dependence and vied with him for power. The guards' murder of one of al-Mu'tasin's successors, the caliph al-Mutawakkil (r. 847–861), reduced the caliphate to virtual insignificance.

In the later ninth century, rebellions shook Arabia, Syria, and Persia, and a slave revolt devastated Iraq. These disorders hurt agricultural productivity and in turn cut tax receipts. Having severely taxed the urban mercantile groups, the caliphate had already alienated the commercial classes. Disorder and the danger of disintegration threatened the Muslim state.

In the meantime, the luxury and extravagance of the caliphal court imposed a terrible financial burden. The caliphs lived in surroundings of awesome and ostentatious ceremony and wealth. In the palace complexes, maintained by staffs numbering in the tens of thousands, an important visitor would be conducted through elaborate rituals and confronted with indications of the caliph's majesty and power: rank upon rank of lavishly appointed guards, pages, servants, slaves, and other retainers; lush parks full of exotic wild beasts; fantastic arrays of gold and silver objects, ornamented furniture, precious carpets and tapestries, pools of mercury, and ingenious mechanical devices. The most famous of the mechanical devices was a gold and silver tree with leaves that rustled, branches that swayed, and mechanical birds that sang as the breezes blew.[12]

Some caliphs in the early tenth century worked to halt the process of decay. But by the time that ibn-Ra'ig, the governor of Wasit, a city in Iraq, compelled the caliph to give him the title *amir al-umara,* emir of emirs—which in effect bestowed precedence over other generals in Iraq—the caliphate had been reduced to a titular office symbolizing only the religious unity of Islam.

In 945, the Buyids, a Shi'ite clan originating in Daylam, the mountainous region on the southern shores of the Caspian Sea, overran Iraq and occupied Baghdad. The caliph, al-Mustakfi, was forced to recognize the Buyid leader Mu'izz al-Dawla as *amir al-umara* and to allow the celebration of Shi'ite festivals—though the caliph and most of the people were Sunnites. A year later the caliph was accused of plotting against his new masters. He was snatched from his throne, dragged through the streets to Mu'izz al-Dawla's palace, and blinded. Blinding was a practice that the Buyids adopted from the Byzantines as a way of rendering a ruler incapable of carrying out his duties. This incident marks the practical collapse of the Abbasid caliphate, although the caliphs remained as puppets of the Buyids and symbols of Muslim unity until the Mongols killed the last of them in 1258.

The Assault of the Turks and Mongols

In the mid-tenth century, the Islamic world began to be besieged by the Seljuk Turks. Originating in Turkestan in central Asia and displaying great physical endurance and mobility, the Turks surged westward. They accepted Sunnite Islam near Bukhara (then a great Persian commercial and intellectual center), swarmed over the rest of Persia, and pushed through Iraq and Syria. Baghdad fell to them on December 18, 1055, and the caliph became a puppet of the Turkish *sultan*—literally, "he with authority." The sultan replaced the Buyids as masters of the Abbasid caliphate. Caliphs retained their office, but Turkish sultans held the power. The Turks did not acquire all of the former Abbasid state. To the west, the Shi'ite Fatimids, so-called because they claimed descent from Muhammad's daughter Fatima, had conquered present-day central Algeria, Sicily, and, in 969, Egypt.

Thus by the middle of the eleventh century, there were three centers of Muslim power: Cor-

doba in Spain, Cairo in Egypt, and Baghdad in Iraq. Within the Baghdad caliphate the construction of mosques, schools, canals, and roads for commerce and pilgrimages by Nizam al-Mulk (1018–1092), the vizier of three sultans, signaled new intellectual and spiritual vitality. A Turkish sultan, rather than an Arab caliph, ruled the Baghdad caliphate, but it remained a Muslim state.

Into this world in the early thirteenth century exploded the Mongols, a people descended from an ethnic group that originated in the area that is present-day Siberia. The Mongols adhered to shamanism, a religion in which unseen gods, demons, and ancestral spirits are thought to be responsive only to *shamans,* or priests. In 1206 their leader Jenghiz Khan (1162–1227), having welded the Mongols and related Turkish tribes into a strong confederation, swept westward.

Whether the Mongols were driven by economic or military pressures, or were attracted by the sophisticated life to the west, scholars do not know. With perhaps sixty thousand highly disciplined soldiers, the Mongols left a trail of blood and destruction. They used terror as a weapon, and out of fear the rich commercial centers of central Asia—Khwarizm, Bukhara (whose mosques were turned into stables), Herat, Samarkand, Baikal

Embassy to the Court of Ethiopia   Describing an event that happened centuries before, a fourteenth-century artist depicts a Muslim embassy to the king of Ethiopia to arrange for the extradition of early converts to Islam who had fled to Ethiopia. The easy movement of the figures suggests the influence of Chinese artists who immigrated to Baghdad and Persia during the Mongol period. Both Chinese and Muslim artists believed the blacks dressed very simply. *(Source: Edinburgh University Library)*

(whose peoples were all slaughtered or enslaved)—fell before them. When Jenghiz Khan died, his empire stretched from northern China and Korea to the Caspian Sea, and from the Danube River to the Arctic. In 1242 the Mongols sacked Kiev. By 1250 they controlled all of southern Russia under the title "Khanate of the Golden Horde," and they ruled it for two hundred years (see page 634).

Under Jenghiz Khan's grandsons, Hulagu (1217–1265) and Kublai Khan (1216–1294), the Mongol Empire expanded farther. In the west, Hulagu sacked and burned Baghdad and killed the last Abbasid caliph (1258). His hordes captured Damascus in 1260, and only a major defeat at Ayn Jalut in Syria saved Egypt and the Muslim lands in North Africa and perhaps Spain. In the east, meanwhile, Kublai Khan campaigned in China. His defeat of the Sung Dynasty and establishment of the Yuan Dynasty (see page 320) marked the greatest territorial extent of the Mongol Empire. Kublai Khan ruled China from his capital at Peking.

Hulagu tried to eradicate Muslim culture, but his descendant Ghazan embraced Islam in 1295 and worked for the revival of Muslim culture. As the Turks had done earlier, so the Mongols, once converted, injected new vigor into the faith and spirit of Islam. In the Middle East the Mongols governed through Persian viziers and native financial officials.

THE LIFE OF THE PEOPLE

When the Prophet appeared, Arab society consisted of independent Bedouin tribal groups loosely held together by loyalty to a strong leader and by the belief that all members of a tribe were descended from a common ancestor. Heads of families elected the *sheik,* or tribal chief. He was usually chosen from among aristocratic warrior families whose members had a strong sense of their superiority. Birth determined aristocracy.

According to the Qur'an, however, birth counted for nothing; zeal for Islam was the only criterion for honor: "O ye folk, verily we have created you male and female. . . . Verily the most honourable of you in the sight of God is the most pious of you."[13] The idea of social equality

founded on piety was a basic Muslim doctrine. As a thirteenth-century commentator explained:

We have created everyone of you by means of a father and mother. All are equal in this and there is no reason therefore for boasting of one's lineage (the old Arab view being that in lineage lay honour). Through piety are souls brought to perfection and persons may compete for excellence in it; and let him who desires honour seek it in piety.[14]

When Muhammad defined social equality, he was thinking about equality among Muslims alone. But even among Muslims a sense of pride in ancestry could not be destroyed by a stroke of the pen. Claims of birth remained strong among the first Muslims; and after Islam spread outside of Arabia, full-blooded Bedouin tribesmen regarded themselves as superior to foreign converts.

The Classes of Society

In the Umayyad period, Muslim society consisted of four classes. At the top were the caliph's household and the ruling Arab Muslims. Descended from Bedouin tribespeople and composed of warriors, veterans, governing officials, and town settlers, this class constituted the aristocracy. Because birth continued to determine membership, it was more a caste than a class. It was also a relatively small group, greatly outnumbered by villagers and country people.

Converts constituted the second class in Islamic society. In theory, converts gained full citizenship when they accepted Islam. In practice, they did not: converts had to attach themselves to one of the Arab tribes as clients. This they greatly resented doing on economic, social, and cultural grounds, for they believed that they represented a higher culture than the Arab tribespeople. From this class of Muslim converts eventually came the members of the commercial and learned professions—merchants, traders, teachers, doctors, artists, and interpreters of the *shari'a.* Second-class citizenship led some Muslim converts to adopt Shi'ism (see page 274) and other unorthodox doctrines inimical to the state. Over the centuries, Berber, Copt, Persian, Aramaean, and other converts to Islam intermarried with their Muslim conquerors. Gradually assimilation united peoples of

Harvesting Dates Dates played a major part in fruit cultivation, and the Arabs developed many varieties with certain species famous for flavor, sweetness, or moisture. This detail from an ivory casket given to a Cordoban prince reflects the importance of fruit cultivation in the Muslim-inspired agricultural expansion in southern Europe during the ninth and tenth centuries. *(Source: Louvre/Cliché des Musées Nationaux, Paris)*

various ethnic and "national" backgrounds. However, "an Arabian remained a native of the peninsula, but an Arab became one who professed Islam and spoke Arabic, regardless of national origin."[15]

Dhimmis, or "protected people"—Jews, Christians, and Zoroastrians living under Muslim rule—formed the third class. The term *dhimmis* derives from an Arabic word meaning "pact." The pact allowed Christians and Jews to practice their religions, maintain their houses of worship, and conduct their business affairs, provided they gave unequivocal recognition to Muslim political supremacy. Here is a formula drawn up in the ninth century as a pact between Muslims and their nonbelieving subjects:

If the Iman wishes to write a document for the poll tax [jizya] of non-Muslims, he should write:

. . . I accord to you and to the Christians of the city of so-and-so that which is accorded to the dhimmis *. . . safe-conduct . . . namely:*

You will be subject to the authority of Islam and to no contrary authority. You will not refuse to carry out any obligation which we think fit to impose upon you by virtue of this authority.

If any one of you speaks improperly of Muhammed, may God bless and save him, the Book of God, or of His religion, he forfeits the protection [dhimma] of God, of the Commander of the Faithful, and of all the Muslims; he has contravened the conditions upon which he was given his safe-conduct; his property and his life are at the disposal of the Commander of the Faithful. . . .

If any one of them commits fornication with a Muslim woman or goes through a form of marriage with her or robs a Muslim on the highway or subverts a Muslim from his religion or aids those who made war against the Muslims by fighting with them or by showing them the weak points of the Muslims, or by harboring their spies, he has contravened his pact . . . and his life and his property are at the disposal of the Muslims. . . .

We shall not supervise transactions between you and your coreligionists or other unbelievers nor inquire into them as long as you are content. . . .

You may not display crosses in Muslim cities, nor proclaim polytheism, nor build churches or meeting places for your prayers . . . nor proclaim your polytheistic beliefs on the subject of Jesus [beliefs relating to the Trinity]. . . .

Every adult male of sound mind among you shall have to pay a poll tax [jizya] of one dinar, in good coin, at the beginning of each year. . . . Poverty does not free you from any obligation, nor does it abrogate your pact.[16]

Restrictions placed on Christians and Jews were not severe, and they seem to have thrived under Muslim rule. Rare outbursts of violence against Christians and Jews occurred only when Muslims felt that the *dhimmis* had stepped out of line and broken the agreement. The social position of the "protected people" deteriorated during the Crusades (see pages 362–367) and the Mongol invasions, when there was a general rise of religious loyalties. At those times Muslims suspected the *dhimmis,* often rightly, of collaborating with the enemies of Islam.

At the bottom of the social scale were slaves. The Qur'an's acceptance of slavery parallels that of the Old and New Testaments. The Qur'an forbids the enslavement of Muslims or "protected peoples," and Muhammad had recommended the humane treatment of slaves. Emancipation was a meritorious act, but the Qur'an did not grant freedom to slaves who accepted Islam. The Muslim duty of the holy war ensured a steady flow of slaves. Prisoners of war or people captured in raids or purchased in the slave markets, slaves constituted very large numbers in the Muslim world. The great Muslim commander Musa ibn Nusayr, the son of a Christian enslaved in Iraq, is reputed to have taken 300,000 prisoners of war in his North African campaigns (708–718) and 30,000 virgins from the Visigothic nobility of Spain, though these numbers are surely greatly inflated. Every soldier, from general to private, had a share of slaves from the captured prisoners. In the slave markets of Damascus and Baghdad in the tenth and eleventh centuries, a buyer could select from white slaves brought from Spain, Sicily, and southeastern Europe, yellow slaves from central Asia, brown slaves from India, and black slaves from sub-Saharan Africa.

Most slaves in the Islamic world went into the army or worked as household servants. Some were

Muslim Slave Market Slaves of several races were available at this thirteenth-century market at Zabid in Yemen. Women and children were wanted more than men: boys for military or administrative service, attractive women for the harem. Emancipation or the attainment of high political or military positions worked against the growth of class consciousness among slaves. *(Source: Bibliothèque Nationale, Paris)*

entrusted with business or administrative responsibilities. Few performed the kinds of agricultural labor commonly associated with slavery in the Western Hemisphere. Islamic law declared the children of a female slave to be slaves, but the offspring of a free male and a slave woman were free because lineage was in the paternal line. Many Muslims took slave women as concubines; the children belonged to the father and were free. In classical Islamic civilization, slaves played a large and sometimes distinguished role in the military, politics, religion, and the arts and sciences. Many caliphs were the emancipated sons of Turkish, Greek, and black slave women.

By the beginning of the tenth century, Islamic society had undergone significant change. The courtier al-Fadl b. Yahya writing in 903 divided humankind into four classes:

Firstly, rulers elevated to office by their deserts; secondly, viziers, distinguished by their wisdom and understanding; thirdly, the upper classes, elevated by their wealth; and fourthly, the middle classes to which belong men marked by their culture. The remainder are filthy refuse, a torrent of scum, base cattle, none of whom thinks of anything but his food and sleep.[17]

The last category hardly reflects compassion for the poor and unfortunate. However, it is clear that birth as a sign of social distinction had yielded to wealth and talent.

Women in Classical Islamic Society

Arab tribal law gave women virtually no legal status. According to tribal law, at birth girls could be buried alive by their fathers. They were sold into marriage by their guardians for a price. Their husband could terminate the union at will. And women had virtually no property or succession rights. The Qur'an sought to improve the social position of women.

The Qur'an, like the religious writings of all traditions, represents moral precept rather than social practice, and the texts are open to different interpretations. Yet modern scholars tend to agree that the Islamic sacred book intended women as the spiritual and sexual equals of men and gave women considerable economic rights. In the early Umayyad period, moreover, women played an active role in the religious, economic, and political

life of the community. They owned property. They had freedom of movement and traveled widely. They participated in the politics of the caliphal succession. With men, women shared in the public religious rituals and observances. But this Islamic ideal of women and men of equal value to the community did not last.[18] As Islamic society changed, the precepts of the Qur'an were interpreted to meet different circumstances.

In the later Umayyad period, the status of women declined. The rapid conquest of vast territories led to the influx of large numbers of slave women. As wealth replaced birth as the criterion of social status, men more and more viewed women as possessions, as a form of wealth. The increasingly inferior status of women is revealed in three ways: in the relationship of women to their husbands, in the practice of veiling women, and in the seclusion of women in harems.

On the rights and duties of a husband to his wife, the Qur'an states that "men are in charge of women because Allah hath made the one to excel the other, and because they (men) spend of their property (for the support of women). So good women are obedient, guarding in secret that which Allah hath guarded."[19] A tenth-century interpreter, Abu Ja'far Muhammad ibn-Jarir al-Tabari, commented on that passage as follows:

Men are in charge of their women with respect to disciplining (or chastising) them, and to providing them with restrictive guidance concerning their duties toward God and themselves (i.e., the men), by virtue of that by which God has given excellence (or preference) to the men over their wives: i.e., the payment of their dowers to them, spending of their wealth on them, and providing for them in full. This is how God has given excellence to (the men) over (the women), and hence (the men) have come to be in charge of (the women) and hold authority over them.[20]

A thirteenth-century commentator on the same Qur'anic passage goes into more detail and argues that women are incapable of and unfit for any public duties, such as participating in religious rites, giving evidence in the law courts, or being involved in any public political decisions.[21] Muslim society fully accepted this view, and later interpreters further categorized the ways in which men were superior to women.

Interpretations of the Qur'an's statements on polygamy give another example of the declining

Man Playing a Lyre   Major Persian pottery centers at Rayy and Kashan produced ceramic masterpieces, often in styles influenced by imported Chinese porcelains. In this delicate bowl of off-white paste with an opaque cobalt glaze from the early twelfth century, a gentleman serenades a lady on a lyre. (*Source: Courtesy of the Freer Gallery of Art, Smithsonian Institution*)

status of women. The Qur'an permitted a man to have four wives, provided "that all are treated justly. . . . Marry of the women who seem good to you, two or three or four; and if ye fear that you cannot do justice (to so many) then one (only) or the captives that your right hand possess. Thus it is more likely that you will do injustice."[22] This passage suggests the availability of large numbers of slave women. Where the Qur'an permitted polygamy, Muslim jurists interpreted the statement as having legal force. The Prophet's emphasis on justice to the several wives, however, was understood as a mere recommendation.[23] Although the Qur'an allowed polygamy, only very wealthy men could afford several wives. The vast majority of

Muslim males were monogamous because women could not earn money, and it was all men could do to support one wife.

In contrast to the Christian view of sexual activity as something inherently shameful and even within marriage only a cure for sexual desire, Islam maintained a healthy acceptance of sexual pleasure for both males and females. Islam held that sexual satisfaction for both partners in marriage was necessary to prevent extramarital activity. A sexually frustrated person was considered dangerous to the community. Thus Islam opposed asceticism and required believers with pious vocations to acquire pious wives. Abstinence and chastity were vehemently discouraged.

Although men and women were thought to have similar sexual instincts, men were entitled to as many as four legal partners but women had to be content with one. Because satisfaction of the sexual impulse for males allows polygamy,

one can speculate that fear of its inverse—one woman with four husbands—might explain the assumption of women's insatiability, which is at the core of the Muslim concept of female sexuality. Since Islam assumed that a sexually frustrated individual is a very problematic believer and a troublesome citizen, . . . the distrust of women is even greater.[24]

Modern sociologists contend that polygamy affects individuals' sense of identity. It supports men's self-images as primarily sexual beings, whereas—by emphasizing wives' inability to satisfy their husbands—it undermines women's confidence in their sexuality. The function of polygamy as a device to humiliate women is evident in an aphorism from Moroccan folklore: "Debase a woman by bringing in (the house) another one."[25]

In many present-day Muslim cultures, few issues are more sensitive than those of veiling and the seclusion of women. These practices have their roots in pre-Islamic times, and they took firm hold in classical Islamic society. The head veil seems to have been the mark of free-born urban women; wearing the veil distinguished free women from slave women. Country and desert women did not wear veils because they interfered with work.

Probably of Byzantine or Persian origin, the veil indicated respectability and modesty. As the Arab conquerors subjugated various peoples, they adopted some of the vanquished peoples' customs, one of which was veiling. The Qur'an contains no specific rule about the veil, but its few vague references have been interpreted as sanctioning the practice. Gradually, all parts of a woman's body were considered *pudendal* (shameful because they were capable of arousing sexual desire) and were not allowed to be seen in public.

Even more restrictive of the freedom of women than veiling was the practice of *purdah*, literally seclusion behind a screen or curtain—the harem system. The English word *harem* comes from the Arabic *haram*, meaning "forbidden" or "sacrosanct," which the women's quarters of a house or palace were considered to be. The practice of secluding women in a harem also derives from Arabic contacts with other Eastern cultures. Scholars do not know precisely when the harem system began, but within "one-and-a-half centuries after the death of the Prophet, the (harem) system was fully established. . . . Amongst the richer classes, the women were shut off from the rest of the household."[26] The harem became another symbol of male prestige and prosperity, as well as a way to distinguish and set apart upper-class women from peasants.

Sufism

In the ninth and tenth centuries, in Arabia, Syria, Egypt, and Iraq, a popular religious movement arose within Islam. For some especially devout individuals within the community, the traditional way of religious life through observance of the precepts of the Qur'an was not fully satisfying. They rejected what they considered the increasing materialism of Muslim life and sought a return to the simplicity of the Prophet's time. Called *Sufis* from the simple coarse woolen *(suf)* garments they wore, these men and women followed an ascetic lifestyle, dedicating themselves to fasting, prayer, and meditation on the Qur'an. Through asceticism and a deep love of God, Sufis sought a direct or mystical union with God. Sufi ideals—careful following of the Qur'an, the avoidance of sin, and a humble yearning toward God—were embodied in the word *zuhd*, renunciation.

The woman mystic Rabia (d. 801) epitomizes this combination of renunciation and devotionalism. An attractive woman who refused marriage so that nothing would distract her from a total commitment to God, Rabia attracted followers, whom she served as a spiritual guide. Her poem in the form of prayer captures her deep devotion:

O my lord, if I worship thee from fear of hell, and if I worship thee in hope of paradise, exclude me thence, but if I worship thee for thine own sake, then withhold not from me thine eternal beauty.

Sufism grew into a mass movement that drew people from all social classes. Though its sources were the Qur'an and the Sunna, Sufism accepted ideas from Christian and Buddhist monasticism and from Hindu devotionalism. Consequently, the *ulema*, the religious scholars who interpreted the Qur'an and Muslim law, looked on Sufism as a heretical movement and an unnecessary devi-

Sufi Collective Ritual   Collective or group rituals, in which sufis tried through ecstatic experiences to come closer to God, have always fascinated outsiders, including non-sufi Muslims. Here the sixteenth-century Persian painter Sultan Muhammad illustrates the writing of the fourteenth-century lyric poet Hafiz. Just as Hafiz's poetry moved back and forth between profane and mystical themes, so it is difficult to determine whether the ecstasy achieved here is alcoholic or spiritual. Many figures seem to enjoy wine. Note the various musical instruments and the delicate floral patterns so characteristic of Persian art. *(Source: Courtesy of The Arthur M. Sackler Museum, Harvard University)*

ation from orthodoxy. The *ulema* also felt that the Sufis challenged their religious authority. Just as ecclesiastical authorities in Europe looked on Christian mystics with suspicion because the direct mystical union with God denied the need for the institutional Church, so the Muslim *ulema* condemned and persecuted extreme Sufis for their rejection of religious formalism.

Trade and Commerce

Trade and commerce played a prominent role in the Islamic world. Muhammad had earned his livelihood in business as a representative of the city of Mecca, which carried on a brisk trade from south-ern Palestine to southwestern Arabia. Although Bedouin nomads were among the first converts to Islam, Islam arose in a mercantile, not an agricultural, setting. The merchant had a respectable place in Muslim society. According to the sayings of the Prophet:

The honest, truthful Muslim merchant will stand with the martyrs on the Day of Judgment.

I commend the merchants to you, for they are the couriers of the horizons and God's trusted servants on earth.

If God permitted the inhabitants of paradise to trade, they would deal in cloth and perfume.[27]

Muslim Dhow Hundreds of these lateen-rigged Arab vessels gave Islam mastery of the Indian Ocean. The Muslim fleet in the Mediterranean never equaled the one in the Indian Ocean, a circumstance that helps to explain Venetian and Genoese power in the Mediterranean in the thirteenth century. *(Source: Bibliothèque Nationale, Paris)*

In contrast to the social values of the medieval West and of Confucian China, Muslims tended to look with disdain on agricultural labor and to hold trade in esteem. The Qur'an, moreover, had no prohibition against trade with Christians or other unbelievers.

Western scholars have tended to focus attention on the Mediterranean Sea as the source of Islamic mercantile influence on Europe in the Middle Ages. From the broad perspective of Muslim commerce, however, the Mediterranean held a position much subordinate to other waterways: the Black Sea; the Caspian Sea and the Volga River, which gave access deep into Russia; the Aral Sea, from which region caravans departed for China; the Gulf of Aden; and the Arabian Sea and the Indian Ocean, which linked the Arabian gulf region with eastern Africa, the Indian subcontinent, and eventually Indonesia and the Philippines. These served as the main commercial seaways of the Islamic world.

By land Muslim traders pushed south from North Africa across the Sahara Desert into west central Africa (see Map 10.2) and by the tenth century had penetrated as far east as China and possibly Korea. They were pursuing silk, which was the earliest Chinese gift to the world. Travelers called the land route going through Samarkand, Bukhara, and other Turkestan towns the "great silk way," and along that way caravans collected the merchandise of Transoxiana and Turkestan. The following is a selection from a private ninth-century list of commodities transported into and through the Islamic world by land and by sea:

Imported from India: tigers, leopards, elephants, leopard skins, red rubies, white sandalwood, ebony, and coconuts

From China: aromatics, silk, porcelain, paper, ink, peacocks, fiery horses, saddles, felts, cinnamon

From the Byzantines: silver and gold vessels, embroidered cloths, fiery horses, slave girls, rare articles in red copper, strong locks, lyres, water engineers, specialists in plowing and cultivation, marble workers, and eunuchs

From Arabia: Arab horses, ostriches, thoroughbred she-camels, and tanned hides

From Barbary and Maghrib (the Arabic name for northwest Africa, an area that included Morocco, Algeria, and Tunisia): leopards, acacia, felts, and black falcons

From the Yemen: cloaks, tanned hides, giraffes, breastplates, cornelian incense, indigo, and turmeric

From Egypt: ambling donkeys, fine cloths, papyrus, balsam oil, and, from its mines, high-quality topaz

From the Khazars (a people living on the northern shore of the Black Sea): slaves, slave women, armor, helmets, and hoods of mail

From the land of Khwarizm (a state in central Asia): musk, ermine, sable, squirrel, mink, and excellent sugar cane

From Samarkand: paper

From Isfahan (a city in central Persia): honeycombs, honey, quinces, Chinese pears, apples, saffron, potash, white lead, antimony (a metallic element), fine cloths, and fruit drinks

From Ahwaz (a city in southwestern Persia): sugar, silk brocades, castanet players and dancing girls, kinds of dates, grape molasses, and candy.[28]

What made long-distance land transportation possible? Camels. Stupid and vicious, camels had to be loaded on a daily, sometimes twice-daily, basis. Nevertheless, they proved more efficient for desert transportation than horses or oxen. The use of the camel to carry heavy and bulky freight facilitated the development of world commerce.

Between the eighth and twelfth centuries, the Islamic world functioned virtually as a free-trade area in which goods circulated freely. The Muslims developed a number of business techniques that facilitated the expansion of trade. For example, they originated the concept of the bill of exchange, which made the financing of trade more flexible. The Muslims also seem to have come up with the idea of the joint stock company—an arrangement that lets a group of people invest in a venture and share in its profits and losses in proportion to the amount each has invested. Also, many financial and business terms—check, coffer, cipher, nadir, zenith, zero, and risk—entered the English language from Arabic.

Vigorous long-distance trade had significant consequences. Commodities produced in one part of the world became available in many other places, providing a uniformity of consumer goods among diverse peoples living over a vast area. Trade promoted scientific advances in navigation, shipbuilding, and cartography. For example, from the Chinese, Arabic sailors seem to have learned about the compass, an instrument used by mariners to determine directions on the earth's surface by means of a magnetic needle. Muslims carried the compass to Europe, and in the twelfth century it came into wide navigational use. Muslim mariners also developed the astrolabe, an instrument used to determine latitude and the time of day.

Long-distance trade brought some merchants fabulous wealth. A jeweler in Baghdad remained rich even after the caliph al-Muqtadir (r. 908–937) had seized 16 million dinars of his property. A long-distance trader in Bashr had an annual income of over 1 million dirhams. Many merchants in Siraf owned homes worth 30,000 dinars and had fortunes of 4 million dinars.[29] To appreciate the value of these sums in terms of present-day buying power, more information about the cost of living in tenth- and eleventh-century Muslim cities is needed. Nevertheless, it can be said that the sums represent very great riches.

Did Muslim economic activity amount to a kind of capitalism? If by capitalism is meant private (not state) ownership of the means of production, the production of goods for market sale, profit as the main motive for economic activity, competition, a money economy, and the lending of money at interest, then, unquestionably, the medieval Muslim economy had capitalistic features. Students of Muslim economic life have not made a systematic and thorough investigation of Muslims' industries, businesses, and seaports, but the impressionistic evidence is overwhelming:

despite all the uncertainty of our knowledge, a level (of economic development) does seem to have been reached in the Muslim world which is not to be found elsewhere at the same time or earlier. The density of commercial relations within the Muslim world constituted a sort of world market . . . of unprecedented dimensions. The development of exchange had made possible regional specialization in industry as well as in agriculture, bringing about relationships that some-times extended over great distances. A world market of the same type was formed in the Roman Empire, but the Muslim "common market" was very much bigger. Also, it seems to have been more "capitalist," in the sense that private capital played a greater part in forming it, as compared with the part played by the state, than was the case in the Roman Empire. Not only did the Muslim world know a capitalist sector, but this sector was apparently the most extensive in history before the establishment of the world market created by the Western European bourgeoisie, and this did not outstrip it in importance until the sixteenth century.[30]

Urban Centers

Long-distance trade also provided the wealth that made possible a gracious and sophisticated culture in the cities of the Muslim world. Although cities and mercantile centers dotted the entire Islamic Empire, the cities of Baghdad and Cordoba at their peak in the tenth century stand out as the finest examples of cosmopolitan Muslim civilization. Founded in 762 by the second Abbasid caliph, al-Mansur, on the Tigris river, astride the major overland highways, Baghdad became the administrative, strategic, and commercial capital of the Muslim world. The presence of the caliph and his court and administration, caliphal patronage of learning and the arts, and Baghdad's enormous commercial advantages gave the city international prestige. On its streets thronged a kaleidoscope of races, creeds, costumes, and cultures, an almost infinite variety of peoples: returning travelers, administrative officials, slaves, visitors, merchants from Asia, Africa, and Europe. Shops and marketplaces offered the rich and extravagant a dazzling and exotic array of goods from all over the world.

The caliph Harun al-Rashid (r. 786–809) presided over a glamorous court. His vast palace with hundreds of officials, his harems with thousands of slave girls, his magnificent banquets, receptions, and ceremonies—all astounded foreign visitors. Harun al-Rashid invited writers, dancers, musicians, poets, and artists to live in Baghdad, and he is reputed to have rewarded one singer with 100,000 silver pieces for a single song. This brilliant era provided the background for the tales that appear in *A Thousand and One Nights*, the great folk classic of Arabic literature.

The central plot of the tales involves the efforts of Scheherazade to keep her husband, Schariar, legendary king of Samarkand, from killing her. She entertains him with one tale a night for 1,001 nights. The best-known tales are "Aladdin and His Lamp," "Sinbad the Sailor," and "Ali Baba and the Forty Thieves." Also known as *The Arabian Nights,* this book offers a sumptuous collection of caliphs, viziers, and genies, varieties of sexual experiences, and fabulous happenings. *The Arabian Nights,* although fictional, has provided a large store of the words and images that Europeans have used since the eighteenth century to describe the Islamic world. *The Arabian Nights* remains one of the great works of world literature.

Cordoba in southern Spain competed with Baghdad for the cultural leadership of the Islamic world. In the tenth century, no city in Asia or Europe could equal dazzling Cordoba. Its streets were well paved and lighted, and the city had an abundant supply of fresh water. With a population of about 1 million, Cordoba contained 1,600 mosques, 900 public baths, 213,177 houses for ordinary people, and 60,000 mansions for generals, officials, and the wealthy. In its 80,455 shops, 13,000 weavers produced silks, woolens, and brocades that were internationally famous. The English language has memorialized the city's leather with the word *cordovan.* Cordoba invented the process of manufacturing crystal. Cordoba was a great educational center with 27 free schools and a library containing 400,000 volumes. (By contrast, the great Benedictine abbey of Saint-Gall in Switzerland had about 600 books. The use of paper—whose manufacture the Muslims had learned from the Chinese—instead of vellum, gave rise to this great disparity.) Through Iran and Cordoba the Indian game of chess entered western Europe. Cordoba's scholars made contributions in chemistry, medicine and surgery, music, philosophy, and mathematics. Cordoba's fame was so great it is no wonder that the contemporary Saxon nun Hrosthwita of Gandersheim (d. 1000) could describe the city as the "ornament of the world."[31]

Intellectual Life

The wealth of Baghdad, the generous patronage of Harun al-Rashid, and the "international" character of Islamic culture launched a period of intellectual vitality. The cosmopolitan nature of the Mus-

Mosque of Cordoba Ordered by Abd al-Rahman (r. 756–768), founder of the independent Umayyad dynasty in Spain, the mosque at the market city and river port of Cordoba is located on the site of a Roman temple and Visigothic church. The vaulting is supported by twelve aisles of columns rhythmically repeated in every direction. Some architectural historians consider this mosque the most spectacular Islamic building in the world. *(Source: MAS, Barcelona)*

Public Library at Hulwan near Baghdad   In this scene from everyday life, the teacher, second from right with open book, instructs students by commenting on the text. Library books rest on the shelves in the background. *(Source: Bibliothèque Nationale, Paris)*

lim world facilitated this development. In spite of schism, warfare, and dynastic conflicts, several factors promoted Islamic unity: the sacred Arabic language of the Qur'an, the obligatory pilgrimage to Mecca, and dedication to scholarship and learning that combined Semitic, Hellenic, and Persian knowledge. "A scholar might publish in Samarkand the definitive work on arithmetic used in the religious schools of Cairo. Or, in a dialogue with colleagues in Baghdad and Hamadan, he could claim to have recovered the unalloyed teachings of Aristotle in the libraries of Fez and Cordoba."[32] Modern scholars consider Muslim creativity and vitality from about 900 to 1200 one of the most brilliant periods in the world's history.

Translations from Greek, Syrian, and Persian sources enabled Muslim scholars to absorb the major features of Semitic, Hellenic, Indian, and Persian civilizations. The Persian scholar al-Khwarizmi (d. ca 850) harmonized Greek and Indian findings to produce astronomical tables that formed the basis for later Eastern and Western research. Al-Khwarizmi also studied mathematics, and his textbook on algebra (from the Arabic *al-Jabr*) was the first work in which the word *algebra* is used to mean the "transposing of negative terms in an equation to the opposite side."

Muslim medical knowledge far surpassed that of the West. By the ninth century, Arab physicians had translated most of the treatises of Hippocrates. The Baghdad physician al-Razi (865–925) produced an encyclopedic treatise on medicine that was translated into Latin and circulated widely in the West. Al-Razi was the first physician to make the clinical distinction between measles and smallpox. The prevalence of eye diseases in the Muslim world encouraged medical people to study the eye. One result was the earliest book on ophthalmology. The great surgeon of Cordoba, al-Zahrawi (d. 1013), produced an important work in which he discussed the cauterization of wounds (searing with a branding iron) and the crushing of stones in the bladder. In Ibn Sina of Bukhara (980–1037), known in the West as "Avicenna," a physician, philologist, philosopher, poet, and scientist, Muslim science reached its peak. His *al-Qanun* codified all Greco-Arabic medical thought, described the contagious nature of tuberculosis and the spreading of diseases, and listed 760 pharmaceutical drugs. Muslim scholars also wrote works on geography and jurisprudence.

Likewise, in philosophy the Muslims made significant contributions. The Arabs understood philosophy not as a separate and distinct discipline but as a branch of theology related, like theology, to the study of the Qur'an. The Abbasid caliph al-Ma'mun (r. 813–833) established at Baghdad in 830 the House of Wisdom, a center for research and translation. Under the direction of Humayn ibn-Ishaq (d. 873), the House of Wisdom made a systematic effort to acquire and translate the chief works of ancient Greek philosophy and science. Humayn supervised the translation of almost all of Aristotle's works and the complete medical writings of Hippocrates. At the same research center al-Kindi (d. ca 870) was the first Muslim thinker to try to harmonize Greek philosophy and the religious precepts of the Qur'an. Al-Kindi sought to

Man Bitten by a Mad Dog Alert to the dangers of diseases transmitted by animals, such as rabies, the author of this text discusses pharmaceutical remedies. Medical manuscripts were greatly valued. *(Source: Courtesy of the Freer Gallery of Art, Smithsonian Institution)*

integrate Islamic concepts of human beings and their relations to God and the universe with the principles of ethical and social conduct discussed by Plato and Aristotle. Inspired by Plato's *Republic* and Aristotle's *Politics,* the distinguished philosopher al-Farabi (d. 950) wrote a political treatise describing an ideal city whose ruler is morally and intellectually perfect and who has as his goal the citizens' complete happiness. Avicenna maintained that the truths found by human reason cannot conflict with the truths of revelation as given in the Qur'an.

Ibn Rushid, or Averroës (1126–1198), of Cordoba was perhaps Islam's greatest Aristotelian philosopher. A judge in Seville and later royal court physician, Averroës paraphrased and commented on the works of Aristotle. He insisted on the right to subject all knowledge, except the dogmas of faith, to the test of reason.

The profound significance of these Muslim philosophers lies in the fact that through Latin translations of their Arabic and Hebrew writings, Greek philosophy was transmitted to the European West (see page 428). The leading philosophical system of medieval Europe, Scholasticism (see page 428), leaned heavily on Aristotelian thought. Europeans gained their knowledge of Aristotle primarily from Muslim translators and commentators.

The Muslim View of the West

Europeans and Muslims of the Middle East were geographical neighbors. The two peoples shared a common cultural heritage from the Judeo-Christian past. But a thick psychological iron curtain restricted contact between them. The Muslim assault on Christian Europe in the eighth and ninth centuries—with villages burned, monasteries sacked, and Christians sold into slavery (see page 352)—left a legacy of bitter hostility. Europeans' fierce intolerance also helped form the barrier between the two peoples. Christians felt threatened by a faith that acknowledged God as creator of the universe but denied the doctrine of the Trinity; that accepted Christ as a prophet but denied his divinity; that believed in the Last Judgment but seemed to make sex heaven's greatest reward. Popes preached against the Muslims; theologians penned tracts against them; and church councils condemned them. Europeans' perception

of Islam as a menace helped inspire the Crusades of the eleventh through thirteenth centuries (see pages 362–367). The knightly class believed that it had a sacred obligation to fight the Muslims, as a popular song during the Second Crusade put it:

God has brought before you his suit against the Turks and Saracens [Crusaders' hostile term for Muslims], who have done him great despite [injury]. They have seized his fiefs, where God was first served [that is, the holy places in Palestine] and recognized as Lord.[33]

During the Crusades, Europeans imposed Christianity on any lands they conquered from Islam, and they compelled Muslims to choose among conversion, exile, and death.

By the thirteenth century, Western literature portrayed the Muslims as the most dreadful of Europe's enemies, guilty of every kind of crime. In his *Divine Comedy,* the great Florentine poet Dante (see pages 432–433) placed the Muslim philosophers Avicenna and Averroës with other virtuous "heathens," among them Socrates and Aristotle, in the first circle of Hell, where they endured only moderate punishment. Muhammad, however, Dante consigned to the ninth circle, near Satan himself, where Muhammad was condemned as a spreader of discord and scandal. His punishment was to be continually torn apart from his chin to his anus.

Muslims had a strong aversion to travel in Europe. They were quite willing to trade with Europeans, but they rejected European culture. Medieval Europe had no resident Muslim communities where a traveler could find the mosques, food, or other things needed for the Muslim way of life. Muslims generally had a horror of going among those they perceived as infidels, and often when compelled to make diplomatic or business contacts, they preferred to send Jewish or Christian intermediaries, the *dhimmis.* Commercially, from the Muslim perspective, Europe had very little to offer. Apart from fine English woolens, which the Muslims admired, there was only a trickle of slaves from central and southeastern Europe.

Did Western culture have any impact on Islam? Muslims considered Christianity to be a flawed religion superseded by Islam. "For the Muslim, Christ was a precursor, for the Christian Muhammad was an impostor. For the Muslim, Christianity was an early, incomplete, and obsolete form of the true religion."[34] Religion dominated the Islamic perception of Europe. Muslims understood Europe not as Western, European, or white, but as Christian. And the fact that European culture was Christian immediately discredited it in Muslim eyes. Christians were presumed to be hostile to Islam and were thought to be culturally inferior. Thus Muslims had no interest in them.

An enormous quantity of Muslim historical writing survives from the period between about 800 and 1600. Although the material reflects some knowledge of European geography, it shows an almost total lack of interest among Muslim scholars in European languages, life, and culture. Before the nineteenth century, not a single grammar book or dictionary of any Western language existed in the Muslim world. By contrast, Western scholarship on the Middle East steadily advanced. By the early seventeenth century, a curious European student could find an extensive literature on the history, religion, and culture of the Muslim peoples. In 1633, a professorship in Arabic studies was founded at Cambridge University in England.)[35]

As in language and literature, so in science, engineering, and medicine: the medieval West had no influence on the Muslim world. Muslims had only contempt for Western science. Here is a twelfth-century account of a Muslim's impression of European medical practice:

The Lord of Munaytira (a Crusading Baron) wrote to my uncle asking him to send a physician to treat one of his companions who was sick. He sent him a . . . physician called Thabit. He had hardly been away for ten days, when he returned, and we said to him: "How quickly you have healed the sick!" and he replied, "They brought me two patients, a knight with an abscess on his leg, and a woman afflicted with a mental disorder. I made the knight a poultice, and the abscess burst and he felt better. I put the woman on a diet and kept her humour moist. Then a Frankish physician came to them and said to them: 'This man knows nothing about how to treat them!' Then he said to the knight: 'Which do you prefer, to live with one leg or to die with two?' and the knight said: 'To live with one.' Then the physician said: 'Bring me a strong knight and an ax,' and they brought them. Meanwhile I stood by. Then he put the sick man's leg on a wooden block and said to the knight: 'Strike his leg with the ax and cut it off with one blow!' Then, while I watched, he

struck one blow, but the leg was not severed; then he struck a second blow, and the marrow of the leg spurted out, and the man died at once.

"The physician then turned to the woman, and said: 'This woman has a devil in her head who has fallen in love with her. Shave her hair off.' So they shaved her head, and she began once again to eat their usual diet, with garlic and mustard and such like. Her disorder got worse, and he said:

" 'The devil has entered her head.' Then he took a razor, incised a cross on her head and pulled off the skin in the middle until the bone of the skull appeared; this he rubbed with salt, and the woman died forthwith.

"Then I said to them: 'Have you any further need of me?' and they said no and so I came home, having learned things about their medical practice which I did not know before." [36]

Only in the art of warfare did Muslims show an interest in European knowledge. During the Crusades, the Muslims adopted Frankish weapons and methods of fortification. Overall, though, medieval Muslims considered Christian Europe a backward land and almost always described Europeans as "ignorant infidels."[37]

SUMMARY

Islam is an extraordinary phenomenon in world history. Its universal monotheistic creed helps to explain its initial attractiveness to Bedouin tribes. Driven by the religious zeal of the *jihad,* Muslims carried their faith from the Arabian peninsula through the Middle East to North Africa, Spain, and southern France in the west and to the borders of China and northern India in the east—within the short span of one hundred years. Economic need, the political weaknesses of their enemies, strong military organization, and the practice of establishing army cities in newly conquered territories account for their expansion.

Two successive dynasties—the Umayyad, centered at Damascus in Syria, and the Abbasid, located at Baghdad in Iraq—governed the Islamic state. A large imperial bureaucracy headed by a vizier supervised the administration of the state. All government agencies evolved from the diwan. As provincial governors acquired independent power, which the caliphs could not check, centralized authority within the Islamic state disintegrated.

Commerce and trade also spread the faith of Muhammad. Although its first adherents were nomads, Islam developed and flourished in a mercantile milieu. By land and sea, Muslim merchants transported a rich variety of goods across Asia, the Middle East, Africa, and western Europe. Muslim business procedures and terminology have greatly influenced the West.

On the basis of the wealth that trade generated, a gracious, sophisticated, and cosmopolitan culture developed with centers at Baghdad and Cordoba. In the tenth and eleventh centuries, the Islamic world witnessed enormous intellectual vitality and creativity. Muslim scholars produced important work in many disciplines, especially mathematics, medicine, and philosophy. Muslim civilization in the Middle Ages was far in advance of that of Christian Europe, and Muslims, with some justification, looked on Europeans as ignorant barbarians.

NOTES

1. See F. McG. Donner, *The Early Islamic Conquests* (Princeton, N.J.: Princeton University Press, 1981), pp. 14–37.
2. J. L. Esposito, *Islam: The Straight Path* (New York: Oxford University Press, 1988), pp. 6–17. The quotation is on p. 15.
3. Donner, pp. 57–60.
4. Quoted in J. O'Faolain and L. Martines, eds., *Not in God's Image: Women in History from the Greeks to the Victorians* (New York: Harper & Row, 1973), pp. 108–115.
5. Quoted in P. K. Hitti, *The Near East in History* (Princeton, N.J.: Van Nostrand, 1961), p. 211.
6. Quoted in B. Lewis, ed. and trans., *Islam: From the Prophet Muhammad to the Capture of Constantinople,* vol. 1, *Politics and War* (New York: Harper & Row, 1974), p. 239.
7. Donner, pp. 92–101.
8. Quoted ibid., p. 217.
9. See B. Lewis, *The Muslim Discovery of Europe* (New York: Norton, 1982), pp. 59–63. Discussion herein is based heavily on this important work by Lewis.
10. See G. E. von Grunebaum, *Medieval Islam: A Study in Cultural Orientation* (Chicago: University of Chicago Press, 1954), pp. 142–150.
11. Quoted in Lewis, *Politics and War,* p. 201.
12. L. I. Conrad, "Caliphate," in *Dictionary of the Middle Ages,* vol. 3, ed. J. R. Strayer (New York: Scribner's, 1983), p. 45.
13. Quoted in R. Levy, *The Social Structure of Islam,* 2d ed. (Cambridge, England: Cambridge University Press, 1957), p. 55.
14. Ibid.
15. Hitti, *Near East in History,* p. 229.
16. B. Lewis, ed. and trans., *Islam: From the Prophet Muhammad to the Capture of Constantinople,* vol. 2, *Religion and Society* (New York: Harper & Row, 1975), pp. 219–221.
17. Quoted in Levy, p. 67.
18. N. Coulson and D. Hinchcliffe, "Women and Law Reform in Contemporary Islam," in *Women in the Muslim World,* ed. L. Beck and N. Keddie (Cambridge, Mass.: Harvard University Press, 1982), p. 37.
19. Quoted in B. F. Stowasser, "The Status of Women in Early Islam," in *Muslim Women,* ed. F. Hussain (New York: St. Martin's Press, 1984), p. 25.
20. Quoted ibid., pp. 25–26.
21. Quoted ibid., p. 26.
22. Quoted ibid., p. 16.
23. G. Nashat, "Women in Pre-Revolutionary Iran: A Historical Overview," in *Women and Revolution in Iran,* ed. G. Nashat (Boulder, Colo.: Westview Press, 1983), pp. 47–48.
24. F. Mernissi, *Beyond the Veil: Male-Female Dynamics in Modern Muslim Society* (New York: Schenkman, 1975), p. 16.
25. Ibid.
26. Quoted in D. J. Gerner, "Roles in Transition: The Evolving Position of Women in Arab Islamic Countries," in Hussain, *Muslim Women,* p. 73.
27. Lewis, *Religion and Society,* pp. 126–127.
28. Adapted from Lewis, *Religion and Society,* pp. 154–157.
29. Hitti, p. 278.
30. M. Rodinson, *Islam and Capitalism,* trans. Brian Pearce (Austin: University of Texas Press, 1981), p. 56.
31. R. Hillenbrand, "Cordoba," in Strayer, *Dictionary of the Middle Ages,* vol. 3, pp. 597–601.
32. P. Brown, "Understanding Islam," *The New York Review of Books,* February 22, 1979, pp. 30–33.
33. Quoted in R. W. Southern, *The Making of the Middle Ages* (New Haven, Conn.: Yale University Press, 1961), p. 55.
34. Lewis, *The Muslim Discovery of Europe,* p. 297.
35. Ibid., pp. 296–297.
36. Quoted ibid., p. 222.
37. Ibid.

SUGGESTED READING

In recent years, the literature on classical Islam has expanded greatly, and many studies are available in English. In addition to the works cited in the Notes, the curious student should see A. Hourani, *A History of the Arab Peoples* (1991), a highly readable and profound synthesis, and S. Fisher and W. Ochsenwald, *The Middle East: A History* (1990), which contains excellent bibliographical sections. The older studies of H. A. R. Gibb, *Mohammedanism: An Historical Survey,* 2d ed. (1970), and J. J. Saunders, *A History of Medieval Islam* (1965), are still useful. For the Prophet, see W. M. Watt, *Muhammad at Mecca* (1953) and *Muhammad at Medina* (1956), and M. Rodinson, *Mohammed* (trans. A. Carter, 1971). M. G. S. Hodgson, *The Classical Age of Islam,* vol. 1 of *The Venture of Islam* (1964), is comprehensive but written for the specialist. K. Cragg and R. M. G. Speight, eds., *Islam from Within: Anthology of a Religion* (1980), offers a fine collection of primary material on the beginnings of Islam. For the cultural impact of Islam, G. E. von Grunebaum, *Classical Islam: A History, 600–1258* (trans. K. Watson, 1970), remains valuable.

For law and religious authority within Islam, see N. J. Coulson, *A History of Islamic Law* (1964); J. N. D. Anderson, *Islamic Law in the Modern World* (1959); R. P. Mottahedeh, *Loyalty and Leadership in an Early Islamic Society* (1986); C. Cahen, "The Body Politic," in G. E. von Grunebaum, ed., *Unity and Variety in Muslim Civilization* (1955); A. K. S. Lambton, *State and Government in Medieval Islam (1981);* and S. D. Gottein, *Studies in Islamic History and Institutions* (1966). The best recent study of Muslim expansion is F. M. Donner, *The Early Islamic Conquests* (1986).

A. M. Watson, *Agricultural Innovation in the Early Islamic World* (1983) provides the best study of farming techniques and the diffusion of crops before 1100, while A. L. Udovitch, *Partnership and Profit in Medieval Islam* (1970) treats commercial practices in light of Islamic law and should be compared with the title by Rodinson cited in the Notes. For slavery in the Arab world, see B. Lewis, *Race and Slavery in the Middle East* (1990), which demythologizes the Western view of the Middle East as free of racial prejudice, and G. Murray, *Slavery in the Arab World* (1989), which explains the persistence of slavery in Muslim societies in sexual, not economic, terms.

W. M. Watt, *Islam and the Integration of Society* (1961), is an important sociological study of the economic and social factors that led to the unity of very diverse peoples. A. Talbot Rice, *Islamic Art,* rev. ed. (1985), provides a solid and well-illustrated introduction to the many media of Islamic art. O. Grabar, *The Formation of Islamic Art* (1973), offers a critical analysis of the themes in the development of Islamic art. R. E. Dunn, *The Adventures of Ibn Battuta: A Muslim Traveler of the Fourteenth Century* (1987), contains a fascinating account of Asian and African societies by a Muslim world traveler.

On the Mongols, see D. Morgan, *The Mongols* (1986), a highly readable sketch, and M. Rossabi, *Khubilai Khan: His Life and Times* (1988), which combines biography with a fine appreciation of Eurasian history in the thirteenth century.

11

Tradition and Change in Asia, ca 320–1400

Portrait of the poet Kodai-no-Kimi, or Koogimi

Between approximately 320 and 1400 the various societies of Asia continued to evolve their own distinct social, political, and religious institutions. These years saw momentous changes sweep across Asia. The tide of change surged back and forth between East and West. In the first half of the period Arab conquerors and their new Muslim faith reached the Indian subcontinent and Afghanistan. In central Asia they met the Turks moving westward from the borders of China. The result of this contact was widespread conversion of the Turks to Islam. Muslim Turks then spread their new religion to northern India, which they conquered. Others continued westward, settling in Anatolia and sinking the ethnic and cultural roots of modern Turkey. Meanwhile, Japan emerged into the light of history. Although affected by Chinese culture, philosophy, and religion, the Japanese adapted these influences to their way of life.

In the second half of the period the Mongols swept from their homeland north of China. They conquered China and unsuccessfully hurled two vast fleets at Japan. Toward the end of the period, the travels of the Venetian merchant Marco Polo to Peking gave promise of a new era of East-West contact.

This chapter explores three main questions:

- What effect did these great movements of peoples have on the traditional societies of Asia?
- How were new religious and cultural ideas received by the long-established cultures of the East?
- What political and economic effects did these events have on newcomer and native alike?

INDIA, FROM TRIUMPH TO INVASION (CA 320–1400)

Under the Gupta kings, India enjoyed one of the most magnificent cultural flowerings in its long history. By about 800 the caste system had fully evolved, dividing Indian society into thousands of self-contained subcastes. The incursion of the Muslim Turks—the second permanent foreign influence on India—introduced a new religion that also accelerated the decline of Buddhism in India.

The Gupta Empire (ca 320–480)

For years after the fall of Mauryan power, India suffered fragmentation and foreign domination, but even political turmoil did not interrupt the evolution of Indian culture. Not until about 320 did another line of Indian kings, the Guptas, extend their authority over much of the subcontinent. Founded by Chandragupta—unrelated to the founder of the Mauryan Empire by the same name—the Guptas' original home was in the area of modern Bihar in the Ganges Valley. The Guptas consciously modeled their rule after that of the Mauryan Empire. Although the Guptas failed to restore Ashoka's empire, they united northern India and received tribute from states in Nepal and the Indus Valley. They also gave large parts of India a period of peace and political unity.

The real creator of the Gupta Empire was Chandragupta's son Samudragupta (ca 335–375), who defeated many of the rulers of southern India and then restored them to their thrones as his subjects. With frontier states he made alliances, and over them he extended his protection. By means of military conquest and political shrewdness, Samudragupta brought much of India from the Himalayas in the north to the Vindhya Mountains in the south under his government (Map 11.1).

Once firmly in power, Samudragupta preferred leniency and diplomacy to force of arms. Like Ashoka, he adhered to the ideal of a just king who ruled according to *dharma* (the moral law). Following Ashoka's example (see page 81), he proclaimed the glories of his reign on rocks and pillars throughout the land. In one of his most important pronouncements, inscribed on a stone pillar erected by Ashoka some six hundred years earlier, Samudragupta extolled his own fame, power, and personal qualities:

His far-reaching fame, deep-rooted in peace, emanated from the restoration of the sovereignty of many fallen royal families. . . . He, who had no equal in power in the world, eclipsed the fame of the other kings by the radiance of his versatile virtues, adorned by innumerable good actions. He, who was enigmatic, was the real force that generated good and destroyed the evil. Having a compassionate heart, he could easily be won over by faithfulness, loyalty, and homage.[1]

Samudragupta had reason to boast of his accomplishments. By putting an end to weakness and

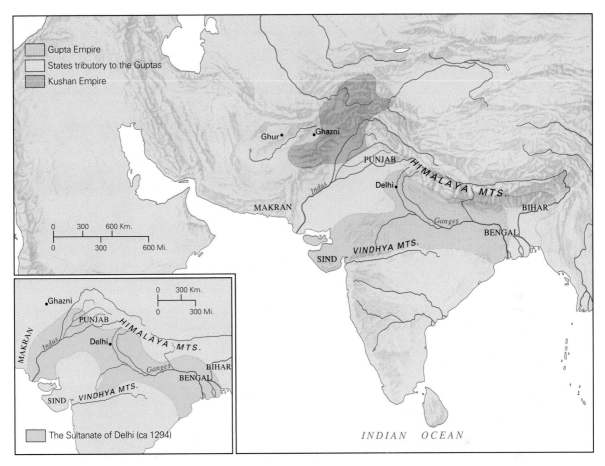

MAP 11.1 Political Map of India, ca 400–ca 1294   This map and inset show the political face of India from the time of the imperial Guptas to the arrival of Muslim invaders. They also demonstrate the importance of the Indus and Ganges river valleys, perhaps the most coveted area in India.

fragmentation, he laid the foundations of India's golden age.

Samudragupta's many achievements were matched by those of his son Chandragupta II (ca 375–415), under whom the glory of the Guptas reached its height. Perhaps Chandragupta's most significant exploit was the overthrow of the Shakas (invaders from the borders of China) in western India. As a result of that victory, the busy maritime trade conducted by the rich seaports of western India with the Middle East and China came under the protection of the Guptas. Chandragupta II put the Indian people into direct touch with the wider world once again, and as in the past this contact involved ideas as well as goods.

The great crisis of the Gupta Empire was the invasion of the Huns, the nomads whose migration

from central Asia shook the known world. By at least 450 a group of them known as the "White Huns" thundered into India. Mustering his full might, the ruler Skandagupta (ca 455–467) threw back the invaders; only a few Huns settled in northern India, where they were in time absorbed by the native population. Although the Huns failed to uproot the Gupta Empire, they dealt the dynasty a fatal blow. By 500 the glory of the Gupta kings was past. Later kings, like the great Harsha (ca 606–647), made valiant efforts to reunite the Gupta Empire, but the country once again reverted to a pattern of local kingdoms in constant conflict.

Even though they failed to unite India permanently, the Guptas set the stage for one of the most splendid epochs in Indian cultural history. Interest

The Mriga Jataka The Buddhist caves at Ajanta contain the most important surviving collection of wall paintings from the Gupta period. Religious in inspiration, they are also spontaneous and unrestrained, as this detail of a royal servant holding an energetic dog on a leash reflects. *(Source: Satish Pavashav/Dinodia Picture Agency)*

in Sanskrit literature, the literature of the Aryans, was a prominent feature. Sanskrit was also the spoken language of India, one that was written in its own script. Sanskrit masterpieces were preserved, and traditional epic poems and verses on mythological themes were reworked and polished to a higher sheen. The Gupta period also saw the rise of Indian drama. India's greatest poet, Kalidasa (ca 380–450), like Shakespeare, melded poetry and drama. Poets composed epics for the courts of the Gupta kings, and other writers experimented with prose romances and popular tales.

In science, too, the Gupta period could boast of impressive intellectual achievements. Science never appealed to the Indians as much as religion, but Indian mathematicians arrived at the concept of zero, which is necessary for higher mathematics. Other scientific thinkers wrestled with the concept of gravitation long before the day of Sir Isaac Newton.

The greatness of the Guptas is neither limited to their political achievements nor diminished by their ultimate failure. They saved India for a period from political fragmentation, foreign domination, and confusion. The peace they established released cultural and intellectual energies that shaped one of the sunniest epochs in India's long history.

Daily Life in India

The first reliable and abundant information about the daily life of the Indian people dates from the period of the Gupta Empire. One of the most instructive and, to modern minds, amazing characteristics of Indian society is its remarkable stability and veneration for its age-old customs and traditions. Since Indian society changed slowly and gradually, it is possible to take a good long look at daily life and social customs in the millennium between the fourth and the fourteenth centuries.

Although Indian agriculture ranged from subsistence farming to the working of huge estates, agricultural life ordinarily meant village life. The average farmer worked a small plot of land outside the village, aided by the efforts of the extended family. All the family members pooled their resources—human, animal, and material—under the direction of the head of the family. Shared work, shared sacrifice, and joint confrontation of hazards strengthened family ties. The Indian farming

family usually lived close to the bone: bad weather and heavy taxes frequently condemned its members to a lean year of poverty and hardship.

To all Indian farmers, rich and poor, water supply was crucial. India's great scourge is its merciless droughts, which cause plants to wither, the earth to crack, and famine to stalk the countryside. Indian farmers quickly learned to drill deep into the ground to tap permanent sources of water. They also irrigated their fields by diverting rivers and digging reservoirs and canals. As in Hammurabi's Mesopotamia, maintenance of waterworks demanded constant effort, and disputes over water rights often led to local quarrels.

The agricultural year began with spring plowing. The ancient plow, drawn by two oxen wearing yokes and collars, had an iron-tipped share and a handle with which the farmer guided it. Similar plows are still used in parts of India. Once plowed and sown, the land yielded a rich variety of crops. Rice, the most important and popular grain, was sown at the beginning of the long rainy season. Beans, lentils, and peas were the farmer's friends, since they grew during the cold season and were harvested in the spring when fresh food was scarce. Cereal crops like wheat, barley, and millet provided carbohydrates and other nutrients, and large estates grew sugar cane. Some families cultivated vegetables, spices, and flowers in their gardens. Village orchards kept people supplied with fruit, and the inhabitants of well-situated villages could eat their fill of fresh and dried fruit and sell the surplus at a nearby town.

Indian farmers raised and bred livestock, the most highly valued of which were cattle. Cattle were used for plowing and esteemed for their milk. Their hides and horns were precious raw materials, as were the fleeces of sheep. All the animals of the community were in the hands of the village cowherd or shepherd, who led them to and from pasture and protected them from wild animals and thieves.

Farmers fortunate enough to raise surpluses found ready markets in towns and cities. There they came into contact with merchants and traders, some of whom dealt in local commodities and others in East-West trade. Like their Muslim counterparts, Indian merchants enjoyed a respectable place in society. Given India's central geographical position between China and the West, there were huge profits to be made in foreign commerce. Daring Indian sailors founded new trading centers along the coasts of Southeast Asia, and in the process spread Indian culture. Other Indian merchants specialized in the caravan trade that continued to link China, Iran, India, and the West. These hardy merchants conducted cargoes from Indian seaports northward to the overland routes across central Asia.

Local craftsmen and tradesmen lived and worked in specific parts of the town or village. Their shops were open to the street; the family lived on the floor above. The busiest tradesmen dealt in milk and cheese, oil, spices, and perfumes. Equally prominent but disreputable were tavern-keepers. Indian taverns were haunts of criminals and con artists, and in the worst of them fighting was as common as drinking. In addition to these tradesmen and merchants a host of peddlers shuffled through towns and villages selling everything from bath salts to fresh-cut flowers.

Although leatherworkers were economically important, their calling was considered beneath the dignity of anyone but *outcastes* (those without places in the traditional social structure). Indian religious and social customs condemned those who made a living handling the skins of dead animals. Masons, carpenters, and brickmakers were more highly respected. As in all agricultural societies, blacksmiths were essential. Pottery was used in all households, but Indian potters, unlike their counterparts in the ancient Near East and the Greco-Roman world, neither baked their wares in kilns nor decorated them. Indian potters restricted themselves to the functional. The economic life of the village, then, consisted of a harmonious balance of agriculture and small business.

What of the village itself—its people and its daily sights? Encircled by walls, the typical village was divided into quarters by two main streets that intersected at the center of the village. The streets were unpaved, and the rainy season turned them into a muddy soup. Cattle and sheep roamed as freely as people. The villagers shared their simple houses with such household pets as cats, parrots, and geese. Half-wild mongooses served as effective protection against snakes. The pond outside the village, which served as its main source of water, also bred fish, birds, and mosquitoes. Women drawing water frequently encountered water buffaloes wallowing in the shallows. After the farmers returned from the fields in the evening, the village gates were closed until morning.

Towns and cities were also typically laid out in a square or rectangular pattern, always situated near a lake or river. They, too, were fortified by walls and towers and entered through gates. A city was usually surrounded by a moat, into which the gutters flowed; the moat often served as a source of drinking water. The streets of cities and towns were paved and flanked by gutters. Every sizable city or town had a marketplace where villagers could sell their surplus to townspeople and peddlers hawked their wares. Nearby were temples, houses, and the usual shops and craftsmen's stalls. Part of every major city was devoted to parks, fountains, and gardens. The populations of particularly prosperous cities often spilled over outside the walls into crowded and squalid slums. Here worked some of the most despised elements of the population: butchers, public executioners, and undertakers. Sometimes the slums evolved into cities that ringed the original city.

The period following the fall of the Guptas saw the slow proliferation and hardening of the caste system. Early Indian society was divided into four major groups: priests (Brahmans), warriors (Kshatriyas), peasants (Vaishyas) and serfs (Shudras) (see page 70). Further subdivisions arose, reflecting differences in trade or profession, tribal or racial affiliation, religious belief, and place of residence. By about 800 these distinctions had solidified into an approximation of the caste system as it is known today. Eventually Indian society comprised perhaps as many as three thousand castes. A caste sustained its members, giving them a sense of belonging and helping to define their relations to members of other castes. Yet the caste system further fragmented society. Each caste had its own governing body, which enforced the rules of the caste. Those incapable of living up to the rules were expelled, becoming outcastes. These unfortunates lived hard lives, performing tasks that others considered unclean or lowly.

For all members of Indian society, regardless of caste, marriage and the family were the focus of life. Once again, far more is known about the upper levels of society than about the lower. As in earlier eras, the Indian family of this period was an extended family: grandparents, uncles and aunts, cousins, and nieces and nephews lived together in the same house or compound. The joint family was under the authority of the eldest male, who might take several wives. The family affirmed its

Indian Monastic Life Some of the most important duties in a monastery were purely ritualistic. Students often had the duty to keep the sacred fire burning. Some students chopped wood and others carried the logs, which still others placed on the fire. Each played a part in the symbolic ritual. *(Source: Musée Guimet, Cliché des Musées Nationaux)*

solidarity by the religious ritual of honoring its dead ancestors, which linked the living and the dead.

Special attention was devoted to the raising of sons, but all children were pampered. The great poet Kalidasa depicts children as the greatest joy of their father's life:

With their teeth half-shown in causeless laughter,
and their efforts at talking so sweetly uncertain,
when children ask to sit on his lap
a man is blessed, even by the dirt on their bodies.[2]

In poor households children worked as soon as they were able. In wealthier homes children faced the age-old irritations of reading, writing, and arithmetic. Less attention was paid to daughters, though in the most prosperous families they were usually literate.

The three upper castes welcomed boys fully into the life of the caste and society with a religious initiation symbolizing a second birth. Ideally, a boy then entered into a period of asceticism and religious training during which he mastered at least part of one Veda. Such education was at the hands of *gurus*, Brahman teachers with whom the boys boarded. In reality, relatively few went through this expensive education.

Having completed their education, young men were ready to lead adult lives, the first and foremost step in which was marriage. Child-marriage, unknown in earlier periods, later became customary. Indians considered child-marriage desirable, in part because of their attitudes toward women. Girls were thought to be unusually fascinated by sex. Lawgivers feared that young girls left to their own whims would take lovers as soon as they reached puberty and become pregnant before they were married. Girls who had lost their virginity could seldom hope to find good husbands; most became financial burdens and social disgraces to their families. Indian law even warned fathers that they sinned grievously unless they betrothed a daughter before her first menstrual period. Indian custom also held that in the best marriages the husband was at least three times as old as his wife. Daughters were customarily betrothed before they reached puberty, often to men whom they had never seen. The wedding and consummation of the marriage did not take place, however, until after a girl had reached puberty and could start a family.

After an elaborate wedding ceremony, a newly married couple set up quarters in the house or compound of the bridegroom's father. In contrast to ancient Jewish practice, newlyweds were not expected to consummate their marriage on the first night. Indian custom delicately acknowledged that two strangers, though married, might need some time to adjust to their new mode of life. Hindu ritual advised couples to forgo sex for the first three nights so that they could become acquainted.

An Indian wife had two main duties: to manage the house and to produce children, preferably sons. Her husband was her master, to whom she owed obedience; Indian women spent their entire lives, from childhood to old age, under the authority of men. Indian law was blunt:

A woman is not independent, the males are her masters. . . . Their fathers protect them in childhood, their husbands protect them in youth, and their sons protect them in age; a woman is never fit for independence.[3]

Denied a significant role in life outside the home, wives made the household their domain. All domestic affairs were under their control. As a rule, women rarely left the house, and then only with a chaperone. They did accompany their husbands to weddings, great festivals, and quiet outings with the family. Among one stratum of high-caste Hindus, the Kshatriyas, wives' bonds with their husbands were so strong that a widow was expected to perform the act of *sati,* throwing herself on his fu-

neral pyre. In medieval periods it was strongly felt that a true and faithful wife—a *sati,* for whom the practice of self-immolation was named—should have no life apart from her husband, yet there is reason to think that this custom did not become common practice.

Within the home, the position of a wife often depended chiefly on her own intelligence and strength of character. In the best of cases a wife was considered a part of her husband, his friend and comforter as well as his wife. Wives were traditionally supposed to be humble, cheerful, and diligent even toward worthless husbands. In reality, some women took matters into their own hands. Far from being docile, they ruled the roost. An Indian verse paints a vivid picture of what a henpecked husband could expect:

But when she has him in her clutches
it's all housework and errands!
"Fetch a knife to cut this gourd!"
"Get me some fresh fruit!"

"We want wood to boil the greens,
and for a fire in the evening!"
"Now paint my feet!"
"Come and massage my back!"

So . . . resist the wiles of women,
avoid their friendship and company
The little pleasure you get from them
will only lead you into trouble![4]

Most women, however, were frankly and unashamedly subservient to their husbands. Nevertheless, despite the severe limitations of her society, the typical wife lived her days honored, cherished, and loved by her husband and family.

The most eagerly desired event was the birth of children. Marriage had no other purpose. Before consummating their marriage, the newlyweds repeated traditional prayers for the wife immediately to become pregnant. While pregnant, the wife was treated like a queen, nearly suffocated with affection and attention, and rigorously circumscribed by religious ritual. Members of the family carefully watched her diet and exercise, and women of her caste prayed that she would bear sons. Labor and birth were occasions of religious ceremony. While the women of the household prepared for the birth, the husband performed rituals intended to guarantee an easy delivery and a healthy child. After the child's birth, the parents performed rituals intended to bring the baby happiness, prosperity, and desirable intellectual, physical, and moral qualities. Infants were pampered until they reached the age of schooling and preparation for the adult world.

India and Southeast Asia

Between about 650 and 1250, Indian merchants and missionaries disseminated Indian culture throughout Southeast Asia, the area stretching eastward roughly from Burma to Vietnam and southward to Malaysia and Indonesia. The earlier history of the area is the product of archeological studies. So far the evidence has allowed scholars to trace the movements of numerous peoples without being able to tell very much about them. It is known that Indian penetration of Southeast Asia changed things considerably, and Sanskrit gave peoples a common mode of written expression.

The impact of the Indians was so pervasive that historians often refer to this phenomenon as the "Indianization of Southeast Asia." The phrase, though useful, must not be applied too sweepingly. The demands of trade frequently led to small Indian settlements, generally located on the coast, stretching from modern Thailand in the west to the Mekong Delta of modern Vietnam (Map 11.2). In these trading posts Indians met natives, and the result was often intermarriage and the creation of a culture fertilized by both. The greatest influence of India on Southeast Asian societies came in the courts of local rulers, who often adopted Indian customs and values, embraced Hinduism and Buddhism, and learned Sanskrit.

Although there is no denying Indian influence on Southeast Asia, its strength should not be exaggerated. Indian culture never supplanted the various native cultures that it encountered. Outside the courts of the rulers, native societies maintained their own cultural identity, even when they assimilated various Indian customs. Perhaps two

MAP 11.2 The States of Southeast Asia   This map illustrates the greatest extent of several major Southeast Asian states between ca 650 and ca 1250. The boundaries are somewhat approximate, for states gained and lost territory several times during this long period.

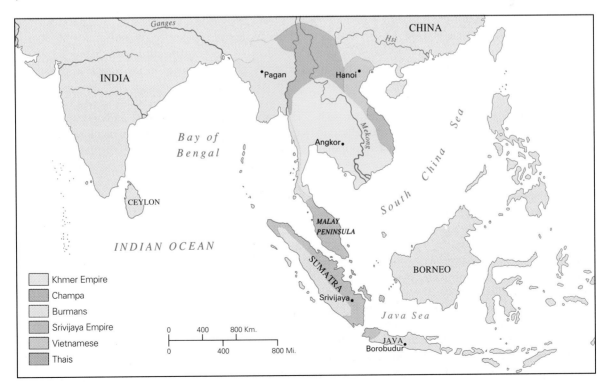

examples can illustrate the process. Among other things, Indian merchants brought to Java their literary epics. There they introduced the *Ramayana,* an epic poem describing the deeds of the Vedic heroes. The tale appealed to the Javanese, who retained the essentials of the Indian narrative but added to it native Javanese legends, thus creating a work that did not belong solely to either culture. So, too, with religion. Early peoples in the region of Cambodia (modern Kampuchea) adapted Buddhism to their own customs and beliefs, as did the peoples of ancient Tibet. They both became Buddhist societies, but their forms of Buddhism varied markedly because each people applied its native values and attitudes to the imported religion. In both cases local tradition changed Buddhism in its own likeness.

When the Indians entered Southeast Asia, they encountered both indigenous peoples and newcomers moving southward from the frontiers of China. Their relations with these peoples varied greatly. Contact with the vigorous tribes moving into the southern areas of the mainland was generally peaceful. But with the native states in the Malay Peninsula and the islands of the Indian Ocean, commercial rivalry sometimes led to active warfare. Although many of the events of these years are imperfectly known, a fairly clear picture has emerged of the Indianization of the Vietnamese, Thais, Burmans, Kampucheans, and the native peoples of the islands (see Map 11.2).

On the mainland three major groups of newcomers pushed southward toward the Indian Ocean from the southern borders of China. Their movements entailed prolonged fighting as each people strove to win a homeland. As in other such extensive migrations, the newcomers fought one another as often as they fought the native populations. The Vietnamese established themselves on the eastern coast of the mainland. In 939 they became independent of China and extended their power southward along the coast of present-day Vietnam. Of all these peoples, the Vietnamese were the least influenced by Indian culture. The Thais lived to the west in what is today southwestern China and northern Burma. In the eighth century the Thai tribes united in a confederacy and even expanded northward against T'ang China; like China, however, the Thai confederacy fell to the Mongols in 1253. Still farther west another tribal people, the Burmans, migrated in the eighth century to the area of modern Burma. They too

established a state, which they ruled from their capital, Pagan, and came into contact with India and Ceylon.

The most important mainland state was the Khmer Empire of Kampuchea, which controlled the heart of the region. The Khmers were indigenous to the area, and around 400 they had created an independent state. Their empire, founded in 802, eventually extended its southern borders to the sea and the northeastern Malay Peninsula. Generally successful in a long series of wars with the Vietnamese, Khmer power reached its peak, then declined after 1219.

Far different from these land-based states was the maritime empire of Srivijaya, which originated as a city-state on the island of Sumatra. Like the Khmers, the people of Srivijaya were indigenous. Their wealth was based on seaborne trade and tolls on ships passing through their waters. To protect their commercial interests, they created a navy strong enough to rule the waters around Sumatra, Java, and Borneo. At its height the Srivijaya Empire controlled the eastern coast of Sumatra, the southern half of the Malay Peninsula, and the western tip of Java. Though long predominant in the area, Srivijaya suffered a stunning blow in 1025: a commercial rival in southern India launched a large naval raid that succeeded in capturing the king and capital of the empire. Unable to hold their gains, the Indians retreated, but the Srivijaya Empire never recovered its former vigor. By the mid-thirteenth century it was further weakened by the arrival of Chinese traders and eventually fell to local rivals.

Although the political histories of all these peoples varied, their responses to Indian culture were similar. The coastal states, influenced by the presence of trading stations, were the first to adopt and adapt Indian ways. The very concept of kingship came from India. Local rulers and their elites, like good Indian kings, began to observe dharma and to govern their peoples by its precepts. Sanskrit, both the Indian language and the script in which it was written, surmounted the barriers raised by the many different native languages of the region. Indian mythology took hold, as did Indian architecture and sculpture. Some of the world's greatest edifices were erected in central Java and Kampuchea, inspired by Indian building principles, techniques, and cultural ideals. Kings and their courts, the first to embrace Indian culture, consciously spread it to their subjects.

Angkor Wat The great artistic achievement of the Khmers was the planning and building of Angkor Wat, an enormous and lavishly decorated temple. The temple also reflects Indian influence, for the god chiefly honored here is Vishnu. *(Source: Jean-Claude Labbé/Gamma-Liaison)*

Indian religion was also instrumental in this process. Certain aspects of Hinduism proved popular, but Buddhism took Southeast Asia by storm. Buddhism emphasized the value of popular education, and its temples, monasteries, and missionaries helped bring education to the common people. Especially influential was the Buddhist concept of the *bodhisattva,* a buddha-in-becoming (see page 78). Inspired by this ideal, many kings and local rulers strove to give their subjects good and humane government. Buddhist missionaries from India played a prominent role in these developments. Local converts continued the process by making pilgrimages to India and Ceylon to worship and to observe Indian life for themselves.

By the twelfth century, Indian culture, secular and religious, had found a permanent new home in Southeast Asia. A major consequence was that the Indianization of Southeast Asia was for the most part peaceful in that unlike western newcomers in modern times no truly forced colonization seems to have occurred. Chinese influence flourished more strongly among the Vietnamese, and Islam would later rival Buddhism; but Indian culture persisted, especially in the southern part of the region. Seldom has the world seen such a protracted and pervasive cultural diffusion. It stands as a monument to the vitality and magnetism of Indian civilization.

India Under Siege

Between roughly 650 and 1400 India experienced turmoil and invasion, as wave after wave of foreign armies moved into the subcontinent. Arabs, Turks, and Mongols all swept into India. Particularly during the six centuries from 636 to 1296, invaders beat against India and its neighbors. This complex and imperfectly understood phenomenon had four distinct phases. The Muslim Arabs' attack on the Sind area (636–713) was followed by the battle for Afghanistan (643–870). Muslims next pushed into the Punjab (870–1030) and finally conquered the valley of the Ganges (1175–1206). Between onslaughts, conflict persisted between newcomer and native.

Arabs under the leadership of Muhammad ibn-Qasim reached the western coast of modern Pakistan in 636 and pushed on into the Sind and the Indus Valley (see Map 11.1). But the Islamic conquest of northern India came at the hands of Turkish converts to Islam, not these first Arab invaders. While huge numbers of Turks advanced on the Byzantine Empire and won control of Asia Minor, others also remained in the East. One group established a small kingdom in northeastern Iran and Afghanistan, with its capital at Ghazni. In 986 Sabuktigin, a Turkish chieftain and devout Mus-

Arab Invasion Arab cavalry, mounted on camels, stormed into India. The camels allowed the Arabs, who were armed with lances and swords, to strike quickly over great distances. *(Source: Edinburgh University Library)*

lim, launched his initial raid into the Punjab. Once again, India suffered its age-old fate: invasion by a strong and confident power through the northwestern corridor. Sabuktigin's son Mahmud stepped up the frequency and intensity of the raids until he had won the Punjab. Then, like other invaders before him, he began pushing toward the Ganges. Mahmud systematically looted secular palaces and Hindu shrines, and he destroyed Indian statues as infidel idols. Even the Arab conquerors of the Sind fell to him. The Indus Valley, the Punjab, and the rest of northwestern India were in the grip of the invader.

Mahmud's death gave India roughly a century and a half of fitful peace marred by local conflicts. Then a new line of Turkish rulers that had arisen in Afghanistan, with its capital at Ghur (see Map 11.1), southwest of modern Kabul, renewed Muslim attacks on India. Muhammad of Ghur planned to annex the land he attacked, rather than merely plunder it. After conquering Mahmud's Indian holdings, he struck eastward toward the Ganges in 1192. Muhammad's generals captured Delhi and by the end of the twelfth century had extended their control nearly throughout northern India. Like Mahmud, Muhammad and his generals considered Hindu and Buddhist religious statues nothing more than idols; Muslim troops destroyed them in vast numbers. Buddhist centers of worship and learning suffered grievously. The great Buddhist university at Nalanda in Bihar was destroyed by a Turkish raiding party in 1193. Most Buddhists took refuge from this dual military and religious assault in Tibet and places farther east. Buddhism, which had thrived so long in peaceful and friendly competition with Hinduism, was pushed out of its native soil by the invaders.

When Muhammad fell to an assassin in 1206, one of his generals, the former slave Qutb-ud-din, seized the reins of power and made his capital at Delhi. Qutb-ud-din established the sultanate of Delhi, a Muslim kingdom that ruled northern India from the Indus to Bengal from 1206 to 1526 (see inset, Map 11.1). As early as 1327 the Muslim sultans of Delhi had brought a large portion of India under their control. The Muslims, like the Aryans centuries before them (see pages 68–73), were a conquering minority. To prevent assimilation by the far more numerous Indians, they recruited Turks and Iranians from outside India; they also provided a haven for elite Muslim refugees fleeing the widespread Mongol devastation of Iran and

INDIA, CA 320–CA 1400

ca 320–480	Gupta Empire
ca 380–450	Kalidasa, India's greatest poet
636–1206	Muslim invasions of India
1192	Destruction of Buddhism in India
1290–1320	Sultanate of Delhi
1398	Timur conquers the Punjab and Delhi

the Middle East. Both groups of newcomers reinforced the Islamic impact on India. Under the sultanate of Delhi, Iranian influences deeply affected Hindu art and architecture. Iranians introduced the minaret—an essential architectural feature of the mosque—as well as the arch and the dome. So great was the impact of Iranian Muslims that Urdu, the official language of modern Pakistan, evolved as a mixture of Persian with Arabic and Hindi.

The most lasting impact of the invader was religious. Islam replaced Hinduism and Buddhism in the Indus Valley (modern Pakistan) and in Bengal at the mouth of the Ganges (modern Bangladesh). Elsewhere in India, where Muslim influence was far less powerful, Hinduism resisted the newcomers and their religion. Most Indians looked on the successful invaders simply as a new ruling caste, capable of governing and taxing them but otherwise peripheral to their lives. Hinduism was bolstered in this attitude by the caste system: the myriad castes largely governed themselves, isolating the newcomers. Hinduism also enjoyed profound devotion on the part of the Indian people. The years of war and invasion had not hindered the development of a pious, devotional Hinduism called Bhakti. Bhakti emphasized personal reverence for and worship of a Hindu deity such as Krishna, Shiva, or Rama. Bhakti nourished impassioned love of the Hindu gods among ordinary folk. In some instances the Bhakti tradition sought synthesis with Islam; in others, converts to Islam retained much of Hindu tradition. In all cases there was a certain amount of mutual borrowing. In general, Hinduism's beliefs and social organization had a strong hold over the people of India; roughly 75 percent remained Hindu.

Muslim control over most of the subcontinent was short-lived. By 1336 a native Indian kingdom in the south effectively resisted the Muslims. In the north, the Muslims were dominant longer but still suffered the traditional fate of foreign conquerors of the north. In 1398 the Turkish chieftain Timur, lord of central Asia, Iran, and Mesopotamia, pushed into the Punjab and captured Delhi. To Timur, India was merely a source of loot. When his troops were sated with destruction and slaughter, Timur retired from India, leaving the Muslims and Hindus to pick up the pieces.

By about 1400 India was as politically divided as it had been before the Gupta Empire. Yet the events of the preceding millennium had had more than political and military significance. The march of armies had brought Islam into India and driven Buddhism out. Meanwhile Hinduism had flourished. These developments were to be critically important for the future of the entire region, for in them lie the origins of the modern nations of India, Pakistan, and Bangladesh.

CHINA'S GOLDEN AGE (580–CA 1400)

The years between the fall of the Han Dynasty in the third century and the rise of the Ming in the fourteenth brought some of China's brightest days and some of its darkest. During this period the Chinese absorbed foreign influences, notably Buddhism, that fundamentally shaped their society. Chinese cultural traditions, especially Confucianism, drew new strength and vitality from abroad. This was a golden era of enormous intellectual and artistic creativity in Chinese history.

Sui, T'ang, and Sung emperors and statesmen reunited the empire, repaired the foundations of national strength, and once again made China one of the world's unrivaled states. Even later political disruption, particularly the invasion of the Mongols, could not undo the achievements of those who shaped the history of these years. Nor were invasions and internal chaos enough to break the spirit of the Chinese people. The Mongols were the first foreigners ever to rule all of China, but their domination lasted only ninety-seven years, until the Ming emperors once again united the land under a native dynasty.

Buddhism Reaches China

Between the fall of the Han Dynasty in 220 and the rise of the Sui in 589, Buddhism reached China from the west. Merchants and travelers from India spread word of the new religion in the north while Indian sailors were introducing it into China's southern ports. Buddhism reached China at a time when many thinkers were doubting the value of traditional Confucian thought and many ordinary people wanted a message of hope. Buddhism initially won a place for itself in China because it offered a refreshing and novel solution to social disruption and political chaos (see pages 76–78). Buddhism was ultimately successful in China because it had powerful appeal for many different segments of society. To Chinese scholars, the Buddhist concepts of transmigration of souls, karma, and nirvana posed a stimulating intellectual challenge. For rulers the Buddhist church was a source of magical power and a political tool: since it was neither barbarian nor Chinese, this foreign faith could embrace both groups equally. To the middle and lower classes, Buddhism's egalitarianism—the teaching that enlightenment was available to all—came as a breath of fresh air. Buddhism spoke to all, regardless of their social class. Thus the lower orders of society believed that they had as much chance as the elites to live according to Buddha's precepts. For them especially, simple faith and devotion alone could win salvation. For many, regardless of social status, Buddhism's promise of eternal bliss as the reward for a just and upright life was deeply comforting. In a rough and tumultuous age, moreover, Buddhism's emphasis on kindness and the value of human life offered hope of a better future on earth. Similarly, Buddhist teachings on the value of charity and good works had a profound impact on Chinese morality. Besides holding out a path to salvation in the next world, Buddhism offered a practical program for improving life in this world.

If Buddhism changed Chinese life, China likewise changed Buddhism. Mahayana Buddhism, the more flexible and widespread of Buddhism's two schools (see page 78), gave rise to several new sects responsive to specific Chinese needs. The T'ien-t'ai sect, which later gave rise to the Tendai sect in Japan (see page 325), was favored by Chinese scholars, who attempted to resolve the numerous intellectual problems in Buddhism and to organize its doctrines in keeping with traditional Chinese thought. Most popular was the Pure Land sect, which retained many of the most appealing aspects of Mahayana Buddhism. It too would later have a vast impact on Japanese society. Like its Indian counterpart, this sect was very lenient. Instead of following Buddha's Eightfold Path, people had only to declare their sincere faith in Buddha to reach paradise, the "pure land." Many simple and uneducated people found in the Pure Land sect a comforting route to joy scarcely attainable on earth. Meanwhile the True Word sect, which won more popularity in Japan than in China, promised adherents immortality through magic, rituals, and chants. Last, the Ch'an sect, the forerunner of Zen Buddhism in Japan, combined elements of Taoism and Buddhism. Like Taoism itself, Ch'an dreamed of a return to nature and simplicity and preached that individuals were responsible for their own ultimate enlightenment. In this respect Ch'an was quite similar to Buddha's teaching that each person must tread the path of enlightenment alone. Ch'an emphasized meditation and the individual search for enlightenment instead of the learning and scholarship of the T'ien-t'ai sect. One of the prime reasons for Buddhism's success in China was its extraordinary ability to accommodate itself to local thought, beliefs, and conditions.

Buddhist monks from abroad introduced monasticism to China, and the resulting monasteries became more than merely centers for religious practice and study. Like their Christian counterparts in medieval Europe (see pages 355–357), Buddhist monasteries played an active role in social, economic, and political life. Buddhist missionary monks traveled the trade routes with Buddhist merchants, who gave the newly formed

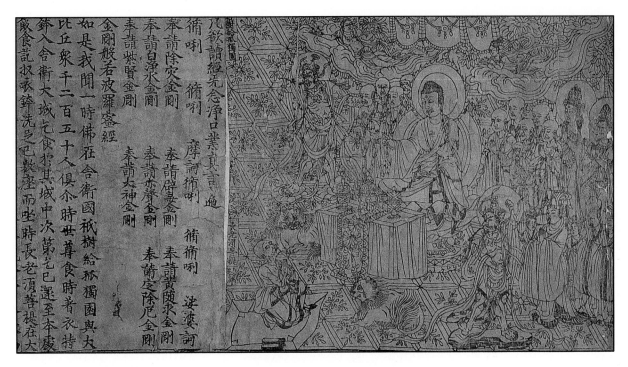

Buddhism Reaches China   This scene brilliantly illustrates the spread of Buddhism from India to China. The writing at the left, printed in Chinese characters, is a translation of a Buddhist text originally written in Sanskrit. This scene of Buddha addressing a follower is also the earliest dated example of blockprinting. *(Source: The British Library)*

monasteries a secular function: increasingly, they entrusted their money and wares to the monasteries for safekeeping, in effect transforming the monasteries into banks and warehouses. Buddhist merchants often endowed monks with money or land to support temples and monasteries. The monks, who thus became powerful landlords, hired peasants to work the monastic and temple lands, and the tenants in turn became ready converts to Buddhism. Formidable in wealth and numbers, monasteries became influential participants in politics, rivaling the power of the traditional Chinese landlords. The monasteries' prosperity and political power further protected converts from local Chinese lords and reinforced the spread of Buddhism.

Buddhism also had a profound impact on the artistic life of China. Buddhist art, like the faith's religious message, first reached China along the Silk Road. At Tun-huang in northwestern China, thousands of artists worked for centuries to transform a mile-long stretch of hillside into a monumental shrine. The life of Buddha also offered

Chinese painters and sculptors a wealth of new themes. From the fourth century on, Buddha and his life became inseparable from Chinese art.

Thus Buddhism's appeal to the Chinese was religious, social, and artistic. Its message struck a sympathetic chord among nobles and peasants alike. It endowed China with a new view of human dignity, the promise of personal salvation, and a compelling vision of peace.

The T'ang Dynasty (618–907)

The T'ang emperors rose to greatness on the shoulders of their predecessors, the Sui Dynasty (ca 581–618). The Sui resembled the Ch'in of the third century B.C. (see pages 99–100) in that both were short-lived dynasties that restored political order to a storm-tossed land and set the stage for splendid successors. Sui land reforms helped to restore prosperity, and Sui waterworks strengthened ties between northern and southern China. The crowning achievement of the Sui was the Grand

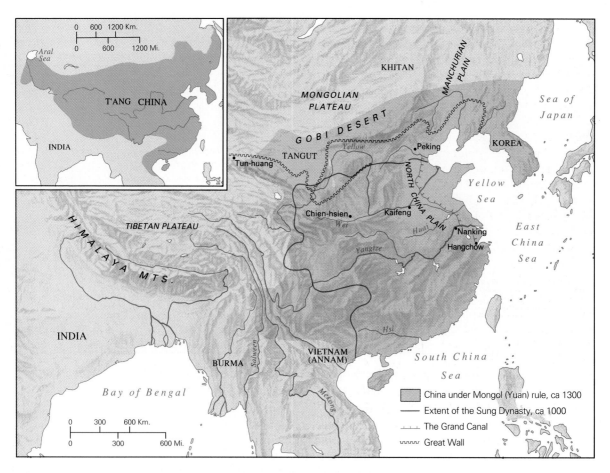

MAP 11.3 The Political Divisions of China from the T'ang to Yuan Dynasties, 618–1368 This map and inset illustrate how the T'ang Dynasty and its successors were able to sustain the expanded frontiers of the Han Dynasty, although their hold in the west was always somewhat tenuous.

Canal, connecting the eastern reaches of the Yellow River to the eastern waters of the Huai and Yangtze rivers (Map 11.3). The canal facilitated the shipping of tax grain from the recently developed Yangtze Delta to the centers of political and military power in northern China. Henceforth the rice-growing Yangtze Valley and southern China generally played an ever more influential role in the country's economic and political life, strengthening China's internal cohesion.

Though successful as reformers, the Sui emperors fell prey to a grim combination of military defeat and massive peasant uprisings. From these unlikely conditions rose the T'ang Dynasty (618–907), probably the greatest dynasty in Chinese history. Its founder, who took the imperial name T'ai Tsung, was far more than a mere upstart who eliminated the last Sui emperor. In addition

to being an able general and astute politician, T'ai Tsung was also an educated and far-sighted administrator who followed conscientiously the lessons of Chinese history. Having seen the results of oppression, T'ai Tsung avoided extravagance and continued Sui reforms.

T'ai Tsung tried first to alleviate the poverty of the peasants. Building on the Sui system, he ordered that land be divided among the peasants as equally as possible and that imperial officials safeguard the peasants' holdings. A prosperous peasantry, in T'ai Tsung's view, would provide a secure and steady base of income for the empire. In practice, the attempt to equalize landholdings quickly broke down, and by 780 the law was revoked. Even so, T'ai Tsung's efforts were not entirely in vain: he had done enough to give agriculture a much-needed boost, and productivity increased in both grain and livestock. Not since the Han Dynasty had the peasants been so well off.

In the civil sphere, T'ang accomplishments far outstripped anything known in Europe until the growth of national states in the seventeenth century (see Chapter 19). T'ang emperors subdivided the administration of the empire into departments, much like the numerous agencies of modern governments. T'ang departments oversaw military organization, maintenance and supply of the armies, foreign affairs, administration of justice, finance, building and transportation, education, and much else. During this period no other state on earth was as politically sophisticated as the T'ang Empire.

A bureaucracy of this scope demanded huge numbers of educated and trained personnel; as in earlier eras of strong central government, the imperial administration offered a lucrative career to talented Chinese. T'ang emperors revived and expanded the Han method of hiring and promoting government officials on the basis of education, ability, and merit. This process reinforced Confucian values, ethics, and emphasis on scholarship. Candidates for official positions were expected to learn the Confucian classics, to master the rules of poetry, and to discuss practical administrative and political matters. Universities were founded to train able and dedicated young men. Graduates passed a demanding battery of oral and written examinations to prove their ability. Training was hard and long; although students did not endure the physical discipline of Mesopotamian scribes, they sacrificed much to achieve success.

Students who passed the official examinations had unlimited futures ahead of them. Talent, education, and a bureaucracy theoretically based on merit promised them high office, wealth, and prestige. Although the rich and powerful often sidestepped the system of formal examinations, the T'ang created an effective civil service long before anything comparable developed elsewhere in the world. The T'ang emperors deserve full credit for the mandarin system of professional public service. Despite weaknesses and loopholes for the influential, the T'ang administrative system was so effective that it lasted into the twentieth century.

Mandarin scholar-officials also played an important cultural role. Since much of an official's training involved the study of literature, history, and politics, China's literary heritage became integral to contemporary life. Because nearly any literate man in the empire could take the examinations, centers for study sprouted throughout China. Knowledge of the classics spread throughout the empire, encouraging cultural unity. The weakness of the mandarin system was its narrow outlook and inflexibility, which stifled originality

Portrait of T'ai Tsung The founder of the T'ang dynasty, T'ai Tsung was an emperor possessing character and vision. He initiated reforms that were intended to help the peasants and increase agricultural productivity. Here he is portrayed as a determined and cultured leader. *(Source: Wan-go Weng/National Palace Museum, Taipei)*

and independence of thought. Nonetheless, the mandarin system was an institution in which people from every part of China could meet on a common ground.

In foreign affairs the T'ang turned their attention first to the Turks, who had spread their power from the northern borders of China to the Byzantine Empire in Asia Minor. By T'ai Tsung's death in 649, Chinese armies had conquered all of Turkestan in the west. The T'ang also turned to Korea, but they had much less success there than the Han had had seven centuries earlier. Chinese influence in Tibet came somewhat more peacefully, despite some Sino-Tibetan rivalries and wars. For years the Tibetans had lived a partly nomadic and partly agricultural life on China's western border. Then in the early seventh century one of their chieftains unified the Tibetan tribes and sought a marriage alliance with T'ai Tsung. The emperor sent his daughter to Tibet with musicians, craftsmen, and technicians to introduce new tools and techniques, along with books on Chinese agricultural methods. The Tibetans modeled their culture partially on the T'ang; the Koreans and Japanese adopted Chinese culture more enthusiastically. China's script and literature, Buddhism, crafts, and political ideas and techniques spread widely, making Chinese culture dominant throughout eastern Asia.

The Sung Dynasty (960–1279)

In the middle of the eighth century, T'ang foreign policy collapsed in rout and rebellion. The defeat of Chinese armies in central Asia and on the southwestern border undercut the emperor's authority. The sources of this crisis varied from the changing demands of frontier defense to stupid imperial decisions. At last in 755 a powerful general, An Lu-shan, revolted in response to imperial maltreatment. An Lu-shan was defeated, but other generals followed his example. The T'ang Dynasty ended in a conflagration of military rebellions, peasant uprisings, and barbarian invasions. The period from 907 to 960, known as the "Era of the Five Dynasties," resembled the age of the barracks emperors of the Roman Empire (see page 217). In northern China rival generals struggled against barbarians and against one another to establish permanent dynasties. Southern China fragmented into ten independent states. Weak and distracted, China presented an easy target to the barbarians, and one group of nomads, known as the "Khitan," captured Peking and most of northeastern China and Manchuria.

The founder of the Sung Dynasty, the northern general Chao K'uang-yin, made his bid for empire in 960. Unsuccessful against the Khitans in the northeast and the Tanguts, a now-extinct ethnic group, in the northwest, Chao K'uang-yin recognized that he lacked the resources to engage all his enemies simultaneously. He thus sought peace with the Khitan and Tanguts by paying them both annual tribute. He then mapped out a broad strategy to annex the economically prosperous southern states, most of which fell to him easily. Gradually Chao K'uang-yin—known as "Emperor Sung T'ai Tsu"—unified southern China and extended his influence as far as Indonesia.

Despite sporadic warfare, the early Sung period enjoyed broad-based economic prosperity for a variety of demographic and economic reasons. The population had increased to an unprecedented 100 million. Rapidly increasing urbanization went hand in hand with greatly expanded agricultural productivity. Advances in the technology and production of coal and iron also played quite a significant part, as did improvements in communications. Efficient water transport fostered the development of a national market for domestic products. The tea trade boomed: in the Han period tea had been a luxury item, but under the T'ang period tea had become immensely popular throughout China. Trade was brisk in other commodities as well. Porcelain continued to be a prime export and domestic product. Salt continued to be a state monopoly. By bringing political stability to southern China, the Sung fostered commercial expansion.

The political and economic success of the Sung permitted the technological innovations of the T'ang period to reach full growth. Foremost among them was the invention of printing, which changed the history of China and the entire world. T'ang craftsmen developed the art of carving words and pictures onto wooden blocks, inking them, and then pressing the blocks onto paper. Each block consisted of an entire page of text and illustrations. Such whole-page blocks were being printed as early as the middle of the ninth century, and in the eleventh century movable type was invented. Movable type was never widely used in China, but when this Chinese invention reached

Europe in the fifteenth century (see page 520), it revolutionized the communication of ideas. In China as in Europe, the invention and spread of printing dramatically increased the availability of books and lowered their price. Scholarship flourished, and literacy spread rapidly among the general population.

The T'ang and Sung periods were rich in technological innovation. The T'ang invented gunpowder, originally for use in fireworks. By the early Sung period people were using gunpowder to propel arrows—in effect, the first rockets. Later, projectiles were given a gunpowder charge so that they exploded on impact. Although the cannon still lay in the future, the Chinese began to develop artillery long before it was known in other parts of the world.

Other inventions included the abacus, which allowed quick computation of complicated sums. The combination of the water wheel and the bellows enabled smelters to increase the output of pig iron. Under the Sung, government-operated spinning and weaving mills produced cheap, durable, and comfortable cotton clothing.

Economic vitality and the consolidation of Sung rule gave a great impetus to urbanization. In fact, city dwellers were becoming economically more important than the landed gentry. Rich urbanites indulged in increasingly costly dress and food. Women suffered a severe decline in social standing, the most obvious expression of which was the custom of footbinding. As long as women's labor was needed to help keep starvation from the door, women possessed a certain status, albeit lowly. In prosperous urban households, however, women no longer fulfilled an economic function and became ornaments of status. To show the world that they need not work, mothers bound the feet of their infant daughters until the arches broke and the foot healed to half its normal growth. Not until the twentieth century was this custom abandoned.

Although the Sung unified central and southern China and created the climate for new prosperity, they never fully solved the problem of political relations with the Khitan and Tangut states in the north.

Whenever possible, the Sung used diplomacy to avoid war and play off one state against the other. In 1114, however, the political situation became more complex. The Jurchen, a people from the northeastern frontier, threw off the yoke of the

Head of the Dragon This elaborate tower is the creation of the astronomer Guo Shoujing, who in 1283 used it to calculate the length of the solar year. He was accurate to within twenty seconds. *(Source: Patrick Lui & Associates)*

Khitan state and in 1125 toppled their former overlords. Flushed with success, the Jurchen marched against the Sung, and in 1126 they sacked the Sung capital and drove the remnants of the imperial court to the southern city of Hangchow.

The Sung emperors who governed from Hangchow, commonly known as the "Southern Sung Dynasty," held on to the area below the Yangtze River from 1127 to 1279. The Southern Sung resisted the northerners but established a stable border with them. Although there never was genuine peace between the two, fighting was usually limited to border areas. For 152 years the Southern Sung flourished, despite the annual tribute they paid to the northerners.

CHINA, CA 320–CA 1400

220–589	Buddhism reaches China
580–618	Sui Dynasty and restoration of public order
618–907	T'ang Dynasty: economic, political, and artistic flowering
907–960	Era of the Five Dynasties: warfare and revolt
960–1279	Sung Dynasty and Neo-Confucian thought
1021–1086	Wang An-shih, author and political reformer
1215–1368	Mongol conquest of China
ca 1300	Marco Polo travels in China

The Southern Sung period is especially notable for a great increase in the volume of maritime trade, both oceanic and coastal. Chinese shipwrights built large, stable junks with huge cargo capacity. These ships enabled Chinese merchants to sail directly to Korea and Japan, which became eager importers of Chinese goods. Ocean voyages were rendered considerably easier and safer by the Chinese invention of the magnetic compass, which was widely used in China at least two centuries earlier than in the rest of the world. The shipping of Chinese goods to the West was mostly in the hands of Arabs, who like their Roman and Indian predecessors, used the annual monsoon winds to sail to ports in India and East Africa. Thus southern China under the Sung entered fully and prosperously into a commercial network that stretched from Japan all the way to the Mediterranean.

The invention of printing and the increased volume of trade led to two momentous innovations: the use of paper money and the development of banking. The standardized currency introduced under the First Emperor in the third century had been bulky copper coinage (see page 99). Paper money originated under the Sung as notes of deposit—documents certifying that a person had deposited a specific amount of copper coinage with the government. Notes of deposit rapidly gave way to true paper money, which anyone could cash in for copper coins. The legendary Venetian merchant and adventurer Marco Polo (ca 1254–1342) wrote one of the earliest descriptions of how Chinese paper money was issued:

The coinage of this paper money is authenticated with as much form and ceremony as if it were actually of pure gold or silver; for to each note a number of officers, specially appointed, not only subscribe their names, but affix their signets also; and when this has been regularly done by the whole of them, the principal officer . . . having dipped into vermillion the royal seal committed to his custody, stamps with it the piece of paper, so that the form of the seal tinged with the vermillion remains impressed upon it.[5]

To this day American paper money carries the signatures of federal officials, the seals of the Federal Reserve Bank, and the Great Seal of the United States; only the vermillion is absent.

Merchants increasingly used the convenient and portable paper money as a medium of exchange. The popularity of paper money also gave rise to the new profession of counterfeiting; Chinese counterfeiters risked their heads, for those inept or unlucky enough to be caught were decapitated. Paper money in turn gave rise to a system of credit and banking that enabled merchants to deposit money, take out loans, and invest in commercial ventures. Facilitated by the new monetary and banking systems, trade burgeoned so much that the Sung government derived more revenue from trade and taxes on trade than from the traditional land tax.

Yet despite their political and economic success, the Southern Sung emperors were living in the twilight of a great era: in the north a new and unforeseen danger, the Mongols, was on the verge of shaking the world from China to Hungary.

Cultural Blossoming of the T'ang and Sung

The economic reforms, political stability, and military successes of the T'ang and Sung nourished a splendid era in the history of Chinese culture. Although the T'ang period is best known for its poetry, many forms of art flourished during these years. Potters produced porcelain of extraordinarily high quality and delicate balance. The finest porcelain was produced in state factories for use at court or as royal gifts to foreign dignitaries. Later, porcelain of uniformly high quality became a major item of export to western Asia and Europe.

Within the past seventeen years the excavations of T'ang imperial tombs at Chien-hsien in Shensi province have shed welcome light on the sculpture and painting of this vibrant period. T'ang emperors were customarily accompanied to their graves by a crowd of monumental stone figures and ceramic statuettes. At Chien-hsien scores of life-size statues of horses and warriors guard the tombs while rows of statues of dignitaries, lions, and sheep stand in silent audience. Inside the tombs, ceramic statuettes of ceremonial troops serve as guardians.

The royal tombs display T'ang painting at its best. The walls are graced with the painted figures of respectful mandarins, court ladies, and warrior guards. Scenes of hunting and polo lend an air of energy and vivacity. Mythological creatures ward off evil spirits. Realistic and graceful in form, the paintings exhibit a sophisticated sense of perspective. The total effect is joyous, even gay. T'ang painters captured life accurately and with a deft touch.

New developments in the T'ang period widened the horizons of prose writing. The translation of Buddhist texts originally written in Indian and central Asian languages introduced new concepts, styles of writing, and literary devices to the Chinese language. In turn, translators had to adapt Chinese to these foreign languages. Mandarins, too, needed a flexible literary medium in which to write their official reports. Writers consciously

Chinese River Festival   All of the beauty and delicacy of Chinese painting is obvious in this lively scene of people enjoying a river festival. Like the great poets, Chinese painters delighted in scenes from daily life. *(Source: The Metropolitan Museum of Art, Fletcher Fund, 1947, The A. W. Bahr Collection)*

aimed at greater clarity and easier means of expression. Some writers used this new flexibility to create the prose essay as a literary form. Prose in the T'ang period became a more useful tool for the bureaucracy and a distinctive literary genre.

The glory of T'ang literature was its poetry, which achieved unmatched elegance and brilliance. T'ang poetry was sophisticated, urbane, and learned. Thoroughly familiar with earlier poetry and with history, T'ang poets were also influenced by Chinese and foreign folk songs. They were consummate masters of meter and rhythm, their poems often gemlike. Though formal and rigorous in composition, T'ang poetry expresses genuine emotion, frequently with humor and sensitivity. Some poets strung songs together to accompany drama, in effect creating Chinese opera. T'ang poets created new vehicles for verse, and they themselves became the models for their Sung successors and all later Chinese poets.

One of the most delightful of the T'ang poets was Li Po (701–762), whose poetry is polished, learned, and good-natured. Unlike most T'ang poets, Li Po was never a mandarin official, although he was familiar with the cultivated life of the imperial court. He was a member in good standing of the literary circle known as the "Eight Immortals of the Wine Cup," and his poems allude often to his love of wine. Even banishment from the court did not dampen his spirits, for Li Po loved his wine, his art, and all of nature too much ever to become morose. One of his most famous poems describes an evening of drinking with only the moon and his shadow for company:

A cup of wine, under the flowering trees;
I drink alone, for no friend is near.
Raising my cup I beckon the bright moon,
For he, with my shadow, will make three men.
The moon, alas, is no drinker of wine;
Listless, my shadow creeps about at my side.

. . .

Now we are drunk, each goes his way.
May we long share our odd, inanimate feast,
And we meet at last on the cloudy River of the sky.[6]

Another poem captures a moment of joy while walking in the mountains on a summer day:

Gently I stir a white feather fan,
With open shirt sitting in a green wood.

I take off my cap and hang it on a jutting stone;
A wind from the pine-trees trickles on my bare head.[7]

Li Po is said to have died one night in the company of his old friend the moon.

Less cheerful but no less talented was Po Chü-i (772–846), whose poems often reflect the concerns of a scholar-official. He felt the weight of his responsibilities as governor of several small provinces and sympathized with the people whom he governed. At times Po Chü-i worried about whether he was doing his job justly and well:

From my high castle I look at the town below
Where the natives of Pa cluster like a swarm of flies.
How can I govern these people and lead them
*   aright?*
I cannot even understand what they say.

But at least I am glad, now that the taxes are in,
To learn that in my province there is no discontent.[8]

Watching the reapers in the fields, he described their work and wondered about their fate and his:

Tillers of the soil have few idle months;

. . .

Suddenly the hill is covered with yellow corn.
Wives and daughters shoulder baskets of rice;
Youths and boys carry the flasks of wine.
Following after they bring a wage of meat
To the strong reapers toiling on the southern hill,
Whose feet are burned by the hot earth they tread,
Whose backs are scorched by flames of the shining
*   sky.*

. . .

And I to-day . . . by virtue of what right
Have I never once tended field or tree?

. . .

Thinking of this, secretly I grew ashamed;
And all day the thought lingered in my head.[9]

Like most other T'ang poets, Po Chü-i keenly appreciated nature. Though a high official, he enjoyed such simple things as the pine trees growing around his house and a river babbling over its stony bed. Forced to retire from official life because of ill health, he took discomfort and retirement in graceful stride. At age seventy-four he died of a stroke, comforted by his wine and poetry. He had lived a long life with few regrets.

The artists and thinkers of the Sung period brought to fulfillment what the T'ang had so brilliantly begun. Buoyed by political stability and economic prosperity, the Sung explosion of learning and thought was a direct result of the invention of printing. The availability of books enabled scholars to amass their own libraries and thus to pursue their studies more easily and deeply. Sung scholars formed circles to discuss their interests and ideas and to share their work with others. Sung publishers printed the classics of Chinese literature in huge editions to satisfy scholarly appetites. Works on philosophy, science, and medicine were also consumed avidly. Han and T'ang poetry and historical works became the models for Sung writers' own work. One popular literary innovation was the encyclopedia, which first appeared in the Sung period, at least five centuries before publication of a European encyclopedia.

One of the most influential Sung schools of thought (which gave rise to an intellectual trend known as Neo-Confucianism) was that of Wang An-shih (1021–1086), whose interests embraced economics, politics, literary style, and the classics of Chinese literature. As a Sung minister of state, Wang An-shih launched a series of political and economic innovations with his "New Laws." The "Young Shoots" law extended low-interest loans to poor farmers, as some governments do today. Another law substituted a graduated tax for forced labor on state work projects. Like the Roman emperor Diocletian (see page 218), Wang An-shih introduced official price controls and limitations on profits; he went further than Diocletian by coupling this measure with a plan to equalize the land tax. Though marked by realism and good sense, Wang An-shih's innovations ultimately failed. When his imperial patron died, he was left powerless and defenseless. Ideological warfare and heavy bureaucratic infighting among officials stifled action. The New Laws also met with serious opposition from wealthy merchants and great landowners.

Other schools of Neo-Confucian thought confronted purely intellectual problems and left a more enduring imprint. The Ch'eng-Chu school achieved one of the greatest intellectual feats of a great age by adding a metaphysical dimension to traditional Confucianism's secular approach to human life and the universe. Metaphysics—the theoretical philosophy of being—gave Confucianism an intellectual depth and sophistication that equipped it to challenge what had long been a Buddhist monopoly of ultimate truth.

Neo-Confucians mined Confucian, Buddhist, and Taoist thought to create this new metaphysics. Meanwhile one of the finest minds of the age, Chu Hsi (1120–1200), addressed himself to the metaphysical problem of evil, evolving ideas that correspond roughly to Plato's theory of forms (see page 141). Like Plato, Chu Hsi concluded that everything that exists has a specific form, or *li*. *Ch'i*, or matter, combines with li to make up the material world. When the two are out of balance, the result is evil. People can correct this imbalance, Chu Hsi taught, through Confucian study and Buddhist meditation. In effect, Chu Hsi explained not only how evil develops in the world but how it can be corrected.

Chu Hsi's talents extended to the classics of Chinese literature, on which he wrote learned commentaries. He was also the premier historian of his day. In striving for a unified view of life and the universe, he interpreted history and literature in support of his philosophical ideas. Unparalleled among Neo-Confucians, Chu Hsi's writings became classics; they have been read, revered, and imitated for centuries. He and other intellectuals breathed new life into Confucianism to meet the challenge of Buddhism.

Sung poets and painters matched the greatness of their T'ang predecessors. The Sung particularly excelled at painting. Two dramatically dissimilar approaches to art arose: some painters, like Li Lung-mien (ca 1040–1106), stressed exact realism; others, like Mi Fei (ca 1051–1107), pursued a mystical romanticism in which space and natural elements were suggested with a few brush strokes.

The culture of the T'ang and Sung periods is remarkable for its breadth and variety, as well as its brilliance. From painting to poetry, from philosophy to history, these years gave rise to exquisite masterpieces.

The Mongol Conquest (1215–1368)

In 1215 the Southern Sung and their northern neighbors felt the first tremor of what was to be among the most remarkable movements of people in all history. Jenghiz Khan (1162–1227) and his huge band of Mongols, Tatars, and Turks (see pages 278–279) burst into northern China. Marco Polo left a vivid description of their endurance and military skill:

They are brave in battle, almost to desperation, setting little value upon their lives, and exposing themselves without hesitation to all manner of danger. Their disposition is cruel. They are capable of supporting every kind of privation, and when there is a necessity for it, can live for a month on the milk of their mares, and upon such wild animals as they may chance to catch. Their horses are fed upon grass alone, and do not require barley or other grain. The men are habituated to remain on horseback during two days and two nights, without dismounting, sleeping in that situation whilst their horses graze. No people on earth can surpass them in fortitude under difficulties, nor show greater patience under wants of every kind.[10]

In 1215 the Mongols overwhelmed the Jurchens in the north and captured Peking. All

Marble Gate near the Great Wall This majestic arch, erected in 1345, marks the site where the Mongol leader Jenghiz Khan fought and won a major battle against the Chinese. Although it is the monument of a foreign ruler, the arch is typically Chinese in its design and decoration. *(Source: Courtesy Smith College)*

of northern China fell in 1234. The Southern Sung held out tenaciously against the invaders, but Jenghiz Khan's grandson Kublai Khan (1216–1294) extinguished the dynasty and annexed all of southern China by 1279 (see Map 11.3). For the first time in history, all of China was ruled by foreigners. By 1271 Kublai Khan (also known as the Great Khan) had proclaimed himself emperor of China and founder of the Yuan Dynasty (1271–1368).

The Mongols distrusted the traditional mandarin class yet needed their bureaucratic system. They compromised by assigning foreigners—Turks, Muslims from central Asia, and even a handful of European adventurers—to the highest administrative posts and allowing Chinese to hold lower offices. The Mongol conquest did not hinder China's trade, which continued the expansion begun under the Sung. By establishing his capital at Peking, Kublai Khan helped reunite northern and southern China commercially: the wealth of the south flowed north to sustain the capital.

A conquering minority, the Mongols proclaimed repressive laws against the far more numerous Chinese. They divided society into four classes with varying rights, privileges, and legal protection. The Mongols themselves enjoyed full protection under the law; below them were their foreign administrators. The northern Chinese, who had been conquered first, had broader political and legal rights than the southerners but bore a far heavier burden of taxes and services. The southern Chinese shouldered a very light tax load but suffered heavy legal and political discrimination. The Mongols disarmed the Chinese people and forbade them to assemble in large numbers and even to travel by night. The Chinese were captives in their own country.

Yet in internal affairs the Mongols welcomed contact with the outside world. Historians have begun to debate whether Mongol rule was really as harsh as it is usually depicted. Some scholars argue that the Mongols provided a climate of peace and toleration that facilitated friendly relations with those involved in long-distance trade. They see the Mongols as opening China to the West. Other historians point to the restrictions placed on the Chinese as evidence that the Mongols were anything but philanthropists. A realistic, or even cynical, view is that it served the Mongols, who were outsiders, very handsomely to seek outside economic support for their rule, all the while

The Silk Road   The Mongol conquest at least secured the safety of merchants traveling the Silk Road. There were few inns or hostels along the route, except in the cities, and most merchants, like those here, pitched camp each night by their camels. *(Source: National Palace Museum, Taiwan)*

keeping the Chinese in their place. The Mongols were hardly altruists, but they did keep the peace in China.

Into this world wandered Marco Polo with his father and uncle. The three Polos had journeyed by land across Asia to the court of Kublai Khan, who received them with warmth and curiosity. Adept in four Asian languages, Marco Polo was uniquely equipped to collect accurate information about China. He probably never traveled far from Peking but instead drew heavily on Chinese accounts. He trained his insatiable curiosity on the land of China, its people and their customs, and everything likely to stimulate commerce. After seventeen years in China, the Polos returned to Italy, where Marco wrote a vivid account of their travels. At first considered sheer fantasy, his book

was widely read and contributed enormously to familiarizing Europeans with Asia.

Mongol repression bred bitter resentment throughout China. By the middle of the fourteenth century, moreover, the Mongol hold on East Asia was weakening. Struggles among claimants to the Yuan throne seriously compromised the Great Khan's power and prestige, and Kublai Khan's successors proved weak and incompetent. In this atmosphere of crisis, some Chinese formed secret societies—underground resistance groups dedicated to overthrowing the oppressor. The most effective secret society, known as the "Red Turbans," consisted of peasants and artisans, who had suffered the most from Mongol rule. In 1351 the rebels were ready to strike. Their rebellion caught the Mongols totally off guard. One of the rebels, a poor peasant and former monk best known to history as Hung Wu, later became the first Ming emperor.

In 1356 Hung Wu and his followers stormed the important city of Nanking. Securing control over southern and central China, they pushed the Mongols northward, and by 1368 the Chinese had driven the Mongols completely out of China. Hung Wu established the Ming Dynasty (1368–1644). Once again China was united under one of its sons. In the following years Ming emperors would continue to push the Mongols north. They also rebuilt the Chinese economy by reclaiming abandoned farmland, by repairing neglected dikes and canals that were essential to fruitful agriculture, and by reforesting the countryside. As a result, under Ming rule China again prospered.

JAPAN, DAWN OF THE RISING SUN

Japan entered the light of history late, and Japanese historical writing originated even later. The earliest reliable information on Japan comes from sporadic notices in Chinese histories, the first of which dates only from A.D. 57. Little is known about the origins and formative years of the Japanese people. By the time of their first appearance in history, they had already had extensive exposure to Chinese culture. Yet though the Japanese derived much from the Chinese, they molded their borrowings to suit their special needs. Early Japan saw the growth of an indigenous culture that was influenced but never overwhelmed by the Chinese.

The Japanese Islands

The heart of Japan is four major islands, the largest and most important of which is Honshu. The three southern islands surround the Inland Sea, a narrow stretch of water dotted with smaller islands (Map 11.4). All four major islands are mountainous, with craggy interiors and some active volcanoes. Rugged terrain divides the land into numerous small valleys watered by streams. There is little flat land, and only 16 percent of the total area is arable. Japan's climate ranges from subtropical in the south, which the Pacific bathes in warm cur-

rents, to a region of cold winters in the north. Rainfall is abundant, favoring rice production. Yet nature can be harsh: Japan is a land buffeted by earthquakes, typhoons, and tidal waves.

Despite occasional rages, the sea provides a rich harvest, and the Japanese have traditionally been fishermen and mariners. Since the land is rugged and lacking in navigable waterways, political unification by land was difficult until the modern period. The Inland Sea, like the Aegean in Greece, was the readiest avenue of communication. Hence the land bordering the Inland Sea developed as the political and cultural center of early Japan. Geography also blessed Japan with a moat, the Korean Strait, and the Sea of Japan. Great powers like the Han and T'ang dynasties and the Mongols might overrun the Asian continent, but their grasp never reached to the Japanese islands. Japan did not suffer a single successful invasion until the Second World War, when American and Allied troops stepped ashore after the Japanese surrender in 1945. Consequently, the Japanese have for long periods been free to develop their way of life without external interference. Continuity has been a hallmark of Japanese history.

Early Japan and the Yamato State

The beginnings of Japanese history are lost in the mists of legend. The Chinese historian Wei Chih wrote one of the earliest reliable descriptions of Japanese life in A.D. 297:

The land of Wa [Japan] is warm and mild. In winter as in summer the people live on raw vegetables and go barefooted. They live in houses; father and mother, elder and younger, sleep separately. They smear their bodies with pink and scarlet, just as the Chinese use powder. They serve food on bamboo and wooden trays, helping themselves with their fingers.[11]

The society that Wei Chih and other Chinese sources portray was based on agriculture and dominated by a warrior aristocracy. Clad in helmet and armor, these warriors wielded swords and battle-axes and often the bow. Some of them rode into battle on horseback. Social stratification was rigid, peasants serving at the command of nobles. At the bottom of the social scale were slaves—usually house servants. Slaves may have accounted for about 5 percent of the total population.

Early Japan was divided into numerous political units, although by about 513 their number had been greatly reduced. Each pocket of local authority was under the rule of a particular clan—a large group of families that claimed descent from a common ancestor and worshiped a common deity. Each clan had its own chieftain, who marshaled clan forces for battle and served as clan chief priest. In Japan as in many other ancient societies, political power was a function of family strength, organization, and cohesion.

By the third century A.D. the Yamato clan had seized the fertile area south of Kyoto, near Osaka Bay (see Map 11.4). At the center of the Yamato holdings was a rich plain, which constituted the chief economic resource of the clan. Gradually the Yamato clan, which traced its descent from the sun-goddess, subordinated a huge number of other clans to create the Yamato state. The chieftain of the Yamato clan proclaimed himself emperor and ruler over the other chieftains. The Yamato harnessed the loyalty of their subordinates by giving them specific duties, functions, and gifts and by including them in a religious hierarchy. Clans that recognized Yamato dominion continued to exercise local authority, and some clans were given specific military or religious functions to fulfill. In an effort to centralize further the administration of the state, the emperor created a council of chieftains, whose members were treated as though they were appointed officials.

The Yamato also used their religion to subordinate the gods of their supporters, much as Hammurabi had used Marduk (see page 19). Creating a hierarchy of gods under the authority of their sun-goddess, the Yamato established her chief shrine in eastern Honshu, where the sun-goddess could catch the first rays of the rising sun. Around the shrine there grew up local clan cults, giving rise to a native religion known as "Shinto," the Way of the Gods. Shinto was a unifying force: the chief deity of Shinto, the sun-goddess, became the nation's protector. Shinto also stressed the worship of ancestors, thus strengthening the link between the present and the past. Much of its appeal rose from the fact that it was a happy religion. Its rituals celebrated the beauty of nature instead of invoking the hazards of fate or divine wrath. Shinto emphasized ritual cleanliness, and its festivals were marked by wine, song, and good cheer.

By the sixth century the powerful Yamato state was struggling to dominate Korea. From the dawn

MAP 11.4 The Islands of Japan, ca 1185   The map illustrates the importance of the island of Honshu and the Inland Sea in the development of early Japanese society.

of their history the Japanese had held parts of Korea, but by 562 the Koreans had driven them out. Yet Japanese-Korean contact was not entirely hostile or limited to warfare. Early Japanese society easily absorbed migrating Koreans, and its holdings in Korea enriched the Japanese economically.

Much more important, however, was Korea's role as the avenue through which Chinese influence reached Japan. Chinese impact on the Japanese was profound and wide ranging. The Japanese adapted the Chinese systems of writing and record keeping, which allowed for bureaucratic administration along Chinese lines and set the stage for literature, philosophy, and written history.

Another influence was of lasting importance to the Japanese: Buddhism. In 538 a Korean king sent the Yamato court Buddhist images and scriptures. The new religion immediately became a political football, one faction of the ruling clan

Creation of Japan This Japanese painting portrays two deities standing in the clouds above the Pacific Ocean. The god, sword at his side, stirs the waters with a lance and thereby creates the home islands of Japan. (*Source: Courtesy, Museum of Fine Arts, Boston, Bigelow Collection*)

favoring its official adoption and other factions opposing it. The resulting turmoil, both religious and political, ended only in 587, when the pro-Buddhists defeated their opponents on the battlefield. Buddhism proved important to Japanese life for three broad reasons. First, it was a new and sophisticated but appealing religion that met needs not envisaged by Shinto. Second, it served as an influential carrier of Chinese culture. Finally, its acceptance by Japan's rulers enabled it to play an influential role in politics.

The victorious pro-Buddhists undertook a sweeping reform of the state, partly to strengthen Yamato rule and partly to introduce Chinese political and bureaucratic concepts. The architect of this effort was Prince Shotoku (574–622), the author of the "Seventeen Article Constitution," a triumph of Buddhist ethical and Confucian political thought. Issued in 604, the constitution was not a blueprint for government but a list of moral and ethical Buddhist precepts stressing righteous political conduct. It upheld the rights of the ruler and commanded his subjects to obey him. The constitution recommended an intricate bureaucracy like China's and admonished the nobility to avoid strife and opposition. Although the Seventeen Article Constitution never became the law of the entire land, it spelled out what Shotoku considered the proper goals of government and pointed the way to future reform.

Shotoku realized that Japan lacked the trained personnel to put his reforms into effect. To build a corps of professional administrators he sent a large group of talented Japanese to T'ang China in 607 to learn Chinese methods and arts at the source. Other students studied at Buddhist monasteries in China and then carried the message of Buddha accurately and fully to Japan. At first their numbers were small, but over the course of years thousands of young men studied in China and returned home to share what they had learned.

The death of Shotoku in 622 set off some twenty years of political chaos. Finally in 645 supporters of his policies, aided by students trained in China, overthrew the government. The following year they proclaimed the "Taika Reforms," a bold effort to create a complete imperial and bureaucratic system like that of the T'ang Empire. For all their hopes, the Taika Reforms failed to make Japan a small-scale copy of T'ang China. Nonetheless, the reformers created a nation with all the political trappings of its neighbors. The symbol of this new political awareness was the establishment in 710 of Japan's first true capital and first city, modeled on the T'ang capital, at Nara, just north of modern Osaka. Nara gave its name to an era that lasted until 794, an era characterized by the continued importation of Chinese ideas and methods. Buddhism triumphed both religiously and politically. The Buddhist monasteries that ringed the capital were both religious centers and wealthy landlords, and the monks were active in the political life of the capital. In the Nara era, Buddhism and the imperial court went hand in hand.

The Heian Era (794–1185)

Buddhist influence at Nara showed its dark side when in 770 a Buddhist priest tried to usurp the throne. The results were twofold. The imperial family removed the capital to Heian—modern Kyoto—where it remained until 1867. And a strong reaction against Buddhism and Chinese culture soon set in, strikingly symbolized by the severance of relations with China after 838. Thereafter the Japanese assimilated and adapted what they had imported. In a sense their intellectual and cultural childhood had come to an end, and they were ready to go their own way.

Though under a cloud, Buddhism not only survived the reaction but actually made gains. Before closing the door on China, the Japanese admitted two new Buddhist cults that gradually became integral parts of Japanese life. In 805 a Japanese monk introduced the Tendai (Chinese T'ien-t'ai) sect (see page 310). Though a complex product of China's high culture, Tendai proved popular because it held out the possibility of salvation to all. In addition to its religious message, Tendai preached the Confucian ideal of service to the state. The Shingon (True Word) sect arrived in 806 on the heels of Tendai. Like its Chinese precursor, this Japanese sect promised salvation through ritual, magical incantations, and masses for the dead.

Patronized initially by the nobility, both sects held the seeds of popular appeal. The common people cared nothing for Tendai and Shingon as metaphysical and intellectual systems but were strongly attracted by their magic and the prospect of personal salvation. As Tendai and Shingon spread Buddhism throughout Japan, they were gradually transformed into distinctively Japanese

religions. Furthermore, Buddhist art extended an esthetic appeal to the Japanese people.

Only later, during the Kamakura Shogunate (1185–1333), did Buddhism begin a vigorous proselytizing campaign. The emphasis on equality and salvation that was the hallmark of both Tendai and Shingon prepared the way for two sects that promised their followers sure and immediate salvation. The Pure Land sect (see page 310) preached that Buddha's paradise of eternal bliss, the pure land, could be reached through simple faith in Buddha. Neither philosophical understanding of Buddhist scriptures nor devotion to rituals was necessary. People had only to repeat Buddha's name to be saved. The second sect, an offshoot of the first, was the Lotus sect of Nichiren

Prince Shotoku Prince Shotoku, the author of the "Seventeen Article Constitution," is shown here with many of the attributes of a Chinese mandarin official. His sword shows that he was more than a mere administrator, and was ready to resist those who opposed his reforms. *(Source: Imperial Household Collection, Kyoto)*

(1222–1281), a fiery and intolerant preacher who reduced Buddhism to a single moment of faith. To be saved, according to Nichiren, people had only to call sincerely on Buddha. Nothing else was necessary. Stripped of its intellectual top-weight, Buddhism made greater headway in the countryside than ever before.

The eclipse of Chinese influence liberated Japanese artistic and cultural impulses. The Japanese continued to draw on Chinese models but forged new paths of their own. Japanese architects evolved a light, simple, and graceful style of building beautifully in keeping with the country's natural surroundings. The Heian era fostered a unique development in painting, the "Yamato pictures," paintings of everyday scenes in which figures and objects are outlined and then painted with bright colors. Equally great strides were made in writing. In order to express themselves more easily and clearly, Japanese scholars modified the Chinese script that they had adopted during the Yamato period. The Japanese produced two *syllabaries,* sets of phonetic signs that stand for syllables instead of whole words or letters. This development made it possible for the first time to write the Japanese language in the native syntax.

The reform of their written language unshackled Japanese writers. No longer bound in the straitjacket of Chinese, they created their own literary style and modes of expression. The writing of history, which had begun in the Nara era, received a huge boost, as did poetry. Completely original was the birth of the novel, one of the finest of which is *The Tale of Genji*. This ageless novel by the court lady Murasaki Shikibu (978–ca 1016) treats court life, paying minute attention to dialogue and exploring personalities. Not merely a novelist, Murasaki also wrote about the mission of the novelist and the purpose of the novel. The novel was taken up by other writers; Sei Shonagon's *Pillow Book* is another masterpiece. These works bore no resemblance to any works in Chinese literature. The Japanese had launched their own independent and fertile literary tradition.

Politically, the Heian era gave rise to two opposing tendencies: while the emperors were trying to extend their power and centralize their authority, aristocrats were striving to free themselves from imperial control. The aristocrats quickly won out over the emperors. The biggest winners were the Fujiwara family, who in the ninth century had regularly served as regents for the emperors. They

were also the most successful, for they married and connived their way into almost complete domination of the imperial line of rulers. As other families too rose to prominence, setting the stage for intrigue and infighting at court, the effectiveness of the imperial government was further diminished.

The emperors contributed to their own eclipse by decreeing disastrous land laws. The imperial government's efforts to appropriate land and redistribute it to peasants wrecked its own economic base. The government was too weak to overcome widespread resistance and evasion of the laws, and the emperors themselves permitted too many loopholes. The result was precisely the opposite of what the central government intended: vast tracts of land were made exempt from taxation and imperial control, and land became consolidated in fewer hands. Those who profited most were local lords and high government officials, members of the imperial court and Buddhist monasteries, all of whom became great landlords at the emperor's expense. Instead of a peasantry of small landholders paying taxes to the imperial treasury, the emperors and even the Fujiwara regents had to contend with strong aristocratic families who were increasingly difficult to control.

In 1156, fed by declining central power, feuds among the great families, and the ambitions of local lords, open rebellion and civil war erupted. The two most powerful contenders in the struggle were the Taira and Minamoto clans, who quickly outstripped both the emperor and the Fujiwara. The Taira drew their political strength from their vast landholdings; the Minamoto dominated the Kanto Plain, a rich agricultural area near modern Tokyo. Both clans relied on *samurai,* skilled warriors who were rapidly consolidating as a new social class. By 1192 the Minamoto had vanquished all opposition, and their leader Yoritomo (1147–1199) became *shogun,* or general-in-chief. With him began the Kamakura Shogunate, which lasted until 1333.

The Land and the Samurai

The twelfth-century events that culminated in the Kamakura Shogunate involved a new relation between the samurai and the land that eventually led to a fusion of the military, civil, and judicial aspects of government into a single authority. The Japanese samurai were a very important part of a larger system. Without an independent income of its own, a warrior class needs the economic support of others, and here the samurai were no different. They depended economically on the *shoen,* a private domain outside imperial control. The shoen typically consisted of a village and its farmland, normally land capable of growing rice. Land was essential to the maintenance of the samurai.

Samurai and shoen were basic elements of early Japanese history, but what conditions bonded them so closely? Both owed their origins directly to the gradual breakdown of central authority in the Heian era. The shoen had its roots in the ninth century, when local lords began escaping imperial taxes and control by formally giving their land to a Buddhist monastery, which was exempt from taxes, or to a court official who could get special privileges from the emperor. The local lord then received his land back as a tenant who paid his protector a nominal rent. The monastery or official received a steady income from the land, and the tenant was thereafter free of imperial taxes and jurisdiction. The local lord continued to exercise actual authority over the land—all the more so, in fact, since imperial officials could no longer touch him. In spite of his legal status as a tenant, he was the real boss of the estate.

The many other people who were economically, politically, and legally dependent on the shoen, and who had various and often overlapping rights and functions within it, enjoyed the rights of the *shiki,* a share of the produce of the land. The lord often entrusted the actual running of the estate to a manager, who received a share of the estate's produce in payment. The shoen was cultivated by independent farmers *(myoshu)* who owned specific fields, by dependent farmers, or, typically, by a combination of both. Unlike peasants in medieval Europe, dependent farmers never became serfs.

To keep order on the shoen and to protect it from harm, lords organized private armies. As the central government weakened, local lords and their armies—the only source of law and order in the countryside—grew stronger. Thus the inability of central authority to defend its subjects sparked the rise of local armies of professional soldiers—the samurai.

The samurai and his lord had a double bond. The lord extended his authority over the samurai in return for the latter's loyalty and service. The samurai originally received from his lord only *shiki rights*—a certain portion of an estate's produce—

Five-Story Pagoda This splendid pagoda is a good example of Japanese architecture of the Heian period. Such buildings were intended to complement their natural surroundings. *(Source: Courtesy, Horyuji Temple)*

not a grant of land. Only later did samurai receive land for their service. Each samurai entered into his lord's service in a formal ceremony that included a religious element. Initially, the lord-samurai relationship existed alongside the anemic imperial system. Not until the Ashikaga Shogunate, which lasted from 1338 to 1573 (see page 330), did the military aristocracy take over from imperial officers.

The samurai had his own military and social code of conduct, later called *Bushido,* or "Way of the Warrior." The bedrock of the samurai's code was loyalty to his lord, to which everything else was secondary. Yoritomo founded the Kamakura

---

JAPAN, CA 320–CA 1400

3d century A.D.	Creation of the Yamato state
538	Introduction of Buddhism
604	Shotoku's Seventeen Article Constitution
655	Taika reforms
710	Establishment of Nara as Japan's first capital and first city
710–784	Nara era
794–1185	Heian era and literary flowering
1185–1333	Kamakura Shogunate and Japanese feudalism
1274 and 1281	Unsuccessful Mongol invasions of Japan

Shogunate on the samurai and his code, and attitudes that blossomed in Yoritomo's lifetime long outlasted the political system he built. Perhaps the scholar George Sansom has best caught the flavor of the samurai's devotion to lord and duty:

The warrior does not question the commands of his lord, but obeys them regardless of his own life, his family, and all his private interests. In defeat he must bear in mind what he owes for past favors and must be ready to die in the cause of his lord, or in the cause of the family or clan of which he is a member. It follows that a warrior's life belongs to his lord, and he may not dispose of it to suit his own ends, or merely to preserve his own reputation.[12]

Preferring death to dishonor, the samurai showed complete dedication in the act of *seppuku* (sometimes incorrectly called *harakiri*), ritual suicide by disemboweling oneself.

By the end of the twelfth century the samurai had left their mark on cultural life as well as on military affairs. They constituted the ruling class at the local level, warrior-aristocrats who were close to the land and to those who worked it. Although samurai's values were not the values of the court aristocracy, their code of conduct was by no means rude or vulgar. The principles of the samurai embraced religion, personal conduct, and practical affairs. As articulated in the *Bushido*, samurai were expected to respect the gods, keep honorable company, be fair and even generous to others, and be sympathetic to the weak and helpless.

The symbols of the samurai were their swords, with which they were expected to be expert, and the cherry blossom, which falls with the spring wind, signifying the way in which samurai gave

their lives for their lords. Like knights, samurai went into battle in armor and often on horseback. Like the ancient Spartans, samurai were expected to make do with little and like it. Physical hardship became routine, and soft living was despised as weak and unworthy. Although the full-blown samurai code did not take final shape until the later Ashikaga Shogunate, samurai were making an irresistible impact on Japanese life by the end of the twelfth century.

The Kamakura Shogunate (1185–1333)

The Kamakura Shogunate derives its name from Kamakura, the seat both of the Minamoto clan and of Yoritomo's shogunate. Yoritomo's victory meant that the emperor was still an ornament, honored and esteemed but mostly powerless.

Based on the loyalty of his followers, Yoritomo's rule was an extension of the way in which he ran his own estate. Having established his *bakufu* (tent government) at Kamakura, Yoritomo created three bodies, staffed by his retainers, to handle political and legal matters. His administrative board drafted government policy. Another board regulated lords and samurai, and a board of inquiry served as the court of the land.

For administration at the local level, Yoritomo created two groups of officials: military land stewards and military governors. The military land stewards were responsible for the collection of taxes. Charged with governing most estates, they saw to the estates' proper operation and maintained law and order in return for a share of the produce. The military governors oversaw the military and police protection of the provinces. They supervised the conduct of the military land stewards in peacetime and commanded the provincial samurai in war.

Yoritomo's system suffered from a weakness. Before the end of the twelfth century, the military land stewards and military governors had become hereditary officials—local rulers in their own right—whose allegiance to the Kamakura Shogunate was waning.

Yoritomo's successors did not inherit his ability, and in 1219 the Hojo family, a powerful vassal, reduced the shogun to a figurehead. Until 1333, the Hojo family held the reins of power by serving as regents of the shogun. The shogun had joined the emperor as a political figurehead.

Internal affairs continued unchanged during the Hojo Regency, but a formidable challenge appeared from abroad. Japan's self-imposed isolation was rudely interrupted in the thirteenth century by a massive seaborne invasion whose lingering effects weakened the Hojo Regency and eventually led to the downfall of the Kamakura Shogunate. The Mongol leader Kublai Khan, having overrun China and Korea, turned his eyes toward Japan. In 1274 and again in 1281 he sent huge numbers of ships and men to storm the islands. On both occasions the Mongols managed to land but were beaten back by samurai. What proved decisive, however, were two fierce storms that destroyed the Mongol fleets. Marco Polo recounted what he heard about one invasion force:

The expedition sailed from the ports of Zai-tun and Kin-sai, and crossing the intermediate sea, reached the island in safety. . . . It happened, after some time, that a north wind began to blow with great force, and the ships of the Tartars, which lay near the shore of the island, were driven foul of each other. . . . The gale, however, increased to so violent a degree that a number of vessels foundered. The people belonging to them, by floating upon the pieces of the wreck, saved themselves upon an island lying about four miles from the coast of Zipangu [Japan].[13]

The Japanese claimed that they were saved by the *kamikaze*, the "Divine Wind"—which lent its name to the thousands of Japanese aviators who tried to become a second divine wind in World War Two by crashing their airplanes on American warships.

Although the Hojo regents had successfully defended Japan, they could not reward their vassals satisfactorily because little booty was found among the wreckage. Discontent grew among the samurai, and by the fourteenth century the entire

Resisting the Mongols   Although this scene shows the Japanese samurai prepared behind a defensive wall for an attack by the Mongols, Kubla Khan's invasion plans were actually ruined by fierce storms, which the Japanese called the *kamikaze*, or "Divine Wind." *(Source: Imperial Household Collection, Tokyo)*

political system was breaking down. Both the imperial and the shogunate families were divided among themselves, and discontent increased among the samurai, who were rapidly growing in number. Since the land could not adequately support more samurai, many samurai families became increasingly impoverished. This phenomenon had two results. First, poverty created a pool of warriors ready for plunder. Second, the samurai shifted their loyalty from the Kamakura Shogunate to local officials who could offer them adequate maintenance.

The combination of factional disputes among Japan's leading families and the samurai remained explosive until 1331, when the emperor Go-Daigo tried to recapture real power. His attempt sparked an uprising by the great families, local lords, samurai, and even Buddhist monasteries, which commanded the allegiance of thousands of samurai. Go-Daigo destroyed the Kamakura Shogunate in 1333 but lost the loyalty of his followers. One of his most important military leaders, Ashikaga Takauji, made his own bid for power. By 1338 the rebel had defeated the emperor and established the Ashikaga Shogunate, which lasted until 1573. Takauji's victory was also a victory for the samurai, who took over civil authority throughout Japan. The day of the samurai had fully dawned.

SUMMARY

By about 1400, traditional religious, social, and intellectual values had been challenged and fertilized by new peoples and new ideas throughout Asia. Most of India clung to Hinduism while Islam took root in modern Pakistan and Bangladesh. China incorporated and distilled Buddhism, which won a place next to Confucianism in Chinese life. Japan imported much of Chinese culture only to mold it into something distinctly Japanese. Finally, firm economic and cultural links made it virtually impossible for any Asian people to continue to develop in isolation.

NOTES

1. O. P. Singh Bhatia, trans., *The Imperial Guptas* (New Delhi: New India Press, 1962), p. 79.

2. A. L. Basham, trans., *The Wonder That Was India* (New York: Grove Press, 1954), p. 161.
3. *Vasishtha,* 4.5.1–2, trans. G. Bühler, in *The Sacred Laws of the Aryas,* part 2, *Vasishtha and Baudhayana* (Oxford: Clarendon Press, 1882), p. 31.
4. *Sutrakritanga,* 1.4.2, quoted in Basham, *The Wonder That Was India,* pp. 459–460.
5. *The Travels of Marco Polo, the Venetian* (London: J. M. Dent and Sons, 1908), p. 203.
6. A. Waley, trans., *More Translations from the Chinese* (New York: Knopf, 1919), p. 27.
7. Ibid., p. 29.
8. Ibid., p. 71.
9. Ibid., p. 41.
10. *The Travels of Marco Polo,* p. 128.
11. R. Tsunoda et al., *Sources of the Japanese Tradition* (New York: Columbia University Press, 1958), p. 6.
12. G. Sansom, *A History of Japan to 1334* (Stanford, Calif.: Stanford University Press, 1958), p. 360.
13. *The Travels of Marco Polo,* pp. 325–326.

SUGGESTED READING

The reign of the Guptas is especially well documented. O. P. Singh Bhatia, *The Imperial Guptas* (1962), treats the entire dynasty. In a series of works S. K. Maity covers many facets of the period: *Gupta Civilization: A Study* (1974), *The Imperial Guptas and Their Times* (1975), and *Economic Life in North India in the Gupta Period* (1975). D. H. H. Ingalls, "Kalidasa and the Attitudes of the Golden Age," *Journal of the American Oriental Society* 96 (1976): 15–26, studies the writings of India's greatest poet and dramatist in their historical context.

Good treatments of Indian society and daily life can be found in A. L. Basham, *The Wonder That Was India* (1954), chap. 6, and J. Auboyer, *Daily Life in Ancient India from 200 B.C. to A.D. 700* (1965).

O. W. Wolters, *Early Indonesian Commerce: A Study of the Origins of Srivijaya* (1967), is perhaps the most comprehensive treatment of that kingdom. Much broader in scope are two books by H. G. Q. Wales: *The Indianization of China and of South-East Asia* (1967), and *The Making of Greater India,* 3d ed. (1974).

An extensive survey of the Islamic invasions of India is J. F. Richards, "The Islamic Frontier in the East: Expansion into South Asia," *South Asia* 4 (1974): 90–109, in which Richards makes the point that many Indian princes put up stiff resistance to the invaders. Much broader studies of the impact of Islam on the subcontinent are A. Embree, ed., *Muslim Civilization in India* (1964), and I. H. Qureshi, *History of the Muslim Community of the Indo-Pakistan Subcontinent* (1961), which is very pro-Pakistan. A good treatment of early Islam in

India is K. A. Nizami, *Some Aspects of Religion and Politics in India During the Thirteenth Century* (reprinted 1970). In two books, *Islam in the Indian Subcontinent* (1980) and *Islam in India and Pakistan* (1982), A. Schimmel surveys many aspects of Islam, including architecture, life, art, and traditions in the subcontinent. G. S. Pomerantz, "The Decline of Buddhism in India," *Diogenes* 96 (1976): 38–66, treats the demise of Buddhism on its native soil.

Two works concentrate on the sultanate of Delhi: M. Habib and K. A. Nizami, eds., *Comprehensive History of India,* vol. 5, *Delhi Sultanate* (1970), and P. Hardy, "The Growth of Authority over a Conquered Political Elite: The Early Delhi Sultanate as a Possible Case Study," in J. F. Richards, ed., *Kingship and Authority in South Asia* (1978).

The standard work on the arrival of Buddhism in China is E. Zürcher, *The Buddhist Conquest of China,* 2 vols. (1959). Also good on the intellectual climate of the time are E. Balazs, *Chinese Civilization and Bureaucracy* (1964), and H. Welch and A. Seidel, eds., *Facets of Taoism* (1979). Shorter and more popular is A. Wright, *Buddhism in Chinese History* (1959). Two books by K. Ch'en, *Buddhism in China* (1964) and *The Chinese Transformation of Buddhism* (1973), cover the early evolution of Buddhism in China. B. Gray, *Buddhist Cave Paintings at Tunhuang* (1959), is the place to begin study of the artistic impact of Buddhism on China.

Political events from the time of the Sui to the Sung Dynasty are particularly well covered. A. F. Wright, *The Sui Dynasty* (1978), has become the standard work on this important dynasty. Though old, W. Bingham, *The Founding of the T'ang Dynasty: The Fall of Sui and Rise of T'ang* (1941), is still useful. C. P. Fitzgerald, *Son of Heaven: A Biography of Li Shih-min, Founder of the T'ang Dynasty* (1933), is likewise an old treatment of the first T'ang emperor. Newer and broader is J. Perry and B. Smith, eds., *Essays on T'ang Society* (1976). The career of An Lu-shan is admirably discussed by E. G. Pullyblank, *The Background of the Rebellion of An Lu-shan* (1955). The difficult period of the Five Dynasties is well covered by G. Wang, *The Structure of Power in North China During the Five Dynasties* (1963). Various aspects of Sung developments receive attention in J. T. C. Liu and P. Golas, eds., *Changes in Sung China* (1969), and E. A. Kracke, Jr., *Civil Service in Early Sung China (960–1067)* (1953).

A brief treatment of the T'ang tombs at Chien-hsien, well illustrated with color plates, is N. H. Dupree, "T'ang Tombs in Chien County, China," *Archaeology* 32, no. 4 (1979): 34–44. Those interested in further discussion of the great poets of the period can find no better place to start than the work of A. Waley, a gifted translator: *The Life and Times of Po Chü-i* (1949) and *The Poetry and Career of Li Po, 701–762* (1950). Wang

An-shih still generates controversy, and a variety of views can be found in J. T. C. Liu, *Reform in Sung China: Wang An-shih (1021–1086) and His New Policies* (1959), and J. Meskill, ed., *Wang An-shih—Practical Reformer?* (1963).

For the Mongols in their native setting, see L. Kwanten, *Imperial Nomads: A History of Central Asia, 500–1500 A.D.* (1979), a comprehensive picture of central Asian developments. H. D. Martin, *The Rise of Chinghis Khan and His Conquest of North China* (1950), studies the rise of the Mongols to greatness. J. Dardess's "From Mongol Empire to Yuan Dynasty: Changing Forms of Imperial Rule in Mongolia and Central Asia," *Monumenta Serica* 30 (1972–1973): 117–165, traces the evolution of Mongol government. His *Conquerors and Confucians: Aspects of Political Change in Late Yuan China* (1973) continues the study for a somewhat later period. Dardess's "The Transformations of Messianic Revolt and the Founding of the Ming Dynasty," *Journal of Asian Studies* 29 (1970): 539–558, treats some of the factors behind the overthrow of the Yuan Dynasty.

Among the many fine general works on Japan, the following are especially recommended in addition to those cited in the Notes: G. Trewartha, *Japan: A Geography* (1965); and E. O. Reischauer and J. K. Fairbank, *East Asia: The Great Tradition* (1960). More recent works include C. Schirokauer, *A Brief History of Chinese and Japanese Civilizations,* 2d ed. (1989); J. K. Fairbank, E. O. Reischauer, and A. Craig, *East Asia: Tradition and Transformation,* rev. ed. (1989); C. Totman, *Japan Before Perry* (1981); and A. Tiedmann, ed., *An Introduction to Japanese Civilization* (1974)

For early Japanese history, G. J. Groot, *The Prehistory of Japan* (1951), is still useful though rapidly becoming dated. The same is true of J. E. Kidder, *Japan Before Buddhism* (1959). Newer and quite readable is Kidder, *Early Buddhist Japan* (1972), which is well illustrated. J. M. Kitagawa, *Religion in Japanese History* (1966), discusses both Shinto and Buddhism.

Early Japanese literary flowering has attracted much attention. I. Morris, *The World of the Shining Prince: Court Life in Ancient Japan* (1964), provides a general treatment of the climate in which early Japanese artists lived. Murasaki Shikibu, *The Tale of Genji* has been recently translated by R. Bowring (1988); I. Morris translated *The Pillow Book of Sei Shonagon,* 2 vols. (1967).

Japanese feudalism, like its medieval European counterpart, continues to excite discussion and disagreement. Some provocative works include K. Asakawa, *Land and Society in Medieval Japan* (1965); P. Duus, *Feudalism in Japan,* 2d ed. (1976); J. W. Hall, *Government and Local Power in Japan: 500–1700: A Study Based on Bizen Province* (1966); and E. O. Reischauer, "Japanese Feudalism," in R. Coulborn, ed., *Feudalism in History* (1956), pp. 26–48.

12

Europe in the Early and High Middle Ages

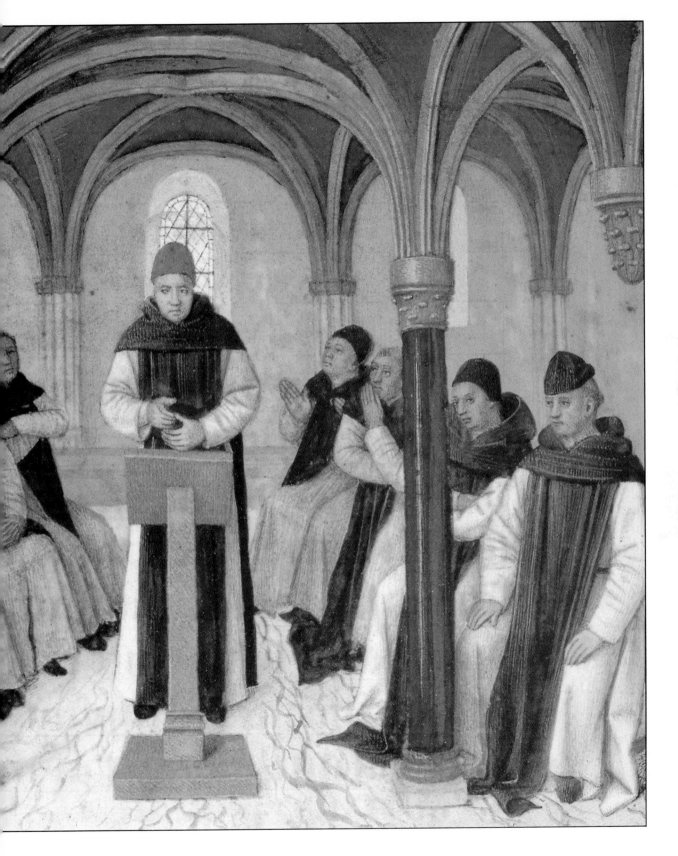

St. Bernard, Abbot of Clairvaux, preaching to his fellow Cistercians

*T*he Frankish chieftain Charles Martel defeated Muslim invaders in 733 at the Battle of Tours in central France.[1] Although at the time the battle seemed only another skirmish in the struggle between Christians and Muslims, in retrospect it looms as one of the great battles of history: this Frankish victory halted Muslim expansion in northern Europe.

Between 733 and 843 a distinctly European society emerged. A new kind of social and political organization, later called "feudalism," appeared. And for the first time since the collapse of the Roman Empire, most of western Europe was united under one government, which reached its peak under Charles Martel's grandson, Charlemagne. Christian missionary activity among the Germanic peoples continued, and strong ties were forged with the Roman papacy. A revival of study and learning, sometimes styled the "Carolingian Renaissance," occurred under Charlemagne.

In 843 Charlemagne's three grandsons, after a bitter war, concluded the Treaty of Verdun, dividing the European continent among themselves. Against this background, invasion and disorder wracked Europe for about 150 years.

By the last quarter of the tenth century, after a long and bitter winter of discontent, the first signs of European spring appeared. That spring lasted from the early eleventh century to the end of the thirteenth. This period from about 1050 to 1300 has often been called the "High Middle Ages." The term designates a time of crucial growth and remarkable cultural achievement between two eras of economic, political, and social crisis.

- How did Charlemagne acquire and govern his vast empire?

- What was the Carolingian Renaissance?

- What factors contributed to the disintegration of the Carolingian Empire?

- What was feudalism, and how did it begin?

- What were the ingredients of the revival that followed the great invasions of the ninth century?

- What was the social and political impact of the recovery of Europe?

- How did the Christian church's development during the early and High Middle Ages affect relations between the church and civil authorities?

- What were the Crusades, and how did they manifest the influence of the church and the ideals of medieval society?

These are the questions that frame discussion in this chapter.

THE FRANKISH ARISTOCRACY AND THE RISE OF THE CAROLINGIAN DYNASTY

Through a series of remarkable victories over other Germanic tribes, the Franks under Clovis (r. 481–511) had emerged as the most powerful people in Europe by the early sixth century (see page 247). The Frankish kingdom included most of what is now France and a large section of the southern half of western Germany. Clovis's baptism into orthodox Christianity in 496 won him church support against other Germanic tribes, most of them Arian Christians. Clovis died in 511, and the Merovingian dynasty went on to rule for the next two centuries.

Rule is, of course, too strong a verb. Conquering the vast territories proved easier than governing them for the Merovingians, given their inadequate political institutions. The size of Clovis's kingdom forced him to divide it among his four sons, because no one person could govern it effectively. Practically, however, Clovis's decision was disastrous. The Merovingians bitterly hated one another, and each king fought to deprive his relatives of their portions of the kingdom. Violence and assassination ceased only when one man had killed off all his rivals. Thus in 558 Clovis's youngest son, Lothair, acquired the whole kingdom after he had murdered two nephews and eliminated one rebellious son by burning him and his family alive. After Lothair died, his sons continued the civil war until one king survived.

Civil war in the Frankish kingdom may have provided the opportunity for a distinct aristocratic class to emerge. Recent research in Frankish family history has revealed that a noble ruling class existed before the mid-sixth century. Members of this class belonged to families of high reputation who gradually intermarried with members of the old Gallo-Roman senatorial class. They possessed wealth and great villas where they led an aristo-

Merovingian Army This sixth- or seventh-century ivory depicts a nobleman in civilian dress followed by seven warriors. Note that the mounted men do not have stirrups and that they seem to have fought with spears and bows and arrows. The power of the Frankish aristocracy rested on these private armies. *(Source: Rheinisches/Landesmuseum, Trier)*

cratic lifestyle. They exercised rights of lordship over their lands and tenants, dispensing local customary, not royal, law. These families provided almost all the bishops of the church. Because they had a self-conscious awareness of their social, economic, and political distinctiveness, they constituted a noble class.[2]

In the seventh century, the central government of the Merovingians could not control these nobles. Primitive and disorganized, the government consisted of a few household officials, the most important of whom was the mayor of the palace. He was in charge of administration and acted as the king's deputy; he also represented the interests of the nobility. Because the Frankish kingdom was divided into East Frankland, West Frankland, and Burgundy, and because some territories such as Bavaria were virtually independent, the Merovingian kingdom slowly disintegrated.

Reconstruction of the Frankish kingdom began with the efforts of Pippin of Landen, a member of one aristocratic family. In the early seventh century, he was mayor of the palace in East Frankland. His grandson, Pippin II (d. 714), gained the position of mayor of the palace in both East and West Frankland. It was Pippin II's son Charles Martel (714–741) who defeated the Muslims at Tours and thus checked Arab expansion in northern Europe. Charles's wars against the Saxons, Burgundians, and Frisians broke those weakening forces. His victory over the Muslims and his successful campaigns in the Frankish kingdom added to his family's prestige a reputation for great military strength. Charles Martel held the real power in the Frankish kingdom; the Merovingians were kings in name only.

The rise of the Carolingian dynasty, whose name derives from the Latin *Carolus,* meaning "Charles," was partly due to papal support. In the early eighth century, missionaries supported Charles Martel and his son Pippin III as they attempted to bring the various Germanic tribes under their jurisdiction. The most important missionary was the Anglo-Saxon Wynfrith, or Boniface (680–754), as he was later called. Given the semibarbaric peoples with whom he was dealing, Boniface's achievements were remarkable. He helped shape the structure of the German church.

He established *The Rule of Saint Benedict* in all the monastaries that he founded or reformed. And with the full support of Pippin III, he held several councils that reformed the Frankish church.

Saint Boniface preached throughout Germany against divorce, polygamous unions, and incest. On these matters German custom and ecclesiastical law completely disagreed. The Germans allowed divorce simply by the mutual consent of both parties. The Germanic peoples also practiced polygamy (the practice of having more than one wife) and incest (sexual relations between brothers and sisters or parents and children) on a wide scale. Church councils and theologians stressed that marriage, validly entered into, could not be ended, and they firmly condemned incest.

Boniface's preaching was not without impact, for in 802 Charlemagne prohibited incest and decreed that a husband might separate from an adulterous wife. The woman could be punished, and the man could not remarry in her lifetime. Charlemagne also encouraged severe punishment for adulterous men. In so doing, he contributed to the dignity of marriage, the family, and women.

Charles Martel and Pippin III protected Boniface, and he preached Christian obedience to rulers. Because of Boniface's staunch adherence to Roman ideas and the Roman pope, the Romanization of Europe accompanied its Christianization.

Charles Martel had been king of the Franks in fact but not in title. His son Pippin III (r. 751–768) made himself king in title as well as in fact. In Germanic custom—and custom was law—the kingship had to pass to someone of royal blood. Pippin did not want to murder the ineffectual Merovingian king, but he did want the kingship. Because the missionary activity of Boniface had enhanced papal influence in the Frankish kingdom, Pippin decided to consult the pope. Accordingly, Pippin sent envoys to Rome to ask the pope whether the man with the power was entitled to be king. Pope Zacharias (r. 741–752), guided by the Augustinian principle that the real test of kingship is whether it provides for order and justice, responded in 751 that he who has the power should also have the title. This answer constituted recognition of the Carolingians. The Merovingian king was deposed and forced to become a monk.

Just as the emperors Constantine and Theodosius had taken actions in the fourth century that would later be cited as precedents in church-state relations (see pages 221, 231), so Pippin III in the mid-eighth century took papal confirmation as official approval of his title. In 751 Pippin III was formally elected king of the Franks by the *magnates*, or great lords, of the Frankish territory. Three years later, Pope Stephen II (r. 752–757)—who needed Pippin's protection from the Lombards—came to Gaul and personally anointed Pippin king at Paris. Thus an important alliance was struck between the papacy and the Frankish ruler. In 754 Pope Stephen gave Pippin the title "Protector of the Roman Church." Pippin in turn agreed to restore to the papacy territories in northern Italy recently seized by the Lombards, and he promptly marched into Italy and defeated the Lombards. The Carolingian family had received official recognition and anointment from the leading spiritual power in Europe, and the papacy had gained a powerful military protector.

On a second successful campaign in Italy in 756, Pippin made a large donation to the papacy. The gift was estates in central Italy that technically belonged to the Byzantine emperor. Known as the "Papal States," they existed over a thousand years, until the newly formed kingdom of Italy abolished them in 1870.

Because of Pippin's anointment, his kingship took on a special spiritual and moral character. Before Pippin, only priests and bishops had received anointment. Pippin became the first to be anointed with the sacred oils and acknowledged as *rex et sacerdos* ("king and priest"). Anointment, rather than royal blood, set the Christian king apart. Pippin also cleverly eliminated possible threats to the Frankish throne, and the pope promised him support in the future. When Pippin died, his son Charles succeeded him.

THE EMPIRE OF CHARLEMAGNE

Charles the Great (r. 768–814) built on the military and diplomatic foundations of his ancestors. Charles's secretary and biographer, a Saxon by the name of Einhard, wrote a lengthy description of this warrior-ruler. It has serious flaws, partly because it is modeled directly on the Roman author Suetonius's *Life of the Emperor* Augustus. Still, it is the earliest medieval biography of a layman, and historians consider it generally accurate:

Charles was large and strong, and of lofty stature, though not disproportionately tall ... the upper part of his head was round, his eyes very large and animated, nose a little long, hair fair, and face laughing and merry. Thus his appearance was always stately and dignified ... although his neck was thick and somewhat short, and his belly rather prominent; but the symmetry of the rest of his body concealed these defects. His gait was firm, his whole carriage manly, and his voice clear, but not so strong as his size led one to expect. In accordance with the national custom, he took frequent exercise on horseback and in the chase, accomplishments in which scarcely any people in the world can equal the Franks. He enjoyed the exhalations from natural warm springs, and often practiced swimming, in which he was such an adept that none could surpass him.[3]

Though crude and brutal, Charlemagne was a man of enormous intelligence. He appreciated good literature, such as Saint Augustine's *City of God,* and Einhard considered him an unusually effective speaker. On the other hand, he could not even write his own name.

The security and continuation of his dynasty and the need for diplomatic alliances governed Charlemagne's complicated marriage pattern. The high rate of infant mortality required many sons. Married first to the daughter of Desiderius, king of the Lombards, Charlemagne divorced her on grounds of sterility. His second wife, Hildegard, produced nine children in twelve years. When she died, Charlemagne married Fastrada, daughter of an East Frankish count whose support Charles needed in his campaign against the Saxons. Charlemagne had a total of four legal wives and six concubines, and even after the age of sixty-five continued to sire children. Though three sons reached adulthood, only one outlived him. His three surviving grandsons, however, ensured perpetuation of the family.

Territorial Expansion

The most striking feature of Charlemagne's character was his phenomenal energy, which helps to explain his tremendous military achievements.[4]

Continuing the expansionist policies of his ancestors, Charlemagne fought more than fifty campaigns and became the greatest warrior of the early Middle Ages. He subdued all of the north of modern France (Map 12.1). In the south, the lords of the mountainous ranges of Aquitaine—

Equestrian Statue of Charlemagne A medieval king was expected to be fierce (and successful) in battle, to defend the church and the poor, and to give justice to all. This majestic and idealized figure of Charlemagne conveys these qualities. The horse is both the symbol and the means of his constant travels. *(Source: Girandon/Art Resource)*

MAP 12.1 The Carolingian World The extent of Charlemagne's nominal jurisdiction was extraordinary: it was not equaled until the nineteenth century.

what is now called "Basque country"—fought off his efforts at total conquest. The Muslims in northeastern Spain were checked by the establishment of strongly fortified areas known as *marches*.

Charlemagne's greatest successes occurred in modern-day Germany. There his concerns were basically defensive. In the course of a thirty-year war against the semibarbaric Saxons, he added most of the northwestern German tribes to the Frankish kingdom. Because of their repeated rebellions, Charlemagne (according to Einhard) ordered more than four thousand Saxons slaughtered in one day.

To the south, he also achieved spectacular results. In 773 and 774 the Lombards in northern Italy again threatened the papacy. Charlemagne marched south, overran fortresses at Pavia and Spoleto, and incorporated Lombardy into the Frankish kingdom. Charlemagne also ended Bavarian independence and defeated the nomadic Avars, opening the plain of the Danube for later settlement. He successfully fought the Byzantine Empire for Venetia (excluding the city of Venice itself), Istria, and Dalmatia and temporarily annexed those areas to his kingdom.

Charlemagne tried to occupy Basque territory in northwestern Spain between the Ebro River and the Pyrenees. When he was forced to retreat, his rear guard under Count Roland was annihilated by the Basques at Roncevalles (778). Although the foray had little political significance, the campaign in Spain inspired the great medieval epic, *The Song of Roland*. Based on legend and written down around 1100 at the beginning of the European crusading movement, the poem portrays Roland as the ideal chivalric knight and Charlemagne as having devoted his life to fighting the Muslims. Although considerably removed from the historical evidence, *The Song of Roland* is important because it reveals the popular image of Charlemagne in later centuries.

By around 805, the Frankish kingdom included all of continental Europe except Spain, Scandinavia, southern Italy, and the Slavic fringes of the East (see Map 12.1). Not since the third century A.D. had any ruler controlled so much of the Western world. Not until Napoleon Bonaparte's era in the early nineteenth century was the feat to be repeated.

The Government of the Carolingian Empire

Charlemagne ruled a vast rural world dotted with isolated estates and characterized by constant petty violence. His empire was definitely not a state as people today understand that term; it was a collection of primitive peoples and semibarbaric tribes. Apart from a small class of warrior-aristocrats and clergy, almost everyone engaged in agriculture. Trade and commerce played only a small part in the economy. Cities served as the headquarters of bishops and as ecclesiastical centers.

By constant travel, personal appearances, and the sheer force of his personality, Charlemagne sought to awe conquered peoples with his fierce presence and terrible justice. By confiscating the estates of great territorial magnates, he acquired lands and goods with which to gain the support of lesser lords, further expanding the territory under his control.

The political power of the Carolingians rested on the cooperation of the dominant social class, the Frankish aristocracy. By the seventh century, through mutual cooperation and frequent marriage alliances, these families exercised great power that did not derive from the Merovingian kings. The Carolingians themselves had emerged from this aristocracy, and their military and political success depended on its support. The lands and booty with which Charles Martel and Charlemagne rewarded their followers in these noble families enabled the nobles to improve their economic position; but it was only with noble help that the Carolingians were able to wage wars of expansion and suppress rebellions. In short, Carolingian success was a matter of reciprocal help and reward.[5]

Two or three hundred counts, powerful members of the imperial nobility, governed at the local level. They had full military and judicial power and held their offices for life but could be removed for misconduct. As a link between local authorities and the central government of the emperor, Charlemagne appointed officials called *missi dominici,* "agents of the lord king." The empire was divided into visitorial districts. Each year, beginning in 802, two missi, usually a count and a bishop or abbot, visited assigned districts. They held courts and investigated the district's judicial, financial, and clerical activities. They held commissions to regulate crime, moral conduct, education, the clergy, the poor, and many other matters. The missi checked up on the counts and worked to prevent the counts' positions from becoming hereditary: strong counts with hereditary estates would have weakened the emperor's power. In especially barbarous regions, such as the Spanish and Danish borders, Charles set up areas called "marks," where officials called "margraves" had extensive powers to govern.

A modern state has institutions of government, such as a civil service, courts of law, financial agencies for apportioning and collecting taxes, and police and military powers with which to maintain order internally and defend against foreign attack. These did not exist in Charlemagne's empire.

A Dual Investiture As Christ gave authority to St. Peter (Matthew 16:18–20), so Peter invests Pope Leo III (r. 795–816) with the pallium, symbol of archiepiscopal authority, and Charlemagne with the Roman standard, representing civil authority in the West. Leo III commissioned this mosaic to celebrate papal power. *(Source: Scala/Art Resource)*

What held society together were dependent relationships cemented by oaths promising faith and loyalty.

Although the empire lacked viable institutions, some Carolingians involved in governing did have vigorous political ideas. The abbots and bishops who served as Charlemagne's advisers worked out what was for their time a sophisticated political ideology based on high ideals of behavior and of government. They wrote that a ruler may hold power from God but is responsible to the law. Just as all subjects of the empire were required to obey him, so he, too, was obliged to respect the law. They envisioned a unified Christian society presided over by a king who was responsible for maintaining peace. These views derived largely from Saint Augustine's theories of kingship (see page 241). Inevitably, they could not be realized in an illiterate, half-Christianized, preindustrial society. But they were the foundations from which medieval and even modern ideas of government were to develop.

The Imperial Coronation of Charlemagne (800)

In the autumn of the year 800, Charlemagne paid a momentous visit to Rome. Einhard gave this account of what happened:

His last journey there to Rome was due to another factor, namely that the Romans, having inflicted many injuries on Pope Leo—plucking out his eyes and tearing out his tongue, he had been compelled to beg the assistance of the king. Accordingly, coming to Rome in order that he might set in order those things which had exceedingly disturbed the condition of the Church, he remained there the whole winter. It was at the time that he accepted the name of Emperor and Augustus. At first he was so much opposed to this that he insisted that although that day was a great [Christian] feast, he would not have entered the Church if he had known beforehand the pope's intention. But he bore very patiently the jealousy of the Roman Emperors [that is, the Byzantine rulers] who were indignant when he received these titles. He overcame their arrogant haughtiness with magnanimity, a virtue in which he was considerably superior to them, by sending frequent ambassadors to them and in his letters addressing them as brothers.[6]

Did Charles plan the imperial coronation ceremony in Saint Peter's Cathedral on Christmas Day or did he merely accept the imperial title? What did he have to gain from it? Did Charlemagne use the imperial title? Did Pope Leo III (r. 795–816) arrange the coronation in order to identify the Frankish monarchy with the papacy and papal policy? Final answers will probably never be found, but several things seem certain.

First, Charlemagne considered himself a Christian king ruling a Christian people. His motto, *Renovatio Romani Imperi* ("Revival of the Roman Empire"), "implied a revival of the Western Empire in the image of Augustinian political philosophy," according to one historian.[7] Charles was consciously perpetuating old Roman imperial notions while at the same time identifying with the new Rome of the Christian church. Charlemagne and his government represented a combination of Frankish practices and Christian ideals, the two basic elements of medieval European society.

Second, later German rulers were eager to gain the imperial title and to associate themselves with the legends of Charlemagne and ancient Rome. Finally, ecclesiastical authorities continually cited the event as proof that the dignity of the imperial crown could be granted only by the pope. Whether planned by the Carolingian court or by the pope, the imperial coronation of Charlemagne was to have a profound effect on the course of German history and on the later history of Europe.

THE CAROLINGIAN INTELLECTUAL REVIVAL

It is ironic that Charlemagne's most enduring legacy was the stimulus he gave to scholarship and learning. Barely literate himself, preoccupied with the control of vast territories, much more a warrior than a thinker, he nevertheless set in motion a cultural revival that had "international" and long-lasting consequences. The revival of learning associated with Charlemagne and his court at Aachen drew its greatest inspiration from seventh- and eighth-century intellectual developments in the Anglo-Saxon kingdom of Northumbria, situated at the northernmost tip of the old Roman world (see Map 12.1).

Northumbrian Culture

Despite the victory of the Roman forms of Christian liturgy at the Synod of Whitby in 664 (see page 235), Irish-Celtic culture permeated the Roman church in Britain and resulted in a flowering of artistic and scholarly activity. Northumbrian creativity owes a great deal to the intellectual curiosity and collecting zeal of Saint Benet Biscop (ca 628–689). A strong supporter of Benedictine monasticism, Benet Biscop introduced the Roman ceremonial form into new religious houses that he founded and encouraged it in older ones. Benet Biscop made five dangerous trips to Italy, raided libraries, and brought back to Northumbria manuscripts, relics, paintings, and other treasures that formed the libraries on which much later study was based.

Northumbrian monasteries produced scores of books: missals (used for the celebration of the mass), psalters (which contained the 150 psalms and other prayers used by the monks in their devotions), commentaries on the Scriptures, illuminated manuscripts, law codes, and letters and sermons. The finest product of Northumbrian art is probably the Gospel book produced at Lindisfarne around 700. The incredible expense involved in the publication of such a book—for vellum, coloring, gold leaf—represents in part an aristocratic display of wealth. The script, *uncial,* is a Celtic version of contemporary Greek and Roman handwriting. The illustrations have an Eastern quality, combining the abstract style of the Christian Middle East and the narrative approach of classical Roman art. Likewise, the use of geometrical decorative designs shows the influence of Syrian art. Many scribes, artists, and illuminators must have participated in the book's preparation.

The finest representative of Northumbrian and indeed all Anglo-Saxon scholarship is the Venerable Bede (ca 673–735). Bede spent his life in Benet Biscop's monastery, surrounded by the books Benet Biscop had brought from Italy. Bede's scrupulous observance of *The Rule of Saint Benedict* showed his deep piety. As a scholar, his patience and diligence reflected a profound love of learning. Contemporaries revered Bede for his learned commentaries on the Scriptures and for the special holiness of his life, which earned him the title "Venerable." He was the most widely read author in the Middle Ages.

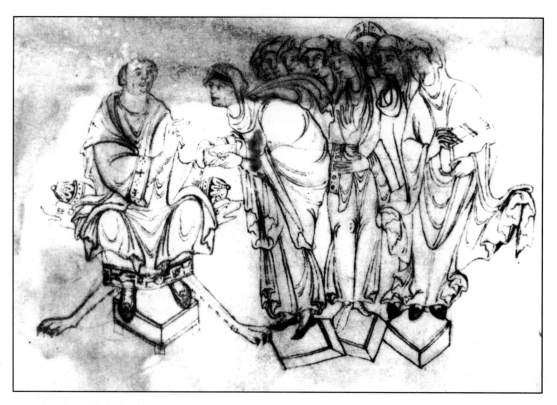

St. Hilda   The superior of a mixed monastery of men and women at Whitby in Northumbria, St. Hilda (614–680) here receives a copy of the scholar Aldhelm's treatise *In Praise of Holy Virgins.* The simple drapery of the nuns' clothing with its nervous quality is characteristic of the eleventh-century Anglo-Saxon scriptoria. *(Source: His Grace the Archbishop of Canterbury and the Trustees of Lambeth Palace Library)*

Modern scholars praise Bede for his *Ecclesiastical History of the English Nation.* Broader in scope than the title suggests, it is the chief source of information about early Britain. Bede searched far and wide for his information, discussed the validity of his evidence, compared various sources, and exercised a rare critical judgment. For these reasons, he has been called the "first scientific intellect among the Germanic peoples of Europe."[8]

Bede also popularized the system of dating events from the birth of Christ. He introduced the term *anno Domini,* "in the year of the Lord" (abbreviated A.D.), and fit the entire history of the world into this new dating method. Saint Boniface introduced this system of reckoning time throughout the Frankish kingdom.

The physical circumstances of life in the seventh and eighth centuries make Northumbrian cultural achievements all the more remarkable. Learning was pursued under terribly primitive conditions.

Monasteries such as Jarrow and Lindisfarne stood on the very fringes of the European world (see Map 12.1). The barbarian Picts, just an afternoon's walk from Jarrow, were likely to attack at any time.

Food was not the greatest problem. The North Sea and nearby rivers, the Tweed and the Tyne, yielded abundant salmon and other fish, which could be salted or smoked for winter, a nutritious if monotonous diet. Climate was another matter. Winter could be extremely harsh. In 664, for example, deep snow was hardened by frost from early winter until mid-spring. When it melted away, many animals, trees, and plants were found dead. To make matters worse, disease could take terrible tolls, as Bede described: "Also in that year 664 a sudden pestilence first depopulated the southern parts of Britain and then attacked the kingdom of the Northumbrians as well. Raging far and wide for a long time with cruel devastation it struck down a great multitude of men."[9] Damp cold with bitter winds blowing across the North Sea must have pierced everything, even stone monasteries. Inside, only one room, the *calefactory*, or "warming room," had a fire. Scribes in the *scriptorium*, or "writing room," had to stop frequently to rub circulation back into their numb hands. These monk-artists and monk-writers paid a high physical price for what they gave to posterity.

Had Northumbrian cultural achievements remained entirely insular, they would have been of slight significance. As it happened, an Englishman from Northumbria played a decisive role in the transmission of English learning to the Carolingian Empire and continental Europe.

The Carolingian Renaissance

Charlemagne's empire began to disintegrate shortly after his death in 814. But the support Charlemagne gave to education and learning helped preserve the writings of the ancients and laid the foundations for all subsequent medieval culture in Europe. Charlemagne promoted a revival that scholars have named the "Carolingian Renaissance."

At his court at Aachen, Charlemagne assembled learned men from all over Europe. The most important scholar and the leader of the palace school was a Northumbrian, Alcuin (ca 735–804). From 781 until his death, Alcuin was the emperor's chief adviser on religious and educational matters. An unusually prolific scholar, Alcuin prepared some of the emperor's official documents and wrote many moral *exempla*, or "models," which set high standards for royal behavior and constitute a treatise on kingship. Alcuin's letters to Charlemagne set forth political theories on the authority, power, and responsibilities of a Christian ruler.

What did the scholars at Charlemagne's court do? They copied books and manuscripts and built up libraries. They developed the beautifully clear handwriting known as "Carolingian minuscule," from which modern Roman type is derived. (This script is called "minuscule" because it has lower-case letters; the Romans had only capitals.) They established schools all across Europe, attaching them to monasteries and cathedrals. They placed great emphasis on the education of priests, trying to make all of them at least able to read, write, and do simple arithmetic.

The revival of learning inspired by Charlemagne and directed by Alcuin halted the threat of barbaric illiteracy on the European continent. Although hardly widespread by later standards, basic literacy was established among the clergy and even among some of the nobility. The greatest contribution of the scholars at Aachen was not so much the originality of their ideas as their hard work of salvaging and preserving the language, thought, and writings of classical Greece and Rome.

Meanwhile, the common people spoke their local vernacular languages. Thus the Saxons and Bavarians, for example, despite their geographical

The Venerable Bede This twelfth-century representation of the eighth-century monk cannot pretend to an accurate likeness but shows that later ages respected Bede as a scholar. Note the knife in one hand to sharpen the pen in the other. *(Source: The British Library)*

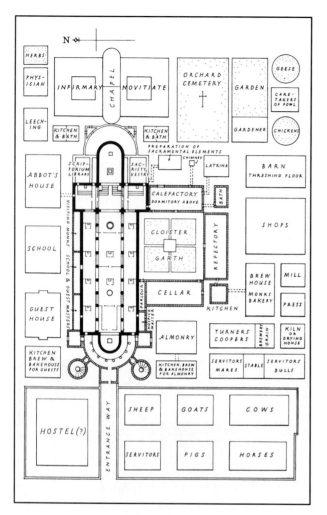

Plan for an Ideal Monastery This is a ninth-century architectural design for a self-supporting monastic community of two hundred and seventy members. The monks' lives mainly focused on the church and the cloister, which appropriately appear in the center of the plan. Note the herb garden close to the physician's quarters. The western entrance for visitors was surrounded by the hostel for poor guests and pens for farm animals—with all the inevitable smells. *(Source: Kenneth John Conant,* Carolingian and Romanesque Architecture, 800–1200. Pelican History of Art, *2nd rev. ed. (New York: Pelican, 1978), p. 57)*

a great outpouring of more sophisticated books. Ecclesiastical writers, imbued with the legal ideas of ancient Rome and the theocratic ideals of Saint Augustine, instructed the semibarbaric rulers of the West. And it is no accident that systematic medical study in the West began, at Salerno in southern Italy, in the late ninth century, *after* the Carolingian Renaissance.

Alcuin completed the work of his countryman Boniface: the Christianization of northern Europe. Latin Christian attitudes penetrated deeply into the consciousness of European peoples. By the tenth century, the patterns of thought and lifestyles of educated Western Europeans were those of Rome and Latin Christianity. Even the violence and destruction of the great invasions of the ninth century and the conflicts of the tenth could not destroy the strong foundations laid by Alcuin and his colleagues.

HEALTH AND MEDICAL CARE IN THE EARLY MIDDLE AGES

In a society devoted to fighting, warriors and civilians alike stood a strong chance of wounds from sword, spear, battle-ax, or blunt instrument. Trying to eke a living from poor soil with poor tools, perpetually involved in pushing back forest and wasteland, the farmer and his family daily ran the risk of accidents. Poor diet weakened everyone's resistance to disease. People bathed rarely. Low standards of personal hygiene increased the danger of infection. This being the case, what medical attention was available to medieval people? Scholars' examination of medical treatises, prescription (or herbal) books, manuscript illustrations, and archeological evidence has recently revealed a surprising amount of information about medical treatment in the early Middle Ages.

The Germanic peoples had no rational understanding of the causes and cures of disease. They believed that sickness was due to one of three factors: elf-shot, darts hurled by elves, that produced disease and pain; wormlike creatures in the body; and the number 9. Treatments included charms, amulets, priestly incantations, and potions. Drinks prepared from mistletoe, for example, were thought to serve as an antidote to poison and to make women fertile.

proximity (see Map 12.1), could not understand each other. Communication among the diverse peoples of the Carolingian Empire was possible only through the medium of Latin.

Once basic literacy was established, monastic and other scholars went on to more difficult work. By the middle years of the ninth century, there was

Medical practice consisted primarily of drug and prescription therapy. Through the monks' efforts and recovery of Greek and Arabic manuscripts, a large body of the ancients' prescriptions was preserved and passed on. For almost any ailment, several recipes were likely to exist in the prescription lists. Balsam was recommended for coughs. For asthma, an ointment combining chicken, wormwood, laurel berries, and oil of roses was rubbed on the chest. The scores of prescriptions to rid the body of lice, fleas, and other filth reflect frightful standards of personal hygiene. The large number of prescriptions for eye troubles suggests that they, too, must have been common. This is understandable, given the widespread practice of locating the fireplace in the center of the room. A lot of smoke and soot filtered into the room, rather than going up the chimney. One remedy calls for bathing the eyes in a solution of herbs mixed with honey, balsam, rainwater, salt water, or wine.

Poor diet caused frequent stomach disorders and related ailments such as dysentery, constipation, and diarrhea. The value of dieting and avoiding greasy foods was recognized. For poor circulation, a potion of meadow wort, oak rind, and lustmock was recommended. Pregnant women were advised to abstain from eating the flesh of almost all male animals because their meat might deform the child. Men with unusually strong sexual appetites were advised to fast and to drink at night the juice of agrimony (an herb of the rose family) boiled in ale. If a man suffered from lack of drive, the same plant boiled in milk gave him "courage."

Physicians did not examine patients. The physician, or "leech," as he was known in Anglo-Saxon England, treated only what he could see or deduce from obvious symptoms. The physician knew little about physiological functions, internal medicine, or the pathology of disease. He had no accurate standards of weights and measures. Prescriptions called for "a pinch" or "a handful" or "an eggshell full."

All wounds and open injuries invited infection, and infection invited gangrene. Several remedies were known for wounds. Physicians appreciated the antiseptic properties of honey, and prescriptions recommended that wounds be cleaned with it. When an area or limb had become gangrenous, a good technique of amputation existed. The physician was instructed to cut above the diseased flesh—that is, to cut away some healthy tissue and

bone—in order to hasten cure. The juice of white poppy plants—the source of heroin—could be added to wine and drunk as an anesthetic. White poppies, however, grew only in southern Europe and North Africa. If a heavy slug of wine was not enough to dull the patient, he or she had to be held down forcibly while the physician cut. Butter and egg whites, which have a soothing effect, were prescribed for burns.

Teeth survive long periods of burial and give reasonably good information about disease. Evidence from early medieval England shows that in the adult population, the rate of cavities was only

The Wound Man This illustration from a fifteenth-century manuscript depicts a "wound man" displaying weapons, sources of injuries, and sores. It may have been used to prompt the aspiring surgeon's memory. *(Source: Courtesy, The Wellcome Institute)*

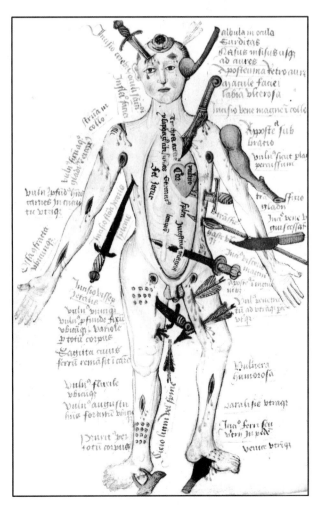

one-sixth that of today. Cavities below the gum line, however, were very common because of the prevalence of carbohydrates in the diet. The resulting abscesses of the gums, and other forms of periodontal disease, were widespread after the age of thirty.[10]

The spread of Christianity in the Carolingian era had a beneficial effect on medical knowledge and treatment. Several of the church fathers expressed serious interest in medicine. Some of them even knew something about it. The church was deeply concerned about human suffering, whether physical or mental. Christian teaching vigorously supported concern for the poor, sick, downtrodden, and miserable. Churchmen taught that, while all knowledge came from God, he had supplied it so that people could use it for their own benefit.

In the sixth and seventh centuries, the period of the bloodiest violence, medical treatment was provided by monasteries. No other places offered the calm, quiet atmosphere necessary for treatment and recuperation. Monks took care of the sick. They collected and translated the ancient medical treatises. They cultivated herb gardens from which medicines were prepared.

The founding of a school at Salerno sometime in the ninth century gave a tremendous impetus to medical study by lay people. Its location attracted Arabic, Greek, and Jewish physicians from all over the Mediterranean region. Students flocked there from northern Europe. The Jewish physician Shabbathai Ben Abraham (931–982) left behind pharmacological notes that were widely studied in later centuries.

By the eleventh century, the medical school at Salerno enjoyed international fame. Its most distinguished professor was Constantine the African. A native of Carthage, he had studied medicine throughout the Middle East and, because of his thorough knowledge of Oriental languages, served as an important transmitter of Arabic culture to the West. Constantine taught and practiced medicine at Salerno for some years before becoming a monk.

Several women physicians also contributed to the celebrity of the school. Trotula, for example, an authority on gynecological problems, wrote a book called *On Female Disorders*. Though not connected with the Salerno medical school, the abbess Hildegard (1098–1179) of Rupertsberg in Hesse, Germany, reputedly treated the emperor Frederick Barbarossa. Hildegard's treatise *On the Physical Elements* shows a remarkable degree of careful scientific observation.

How available was medical treatment? Most people lived on isolated rural estates and had to take such advice and help as were available locally. Physicians were few in the early Middle Ages. They charged a fee that only the rich could afford. Apparently, most illnesses simply took their course. People had to develop a stoical attitude. Death came early. A person of forty was considered old. People's vulnerability to ailments for which there was no cure contributed to a fatalistic acceptance of death at a young age. Early medical literature shows that attempts to relieve pain were crude; still, they *were* made.

DIVISION AND DISINTEGRATION OF THE CAROLINGIAN EMPIRE (814–987)

Charlemagne left his vast empire to his only surviving son, Louis the Pious (r. 814–840), who had actually been crowned emperor in his father's lifetime. Deeply religious and well educated, Louis was no soldier. Thus he could not retain the respect and loyalty of the warrior-aristocracy on whom he depended for troops and for administration of his territories. Disintegration began almost at once.

The basic reason for the collapse of the Carolingian Empire is simply that it was too big. In Charlemagne's lifetime it was held together by the sheer force of his personality and driving energy. After his death, it began to fall apart. The empire lacked a bureaucracy like that of the Roman Empire—the administrative machinery necessary for strong and enduring government. It was a collection of tribes held together at the pleasure of warrior-aristocrats, men most interested in strengthening their own local positions and ensuring that they could pass on to their sons the offices and estates that they had amassed. Counts, abbots, bishops—both lay and ecclesiastical magnates—needed estates to support themselves and reward their followers. In their localities, they simply assumed judicial, military, and financial functions. Why should they obey an unimpressive distant ruler who represented a centralizing power that threatened their local interests?

Bad roads swarming with thugs and rivers infested with pirates made communication within the empire very difficult. Added to this was the Frankish custom of dividing estates among all male heirs. Between 817 and his death in 840, Louis the Pious made several divisions of the empire. Dissatisfied with their portions and anxious to gain the imperial title, Louis's sons—Lothair, Louis the German, and Charles the Bald—fought bitterly among themselves. Finally, in the Treaty of Verdun of 843, the brothers agreed to partition the empire (Map 12.2).

Lothair, the eldest, received the now-empty title of emperor and the "middle kingdom," which included Italy and the territories bordered by the Meuse, Saône, and Rhône rivers in the west and the Rhine in the east. Almost immediately, this kingdom broke up into many petty principalities extending diagonally across Europe from Flanders to Lombardy. From the tenth century to the twelfth and thirteenth centuries, when French and German monarchs were trying to build strong central governments, this area was constantly contested between them. Even in modern times, the "middle kingdom" of Lothair has been bloodsoaked.

The eastern and most Germanic part of the Carolingian Empire passed to Louis the German. The western kingdom went to Charles the Bald; it included the provinces of Aquitaine and Gascony and formed the basis of medieval and modern France. The descendants of Charles the Bald held on in the west until 987, when the leading magnates elected Hugh Capet as king. The heirs of Louis the German ruled the eastern kingdom until 911, but real power was in the hands of local chieftains. Everywhere in the tenth century, fratricidal warfare among the descendants of Charlemagne accelerated the spread of feudalism.

FEUDALISM

The adjective *feudal* is often used disparagingly today to describe something antiquated and barbaric. It is similarly commonplace to think of medieval feudalism as a system that let a small group of lazy military leaders exploit the producing class, the tillers of the soil. This is not a very useful approach. Preindustrial societies ranging from ancient Greece to the American South before the Civil War to some twentieth-century Latin American countries have been characterized by sharp di-

MAP 12.2 Division of the Carolingian Empire, 843 The Treaty of Verdun (843), which divided the empire among Charlemagne's grandsons, is frequently taken as the start of the separate development of Germany, France, and Italy. The "middle kingdom" of Lothair, however, lacking defensive borders and any political or linguistic unity, quickly broke up into numerous small territories.

visions between "exploiters" and "exploited." To call all such societies "feudal" strips the term of significant meaning and distorts understanding of medieval feudalism. Many twentieth-century scholars have demonstrated that, when feudalism developed, it served the needs of medieval society.

The Two Levels of Feudalism

Webster's *Third New International Dictionary* defines *government* as "the officials collectively comprising the governing body of a political unit and constituting the organization as an active agency." Although the term *feudalism* was not coined until the seventeenth century, feudalism emerged in western Europe in the ninth century and was a type of government "in which political power was treated as a private possession and was divided among a large number of lords."[11] This kind of government characterized western Europe from about 900 to 1300.

Feudalism actually existed at two social levels: first, at the level of armed retainers who became knights; second, at the level of royal officials, such as counts, who ruled great feudal principalities. A wide and deep gap in social standing and political function separated these armed retainers and royal officials.

In the early eighth century, the Carolingian kings and other powerful men needed bodyguards and retainers, armed men who could fight effectively on horseback. The arrival in western Europe around this time of a Chinese technological invention, the stirrup, revolutionized warfare. The stirrup welded horse and rider into a powerful fighting unit. A rider without stirrups could seldom impale an adversary, but a rider in stirrups could utilize the force of the galloping animal to strike and wound the enemy. Charles Martel recognized the potential of heavily armed cavalry equipped with stirrups, and the invention prompted him to gather a large number of retainers. Horses and armor were terribly expensive, and few could afford them. It also took considerable time to train a man to be an effective cavalryman. As the value of retainers increased, Charles Martel and other powerful men bound their retainers by oaths of loyalty and ceremonies of homage. Here is an oath of *fealty* (or faithfulness) from the ninth century:

Thus shall one take the oath of fidelity:

By the Lord before whom this sanctuary [some religious place] is holy, I will to N. be true and faithful, and love all which he loves and shun all which he shuns, according to the laws of God and the order of the world. Nor will I ever with will or action, through word or deed, do anything which is unpleasing to him, on condition that he will hold to me as I shall deserve it, and that he will perform everything as it was in our agreement when I submitted myself to him and chose his will.[12]

Lords also tried to ensure the support of their retainers with gifts of weapons and jewelry. Some great lords gave their armed cavalrymen, or *vassals,* estates, or *fiefs,* that produced income to maintain the retainer and his family. Because knights were not involved in any government activity, and because only men who exercised political power were considered noble, knights were not part of the noble class. Down to the eleventh century, political power was concentrated in a small group of counts.

This group of counts, descended from the old Frankish aristocracy (see page 334), constituted the second level of feudalism. Under Charles Martel and his heirs, counts monopolized the high offices in the Carolingian Empire. At the local level, they had full judicial, military, and financial power. They held courts that dispensed justice, waged wars, and collected taxes. For most ordinary people, the counts were the government. Charlemagne regularly sent missi to inspect the activities of the counts, but there was slight chance of a corrupt count being removed from office.

Although countships were not hereditary in the eighth century, they tended to remain within the same family. In the eighth and early ninth centuries, regional concentrations of power depended on family connections and political influence at the king's court. The disintegration of the Carolingian Empire, however, served to increase the power of regional authorities. Civil wars weakened the power and prestige of kings because they could do little about domestic violence. Likewise, the great invasions of the ninth century, especially the Viking invasions (see pages 350–352), weakened royal authority. The West Frankish kings could do little to halt the invaders, and the aristocracy had to assume responsibility for defense. Common people turned for protection to the strongest local power, the counts, whom they considered their rightful rulers. Thus, in the ninth and tenth centuries, great aristocratic families governed virtually independent territories in which distant and weak kings could not interfere. "Political power had become a private, heritable property for great counts and lords."[13] This is what is meant by feudalism as a form of government.

Because feudal society was a military society, men held the dominant positions in it. The legal and social position of women was not as insignificant as might be expected, however. Charters recording gifts to the church indicate that women held land in many areas. Women frequently endowed monasteries, churches, and other religious establishments. The possession of land obviously meant economic power. Moreover, women inherited land. In southern France and Catalonia in Spain, women inherited feudal property as early as the tenth century. Other kinds of evidence attest to women's status. For example, in parts of northern France, children sometimes identified themselves in legal documents by their mother's name rather than their father's, indicating that the mother's social position in the community was higher than the father's.

Commendation and Initiation Just as the spiritual power of priests is bequeathed by the laying of the priests' hands on the candidate's head at ordination, so the military virtues of strength and loyalty were conveyed to the warrior by the act of commendation when he placed his clasped hands between the hands of his lord. A kiss, symbolizing peace, often concluded the ceremony. *(Source: Universitätsbibliothek, Heidelberg)*

In a treatise he wrote in 822 on the organization of the royal household, Archbishop Hincmar of Reims placed the queen directly above the treasurer. She was responsible for giving the knights their annual salaries. She supervised the manorial accounts. Thus, in the management of large households with many knights to oversee and complicated manorial records to supervise, the lady of the manor had highly important responsibilities. With such responsibility went power and influence.[14]

Manorialism

Feudalism concerned the rights, powers, and lifestyle of the military elite; *manorialism* involved the services and obligations of the peasant classes. The economic power of the warring class rested on landed estates worked by peasants. Hence feudalism and manorialism were inextricably linked. Peasants needed protection, and lords demanded something in return for providing that protection. Free peasants surrendered themselves and their lands to the lord's jurisdiction. The land was given back, but the peasants became tied to the land by various payments and services. In France, England, Germany, and Italy, local custom determined precisely what those services were, but certain practices became common everywhere. The peasant was obliged to turn over to the lord a percentage of the annual harvest, usually in produce, sometimes in cash. The peasant paid a fee to marry someone from outside the lord's estate. He paid a fine, often his best beast, to inherit property. Above all, the peasant became part of the lord's permanent labor force. With vast stretches of uncultivated virgin land and a tiny labor population, lords encouraged population growth and immigration. The most profitable form of capital was not land but laborers.

In entering into a relationship with a feudal lord, a free farmer lost status. His position became servile, and he became a *serf*—that is, he was bound to the land and could not leave it without the lord's permission. He was also subject to the jurisdiction of the lord's court in any dispute over property or if he was suspected of criminal behavior.

The transition from freedom to serfdom was slow; its speed was closely related to the degree of political order in a given region. Even in the late eighth century there were still many free peasants. And within the legal category of serfdom there were many economic levels, ranging from the highly prosperous to the desperately poor. Nevertheless, a social and legal revolution was taking place. By the year 800, perhaps 60 percent of the population of western Europe—completely free a century before—had been reduced to serfdom. The ninth-century Viking assaults on Europe created extremely unstable conditions and individual insecurity, leading to additional loss of personal freedom. The lives of the peasants are described in detail on pages 374–385.

Scandinavian Sword Hilt (late sixth century) Scandinavian artists attained a high level of achievement in the zoomorphic (or animal) style, though the animals are not recognizable in this fine example of metalwork. The Scandinavians later learned to work in wood and leather from Merovingian, Northumbrian, and Irish artists, but few examples of these techniques survive. *(Source: University Museum of National Antiquities, Oslo)*

GREAT INVASIONS OF THE NINTH CENTURY

After the Treaty of Verdun (843) and the division of Charlemagne's empire among his grandsons, continental Europe presented an easy target for foreign invaders. All three kingdoms were torn by domestic dissension and disorder. No European political power was strong enough to put up effective resistance to external attacks. Frontier and coastal defenses erected by Charlemagne and maintained by Louis the Pious were completely neglected.

From the moors of Scotland to the mountains of Sicily there arose in the ninth century the Christian prayer "Save us, O God, from the violence of the Northmen." The Northmen, also known as "Normans" or "Vikings," were Germanic peoples from Norway, Sweden, and Denmark who had remained beyond the sway of the Christianizing and civilizing influences of the Carolingian Empire. Some scholars believe that the name "Viking" derives from the Old Norse word *vik,* meaning "creek." A *Viking,* then, was a pirate who waited in a creek or bay to attack passing vessels.

Charlemagne had established marches, fortresses, and watchtowers along his northern coasts to defend his territory against Viking raiders. Their assaults began around 787, and by the mid-tenth century they had brought large chunks of continental Europe and Britain under their sway (Map 12.3). In the east they pierced the rivers of Russia as far as the Black Sea. In the west they sailed as far as Iceland, Greenland, and even

MAP 12.3 The Great Invasions of the Ninth Century Note the Viking penetration of eastern Europe and their probable expeditions to North America. What impact did their various invasions have on European society?

the coast of North America, perhaps as far south as Long Island Sound.

The Vikings were superb seamen. Advanced construction methods gave their ships great speed and maneuverability. Propelled either by oars or by sails, deckless, and about 65 feet long, a Viking ship could carry between forty and sixty men—quite enough to harass an isolated monastery or village. These boats, navigated by thoroughly experienced and utterly fearless sailors, moved through the most complicated rivers, estuaries, and waterways in Europe. The Carolingian Empire, with no navy and no notion of the importance of sea power, was helpless. The Vikings moved swiftly, attacked, and escaped to return again.

Scholars disagree about the reasons for these migrations. Some maintain that overpopulation forced the Vikings to emigrate. Others argue that climatic conditions and crop failures forced migration. Still others insist that the Northmen were looking for trade and new commercial contacts, as well as plunder.

Plunder they did. Viking attacks were savage. At first they attacked and sailed off laden with booty. Later, on returning, they settled down and colonized the areas they had conquered. For example, the Vikings overran a large part of northwestern France and called the territory "Norsemanland," from which the word *Normandy* derives (see Map 12.3).

Scarcely had the savagery of the Viking assaults begun to subside when Europe was hit from the east and south. Beginning about 890, Magyar tribes crossed the Danube and pushed steadily westward. (Since people thought of them as returning Huns, the Magyars came to be known as "Hungarians.") They subdued northern Italy, compelled Bavaria and Saxony to pay tribute, and penetrated even into the Rhineland and Burgundy. These roving bandits attacked isolated villages and monasteries, taking prisoners and selling them in the Eastern slave markets. The Magyars were not colonizers; their sole object was booty and plunder.

The Vikings and Magyars depended on fear. In their initial attacks on isolated settlements, every man, woman, and child was put to the sword. A few attractive women might be spared to satisfy the conquerors' lusts or to be sold into slavery. The Scandinavians and Hungarians struck such terror in defenseless rural peoples that those peoples often gave up without a struggle. Many communities bought peace by paying tribute.

From the south the Muslims began new encroachments, concentrating on the two southern European peninsulas, Italy and Spain. They drove northward and sacked Rome in 846. Expert seamen, they sailed around the Iberian Peninsula and braved the notoriously dangerous shoals and winds of the Atlantic coast. In 859 they attacked the settlements along the coast of Provence. Muslim attacks on the European continent in the ninth and tenth centuries were less destructive than those of the Vikings and Magyars. Compared to the rich, sophisticated culture of the Arab capi-

tals, northern Europe was primitive, backward, and offered little.

What was the effect of these invasions on the structure of European society? Viking, Magyar, and Muslim attacks accelerated the development of feudalism. Lords capable of rallying fighting men, supporting them, and putting up resistance to the invaders did so. They also assumed political power in their territories. Weak and defenseless people sought the protection of local strongmen. Free men sank to the level of serfs. Consequently, European society became further fragmented. Public power became increasingly decentralized.

POLITICAL REVIVAL

The eleventh century witnessed the beginnings of political stability in western Europe. People grew increasingly secure in their persons and property. Political stability and security contributed to a slow increase in population and provided the foundation for economic recovery.

The Decline of Invasion and Civil Disorder

The most important factor in the revival of Europe after the disasters of the ninth century was the gradual decline in foreign invasions and the reduction of domestic violence. In France, for example, the Norwegian leader Rollo in 911 subdued large parts of what was later called "Normandy." The West Frankish ruler Charles the Simple, unable to oust the Northmen, went along with that territorial conquest. He recognized Rollo as duke of Normandy on the condition that Rollo swear allegiance to him and hold the territory as a sort of barrier against future Viking assaults. This agreement, embodied in the Treaty of Saint-Clair-sur-Epte, marks the beginning of the rise of Normandy.

Rollo kept his word. He exerted strong authority over Normandy and in troubled times supported the weak Frankish king. Rollo and his soldiers were baptized as Christians. Although additional Viking settlers arrived, they were easily pacified. The tenth and eleventh centuries saw the steady assimilation of Normans and French. Major attacks on France ended. By 1066—the year Rollo's descendant Duke William I (1035–1087) and the Normans invaded England—the duchy of Normandy was the strongest and most peaceful territory in western Europe.

The civil wars and foreign invasions of the ninth and tenth centuries left the territories now called "France" divided into provinces and counties where local feudal lords held actual power. After the death of the last Carolingian ruler in 987, an assembly of nobles met to choose a successor. The nobles selected Hugh Capet, head of a powerful clan in the West Frankish kingdom. The Capetian kings subsequently saved France from further division. But that they would do so was hardly apparent in 987. Compared with the dukes of Normandy and Aquitaine, the first Capetians were weak, but by hanging on to what they had, they laid the foundations for later political stability.

Recovery followed a different pattern in Anglo-Saxon England. The Danes (or Vikings) had made a concerted effort to conquer and rule the whole island, and probably no region of Europe suffered more. By 877 only parts of Wessex survived. The victory of the remarkable Alfred, king of the West Saxons (or Wessex), over Guthrun the Dane at Edington in 878 inaugurated a great political revival. Alfred and his immediate successors built a system of local defenses and slowly extended royal rule beyond Wessex to other Anglo-Saxon peoples until one law, royal law, replaced local custom.

The Danish ruler Canute, king of England (r. 1016–1035) and after 1030 king of Norway as well, made England the center of his empire. Canute promoted a policy of assimilation and reconciliation between Anglo-Saxons and Vikings. Slowly the two peoples were molded together. The assimilation of Anglo-Saxon and Viking was personified by King Edward the Confessor (r. 1042–1066), the son of an Anglo-Saxon father and a Norman mother who had taken Canute as her second husband.

In the east, the German king Otto I (r. 936–973) inflicted a crushing defeat on the Hungarians at the banks of the Lech River in 955. This battle halted the Magyars' westward expansion and threat to Germany and made Otto a great hero to the Germans. It also signified the revival of the German monarchy and demonstrated that Otto was a worthy successor to Charlemagne.

When chosen king, Otto had selected Aachen as the site of his coronation to symbolize his intention to continue the tradition of Charlemagne.

Vikings Invade Britain   In this twelfth-century representation of the Viking invasions, warriors appear to be armed with helmets, spears, and shields. Crossing the rough North Sea and English Channel in open, oar-propelled boats, they had great courage. *(Source: The Pierpont Morgan Library)*

The basis of his power was to be alliance with and control of the church. Otto asserted the right of effective control over ecclesiastical appointments. Before receiving religious consecration, bishops and abbots had to perform feudal homage for the lands that accompanied the church office. (This practice was to create a grave crisis in the eleventh century; see pages 359–361.)

Otto realized that he had to use the financial and military resources of the church to halt feudal anarchy. He used the higher clergy extensively in

Christ Enthroned with Saints and the Emperor Otto I
(tenth century) Between 933 and 973, Emperor Otto I
founded the church of St. Mauritius in Magdeburg. As a
memorial to the event, Otto commissioned the production of this ivory plaque showing Christ accepting a
model of the church from the emperor. Ivory was a favorite medium of Ottonian artists, and squat figures in a
simple geometrical pattern characterize their work.
*(Source: The Metropolitan Museum of Art, Bequest of
George Blumenthal, 1941 (41.100.157))*

his administration, and the bulk of his army came
from monastic and other church lands. Between
936 and 955, Otto succeeded in breaking the territorial power of the great German dukes.

Otto's coronation by the pope in 962 revived
the imperial dignity and laid the foundation for
what was later called the "Holy Roman Empire."
The coronation showed that Otto had the support
of the church in Germany and Italy. The uniting
of the kingship with the imperial crown advanced
German interests. Otto filled a power vacuum in
northern Italy and brought peace among the great
aristocratic families. The level of order there improved for the first time in over a century. Peace
and political stability in turn promoted the eco-

nomic revival of Venice and other northern Italian
cities.

By the start of the eleventh century, the Italian
maritime cities were seeking a place in the rich
Mediterranean trade. Pisa and Genoa fought to
break Muslim control of the trade and shipping
with the Byzantine Empire and the Far East. Once
the Muslim fleets had been destroyed, the Italian
cities of Venice, Genoa, and Pisa embarked on the
road to prosperity. The eleventh century witnessed
a steady rise in their strength and wealth. Freedom
from invasion and domestic security made economic growth possible all over western Europe.
In Spain, the *reconquista*—the reconquest of
Muslim-controlled lands—gained impetus.

Increasing Population and Mild Climate

A steady growth of population also contributed to
Europe's general recovery. The decline of foreign
invasions and internal civil disorder reduced the
number of people killed and maimed. Feudal
armies in the eleventh through thirteenth centuries continued their destruction, but they were
very small by modern standards and fought few
pitched battles. Most medieval conflicts consisted
of sieges on castles or fortifications. As few as
twelve men could defend a castle. Monastic chroniclers, frequently bored and almost always writing
from hearsay evidence, tended to romanticize medieval warfare (as long as it was not in their own
neighborhoods). Most conflicts were petty skirmishes with slight loss of life. The survival of more
young people, those most often involved in war
and usually the most sexually active, meant a population rise.

Nor did nature or biology hinder population expansion. Between the tenth and fourteenth centuries, no major plague or other medical scourge hit
Europe, though leprosy and malaria did strike
down some people. Leprosy had entered Europe in
the early Middle Ages. Caused by a virus, the disease was not very contagious and, if contracted,
worked slowly. Lepers presented a frightful appearance: the victim's arms and legs rotted away, and
gangrenous sores emitted a horrible smell. Physicians had no cure. Eventually, medieval lepers were
segregated in hospitals called "leprosaria." Malaria, spread by protozoa-carrying mosquitoes that
infested swampy areas, is characterized by alternate

chills and fevers and leaves the afflicted person extremely weak.

During the High Middle Ages, relatively few people caught leprosy or malaria. Crop failure and the ever-present danger of starvation were much more pressing threats. Here, the weather cooperated with the revival. The century between 1080 and 1180 witnessed exceptionally clement weather in England, France, and Germany, with mild winters and dry summers. Good weather helps to explain advances in land reclamation and agricultural yield. And increased agricultural output had a profound impact on society: it affected Europeans' health, commerce, industry, and general lifestyle.

REVIVAL AND REFORM IN THE CHRISTIAN CHURCH

The eleventh century witnessed the beginnings of a remarkable religious revival. Monasteries, always the leaders in ecclesiastical reform, remodeled themselves under the leadership of the Burgundian abbey of Cluny. Subsequently, new religious orders, such as the Cistercians, were founded and became a broad spiritual movement.

The papacy itself, after a century of corruption and decadence, was cleaned up. The popes worked to clarify church doctrine and codify church law. They and their officials sought to communicate with all the clergy and peoples of Europe through a clearly defined, obedient hierarchy of bishops. The popes wanted the basic loyalty of all members of the clergy. Ultimately, assertions of papal power caused profound changes and serious conflicts with secular authorities. The revival of the church was manifested in the twelfth and thirteenth centuries by a flowering of popular piety and the building of magnificent cathedrals (see pages 429–432).

Monastic Decline and Revival

In the early Middle Ages, the best Benedictine monasteries had been citadels of good Christian living and centers of learning. Between the seventh and ninth centuries, religious houses copied and preserved manuscripts, maintained schools, and set high standards of monastic observance. Charlemagne had encouraged and supported these monastic activities, and the collapse of the Carolingian Empire had disastrous effects.

Viking, Magyar, and Muslim invaders attacked and ransacked many monasteries across Europe. Some communities fled and dispersed. In the period of political disorder that followed the disintegration of the Carolingian Empire, many religious houses fell under the control of local feudal lords. Powerful laymen appointed themselves or their relatives as abbots, while keeping their wives or mistresses. They took for themselves the lands and goods of monasteries, spending monastic revenues and selling monastic offices. All over Europe, temporal powers dominated the monasteries. The level of spiritual observance and intellectual activity declined.

In 909 William the Pious, duke of Aquitaine, established the abbey of Cluny near Mâcon in Burgundy. In his charter of endowment, Duke William declared that Cluny was to enjoy complete independence from all feudal or secular lordship. The new monastery was to be subordinate only to the authority of Saints Peter and Paul as represented by the pope. The duke then renounced his own possession of and influence over Cluny.

In the church as a whole, Cluny gradually came to stand for clerical celibacy and the suppression of *simony*—the sale of church offices. In the eleventh century, Cluny was fortunate in having a series of highly able abbots who ruled for a long time. These abbots paid careful attention to sound economic management. In a disorderly world, Cluny gradually came to represent religious and political stability. Moreover, properties and monasteries under Cluny's jurisdiction enjoyed special protection, at least theoretically, from violence.[15] Thus laypersons placed lands in its custody and monastic priories under its jurisdiction for reform. In this way hundreds of monasteries, primarily in France and Spain, came under Cluny's authority.

By the last quarter of the eleventh century, some monasteries enjoyed wide reputations for the beauty and richness of their chant and the piety of their monks' lives. Deeply impressed laymen showered gifts on them. Jewelry, rich vestments, elaborately carved sacred vessels, even lands and properties poured into some houses. With this wealth came lay influence. As the monasteries grew richer, the monks' lifestyle became increasingly

Mont St.-Michel At the summit of a 250-foot cone of rock rising out of the sea and accessible only at low tide, Mont St.-Michel combined fortified castle and monastery. Thirteenth-century monarchs considered it crucial to their power in northwestern France, and it played a decisive role in French defenses against the English during the Hundred Years' War. The abbots so planned the architecture that monastic life went on undisturbed by military activity. *(Source: Giraudon/Art Resource)*

luxurious. Conversely, monastic observance and spiritual fervor declined.

Once again the ideals of the pristine Benedictine life were threatened. Fresh demands for reform were heard, and the result was the founding of new religious orders in the late eleventh and early twelfth centuries. The best representatives of the new reforming spirit were the Cistercians.

In 1098 a group of monks left the rich abbey of Molesmes in Burgundy and founded a new house in the swampy forest of Cîteaux. They planned to avoid all involvement with secular feudal society. They decided to accept only uncultivated lands far from regular habitation. They intended to refuse all gifts of mills, serfs, tithes, and ovens—the traditional manorial sources of income. The early Cistercians determined to avoid elaborate liturgy and ceremony and to keep their chant simple. Finally, because they knew that lay influence was usually harmful to careful observance, they refused to allow the presence of powerful laymen in their monasteries. The Cistercians were creating a new kind of commune. It was to be simple, isolated, austere, and purified of all the economic and religious complexities found in the Benedictine houses.

These Cistercian goals coincided perfectly with the needs of twelfth-century society. The late eleventh and early twelfth centuries witnessed energetic agricultural expansion and land reclamation all across Europe. The early Cistercians wanted to farm only land that had previously been uncultivated, swampland, or fenland, and that was exactly what needed to be done. They thus became the great pioneers of the twelfth century.

The first monks at Cîteaux experienced sickness, a dearth of recruits, and terrible privations. But their obvious sincerity and high idealism eventually attracted attention. In 1112, a twenty-three-year-old nobleman called Bernard and thirty of his aristocratic companions joined the community at Cîteaux. Thereafter, this reforming movement gained impetus. The Cistercians founded 525 new monasteries in the course of the twelfth century, and their influence on European society was profound. Unavoidably, however, the Cistercians' success brought wealth, and wealth brought power. By the end of the twelfth century, economic prosperity and political power had begun to compromise the primitive Cistercian ideals.

Reform of the Papacy

In the tenth century the papacy provided little leadership to the Christian peoples of Western Europe. Factions in Rome sought to control the papacy for their own material gain. Popes were appointed to advance the political ambitions of their families—the great aristocratic families of the city—and not because of special spiritual qualifications. The office of pope, including its spiritual powers and influence, was frequently bought and sold even though the crime of simony had been condemned by Saint Peter. The licentiousness and debauchery of the papal court weakened the popes' religious prestige and moral authority. According to a contemporary chronicler, for example, Pope John XII (r. 955–963), who had secured the papal office at the age of eighteen, wore himself out with sexual excesses before he reached his twenty-eighth year.

At the local parish level there were many married priests. Taking Christ as the model for the priestly life, the Roman church had always encouraged clerical celibacy, and celibacy had been an obligation for ordination since the fourth century.

Consecration of the Church of Cluny   Pope Urban II surrounded by mitred bishops appears on the left, Abbot Hugh of Cluny with cowled monks on the right. A French nobleman who had been a monk at Cluny, Urban coined the term *curia* as the official designation of the central government of the church. *(Source: Bibliothèque Nationale, Paris)*

But in the tenth and eleventh centuries, probably a majority of European priests were married or living with a woman. Such priests were called "Nicolaites," from a reference in the Book of Revelation to early Christians who advocated a return to pagan sexual practices.

Several factors may account for the lack of clerical celibacy. The explanation may lie in the basic need for warmth and human companionship. Perhaps village priests could not survive economically on their small incomes and needed the help of a mate. Perhaps the tradition of a married clergy was so deep-rooted by the tenth century that each generation simply followed the example of its predecessor. In any case, the disparity between law and reality shocked the lay community and bred disrespect for the clergy.

Serious efforts at reform began under Pope Leo IX (r. 1049–1054). Not only was Leo related to Holy Roman Emperor Henry III (r. 1039–1056)

but, as bishop of Toul and a German, he was also an outsider who owed nothing to any Roman faction. Leo traveled widely and at Pavia, Reims, and Mainz held councils that issued decrees against simony, Nicolaism, and violence. Leo's representatives held church councils across Europe, pressing for moral reform. They urged those who could not secure justice at home to appeal to the pope, the ultimate source of justice.

Papal reform continued after Leo IX. In the short reign of Nicholas II (r. 1058–1061), a council held in Rome in the ancient church of Saint John Lateran in 1059 devised a new method for electing the pope. Since the eighth century, the priests of the major churches in and around Rome had constituted a special group, called a "college," that advised the pope. These chief priests were called "cardinals" from the Latin *cardo*, meaning "hinge." The Lateran Synod of 1059 decreed that the authority and power to elect the pope rested

Rievaulx Abbey Taking its name from the nearby Rie River and the valley in which it is situated, both this vast abbey church (completed in 1145) and the accompanying monastic complex were financed by the extremely fine wool produced from the sheep who grazed on these hillsides. The wool clip also supported a monastic community of over 600 in the mid-twelfth century. *(Source: English Heritage. Crown Copyright)*

solely in this college of cardinals. The college retains that power today.

The object of this decree was to reduce royal influence and remove this crucial decision from the secular squabbling of Roman aristocratic factions. When the office of pope was vacant, the cardinals were responsible for governing the church. By 1073 the progress of reform in the Christian church was well advanced. The election of Cardinal Hildebrand as Pope Gregory VII (r. 1073–1085) changed the direction of reform from a moral to a political one.

THE GREGORIAN REVOLUTION

The papal reform movement of the eleventh century is frequently called the "Gregorian reform movement," after Pope Gregory VII. The label is not accurate, for reform began long before Gregory's pontificate and continued after it. Gregory's reign, however, did inaugurate a radical or revolutionary phase that had important political and social consequences.

Pope Gregory VII's Ideas

Once Hildebrand became pope, the reform of the papacy took on a new dimension. Its goal was not just the moral regeneration of the clergy and centralization of the church under papal authority. Gregory and his assistants began to insist on the "freedom of the church." By this they meant freedom from control and interference by laymen.

The concept of freedom of the church signaled the end of *lay investiture*—the selection and appointment of church officials by secular authority. Traditionally, bishops and abbots were invested with a staff representing pastoral jurisdiction and a ring signifying union with a diocese or monastic community. Laymen, such as kings, who gave these symbols appeared to be distributing spiritual authority. Ecclesiastical opposition to lay investiture had been part of church theory for centuries. But Gregory's attempt to put theory into practice was a radical departure from tradition. Because feudal monarchs depended on churchmen for the operation of their governments, Gregory's program seemed to spell disaster for stable royal administration. It provoked a terrible crisis.

The Controversy over Lay Investiture

In February 1075, Pope Gregory held a council at Rome. It published decrees not only against Nicolaism and simony but also against lay investiture:

If anyone henceforth shall receive a bishopric or abbey from the hands of a lay person, he shall not be considered as among the number of bishops and abbots. . . . Likewise if any emperor, king. . . . or any one at all of the secular powers, shall presume to perform investiture with bishoprics or with any other ecclesiastical dignity . . . he shall feel the divine displeasure as well with regard to his body as to his other belongings.[16]

In short, clerics who accepted investiture from laymen were to be deposed, and laymen who invested clerics were to be *excommunicated*—that is, cut off from the sacraments and from all Christian worship.

The church's penalty of excommunication relied for its effectiveness on public opinion. Since most Europeans favored Gregory's moral reforms, he believed that excommunication would compel rulers to abide by his changes. Immediately, however, Henry IV in the Holy Roman Empire, William the Conqueror in England, and Philip I in France protested.

The strongest reaction came from the Holy Roman Empire. Most eleventh-century rulers could not survive without the literacy and administrative knowledge of bishops and abbots. Naturally, then, kings selected and invested most of the bishops and abbots. In this respect, as recent research has shown, German kings scarcely varied from other rulers. In two basic ways, however, the German kings had the most to lose from the prohibition on lay investiture, for the pope granted the imperial crown, and both the empire and the Papal States claimed northern Italy.

Over and above the subject of lay investiture, a more fundamental issue was at stake. Gregory's decree raised the question of the proper role of the monarch in a Christian society. Did a king have ultimate jurisdiction over all his subjects, including the clergy? For centuries, tradition had answered this question in favor of the ruler. Thus it is no wonder that Henry protested the papal assertions about investiture. Indirectly, they undermined imperial power and sought to make papal authority supreme.

Henry IV and Gregory VII The twelfth-century Cistercian chronicler Otto at Freising depicts Gregory VII expelled from Rome while Henry IV sits beside an anti-pope. Grandson of Henry IV, Otto did not sympathize with Gregory, whom he thought had sown disorder in the church. *(Source: Sächsische Landesbibliothek/Deutsche Fotothek)*

An increasingly bitter exchange of letters ensued. Gregory accused Henry IV (r. 1056–1106) of lack of respect for the papacy and insisted that disobedience to the pope was disobedience to God. Henry protested in a now-famous letter beginning, "Henry King not by usurpation, but by the pious ordination of God, to Hildebrand, now not Pope, but false monk."

Within the empire, those who had most to gain from the dispute quickly took advantage of it. In January 1076, the German bishops who had been invested by Henry withdrew their allegiance from the pope. Gregory replied by excommunicating them and suspending Henry from the kingship. With Henry IV excommunicated and cast outside the Christian fold, lay nobles did not have to obey him and could advance their own interests. Gregory hastened to support the nobles. The Christmas season of 1076 witnessed an ironic situation in Germany: the clergy supported the king, and the great nobility favored the pope.

Henry outwitted Gregory. Crossing the Alps in January 1077, he approached the pope's residence at Canossa in northern Italy. According to legend, for three days Henry stood in the snow seeking forgiveness. As a priest, Pope Gregory was obliged to grant absolution and to readmit the emperor to the Christian community.

Henry's trip to Canossa is often described as the most dramatic incident in the High Middle Ages. Some historians claim that it marked the peak of papal power because the most powerful ruler in Europe, the emperor, had bowed before the pope. Actually, Henry scored a temporary victory. When the sentence of excommunication was lifted, Henry regained the kingship and authority over his rebellious subjects. But in the long run, in Germany and elsewhere, secular rulers were reluctant to pose a serious challenge to the papacy for the next two hundred years.

For Germany the incident at Canossa settled nothing. In 1080 Gregory VII again excommunicated and deposed Henry IV; Henry then invaded Italy, captured Rome, and controlled the city when Gregory died in exile in 1085. But Henry's victory did not last. Gregory's successors encouraged Henry's sons to revolt against their father. With lay investiture the ostensible issue, the conflict between the papacy and Henry IV's successors continued into the twelfth century.

The struggle did have profound social consequences for Germany. The nobility triumphed. Recent research has revealed that by the eleventh century many great German families had achieved a definite sense of themselves as noble. The long struggle between pope and emperor preoccupied the monarchy and allowed emerging noble dynasties to enhance their position. When the papal-imperial conflict ended in 1122, the nobility held the balance of power in Germany.[17] Later efforts by Frederick Barbarossa (r. 1152–1190) (see page 409) and other German kings to strengthen the monarchy against the princely families failed. For centuries, the German nobility remained the dominant social class and political force. The German aristocracy subordinated the knights and reinforced their dependency with strong feudal ties. The aristocracy reduced free men and serfs to servile position. Henry IV and then Henry V (r. 1106–1125) were compelled to surrender rights and privileges to the nobility. Particularism, localism, and feudal independence characterized the Holy Roman Empire in the High Middle Ages. The investiture controversy had a catastrophic effect there, severely retarding the development of a strong centralized monarchy.

A long and exhausting propaganda campaign followed the confrontation at Canossa. Finally in 1122, at a conference held at Worms, the issue was settled by compromise. Bishops were to be chosen according to *canon law*—that is, church law—in the presence of the emperor or his delegate. The emperor surrendered the right of investing bishops with the ring and staff. But since lay rulers were permitted to be present at ecclesiastical elections and to accept or refuse feudal homage from the new prelates, they still possessed an effective veto over ecclesiastical appointments. At the same time, the papacy achieved technical success, because rulers could no longer invest. Papal power was enhanced and neither side won a clear victory. The real winners in Germany were the great princes and the lay aristocracy.

William the Conqueror of England and Philip I of France were just as guilty of lay investiture as the German emperor, and both quarreled openly with Gregory. However, Rome's conflict with the Western rulers never reached the proportions of the dispute with the German emperor. Gregory VII and his successors had the diplomatic sense to avoid creating three enemies at once.

The Papacy in the High Middle Ages

In the late eleventh century and throughout the twelfth, the papacy pressed Gregory's campaign for reform of the church. Pope Urban II (r. 1088–1099) laid the real foundations for the papal monarchy by reorganizing the central government of the Roman church, the papal writing office (the chancery), and papal finances. He recognized the college of cardinals as a definite consultative body. These agencies, together with the papal chapel, constituted the papal court, or *curia*—the papacy's administrative bureaucracy and its court of law. The papal curia, although not fully developed until the mid-twelfth century, was the first well-organized institution of monarchial authority in medieval Europe.

The Roman curia had its greatest impact as a court of law. As the highest ecclesiastical tribunal, it formulated canon law for all of Christendom. It was the instrument with which the popes pressed the goals of reform and centralized the church. The curia sent legates to hold councils in various parts of Europe. Councils published decrees and sought to enforce the law. When individuals in any part of Christian Europe felt that they were being denied justice in their local church courts, they could appeal to Rome. Slowly but surely, in the High Middle Ages the papal curia developed into the court of final appeal for all of Christian Europe.

In the course of the twelfth century, appeals to the curia steadily increased. The majority of cases related to disputes over church property or ecclesiastical elections and above all to questions of marriage and annulment. Significantly, most of the popes in the twelfth and thirteenth centuries were canon lawyers. The most famous of them, the man whose pontificate represented the height of medieval papal power, was Innocent III (r. 1198–1216).

Innocent judged a vast number of cases and exerted papal authority in many areas. He compelled King Philip Augustus of France to take back his wife, Ingeborg of Denmark. He arbitrated the rival claims of two disputants to the imperial crown of Germany. He forced King John of England to accept as archbishop of Canterbury a man whom John did not really want.

By the early thirteenth century, papal efforts at reform begun more than a century before had attained phenomenal success. The popes themselves were men of high principles and strict moral behavior. The frequency of clerical marriage and the level of violence had declined considerably. Simony was much more the exception than the rule.

Yet the seeds of future difficulties were being planted. As the volume of appeals to Rome multiplied, so did the size of the papal bureaucracy. As the number of lawyers increased, so did concern for legal niceties and technicalities, fees, and church offices. As early as the mid-twelfth century, John of Salisbury, an Englishman working in the papal curia, had written that the people condemned the curia for its greed and indifference to human suffering. Nevertheless, the power of the curia continued to grow, as did its bureaucracy.

Thirteenth-century popes devoted their attention to the bureaucracy and their conflicts with the German emperor Frederick II (see pages 411–412). Some, like Gregory IX (r. 1227–1241), abused their prerogatives to such an extent that their moral impact was seriously weakened. Even worse, Innocent IV (r. 1243–1254) used secular weapons, including military force, to maintain his leadership. These popes badly damaged papal prestige and influence. By the early fourteenth century, the seeds of disorder would grow into a vast and sprawling tree, and once again cries for reform would be heard.

THE CRUSADES

The Crusades of the eleventh and twelfth centuries were the most obvious manifestation of the papal claim to the leadership of Christian society. The enormous popular response to papal calls for crusading reveals Europe's religious enthusiasm and the influence of the reformed papacy. The Crusades also reflect the church's new understanding of the noble warrior class. As a distinguished scholar of the Crusades wrote:

At around the turn of the millennium [the year 1000], the attitude of the church toward the military class underwent a significant change. The contrast between militia Christi *[war for Christ] and* militia saecularis *[war for worldly purposes] was overcome and just as rulership earlier had been Christianized . . . , so now was the military profession; it acquired a direct eccle-*

siastical purpose, for war in the service of the church or for the weak came to be regarded as holy and was declared to be a religious duty not only for the king but also for every individual knight.[18]

The Crusades in the late eleventh and early twelfth centuries were holy wars sponsored by the papacy for the recovery of the Holy Land from the Muslim Arabs or the Turks. They grew out of the long-standing conflict between Christians and Muslims in Spain, where by about 1250 Christian kings had regained roughly 90 percent of the peninsula. Throughout this period, Christians alone and in groups left Europe in a steady trickle for the Middle East. Although people of all ages and classes participated in the Crusades, so many knights did so that crusading became a distinctive feature of the upper-class lifestyle. In an aristocratic military society, men coveted reputations as Crusaders; the Christian knight who had been to the Holy Land enjoyed great prestige. The Crusades manifested the religious and chivalric ideals—as well as the tremendous vitality—of medieval European society.

By the late eleventh century the Roman papacy had strong reasons for wanting to launch an expedition against Muslim infidels in the Middle East. The papacy had been involved in a bitter struggle over investiture with the German emperors. If the pope could muster a large army against the enemies of Christianity, his claim to be leader of Christian society in the West would be strengthened.

Moreover, in 1054 a serious theological disagreement had split the Greek church of Byzantium and the Roman church of the West. The pope believed that a crusade would lead to strong Roman influence in Greek territories and eventually the reunion of the two churches. Then, in 1071 at Manzikert in eastern Anatolia (Map 12.4), Turkish soldiers in the pay of the Arabs defeated a Greek army and occupied much of Asia Minor. The emperor at Constantinople appealed to the West for support. Shortly afterward, the holy city of Jerusalem, the scene of Christ's preaching and burial, fell to the Turks. Pilgrimages to holy places in the Middle East became very dangerous, and the papacy was outraged that the holy city was in the hands of infidels.

In 1095 Pope Urban II (r. 1088–1099) journeyed to Clermont in France and called for a great

EUROPE IN THE MIDDLE AGES

ca 700	Publication of the Lindisfarne Gospel, Bede's *Ecclesiastical History of the English Nation*, and *Beowulf*
ca 710–750	Missionary work of Wynfrith (Boniface) supports the efforts of Charles Martel and Pippin III to assimilate Germanic tribes
733	Charles Martel defeats Muslims at Battle of Tours
752	Pippin III elected king by Frankish magnates
754	Pope Stephen anoints Pippin III king at Paris, establishing an important alliance between the Christian church and the Frankish ruler
756	Pippin III donates the Papal States to the papacy
768	Charlemagne succeeds to the Frankish crown
768–805	Charlemagne conquers all of continental Europe except Spain, Scandinavia, southern Italy, and Slavic fringes of the East
781	Alcuin enters Charlemagne's court at Aachen as chief adviser on religious and educational matters; encourages Christianization of northern Europe and directs the revival of learning inspired by Charlemagne
ca 787	Viking raids of Carolingian territories begin
800	Imperial coronation of Charlemagne
814	Louis the Pious succeeds to Charlemagne's empire
843	Treaty of Verdun: Charlemagne's empire divided among his grandsons Lothair, Louis the German, and Charles the Bald
ca 845–900	Series of Viking, Magyar, and Muslim invasions complete the disintegration of the Carolingian Empire
878	King Alfred's victory over Guthrun inaugurates political recovery in Anglo-Saxon England
909	Abbey of Cluny, a source of vast religious influence, founded; first step in the revival of monasticism and reform of the Church
955	Otto I's victory at Lech River ends Magyar incursions in Germany
962	Otto's coronation lays the foundation for the Holy Roman Empire
987	Election of Hugh Capet as king of the West Frankish kingdom
1049	Pope Leo IX begins serious reform of the Church
1059	Lateran Synod gives power of papal election to the college of cardinals
1073	Cardinal Hildebrand becomes Pope Gregory VII
1075	Church issues decree against lay investiture that leads to conflict between the pope and the rulers of Germany, England, and France
1096–1099	The First Crusade
1098	The Cistercians found an austere order of monks that would influence societies throughout Europe
1122	Compromise at Worms removes power of investiture from lay rulers but grants them effective veto over eccleciastical appointments
1147–1149	The Second Crusade
1189–1192	The Third Crusade
1202–1204	The Fourth Crusade; sacking of Constantinople cements the split between Eastern and Western churches

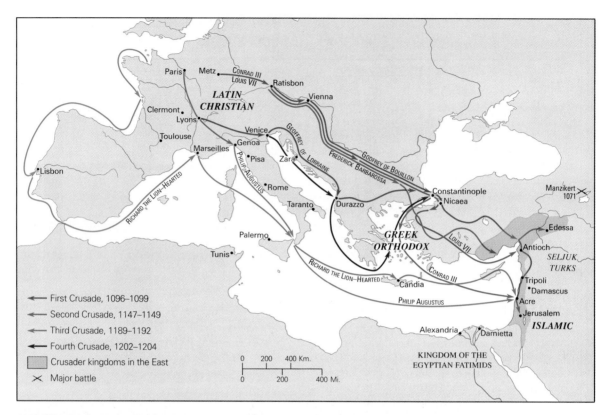

MAP 12.4 The Routes of the Crusades   The Crusades led to a major cultural encounter between Muslim and Christian values. What significant intellectual and economic effects resulted?

Christian holy war against the infidels. He stressed the sufferings and persecution of Christians in Jerusalem. He urged Christian knights who had been fighting one another to direct their energies against the true enemies of God, the Muslims. Urban proclaimed an *indulgence*, or remission of the temporal penalties imposed by the church for sin, to those who would fight for and regain the holy city of Jerusalem. Few speeches in history have had such a dramatic effect as Urban's call at Clermont for the First Crusade.

The response was fantastic. Godfrey of Bouillon, Geoffrey of Lorraine, and many other great lords from northern France immediately had the cross of the Crusader sewn on their tunics. Encouraged by popular preachers like Peter the Hermit and by papal legates in Germany, Italy, and England, thousands of people of all classes joined the crusade. Although most of the Crusaders were French, pilgrims from all countries streamed southward from the Rhineland, through Germany and the Balkans.

Religious convictions inspired many, but mundane motives were also involved. Except for wives, who had to remain at home to manage estates, many people expected to benefit from the crusade. For the curious and the adventurous, it offered foreign travel and excitement. The crusade provided kings, who were trying to establish order and build states, the perfect opportunity to get rid of trouble-making knights. It gave land-hungry younger sons a chance to acquire fiefs in the Middle East. Even some members of the middle class who stayed at home profited from the crusade. Many nobles had to borrow money from the townspeople to pay for their expeditions, and they put up part of their land as security. If a noble did not return home or could not pay the interest on the loan, the middle-class creditor took over the land.

The First Crusade (1096–1099) was successful mostly because of the dynamic enthusiasm of the participants. The Crusaders had little more than religious zeal. They knew nothing about the geography or climate of the Middle East. Although there were several counts with military experience among the throng, the Crusaders could never agree on a leader, and the entire expedition was marked by disputes among the great lords. Lines of supply were never set up. Starvation and disease wracked the army, and the Turks slaughtered hundreds of noncombatants. Nevertheless, convinced that "God wills it"—the war cry of the Crusaders—the army pressed on and in 1099 captured Jerusalem. Although the Crusaders fought bravely, Arab disunity was a chief reason for their victory. At Jerusalem, Edessa, Tripoli, and Antioch (see Map 12.4), Crusader kingdoms were founded on the Western feudal model.

Between 1096 and 1270, the crusading ideal was expressed in eight papally approved expeditions to the East. In addition, in 1208 two expeditions of children set out on a crusade to the Holy Land. One contingent turned back; the other was captured and sold into slavery. None of the crusades against the Muslims achieved very much. The third (1189–1192) was precipitated by the recapture of Jerusalem by the sultan Saladin in 1187. Frederick Barbarossa of the Holy Roman Empire, Richard the Lion-Hearted of England, and Philip Augustus of France participated. The Third Crusade was better financed than previous ones, but disputes among the leaders and strategic problems prevented any lasting results.

During the Fourth Crusade (1202–1204), careless preparation and inadequate financing had disastrous consequences for Byzantine-Latin relations. Hoping to receive material support from the Greeks, the leaders of the crusade took the expedition to Constantinople. Once there, they sacked

Crusading Scene Heavily armored Western knights face unencumbered Muslims. Some scholars believe that their dress gave the Muslims a decided advantage in certain battles. (*Source: Bibliothèque Nationale, Paris*)

the city and established the Latin Empire of Constantinople. The empire lasted only from 1204 to 1261. This assault by one Christian people on another, when one of the goals of the Crusades was the reunion of the Greek and Latin churches, made the split between the Western and Eastern churches permanent. It also helped to discredit the entire crusading movement. Two later crusades, undertaken by King Louis IX of France (r. 1226–1270), added to his prestige as a pious ruler.

Apart from that, the last of the official crusades accomplished nothing at all.

Crusades were also mounted against groups perceived as Christian Europe's social enemies. In 1208 Pope Innocent III (r. 1198–1216) proclaimed a crusade against the Albigensians, a heretical sect in southern France (see page 435). The popes in the mid-thirteenth century, fearful of encirclement by imperial territories, promoted crusades against Emperor Frederick II (r. 1215–

The Capture of Jerusalem in 1099   As engines hurl stones to breach the walls, Crusaders enter on scaling ladders. Scenes from Christ's passion (above) identify the city as Jerusalem. *(Source: Bibliothèque Nationale, Paris)*

1250). This use of force against a Christian ruler backfired, damaging the credibility of the papacy as the sponsor of peace.

Although the Crusades introduced some Europeans to Eastern luxury goods, the Crusades' overall cultural impact on the West remains debatable. By the late eleventh century, strong economic and intellectual ties with the East had already been made. The Crusades testify to the religious enthusiasm of the High Middle Ages. But, as Steven Runciman, a distinguished scholar of the Crusades, concluded in his three-volume history:

The triumphs of the Crusade were the triumphs of faith. But faith without wisdom is a dangerous thing. . . . In the long sequence of interaction and fusion between Orient and Occident out of which our civilization has grown, the Crusades were a tragic and destructive episode. . . . High ideals were besmirched by cruelty and greed, enterprise and endurance by a blind and narrow self-righteousness; and the Holy War itself was nothing more than a long act of intolerance in the name of God, which is the sin against the Holy Ghost.[19]

From the Muslim perspective, the Western assaults on the eastern Mediterranean from the eleventh to the thirteenth century represented only a minor event: the Crusades were never a serious threat to Islam. Pressures within European society launched and continued the Crusades, and the European historical tradition has portrayed the relationship between Christianity and Islam in terms of glamorous military conflict. Islam, however, considered the Crusades merely a nuisance.

The feudal states set up by the Crusades along the Syrian and Palestinian coasts (see Map 12.4) managed to survive for about two centuries before the Muslims reconquered them. The Crusaders, however, left in the Middle East two more permanent legacies. First, the long struggle between Islam and Christendom and the example of persecution set by Christian kings and prelates left an inheritance of deep bitterness; relations between Muslims and their Christian and Jewish subjects worsened. Second, European merchants, primarily Italians, had established communities in the Crusader states. After those kingdoms collapsed, Muslim rulers still encouraged trade with European businessmen. Commerce with the West benefited both Muslims and Europeans, and it continued to flourish.[20]

SUMMARY

The civilization that emerged in Europe between 733 and 843 had definite characteristics: it was feudal, Christian, and infused with Latin ideas and models. Despite the disasters of the ninth and tenth centuries, these features remained basic aspects of European culture for centuries to come.

The century and a half after the death of Charlemagne in 814 witnessed a degree of disintegration, destruction, and disorder unparalleled in Europe until the twentieth century. No civil or religious authority could maintain stable government over a very wide area. Local strongmen provided what little security existed. Commerce and long-distance trade were drastically reduced. Leadership of the church became the political football of aristocratic Roman families. The rich became warriors; the poor sought protection. The result was that society became feudal.

The end of the great invasions signaled the beginning of profound changes in European society. In the year 1000, having enough to eat was the rare privilege of a few nobles, priests, and monks. But in the eleventh century, manorial communities slowly improved their agricultural equipment; this advance, aided by warmer weather, meant more food and increasing population.

In the eleventh century also, rulers and local authorities gradually imposed some degree of order within their territories. Peace and domestic security, vigorously promoted by the church, meant larger crops and improved trading conditions. The church overthrew the domination of lay influences, and the spread of the Cluniac and Cistercian orders marked the ascendancy of monasticism. Having put its own house in order, the Roman papacy in the twelfth and thirteenth centuries built the first strong government bureaucracy in medieval Europe. In the High Middle Ages, the church exercised general leadership of European society. The early Crusades exhibited that leadership and the enormous, if misguided, vitality of medieval society.

NOTES

1. For the date of this battle, October 17, 733, see L. White, *Medieval Technology and Social Change* (Oxford: Clarendon Press, 1962), p. 3, n. 3, and p. 12.

2. See F. Irsigler, "On the Aristocratic Character of Early Frankish Society," in *The Medieval Nobility: Studies on the Ruling Class of France and Germany from the Sixth to the Twelfth Century,* ed. and trans. T. Reuter (New York: North-Holland, 1978), pp. 105–136, esp. p. 123.

3. Einhard, *The Life of Charlemagne,* with a foreword by S. Painter (Ann Arbor: University of Michigan Press, 1960), pp. 50–51.

4. P. Stafford, *Queens, Concubines, and Dowagers: The King's Wife in the Early Middle Ages* (Athens, Ga.: University of Georgia Press, 1983), pp. 60–62.

5. See K. F. Werner, "Important Noble Families in the Kingdom of Charlemagne," in Reuter, pp. 174–184.

6. Quoted in B. D. Hill, ed., *Church and State in the Middle Ages* (New York: Wiley, 1970), pp. 46–47.

7. P. Geary, "Carolingians and the Carolingian Empire," in *Dictionary of the Middle Ages,* vol. 3, ed. J. R. Strayer (New York: Scribner's, 1983), p. 110.

8. R. W. Southern, *Medieval Humanism and Other Studies* (Oxford: Basil Blackwell, 1970), p. 3.

9. L. Sherley-Price, trans., *Bede: A History of the English Church and People* (Baltimore: Penguin Books, 1962), bk. 3, chap. 27, p. 191.

10. See S. Rubin, *Medieval English Medicine, 500–1300* (New York: Barnes & Noble, 1974).

11. J. R. Strayer, "The Two Levels of Feudalism," in *Medieval Statecraft and the Perspectives of History,* ed. J. R. Strayer (Princeton, N.J.: Princeton University Press, 1971), p. 63. This section leans heavily on Strayer's seminal study.

12. E. P. Cheney, trans., in *University of Pennsylvania Translations and Reprints,* vol. 4, no. 3 (Philadelphia: University of Pennsylvania Press, 1898), p. 3.

13. Strayer, "Two Levels of Feudalism," pp. 65–76, esp. p. 71.

14. See D. Herlihy, "Land, Family, and Women in Continental Europe, 701–1200," in *Women in Medieval Society,* ed. S. M. Stuart (Philadelphia: University of Pennsylvania Press, 1976), pp. 13–45.

15. See B. Rosenwein, *Rhinoceros Bound: Cluny in the Tenth Century* (Philadelphia: University of Pennsylvania Press, 1982), chap. 2.

16. Quoted in Hill, p. 68.

17. See J. B. Freed, "The Counts of Falkenstein: Noble Self-Consciousness in Twelfth Century Germany," *Transactions of the American Philosophical Society,* vol. 74, pt. 6 (1984): 9–11.

18. C. Erdmann, *The Origin of the Idea of the Crusade,* trans. M. Baldwin and W. Goffart (Princeton, N.J.: Princeton University Press, 1977), p. 57.

19. S. Runciman, *A History of the Crusades,* vol. 3, The Kingdom of Acre (Cambridge, England: Cambridge University Press, 1955), p. 480.

20. B. Lewis, *The Muslim Discovery of Europe* (New York: Norton, 1982), pp. 23–25.

SUGGESTED READING

A good general introduction to the entire period is C. Dawson, *The Formation of Christendom* (1967). The same author's *Religion and the Rise of Western Culture* (1958) emphasizes the religious bases of Western culture. C. H. Talbot, ed., *The Anglo-Saxon Missionaries in Germany* (1954), gives an exciting picture, through biographies and correspondence, of the organization and development of the Christian church in the Carolingian Empire. J. B. Russell, *A History of Medieval Christianity: Prophesy and Order* (1968), describes the mind of the Christian church and how it gradually had an impact on pagan Germanic peoples. The monumental work of F. Kempf et al., *The Church in the Age of Feudalism* (trans. A. Biggs, 1980), volume 3 of the *History of the Church* series edited by H. Jedin and J. Dolan, contains a thorough treatment of the institutional church in both East and West based on the latest scholarship; this book is primarily for scholars. Significant aspects of spirituality are traced in B. McGinn and J. Meyendorff, eds., *Christian Spirituality: From the Apostolic Fathers to the Twelfth Century* (1985).

Einhard's *The Life of Charlemagne* (see Notes) is a good starting point for study of the great chieftain. The best general biography of Charlemagne is D. Bullough, *The Age of Charlemagne* (1965). P. Riché, *Daily Life in the World of Charlemagne* (trans. J. McNamara, 1978), is a richly detailed study of many facets of Carolingian society. The same scholar's *Education and Culture in the Barbarian West: From the Sixth Through the Eighth Century* (trans. J. J. Contreni, 1976) provides an excellent, if technical, treatment of Carolingian intellectual activity. Both volumes contain solid bibliographies. For agricultural and economic life, G. Duby, *Early Growth of the European Economy: Warriors and Peasants from the Seventh to the Twelfth Century* (1977), relates economic behavior to other aspects of human experience in a thoroughly readable style. He also shows how social structure and attitudes evolved. The importance of technological developments in the Carolingian period is described by L. White, *Medieval Technology and Social Change* (1962), now a classic work. For the meaning of war to the Merovingian and Carolingian kings, see "War and Peace in the Early Middle Ages," in J. M. Wallace-Hadrill, *Early Medieval History* (1975). The book also contains interesting essays on Bede, Boniface, Charlemagne, and England. As the title implies, G. Barraclough, *The Crucible of Europe: The Ninth and Tenth Centuries in European History* (1976), sees those centuries as crucial in the formation of European civilization. The author also stresses the importance of stable government. E. James, *The Origins of France: From Clovis to the Capetians, 500–1000* (1982), is a solid introductory survey of early French history, with emphasis on family relationships.

For the eighth-century revival of learning, see M. L. W. Laistner, *Thought and Letters in Western Europe, 500–900* (1931), and the beautifully written evocation by P. H. Blair, *Northumbria in the Days of Bede* (1976). The best treatment of the theological and political ideas of the period is probably K. F. Morrison, *The Two Kingdoms: Ecclesiology in Carolingian Political Thought* (1964), a difficult book.

Those interested in the role of women and children in early medieval society should see the article by D. Herlihy cited in the Notes, as well as E. Coleman, "Infanticide in the Early Middle Ages," in the same volume. The best available study of women in this period is S. F. Wemple, *Women in Frankish Society: Marriage and the Cloister, 500 to 900* (1981). In addition to the work by Stafford cited in the Notes, the following studies are also useful: J. McNamara, "A Legacy of Miracles: Hagiography and Nunneries in Merovingian Gaul," in J. Kirshner and S. Wemple, eds., *Women of the Medieval World: Essays in Honor of John H. Mundy* (1985); and C. Fell, *Women in Anglo-Saxon England* (1984).

For health and medical treatment in the early Middle Ages, the curious student should consult S. Rubin, *Medieval English Medicine, A.D. 500–1300* (1974), especially pp. 97–149; W. H. McNeill, *Plagues and Peoples* (1976); A. Castiglioni, *A History of Medicine* (trans. E. B. Krumbhaar, 1941); and the important article by J. M. Riddle, "Theory and Practice in Medieval Medicine," *Viator* 5 (1974): 157–184. J. C. Russell, *The Control of Late Ancient and Medieval Population* (1985), discusses diet, disease, and demography.

For feudalism and manorialism see, in addition to the references given in the Notes, F. L. Ganshof, *Feudalism* (1961), and J. R. Strayer, "Feudalism in Western Europe," in R. Coulborn, ed., *Feudalism in History* (1956). M. Bloch, *Feudal Society* (trans. L. A. Manyon, 1961), remains important. The more recent treatment of P. Anderson, *Passages from Antiquity to Feudalism* (1978), stresses the evolution of social structures and mental attitudes. For the significance of the ceremony of vassalage, see J. Le Goff, "The Symbolic Ritual of Vassalage," in his *Time, Work, & Culture in the Middle Ages* (trans. A. Goldhammer, 1982). The best broad treatment of peasant life and conditions is G. Duby, *Rural Economy and Country Life in tne Medieval West* (trans. C. Postan, 1968).

J. Brondsted, *The Vikings* (1960), is an excellently illustrated study of the culture of the Northmen. G. Jones, *A History of the Vikings*, rev. ed. (1984), provides a comprehensive survey of the Viking world based on archeological findings and numismatic evidence.

In addition to the references in the Notes, the curious student will find a fuller treatment of the High Middle Ages in the following works:

C. D. Burns, *The First Europe* (1948), surveys the entire period and emphasizes the transformation from a time of anarchy to one of great creativity. G. Barraclough, *The Origins of Modern Germany* (1963), is essential for central and eastern Europe.

For the Christian church, the papacy, and ecclesiastical developments, the best recent study is I. S. Robinson, *The Papacy, 1073–1198: Continuity and Innovation* (1990), while G. Barraclough's richly illustrated *The Medieval Papacy* (1968) is a good general survey that emphasizes the development of administrative bureaucracy. W. Ullmann's *The Growth of Papal Government in the Middle Ages*, rev. ed. (1970), traces the evolution of papal law and government. G. Tellenbach, *Church, State, and Christian Society at the Time of the Investiture Contest* (1959), emphasizes the revolutionary aspects of the Gregorian reform program. The relationship of the monks to the ecclesiastical crisis of the late eleventh century is discussed by N. F. Cantor, "The Crisis of Western Monasticism," *American Historical Review* 66 (1960), but see also the essential analysis of J. Van Engen, "The 'Crisis of Cenobitism' Reconsidered: Benedictine Monasticism in the Years 1050–1150," *Speculum*, vol. 61, no. 2 (1986): 269–304, as well as H. E. J. Cowdrey, *The Cluniacs and the Gregorian Reform* (1970), an impressive but difficult study. Cowdrey's recent *The Age of Abbot Desiderius: Monte Cassino, the Papacy, and the Normans in the Eleventh and Early Twelfth Centuries* (1983) focuses on Monte Cassino. J. B. Russell, *A History of Medieval Christianity* (1968), offers an important and sensitively written survey. The advanced student will benefit considerably from the works by C. Erdmann, J. B. Freed, and B. Rosenwein that are cited in the Notes.

The following studies provide exciting and highly readable general accounts of the Crusades: J. Riley-Smith, *What Were the Crusades?* (1977); R. C. Finucane, *Soldiers of the Faith: Crusaders and Muslims at War* (1983); and R. Payne, *The Dream and the Tomb: A History of the Crusades* (1984). There are excellent articles on many facets of the Crusades, including "The Children's Crusade," "Crusade Propaganda," "Crusader Art and Architecture," and "The Political Crusades," all written by authorities and based on the latest research, in J. R. Strayer, ed., *Dictionary of the Middle Ages*, vol. 4 (1984). These articles also contain good bibliographies. C. M. Brand, *Byzantium Confronts the West, 1180–1204* (1968), provides the Greek perspective on the Crusades. Serious students will eventually want to consult the multivolume work of K. M. Setton, gen. ed., *A History of the Crusades* (1955–1977).

PERIOD (CA 200–1200)	AFRICA AND THE MIDDLE EAST	THE AMERICAS
200	Camel first used for trans-Saharan transport, ca 200 Expansion of Bantu people, ca 200–900 Axum (Ethiopia) controls Red Sea trade, ca 250	Olmec civilization, ca 1500 B.C.–A.D. 300
300	Axum accepts Christianity, ca 4th century	Maya civilization in Central America, ca 300–1500 Classic period of Teotihuacán civilization in Mexico, ca 300–900
500	Political and commercial ascendency of Axum, ca 6th–7th centuries Muhammad, 570–632; the *hijra,* 622 Extensive slave trade from sub-Saharan Africa to Mediterranean, ca 600–1500 Umayyad Dynasty, 661–750; continued expansion of Islam	Tiahuanaco civilization in South America, ca 600–1000
700	Abbasid Dynasty, 750–1258; Islamic capital moved to Baghdad Decline of Ethiopia, ca 9th century Golden age of Muslim learning, ca 900–1100 Kingdom of Ghana, ca 900–1100 Mahmud of Ghazna, 998–1030	"Time of Troubles" in Mesoamerica, 800–1000
1000	Islam penetrates sub-Saharan Africa, ca 11th century Kingdom of Benin, ca 1100–1897 Kingdom of Mali, middle Niger region, ca 1200–1450 Mongol invasion of Middle East, ca 1220	Inca civilization in South America, ca 1000–1500 Toltec hegemony, ca 1000–1300 Aztecs arrive in Valley of Mexico, ca 1325

EAST ASIA	INDIA AND SOUTHEAST ASIA	EUROPE
Creation of Yamato state in Japan, ca 3rd century Buddhism gains popularity in China and Japan, ca 220–590 Fall of Han Dynasty, 220 Three Kingdoms Era in China, 221–280	Kushan rule in northwestern India, A.D. 2nd–3rd centuries Fall of the Parthian Empire, rise of the Sassanids, ca 225	Breakdown of the *Pax Romana*, ca 180–284; civil wars, economic decline, invasions Reforms by Diocletian, 284–305
Barbarian invasions, 4th–5th centuries	Chandragupta I founds Gupta Dynasty in India, ca 320–500 Chandragupta II conquers western India, establishes trade with Middle East and China, ca 400 Huns invade India, ca 450	Reign of Constantine, 306–337; Edict of Milan, 313; Council of Nicaea, 325; founding of Constantinople, 330 Theodosius recognizes Christianity as official state religion, 380 Germanic raids of Western Europe, 5th century Clovis unites Franks and rules Gauls, 481–511
Sui Dynasty in China, 580–618; restoration of public order "Constitution" of Shotoku in Japan, 604 T'ang Dynasty, 618–907; cultural flowering	Sanskrit drama, ca 600–1000 Muslim invasions of India, ca 636–1206	St. Benedict publishes his *Rule,* 529 Law Code of Justinian, 529 Synod of Whitby, 664
Taika Reform Edict in Japan, 655 Nara era, creation of Japan's first capital, 710–784 Heian era in Japan, 794–1185; literary flowering Era of the Five Dynasties in China, 907–960; warfare, revolt Sung Dynasty, 960–1279	Khmer Empire (Kampuchea) founded, 802	Charles Martel defeats Muslims at Tours, 733 Charles the Great (Charlemagne), 768–814 Invasions of Carolingian Empire, 9th–10th centuries Treaty of Verdun divides Carolingian Empire, 843 Cluny monastery founded, 910
Vietnam gains independence from China, ca 1000 China divided between empires of Sung (south) and Chin (north), 1127 Kamakura Shogunate, 1185–1333 Mongol conquest of China, 1215–1368	Construction of Angkor Wat, ca 1100–1150 Muslim conquerors end Buddhism in India, 1192 Peak of Khmer Empire in southeast Asia, ca 1200 Turkish sultanate at Delhi, 1206–1526; Indian culture divided into Hindu and Muslim	Yaroslav the wise, 1019–1054; peak of Kievan Russia Schism between Latin and Greek churches, 1054 Norman Conquest of England, 1066 Investiture struggle, 1073–1122 The Crusades, 1096–1270 Growth of trade and towns, 12th–13th centuries Frederick Barbarossa invades Italy, 1154–1158

13

Life in Christian Europe
in the High Middle Ages

"April," from *Hours of the Virgin*

lose links existed between educated circles on both sides of the English Channel. In one of the writings produced at the court of the late-ninth-century Anglo-Saxon king, Alfred (r. 871–899), Christian society is said to be composed of those who work (the peasants), those who fight (the nobles), and those who pray (the monks). In France, Bishop Adalbero of Laon used the same three social divisions in a poem written about 1028. This image of a society in which function determined social classification gained wide circulation in the High Middle Ages.[1] It did not take into consideration the emerging commercial classes; but that omission is not surprising, for traders and other city dwellers were not typical members of early medieval society. Moreover, medieval Europeans were usually contemptuous (at least officially) of profit-making activities; and even after the appearance of urban commercial groups, the general sociological view of medieval Christian society remained the one first formulated during the ninth century and given expression in King Alfred's court.

In the High Middle Ages, the most representative figures of Christian society were peasants, nobles, and monks.

■ How did these people actually live?

■ What were their preoccupations and lifestyles?

■ To what extent was social mobility possible for them?

These are among the questions that are explored in this chapter.

THOSE WHO WORK

The largest and economically most productive group in medieval European society was the peasants. The men and women who worked the land in the twelfth and thirteenth centuries made up the overwhelming majority of the population, probably more than 90 percent. Yet it is difficult to form a coherent picture of them. The records that serve as historical sources were written by and for the aristocratic classes. Since peasants did not perform what were considered "noble" deeds, the aristocratic monks and clerics did not waste time or precious writing materials on them. When peasants were mentioned, it was usually with contempt or in terms of the services and obligations they owed.

Usually—but not always. In the early twelfth century, Honorius, a monk and teacher at Autun, France, wrote: "What do you say about the agricultural classes? Most of them will be saved because they live simply and feed God's people by means of their sweat."[2] This sentiment circulated widely. Honorius's comment suggests that peasant workers may have been appreciated and in a sense respected more than is generally believed.

In the past twenty-five years, historians have made remarkable advances in their knowledge of the medieval European peasantry. They have been able to do so by bringing fresh and different questions to old documents, by paying greater attention to such natural factors as geography and climate, and by studying demographic changes. Nevertheless, this new information raises additional questions, and a good deal remains unknown.

In 1932 a distinguished economic historian wrote, "The student of medieval social and economic history who commits himself to a generalization is digging a pit into which he will later assuredly fall and nowhere does the pit yawn deeper than in the realm of rural history."[3] This remark is as true today as when it was written. It is therefore important to remember that peasants' conditions varied widely across Europe, that geographical and climatic features as much as human initiative and local custom determined the peculiar quality of rural life. The problems that faced the English farmer in Yorkshire, where the soil was rocky and the climate rainy, were very different from those that faced the Italian peasant in the sun-drenched Po Valley.

Another difficulty has been historians' tendency to group all peasants into one social class. Doing so is a serious mistake. Even though medieval theologians lumped everyone who worked the land into the category of "those who work," there were many levels of peasants, ranging from complete slaves to free and very rich farmers. The period from 1050 to 1250 was one of considerable fluidity with no little social mobility. The status of the peasantry varied widely all across Europe.

The Three Classes Medieval people believed that their society was divided among warriors, clerics, and workers, here represented by a monk, a knight, and a peasant. The new commercial class had no recognized place in the agrarian military world. *(Source: The British Library)*

Slavery, Serfdom, and Upward Mobility

Slaves were found in western Europe in the High Middle Ages, but in steadily declining numbers. That the word *slave* derives from "Slav" attests to the widespread trade in men and women from the Slavic areas in the early Middle Ages. Around the year 1200, there were in aristocratic and upper-middle-class households in Provence, Catalonia, Italy, and Germany a few slaves—blond Slavs from the Baltic, olive-skinned Syrians, and blacks from Africa.

Since ancient times, it had been a universally accepted practice to enslave conquered peoples. The church had long taught that all baptized Christians were brothers in Christ and that all Christians belonged to one "international" community. Although the church never issued a blanket condemnation of slavery, it vigorously opposed the enslaving of Christians. In attacking the enslavement of Christians and in criticizing the reduction of pagans and infidels to slavery, the church made a contribution to the development of human liberty.

In Western Europe during the Middle Ages, legal language differed considerably from place to place, and the distinction between slave and serf was not always clear. Both lacked freedom—the power to do as one wished—and were subject to the arbitrary will of one person, the lord. A serf, however, could not be bought and sold like an animal or an inanimate object, as the slave could.

A serf was required to perform labor services on the lord's land. The number of workdays per week varied, but it was usually three days except in the planting or harvest seasons, when it was more. Serfs had to pay many arbitrary levies. When a man married, he had to pay his lord a fee. When he died, his son or heir had to pay an inheritance tax to inherit his parcels of land. The precise amounts of tax paid to the lord on these important occasions depended on local custom and tradition. Every manor had its particular obligations. A free peasant had to do none of those things. For his or her landholding, rent had to be paid to the lord, and that was often the sole obligation. A free person could move and live as he or she wished.

Serfs were tied to the land, and serfdom was a hereditary condition. A person born a serf was likely to die a serf, though many did secure their freedom. About 1187 Glanvill, an official of King Henry II and an expert on English law, described how *villeins* (literally, "inhabitants of small villages")—as English serfs were called—could be made free:

A person of villein status can be made free in several ways. For example, his lord, wishing him to achieve freedom from the villeinage by which he is subject to him, may quit-claim [release] him from himself and his heirs; or he may give or sell him to another with intent to free him. It should be noted, however, that no person of villein status can seek his freedom with his own money, for in such a case he could, according to the law and custom of the realm, be recalled to villeinage by his lord, because all the chattels of a villein are deemed to such an extent the property of his lord that he cannot redeem himself from villeinage with his own money, as against his lord. If, however, a third party provides the money and buys the villein in order to free him, then he can maintain himself for ever in a state of
freedom as against his lord who sold him. . . . If any villein stays peaceably for a year and a day in a privileged town and is admitted as a citizen into their commune, that is to say, their gild, he is thereby freed from villeinage.[4]

Many energetic and hard-working serfs acquired their freedom in the High Middle Ages. More than anything else, the economic revival that began in the eleventh century advanced the cause of individual liberty (see pages 417–426). The revival saw the rise of towns, increased land productivity, the growth of long-distance trade, and the development of a money economy. With the advent of a money economy, serfs could save money and, through a third-person intermediary, buy their freedom.

Another opportunity for increased personal freedom, or at least for a reduction in traditional manorial obligations and dues, was provided by the reclamation of wasteland and forest land in the eleventh and twelfth centuries. Resettlement on newly cleared land offered unusual possibilities for younger sons and for those living in areas of acute land shortage or on overworked, exhausted soil. Historians still do not know very much about this movement: how the new frontier territory was advertised, how men were recruited, how they and their households were transported, and how the new lands were distributed. It is certain, however, that there was significant migration and that only a lord with considerable authority over a wide territory could sponsor such a movement. Great lords supported the fight against the marshes of northern and eastern Germany and against the sea in the Low Countries (present-day Holland, Belgium, and French Flanders). For example, in the twelfth century the invitation of German and Slavic rulers led to peasant settlements in "the territory between the Saale and the upper Elbe" rivers.[5] The thirteenth century witnessed German peasant migrations into Brandenburg, Pomerania, Prussia, and the Baltic states.

In the thirteenth century, the noble class frequently needed money to finance crusading building, or other projects. For example, in 1240 when Geoffrey de Montigny became abbot of Saint-Pierre-le-Vif in the Senonais region of France, he found the abbey church in disrepair. Geoffrey also discovered that the descendants of families who had once owed the abbey servile obligations now refused to recognize their bondage. Some of these peasants had grown wealthy. When the abbot determined to reclaim these peasants in order to get the revenues to rebuild his church, a legal struggle ensued. In 1257 a compromise was worked out whereby Geoffrey manumitted 366 persons who in turn agreed to pay him 500 pounds a year over a 12-year period.[6]

As land long considered poor was brought under cultivation, there was a steady nibbling away at the wasteland on the edges of old villages. Clearings were made in forests. Marshes and fens were drained and slowly made arable. This type of agricultural advancement improved many peasants' social and legal condition. A serf could clear a patch of fen or forest land, make it productive, and, through prudent saving, buy more land and eventually purchase freedom. There were in the thirteenth century many free tenants on the lands of the bishop of Ely in eastern England, tenants who had moved into the area in the twelfth century and drained the fens. Likewise, settlers on the lowlands of the abbey of Bourbourg in Flanders, who had erected dikes and extended the arable lands, possessed hereditary tenures by 1159. They secured personal liberty and owed their overlord only small payments.

Peasants who remained in the villages of their birth often benefited because landlords, threatened with the loss of serfs, relaxed ancient obligations and duties. While it would be unwise to exaggerate the social impact of the settling of new territories, frontier lands in the Middle Ages did provide opportunities for upward mobility.

The Manor

In the High Middle Ages, most European peasants, free and unfree, lived on estates called "manors." The word *manor* derives from a Latin term meaning "dwelling," "residence," or "homestead." In the twelfth century it meant the estate of a lord and his dependent tenants.

The manor was the basic unit of medieval rural organization and the center of rural life. All other generalizations about manors and manorial life have to be limited by variations in the quality of the soil, local climatic conditions, and methods of cultivation. Some manors were vast, covering several thousand acres of farmland; others were no

larger than 120 acres. A manor might include several villages or none at all, but usually it contained a single village and was subject to one lord (Figure 13.1).

The arable land of the manor was divided into two sections. The *demesne,* or home farm, was cultivated for the lord. The other part was held by the peasantry. Usually, the peasants' portion was larger, held on condition that they cultivate the lord's demesne. All the arable land, both the lord's and the peasants', was divided into strips, and the strips belonging to any given individual were scattered throughout the manor. All peasants cooperated in the cultivation of the land, working it as a group. This meant that all shared in any disaster as well as in any large harvest.

A manor usually held pasture or meadow land for the grazing of cattle, sheep, and sometimes goats. Many manors had some forest land as well. Forests had enormous economic importance. They were the source of wood for building and fuel, bark for the manufacture of rope, resin for lighting, ash for candles, and ash and lime for fertilizers and all sorts of sterilizing products. The forests were also used for feeding pigs, cattle, and domestic animals on nuts, roots, and wild berries. If a manor was intersected by a river, it had a welcome source of fish and eels.

Agricultural Methods

The fundamental objective of all medieval agriculture was the production of an adequate food supply. According to the method that historians have called the "open-field system," at any one time half of the manorial land was under cultivation and the other half lay fallow; the length of the fallow period was usually one year. Every peasant farmer had strips scattered in both halves. One part of the land under cultivation was sown with winter cereals, such as wheat and rye, the other with spring crops, such as peas, beans, and barley. What was planted in a particular field varied each year, when the crops were rotated.

Local needs, the fertility of the soil, and dietary customs determined what was planted and the method of crop rotation. Where one or several manors belonged to a great aristocratic establishment, such as the abbey of Cluny, that needed large quantities of oats for horses, more of the ar-

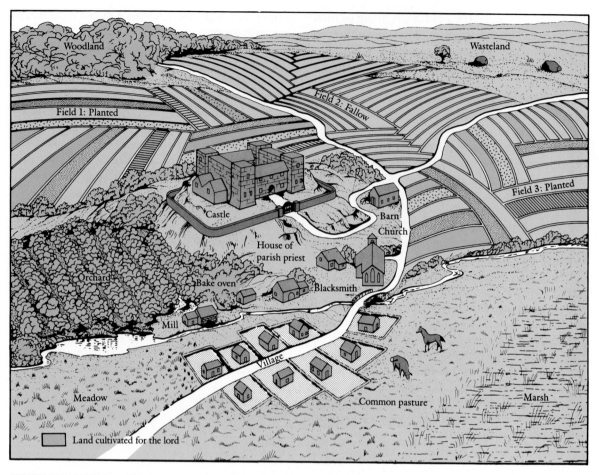

FIGURE 13.1 A Medieval Manor   The basic unit of rural organization and the center of life for most people, the manor constituted the medieval peasants' world. Since manors had to be economically self-sufficient, life meant endless toil.

able land would be planted in oats than in other cereals. Where the land was extremely fertile, such as the Alsace region of Germany, a biennial cycle was used: one crop of wheat was sown and harvested every other year, and in alternate years all the land lay fallow. The author of an English agricultural treatise advised his readers to stick to a two-field method of cultivation and insisted that a rich harvest every second year was preferable to two mediocre harvests every three years.

Farmers were aware of the value of animal fertilizers. Chicken manure, because of its high nitrogen content, was the richest but was limited in quantity. Sheep manure was also valuable. Gifts to English Cistercian monasteries were frequently given on condition that the monks' sheep be allowed to graze at certain periods on the benefactor's demesne. Because cattle were fed on the com-

mon pasture and were rarely stabled, gathering their manure was laborious and time consuming. Nevertheless, whenever possible, animal manure was gathered and thinly spread. So also was house garbage—eggshells, fruit cores, onion skins—that had disintegrated on a compost heap.

Tools and farm implements are often shown in medieval manuscripts. But accepting such representations at face value is unwise. Rather than going out into a field to look at a tool, medieval artists simply copied drawings from classical and other treatises. Thus a plow or harrow (used to smooth out the soil after it had been broken up) pictured in a book written in the Île-de-France may actually have been used in England or Italy a half-century before.

In the early twelfth century, the production of iron increased greatly. There is considerable evidence for the manufacture of iron plowshares (the part of the plow that cuts the furrow into and grinds up the earth). In the thirteenth century, the wooden plow continued to be the basic instrument of agricultural production, but its edge was strengthened with iron. Only after the start of the fourteenth century, when lists of manorial equipment began to be kept, is there evidence for pitchforks, spades, axes, and harrows. Harrows were usually made of wood and weighted down with stones to force a deeper cut into the earth.

Plow and harrow were increasingly pulled by horses. The development of the padded horse collar, resting on the horse's shoulders and attached to the load by shafts, led to an agricultural revolution. The horse collar meant that the animal could put its entire weight into the task of pulling. The use of horses, rather than oxen, spread in the twelfth century. Horses' greater strength brought greater efficiency to farming.[7] Horses were an enormous investment, perhaps comparable to a modern tractor. They had to be shod (another indication of increased iron production), and the

oats they ate were costly. But horses were a crucial element in the improvement of the medieval agricultural economy. Some scholars believe that the use of the horse in agriculture is one of the decisive ways in which western Europe advanced over the rest of the world. But horses were not universally adopted. The Mediterranean countries, for example, did not use horsepower. And tools and farm implements still remained primitive.

Agricultural yields varied widely from place to place and from year to year. Even with good iron tools, horsepower, and careful use of seed and fertilizer, medieval peasants were at the mercy of the weather. Even today, lack of rain or too much rain can cause terrible financial loss and extreme hardship. How much more vulnerable was the medieval peasant with his primitive tools! By twentieth-century standards, medieval agricultural yields were very low. Inadequate soil preparation, poor seed selection, lack of manure—all made this virtually inevitable.

Yet there was striking improvement over time. Between the ninth and early thirteenth centuries,

Late Medieval Wheelless Plow This plow has a sharp-pointed colter, which cut the earth while the attached mold-board lifted, turned, and pulverized the soil. As the man steers the plow, his wife prods the oxen. The caption reads, "God speed the plow, and send us corn (wheat) enough." *(Source: Trinity College Library, Cambridge)*

it appears that yields of cereals approximately doubled, and on the best-managed estates, for every bushel of seed planted, the farmer harvested five bushels of grain. This is a tentative conclusion. Because of the scarcity of manorial inventories before the thirteenth century, the student of medieval agriculture has great difficulty determining how much the land produced. The author of a treatise on land husbandry, Walter of Henley, who lived in the mid-thirteenth century, wrote that the land should yield three times its seed; that amount was necessary for sheer survival. The surplus would be sold to grain merchants in the nearest town. Townspeople were wholly dependent on the surrounding countryside for food, which could not be shipped a long distance. A poor harvest meant that both town and rural people suffered.

Grain yields were probably greatest on large manorial estates, where there was more professional management. For example, the estates of Battle Abbey in Sussex, England, enjoyed a very high yield of wheat, rye, and oats in the century and a half between 1350 and 1499. This was due to heavy seeding, good crop rotation, and the use of manure from the monastery's sheep flocks. Battle Abbey's yields seem to have been double those of smaller, less efficiently run farms. A modern Illinois farmer expects to get 40 bushels of soybeans, 150 bushels of corn, and 50 bushels of wheat for every bushel of seed planted. Of course, modern costs of production in labor, seed, and fertilizer are quite high, but this yield is at least ten times that of the farmer's medieval ancestor. The average manor probably got a yield of 5 to 1 in the thirteenth century.[8] As low as that may seem by current standards, it marked a rise in productivity equal to that of the years just before the great agricultural revolution of the eighteenth century.

Life on the Manor

Life for most people in medieval Europe meant country life. Most people's horizons were restricted to the manor on which they were born. True, peasants who colonized such sparsely settled regions as eastern Germany must have traveled long distances. But most people rarely traveled more than twenty-five miles beyond their villages. Everyone's world was small, narrow, and provincial in the original sense of the word: limited by the boundaries of the province. This way of life did not have entirely unfortunate results. A farmer had a strong sense of family and the certainty of its support and help in time of trouble. People knew what their life's work would be—the same as their mother's or father's. They had a sense of place, and pride in that place was reflected in adornment of the village church. Religion and the village gave people a sure sense of identity and with it psychological peace. Modern people—urban, isolated, industrialized, rootless, and thoroughly secularized—have lost many of these reinforcements.

On the other hand, even aside from the unending physical labor, life on the manor was dull. Medieval men and women must have had a crushing sense of frustration. They lived lives of quiet desperation. Often they sought escape in heavy drinking. English judicial records of the thirteenth century reveal a surprisingly large number of "accidental" deaths. Strong, robust, commonsensical farmers do not ordinarily fall on their knives and stab themselves, or slip out of boats and drown, or get lost in the woods on a winter's night, or fall from horses and get trampled. They were probably drunk. Many of these accidents occurred, as the court records say, "coming from an ale." Brawls and violent fights were frequent at taverns.

Scholars have recently spent much energy investigating the structure of medieval peasant households. Because little concrete evidence survives, conclusions are very tentative. It appears, however, that a peasant household consisted of a simple nuclear family: a married couple alone, a couple with children, or widows or widowers with children. Peasant households were *not* extended families containing grandparents or married sons and daughters and their children, as was common in Asian countries, such as China. The simple family predominated in thirteenth-century England, in northern France in the fourteenth century, and in fifteenth-century Tuscany. Before the first appearance of the Black Death, perhaps 94 percent of peasant farmers married, and bride and groom were both in their twenties. The "typical" household numbered about five people: the parents and three children.[9]

Women played a significant role in the agricultural life of medieval Europe. This obvious fact is often overlooked by historians. Women shared with their fathers and husbands the backbreaking labor in the fields, work that was probably all the more difficult for them because of weaker muscular development and frequent pregnancies. The adage from the Book of Proverbs "Houses and riches are the inheritances of fathers: but a prudent wife is from the Lord" was seldom more true than in an age when the wife's prudent management was often all that separated a household from starvation in a year of crisis. And starvation was a very real danger to the peasantry until the eighteenth century.

Women managed the house. The size and quality of peasants' houses varied according to their relative prosperity, and that prosperity usually depended on the amount of land held. Poorer peasants lived in windowless cottages built of wood or wattle (poles intertwined with twigs or reeds) and clay and thatched with straw. These cottages consisted of one large room that served as the kitchen and living quarters for all. Everyone slept there. The house had an earthen floor and a fireplace. The lack of windows meant that the room was very sooty. A trestle table, several stools, one or two beds, and a chest for storing clothes constituted the furniture. A shed attached to the house provided storage for tools and shelter for animals. Prosperous peasants added rooms and furniture as they could be afforded, and some wealthy peasants in the early fourteenth century had two-story houses with separate bedrooms for parents and children.

Every house had a small garden and an outbuilding. Onions, garlic, turnips, and carrots were grown and stored through the winter in the main room of the dwelling or in the shed attached to it. Cabbage was raised almost everywhere and, after being shredded, salted, and packed in vats in hot water, was turned into kraut. Peasants ate vegetables, not because they appreciated their importance for good health but because there was usually little else. Some manors had fruit trees—apple, cherry, and pear in northern Europe; lemon, lime, and olive in the south. But because of the high price of sugar, when it was available, fruit could not be preserved. Preserving and storing other foods were the basic responsibility of the women and children.

Women also had to know the correct proportions of barley, water, yeast, and hops to make beer—the universal drink of the common people in northern Europe. By modern American standards the rate of beer consumption was heroic. Each monk of Abingdon Abbey in England in the twelfth century was allotted three gallons a day,

Woman's Work Carrying a heavy sack of grain to the mill was part of this medieval woman's everyday work. *(Source: The Pierpoint Morgan Library)*

and a man working in the fields for ten or twelve hours a day probably drank much more.[10]

The mainstay of the diet for peasants everywhere—and for all other classes—was bread. It was a hard, black substance made of barley, millet, and oats, rarely of expensive wheat flour. The housewife usually baked the household supply once a week. Where sheep, cows, or goats were raised, she also made cheese. In places like the Bavarian Alps of southern Germany, where hundreds of sheep grazed on the mountainsides, or at Cheddar in southwestern England, cheese was a staple.[11]

The diet of those living in an area with access to a river, lake, or stream was supplemented with fish, which could be preserved by salting. In many places there were severe laws against hunting and trapping in the forests. Deer, wild boars, and other game were strictly reserved for the king and nobles. These laws were flagrantly violated, however, and stolen rabbits and wild game often found their way to the peasants' tables. Woods and forests also provided nuts, which housewives and small children would gather in the fall.

Lists of peasant obligations and services to the lord, such as the following from Battle Abbey, commonly included the payment of chickens and eggs:

382 CHAPTER 13 LIFE IN CHRISTIAN EUROPE IN THE HIGH MIDDLE AGES

John of Coyworth holds a house and thirty acres of land, and owes yearly 2 p at Easter and Michaelmas; and he owes a cock and two hens at Christmas, of the value of 4 d.[12]

Chicken and eggs must have been highly valued in the prudently managed household. Except for the rare chicken or illegally caught wild game, meat appeared on the table only on the great feast days of the Christian year: Christmas, Easter, and Pentecost. Then the meat was likely to be pork from the pig slaughtered in the fall and salted for the rest of the year. Some scholars believe that by the mid-thirteenth century there was a great increase in the consumption of meat generally. If so, this change in diet is further evidence of an improved standard of living.

Breakfast, eaten at dawn before the farmer departed for his work, might consist of bread, an onion (easily stored through the winter months), and a piece of cheese, washed down with milk or beer. Farmers, then as now, ate their main meal around noon. This was often soup—a thick *potage* of boiled cabbage, onions, turnips, and peas, seasoned with a bone or perhaps a sliver of meat. The evening meal, taken at sunset, consisted of leftovers from the noon meal, perhaps with bread, cheese, milk, or beer.

Once children were able to walk, they helped their parents in the hundreds of chores that had to be done. Small children were set to collecting eggs, if the family had chickens, or gathering twigs and sticks for firewood. As they grew older, children had more responsibility—weeding the family vegetable garden, milking the cows, shearing the sheep, cutting wood for fires, helping with the planting or harvesting, and assisting their mothers in the endless tasks of baking, cooking, and preserving. Because of poor diet, terrible sanitation, and lack of medical care, the death rate among children was phenomenally high.

Popular Religion

Apart from the land, the weather, and the peculiar conditions that existed on each manor, the Christian religion had its greatest impact on the daily lives of ordinary people in the High Middle Ages. Religious practices varied widely from country to country and even from province to province. But nowhere was religion a one-hour-on-Sunday or only-on-high holy days affair. Christian practices and attitudes permeated virtually all aspects of everyday life.

In the ancient world, participation in religious rituals was a public and social duty. As the Germanic and Celtic peoples were Christianized, their new religion became a fusion of Jewish, pagan, Roman, and Christian practices. By the High Middle Ages, religious rituals and practices represented a synthesis of many elements, and all people shared as a natural and public duty in the religious life of the community.

The village church was the center of manorial life—social, political, and economic as well as religious. Most of the important events in a person's life took place in or around the church. A person was baptized there, within hours of birth. Men and women confessed their sins to the village priest there and received, usually at Easter and Christmas, the sacrament of the Eucharist. In front of the church, the bishop reached down from his horse and confirmed a person as a Christian by placing his hands over the candidate's head and making the sign of the cross on the forehead. (Bishops Thomas Becket of Canterbury and Hugh of Lincoln were considered especially holy men because they got down from their horses to confirm.) Young people courted in the churchyard and, so the sermons of the priests complained, made love in the church cemetery. Priests urged couples to marry publicly in the church, but many married privately, without witnesses (see page 450).

The stone in the church altar contained relics of the saints, often a local saint to whom the church itself had been dedicated. In the church, women and men could pray to the Virgin and the local saints. The saints had once lived on earth and thus could well understand human problems. They could be helpful intercessors with Christ or God the Father. According to official church doctrine, the center of the Christian religious life was the mass, the re-enactment of Christ's sacrifice on the cross. Every Sunday and on holy days, villagers stood at mass or squatted on the floor (there were no chairs), breaking the painful routine of work. Finally, people wanted to be buried in the church cemetery, close to the holy place and the saints believed to reside there.

The church was the center of village social life. The feasts that accompanied baptisms, weddings, funerals, and other celebrations were commonly held in the churchyard. Medieval drama originated within the church. Mystery plays, based on biblical episodes, were performed first in the sanctuary, then on the church porch, and finally in the village square, which was often in front of the west door.

From the church porch the priest read to his parishioners orders and messages from royal and ecclesiastical authorities. Royal judges traveling on circuit opened their courts on the church porch. The west front of the church, with its scenes of the Last Judgment, was the background against which the justices disposed of civil and criminal cases. Farmers from outlying districts pushed their carts to the marketplace in the village square near the west front. In busy mercantile centers such as London, business agreements and commercial exchanges were made in the aisles of the church itself, as at Saint Paul's.

Popular religion consisted of rituals heavy with symbolism. Before slicing a loaf of bread, the good wife tapped the sign of the cross on it with her knife. Before the planting, the village priest customarily went out and sprinkled the fields with holy water, symbolizing refreshment and life. Shortly after a woman had successfully delivered a child, she was "churched" in a ceremony of thanksgiving based on the Jewish rite of purification. When a child was baptized, a few grains of salt were dropped on its tongue. Salt had been the symbol of purity, strength, and incorruptibility for the ancient Hebrews, and the Romans had used it in their sacrifices. It was used in Christian baptism to drive away demons and to strengthen the infant in its new faith.

The entire calendar was designed with reference to Christmas, Easter, and Pentecost. Saints' days were legion. Everyone participated in village processions. The colored vestments worn by the priests at mass gave the villagers a sense of the changing seasons of the church's liturgical year. The signs and symbols of Christianity were visible everywhere.

Was popular religion entirely a matter of ritualistic formulas and ceremonies? What did the peasants actually *believe*? They accepted what family, custom, and the clergy ingrained in them. They learned the fundamental teachings of the church from the homilies of the village priests. The mass was in Latin, but the priest delivered sermons on the Gospel in the vernacular. People grasped the meaning of biblical stories and church doctrines

from the paintings on the village church wall. If their parish was wealthy, scenes depicted in the church's stained-glass windows instructed them. Illiterate and uneducated, they certainly could not reason out the increasingly sophisticated propositions of clever theologians. Still, scriptural references and proverbs dotted everyone's language. The everyday English farewell, "Goodbye" (French *adieu,* Spanish *adios*), meaning "God be with you" or "Godspeed," reflects the religious influence in ordinary speech. Christianity was a basic element in the common people's culture; indeed, it was a foundation of their culture.

Christianity has always absorbed the rituals and practices of other faiths, investing them with Christian significance. The rosary provides a good example of the adaptation of an Asian device. Since the beginnings of Christianity, one feature of everyday Christian spirituality was the continuous repetition of prayers and biblical verses. Pebbles, beads, and gems strung on a rope or chain were used to assist in counting these repetitions. This rope of beads originated in Hindu India (see page 73) and from Hinduism it spread to Buddhism and later to Islam. Muslims finger tasseled worry beads to calm their nerves, and in the twelfth century Western Crusaders returning from the Middle East spread this practice, which they had learned from the Muslims. In the Muslim world the beads have a secular character; in the West the practice is strictly religious.[13]

Scholars do not know when the practice of reciting the rosary actually entered Western Christianity. A rosary was found in the grave of the Abbess Gertrude (d. 659), daughter of King Pippin I of the Franks; and when Lady Godiva of Coventry died in 1041, her will mentioned a circlet of gems on which she had said her prayers. Popular tradition holds that Saint Dominic (1170?–1221) (see page 435) invented the rosary after a miraculous vision of the Virgin Mary, but this religious practice obviously existed much earlier.

Christians had long had special reverence and affection for the Virgin Mary as the Mother of Christ. In the eleventh century, theologians began to emphasize the depiction of Mary at the crucifixion in the Gospel of John:

But standing by the cross of Jesus were his mother, and his mother's sister, Mary the wife of Clopas, and Mary Magdalene. When Jesus saw his mother and the disciple whom he loved standing near, he said to his

Medieval Vision of Hell (Winchester Psalter) Frightful demons attack the damned souls—including kings, queens, and monks—in this twelfth-century portrayal of hell. The inscription at the top reads, "Here is hell and the angel closes the gates." *(Source: The British Library)*

mother, "Woman, behold, your son!" Then he said to the disciple, "Behold, your mother!" [14]

Medieval scholars interpreted this passage as expressing Christ's compassionate concern for all humanity and Mary's spiritual motherhood of all Christians. The huge outpouring of popular devotions to Mary concentrated on her role as Queen of Heaven and, because of her special relationship to Christ, as all-powerful intercessor with him. Masses on Saturdays specially commemorated her; sermons focused on her unique influence with Christ; and hymns and prayers to her multiplied. The most famous prayer, "Salve Regina," perfectly expresses the confidence that medieval people placed in Mary, their advocate with Christ:

Hail, holy Queen, Mother of Mercy! Our life, our sweetness, and our hope. To thee we cry, poor banished children of Eve; to thee we send up our sighs, mourning and weeping in this valley of tears. Turn, then, most gracious advocate, thy merciful eyes upon us; and after this our exile show us the blessed fruit of thy womb, Jesus. O merciful, O loving, O sweet Virgin Mary!

Peasants had a strong sense of the universal presence of God. They believed that God intervened directly in human affairs and could reward the virtuous and bring peace, health, and material prosperity. They believed, too, that God punished men and women for their sins with disease, poor harvests, and the destructions of war. Sin was caused by the Devil, who lurked everywhere. The Devil constantly incited people to evil deeds and sin, especially sins of the flesh. Sin frequently took place in the dark. Thus evil and the Devil were connected in the peasant's mind with darkness or blackness. In medieval literature the Devil is sometimes portrayed as a black, an identification that has had a profound and sorry impact on Western racial attitudes.

For peasants, life was not only hard but short. Few lived beyond the age of forty. They had a great fear of nature: storms, thunder, and lightning terrified them. They had a terror of hell, whose geography and awful tortures they knew from sermons. And they certainly saw that the virtuous were not always rewarded but sometimes suffered considerably on earth. These things, which they could not explain, bred a deep pessimism.

No wonder, then, that pilgrimages to shrines of the saints were so popular. They offered hope in a world of gloom. They satisfied a strong emotional need. They meant change, adventure, excitement. The church granted indulgences to those who visited the shrines of great saints. *Indulgences* were remissions of the penalties that priests imposed on penitents for grave sin. People, however, equated indulgences with salvation itself. They generally believed that an indulgence cut down the amount of time one would spend in hell. Thus indulgences and pilgrimages "promised" salvation. Vast numbers embarked on pilgrimages to the shrines of Saint James at Santiago de Compostella in Spain, Thomas Becket at Canterbury, Saint-Gilles de Provence, and Saints Peter and Paul at Rome.

THOSE WHO FIGHT

The nobility, though a small fraction of the total population, strongly influenced all aspects of medieval culture—political, economic, religious, educational, and artistic. For that reason, European society in the twelfth and thirteenth centuries may be termed "aristocratic." Despite political, scientific, and industrial revolutions, the nobility continued to hold real political and social power in Europe down to the nineteenth century. In order to account for this continuing influence, it is important to understand its development in the High Middle Ages.

During the past twenty years, historians have discovered a great deal about the origins and status of the medieval European nobility. It is now known, for example, that ecclesiastical writers in the tenth and eleventh centuries frequently used the term *nobilitas* in reference to the upper classes but did not define it. Clerical writers, however, had no trouble distinguishing who was and was not noble. By the thirteenth century, nobles were broadly described as "those who fight"—those who had the profession of arms. What was a noble? How did the social status and lifestyle of the nobility in the twelfth and thirteenth centuries differ from their tenth-century forms? What political and economic role did the nobility play?

First, in the tenth and eleventh centuries, the social structure in different parts of Europe varied considerably. There were distinct regional customs and social patterns. Broad generalizations about the legal and social status of the nobility, therefore, are dangerous, because they are not universally applicable. For example, in Germany until about 1200, approximately one thousand families, descended from the Carolingian imperial aristocracy and perhaps from the original German tribal nobility, formed the ruling social group. The members of this group intermarried and held most of the important positions in church and state.[15] Between free and nonfree individuals there were rigid distinctions, which prevented the absorption of those of servile birth into the ranks of the nobility.

Likewise, in the region around Paris from the tenth century on, a group of great families held public authority, was self-conscious about its ancestry and honorable status, was bound to the royal house, and was closed to the self-made man. From this aristocracy descended the upper nobility of the High Middle Ages.[16] To the west, however, in the provinces of Anjou and Maine, men of fortune who gained wealth and power became part of the closely related web of noble families by marrying into those families; in these regions, considerable upward mobility existed. Some scholars argue that before the thirteenth century the French nobility was an open caste.[17] Across the English Channel, the English nobility in the High Middle Ages derived from the Norman, Breton, French, and Flemish warriors who helped Duke William of Normandy defeat the Anglo-Saxons at the Battle of Hastings in 1066 (see page 405).

In most places, for a son or daughter to be considered a noble, both parents had to be noble. Non-noble women could not usually enter the nobility through marriage, though evidence from Germany shows that some women were ennobled because they had married nobles. There is no evidence of French or English women being raised to the nobility.

Members of the nobility enjoyed a special legal status. A noble was free personally and in his possessions. He had immunity from almost all outside authorities. He was limited only by his military obligation to king, duke, or prince. As the result of his liberty, he had certain rights and responsibilities. He raised troops and commanded them in the field. He held courts that dispensed a sort of justice. Sometimes he coined money for use within his territories. He conducted relations with outside powers. He was the political, military, and judicial lord of the people who settled on his lands. He made political decisions that affected them, resolved disputes among them, and protected them in time of attack. The liberty of the noble and the privileges that went with his liberty were inheritable, perpetuated by blood and not by wealth alone.

The noble was a professional fighter. His social function, as churchmen described it, was to protect the weak, the poor, and the churches by force of arms. He possessed a horse and a sword. These, and the leisure time in which to learn how to use them in combat, were the visible signs of his nobility. He was encouraged to display chivalric virtues. Chivalry was a code of conduct originally devised by the clergy to transform the crude and brutal behavior of the knightly class. A knight was sup-

posed to be brave, eager to win praise, courteous, loyal to his commander, generous, and gracious. The medieval nobility developed independently of knighthood and preceded it; all nobles were knights, but not all knights were noble.[18]

During the eleventh century, the term *chevalier,* meaning "horseman" or "knight," gained wide currency in France. Non-French people gradually adopted it to refer to the nobility, "who sat up high on their war-horses, looking down on the poor masses and terrorizing the monks."[19] In France and England by the twelfth century, the noble frequently used the Latin term *miles,* or "knight." By this time the word connoted moral values, a consciousness of family, and participation in a superior hereditary caste.

Those who aspired to the aristocracy desired a castle, the symbol of feudal independence and military lifestyle. Through military valor, a fortunate marriage, or outstanding service to king or lord, poor knights could and did achieve positions in the upper nobility. This was not so in Germany, however, where a large class of unfree knights, or *ministerials,* existed. Recruited from the servile dependents of great lords, ministerials were stewards who managed nobles' estates or households or who fought as warriors. In the twelfth century, ministerials sometimes acquired fiefs and wealth. The most important ministerials served the German kings and had significant responsibilities. Legally, however, they remained of servile status: they were not noble.[20]

Infancy and Childhood

Most information about childbirth in the Middle Ages comes from manuscript illuminations that depict the birth process from the moment of coitus through pregnancy to delivery. An interesting thirteenth-century German miniature from Vienna shows a woman in labor. She is sitting on a chair or stool surrounded by four other women, who are present to help her in the delivery. They could be relatives or neighbors. If they are midwives, the woman in labor is probably noble or rich, since midwives charged a fee. Two midwives seem to be shaking the mother up and down to hasten delivery. One of the women is holding a coriander seed near the mother's vagina. Coriander is an herb of the carrot family, and its seeds were used for cleaning purposes. They were thought to be helpful for expelling gas from the alimentary canal—hence their purported value in speeding up delivery.

The rate of infant mortality (the number of babies who would die before their first birthday) in the High Middle Ages must have been staggering. Such practices as jolting a pregnant woman up and down and inserting a seed into her surely contributed to the death rate of both the newborn and the mother. Natural causes—disease and poor or insufficient food—also resulted in many deaths. Infanticide, however, which was common in parts of the ancient world, seems to have declined in the High Middle Ages. Ecclesiastical pressure worked steadily against it. Infanticide in medieval Europe is another indication of the slow and very imperfect Christianization of European peoples. High mortality due to foreign invasions and the generally violent and unstable conditions of the ninth and tenth centuries made unnecessary the deliberate killing of one's own children. On the other hand, English court records from the counties of Warwickshire, Staffordshire, and Gloucestershire for 1221 reveal a suspiciously large number of children dying from "accidental" deaths—drowning, falling from carts, disappearing into the woods, falling into the fire. Still, accidental deaths in rural conditions are more common than is usually thought. More research is needed to determine the actual prevalence of infanticide in the High Middle Ages.

The abandonment of infant children seems to have been the most favored form of family limitation, widely practiced throughout the entire Middle Ages. Abandonment was "the voluntary relinquishing of control over children by their natal parents or guardians, whether by leaving them somewhere, selling them, or legally consigning authority to some other person or institution."[21] Why did parents do this? What became of the children? What was the rate of abandonment? What attitudes did medieval society have toward this practice?

Poverty or local natural disaster led some parents to abandon their children because they could not support them. Before the eleventh century, food was so scarce that few parents could feed themselves, let alone children. Thus Saint Patrick wrote that, in times of famine, fathers would sell their sons and daughters so that the children could be fed. Parents sometimes gave children away because they were illegitimate or the result of incestuous unions. An eighth-century penitential collection describes the proper treatment for a woman who exposes her unwanted child—that is, leaves it in the open to die—because she has been raped by an enemy or is unable to nourish it. She is not to be blamed, but she should do penance.[22]

Sometimes parents believed that someone of greater means or status might find the child and bring it up in better circumstances than the natal parents could provide. Disappointment in the sex of the child, or its physical weakness or deformity, might also lead parents to abandon it. Finally, some parents were indifferent—they "simply could not be bothered" with the responsibilities of parenthood.[23]

The Christian Middle Ages witnessed a significant development in the disposal of superfluous children: they were given to monasteries as *oblates*.

Children Given to Creditors Ecclesiastical laws against lending money at interest were widely flouted, and many nobles, having borrowed beyond their ability to repay, fell heavily into debt. As illustrated here, the selling or giving of children to creditors was one solution to indebtedness. *(Source: The Bodleian Library, Oxford)*

The word *oblate* derives from the Latin *oblatio,* meaning "offering." Boys and girls were given to monasteries or convents as permanent gifts. Saint Benedict (see pages 242–244), in the fifty-ninth chapter of his *Rule,* takes oblation as a normal method for entrance into the monastic life. By the seventh century, church councils and civil codes had defined the practice: "Parents of any social status could donate a child, of either sex, at least up to the age of ten." Contemporaries considered oblation a religious act, since the child was offered to God often in recompense for parental sin. But oblation also served social and economic functions. The monastery nurtured and educated the child in a familial atmosphere, and it provided career opportunities for the mature monk or nun despite his or her humble origins. Oblation has justifiably been described as "in many ways the most humane form of abandonment ever devised in the West."[24]

The fragmentary medieval evidence prevents the modern student from gaining precise figures on the rate of abandonment. Recent research suggests, however, that abandonment was very common until about the year 1000. The next two hundred years, which saw great agricultural change and relative prosperity, witnessed a low point in abandonment. On the other hand, in the twelfth and thirteenth centuries, the incidence of noble parents giving their younger sons and daughters to religious houses increased dramatically; nobles wanted to preserve the estate intact for the eldest son. Consequently, oblates composed a high percentage of monastic populations. At Winchester in England, for example, 85 percent of the new monks between 1030 and 1070 were oblates. In the early thirteenth century, the bishop of Paris observed that children were

. . . cast into the cloister by parents and relatives just as if they were kittens or piglets whom their mothers could not nourish; so that they may die to the world not spiritually but . . . civilly, that is—so that they may be deprived of their hereditary position and that it may devolve on those who remain in the world.

The abandonment of children remained a socially acceptable practice. Ecclesiastical and civil authorities never legislated against it. Moralists reproached parents for abandoning children because they viewed the child as proof of careless sexuality—not because parents had special obligations to the child. By stressing that all sexual acts have a procreational purpose, and by providing a monastic oblation a humane solution for abandonment, the Christian church may have actually increased the rate of abandonment.[25]

For children of aristocratic birth, the years from infancy to around the age of seven or eight were primarily years of play. Infants had their rattles, as the twelfth-century monk Guibert of Nogent reports, and young children their special toys. Of course, then as now, children would play with anything—handballs, rings, pretty stones, horns, any small household object. Gerald of Wales, who later became a courtier of King Henry II, describes how as a child he built monasteries and churches in the sand while his brothers were making castles and palaces. Vincent of Beauvais, who composed a

Child Oblate   As St. Benedict allowed (*Rule,* Chap. 59), medieval monasteries frequently received oblates, or children offered by their parents, as permanent members. In this twelfth-century manuscript, a father presents his young son, along with the required dowry, to the abbot (shown with staff). *(Source: Giraudon/Art Resource)*

great encyclopedia around 1250, recommended that children be bathed twice a day, fed well, and given ample play time.

Guibert of Nogent speaks in several places in his autobiography of "the tender years of childhood"—the years from six to twelve. Describing the severity of the tutor whom his mother assigned to him, Guibert wrote:

Placed under him, I was taught with such purity and checked with such honesty from the vices which commonly spring up in youth that I was kept from ordinary games and never allowed to leave my master's company, or to eat anywhere else than at home, or to accept gifts from anyone without his leave; in everything I had to show self-control in word, look, and deed, so that he seemed to require of me the conduct of a monk rather than a clerk. While others of my age wandered everywhere at will and were unchecked in the indulgence of such inclinations as were natural at their age, I, hedged in with constant restraints and dressed in my clerical garb, would sit and look at the troops of players like a beast awaiting sacrifice. Even on Sundays and saints' days I had to submit to the severity of school exercises.[26]

Guibert's mother had intended him for the church. Other boys and girls had more play time and freedom.

Nobles naturally wanted to ensure the continuation of the family and to preserve intact its landed patrimony. Scholars disagree about how nobles achieved this. According to one authority, "The struggle to preserve family holdings intact led them to primogeniture [the exclusive right of the first-born son to inherit] and its corollary, wet nursing, which guaranteed a considerable number of children, males among them."[27] Another student has argued persuasively that nobles deliberately married late or limited the number of their children who could marry by placing them in the church or forbidding them to marry while still laypersons. Or, nobles may have practiced birth control. For example, the counts of Falkenstein, who held lordships in upper Bavaria and lower Austria, adopted the strategy of late marriages and few children. This custom plus a violent lifestyle ultimately backfired and extinguished the dynasty.[28] Another student, using evidence from tenth-century Saxony, maintains that parents while alive commonly endowed sons with estates.

This practice allowed sons to marry at a young age and to demonstrate their military prowess.[29] Until more is known about family size and local customs in the High Middle Ages, generalizations about child-rearing practices must be avoided.

Parents decided on the futures of their children as soon as they were born or when they were still toddlers. Sons were prepared for one of the two positions considered suitable to their birth and position. Careers for the youngest sons might be found in the church; for the rest, a suitable position meant a military career. Likewise, parents determined early which daughters would be married—and to whom—and which would become nuns.

At about the age of seven, a boy of the noble class who was not intended for the church was placed in the household of one of his father's friends or relatives. There he became a servant to the lord and received his formal training in arms. He was expected to serve the lord at the table, to assist him as a private valet when called on to do so, and, as he gained experience, to care for the lord's horses and equipment. The boy might have a great deal of work to do, depending on the size of the household and the personality of the lord. The work that children did, medieval people believed, gave them experience and preparation for later life.

Training was in the arts of war. The boy learned to ride and to manage a horse. He had to acquire skill in wielding a sword, which sometimes weighed as much as twenty-five pounds. He had to be able to hurl a lance, shoot with a bow and arrow, and care for armor and other equipment.

Increasingly, in the eleventh and twelfth centuries, noble youths learned to read and write some Latin. Still, on thousands of charters from that period nobles signed with a cross (+) or some other mark. Literacy for the nobility became more common in the thirteenth century. Formal training was concluded around the age of twenty-one with the ceremony of knighthood.

The custom of knighting, though never universal, seems to have been widespread in France and England but not in Germany. The ceremony of knighthood was one of the most important in a man's life. Once knighted, a young man was supposed to be courteous, generous, and, if possible, handsome and rich. Above all, he was to be loyal to his lord and brave in battle. In a society lacking

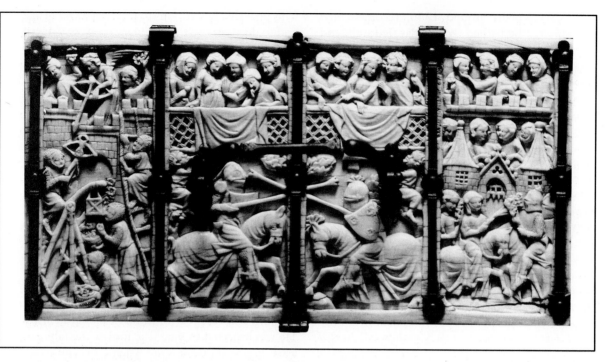

A Knightly Tournament or the Battle of the Sexes The lid of this exquisitely carved French ivory casket shows ladies and gentlemen on a balcony watching a tournament among mounted knights, while men storm the castle of love (left) and a lady and knight tilt with branches of flowers (right). *(Source: Walters Art Gallery, Baltimore)*

strong institutions of government, loyalty was the cement that held aristocratic society together. That is why the greatest crime was called a "felony," which meant treachery to one's lord.

Power and Responsibility

A member of the nobility became an adult when he came into the possession of his property. He then acquired vast authority over lands and people. With it went responsibility. In the words of Honorius of Autun:

Soldiers: You are the arm of the Church, because you should defend it against its enemies. Your duty is to aid the oppressed, to restrain yourself from rapine and fornication, to repress those who impugn the Church with evil acts, and to resist those who are rebels against priests. Performing such a service, you will obtain the most splendid of benefices from the greatest of Kings.[30]

Nobles rarely lived up to this ideal, and there are countless examples of nobles attacking the church. In the early thirteenth century, Peter of Dreux, count of Brittany, spent so much of his time attacking the church that he was known as the "Scourge of the Clergy."

The nobles' conception of rewards and gratification did not involve the kind of postponement envisioned by the clergy. They wanted rewards immediately. Since by definition a military class is devoted to war, those rewards came through the pursuit of arms. When nobles were not involved in local squabbles with neighbors—usually disputes over property or over real or imagined slights—they participated in tournaments.

Complete jurisdiction over properties allowed the noble, at long last, to gratify his desire for display and lavish living. Since his status in medieval society depended on the size of his household, he would be eager to increase the number of his household retainers. The elegance of his clothes, the variety and richness of his table, the number of his horses and followers, the freedom with which he spent money—all were public indications of his social standing. The aristocratic lifestyle was luxurious and extravagant. To maintain it, nobles often had to borrow from financiers or wealthy monasteries.

At the same time, nobles had a great deal of work to do. The responsibilities of a noble in the High Middle Ages depended on the size and extent of his estates, the number of his dependents, and his position in his territory relative to others of his class and to the king. As a vassal he was required to fight for his lord or for the king when called on to do so. By the mid-twelfth century, this service was limited in most parts of western Europe to forty days a year. He might have to perform guard duty at his lord's castle for a certain number of days a year. He was obliged to attend his lord's court on important occasions when the lord wanted to put on great displays, such as at Easter, Pentecost, and Christmas. When the lord knighted his eldest son or married off his eldest daughter, he called his vassals to his court. They were expected to attend and to present a contribution known as a "gracious aid."

Throughout the year, a noble had to look after his own estates. He had to appoint prudent and honest overseers and make sure that they paid him the customary revenues and services. Since a great lord's estates were usually widely scattered, he had to travel frequently.

Until the late thirteenth century, when royal authority intervened, nobles in France and England had great power over the knights and peasants on their estates. They maintained order among them and dispensed justice to them. Holding the manorial court, which punished criminal acts and settled disputes, was one of their gravest obligations. The quality of justice varied widely: some lords were vicious tyrants who exploited and persecuted their peasants; others were reasonable and evenhanded. In any case, the quality of life on the manor and its productivity were related in no small way to the temperament and decency of the lord—and his lady.

Women played a large and important role in the functioning of the estate. They were responsible for the practical management of the household's "inner economy"—cooking, brewing, spinning, weaving, overseeing servants, caring for yard animals. The lifestyle of the medieval warrior-nobles required constant travel, both for purposes of war and for the supervision of distant properties. When the lord was away for long periods, the women frequently managed the herds, barns, granaries, and outlying fields as well.

Frequent pregnancies and reluctance to expose women to hostile conditions kept the lady at home and therefore able to assume supervision of the family's fixed properties. When a husband went away on crusade—his absence could last anywhere from two to five years, if he returned at all—his wife was often the sole manager of the family properties. When her husband went to the Holy Land between 1060 and 1080, the lady Hersendis was the sole manager of the family properties in northern France.

Women's activities were not confined to managing households and estates in their husbands' absence. Medieval warfare was largely a matter of brief skirmishes, and few men were killed in any single encounter. But altogether the number slain ran high, and there were many widows. Aristocratic widows frequently controlled family properties and fortunes and exercised great authority. Although the evidence is scattered and sketchy, there are indications that women performed many of the functions of men. In Spain, France, and Germany they bought, sold, and otherwise transferred property. Gertrude, labeled "Saxony's almighty widow" by the chronicler Ekkehard of Aura, took a leading role in conspiracies against the emperor Henry V. And Eilika Billung, widow of Count Otto of Ballenstedt, built a castle at Burgwerben on the Saale River and, as advocate of the monastery of Goseck, removed one abbot and selected his successor. From her castle at Bernburg, the countess Eilika was also reputed to ravage the countryside.

Throughout the High Middle Ages, fighting remained the dominant feature of the noble lifestyle. The church's preachings and condemnations reduced but did not stop violence. Late inheritances, which deprived the nobles of constructive outlets for their energy, together with the military ethos of their culture, encouraged petty warfare and disorder (see pages 346–347). The nobility thus were a constant source of trouble for the monarchy. In the thirteenth century, kings drew on the financial support of the middle classes to build the administrative machinery that gradually laid the foundations for strong royal government.

The Crusades relieved the rulers of France, England, and the German Empire of some of their most dangerous elements. Complete royal control of the nobility, however, came only in modern times.

THOSE WHO PRAY

Medieval Europeans believed that monks performed the most important social service, prayer. In the Middle Ages, prayer was looked on as a vital social service, as crucial as the labor of peasants and the military might of nobles. Just as the peasants provided sustenance through their toil and the knights protected and defended society with the sword, so the monks with their prayers and chants worked to secure God's blessing for society.

Monasticism represented some of the finest aspirations of medieval civilization. The monasteries were devoted to prayer, and their standards of Christian behavior influenced the entire church. The monasteries produced the educated elite that was continually drawn into the administrative service of kings and great lords. Monks kept alive the remains of classical culture and experimented with new styles of architecture and art. They introduced new techniques of estate management and land reclamation. Although relatively few in number in the High Middle Ages, the monks played a significant role in medieval society.

Recruitment

Toward the end of his *Ecclesiastical History of England and Normandy,* when he was well into his sixties, Orderic Vitalis (ca 1075–1140), a monk of the Norman abbey of Saint Evroul, interrupted his narrative to explain how he happened to become a monk:

And so, O glorious God, you didst inspire my father Odeleric to renounce me utterly and submit me in all things to thy governance. So, weeping, he gave me, a weeping child, into the care of the monk Reginald, and sent me away into exile for love of thee, and never saw me again. And I, a mere boy, did not presume to oppose my father's wishes, but obeyed him in all things, for he promised me for his part that if I became a monk I should taste of the joys of Heaven with the In-

nocents after my death.... And so, a boy of ten, I crossed the English channel and came into Normandy as an exile, unknown to all, knowing no one. Like Joseph in Egypt I heard a language which I could not understand. But thou didst suffer me through thy grace to find nothing but kindness among strangers. I was received as an oblate in the abbey of St. Evroul by the venerable abbot Mainier in the eleventh year of my life.... The name of Vitalis was given me in place of my English name, which sounded harsh to the Normans.[31]

Orderic Vitalis was one of the leading scholars of his times. As such, he is not a representative figure or even a typical monk. Intellectuals, those who earn their living or spend most of their time working with ideas, are never typical figures of their times. In one respect, however, Orderic was quite representative of the monks of the High Middle Ages: although he had no doubt that God wanted him to be a monk, the decision was actually made by his parents, who gave him to a monastery as a child-oblate. Orderic was the third son of Odeleric, a knight who fought for William the Conqueror at the Battle of Hastings (1066). For his participation in the Norman conquest of England, Odeleric was rewarded with lands in western England. Concern for the provision of his two older sons probably led him to give his youngest to the monastery.

Medieval monasteries were religious institutions whose organization and structure fulfilled the social needs of the feudal nobility. Between the tenth and thirteenth centuries, economic necessities compelled great families, or aspiring ones, to seek a life in the church for some members. There simply were not sufficient resources or career opportunities to provide suitable, honorable positions in life for all the children in aristocratic families. The monasteries provided these children with both an honorable and aristocratic life and opportunities for ecclesiastical careers.[32]

Until well into modern times, and certainly in the Middle Ages, almost everyone believed in the thorough subjection of children to their parents. This belief was the logical consequence of the fact that young noblemen were not expected to work and were therefore totally dependent on their fathers. Some men did become monks as adults, apparently for a wide variety of reasons: belief in a direct call from God, disgust with the materialism and violence of the secular world, the encourage-

French Castle Under Siege Most medieval warfare consisted of small skirmishes and the besieging of castles. If surrounded by a moat and supplied with food and water, a few knights could hold a castle against large armies for a long time. Notice the use of engines to hurl missiles. *(Source: The British Library)*

ment and inspiration of others, economic failure or lack of opportunity, poverty, sickness, fear of hell. However, most men who became monks, until about the early thirteenth century, seem to have been given as child-oblates by their parents.

In the thirteenth century, the older Benedictine and Cistercian orders had to compete with the new orders of friars—the Franciscans and Dominicans (see pages 435–437). More monks had to be recruited from the middle class—that is, from small landholders or traders in the district near the abbey. As medieval society changed economically, and as European society ever so slowly developed middle-class traits, the monasteries almost inevitably drew their manpower, when they were able, from the middle classes. Until that time, they were preserves of the aristocratic nobility.

The Nuns

Throughout the Middle Ages, social class also defined the kinds of religious life open to women. Kings and nobles usually established convents for their daughters, sisters, aunts, or aging mothers. Entrance was restricted to women of the founder's class. Since a well-born lady could not honorably be apprenticed to a tradesperson, and since her dignity did not permit her to do any kind of manual labor, the sole alternative to life at home was the religious life.

The founder's endowment and support greatly influenced the later social, economic, and political status of the convent. Social and religious bonds between benefactors and communities of nuns frequently continued over many generations. A few

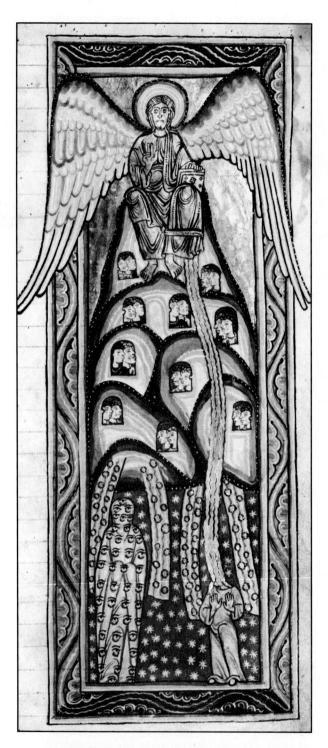

Hildegard of Bingen To describe her gift of visions, Hildegard wrote *Scivias (Know the Ways)*, an encyclopedia of Christian salvation. In this first vision, God, enthroned in light at the top of a mountain symbolizing the divine kingdom, embraces all of creation and promises eternal life. *(Source: Rheinisches Bildarchiv)*

convents received large endowments and could accept many women. Amesbury Priory in Wiltshire, England, for example, received a handsome endowment from King Henry II in 1177, and his successors Henry III and Edward I also made lavish gifts. In 1256 Amesbury supported a prioress and 76 nuns, 7 priests, and 16 lay brothers. It owned 200 oxen, 23 horses, 7 cows, 4 calves, 300 pigs, and 4,800 sheep. The convent raised 100 pounds in annual rents and 40 pounds from the wool clip, very large sums at the time. The entrance of such high-born ladies as the dowager queen Eleanor (widow of Henry III), Edward I's daughter Mary, and his niece Isabella of Lancaster stimulated the gift of additional lands and privileges. By 1317 Amesbury had 177 nuns.[33] Most houses of women, however, possessed limited resources and remained small in numbers.

The office of abbess or prioress, the house's superior, customarily went to a nun of considerable social standing. Thus William the Conqueror's daughter Cecelia became abbess of her mother's foundation, Holy Trinity Abbey in Caen, and Henry II's daughter became abbess of Barking. Since an abbess or prioress had responsibility for governing her community and for representing it in any business with the outside world, she was a woman of local power and importance. Sometimes her position brought national prominence. In 1306 Edward I of England summoned several abbesses to Parliament; he wanted their financial support for the expenses connected with knighting his eldest son.

What kind of life did the nuns lead? Religious duties held prime importance. Then there were business responsibilities connected with lands, properties, and rents that preoccupied those women of administrative ability. Sewing, embroidery, and fine needlework were considered the special pursuits of gentlewomen. Nuns in houses with an intellectual tradition copied manuscripts. Although the level of intellectual life in the women's houses varied widely, the careers of two nuns—Hildegard of Bingen and Isabella of Lancaster—suggest the activities of some nuns in the High Middle Ages.

The tenth child of a lesser noble family, Hildegard (1098–1179) was given when eight years old as an oblate to an abbey in the Rhineland, where she learned Latin and received a good education. Obviously possessed of leadership and administrative talents, Hildegard was sent in 1147 to found the convent of Rupertsberg near Bingen. There she produced a body of writings including the *Scivias (Know the Ways),* a record of her mystical visions that incorporates vast theological learning; the *Physica (On the Physical Elements),* a classification of the natural elements, such as plants, animals, metals, and the movements of the heavenly bodies; a mystery play; and a medical work that led a distinguished twentieth-century historian of science to describe Hildegard as "one of the most original writers of the Latin West in the twelfth century." At the same time, she carried on a vast correspondence with scholars, prelates, and ordinary people and had such a reputation for wisdom that a recent writer has called her "the Dear Abby of the twelfth century to whom everyone came or wrote for advice or comfort."[34] An exceptionally gifted person, Hildegard represents the Benedictine ideal of great learning combined with a devoted monastic life.

Like intellectual monks, however, intellectual nuns were not typical of the era. The life of the English nun Isabella of Lancaster better exemplifies the careers of high-born women who became nuns. The niece of King Edward I, she was placed at Amesbury Priory in early childhood, grew up there, made her profession of commitment to the convent life, and became abbess in 1343. Isabella seems to have been a conventional but not devout nun. She traveled widely, spent long periods at the royal court, and with the support of her wealthy relations maintained a residence apart from the priory. She was, however, an able administrator who handled the community finances with prudent skill. Amesbury lacked the intellectual and spiritual standards of Bingen. Isabella's interests were secular and her own literary production was a book of romances.

Prayer and Other Work

The pattern of life within individual monasteries varied widely from house to house and from region to region. Each monastic community was shaped by the circumstances of its foundation and endowment, by tradition, by the interests of its abbots and members, and by local conditions. It would thus be a mistake to think that Christian monasticism in the High Middle Ages was every-

where the same. One central activity, however—the work of God—was performed everywhere. Daily life centered around the liturgy.

Seven times a day and once during the night, the monks went to choir to chant the psalms and other prayers prescribed by Saint Benedict. Prayers were offered for peace, rain, good harvests, the civil authorities, and the monks' families and benefactors. Monastic patrons in turn lavished gifts on the monasteries, which often became very wealthy.

Prayer justified the monks' spending a large percentage of their income on splendid objects to enhance the liturgy; monks praised God, they believed, not only in prayer but in everything connected with prayer. They sought to accumulate priestly vestments of the finest silks, velvets, and embroideries, and sacred vessels of embossed silver and gold. Thuribles (vessels) containing sweet-smelling incense brought at great expense from the East were used for the incensing of the altars, following ancient Jewish ritual. The pages of Gospel books were richly decorated with gold leaf, and the books' bindings were ornamented and bejeweled. Every monastery tried to acquire the relics of its patron saint, which if acquired needed to be housed in a beautifully crafted reliquary. The liturgy inspired a great deal of art, and the monasteries became the storehouses of art in Western Christendom.

The monks fulfilled their social responsibility by praying. It was generally agreed that they could best carry out this duty if they were not distracted by worldly matters. Thus great and lesser lords gave the monasteries lands that would supply the community with necessities. Each manorial unit was responsible for provisioning the local abbey for a definite period of time, and the expenses of each abbey were supposed to equal its income.

The administration of an abbey's estates and properties consumed considerable time. The operation of a large establishment, such as Cluny in Burgundy or Bury Saint Edmunds in England, which by 1150 had several hundred monks, involved planning, prudence, and wise management. Although the abbot or prior had absolute authority in making assignments, common sense advised that tasks be allotted according to the talents of individual monks.

The usual method of economic organization was the manor. Many monastic manors were small enough and close enough to the abbey to be supervised directly by the abbot. But if a monastery held and farmed vast estates, the properties were divided into administrative units under the supervision of one of the monks of the house. The lands of the German abbey of Saint Emmeran at Regensburg, for example, were divided into thirty-three manorial centers.

Because the *choir monks* were aristocrats, they did not till the land themselves. In each house one monk, the *cellarer* or general financial manager, was responsible for supervising the lay brothers or peasants who did the actual agricultural labor. *Lay brothers* were vowed religious drawn from the servile classes; they had simpler religious and intellectual obligations than those of the choir monks. The cellarer had to see to it that the estates of the monastery produced enough income to cover its expenses. Another monk, the *almoner,* was responsible for feeding and caring for the poor of the neighborhood. At the French abbey of Saint-Requier in the eleventh century, 110 persons were fed every day. At Corbie, fifty loaves of bread were distributed daily to the poor.

The *precentor* or *cantor* was responsible for the library and the careful preservation of books. The *sacristan* of an abbey had in his charge all the materials and objects connected with the liturgy—vestments, candles, incense, sacred vessels, altar cloths, and hangings. The *novice master* was responsible for the training of recruits, instructing them in the *Rule,* the chant, the Scriptures, and the history and traditions of the house. For a few of the monks, work was some form of intellectual activity, such as the copying of books and manuscripts, the preparation of manuals, and the writing of letters.

Although several orders forbade monks to study law and medicine, that rule was often ignored. In the twelfth and thirteenth centuries, many monks gained considerable reputations for their knowledge and experience in the practice of both the canon law of the church and the civil law of their countries. For example, the Norman monk Lanfranc, because of his legal knowledge and administrative ability, became the chief adviser of William the Conqueror.

Although knowledge of medicine was primitive by twentieth-century standards, monastic practitioners were less ignorant than one would suspect. Long before 1066, a rich medical literature had been produced in England. The most important of these treatises was *The Leech Book of Bald* (*leech* means "medical"). This work exhibits a wide knowledge of herbal prescriptions, ancient authorities, and empirical practice. Bald discusses diseases of the lungs and stomach together with their remedies and demonstrates his acquaintance with surgery. Medical knowledge was sometimes rewarded. King Henry I of England (r. 1100–1135) enriched several of his physicians, and Henry II (r. 1154–1189) made his medical adviser, the monk Robert de Veneys, abbot of Malmesbury.

The religious houses of medieval Europe usually took full advantage of whatever resources and opportunities their location offered. For example, the raising of horses could produce income in a world that depended on horses for travel and for warfare. Some monasteries, such as the Cistercian abbey of Jervaulx in Yorkshire, became famous for and quite wealthy from their production of prime breeds. In the eleventh and twelfth centuries, a period of considerable monastic expansion, large tracts of swamp, fen, forest, and wasteland were brought under cultivation—principally by the Cistercians (see page 356).

The Cistercians, whose constitution insisted that they accept lands far from human habitation and forbade them to be involved in the traditional feudal-manorial structure, were ideally suited to the agricultural needs and trends of their times. In the Low Countries they built dikes to hold back the sea, and the reclaimed land was put to the production of cereals. In the eastern parts of Germany—Silesia, Mecklenburg, and Pomerania—they took the lead in draining swamps and cultivating wasteland. Because of a labor shortage, they advertised widely across Europe for monks and lay brothers. Through their efforts, the rich, rolling land of French Burgundy was turned into lush vineyards. In northern and central England, the rocky soil and damp downs of Lincolnshire, poorly suited to agriculture, were turned into sheep runs. By the third quarter of the twelfth century, the Cistercians were raising sheep and playing a large role in the production of England's staple crop, wool.

Some monasteries got involved in iron and lead mining. In 1291 the Cistercian abbey of Furness operated at least forty forges. The German abbeys of Königsbronn, Waldsassen, and Saabergen also mined iron in the thirteenth century. The monks entered this industry first to fill their own needs, but in an expanding economy they soon discovered a large market. Iron had hundreds of uses. Nails, hammers, plows, armor, axes, stirrups, horseshoes, and spears and many other weapons of war were all made from this basic metal. When King Richard of England was preparing to depart on crusade in 1189, he wanted to take fifty thousand horseshoes with him. Lead also had a great variety of uses. It could be used for roofing; as an alloy for strengthening silver coinage; for framing pane-glass windows in parish, monastery, and cathedral churches; and even for lavatory drainpipes.

Whatever work particular monks did and whatever economic activities individual monasteries were involved in, monks also performed social services and exerted an influence for the good. Monasteries often ran schools that gave primary education to young boys. Abbeys like Saint Albans, situated north of London on a busy thoroughfare, served as hotels and resting places for travelers. Monasteries frequently operated "hospitals" and leprosaria, which provided care—primitive care, it is true, but often all that was available—and attention to the sick, the aged, and the afflicted. In short, monasteries performed a variety of social services in an age when there was no "state" and no conception of social welfare as a public responsibility.

Economic Difficulties

In the twelfth century, expenses in the older Benedictine monastic houses increased more rapidly than did income. The result was a steadily worsening economic situation. Cluny is a good example. Life at Cluny was lavish and extravagant. There were large quantities of rich food. The monks' habits were made of the best cloth available. Cluny's abbots and priors traveled with sizable retinues, as great lords were required to do. The abbots worked to make the liturgy ever more magnificent, and large sums were spent on elaborate vestments and jeweled vessels. Abbot Hugh embarked on an extraordinarily expensive building program. He entirely rebuilt the abbey church, and when Pope Urban II consecrated it in 1095, it was the largest church in Christendom. The monks lived like lords, which in a sense they were.

Revenue came from the hundreds of monasteries scattered across France, Italy, Spain, and England that Cluny had reformed in the eleventh century; each year they paid Cluny a cash sum. Novices were expected to make a gift of land or cash when they entered. For reasons of security, knights departing on crusade often placed their estates under Cluny's authority. Still this income was not enough. The management of Cluny's manors across Europe was entrusted to bailiffs or wardens who were not monks. Many of these bailiffs were poor managers and produced no profits; but, because they had lifetime contracts, they could not be removed and replaced. In order to meet expenses, Cluny had to rely on cash reserves. Cluny's estates produced only a small percentage of needed food supplies; the rest had to be paid for from cash reserves.

Cluny had two basic alternatives: improve management to cut costs or borrow money. The abbey could have placed the monastic manors under the jurisdiction of monks, rather than hiring bailiffs who would grow rich as middlemen. It could have awarded annual rather than lifetime contracts, supervised all revenues, and tried to cut costs within the monastery. Cluny chose the second alter-

Bee Keeping at Monte Cassino Because of the scarcity and expense of sugar, honey was the usual sweetener for pastries and liquids throughout the Middle Ages. This illustrator had never actually seen the process: without veils, nets, and gloves, the bee keepers would be badly stung. *(Source: Biblioteca Apostolica Vaticana)*

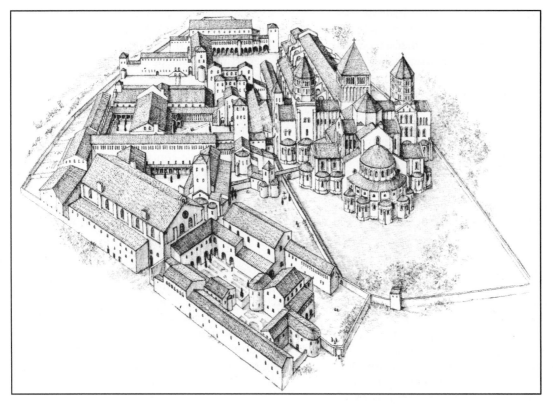

Cluny, ca 1157   Begun in 1085 and supported by the generosity of kings and peasants, the church (right center) and monastery of Cluny was the administrative center of a vast monastic and feudal empire. Note the apse around the east end of the church and the large foreground complex, which served as monastic infirmary and guest hostel. *(Source: The Medieval Academy of America)*

native—borrowing. Consequently, the abbey spent hoarded reserves of cash and fell into debt.

In contrast to the abbot of Cluny, Suger (1122–1151), the superior of the royal abbey of Saint-Denis near Paris, was a shrewd manager. Though he, too, spared no expense to enhance the beauty of his monastery and church, Suger kept an eye on costs and made sure that his properties were soundly managed. But the management of Saint-Denis was unusual. Far more typical was the economic mismanagement at Cluny. By the later twelfth century, small and great monasteries were facing comparable financial difficulties.

SUMMARY

Generalizations about peasant life in the High Middle Ages must always be qualified by manorial customs, by the weather in a given year, and by the personalities of local lords. Everywhere, however, the performance of agricultural services and the payment of rents preoccupied peasants. Though they led hard lives, peasants could achieve some social mobility through exceedingly hard work, luck, or flight to a town.

By 1100 the knightly class was united in its ability to fight on horseback, its insistence that each member was descended from a valorous ancestor, its privileges, and its position at the top of the social hierarchy. The nobility possessed a strong class consciousness. Aristocratic values and attitudes shaded all aspects of medieval culture. However, these characteristics were not typical of Germany, where a sharp distinction existed between nobles and their servile warriors, the ministerials.

Monks exercised a profound influence on matters of the spirit. In their prayers, monks battled for the Lord just as chivalrous knights fought on the battlefield. In their chant and rich ceremonial, in their architecture, and in the example of many monks' lives, the monasteries inspired Christian peoples to an incalculable degree. As the storehouses of sacred art, the monasteries became cultural centers of Christian Europe.

NOTES

1. G. Duby, *The Chivalrous Society,* trans. C. Postan (Berkeley: University of California Press, 1977), pp. 90–93.
2. Honorius of Autun, "Elucidarium sive Dialogus de Summa Totius Christianae Theologiae," in *Patrologia Latina,* vol. 172, ed. J. P. Migne (Paris: Garnier Brothers, 1854), col. 1149.
3. E. Power, "Peasant Life and Rural Conditions," in *The Cambridge Medieval History,* vol. 7, eds. J. R. Tanner et al. (Cambridge, England: Cambridge University Press, 1958), p. 716.
4. Glanvill, "De Legibus Angliae," bk. 5, chap. 5, in *Social Life in Britain from the Conquest to the Reformation,* ed. G. G. Coulton (London: Cambridge University Press, 1956), pp. 338–339.
5. J. B. Freed, *The Friars and German Society in the Thirteenth Century* (Cambridge, Mass.: Mediaeval Academy of America, 1977), p. 55.
6. See W. C. Jordan, *From Servitude to Freedom: Manumission in the Senonais in the Thirteenth Century* (Philadelphia: University of Pennsylvania Press, 1986), esp. chap. 3, pp. 37–58.
7. See L. White, Jr., *Medieval Technology and Social Change* (Oxford: Clarendon Press, 1962), pp. 59–63.
8. G. Duby, *Early Growth of the European Economy: Warriors and Peasants from the Seventh to the Twelfth Century* (Ithaca, N.Y.: Cornell University Press, 1978), pp. 213–219.
9. See B. A. Hanawalt, *The Ties That Bound: Peasant Families in Medieval England* (New York: Oxford University Press, 1986), pp. 90–100.
10. On this quantity and medieval measurements, see "The Measures of Monastic Beverages," in D. Knowles, *The Monastic Order in England* (Cambridge, England: Cambridge University Press, 1962), p. 717.
11. G. Duby, *Rural Economy and Country Life in the Medieval West,* trans. C. Postan (London: Edward Arnold, 1968), pp. 146–147.
12. S. R. Scargill-Bird, ed., *Custumals of Battle Abbey in the Reigns of Edward I and Edward II* (London: Camden Society, 1887), p. 213.
13. M. Warner, *Alone of Her Sex: The Myth and Cult of the Virgin Mary* (New York: Knopf, Wallaby Books, 1978), pp. 305–306 and p. 390.
14. John 19:25–27.
15. J. B. Freed, "The Origins of the European Nobility: The Problem of the Ministerials," *Viator 7* (1976): 213.
16. Duby, *Chivalrous Society,* pp. 104–105.
17. See C. Bouchard, "The Origins of the French Nobility," *The American Historical Review,* vol. 86 (1981): 501–532.
18. Duby, *Chivalrous Society,* p. 98.
19. G. Duby, *The Age of the Cathedrals: Art and Society, 980–1420,* trans. E. Levieux and B. Thompson (Chicago: University of Chicago Press, 1981), p. 38.
20. Freed, "Origins of European Nobility," p. 214.
21. J. Boswell, *The Kindness of Strangers: The Abandonment of Children in Western Europe from Late Antiquity to the Renaissance* (New York: Pantheon Books, 1989), p. 24. This section relies heavily on Boswell's important work.
22. Ibid., pp. 214, 223.
23. Ibid., pp. 428–429.
24. Ibid., pp. 238–239.
25. Ibid., pp. 297, 299, and the Conclusion.
26. F. Benton, ed. and trans., *Self and Society in Medieval France: The Memoirs of Abbot Guibert Nogent* (New York: Harper & Row, 1970), p. 46.
27. J. C. Russell, *Late Ancient and Medieval Population Control* (Philadelphia: American Philosophical Society, 1985), p. 180.
28. See J. B. Freed, "The Counts of Falkenstein: Noble Self-Consciousness in Twelfth-Century Germany," *Transactions of the American Philosophical Society,* vol. 74, pt. 6 (1984): 63–67.
29. See R. J. Leyser, *Rule and Conflict in an Early Medieval Society: Ottonian Saxony* (Bloomington, Ind.: Indiana University Press, 1979), pp. 49–62, esp. p. 59.
30. Honorius of Autun, in *Patrologia Latina,* vol. 172, col. 1148.
31. M. Chibnall, ed. and trans., *The Ecclesiastical History of Orderic Vitalis,* vol. 2 (Oxford: Oxford University Press, 1972), p. xiii.
32. R. W. Southern, *Western Society and the Church in the Middle Ages* (Baltimore: Penguin Books, 1970), pp. 224–230, esp. p. 228.
33. See M. W. Labarge, *A Small Sound of the Trumpet: Women in Medieval Life* (Boston: Beacon Press, 1986), pp. 104–105.
34. J. M. Ferrante, "The Education of Women in the Middle Ages in Theory, Fact, and Fantasy," in *Beyond Their Sex: Learned Women of the European Past,* ed. P. H. Labalme (New York: New York University Press, 1980), pp. 22–24.

SUGGESTED READING

The best short introduction to the material in this chapter is C. Brooke, *The Structure of Medieval Society* (1971), a beautifully illustrated book. The student interested in aspects of medieval slavery, serfdom, or the peasantry should begin with M. Bloch, "How Ancient Slavery Came to an End" and "Personal Liberty and Servitude in the Middle Ages, Particularly in France," in *Slavery and Serfdom in the Middle Ages: Selected Essays* (trans. W. R. Beer, 1975). There is an excellent discussion of these problems in the magisterial work of G. Duby, *Rural Economy and Country Life in the Medieval West* (see the Notes). G. C. Homans, *English Villagers of the Thirteenth Century* (1975), is a fine combination of sociological and historical scholarship; and the older study of H. S. Bennett, *Life on the English Manor: A Study of Peasant Conditions* (1960), contains much useful information presented in a highly readable fashion. E. L. Ladurie, *Montaillou: Cathars and Catholics in a French Village, 1294–1324* (trans. B. Bray, 1978), is a fascinating glimpse of village life. Also cited in the Notes, G. Duby, *Early Growth of the European Economy,* is a superb synthesis by a leading authority. Advanced students should see the same author's *The Three Orders: Feudal Society Imagined* (1980), a brilliant but difficult book.

For the religion of the people, two recent studies are highly recommended: R. Brooke and C. Brooke, *Popular Religion in the Middle Ages* (1984), a highly readable synthesis, and B. Ward, *Miracles and the Medieval Mind* (1982), an important and scholarly study. For the development of lay literacy, see M. T. Clanchy, *From Memory to Written Record: England, 1066–1307* (1979).

For the origins and status of the nobility in the High Middle Ages, students are strongly urged to see the recent and important studies by Bouchard, Duby, and Freed cited in the Notes. See, in addition, the following articles, which appear in F. L. Cheyette, ed., *Lordship and Community in Medieval Europe: Selected Readings* (1968): L. Genicot, "The Nobility in Medieval Francia: Continuity, Break, or Evolution?"; A. Borst, "Knighthood in the High Middle Ages: Ideal and Reality"; and two studies by G. Duby, "The Nobility in Eleventh and Twelfth Century Maconnais" and "Northwestern France: The 'Youth' in Twelfth Century Aristocratic Society." Social mobility among both peasants and nobles is discussed in T. Evergates, *Feudal Society in the Bailliage of Troyes Under the Counts of Champagne, 1152–1284* (1976). Also fundamental are K. F. Bosl, "Kingdom and Principality in Twelfth-Century France" and " 'Noble Unfreedom': The Rise of the Ministerials in Germany," in T. Reuter, ed., *The Medieval Nobility: Studies on the Ruling Classes of France and Germany from the Sixth to the Twelfth Century* (1978), are also fundamental. The older study of M. Bloch, *Feudal Society* (1966), is now somewhat dated. The career of the man described by contemporaries as "the greatest of knights" is celebrated in G. Duby, *William Marshal: The Flowering of Chivalry* (trans. R. How ard, 1985), a remarkable rags-to-riches story.

E. Power, *Medieval Women* (1976), is a nicely illustrated sketch of the several classes of women. For women, marriage, and the family in the High Middle Ages, see D. Herlihy, *Medieval Households* (1985), which describes how medieval families developed ties of kinship and emotional unity; J. McNamara and S. F. Wemple, "Sanctity and Power: The Dual Pursuit of Medieval Women," in R. Bridenthal and C. Koonz, eds., *Becoming Visible: Women in European History* (1977); and E. R. Coleman, "Medieval Marriage Characteristics: A Neglected Factor in the History of Medieval Serfdom," in T. K. Rabb and R. I. Rotberg, eds., *The Family in History: Interdisciplinary Essays* (1973). For health and medical care, see B. Rowland, *Medieval Woman's Guide to Health* (1981).

There is no dearth of good material on the monks in medieval society. The titles listed in Suggested Reading for Chapter 9 represent a good starting point for study. A. Boyd, *The Monks of Durham* (1975), is an excellently illustrated introductory sketch of many facets of monastic culture in the High Middle Ages. B. D. Hill, "Benedictines" and "Cistercian Order," in J. R. Strayer, ed., *Dictionary of the Middle Ages,* vols. 2 and 3 (1982 and 1983), provide broad surveys of the premier monastic orders and contain useful bibliographies. L. J. Lekai, *The Cistercians: Ideals and Reality* (1977), synthesizes recent research on the Cistercians and carries their story down to the twentieth century. P. D. Johnson, *Prayer, Patronage, and Power: The Abbey of La Trinité, Vendôme, 1032–1187* (1981), examines one important French monastery in its social environment; this book is a valuable contribution to medieval local history. T. Verdon, ed., *Monasticism and the Arts* (1984), is a rich compilation of papers on various aspects of monastic culture, some of them written by leading scholars. J. Leclercq, *Monks on Marriage: A Twelfth Century View* (1982), studies marital love literature and gives new insights on medieval attitudes toward sex and marital love. Duby's *The Age of the Cathedrals,* cited in the Notes, is especially strong on the monastic origins of medieval art. Both W. Braunfels, *Monasteries of Western Europe: The Architecture of the Orders* (1972), and C. Brooke, *The Monastic World* (1974), have splendid illustrations and good bibliographies. The best study of medieval English Cistercian architecture is P. Fergusson, *Architecture of Solitude: Cistercian Abbeys in Twelfth Century England* (1984).

14

Creativity and Crisis
in the High and Later
Middle Ages

Caracassone, southern France

The High Middle Ages witnessed several of the most remarkable achievements in the entire history of Western society. Political rulers tried to establish contact with all their peoples, developed new legal and financial institutions, and slowly consolidated power in the hands of the monarchy. The kings of France and England succeeded in laying the foundations of modern national states. The European economy underwent a remarkable recovery, as towns grew and long-distance trade revived. In arts and letters, medieval people expressed their appreciation for the worlds of nature, man, and God, and in the Gothic cathedral they manifested their sense of community and their deep Christian faith.

In the fourteenth century, however, a string of disasters sapped the vitality of European society. Between 1300 and 1450, Europeans experienced a frightful series of shocks: economic dislocation, plague, war, and social upheaval. During the later Middle Ages, the last book of the New Testament—the Book of Revelation, dealing with visions of the end of the world, disease, war, famine, and death—inspired thousands of sermons and hundreds of religious tracts. Death and preoccupation with death make the fourteenth century one of the most wrenching periods of Western civilization.

The progression from the vitality of the High Middle Ages to the crisis of the later Middle Ages brings to mind a number of questions:

- How did medieval rulers in England, France, and Germany work to solve their problems of government, thereby laying the foundations of the modern state?
- How did medieval towns originate, and how do they reveal the beginnings of radical change in medieval society?
- What social needs and attitudes did the development of universities, the Gothic cathedral, and a vernacular literature indicate?
- Why did medieval towns become the center of religious heresy, and what was the church's response?
- How did economic difficulties, plague, and war affect Europeans socially, economically, and politically in the fourteenth century?

- What provoked the division of the church in the fourteenth century, and how did the schism affect the faith of medieval people?
- What dominant features characterized the lives of ordinary people in the late Middle Ages?

This chapter focuses on these questions.

MEDIEVAL ORIGINS OF THE MODERN STATE

Rome's great legacies to Western civilization were the concepts of the state and the law; but for almost five hundred years after the disintegration of the Roman Empire in the West, the state as a reality did not exist. Political authority was completely decentralized. Power was spread among many feudal lords, who gave their localities such protection and security as their strength allowed. The fiefdoms, kingdoms, and territories that covered the continent of Europe did not have the qualities or provide the services of a modern state. They did not have jurisdiction over many people, and their laws affected a relative few. In the mid-eleventh century, there existed many layers of authority—earls, counts, barons, knights—between a king and the ordinary people.

In these circumstances, medieval kings had common goals. The rulers of England, France, and Germany wanted to strengthen and extend royal authority within their territories. They wanted to establish an effective means of communication with all peoples in order to increase public order. They wanted more revenue and efficient bureaucracies. The solutions they found to these problems laid the foundations for modern national states.

The modern state is an organized territory with definite geographical boundaries that are recognized by other states. It has a body of law and institutions of government. If the state claims to govern according to law, it is guided in its actions by the law. The modern national state counts on the loyalty of its citizens, or at least on that of a majority of them. In return, it provides order so that citizens can go about their daily work and other activities. It protects its citizens in their persons and property. The state tries to prevent violence and to apprehend and punish those who commit it. It supplies a currency or medium of exchange that permits financial and commercial transactions. The state conducts relations with foreign governments. In order to accomplish even these minimal functions, the state must have officials, bureaucracies, laws, courts of law, soldiers, information, and money. States with these attributes are relatively recent developments.

Unification and Communication

Under the pressure of the Danish (or Viking) invasions of the ninth and tenth centuries, the seven kingdoms of Anglo-Saxon England united under one king (see page 353). At the same time, England was divided into local units called *shires,* or counties, each under the jurisdiction of a sheriff appointed by the king. The Danish king Canute (r. 1016–1035) and his successor, Edward the Confessor (r. 1042–1066), exercised broader authority than any contemporary ruler on the Continent. All the English *thegns,* or local chieftains, recognized the central authority of the kingship. The

kingdom of England, therefore, had a political head start on the rest of Europe.

When Edward the Confessor died, his cousin Duke William of Normandy—known in English history as "William the Conqueror"—claimed the English throne and in 1066 he defeated the Anglo-Saxon claimant on the battlefield of Hastings. As William subdued the rest of the country, he distributed lands to his Norman followers and assigned specific military quotas to each estate. He also required all feudal lords to swear an oath of allegiance to him as king.

William the Conqueror (r. 1066–1087) preserved the Anglo-Saxon institution of sheriffs representing the king at the local level but replaced Anglo-Saxon sheriffs with Normans. A sheriff had heavy duties. He maintained order in the shire. He caught criminals and punished them in the shire court, over which he presided. He collected taxes and, when the king ordered him to do so, raised an army of foot soldiers. The sheriff also organized adult males in groups of ten, with each member liable for the good behavior of the others. William thus made local people responsible for order in

The Bayeux Tapestry Measuring 231 feet by 19½ inches, the Bayeux Tapestry gives a narrative description of the events surrounding the Norman Conquest of England. The tapestry provides an important historical source for the clothing, armor, and lifestyles of the Norman and Anglo-Saxon warrior class. *(Source: Tapisserie de Bayeux et avec autorisation spéciale de la Ville de Bayeux)*

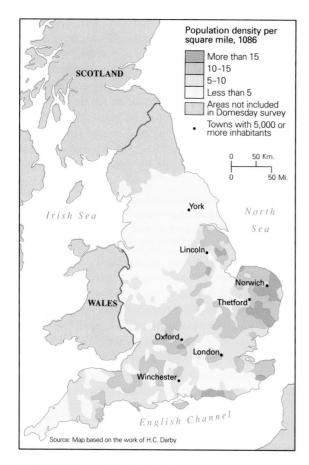

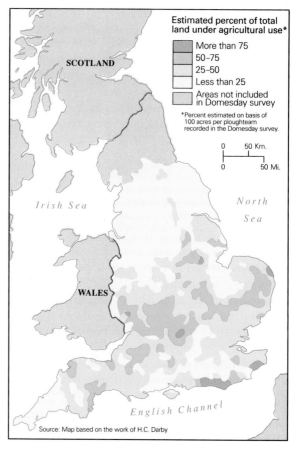

MAP 14.1 Domesday Population and Agriculture, 1086 The incomparably rich evidence of *Domesday Book* enables modern demographers and historians to calculate the English population and land under cultivation in the eleventh century.

their communities. For all his efforts, the sheriff received no pay. This system, whereby unpaid officials governed the county, served as the basic pattern of English local government for many centuries. It cost the Crown nothing, but it restricted opportunities for public service to the well-to-do.

William also retained another Anglo-Saxon device, the *writ*. This brief administrative order, written in the vernacular (Anglo-Saxon) by a government clerk, was the means by which the central government communicated with people at the local level. Sheriffs were empowered to issue writs relating to matters in their counties.

William introduced into England a major innovation, the Norman inquest. To determine how much wealth there was in his new kingdom, who held what land, and what lands had been disputed among his vassals since the conquest of 1066, William in 1086 sent groups of royal officials or judges to every part of the country. In every village and farm, the priest and six local people were put under oath to answer the questions of the king's commissioners truthfully. In the words of a contemporary chronicler:

He sent his men over all England into every shire and had them find out how many hundred hides there were in the shire [a hide was a measure of land large enough to support one family], or what land and cattle the king himself had, or what dues he ought to have in twelve months from the shire. Also . . . what or how much everybody had who was occupying land in England, in land or cattle, and how much money it was worth. So very narrowly did he have it investigated, that there was no single hide nor yard of land, nor indeed . . . one ox nor one cow nor one pig was there left out, and not put down in his record: and all these records were brought to him afterwards.[1]

The resulting record, called *Domesday Book* from the Anglo-Saxon word *doom* meaning "judgment," still survives. It is an invaluable source of social and economic information about medieval England (Map 14.1).

Domesday Book, a unique document, provided William and his descendants with information vital for the exploitation and government of the country. Knowing the amount of wealth every area possessed, the king could tax accordingly. Knowing the amount of land his vassals had, he could allot knight service fairly. The inclusion of material covering all of England helped English kings to regard their country as one unit.

In 1128 William's granddaughter Matilda married Geoffrey of Anjou. Their son, who became Henry II of England and inaugurated the Angevin (from Anjou, his father's county) dynasty, inherited the French provinces of Normandy, Anjou, Maine, and Touraine in northwestern France. When Henry married the great heiress Eleanor of Aquitaine in 1152, he claimed lordships over Aquitaine, Poitou, and Gascony in southwestern France. The territory some students call the "Angevin empire" included most of the British Isles and half of France (see Map 14.2). The histories of England and France in the High Middle Ages were thus closely intertwined.

In the early twelfth century, France consisted of a number of virtually independent provinces. Each was governed by its local ruler; each had its own laws and customs; each had its own coinage; each had its own dialect. Unlike the king of England, the king of France had jurisdiction over a very small area. Chroniclers called King Louis VI (r. 1108–1137) *roi de Saint-Denis,* king of Saint-Denis, because the territory he controlled was limited to Paris and the Saint-Denis area surrounding the city. This region, called the *Île-de-France* or royal domain, became the nucleus of the French state. The term *Saint-Denis* had political and religious charisma, which the Crown exploited. Saint Denis was a deeply revered saint whom the French believed protected the country from danger. The Capetian kings identified themselves with the cult of Saint Denis in order to tap "national" devotion to him and tie that devotion and loyalty to the monarchy.[2] The clear goal of the medieval French king was to increase the royal domain and extend his authority (Map 14.2).

The work of unifying France began under Louis VI's grandson Philip II (r. 1180–1223). Rigord,

Philip's biographer, gave him the title "Augustus" (from a Latin word meaning "to increase") because he vastly enlarged the territory of the kingdom of France. By defeating a baronial plot against the Crown, Philip Augustus acquired the northern counties of Artois and Vermandois. When King John of England, who was Philip's vassal for the rich province of Normandy, defaulted on his feudal obligation to come to the French court, Philip declared Normandy forfeit to the French crown. He enforced his declaration militarily, and in 1204 Normandy fell to the French. Within two years Philip also gained the farmlands of Maine, Touraine, and Anjou. By the end of his reign Philip was effectively master of northern France.

In the thirteenth century, Philip Augustus's descendants acquired important holdings in the south, including the county of Poitou, the Mediterranean province of Provence, and Languedoc. By the end of the thirteenth century, most of the provinces of modern France had been added to the royal domain through diplomacy, marriage, war, and inheritance. The king of France was stronger than any group of nobles who might try to challenge his authority.

Philip Augustus devised a method of governing the provinces and providing for communication between the central government in Paris and local communities. Philip decided that each province would retain its own institutions and laws. But royal agents, called *baillis* in the north and *seneschals* in the south, were sent from Paris into the provinces as the king's official representatives with authority to act for him. Often middle-class lawyers, these men possessed full judicial, financial, and military jurisdiction in their districts. The baillis and seneschals were appointed by, paid by, and responsible to the king. Unlike the English sheriffs, they were never natives of the provinces to which they were assigned, and they could not own land there. This policy reflected the fundamental principle of French administration: royal interests superseded local interests.

English government administration was based on the services of unpaid local officials, but France was administered by a professional royal bureaucracy. As new territories came under royal control, the bureaucracy expanded. So great was the variety of customs, laws, and provincial institutions that any attempt to impose uniformity would have touched off a rebellion. The French system was

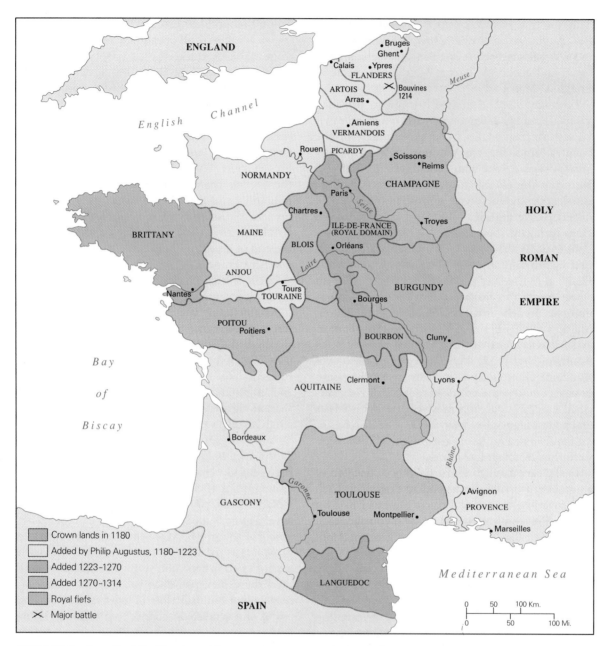

MAP 14.2 The Growth of the Kingdom of France Some scholars believe that Philip II received the title "Augustus" (from a Latin word meaning "to increase") because he vastly expanded the territories of the kingdom of France.

characterized by diversity at the local level and centralization at the top. Although it sometimes fell into disrepair, the basic system that Philip Augustus created worked so well that it survived until the Revolution of 1789.

The political problems of Germany were considerably different from those of France and England. The eleventh-century investiture controversy

between the German emperor and the Roman papacy had left Germany shattered and divided (see pages 359–361). In the twelfth and thirteenth centuries, Germany was split into hundreds of independent provinces, principalities, bishoprics, duchies, and free cities. Princes, dukes, and local rulers maintained power over small areas.

There were several barriers to the development of a strong central government. The German rulers lacked a strong royal domain, like that of the French kings, to use as a source of revenue and a base from which to expand royal power. No accepted principle of succession to the throne existed; as a result, the death of the emperor was often followed by disputes, civil war, and anarchy. Moreover, German rulers were continually attracted south by the wealth of the northern Italian cities or by dreams of restoring the imperial glory of Charlemagne. Time after time the German kings got involved in Italian affairs, and in turn the papacy, fearful of a strong German power in northern Italy, interfered in German affairs. German princes took bribes from whichever authority—the emperor or the pope—best supported their own particular ambitions. Consequently, in medieval Germany, power remained in the hands of numerous princes instead of the king.

When Conrad III died in 1152, the resulting anarchy was so terrible that the *electors*—the seven princes responsible for choosing the emperor—decided the only alternative to continued chaos was the selection of a strong ruler. They chose Frederick Barbarossa of the house of Hohenstaufen.

Frederick Barbarossa (r. 1152–1190) tried valiantly to unify the empire. Just as the French rulers branched out from their compact domain in the Île-de-France, Frederick tried to use his family duchy of Swabia in southwestern Germany as a power base (Map 14.3). Just as William the Conqueror had done, Frederick required all vassals in Swabia to take an oath of allegiance to him as emperor, no matter who their immediate lord might be. He appointed ministerials (see page 386) to exercise the full imperial authority over administrative districts of Swabia. Ministerials linked the emperor and local communities.

Outside of Swabia, Frederick tried to make feudalism work as a system of government. He made alliances with the great lay princes and the great churchmen, who acknowledged that their lands were fiefs of the emperor. Frederick solved the problem of chronic violence by making the princes responsible for the establishment of peace within their territories. At a great assembly held at Roncaglia in 1158, private warfare was forbidden in Italy, and severe penalties were laid down for violations of the peace.

Unfortunately, Frederick Barbarossa did not concentrate his efforts and resources in one area.

He, too, wanted to restore the Holy Roman Empire, joining Germany and Italy and cashing in on the wealth of the northern Italian trading cities. Frederick saw that although the Italian cities were populous and militarily strong, they lacked stable governments and were often involved in struggles with one another. The emperor did not realize that the merchant oligarchs who ran the city governments of Milan, the Venetian republic, and Florence prized their independence and were determined to fight for it. Frederick's desire to control the papacy also attracted him southward. Between 1154 and 1188, Frederick made six expeditions into Italy. After some initial success, he was defeated in 1176 at Legnano (see Map 14.3). Frederick was forced to recognize the municipal autonomy of the northern Italian cities. Germany and Italy remained separate countries and followed separate courses of development.

Frederick Barbarossa's Italian ventures contributed nothing to the unification of the German states. Because the empire lacked a stable bureaucratic system of government, his presence was essential for the maintenance of peace. In Frederick's absences, the fires of independence and disorder spread. The princes and magnates consolidated their power, and the unsupervised royal ministerials gained considerable independence. By 1187 Frederick had to accept again the reality of private warfare. The power of the princes cost the growth of a centralized monarchy.

Finance

As medieval rulers expanded territories and extended authority, they required more officials, larger armies, and more money. Officials and armies had to be paid, and kings had to find ways to raise revenue.

In England, William the Conqueror's son Henry I (r. 1100–1135) established a bureau of finance called the "Exchequer" (for the checkered cloth at which his officials collected and audited royal accounts). Henry's income came from a variety of sources, including taxes paid by peasants living on the king's estates and money paid to the Crown for settling disputes. Henry also received income because of his position as feudal lord, and from the knights he took *scutage,* money paid in lieu of the performance of military service. With the scutage collected, Henry could hire mercenary

0   100   200   300 Km.
0   100   200   300 Mi.

Lübeck
HOLSTEIN
POMERANIA
Bremen
BRANDENBURG
FRISIA
SAXONY
Brandenburg
POLAND
LUSATIA
Goslar
LOWER
LORRAINE
Cologne
THURINGIA
MEISSEN
Aix-la-Chapelle
FRANCONIA
Mainz
Prague
Trier
BOHEMIA
Worms
MORAVIA
Verdun
UPPER
LORRAINE
Toul
AUSTRIA
Augsburg
BAVARIA
SWABIA
Salzburg
STYRIA
FRANCE
Besançon
CARINTHIA
CARNIOLA
HUNGARY
BURGUNDY-
ARLES
VERONA
Legnano 1176
Venice
LOMBARDY
Milan
Pavia
Roncaglia
REPUBLIC OF VENICE
Avignon
Arles
Florence
Marseilles
TUSCANY
PAPAL
STATES
CORSICA
Rome
Capua
APULIA
Naples
Salerno
SARDINIA
KINGDOM OF SICILY
Messina
Palermo
SICILY

✕   Major battle
     Holy Roman Empire, ca 1200
     Kingdom of Sicily
     Republic of Venice

troops. The sheriff in each county was responsible for collecting all these sums and paying them twice a year to the king's Exchequer. Henry, like other medieval kings, made no distinction between his private income and state revenues.

An accurate record of expenditures and income is needed to ensure a state's solvency. Henry assigned a few of the barons and bishops at his court to keep careful records of the moneys paid into and out of the royal treasury. These financial officials, called "barons of the Exchequer," gradually developed a professional organization with its own rules, procedures, and esprit de corps. The Exchequer, which sat in London, became the first institution of England's government bureaucracy.

The development of royal financial agencies in most continental countries lagged behind the English Exchequer. Twelfth-century French rulers derived their income from their royal estates in the Île-de-France. As Philip Augustus and his successors added provinces to the royal domain, the need for money became increasingly acute. Philip made the baillis and seneschals responsible for collecting taxes in their districts, primarily from fines and confiscations imposed by the courts.

In the thirteenth century, French rulers found additional sources of revenue. They acquired some income from the church, and townspeople paid *tallage* or the *taille*—a tax arbitrarily laid by the king. Louis IX converted feudal vassals' military obligation into a cash payment, called "host tallage." Moreover, pervasive anti-Semitism allowed Philip Augustus, Louis VIII, and Louis IX to tax their Jewish subjects mercilessly.

Medieval people believed that a good king lived on the income of his own land and taxed only in time of a grave emergency—a just war. Taxation meant war financing. The French monarchy could not continually justify taxing the people for the needs of war. Thus French kings were slow to develop an efficient bureau of finance. French localism—in contrast to England's early unification—also retarded the growth of a central financial agency. Not until the fourteenth century, as a result of the Hundred Years' War, did a state financial bureau emerge—the Chamber of Accounts.

In the twelfth century, in finance, law, and bureaucratic development, the papal curia represented the most advanced government. The one secular government other than England that developed a financial bureaucracy was the kingdom of Sicily. Sicily is a good example of how strong government could be built on a feudal base by determined rulers.

Like England, Sicily had come under Norman domination. Between 1061 and 1091, a bold Norman knight, Roger de Hauteville, with a small band of mercenaries had defeated the Muslims and Greeks who controlled the island. Like William the Conqueror in England, Roger introduced Norman feudalism in Sicily and made it work as a system of government. Roger distributed scattered fiefs to his followers, so no vassal had a centralized power base. He took an inquest of royal properties and rights, and he forbade private warfare. Roger adapted his Norman experience to Arabic and Greek government practices. Thus he retained the Muslims' main financial agency, the *diwan,* a sophisticated bureau for record keeping.

His son and heir, Count Roger II (r. 1130–1154), continued the process of state building. He had himself crowned king of Sicily and organized the economy in the interests of the state; for example, the Crown secured a monopoly on the sale of salt and lumber. With the revenues thus acquired, Roger hired mercenary troops. His judiciary welcomed appeals from local communities. The army, the judiciary, and the diwan were staffed by Greeks and Muslims as well as Normans.

Frederick II Hohenstaufen (r. 1212–1250), grandson of Roger II and grandson and heir of Frederick Barbarossa, was a brilliant legislator and administrator, and he constructed the most advanced bureaucratic state in medieval Europe. The institutions of the kingdom of Sicily were harnessed in the service of the state as represented by the king.

Frederick banned private warfare and placed all castles and towers under royal administration. He also replaced town officials with royal governors. In 1231 he published the *Constitutions of Melfi,* a collection of laws that vastly enhanced royal authority. Both feudal and ecclesiastical courts were subordinated to the king's courts. Thus churchmen accused of crimes were tried in the royal courts. Royal control of the nobility, of the towns, and of the judicial system added up to great centralization, which required a professional bureaucracy and sound state financing.

MAP 14.3 The Holy Roman Empire, ca 1200

Frederick's financial experts regulated agriculture, public works, even business. His customs service supervised all imports and exports, collecting taxes on all products. Moreover, Frederick secured the tacit consent of his people to regular taxation. This was an amazing achievement, for most people believed that taxes should be levied only in time of grave emergency, the just war. Frederick defined *emergency* broadly. For much of his reign he was involved in a bitter dispute with the papacy. Churchmen hardly considered the emperor's wars with the popes as just, but Frederick was so strong that he could ignore criticism and levy taxes.

Frederick's contemporaries called him the "Transformer of the World." He certainly transformed the kingdom of Sicily, creating a state that was in many ways modern. But Frederick was highly ambitious: he wanted to control the entire peninsula of Italy. The popes, fearful of being encircled, waged a long conflict to prevent that. The kingdom of Sicily required constant attention, and

Frederick's absences took their toll. Shortly after he died, the unsupervised bureaucracy that he had built fell to pieces. The pope, as the feudal overlord of Sicily, called in a French prince to rule.

Frederick showed little interest in Germany. He concentrated on Sicily rather than on the historic Hohenstaufen stronghold in Swabia, and the focus of imperial concerns shifted southward. When he visited the empire, expecting to secure German support for his Italian policy, he made sweeping concessions to the princes, bishops, duchies, and free cities. In 1220, for example, he exempted German churchmen from taxation and from the jurisdiction of imperial authorities. In 1231 he gave lay princes the same exemptions and even threw in the right to coin money. Frederick gave away so much that imperial authority was seriously weakened. In the later Middle Ages, lay and ecclesiastical princes held sway in the Holy Roman Empire. The centralizing efforts of Frederick Barbarossa were destroyed by his grandson Frederick II.

The Chancellery at Palermo Reflecting the fact that Vandals, Ostrogoths, Greeks, Muslims, and Normans had left their imprint on Sicily, the imperial court bureaucracy kept official records in Greek, Arabic, and Latin, as this manuscript illustration shows. *(Source: Burgerbibliothek Bern)*

Law and Justice

Throughout Europe in the twelfth and thirteenth centuries, the law was a hodgepodge of Germanic customs, feudal rights, and provincial practices. Kings wanted to blend these elements into a uniform system of rules acceptable and applicable to all their peoples. In France and England, kings successfully contributed to the development of national states through the administration of their laws. Legal developments in continental countries like France were strongly influenced by Roman law. England slowly built up a unique, unwritten common law.

The French king Louis IX (r. 1226–1270) was famous in his time for his concern for justice. Each French province, even after being made part of the kingdom of France, retained its unique laws and procedures, but Louis IX created a royal judicial system. He established the Parlement of Paris, a kind of supreme court that welcomed appeals from local administrators and from the courts of feudal lords throughout France. By the very act of appealing the decisions of feudal courts to the Parlement of Paris, French people in far-flung provinces were recognizing the superiority of royal justice.

Louis sent royal judges to all parts of the country to check up on the work of the baillis and seneschals and to hear complaints of injustice. He was the first French monarch to publish laws for the entire kingdom. The Parlement of Paris registered (or announced) these laws, which forbade private warfare, judicial duels, gambling, blaspheming, and prostitution. Louis sought to identify justice with the kingship, and gradually royal justice touched all parts of the kingdom.

Under Henry II (r. 1154–1189), England developed and extended a *common law,* a law common to and accepted by the entire country. No other country in medieval Europe did so. Henry I had occasionally sent out *circuit judges* (royal officials who traveled a given circuit or district) to hear civil and criminal cases. Henry II made this way of extending royal justice an annual practice. Every year, royal judges left London and set up court in the counties. Wherever the king's judges sat, there sat the king's court. Slowly, the king's court gained jurisdiction over all property disputes and criminal actions.

Henry also improved procedure in criminal justice. In 1166 he instructed the sheriffs to summon local juries to conduct inquests and draw up lists of known or suspected criminals. These lists, sworn to by the juries, were to be presented to the royal judges when they arrived in the community. This accusing jury is the ancestor of the modern grand jury.

An accused person formally charged with a crime did *not* undergo trial by jury. He or she was tried by ordeal. The accused was tied hand and foot and dropped in a lake or river. People believed that water was a pure substance and would reject anything foul or unclean. Thus a person who sank was considered innocent, and a person who floated was considered guilty. God determined innocence or guilt, and a priest had to be present to bless the water.

Henry II and others considered this ancient Germanic method irrational and a poor way of determining results, but they knew no alternative. In 1215 the Fourth Lateran Council of the church forbade the presence of priests at trials by ordeal and thus effectively abolished them. Gradually, in the course of the thirteenth century, the king's judges adopted the practice of calling on twelve people (other than the accusing jury) to consider the question of innocence or guilt. This became the jury of trial, but it was very slowly accepted because medieval people had more confidence in the judgment of God than in the judgment of twelve ordinary people.

One aspect of Henry's judicial reforms encountered stiff resistance from an unexpected source: a friend and former chief adviser whom Henry had made archbishop of Canterbury—Thomas Becket. In the 1160s many literate people accused of crimes claimed "benefit of clergy" even though they were not clerics and often had no intention of being ordained. Benefit of clergy gave the accused the right to be tried in church courts, which meted out mild punishments. A person found guilty in the king's court might suffer mutilation—loss of a hand or foot, castration—or even death. Ecclesiastical punishments tended to be an obligation to say certain prayers or to make a pilgrimage. In 1164 Henry II insisted that everyone, including clerics, be subject to the royal courts. Becket vigorously protested that church law required clerics to be subject to church courts. The disagreement dragged on for years. The king grew increasingly bitter that his appointment of Becket had proved to be such a mistake. Late in December 1170, in a fit of rage, Henry expressed the wish that Becket

The Martyrdom of Thomas Becket Becket's murder evoked many illustrations in the thirteenth century. This illumination faithfully follows the manuscript sources: while one knight held off the archbishop's defenders, the other three attacked. With a powerful stroke, the crown of Becket's head was slashed off and his brains scattered on the cathedral floor. *(Source: Walters Art Gallery, Baltimore)*

be destroyed. Four knights took the king at his word, went to Canterbury, and killed the archbishop in his cathedral as he was leaving evening services.

What Thomas Becket could not achieve in life, he gained in death. The assassination of an archbishop in his own church during the Christmas season turned public opinion in England and throughout western Europe against the king. Within months, miracles were recorded at Becket's tomb, and in a short time Canterbury Cathedral became a major pilgrimage and tourist site. Henry had to back down. He did public penance for the

murder and gave up his attempts to bring clerics under the authority of the royal court.

Henry II's sons Richard I, who was known as "the Lion-Hearted" (r. 1189–1199), and John (r. 1199–1216) lacked their father's interest in the work of government. Handsome, athletic, and with an international reputation for military prowess, Richard looked on England as a source of revenue for his military enterprises. Soon after his accession, he departed on a crusade to the Holy Land. During his reign he spent only six months in England, and the government was run by ministers trained under Henry II.

Unlike Richard, King John was incompetent as a soldier and unnecessarily suspicious that the barons were plotting against him. His basic problems, however, were financial. King John inherited a heavy debt from his father and brother. The country had paid dearly for Richard's crusading zeal. While returning from the Holy Land, Richard had been captured, and England had paid an enormous ransom to secure his release. In 1204 John lost the rich province of Normandy to Philip Augustus of France and then spent the rest of his reign trying to get it back. To finance that war, John squeezed as much money as possible from his position as feudal lord. He took scutage and each time increased the amount due. He forced widows to pay exorbitant fines to avoid unwanted marriages. He sold young girls who were his feudal wards to the highest bidder. These actions antagonized the nobility.

John also alienated the church and the English townspeople. He rejected Pope Innocent III's nominee to the see of Canterbury. And he infuriated the burghers of the towns by extorting money from them and threatening to revoke their charters of self-government.

All the money that John raised did not bring him success. In July 1214, John's coalition of Flemish, German, and English cavalry suffered a severe defeat at the hands of Philip Augustus of France at Bouvines in Flanders (see Map 14.2). This battle ended English hopes for the recovery of territories from France and also strengthened the barons' opposition to John. On top of his heavy taxation, his ineptitude as a soldier in a society that idealized military glory was the final straw. Rebellion begun by a few hotheaded northern barons eventually grew to involve many of the English nobility. After lengthy negotiations, John was forced to sign the treaty called "Magna

THE EMERGENCE OF STATES

1066	Norman Conquest of England; William the Conqueror requires oath of allegiance from all feudal lords
1085	William introduces the Norman inquest, thereby enabling a systematic investigation of the whole of England
1086	Publication of *Domesday Book*
1095	Pope Urban II calls for the First Crusade
1096–1270	Papacy sponsors the Crusades to recover Jerusalem from the Muslims
1120	Publication of Abelard's *Sic et Non*
1130	Henry I of England establishes the Exchequer, the first governmental bureau of finance in England
	Roger II crowned king of Sicily; establishes a professional royal army
1144	Consecration of the first Gothic church, the abbey church of Saint-Denis
ca 1150–1300	Expansion of church building throughout Europe mirrors growth of towns and expansion of commerce
1152	Henry II marries Eleanor of Aquitaine, thereby gaining control over half of France as well as most of the British Isles (the "Angevin empire")
	Frederick Barbarossa chosen emperor by the German princes; requires oath of allegiance from his vassals
1154–1158	Frederick Barbarossa attempts to restore Holy Roman Empire by invading Italy
1159	Founding of the city of Lübeck, origin of the Hanseatic League
1166	Institution of the accusing jury in England
1170	Assassination of Thomas Becket by Henry II's knights
1176	Battle of Legnano, the first defeat of armed knights by bourgeois infrantrymen; Frederick Barbarossa forced to recognize the autonomy of the northern Italian cities
1180–1223	Philip II (Augustus) extends authority of the French monarchy by conquering most of northern France; hires agents to represent the Crown's interests in the provinces, thus establishing a professional royal bureaucracy
1200	Philip Augustus officially recognizes the University of Paris
1214	John of England defeated by Philip Augustus at Battle of Bouvines; baronial opposition to John increases
1215	Signing of the Magna Carta
1224	Frederick II Hohenstaufen founds the University of Naples
1231	Frederick II enhances royal authority in Sicily by publishing the Constitutions of Melfi, which subordinate feudal and ecclesiastical to royal courts; to gain German support of his efforts to control Italy, he exempts princes from taxation and imperial jurisdiction, thereby weakening royal authority in Germany
1235	Publication of Aquinas's *Summa Theologica*
1296	War opens between Edward I of England and Philip the Fair of France; Pope Boniface VIII attempts to deny kings the power to levy taxes on the Church
1302	Boniface writes *Unam Sanctam*, a letter asserting papal supremacy over monarchies
1303	Philip the Fair orders the arrest of Boniface at Anagni

Carta," which became the cornerstone of English justice and law.

Magna Carta set forth the principle that everyone—including the king and the government—must obey the law. It defends the interests of widows, orphans, townspeople, free men, and the church. Some clauses contain the germ of the ideas of due process of law and the right to a fair and speedy trial. Every English king in the Middle Ages reissued Magna Carta as evidence of his promise to observe the law. Later generations appealed to it as a written statement of English liberties, and it acquired an almost sacred importance as a guarantee of law and justice.

In the thirteenth century, the judicial precedents set under Henry II slowly evolved into permanent institutions. English people found the king's justice more rational and evenhanded than the justice meted out in the baronial courts. Respect for the king's law and courts promoted loyalty to the Crown. By the time of Henry's great-grandson Edward I (r. 1272–1307), one law, the common law, operated all over England.

In the later Middle Ages, the English common law developed features that differed strikingly from the system of Roman law operative in continental Europe. The common law relied on precedents: a decision in an important case served as an authority for deciding similar cases. By contrast, continental judges, trained in Roman law, used the fixed legal maxims of the Justinian *Code* (see pages 256–257) to decide their cases. Thus the common-law system evolved according to the changing experience of the people, and the Roman-law tradition tended toward an absolutist approach. In countries influenced by the common law, such as Canada and the United States, the court is open to the public; in countries with Roman-law traditions, such as France and the Latin American nations, courts need not be public. Under the common law, people accused in criminal cases have a right to access to the evidence against them; under the other system, they need not see the evidence. The common law urges judges to be impartial; in the Roman-law system, judges interfere freely in activities in their courtrooms. Finally, whereas torture is foreign to the common-law tradition, it was once widely used in the Roman legal system.

The extension of law and justice led to a phenomenal amount of legal codification all over Europe. Legal texts and encyclopedias exalted royal authority, consolidated royal power, and emphasized political and social uniformity. The pressure for social conformity in turn contributed to a rising hostility toward minorities, Jews, and homosexuals.

By the late eleventh century, many towns in western Europe had small Jewish populations. Jews typically earned their livelihoods in the lesser trades or by lending money at interest. The laws of most countries forbade Jews to own land, though they could hold land pledged to them for debts. By the twelfth century, many Jews were usurers: they lent to consumers but primarily to new or growing business enterprises. New towns and underdeveloped areas where cash was scarce welcomed Jewish settlers. Like other business people, the Jews preferred to live near their work; they also settled close to their synagogue or school. Thus originated the Jews' street or quarter or ghetto. Such neighborhoods gradually became legally defined sections where Jews were required to live.

Through the twelfth century, Jews had been generally tolerated and had become important participants in urban economies through trade and finance. The later twelfth and entire thirteenth centuries, however, witnessed increasingly ugly anti-Semitism. Shifting agricultural and economic patterns aggravated social tensions. The indebtedness of peasants and nobles to Jews in an increasingly cash-based economy; the xenophobia that accompanied and followed the Crusades; Christian merchants' and financiers' resentment of Jewish business competition; the spread of vicious accusations of ritual murders or sacrileges against Christian property and persons; royal and papal legislation aimed at social conformity—these factors all contributed to rising anti-Semitism. Thus, from 1180 to 1182, Philip Augustus of France used hostility to Jews as an excuse to imprison them and then to demand heavy ransom for their release. The Fourth Lateran Council (1215) forbade Jews to hold public office, restricted their financial activities, and required them to wear distinctive clothing. In 1290 Edward I of England capitalized on mercantile and other resentment of Jews to expel them from the country in return for a large parliamentary grant. In 1302 Philip IV of France followed suit by expelling the Jews from his kingdom and confiscating their property. Fear, ignorance, greed, stupidity, and the pressure for social conformity all played a part in anti-Semitism of the High Middle Ages.

Early Christians displayed no special prejudice against homosexuals (see page 239). Some of the church fathers, such as Saint John Chrysostom (347–407), preached against them, but a general indifference to homosexual activity prevailed throughout the early Middle Ages. In the early twelfth century, a large homosexual literature circulated. Publicly known homosexuals such as Ralph, archbishop of Tours (1087–1118), and King Richard I of England held high ecclesiastical and political positions.

Beginning in the late twelfth century, however, a profound change occurred in public attitudes toward homosexual behavior. Why did this happen, if prejudice against homosexuals cannot be traced to early Christianity? Scholars have only begun to investigate this question, and the root cause of intolerance rarely yields to easy analysis. In the thirteenth century, heretics were the most despised minority in an age that stressed religious and social uniformity, and the notion spread that both Muslims and heretics—the great foreign and domestic menaces to the security of Christian Europe—were inclined to homosexual relations. Finally, the systematization of law and the rising strength of the state made any religious or sexual distinctiveness increasingly unacceptable. Whatever the precise cause, "between 1250 and 1300 homosexual activity passed from being completely legal in most of Europe to incurring the death penalty in all but a few legal compilations."[3] Spain, France, England, Norway, and several Italian city-states adopted laws condemning homosexual acts. Most of these laws remained on statute books until the twentieth century. Anti-Semitism and hostility to homosexuals reflect a dark and evil side to high medieval culture, not the general creativity and vitality of the period.

ECONOMIC REVIVAL

A salient manifestation of Europe's recovery after the tenth-century disorders and of the vitality of the High Middle Ages was the rise of towns and the development of a new business and commercial class. This development was to lay the foundations for Europe's transformation, centuries later, from a rural agricultural society into an industrial urban society—a change with global implications.

Why and how did these developments occur when they did? Part of the answer has already been given. Without increased agricultural output, there would not have been an adequate food supply for new town dwellers. Without a rise in population, there would have been no one to people the towns. Without a minimum of peace and political stability, merchants could not have transported and sold goods.

The Rise of Towns

Early medieval society was traditional, agricultural, and rural. The emergence of a new class that

was none of these constituted a social revolution. The new class—artisans and merchants—came from the peasantry. They were landless younger sons of large families, driven away by land shortage. Or they were forced by war and famine to seek new possibilities. Or they were unusually enterprising and adventurous, curious and willing to take a chance.

Some scholars believe that towns began as *boroughs*—that is, as fortifications erected during the ninth-century Viking invasions. According to this view, towns were at first places of defense into which farmers from the surrounding countryside moved when their area was attacked. Most residents of early towns made their living by farming outside the town.

Later, merchants were attracted to the fortifications because they had something to sell and wanted to be where customers were. Usually traders settled just outside the walls, in the *faubourgs* or *suburbs*—both of which mean "outside" or "in the shelter of the walls." As their markets prospered and as their number outside the walls grew, the merchants built a new wall around themselves, every century or so. According to Belgian historian Henri Pirenne, a medieval town consisted architecturally of a number of concentric walls.

The great cathedrals and monasteries, too, played a part, representing a demand for goods and services. Cathedrals such as Notre Dame in Paris conducted schools that drew students from far and wide. Consequently, traders and merchants settled near religious establishments to cater to the residents' economic needs.

Few towns of the tenth and eleventh centuries were "new" in the sense that American towns and cities were new in the seventeenth and eighteenth centuries. They were not carved out of forest and wilderness. Some medieval towns that had become flourishing centers of trade by the mid-twelfth century had originally been Roman army camps. York in northern England and Cologne in west central Germany are good examples of ancient towns that underwent revitalization in the eleventh century. Some Italian seaport cities, such as Venice, Pisa, and Genoa, had been centers of shipping and commerce in earlier times. Muslim attacks and domestic squabbles had cut their populations and drastically reduced the volume of their trade in the early Middle Ages, but trade with Constantinople and the East had never stopped entirely. The restoration of order and political stability promoted rebirth and new development. The twelfth century also witnessed the foundation of completely new towns, such as Lübeck, Berlin, and Munich.

Whether evolving from a newly fortified place or an old Roman army camp, from a cathedral site or a river junction or a place where several overland routes met, medieval towns had a few common characteristics. Walls enclosed the town. The terms *burgher* and *bourgeois* derive from the Old English and Old German words *burg, burgh, borg,* and *borough* for "a walled or fortified place." Thus a burgher or bourgeois was originally a person who lived or worked inside the walls. The town had a marketplace. It often had a mint for the coining of money and a court to settle disputes.

In each town, many people inhabited a small, cramped area. As population increased, towns rebuilt their walls, expanding the living space to accommodate growing numbers. Through an archeological investigation of the amount of land gradually enclosed by walls, historians have gained a rough estimate of medieval town populations. For example, the walled area of the German city of Cologne equaled 100 hectares in the tenth century (1 hectare = 2.471 acres), about 185 hectares in 1106, about 320 in 1180, and 397 in the fourteenth century. In 1180 Cologne's population was at least 32,000; in the mid-fourteenth century, perhaps 40,000.[4] (By contrast, in the twelfth century some cities in the western Sudan in Africa such as Kumbi, Timbuctu, and Gao may have had populations of between 15,000 and 20,000.) The concentration of the textile industry in the Netherlands brought into being the most populous cluster of cities in western Europe: Ghent with about 56,000 people, Bruges with 27,000, Tournai and Brussels, each with perhaps 20,000.[5] Paris, together with Milan, Venice, and Florence, each with about 80,000, led all Europe in population.

In their backgrounds and abilities, townspeople represented diversity and change. They constituted an entirely new element in medieval society. They fit into none of the traditional categories. Their occupations, their preoccupations, were different from those of the feudal nobility and the laboring peasantry.

The aristocratic nobility glanced down with contempt and derision at the money-grubbing townspeople but were not above borrowing from them. The rural peasantry peered up with suspicion and fear at the town dwellers. Though some fled to the towns seeking wealth and freedom, what was the point, most farmers wondered, of making money? Only land had real permanence. Nor did the new commercial class make much sense initially to churchmen. The immediate goal of the middle class was obviously not salvation. It was to be a good while before churchmen developed a theological justification for the new class.

Town Liberties

In the words of the Greek poet Alcaeus, "Not houses finely roofed or well built walls, nor canals or dockyards make a city, but men able to use their opportunity."[6] Men and opportunity. That is fundamentally what medieval towns meant—concentrations of people and varieties of chances. No matter where groups of traders congregated, they settled on someone's land and had to secure from king or count, abbot or bishop, permission to live and trade. Aristocratic nobles and churchmen were suspicious of and hostile to the middle class. They soon realized, however, that profits and benefits flowed to them and their territories from the markets set up on their land.

The history of towns in the eleventh through thirteenth centuries consists largely of merchants' efforts to acquire liberties. In the Middle Ages, *liberties* meant special privileges. For the town dweller, liberties included the privilege of living and trading on the lord's land. The most important privilege a medieval townsperson could gain was personal freedom. It gradually developed that an individual who lived in a town for a year and a day, and was accepted by the townspeople, was free of servile obligations and status. More than anything else, perhaps, the liberty of personal freedom that came with residence in a town contributed to the emancipation of the serfs in the High Middle Ages. Liberty meant citizenship, and citizenship in a town implied the right to buy and sell goods there. Unlike foreigners and outsiders of any kind, a full citizen did not have to pay taxes and tolls in the market. Obviously, this increased profits.

In the twelfth and thirteenth centuries, towns fought for, and slowly gained, legal and political rights. Since the tenth century, some English boroughs had held courts with jurisdiction over members of the town in civil and criminal matters. In the twelfth century, such English towns as Lon-

Hammering Cobblestones into place on a roadbed made of loose earth, laborers pave the highways leading from the walled city of Bavay in France. Upkeep of the roads and walls were often a town's greatest expenses. *(Source: Bibliothèque royale Albert 1ᵉʳ, Brussels)*

don and Norwich developed courts that applied a special kind of law, called "law merchant." It dealt with commercial transactions, debt, bankruptcy, proof of sales, and contracts. Gradually, towns across Europe acquired the right to hold municipal courts that alone could judge members of the town. In effect, this right gave them judicial independence.[7]

In the acquisition of full rights of self-government, the *merchant guilds* played a large role. Medieval people were long accustomed to communal enterprises. In the late tenth and early eleventh centuries, those who were engaged in foreign trade joined together in merchant guilds; united enterprise provided them greater security and less

risk of losses than did individual action. At about the same time, the artisans and craftsmen of particular trades formed their own guilds. These were the butchers, bakers, and candlestick makers. Members of the *craft guilds* determined the quality, quantity, and price of the goods produced and the number of apprentices and journeymen affiliated with the guild.

Recent research indicates that by the fifteenth century, women composed the majority of the adult urban population. Many women were heads of households.[8] They engaged in every kind of urban commercial activity, both as helpmates to their husbands and independently. Craft guilds provided greater opportunity for women than did merchant guilds. In many manufacturing trades women predominated, and in some places women were a large percentage of the labor force. In fourteenth-century Frankfurt, for example, about 33 percent of the crafts and trades were entirely female. In late-twelfth-century Cologne, women and men had equal rights in the turners' guild (the guild for those who made wooden objects on a lathe). Most members of the Paris silk and woolen trades were women, and some achieved the mastership. Widows frequently followed their late husbands' professions, but if they remarried outside the craft, they lost the mastership. Guild records show that women received lower wages than men for the same work, on the grounds that they needed less income.

By the late eleventh century, especially in the towns of the Low Countries and northern Italy, the leaders of the merchant guilds were quite rich and powerful. They constituted an oligarchy in their towns, controlling economic life and bargaining with kings and lords for political independence. Full rights of self-government included the right to hold a town court, the right to select the mayor and other municipal officials, and the right to tax and collect taxes. Kings often levied on their serfs and unfree townspeople the arbitrary tax, tallage. Such a tax (also known as "customs") called attention to the fact that men were not free. Citizens of a town much preferred to levy and collect their own taxes.

A charter that King Henry II of England granted to the merchants of Lincoln around 1157 nicely illustrates the town's rights. The passages that follow clearly suggest that the merchant guild had been the governing body in the city for almost a century and that anyone who lived in Lincoln for a year and a day was considered free:

Henry, by the grace of God, etc. . . . Know that I have granted to my citizens of Lincoln all their liberties and customs and laws which they had in the time of Edward [King Edward the Confessor] and William and Henry, kings of England. And I have granted them their gild-merchant, comprising men of the city and other merchants of the shire, as well and freely as they had it in the time of our aforesaid predecessors, kings of England. . . . I also confirm to them that if anyone has lived in Lincoln for a year and a day without dispute from any claimant, and has paid the customs, and if the citizens can show by the laws and customs of the city that the claimant has remained in England during

that period and has made no claim, then let the defendant remain in peace in my city of Lincoln as my citizen, without [having to defend his] right.[9]

Kings and lords were reluctant to grant towns self-government, fearing loss of authority and revenue if they gave the merchant guilds full independence. But the lords discovered that towns attracted increasing numbers of people to an area—people whom the lords could tax. Moreover, when burghers bargained for a town's political independence, they offered sizable amounts of ready cash. Consequently, feudal lords ultimately agreed to self-government.

Town Life

Protective walls surrounded almost all medieval towns and cities. The valuable goods inside a town were too much of a temptation to marauding bands for the town to be without the security of bricks and mortar. The walls were pierced by gates, and visitors waited at the gates to gain entrance to the town. When the gates were opened early in the morning, guards inspected the quantity and quality of the goods brought in and collected the customary taxes. Part of the taxes went to the king or lord on whose land the town stood, part to the town council for civic purposes. Constant repair of the walls was usually the town's greatest expense.

Peasants coming from the countryside and merchants traveling from afar set up their carts as stalls just inside the gates. The result was that the road nearest the gate was the widest thoroughfare. It was the ideal place for a market, because everyone coming in or going out used it. Most streets in a medieval town were marketplaces as much as passages for transit. Yet they were generally narrow, just wide enough to transport goods.

Medieval cities served, above all else, as markets. In some respects the entire city was a marketplace. The place where a product was made and sold was also typically the merchant's residence. Usually the ground floor was the scene of production. A window or door opened from the main workroom directly onto the street. The window displayed the finished product, and passers-by could look in and see the goods being produced. The merchant's family lived above the business on the second or third floor. As the business and the family expanded, the merchant built additional stories on top of the house.

Because space within the town walls was limited, expansion occurred upward. Second and third stories were built jutting out over the ground floor and thus over the street. Neighbors on the opposite side did the same. Since the streets were narrow to begin with, houses lacked fresh air and light. Initially, houses were made of wood and thatched with straw. Fire represented a constant danger, and because houses were built so close together, fires spread rapidly. Municipal governments consequently urged construction in stone or brick.

Most medieval cities developed haphazardly. There was little town planning. As the population increased, space became more and more limited. Air and water pollution presented serious problems. Many families raised pigs for household consumption in sties next to the house. Horses and oxen, the chief means of transportation and power, dropped tons of dung on the streets every

Hamburg Cattle Market In the twelfth and thirteenth centuries, Hamburg, located on the Elbe near the river's mouth on the North Sea, gained great commercial importance, and its alliance (1241) with Lübek became the basis of the Hanseatic League. Pigs and cattle were among the vast merchandise offered for sale. The market court (background) sold licenses, set prices, and settled disputes. *(Source: Staatsarchiv Hamburg)*

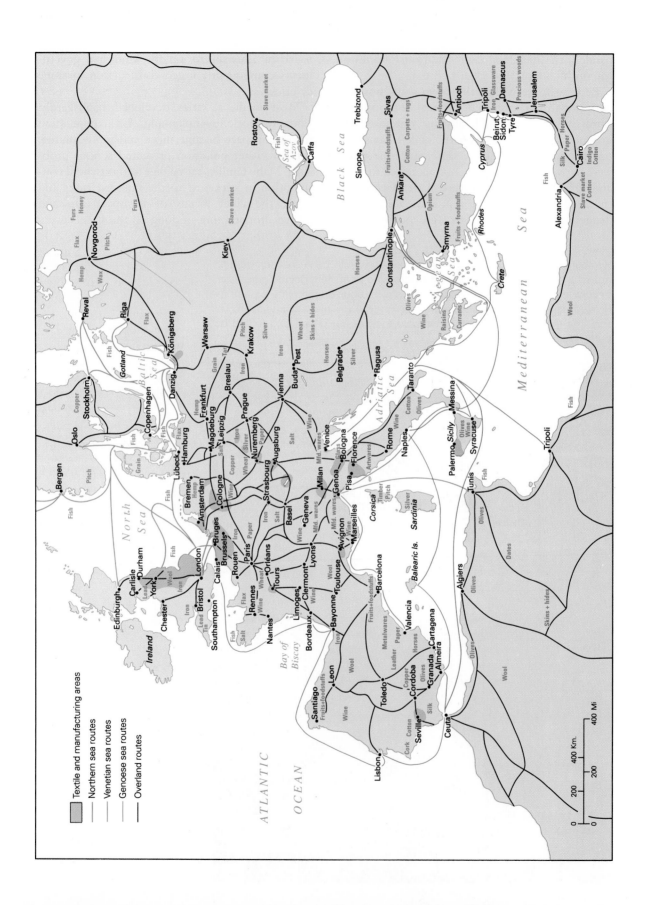

Textile and manufacturing areas

—— Northern sea routes
—— Venetian sea routes
—— Genoese sea routes
—— Overland routes

ATLANTIC

OCEAN

Bay of Biscay

Ireland

North Sea

Baltic Sea

Gotland

Black Sea

Sea of Azov

Aegean Sea

Mediterranean Sea

Adriatic Sea

Corsica

Sardinia

Balearic Is.

Sicily

Crete

Cyprus

Rhodes

Bergen

Oslo

Stockholm

Copenhagen

Reval

Riga

Novgorod

Rostov

Kiev

Königsberg

Warsaw

Krakow

Danzig

Lübeck

Hamburg

Bremen

Amsterdam

Bruges

Brussels

London

York

Durham

Carlisle

Edinburgh

Chester

Bristol

Southampton

Calais

Rouen

Paris

Orléans

Rennes

Nantes

Tours

Limoges

Bordeaux

Bayonne

Clermont

Toulouse

Lyons

Geneva

Basel

Strasbourg

Cologne

Frankfurt

Magdeburg

Leipzig

Prague

Nuremberg

Augsburg

Vienna

Buda

Pest

Belgrade

Ragusa

Breslau

Milan

Genoa

Pisa

Florence

Bologna

Venice

Rome

Naples

Taranto

Palermo

Messina

Syracuse

Tunis

Algiers

Tripoli

Marseilles

Avignon

Barcelona

Valencia

Cartagena

Almería

Granada

Córdoba

Seville

Ceuta

Toledo

Leon

Santiago

Lisbon

Constantinople

Sinope

Trebizond

Caffa

Ankara

Sivas

Smyrna

Antioch

Tripoli

Beirut

Sidon

Tyre

Damascus

Jerusalem

Cairo

Alexandria

Furs
Honey
Flax
Hemp
Wax
Pitch
Fish
Slave market
Fish
Furs
Copper
Pitch
Grain
Fish
Flax
Flax
Hemp
Grain
Pitch
Silver
Iron
Wheat
Skins + hides
Horses
Silver
Wine
Olives
Wine
Wine
Raisins
Currants
Olives
Wine
Olives
Wine
Cotton
Olives
Fish
Fish
Olives
Dates
Skins + hides
Wool
Olives
Wool
Olives
Olives
Fish
Wool
Wool
Olives
Metalwares
Paper
Leather
Horses
Silk
Copper
Olives
Cork
Cotton
Fruits+foodstuffs
Wine
Fruits+foodstuffs
Fruits+foodstuffs
Wool
Wheat
Wine
Iron
Salt
Fish
Lead
Tin
Iron
Lead
Iron
Wool
Flax
Salt
Wine
Paper
Iron
Copper
Salt
Wheat
Wine
Salt
Silver
Iron
Paper
Mfd. wares
Mfd. wares
Glass
Artwares
Timber
Pitch
Silver
Cotton
Olives
Wine
Fish
Wool
Fish
Fruits+foodstuffs
Opium
Fruits+foodstuffs
Fruits+foodstuffs
Cotton
Carpets + rugs
Fruits+foodstuffs
Iron
Glassware
Precious woods
Silk
Paper
Horses
Slave market
Cotton
Indigo
Cotton
Horses
Grain
Wheat
Iron
Iron
Salt
Tar
Salt
Silver
Hemp

0   200   400 Km.
0   200   400 Mi

year. It was universal practice in the early towns to dump household waste, both animal and human, into the road in front of one's house. The stench must have been abominable. In 1298 the burgesses of the town of Boutham in Yorkshire, England, received the following order (one long, vivid sentence):

To the bailiffs of the abbot of St. Mary's York, at Boutham. Whereas it is sufficiently evident that the pavement of the said town of Boutham is so very greatly broken up . . . , and in addition the air is so corrupted and infected by the pigsties situated in the king's highways and in the lanes of that town and by the swine feeding and frequently wandering about . . . and by dung and dunghills and many other foul things placed in the streets and lanes, that great repugnance overtakes the king's ministers staying in that town and also others there dwelling and passing through, the advantage of more wholesome air is impeded, the state of men is grievously injured, and other unbearable inconveniences . . . , to the nuisance of the king's ministers aforesaid and of others there dwelling and passing through, and to the peril of their lives . . . : the king, being unwilling longer to tolerate such great and unbearable defects there, orders the bailiffs to cause the pavement to be suitably repaired within their liberty before All Saints next, and to cause the pigsties, aforesaid streets and lanes to be cleansed from all dung and dunghills, and to cause them to be kept thus cleansed hereafter, and to cause proclamation to be made throughout their bailiwick forbidding any one, under pain of grievous forfeiture, to cause or permit their swine to feed or wander outside his house in the king's streets or the lanes aforesaid.[10]

A great deal of traffic passed through Boutham in 1298 because of the movement of English troops to battlefronts in Scotland. Conditions there were probably not typical. Still, this document suggests that space, air pollution, and sanitation problems bedeviled urban people in medieval times, as they do today.

As members of the bourgeoisie gained in wealth, they expressed their continuing Christian

MAP 14.4 Trade and Manufacturing in Medieval Europe Note the number of cities and the sources of silver, iron, copper, lead, paper, wool, carpets and rugs, and slaves.

faith by refurbishing old churches, constructing new ones, and giving stained-glass windows, statues, and carvings. The twelfth-century chronicler William of Newburgh could proudly boast that the city of London had 126 parish churches, in addition to 13 monastic churches and the great cathedral of Saint Paul's.

The Revival of Long-Distance Trade

The eleventh century witnessed a remarkable revival of trade as artisans and craftsmen manufactured goods for local and foreign consumption (Map 14.4). Because long-distance trade was risky and required large investments of capital, it could be practiced only by professionals. The transportation of goods involved serious risks. Shipwrecks were common. Pirates infested the sea lanes, and robbers and thieves roamed virtually all of the land routes. Since the risks were so great, merchants preferred to share them. A group of people would thus pool some of their capital to finance an expedition to a distant place. When the ship or caravan returned and the goods brought back were sold, the investors would share the profits. If disaster struck the caravan, an investor's loss was limited to the amount of that individual's investment.

In the late eleventh century, the Italian cities, especially Venice, led the West in trade in general and completely dominated the Eastern market. Ships carried salt from the Venetian lagoon, pepper and other spices from North Africa, and silks and purple textiles from the East to northern and western Europe. In the thirteenth century, Venetian caravans brought slaves from the Crimea and Chinese silks from Mongolia to the West. Lombard and Tuscan merchants exchanged those goods at the town markets and regional fairs of France, Flanders, and England. (Fairs were periodic gatherings that attracted buyers, sellers, and goods from all over Europe.) Flanders controlled the cloth industry. The towns of Bruges, Ghent, and Ypres built up a vast industry in the manufacture of cloth. Italian merchants exchanged their products for Flemish tapestries, fine broadcloth, and various other textiles.

Two circumstances help to explain the lead in long-distance trade gained by Venice and the Flemish towns. Both enjoyed a high degree of peace and political stability. Geographical factors were equally, if not more, important. Venice was ideally located at the northwestern end of the Adriatic Sea, with easy access to the transalpine land routes as well as the Adriatic and Mediterranean sea lanes. The markets of North Africa, Byzantium, and Russia and the great fairs of Ghent in Flanders and Champagne in France provided commercial opportunities that Venice quickly seized. The geographical situation of Flanders also offered unusual possibilities. Just across the channel from England, Flanders had easy access to English wool. Indeed, Flanders and England developed a very close economic relationship.

Wool was the cornerstone of the English medieval economy. Population growth in the twelfth century and the success of the Flemish and Italian textile industries created foreign demand for English wool. This demand stimulated Flemish manufacturing, and the expansion of the Flemish cloth industry in turn spurred the production of English wool. The availability of raw wool also encouraged the development of cloth manufacture in England. The towns of Lincoln, York, Leicester, Northampton, Winchester, and Exeter became important cloth-producing towns. The port cities of London, Hull, Boston, and Bristol thrived on the wool trade. In the thirteenth century, commercial families in these towns grew fabulously rich.

The wool and cloth trades serve as a good barometer of the economic growth and decline of English towns. The supply of wool depended on such natural factors as weather, the amount of land devoted to grazing, and the prevalence of sheep disease, or *scab*. The price of wool, unlike the price of wheat or other foodstuffs, was determined not by supply but by demand. Changes in demand—often the result of political developments over which merchants had no control—could severely damage the wool trade. In the 1320s, for example, violent disorder exploded in the Flemish towns, causing a sharp drop in demand for English wool. When wool exports fell, the economies of London, Hull, and Southampton slumped. Then, during the Hundred Years' War (see pages 441–446), the English crown laid increasingly high export taxes on raw wool, and again the wool trade suffered. On the other hand, the decline of wool exports encouraged the growth of domestic cloth manufacturing and led in the fourteenth century to some population growth along with considerable prosperity in English centers of cloth production.

The Commercial Revolution

A steadily expanding volume of international trade from the late eleventh through the thirteenth centuries was a sign of the great economic surge, but it was not the only one. In cities all across Europe, trading and transportation firms opened branch offices. Credit was widely extended, considerably facilitating exchange. Merchants devised the letter of credit, which made unnecessary the slow and dangerous shipment of coin for payment.

A new capitalistic spirit developed. Professional merchants were always on the lookout for new markets and opportunities. They invested surplus capital in a wide variety of operations. The typical prosperous merchant in the late thirteenth century might be involved in buying and selling, shipping, lending some capital at interest, and engaging in other types of banking. Medieval merchants were fiercely competitive.

Some scholars consider capitalism a modern phenomenon, beginning in the fifteenth or sixteenth century. But in their use of capital to make more money, in their speculative pursuits and willingness to gamble, in their competitive spirit, and in the variety of their interests and operations, medieval businessmen displayed capitalistic traits.

The ventures of the German Hanseatic League illustrate these impulses. The Hanseatic League was a mercantile association of towns. Though scholars trace the league's origin to the foundation of the city of Lübeck in 1159, the mutual protection treaty later signed between Lübeck and Hamburg marks the league's actual expansion. During the next century, perhaps two hundred cities from Holland to Poland, including Cologne, Brunswick, Dortmund, Danzig, and Riga, joined the league, but Lübeck always remained the dominant member. From the thirteenth to the sixteenth century, the Hanseatic League controlled trade over a Novgorod-Reval-Lübeck-Hamburg-Bruges-London axis—that is, the trade of northern Europe (see Map 11.4). In the fourteenth century, Hanseatic merchants branched out into southern Germany and Italy by land and into French, Spanish, and Portuguese ports by sea.

Across regular, well-defined trade routes along the Baltic and North seas, the ships of league cities carried furs, wax, copper, fish, grain, timber, and wine. These goods were exchanged for finished products, mainly cloth and salt, from western cities. At cities such as Bruges and London, Hanseatic merchants secured special trading concessions exempting them from all tolls and allowing them to trade at local fairs. Hanseatic merchants established foreign trading centers called "factories." The most famous of these was the London Steelyard, a walled community with warehouses, offices, a church, and residential quarters for company representatives.[11]

By the late thirteenth century, Hanseatic merchants had developed an important business technique, the business register. Merchants publicly recorded their debts and contracts and received a league guarantee for them. This device proved a decisive factor in the later development of credit and commerce in northern Europe.[12] These activities required capital, risk taking, and aggressive pursuit of opportunities—the essential ingredients of capitalism. They also yielded fat profits.

These developments added up to what one modern scholar who knows the period well has called "a commercial revolution, . . . probably the greatest turning point in the history of our civilization."[13] This is not a wildly extravagant statement. In the long run, the commercial revolution of the High Middle Ages brought about radical change in European society. One remarkable aspect of this change is that the commercial classes did not constitute a large part of the total population—never more than 10 percent. They exercised an influence far in excess of their numbers.

The commercial revolution created a great deal of new wealth. Wealth meant a higher standard of living. The new availability of something as simple as spices, for example, allowed for variety in food. Dietary habits gradually changed. Tastes became more sophisticated. Contact with Eastern civilizations introduced Europeans to eating utensils such as forks. Table manners improved. Nobles learned to eat with forks and knives instead of tearing the meat from a roast with their hands. They began to use napkins instead of wiping their greasy fingers on the dogs lying under the table.

The existence of wealth did not escape the attention of kings and other rulers. Wealth could be taxed, and through taxation kings could create strong and centralized states. In the years to come, alliances with the middle classes were to enable kings to defeat feudal powers and aristocratic interests and to build the states that came to be called "modern."

The commercial revolution also provided the opportunity for thousands of serfs to improve

Hanseatic League Merchants at Hamburg In the thirteenth century, the merchants of Hamburg and other cities in northern Germany formed an association for the suppression of piracy and the acquisition of commercial privileges in foreign countries. Members of the Hansa traded in furs, fish, wax, and oriental luxury goods. *(Source: Staatsarchiv Hamburg)*

their social position. The slow but steady transformation of European society from almost completely rural and isolated to relatively more sophisticated constituted the greatest effect of the commercial revolution that began in the eleventh century.

Even so, merchants and business people did not run medieval communities, except in central and northern Italy and in the county of Flanders. Most towns remained small. The castle, the manorial village, and the monastery dominated the landscape. The feudal nobility and churchmen determined the preponderant social attitudes, values, and patterns of thought and behavior. The commercial changes of the eleventh through thirteenth centuries did, however, lay the economic foundations for the development of urban life and culture.

MEDIEVAL UNIVERSITIES

Just as the first strong secular states emerged in the thirteenth century, so did the first universities. This was no coincidence. The new bureaucratic states and the church needed educated administrators, and universities were a response to this need. The word *university* derives from the Latin *universitas*, meaning "corporation" or "guild." Medieval universities were educational guilds that produced educated and trained individuals. They were also an expression of the tremendous vitality and creativity of the High Middle Ages. Their organization, methods of instruction, and goals continue to influence institutionalized learning in the Western world.

Origins

In the early Middle Ages, anyone who received education got it from a priest. Few boys acquired elementary literacy, and girls did not obtain even that. Few schools were available. Society was organized for war and defense and gave slight support to education. But by the late eleventh century, social conditions had markedly improved. There was greater political stability, and favorable economic conditions had advanced many people beyond the level of bare subsistence. The curious and able felt the lack of schools and teachers.

Since the time of the Carolingian Empire, monasteries and cathedral schools had offered the only formal instruction available. Monasteries, geared to religious concerns, wished to maintain an atmosphere of seclusion and silence and were unwilling to accept large numbers of noisy lay students. In contrast, schools attached to cathedrals and run by the bishop and his clergy were frequently situated in bustling cities, and by the eleventh century in Italian cities like Bologna, wealthy businessmen had established municipal schools. Cities inhabited by peoples of many backgrounds and "nationalities" stimulated the growth and exchange of ideas. In the course of the twelfth century, cathedral schools in France and municipal schools in Italy developed into universities (Map 14.5). The first European universities appeared in Italy, at Bologna and Salerno.

The growth of the University of Bologna coincided with a revival of interest in Roman law. The study of Roman law as embodied in the Justinian *Code* had never completely died out in the West, but this sudden burst of interest seems to have been inspired by Irnerius (d. 1125), a great teacher at Bologna. His fame attracted students from all over Europe. Irnerius not only explained the Roman law of the Justinian *Code*, he applied it to difficult practical situations.

At Salerno, interest in medicine had persisted for centuries. Greek and Muslim physicians there had studied the use of herbs as cures and experimented with surgery. The twelfth century ushered in a new interest in Greek medical texts and in the work of Arab and Greek doctors. Students of medicine poured into Salerno and soon attracted royal attention. In 1140, when King Roger II of Sicily took the practice of medicine under royal control, his ordinance stated:

Who, from now on, wishes to practice medicine, has to present himself before our officials and examiners, in order to pass their judgment. Should he be bold enough to disregard this, he will be punished by imprisonment and confiscation of his entire property. In this way we are taking care that our subjects are not endangered by the inexperience of the physicians.[14]

In the first decades of the twelfth century, students converged on Paris. These men crowded into the cathedral school of Notre Dame and spilled over into the area later called the "Latin Quarter"—whose name probably reflects the Italian origin of many of the students attracted to Paris by the surge of interest in the classics, logic, and theology. The cathedral school's international reputation had already drawn to Paris scholars from all over Europe. One of the most famous of them was the teacher Peter Abelard.

Peter Abelard (1079–1142) was fascinated by logic, which he believed could be used to solve most problems. He had a brilliant mind and, al-

Map 14.5 Intellectual Centers of Medieval Europe Universities provided more sophisticated instruction than did monastic and cathedral schools.

SCOTLAND

St. Andrews
Glasgow

North Sea

DENMARK
Copenhagen

Baltic Sea

IRELAND

Durham Jarrow
Rivaulx
York

ENGLAND

Petersborough
Cambridge Bury
Oxford St. Edmunds
Canterbury

Salisbury
Winchester

ATLANTIC OCEAN

Magdeburg Berlin

Louvain Cologne
Ypres
Brussels Leipzig

HOLY

Amiens Fulda
Laon Mainz
Bec Reims Bamberg
Jumièges Heidelberg

ROMAN

Mont
St. Michel Notre
Dame St.-Denis
Paris Hirsau Lorch Regensburg
Savigny Chartres Beauvais
Orléans Fleury Clairvaux Vienna
Tours Basel Munich
Bourges Cîteaux St.-Gall

EMPIRE

Poitiers

Cluny

FRANCE

Bordeaux

Prague

Padua
Grenoble Pavia Piacenza

Cahors

Toulouse Montpellier Avignon

Bologna
Florence Vallombrosa
Perugia

Valladolid

Salamanca
Coimbra

SPAIN

Toledo

Corsica

Rome Monte
Cassino
Naples
Salerno

Sardinia

Seville

Palermo

Mediterranean Sea

Sicily

◆ University
■ Monastery school
⛪ Cathedral school

0   100   200   300 Km.
0   100   200   300 Mi.

though orthodox in his philosophical teaching, appeared to challenge ecclesiastical authorities. His book *Sic et Non* (*Yes and No*) was a list of apparently contradictory propositions drawn from the Bible and the writings of the church fathers. One such proposition, for example, stated that sin is pleasing to God and is not pleasing to God. Abelard used a method of systematic doubting in his writing and teaching. As he put it in the preface of *Sic et Non,* "By doubting we come to questioning, and by questioning we perceive the truth." While other scholars merely asserted theological principles, Abelard discussed and analyzed them. Through reasoning he even tried to describe the attributes of the three persons of the Trinity, the central mystery of the Christian faith. Abelard was severely censured by a church council, but his cleverness, boldness, and imagination made him a highly popular figure among students.

The influx of students eager for learning, together with dedicated and imaginative teachers, created the atmosphere in which universities grew. In northern Europe—at Paris and later at Oxford and Cambridge in England—associations or guilds of professors organized universities. They established the curriculum, set the length of time for study, and determined the form and content of examinations.

Instruction and Curriculum

University faculties grouped themselves according to academic disciplines, called "schools"—law, medicine, arts, and theology. The professors, known as "schoolmen" or "Scholastics," developed a method of thinking, reasoning, and writing in which questions were raised and authorities cited on both sides of the issue. The goal of the Scholastic method was to arrive at definitive answers and to provide a rational explanation for what was believed on faith. Schoolmen held that reason and faith constitute two harmonious realms in which the truths of faith and reason complement each other. The Scholastic approach rested on the recovery of classical philosophical texts.

Ancient Greek and Arabic texts had come into Europe in the early twelfth century, primarily through Toledo in Muslim Spain. Thirteenth-century philosophers relied on Latin translations of these texts, especially translations of Aristotle.

Aristotle had stressed direct observation of nature, as well as the principles that theory must follow fact and that knowledge of a thing requires an explanation of its causes. The schoolmen reinterpreted Aristotelian texts in a Christian sense.

In exploration of the natural world, Aristotle's axioms were not precisely followed. Medieval scientists argued from authority—such as the Bible, the Justinian *Code,* or an ancient scientific treatise—rather than from direct observation and experimentation, as modern scientists do. Thus the conclusions of medieval scientists were often wrong. Nevertheless, natural science gradually emerged as a discipline distinct from philosophy. Scholastics made important contributions to the advancement of knowledge. They preserved the Greek and Arabic texts that contained the body of ancient scientific knowledge, which would otherwise have been lost. And, in asking questions about nature and the universe, Scholastics laid the foundations for later scientific work.

Many of the problems raised by Scholastic philosophers dealt with theological issues. For example, they addressed the question that interested all Christians, educated and uneducated: how is a person saved? Saint Augustine's thesis—that, as a result of Adam's fall, human beings have a propensity to sin—had become a central feature of medieval church doctrine. The church taught that it possessed the means to forgive the sinful: grace conveyed through the sacraments. However, although grace provided a predisposition to salvation, the Scholastics held that one must *decide to use* the grace received. In other words, a person must use his or her reason to advance to God.

Thirteenth-century Scholastics devoted an enormous amount of time to collecting and organizing knowledge on all topics. These collections were published as *summa,* or reference books. There were summa on law, philosophy, vegetation, animal life, and theology. Saint Thomas Aquinas (1225–1274), a professor at Paris, produced the most famous collection, the *Summa Theologica,* which deals with a vast number of theological questions.

Aquinas drew an important distinction between faith and reason. He maintained that although reason can demonstrate many basic Christian principles such as the existence of God, other fundamental teachings such as the Trinity and original sin cannot be proved by logic. That reason cannot establish them does not, however, mean that they are contrary to reason. Rather, people understand such doctrines through revelation embodied in Scripture. Scripture cannot contradict reason, nor reason Scripture:

The light of faith that is freely infused into us does not destroy the light of natural knowledge [reason] implanted in us naturally. For although the natural light of the human mind is insufficient to show us these things made manifest by faith, it is nevertheless impossible that these things which the divine principle gives us by faith are contrary to these implanted in us by nature [reason]. Indeed, were that the case, one or the other would have to be false, and, since both are given to us by God, God would have to be the author of untruth, which is impossible. . . . It is impossible that those things which are of philosophy can be contrary to those things which are of faith.[15]

Aquinas also investigated *epistemology*, which is the branch of philosophy concerned with how a person knows something. Aquinas stated that one knows, first, through sensory perception of the physical world—seeing, hearing, touching, and so on. He maintained that there can be nothing in the mind that is not first in the senses. Second, knowledge comes through reason, the mind exercising its natural abilities. Aquinas stressed the power of human reason to know, even to know God. Proofs of the existence of God exemplify the Scholastic method of knowing.

Aquinas began with the things of the natural world—earth, air, trees, water, birds. Then he inquired about their original source or cause: the mover, creator, planner who started it all. Everything, Aquinas maintained, has an ultimate and essential explanation, a reason for existing. Here he was following Aristotle. Aquinas went further and identified the reason for existing, or the first mover, with God. Thomas Aquinas and all medieval intellectuals held that the end of both faith and reason was the knowledge of, and union with, God. His work later became the fundamental text of Roman Catholic doctrine.

At all universities, the standard method of teaching was the *lecture*—that is, a reading. The professor read a passage from the Bible, the Justinian *Code,* or one of Aristotle's treatises. He then explained and interpreted the passage; his interpretation was called a *gloss.* Students wrote down everything. Texts and glosses were sometimes collected and reproduced as textbooks. But because

books had to be copied by hand, they were extremely expensive and few students could afford them. Thus students depended for study on their own or friends' notes accumulated over a period of years. The choice of subjects was narrow. The syllabus at all universities consisted of a core of ancient texts that all students studied and, if they wanted to get ahead, mastered.

There were no examinations at the end of a series of lectures. Examinations were given after three, four, or five years of study, when the student applied for a degree. The professors determined the amount of material students had to know for each degree, and students frequently insisted that the professors specify precisely what that material was. When a candidate for a degree believed himself prepared, he presented himself to a committee of professors for examination. (No evidence survives of women sitting for an examination.)

Examinations were oral and very difficult. If the candidate passed, he was awarded the first, or bachelor's, degree. Further study, about as long, arduous, and expensive as it is today, enabled the graduate to try for the master's and doctor's degrees. All degrees certified competence in a given subject, and degrees were technically licenses to teach. Most students, however, did not become teachers.

THE CREATIVE OUTBURST

The creative energy that characterized the High Middle Ages was manifested in ways sacred and secular. As architecture, drama, art, and literature evolved in adaptation to the changing conditions of the High and late Middle Ages, they both expressed and satisfied the needs of medieval people.

From Romanesque Gloom to "Uninterrupted Light"

Medieval churches stand as the most spectacular manifestations of medieval vitality and creativity. It is difficult for twentieth-century people to appreciate the extraordinary amounts of energy, imagination, and money involved in building them. Between 1180 and 1270 in France alone, eighty cathedrals, about five hundred abbey churches, and tens of thousands of parish churches were constructed. This construction represents a remarkable investment for a country of scarcely eighteen million people. More stone was quarried for churches in medieval France than had been mined in ancient Egypt, where the Great Pyramid alone consumed 40.5 million cubic feet of stone. All these churches displayed a new architectural style. Fifteenth-century critics called the new style "Gothic" because they mistakenly believed that the fifth-century Goths had invented it. It actually developed partly in reaction to the earlier "Romanesque" style, which resembled ancient Roman architecture.

Gothic cathedrals were built in towns and reflect both bourgeois wealth and enormous civic pride. The manner in which a society spends its wealth expresses its values. Cathedrals, abbeys, and village churches testify to the religious faith and piety of medieval people. If the dominant aspect of medieval culture had not been Christianity, the builder's imagination and the merchant's money would have been used otherwise.

The relative political stability and increase of ecclesiastical wealth in the eleventh century encouraged the arts of peace. In the ninth and tenth centuries, the Vikings and Magyars had burned hundreds of wooden churches. In the eleventh century, the abbots wanted to rebuild in a more permanent fashion, and after the year 1000, church building increased on a wide scale. Because fireproofing was essential, ceilings had to be made of stone. The stone ceilings, called "vaults," were heavy; only thick walls would support them. Because the walls were so thick, the windows were small, allowing little light into the interior of the church. In northern Europe, twin bell towers often crowned these Romanesque churches, giving them a powerful, fortresslike appearance, reflecting the quasi-military, aristocratic, and pre-urban society that built them.

The inspiration for the Gothic style originated in the brain of one monk, Suger, abbot of Saint-Denis (1122–1151). When Suger became abbot, he decided to reconstruct the old Carolingian abbey church at Saint-Denis. Work began in 1137. On June 11, 1144, King Louis VII and a large crowd of bishops, dignitaries, and common people witnessed the solemn consecration of the first Gothic church in France.

The basic features of Gothic architecture—the pointed arch, the ribbed vault, and the flying buttress—were not unknown before 1137. What was without precedent was the interior lightness they made possible. Since the ceiling of a Gothic church weighed less than that of a Romanesque church, the walls could be thinner. Stained-glass windows were cut into the stone, flooding the church with light. The bright interior was astounding. Suger, describing his achievement, exulted at "the wonderful and uninterrupted light of most sacred windows, pervading the interior beauty."[16]

Begun in the Île-de-France, Gothic architecture spread throughout France with the expansion of royal power. French architects were soon invited to design and supervise the construction of churches in other parts of Europe, and the new style traveled rapidly over the continent.

Community Expression

The construction of a Gothic cathedral represented a gigantic investment of time, money, and corporate effort. The bishop and the clergy of the cathedral made the decision to build, but they depended on the support of all the social classes. Bishops raised revenue from contributions by people in their dioceses, and the clergy appealed to the king and the nobility. The French kings, for example, were generous patrons of many cathedrals. Noble families often gave contributions in order to have their crests in the stained-glass windows. Above all, the church relied on the financial help of those with the greatest amount of ready cash, the commercial classes.

Money was not the only need. A great number of craftsmen had to be assembled, from quarrymen and sculptors, to blacksmiths and glassmakers, and unskilled laborers had to be recruited for the heavy work. The construction of a large cathedral was rarely completed in one lifetime; many cathedrals were never finished at all. Because generation after generation added to the building, many Gothic churches show the architectural influences of two or even three centuries.

Since cathedrals were symbols of bourgeois civic pride, towns competed to build the largest and most splendid church. The people of Beauvais, in France, exceeded everyone: their church, started in 1247, reached the exceptional height of 157 feet. Unfortunately, the weight imposed on the vaults was too great, and the building collapsed in

1284. Medieval people built cathedrals to glorify God—and if mortals were impressed, so much the better.[17]

Cathedrals served secular as well as religious purposes. The sanctuary containing the altar and the bishop's chair belonged to the clergy, but the rest of the church belonged to the people. In addition to marriages, baptisms, and funerals, there were scores of feast days on which the entire town gathered in the cathedral for festivities. Local guilds met in the cathedrals, and magistrates and municipal officials held political meetings there. Some towns never built town halls because all civic functions took place in the cathedral. Pilgrims

West Front of Notre Dame Cathedral   In this powerful vision of the Last Judgment, Christ sits in judgment surrounded by angels, the Virgin, and Saint John. Scenes of paradise fill the arches on Christ's right, scenes of hell on the left. In the lower lintel, the dead arise incorruptible, and in the upper lintel (below Christ's feet), the saved move off to heaven, while devils push the damned to hell. Below, the twelve apostles line the doorway. *(Source: Alinari/Scala/Art Resource)*

slept there, lovers courted there, traveling actors staged plays there. The cathedral belonged to all.

First and foremost, however, the cathedral was intended to teach the people the doctrines of Christian faith through visual images. Architecture became the servant of theology. The main altar was at the east end, pointing toward Jerusalem, the city of peace. The west front of the cathedral faced the setting sun, and its wall was usually devoted to the scenes of the Last Judgment. The north side, which received the least sunlight, displayed events from the Old Testament. The south side, washed in warm sunshine for much of the day, depicted scenes from the New Testament. This symbolism implied that the Jewish people of the Old Testament lived in darkness and that the Gospel brought by Christ illuminated the world. Every piece of sculpture, furniture, and stained glass had some religious or social significance.

Stained glass beautifully reflects the creative energy of the High Middle Ages. It is both an integral part of Gothic architecture and a distinct form of painting. The glassmaker "painted" the picture with small fragments of glass held together with strips of lead. As Gothic churches became more skeletal and had more windows, stained glass replaced manuscript illumination as the leading kind of painting. Thousands of scenes in the cathedrals celebrate nature, country life, and the activities of ordinary people. All members of medieval society had a place in the City of God, which the Gothic cathedral represented. No one, from king to peasant, was excluded.

Tapestry making also came into its own in the fourteenth century. Heavy woolen tapestries were first made in the monasteries and convents as wall hangings for churches. Because they could be moved and lent an atmosphere of warmth, they subsequently replaced mural paintings. Early tapestries depicted religious scenes, but later hangings produced for the knightly class bore secular designs, especially romantic forests and hunting spectacles.

During the same period drama, derived from the church's liturgy, emerged as a distinct art form. For centuries, skits based on Christ's Nativity and Resurrection had been performed in monasteries and cathedrals. Beginning in the thirteenth century, plays based on these and other biblical themes and on the lives of the saints were performed in the church square and later in the town marketplace. Guilds financed these "mystery plays," so called because they were based on the mysteries of the Christian faith. By combining comical farce based on ordinary life with serious religious scenes, they allowed the common people to understand and identify with religious figures and the mysteries of their faith. Provoking the individual conscience to reform, mystery plays were also an artistic manifestation of local civic pride.

Vernacular Literature

Few developments expressed the emergence of national consciousness more vividly than the emergence of national literatures. Across Europe people spoke the language and dialect of their particular locality and class. In England, for example, the common people spoke regional English dialects, and the upper classes conversed in French. Official documents and works of literature were written in Latin or French. Beginning in the fourteenth century, however, national languages—the vernacular—came into widespread use not only in verbal communication but in literature as well. Three masterpieces of European culture, Dante's *Divine Comedy* (1310–1320), Chaucer's *Canterbury Tales* (1387–1400), and Villon's *Grand Testament* (1461), brilliantly manifested this new national pride.

Dante Alighieri (1265–1321) descended from an aristocratic family in Florence, where he held several positions in the city government. Dante called his work a "comedy" because he wrote it in Italian and in a different style from the "tragic" Latin; a later generation added the adjective "divine," referring both to its sacred subject and to Dante's artistry. The *Divine Comedy* is an allegorical trilogy of one hundred cantos (verses) whose three equal parts (1 + 33 + 33 + 33) each describe one of the realms of the next world: Hell, Purgatory, and Paradise. Dante recounts his imaginary journey through these regions toward God. The Roman poet Virgil, representing reason, leads Dante through Hell, where he observes the torments of the damned and denounces the disorders of his own time, especially ecclesiastical ambition and corruption. Passing up into Purgatory, Virgil shows the poet how souls are purified of their disordered inclinations. From Purgatory, Beatrice, a woman whom Dante once loved and the symbol of divine revelation in the poem, leads him to Paradise. In Paradise, home of the angels and saints,

Dante Alighieri   In this fifteenth-century fresco the poet, crowned with the wreath of poet laureate, holds the book containing the opening lines of his immortal *Commedia*. On the left is Hell and the mountain of purgatory; on the right, the city of Florence. *(Source: Scala/Art Resource)*

Saint Bernard—representing mystic contemplation—leads Dante to the Virgin Mary. Through her intercession Dante at last attains a vision of God.

The *Divine Comedy* portrays contemporary and historical figures, comments on secular and ecclesiastical affairs, and draws on Scholastic philosophy. Within the framework of a symbolic pilgrimage to the City of God, the *Divine Comedy* embodies the psychological tensions of the age. A profoundly Christian poem, it also contains bitter criticism of some church authorities. In its symmetrical structure and use of figures from the ancient world, such as Virgil, the poem perpetuates the classical tradition, but as the first major work of literature in the Italian vernacular, it is distinctly modern.

Geoffrey Chaucer (1340–1400), the son of a London wine merchant, was an official in the administrations of the English kings Edward III and Richard II and wrote poetry as an avocation. Chaucer's *Canterbury Tales* is a collection of stories in lengthy, rhymed narrative. On a pilgrimage to the shrine of Saint Thomas Becket at Canterbury (see page 413), thirty people of various social backgrounds each tell a tale. The Prologue sets the scene and describes the pilgrims, whose characters are further revealed in the story each one tells. For example, the gentle Christian Knight relates a chivalric romance; the gross Miller tells a vulgar story about a deceived husband; the earthy Wife of Bath, who has buried five husbands, sketches a fable about the selection of a spouse. In depicting the interests and behavior of all types of people, Chaucer presents a rich panorama of English social life in the fourteenth century. Like the *Divine Comedy*, *Canterbury Tales* reflects the cultural tensions of the times. Ostensibly Christian, many of the pilgrims are also materialistic, sensual, and worldly, suggesting the ambivalence of the broader society's concern for the next world and frank enjoyment of this one.

Present knowledge of François Villon (1431–1463), probably the greatest poet of late medieval France, derives from Paris police records and his own poetry. Although born to desperately poor parents, Villon earned the master of arts degree at the University of Paris. A rowdy and free-spirited student, in 1455 he killed a man in a street brawl. Banished from Paris, he joined one of the bands of wandering thieves that harassed the countryside after the Hundred Years' War. For his fellow bandits he composed ballads in thieves' jargon.

Villon's *Lais* (1456), a pun on the word *legs* ("legacy"), is a series of farcical bequests to friends and enemies. "Ballade des Pendus" ("Ballad of the Hanged") was written while Villon was contemplating that fate in prison. (His execution was commuted.) Villon's greatest and most self-revealing work, the *Grand Testament,* contains another string of bequests, including a legacy to a prostitute, and describes his unshakable faith in the beauty of life on earth. The *Grand Testament* possesses elements of social rebellion, bawdy humor, and rare emotional depth. The themes of Dante's and Chaucer's poetry are distinctly medieval, but Villon's celebration of the human condition brands him as definitely modern. He used medieval forms of versification, but his language was the vernacular of the poor and the criminal.

Perhaps the most versatile and prolific French writer of the later Middle Ages was Christine de Pisan (1363?–1434?). The daughter of a professor of astrology at Bologna whose international reputation won him a post at the French royal court where she received her excellent education, Christine had a broad knowledge of Greek, Latin, French, and Italian literature. The deaths of her father and husband left her with three small children and her mother to support, and she resolved to earn her living with her pen. In addition to poems and books on love, religion, and morality, Christine produced the *Livre de la mutacion de fortune,* a major historical work; a biography of King Charles V; the *Ditié,* celebrating Joan of Arc's victory; and many letters. *The City of Ladies* lists the great women of history and their contributions to society, and *The Book of Three Virtues* provides prudent and practical advice on household management for women of all social classes and at all stages of life. Christine de Pisan's wisdom and wit are illustrated in her autobiographical *Avison-*

Christine. She records that a man told her that an educated woman is unattractive, since there are so few, to which she responded that an ignorant man was even less attractive, since there are so many.

HERESY AND THE FRIARS

As the commercial revolution of the High Middle Ages fostered urban development, the towns experienced an enormous growth of heresy. In fact, in the twelfth and thirteenth centuries, "the most economically advanced and urbanized areas: northern Italy, southern France, Flanders-Brabant, and the lower Rhine Valley" witnessed the strongest heretical movements.[18] Why did heresy flourish in such places? The bishops, usually drawn from the feudal nobility, did not understand urban culture and were suspicious of it. Christian theology, formulated for an earlier, rural age, did not address the problems of the more sophisticated mercantile society. The new monastic orders of the twelfth century, deliberately situated in remote, isolated areas, had little relevance to the towns.[19] Finally, townspeople wanted a pious clergy capable of preaching the Gospel in a manner that satisfied their spiritual needs. They disapproved of clerical ignorance and luxurious living. Critical of the clergy, neglected, and spiritually unfulfilled, townspeople turned to heretical sects.

The term *heresy,* which derives from the Greek *hairesis,* meaning "individual choosing," is older than Christianity. Civil authority in early Christian times could (and did) punish heresy (see page 232). In the early Middle Ages, the term came to be applied to the position of a Christian who chose and stubbornly held to doctrinal error in defiance of church authority.[20]

Ironically, the eleventh-century Gregorian reform movement, which had worked to purify the church of disorder, led to some twelfth- and thirteenth-century heretical movements. Papal efforts to improve the sexual morality of the clergy, for example, had largely succeeded. But Gregory VII did not foresee the consequences of his order forbidding married priests to celebrate church ceremonies. Laypersons assumed that they could remove immoral priests. Critics and heretics accused clergymen of immorality and thus weakened their influence. The clergy's inability to provide adequate instruction weakened its position.

In northern Italian towns, Arnold of Brescia, a vigorous advocate of strict clerical poverty, denounced clerical wealth. In France, Peter Waldo, a rich merchant of Lyon, gave his money to the poor and preached that only prayers, not sacraments, were needed for salvation. The "Waldensians"—as Peter Waldo's followers were called—bitterly attacked the sacraments and church hierarchy, and they carried these ideas across Europe.

Another group, known as the "Cathars" (from the Greek *katharos,* meaning "pure") and as the "Albigensians" (from the town of Albi in southern France), rejected not only the hierarchical organization and the sacraments of the church but the Roman church itself. The Albigensians' primary tenet was the dualist belief that God had created spiritual things and the Devil had created material things; thus the soul was good and the body evil. Albigensians believed that forces of good and evil battled constantly and that leading a perfect life meant being stripped of all physical and material things. Thus sexual intercourse was evil because it led to the creation of more physical bodies. Albigensians were divided into the "perfect," who followed the principles of Catharism, and the "believers," who led ordinary lives until their deaths, when they repented and were saved.

The Albigensian heresy won many adherents in southern France. Townspeople admired the virtuous lives of the "perfect," which contrasted very favorably with the luxurious living of the Roman clergy. Women were attracted because the Albigensians treated them as men's equals. Nobles were drawn because they coveted the clergy's wealth.

Faced with widespread defection in southern France, in 1208 Pope Innocent III proclaimed a crusade against the Albigensian heretics. When the papal legate was murdered by a follower of Count Raymond of Toulouse, the greatest lord in southern France and a suspected heretic, the crusade took on a political character; heretical beliefs became fused with feudal rebellion against the French crown. Northern French lords joined the crusade and inflicted severe defeats on the towns of the large southern province of Languedoc. The Albigensian crusade, however, was a political rather than a religious success; the heresy simply went underground.

In its continuing struggle against heresy, the church gained the support of two remarkable men, Saint Dominic and Saint Francis, and of the orders they founded.

Born in Castile, the province of Spain famous for its zealous Christianity and militant opposition to Islam, Domingo de Gúzman (1170?–1221) received a sound education and was ordained a priest. In 1206 he accompanied his bishop on a mission to preach to the Albigensian heretics in Languedoc. Although the austere simplicity in

St. Dominic and the Inquisition The fifteenth-century court painter to the Spanish rulers Ferdinand and Isabella, Pedro Berruguete here portrays an event from the life of St. Dominic: Dominic presides at the trial of Count Raymond of Toulouse, who had supported the Albigensian heretics. Raymond, helmeted and on horseback, repented and was pardoned; his companions, who would not repent, were burned. Smoke from the fire has put one of the judges to sleep, and other officials, impervious to the human tragedy, chat among themselves. *(Source: Museo del Prado, Madrid)*

which they traveled contrasted favorably with the pomp and display of the papal legate in the area, Dominic's efforts had little practical success. Determined to win the heretics back with ardent preaching, Dominic subsequently returned to France with a few followers. In 1216 the group—known as the "Preaching Friars"—won papal recognition as a new religious order. Their name indicates their goal: they were to preach. In order to preach effectively, they had to study; so Dominic sent his recruits to the universities for training in theology.

Francesco di Bernardone (1181–1226), son of a wealthy cloth merchant from the northern Italian town of Assisi, was an extravagant wastrel until he had a sudden conversion. Then he determined to devote himself entirely to living the Gospel. Directed by a vision to rebuild the dilapidated chapel of Saint Damiano in Assisi, Francis sold some of his father's cloth to finance the reconstruction. His enraged father insisted that he return the money and enlisted the support of the bishop. When the bishop told Francis to obey his father, Francis took off all his clothes and returned them to his father. Thereafter he promised to obey only his Father in heaven.

Francis was particularly inspired by two biblical texts: "If you seek perfection, go, sell your possessions, and give to the poor. You will have treasure in heaven. Afterward, come back and follow me" (Matthew 19:21); and Jesus's advice to his disciples as they went out to preach, "Take nothing for the journey, neither walking staff nor travelling bag, no bread, no money" (Luke 9:3). Over the centuries, these words had stimulated countless young people. Francis, however, intended to observe them literally and without compromise. He set out to live and preach the Gospel in absolute poverty.

The simplicity, humility, and joyful devotion with which Francis carried out his mission soon attracted companions. Although he resisted pressure to establish an order, his followers became so numerous that he was obliged to develop some formal structure. In 1221 the papacy approved the "Rule of the Little Brothers of Saint Francis," as the Franciscans were known.

The new Dominican and Franciscan orders differed significantly from older monastic orders such as the Benedictines and the Cistercians. First, the Dominicans and Franciscans were friars, not monks. They lived and worked in the cities and university towns, the busy centers of commercial and intellectual life, not in the secluded and cloistered world of the monastery. Second, the friars stressed apostolic poverty, a life based on the Gospel's teachings. They owned no property and depended on Christian people for their material needs; thus they were called *mendicants,* begging friars. Benedictine and Cistercian abbeys, by contrast, held land—not infrequently great tracts of land. Finally, the friars drew most of their members from the burgher class, from small property owners and shopkeepers. The monastic orders, by contrast, gathered their members (at least until the thirteenth century) overwhelmingly from the nobility.[21]

The friars represented a response to the spiritual and intellectual needs of the thirteenth century. Research on the German friars has shown that although the Franciscans initially accepted uneducated men, the Dominicans always showed a marked preference for university graduates.[22] A more urban and sophisticated society required a highly educated clergy. The Dominicans soon held professorial chairs at leading universities, and they count Thomas Aquinas, probably the greatest medieval philosopher in Europe, as their most famous member. But the Franciscans followed suit at the universities and also produced intellectual leaders. The Franciscans' mission to the towns and the poor, their ideal of poverty, and their compassion for the human condition made them vastly popular. The friars interpreted Christian doctrine for the new urban classes. By living Christianity as well as by preaching it, they won the respect of the medieval bourgeoisie.

Dominic started his order to combat heresy. Francis's followers were motivated by the ideal of absolute poverty. The papacy used the friars to staff a new (1233) ecclesiastical court, the Inquisition. Popes selected the friars to direct the Inquisition because bishops proved unreliable and because special theological training was needed. *Inquisition* means "investigation," and the Franciscans and Dominicans developed expert methods of rooting out unorthodox thought. Modern Americans consider the procedures of the Inquisition exceedingly unjust, and there was substantial criticism of it in the Middle Ages. The accused did not learn the evidence against them or see their accusers; they were subjected to lengthy interrogations often designed to trap them; and torture could be used to extract confessions. Those who supported the Inquisition, however, believed that heretics destroyed the souls of their neighbors. By attacking religion, it was also thought, heretics destroyed the very bonds of society. So successful was the Inquisition that heresy was virtually extinguished within a century.

THE BLACK DEATH

Societies, like individuals, cannot maintain a high level of energy indefinitely. In the later years of the thirteenth century, Europeans seemed to run out of steam. The crusading movement gradually fizzled out. Few new cathedrals were constructed, and if a cathedral had not been completed by 1300, the chances were high that it never would be. The vigor of the strong rulers of England and France did not pass to their immediate descendants. And the church, which for two centuries had guided Christian society, began to face grave difficulties.

Economic problems originating in the later thirteenth century were fully manifest by the start of the fourteenth. In the first decade, the countries of northern Europe experienced considerable price inflation. The costs of grain, livestock, and dairy products rose sharply. Bad weather made a serious situation worse. An unusual number of storms brought torrential rains, ruining the wheat, oat, and hay crops on which people and animals depended almost everywhere. Poor harvests—and one in four was likely to be poor—led

MAP 14.6 The Course of the Black Death in Fourteenth-Century Europe   Note the routes that the bubonic plague took across Europe. How do you account for the fact that several regions were spared the "dreadful death"?

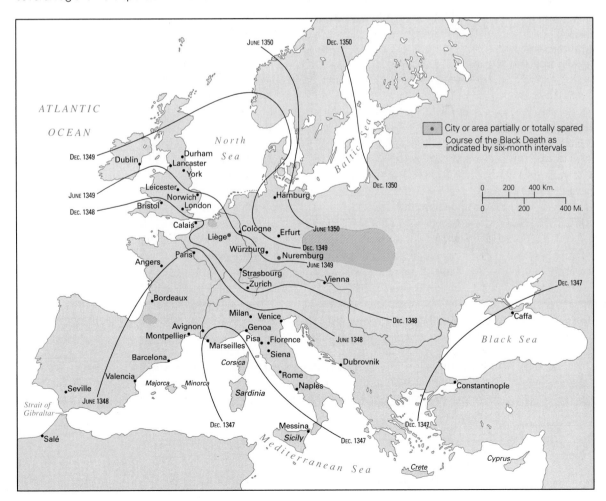

The Plague-Stricken Even as the dead were wrapped in shrouds and collected in carts for mass burial, the disease struck others. The man collapsing has the symptomatic buba on his neck. As Saint Sebastian pleads for mercy (above), a winged devil, bearer of the plague, attacks an angel. *(Source: Walters Art Gallery, Baltimore)*

to scarcity and starvation. Almost all of northern Europe suffered a terrible famine in the years 1315 to 1317. Meanwhile, an epidemic of typhoid fever carried away thousands. In 1316, 10 percent of the population of the city of Ypres may have died between May and October alone. Then in 1318 disease hit cattle and sheep, drastically reducing the herds and flocks. Another bad harvest in 1321 brought famine, starvation, and death.

These catastrophes had devastating social consequences. Population had steadily increased in the twelfth and thirteenth centuries, and large amounts of land had been put under cultivation. The amount of food yielded, however, did not keep up with the level of population growth. Bad weather had disastrous results, and population fell. Meanwhile, the international character of trade and commerce meant that a disaster in one country had serious implications elsewhere. For example, the infection that attacked English sheep in 1318 caused a sharp decline in wool exports in the following years. Without wool, Flemish weavers could not work. Without woolen cloth, the businesses of Flemish, French, and English merchants suffered. Unemployment encouraged many men to turn to crime. Economic and social problems were aggravated by the appearance in western Europe of a frightful disease.

Scholars dispute the origins of the bubonic plague, often known as the "Black Death." Some students hold that it broke out in China or central Asia around 1331 and that during the next fifteen years merchants and soldiers carried it over the caravan routes until in 1346 it reached the Crimea in southern Russia. Other scholars believe that the plague was endemic in southern Russia. In either case, from the Crimea the plague had easy access to Mediterranean lands and western Europe.

In October 1347, Genoese ships brought the plague to Messina. From there it spread across Sicily. Venice and Genoa were hit in January 1348, and from the port of Pisa the disease spread south to Rome and east to Florence and all Tuscany. By late spring, southern Germany was attacked. Frightened French authorities chased a galley bearing the disease from the port of Marseilles, but not before plague had infected the city, from where it spread to Languedoc and Spain. In June 1348 two ships entered the Bristol Channel and introduced it into England. All Europe felt the scourge of this horrible disease (Map 14.6).

Pathology

Modern understanding of the bubonic plague rests on the research of two bacteriologists, one French and one Japanese, who in 1894 independently identified the bacillus that causes the plague, *Pasteurella pestis* (so labeled after the French scientist's teacher, Louis Pasteur). The bacillus liked to live in the bloodstream of an animal or, ideally, in the stomach of a flea. The flea in turn resided in the hair of a rodent, sometimes a squirrel but preferably the hardy, nimble, and vagabond black rat. Why the host black rat moved so much, scientists still do not know, but it often traveled by ship. There the black rat could feast for months on a cargo of grain or live snugly among bales of cloth. Fleas bearing the bacillus also had no trouble nesting in saddlebags.[23] Comfortable, well fed, and often having greatly multiplied, the black rats ended their ocean voyage and descended on the great cities of Europe. Once in the population, the plague also was communicated directly from one person to another.

Although by the fourteenth century urban authorities from London to Paris to Rome had begun to try to achieve a primitive level of sanitation, urban conditions remained ideal for the spread of disease. In the narrow streets filled with mud, refuse, and human excrement, dead animals and sore-covered beggars greeted the traveler. Extreme overcrowding was commonplace. All members of an aristocratic family lived and slept in one room. In a middle-class or poor household, six or eight persons slept in one bed—if they had one. Closeness, after all, provided warmth. Houses were beginning to be constructed of brick, but many remained of wood, clay, and mud. A determined rat had little trouble entering such a house.

Standards of personal hygiene remained frightfully low. Most large cities had public bathhouses, but there is no way of knowing how frequently ordinary people used them. People probably bathed rarely. Lack of personal cleanliness, combined with any number of temporary ailments such as diarrhea and the common cold, weakened the body's resistance to serious disease. Fleas and body lice were universal afflictions: everyone from peasants to archbishops had them. One more bite did not cause much alarm. But if that nibble came from a bacillus-bearing flea, an entire household or area was doomed.

The symptoms of the bubonic plague started with a growth the size of a nut or an apple in the armpit, in the groin, or on the neck. This was the boil, or *buba,* that gave the disease its name and caused agonizing pain. If the buba was lanced and the pus thoroughly drained, the victim had a chance of recovery. The secondary stage was the appearance of black spots or blotches caused by bleeding under the skin. Finally, the victim began to cough violently and spit blood. This stage, indicating the presence of thousands of bacilli in the bloodstream, signaled the end, and death followed in two or three days. Rather than evoking compassion for the victim, a French scientist has written, everything about the bubonic plague provoked horror and disgust: "All the matter which exuded from their bodies let off an unbearable stench; sweat, excrement, spittle, breath, so fetid as to be overpowering; urine turbid, thick, black or red."[24]

Medieval people had no rational explanation for the disease nor any effective medical treatment for it. Most people—lay, scholarly, and medical—believed that the Black Death was caused by some "vicious property in the air" that carried the disease from place to place. When ignorance was joined to fear and ancient bigotry, savage cruelty sometimes resulted. Many people believed that the Jews had poisoned the wells of Christian communities and thereby infected the drinking water. This charge led to the murder of thousands of Jews across Europe.

The Italian writer Giovanni Boccaccio (1313–1375), describing the course of the disease in Florence in the preface to his book of tales, *The Decameron,* pinpointed the cause of the spread:

Moreover, the virulence of the pest was the greater by reason that intercourse was apt to convey it from the sick to the whole, just as fire devours things dry or greasy when they are brought close to it. Nay, the evil went yet further, for not merely by speech or association with the sick was the malady communicated to the healthy with consequent peril of common death, but any that touched the clothes of the sick or aught else that had been touched or used by them, seemed thereby to contract the disease.[25]

The rat that carried the disease-bearing flea avoided travel outside the cities. Thus the countryside was relatively safe. City dwellers who could afford to move fled to the country districts.

Only educated guesses, subject to enormous scholarly controversy, can be made about the plague's mortality rate. Of a total English population of perhaps 4.2 million, probably 1.4 million died of the Black Death in its several visits.[26] Densely populated Italian cities endured incredible losses. Florence, for example, lost between half and two-thirds of its 1347 population of 85,000 when the plague visited in 1348. The disease recurred intermittently in the 1360s and 1370s and reappeared many times down to 1700. There have been twentieth-century outbreaks in such places as Hong Kong, Bombay, and Uganda.

Social and Psychological Consequences

Predictably, the poor died more rapidly than the rich, because the rich enjoyed better health to begin with; but the powerful were not unaffected. In England two archbishops of Canterbury fell victim to the plague in 1349, King Edward III's daughter Joan died, and many leading members of the London guilds followed her to the grave.

It is noteworthy that in an age of mounting criticism of clerical wealth, the behavior of the clergy during the plague was often exemplary. Priests, monks, and nuns cared for the sick and buried the dead. In places like Venice, from where even physicians fled, priests remained to give what ministrations they could. Consequently, their mortality rate was phenomenally high. The German clergy, especially, suffered a severe decline in personnel in the years after 1350. With the ablest killed off, the wealth of the German church fell into the hands of the incompetent and weak. The situation was ripe for reform.

Economic historians and demographers sharply dispute the impact of the plague on the economy in the late fourteenth century. The traditional view that the plague had a disastrous effect has been greatly modified. The clearest evidence comes from England, where the agrarian economy showed remarkable resilience. Although the severity of the disease varied from region to region, it appears that by about 1375 most landlords enjoyed revenues near those of the pre-plague years. By the early fifteenth century seigneurial prosperity reached a medieval peak. Why? The answer appears to lie in the fact that England and many parts of Europe suffered from overpopulation in the early fourteenth century. Population losses caused by the Black Death "led to increased productivity by restoring a more efficient balance between labour, land, and capital."[27] Population decline meant a sharp increase in per capita wealth. Increased demand for labor meant greater mobility among peasant and working classes. Wages rose, providing better distribution of income and putting landlords on the defensive. Some places, such as Florence, experienced economic prosperity as a long-term consequence of the plague.

Even more significant than the social effects were the psychological consequences. The knowledge that the disease meant almost certain death provoked the most profound pessimism. Imagine an entire society in the grip of the belief that it was at the mercy of a frightful affliction about which nothing could be done, a disgusting disease from which family and friends would flee, leaving one to die alone and in agony. It is not surprising that some sought release in orgies and gross sensuality while others turned to the severest forms of asceticism and frenzied religious fervor. Some extremists joined groups of *flagellants,* men and women who collectively whipped and scourged themselves as penance for their and society's sins, in the belief that the Black Death was God's punishment for humanity's wickedness.

The literature and art of the fourteenth century reveal a terribly morbid concern with death. One highly popular artistic motif, the Dance of Death, depicted a dancing skeleton leading away a living person. No wonder survivors experienced a sort of shell shock and a terrible crisis of faith. Lack of confidence in the leaders of society, lack of hope for the future, defeatism, and malaise wreaked enormous anguish and contributed to the decline of the Middle Ages. A prolonged international war added further misery to the frightful disasters of the plague.

THE HUNDRED YEARS' WAR (CA 1337–1453)

On and off from 1337 to 1453, another phase of the centuries-old struggle between the English and French monarchies was fought. The Hundred Years' War had both distant and immediate causes. In 1259 France and England signed the Treaty of Paris, in which the English king agreed to become—for himself and his successors—vassal of the French crown for the duchy of Aquitaine. The English claimed Aquitaine as an ancient inheritance. French policy, however, was strongly expansionist, and the French kings resolved to absorb the duchy into the kingdom of France. In 1329 Edward III (r. 1327–1377) paid homage to Philip VI (r. 1328–1350) for Aquitaine. In 1337 Philip, determined to exercise full jurisdiction there, confiscated the duchy. This was the immediate cause of the war. Edward III maintained that the only way he could exercise his rightful sovereignty over Aquitaine was by assuming the title of king of France.[28] As the eldest surviving male descendant of the French king Philip the Fair (r. 1285–1314), he believed that he could rightfully make this claim. Moreover, the dynastic argument had feudal implications: in order to increase their independent power, French vassals of Philip VI used the excuse that they had to transfer their loyalty to a more legitimate overlord, Edward III. One reason the war lasted so long was that it became a French civil war, with French barons supporting English monarchs in order to thwart the centralizing goals of the French crown.

Economic factors involving the wool trade and the control of Flemish towns had served as justifications for war between France and England for centuries. The causes of the conflicts known as the "Hundred Years' War" were thus dynastic, feudal, political, and economic. Recent historians have stressed economic factors. The wool trade between England and Flanders served as the cornerstone of both countries' economies; they were closely interdependent. Flanders was a fief of the French crown, and the Flemish aristocracy was highly sympathetic to the monarchy in Paris. But the wealth of Flemish merchants and cloth manufacturers depended on English wool, and Flemish burghers strongly supported the claims of Edward III. The disruption of commerce with England threatened their prosperity.

It is impossible to measure the precise influence of the Flemings on the cause and course of the war. Certainly Edward could not ignore their influence, because it represented money he needed to carry on the war. Although the war's impact on commerce fluctuated, over the long run it badly hurt the wool trade and the cloth industry.

One historian has written in jest that if Edward III had been locked away in a castle with a pile of toy knights and archers to play with, he would have done far less damage.[29] The same might be said of Philip VI. Both rulers glorified war and saw it as the perfect arena for the realization of their chivalric ideals. Neither king possessed any sort of policy for dealing with his kingdom's social, economic, or political ills.

The Popular Response

The governments of both England and France manipulated public opinion to support the war. Whatever significance modern students ascribe to the economic factor, public opinion in fourteenth-century England held that the war was waged for one reason: to secure for King Edward the French crown that he had been denied.[30] Edward III issued letters to the sheriffs describing in graphic terms the evil deeds of the French and listing royal needs. Kings in both countries instructed the clergy to deliver sermons filled with patriotic sentiment. The royal courts sensationalized the wickedness of the other side and stressed the great fortunes to be made from the war. Philip VI sent agents to warn communities about the dangers of invasion and to stress the French crown's revenue needs to meet the attack.

The royal campaign to rally public opinion was highly successful, at least in the early stage of the war. Edward III gained widespread support in the 1340s and 1350s. The English developed a deep hatred of the French and feared that King Philip intended "to have seized and slaughtered the entire realm of England." As England was successful in the field, pride in the country's military proficiency increased.

Most important of all, the Hundred Years' War was popular because it presented unusual opportunities for wealth and advancement. Poor knights and knights who were unemployed were promised regular wages. Criminals who enlisted were granted pardons. The great nobles expected to be rewarded with estates. Royal exhortations to the troops before battles repeatedly stressed that, if victorious, the men might keep whatever they seized. The French chronicler Jean Froissart wrote that at the time of Edward III's expedition of 1359, men of all ranks flocked to the English king's banner. Some came to acquire honor, but many came in order "to loot and pillage the fair and plenteous land of France."[31]

The Course of the War to 1419

Armies in the field were commanded by rulers themselves; by princes of the blood such as Edward III's son Edward, the "Black Prince"—so called because of the color of his armor—or by great aristocrats. Knights formed the cavalry; the peasantry served as infantrymen, pikemen, and archers. By medieval standards, the force was astronomically large. The costs of these armies stretched French and English resources to the breaking point.

The war was fought almost entirely in France and the Low Countries (Map 14.7). It consisted mainly of a series of random sieges and cavalry raids. In 1335 the French began supporting Scottish incursions into northern England, ravaging the countryside in Aquitaine, and sacking and burning Southampton and other English coastal towns. Naturally such tactics lent weight to Edward III's propaganda campaign. In fact, royal propaganda on both sides fostered a kind of early nationalism.

During the war's early stages, England was highly successful. At Crécy in northern France in 1346, English longbowmen scored a great victory over French knights and crossbowmen. Although the fire of the longbow was not very accurate, the longbow could be reloaded rapidly; thus English archers could send off three arrows to the French crossbowmen's one. The result was a blinding shower of arrows that unhorsed the French knights and caused mass confusion. The firing of cannon—probably the first use of artillery in the West—created further panic; thereupon the English horsemen charged and butchered the French.

This was not war according to the chivalric rules that Edward III would have preferred. The English victory at Crécy rested on the skill and swiftness of the yeomen archers, who had nothing at all to do with the chivalric ideals of aristocratic military glory for which the war was being fought. Ten years later, Edward the Black Prince, using the same tactics as at Crécy, smashed the French at

MAP 14.7 English Holdings in France During the Hundred Years' War The year 1429 marked the greatest extent of English holdings in France. Why was it unlikely that England could have held these territories permanently?

1337
(before the Battle of Crécy)

Held by the kings of England

1360
(after the Battle of Poitiers)

Held by the kings of England

✕ Major battles

ca 1429
(after the siege of Orléans)

Held by the kings of England

✕ Major battle

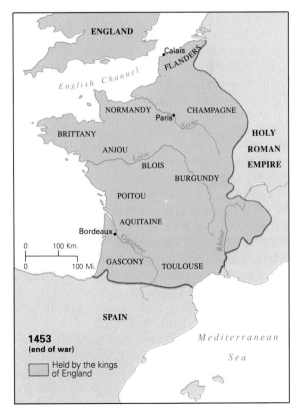

1453
(end of war)

Held by the kings of England

Poitiers, captured the French king, and held him for ransom. Again, at Agincourt in 1415, the chivalric English soldier-king Henry V (r. 1413–1422) gained the field over vastly superior numbers. Henry followed up his triumph at Agincourt with the reconquest of Normandy. By 1419 the English had advanced to the walls of Paris (see Map 14.7).

The French cause, however, was not lost. Although England had scored the initial victories, France won the war.

Joan of Arc and France's Victory

The ultimate success of France rests heavily on the actions of an obscure French peasant girl, Joan of Arc, whose vision and work revived French fortunes and led to victory. A great deal of pious and popular legend surrounds Joan the Maid because of her peculiar appearance on the scene, her astonishing success, her martyrdom, and her canonization by the Catholic church. The historical fact is that she saved the French monarchy.

Born in 1412 to well-to-do peasants in the village of Domrémy in Champagne, Joan of Arc grew up in a religious household. During adolescence she began to hear voices, which she later said belonged to Saint Michael, Saint Catherine, and Saint Margaret. In 1428 these voices spoke to her with great urgency, telling her that the dauphin (the uncrowned King Charles VII) had to be crowned and the English expelled from France. Joan went to the French court, persuaded the king to reject the rumor that he was illegitimate, and secured his support for her relief of the besieged city of Orléans.

Joan arrived before Orléans on April 28, 1429. Seventeen years old, she knew little of warfare and believed that if she could keep the French troops from swearing and frequenting whorehouses, victory would be theirs. On May 8 the English, weakened by disease and lack of supplies, withdrew from Orléans. Ten days later, Charles VII was crowned king at Reims. These two events marked the turning point in the war.

In 1430 England's allies, the Burgundians, captured Joan and sold her to the English. When the English handed her over to the ecclesiastical authorities for trial, the French court did not intervene. The English wanted Joan eliminated for obvious political reasons, but sorcery (witchcraft) was the ostensible charge at her trial. Her claim of direct inspiration from God, thereby denying the authority of church officials, constituted heresy. In 1431 the court condemned her as a heretic and burned her at the stake in the marketplace at Rouen. A new trial in 1456 rehabilitated her name. In 1920 she was canonized and declared a holy maiden, and today she is revered as the second patron saint of France.

The relief of Orléans stimulated French pride and rallied French resources. At the same time, as the war dragged on, English demoralization increased. Slowly the French reconquered Normandy and, finally, ejected the English from Aquitaine. At the war's end in 1453, only the town of Calais remained in English hands.

Costs and Consequences

For both France and England, the war proved a disaster. In France the English had slaughtered thousands of soldiers and civilians. In the years after the sweep of the Black Death, this additional killing meant a grave loss of population. The English had laid waste to hundreds of thousands of acres of rich farmland, leaving the rural economy of many parts of France a shambles. The war had disrupted trade and the great fairs, drastically reducing French participation in international commerce. Defeat in battle and heavy taxation contributed to widespread dissatisfaction and aggravated peasants' grievances.

In England only the southern coastal ports experienced much destruction, and the demographic effects of the Black Death actually worked to restore the land-labor balance (see pages 440–441). The costs of the war, however, were tremendous. England spent over £5 million on the war effort, a huge sum in the fourteenth and fifteenth centuries. Manpower losses had great social consequences. The knights who ordinarily handled the work of local government as sheriffs, coroners, jurymen, and justices of the peace were abroad, and their absence contributed to the breakdown of order at the local level. The English government attempted to finance the war effort by raising taxes on the wool crop. Because of steadily increasing costs, the Flemish and Italian buyers could not afford English wool. Consequently, exports of raw wool slumped drastically between 1350 and 1450.

The long war also had a profound impact on the political lives of the two countries. Most notably, it stimulated the development of the English Parliament. Between 1250 and 1450, representative assemblies from several classes of society flourished in many European countries. Edward III's constant need for money to pay for the war compelled him to summon not only the great barons and bishops but knights of the shires and burgesses from the towns as well. Between the outbreak of the war in 1337 and the king's death in 1377, parliamentary assemblies met twenty-seven times.[32]

The frequency of the meetings is significant. Representative assemblies were becoming a habit. Knights and burgesses—or the "Commons," as they came to be called—recognized their mutual interests and began to meet apart from the great lords. The Commons gradually realized that they held the country's purse strings, and a parliamentary statute of 1341 required that all nonfeudal levies have parliamentary approval. When Edward III signed the law, he acknowledged that the king of England could not tax without Parliament's consent. Increasingly, during the war, money grants were tied to royal redress of grievances: if the government was to raise money, it had to correct the wrongs that its subjects protested.

In England theoretical consent to taxation and legislation was given in one assembly for the entire country. France had no such single assembly; instead, there were many regional or provincial assemblies. Why did a national representative assembly fail to develop in France? In fact, no one in France wanted a national assembly. Provincial differences and identities were very strong and provincial assemblies highly jealous of their independence. The French monarchy found the idea of representative assemblies thoroughly distasteful. Large gatherings of the nobility potentially or actually threatened the king's power. The advice of a councilor to King Charles VI (r. 1380–1422), "above all things be sure that no great assemblies of nobles or of *communes* take place in your kingdom," was accepted.[33] Charles VII (r. 1422–1461) even threatened to punish those proposing a national assembly.

The English Parliament was above all else a court of law, a place where justice was done and grievances remedied. No French assembly (except that of Brittany) had such competence. The national assembly in England met frequently. In France general assemblies were so rare that they never got the opportunity to develop precise procedures or to exercise judicial functions.

In both countries, however, the war did promote the growth of *nationalism*—the feeling of unity and identity that binds together a people who speak the same language, have a common ancestry and customs, and live in the same area. In the fourteenth century, nationalism took the form of hostility toward foreigners. Both Philip VI and Edward III drummed up support for the war by portraying the enemy as an alien, evil people. Edward III sought to justify his personal dynastic quarrel by linking it with England's national interests. As the Parliament Roll of 1348 states:

The Knights of the shires and the others of the Commons were told that they should withdraw together

Joan of Arc   This is how the court scribe who made this sketch in 1429, the year Joan raised the siege of Orleans, imagined her. He had never seen her. *(Source: Archives Nationales, Paris)*

and take good counsel as to how, for withstanding the malice of the said enemy and for the salvation of our said lord the King and his Kingdom of England . . . the King could be aided.[34]

After victories, each country experienced a surge of pride in its military strength. Just as English patriotism ran strong after Crécy and Poitiers, so French national confidence rose after Orléans. French national feeling demanded the expulsion of the enemy not merely from Normandy and Aquitaine but from French soil. Perhaps no one expressed this national consciousness better than Joan of Arc, when she exulted that the enemy had been "driven out of *France.*"

THE DECLINE OF THE CHURCH'S PRESTIGE

In times of crisis or disaster, people of all faiths have sought the consolation of religion. In the fourteenth century, however, the official Christian church offered very little solace. In fact, the leaders of the church added to the sorrow and misery of the times.

First, a violent dispute between the papacy and the kings of England and France badly damaged the prestige of the pope. In 1294 King Edward I of England and Philip the Fair of France declared war on each other. To finance this war, both kings laid taxes on the clergy. Kings had been taxing the church for decades. Pope Boniface VIII (r. 1294–1303), arguing from precedent, insisted that kings gain papal consent for taxation of the clergy and forbade churchmen to pay the taxes. But Edward and Philip refused to accept this decree, partly because it hurt royal finances and partly because the papal order threatened royal authority within their countries. Edward immediately denied the clergy the protection of the law, an action that meant its members could be attacked with impunity. Philip halted the shipment of all ecclesiastical revenue to Rome. Boniface had to back down.

Philip the Fair and his ministers continued their attack on all powers in France outside royal authority. Philip arrested a French bishop who was also the papal legate. When Boniface defended the ecclesiastical status and diplomatic immunity of the bishop, Philip replied with the trumped-up charge that the pope was a heretic. The papacy and the French monarchy waged a bitter war of propaganda. Finally, in 1302, in a letter entitled *Unam Sanctam* (because its opening sentence spoke of one holy Catholic church), Boniface insisted that all Christians are subject to the pope. Although the letter made no specific reference to Philip, it held that kings should submit to papal authority. Philip's university-trained advisers responded with an argument drawn from Roman law. They maintained that the king of France was completely sovereign in his kingdom and responsible to God alone. French mercenary troops went to Italy and arrested the aged pope. Although Boniface was soon freed, he died shortly afterward.

In order to control the church and its policies, Philip pressured Pope Clement V (r. 1305–1314) to settle in the city of Avignon, in southeastern France. Clement, critically ill with cancer, lacked the will to resist Philip.

The Babylonian Captivity

From 1309 to 1376, the popes lived in Avignon. This period in church history is often called the "Babylonian Captivity" (referring to the seventy years the ancient Hebrews were held captive in Mesopotamian Babylon). The Babylonian Captivity badly damaged papal prestige. The Avignon papacy reformed its financial administration and centralized its government. But the seven popes who resided at Avignon concentrated on bureaucratic matters to the exclusion of spiritual objectives. Some of them led austere lives there, but the general atmosphere was one of luxury and extravagance. The leadership of the church was cut off from its historic roots and the source of its ancient authority, the city of Rome. In the absence of the papacy, the Papal States in Italy lacked stability and good government. As long as the French crown dominated papal policy, papal influence in England (with which France was intermittently at war) and in Germany declined.

Many devout Christians urged the popes to return to Rome, and in 1377 Pope Gregory XI (r. 1370–1378) brought the papal court back to Rome. Unfortunately, he died shortly after the return. At Gregory's death, Roman citizens demanded an Italian pope who would remain in Rome. Determined to influence the papal *conclave* (the assembly of cardinals who chose the new pope) to elect an Italian, a Roman mob surrounded Saint Peter's Basilica, blocked the roads leading out of the city, and seized all boats on the Tiber River. Between the time of Gregory's death and the opening of the conclave, great pressure was put on the cardinals to elect an Italian. At the time, none of them protested this pressure. On April 7, 1378, after two ballots, they unanimously chose a distinguished administrator, the archbishop of Bari, Bartolomeo Prignano, who took the name Urban VI. Each of the cardinals swore that Urban had been elected "sincerely, freely, genuinely, and canonically."

Urban VI (r. 1378–1389) had excellent intentions for church reform. He wanted to abolish simony, *pluralism* (holding several church offices at the same time), absenteeism, clerical extravagance, and ostentation. These were the very abuses being increasingly criticized by Christian people across Europe. Unfortunately, Pope Urban went about the work of reform in a tactless, arrogant, and bullheaded manner. In the weeks following his coronation, Urban attacked clerical luxury, denouncing individual cardinals by name. He threatened to strike the cardinal archbishop of Amiens. Urban even threatened to excommunicate certain cardinals, and when he was advised that such excommunications would not be lawful unless the guilty had been warned three times, he shouted, "I can do anything, if it be my will and judgment."[35] Urban's quick temper and irrational behavior have led scholars to question his sanity. Whether he was medically insane or just drunk with power is a moot point. In any case, Urban's actions brought on disaster.

The cardinals declared Urban's election invalid because it had come about under threats from the Roman mob, and they asserted that Urban himself was excommunicated. Then they elected Cardinal Robert of Geneva, the cousin of King Charles V of France, as pope. Cardinal Robert took the name Clement VII. There were thus two popes: Urban at Rome and the "antipope" Clement VII (r. 1378–1394), who set himself up at Avignon in opposition to the legally elected Urban. So began the Great Schism, which divided Western Christendom until 1417.

The Great Schism

The powers of Europe aligned themselves with Urban or Clement along strictly political lines. France naturally recognized the French antipope, Clement. England, France's historic enemy, recognized Pope Urban. Scotland, whose attacks on England were subsidized by France, followed the French and supported Clement. The Holy Roman emperor, who bore ancient hostility to France, recognized Urban VI. At first the Italian city-states recognized Urban; but when he alienated them, they opted for Clement.

John of Spoleto, a professor at the law school at Bologna, eloquently summed up intellectual opinion of the schism: "The longer this schism lasts, the more it appears to be costing, and the more harm it does; scandal, massacres, ruination, . . . wars, rising tyranny, decreasing freedom.[36] The scandal "rent the seamless garment of Christ," as the church was called, and provoked horror and vigorous cries for reform. The common people, wracked by inflation, wars, and plague, were thoroughly confused about which pope was legitimate. At a time when ordinary Christians needed the consolation of religion and confidence in religious leaders, church officials were fighting among themselves for power.

The Conciliar Movement

Calls for church reform were not new. A half-century before the Great Schism, in 1324, Marsiglio of Padua, then rector of the University of Paris, had published *Defensor Pacis (The Defender of the Peace)*. Dealing as it did with the authority of state and church, *Defensor Pacis* proved to be one of the most controversial works written in the Middle Ages.

Marsiglio argued that the state was the great unifying power in society and that the church was subordinate to the state. He put forth the revolutionary ideas that the church had no inherent jurisdiction and should own no property. Authority in the Christian church, according to Marsiglio, should rest in a general council made up of laymen as well as priests and superior to the pope. These ideas directly contradicted the medieval notion of a society governed by the church and the state, with the church supreme. *Defensor Pacis* was condemned by the pope, and Marsiglio was excommunicated.

Even more earthshaking than the theories of Marsiglio of Padua were the ideas of the English scholar and theologian John Wyclif (1329–1384). Wyclif wrote that papal claims of temporal power had no foundation in the Scriptures and that the Scriptures alone should be the standard of Christian belief and practice. Sincere Christians, according to Wyclif, should read the Bible for themselves. In response to that idea, the first English translation of the Bible was produced and circulated.

Wyclif's views had broad social and economic significance. Wyclif urged that the church be stripped of its property. His idea that every Christian free of mortal sin possessed lordship was seized on by peasants in England during a revolt in 1381 and used to justify their goals. In advancing these views, Wyclif struck at the roots of medieval church structure and religious practices. Consequently, he has been hailed as a precursor of the Reformation of the sixteenth century. Although Wyclif's ideas were vigorously condemned by ecclesiastical authorities, they were widely disseminated by humble clerics and enjoyed great popularity in the early fifteenth century. In Bohemia, they were spread by John Hus (1369?–1415), rector of the University of Prague.

In response to continued calls throughout Europe for a council, the two colleges of cardinals— one at Rome, the other at Avignon—summoned a council at Pisa in 1409. A distinguished gathering of prelates and theologians deposed both popes and selected another. Neither the Avignon pope nor the Roman pope would resign, however, and the appalling result was a threefold schism.

Finally, because of the pressure of the German emperor Sigismund (r. 1411–1437), a great council met at the imperial city of Constance from 1414 to 1418. It had three objectives: to end the schism, to reform the church "in head and members" (from top to bottom), and to wipe out heresy. The council condemned John Hus, and he was burned at the stake. The council accepted the resignation of the Roman pope and deposed the pope chosen at Pisa and the antipope at Avignon. A conclave elected a new leader, the Roman cardinal Colonna, who took the name Martin V (r. 1417–1431).

Martin proceeded to dissolve the council. Nothing was done about reform. The schism was over, and though councils subsequently met at Basel and at Ferrara-Florence, in 1450 the papacy held a jubilee, celebrating its triumph over the conciliar movement. Later in the fifteenth century, the papacy concentrated on Italian problems to the exclusion of universal Christian interests. But the schism and the conciliar movement had exposed the crying need for ecclesiastical reform, thus laying the foundations for the great reform efforts of the sixteenth century.

THE LIFE OF THE PEOPLE

In the fourteenth century, economic and political difficulties, disease, and war profoundly affected the lives of European peoples. Decades of slaughter and destruction, punctuated by the decimating visits of the Black Death, made a grave economic situation virtually disastrous. In many parts of France and the Low Countries, fields lay in ruin or untilled for lack of labor power. In England, as taxes increased, criticisms of government policy and mismanagement multiplied. Crime, always a factor in social history, aggravated economic troubles, and throughout Europe the frustrations of the common people erupted into revolts. Nevertheless, marriage and the local parish church continued to be the center of life for most people.

Marriage

Life for those who were not clerics or nuns meant married life. The community expected people to marry. For a boy, childhood and youth included farm experience or training in a trade or skill; for a girl, childhood was preparation for marriage. In addition to the thousands of chores involved in running a household, girls learned obedience, or at least subordination. Adulthood for women meant living as a wife or widow.

In any case, sweeping statements about marriage in the Middle Ages have limited validity. Most peasants were illiterate and left slight record of their feelings toward their spouses or about marriage as an institution. The gentry, however, often could write, and letters exchanged between Margaret and John Paston, upper-middle-class people who lived in Norfolk, England, in the fifteenth century, provide important evidence of the experience of one couple.

John and Margaret Paston were married about 1439, after an arrangement concluded entirely by their parents. John spent most of his time in London fighting through the law courts to increase his family properties and business interests. Margaret remained in Norfolk to supervise the family lands. Her responsibilities involved managing the Paston estates, hiring workers, collecting rents, ordering supplies for the large household, hearing complaints and settling disputes among tenants, and marketing her crops. In these duties she proved herself a shrewd business person. Moreover, when an army of over a thousand men led by the aristocratic thug Lord Moleyns attacked her house, she successfully withstood the siege. When the Black Death entered her area, Margaret moved her family to safety.

Margaret Paston did all this on top of raising eight children (there were probably other children who did not survive childhood). Her husband died before she was forty-three, and she later conducted the negotiations for the children's marriages. Her children's futures, like her estate management, were planned with an eye toward economic and social advancement. When one daughter secretly married the estate bailiff, an alliance considered beneath her, the girl was cut off from the family as if she were dead.[37]

The many letters surviving between Margaret and John reveal slight tenderness toward their children. They seem to have reserved their love for each other, and during many of John's frequent absences they wrote to express mutual affection and devotion. How typical the Paston relationship was, modern historians cannot say, but the marriage of John and Margaret, though completely arranged by their parents, was based on respect, responsibility, and love.[38]

At what age did people usually marry? For girls, population surveys at Prato, in Italy, place the age at 16.3 years in 1372 and 21.1 in 1470. Chaucer's Wife of Bath says that she married first in her twelfth year. Recent research has indicated that in the Hohenzollern family in the later Middle Ages "five brides were between 12 and 13; five about 14, and five about 15."

Men were older when they married. An Italian chronicler writing about 1354 says that men did not marry before the age of 30. Chaucer's Wife of Bath describes her first three husbands as "goode

Prostitute Invites a Traveling Merchant Poverty and male violence drove women into prostitution, which, though denounced by moralists, was accepted as a normal part of the medieval social fabric. In the cities and larger towns where prostitution flourished, public officials passed laws requiring prostitutes to wear a special mark on their clothing, regulated hours of business, forbade women to drag men into their houses, and denied business to women with the "burning sickness," gonorrhea. *(Source: The Bodleian Library, Oxford)*

men, and rich, and old." Among seventeen males in the noble Hohenzollern family, eleven were over 20 years when married, five between 18 and 19, one 16. The general pattern in late medieval Europe was marriage between men in their middle or late twenties and women under twenty.[39] The later marriage age of men affected the number of children a couple had.

With marriage for men postponed, was there any socially accepted sexual outlet? Recent research on the southern French province of Languedoc in the fourteenth and fifteenth centuries has revealed the establishment of legal houses of prostitution.[40] Municipal authorities in Toulouse, Montpellier, Albi, and other towns set up houses or red-light districts either outside the city walls or away from respectable neighborhoods. The towns of Languedoc were not unique. In the cities and larger towns where prostitution flourished, public officials passed laws requiring prostitutes to wear a special mark on their clothing, regulating hours of business, forbidding women to drag men into their houses, and denying business to women with the "burning sickness," gonorrhea. Prostitution thus passed from being a private concern to a social matter requiring public supervision. Prostitution was an urban phenomenon because only populous towns had large numbers of unmarried young men, communities of transient merchants, and a culture accustomed to a cash exchange.

Although the risk of disease limited the number of years a woman could practice this profession, many women prospered. Archives in several cities show expensive properties bought by women who named their occupation as prostitution. Legalized prostitution suggests that public officials believed the prostitute could make a positive contribution to the society; it does not mean the prostitute was respected. Rather, she was scorned and distrusted. Legalized brothels also reflect a greater tolerance for male than for female sexuality.[41]

In the later Middle Ages, as earlier—indeed, until the late nineteenth century—economic factors rather than romantic love or physical attraction determined whom and when a person married. A young agricultural laborer on a manor had to wait until he had sufficient land. A journeyman craftsman in an urban guild faced the same material difficulties. Most men had to wait until their fathers died or yielded their holding. Prudent young men selected (or their parents selected for them) girls who would bring the most land or money to the union. Once a couple married, the union ended only with the death of one partner.

Deep emotional bonds knit members of medieval families. Most parents delighted in their children, and the church encouraged a cult of paternal care. The church stressed its right to govern and sanctify marriage, and it emphasized monogamy. Tight moral and emotional unity within marriages resulted.[42]

Divorce did not exist in the Middle Ages, although annulments were granted in extraordinary circumstances, such as male impotence, on the grounds that a lawful marriage had never existed. The church held that a marriage validly entered into could not be dissolved. A valid marriage consisted of the mutual oral consent or promise of two parties. Church theologians of the day urged that marriage be publicized by *banns*, or announcements made in the parish church, and that the couple's union be celebrated and witnessed in a church ceremony and blessed by a priest.

A great number of couples did not observe the church's regulations. Some treated marriage as a private act. They made the promise and spoke the words of marriage to each other without witnesses and then proceeded to enjoy the sexual pleasures of marriage. This practice led to a great number of disputes, for one or the other of the two parties could later deny having made a marriage agreement. The records of the ecclesiastical courts reveal many cases arising from privately made contracts. Evidence survives of marriages contracted in a garden, in a blacksmith's shop, at a tavern, and, predictably, in a bed.[43]

Life in the Parish

In the later Middle Ages, the land and the parish remained the focus of life for the European peasantry. Work on the land continued to be performed collectively. All men, for example, cooperated in the annual tasks of planting and harvesting. The close association of the cycle of agriculture and the liturgy of the Christian calendar endured. The parish priest blessed the fields before the annual planting, offering prayers on behalf of the people for a good crop. If the harvest was a rich one, the priest led the processions and celebrations of thanksgiving.

How did the common people feel about their work? Since the vast majority were illiterate and inarticulate, it is difficult to say. It is known that the peasants hated the ancient services and obligations on the lords' lands and tried to get them commuted for money rents. When lords attempted to reimpose service duties, the peasants revolted.

In the thirteenth century, the craft guilds provided the small minority of men and women living in towns and cities with the psychological satisfaction of involvement in the manufacture of a superior product. The craft guilds set high standards for their merchandise. Guild members also had economic security. The guilds looked after the sick, the poor, the widowed, and the orphaned. Masters and employees worked side by side.

In the fourteenth century, those ideal conditions began to change. The fundamental objective of the craft guild was to maintain a monopoly on its product, and to do so recruitment and promotion were carefully restricted. Some guilds required a high entrance fee for apprentices; others admitted only relatives of members. Apprenticeship increasingly lasted a long time, seven years. Even after a young man had satisfied all the tests for full membership in the guild and had attained the rank of master, he might need special connections just to join a guild. Women began to experience exclusion. A careful study of the records of forty-two craft guilds in Cologne, for example, shows that in the fifteenth century all but six became virtual male preserves, either greatly restricting women's participation or allowing so few female members that they cannot be considered mixed guilds.[44] The larger a particular business was, the greater was the likelihood that the master did not know his employees. The separation of master and journeyman and the decreasing number of openings for master craftsmen created serious frustrations. Strikes and riots occurred in the Flemish towns, in France, and in England.

The recreation of all classes reflected the fact that late medieval society was organized for war and violence was common. The aristocracy engaged in tournaments or jousts; archery and wrestling were popular among ordinary people. Everyone enjoyed the cruel sports of bullbaiting and bearbaiting. The hangings and mutilations of criminals were exciting and well-attended festive events. Chroniclers exulted in describing executions, murders, and massacres. Here a monk gleefully describes the gory execution of William Wallace in 1305:

Wilielmus Waleis, a robber given to sacrilege, arson and homicide . . . was condemned to most cruel but justly deserved death. He was drawn through the streets of London at the tails of horses, until he reached a gallows of unusual height, there he was suspended by a halter; but taken down while yet alive, he

Domestic Brawl   In all ages the hen-pecked husband has been a popular subject for jests. This elaborate woodcarving from a fifteenth-century English choir stall shows the husband holding distaff and ball of thread, symbolic of wife's work as "spinster," while his wife thrashes him. *(Source: Royal Commission on the Historical Monuments of England)*

was mutilated, his bowels torn out and burned in a fire, his head then cut off, his body divided into four, and his quarters transmitted to four principal parts of Scotland.[45]

Violence was as English as roast beef and plum pudding, as French as bread, cheese, and *potage*.

If violent entertainment was not enough to dispel life's cares, alcohol was also available. Beer or ale commonly provided solace to the poor, and the frequency of drunkenness reflects their terrible frustrations.

Upper-class violence and crime played a part in parish life. Many nobles turned to crime as a way of raising money. The fourteenth and fifteenth centuries witnessed a great deal of "fur-collar crime," so called for the miniver fur that members of the nobility alone were allowed to wear on their collars. England provides a good case study of upper-class crime.

Fur-collar crime rarely involved such felonies as homicide, robbery, rape, and arson. Instead, nobles used their superior social status to rob and extort from the weak and then to corrupt the judicial process. The rich suffered too. Attacks on the rich often took the form of kidnapping and extortion. Individuals were grabbed in their homes, and wealthy travelers were seized on the highways and held for ransom.[46]

Fur-collar criminals were terrorists, but like some twentieth-century white-collar criminals who commit nonviolent crimes, medieval aristocratic criminals got away with their outrages. When accused of wrongdoing, fur-collar criminals intimidated witnesses. They threatened jurors. They used "pull" or cash to bribe judges. As a fourteenth-century English judge wrote to a young nobleman, "For the love of your father I have hindered charges being brought against you and have prevented execution of indictment actually made."[47] Criminal activity by nobles continued decade after decade because governments were too weak to stop it.

During the fourteenth and fifteenth centuries, the laity began to exercise increasing control over parish affairs. Churchmen were criticized. The constant quarrels of the mendicant orders (the Franciscans and Dominicans), the mercenary and grasping attitude of the parish clergy, the scandal of the Great Schism and a divided Christendom— all these did much to weaken the spiritual mystique of the clergy in the popular mind. The laity

steadily took responsibility for the management of parish lands. Lay people organized associations to vote on and purchase furnishings for the church. And ordinary lay people secured jurisdiction over the structure of the church building, its vestments, books, and furnishings. These new responsibilities of the laity reflect the increased dignity of parishioners in the late Middle Ages.[48]

Peasant Revolts

Peasant revolts occurred often in the Middle Ages. Early in the thirteenth century, the French preacher Jacques de Vitry asked rhetorically, "How many serfs have killed their lords or burnt their castles?"[49] And in the fourteenth and fifteenth centuries, social and economic conditions caused a great increase in peasant uprisings (Map 14.8).

In 1358, when French taxation for the Hundred Years' War fell heavily on the poor, the frustrations of the French peasantry exploded in a massive uprising called the *Jacquerie,* after a supposedly happy agricultural laborer, Jacques Bonhomme (Good Fellow). Peasants in Picardy and Champagne went on the rampage. Crowds swept through the countryside slashing the throats of nobles, burning their castles, raping their wives and daughters, killing or maiming their horses and cattle. Peasants blamed the nobility for oppressive taxes, for the criminal brigandage of the countryside, for defeat in war, and for the general misery. Artisans, small merchants, and parish priests joined the peasants. Urban and rural groups committed terrible destruction, and for several weeks the nobles were on the defensive. Then the upper class united to repress the revolt with merciless ferocity. Thousands of the "Jacques," innocent as well as guilty, were cut down.

This forcible suppression of social rebellion, without some effort to alleviate its underlying causes, could only serve as a stopgap measure and drive protest underground. Between 1363 and 1484, serious peasant revolts swept the Auvergne; in 1380 uprisings occurred in the Midi; and in 1420 they erupted in the Lyonnais region of France.

The Peasants' Revolt in England in 1381, involving perhaps a hundred thousand people, was probably the largest single uprising of the entire Middle Ages (see Map 14.8). The causes of the rebellion were complex and varied from place to

The Jacquerie   Because social revolt on the part of the war-weary, frustrated poor seemed to threaten the natural order of Christian society during the fourteenth and fifteenth centuries, the upper classes everywhere exacted terrible vengeance on peasants and artisans. In this scene some *jacques* are cut down, some beheaded, and others drowned. *(Source: Bibliothèque Nationale, Paris)*

place. In general, though, the thirteenth century had witnessed the steady commutation of labor services for cash rents, and the Black Death had drastically cut the labor supply. As a result, peasants demanded higher wages and fewer manorial obligations. Thirty years earlier the parliamentary Statute of Laborers (1351) had declared:

Whereas to curb the malice of servants who after the pestilence were idle and unwilling to serve without securing excessive wages, it was recently ordained . . . that such servants, both men and women, shall be bound to serve in return for salaries and wages that were customary . . . five or six years earlier.[50]

This statute was an attempt by landlords to freeze wages and social mobility. It could not be enforced. As a matter of fact, the condition of the English peasantry steadily improved in the course of the fourteenth century. Some scholars believe that the peasantry in most places was better off in the period 1350 to 1450 than it had been for centuries before or was to be for four centuries after.

Why then was the outburst in 1381 so serious? It was provoked by a crisis of rising expectations. The relative prosperity of the laboring classes led to demands that the upper classes were unwilling to grant. Unable to climb higher, the peasants found release for their economic frustrations in revolt. But economic grievances combined with other factors. The south of England, where the revolt broke out, had been subjected to frequent and destructive French raids. The English government did little to protect the south, and villages grew increasingly scared and insecure. Moreover, decades of aristocratic violence, much of it perpetrated against the weak peasantry, had bred hostility and bitterness.

MAP 14.8 Fourteenth-Century Peasant Revolts In the later Middle Ages and early modern times, peasant and urban uprisings were endemic, as common as factory strikes in the industrial world. The threat of insurrection served to check unlimited exploitation.

The straw that broke the camel's back in England was the reimposition of a head tax on all adult males. Although the tax met widespread opposition in 1380, the royal council ordered the sheriffs to collect it again in 1381 on penalty of a huge fine. Beginning with assaults on the tax collectors, the uprising in England followed much the same course as had the Jacquerie in France. Castles and manors were sacked; manorial records were destroyed. Many nobles, including the archbishop of Canterbury, who had ordered the collection of the tax, were murdered.

Although the center of the revolt lay in the highly populated and economically advanced south and east, sections of the north and the Midlands also witnessed rebellions. Violence took different forms in different places. The townspeople of Cambridge expressed their hostility toward the university by sacking one of the colleges and building a bonfire of academic property. In towns containing skilled Flemish craftsmen, fear of competition led to their being brutalized. Urban discontent merged with rural violence. Apprentices and journeymen, frustrated because the highest guild positions were closed to them, rioted.

The boy-king Richard II (r. 1377–1399) met the leaders of the revolt, agreed to charters ensuring peasants' freedom, tricked them with false promises, and then proceeded to crush the uprising. Although the nobility tried to restore ancient duties of serfdom, virtually a century of freedom had elapsed, and the commutation of manorial services continued. Rural serfdom had disappeared in England by 1550.

Albrecht Dürer: The Four Horsemen of the Apocalypse   From right to left, representatives of war, strife, famine, and death gallop across Christian society, leaving thousands dead or in misery. The horrors of the age made this subject extremely popular in art, literature, and sermons. *(Source: Courtesy, Museum of Fine Arts, Boston)*

Conditions in England and France were not unique. In Florence in 1378, the *ciompi,* the poor propertyless workers, revolted. Serious social trouble also occurred in Lübeck, Brunswick, and other German cities. In Spain in 1391, aristocratic attempts to impose new forms of serfdom, combined with demands for tax relief, led to massive working-class and peasant uprisings in Seville and Barcelona. These took the form of vicious attacks on Jewish communities. Rebellions and uprisings everywhere reveal deep peasant and working-class frustration and the general socioeconomic crisis of the time.

SUMMARY

The High Middle Ages was one of the most creative periods in the history of Western society. Advances were made in the evolution of strong government and urban life, economic development, architectural design, and education. Through the instruments of justice and finance, the kings of England and France attacked feudal rights and provincial practices and built centralized bureaucracies. In so doing, these rulers laid the foundations for modern national states. The German emperors, preoccupied with Italian affairs and with a quest for the imperial crown, allowed feudal and local interests to triumph.

Medieval cities recruited people from the countryside and brought into being a new social class, the middle class. Cities provided economic opportunity, which, together with the revival of long-distance trade and a new capitalistic spirit, led to greater wealth, a higher standard of living, and upward social mobility. Medieval townspeople built soaring Gothic cathedrals, and universities, institutions of higher learning unique to the West, emerged from cathedral and municipal schools.

By the later Middle Ages, however, preachers likened the crises of their times to the Four Horsemen of the Apocalypse in the Book of Revelation, who brought famine, war, disease, and death. The crises of the fourteenth and fifteenth centuries were acids that burned deeply into the fabric of traditional medieval European society. Bad weather brought poor harvests, which contributed to the international economic depression. Disease, over which people also had little control, fostered

widespread depression and dissatisfaction. Population losses caused by the Black Death and the Hundred Years' War encouraged the working classes to try to profit from the labor shortage by selling their services higher: they wanted to move up the economic ladder. The ideas of thinkers like John Wyclif fanned the flames of social discontent. When peasant frustrations exploded in uprisings, the frightened nobility and upper middle class joined to crush the revolts and condemn heretical preachers as agitators of social rebellion. But the war had heightened social consciousness among the poor.

The Hundred Years' War served as a catalyst for the development of representative government in England. The royal policy of financing the war through Parliament-approved taxation gave the middle classes an increased sense of their economic power. They would pay taxes in return for some influence in shaping royal policies.

In France, by contrast, the war stiffened opposition to national assemblies. The disasters that wracked France decade after decade led the French people to believe that the best solutions to complicated problems lay not in an assembly but in the hands of a strong monarch.

Religion remained the cement that held society together. European culture was a Christian culture. But although the Church exercised leadership of Christian society in the High Middle Ages, the clash between the papacy and the kings of France and England at the end of the thirteenth century seriously challenged papal power. And the Great Schism weakened the prestige of the church and people's faith in papal authority. The conciliar movement, by denying the church's universal sovereignty, strengthened the claims of secular rulers to jurisdiction over all their peoples. The later Middle Ages witnessed a steady shift of basic loyalty from the church to the emerging national states.

NOTES

1. D. C. Douglas and G. E. Greenaway, eds., *English Historical Documents,* vol. 2 (London: Eyre & Spottiswoode, 1961), p. 853.
2. See G. M. Spiegel, "The Cult of Saint Denis and Capetian Kingship," *Journal of Medieval History* 1 (April 1975): 43–65, esp. 59–64.

3. J. Boswell, *Christianity, Social Tolerance, and Homosexuality: Gay People in Western Europe from the Beginning of the Christian Era to the Fourteenth Century* (Chicago: University of Chicago Press, 1980), pp. 270–293; the quotation is from p. 293. For alternative interpretations, see K. Thomas, "Rescuing Homosexual History," *New York Review of Books,* December 4, 1980, pp. 26ff.; and J. DuQ. Adams, *Speculum* 56 (April 1981): 350ff. For the French monarchy's persecution of the Jews, see J. W. Baldwin, *The Government of Philip Augustus: Foundations of French Royal Power in the Middle Ages* (Berkeley: University of California Press, 1986), pp. 51–52; and W. C. Jordan, *The French Monarchy and the Jews* (Philadelphia: University of Pennsylvania Press, 1989).

4. J. C. Russell, *Medieval Regions and Their Cities* (Bloomington: University of Indiana Press, 1972), p. 91.

5. Ibid., pp. 113–117.

6. Quoted in R. S. Lopez, "Of Towns and Trade," in *Life and Thought in the Early Middle Ages,* ed. R. S. Hoyt (Minneapolis: University of Minnesota Press, 1967), p. 33.

7. H. Pirenne, *Economic and Social History of Medieval Europe* (New York: Harcourt, Brace, 1956), p. 53.

8. See D. Herlihy, *Medieval and Renaissance Pistoia: The Social History of an Italian Town, 1200–1430* (New Haven, Conn.: Yale University Press, 1967), p. 257.

9. Douglas and Greenaway, pp. 969–970.

10. H. Rothwell, ed., *English Historical Documents,* vol. 3 (London: Eyre & Spottiswoode, 1975), p. 854.

11. See P. Dollinger, *The German Hansa,* trans. and ed. D. S. Ault and S. H. Steinberg (Stanford, Calif.: Stanford University Press, 1970).

12. C. M. Cipolla, *Before the Industrial Revolution: European Society and Economy, 1000–1700,* 2d ed. (New York: Norton, 1980), p. 197.

13. R. S. Lopez, "The Trade of Medieval Europe: The South," in *The Cambridge Economic History of Europe,* vol. 2, ed. M. M. Postan and E. E. Rich (Cambridge, England: Cambridge University Press, 1952), p. 289.

14. Quoted in H. E. Sigerist, *Civilization and Disease* (Chicago: University of Chicago Press, 1943), p. 102.

15. Quoted in J. H. Mundy, *Europe in the High Middle Ages, 1150–1309* (New York: Basic Books, 1973), pp. 474–475.

16. E. Panofsky, trans. and ed., *Abbot Suger on the Abbey Church of St. Denis and Its Art Treasures* (Princeton, N.J.: Princeton University Press, 1946), p. 101.

17. See J. Gimpel, *The Cathedral Builders* (New York: Grove Press, 1961), pp. 42–49.

18. J. B. Freed, *The Friars and German Society in the Thirteenth Century* (Cambridge, Mass.: Mediaeval Academy of America, 1977), p. 8.

19. Ibid., p. 9.

20. See F. Oakley, *The Western Church in the Later Middle Ages* (Ithaca, N.Y.: Cornell University Press, 1979), p. 175.

21. See Freed, pp. 119–128.

22. Ibid., esp. p. 125.

23. W. H. McNeill, *Plagues and Peoples* (New York: Doubleday, 1976), pp. 151–168.

24. Quoted in P. Ziegler, *The Black Death* (Harmondsworth, England: Pelican Books, 1969), p. 20.

25. J. M. Rigg, trans., *The Decameron of Giovanni Boccaccio* (London: J. M. Dent & Sons, 1903), p. 6.

26. Ziegler, pp. 232–239.

27. J. Hatcher, *Plague, Population and the English Economy, 1348–1530* (London: Macmillan Education, 1986), p. 33.

28. See G. P. Cuttino, "Historical Revision: The Causes of the Hundred Years' War," *Speculum 31* (July 1956): 463–472.

29. N. F. Cantor, *The English: A History of Politics and Society to 1760* (New York: Simon & Schuster, 1967), p. 260.

30. J. Barnie, *War in Medieval English Society: Social Values and the Hundred Years' War* (Ithaca, N.Y.: Cornell University Press, 1974), p. 6.

31. Quoted in Barnie, p. 34.

32. See M. M. Postan, "The Costs of the Hundred Years' War," *Past and Present 27* (April 1964): 34–63; G. O. Sayles, *The King's Parliament of England* (New York: Norton, 1974), esp. pp. 137–141.

33. Quoted in P. S. Lewis, "The Failure of the Medieval French Estates," *Past and Present 23* (November 1962): 6.

34. C. Stephenson and G. F. Marcham, eds., *Sources of English Constitutional History,* rev. ed. (New York: Harper & Row, 1972), p. 217.

35. Quoted in J. H. Smith, *The Great Schism 1378: The Disintegration of the Medieval Papacy* (New York: Weybright & Talley, 1970), p. 141.

36. Ibid., p. 15.

37. A. S. Haskell, "The Paston Women on Marriage in Fifteenth Century England," *Viator* 4 (1973): 459–469.

38. Ibid., p. 471.

39. See D. Herlihy, *Medieval Households* (Cambridge, Mass.: Harvard University Press, 1985), pp. 103–111.

40. L. L. Otis, *Prostitution in Medieval Society: The History of an Urban Institution in Languedoc* (Chicago: University of Chicago Press, 1987), p. 2.

41. Ibid., pp. 25–27, 64–66, 100–106.

42. Herlihy, *Medieval Households,* pp. 118–130.

43. See R. H. Helmholz, *Marriage Litigation in Medi-*

eval England (Cambridge: Cambridge University Press, 1974), pp. 28–29, et passim.

44. See M. C. Howell, *Women, Production, and Patriarchy in Late Medieval Cities* (Chicago: University of Chicago Press, 1986), pp. 134–135.

45. A. F. Scott, ed., *Everyone a Witness: The Plantagenet Age* (New York: Thomas Y. Crowell, 1976), p. 263.

46. B. A. Hanawalt, "Fur Collar Crime: The Pattern of Crime Among the Fourteenth-Century English Nobility," *Journal of Social History* 8 (Spring 1975): 1–14.

47. Quoted ibid., p. 7.

48. See E. Mason, "The Role of the English Parishioner, 1000–1500," *Journal of Ecclesiastical History* 27 (January 1976): 17–29.

49. Quoted in M. Bloch, *French Rural History,* trans. J. Sondeimer (Berkeley: University of California Press, 1966), p. 169.

50. Stephenson and Marcham, p. 225.

SUGGESTED READING

The achievements of the High Middle Ages have attracted considerable scholarly attention. Three general surveys of the period 1050 to 1300 are especially recommended: J. R. Strayer, *Western Europe in the Middle Ages* (1955), a masterful synthesis; J. W. Baldwin, *The Scholastic Culture of the Middle Ages* (1971); and F. Heer, *The Medieval World* (1963).

R. A. Brown, *The Normans* (1983), revitalizes the old thesis that the conquerors of England and Sicily were an exceptionally creative force in the eleventh and twelfth centuries. D. Howarth, *1066: The Year of the Conquest* (1981), is a lively and cleverly written account, from Norman, Scandinavian, and English perspectives, of the Norman conquest of England. G. O. Sayles, *The Medieval Foundations of England* (1961), traces political and social conditions to the end of the twelfth century.

Students interested in crime, society, and legal developments will find the following works useful and sound: J. B. Given, *Society and Homicide in Thirteenth-Century England* (1977); J. M. Carter, *Rape in Medieval England: An Historical and Sociological Study* (1985); R. C. Palmer, *The County Courts of Medieval England, 1150–1350* (1982); and the same scholar's *The Whilton Dispute, 1264–1380: A Social-Legal Study of Dispute Settlement in Medieval England* (1984). Elizabeth M. Hallam, *Domesday Book Through Nine Centuries* (1986), is an excellent recent appreciation of that important document. J. R. Strayer, *On the Medieval Origins of the Modern State* (1970), is a fine synthesis of political, legal, and administrative developments.

For France, both E. Hallam, *The Capetian Kings of France, 987–1328* (1980), and R. Fawtier, *The Capetian*

Kings of France (1962), are readable introductions. On Germany, G. Barraclough, *The Origins of Modern Germany* (1963), provides an excellent explanation of the problems and peculiarities of the Holy Roman Empire; this is a fine example of the Marxist interpretation of medieval history. M. Pacaut, *Frederick Barbarossa* (trans. A. J. Pomerans, 1980), is perhaps the best one-volume treatment of that important ruler, but P. Munz, *Frederick Barbarossa* (1979), is also important.

For the economic revival of Europe, see, in addition to the titles by Dollinger, Herlihy, Lopez, and Russell given in the Notes, G. J. Hodgett, *A Social and Economic History of Medieval Europe* (1974), a broad survey; C. M. Cipolla, *Before the Industrial Revolution: European Society and Economy, 1000–1700* (1980), which draws on recent research to treat demographic shifts, technological change, and business practices; and R. Lopez, *The Commercial Revolution of the Middle Ages* (1976). The effect of climate on population and economic growth is discussed in the remarkable work of E. L. Ladurie, *Times of Feast, Times of Famine: A History of Climate Since the Year 1000* (trans. B. Bray, 1971).

Students interested in the origins of medieval towns and cities will learn how historians use the evidence of coins, archeology, tax records, geography, and laws in J. F. Benton, ed., *Town Origins: The Evidence of Medieval England* (1968). H. Pirenne, *Early Democracy in the Low Countries* (1932), is an important and standard work. H. Saalman, *Medieval Cities* (1968), gives a fresh description of the layouts of medieval cities, with an emphasis on Germany, and shows how they were places of production and exchange. R. Muir, *The English Village* (1980), surveys many aspects of ordinary people's daily lives. For readability, few works surpass J. and F. Gies, *Life in a Medieval City* (1973).

For the new currents of thought in the High Middle Ages, see C. Brooke, *The Twelfth Century Renaissance* (1970), a splendidly illustrated book with copious quotations from the sources; E. Gilson, *Héloise and Abélard* (1960), which treats the medieval origins of modern humanism against the background of Abelard the teacher; C. H. Haskins, *The Renaissance of the Twelfth Century* (1971), a classic; and C. W. Hollister, ed., *The Twelfth Century Renaissance* (1969), a well-constructed anthology with source materials on many aspects of twelfth-century culture. N. Orme, *English Schools in the Middle Ages* (1973), focuses on the significance of schools and literacy in English medieval society. J. Leclercq, *The Love of Learning and the Desire of God* (1974), discusses monastic literary culture. For the development of literacy among lay people and the formation of a literate mentality, the advanced student should see M. T. Clanchy, *From Memory to Written Record: England, 1066–1307* (1979).

On the medieval universities, C. H. Haskins, *The Rise of the Universities* (1959), is a good introduction; H.

Rashdall, *The Universities of Europe in the Middle Ages* (1936), is the standard scholarly work. G. Leff, *Paris and Oxford Universities in the Thirteenth and Fourteenth Centuries* (1968), includes a useful bibliography.

N. Pevsner, *An Outline of European Architecture* (1963), provides a good general introduction to Romanesque and Gothic architecture. The following studies are all valuable for the evolution and development of the Gothic style: J. Harvey, *The Gothic World* (1969); the same author's *The Master Builders* (1971); P. Frankl, *The Gothic* (1960); O. von Simson, *The Gothic Cathedral* (1973); and J. Bony, *French Gothic Architecture of the 12th and 13th Centuries* (1983). D. Grivot and G. Zarnecki, *Gislebertus, Sculptor of Autun* (1961), is the finest appreciation of Romanesque architecture written in English. For the actual work of building, see D. Macaulay, *Cathedral: The Story of Its Construction* (1973), a prize-winning, simply written, and cleverly illustrated re-creation of the problems and duration of cathedral building. J. Gimpel, *The Cathedral Builders* (1961), explores the engineering problems involved in cathedral building and places the subject within its social context. E. G. Holt, ed., *A Documentary History of Art* (1957), contains source materials useful for writing papers. J. Gimpel, *The Medieval Machine: The Industrial Revolution of the Middle Ages* (1977), an extremely useful book, discusses the mechanical and scientific problems involved in early industrialization.

For the Black Death, see P. Ziegler, *The Black Death* (1969), a fascinating and highly readable study. For the social implications of disease, see W. H. McNeill, *Plagues and Peoples* (1976); F. F. Cartwright, *Disease and History* (1972); and H. E. Sigerist, *Civilization and Disease* (1970). For the economic effects of the plague, see J. Hatcher, *Plague, Population, and the English Economy, 1348–1550* (1977).

The standard study of the long military conflicts of the fourteenth and fifteenth centuries remains E. Perroy, *The Hundred Years' War* (1959). J. Barnie's *War in Medieval English Society,* treats the attitudes of patriots, intellectuals, and the general public. D. Seward, *The Hundred Years' War: The English in France, 1337–1453* (1981), tells an exciting story, and J. Keegan, *The Face of Battle* (1977), chap. 2, "Agincourt," describes what war meant to the ordinary soldier. B. Tuchman, *A Distant Mirror: The Calamitous Fourteenth Century* (1980), gives a vivid picture of many facets of fourteenth-century life while concentrating on the war. The best treatment of the financial costs of the war is probably M. M. Postan, "The Costs of the Hundred Years' War." E. Searle and R. Burghart, "The Defense of England and the Peasants' Revolt," *Viator* 3 (1972), is a fascinating study of the peasants' changing social attitudes. R. Barber, *The Knight and Chivalry* (1982), and M. Keen, *Chivalry* (1984), give fresh interpretations of the cultural importance of chivalry.

For political and social conditions in the fourteenth and fifteenth centuries, see the works by Lewis, Sayles, Bloch, Hanawalt, and Helmholz cited in the Notes. The following studies are also useful: P. S. Lewis, *Later Medieval France: The Polity* (1968); L. Romier, *A History of France* (1962); A. R. Meyers, *Parliaments and Estates in Europe to 1789* (1975); R. G. Davies and J. H. Denton, eds., *The English Parliament in the Middle Ages* (1981); I. Kershaw, "The Great Famine and Agrarian Crisis in England, 1315–1322," *Past and Present* 59 (May 1973); K. Thomas, "Work and Leisure in Pre-industrial Society," *Past and Present* 29 (December 1964); R. Hilton, *Bond Men Made Free: Medieval Peasant Movements and the English Rising of 1381* (1973), a comparative study; M. Keen, *The Outlaws of Medieval Legend* (1961) and "Robin Hood—Peasant or Gentleman?" *Past and Present* 19 (April 1961): 7–18; and P. Wolff, "The 1391 Pogrom in Spain: Social Crisis or Not?" *Past and Present* 50 (February 1971): 4–18. Students are especially encouraged to consult the brilliant achievement of E. L. Ladurie, *The Peasants of Languedoc* (trans. J. Day, 1976). R. H. Hilton, ed., *Peasants, Knights, and Heretics: Studies in Medieval English Social History* (1976), contains a number of valuable articles primarily on the social implications of agricultural change. J. C. Holt, *Robin Hood* (1982), is a soundly researched and highly readable study of the famous outlaw.

For women's economic status in the late medieval period, see the important study of M. C. Howell, *Women, Production, and Patriarchy in Late Medieval Cities* (1986). B. Hanawalt, *The Ties That Bind: Peasant Families in Medieval England* (1986), gives a living picture of the family lives of ordinary people in rural communities. D. Nicholas, *The Domestic Life of a Medieval City: Women, Children, and the Family in Fourteenth-Century Ghent* (1985), focuses on an urban society.

The poetry of Dante, Chaucer, and Villon may be read in the following editions: D. Sayers, trans., *Dante: The Divine Comedy,* 3 vols. (1963); N. Coghill, trans., *Chaucer's Canterbury Tales* (1977); P. Dale, trans., *The Poems of Villon* (1973). The social setting of *Canterbury Tales* is brilliantly evoked in D. W. Robertson, Jr., *Chaucer's London* (1968).

For the religious history of the period, F. Oakley, *The Western Church in the Later Middle Ages* (1979), is an excellent introduction, while R. N. Swanson, *Church and Society in Late Medieval England* (1989) provides a good synthesis of English conditions. S. Ozment, *The Age of Reform, 1250–1550* (1980), discusses the Great Schism and the conciliar movement in the intellectual context of the ecclesio-political tradition of the Middle Ages. Students seeking a highly detailed and comprehensive work should consult H. Beck et al., *From the High Middle Ages to the Eve of the Reformation,* trans. A. Biggs, vol. 14 in the History of the Church series edited by H. Jedin and J. Dolan (1980).

15

Africa Before European Intrusion, ca 400–1500

Ruins of Great Zimbabwe

Between about 400 and 1500, Africa witnessed the development of highly sophisticated civilizations alongside a spectrum of more simply organized societies. Until fairly recently, ethnocentrism, Eurocentrism, and white racism have limited what Asians, Europeans, and Americans have known about Africa. The more that historians, sociologists, and anthropologists have learned about early African civilizations, the more they have come to appreciate the richness, diversity, and dynamism of those cultures.

In a discussion of the major civilizations of Africa before 1500, this chapter explores the following questions:

- What patterns of social and political organization prevailed among the peoples of Africa?

- What types of agriculture and commerce did Africans engage in?

- What values do Africans' art, architecture, and religions express?

THE LAND AND PEOPLES OF AFRICA

Africa is immense. The world's second largest continent (after Asia), it is three times as big as Europe and covers 20 percent of the earth's land surface. Since much of the continent lies far from the ocean, Africa's peoples tend to be isolated from the populations of other continents. Five climatic zones roughly divide the continent (Map 15.1). Fertile land though with unpredictable rainfall borders parts of the Mediterranean coast in the north and the southwestern coast of the Cape of Good Hope in the south. Inland from these areas lies dry steppe country with little plant life. The southern fringe of this area is called the "Sabel." The steppes gradually give way to Africa's great deserts: the Sahara in the north and the Namib and Kalahari to the south. The vast Sahara—3.5 million square miles—takes its name from the Arabic word for "tan," the color of the desert. (Folk etymology ascribes the word *Sahara* to an ancient Arabic word that sounds like a parched man's gasp for water.) Dense, humid, tropical rain forests stretch along coastal West Africa and on both sides of the equator in central Africa until they are stopped by volcanic mountains two-thirds of the way across the continent. Savanna—flat grasslands —extends in a swath across the widest part of the continent, as well as across parts of south central Africa and along the eastern coast. One of the richest habitats in the world, the savanna has always invited migration and cultural contacts. Thus it is the most important region of West Africa historically.

The climate in most of Africa is tropical. Subtropical climates are limited to the northern and southern coasts and to regions of high elevation. Rainfall is seasonal in most parts of the continent and is very sparse in desert and semidesert areas.

Geography and climate have shaped the economic development of the peoples of Africa just as they have shaped the lives of people everywhere else. In the eastern African plains, the earliest humans hunted wild animals. The drier steppe regions favored the development of herding. Wetter savanna regions, like the Nile Valley, encouraged the rise of grain-based agriculture. The tropical forests favored hunting and gathering and, later, root-based agriculture. Regions around rivers and lakes supported economies based on fishing.

The peoples of Africa are as diverse as the topography of the continent. In North Africa, contacts with Asian and European civilizations date back to the ancient Phoenicians, Greeks, and Romans. The native Berbers, who lived along the Mediterranean, intermingled with many different peoples—with Muslim Arabs, who first conquered the region of North Africa in the seventh and eighth centuries A.D.; with Spanish Muslims and Jews, many of whom settled in North Africa after their expulsion from Spain in 1492 (see pages 532–533); and with sub-Saharan blacks.[1]

The Egyptians were a cultural rather than a racial group. Geography isolated them from the rest of the continent and brought them into contact with the ancient Greeks and other Mediterranean civilizations.

Black Africans inhabited the region south of the Sahara, an area of savanna and rain forest. In describing them, the ancient Greeks used the term

MAP 15.1 Africa Before 1500 For centuries trade linked West Africa with Mediterranean and Asian societies. Note the major climatic zones, the several trans-Saharan trade routes, and the routes along the East African coast.

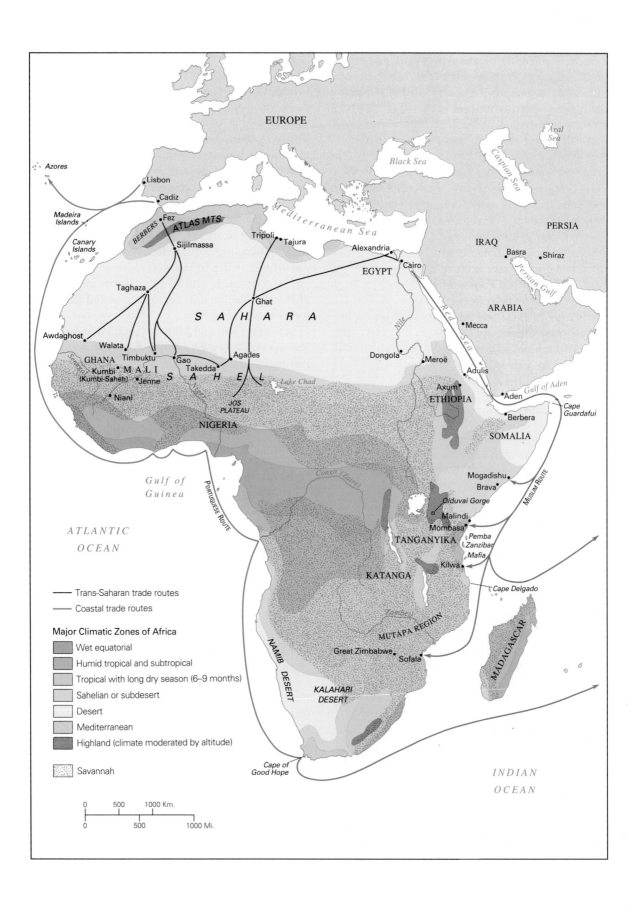

EUROPE

Azores

Lisbon

Cadiz

Madeira Islands

Canary Islands

BERBERS Fez ATLAS MTS.

Sijilmassa

Tripoli Tajura

Mediterranean Sea

Black Sea

Aral Sea

Caspian Sea

PERSIA

IRAQ

Basra

Shiraz

Alexandria

Cairo

EGYPT

Nile

Persian Gulf

ARABIA

Mecca

Taghaza

Ghat

S A H A R A

Awdaghost

Walata

GHANA   Timbuktu   Gao

Kumbi   MALI   Takedda

(Kumbi-Saheh)   Jenne

Niani

Agades

S A H E L

Lake Chad

JOS PLATEAU

NIGERIA

Red Sea

Dongola

Meroë

Adulis

Axum

ETHIOPIA

Berbera

Gulf of Aden

Cape Guardafui

SOMALIA

Gulf of Guinea

PORTUGUESE ROUTE

Congo (Zaire)

Mogadishu

Brava

MUSLIM ROUTE

ATLANTIC OCEAN

Olduvai Gorge

Malindi

Mombasa

TANGANYIKA   *Pemba*

Zanzibar

Mafia

Kilwa

KATANGA

Cape Delgado

Zambezi

MUTAPA REGION

NAMIB DESERT

Great Zimbabwe   Sofala

KALAHARI DESERT

MADAGASCAR

Trans-Saharan trade routes

Coastal trade routes

Major Climatic Zones of Africa

Wet equatorial

Humid tropical and subtropical

Tropical with long dry season (6–9 months)

Sahelian or subdesert

Desert

Mediterranean

Highland (climate moderated by altitude)

Savannah

Cape of Good Hope

INDIAN OCEAN

0   500   1000 Km.

0   500   1000 Mi.

Ethiopians, which meant "people with burnt faces." The Berbers coined the term *Akal-n-Iquina-wen,* which survives today as *Guinea.* The Arabs introduced another term, *Bilad al-Sudan,* which survives as *Sudan.* The Berber and Arab words both mean the "land of the blacks." Short-statured peoples sometimes called "Pygmies" inhabited the equatorial rain forests. South of those forests, in the southern third of the continent, lived the Khoisan, a small people of yellow-brown skin color who primarily were hunters.

EARLY AFRICAN SOCIETIES

Africa was one of the sites where agriculture began. Archeological investigations suggest that knowledge of cultivation moved west from ancient

Settled Agriculture This scene of cattle grazing near the group of huts (represented by stylized white ovals) reflects the domestication of animals and the development of settled pastoral agriculture. Note that it is the women and children (background) who perform the domestic chores. *(Source: Henri Lhote, Montrichard, France)*

Judaea (southern Palestine) and arrived in the Nile Delta in Egypt about the fifth millennium before Christ. Settled agriculture then traveled down the Nile Valley and moved west across the southern edge of the Sahara to the central and western Sudan. By the first century B.C. settled agriculture existed in West Africa. From there it spread to the equatorial forests. African farmers learned to domesticate plants, including millet, sorghum, and yams. Cereal-growing people probably taught forest people to plant regular fields. Gradually African farmers also learned to clear land by burning. Slowly they evolved a sedentary way of life: living in villages, clearing fields, relying on root crops, and fishing. As the importance of hunting declined in their lives, so did the need for periodic migrations.

Between 1500 and 1000 B.C., settled agriculture also spread southward from Ethiopia along the Rift Valley of present-day Kenya and Tanzania. Archeological evidence reveals that the peoples of this region grew cereals, raised cattle, and used tools made of wood and stone. Cattle raising spread more quickly than did planting. Early African peoples prized cattle highly. Many trading agreements, marriage alliances, political compacts, and treaties were negotiated in terms of cattle.

Scholars speculate that traders brought bananas, taros (a type of yam), sugar cane, and coconut palms to Africa from Southeast Asia. Because tropical forest conditions were ideal for banana trees, their cultivation spread rapidly; they were easier to raise than cereal grains. Donkeys, pigs, chickens, geese, and ducks were also domesticated.

The evolution to a settled life had profound effects. In contrast to nomadic conditions, settled societies made shared or common needs more apparent, and those needs strengthened ties among extended families. Population also increased:

The change from a hunter-gatherer economy to a settled farming economy affected population numbers. . . . Certainly in the agricultural economy there was more food available, if only because . . . it enabled more food to be extracted from a given piece of land. What remains uncertain is whether in the agricultural economy there were more people, better fed, or more people, less well fed. . . . In precolonial Africa agricultural and pastoral populations may not have increased steadily over time, but fluctuated cyclically, growing and declining, though overall slowly growing.²

Scholars dispute the route by which ironworking spread to sub-Saharan Africa. Some believe that the Phoenicians brought the technique for smelting iron to northwestern Africa and that from the north it spread southward. Others insist that it spread from the Meroe region on the Nile westward. Since most of West Africa had acquired knowledge of ironworking by 250 B.C., and since archeologists believe that Meroe achieved pre-eminence as an iron-smelting center only in the first century B.C., a stronger case can probably be made for the Phoenicians. The great African overland trade routes may have carried a knowledge of ironworking southward; in any case, by about A.D. 600 it was widely understood in sub-Saharan Africa. Ancient iron tools found at the village of Nok on the Jos Plateau in present-day Nigeria seem to prove a knowledge of ironworking in West Africa. Nok culture (ca 800 B.C.–A.D. 200) enjoys enduring fame for its fine terra-cotta (baked clay) sculptures.

Around the time of Christ, Bantu-speakers—a small group of people who had long occupied modern-day Nigeria on Africa's west coast—began to move southeastward, settling for a time in central Africa, south of the equatorial rain forests. Because much of central Africa is a plateau, its topsoil is thin and ground water is scarce. These conditions promote migratory rather than settled agriculture. The Bantu continued to move gradually south and east, reaching present-day Zimbabwe by the eighth century and the southeastern coast by the sixteenth century. Knowledge of ironworking gave the Bantu a distinct advantage over hunters and gatherers such as the Pygmy and Khoisan people they encountered, whom they absorbed and displaced.

Describing the village life of Bantu people in the nineteenth century, the Scottish missionary-explorer David Livingstone (1813–1873) wrote, "Food abounds, and very little labor is required for its cultivation. . . . When a garden becomes too poor for good crops . . . the owner removes a little farther into the forest, applies fire round the roots of the larger trees to kill them, cuts down the smaller, and a new, rich garden is ready for the seed."[3] One must be cautious in accepting at face value Livingstone's evaluation of the slight effort involved in cultivating the soil. Farming always requires considerable skill and labor—even more effort if performed by women, as much of it was in Africa.

AFRICAN KINGDOMS IN THE WESTERN SUDAN (CA 1000 B.C.–A.D. 200)

The region bounded on the north by the Sahara, on the south by the Gulf of Guinea, on the west by the Atlantic, and on the east by the mountains of Ethiopia is known as the "Sudan." In the savanna lands of the western Sudan—where the Bantu migrations originated—a series of dynamic kingdoms emerged in the millennium before European intrusion.

Between 1000 B.C. and A.D. 200, the peoples of the western Sudan made the momentous shift from nomadic hunting to settled agriculture. They cultivated crops with iron tools and domesticated animals for food. The rich savanna proved ideally suited to the production of cereals, especially rice, millet, and sorghum, and people situated near the Senegal River and Lake Chad supplemented their diet with fish. Food supply tends to affect population, and the peoples of the region—known as the "Mande" and the "Chadic speakers," or "Sao"—increased dramatically in number. By A.D. 400 the entire savanna, particularly the areas around Lake Chad, the Niger River bend, and present-day central Nigeria (see Map 15.1) had a large population.

Families and clans affiliated by blood kinship lived together in villages or small city-states. The basic social unit was the extended family. The village was governed by a chief in consultation with a council of elders. Some city-states and villages seem to have formed kingdoms. Village chiefs were responsible to regional heads, who answered to provincial governors, who were in turn responsible to a king. The various chiefs and their families formed an aristocracy. Kingship in the Sudan may have emerged from the priesthood, whose members were believed to make rain and to have contact with spirit powers. African kings always had religious sanction or support for their authority and were often considered divine. (In this respect, early African kingship bears a strong resemblance to Germanic kingship of the same period: the authority of the king rested in part on the ruler's ability to negotiate with outside powers, such as the gods.) The most prominent feature of early African society was a strong sense of community, based on the blood relationship and on religion.

African religions were animistic. Most people believed that a supreme being had created the universe and was the source of all life but individual men and women could not know or communicate with that being. The supreme being breathed spirit into all living things, and the *anima,* or spirit, residing in such things as trees, water, and earth had to be appeased. In the cycle of the agricultural year, for example, all the spirits had to be propitiated from the time of clearing the land through sowing the seed to the final harvest. Because special ceremonies and rituals were necessary to satisfy the spirits, special priests with the knowledge and power to communicate with them were needed. Thus the practice of African religion consisted primarily of sacred rituals performed by priests who were also the heads of families and villages. The head of each family was also responsible for maintaining the family ritual cults—ceremonies honoring the dead and living members of the family.[4]

In sum, extended families made up the villages that collectively formed small kingdoms. What spurred the expansion of these small kingdoms into formidable powers controlling sizable territory was the development of long-distance trade. And what made long-distance or trans-Saharan trade possible was the camel.

THE TRANS-SAHARAN TRADE

The camel had an impact on African trade comparable to the impact of the horse on European agriculture (see page 379). Although scholars dispute exactly when the camel was introduced from central Asia—first into North Africa, then into the Sahara and the Sudan—they agree that it was before A.D. 200. Camels can carry about 500 pounds as far as 25 miles a day and can go for days without drinking, living on the water stored in their stomachs. Camels were (and are) stupid and vicious. They had to be loaded on a daily, sometimes twice-daily, basis. And much of the cargo for a long trip consisted of provisions for the journey itself. Nevertheless, camels proved more efficient for desert transportation than horses or oxen. The use of this beast to carry heavy and bulky freight affected not only African economic and social change but the development of world commerce.

Sometime in the fifth century the North African Berbers adopted a saddle for use on the camel. The North African saddle had no direct effect on commercial operations, for a merchant usually walked and guided the camel on foot. But the saddle gave the Berbers and later the Arabian inhabitants of the region maneuverability on the animal and thus a powerful political and military advantage: they came to dominate the desert and to create lucrative routes across it. The Berbers determined who could enter the desert, and they levied heavy protection money on merchant caravans.

Between A.D. 700 and 900 the Berbers developed a network of caravan routes between the Mediterranean coast and the Sudan (see Map 15.1). The Morocco-Niger route ran from Fez to Sijilmasa on the edge of the desert and then south by way of Taghaza and Walata and back to Fez. Another route originated at Sijilmasa and extended due south to Timbuktu with a stop at Taghaza. A third route ran south from Tripoli to Lake Chad. A fourth ran from Egypt to Gao by way of the Saharan oases of Ghat and Agades and then on to Takedda.

The long expedition across the Sahara testifies to the spirit of the traders and to their passion for wealth. Ibn Battuta, an Arab traveler who made the journey in the fourteenth century when trans-Saharan traffic was at its height, wrote an account of the experience. Because of the blistering sun and daytime temperatures of 110, the caravan drivers preferred to travel at night, when the temperature might drop to the low 20s. Nomadic raiders, the Tuareg Berbers, posed a serious threat. The Tuaregs lived in the desert uplands and preyed on the caravans as a way of life. Consequently, merchants made safe-conduct agreements with them and selected guides from among them. Caravans of twelve thousand camels were reported in the fourteenth century. Large numbers of merchants crossed the desert together to discourage attack. Blinding sandstorms often isolated part of a line of camels and on at least one occasion buried alive some camels and drivers. Water was the biggest problem. The Tuaregs sometimes poisoned wells to wipe out caravans and steal their goods. In order to satisfy normal thirst and to compensate for constant sweating, a gallon of water a day per person was required. Desperate thirst sometimes forced the traders to kill camels and drink the foul, brackish water in their stomachs. It took Ibn Battuta twenty-five days to travel from Sijilmasa to the oasis of Taghaza and another sixty-five days to travel from Taghaza to the important market town of Walata. The entire trip took almost three months.

The Arab-Berber merchants from North Africa who controlled the caravan trade carried manufactured goods—silk and cotton cloth, beads, mirrors—as well as dates and salt (essential in tropical climates to replace the loss from perspiration) from the Saharan oases and mines to the Sudan. These products were exchanged for the much-coveted commodities of the West African savanna—gold, ivory, gum, kola nuts (eaten as a stimulant), and slaves.

The steady growth of trans-Saharan trade had three important effects on West African society. The trade stimulated gold mining and the search for slaves. Parts of modern-day Senegal, Nigeria, and Ghana contained rich veins of gold. Both sexes shared in mining it: the men sank the shafts and hacked out gold-bearing rocks and crushed them, separating the gold from the soil; the women washed the gold in gourds. Alluvial gold (mixed with soil, sand, or gravel) was separated from the soil by panning. Scholars estimate that by the eleventh century nine tons were exported to Europe annually, a prodigious amount, since even with modern machinery and sophisticated techniques the total gold exports from the same region in 1937 amounted to only twenty-one tons. A large percentage of this metal went to Egypt. From there it was transported down the Red Sea to India to pay for the spices and silks demanded by Mediterranean commerce. West African gold proved "absolutely vital for the monetization of the medieval Mediterranean economy and for the maintenance of its balance of payments with South Asia."[5] African gold linked the entire world, exclusive of the Western Hemisphere.

West Africa's second most valuable export was slaves. It seems that African slaves, like their early European and Asian counterparts, were peoples captured in war. In the Muslim cities of North Africa, southern Europe, and southwestern Asia, the demand for household slaves was high among the elite. Slaves were also needed to work the gold and salt mines. Recent research suggests, moreover, that large numbers of black slaves were recruited through the trans-Saharan trade for Muslim military service. The armed forces of medieval Islamic regimes in Morocco and Egypt consisted largely of slaves. High death rates from disease, manumission, and the assimilation of some blacks into Muslim society meant that the demand for

Ashanti Weight The Ashanti of Ghana used brass or bronze weights to measure gold dust, their major export. This weight, one of the largest found, probably was used in a chief's treasury. The weights often illustrated folk legends, proverbs, or scenes from everyday life. *(Source: Museum of Mankind (British Museum)/ Michael Holford)*

slaves remained high for centuries. Table 15.1 shows one scholar's tentative conclusions, based on many kinds of evidence, about the scope of the trans-Saharan slave trade. The total number of blacks enslaved over an 850-year period may be tentatively estimated at over 4 million.[6]

Slavery in Muslim societies, as in European and Asian countries before the fifteenth century, was not based strictly on skin color. The slaves exported from West Africa were all black, but Muslims also enslaved Caucasians who had been purchased, seized in war, or kidnapped from Europe. The households of wealthy Muslims in Cordoba, Alexandria, or Tunis often included slaves of a number of races, all of whom had been completely cut off from their cultural roots. Likewise, West African kings who sold blacks to traders from the north also bought a few white slaves—Slavic, British, and Turkish—for their domestic needs. Race had very little to do with the phenomenon of slavery.[7]

The trans-Saharan trade also stimulated the development of vigorous urban centers in West Africa. Scholars date the growth of African cities

TABLE 15.1   ESTIMATED MAGNITUDE OF TRANS-SAHARAN SLAVE TRADE, 650–1500

Years	Annual Average of Slaves Traded	Total
650–800	1,000	150,000
800–900	3,000	300,000
900–1100	8,700	1,740,000
1100–1400	5,500	1,650,000
1400–1500	4,300	430,000

Source: From R. A. Austen, "The Trans-Saharan Slave Trade: A Tentative Census," in The Uncommon Market: Essays in the Economic History of the Atlantic Slave Trade, *ed. H. A. Gemery and J. S. Hogendorn (New York: Academic Press, 1979). Used with permission.*

from around the beginning of the ninth century. Families that had profited from trade tended to congregate in the border zones between the savanna and the Sahara. They acted as middlemen between the miners to the south and Muslim merchants from the north. By the early thirteenth century, these families had become powerful black merchant dynasties. Muslim traders from the Mediterranean settled permanently in the trading depots, from which they organized the trans-Saharan caravans. The concentration of people stimulated agriculture and the craft industries. Gradually cities of sizable population emerged. Jenne, Gao, and Timbuktu, which enjoyed commanding positions on the Niger River bend, became centers of the export-import trade. Sijilmasa grew into a thriving market center. Kumbi, with between 15,000 and 20,000 inhabitants, was probably the largest city in the western Sudan in the twelfth century. (By European standards Kumbi was a metropolis; London and Paris achieved its size only in the late thirteenth century.) Between 1100 and 1400 these cities played a dynamic role in the commercial life of West Africa and Europe and became centers of intellectual creativity.

Perhaps the most influential consequence of the trans-Saharan trade was the introduction of Islam to West African society. Muslim expansion began soon after Muhammad's death in 632 (see pages

268–270). By the tenth century, Muslim Berbers controlled the north-south trade routes to the savanna. By the eleventh century, African rulers of Gao and Timbuktu had accepted Islam. The king of Ghana was also influenced by Islam. Muslims quickly became integral to West African government and society.

Conversion to Islam introduced West Africans to a rich and sophisticated culture. By the late eleventh century, Islam encompassed not only theological doctrines and a way of life but a body of legal traditions and writings, efficient techniques of government and statecraft, advanced scientific knowledge and engineering skills, and collections of lyric poetry and popular romances (see pages 289–292). At approximately the same time, Muslims were aiding Roger of Sicily in the construction of his state bureaucracy (see page 411) and guiding the ruler of Ghana in the operation of his administrative machinery. The king of Ghana adopted the Muslim *diwan*, the agency for keeping financial records. Because efficient government depends on the preservation of records, the arrival of Islam in West Africa marked the advent of written documents there. Arab Muslims also taught the rulers of Ghana how to manufacture bricks, and royal palaces and mosques began to be built of brick. African rulers corresponded with Muslim architects, theologians, and other intellectuals, who advised them on statecraft and religion. In sum, Islam accelerated the development of the African empires of the ninth through fifteenth centuries.

AFRICAN KINGDOMS AND EMPIRES (CA 800–1450)

All African societies shared one basic feature: a close relationship between political and social organization. Ethnic or blood ties bound clan members together. What scholars call "stateless societies" were culturally homogeneous ethnic societies. The smallest ones numbered fewer than a hundred people and were nomadic hunting groups. Larger stateless societies of perhaps several thousand people lived a settled and often agricultural or herding life.

The period from about 800 to 1450 witnessed the flowering of several powerful African states. In the western Sudan, the large empires of Ghana and Mali developed, complete with massive royal bureaucracies. On the east coast emerged powerful city-states based on sophisticated mercantile activities and, like the Sudan, very much influenced by Islam. In Ethiopia, in central East Africa, kings relied on the Christian faith of their people to strengthen political authority. In South Africa the empire of Great Zimbabwe, built on the gold trade with the east coast, flourished.

The Kingdom of Ghana (ca 900–1100)

So remarkable was the kingdom of Ghana during the age of Africa's great empires that writers throughout the medieval world, such as the fourteenth-century Muslim historian Ibn Khaldun, praised it as a model for other rulers. Medieval Ghana also holds a central place in the historical consciousness of the modern state of Ghana. Since this former British colony attained independence in 1957, its political leaders have hailed the medieval period as a glorious heritage. The name of the modern republic of Ghana—which in fact lies far from the site of the old kingdom—was selected to signify the rebirth of an age of gold in black Africa.

The nucleus of the territory that became the kingdom of Ghana was inhabited by Soninke people who called their ruler *ghana*, or war chief. By the late eighth century Muslim traders and other foreigners applied the word to the region where the Soninke lived, the black kingdom south of the Sahara. The Soninke themselves called their land "Aoukar" or "Awkar," by which they meant the region north of the Senegal and Niger rivers. Only the southern part of Aoukar received enough rainfall to be agriculturally productive, and it was in this area that the civilization of Ghana developed. Skillful farming and an efficient system of irrigation led to the production of abundant crops, which eventually supported a population of as many as 200,000.

The Soninke name for their king—war chief—aptly describes the king's major preoccupation in the tenth century. In 992 Ghana captured the Berber town of Awdaghast, strategically situated on the trans-Saharan trade route. Thereafter Ghana controlled the southern portion of a major caravan route. Before the year 1000 the rulers of Ghana

had extended their influence almost to the Atlantic coast and had captured a number of small kingdoms in the south and east. By the beginning of the eleventh century, the king exercised sway over a vast territory approximately the size of Texas. No other African power could successfully challenge him.

Throughout this vast area, all authority sprang from the king. The people considered him semisacred. Religious ceremonies and court rituals emphasized his sacredness and were intended to strengthen his authority. The king's position was hereditary in the matrilineal line—that is, the heir of the ruling king was one of his sister's sons (presumably the eldest or fittest for battle). According to the eleventh-century Spanish Muslim geographer al-Bakri (1040?–1094): "This is their custom . . . the kingdom is inherited only by the son of the

Arab Merchant-Scholars The Islamic faith and the Arabic language lent the Muslim world a unity that fostered the wide circulation of trade and ideas. *(Source: Bibliothèque Nationale/Sonia Halliday)*

king's sister. He the king has no doubt that his successor is a son of his sister, while he is not certain that his son is in fact his own."[8]

A council of ministers assisted the king in the work of government, and from the ninth century on most of these ministers were Muslims. Detailed evidence about the early Ghanaian bureaucracy has not survived, but scholars suspect that separate agencies were responsible for taxation, royal property, foreigners, forests, and the army. The royal administration was well served by Muslim ideas, skills, and especially literacy. The king and his people, however, clung to their ancestral religion, and the basic political institutions of Ghana remained African.

The king of Ghana held his court in Kumbi. Al-Bakri provides a valuable picture of the city in the eleventh century:

The city of Ghana consists of two towns lying on a plain, one of which is inhabited by Muslims and is large, possessing twelve mosques—one of which is a congregational mosque for Friday prayer; each has its imam, its muezzin and paid reciters of the Quran. The town possesses a large number of jurisconsults and learned men.[9]

The town inhabited by the king is six miles from the Muslim one and is called Al Ghana. . . . The residence of the king consists of a palace and a number of dome-shaped dwellings, all of them surrounded by a strong enclosure, like a city wall. In the town . . . is a mosque, where Muslims who come on diplomatic missions to the king pray. The town where the king lives is surrounded by domed huts, woods, and copses where priest-magicians live; in these woods also are the religious idols and tombs of the kings. Special guards protect this area and prevent anyone from entering it so that no foreigners know what is inside. Here also are the king's prisons, and if anyone is imprisoned there, nothing more is heard of him.[10]

The Muslim community in Ghana must have been large and prosperous to have supported twelve mosques. Either for their own protection or to preserve their special identity, the Muslims lived separate from the African artisans and tradespeople. The *imam* was the religious leader who conducted the ritual worship, especially the main prayer service on Fridays. Since Islamic worship had political connotations as well as religious

meaning, the imam was then, as now, both a political and a religious authority in the community. The *muezzin* leads the prayer responses after the imam; he must have a strong voice so that those at a distance and the women in the harem, or enclosure, can hear. Muslim religious leaders exercised civil authority over their coreligionists. Their presence and that of other learned Muslims also suggests vigorous intellectual activity.

Al-Bakri also describes the royal court:

The king adorns himself, as do the women here, with necklaces and bracelets; on their heads they wear caps decorated with gold, sewn on material of fine cotton stuffing. When he holds court in order to hear the people's complaints and to do justice, he sits in a pavilion around which stand ten horses wearing golden trappings; behind him ten pages stand, holding shields and swords decorated with gold; at his right are the sons of the chiefs of the country, splendidly dressed and with their hair sprinkled with gold. The governor of the city sits on the ground in front of the king with other officials likewise sitting around him. Excellently pedigreed dogs guard the door of the pavilion: they never leave the place where the king is; they wear collars of gold and silver studded with bells of the same material. The noise of a sort-of drum, called a daba, and made from a long hollow log, announces the start of the royal audience. When the king's coreligionists appear before him, they fall on their knees and toss dust on their heads—this is their way of greeting their sovereign. Muslims show respect by clapping their hands.[11]

What sort of juridical system did Ghana have? How was the guilt or innocence of an accused person determined? Justice derived from the king, who heard cases at court or on travels throughout his kingdom. As al-Bakri recounts:

When a man is accused of denying a debt or of having shed blood or some other crime, a headman (village chief) takes a thin piece of wood, which is sour and bitter to taste, and pours upon it some water which he then gives to the defendant to drink. If the man vomits, his innocence is recognized and he is congratulated. If he does not vomit and the drink remains in his stomach, the accusation is accepted as justified.[12]

This appeal to the supernatural for judgment was very similar to the justice by ordeal that prevailed among the English and Germanic peoples of western Europe at the same time. Complicated cases in Ghana seem to have been appealed to the king, who often relied on the advice of Muslim legal experts.

The king's elaborate court, the administrative machinery he built, and the extensive territories he governed were all expensive. The king of Ghana needed a lot of money, and he apparently had four main sources of support. The royal estates—some hereditary, others conquered in war—produced annual revenue, mostly in the form of foodstuffs for the royal household. The king also received tribute annually from subordinate chieftains. (Lack of evidence prevents an estimate of the value of this tax.) The third and probably largest source of income was customs duties on goods entering and leaving the country. Salt was the largest import. According to al-Bakri, "for every donkey that enters the country, the king takes a duty of one gold dinar and two for one that leaves."[13] Berber merchants paid a tax to the king on the cloth, metalwork, weapons, and other goods that they brought into the country from North Africa; in return these traders received royal protection from bandits. African traders bringing gold into Ghana from the south also paid the customs duty.

Finally, the royal treasury held a monopoly on the export of gold. The gold industry was undoubtedly the king's largest source of income. It was on gold that the fame of medieval Ghana rested. The eighth-century astronomer al-Fazari called Ghana the "land of gold"; the ninth-century geographer al-Ya-qubi wrote, "its king is mighty, and in his lands are gold mines. Under his authority are various other kingdoms—and in all this region there is gold."[14]

The governing aristocracy—the king, his court, and Muslim administrators—occupied the highest rank on the Ghanaian social ladder. The next rung consisted of the merchant class. Considerably below the merchants stood the farmers, cattle breeders, supervisors of the gold mines, and skilled craftsmen and weavers—what today might be called the "middle class." Some merchants and miners must have enjoyed great wealth, but, as in all aristocratic societies, money alone did not suffice. High status was based on blood and royal service. At the bottom of the social scale were the slaves, who worked in households, on farms, and in the mines. As in Asian and European societies

Royal Woman from Benin The elaborate gold headdress, the gold braided in her hair, and the heavy gold necklace indicate that this woman is from the royal class and attest to the wealth of the region. *(Source: Courtesy of the Trustees of the British Museum)*

of the time, slaves accounted for only a small percentage of the population.

Apart from these social classes stood the army. According to al-Bakri, "the king of Ghana can put 200,000 warriors in the field, more than 40,000 being armed with bow and arrow."[15] Like most medieval estimates, this is probably a gross exaggeration. Even a modern industrialized state with sophisticated means of transportation, communication, and supply lines would have enormous difficulty mobilizing so many men for battle. The king of Ghana, however, was not called "war chief" for nothing. He maintained at his palace a crack standing force of a thousand men, comparable to the Roman Praetorian Guard (see page 207). These thoroughly disciplined, well-armed,

Mali Horsemen Recent archeological excavations have uncovered evidence of an ancient artistic tradition in wood carving. In spite of the threats of weather, termites, and other insects, these wooden horses survived—showing that they were extensively decorated. *(Source: Australian National Gallery, Canberra)*

totally loyal troops protected the king and the royal court. They lived in special compounds, enjoyed the favor of the king, and sometimes acted as his personal ambassadors to subordinate rulers. In wartime, this regular army was augmented by levies of soldiers from conquered peoples and by the use of slaves and free reserves. The force that the king could field was sizable, if not as huge as al-Bakri estimated.

The Kingdom of Mali (ca 1200–1450)

During the century after the collapse of Kumbi, a cloud of obscurity hung over the western Sudan. The kingdom of Ghana split into several small kingdoms that feuded among themselves. One people, the Mandinke, lived in the kingdom of Kangaba on the upper Niger River. The Mandinke had long been part of the Ghanaian empire, and the Mandinke and Soninke belonged to the same language group. Kangaba formed the core of the new empire of Mali. Building on Ghanaian foundations, Mali developed into a better-organized and more powerful state than Ghana.

The kingdom of Mali (Map 15.2) owed its greatness to two fundamental assets. First, its strong agricultural and commercial base provided for a large population and enormous wealth. Second, Mali had two rulers, Sundiata and Mansa Musa, who combined military success with exceptionally creative personalities.

The earliest surviving evidence about the Mandinke, dating from the early eleventh century, indicates that they were extremely successful at agriculture. Consistently large harvests throughout the twelfth and thirteenth centuries meant a plentiful supply of food, which encouraged steady population growth. The geographical location of Kangaba also placed the Mandinke in an ideal position in West African trade. Earlier, during the period of Ghanaian hegemony, the Mandinke had acted as middlemen in the gold and salt traffic flowing north and south. In the thirteenth century Mandinke traders formed companies, traveled widely, and gradually became a major force in the entire West African trade.

Sundiata (ca 1230–1255) set up his capital at Niani, transforming the city into an important financial and trading center. He then embarked on a policy of imperial expansion. Through a series of military victories, Sundiata and his successors absorbed into Mali other territories of the former kingdom of Ghana and established hegemony over the trading cities of Gao, Jenne, and Walata.

These expansionist policies were continued in the fourteenth century by Sundiata's descendant Mansa Musa (ca 1312–1337), early Africa's most famous ruler. In the language of the Mandinke, *mansa* means "emperor." Mansa Musa fought many campaigns and checked every attempt at rebellion. Ultimately his influence extended northward to several Berber cities in the Sahara, eastward to Timbuktu and Gao, and westward as far as the Atlantic Ocean. Throughout his territories he maintained strict royal control over the rich trans-Saharan trade. Thus this empire, roughly twice the size of the Ghanaian kingdom and containing perhaps 8 million people, brought Mansa Musa fabulous wealth.

Mansa Musa built on the foundations of his predecessors. The stratified aristocratic structure of Malian society perpetuated the pattern set in Ghana, as did the system of provincial administration and annual tribute. The emperor took responsibility for the territories that formed the heart of the empire and appointed governors to rule the outlying provinces or dependent kingdoms. Here Mansa Musa made a significant innovation: in a practice strikingly similar to the French *appanages* of the time, he chose members of the royal family as provincial governors. He could count on their loyalty, and they received valuable experience in the work of government.

In another aspect of administration, Mansa Musa also differed from his predecessors. He became a devout Muslim. While most of the Mandinke clung to their ancestral animism, Islamic practices and influences in Mali multiplied.

The most celebrated event of Mansa Musa's reign was his pilgrimage to Mecca in 1324–1325, during which he paid a state visit to the sultan of Egypt. Mansa Musa's entrance into Cairo was magnificent. Preceded by five hundred slaves, each carrying a six-pound staff of gold, he followed with a huge host of retainers including one hundred elephants each bearing one hundred pounds of gold. Several hundred additional camels carrying food, supplies, and weapons brought up the rear. The emperor lavished his wealth on the citizens of the Egyptian capital. Writing twelve years later, al-Omari, one of the sultan's officials, recounts:

This man Mansa Musa spread upon Cairo the flood of his generosity: there was no person, officer of the court, or holder of any office of the Sultanate who did not receive a sum of gold from him. The people of Cairo earned incalculable sums from him, whether by buying and selling or by gifts. So much gold was current in Cairo that it ruined the value of money. . . . Let me add that gold in Egypt had enjoyed a high rate of exchange up to the moment of their arrival. . . . But from that day onward, its value dwindled; the exchange was ruined, and even now it has not recovered.[16]

Mansa Musa's gold brought about terrible inflation throughout Egypt. For the first time, the Mediterranean world gained concrete knowledge of the wealth and power of the black kingdom of Mali, and it began to be known as one of the great empires of the world. Mali retained this international reputation into the fifteenth century.

Musa's pilgrimage also had significant consequences within Mali. He gained some understanding of the Mediterranean countries and opened diplomatic relations with the Muslim rulers of Morocco and Egypt. His zeal for the Muslim faith and Islamic culture increased. Musa brought back from Arabia the distinguished architect al-Saheli, whom he commissioned to build new mosques at Timbuktu and other cities. These mosques served as centers for the conversion of Africans. Musa employed Muslim engineers to build in brick where pounded clay had formerly been used. He also encouraged Malian merchants and traders to wear the distinctive flowing robes and turbans of Muslim males.

Timbuktu began as a campsite for desert nomads. Under Mansa Musa it grew into a thriving entrepôt, attracting merchants and traders from

MAP 15.2 The Kingdom of Mali The economic strength of the kingdom of Mali rested heavily on the trans-Saharan trade.

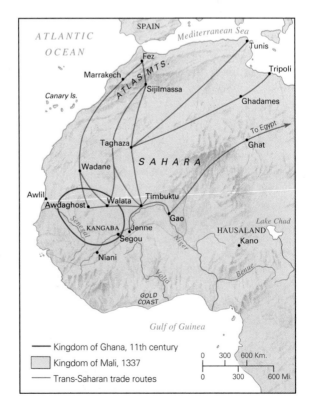

North Africa and all parts of the Mediterranean world. These people brought with them cosmopolitan attitudes and ideas. In the fifteenth century Timbuktu developed into a great center for scholarship and learning. Architects, astronomers, poets, lawyers, mathematicians, and theologians flocked there. One hundred and fifty schools were devoted to the study of the Qur'an. The school of Islamic law enjoyed a distinction in Africa comparable to the prestige of the law school at Bologna. A vigorous trade in books flourished in Timbuktu. Leo Africanus, a sixteenth-century Muslim traveler and writer who later converted to Christianity, recounts that around 1500 Timbuktu had a "great store of doctors, judges, priests, and other learned men that are bountifully maintained at the king's cost and charges. And hitherto are brought diverse manuscripts or written books out of Barbarie the north African states, from Egypt to the Atlantic Ocean which are sold for more money than any other merchandise." It is easy to understand why the university at Timbuktu was called by a contemporary writer "the Queen of the Sudan." Timbuktu's tradition and reputation for scholarship lasted until the eighteenth century.

In the fourteenth and fifteenth centuries many Muslim intellectuals and Arabic traders married native African women. These unions brought into being a group of racially mixed people. The necessity of living together harmoniously, the traditional awareness of diverse cultures, and the cosmopolitan atmosphere of Timbuktu all contributed to a rare degree of racial toleration and understanding. After visiting the court of Mansa Musa's successor in 1352–1353, Ibn Battuta observed that

the Negroes possess some admirable qualities. They are seldom unjust, and have a greater abhorrence of injustice than any other people. Their sultan shows no

Timbuktu Begun as a Tuareg seasonal camp in the eleventh century, Timbuktu emerged as a great commercial entrepôt in the fourteenth century and as an important Muslim educational center in the sixteenth. A strong agricultural base, watered by the nearby Niger River, supported a sizable population. *(Source: Library of Congress)*

Mosque at Timbuktu   This fascinating piece of architecture attests to the strong Muslim religious and intellectual influence at Timbuktu. Another mosque served as the university center there. *(Source: George Holton/Photo Researchers)*

mercy to anyone who is guilty of the least act of it. There is complete security in their country. Neither traveler nor inhabitant in it has anything to fear from robbers. . . . They do not confiscate the property of any white man who dies in their country, even if it be uncounted wealth. On the contrary, they give it into the charge of some trustworthy person among the whites, until the rightful heir takes possession of it. They are careful to observe the hours of prayer, and assiduous in attending them in congregations, and in bringing up their children to them. On Fridays, if a man does not go early to the mosque, he cannot find a corner to pray in, on account of the crowd.[17]

The East African City-States

In the first century A.D., a merchant-seaman from Alexandria in Egypt, possibly acting as an agent of the Roman imperial government, sailed down the Red Sea and out into the Indian Ocean. Along the coasts of East Africa and India he found seaports. He took careful notes on all he observed, and the result, *Periplus of the Erythraean Sea* (as the Greeks called the Indian Ocean), is the earliest surviving literary evidence of the city-states of the East African coast. Although primarily preoccupied with geography and navigation, the *Periplus* includes accounts of the local peoples and their commercial activities. Even in the days of the Roman emperors, the *Periplus* testifies, the East African coast had strong commercial links with India and the Mediterranean.

Greco-Roman ships traveled from Adulis on the Red Sea around the tip of the Gulf of Aden and down the African coast that the Greeks called "Azania," in modern-day Kenya and Tanzania (see Map 15.3). These ships carried manufactured goods—cotton cloth, copper and brass, iron tools, and gold and silver plate. At the African coastal emporiums, Mediterranean merchants exchanged these goods for cinnamon, myrrh and frankincense, slaves, and animal by-products such as ivory, rhinoceros horns, and tortoise shells. Somewhere around Cape Guardafui on the Horn of Africa, the ships caught the monsoon winds eastward to India, where ivory was in great demand.

An omission in the *Periplus* has created a debate over the racial characteristics of the native peoples in East Africa and the dates of Bantu migrations into the area. The author, writing in the first century, did not describe the natives; apparently he did not find their skin color striking enough to comment on. Yet in the fifth century, there are references to these peoples as "Ethiopians." Could this mean that migrating black Bantu-speakers reached the east coast between the first and the fifth centuries? Possibly. The distinguished archeologist Neville Chittick, however, thinks not:

The Periplus . . . *tells us nothing about the physical characteristics of the native inhabitants of the East African coast save that they were very tall. The fact that nothing is said about their color has been taken as indicating that they were not Negroid. But we are not really justified in drawing such a conclusion. The writer of the* Periplus *made few comments on the physical nature of the inhabitants of the countries which he described . . . therefore nothing can be based on the mere omission of any mention of skin color.*[18]

In the first few centuries of the Christian era, many merchants and seamen from the Mediterranean settled in East African coastal towns. Succeeding centuries saw the arrival of more traders. The great emigration from Arabia after the death of Muhammad accelerated Muslim penetration of the area, which the Arabs called the *Zanj,* "land of the blacks." Arabic Muslims established along the coast small trading colonies whose local peoples were ruled by kings and practiced various animistic religions. Eventually—whether through Muslim political hegemony or gradual assimilation—the coastal peoples slowly converted to Islam. Indigenous African religions, however, remained strong in the interior of the continent.

Beginning in the late twelfth century, fresh waves of Arabs and of Persians from Shiraz poured down the coast, first settling at Mogadishu, then pressing southward to Kilwa (see Map 15.3). Everywhere they landed, they introduced Islamic culture to the indigenous population. Similarly, Indonesians crossed the Indian Ocean and settled on the African coast and on the large island of Madagascar or Malagasy, an Indonesian word from the earliest Christian centuries through the Middle Ages. All these immigrants intermarried with Africans, and the resulting society combined Asian, African, and especially Islamic traits.

The East African coastal culture was called "Swahili," after a Bantu language whose vocabulary and poetic forms exhibit a strong Arabic influence. The thirteenth-century Muslim mosque at Mogadishu and the fiercely Muslim populations of Mombasa and Kilwa in the fourteenth century attest to strong Muslim influence.

Much current knowledge about life in the East African trading societies rests on the account of Ibn Battuta. The coastal cities were great commercial empires in the fourteenth and fifteenth centuries, comparable to Venice and Genoa. Like those Italian city-states, Kilwa, Mombasa, and Mafia were situated on offshore islands; the tidal currents that isolated them from the mainland also protected them from landside attack.

When Ibn Battuta arrived at Mogadishu, he was impressed, in the words of a modern historian,

with the size of the town, the . . . richly appointed palace. Traveling on to Kilwa, he found the city large and elegant, its buildings, as was typical along the coast, constructed of stone and coral rag [roofing slate]. Houses were generally single storied, consisting of a number of small rooms separated by thick walls supporting heavy stone roofing slabs laid across mangrove poles. Some of the more formidable structures contained second and third stories, and many were embellished with cut stone decorative borders framing the entranceways. Tapestries and ornamental niches covered the walls and the floors were carpeted. Of course, such appointments were only for the wealthy; the poorer classes occupied the timeless mud and straw huts of Africa, their robes a simple loincloth, their dinner a millet porridge.[19]

On the mainland were fields and orchards of rice, millet, oranges, mangoes, and bananas, and pastures and yards for cattle, sheep, and poultry. Yields were apparently high; Ibn Battuta noted that the rich enjoyed three enormous meals a day and were very fat.

From among the rich mercantile families that controlled the coastal cities arose a ruler who by the fourteenth century had taken the Arabic title *sheik,* which by this time had come to mean "sultan." The sheik governed both the island city and the nearby mainland. Farther inland, tribal chiefs ruled with the advice of councils of elders. By the late thirteenth century Kilwa had become the most powerful city on the coast, exercising political hegemony as far north as Pemba and as far south as Sofala (see Map 15.3).

The Portuguese, approaching the East African coastal cities in the late fifteenth century (see Map 15.1), were astounded at their enormous wealth and prosperity. This wealth rested on monopolistic control of all trade in the area. Some coastal cities manufactured goods for export: Mogadishu produced a cloth for the Egyptian market; Mom-

Church of St. George, Lalibela Shortly before A.D. 1100 the political capital of Ethiopia was moved south from Axum to Lalibela. Legend holds that St. George, the third-century Christian martyr, ordered villagers here to construct a church in his honor. They carved it from a hillside of volcanic rock. Worshipers entered through the subterranean trench to the left of the building, while concentric Greek crosses, formed of four equal arms and symbolizing the universal Christian Church, made up the roof. *(Source: Kal Mueller/Woodfin Camp & Associates)*

basa and Malindi processed iron tools; and Sofala made Cambay cottons for the interior trade. The bulk of the cities' exports, however, were animal products—leopard skins, tortoise shell, ambergris, ivory, and gold. The gold originated in the Mutapa region south of the Zambezi River, where the Bantu mined it. As in tenth-century Ghana, gold was a royal monopoly in the fourteenth-century coastal city-states. The Mutapa kings received it as annual tribute, prohibited outsiders from entering the mines or participating in the trade, and controlled shipments down the Zambezi to the coastal markets. The prosperity of Kilwa rested on its traffic in gold.

African goods satisfied the widespread aristocratic demand for luxury goods. In Arabia, leopard skins were made into saddles and shells into combs, and ambergris was used in the manufacture of perfumes. Because the tusks of African elephants were larger and more durable than the tusks of Indian elephants, African ivory was in great demand in India for sword and dagger handles, carved decorative objects, and the ceremonial bangles used in Hindu marriage rituals. In China, the wealthy valued African ivory for use in the construction of sedan chairs.

In exchange for these natural products, the Swahili cities bought pottery, glassware and beads, and many varieties of cloth. Swahili kings imposed enormous duties on imports, perhaps more than 80 percent of the value of the goods themselves. Even so, traders who came to Africa made fabulous profits.

Slaves were another export from the East African coast. Reports of slave trading began with the *Periplus,* accelerated with the establishment of Muslim settlements in the eighth century, and continued down to the arrival of the Portuguese in the late fifteenth century. (In fact, the East African coastal trade in slaves persisted at least to the beginning of the twentieth century.) The Arabs called the northern Somali coast *Ras Assir* ("Cape of Slaves"). From the ports of Brava, Mogadishu, Berbera, and Tajura, Arab traders transported slaves northward up the Red Sea and the Caspian Sea to the markets of Arabia, Persia, and Iraq. Muslim dealers also shipped blacks from the region of Zanzibar across the Indian Ocean to markets in India. Rulers of the Deccan in central India used large numbers of black soldier-slaves in their military campaigns. Slaves also worked on the docks and *dhows* (typical Arab lateen-rigged ves-

sels) in the Muslim-controlled Indian Ocean and as domestic servants and concubines throughout South and East Asia. As early as the tenth century, sources mention persons with "lacquer-black bodies" in the possession of wealthy families in Sung China.[20]

As in West Africa, African merchants recruited slaves primarily through raids and kidnappings in the interior. These businessmen responded to the demand for slaves: profit was their obvious motive. In the East African, Indian, and Chinese markets, however, slaves were never as valuable a commodity as ivory. Thus the volume of the eastern slave trade never approached that of the trans-Saharan trade.

Ethiopia: The Christian Kingdom of Axum

Egyptian culture exerted a profound influence on the sub-Saharan kingdom of Nubia in northeastern Africa (see Map 15.3). Nubia's capital was at Meroe; thus the country is often referred to as the Nubian kingdom of Meroe. The elaborate pyramids and temples that survive at Meroe attest to the strong Egyptian influence. As part of the Roman Empire, Egypt was naturally subject to Hellenistic and Roman cultural forces, and it became an early center of Christianity. Nubia, however, was never part of the Roman Empire; its people clung to ancient Egyptian religious ideas. Christian missionaries went to the upper Nile region and succeeded in converting the Nubian rulers around A.D. 600. By that time there were three separate Nubian states, of which the kingdom of Nobatia, centered at Dongola, was the strongest. The Christian rulers of Nobatia had close ties with the kingdom of Ethiopia.

The kingdom of Ethiopia, centered at Axum (Map 15.3), had had important commercial contacts with the Roman world. Perhaps partly for that reason, Axum officially adopted Christianity in A.D. 350, just a short time after Christianity became legal within the Roman Empire itself. Ethiopia adopted the Egyptian or Coptic form of Christianity. According to its Monophysitic doctrine, Christ has only one, divine, nature. Orthodox teaching holds that Christ's nature is both human and divine. The Egyptian patriarch of Alexandria appointed the first bishop of Axum, an appointment that led to close religious ties between Egypt and Ethiopia. At the time Axum was a powerful

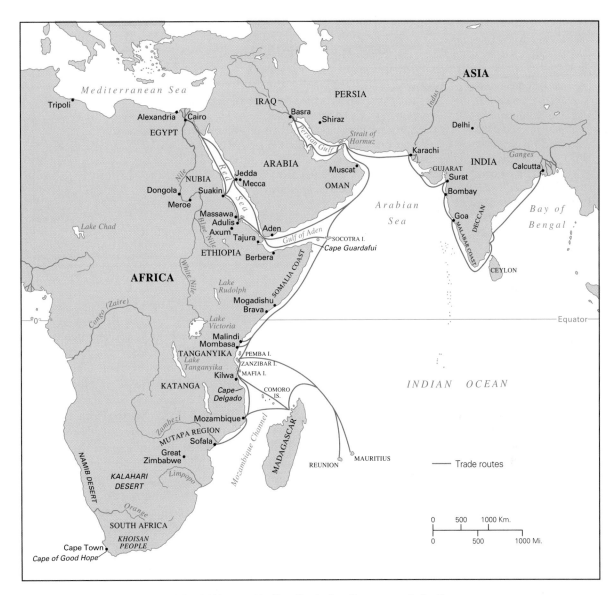

MAP 15.3 Trade Routes Between East Africa and India   The Indian Ocean, controlled by the Muslim merchant fleet until the arrival of the Portuguese in the late fifteenth century, was of far greater importance for world trade than the Mediterranean. Gold from Great Zimbabwe passed through the cities on the East African coast before shipment north to the Middle East and east to India and China.

cosmopolitan center whose mercantile activities played a major part in international commerce and whose military and political power was the dominant influence in East Africa.

The expansion of Islam in the eighth century severed Axum's commercial contacts with the Byzantine Empire and ended its control of the Red Sea routes. The kingdom declined as a major power. Ethiopia's high mountains encouraged an inward concentration of attention and hindered access from the outside. Twelfth-century crusaders returning from the Middle East told of a powerful Christian ruler, Prester John, whose lands lay behind Muslim lines and who was eager to help restore the Holy Land to Christian control. Europeans identified that kingdom with Ethiopia. In the later thirteenth century, the dynasty of the Solomonid kings witnessed a literary and artistic

AFRICA, CA 400–1500

ca 1st century A.D.	Beginning of Bantu migrations
ca A.D. 200	First use of the camel for trans-Saharan transportation
4th century	Ethiopia accepts Christianity
600–1500	Extensive slave trade from sub-Saharan Africa to the Mediterranean
6th and 7th centuries	Political and commercial ascendancy of Ethiopia
9th century	Decline of Ethiopia
11th century	Islam penetrates sub-Saharan Africa
	Height of the kingdom of Ghana
13th and 14th centuries	Kingdom of Mali
1312–1337	Mansa Musa, medieval Africa's most famous ruler
14th and 15th centuries	Height of the Swahili (East African) city-states

renaissance particularly notable for works of hagiography (biographies of saints), biblical exegesis, and manuscript illumination. The most striking feature of Ethiopian society in the period from 500 to 1500 was the close relationship between the church and the state. Coptic Christianity inspired a fierce devotion and tended to equate doctrinal heresy with political rebellion, thus reinforcing central monarchial power.

South Africa

South Africa, the region bordered on the northwest by tropical grasslands and on the northeast by the Zambezi River (see Map 15.3), enjoys a mild and temperate climate. Desert conditions prevail along the Atlantic coast, which gets less than five inches of annual rainfall. Eastward rainfall increases, though some areas still receive less than twenty inches a year. Although the Limpopo Valley in the east is very dry, temperate grasslands characterize the highlands of the region of the modern Orange Free State, the Transvaal, and Zimbabwe. Considerable climatic variations occur throughout much of South Africa from year to year.

Located at the southern extremity of the Afro-Eurasian land mass, South Africa has a history that is very different from the histories of West Africa, the Nile Valley, and the east coast. Over the centuries, North and West Africa felt the influences of Phoenician, Greek, Roman, and

Muslim cultures; the Nile Valley experienced the impact of major Egyptian, Assyrian, Persian, and Muslim civilizations; and the East African coast had important contacts across the Indian Ocean with southern and eastern Asia and across the Red Sea with Arabia and Persia. South Africa, however, remained far removed from the outside world until the arrival of the Portuguese in the late fifteenth century. With an important exception. Bantu-speaking people reached South Africa in the eighth century. They brought with them skills in ironworking and mixed farming (settled crop production plus cattle and sheep raising) and an immunity to the kinds of diseases that later decimated the Amerindians of South America (see pages 573–574).

The earliest residents of South Africa were hunters and gatherers. In the first millennium after the birth of Christ, new farming techniques from the north arrived. A lack of water and timber (which were needed to produce the charcoal used in iron smelting) slowed the spread of iron technology and tools and thus of crop production in western South Africa. These advances, however, reached the western coastal region by 1500. By that date Khoisan-speakers were farming in the arid western regions. To the east, descendants of Bantu immigrants grew sorghum, raised sheep and cattle, and fought with iron-headed spears. They practiced polygamy and traced their descent in the male line.

In 1871 a German explorer discovered the ruined city of Great Zimbabwe southeast of the modern Rhodesian town of Fort Victoria. Archeologists consider Great Zimbabwe the most powerful monument in Africa south of the Nile Valley and the Ethiopian highlands. The ruins consist of two vast complexes of dry-stone buildings, a fortress, and an elliptically shaped enclosure commonly called "the Temple." Stone carvings, gold and copper ornaments, and Asian ceramics once decorated the buildings. The ruins extend over sixty acres and are encircled by a massive wall. The entire city was built from local granite between the eleventh and fifteenth centuries without any outside influence.

These ruins tell a remarkable story. Great Zimbabwe was the political and religious capital of a vast empire. During the first millennium A.D., settled crop cultivation, cattle raising, and work in metal led to a steady build-up in population in the Zambezi-Limpopo region. The area also contained a rich gold-bearing belt. Gold ore lay near the surface; alluvial gold lay in the Zambezi River tributaries. In the tenth century the inhabitants collected the alluvial gold by panning and washing; after the year 1000 the gold was worked in open mines with iron picks. Traders shipped the gold eastward to Sofala (see Map 15.3). The wealth and power of Great Zimbabwe rested on this gold trade.[21]

Great Zimbabwe declined in the fifteenth century, perhaps because the area had become agriculturally exhausted and could no longer support the large population. Some people migrated northward and settled in the valley of the Mazoe River, a tributary of the Zambezi. This region also contained gold. The settlers built a new empire in the tradition of Great Zimbabwe. Rulers of this

Ruins of Great Zimbabwe   Considered the most impressive monument in the African interior south of the Ethiopian highlands, these ruins of Great Zimbabwe consist of two complexes of dry-stone buildings, some surrounded by a massive serpentine wall 32 feet high and 17 feet thick at its maximum. Great Zimbabwe was the center of a state whose wealth rested on gold. *(Source: Robert Aberman/Werner Forman Archive)*

empire were called "Mwene Mutapa," and their power too was based on the gold trade carried on by means of the Zambezi River and Indian Ocean ports. It was this gold that the Portuguese sought when they arrived on the East African coast in the late fifteenth century.

SUMMARY

In the fifteenth century, the African continent contained a number of very different societies and civilizations. In West Africa, Mali continued the brisk trade in gold, salt, and slaves that had originated many centuries earlier. Islam, which had spread to sub-Saharan Africa through the caravan trade, had tremendous influence on the peoples of the western Sudan, their administrative forms, and their cities. The impact of the Islamic faith was also felt in East Africa, whose bustling port cities were in touch with the cultures of the Mediterranean and the Indian Ocean. While the city-states of the eastern coast conducted complicated mercantile activities with foreign powers, the Christian kingdom of Ethiopia led an isolated, inward-looking existence. In South Africa, the vast empire of Great Zimbabwe was giving way to yet another kingdom whose power was based on precious gold.

NOTES

1. See J. Hiernaux, *The People of Africa* (New York: Scribner's, 1975), pp. 46–48.
2. "African Historical Demography" (Proceedings of a seminar held in the Centre of African Studies, University of Edinburgh, April 29–30, 1977), p. 3.
3. Quoted in R. W. July, *Precolonial Africa: An Economic and Social History* (New York: Scribner's, 1975), p. 135.
4. J. S. Trimingham, *Islam in West Africa* (Oxford: Oxford University Press, 1959), pp. 6–9.
5. R. A. Austen, *Africa in Economic History* (London: James Currey/Heinemann, 1987), p. 36
6. R. A. Austen, "The Trans-Saharan Slave Trade: A Tentative Census," in *The Uncommon Market: Essays in the Economic History of the Atlantic Slave Trade,* ed. H. A. Gemery and J. S. Hogendorn

(New York: Academic Press, 1979), pp. 1–71, esp. p. 66.
7. July, pp. 124–129.
8. Quoted in J. O. Hunwick, "Islam in West Africa, A.D. 1000–1800," in *A Thousand Years of West African History,* ed. J. F. Ade Ajayi and I. Espie (New York: Humanities Press, 1972), pp. 244–245.
9. Quoted in A. A. Boahen, "Kingdoms of West Africa, c. A.D. 500–1600," in *The Horizon History of Africa* (New York: American Heritage, 1971), p. 183.
10. Al-Bakri, *Kitab al-mughrib fdhikr bilad Ifriqiya wa'l-Maghrib (Description de l'Afrique Septentrionale),* trans. De Shane (Paris: Adrien-Maisonneuve, 1965), pp. 328–329.
11. Quoted in R. Oliver and C. Oliver, eds., *Africa in the Days of Exploration* (Englewood Cliffs, N.J.: Prentice-Hall, 1965), p. 10.
12. Quoted in Boahen, p. 184.
13. Quoted in ibid.
14. Quoted in E. J. Murphy, *History of African Civilization* (New York: Delta, 1972), p. 109.
15. Quoted ibid., p. 111.
16. Quoted ibid., p. 120.
17. Quoted in Oliver and Oliver, p. 18.
18. H. N. Chittick, "The Peopling of the East African Coast," in *East Africa and the Orient: Cultural Syntheses in Pre-Colonial Times.* ed. H. N. Chittick and R. I. Rotberg (New York: Africana Publishing, 1975), p. 19.
19. July, p. 209.
20. See Austen, "The Trans-Saharan Slave Trade," p. 65; J. H. Harris, *The African Presence in Asia* (Evanston, Ill.: Northwestern University Press, 1971), pp. 3–6, 27–30; and P. Wheatley, "Analecta Sino-Africana Recensa," in *East Africa and the Orient,* ed. Chittick and Rotberg, p. 109.
21. P. Curtin et al., *African History* (New York: Longman, 1984), rev. ed., pp. 284–287.

SUGGESTED READING

The titles by Austen, Chittick, Curtin et al., Hiernaux, and Wheatley listed in the Notes represent some of the recent scholarship on early African history, and they are especially recommended. Most contain useful bibliographies. In addition, the enterprising student should see H. P. White and M. B. Gleave, *An Economic Geography of West Africa* (1971), and N. C. Pollock and S. Agnew, *An Historical Geography of South Africa* (1963). Colin M. Turnbull, *Man in Africa* (1976), and R. E. Leakey and R. Lewin, *Origins: What New Discoveries Reveal*

About the Emergence of Our Species and Its Possible Future (1977), are important for the discoveries of the earliest human skeletons. R. Olaniyan, *African History and Culture* (1982), is a useful general survey. For the importance of the camel to African trade, see R. W. Bulliet, *The Camel and the Wheel* (1975).

For specific topics raised in early African history, see, in addition to the titles listed in the Notes, R. Oliver and G. Mathew, eds., *History of East Africa* (1963), the standard work on the eastern part of the continent, which has a valuable chapter on the coastal city-states; G. S. P. Freeman-Grenville, *The East African Coast: Select Documents from the First to the Earlier Nineteenth Century* (1962), which contains excellent material from Arabic, Chinese, and Portuguese perspectives; D. Conrad and H. Fisher, "The Conquest That Never Was: Ghana and the Almoravids," *History of Africa* 9 (1982): 21–59; M. Klein and P. E. Lovejoy, "Slavery in West Africa," in Gemery and Hogendorn's *The Uncommon Market* (see the Notes); and R. S. Smith, *Warfare and Diplomacy in Pre-colonial West Africa* (1976). On the important topic of Islam, see J. S. Trimingham's *A History of Islam in West Africa* (1970) and *Islam in East Africa* (1974), which are standard works. J. Kritzeck and W. H. Lewis, eds., *Islam in Africa* (1969), and M. Lombard, *The Golden Age of Islam* (1975), are also helpful.

16

The Americas Before European Intrusion, ca 400–1500

Toltec statuary

In 1501–1502 the Florentine explorer Amerigo Vespucci (1451–1512) sailed down the eastern coast of South America to Brazil. Convinced that he had found a new world, Vespucci published an account of his voyage. Shortly thereafter the German geographer Martin Waldseemüller proposed that this new world be called "America" to preserve Vespucci's memory. Initially applied only to South America, by the end of the sixteenth century the term *America* was used for both continents in the Western Hemisphere.

To the people of the Americas, the notion of a discovery meant nothing. The New World was, in a sense, a European invention. And even for Europeans the concept of discovery presented problems. In matters of geography, as in other branches of knowledge, medieval Europeans believed that all human knowledge was contained in the Scriptures, the writings of the church fathers, and the Greek and Roman authors, none of whom mentioned a new world. The adventurous explorers of the fifteenth and sixteenth centuries sailed west searching for Asia and Africa because Europeans believed that those continents and Europe were the only world that existed. They did not expect to find new continents. Long before the arrival of Europeans, however, sophisticated civilizations were flourishing in Central and South America.

- What is the geography of the Americas and how did it shape the lives of the peoples?
- What patterns of social and political organization did Amerindian peoples display before the European intrusion?
- What are the significant cultural achievements of the Mayas, Aztecs, and the Incas?

This chapter considers these questions.

THE GEOGRAPHY AND PEOPLES OF THE AMERICAS

The distance from the Bering Strait, which separates Asia from North America, to the southern tip of South America is about eleven thousand miles. A mountain range extends all the way from Alaska to the tip of South America, crossing Central America from northwest to southeast and making for rugged country along virtually the entire western coast of both continents.

Scholars use the term *Mesoamerica* to designate the area of present-day Mexico and Central America. Mexico is dominated by high plateaus bounded by coastal plains. Geographers have labeled the plateau regions "cold lands," the valleys between the plateaus "temperate lands," and the Gulf and Pacific coastal regions "hot lands." The Caribbean coast of Central America—modern Belize, Guatemala, Honduras, Nicaragua, El Salvador, Costa Rica, and Panama—is characterized by thick jungle lowlands, heavy rainfall, and torrid heat; it is an area generally unhealthy for humans. Central America's western uplands, with their more temperate climate and good agricultural land, support the densest population in the region.

The continent of South America, south of the Isthmus of Panama, contains thirteen nations: in descending order of size, Brazil, Argentina, Peru, Colombia, Bolivia, Venezuela, Paraguay, Chile, Ecuador, Guyana, Uruguay, Surinam, and French Guiana. Brazil—three times the size of Argentina and almost one hundred times larger than French Guiana—is about the same size as the United States including Alaska.

Like Africa, South America is a continent of extremely varied terrain. The entire western coast is edged by the Andes, the highest mountain range in the Western Hemisphere. Mount Alcanqua in Argentina rises 23,000 feet, 3,000 feet higher than the tallest mountain in the United States. On the east coast another mountain range, called the "Brazilian Highlands," accounts for one-fourth of the area of Brazil. Yet three-fourths of South America—almost the entire periphery of the continent—is plains. The Amazon River, at 4,000 miles the second longest river in the world, bisects the north central part of the continent. The Amazon drains 2.7 million square miles of land in Brazil, Colombia, and Peru. Tropical lowland rain forests, characterized by dense growth and annual rainfall in excess of 80 inches, extend from the Amazon and Orinoco river basins northward all the way to southern Mexico. This jungle, the largest in the world, covers parts of Brazil, Venezuela, and Ecuador.

Most scholars believe that people began crossing the Bering Strait from Russian Siberia between

50,000 and 20,000 years ago, when the strait was narrower than it is today. Skeletal finds indicate that these immigrants belonged to several ethnic groups. Anthropologists classify the earliest of them as Amurians, short-statured people with long flat heads and coppery skin—a physical type once common in Asia and Europe. The last to arrive, at about the time of Christ, had strong Mongoloid features, large faces, and yellowish skin. The American Indians, or Amerindians, represent a hybrid of Amurians and Mongoloids.

Nomadic and technologically primitive, Amerindians lived by hunting small animals, fishing, and gathering wild fruits. As soon as an area had been exploited and the group had grown too large for the land to support, some families moved on, usually southward. Gradually the newcomers spread throughout the Americas, losing contact with one another.

At the time the Europeans arrived, most of the peoples of North America and the huge Amazon Basin were Neolithic hunters and farmers, some migratory and some living in villages. Big-game hunters, armed with heavy stone missiles, necessarily traveled in small groups. Sizable populations, however, grew among the peoples who learned to cultivate the soil. By necessity or experimentation or accident, they discovered how to domesticate plants. Archeological excavations in Mexico City indicate that corn was grown there around 2500 B.C. Before 2300 B.C. the Amerindians also were raising beans, squash, pumpkins, and, in the area of modern Peru, white potatoes.

In central Mexico, the Amerindians built *chinampas,* floating gardens, by dredging soil from the bottom of a lake or pond, placing the soil on mats of woven twigs, and planting crops in the soil. Chinampas were enormously productive, yielding up to three harvests a year. So extensive was this method of agriculture that central Mexico became known as the "chinampas region." In Peru, meanwhile, the Andean mountain slopes were terraced with stone retaining walls to keep the hillsides from sliding. Both chinampas and terraced slopes required large labor forces, making stable settlement essential.

Careful cultivation of the land meant a reliable and steady food supply, which contributed to a relatively high fertility rate and in turn to a population boom. Because corn and potatoes require much less labor than does grain, Amerindian civilizations were able to use their large labor forces in the construction of religious and political buildings and as standing armies.[1] Agricultural advancement thus had definitive social and political consequences.

MESOAMERICAN CIVILIZATIONS FROM THE OLMEC TO THE TOLTEC

The period between ca 1500 B.C. and ca 900 A.D. witnessed the rise of several ancient American civilizations. Archeological investigations of these civilizations are still underway, and more questions

Olmec Mother and Child The Olmecs excelled in sculpture and modeled in clay, jade, and basalt. Much of their work reflects a religious impulse. *(Source: The Metropolitan Museum of Art)*

than answers about them remain, but students generally accept a few basic conclusions. Scholars believe the Olmec represent the most ancient advanced Amerindian civilization. Their culture spread over regions in central Mexico that lie thousands of miles apart. The Olmec tradition of building scattered ceremonial centers based on an extensive agricultural foundation found its highest cultural expression in the civilization of the Maya. The Maya occupied an area comprising the present-day Yucatán, the highland crescent of eastern Chiapas in Mexico, much of Guatemala and western Honduras. In the central plateau of Mexico an "empire" centered at Teotihuacán arose. Scholars hotly debate whether the Teotihuacán territory constituted an empire, but they agree that Teotihuacán society was heavily stratified and that it exercised military, religious, and political power over a wide area. The Toltec, whose culture adopted many features of Teotihuacán and Olmec civilizations, was the last advanced Amerindian civilization before the rise of the Aztec.

The Olmec

Population growth led to the development of the first distinct Mesoamerican civilization, the Olmec, which scholars estimate to have thrived from approximately 1500 B.C. to A.D. 300. All subsequent Mesoamerican cultures have rested on the Olmec. Originating at present-day San Lorenzo in the region of southern Veracruz and Tabasco (see Map 16.2), Olmec society revolved around groups of large stone buildings where the political elite and the priestly hierarchy resided with their retainers. Peasant farmers inhabited the surrounding countryside. From careful study of the surviving architectural monuments and their richly carved jade sculptures, scholars have learned that a small hereditary elite governed the mass of workers and that the clustered buildings served as sites for religious ceremonies and as marketplaces for the exchange of agricultural produce and manufactured goods. The Olmecs also possessed a form of writing. Around 900 B.C. San Lorenzo was destroyed, probably by migrating peoples from the north, and power passed to La Venta in Tabasco.

At La Venta, archeological excavation has uncovered the huge volcano-shaped Great Pyramid. Built 110 feet high at an inaccessible site on an is-

land in the Tonala River, the Great Pyramid was the center of the Olmec religion. The upward thrust of this monument, like that of the cathedrals of medieval Europe, may have represented the human effort to get closer to the gods. Built of huge stone slabs, the Great Pyramid required, scholars have estimated, some 800,000 man-hours of labor. It testifies to the region's bumper harvests, which supported a labor force large enough to build such a monument. Around 300 B.C., however, La Venta fell. Tres Zapotes, 100 miles to the northwest, became the leading Olmec site. Olmec ceremonialism, magnificent sculpture, skillful stone work, social organization, and writing were important cultural advances that paved the way for the developments of the Classic period (A.D. 300–900), the golden age of Mesoamerican civilization.

The Maya of Central America

In the Classic period another Amerindian people, the Maya, attained a level of intellectual and artistic achievement equaled by no other Indian people in the Western Hemisphere and by few peoples throughout the world. The Maya developed a sophisticated system of writing perhaps derived partly from the Olmec. They also invented a calendar considered more accurate than the European Gregorian calendar. And the Maya made advances in mathematics that Europeans did not match for several centuries. Who were the Maya and where did they come from? What was the basis of their culture? What is the significance of their intellectual and artistic achievement?

The word *Maya* seems to derive from *Zamna*, the early Maya culture god. On the basis of linguistic evidence, scholars believe that the first Maya were a small North American Indian group who emigrated from southern Oregon and northern California to the western highlands of Guatemala. Between the third and second millennia B.C. various groups, including the Cholans and Tzeltalans, broke away from the parent group, moving north and east into the Yucatán Peninsula. The Cholan-speaking Maya, who occupied the area during the time of great cultural achievement, apparently created the culture.

Maya culture rested on agriculture. As rice proved the staple of the diet in Asia and wheat in

Europe, so in Mesoamerica maize (corn) became the basic or staple crop. In 1972, a geographer and an aerial photographer studying the Campeche region (Map 16.1) proved that the Maya practiced intensive agriculture in raised fields, narrow rectangular plots built above the low-lying, seasonally inundated lands bordering rivers. Because of poor soil caused by heavy tropical rainfall and the fierce sun, farmers may also have relied on *milpa* for growing maize. Using this method, farmers cut down a patch of forest land and set the wood and brush afire. They then used a stick to poke holes through the ash and planted maize seed in the holes. A milpa (meaning both the area and the method) produced for only two years, after which it had to lie fallow for between four and seven years.

In addition to maize, the Maya grew beans, squash, chili peppers, some root crops, and fruit trees. Turkeys were domesticated, but barkless dogs that were fattened on corn seem to have been the main source of protein. In the Yucatán, men trapped fish along the shores. Cotton was widely exported, as the discovery of rich Maya textiles all over Mesoamerica attests.

The raised-field and milpa systems of intensive agriculture yielded food sufficient to support large population centers. The entire Maya region could have had as many as 14 million inhabitants. At Uxmal, Uaxactún, Copan, Piedras Negras, Tikal, Palenque, and Chichén Itza (see Map 16.1), archeologists have uncovered the palaces of nobles, elaborate pyramids where nobles were buried, engraved steles (stone-slab monuments), masonry temples, altars, sophisticated polychrome pottery, and courts for games played with a rubber ball. The largest site, Tikal, may have had 40,000 people. Since these centers lacked commercial and industrial activities, scholars avoid calling them "cities." Rather they were religious and ceremonial centers.

Although Maya sources rarely mention marketplaces in Maya population centers, the Maya carried on extensive long-distance trade with other Mesoamerican peoples. The shipment of products from various local regions to areas where they were needed helped hold the Maya settlements together. Wealth seems to have been concentrated in a few hands, probably in one clan or lineage that enjoyed great power, but the Maya apparently had no distinct mercantile class. They did have sharply

MAP 16.1 The Maya World, A.D. 300–900 Archeologists have discovered the ruins of dozens of Maya city-states, only the largest of which are shown here. Called the "Greeks of the New World," the Maya perfected the only written language in the Western Hemisphere, developed a sophisticated political system and a flourishing trade network, and created elegant art.

defined social classes, however. A hereditary elite owned private land, defended society, carried on business activities, directed religious rituals, and held all political power. The intellectual class also belonged to the ruling nobility. The rest of the people were free workers, serfs, and slaves.

The Maya developed a system of hieroglyphic writing with 850 characters and used it to record chronology, religion, and astronomy in books made of bark paper and deerskin. The recent deciphering of this writing has demonstrated that inscriptions on steles are actually historical documents recording the births, accessions, marriages, wars, and deaths of Maya kings. An understanding of the civilization's dynastic history allows scholars to interpret more accurately Maya pictorial imagery and to detect patterns in Maya art. They are finding that the imagery explicitly portrays the text in pictorial scenes and on stelar carvings.[2]

Cylindrical Vessel Because the Maya suffered a high death rate from warfare, sacrificial ritual, and natural causes, the subject of death preoccupied them. Many art objects depict death as a journey into Xibalba, the Maya hell, and to rebirth for the Maya in children and grandchildren who replace them. Here three Xibalbans receive a sacrificial head on a drum. The scrawny torso of one has the look of starvation, and the excrement implies a revolting smell. The next figure, with a skeletal head, insect wings, and a distended stomach suggests a parasitic disease. A common if nauseating scene. *(Source: © Justin Kerr 1985. Courtesy Houston Art Museum)*

A method of measuring and recording time to arrange and commemorate events in the life of a society and to plan the agricultural and ceremonial year is a basic feature of all advanced societies. From careful observation of the earth's movements around the sun, the Maya invented a calendar of eighteen 20-day months and one 5-day month, for a total of 365 days. Using a system of bars (— = 5) and dots (° = 1), the Maya devised a form of mathematics based on the vigesimal (20) rather than the decimal (10) system. The Maya proved themselves masters of abstract knowledge—notably in astronomy, mathematics, calendric development, and the recording of history.

Maya civilization lasted about a thousand years, reaching its peak in about A.D. 500–800, the period when the T'ang Dynasty was flourishing in China, Islam was spreading in the Middle East, and Carolingian rulers were extending their sway in Europe. Between the eighth and tenth centuries, the Maya abandoned their cultural and ceremonial centers, and Maya civilization collapsed. Why?

Archeologists and historians have advanced several theories: foreign invasions led by peoples attracted to the wealth of the great centers, domestic revolts of subject peoples, disease, overpopulation caused by crop failures, the acquisition of such broad territories by expansionist kings that rulers could not govern them effectively. Just as students give no single reason for the decline and fall of the Roman Empire in Europe, so current scholarship holds that the fall of Maya civilization involved many factors. But the Maya were not totally vanquished. Having resisted Indian invaders and the encroachments of Spanish American civilization, about two million Maya survive today in the Yucatán peninsula of Mexico.

Teotihuacán and Toltec Civilizations

During the Classic period the Teotihuacán Valley in central Mexico witnessed the flowering of a remarkable civilization. The culture of Teotihuacán seems to have been built by a new people from regions east and south of the Valley of Mexico. The city of Teotihuacán had a population of over 200,000—larger than any European city at the time. The inhabitants were stratified into distinct social classes. The rich and powerful elite resided in a special precinct, in houses of palatial splendor. Ordinary working people, tradespeople, artisans, and obsidian craftsmen lived in apartment compounds, or *barrios,* on the edge of the city. Around A.D. 600 each of these compounds housed about a hundred people; archeological research is slowly yielding information about their standard of living. The inhabitants of the barrios seem to have been very poor and related by kinship ties and perhaps by shared common ritual interests. Agricultural laborers lived outside the city. Teotihuacán was a great commercial center, the entrepôt for trade and culture for all of Mesoamerica. It was also the ceremonial center of an entire society, a capital filled with artworks, a mecca that attracted thousands of pilgrims a year.

In the center of the city stood the pyramids of the Sun and Moon. The Pyramid of the Sun, each of whose sides is 700 feet long and 200 feet high, was built of sun-dried bricks and faced with stone. The smaller Pyramid of the Moon was similar in construction. In lesser temples, natives and outlanders worshiped the rain-god and the feathered serpent, later called "Quetzalcoatl." These gods were associated with the production of corn, the staple of the people's diet.

Although Teotihuacán dominated Mesoamerican civilization during the Classic period, other centers also flourished. In the isolated valley of Oaxaca at modern-day Monte Albán (see Map 16.2), for example, Zapotecan-speaking peoples established a great religious center whose temples and elaborately decorated tombs testify to the wealth of the nobility. The art—and probably the entire culture—of Monte Albán and other centers derived from Teotihuacán.

As had happened to San Lorenzo and La Venta, Teotihuacán collapsed before invaders. Around A.D. 700 semibarbarian hordes from the southwest burned Teotihuacán; Monte Albán fell shortly afterward. By 900 the golden age of Mesoamerica had ended.

There followed an interregnum known as the "Time of Troubles" (ca A.D. 800–1000), characterized by disorders and an extreme militarism. Whereas nature gods and their priests seem to have governed the great cities of the earlier period, militant gods and warriors dominated the petty states that now arose. Among these states, the most powerful heir to Teotihuacán was the Toltec confederation, a weak union of strong states. The Toltecs admired the culture of their predecessors and sought to absorb and preserve it; through intermarriage, they assimilated with the Teotihuacán people. In fact, every new Mesoamerican confederation became the cultural successor of earlier ones.

Under Toliptzin (ca 980–1000), the Toltecs extended their hegemony over most of central Mexico. He established his capital at Tula, whose splendor and power became legendary during his reign. Apparently Toliptzin took the name "Quetzalcoatl," signifying his position as high priest of the Teotihuacán god worshiped by the Toltecs. According to the "Song of Quetzalcoatl," a long Aztec glorification of Toliptzin,

he was very rich and had everything necessary to eat and drink, and the corn under his reign was in abundance, and the squash very fat, an arm's length around, and the ears of corn were so tall that they were carried with both arms. . . . And more than that the said Quetzalcoatl had all the wealth of the world, gold and silver and green stones jade and other precious things and a great abundance of coca trees in different colors, and the said vassals of the said Quetzalcoatl were very rich and lacked nothing. . . . Nor did they lack corn, nor did they eat the small ears but rather they used them like firewood to heat up their baths.[3]

Later, Aztec legends would describe a powerful struggle between the Toltecs' original tribal god, Tezcatlipoca, who required human sacrifices, and the newer Toltec-Teotihuacán god, Quetzalcoatl, who gave his people bumper corn crops, fostered learning and the arts, and asked only the sacrifice of animals like butterflies and snakes. Tezcatlipoca won this battle, and the priest-king Toliptzin-Quetzalcoatl was driven into exile. As he departed, he promised to return and regain his kingdom.

Whatever reality lies behind this legend, it became a cornerstone of Aztec tradition. It also played a profound role in Mexican history: by a remarkable coincidence, the year that Quetzalcoatl had promised to return happened to be the year when the Spanish explorer Hernando Cortés landed in Mexico. Belief in the Quetzalcoatl legend helps explain the Aztec emperor Montezuma's indecisiveness about the Spanish adventurers and his ultimate fate (pages 571–572).

After the departure of Toliptzin-Quetzalcoatl, troubles beset the Toltec state. Drought led to crop failure. Northern barbarian peoples, the Chichimec, attacked the borders in waves. Weak, incompetent rulers could not quell domestic uprisings. When the last Toltec king committed suicide in 1174, the Toltec state collapsed. In 1224 the Chichimec captured Tula.

The last of the Chichimec to arrive in central Mexico were the Aztecs. As before, the vanquished strongly influenced the victors: the Aztecs ab-

Tezcatlipoca and Quetzalcoatl The Aztecs were deeply concerned with the passage of time, and like the Maya they had a solar year of 365 days divided into 18 months of 20 days each. The Aztec *tonalamatl,* or sacred "book of days," included a ritual calendar that portrayed thirteen Lords of the Day and nine Lords of the Night, each of them associated with a particular bird. This early sixteenth-century illustration of a book of days shows Tezcatlipoca and Quetzalcoatl, who were major Lords of the Day. *(Source: Bibliothèque de l'Assemblée, Paris)*

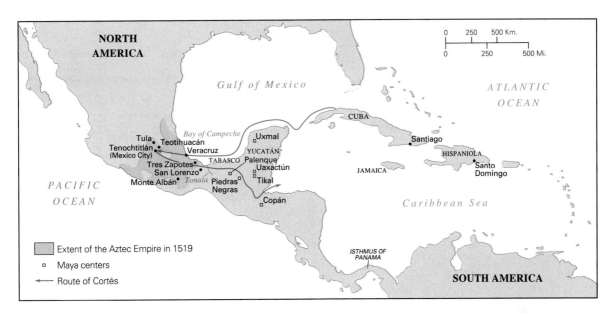

MAP 16.2 The Aztec Empire, 1519 Aztecs controlled much of central Mexico, while the Maya survived in the Yucatán Peninsula and some of present-day Guatemala. Note the number of cities.

sorbed the cultural achievements of the Toltecs. The Aztecs—building on Olmec, Maya, Teotihuacán, and Toltec antecedents—created the last unifying civilization in Mexico before the arrival of the Europeans.

AZTEC SOCIETY: RELIGION AND WAR

When the Aztecs appeared in the Valley of Mexico, they spoke the same Nahuatl language as the Toltecs; otherwise, they had nothing in common with their advanced predecessors. Poor, unwelcome, looked on as foreign barbarians, they had to settle on a few swampy islands in Lake Texcoco. There, in 1325, they founded a city consisting of a few huts and an altar for their war-god Huitzilopochtli, who had protected them during 150 years of wandering. From these unpromising beginnings the Aztecs rapidly assimilated the cultural legacy of the Toltecs and in 1428 embarked on a policy of territorial expansion. By the time Cortés arrived in 1519, the Aztec confederation encompassed all of central Mexico from the Gulf of Mexico to the Pacific Ocean as far south as Guatemala (Map 16.2). The rulers of neighboring Texcoco

and Tlacopan bowed to the Aztec king, and thirty-eight subordinate provinces paid tribute to him.

The growth of a strong mercantile class led to an influx of tropical wares and luxury goods: cotton, feathers, cocoa, skins, turquoise jewelry, and gold. The upper classes enjoyed an elegant and extravagant life style; the court of Emperor Montezuma II (r. 1502–1520) was more magnificent than anything in Western Europe. How, in less than two hundred years, had the Mexicans (from the Aztec word *mizquitl,* meaning "desolate land," or from *Mixitli,* the Aztec god of war) grown from an insignificant tribe of wandering nomads to a people of vast power and fabulous wealth?

The Aztecs' pictorial records attribute their success to the power of Huitzilopochtli and to the Aztecs' drive and indomitable will power. Will and determination they unquestionably had, but there is another explanation: the Aztec state was geared for war. In the course of the fifteenth century, the primitive tribesmen who had arrived in the Valley of Mexico in 1325 transformed themselves into professional soldiers. As the territory under Aztec control gradually expanded and military campaigns continued, warriors had to be in perpetual readiness. They were constantly subduing new states and crushing rebellions. A strong standing army was the backbone of the Mexican state, and war had become the central feature of Mexican culture.

War and Human Sacrifice

In Aztec society, war shaped the social hierarchy, education, and economic prosperity. War was also an article of religious faith.

Chief among the Aztecs' many gods was Huitzilopochtli, who symbolized the sun blazing at high noon. The sun, the source of all life, had to be kept moving in its orbit if darkness was not to overtake the world. To keep it moving, Aztecs believed, the sun had to be frequently fed precious fluids—that is, human blood. Human sacrifice was a sacred duty, essential for the preservation and prosperity of humankind. Black-robed priests carried out the ritual:

The victim was stretched out on his back on a slightly convex stone with his arms and legs held by four priests, while a fifth ripped him open with a flint knife and tore out his heart. The sacrifice also often took place in a manner which the Spanish described as gladiatorio: *the captive was tied to a huge disk of stone . . . by a rope that left him free to move; he was armed with wooden weapons, and he had to fight several normally-armed Aztec warriors in turn. If, by an extraordinary chance, he did not succumb to their attacks, he was spared; but nearly always the "gladiator" fell, gravely wounded, and a few moments later he died on the stone, with his body opened by the black-robed, long-haired priests.*[4]

Mass sacrifice was also practiced:

Mass sacrifices involving hundreds and thousands of victims could be carried out to commemorate special events. The Spanish chroniclers were told, for example, that at the dedication in 1487, of the great pyramid of Tenochititlán four lines of prisoners of war stretching for two miles each were sacrificed by a team of executioners who worked night and day for four days. Allotting two minutes for sacrifice, the demographer and historian Sherbourne Cook estimated that the number of victims associated with that single event was 14,100. The scale of these rituals could be dismissed as exaggerations were it not for the encoun-ters of Spanish explorers with . . . rows of human skulls in the plazas of the Aztec cities. . . . In the plaza of Xocotlan "there were . . . more than one hundred thousand of them."[5]

Anthropologists have proposed several explanations, none of them completely satisfactory, of the Aztecs' practice of human sacrifice and the cannibalism that often accompanied it. Some suggest that human sacrifice served to regulate population growth. Yet ritual slaughter had been practiced by earlier peoples—the Olmecs, the Maya, the dwellers of Teotihuacán, and the Toltecs—in all likelihood before population density had reached the point of threatening the food supply. Moreover, since almost all those sacrificed were men—warriors captured in battle—population growth could still have exceeded the death rate. Executing women of child-bearing age would have had more effect on population growth.

According to a second hypothesis, the ordinary people were given victims' bodies as a source of protein.[6] These people lived on a diet of corn, beans, squash, tomatoes, and peppers. Wildlife was scarce, and dog meat, chicken, turkey, and fish were virtually restricted to the upper classes. The testimony of modern nutritionists that beans supply ample protein, and the evidence that, in an area teeming with wild game, the Huron Indians of North America ritually executed captives and feasted on their stewed bodies, weaken the validity of this theory.

A third, more plausible, theory holds that ritual human sacrifice was an instrument of state terrorism—that the Aztec rulers crushed dissent with terror. The Aztecs controlled a large confederation of city-states by sacrificing prisoners seized in battle; by taking hostages from among defeated peoples as ransom against future revolt; and by demanding from subject states an annual tribute of people to be sacrificed to Huitzilopochtli. Unsuccessful generals, corrupt judges, and careless public officials, even people who accidentally entered forbidden precincts of the royal palaces, were routinely sacrificed. When the supply of such victims ran out, slaves, plebeians, even infants torn from their mothers suffered ritual execution. The emperor Montezuma II, who celebrated his coronation with the sacrifice of 5,100 people, could be said to have ruled by holocaust. Trumpets blasted and drums beat all day long announcing the sacrifice of yet another victim. Blood poured down the steps of the pyramids. Death and fear stalked everywhere. Ordinary people appear to have endured this living nightmare by escaping into intoxicating drink and drugs.[7]

The Life of the People

A wealth of information has survived about fifteenth- and sixteenth-century Mexico. The Aztecs were deeply interested in their own past, and in their pictographic script they wrote many books recounting their history, geography, and religious practices. They loved making speeches, and every public or social occasion gave rise to lengthy orations, which scribes copied down. The Aztecs also preserved records of their legal disputes, which alone amounted to vast files. The Spanish conquerors subsequently destroyed much of this material. But enough documents remain to construct a picture of the Mexican people at the time of the Spanish intrusion.

During their early migrations, no sharp social distinctions existed among the Aztecs. All were equally poor. The head of a family was both provider and warrior, and a sort of tribal democracy prevailed in which all adult males participated in important decision making. By the early sixteenth century, however, a stratified social structure had come into being, and the warrior aristocracy exercised great authority.

Scholars do not yet understand precisely how this social stratification evolved. According to Aztec legend, the Mexicans admired the Toltecs and chose their first king, Acamapichti, from among them. The many children he fathered with Aztec women formed the nucleus of the noble class. At the time of the Spanish intrusion into Mexico, men who had distinguished themselves in war occupied the highest military and social positions in the state. Generals, judges, and governors of provinces were appointed by the emperor from among his servants who had earned reputations as war heroes. These great lords, or *tecuhtli,* dressed luxuriously and lived in palaces. Like feudal lords, the provincial governors exercised full political, judicial, and military authority on the emperor's behalf. In their territories they maintained order, settled disputes and judged legal cases; oversaw the cultivation of land; and made sure that trib-

ute—in food or gold—was paid. The governors also led troops in wartime. These functions resembled those of feudal lords in western Europe during the Middle Ages (see pages 347–348). Just as only nobles of France and England could wear fur and carry a sword, so in Aztec society, only the tecuhtli could wear jewelry and embroidered cloaks.

Beneath the great nobility of soldiers and imperial officials was the class of warriors. Theoretically every freeman could be a warrior, and parents dedicated their male children to war: parents buried a male child's umbilical cord with some arrows and a shield on the day of his birth. In actuality the sons of nobles enjoyed advantages deriving from their fathers' position and influence in the state. At the age of six, boys entered a school that trained them for war. Future warriors were taught to fight with a *macana,* a paddle-shaped wooden club edged with bits of obsidian (a volcanic rock similar to granite but as sharp as glass). This weapon could be brutally effective: during the Spanish invasion, Aztec warriors armed with macanas slashed off the heads of horses at one blow. Youths were also trained in the use of spears, bows and arrows, and lances fitted with obsidian points. They learned to live on little food and sleep and to accept pain without complaint. At about age eighteen a warrior fought his first campaign. If he captured a prisoner for ritual sacrifice, he acquired the title iyac, or warrior; if in later campaigns he succeeded in killing or capturing four of the enemy, he became a *tequiua*—one who shared in the booty and thus was a member of the nobility. Warriors enjoyed a privileged position in Mexican society because they provided the state with the victims necessary for its survival. If a young man failed in several campaigns to capture the required four prisoners, he joined the *maceualtin,* the plebeian or working class.

The maceualtin were the ordinary citizens, the backbone of Aztec society and the vast majority of the population. The word *maceualti* means "worker" and implied boorish speech and vulgar behavior. Members of this class performed all sorts of agricultural, military, and domestic services and carried heavy public burdens not required of noble warriors. Government officials assigned the maceualtin work on the temples, roads, and bridges. Army officers called them up for military duty, but Mexicans considered this an honor and a religious rite, not a burden. Unlike nobles, priests, orphans, and slaves, maceualtin paid taxes. Maceualtin in the capital, however, possessed certain rights: they held their plots of land for life, and they received a small share of the tribute paid by the provinces to the emperor. Maceualtin in subject provinces enjoyed none of those rights.

Beneath the maceualtin were the *thalmaitl*, the landless workers or serfs. Some social historians speculate that this class originated during the

The Goddess Tlazolteotl The Aztecs believed that Tlazolteotl (sometimes called "Mother of the Gods"), in her eating refuse, consumed the sins of humankind, thus leaving them pure. As the goddess of childbirth, Tlazolteotl was extensively worshiped. Note the squatting position for childbirth, then common all over the world. *(Source: Dumbarton Oaks Research Library and Collections, Washington, D.C.)*

"Time of Troubles," a period of migrations and upheavals in which weak and defenseless people placed themselves under the protection of strong warriors. The thalmaitl provided agricultural labor at times of planting and harvesting, paid rents in kind, and were bound to the soil—they could not move off the land. The thalmaitl resembled in many ways the serfs of Western Europe, but unlike serfs they performed military service when called on to do so. They enjoyed some rights as citizens and generally were accorded more respect than slaves.

Slaves were the lowest social class. Like European and African slaves, most were prisoners captured in war or kidnapped from enemy tribes. Aztecs who stole from a temple or private house or plotted against the emperor could also be enslaved. Also people in serious debt sometimes voluntarily sold themselves into slavery. Female slaves often became their masters' concubines. Mexican slaves, however, differed fundamentally from European ones: "Tlatlocotin slaves could possess goods, save money, buy land and houses and even slaves for their own service."[8] Slaves could purchase their freedom. If a male slave married a free woman, their offspring were free, and a slave who escaped and managed to enter the emperor's palace was automatically free. Most slaves eventually gained their freedom. Mexican slavery, therefore, had humane qualities, in marked contrast with the methods that the Spanish later introduced into South America and those that the English imposed in North America.

Alongside the secular social classes stood the temple priests. Huitzilopochtli and each of the numerous lesser gods had many priests to oversee the upkeep of the temple, assist at religious ceremonies, and perform ritual sacrifices. The priests also did a brisk business in divination, foretelling the future on the basis of signs and omens. Aztecs were deeply concerned about coming events. They consulted priests on the selection of wives and husbands, on the future careers of newborn babies, and before leaving on journeys or for war. Because the emperor and the wealthy showered gifts on the gods, temples possessed enormous wealth in gold and silver ceremonial vessels, statues, buildings, and land. For example, fifteen provincial villages had to provide food for the temple at Texcoco and wood for its eternal fires. The priests who had custody of all this property did not marry and were expected to live moral and upright lives. From the temple revenues and resources, the priests supported schools, aided the poor, and maintained hospitals. The chief priests had the ear of the emperor and often exercised great power and influence.

At the peak of the social pyramid stood the emperor. The various Aztec historians contradict one another about the origin of the imperial dynasty, but modern scholars tend to accept the verdict of one sixteenth-century authority that the "custom has always been preserved among the Mexicans (that) the sons of kings have not ruled by right of inheritance, but by election."[9] The monarchy passed from the emperor to the ablest son of one of his legitimate wives (not his many concubines); a small oligarchy of the chief priests, warriors, and state officials made the selection. If none of the sons proved satisfactory, a brother or nephew of the emperor was chosen, but election was always restricted to the royal family.

The Aztec emperor was expected to be a great warrior; one of his titles was *tlacatecuhtli,* "lord of the men." He led Mexican and allied armies into battle. All his other duties pertained to the welfare of his people. It was up to the emperor to see that justice was done—he was the final court of appeal. He also held ultimate responsibility for ensuring an adequate food supply and for protecting against famine and other disasters. The emperor Montezuma I (r. 1440–1467) distributed twenty thousand loads of stockpiled grain when a flood hit the city. The records show that the Aztec emperors took their public duties seriously.

The Cities of the Aztecs

When the Spanish entered Tenochtitlán (which they called "Mexico City") in November 1519, they could not believe their eyes. According to Bernal Díaz, one of Cortés's companions,

when we saw all those cities and villages built in the water, and other great towns on dry land, and that straight and level causeway leading to Mexico, we were astounded. These great towns and cues (temples) and buildings rising from the water, all made of stone, seemed like an enchanted vision. . . . Indeed, some of our soldiers asked whether it was not all a dream.[10]

Tenochtitlán had about 60,000 households. The upper class practiced polygamy and had many children, and many households included servants and slaves. The total population probably numbered at least 500,000. At the time, no European city and few Asian ones could boast a population even half that size. The total Aztec empire has been estimated at around 5 million inhabitants.

Originally built on salt marshes, Tenochtitlán was approached by four great highways that connected it with the mainland. Wide straight streets and canals crisscrossed the city, and the bridges over the canals were so broad and solidly built that ten horsemen could ride abreast over them. Boats and canoes plied the canals. Lining the roads and canals stood thousands of rectangular one-story houses of mortar faced with stucco. Although space was limited, many houses had small gardens, which along with the numerous parks dazzled with the colors and scents of flowers. The Mexicans loved flowers and used them in ritual ceremonies.

A large aqueduct whose sophisticated engineering astounded Cortés carried pure water from distant springs and supplied fountains in the parks. Streets and canals opened onto public squares and marketplaces. Tradespeople offered every kind of merchandise: butchers hawked turkeys, ducks, chickens, rabbits, and deer, while grocers sold kidney beans, squash, avocados, corn, and all kinds of peppers. Artisans sold intricately designed gold, silver, and feathered jewelry. Seamstresses offered sandals, loincloths and cloaks for men, and blouses and long skirts for women—the traditional dress of ordinary people—and embroidered robes and cloaks for the rich. Slaves for domestic service, wood for building, herbs for seasoning and medicinal purposes, honey and sweets, knives, jars and utensils, smoking tobacco, even human excrement used to cure animal skins—all these wares made a dazzling spectacle.

At one side of the central square of Tenochtitlán stood the great temple of Huitzilopochtli. Built as a pyramid and approached by three flights of 120 steps each, the temple was about 100 feet high and dominated the city's skyline. According to Cortés it was

so large that within the precincts, which are surrounded by a very high wall, a town of some five hundred inhabitants could easily be built. All round

Tenochtitlán The great Mexican archeologist Ignacio Marquina reconstructed the central plaza of the Aztec capital as it looked in 1519. The huge temple of the God of War dominates the area, with royal palaces on each side. On the right stands the rack with tens of thousands of human skulls; in the center is the platform where captives met sacrificial death. *(Source: Library of Congress)*

inside this wall there are very elegant quarters with very large rooms and corridors where their priests live. There are as many as forty towers, all of which are so high that in the case of the largest there are fifty steps leading up to the main part of it . . . They are so well constructed in both their stone and woodwork that there can be none better in any place.[11]

Describing the Aztec way of life for the emperor Charles V, Cortés concluded: "I will say only that these people live almost like those in Spain, and in such harmony and order as there, and considering that they are barbarous and so far from the knowledge of God and cut off from all civilized nations, it is truly remarkable to see what they have achieved in all things."[12] Certainly Cortés's views reflect his own culture and outlook, but it is undeniable that Aztec culture was remarkable.

THE INCAS OF PERU

In the late 1980s archeologists working in the river valleys on the west coast of Peru uncovered stunning evidence of complex societies that flourished between 5,000 and 3,000 years ago—roughly the same period as the great pyramids of Egypt (see page 28). In spite of the altitude and aridity of the semidesert region, scores of settlements existed, perhaps the largest being at Cardal south of Lima, Aspero on the coast, Sechin Alto north of Lima, and the most spectacular, Pampa de las Llamas-Moxeke in the Casma Valley (Map 16.3). Stepped pyramids and U-shaped buildings, some more than ten stories high, dominated these settlements. Were these monuments warehouses for storing food or cultic temples? Were these settlements connected in some sort of political association? Was there sufficient commercial activity to justify calling them cities? Further investigation may answer these questions. The people depended on the sea for food and lived on a diet of fish, sweet potatoes, beans, and peanuts. Why did these peoples suddenly abandon their settlements and move into the Andean highlands? Scholars have only begun to process these vast remains, but radio carbon dating has already demonstrated that the settlements are older than the Maya and Aztec monuments.[13]

The Aztec civilization of Mexico had already passed its peak when the Spanish landed in America. So too had a greater culture to the south, that of the Incas of Peru. Like the Aztecs, the Incas were "a small militaristic group that came to power late, conquered surrounding groups, and established one of the most extraordinary empires in the world."[14] Gradually, Inca culture spread throughout Peru. Modern knowledge of the Incas is concentrated on the last century before Spanish intrusion (1438–1532); today's scholars know far less about earlier developments.

Peru consists of three radically different geographical regions: a 2,000-mile-long semidesert coastland skirting the Pacific Ocean; tropical jungle lowlands bordering modern Bolivia and Brazil; and, in the center, the cold highlands of the Andes Mountains. Six valleys of fertile and wooded land at altitudes of 8,000 to 11,000 feet punctuate highland Peru. The largest of these valleys are Huaylas, Cuzco, and Titicaca. It was there that Inca civilization developed and flourished.

Archeologists still do not understand how people of the Andean region acquired a knowledge of agriculture. Around 2500 B.C. they were relying on fish and mussels for food. Early agriculture seems to have involved cultivating cotton for ordinary clothing, ceremonial dress, and for fish nets. Beautifully dyed cotton textiles, swatches of which have been found in ancient gravesites, may also have served as articles for trade. The central highland region of the Andes is much less suited to agriculture than is Mesoamerica; in the Andes arable land is scarce. Yet between A.D. 600 and 1000, remarkable agricultural progress was made.

The Incas constructed great terraces along the mountain slopes and shored them up with walls to retain moisture. Terracing proved ideal for the cultivation of white potatoes. With only a foot plow, bronze hoe, and *guano* (the dried excrement of sea birds) as fertilizer, the Amerindians of Peru produced bumper crops of potatoes. They also learned an excellent method of preserving them. Potatoes ordinarily cannot be stored for long periods, but the Inca of the Andean highlands developed a product called *chuñu,* freeze-dried potatoes, made by subjecting potatoes alternately to nightly frosts and daily sun. Chuñu will keep unspoiled for several years. The construction of irrigation channels also facilitated the cultivation of corn, the other important Andean crop (much less important than the potato, however). Potatoes and corn required

MAP 16.3 The Inca Empire, 1463–1532 South America, which extends 4,750 miles in length and 3,300 miles from east to west at its widest point, contains every climatic zone and probably the richest variety of vegetation on earth. Note the system of Inca roads that linked most of the Andean region.

THE AMERICAS, CA 400–1500

ca 20,000 B.C.	Migration across the Bering Sea to the Americas
ca 1500 B.C.–A.D. 300	Rise of Olmec culture
A.D. 300–900	Classic period of Teotihuacán civilization
ca 600–900	Peak of Maya civilization
ca 800–1000	"Time of Troubles" in Mesoamerica
ca 1000	Beginning of Inca expansion
ca 1000–1300	Toltec hegemony
ca 1325	Arrival of the Aztecs in the Valley of Mexico
mid-15th century	Height of Aztec culture
1438–1493	Great Age of Inca imperialism
1519	Arrival of the Spanish
1521	Collapse of the Aztecs
1532	Spanish execution of the Inca king and collapse of Inca empire

far less labor and time than did the cultivation of wheat in Europe or rice in China.

By the fifteenth century, enough corn, beans, chili peppers, squash, tomatoes, sweet potatoes, peanuts, avocados, and white potatoes were harvested to feed not only the farmers themselves but also massive armies and administrative bureaucracies and thousands of industrial workers. Wild animals had become almost extinct in the region and were the exclusive preserve of the nobility; common people rarely ate any meat other than guinea pigs, which most families raised. Chicha, a beer fermented from corn, was the staple drink.

Inca Imperialism

Who were the Incas? *Inca* was originally the name of the governing family of an Amerindian group that settled in the basin of Cuzco (see Map 16.3). From that family, the name was gradually extended to all Indians living in the Andes valleys. The Incas themselves used the word to identify their chief or emperor. Here the term is used for both the ruler and the people.

Around A.D. 1000 the Incas were one of many small groups fighting among themselves for land and water. As they began to conquer their neighbors, a body of religious lore came into being that ascribed divine origin to their earliest king, Manco

Capac (ca 1200) and promised warriors the gods' favor and protection. Strong historical evidence dates only from the reign of Pachacuti Inca (1438–1471), who launched the imperialist phase of Inca civilization. By threats, promises, and brute conquest, Pachacuti and his son Topa Inca (1471–1493) extended the Incas' domination to the frontier of present-day Ecuador and Colombia in the north and to the Maule River in present-day Chile in the south (see Map 16.3), an area of about 350,000 square miles. Some authorities rank Pachacuti and Topa Inca with Alexander the Great and Napoleon among the world's great conquerors. By the time of the Spanish conquest in 1532, about 16 million people owed allegiance to the Inca ruler.

Inca civilization was the culmination of the fusion and assimilation of earlier Amerindian cultures in the Andes valleys. Each group that had entered the region had its own distinct language. These languages were not written and have become extinct. Scholars will probably never understand the linguistic condition of Peru before the fifteenth century when Pachacuti made Quechua (pronounced "keshwa") the official language of his people and administration. Quechua-speaking peoples were sent as colonists to subject regions, and conquered peoples were forced to adopt the language. Quechua thus superseded native dialects and spread the Inca way of life throughout the

Andes. Although not written until the Spanish in Peru adopted it as a second official language, Quechua had replaced local languages by the seventeenth and eighteenth centuries and is still spoken by most Peruvians today.

Whereas the Aztecs controlled their subject peoples through terror, the Incas governed by means of imperial unification. They imposed not only their language but their entire panoply of gods: the sun-god, divine ancestor of the royal family; his wife the moon-god; and the thunder-god, who brought life-giving rain. Magnificent temples scattered throughout the expanding empire housed idols of these gods and the state-appointed priests who attended them. Priests led prayers and elaborate rituals, and, on such occasions as a terrible natural disaster or a great military victory, they sacrificed human beings to the gods. Subject peoples were required to worship the state gods. Imperial unification was also achieved through the forced participation of local chieftains in the central bureaucracy and through a policy of colonization called *mitima*. To prevent rebellion in newly conquered territories, Pachacuti transferred all their inhabitants to other parts of the empire, replacing them with workers who had lived longer

Machu Picchu   The citadel of Machu Picchu, surrounded by mountains in the clouds, clings to a spectacular crag in upland Peru. It was discovered only in 1911, by the young American explorer Hiram Bingham. Both its origin and the reason for its abandonment remain unknown. *(Source: Carl Frank/Photo Researchers)*

under Inca rule and whose independent spirit had been broken.[15] An excellent system of roads—averaging three feet in width, some paved and others not—provided for the transportation of armies and the rapid communication of royal orders by runners. Inca roads followed straight lines wherever possible, but they also crossed marshes and causeways and rivers and streams on pontoon bridges and tunneled through hills. This great feat of engineering bears striking comparison with ancient Roman roads, which also linked an empire.

Inca Society

The fundamental unit of early Inca society was the *ayllu,* or clan, which consisted of all those who claimed a common male ancestor. A village typically consisted of several ayllus. Each ayllu had its own farmland and woodland, which all members tended. The chief, or *curacas,* of an ayllu, to whom all members owed allegiance, conducted relations with outsiders.

In the fifteenth century, Pachacuti and Topa Incas superimposed imperial institutions on those of kinship. The Incas ordered allegiance to be paid to the ruler at Cuzco rather than to the curacas. They drafted local men for distant wars and changed the entire populations of certain regions through the system of mitima. Entirely new ayllus were formed, based on residence rather than kinship.

The emperors sometimes gave newly acquired lands to victorious generals, distinguished civil servants, and favorite nobles. These lords subsequently exercised authority previously held by the native curacas. Whether long-time residents or new colonists, all had the status of peasant farmers, which entailed heavy agricultural or other obligations. Just as in medieval Europe peasants worked several days each week on their lord's lands, so the Inca people had to work on state lands (that is, the emperor's lands) or on lands assigned to the temple. Peasants also labored on roads and bridges; terraced and irrigated new arable land; served on construction crews for royal palaces, temples, and public buildings such as fortresses; acted as runners on the post roads; and excavated in the imperial gold, silver, and copper mines. The imperial government annually determined the number of laborers needed for these various undertakings,

and each district had to supply an assigned quota. The government also made an ayllu responsible for the state-owned granaries and for the production of cloth for army uniforms.

The state required everyone to marry, and even decided when and sometimes whom a person should marry. A person was not considered an adult until he or she married, started a household, and became liable for public responsibilities. Men married around the age of twenty, women a little younger. A young man who wanted a certain girl "hung around" her father's house and shared in the work. The Incas did not especially prize virginity; premarital sex was common. The marriage ceremony consisted of the joining of hands and the exchange of a pair of sandals. This ritual was followed by a large wedding feast, at which the state presented the bride and groom with two complete sets of clothing, one for everyday wear and one for festive occasions. If a man or woman did not find a satisfactory mate, the provincial governor selected one for him or her. Travel was forbidden, so couples necessarily came from the same region. Like most warring societies with high male death rates, the Incas practiced polygamy, though the cost of supporting many wives restricted it largely to the upper classes.

In many aspects of daily life, the common people were regimented, denied both choice and initiative. The Incas, however, took care of the poor and aged who could not look after themselves, distributed grain in time of shortage and famine, and supplied assistance in natural disasters. Scholars have debated whether Inca society was socialistic, totalitarian, or a forerunner of the welfare state; it may be merely a matter of definition. Although the Inca economy was strictly regulated, there certainly was not an equal distribution of wealth. Everything above and beyond the masses' basic needs went to the emperor and the nobility. The backbreaking labor of ordinary people in the fields and mines made possible the luxurious lifestyle of the great Inca nobility. The nobles—called "Big Ears," or *Orejones* by the Spanish, because they pierced their ears and distended the lobes with heavy jewelry—were the ruling Inca's kinsmen. Lesser nobles included the curacas, royal household servants, public officials, and entertainers. As the empire expanded in the fifteenth century, there arose a noble class of warriors, governors, and local officials, whose support the ruling Inca

Inca Tunic This colorful Inca fabric of many designs, perhaps once part of an emperor's tunic, suggests the remarkable Inca expertise in the dyeing and weaving of textiles. *(Source: Dumbarton Oaks Research Library and Collections, Washington, D.C.)*

secured with gifts of land, precious metals, and llamas and alpacas (llamas were used as beasts of burden; alpacas were raised for their long fine wool). The nobility was exempt from agricultural work and other kinds of public service.

SUMMARY

Across the Atlantic, several great Amerindian cultures had flourished in the years between 400 and 1500. The Maya are justly renowned for their art and their accomplishments in abstract thought. The Aztecs built a unified civilization based

heavily on the Toltec heritage and distinguished by achievements in engineering, sculpture, and architecture. The Incas revealed a genius for organization, and their state was virtually unique in its time in assuming responsibility for the social welfare of all its people.

NOTES

1. See F. Braudel, *The Structures of Everyday Life: Civilization and Capitalism, 15th–18th Century,* vol. I, trans. S. Reynolds (New York: Harper & Row, 1981), pp. 160–161.

2. See L. Schele and M. E. Miller, *The Blood of Kings: Dynasty and Ritual in Maya Art* (New York: Braziller, 1986), pp. 14–15, *passim.*

3. Quoted in I. Bernal, *Mexico Before Cortez: Art, History, and Legend,* rev. ed., trans. Willis Barnstone (New York: Anchor Books, 1975), p. 68.

4. J. Soustelle, *Daily Life of the Aztecs on the Eve of the Spanish Conquest,* trans. P. O'Brian (Stanford, Calif.: Stanford University Press, 1970), p. 97.

5. See M. Harris, *Cannibals and Kings* (New York: Random House, 1977), pp. 99–110; the quotation is from p. 106.

6. Ibid., pp. 109–110.

7. See R. Padden, *The Hummingbird and the Hawk* (Columbus, Ohio: Ohio State University Press, 1967), pp. 76–99.

8. Soustelle, p. 74.

9. Quoted ibid., p. 89.

10. B. Díaz, *The Conquest of New Spain,* trans. J. M. Cohen (New York: Penguin Books, 1978), p. 214.

11. Quoted in J. H. Perry, *The Discovery of South America,* (New York: Taplinger, 1979), pp. 161–163.

12. Quoted ibid., p. 163.

13. William K. Stevens, "Andean Culture Found to Be as Old as the Great Pyramids," in *The New York Times,* October 3, 1989, p. C1.

14. J. A. Mason, *The Ancient Civilizations of Peru* (New York: Penguin Books, 1978), p. 108.

15. Ibid., p. 123

SUGGESTED READING

Students interested in exploring aspects of pre-Columbian Central and South America will have no trouble finding a rich literature. F. Katz, *The Ancient American Civilisations* (1972), is now a standard study by a distinguished historian and anthropologist. G. C. Vaillant, *Aztecs of Mexico* (1979), Michael D. Coe, *The Maya,* 4th ed. (1987), and the work by Mason cited in the Notes are all sound and well-illustrated surveys. Coe's *Mexico* (1977) is probably the most comprehensive treatment of Mexican civilizations, with excellent illustrations and a good bibliography. The clever sketches of V. W. Von Hagen, *Realm of the Incas* (1961) and *The Aztec: Man and Tribe* (1961), are popular archeological accounts. Bernal's *Mexico Before Cortez* (listed in the Notes) brings out the social significance of Mexican art. P. Westheim, *The Sculpture of Ancient Mexico,* trans. U. Bernard (1963), also focuses on the importance of art and sculpture for an understanding of Mexican civilization. For any facet of Maya culture and civilization, see the splendid achievement of Schele and Miller cited in the Notes, which is superbly illustrated and the recent treatment of L. Schele and D. Freidel, *A Forest of Kings: The Untold Story of the Ancient Maya* (1990).

More specialized recent studies include M. P. Weaver, *The Aztec, Maya and Their Predecessors* (1981), which is highly readable and splendidly illustrated; K. W. Luckert, *Olmec Religion: A Key to Middle America and Beyond* (1976), an iconographical study of Olmec and Aztec religious symbolism; B. C. Brundage, *A Rain of Darts: The Mexican Aztecs* (1973); N. Davies, *The Aztecs Until the Fall of Tula* (1977), a highly detailed but fascinating book; E. R. Wolf, ed., *The Valley of Mexico: Studies in Pre-Hispanic Ecology and Society* (1976), an important collection of significant articles; L. Baudin, *A Socialist Empire: The Incas of Peru* (1961); and J. Soustelle, *The Olmecs: The Oldest Civilization in Mexico* (1984). Students interested in the importance of the environment to Inca history and development should see S. Masuda, I. Shimada, and C. Morris, eds., *Andean Ecology and Civilization* (1985).

17

European Society in the Age of the Renaissance and Reformation

Andrea Mantegna, *The Court of the Gonzaga Family*

The fourteenth century witnessed the beginnings of remarkable changes in many aspects of Italian society. In the fifteenth century, these phenomena spread beyond Italy and gradually influenced society in northern Europe. These cultural changes have collectively been labeled the "Renaissance."

Many present-day scholars interpret the sixteenth-century Reformation against the background of reforming trends begun in the fifteenth century. The idea of reform is as old as Christianity itself: the need for reform of the individual Christian and of the institutional church is central to the Christian faith. The Christian humanists of the late fifteenth and early sixteenth centuries called for reform of the church on the pattern of the early church, primarily through educational and social change. Men and women of every period believed the early church represented a golden age, and critics in every period called for reform. In the sixteenth century, demands for religious reform became so strong that they became enmeshed with social, political, and economic factors.

- What does the term *renaissance* mean?
- How did the Renaissance manifest itself in politics, government, art, and social organization?
- Why did the theological ideas of Martin Luther trigger political, social, and economic reactions?
- What response did the Catholic church make to the movements for reform?

This chapter explores these questions.

THE EVOLUTION OF THE ITALIAN RENAISSANCE

Economic growth laid the material basis for the Italian Renaissance. The period extending roughly from 1050 to 1300 witnessed phenomenal commercial and financial development, the growing political power of self-governing cities, and great population expansion. Then the period from the late thirteenth to the late sixteenth century was characterized by an incredible efflorescence of artistic energies.[1] Scholars commonly use the term *Renaissance* to describe the cultural achievements of the fourteenth through sixteenth centuries; those achievements rest on the economic and political developments of earlier centuries.

In the great commercial revival of the eleventh century, northern Italian cities led the way. By the middle of the twelfth century, Venice, supported by a huge merchant marine, had grown enormously rich through overseas trade. It profited tremendously from the diversion of the Fourth Crusade to Constantinople (see page 365). Genoa and Milan also enjoyed the benefits of a large volume of trade with the Middle East and northern Europe. These cities fully exploited their geographical positions as natural crossroads for mercantile exchange between the East and West. In the early fourteenth century, furthermore, Genoa and Venice made important strides in shipbuilding, allowing their ships for the first time to sail all year long. Most goods were purchased directly from the producers and sold a good distance away. For example, Italian merchants bought fine English wool directly from the Cistercian abbeys of Yorkshire in northern England. The wool was transported to the bazaars of North Africa either overland or by ship through the Strait of Gibraltar. The risks in such an operation were great, but the profits were enormous. These profits were continually reinvested to earn more.

Scholars tend to agree that the first artistic and literary manifestations of the Italian Renaissance appeared in Florence, which possessed enormous wealth despite geographical constraints: it was an inland city without easy access to water transportation. Toward the end of the thirteenth century, Florentine merchants and bankers acquired control of papal banking. From their position as tax collectors for the papacy, Florentine mercantile families began to dominate European banking on both sides of the Alps. These families had offices in Paris, London, Bruges, Barcelona, Marseilles, Tunis and other North African ports, and, of course, Naples and Rome. The profits from loans, investments, and money exchanges that poured back to Florence were pumped into urban industries. Such profits contributed to the city's economic vitality.

The wool industry, however, was the major factor in Florence's financial expansion and population increase. Florence purchased the best-quality wool from England and Spain, developed remarkable techniques for its manufacture, and employed thousands of workers to turn it into cloth. Florentine weavers produced immense quantities of superb woolen cloth, which brought the highest prices in the fairs, markets, and bazaars of Europe, Asia, and Africa.

By the first quarter of the fourteenth century, the economic foundations of Florence were so strong that even severe crises could not destroy the city. In 1344 King Edward III of England repudiated his huge debts to Florentine bankers and forced some of them into bankruptcy. Florence suffered frightfully from the Black Death, losing perhaps half of its population. Serious labor unrest, such as the ciompi revolts of 1378 (see page 456), shook the political establishment. Still, the basic Florentine economic structure remained stable. Driving enterprise, technical know-how, and competitive spirit saw Florence through the difficult economy of the late fourteenth century.

Communes and Republics

The northern Italian cities were *communes,* sworn associations of free men seeking complete political and economic independence from local nobles. The merchant guilds that formed the communes built and maintained the city walls, regulated trade, raised taxes, and kept civil order. In the course of the twelfth century, communes at Milan, Florence, Genoa, Siena, and Pisa fought for and won their independence from surrounding feudal nobles. The nobles, attracted by the opportunities of long-distance and maritime trade, the rising value of urban real estate, the new public offices available in the expanding communes, and the chances for advantageous marriages into rich commercial families, frequently settled within the cities. Marriage vows often sealed business contracts between the rural nobility and the mercantile aristocracy. This merger of the northern Italian feudal nobility and the commercial aristocracy constituted the formation of a new social class, an urban nobility. Within the nobility, groups tied by blood, economic interests, and social connections formed tightly knit alliances to defend and expand their rights.

This new class made citizenship in the communes dependent on a property qualification, years of residence within the city, and social con-

Business Activities in a Florentine Bank The Florentines early developed new banking devices. One man (left) presents a letter of credit or a bill of exchange, forerunners of the modern check, which allowed credit in distant places. A foreign merchant (right) exchanges one kind of currency for another. The bank profited from the fees it charged for these services. *(Source: Prints Division, New York Public Library; Astor, Lenox and Tilden Foundation)*

nections. Only a tiny percentage of the male population possessed these qualifications and thus could hold office in a commune's political councils. The *pòpolo,* or middle class, bitterly resented its exclusion from power. The pòpolo wanted places in the city government and equality of taxation. Throughout most of the thirteenth century, in city after city, the pòpolo used armed forces and violence to assume power and establish republican governments. However, the pòpolo could not establish civil order within the cities, and these movements for republican government failed. By 1300 *signori* (despots, or one-man rulers) or *oligarchies* (the rule of merchant aristocracies) had triumphed everywhere.[2]

For the next two centuries, the Italian city-states were ruled by signori or by constitutional oligarchies. In the signories, despots pretended to observe the law while actually manipulating it to conceal their basic illegality. Oligarchic regimes possessed constitutions, but through a variety of schemes, a small, restricted class of wealthy merchants exercised the judicial, executive, and legislative functions of government.

In the fifteenth century, political power and elite culture centered at the princely courts of despots and oligarchs. "A court was the space and personnel around a prince as he made laws, received ambassadors, made appointments, took his meals, and proceeded through the streets."[3] At his court a prince flaunted his patronage of learning and the arts by munificent gifts to writers, philosophers, and artists. The princely court afforded the despot or oligarch the opportunity to display his wealth. Ceremonies connected with family births, baptisms, marriages, funerals, or triumphant entrances into the city served as occasions for magnificent pageantry and elaborate ritual—all designed to assert the ruler's wealth and power.

The Balance of Power Among the Italian City-States

Renaissance Italians had a passionate attachment to their individual city-states: political loyalty and feeling centered on the local city. This intense local feeling perpetuated dozens of small states and hindered the development of a unified state. Italy, consequently, was completely disunited.

In the fifteenth century, five powers dominated the Italian peninsula: Venice, Milan, Florence, the Papal States, and the kingdom of Naples (Map 17.1). The rulers of the city-states—whether despots or oligarchs—governed as monarchs. They crushed urban revolts, levied taxes, killed their enemies, and used massive building programs to employ the masses and the arts to overawe them.

Venice, with enormous trade and a vast colonial empire, ranked as an international power. Though Venice had a sophisticated constitution and was a republic in name, an oligarchy of merchant-aristocrats actually ran the city. Milan was also called a "republic," but despots of the Sforza family ruled harshly and dominated the minor city-states of the north. Likewise in Florence the form of government was republican, with authority vested in several councils of state. In reality, however, between 1434 and 1494, power in Florence was held by the great Medici banking family. Though not public officers, Cosimo de' Medici (r. 1434–1464) and Lorenzo de' Medici (r. 1469–1492) ruled from behind the scenes.

Central Italy consisted mainly of the Papal States, which during the Babylonian Captivity had come under the sway of important Roman families

(see pages 446–447). Pope Alexander VI (r. 1492–1503), aided militarily and politically by his son Cesare Borgia, reasserted papal authority in the papal lands. Cesare Borgia became the model for Machiavelli's *The Prince* because he began the work of uniting the peninsula by ruthlessly conquering and exacting total obedience from the principalities making up the Papal States.

South of the Papal States was the kingdom of Naples, consisting of virtually all of southern Italy and, at times, Sicily. The kingdom of Naples had long been disputed by the Aragonese of Spain and by the French. In 1435 it passed to Aragon.

The major Italian city-states controlled the smaller ones, such as Siena, Mantua, Ferrara, and Modena, and competed furiously among themselves for territory. The large cities used diplomacy, spies, paid informers, and any other means to get information that could be used to advance their ambitions. While the states of northern Europe were moving toward centralization and consolidation, the world of Italian politics resembled a jungle where the powerful dominated the weak.

In one significant respect, however, the Italian city-states anticipated relations among competing European states after 1500. Whenever one Italian state appeared to gain a predominant position within the peninsula, other states combined to establish a balance of power against the major threat. In 1450, for example, Venice went to war against Milan to protest Francesco Sforza's acquisition of the title of duke of Milan. Cosimo de' Medici of Florence, a long-time supporter of a Florentine-Venetian alliance, switched his position and aided Milan. Florence and Naples combined with Milan against powerful Venice and the papacy. In the peace treaty signed at Lodi in 1454, Venice received territories in return for recognizing Sforza's right to the duchy. This pattern of shifting alliances continued until 1494. In the formation of these alliances, Renaissance Italians invented the machinery of modern diplomacy: permanent embassies with resident ambassadors in capitals where political relations and commercial ties needed continual monitoring. The resident ambassador is one of the great achievements of the Italian Renaissance.

At the end of the fifteenth century, Venice, Florence, Milan, and the Papal States possessed tremendous wealth and represented high cultural achievement. However, their imperialistic ambitions at one another's expense and their inability

MAP 17.1 The Italian City-States, ca 1494 In the fifteenth century the Italian city-states represented great wealth and cultural sophistication. The political divisions of the peninsula invited foreign intervention.

to form a common alliance against potential foreign enemies made Italy an inviting target for invasion. When Florence and Naples entered into an agreement to acquire Milanese territories, Milan called on France for support.

At Florence the French invasion had been predicted by the Dominican friar Girolamo Savona-rola (1452–1498). In a number of fiery sermons between 1491 and 1494, Savonarola attacked what he considered the paganism and moral vice of the city, the undemocratic government of Lorenzo de' Medici, and the corruption of Pope Alexander VI. For a time Savonarola enjoyed wide popular support among the ordinary people; he

Pallazzo Vecchio, Florence Built during the late thirteenth and early fourteenth centuries as a fortress of defense against both popular uprising and foreign attack, the building housed the *podesta*, the city's highest magistrate, and all the offices of the government. *(Source: Scala/Art Resource)*

fore him. When Piero de' Medici, Lorenzo's son, went to the French camp seeking peace, the Florentines exiled the Medicis and restored republican government.

Charles's success simply whetted French appetites. In 1508 his son Louis XII (r. 1498–1515) formed the League of Cambrai with the pope and the German emperor Maximilian (r. 1486–1519) for the purpose of stripping rich Venice of its mainland possessions. Pope Leo X (r. 1513–1521) soon found the French a dangerous friend, and in a new alliance called on the Spanish and Germans to expel the French from Italy. This anti-French combination was temporarily successful. In 1519 Charles V (r. 1519–1556) succeeded his grandfather Maximilian as Holy Roman emperor. When the French returned to Italy in 1522, there began the series of conflicts called the "Habsburg-Valois Wars" (named for the German and French dynasties), whose battlefield was Italy.

In the sixteenth century, the political and social life of Italy was upset by the relentless competition for dominance between France and the empire. The Italian cities suffered severely from the continual warfare, especially in the frightful sack of Rome in 1527 by imperial forces under Charles V. Thus the failure of the city-states to form some federal system, to consolidate, or at least to establish a common foreign policy led to the continuation of the centuries-old subjection of the peninsula by outside invaders. Italy was not to achieve unification until 1870.

became the religious leader of Florence and as such contributed to the fall of the Medici. Eventually, however, people wearied of his moral denunciations, and he was excommunicated by the pope and executed. Savonarola stands as proof that the common people did not share the worldly outlook of the commercial and intellectual elite. His career also illustrates the internal instability of Italian cities such as Florence, an instability that invited foreign interference.

The invasion of Italy in 1494 by the French king Charles VIII (r. 1483–1498) inaugurated a new period in Italian and European power politics. Italy became the focus of international ambitions and the battleground of foreign armies. Charles swept down the peninsula with little opposition, and Florence, Rome, and Naples soon bowed be

INTELLECTUAL HALLMARKS OF THE RENAISSANCE

Some fourteenth- and fifteenth-century Italians were aware that they were living in a new era. The realization that something new and unique was happening first came to men of letters in the fourteenth century such as Francesco Petrarch (1304–1374), a poet, humanist, and diplomat. Petrarch thought that he was living at the start of a new age, a period of light following a long night of Gothic gloom.

Petrarch believed that the first two centuries of the Roman Empire had represented the peak in the development of human civilization and that the Germanic invasions had caused a sharp cultural break with the glories of Rome and inaugurated what he called the "Dark Ages." Medieval people had believed that they were continuing in the glorious tradition of ancient Rome, and they had perceived no cultural division between the era of the emperors and their own times. But for Petrarch and many of his contemporaries, the thousand-year period between the fourth and the fourteenth centuries constituted a barbarian, or Gothic, or "middle" age. Sculptors, painters, and writers in the fourteenth and fifteenth centuries, contemptuous of their medieval predecessors, identified themselves with the thinkers and artists of Greco-Roman civilization. Petrarch believed that he was witnessing a new golden age of intellectual achievement—a rebirth or, to use the French word that came into English, a *renaissance*.

The division of historical time into periods is often arbitrary and done for the convenience of historians. In terms of the way most people lived and thought, no sharp division existed between the Middle Ages and the Renaissance. Nevertheless, some important writers and artists believed that they were living in a new age.

Characteristic of the Renaissance was a new attitude toward men, women, and the world—an attitude that may be described as "individualism." Humanism characterized by a deep interest in the Latin classics and a deliberate attempt to revive antique lifestyles emerged, as did a bold new secular spirit.

Individualism

The Middle Ages had seen the appearance of remarkable individuals, but recognition of such persons was limited. The examples of Saint Augustine in the fifth century and Peter Abélard and Guibert of Nogent in the twelfth—men who perceived of themselves as unique and produced autobiographical statements—stand out, for Christian humility discouraged self-absorption. In the Renaissance, in contrast, intellectuals developed a new sense of historical distance from earlier periods. A large literature specifically concerned with the nature of individuality emerged. This literature represented the flowering of a distinctly Renaissance individualism.

The Renaissance witnessed the emergence of many distinctive personalities who gloried in their uniqueness. Italians of unusual abilities were self-consciously aware of their singularity and

unafraid to be unlike their neighbors; they had enormous confidence in their ability to achieve great things. Leon Battista Alberti (1404–1474), a writer, architect, and mathematician, remarked, "Men can do all things if they will."[4] The Florentine goldsmith and sculptor Benvenuto Cellini (1500–1574) prefaced his *Autobiography* with a sonnet that declares:

My cruel fate hath warr'd with me in vain:
Life, glory, worth, and all unmeasur'd skill,
Beauty and grace, themselves in me fulfill
That many I surpass, and to the best attain.[5]

Cellini, certain of his genius, wrote so that the whole world might appreciate it.

Individualism stressed personality, genius, uniqueness, and the fullest development of capabilities and talents. Athlete, painter, scholar, sculptor, whatever—a thirst for fame, a driving ambition, a burning desire for success drove such people to the complete achievement of their potential. The quest for glory was central to Renaissance individualism.

The Revival of Antiquity

In the cities of Italy, especially Rome, civic leaders and the wealthy populace showed phenomenal archeological zeal for the recovery of manuscripts, statues, and monuments. Pope Nicholas V (r. 1447–1455), a distinguished scholar, planned the Vatican Library for the nine thousand manuscripts he had collected. Pope Sixtus IV (r. 1471–1484) built that library, which remains one of the richest repositories of ancient and medieval documents.

Patrician Italians consciously copied the lifestyle of the ancients and even searched out pedigrees dating back to ancient Rome. Aeneas Silvius Piccolomini, a native of Siena who became Pope Pius II (r. 1458–1464), once pretentiously declared, "Rome is as much my home as Siena, for my House, the Piccolomini, came in early times from the capital to Siena, as is proved by the constant use of the names Aeneas and Silvius in my family."[6]

The revival of antiquity also took the form of profound interest in and study of the Latin classics. This feature of the Renaissance became known as the "new learning," or simply *humanism,* the term used by the Florentine rhetorician and historian Leonardo Bruni (1370–1444). The words *humanism* and *humanist* derived ultimately from the Latin *humanitas,* which Cicero used to mean the literary culture needed by anyone who would be considered educated and civilized. Humanists studied the Latin classics to learn what they reveal about human nature. Humanism emphasized human beings—their achievements, interests, and capabilities. Although churchmen supported the new learning, by the later fifteenth century Italian humanism was increasingly a secular phenomenon.

Appreciation for the literary culture of the Romans had never died in the West. Scholars like Bede and John of Salisbury had studied and imitated the writings of the ancients. Medieval thinkers, however, had studied the ancients in order to come to know God. They had interpreted the clas-

Brunelleschi: Abraham's Sacrifice of Isaac When the Florentine textile merchants' guild held a competition for designs of the bronze doors of the city Baptistery, Brunelleschi entered this design based on the story in Genesis 22. The Roman altar and the boy removing a thorn from his foot (lower right) show conscious Roman elements in this dramatic, even violent scene. *(Source: Alinari/Art Resource)*

sics in a Christian sense and invested the ancients' poems and histories with Christian meaning.

Renaissance humanists approached the classics differently. Where medieval writers accepted pagan and classical authors uncritically, Renaissance humanists were skeptical of their authority, conscious of the historical distance separating themselves from the ancients, and fully aware that classical writers often disagreed among themselves. Renaissance humanists rejected classical ideas that were opposed to Christianity, or they sought through reinterpretation an underlying harmony between the pagan and secular and the Christian faith.

Deeply Christian like their medieval predecessors, Renaissance humanists studied the classics to understand human nature, and although they fully grasped the moral thought of pagan antiquity, they viewed man from a strongly Christian perspective. In a remarkable essay, "On the Dignity of Man," the Florentine writer Pico della Mirandola (1463–1494) stressed that man possesses great dignity because he was made as Adam in the image of God before the Fall and as Christ after the Resurrection. Man's place in the universe is somewhere between the beasts and the angels, but because of the divine image planted in man, there are no limits to what he can accomplish. The fundamental difference between Renaissance humanists and medieval humanists is that the former were more self-conscious about what they were doing.[7]

The fourteenth- and fifteenth-century humanists loved the language of the classics and considered it superior to the corrupt Latin of the medieval schoolmen. Eventually, Renaissance writers became concerned more about form than about content, more about the way an idea was expressed than about the significance and validity of the idea. Literary humanists of the fourteenth century wrote one another highly stylized letters imitating ancient authors, and they held witty philosophical dialogues in conscious imitation of Plato's Academy of the fourth century B.C. The leading humanists of the early Renaissance were rhetoricians, seeking effective and eloquent communication, both written and oral.

A New Secular Spirit

Secularism is a basic concern with the material world instead of with eternal and spiritual considerations. A secular way of thinking tends to find the ultimate explanation of everything and the final end of human beings within the limits of what the senses can discover. Medieval business people ruthlessly pursued profits while medieval monks fought fiercely over property. Yet medieval society was religious, not secular: the dominant ideals focused on the otherworldly, on life after death. In a secular society, attention is concentrated on the here-and-now, often on the acquisition of material things. The fourteenth and fifteenth centuries witnessed the slow but steady growth of secularism in Italy.

The economic changes and rising prosperity of the Italian cities in the thirteenth century worked a fundamental change in social and intellectual attitudes and values. Worries about shifting rates of interest, shipping routes, personnel costs, and employee relations did not leave much time for thoughts about penance and purgatory. The busy bankers and merchants of the Italian cities calculated ways of making money. Money allowed greater material pleasures, a more comfortable life, leisure to appreciate and patronize the arts. Money could buy many sensual gratifications, and the patricians of Venice, Florence, Genoa, and Rome came to see life more as something to enjoy than as a painful pilgrimage to the City of God.

In *On Pleasure,* the humanist Lorenzo Valla (1406–1457) defended the pleasures of the senses as the highest good. Scholars praise Valla as a father of modern historical criticism. His study *On the False Donation of Constantine* (1444) demonstrated by careful textual examination that an anonymous eighth-century document supposedly giving the papacy jurisdiction over vast territories in western Europe was a forgery. Medieval people had accepted "the donation of Constantine" as a reality, and the proof that it was an invention weakened the foundations of papal claims to temporal authority. Lorenzo Valla's work exemplifies the application of critical scholarship to old and almost-sacred writings, as well as the new secular spirit of the Renaissance. The tales in *The Decameron* (1353) by the Florentine Giovanni Boccaccio (1313–1375), which describe ambitious merchants, lecherous friars, and cuckolded husbands, portray a frankly acquisitive, sensual, and worldly society. The "contempt of the world" theme, so pervasive in medieval literature, had disappeared. Renaissance writers justified the accumulation and enjoyment of wealth with references to ancient authors.

Church leaders did little to combat the new secular spirit. In the fifteenth and early sixteenth centuries, the papal court and the households of the cardinals were just as worldly as those of great urban patricians. Most of the popes and high church officials had come from the bourgeois aristocracy. Renaissance popes beautified the city of Rome and patronized artists and men of letters, expending enormous enthusiasm and huge sums of money. A new papal chancellery, begun in 1483 and finished in 1511, stands as one of the architectural masterpieces of the period that art historians describe as the "High Renaissance" (1500–1527). Pope Julius II (r. 1503–1513) tore down the old Saint Peter's Basilica and began work on the present structure in 1506. Michelangelo's dome for Saint Peter's Basilica is still considered his greatest work. Papal interests, far removed from spiritual concerns, fostered rather than discouraged the new worldly attitude.

The broad mass of the people and the intellectuals and leaders of society remained faithful to the Christian church. Few people questioned the basic tenets of the Christian religion. Italian humanists and their aristocratic patrons were antiascetic, antischolastic, and ambivalent, but they were not agnostics or skeptics. Thousands of pious paintings, sculptures, processions, and pilgrimages prove that strong religious feeling persisted in the Renaissance.

ART AND THE ARTIST

No feature of the Renaissance evokes greater admiration than the masterpieces in painting, architecture, and sculpture created in the 1400s and 1500s. In all the arts, the city of Florence led the way. According to the Renaissance art historian Giorgio Vasari (1511–1574), the painter Perugino once asked why it was in Florence and not elsewhere that men achieved perfection in the arts. The first answer he received was, "There were so many good critics there, for the air of the city makes men quick and perceptive and impatient of mediocrity."[8] But Florence was not the only artistic center. In the High Renaissance Rome took the lead. The main characteristics of High Renaissance art—classical balance, harmony, and restraint—are revealed in the masterpieces of Leonardo da Vinci

(1452–1519), Raphael (1483–1520), and Michelangelo (1475–1564), all of whom worked in Rome at this time.

Art and Power

The subject matter of art through the early fifteenth century, as in the Middle Ages, remained overwhelmingly religious. Religious themes appeared in all media—wood carvings, painted frescoes, stone sculptures, paintings. As in the Middle Ages, art served an educational purpose. A religious picture or statue was intended to spread a particular doctrine, act as a profession of faith, or recall sinners to a moral way of living.

In early Renaissance Italy, art was a sign of corporate power. Powerful urban groups such as guilds and religious confraternities commissioned works of art. The Florentine cloth merchants, for example, delegated Brunelleschi (1377–1466) to build the magnificent dome on the cathedral of Florence and selected Lorenzo Ghiberti (1378–1455) to design the bronze doors of the baptistry. These works represented the merchants' dominant influence in the community. Corporate patronage is also reflected in the Florentine government's decision to hire Michelangelo to sculpt David, the great Hebrew hero and king.

Increasingly in the later fifteenth century, individuals and oligarchs, rather than corporate groups, sponsored works of art. Patrician merchants and bankers, popes, and princes supported the arts as a means of glorifying themselves and their families. Vast sums were spent on family chapels, frescoes, religious panels, and tombs. Paintings cost money and thus were also means of displaying wealth. Writing about 1470, the Florentine oligarch Lorenzo de' Medici, called "the Magnificent," declared that over the past thirty-five years his family had spent the astronomical sum of 663,755 gold florins for artistic and architectural commissions. Yet, he observed, "I think it casts a brilliant light on our estate [public reputation] and it seems to me that the monies were well spent and I am very pleased with this." Powerful men wanted to glorify themselves, their families, and their offices. A magnificent style of living, enriched by works of art, served to prove the greatness and the power of the despot or oligarch.[9]

As the fifteenth century advanced, the subject matter of art became steadily more secular. The study of classical texts deepened understanding of ancient ideas. Classical themes and motifs, such as the lives and loves of pagan gods and goddesses, figured increasingly in painting and sculpture. Religious topics, such as the Annunciation of the Virgin and the Nativity, remained popular among both patrons and artists, but frequently the patron had himself and his family portrayed. People were conscious of their physical uniqueness and wanted their individuality immortalized.

The style of Renaissance art was decidedly different from the style of Medieval art. The individual portrait emerged as a distinct artistic genre. In the fifteenth century, members of the newly rich middle class often had themselves painted in a scene of romantic chivalry or in courtly society. Rather than reflecting a spiritual ideal, as medieval painting and sculpture tended to do, Renaissance portraits mirrored reality. The Florentine painter Giotto (1276–1337) led the way in the depiction of realism; his treatment of the human body and face replaced the formal stiffness and artificiality that had for so long characterized the representation of human features. The sculptor Donatello (1386–1466) probably exerted the greatest influence of any Florentine artist before Michelangelo. His many statues express an appreciation of the incredible variety of human nature. Medieval artists had depicted the nude human body only in a spiritualized and moralizing context. Donatello revived the classical figure with its balance and self-awareness. The short-lived Florentine Masaccio (1401–1428), sometimes called the "father of modern painting," inspired a new style characterized by great realism, narrative power, and remarkable use of light and dark.

Narrative artists depicted the body in a more scientific and natural manner. The female figure is voluptuous and sensual. The male body, as in Michelangelo's *David* and *The Last Judgment*, is strong and heroic. *The Last Supper* of Leonardo da Vinci, with its stress on the tension between Christ and the disciples, is an incredibly subtle psychological interpretation. Brunelleschi and Piero della Francesca (1420–1492) seem to have pioneered artistic *perspective*, the linear representation of distance and space on a flat surface.

As important as realism was the new "international style," so called because of the wandering careers of influential artists, the close communications and rivalry of princely courts, and the increased trade in works of art. Rich color, decorative detail, curvilinear rhythms, and swaying forms characterized the international style. The Venetian painter Titian's portrait of the emperor Charles V (page 543) is a good example of the international style. As the term *international* implies, this style was European, not merely Italian.

The Status of the Artist

In the Renaissance the social status of the artist improved. The lower-middle-class medieval master mason had been viewed in the same light as a mechanic. The artist in the Renaissance was considered a free intellectual worker. An artist did not produce unsolicited pictures or statues for the general public, for doing so could mean loss of status.

Benozzo Gozzoli: *Journey of the Magi*   Few Renaissance paintings better illustrate art in the service of the princely court, in this case the Medici. Commissioned by Piero de' Medici to adorn his palace chapel, everything in this fresco—the large crowd, the feathers and diamonds adorning many of the personages, the black servant in front—serve to flaunt the power and wealth of the House of Medici. There is nothing especially religious about it; the painting could more appropriately be called "Journey of the Medici." The artist has discreetly placed himself in the crowd, the name Benozzo embroidered on his cap. *(Source: Scala/Art Resource)*

He usually worked on commission from a powerful prince. An artist's reputation depended on the support of powerful patrons, and through them some artists and architects achieved not only economic security but very great wealth. All aspiring artists received a practical (not theoretical) education in a recognized master's workshop. For example, Michelangelo was apprenticed at age thirteen to the artist Ghirlandaio (1449–1494), although he later denied the fact to make it appear that he never had any formal training. The more famous the artist, the more he attracted assistants or apprentices. Ghiberti had twenty assistants during the period he was working on the bronze doors of the baptistry in Florence, his most famous achievement.

Ghiberti's salary of two hundred florins a year compared very favorably with that of the head of the city government, who earned five hundred florins. Moreover, at a time when a man could live in a princely fashion on three hundred ducats a year, Leonardo da Vinci was making two thousand annually. Michelangelo was paid three thousand ducats for painting the ceiling of the Sistine Chapel. When he agreed to work on Saint Peter's Basilica, he refused a salary; he was already a wealthy man.[10]

Renaissance society respected and rewarded the distinguished artist. In 1537 the prolific letter writer, humanist, and satirizer of princes Pietro Aretino (1492–1556) wrote to Michelangelo while he was painting the Sistine Chapel:

To the Divine Michelangelo:
Sir, just as it is disgraceful and sinful to be unmindful of God so it is reprehensible and dishonourable for any man of discerning judgement not to honour you as a brilliant and venerable artist whom the very stars use as a target at which to shoot the rival arrows of their favour. You are so accomplished, therefore, that hidden in your hands lives the idea of a new king of creation. . . . And it is surely my duty to honour you with this salutation, since the world has many kings but only one Michelangelo.[11]

When the Holy Roman emperor Charles V visited the workshop of the great Titian (1477–1576) and stooped to pick up the artist's dropped paintbrush, the emperor was demonstrating that the patron himself was honored in the act of honoring the artist. The social status of the artist of genius was immortally secured.

Renaissance artists were not only aware of their creative power; they boasted about it. Describing his victory over five others, including Brunelleschi, in the competition to design Florence's baptistry doors, Ghiberti exulted, "The palm of victory was conceded to me by all the experts and by all my fellow-competitors. By universal consent and without a single exception the glory was conceded to me."[12] Some medieval painters and sculptors had signed their works. Renaissance artists almost universally did so, and many of them incorporated self-portraits, usually as bystanders, in their paintings.

The Renaissance, in fact, witnessed the birth of the concept of the artist as genius. In the Middle Ages, people believed that only God created, albeit through individuals; the medieval conception recognized no particular value in artistic originality. Renaissance artists and humanists came to think that a work of art was the deliberate creation of a unique personality, of an individual who transcended traditions, rules, and theories. A genius had a peculiar gift that ordinary laws should not inhibit. Cosimo de' Medici described a Renaissance painter, because of his genius, as "divine," implying that the artist shared in the powers of God. The word *divine* was widely applied to Michelangelo.

Italian Renaissance culture must not be interpreted in twentieth-century democratic terms. The culture of the Renaissance was that of a small mercantile elite, a business patriciate with aristocratic pretensions. Renaissance culture did not directly affect the broad middle classes, let alone the vast urban proletariat. A small, highly educated minority of literary humanists and artists created the culture of and for an exclusive elite. They cared little for ordinary people, and some thoroughly despised the masses. Renaissance humanists were a smaller and narrower group than the medieval clergy had ever been. High churchmen had commissioned the construction of the Gothic cathedrals but, once finished, the buildings were for all to enjoy. Modern visitors can still see the deep ruts in the stone floors of Chartres and Canterbury where the poor pilgrims slept at night. Nothing comparable was built in the Renaissance by the insecure, social-climbing merchant princes.[13] The Renaissance maintained the gulf between the learned minority and the uneducated multitude—a gulf that has survived for century after century.

SOCIAL CHANGE

The new developments of the Renaissance brought about real breaks with the medieval past. In education, in politics, through printing, and in the experience of women and blacks, the Renaissance changed many aspects of Italian, and subsequently European, society.

Education and Political Thought

One of the central preoccupations of the humanists was education and moral behavior. Humanists poured out treatises, often in the form of letters, on the structure and goals of education and the training of rulers. In one of the earliest systematic programs for the young, Peter Paul Vergerio (1370–1444) wrote Ubertinus, the ruler of Carrara:

For the education of children is a matter of more than private interest; it concerns the State, which indeed regards the right training of the young as, in certain aspects, within its proper sphere. . . . Tutors and comrades alike should be chosen from amongst those likely to bring out the best qualities, to attract by good example, and to repress the first signs of evil. . . . Above all, respect for Divine ordinances is of the deepest importance; it should be inculcated from the earliest years. . . .

We call those studies liberal which are worthy of a free man; those studies by which we attain and practise virtue and wisdom; that education which calls forth, trains and develops those highest gifts of body and of mind which ennoble men, and which are rightly judged to rank next in dignity to virtue only.[14]

Part of Vergerio's treatise specifies subjects for the instruction of young men in public life: history teaches virtue by examples from the past; ethics focuses on virtue itself; and rhetoric or public speaking trains for eloquence.

No book on education had broader influence than Baldassare Castiglione's *The Courtier* (1528). This treatise sought to train, discipline, and fashion the young man into the courtly ideal, the gentleman. According to Castiglione (1478–1529), the educated man of the upper class should have a broad background in many academic subjects, and his spiritual and physical, as well as intellectual, capabilities should be trained. The courtier should have easy familiarity with dance, music, and the arts. Castiglione envisioned a man who could compose a sonnet, wrestle, sing a song and accompany himself on an instrument, ride expertly, solve difficult mathematical problems, and above all speak and write eloquently. With these accomplishments, he would be the perfect Renaissance man. In the sixteenth and seventeenth centuries, *The Courtier* was widely read. It influenced the social mores and patterns of conduct of elite groups in Renaissance and early modern Europe. The courtier became the model of the European gentleman.

No Renaissance book on any topic, however, has been more widely read and studied in all the centuries since its publication in 1513 than the short political treatise *The Prince,* by Niccolò Machiavelli (1469–1527). Some political scientists maintain that Machiavelli was describing the actual competitive framework of the Italian states with which he was familiar. Other thinkers praise *The Prince* because it revolutionized political theory and destroyed medieval views of the nature of the state. Still other scholars consider this work a classic because it deals with eternal problems of government and society.

Born to a modestly wealthy Tuscan family, Machiavelli received a good education in the Latin classics. He entered the civil service of the Florentine government and served on thirty diplomatic missions. When the exiled Medicis returned to power in the city in 1512, they expelled Machiavelli from his position as officer of the city government. In exile he wrote *The Prince*.

The subject of *The Prince* is political power: how a ruler should gain, maintain, and increase it. In this, Machiavelli implicitly addresses the question of the citizen's relationship to the state. As a good humanist, he explores the problems of human nature and concludes that human beings are selfish and out to advance their own interests. This pessimistic view of humanity leads him to maintain that a prince may have to manipulate the people in any way he finds necessary:

For a man who, in all respects, will carry out only his professions of good, will be apt to be ruined amongst so many who are evil. A prince therefore who desires to maintain himself must learn to be not always good, but to be so or not as necessity may require.[15]

A prince should combine the cunning of a fox with the ferocity of a lion to achieve his goals. Asking rhetorically whether it is better for a ruler to be loved or feared, Machiavelli wrote:

This, then, gives rise to the question "whether it be better to be loved than feared, or to be feared than loved." It will naturally be answered that it would be desirable to be both the one and the other; but as it is difficult to be both at the same time, it is much more safe to be feared than to be loved, when you have to choose between the two. For it may be said of men in general that they are ungrateful and fickle, dissemblers, avoiders of danger, and greedy of gain. So long as you shower benefits upon them, they are all yours.[16]

Medieval political theorists and theologians had stressed the way government *ought* to be; they set high moral and Christian standards for the ruler's conduct. Machiavelli maintained that the ruler should be concerned *not* with the way things ought to be but with the way things actually are. The sole test of a "good" government was whether it was effective, whether the ruler increased his power. Machiavelli did not advocate amoral behavior, but he believed that political action cannot be restricted by moral considerations. Amoral action might be the most effective approach in a given situation. In *Discourses on the Ten Books of Titus Livy,* however, Machiavelli showed his strong commitment to republican government. Nevertheless, on the basis of a crude interpretation of *The Prince,* the word *Machiavellian* entered the language as a synonym for devious, corrupt, and crafty politics in which the end justifies the means. Machiavelli's ultimate significance rests on two ideas: first, that one permanent social order reflecting God's will cannot be established; second, that politics has its own laws and ought to be a science.[17]

The Printed Word

Sometime in the thirteenth century, paper money and playing cards from China reached the West. They were *block printed*—that is, Chinese characters or pictures were carved into a wooden block, inked, and the words or illustrations put on paper. Since each word, phrase, or picture was on a separate block, this method of reproduction was extraordinarily expensive and time consuming.

Around 1455, probably through the combined efforts of three men—Johann Gutenberg, Johann Fust, and Peter Schöffer, all experimenting at Mainz—movable type came into being. The mirror image of each letter (rather than entire words or phrases) was carved on relief on a small block. Individual letters, easily movable, were put together to form words in lines of type that made up a page. Since letters could be arranged into any format, an infinite variety of texts could be printed by reusing and rearranging pieces of type.

By the middle of the fifteenth century, paper too was widely available in Europe. Originating in China, the knowledge of manufacturing paper reached the West in the twelfth century, when the Arabs introduced the process into Spain. Europeans quickly learned that durable paper was far less expensive than the vellum (calfskin) and parchment (sheepskin) on which medieval scribes had relied for centuries.

The effects of the invention of movable-type printing were not felt overnight. Nevertheless, within a half century of the publication of Gutenberg's Bible in 1456, movable type brought about radical changes. Between the sixteenth and eighteenth centuries, printing transformed both the private and the public lives of Europeans. Governments that "had employed the cumbersome methods of manuscripts to communicate with their subjects switched quickly to print to announce declarations of war, publish battle accounts, promulgate treaties or argue disputed points in pamphlet form." Printing made propaganda possible, emphasizing differences between various groups, such as crown and nobility, church and state. These differences laid the basis for the formation of distinct political parties. Printed materials reached an invisible public, allowing silent individuals to join causes and groups of individuals widely separated by geography to form a common identity. This new group consciousness could compete with older, localized loyalties.

Printing also stimulated the literacy of lay people and eventually came to have a deep effect on their private lives. Although most of the earliest books and pamphlets dealt with religious subjects, students, housewives, businessmen, and upper- and middle-class people sought books on all subjects. Printers responded with moralizing, medi-

The Print Shop Sixteenth-century printing involved a division of labor. Two persons (left) at separate benches set the pieces of type. Another (center, rear) inks the chase (or locked plate containing the set type). Another (right) operates the press, which prints the sheets. The boy removes the printed pages and sets them to dry. Meanwhile, a man carries in fresh paper on his head. *(Source: Bettman/Hulton)*

cal, practical, and travel manuals. Pornography as well as piety assumed new forms. Broadsides and fly sheets allowed great public festivals, religious ceremonies, and political events to be experienced vicariously by those who stayed at home. Since books and printed materials were read aloud to the illiterate, print bridged the gap between written and oral cultures.[18]

Women in Renaissance Society

The status of upper-class women declined during the Renaissance. If women in the High Middle Ages are compared with those of fifteenth- and sixteenth-century Italy with respect to the kind of work they performed, their access to property and political power, and the role they played in shap-

ing the outlook of their society, it is clear that ladies in the Renaissance ruling classes generally had less power than comparable ladies of the feudal age.

In the cities of Renaissance Italy, girls and boys received a similar education. Young ladies learned their letters and studied the classics. Many read Greek as well as Latin, knew the poetry of Ovid and Virgil, and could speak one or two "modern" languages, such as French or Spanish. In this respect, Renaissance humanism represented a real educational advance for women.

Some women, though a small minority among humanists, acquired great learning and achieved fame in typically humanist genres—letters, orations, treatises, and poems. Laura Cereta (1469–1499) illustrates the successes and failures of educated Renaissance women. Educated by her father,

Sofonisba Anguissola: The Artist's Sister Minerva A nobleman's daughter and one of the first Italian women to become a recognized artist, Sofonisba did portraits of her five sisters and of prominent people. The coiffure, elegant gown, necklaces, and rings depict aristocratic dress in the mid-sixteenth century. *(Source: Milwaukee Art Museum, Gift of the family of Fred Vogel, Jr.)*

study. However, she had to bear the envy of other women and the hostility of men who felt threatened. In response, Laura condemned "empty women, who strive for no good but exist to adorn themselves . . . these women of majestic pride, fantastic coiffures, outlandish ornament, and necks bound with gold or pearls [which] bear the glittering symbols of their captivity to men." For Laura Cereta, women's inferiority was derived not from the divine order of things but from women themselves: "For knowledge is not given as a gift, but through study. . . . The free mind, not afraid of labor, presses on to attain the good."[19] Despite Laura's faith in women's potential, men frequently believed that a woman in becoming learned violated nature and thus ceased to be a woman. Brilliant women such as Laura Cereta were severely attacked by men who feared threats to male dominance in the intellectual realm.

Laura Cereta was a prodigy. Ordinary girls of the urban upper middle class, in addition to a classical education, received some training in painting, music, and dance. What were they to do with this training? They were to be gracious, affable, charming—in short, decorative. Renaissance women were better educated than their medieval counterparts. But whereas education trained a young man to rule and to participate in the public affairs of the city, it prepared a woman for the social functions of the home. An educated lady was supposed to know how to attract artists and literati to her husband's court and grace her husband's household.

Whatever the practical reality, a striking difference also exists between the medieval literature of courtly love—the etiquette books and romances— and the widely studied Renaissance manual on courtesy and good behavior, Castiglione's *The Courtier.* In the medieval books, manners shaped the man to please the lady; in *The Courtier* the lady was to make herself pleasing to the man. With respect to love and sex, the Renaissance witnessed a downward shift in women's status. In contrast to the medieval tradition of relative sexual equality, Renaissance humanists laid the foundations for the bourgeois double standard. Men, and men alone, operated in the public sphere; women belonged in the home. Castiglione, the foremost spokesman of Renaissance love and manners, completely separated love from sexuality. For women, sex was restricted entirely to marriage. Ladies were bound to chastity, to the roles of wife and mother

who was a member of the governing elite of Brescia in Lombardy, she learned languages, philosophy, theology, and mathematics. She also gained self-confidence and a healthy respect for her own potential. By the age of fifteen, when she married, her literary career was already launched, as her letters to several cardinals attest. For Laura Cereta, however, as for all educated women of the period, the question of marriage forced the issue: she could choose a husband, family, and full participation in social life, or she could study and withdraw from the world. Marriage brought domestic responsibilities and usually prevented women from fulfilling their scholarly potential. Laura chose marriage, but she was widowed at eighteen and spent the remaining twelve years of her life in

in a politically arranged marriage. Men, however, could pursue sensual indulgence outside marriage.[20]

Official attitudes toward rape provide another index of the status of women in the Renaissance. A careful study of the legal evidence from Venice in the years 1338 to 1358 is informative. The Venetian shipping and merchant elite held economic and political power and made the laws. Those laws reveal that rape was not considered a particularly serious crime against either the victim or society. Noble youths committed a higher percentage of rapes than their small numbers in Venetian society would imply, despite government-regulated prostitution. The rape of a young girl of marriageable age or a child under twelve was considered a graver crime than the rape of a married woman. Still, the punishment for the rape of a noble, marriageable girl was only a fine or about six months' imprisonment. In an age when theft and robbery were punished by mutilation, and forgery and sodomy by burning, this penalty was very mild indeed. When a youth of the upper class was convicted of the rape of a non-noble girl, his punishment was even lighter. By contrast, the sexual assault on a noblewoman by a man of working-class origin, which was extraordinarily rare, resulted in severe penalties because the crime had social and political overtones.

In the eleventh century, William the Conqueror had decreed that rapists be castrated, implicitly according women protection and a modicum of respect. But in the early Renaissance, Venetian laws and their enforcement show that the governing oligarchy believed that rape damaged, but only slightly, men's property—women.[21]

Evidence from Florence in the fifteenth century sheds light on infanticide, which historians are only now beginning to study in the Middle Ages and the Renaissance. Early medieval penitentials and church councils had legislated against abortion and infanticide, though it is known that Pope Innocent III (r. 1198–1216) was moved to establish an orphanage "because so many women were throwing their children into the Tiber."[22] In the fourteenth and early fifteenth centuries, a considerable number of children died in Florence under suspicious circumstances. Some were simply abandoned outdoors. Some were said to have been crushed to death while sleeping in bed with their parents. Some died from "crib death" or suffocation. These deaths occurred too frequently to

have all been accidental. And far more girls than boys died, thus reflecting societal discrimination against girl children as inferior and less useful than boys. The dire poverty of parents led them to do away with unwanted children.

The gravity of the problem of infanticide, which violated both the canon law of the church and the civil law of the state, forced the Florentine government to build the Foundling Hospital. Supporters of the institution maintained that, without public responsibility, "many children would soon be found dead in the rivers, sewers, and ditches, unbaptized."[23] The unusually large size of the hospital suggests that great numbers of children were abandoned.

Blacks in Renaissance Society

Ever since the time of the Roman Republic, a few black people had lived in Western Europe. They had come, along with white slaves, as the spoils of war. Even after the collapse of the Roman Empire, Muslim and Christian merchants continued to import them. The evidence of medieval art attests to the presence of Africans in the West and Europeans' awareness of them. In the twelfth and thirteenth centuries, a large cult surrounded Saint Maurice, martyred in the fourth century for refusing to renounce his Christian faith, who was portrayed as a black knight. Saint Maurice received the special veneration of the nobility.

The numbers of blacks in Europe had always been small. Beginning in the late fifteenth century, however, hordes of black slaves entered Europe. Portuguese explorers imported perhaps a thousand a year and sold them at the markets of Seville, Barcelona, Marseilles, and Genoa. By the mid-sixteenth century, blacks, slave and free, constituted about 10 percent of the populations of the Portuguese cities of Lisbon and Évora; other cities had smaller percentages. The Venetians controlled the slave trade, which until this time had involved the import of white slaves from southern Russia and the Balkans. But blacks were greatly in demand at the Renaissance courts of northern Italy. What roles did blacks play in Renaissance society? What image did Europeans have of Africans?

The medieval interest in curiosities, the exotic, and the marvelous continued into the Renaissance. Because of their rarity, black servants were highly prized and much sought after. In the late fifteenth century, Isabella, the wife of Gian Galazzo Sforza, took pride in the fact that she had ten blacks. In 1491 Isabella of Este, duchess of Mantua, instructed her agent to secure a black girl between four and eight years old, "shapely and as black as possible." The duchess saw the child as a source of entertainment: she hoped that the little girl would become "the best buffoon in the world."[24] The cruel ancient tradition of a noble household retaining a professional "fool" for the family's amusement persisted through the Renaissance—and even down to the twentieth century.

Adult black slaves filled a variety of positions. Many served as maids, valets, and domestic servants. The Venetians employed blacks—slave and free—as gondoliers and stevedores on the docks. Tradition, stretching back at least as far as the thirteenth century, connected blacks with music and dance. In Renaissance Spain and Italy, blacks performed as dancers, as actors and actresses in courtly dramas, and as musicians, sometimes composing full orchestras.[25]

Until the exploration and observation of the sixteenth, seventeenth, and nineteenth centuries allowed, ever so slowly, for the development of scientific knowledge, the Western conception of Africa and black people remained bound up with religious notions.[26] During the Renaissance, Europeans had little concrete knowledge of Africans and African culture beyond biblical accounts.

The European attitude toward Africans was ambivalent. On the one hand, Europeans perceived Africa as a remote place, the home of strange people isolated by heresy and Islam from "superior" European civilization. They believed that contact, even as slaves with Christian Europeans could only "improve" black Africans. Most Europeans' knowledge of the black as a racial type was based entirely on theological speculation. Theologians taught that God is light. Blackness, the opposite of light, thus represented the hostile forces of the underworld: evil, sin, and the Devil. The Devil was commonly represented as a black man in medieval and early Renaissance art. On the other hand, blackness was also associated with certain positive qualities. It symbolized the vanity of worldly goods, the humility of the monastic way of life. Black clothes permitted a conservative and discreet display of wealth. Black vestments and funeral trappings indicated grief, and Christ had said that those who mourn are blessed. In Renaissance society, blacks, like women, were signs of wealth; both

were used for display. Europeans' image of blacks remained one based on theological ideas.

THE RENAISSANCE IN THE NORTH

In the last quarter of the fifteenth century, students from the Low Countries, France, Germany, and England flocked to Italy, imbibed the "new learning," and carried it back to their countries. Northern humanists interpreted Italian ideas about and attitudes toward classical antiquity, individualism, and humanism in terms of their own traditions. The culture of northern Europe had tended to remain more distinctly Christian, or at least pietistic, than that of Italy. Italians certainly were strongly Christian, but in Italy secular and pagan themes and Greco-Roman motifs received more attention from the humanists than they received in northern Europe. North of the Alps, the Renaissance had a distinctly religious character, and humanists stressed biblical and early Christian themes. What fundamentally distinguished Italian humanists from northern humanists is that the latter had a program for broad social reform based on Christian ideals.

Christian humanists in northern Europe were interested in the development of an ethical way of life. To achieve it, they believed that the best elements of classical and Christian cultures should be combined. For example, the classical ideals of calmness, stoical patience, and broad-mindedness should be joined in human conduct with the Christian virtues of love, faith, and hope. Northern humanists also stressed the use of reason, rather than acceptance of dogma, as the foundation for an ethical way of life. Like the Italians, they were impatient with Scholastic philosophy. Northern humanists had a profound faith in the power of human intellect to bring about moral and institutional reform. They believed that, although human nature had been corrupted by sin, it was fundamentally good and capable of improvement through education, which would lead to piety and an ethical way of life.

The work of the French priest Jacques Lefèvre d'Étaples (ca 1455–1536) is one of the early attempts to apply humanistic learning to religious problems. A brilliant thinker and able scholar, he believed that more accurate texts of the Bible would lead people to live better lives. According to

Lefèvre, a solid education in the Scriptures would increase piety and raise the level of behavior in Christian society. Lefèvre produced an edition of the Psalms and a commentary on Saint Paul's letters.

The Englishman Thomas More (1478–1535) towers above other figures in sixteenth-century English social and intellectual history. More's troubles at the time of the Reformation with King Henry VIII (see page 551) have tended to obscure his contribution to Christian humanism. Trained as a lawyer, More lived as a student in the London Charterhouse, a Carthusian monastery. He subsequently married and practiced law but became deeply interested in the classics. His household served as a model of warm Christian family life and a mecca for foreign and English humanists. In a career pattern similar to that of Italian humanists such as Petrarch, More entered government service. Under Henry VIII he was sent as ambassador to Flanders. There More found the time to write *Utopia* (1516), which presented a revolutionary view of society.

Utopia, which literally means "nowhere," describes an ideal socialistic community on an island somewhere off the mainland of the New World. All its children receive a good education, primarily in the Greco-Roman classics, and learning does not cease with maturity, for the goal of all education is to develop rational faculties. Adults divide their days equally between manual labor or business pursuits and various intellectual activities.

Because the profits from business and property are held strictly in common, there is absolute social equality. The Utopians use gold and silver to make chamber pots or to prevent wars by buying off their enemies. By this casual use of precious metals, More meant to suggest that the basic problems in society were caused by greed. Utopian law exalts mercy above justice. Citizens of Utopia lead an ideal, nearly perfect existence because they live by reason; their institutions are perfect. More punned on the word *Utopia*—which he termed "a good place. A good place which is no place."

More's ideas were profoundly original in the sixteenth century. Contrary to the long-prevailing view that vice and violence exist because women and men are basically corrupt, More maintained that acquisitiveness and private property promoted all sorts of vices and civil disorders. Since society protected private property, *society's* flawed institutions were responsible for corruption and war.

Baldung: Adoration of the Magi Early sixteenth-century German artists produced thousands of adoration scenes depicting a black man as one of the three kings: these paintings were based on direct observation, reflecting the increased presence of blacks in Europe. The elaborate costumes, jewelry, and landscape expressed royal dignity, Christian devotion, and oriental luxury. (Source: Gemäldegalerie, Staatliche Museen Preusischer Kulturbesitz, Berlin)

Today people take this view so much for granted that it is difficult to appreciate how radical it was in the sixteenth century. According to More, the key to improvement and reform of the individual was reform of the social institutions that mold the individual.

Better known by his contemporaries than Thomas More was the Dutch humanist Desiderius Erasmus of Rotterdam (1466?–1536). Orphaned as a small boy, Erasmus was forced to enter a monastery. Although he intensely disliked the monastic life, he developed there an excellent knowledge of the Latin language and a deep appreciation for the Latin classics. The application of the best humanistic learning to the study and explanation of the Bible became Erasmus's life work. As a mature scholar with an international reputation stretching from Cracow to London, Erasmus could boast with truth, "I brought it about that humanism, which among the Italians . . . savored of nothing but pure paganism, began nobly to celebrate Christ."[27]

Erasmus's long list of publications includes *The Adages* (1500), a list of Greek and Latin precepts on ethical behavior; *The Education of a Christian Prince* (1504), which combines idealistic and practical suggestions for the formation of a ruler's character through the careful study of Plutarch, Aristotle, Cicero, and Plato; *The Praise of Folly* (1509), a satire on worldly wisdom and a plea for the simple and spontaneous Christian faith of children; and, most important of all, a critical edition of the Greek New Testament (1516). In the preface to the New Testament, Erasmus explained the purpose of his great work:

Only bring a pious and open heart, imbued above all things with a pure and simple faith. . . . For I utterly dissent from those who are unwilling that the sacred Scriptures should be read by the unlearned translated into their vulgar tongue, as though Christ had taught such subtleties that they can scarcely be understood even by a few theologians. . . . Christ wished his mysteries to be published as openly as possible. I wish that even the weakest woman should read the Gospel— should read the epistles of Paul. And I wish these were translated into all languages, so that they might be read and understood, not only by Scots and Irishmen, but also by Turks and Saracens. . . . Why do we prefer to study the wisdom of Christ in men's writings rather than in the writing of Christ himself?[28]

Two fundamental themes pervade all of Erasmus's scholarly work. First, education was the means to reform, the key to moral and intellectual improvement. The core of education ought to be study of the Bible and the classics. Second, the essence of Erasmus's thought is, in his own phrase, "the philosophy of Christ." By this Erasmus meant that Christianity is an inner attitude of the heart or spirit. Christianity is not formalism, special cer-

emonies, or law. Christianity is Christ—his life and what he said and did—not what theologians have written about him.

The writings of Lefèvre, More, and Erasmus have strong Christian themes and have drawn the attention primarily of scholars. In contrast, the stories of the French humanist François Rabelais (1490?–1553) possess a distinctly secular flavor and have attracted broad readership among the literate public. Rabelais's *Gargantua* and *Pantagruel* (serialized between 1532 and 1552) belong among the great comic masterpieces of world literature. These stories' gross and robust humor introduced the adjective *Rabelaisian* into English.

Gargantua and *Pantagruel* can be read on several levels: as comic romances about the adventures of the giant Gargantua and his son, Pantagruel; as spoofs on contemporary French society; as a program for educational reform; as illustrations of Rabelais's prodigious learning. The reader enters a world of Renaissance vitality, ribald joviality, and intellectual curiosity. On his travels Gargantua meets various absurd characters, and within their hilarious exchanges there occur serious discussions on religion, politics, philosophy, and education. Rabelais had received an excellent humanistic education in a monastery, and Gargantua discusses the disorders of contemporary religious and secular life.

Like Erasmus and More, Rabelais did not denounce institutions directly. Like Erasmus, he satirized hypocritical monks, pedantic academics, and pompous lawyers. But where Erasmus employed intellectual cleverness and sophisticated wit, Rabelais applied wild and gross humor. Like More, Rabelais believed that institutions molded individuals and that education was the key to a moral and healthy life. The middle-class inhabitants of More's Utopia lived lives of restrained moderation. The aristocratic residents of Rabelais's Thélème lived for the full gratification of their physical instincts and rational curiosity.

Thélème, the abbey that Gargantua establishes, parodies traditional religion and other social institutions. Thélème, whose motto is "Do as Thou Wilt," admits men *and* women; allows all to eat, drink, sleep, and work when they choose; provides excellent facilities for swimming, tennis, and football; and encourages sexual experimentation and marriage. Rabelais believed profoundly in the basic goodness of human beings and in the rightness of instinct.

The most roguishly entertaining Renaissance writer, Rabelais was convinced that "laughter is the essence of manhood." A believer in the Roman Catholic faith, he included in Gargantua's education an appreciation for simple and reasonable prayer. Rabelais combined the Renaissance zest for life and enjoyment of pleasure with a classical insistence on the cultivation of the body and the mind.

The distinctly religious orientation of the literary works of the Renaissance in the north also characterized northern art and architecture. Some Flemish painters, notably Jan van Eyck (1366–1441), were the equals of Italian painters. One of the earliest artists successfully to use oil-based paints, van Eyck, in paintings such as *Ghent Altarpiece* and the portrait *Giovanni Arnolfini and His Bride,* shows the Flemish love for detail; the effect is great realism. Van Eyck's paintings also demonstrate remarkable attention to human personality, as is shown in his *Madonna of the Chancellor Rodin.*

Another Flemish painter, Jerome Bosch (ca 1450–1516), frequently used religious themes, but in combination with grotesque fantasies, colorful imagery, and peasant folk legends. Many

Jan van Eyck: Madonna of the Chancellor Rodin The tough and shrewd chancellor who ordered this rich painting visits the Virgin and Christ-Child (though they seem to be visiting him). An angel holds the crown of heaven over the Virgin's head while Jesus, the proclaimed savior of the world, holds a globe in his left hand and raises his right hand in blessing. Through the colonnade, sculpted with scenes from Genesis, is the city of Bruges. Van Eyck's achievement in portraiture is extraordinary; his treatment of space and figures and his ability to capture the infinitely small and very large prompted the art historian Erwin Panofsky to write that "his eye was at one and the same time a microscope and a telescope." *(Source: Louvre/Cliché des Musées Nationaux, Paris)*

of Bosch's paintings reflect the confusion and anguish often associated with the end of the Middle Ages. In *Death and the Miser,* Bosch's dramatic treatment of the dance of death theme, diabolical rats and toads control the miser's gold, increased by usury, and the miser's guardian angel urges the bedfast miser to choose the crucifix, not worldly wealth.

A quasi-spiritual aura likewise infuses architectural monuments in the north. The city halls of wealthy Flemish towns like Bruges, Brussels, Louvain, and Ghent seem more like shrines to house the bones of saints than like settings for the mundane decisions of politicians and businessmen. Northern architecture was little influenced by the classical revival so obvious in Renaissance Rome and Florence.

POLITICS AND THE STATE IN THE RENAISSANCE (1450–1521)

Many basic institutions of the modern state have their origins in the High Middle Ages (see pages 404–417). The linchpin for the development of states, however, was strong monarchy. But in the era of the Hundred Years' War (1337–1453), no ruler in western Europe provided effective leadership. As a result, the resurgent power of feudal nobilities weakened the centralizing work begun in the twelfth and thirteenth centuries.

Beginning in the fifteenth century, however, rulers utilized the aggressive methods implied by Renaissance political ideas to rebuild their governments. First in Italy, then in France, England, and Spain, rulers began to reduce violence, curb unruly nobles and other troublesome elements, and establish domestic order. Within the Holy Roman Empire of Germany, the lack of centralization helps to account for later German distrust of the Roman papacy. Divided into scores of independent principalities, Germany could not deal as an equal with the Roman church.

Jerome Bosch: Death and the Miser   Dutch painters frequently used symbolism, and Bosch (ca 1450–1516) is considered the master artist of symbolism and fantasy. Here rats, which symbolize evil, control the miser's gold. Bosch's imagery appealed strongly to twentieth-century surrealist painters. (*Source: National Gallery of Art, Washington, D.C., Samuel H. Kress Collection*)

The dictators and oligarchs of the Italian city-states, however, together with Louis XI of France, Henry VII of England, and Ferdinand and Isabella of Spain, were tough, cynical, calculating rulers. In their ruthless push for power and strong governments, they subordinated morality to hard results. They preferred to be secure, though feared, rather than loved. They could not have read Machiavelli's *The Prince,* but they acted as if they understood its ideas.

Some historians have called Louis XI (r. 1461–1483), Henry VII (r. 1485–1509), and Ferdinand and Isabella (r. 1474–1516) "new monarchs." The term is only partly appropriate. What was new was a marked acceleration in the acquisition and expansion of power. Renaissance rulers spent precious little time seeking religious justification for their actions. They stressed that monarchy was the one institution that linked all classes and peoples within definite territorial boundaries. Rulers emphasized royal majesty and royal sovereignty and insisted that all must respect and be loyal to them. They ruthlessly suppressed opposition and rebellion, especially from the nobility. They loved the business of kingship and worked hard at it.

In other respects, however, the methods of these rulers, which varied from country to country, were not so new. They reasserted long-standing ideas and practices of strong monarchs in the Middle Ages, seizing on a maxim of the Justinian *Code,* "What pleases the prince has the force of law," to advance their authority. Like some medieval rulers, Renaissance rulers tended to rely on middle-class civil servants. Using tax revenues, medieval rulers had built armies to crush feudal anarchy. Renaissance townspeople with commercial and business interests naturally wanted a reduction of violence and usually were willing to be taxed in order to achieve it. These qualifications of the term "new monarchs" are important in understanding the development of national monarchies in France, England, and Spain in the period 1450 to 1521 and the growth in "international" power of Austria's house of Habsburg.

France

The Hundred Years' War left France badly divided, drastically depopulated, commercially ruined, and agriculturally weak. Nonetheless, the seemingly feeble ruler whom Joan of Arc had seen crowned at Reims, Charles VII (1422–1461), revived the monarchy and France. Charles reorganized the royal council, giving increased influence to middle-class men, and strengthened royal finances through such taxes as the *gabelle* (on salt) and the *taille* (a land tax). Charles created France's first permanent royal army by establishing regular companies of cavalry and archers—recruited, paid, and inspected by the state. In 1438 Charles published the Pragmatic Sanction of Bourges, asserting the superiority of a general church council over the papacy, giving the French crown major control over the appointment of bishops, and depriving the pope of French ecclesiastical revenues. Greater control over the army and the church helped to consolidate the authority of the French crown.

Charles's son Louis XI (r. 1461–1483), called the "Spider King" because of his treacherous and cruel character, was very much a Renaissance prince. Facing the perpetual French problems of unification of the realm and reduction of feudal disorder, he saw money as the answer. Louis promoted new industries, such as silk weaving at Lyon and Tours, and entered into commercial treaties with other countries. The revenues raised through these economic activities and severe taxation went into improving the army, which Louis used to stop aristocratic brigandage and to undercut urban independence.

Luck favored Louis's goal of expanding royal authority and unifying the kingdom. On the timely death of Charles the Bold, duke of Burgundy, in 1477, Louis invaded Burgundy and gained some territories. Three years later, the extinction of the house of Anjou brought Louis the counties of Anjou, Bar, Maine, and Provence.

Some scholars have credited Louis XI with laying the foundations for later French royal absolutism. Indeed, he worked tirelessly to remodel and strengthen the government. In his reliance on finances supplied by the middle classes to fight the feudal nobility, Louis was typical of the new monarchs.

England

English society suffered severely from the disorders of the fifteenth century. The aristocracy came to dominate the government and regularly in-

French Tradesmen   A bootmaker, a cloth merchant (with bolts of material on shelves), and a dealer in gold plate and silver share a stall. Through sales taxes, the French crown received a portion of the profits. *(Source: Giraudon/Art Resource)*

dulged in mischievous violence at the local level. Then, between 1455 and 1471, adherents of the ducal houses of York and Lancaster waged civil war, commonly called the "Wars of the Roses" because the symbol of the Yorkists was a white rose and that of the Lancastrians a red rose. Although only a small minority of the nobility participated in the conflict, the chronic disorder hurt trade, agriculture, and domestic industry. Under the pious but mentally disturbed Henry VI (r. 1422–1461), the authority of the monarchy sank lower than it had been in centuries.

The Yorkist Edward IV (r. 1461–1483) defeated the Lancastrian forces and after 1471 began to reestablish domestic tranquillity, reconstruct the monarchy, and consolidate royal power. Edward, his brother Richard III (r. 1483–1485), and Henry VII (r. 1485–1509) of the Welsh house of Tudor worked to restore royal prestige, to crush the power of the nobility, and to establish order

and law at the local level. All three used methods that Machiavelli would have praised: ruthlessness, efficiency, and secrecy.

The Hundred Years' War had cost the nation dearly, and the money to finance it had been raised by Parliament. Dominated by various baronial factions, Parliament had been the arena where the nobility exerted its power. As long as the monarchy depended on the Lords and Commons for revenue for war, the king had to call Parliament. Thus Edward IV reluctantly established a policy that the monarchy was to follow with rare exceptions down to 1603. Edward, and subsequently the Tudors, except Henry VIII, conducted foreign policy on the basis of diplomacy, avoiding expensive wars and thus undercutting a major source of aristocratic influence.

Although Henry VII did summon several meetings of Parliament in the early years of his reign, the center of royal authority was the royal council, which governed at the national level. There Henry VII revealed his distrust of the nobility. Very few great lords were among the king's closest advisers. Most representatives on the council were from the lesser landowning class, and their education was in law. They were, in a sense, middle class.

In addition to handling the executive, legislative, and judicial business of government, the royal council dealt with real or potential aristocratic threats through a judicial offshoot, the "Court of Star Chamber," so called because of the stars painted on the ceiling of the room in which it met. This court applied principles of Roman law, and its methods were sometimes terrifying: the accused was not entitled to see evidence against him or her; sessions were secret; torture could be applied to extract confessions; and juries were not called. These procedures ran directly counter to English common-law precedents, but they effectively reduced aristocratic troublemaking.

Unlike the continental countries of Spain and France, England had no standing army or professional civil service bureaucracy. The Tudors relied on the support of unpaid local officials, the justices of the peace, who were appointed and supervised by the royal council. These influential landowners in the shires handled all the work of local government. From the royal point of view, they were an inexpensive method of government.

The Tudors won the support of the influential upper middle class because the Crown linked government policy with that group's interests. A commercial or agricultural upper class fears and dislikes disorder and violence. If the Wars of the Roses served any purpose, it was killing off dangerous nobles and thus making the Tudors' work easier. The Tudors promoted peace and social order; and because the government had halted the long period of anarchy, the gentry did not object to methods like those used by the Court of Star Chamber.

Grave, secretive, cautious, and always thrifty, Henry VII rebuilt the monarchy. He encouraged the cloth industry and built up the English merchant marine. English exports of wool and the royal export tax on that wool steadily increased. Henry crushed an invasion from Ireland and secured peace with Scotland through the marriage of his daughter Margaret to the Scottish king. When Henry VII died in 1509, he left a country at peace both domestically and internationally, a substantially augmented treasury, and the dignity and role of the royal majesty much enhanced.

Spain

Political development in Spain followed a pattern different from that in France and England. The central theme in the history of medieval Spain—or, more accurately, of the separate kingdoms that Spain comprised—was disunity and plurality. The various peoples who lived in the Iberian Peninsula lacked a common cultural tradition. Different languages, laws, and religious communities made for a rich diversity. Adding to the Hispanic, Roman, and Visigothic heritage, Muslims and Jews had significantly affected the course of Spanish society.

By the middle of the fifteenth century, the kingdoms of Castile and Aragon dominated the weaker Navarre, Granada, and Portugal (Map 17.2), and the reconquista had won the Iberian Peninsula (except for Granada) for Christianity. The wedding in 1469 of the dynamic and aggressive Isabella, heiress of Castile, and the crafty and persistent Ferdinand, heir of Aragon, was the final major step in the unification and Christianization of Spain. This marriage, however, constituted a dynastic union of two royal houses, not the political union of two peoples. Although Ferdinand and Isabella pursued a common foreign policy, Spain under their rule remained a loose confederation of separate states. Each kingdom continued to maintain its own *cortes* (parliament), laws, courts, bureaucracies, and systems of coinage and taxation.

Isabella and Ferdinand were determined to strengthen royal authority. To curb rebellious and warring aristocrats, they revived an old medieval institution. Popular groups in the towns, called *hermandades,* or "brotherhoods," were given the authority to act both as local police forces and as judicial tribunals. The hermandades repressed violence with such savage punishments that by 1498 they could be disbanded.

The decisive step that Ferdinand and Isabella took to curb aristocratic power was the restructuring of the royal council. The king and queen appointed to the council only people of middle-class background, excluding aristocrats and territorial magnates. The council and various government boards recruited men trained in Roman law, a system that exalted the power of the crown as the embodiment of the state.

In the extension of royal authority and the consolidation of the territories of Spain, the church was the linchpin. The major issue confronting Isabella and Ferdinand was the appointment of the higher clergy. Through a diplomatic alliance with the papacy, especially with the Spanish pope Alexander VI (r. 1492–1503), the Spanish monarchs secured the right to appoint bishops in Spain and in the Hispanic territories in America. This power enabled the "Catholic Kings of Spain," a title granted Ferdinand and Isabella by the papacy, to establish, in effect, a national church and to influence ecclesiastical policy, wealth, and military resources.[29] The Spanish rulers used their power to reform the church, and they used some of the church's wealth for national purposes.

Revenues from ecclesiastical estates provided the means to raise an army to continue the reconquista. The victorious entry of Ferdinand and Isabella into Granada on January 6, 1492, signaled the culmination of eight centuries of Spanish struggle against the Arabs in southern Spain and the conclusion of the reconquista (see Map 17.2). Granada in the south was incorporated into the Spanish kingdom, and in 1512 Ferdinand conquered Navarre in the north.

Although the Arabs had been defeated, there still remained a sizable and, in the view of the Catholic sovereigns, potentially dangerous minority, the Jews. Since ancient times, religious faiths that differed from the official state religion had been considered politically dangerous. Medieval writers quoted the fourth-century Byzantine theologian Saint John Chrysostom, who had asked rhetorically, "Why are the Jews degenerate? Because of their odious assassination of Christ." John Chrysostom and his admirers in the Middle Ages chose to ignore two facts: that it was the Romans who had killed Christ (because they considered him a *political* troublemaker) and that Christ had forgiven his executioners from the cross. France and England had expelled their Jewish populations in the Middle Ages, but in Spain Jews had been tolerated. In fact, Jews had played a decisive role in the economic and intellectual life of the several Spanish kingdoms.

Anti-Semitic riots and pogroms in the late fourteenth century had led many Jews to convert; they were called *conversos*. By the middle of the fifteenth century, many conversos held high positions in Spanish society as financiers, physicians, merchants, tax collectors, and even officials of the church hierarchy. Numbering perhaps 200,000 in a total population of about 7.5 million, Jews exercised an influence quite disproportionate to their numbers. Aristocratic grandees (nobles) who borrowed heavily from Jews resented their financial dependence, and churchmen questioned the sincerity of Jewish conversions. At first, Isabella and Ferdinand continued the policy of royal tolera-

MAP 17.2 The Christianization and Unification of Spain The political unification of Spain was inextricably tied up with conversion or expulsion of the Muslims and the Jews.

tion—Ferdinand himself had inherited Jewish blood from his mother. But many conversos apparently reverted to the faith of their ancestors, prompting Ferdinand and Isabella to secure Rome's permission to revive the Inquisition, a medieval judicial procedure for the punishment of heretics (see page 436).

Although the Inquisition was a religious institution established to ensure the Catholic faith in Spain, it was controlled by the Crown and served primarily as a politically unifying force. Because the Spanish Inquisition commonly applied torture to extract confessions, it gained a notorious reputation. Thus the word *inquisition,* meaning "any judicial inquiry conducted with ruthless severity," came into the English language. The methods of the Spanish Inquisition were cruel, though not as cruel as the investigative methods of certain twentieth-century governments. In 1478 the deeply pious Ferdinand and Isabella introduced the Inquisition into their kingdoms to handle the problem of backsliding conversos. They solved the problem in a dire and drastic manner. Shortly after the reduction of the Moorish stronghold at Granada in 1492, Isabella and Ferdinand issued an edict expelling all practicing Jews from Spain. Of the community of perhaps 200,000 Jews, 150,000 fled. (Efforts were made, through last-minute conversions, to retain good Jewish physicians.) Absolute Catholic orthodoxy served as the foundation of the Spanish national state.

The diplomacy of the Catholic rulers of Spain achieved a success they never anticipated. Partly out of hatred for the French and partly to gain international recognition for their new dynasty, Ferdinand and Isabella in 1496 married their second daughter, Joanna, heiress to Castile, to the archduke Philip, heir through his mother to the Burgundian Netherlands and through his father to the Holy Roman Empire.

Germany and the Rise of the Habsburg Dynasty

The history of the Holy Roman Empire in the later Middle Ages is a story of dissension, disintegration, and debility. Unlike France, England, and Spain, the empire lacked a strong central power. The Golden Bull of 1356 legalized what had long existed—government by an aristocratic federation. Each of seven electors—the archbishops of Mainz,

Trier, and Cologne, the margrave of Brandenburg, the duke of Saxony, the count palatine of the Rhine, and the king of Bohemia—gained virtual sovereignty in his own territory. The agreement ended disputed elections in the empire; it also reduced the central authority of the emperor. Germany was characterized by weak borders, localism, and chronic disorder. The nobility strengthened its territories while imperial power declined.

The marriage in 1477 of Maximilian I of the house of Habsburg and Mary of Burgundy was a decisive event in early modern European history. Through this union with the rich and powerful duchy of Burgundy, the Austrian house of Habsburg, already the strongest ruling family in the empire, became an international power.

"Other nations wage war; you, Austria, marry." Historians dispute the origins of the adage, but no one questions its accuracy. It was the heir of Mary and Maximilian, Philip of Burgundy, who married Joanna of Castile. Through a series of accidents and unexpected deaths, Philip and Joanna's son Charles V (r. 1519–1556) inherited Spain from his mother, together with her possessions in the New World and the Spanish dominions in Italy (Sicily, Sardinia, and the kingdom of Naples). From his father he inherited the Habsburg lands in Austria, southern Germany, the Low Countries, and Franche-Comté in east central France (Map 17.3).

Charles's inheritance was an incredibly diverse collection of states and peoples, each governed in a different manner and held together only by the person of the emperor. Charles's Italian adviser, the grand chancellor Gattinara, told the young ruler: "God has set you on the path toward world monarchy." Charles not only believed this; he was convinced that it was his duty to maintain the political and religious unity of Western Christendom. In this respect Charles V was the last medieval emperor.

Charles needed and in 1519 secured the imperial title. Forward-thinking Germans proposed government reforms. They urged placing the administration in the hands of an imperial council whose president, the emperor's appointee, would have ultimate executive power. Reforms of the imperial finances, the army, and the judiciary were also recommended. Such ideas did not interest the young emperor at all. When he finally arrived in Germany from Spain and opened his first *diet* (assembly of the estates of the empire) at Worms in January 1521, he naively announced that "the

MAP 17.3 The European Empire of Charles V Charles V exercised theoretical jurisdiction over more territory than anyone since Charlemagne. This map does not show his Latin American and Asian possessions.

empire from of old has had not many masters, but one, and it is our intention to be that one." Charles went on to say that he was to be treated as of greater account than his predecessors because he was more powerful than they had been. In view of Germany's long history of aristocratic power, Charles's notions were pure fantasy.

THE CONDITION OF THE CHURCH (1400–1517)

The papal conflict with the German emperor Frederick II (r. 1215–1250) in the thirteenth century, followed by the Babylonian Captivity and then the Great Schism (see pages 446–447), badly damaged the prestige of church leaders. In the fourteenth and fifteenth centuries, conciliarists (proponents of the conciliar view of church government) reflected educated public opinion when they called for the reform of the church "in head and members." The secular humanists of Italy and the Christian humanists of the north denounced and satirized corruption in the church. The records of episcopal visitations of parishes, civil court records, and even such literary masterpieces as Chaucer's *Canterbury Tales* and Boccaccio's *The Decameron* tend to confirm the sarcasms of the humanists.

Signs of Disorder

In the early sixteenth century, critics of the church concentrated their attacks on three disorders: clerical immorality, clerical ignorance, and clerical pluralism and the related problem of absenteeism. There was little pressure for doctrinal change; the emphasis was on moral and administrative reform.

Since the fourth century, church law had required candidates for the priesthood to accept absolute celibacy. The law had always been difficult to enforce. Many priests, especially those ministering to country people, had concubines, and reports of neglect of the rule of celibacy were common. Immorality, of course, included more than sexual transgressions. Clerical drunkenness, gambling, and indulgence in fancy dress were frequent charges. There is no way of knowing how many priests were guilty of such behavior. But because such conduct was so much at odds with the

church's rules and moral standards, it scandalized the educated faithful.

The bishops only casually enforced regulations regarding the education of priests. As a result, standards for ordination were shockingly low. Many priests could barely read and write, and critics laughed at illiterate priests mumbling the Latin words to the mass, which they could not understand. Predictably, clerical ignorance was the disorder that the Christian humanists, with their concern for learning, particularly condemned.

Pluralism and absenteeism constituted the third major abuse. Many clerics, especially higher ecclesiastics, held several benefices simultaneously but seldom visited them, let alone performed the spiritual responsibilities that they entailed. Instead, absentees collected revenues from all of their benefices and paid a poor priest a fraction of the income to fulfill the spiritual duties of a particular local church. King Henry VIII's chancellor Thomas Wolsey was archbishop of York for fifteen years before he set foot in his diocese. The French king Louis XII's famous diplomat Antoine du Prat is perhaps the most notorious example of absenteeism: as archbishop of Sens, the first time he entered his cathedral was in his own funeral procession. Many Italian officials in the papal curia held benefices in England, Spain, and Germany. Revenues from those countries paid the Italian priests' salaries, provoking not only charges of absenteeism but nationalistic resentment. Critics condemned pluralism, absenteeism, and the way money seemed to change hands when a bishop entered into his office.

Although royal governments strengthened their positions and consolidated their territories in the fifteenth and sixteenth centuries, rulers lacked sufficient revenues to pay and reward able civil servants. The Christian church, with its dioceses and abbeys, possessed a large proportion of Europe's wealth. What better way to reward government officials than with high church offices? After all, the practice was sanctioned by centuries of tradition. Thus in Spain, France, England, and the Holy Roman Empire—in fact, all over Europe—church officials who served their monarchs were allowed to govern the church.

The spectacle of proud, aristocratic prelates living in magnificent splendor contrasted very unfavorably with the simple fishermen who were Christ's disciples. Nor did the popes of the period 1450 to 1550 set much of an example. They lived like secular Renaissance princes. Pius II (r. 1458–1464), although deeply learned and a tireless worker, enjoyed a reputation as a clever writer of love stories and Latin poetry. Sixtus IV (r. 1471–1484) beautified the city of Rome, built the Sistine Chapel, and generously supported several artists. Innocent VIII (r. 1484–1492) made the papal court a model of luxury and scandal. All three popes used papal power and wealth to advance the material interests of their own families.

The court of the Spanish pope Rodrigo Borgia, Alexander VI (r. 1492–1503), who publicly acknowledged his mistress and children, reached new heights of impropriety. Because of the prevalence of intrigue, sexual promiscuity, and supposed poisonings, the name *Borgia* became a synonym for moral corruption. Julius II (r. 1503–1513), the nephew of Sixtus IV, donned military armor and personally led papal troops against the French invaders of Italy in 1506. After him, Giovanni de' Medici, the son of Lorenzo the Magnificent, carried on as Pope Leo X (r. 1513–1521)

the Medicean tradition of being a great patron of the arts. Reputedly, Leo opened his pontificate with the words "Now that God has given us the papacy, let us enjoy it."

Signs of Vitality

Calls for reform testify to the spiritual vitality of the church as well as to its problems. In the late fifteenth and early sixteenth centuries, both individuals and groups within the church were working actively for reform. In Spain, Cardinal Jiménez visited religious houses, encouraged the monks and friars to keep their rules and constitutions, and set high standards for the training of the diocesan clergy.

In Holland, beginning in the late fourteenth century, a group of pious lay people called the "Brethren of the Common Life" lived in stark simplicity while daily carrying out the Gospel teaching of feeding the hungry, clothing the naked, and

The Church Contrasted Satirical woodcuts as well as the printed word attacked conditions in the church. Here the attitude of Christ toward money changers is contrasted with the mercenary spirit of the sixteenth-century papacy: Christ drove them from the temple, but the pope kept careful records of revenues owed to the church. *(Source: The Pierpont Morgan Library)*

visiting the sick. The Brethren also taught in local schools. Their goal was to prepare devout candidates for the priesthood and the monastic life. Through prayer, meditation, and the careful study of Scripture, the Brethren sought to make religion a personal, inner experience. The spirituality of the Brethren of the Common Life found its finest expression in the classic *The Imitation of Christ* by Thomas à Kempis. Like later Protestants, the Brethren stressed the centrality of Scripture in the spiritual life.[30] In the mid-fifteenth century, the movement had houses in the Netherlands, central Germany, and the Rhineland; it was a true religious revival.

So, too, were the activities of the Oratories of Divine Love in Italy. The oratories were groups of priests living in communities who worked to revive the church through prayer and preaching. They did not withdraw from the world as medieval monks had done but devoted themselves to pastoral and charitable activities such as founding hospitals and orphanages. Oratorians served God in an active ministry.

The papacy also expressed concern for reform. Pope Julius II summoned an ecumenical (universal) council, which met in the church of Saint John Lateran in Rome from 1512 to 1517. Since most of the bishops were Italian and did not represent a broad cross-section of international opinion, the term *ecumenical* was not appropriate. Nevertheless, the bishops and theologians present strove earnestly to reform the church. They criticized the ignorance of priests and condemned superstitions believed by many of the laity. The council recommended higher standards for education of the clergy and instruction of the common people. The bishops placed the responsibility for eliminating bureaucratic corruption squarely on the papacy and suggested significant doctrinal reforms. But many obstacles stood in the way of ecclesiastical change. The actions of an obscure German friar did not immediately force the issue.

MARTIN LUTHER AND THE BIRTH OF PROTESTANTISM

As the result of a personal religious struggle, a German Augustinian friar named Martin Luther (1483–1546) launched the Protestant Reformation of the sixteenth century. Luther articulated both the widespread desire for reform of the Christian church and a deep yearning for salvation. To the extent that concern for salvation was an important motivating force for Luther and other reformers, the sixteenth-century Reformation was in part a continuation of the medieval religious search.

Martin Luther was born at Eisleben in Saxony, the second son of a hard-working and ambitious copper miner. At considerable sacrifice, his father sent him to school and then to the University of Erfurt. Hans Luther intended his son to proceed to the study of law and a legal career. Badly frightened during a thunderstorm, however, Martin Luther vowed to become a friar. Without consulting his father, he entered the monastery at Erfurt in 1505. Luther was ordained a priest in 1507 and after additional study earned the doctorate of theology. From 1512 until his death in 1546, he served as professor of Scripture at the new University of Wittenberg.

Martin Luther was exceedingly scrupulous in his monastic observances and devoted to prayer, penances, and fasting; nevertheless, the young friar's conscience troubled him constantly. The doubts and conflicts felt by any sensitive young person who has just taken a grave step were especially intense in young Luther. He had terrible anxieties about sin and worried continually about his salvation. Luther intensified his monastic observances but still found no peace of mind.

Luther's wise and kindly professor, Staupitz, directed him to the study of Saint Paul's letters. Gradually, Luther arrived at a new understanding of the Pauline letters and of all Christian doctrine. He came to believe that salvation comes not through external observances and penances but through a simple faith in Christ. Faith is the means by which God sends humanity his grace, and faith is a free gift that cannot be earned. Thus Martin Luther discovered himself, God's work for him, and the centrality of faith in the Christian life.

The Ninety-five Theses

What propelled Martin Luther onto the stage of history was the issue of indulgences. Wittenberg lay within the archdiocese of Magdeburg. Albert, the archbishop of Magdeburg, also held two other high ecclesiastical offices. Such blatant pluralism required papal dispensation, and Pope Leo X, anxious for funds with which to complete Saint Peter's Basilica, allowed Albert to pay for his dispensation by borrowing money from the Fuggers, a wealthy German banking family. Leo also authorized Albert to sell indulgences in Germany to repay the Fuggers.

According to Catholic theology, individuals who sin alienate themselves from God and his love. In order to be reconciled to God, a sinner must confess his or her sins to a priest and do the penance assigned. For example, a man who steals must first return the stolen goods and then perform a penance given by a priest, which is usually certain prayers or good works. The penance given by a priest is known as a "temporal (or earthly) penance," for no one knows what penance God will ultimately require.

The doctrine of indulgence rested on three principles. First, God is merciful but he is also just. Second, Christ and the saints, through their infinite virtue, established a "treasury of merits" on which the church can draw. Third, the church has the authority to grant sinners the spiritual benefits of those merits. Originally an indulgence was a remission of the temporal (priest-imposed) penalties for sin. Beginning in the late eleventh century, popes and bishops had given Crusaders such indulgences. By the later Middle Ages people widely believed that an indulgence secured total remission of penalties for sin—on earth or in purgatory—and ensured swift entry into heaven.

Archbishop Albert hired the Dominican friar John Tetzel to sell indulgences. Tetzel mounted an advertising blitz. One of his slogans—"As soon as coin in coffer rings, the soul from purgatory springs"—brought phenomenal success. Men and women could buy indulgences not only for themselves but for deceased parents, relatives, or friends.

That ignorant people believed that they had no further need for repentance once they had purchased an indulgence severely troubled Luther. Thus, according to historical tradition, on the eve of All Saints' Day (October 31) in 1517, he attached to the door of the church at Wittenberg Castle a list of ninety-five theses (or propositions) on indulgences. By this act Luther intended only to start a theological discussion of the subject and to defend the theses publicly.

Luther firmly rejected the notion that salvation could be achieved by good works, such as indul-

gences. Some of his theses challenged the pope's power to grant indulgences, and others criticized papal wealth: "Why does not the Pope, whose riches are at this day more ample than those of the wealthiest of the wealthy, build the one Basilica of St. Peter's with his own money, rather than with that of poor believers?"[31]

The theses were soon translated into German, printed, and read throughout the empire. Immediately, broad theological issues were raised. When questioned, Luther rested his fundamental argument on the principle that there was no biblical basis for indulgences. But, replied Luther's opponents, to deny the legality of indulgences was to deny the authority of the pope who had authorized them. The issue was drawn: where did authority lie in the Christian church?

In 1519, in a large public debate with the Catholic theologian John Eck at Leipzig, Luther denied both the authority of the pope and the infallibility of a general council. The Council of Constance, he said, had erred when it condemned John Hus (see page 448). The papacy responded with a letter condemning some of Luther's propositions, ordering that his books be burned, and giving him two months to recant or be excommunicated. Luther retaliated by publicly burning the letter. By January 3, 1521, when the excommunication was supposed to become final, the controversy involved more than theological issues. The papal legate wrote, "All Germany is in revolution. Nine-tenths shout 'Luther' as their war-cry; and the other tenth cares nothing about Luther, and cries 'Death to the court of Rome.'"[32]

In this highly charged atmosphere the twenty-one-year-old emperor Charles V held his first diet at Worms and summoned Luther to appear before it. When ordered to recant, Luther replied in language that rang all over Europe:

Unless I am convinced by the evidence of Scripture or by plain reason—for I do not accept the authority of the Pope or the councils alone, since it is established that they have often erred and contradicted themselves—I am bound by the Scriptures I have cited and my conscience is captive to the word of God. I cannot and will not recant anything, for it is neither safe nor right to go against conscience. God help me. Amen.[33]

Charles published the Edict of Worms, in which Luther was declared an outlaw of the empire: he was denied legal protection.

Protestant Thought

Between 1520 and 1530, Luther worked out the basic theological tenets that became the articles of faith for his new church and later for all Protestant groups. The word *Protestant* derives from the protest drawn up by a small group of reforming German princes at the diet of Speyer in 1529. The princes "protested" the decisions of the Catholic majority. At first *Protestant* meant "Lutheran," but with the appearance of many protesting sects, it was applied to all non-Catholic Christians. Lutheran Protestant thought was officially formulated in the Confession of Augsburg in 1530. Ernst Troeltsch, a German student of the sociology of religion, has defined *Protestantism* as a "modification of Catholicism, in which the Catholic formulation of questions was retained, while a different answer was given to them." Luther gave new answers to four basic theological issues.

First, how is a person to be saved? Traditional Catholic teaching held that salvation was achieved by *both* faith *and* good works. Luther held that salvation comes *by faith alone*. Women and men are saved, said Luther, by the arbitrary decision of God, irrespective of good works or the sacraments.

Second, where does religious authority reside? Christian doctrine had long maintained that authority rests both in the Bible and in the traditional teaching of the church. Luther maintained that authority rests in the Word of God as revealed in the Bible alone and as interpreted by an individual's conscience. He urged that each person read and reflect on the Scriptures.

Third, what is the church? Medieval churchmen had identified the church with the clergy. Luther reiterated the Catholic teaching that the church is the entire Christian community.

Finally, what is the highest form of Christian life? The medieval church had stressed the superiority of the monastic and religious life over the secular. Luther argued that all vocations have equal merit, whether ecclesiastical or secular, and that every person should serve God in his or her individual calling.[34] Protestantism, in sum, represented a reformulation of the Christian heritage.

The Social Impact of Luther's Beliefs

As early as 1521, Luther had a vast following. Every encounter with ecclesiastical or political au-

Lucas Cranach the Younger: Luther and the Wittenberg Reformers The massive figure of John Frederick, Elector of Saxony, who protected and supported Luther, dominates this group portrait. Luther is on the far left, his associate Philip Melancthon in the front row on the right. Luther's face shows a quiet determination. *(Source: The Toledo Museum of Art, Toledo, Ohio; Gift of Edward Drummond Libbey)*

thorities attracted attention to him. Pulpits and printing presses spread his message all over Germany. By the time of his death, people of all social classes had become Lutheran. What was the immense appeal of Luther's religious ideas?

Recent historical research on the German towns has shown that two significant late medieval developments prepared the way for Luther's ideas. First,

Grünewald: Crucifixion (ca 1510) The bloodless hands, tortured face, and lacerated body contain an unprecedented depiction of the horrors of physical suffering and reflect the deep emotional piety of northern Europe. Court painter to Albert of Brandenburg, Grünewald later was strongly attracted to Luther's ideas. *(Source: National Gallery of Art, Washington, D.C.; Samuel H. Kress Collection)*

since the fifteenth century, city governments had expressed resentment at clerical privileges and immunities. Priests, monks, and nuns paid no taxes and were exempt from civic responsibilities such as defending the city, yet religious orders frequently held large amounts of urban property. At Zurich in 1467, for example, religious orders held one-third of the city's taxable property. City governments grew determined to integrate the clergy into civic life by reducing clerical privileges and giving the clergy public responsibilities. Accordingly, the Zurich magistracy subjected the religious to taxes, inspected wills so that legacies to the church and legacies left by churchmen could be

controlled, and placed priests and monks under the jurisdiction of the civil courts.

Preacherships also spread Luther's ideas. Critics of the late medieval church, especially informed and intelligent townspeople, condemned the irregularity and poor quality of sermons. As a result, prosperous burghers in many towns established preacherships. Preachers were men of superior education who were required to deliver about a hundred sermons a year, each lasting about forty-five minutes. Luther's ideas attracted many preachers, and in several towns preachers became Protestant leaders. Preacherships also encouraged the Protestant form of worship, in which the sermon, not the Eucharist, was the central part of the service.[35]

In the countryside the attraction of the German peasants to Lutheran beliefs was almost predictable. Luther himself came from a peasant background, and he admired their ceaseless toil. Peasants respected Luther's defiance of church authority. Moreover, they thrilled to the words Luther used in his treatise *On Christian Liberty* (1520): "A Christian man is the most free lord of all and subject to none." Taken by themselves, those words easily contributed to social unrest.

In the early sixteenth century, the economic condition of the peasantry varied from place to place but was generally worse than it had been in the fifteenth century and was deteriorating. Crop failures in 1523 and 1524 aggravated an explosive situation. In 1525 representatives of the Swabian peasants met at the city of Memmingen and drew up the Twelve Articles, which expressed their grievances. The Twelve Articles condemn lay and ecclesiastical lords and summarize the agrarian crisis of the early sixteenth century. The articles complain that nobles had seized village common lands, which traditionally had been used by all; that they had imposed new rents on manorial properties and new services on the peasants working those properties; and that they had forced the poor to pay unjust death duties in the form of the peasants' best horses or cows. Wealthy, socially mobile peasants especially resented these burdens, which they emphasized as new.[36] The peasants believed that their demands conformed to Scripture and cited Luther as a theologian who could prove that they did.

Luther wanted to prevent rebellion. Initially he sided with the peasants, and in a tract, *On Admonition to Peace*, he blasted the lords:

We have no one on earth to thank for this mischievous rebellion, except you lords and princes, especially you blind bishops and mad priests and monks. . . . In your government you do nothing but flay and rob your subjects in order that you may lead a life of splendor and pride, until the poor common folk can bear it no longer.[37]

But, Luther warned the peasants, nothing justified the use of armed force: "The fact that rulers are unjust and wicked does not excuse tumult and rebellion; to punish wickedness does not belong to everybody, but to the worldly rulers who bear the sword."[38] As for biblical support for the peasants' demands, he maintained that Scripture had nothing to do with earthly justice or material gain.

Massive revolts first broke out near the Swiss frontier and then swept through Swabia, Thuringia, the Rhineland, and Saxony. The crowds' slogans came directly from Luther's writings. "God's righteousness" and the "Word of God" were invoked in the effort to secure social and economic justice. The peasants who expected Luther's support were soon disillusioned. He had written of the "freedom" of the Christian, but he had meant the freedom to obey the word of God. "Freedom" for Luther meant independence from the authority of the Roman church; it did not mean opposition to legally established secular powers. The nobility ferociously crushed the revolt. Historians estimate that over 75,000 peasants were killed in 1525.

As it developed, Lutheran theology exalted the state, subordinated the church to the state, and everywhere championed the "powers that be." The consequences for German society were profound and have redounded into the twentieth century. The revolt of 1525 strengthened the authority of lay rulers. Peasant economic conditions, however, moderately improved. For example, in many parts of Germany enclosed fields, meadows, and forests were returned to common use.

Scholars in many disciplines have attributed Luther's fame and success to the invention of the printing press, which rapidly reproduced and made known his ideas. Equally important was Luther's skill with language. Language proved to be the weapon with which this peasant's son changed the world. Like the peasants, educated people and humanists were much attracted by Luther's words. He advocated a simpler, personal religion based on faith, a return to the spirit of the early church, the

centrality of the Scriptures in the liturgy and in Christian life, and abolition of elaborate ceremonial—precisely the reforms that the northern humanists had been calling for. Ulrich Zwingli (1484–1531), for example, a humanist of Zurich, was strongly influenced by Luther's bold stand; it stimulated Zwingli's reforms in that Swiss city. The nobleman Ulrich von Hutten (1488–1523), who had published several humanistic tracts, in 1519 dedicated his life to the advancement of Luther's reformation. And the Frenchman John Calvin (1509–1564), often called "the organizer of Protestantism," owed a great deal to Luther's thought.

The publication of Luther's German translation of the New Testament in 1523 democratized religion. His insistence that everyone should read and reflect on the Scriptures attracted the literate and thoughtful middle classes, partly because Luther appealed to their intelligence. Moreover, the business classes, preoccupied with making money, envied the church's wealth, disapproved of the luxurious lifestyle of some churchmen, and resented tithes and ecclesiastical taxation. Luther's doctrines of salvation by faith and the priesthood of all believers not only raised the religious status of the commercial classes but protected their pocketbooks as well.

For his time Luther held enlightened views on matters of sexuality and marriage. He wrote to a young man, "Dear lad, be not ashamed that you desire a girl, nor you my maid, the boy. Just let it lead you into matrimony and not into promiscuity, and it is no more cause for shame than eating and drinking."[39] Luther was confident that God took delight in the sexual act, and he denied that original sin affected the goodness of creation.

Luther believed, however, that marriage was a woman's career. A student recorded Luther as saying, early in his public ministry, "Let them bear children until they are dead of it; that is what they are for." A happy marriage to a former nun, Katharine von Bora, mellowed him somewhat. Another student later quoted him as saying, "Next to God's Word there is no more precious treasure than holy matrimony. God's highest gift on earth is a pious, cheerful, God-fearing, home-keeping wife, with whom you may live peacefully, to whom you may entrust your goods, and body and life."[40]

Luther deeply loved his "dear Katie," but he believed that women's concerns should revolve exclusively around the children, the kitchen, and the

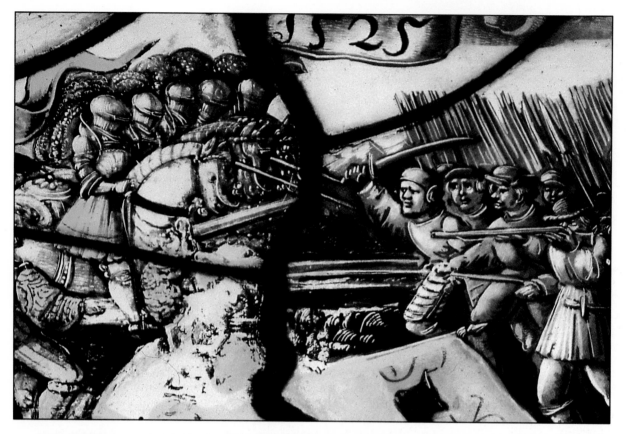

Battle of Gaisbeuren during the Peasants' War, 1525   When peasants' economic and social grievances merged with religious discontent, Luther wrote that the peasants misunderstood the Gospel and could not use it to change the social order. Because his appeal did not persuade the peasants to stop the violence, Luther called on the princes to exercise their right to the sword to end the disorder. A couple of peasants have guns, but most seem armed only with staves. *(Source: Siegfried Lauterwasser)*

church. A happy woman was a patient wife, an efficient manager, and a good mother. Kate was an excellent financial manager (which Luther—much inclined to give money and goods away—was not). A stern if often indulgent father, Luther held that the father should rule his household while the wife controlled its economy. With many relatives and constant visitors, Luther's was a large and happy household, a model for Protestants if an abomination for Catholics.

The Political Impact of Luther's Beliefs

In the sixteenth century, the practice of religion remained a public matter. Everyone participated in the religious life of the community, just as almost everyone shared in the local agricultural work.

Whatever spiritual convictions individuals held in the privacy of their consciences, the emperor, king, prince, magistrate, or other civil authority determined the official form of religious practice within his jurisdiction. Almost everyone believed that the presence of a faith different from that of the majority represented a political threat to the security of the state. Only a tiny minority, and certainly none of the princes, believed in religious liberty.

Against this background, the religious storm launched by Martin Luther swept across Germany. Several elements in his religious reformation stirred patriotic feelings. Anti-Roman sentiment ran high. Humanists lent eloquent intellectual support. And Luther's translation of the New Testament from Latin into German evoked national pride.

For decades devout laymen and churchmen had called on the German princes to reform the church. In 1520 Luther took up the cry in his *Appeal to the Christian Nobility of the German Nation.* Unless the princes destroyed papal power in Germany, Luther argued, reform was impossible. He urged the princes to confiscate ecclesiastical wealth and to abolish indulgences, dispensations, pardons, and clerical celibacy. He told them that it was their public duty to bring about the moral reform of the church. Luther based his argument in part on the papacy's financial exploitation of Germany:

How comes it that we Germans must put up with such robbery and such extortion of our property at the hands of the pope? If the Kingdom of France has pre-vented it, why do we Germans let them make such fools and apes of us? It would all be more bearable if in this way they only stole our property; but they lay waste the churches and rob Christ's sheep of their pious shepherds, and destroy the worship and the Word of God. As it is they do nothing for the good of Christendom; they only wrangle about the incomes of bishoprics and prelacies, and that any robber could do.[41]

Luther's appeal to German patriotism gained him strong support, and national feeling influenced many princes otherwise confused by or indifferent to the complexities of the religious issues.

The church in Germany possessed great wealth. And, unlike other countries, Germany had no strong central government to check the flow of

Titian: The Emperor Charles V (1548) Court painter to Charles V, Titian portrayed him shortly after the emperor's defeat of the league of German Protestant princes at the battle of Mühlberg near Leipzig. In this idealization, one of the earliest equestrian portraits, Charles appears as heroic victor, chivalric knight, and defender of the church. *(Source: Museo del Prado, Madrid)*

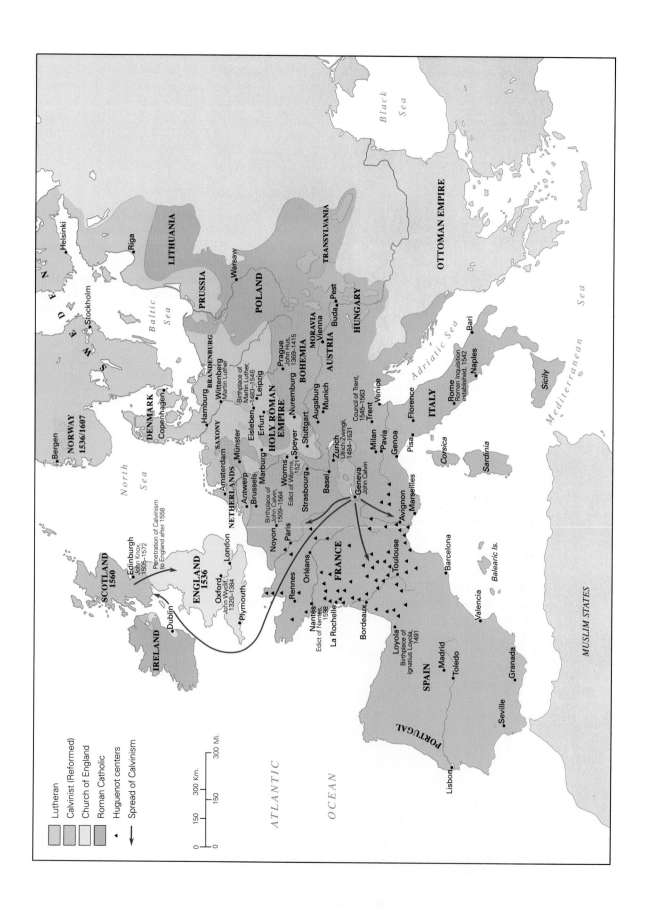

Lutheran

Calvinist (Reformed)

Church of England

Roman Catholic

▲ Huguenot centers

→ Spread of Calvinism

| 0 | 150 | 300 Km. |
| 0 | 150 | 300 Mi. |

ATLANTIC
OCEAN

North
Sea

IRELAND

Dublin

SCOTLAND
1560

Edinburgh
John Knox,
1505–1572

Penetration of Calvinism
to England after 1558

ENGLAND
1536

Oxford
John Wyclif,
1320–1384

London

Plymouth

Rennes

Nantes
Edict of Nantes,
1598

La Rochelle

Bordeaux

Orléans

FRANCE

Toulouse

Loyola
Birthplace of
Ignatius Loyola,
1491

SPAIN

Madrid

Toledo

Seville

Granada

Valencia

Barcelona

Balearic Is.

PORTUGAL

Lisbon

MUSLIM STATES

Mediterranean
Sea

Noyon
Birthplace of
John Calvin,
1509–1564

Paris

Marseilles

Avignon

Geneva
John Calvin

Zurich
Ulrich Zwingli,
1484–1531

Basel

Strasbourg

Worms
Edict of Worms,
1521

Speyer

Stuttgart

Augsburg

Munich

Milan

Pavia

Genoa

Pisa

Corsica

Sardinia

Florence

ITALY

Rome
Roman Inquisition
established, 1542

Naples

Bari

Sicily

Adriatic Sea

Venice

Trent
Council of Trent,
1545–1563

Vienna

AUSTRIA

HUNGARY

Buda Pest

MORAVIA

BOHEMIA

Prague
John Hus,
1369–1415

Nuremberg

Erfurt

Leipzig

Eisleben
Birthplace of
Martin Luther,
1483–1546

Wittenberg
Martin Luther

HOLY ROMAN
EMPIRE

Marburg

Brussels

Antwerp

Amsterdam

NETHERLANDS

Münster

SAXONY

Hamburg

BRANDENBURG

Copenhagen

DENMARK

Baltic
Sea

NORWAY
1536/1607

Bergen

Stockholm

Helsinki

Riga

LITHUANIA

PRUSSIA

Warsaw

POLAND

TRANSYLVANIA

OTTOMAN EMPIRE

Black
Sea

S W E D E N

gold to Rome. Rejection of Roman Catholicism and adoption of Protestantism would mean the legal confiscation of lush farmland, rich monasteries, and wealthy shrines. Some German princes were sincerely attracted to Lutheranism, but many civil authorities realized that they had a great deal to gain by embracing the new faith. A steady stream of duchies, margraviates, free cities, and bishoprics secularized church property, accepted Lutheran theological doctrines, and adopted simpler services conducted in German. The Edict of Worms in 1521, which condemned Luther and his teaching, was not enforced because the German princes did not want to enforce it.

Charles V was a vigorous defender of Catholicism, and contemporary social and political theory denied the possibility of two religions coexisting peacefully in one territory. Thus many princes used the religious issue to extend their financial and political independence. With doctrinal differences linked to political ambitions and financial receipts, the Protestant movement ultimately proved disastrous for Germany.

Charles V must share blame with the German princes for the disintegration of imperial authority in the empire. He neither understood nor took an interest in the constitutional problems of Germany, and he lacked the material resources to oppose Protestantism effectively there. Throughout his reign he was preoccupied with his Flemish, Spanish, Italian, and American territories. Moreover, the Turkish threat prevented him from acting effectively against the Protestants; Charles's brother Ferdinand needed Protestant support against the Turks who besieged Vienna in 1529.

Five times between 1521 and 1555, Charles V went to war with the Valois kings of France. The issue each time was the Habsburg lands acquired by the marriage of Maximilian and Mary of Burgundy. Much of the fighting occurred in Germany. The cornerstone of French foreign policy in the sixteenth and seventeenth centuries was the desire to keep the German states divided. Thus Europe witnessed the paradox of the Catholic king

of France supporting the Lutheran princes in their challenge to his fellow Catholic, Charles V. French policy was successful. The long dynastic struggle commonly called the "Habsburg-Valois Wars" advanced the cause of Protestantism and promoted the political fragmentation of the German empire.

Finally, in 1555, Charles agreed to the Peace of Augsburg, which, in accepting the status quo, officially recognized Lutheranism. Each prince was permitted to determine the religion of his territory. Most of northern and central Germany became Lutheran, while the south remained Roman Catholic (Map 17.4). There was no freedom of religion, however. Princes or town councils established state churches to which all subjects of the area had to belong. Dissidents, whether Lutheran or Catholic, had to convert or leave. The political difficulties that Germany inherited from the Middle Ages had been compounded by the religious crisis of the sixteenth century.

THE GROWTH OF THE PROTESTANT REFORMATION

By 1555 much of northern Europe had broken with the Roman Catholic church. All of Scandinavia, England, Scotland, and such self-governing cities as Geneva and Zurich in Switzerland and Strasbourg in Germany had rejected the religious authority of Rome and adopted new faiths. A common religious faith had been the one element uniting all of Europe for almost a thousand years, so the fragmentation of belief led to profound changes in European life and society. The most significant new form of Protestantism was Calvinism, of which the Peace of Augsburg had made no mention at all.

Calvinism

In 1509, while Luther was studying for the doctorate at Wittenberg, John Calvin (1509–1564) was born in Noyon in northeastern France. Calvin's theological writings would profoundly influence the social thought and attitudes of Europeans and English-speaking peoples all over the world, especially in Canada and the United States.

MAP 17.4 Tne Protestant and the Catholic Reformations The reformations shattered the religious unity of Western Christendom. What common cultural traits predominated in regions where a particular branch of the Christian faith was maintained or took root?

Prior to his ecclesiastical career, Calvin studied law. In 1533 he experienced a religious crisis, as a result of which he converted to Protestantism.

Convinced that God selects certain people to do his work, Calvin believed that God had specifically called him to reform the church. Accordingly, he accepted an invitation to assist in the reformation of the city of Geneva. There, beginning in 1541, Calvin worked assiduously to establish a Christian society ruled by God through civil magistrates and reformed ministers. Geneva, "a city that was a Church," became the model of a Christian community for sixteenth-century Protestant reformers.

To understand Calvin's Geneva, it is necessary to understand Calvin's ideas. These he embodied in *The Institutes of the Christian Religion,* first published in 1536 and definitively issued in 1559. The cornerstone of Calvin's theology was his belief in the absolute sovereignty and omnipotence of God and the total weakness of humanity. Before the infinite power of God, he asserted, men and women are as insignificant as grains of sand.

Calvin did not ascribe free will to human beings because free will would detract from the sovereignty of God. Calvin maintained that men and women cannot actively work to achieve salvation; rather, God in his infinite wisdom decided at the beginning of time who would be saved and who damned. This viewpoint constitutes the theological principle called "predestination":

Predestination we call the eternal decree of God, by which he has determined in himself, what he would have become of every individual of mankind. . . . God has once for all determined, both whom he would admit to salvation, and whom he would condemn to destruction. We affirm that this counsel, as far as concerns the elect, [that is, those whom God has chosen to save], is founded on his gratuitous mercy, totally irrespective of human merit; but that to those whom he devotes to condemnation, the gate of life is closed by a just and irreprehensible, but incomprehensible, judgment. . . . For the will of God is the highest justice; so that what he wills must be considered just, for this very reason, because he wills it.[42]

The doctrine of predestination dates back to Saint Augustine and Saint Paul, but many people have found it a pessimistic view of the nature of God, who they feel revealed himself in the Old and New Testaments as merciful as well as just.

Calvin maintained that although individuals cannot know whether they will be saved—and the probability is that they will be damned—good works are a "sign" of election. In any case, people should concentrate on worshiping God and doing his work and not waste time worrying about whether they will receive salvation.

The Calvinist ethic of the "calling" dignified all work by giving it a religious aspect. Hard work, well done, was believed to be pleasing to God. This doctrine encouraged an aggressive, vigorous activism in the sixteenth and later centuries.

Calvin aroused Genevans to a high standard of morality. His powerful sermons delivered the word of God and thereby monopolized the strongest contemporary means of communication, preaching. Through his *Genevan Catechism,* published in 1541, children and adults memorized set questions and answers and acquired a summary of their faith and a guide for daily living. Calvin's sermons and his *Catechism* gave a whole generation of Genevans thorough instruction in the reformed religion.[43]

In the reformation of the city, the Genevan *consistory* also exercised a powerful role. This body consisted of twelve laymen, plus the Company of Pastors, of which Calvin was the permanent moderator (presider). The duties of the consistory were "to keep watch over every man's life and to admonish amiably those whom they see leading a disorderly life." Although Calvin emphasized that the consistory's activities should be thorough and "its eyes may be everywhere," corrections were only "medicine to turn sinners to the Lord."[44] Thus austere living, public fasting, and evening curfew became the order of the day. Fashionable clothes, dancing, card playing, and heavy drinking were absolutely prohibited. The consistory investigated the private morals of citizens but was unwilling to punish the town prostitutes as severely as Calvin would have preferred. Calvin exercised some political influence through the consistory, but the civil magistrates in Geneva maintained firm control.

Calvin reserved his harshest condemnation for religious dissenters, declaring them "dogs and swine":

God makes plain that the false prophet is to be stoned without mercy. We are to crush beneath our heel all affections of nature when His honor is concerned. The father should not spare his child, nor brother his brother, nor husband his own wife or the friend who is dearer to him than life. No human relationship is more than animal unless it be grounded in God.[45]

Calvin translated his words into action. Executions for heresy were regular occurrences. One example was the Spanish humanist Michael Servetus, who, persecuted by the Spanish Inquisition, escaped to Geneva. In addition to denying the Trinity—which identifies God as three divine persons, Father, Son, and Holy Spirit—Servetus insisted that a person under twenty cannot commit a mortal sin. The city fathers considered this idea dangerous to public morality, "especially in these days when the young are so corrupted." Servetus was burned at the stake.

To many sixteenth-century Europeans, Calvin's Geneva seemed "the most perfect school of Christ since the days of the Apostles." Religious refugees from France, England, Spain, Scotland, and Italy poured into the city. Subsequently, the reformed church of Calvin served as the model for the Presbyterian church in Scotland, the Huguenot church in France, and the Puritan churches in England and New England.

In the *Institutes* Calvin provided a systematic theology for Protestantism. The reformed church of Calvin had a strong and well-organized machinery of government. These factors, together with the social and economic applications of Calvin's theology, made Calvinism the most dynamic force in the sixteenth- and seventeenth-century evolution of Protestantism.

Calvinist Worship   A converted house in Lyons, France, serves as a church for the simple Calvinist service. Although Calvin's followers believed in equality and elected officials administered the church, here men and women are segregated, and some people sit on hard benches while others sit in upholstered pews. Beside the pulpit an hourglass hangs to time the preacher's sermon. (Could the dog sit still for that long?) *(Source: Bibliothèque publique et universitaire, Geneva)*

THE LATER MIDDLE AGES, RENAISSANCE, AND PROTESTANT AND CATHOLIC REFORMATIONS, 1300–1600

As is evident in this chronology, early manifestations of the Renaissance and Protestant Reformation coincided in time with major events of the Later Middle Ages.

1300–1321	Dante, *The Divine Comedy*
1304–1374	Petrarch
1309–1378	Babylonian Captivity of the papacy
1337–1453	Hundred Years' War
1347–1351	The Black Death (returned intermittently until ca 1700)
ca 1350	Boccaccio, *The Decameron*
1356	Golden Bull: transforms the Holy Roman Empire into an aristocratic confederation
1358	The Jacquerie
ca 1376	John Wyclif publishes *Civil Dominion* attacking the church's temporal power and asserting the supremacy of the Scripture
1377–1417	The Great Schism
1378	Laborers' (ciompi) revolt in Florence
1381	Peasants' Revolt in England
1385–1400	Chaucer, *Canterbury Tales*
1414–1418	Council of Constance: ends the schism, postpones reform, executes John Hus
1431	Joan of Arc is burned at the stake
1434	Medici domination of Florence begins
1438	Pragmatic Sanction of Bourges: declares autonomy of the French church from papal jurisdiction
1453	Capture of Constantinople by the Ottoman Turks, ending the Byzantine Empire
1455–1471	Wars of the Roses in England
1456	Gutenberg Bible
1492	Unification of Spain under Ferdinand and Isabela; expulsion of Jews and Muslims from Spain; Columbus reaches the Americas
1494	France invades Italy, inaugurating sixty years of war on Italian soil; Florence expels the Medici and restores republican government

The Anabaptists

The name *Anabaptist* derives from a Greek word meaning "to baptize again." The Anabaptists, sometimes described as the "left wing of the Reformation," believed that only adults could make a free choice about religious faith, baptism, and entry into the Christian community. Thus they considered the practice of baptizing infants and children preposterous and claimed there was no scriptural basis for it. They wanted to rebaptize believers who had been baptized as children. Anabaptists took the Gospel absolutely literally and favored a return to the kind of church that had existed among the earliest Christians—a voluntary association of believers who had experienced an inner light.

Anabaptists believed in the separation of church and state and in religious tolerance. They almost never tried to force their values on others. In an age that believed in the necessity of state-established churches, Anabaptist views on religious liberty were thought to undermine that idea.

Each Anabaptist community or church was entirely independent; it selected its own ministers and ran its own affairs. In 1534 the Anabaptist community at Münster in Germany, for example, established a legal code that decreed the death penalty for insubordinate wives. The Münster community also practiced polygamy and forced all women under a certain age to marry or face expulsion or execution.

However, Anabaptists admitted women to the priesthood. They also shared goods as the early

1509	Erasmus, *The Praise of Folly*
1512	Restoration of the Medici in Florence
1512–1517	Lateran Council undertakes reform of clerical abuses
1513	Balboa discovers the Pacific
	Machiavelli, *The Prince*
1516	Thomas More, *Utopia*
1517	Martin Luther publishes the Ninety-five Theses
1519–1522	Magellan's crew circumnavigates the earth
1523	Luther's translation of the New Testament into German
1525	Peasants' Revolt in Germany
1527	Sack of Rome by mercenaries of Holy Roman Emperor Charles V
1528	Castiglione, *The Courtier*
1530	Confession of Augsburg, official formulation of Lutheran theology
1533	Act in Restraint of Appeals inaugurates the English Reformation
1534–1541	Michelangelo, *The Last Judgment*
1535	Execution of Thomas More for treason
1536	John Calvin, *Institutes of the Christian Religion*
1540	Loyola founds the Society of Jesus (Jesuits)
1541	Calvin establishes a theocracy in Geneva
1543	Copernicus, *On the Revolutions of the Heavenly Spheres*
1545–1563	Council of Trent
1555	Peace of Augsburg: German princes determine the religion of their territories; in effect, official recognition of Lutheranism
1572	St. Bartholemew's Day Massacre
1588	Spanish Armada
1598	Edict of Nantes grants French Protestants freedom of worship in certain towns
1603	Shakespeare, *Hamlet*
1605	Sir Francis Bacon, *The Advancement of Learning*

Christians had done, refused all public offices, and would not serve in the armed forces. In fact, they laid great stress on pacifism. Such beliefs tended to attract the poor, the unemployed, and the uneducated. Geographically, Anabaptists drew their members from depressed urban areas.

Ideas such as absolute pacifism and the distinction between the Christian community and the state brought down on these unfortunate people fanatical hatred and bitter persecution. Both Protestants and Catholics saw—quite correctly—the separation of church and state as leading ultimately to the complete secularization of society. The powerful rulers of Swiss and German society immediately saw the connection between religious heresy and economic dislocation and feared that the combination would lead to civil disturbances.

In Swiss and German cities, Anabaptists were either banished or cruelly executed. Their community spirit and the edifying example of their lives, however, contributed to the survival of Anabaptist ideas.

The English Reformation

As on the Continent, the Reformation in England had social and economic causes as well as religious ones. As elsewhere, too, Christian humanists had for decades been calling for the purification of the church. When the political matter of the divorce of King Henry VIII (r. 1509–1547) became enmeshed with other issues, a complete break with Rome resulted.

Demands for ecclesiastical reform dated back at least to the fourteenth century. The vigorously anticlerical Lollards had been driven underground in the fifteenth century but survived in parts of London, East Anglia, western Kent, and southern England. The work of the English humanist William Tyndale (ca 1494–1536) stimulated cries for reform. In 1525, at Antwerp, Tyndale began printing an English translation of the New Testament. From Antwerp, merchants carried the New Testament into England, where it was distributed by Lollards. Fortified with copies of Tyndale's English Bible and some of Luther's ideas, the Lollards represented the ideal of "a personal, scriptural, non-sacramental, and lay-dominated religion."[46] In this manner, doctrines that would later be called "Protestant" flourished underground in England before any official or state-approved changes.

In the early sixteenth century, the ignorance of much of the parish clergy, and the sexual misbehavior of some, compared unfavorably with the education and piety of lay people. Even more than the ignorance of the lower clergy, the wealth of the English church fostered resentment and anticlericalism. The church controlled perhaps 20 percent of the land and also received an annual tithe of the produce of lay people's estates. Since the church had jurisdiction over wills, the clergy also received mortuary fees, revenues paid by the deceased's relatives. Mortuary fees led to frequent lawsuits, since the common lawyers nursed a deep jealousy of the ecclesiastical courts.

The career of Thomas Wolsey (1474?–1530) provides an extreme example of pluralism in the English church in the early sixteenth century. The son of a butcher, Wolsey became a priest and in 1507 secured an appointment as chaplain to Henry VII. In 1509 Henry VIII made Wolsey a privy councillor. His remarkable ability and energy won him rapid advancement: in 1515 he became a cardinal and lord chancellor; in 1518, papal legate. Wolsey had more power than any previous royal minister, and he used that power to amass a large number of rich church offices. He displayed the vast wealth that these positions brought him with ostentation and arrogance, which in turn fanned the embers of anticlericalism. The divorce of Henry VIII ignited all these glowing coals.

Having fallen in love with Anne Boleyn, Henry wanted to divorce his wife, Catherine of Aragon, the third daughter of Ferdinand and Isabella of Spain. Legal, diplomatic, and theological problems stood in his way, however. When Henry married Catherine, he had secured a dispensation from Pope Julius II to eliminate all doubts and legal technicalities about Catherine's previous marriage to Henry's dead brother, Arthur. For eighteen years Catherine and Henry lived together in what contemporaries thought a happy marriage. Catherine produced six children, but only the princess Mary survived childhood.

Around 1527 Henry began to insist, citing a passage in the Old Testament Book of Leviticus, that God was denying him a male heir to punish him for marrying his brother's widow. Henry claimed that he wanted to spare England the dangers of a disputed succession. He warned that the anarchy and disorders of the Wars of the Roses would surely be repeated if a woman, the princess Mary, inherited the throne.

Henry went about the business of ensuring a peaceful succession in an extraordinary manner. He petitioned Pope Clement VII (r. 1523–1534) to declare that a legal marriage with Catherine had never existed, in which case Princess Mary was illegitimate and thus ineligible to succeed to the throne. Henry argued that Pope Julius's dispensation had contradicted the law of God—that a man may not marry his brother's widow. The English king's request reached Rome at the very time that Luther was widely publishing tracts condemning the papacy as the core of wickedness. By granting Henry's annulment and thereby admitting that a pope had erred, Clement would have given support to the Lutheran assertion that popes substitute their own evil judgments for the law of God. Clement therefore delayed acting on Henry's request.[47] The capture and sack of Rome in 1527 by the emperor Charles V, Queen Catherine's nephew, thoroughly tied the pope's hands.

Henry determined to get his divorce in England. The convenient death of the archbishop of Canterbury allowed Henry to appoint a new archbishop, Thomas Cranmer (1489–1556). Cranmer heard the case in his archiepiscopal court, granted the annulment, and thereby paved the way for Henry's marriage to Anne Boleyn on May 28, 1533. In September the princess Elizabeth was born.

Since Rome had refused to support Henry's matrimonial plans, he decided to remove the English church from papal jurisdiction. Henry used Parliament to legalize the Reformation in Eng-

Henry VIII's "Victory" This cartoon shows Henry VIII, assisted by Cromwell and Cranmer, triumphing over Pope Clement VII. Though completely removed from the historical facts, such illustrations were effectively used to promote antipapal feeling in late sixteenth-century England. *(Source: Fotomas Index)*

land. The Act in Restraint of Appeals (1533) declared the king to be the supreme sovereign in England and went on to forbid all judicial appeals to the papacy, thus establishing the Crown as the highest legal authority in the land. The Act for the Submission of the Clergy (1532) required churchmen to submit to the king and forbade the publication of all ecclesiastical laws without royal permission. The Supremacy Act of 1534 declared the king the supreme head of the Church of England.

Some opposed the king. John Fisher, the bishop of Rochester, a distinguished scholar and humanist, lashed out at the clergy for their cowardice. Another humanist, Thomas More, resigned the chancellorship in protest and would not take an oath recognizing Anne's daughter as heir. Fisher, More, and other dissenters were beheaded.

When Anne Boleyn failed to produce a male child, Henry VIII in 1536 had her beheaded. Parliament promptly proclaimed the princess Elizabeth illegitimate. Henry's third wife, Jane Seymour, gave him the desired son, Edward, and then died in childbirth. Henry went on to three more wives. Before he passed to his reward in 1547, he got Parliament to relegitimate Mary and Elizabeth and fixed the succession first in his son and then in his daughters.

Between 1535 and 1539, under the influence of his chief minister Thomas Cromwell, Henry decided to dissolve the English monasteries because he wanted their wealth. Abruptly, the king ended nine hundred years of English monastic life, dispersed the monks and nuns, and confiscated their lands. Hundreds of properties were later sold to the middle and upper classes and the proceeds spent on war. The dissolution of the monasteries brought the loss of a valuable esthetic and cultural force in English life. The redistribution of land, however, greatly strengthened the upper classes and tied them to the Tudor dynasty.

Holbein: Sir Thomas More   This powerful portrait (1527), revealing More's strong character and humane sensitivity, shows Holbein's complete mastery of detail—down to the stubble on More's chin. The chain was an emblem of More's service to Henry VIII. *(Source: The Frick Collection, New York)*

Recent scholarly research has emphasized that the English Reformation came from above. The surviving evidence does not allow us to gauge the degree of opposition to (or support for) Henry's break with Rome. Sentiment for reform was strong, though only a minority held distinctly Protestant doctrinal views, but certainly many lay people wrote to the king, begging him to spare the monasteries. Most lay people "acquiesced in the Reformation because they hardly knew what was going on, were understandably reluctant to jeopardise life or limb, a career or the family's good name."[48] But all did not quietly acquiesce. Rebellions in 1536 and 1546, despite possessing economic and Protestant components, reflected considerable public opposition to the state-ordered religious changes.[49]

Henry's motives combined personal, political, social, and economic elements. Theologically he retained such traditional Catholic practices and doctrines as auricular confession, clerical celibacy, and *transubstantiation* (the doctrine of the real presence of Christ in the bread and wine of the Eucharist). Meanwhile, Protestant literature circulated, and Henry approved the selection of men with known Protestant sympathies as tutors for his son.

The nationalization of the church and the dissolution of the monasteries led to important changes in government administration. Vast tracts of land came temporarily under the Crown's jurisdiction, and new bureaucratic machinery had to be developed to manage those properties.

Thomas Cromwell reformed and centralized the king's household, the council, the secretariats, the Exchequer (see page 409), and the distribution of government funds. New departments of state were set up. This balancing resulted in greater efficiency and economy. In Henry VIII's reign can be seen the growth of the modern centralized bureaucratic state.

For several decades after Henry's death in 1547, the English church shifted left and right. In the short reign of Henry's sickly son Edward VI (r. 1547–1553), the strongly Protestant ideas of Archbishop Thomas Cranmer exerted a significant influence on the religious life of the country. Cranmer simplified the liturgy, invited Protestant theologians to England, and prepared the first *Book of Common Prayer* (1549). In stately and dignified English, the *Book of Common Prayer* included, together with the Psalter, the order for all services of the Church of England.

The equally brief reign of Mary Tudor (r. 1553–1558) witnessed a sharp move back to Catholicism. The devoutly Catholic daughter of Catherine of Aragon, Mary rescinded the Reformation legislation of her father's reign and fully restored Roman Catholicism. Mary's marriage to her cousin Philip II of Spain (r. 1556–1598), son of the emperor Charles V, proved highly unpopular in England, and her persecution and execution of several hundred devout Protestants further alienated her subjects. During her reign, many Protestants fled to the Continent. Mary's death raised to the throne her sister Elizabeth (r. 1558–1603) and inaugurated the beginnings of religious stability.

At the start of her reign, Elizabeth's position was insecure. Although the populace cheered her accession, many questioned her legitimacy. On the one hand, Catholics wanted a Roman Catholic ruler. On the other hand, a vocal number of returned English exiles—called "Puritans" because they wanted to "purify" the church—wanted all Catholic elements in the Church of England destroyed.

Elizabeth had been raised a Protestant, but if she had genuine religious convictions she kept them to herself. Probably one of the shrewdest politicians in English history, Elizabeth chose a middle course between Catholic and Puritan extremes. She insisted on dignity in church services and political order in the land. She did not care what people believed as long as they kept quiet about it. Avoiding precise doctrinal definitions, Elizabeth had herself styled "Supreme Governor of the Church of England, Etc.," and left it to her subjects to decide what the "Etc." meant.

The parliamentary legislation of the early years of Elizabeth's reign—laws sometimes labeled the "Elizabethan Settlement"—required outward conformity to the Church of England and uniformity in all ceremonies. Everyone had to attend Church of England services; those who refused were fined. In 1563 a convocation of bishops approved the Thirty-nine Articles, a summary in thirty-nine short statements of the basic tenets of the Church of England. During Elizabeth's reign, the "Anglican church" (for the Latin *Ecclesia Anglicana*), as the Church of England was called, moved in a moderately Protestant direction. Serv-

ices were conducted in English, monasteries were not re-established, and the clergy were allowed to marry. But the bishops remained as church officials, and, apart from language, the services were quite traditional.

THE CATHOLIC AND THE COUNTER-REFORMATIONS

Between 1517 and 1547, the reformed versions of Christianity known as "Protestantism" made remarkable advances. Still, the Catholic church made a significant comeback. After about 1540, no new large areas of Europe, except the Netherlands, accepted Protestant beliefs (see Map 17.4).

Historians distinguish between two types of reform within the Catholic church in the sixteenth and seventeenth centuries: the Catholic Reformation and the Counter-Reformation. The Catholic Reformation began before 1517 and sought renewal through the stimulation of a new spiritual fervor. The Counter-Reformation started in the 1530s as a reaction to the rise and spread of Protestantism. The Counter-Reformation involved Catholic efforts to convince or coerce dissidents or heretics to return to the church. The Catholic Reformation and the Counter-Reformation were not mutually exclusive; in fact, after about 1540 they progressed simultaneously.

The Slowness of Institutional Reform

The Renaissance princes who sat on the throne of Saint Peter were not blind to the evils that existed. Modest reform efforts had begun with the Lateran Council called in 1512 by Pope Julius II. The Dutch pope Adrian VI (r. 1522–1523) had instructed his legate in Germany to

say that we frankly confess that God permits this Lutheran persecution of his church on account of the sins of men, especially those of the priests and prelates. . . . We know that in this Holy See now for some years there have been many abominations, abuses in spiritual things, excesses in things commanded, in short that all has become perverted. . . . We have all turned aside in our ways, nor was there, for a long time, any who did right—no, not one.[50]

Why did the popes, spiritual leaders of the Western church, move so slowly? The answers lie in the personalities of the popes themselves, their preoccupation with political affairs in Italy, and the awesome difficulty of reforming so complicated a bureaucracy as the Roman curia.

Clement VII, a true Medicean, was far more interested in elegant tapestries and Michelangelo's painting of the Last Judgment than in theological disputes in barbaric Germany. Indecisive and vacillating, Pope Clement must bear much of the responsibility for the great spread of Protestantism. While Emperor Charles V and the French king Francis I competed for the domination of divided Italy, the papacy worried about the security of the Papal States. Clement tried to follow a middle course, first backing the emperor, then switching from Charles and the Spaniards to Francis I shortly before the emperor's mercenaries sacked Rome in 1527 and captured the pope. Obviously, papal concern about Italian affairs and the Papal States diverted attention from reform.

The idea of reform was closely linked to the idea of a general council representing the entire church. A strong contingent of countries beyond the Alps—Spain, Germany, and France—wanted to reform the vast bureaucracy of Latin officials, reducing offices, men, and revenues. However, popes from Julius II to Clement VII, remembering fifteenth-century conciliar attempts to limit papal authority, resisted calls for a council. The papal bureaucrats who were the popes' intimates warned the popes against a council, fearing loss of power, revenue, and prestige.

The Council of Trent

In the papal conclave that followed the death of Clement VII, Cardinal Alexander Farnese promised two German cardinals that if he were elected pope he would summon a council. He won the election and ruled as Pope Paul III (r. 1534–1549). This Roman aristocrat, humanist, and astrologer, who immediately made his teenage grandsons cardinals, seemed an unlikely person to undertake serious reform. Yet Paul III appointed as cardinals several learned churchmen, such as Caraffa (later Pope Paul IV); established the Inquisition in the Papal States; and—true to his word—called a council, which finally met at Trent, an imperial city close to Italy.

The Council of Trent met intermittently from 1545 to 1563. Lutherans and Calvinists were invited to participate, but their insistence that the Scriptures be the sole basis for discussion made reconciliation impossible. Trent had been selected as the site for the council in the hope it would attract Protestants. In fact, Italian bishops predominated, and no Protestants came; and a number of factors combined to reduce attendance drastically. Portugal, Poland, Hungary, and Ireland sent representatives, but very few German bishops attended.

Other problems bedeviled all the sessions of the council. International politics repeatedly cast a shadow over the theological debates. Charles V opposed discussions on any matter that might further alienate his Lutheran subjects. And the French kings worked against the reconciliation of Roman Catholicism and Lutheranism because they wanted to keep the German states divided.

In spite of these obstacles, the achievements of the Council of Trent are impressive. It established the centralizing tenet that all acts of the council required papal approval, and it dealt with both doctrinal and disciplinary matters. The council gave equal validity to the Scriptures and to tradition as sources of religious truth and authority. It reaffirmed the seven sacraments and the traditional Catholic teaching on transubstantiation, thus rejecting Lutheran and Calvinist positions.

The council tackled the problems arising from ancient abuses by strengthening ecclesiastical discipline. It issued decrees requiring bishops to reside in their own dioceses, suppressing pluralism and simony, and forbidding the sale of indulgences. Clerics who kept concubines were to give them up. The jurisdiction of bishops over all the clergy of their dioceses was made almost absolute, and bishops were ordered to visit every religious house within their dioceses at least once every two years. In a highly original canon, the council required every diocese to establish a seminary for the education and training of the clergy; and it laid great emphasis on preaching and instructing the laity, especially the uneducated.

The Council of Trent did not meet everyone's expectations. Reconciliation with Protestantism was not achieved, nor was reform brought about immediately. Nevertheless, the council laid a solid basis for the spiritual renewal of the church and for the enforcement of correction. For four centuries, the doctrinal and disciplinary legislation of Trent served as the basis for Roman Catholic faith, organization, and practice.

New Religious Orders

The establishment of new religious orders within the church reveals a central feature of the Catholic Reformation. These new orders developed in response to one crying need: to raise the moral and intellectual level of the clergy and people. Education was a major goal of them all.

The Ursuline order of nuns founded by Angela Merici (1474–1540) attained enormous prestige for the education of women. The daughter of a country gentleman, Merici worked for many years among the poor, sick, and uneducated around her native Brescia in northern Italy. In 1535 she established the Ursuline order to combat heresy through Christian education. The first religious order concentrating exclusively on teaching young girls, the Ursulines sought to re-Christianize society by training future wives and mothers. Approved as a religious community by Paul III in

The Council of Trent   This seventeenth-century engraving depicts one of the early and sparsely attended sessions of the Council of Trent. The tridentine sessions of 1562–1563 drew many more bishops and laymen, but there were never many representatives from northern Europe. *(Source: Photo Vatican Museums)*

Pope Paul III's Confirmation of the Jesuit Constitutions On the right Ignatius Loyola receives the constitutions of the Society of Jesus by direct illumination from God. At left the pope approves them. When the constitutions were read to him, Paul III supposedly murmured, "There is the finger of God." *(Source: Historical Picture Service, Chicago)*

1544, the Ursulines rapidly grew and spread to France and the New World. Their schools in North America, stretching from Quebec to New Orleans, provided superior education for young women and inculcated the spiritual ideals of the Catholic Reformation.

The Society of Jesus, founded by Ignatius Loyola (1491–1556), a former Spanish soldier, played a powerful international role in resisting the spread of Protestantism, converting Asians and Latin American Indians to Catholicism, and spreading Christian education all over Europe. While recuperating from a severe battle wound in his legs, Loyola studied a life of Christ and other religious books and decided to give up his military career and become a soldier of Christ. During a year spent in seclusion, prayer, and personal mortification, he gained the religious insights that went into his *Spiritual Exercises*. This work, intended for

study during a four-week period of retreat, directed the individual imagination and will to the reform of life and a new spiritual piety.

Loyola was apparently a man of considerable personal magnetism. After study at the universities in Salamanca and Paris, he gathered a group of six companions and in 1540 secured papal approval of the new Society of Jesus, whose members were called "Jesuits." Their goal was the reform of the church through education, preaching the Gospel to pagan peoples, and fighting Protestantism. Within a short time, the Jesuits attracted many recruits.

The Society of Jesus was a centralized, tightly knit organization. Candidates underwent a two-year novitiate, in contrast to the usual one-year probation required of candidates in most religious orders. Although new members took the traditional vows of poverty, chastity, and obedience, the emphasis was on obedience. Carefully selected members made a fourth vow of obedience to the pope and the governing members of the society. As faith was the cornerstone of Luther's life, so obedience became the bedrock of the Jesuit tradition.

The Jesuits had a modern, quasi-military quality; they achieved phenomenal success for the papacy and the reformed Catholic church. Jesuit schools adopted modern teaching methods. They first concentrated on the children of the poor, but they were soon educating the sons of the nobility. As confessors and spiritual directors to kings, Jesuits exerted great political influence. Indifferent to physical comfort and personal safety and operating on the principle that the end sometimes justifies the means, they were not above spying. Within Europe, the Jesuits brought southern Germany and much of eastern Europe back to Catholicism.

The Sacred Congregation of the Holy Office

In 1542 Pope Paul III established the Sacred Congregation of the Holy Office with jurisdiction over the Roman Inquisition, a powerful instrument of the Counter-Reformation. The Inquisition was a committee of six cardinals with judicial authority over all Catholics and the power to arrest, imprison, and execute. Under the direction of the fanatical Cardinal Caraffa, it vigorously attacked heresy.

The Roman Inquisition operated under the principles of Roman law. It accepted hearsay evidence, was not obliged to inform the accused of charges against them, and sometimes applied torture. Echoing one of Calvin's remarks about heresy, Cardinal Caraffa wrote, "No man is to lower himself by showing toleration towards any sort of heretic, least of all a Calvinist."[51] The Holy Office published the *Index of Prohibited Books,* a catalog of forbidden reading that included the publications of many printers.

Within the Papal States, the Inquisition effectively destroyed heresy (and many heretics). Outside the papal territories, however, its influence was slight. Governments had their own judicial systems for the suppression of treasonable activity, as religious heresy was then considered. In Venice,

for instance, authorities cooperated with the Holy Office only when heresy became a great threat to the security of the republic. The *Index* had no influence on scholarly research in nonreligious areas, such as law, classical literature, and mathematics. As a result of the Inquisition, Venetians and Italians were not cut off from the main currents of European learning.[52]

SUMMARY

The Italian Renaissance, spanning the period from the eleventh through sixteenth centuries, developed in two broad stages. In the first stage, from about 1050 to 1300, a new economy emerged, based on Venetian and Genoese shipping and long-distance trade and on Florentine banking and cloth manufacture. These commercial activities, combined with the struggle of urban communes for political independence from surrounding feudal lords, led to the appearance of a new wealthy aristocratic class. The second stage, extending roughly from 1300 to 1600, witnessed a remarkable intellectual efflorescence. Based on a strong interest in the ancient world, the Renaissance had a classicizing influence on many facets of culture. In the city-states of fifteenth- and sixteenth-century Italy, oligarchic or despotic powers governed; Renaissance culture was manipulated to enhance the power of those rulers. Expanding outside Italy, the intellectual features of this movement affected the culture of all Europe.

In northern Europe, city merchants and rural gentry allied with rising monarchies. Using taxes provided by business people, kings provided a greater degree of domestic peace and order, conditions essential for trade. In Spain, France, and England, rulers also emphasized royal dignity and authority. Feudal monarchies gradually evolved in the direction of nation-states.

In the sixteenth century and through most of the seventeenth, religion and religious issues continued to play a major role in the lives of individuals and in the policies and actions of governments. The age of the Reformation presents very real paradoxes. The break with Rome and the rise of Lutheran, Anglican, Calvinist, and other faiths destroyed the unity of Europe as an organic Christian society. The strength of religious convictions caused political fragmentation, and religion, whether Protestant or Catholic, decisively influenced the growth of national states. Although most reformers rejected religious toleration, they helped pave the way for it.

Scholars have maintained that the sixteenth century witnessed the beginnings of the modern world. They are both right and wrong. The sixteenth-century revolt from the church paved the way for the eighteenth-century revolt from the Christian God, one of the strongest supports of life in Western culture. In this respect, the Reformation marks the beginning of the modern world, with its secularism and rootlessness. At the same time, it can be argued that the sixteenth century represents the culmination of the Middle Ages. Martin Luther's anxieties about salvation show him to be very much a medieval man. His concerns had deeply troubled serious individuals since the time of Saint Augustine. Modern people tend to be less troubled by them.

NOTES

1. See L. Martines, *Power and Imagination: City-States in Renaissance Italy* (New York: Vintage Books, 1980), esp. pp. 332–333.
2. Ibid., pp. 22–61.
3. Ibid., pp. 221–237, esp. p. 221.
4. Quoted in J. Burckhardt, *The Civilization of the Renaissance in Italy* (London: Phaidon Books, 1951), p. 89.
5. *Memoirs of Benvenuto Cellini: A Florentine Artist: Written by Himself* (London: J. M. Dent & Sons, Everyman's Library, 1927), p. 2.
6. Quoted in Burckhardt, p. 111.
7. See C. Trinkaus, *In Our Image and Likeness: Humanity and Divinity in Italian Humanist Thought,* vol. 2 (London: Constable, 1970), pp. 505–529.
8. B. Burroughs, ed., *Vasari's Lives of the Artists* (New York: Simon & Schuster, 1946), pp. 164–165.
9. See Martines, chap. 13, esp. pp. 241, 243.
10. See "The Social Status of the Artists," in A. Hauser, *The Social History of Art,* vol. 2 (New York: Vintage Books, 1959), chap. 3, esp. pp. 60, 68.
11. G. Bull, trans., *Aretino: Selected Letters* (Baltimore: Penguin Books, 1976), p. 109.
12. Quoted in P. Murray and L. Murray, *A Dictionary of Art and Artists* (Baltimore: Penguin Books, 1963), p. 125.
13. Hauser, pp. 48–49.
14. Quoted in W. H. Woodward, *Vittorino da Feltre and Other Humanist Educators* (Cambridge, England: Cambridge University Press, 1897), pp. 96–97.
15. C. E. Detmold, trans., *The Historical, Political and Diplomatic Writings of Niccolò Machiavelli* (Boston: J. R. Osgood & Co., 1882), pp. 51–52.
16. Ibid., pp. 54–55.
17. See F. Gilbert, *Machiavelli and Guicciardini: Politics and History in Sixteenth Century Florence* (New York: Norton, 1985), pp. 197–200.
18. E. L. Eisenstein, *The Printing Press as an Agent of Change: Communications and Cultural Transformations in Early Modern Europe,* vol. 1 (New York: Cambridge University Press, 1979), pp. 126–159, esp. p. 135.
19. M. L. King, "Book-lined Cells: Women and Humanism in the Early Italian Renaissance," in *Beyond Their Sex: Learned Women of the European Past,* ed. P. H. Labalme (New York: New York University Press, 1980), pp. 66–81, esp. p. 73.
20. This account rests on J. Kelly-Gadol, "Did Women Have a Renaissance?" in *Becoming Visible: Women in European History,* ed. R. Bridenthal and C. Koonz, (Boston: Houghton Mifflin, 1977), pp. 137–161, esp. p. 161.
21. G. Ruggerio, "Sexual Criminality in Early Renaissance Venice, 1338–1358," *Journal of Social History* 8 (Spring 1975): 18–31.
22. Quoted in R. C. Trexler, "Infanticide in Florence: New Sources and First Results," *History of Childhood Quarterly,* vol. 1, no. 1 (Summer 1973): 99.
23. Ibid., pp. 100–120.
24. J. Devisse and M. Mollat, *The Image of the Black in Western Art,* vol. 2, trans. W. G. Ryan (New York: Morrow, 1979), pt. 2, pp. 187–188.
25. Ibid., pp. 190–194.
26. Ibid., pp. 255–258.
27. Quoted in E. H. Harbison, *The Christian Scholar and His Calling in the Age of the Reformation* (New York: Scribner's, 1956), p. 109.
28. Quoted in F. Seebohm, *The Oxford Reformers* (London: J. M. Dent & Sons, Everyman's Library, 1867), p. 256.
29. See J. H. Elliott, *Imperial Spain, 1469–1716* (New York: Mentor Books, 1963), esp. pp. 75, 97–108.
30. See R. R. Post, *The Modern Devotion: Confrontation with Reformation and Humanism* (Leiden: E. J. Brill, 1968), esp. pp. 237–238, 255, 323–348.
31. T. C. Mendenhall et al., eds., *Ideas and Institutions in European History: 800–1715* (New York: Henry Holt, 1948), p. 220.
32. Quoted in O. Chadwick, *The Reformation* (Baltimore: Penguin Books, 1976), p. 55.
33. Quoted in E. H. Harbison, *The Age of Reformation* (Ithaca, N.Y.: Cornell University Press, 1963), p. 52.

34. Based heavily on Harbison, *The Age of Reformation,* pp. 52–55.

35. See S. E. Ozment, *The Reformation in the Cities: The Appeal of Protestantism to Sixteenth-Century Germany and Switzerland* (New Haven, Conn.: Yale University Press, 1975), pp. 32–45.

36. See S. E. Ozment, *The Age of Reform, 1250–1550: An Intellectual and Religious History of Late Medieval and Reformation Europe* (New Haven, Conn.: Yale University Press, 1980), pp. 273–279.

37. Quoted ibid., p. 280.

38. Ibid., p. 281.

39. Quoted in H. G. Haile, *Luther: An Experiment in Biography* (Garden City, N.Y.: Doubleday, 1980), p. 272.

40. Quoted in J. Atkinson, *Martin Luther and the Birth of Protestantism* (Baltimore: Penguin Books, 1968), pp. 247–248.

41. *Martin Luther: Three Treatises* (Philadelphia: Muhlenberg Press, 1947), pp. 28–31.

42. J. Allen, trans., *John Calvin: The Institutes of the Christian Religion* (Philadelphia: Westminster Press, 1930), bk. 3, chap. 21, paras. 5, 7.

43. E. W. Monter, *Calvin's Geneva* (New York: Wiley, 1967), pp. 98–108.

44. Ibid., p. 137.

45. Quoted in R. Bainton, *The Travail of Religious Liberty* (New York: Harper & Brothers, 1958), pp. 69–70.

46. A. G. Dickens, *The English Reformation* (New York: Schocken Books, 1964), p. 36.

47. See R. Marius, *Thomas More: A Biography* (New York: Knopf, 1984), pp. 215–216.

48. See J. J. Scarisbrick, *The Reformation and the English People* (Oxford: Basil Blackwell, 1984), pp. 81–84, esp. p. 81.

49. Ibid.

50. Ibid., p. 84.

51. Quoted in Chadwick, p. 270.

52. See P. Grendler, *The Roman Inquisition and the Venetian Press, 1540–1605* (Princeton, N.J.: Princeton University Press, 1977).

SUGGESTED READING

There are many exciting studies available on virtually all aspects of the Renaissance and the Reformation. In addition to the titles given in the Notes, the curious student should see J. H. Plumb, *The Italian Renaissance* (1965), a superbly written book and perhaps the best starting point. J. R. Hales, *Renaissance Europe: The Individual and Society, 1480–1520* (1978), is an excellent treatment of individualism. F. H. New, *The Renaissance and Reformation: A Short History* (1977), gives a balanced, concise, and up-to-date account; however, the older study of M. P. Gilmore, *The World of Humanism* (1962), is still useful. For the city where much of the Renaissance originated, G. A. Brucker, *Renaissance Florence* (1969), provides a fine description of Florentine economic, political, social, and cultural history.

For Machiavelli, the following works are helpful: J. R. Hale, *Machiavelli and Renaissance Italy* (1966), a short, sound biography; G. Bull, trans., *Machiavelli: The Prince* (1975), a readable and easily accessible edition of the political thinker's major work; and F. Guilbert, *Machiavelli and Guicciardini* (1984), a superb analysis of the thought of the two writers.

Renaissance art has inspired vast research. The following titles give some introduction to an enormous literature: A. Martindale, *The Rise of the Artist in the Middle Ages and Early Renaissance* (1972); B. Berenson, *Italian Painters of the Renaissance* (1957); E. Panofsky, *Meaning in the Visual Arts* (1955), by one of the great art historians of the century; L. Steinberg, *The Sexuality of Christ in Renaissance Art and Modern Oblivion* (1983), a brilliant study that relates Christ's sexuality to incarnational theology; C. Hibbert, *Rome: The Biography of a City* (1985), an elegant and entertaining work; and I. A. Richter, ed., *The Notebooks of Leonardo da Vinci* (1985), which gives the artist's scientific and naturalistic ideas and drawings. The magisterial achievement of J. Pope-Hennessy, *Cellini* (1985), is a brilliant evocation of the artist's life and work.

The following works should prove useful for various aspects of Renaissance social history: C. Singleton, trans., *The Courtier* (1959); E. L. Eisenstein, *The Printing Press as an Agent of Change: Communications and Cultural Transformations in Early Modern Europe,* 2 vols. (1979); G. Ruggerio, *Violence in Early Renaissance Florence* (1980), a pioneering study of crime and punishment; D. Weinstein and R. M. Bell, *Saints and Society: The Two Worlds of Christendom, 1000–1700* (1982), an essential work for an understanding of the social origins of saints; and J. C. Brown, *Immodest Acts: The Life of a Lesbian Nun in Renaissance Italy* (1985), and I. Maclean, *The Renaissance Notion of Women* (1980), which are useful for an understanding of the role and status of women. For blacks, see the rich and original achievement of J. Devisse and M. Mollat, *The Image of the Black in Western Art,* vol. 2, pt. 1, *From the Demonic Threat to the Incarnation of Sainthood,* and pt. 2, *Africans in the Christian Ordinance of the World: Fourteenth to Sixteenth Century* (trans. W. G. Ryan, 1979).

The best introduction to the Renaissance in northern Europe and a work that has greatly influenced twentieth-century scholarship is J. Huizinga, *The Waning of the Middle Ages: A Study of the Forms of Life, Thought, and Art in France and the Netherlands in the*

Dawn of the Renaissance (1954), which challenges the whole idea of the Renaissance. French Renaissance civilization is brilliantly evoked in L. Febvre, *Life in Renaissance France* (trans. and ed. M. Rothstein, 1977). The Marius biography of More cited in the Notes is an original study of the English humanist and statesman, but the student may also want to consult E. E. Reynolds, *Thomas More* (1962), and R. W. Chambers, *Thomas More* (1935). Erasmas, the leading northern humanist, is sensitively treated by M. M. Phillips, *Erasmus and the Northern Renaissance* (1956), and J. Huizinga, *Erasmus of Rotterdam* (1952). J. Leclercq, trans., *The Complete Works of Rabelais* (1963), is also easily accessible.

The works by Chadwick and Harbison cited in the Notes are good general introductions to the Reformation, as is H. Hillerbrand, *Men and Ideas in the Sixteenth Century* (1969). L. W. Spitz, *The Protestant Reformation, 1517–1559* (1985), provides a sound and comprehensive survey incorporating much of the latest research. For studies that interpret the Reformation against the background of fifteenth-century reforming developments, see the works by Post and by Ozment (*The Age of Reform*) cited in the Notes and G. Strauss, *Manifestations of Discontent in Germany on the Eve of the Reformation (1971),* an exciting collection of documents.

For the central figure of the early Reformation, see, in addition to the works by Atkinson and Haile cited in the Notes, H. Boehmer, *Martin Luther, Road to Reformation* (1960), a well-balanced work on Luther's formative years. Haile's perceptive study focuses on the mature and aging reformer. Students may expect thorough analyses of Luther's theology in J. Pelikan, *Reformation of Church and Dogma, 1300–1700* (1986); A. E. McGrath, *Luther's Theology of the Cross: Martin Luther on Justification* (1985); and H. Bornkamm, *Luther in Mid-Career, 1521–1530* (1983). The best introduction to Calvin is probably W. J. Bouwsma, *John Calvin: A Sixteenth-Century Portrait* (1988), an authoritative study that situates Calvin within Renaissance culture; R. T. Kendall, *Calvinism and English Calvinism to 1649* (1981), focuses on English conditions; and R. M. Mitchell, *Calvin and the Puritan's View of the Protestant Ethic* (1979), gives the socioeconomic implications of Calvin's thought. For the Anabaptists and the "left

wing" of the Reformation, see the profound but difficult work of G. H. Williams, *The Radical Reformers* (1962).

For England, in addition to the fundamental works by Dickens and Scarisbrick cited in the Notes, see for popular religion K. Thomas, *Religion and the Decline of Magic* (1971), and S. T. Bindoff, *Tudor England* (1959). The best works on the king's divorce are J. J. Scarisbrick, *Henry VIII* (1968); G. Mattingly, *Catherine of Aragon* (1949); and H. A. Kelly, *The Matrimonial Trials of Henry VIII* (1975). On the dissolution of the English monasteries, D. Knowles, *The Religion Orders in England,* vol. 3 (1959), is a superb example of English historical prose. Many aspects of English social history are discussed in J. Youings, *Sixteenth Century England* (1984), a sound and beautifully written work.

For the social history of the Reformation period, see L. P. Buc and J. W. Zophy, eds., *The Social History of the Reformation* (1972), and K. von Greyerz, ed., *Religion and Society in Early Modern Europe, 1500–1800* (1984), both of which contain interesting and important essays; S. E. Ozment, *The Reformation in the Cities* (see the Notes); and G. Strauss, *Luther's House of Learning: The Indoctrination of the Young in the German Reformation* (1978). For women in the period, M. Wiesner, *Women in the Sixteenth Century: A Bibliography* (1983), is a useful reference tool, and S. M. Wyntjes, "Women in the Reformation Era," in Bridenthal and Koonz's *Becoming Visible* (see the Notes), is a good general survey. The best recent treatment of marriage and the family is probably S. E. Ozment, *When Fathers Ruled: Family Life in Reformation Europe* (1983). Ozment's edition of *Reformation Europe: A Guide to Research* (1982) contains many useful articles.

P. Janelle, *The Catholic Reformation* (1951), is a comprehensive treatment of the Catholic Reformation from a Catholic point of view, and A. G. Dickens, *The Counter-Reformation* (1969), gives the Protestant standpoint in a splendidly illustrated book. The virtually definitive study of the Council of Trent is H. Jedin, *A History of the Council of Trent,* 3 vols. (1957–1961). For the Jesuits, see M. Foss, *The Founding of the Jesuits, 1540* (1969), and W. B. Bangert, *A History of the Society of Jesus* (1972).

18

The Age of European Expansion and Religious Wars

Hans Holbein the Younger, *Jean de Dinteville and George de Seluc (The Ambassadors)*

Between 1450 and 1650 two developments dramatically altered the world in which Europeans lived: overseas expansion and the reformations of the Christian churches. Overseas expansion broadened Europeans' geographical horizons and brought them into confrontation with ancient civilizations in Africa, Asia, and the Americas. These confrontations led first to conquest, then to exploitation, and finally to profound social changes in both Europe and the conquered territories. Likewise, the Renaissance and the reformations drastically changed intellectual, political, religious, and social life in Europe. War and religious issues dominated the politics of European states. Although religion was commonly used to rationalize international conflict, wars were fought for power and territorial expansion.

- Why, in the sixteenth and seventeenth centuries, did a relatively small number of people living on the edge of the Eurasian land mass gain control of the major sea lanes of the world and establish political and economic hegemony on distant continents?

- How were a few Spaniards, fighting far from home, able to overcome the powerful Aztec and Inca empires in America?

- What effect did overseas expansion have on Europe and on conquered societies?

- What were the causes and consequences of the religious wars in France, the Netherlands, and Germany?

- How did the religious crises of this period affect the status of women?

- How and why did African slave labor become the dominant form of labor organization in the New World?

- What religious and intellectual developments led to the growth of skepticism?

- What literary masterpieces of the English-speaking world did this period produce?

This chapter addresses these questions.

The Cantino Map (1502), named for the agent secretly commissioned to design it in Lisbon for the duke of Ferrara, an avid Italian map collector, reveals such a good knowledge of the African continent, of the islands of the West Indies, and of the shoreline of present-day Venezuela, Guiana, and Brazil in South America that modern scholars suspect there may have been clandestine voyages to the Americas shortly after Columbus's. (*Source: Biblioteca Estense Universitaria, Modena*)

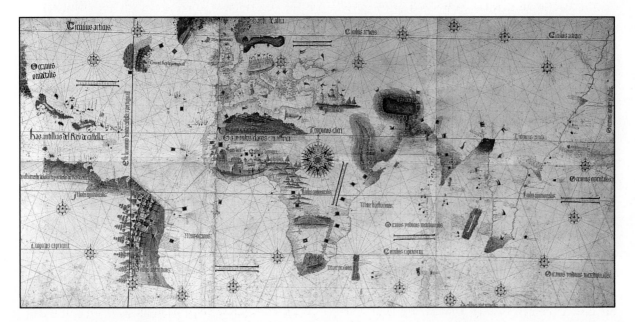

DISCOVERY, RECONNAISSANCE, AND EXPANSION

Historians have called the period from 1450 to 1650 the "Age of Discovery," the "Age of Reconnaissance," and the "Age of Expansion." All three labels are appropriate. "Age of Discovery" refers to the era's phenomenal advances in geographical knowledge and technology, often achieved through trial and error. In 1350 it still took as long to sail from the eastern end of the Mediterranean to the western end as it had taken a thousand years earlier. Even in the fifteenth century, Europeans knew little more about the earth's surface than the Romans had known. By 1650, however, Europeans had made an extensive reconnaissance—or preliminary exploration—and had sketched fairly accurately the physical outline of the whole earth. Much of the geographical information they had gathered was tentative and not fully understood—hence the appropriateness of the label "Age of Reconnaissance."

"Age of Expansion" refers to the migration of Europeans to other parts of the world. This colonization resulted in political control of much of South and North America; of coastal regions of Africa, India, China, and Japan; and of many Pacific islands. Political hegemony was accompanied by economic exploitation, religious domination, and the introduction of European patterns of social and intellectual life. The sixteenth-century expansion of European society launched a new age in world history.

Overseas Exploration and Conquest

The outward expansion of Europe began with the Vikings' voyages across the Atlantic in the ninth and tenth centuries. Vikings led by Eric the Red and Leif Ericson discovered Greenland and the eastern coast of North America. The Crusades of the eleventh through thirteenth centuries were another phase in Europe's attempt to explore, Christianize, and exploit peoples on the periphery of the Continent. But these early thrusts outward resulted in no permanent settlements. The Vikings made only quick raids in search of booty. Lacking stable political institutions in Scandinavia, they had no workable forms of government to impose on distant continents. In the twelfth and thir-

teenth centuries, the lack of a strong territorial base, weak support from the West, and sheer misrule combined to make the medieval Crusader kingdoms short-lived. Even in the mid-fifteenth century, Europe seemed ill prepared for international ventures. By 1450 a grave new threat had appeared in the East—the Ottoman Turks.

Combining excellent military strategy with efficient administration of their conquered territories, the Turks had subdued most of Anatolia and begun to settle on the western side of the Bosporus. The Ottoman Turks under Sultan Muhammad II (r. 1451–1481) captured Constantinople in 1453, pressed into the Balkans. By the early sixteenth century, the eastern Mediterranean was under Turkish control. The Turkish menace badly frightened Europeans. In France in the fifteenth and sixteenth centuries, twice as many books were printed about the Turkish threat as about the American discoveries. The Turks imposed a military blockade on eastern Europe, thus forcing Europeans' attention westward. Yet the fifteenth and sixteenth centuries witnessed a fantastic continuation, on a global scale, of European expansion.

Portugal, situated on the extreme southwestern edge of the European continent, got the start on the rest of Europe. Its taking of Ceuta, an Arab city in northern Morocco, in 1415 marked the beginning of European exploration and control of overseas territory. The objectives of Portuguese policy included the Christianization of Muslims and the search for gold, for an overseas route to the spice markets of India, and for the mythical Christian ruler of Ethiopia, Prester John.

In the early phases of Portuguese exploration, Prince Henry (1394–1460), called "the Navigator" because of the annual expeditions he sent down the western coast of Africa, played the leading role. In the fifteenth century, most of the gold that reached Europe came from the Sudan in West Africa and from Ashanti blacks living near the area of present-day Ghana. Muslim caravans brought the gold from the African cities of Niani and Timbuktu and carried it north across the Sahara to Mediterranean ports. Then the Portuguese muscled in on this commerce in gold. Prince Henry's carefully planned expeditions succeeded in reaching Guinea, and, under King John II (r. 1481–1495), the Portuguese established trading posts and forts on the Guinea coast and penetrated into the continent all the way to Timbuktu (Map 18.1). Portuguese ships brought gold to Lisbon,

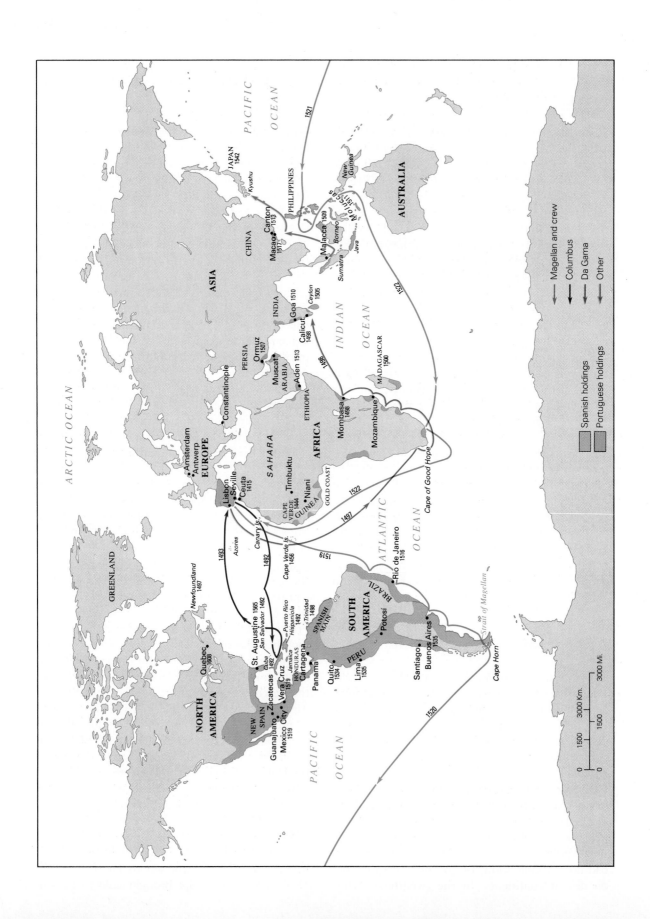

PACIFIC OCEAN

ARCTIC OCEAN

GREENLAND

Newfoundland 1497

NORTH AMERICA

Quebec 1608

NEW SPAIN

Guanajuato
Zacatecas
Mexico City 1519
Vera Cruz 1519

St. Augustine 1565
San Salvador 1492
Cuba 1492
Jamaica
HONDURAS 1519
Cartagena
Panama

Puerto Rico 1492
Hispaniola 1492
Trinidad 1498

SPANISH MAIN

Quito 1534
Lima 1535

PERU

SOUTH AMERICA

BRAZIL

Potosi

Santiago
Buenos Aires 1535

Rio de Janeiro 1516

Cape Horn

Strait of Magellan

ATLANTIC OCEAN

Azores

Canary Is.

Cape Verde Is. 1456

CAPE VERDE 1444
GUINEA
GOLD COAST
Niani
Timbuktu

SAHARA

AFRICA

Ceuta 1415
Lisbon
Seville

EUROPE
Amsterdam
Antwerp

Constantinople

PERSIA
Ormuz 1507

ARABIA
Muscat
Aden 1513

ETHIOPIA

Mombasa 1498

Mozambique

MADAGASCAR 1500

Cape of Good Hope

INDIAN OCEAN

ASIA

INDIA
Goa 1510
Calicut 1498
Ceylon 1505

CHINA
Macao 1517
Canton 1513

JAPAN 1542
Kyushu

PHILIPPINES

Moluccas 1511

Borneo
Java
Sumatra

New Guinea

AUSTRALIA

PACIFIC OCEAN

1521
1522
1519
1520
1497
1498
1492
1493

Magellan and crew
Columbus
Da Gama
Other

Spanish holdings
Portuguese holdings

3000 Mi.
3000 Km.
1500
0

the Portugese capital, and by 1500 Portugal controlled the flow of gold to Europe. The golden century of Portuguese prosperity had begun.

Still the Portuguese pushed farther south down the west coast of Africa. In 1487 Bartholomew Diaz rounded the Cape of Good Hope at the southern tip, but storms and a threatened mutiny forced him to turn back. On a second expedition (1497–1499), the Portuguese mariner Vasco da Gama reached India and returned to Lisbon loaded with samples of Indian wares. King Manuel (r. 1495–1521) promptly dispatched thirteen ships under the command of Pedro Alvares Cabral, assisted by Diaz, to set up trading posts in India. On April 22, 1500, the coast of Brazil in South America was sighted and claimed for the crown of Portugal. Cabral then proceeded south and east around the Cape of Good Hope and reached India. Half of the fleet was lost on the return voyage, but the six spice-laden vessels that dropped anchor in Lisbon harbor in July 1501 more than paid for the entire expedition. Thereafter, convoys were sent out every March. Lisbon became the entrance port for Asian goods into Europe—but not without a fight.

For centuries the Muslims had controlled the rich spice trade of the Indian Ocean, and they did not surrender it willingly. Portuguese commercial activities were accompanied by the destruction or seizure of strategic Muslim coastal forts, which later served Portugal as both trading posts and military bases. Alfonso de Albuquerque, whom the Portuguese crown appointed as governor of India (r. 1509–1515), decided that these bases and not inland territories should control the Indian Ocean. Accordingly, his cannon blasted open the ports of Calicut, Ormuz, Goa, and Malacca, the vital centers of Arab domination of South Asian trade (see Map 18.1). This bombardment laid the foundation for Portuguese imperialism in the sixteenth and seventeenth centuries—a strange way to bring Christianity to "those who were in darkness." As one scholar wrote about the opening of

MAP 18.1 Overseas Exploration and Conquest in the Fifteenth and Sixteenth Centuries The voyages of discovery marked another phase in the centuries-old migrations of European peoples. Consider the major contemporary significance of each of the three voyages depicted on the map.

China to the West, "while Buddha came to China on white elephants, Christ was borne on cannon balls."[1]

Political centralization in Spain helps to explain that country's outward push. In the fifteenth century, Isabella and Ferdinand had consolidated their several kingdoms to achieve a more united Spain. The Catholic rulers reduced the powers of the nobility, revamped the Spanish bureaucracy, and humbled dissident elements, notably the Muslims and the Jews. The Spanish monarchy was stronger than ever before and in a position to support foreign ventures; it could bear the costs and dangers of exploration.

In March 1493, Spanish ships entered Lisbon harbor bearing a triumphant Italian explorer in the service of the Spanish monarchy. Christopher Columbus (1451–1506), a Genoese mariner, had secured Spanish support for an expedition to the East. He sailed from Palos, Spain, to the Canary Islands and crossed the Atlantic to the Bahamas, landing in October 1492 on an island that he named "San Salvador" and believed to be off the coast of India. Like most people of his day, Columbus was deeply religious. The crew of his flagship, *Santa Maria,* recited vespers every night and sang a hymn to the Virgin before going to bed. Nevertheless, the Spanish fleet, sailing westward to find the East, sought wealth as well as souls to convert.

Between 1492 and 1502, Columbus made four voyages to America, discovering all the major islands of the Caribbean—Haiti (which he called "Dominica" and the Spanish named "Hispaniola"), San Salvador, Puerto Rico, Jamaica, Cuba, Trinidad—and Honduras in Central America. Columbus believed until he died that the islands he found were off the coast of India. In fact, he had opened up for the rulers of Spain a whole new world. The Caribbean islands—the West Indies—represented to Spanish missionary zeal millions of Indian natives for conversion to Christianity. Hispaniola, Puerto Rico, and Cuba also offered gold.

The search for precious metals determined the direction of Spanish exploration and expansion into South America. When it became apparent that placer mining (in which ore is separated from soil by panning) in the Caribbean islands was slow and the rewards slim, new routes to the East and new sources of gold and silver were sought.

In 1519 Charles V of Spain commissioned Ferdinand Magellan (1480–1521) to find a direct route to the Moluccan Islands off the southeast coast of Asia. Magellan sailed southwest across the Atlantic to Brazil and then south around Cape Horn into the Pacific Ocean (see Map 18.1). He crossed the Pacific, sailing west, to the Malay Archipelago, which he called the "Western Isles." (These islands were conquered in the 1560s and named the "Philippines" for Philip II of Spain.)

Though Magellan was killed, the expedition continued, returning to Spain in 1522 from the east by way of the Indian Ocean, the Cape of Good Hope, and the Atlantic. Terrible storms, mutiny, starvation, and disease haunted this voyage. Nevertheless, it verified Columbus's theory that the earth was round and brought information about the vastness of the Pacific. Magellan also proved that the earth was much larger than Columbus and others had believed.

In the West Indies, the slow recovery of gold, the shortage of a healthy labor force, and sheer restlessness speeded up Spain's search for wealth. In 1519, the year Magellan departed on his world-wide expedition, a brash and very determined Spanish adventurer, Hernando Cortés (1485–1547), crossed from Hispaniola to mainland Mexico with six hundred men, seventeen horses, and ten cannon. Within three years, Cortés conquered the fabulously rich Aztec Empire, took captive the Aztec emperor Montezuma, and founded Mexico City as the capital of New Spain. The subjugation of northern Mexico took longer, but between 1531 and 1550 the Spanish gained control of Zacatecas and Guanajuato, where rich silver veins were soon tapped.

Francisco Pizarro (1470–1541), another Spanish *conquistador* (explorer), repeated Cortés's feat in Peru. Between 1531 and 1536, with even fewer resources, Pizarro crushed the Inca Empire in northern South America and established the Spanish viceroyalty of Peru with its center at Lima. In 1545 Pizarro opened at Potosí in the Peruvian highlands what became the richest silver mines in the New World.

Between 1525 and 1575, the riches of the Americas poured into Lisbon and the Spanish port of Seville. For all their new wealth, however, Lisbon and Seville did not become important trading centers. It was the Flemish city of Antwerp, controlled by the Spanish Habsburgs, that developed into the great entrepôt for overseas bullion and Portuguese spices and served as the commercial and financial capital of the entire European world.

Since the time of the great medieval fairs, cities of the Low Countries had been important sites for the exchange of products from the Baltic and Italy. Antwerp, ideally situated on the Scheldt River at the intersection of many trading routes (see Map 18.3), steadily expanded as the chief intermediary for international commerce and finance. English woolens; Baltic wheat, fur, and timber; Portuguese spices; German iron and copper; Spanish fruit; French wines and dyestuffs; Italian silks, marble, and mirrors, together with vast amounts of cash—all were exchanged at Antwerp. The city's harbor could dock 2,500 vessels at once, and 5,000 merchants from many nations gathered daily in the *bourse* (exchange).

By the end of the sixteenth century, Amsterdam had overtaken Antwerp as the financial capital of Europe (see page 652). The Dutch had also embarked on foreign exploration and conquest. The Dutch East India Company, founded in 1602, became the major organ of Dutch imperialism and within a few decades expelled the Portuguese from Ceylon and other East Indian islands. By 1650 the Dutch West India Company had successfully intruded on the Spanish possessions in America and gained control of much of the African and American trade.

English and French explorations lacked the immediate, sensational results of the Spanish and Portuguese. In 1497 John Cabot, a Genoese merchant living in London, sailed for Brazil but discovered Newfoundland. The next year he returned and explored the New England coast and perhaps as far south as present-day Delaware. Since these expeditions found no spices or gold, the English king Henry VII lost interest in exploration. Between 1534 and 1541, the Frenchman Jacques Cartier made several voyages and explored the Saint Lawrence region of Canada, but the first permanent French settlement, at Quebec, was not founded until 1608.

The Explorers' Motives

The expansion of Europe was not motivated by demographic pressures. The Black Death had caused serious population losses from which Europe had not recovered in 1500. Few Europeans immigrated to North or South America in the sixteenth century. Half of those who did sail to begin a new life in the Americas died en route; half of

Market of Cartagena   Founded in 1533 as a port on the Caribbean Sea, Cartagena (modern Colombia) became the storage depot for precious metals waiting shipment to Spain. In this fanciful woodcut, male Indians, wearing tunics composed of overlapping feathers, and nude females sell golden necklaces, fish, fruit, and grain. (*Source: Rare Book Division, New York Public Library; Astor, Lenox and Tilden Foundations*)

those who reached the New World eventually returned to their homeland. Why, then, did explorers brave the Atlantic and Pacific oceans, risking their lives to discover new continents and spread European culture?

The reasons are varied and complex. People of the sixteenth century were still basically medieval in the sense that their attitudes and values were shaped by religion and expressed in religious terms. In the late fifteenth century, crusading fervor remained a basic part of the Portuguese and Spanish national ideal. The desire to Christianize Muslims and pagan peoples played a central role in European expansion, as evidenced by Columbus's explanation of his first voyage:

And Your Highnesses, as Catholic Christians and Princes devoted to the Holy Christian Faith and the propagators thereof, and enemies of the sect of Mahomet and of all idolatries and heresies, resolved to send me . . . to the said regions of India, to see the said princes and peoples and lands and to observe the disposition of them and of all, and the manner in which may be undertaken their conversion to our Holy Faith, and ordained that I should not go by land (the usual way) to the Orient, but by the route of the Occident, by which no one to this day knows for sure that anyone has gone.[2]

Queen Isabella of Spain showed a fanatical zeal for converting the Muslims to Christianity, but she concentrated her efforts on the Arabs in Granada in southern Spain. After the abortive crusading attempts of the thirteenth century, Isabella and other rulers realized that they lacked the material resources to mount the full-scale assault on Islam necessary for victory. Crusading impulses thus shifted from the Muslims to the pagan peoples of India, Africa, and the Americas.

Moreover, after the reconquista, enterprising young men of the Spanish upper classes found economic and political opportunities severely limited.

As a recent study of the Castilian city of Ciudad Real shows, the ancient aristocracy controlled the best agricultural land and monopolized urban administrative posts. Great merchants and a few nobles (surprisingly, since Spanish law forbade noble participation in commercial ventures) dominated the textile and leather glove manufacturing industries. Consequently, many ambitious men immigrated to the Americas to seek their fortunes.[3]

Government sponsorship and encouragement of exploration also help to account for the results of the various voyages. Mariners and explorers as private individuals, could not afford the massive sums needed to explore mysterious oceans and to control remote continents. The strong financial support of Prince Henry the Navigator led to Portugal's phenomenal success in the spice trade. Even the grudging and modest assistance of Isabella and Ferdinand eventually brought untold riches—and complicated problems—to Spain. The Dutch in the seventeenth century, through the Dutch East India Company and other government-sponsored trading companies, reaped enormous wealth. Although the Netherlands was a small country in size, it dominated the European economy in 1650. In England, by contrast, Henry VII's lack of interest in exploration delayed English expansion for a century.

Scholars have frequently described the European discoveries as a manifestation of Renaissance curiosity about the physical universe, the desire to know more about the geography and peoples of the world. There is truth to this explanation. Cosmography, natural history, and geography aroused enormous interest among educated people in the fifteenth and sixteenth centuries. Just as science fiction and speculation about life on other planets excite readers today, quasi-scientific literature about Africa, Asia, and the Americas captured the imaginations of literate Europeans. Spanish chronicler Oviedo's *General History of the Indies* (1547), a detailed eyewitness account of plants, animals, and peoples, was widely read.

Spices were another important incentive to voyages of discovery. Introduced into western Europe by the Crusaders in the twelfth century, nutmeg, mace, ginger, cinnamon, and pepper added flavor and variety to the monotonous diet of Europeans. Spices were also used in the preparation of medicinal drugs and incense for religious ceremonies. In the late thirteenth century, the Venetian Marco Polo (ca 1254–1324) had visited the court of the Chinese emperor. The widely publicized account of his travels in the *Book of Various Experiences* stimulated a rich trade in spices between Asia and Italy. The Venetians came to hold a monopoly on the spice trade in western Europe.

Spices were grown in India and China, shipped across the Indian Ocean to ports on the Persian Gulf, and then transported by Arabs across the Arabian Desert to Mediterranean ports. But the rise of the Ming Dynasty in China in the late fourteenth century resulted in the expulsion of foreigners. And the steady penetration of the Ottoman Turks into the eastern Mediterranean and of hostile Muslims across North Africa forced Europeans to seek a new route to the Asian spice markets.

The basic reason for European exploration and expansion, however, was the quest for material profit. Mariners and explorers frankly admitted this. As Bartholomew Diaz put it, his motives were "to serve God and His Majesty, to give light to those who were in darkness and to grow rich as all men desire to do." When Vasco da Gama reached the port of Calicut, India, in 1498, a native asked what the Portuguese wanted. Da Gama replied, "Christians and spices."[4] The bluntest of the Spanish conquistadors, Hernando Cortés, announced as he prepared to conquer Mexico, "I have come to win gold, not to plow the fields like a peasant."[5]

Portuguese and Spanish explorers carried the fervent Catholicism and missionary zeal of the Iberian Peninsula to the New World, and once in America they urged home governments to send clerics. At bottom, however, wealth was the driving motivation. A sixteenth-century diplomat, Ogier Gheselin de Busbecq, summed up this paradoxical attitude well: in expeditions to the Indies and the Antipodes, he said, "religion supplies the pretext and gold the motive."[6] The mariners and explorers were religious and "medieval" in justifying their actions while remaining materialistic and "modern" in their behavior.

Technological Stimuli to Exploration

Technological developments were the key to Europe's remarkable outreach. By 1350 cannon had been fully developed in western Europe. These pieces of artillery emitted frightening noises and great flashes of fire and could batter down fortresses and even city walls. Sultan Muhammad II's siege of Constantinople in 1453 provides a classic illustration of the effectiveness of cannon fire.

Constantinople had very strong walled fortifications. The sultan secured the services of a Western technician who built fifty-six small cannon and a gigantic gun that could hurl stone balls weighing about eight hundred pounds. The gun could be moved only by several hundred oxen and loaded and fired only by about a hundred men working together. Reloading took two hours. This awkward but powerful weapon breached the walls of Constantinople before it cracked on the second day of the bombardment. Lesser cannon finished the job.

Early cannon posed serious technical difficulties. Iron cannon were cheaper than bronze to construct, but they were difficult to cast effectively and were liable to crack and injure the artillerymen. Bronze guns, made of copper and tin, were less subject than iron to corrosion, but they were very expensive. All cannon were extraordinarily difficult to move, required considerable time for reloading, and were highly inaccurate. They thus proved inefficient for land warfare. However, they could be used at sea.

The mounting of cannon on ships and improved techniques of shipbuilding gave impetus to European expansion. Since ancient times, most seagoing vessels had been narrow, open galleys propelled by manpower. Slaves or convicts who had been sentenced to the galleys manned the oars of the ships that sailed the Mediterranean, and both cargo vessels and warships carried soldiers for defense. Though well suited to the placid and thoroughly explored waters of the Mediterranean, galleys could not withstand the rough winds and uncharted shoals of the Atlantic. The need for sturdier craft, as well as population losses caused by the Black Death, forced the development of a new style of ship that would not require soldiers for defense.

In the course of the fifteenth century, the Portuguese developed the *caravel,* a small, light, three-masted sailing ship. Though somewhat slower than the galley, the caravel held more cargo and was highly maneuverable. When fitted with cannon, it could dominate larger vessels, such as the round ships commonly used as merchantmen. The substitution of wind power for manpower, and artillery fire for soldiers, signaled a great technological advance and gave Europeans navigational and military ascendancy over the rest of the world.[7]

Other fifteenth-century developments in navigation helped make possible the conquest of the Atlantic. The magnetic compass, brought to Europe from China by the Muslims, enabled sailors to determine their direction and position at sea. The astrolabe, an instrument developed by Muslim navigators in the twelfth century and used to determine the altitude of the sun and other celestial bodies, permitted mariners to plot their *latitude* (position north or south of the equator). Steadily improved maps and sea charts provided information about distance, sea depths, and general geography.

The Conquest of Aztec Mexico and Inca Peru

Technological development also helps to explain the Spanish conquest of Aztec Mexico and Inca Peru. The strange end of the Aztec nation remains one of the most fascinating events in the annals of human societies. The Spanish adventurer Hernando Cortés landed at Vera Cruz in February 1519. In November he entered Tenochtitlán (Mexico City) and soon had the emperor Montezuma II in custody. In less than two years Cortés destroyed the monarchy, gained complete control of the Mexican capital, and extended his jurisdiction over much of the Aztec Empire. Why did a strong people defending its own territory succumb so quickly to a handful of Spaniards fighting in dangerous and completely unfamiliar circumstances? How indeed, since Montezuma's scouts sent him detailed reports of the Spaniards' movements? The answer lies in the Spaniards' boldness and timing and in the Aztecs' psychology, political structure, attitude toward war, and technology.

The Spaniards arrived in late summer, when the Aztecs were preoccupied with harvesting their crops and not thinking of war. From the Spaniards' perspective, their timing was ideal. A series of natural phenomena, signs, and portents seemed to augur disaster for the Aztecs. A comet was seen in daytime, a column of fire had appeared every midnight for a year, and two temples were suddenly destroyed, one by lightning unaccompanied by thunder. These and other apparently inexplicable events raised the specter of the return of Quetzalcoatl (see page 491) and had a pervasively unnerving effect on the Aztecs. They looked on the Europeans riding "wild beasts" as extraterrestrial forces coming to establish a new social order. Defeatism swept the nation and paralyzed its will.

The Aztecs had never developed an effective method of governing subject peoples. The empire was actually a group of subject communities lacking legal or government ties to what today is called the "state." The Aztecs controlled them through terror, requiring from each clan an annual tribute of humans to be sacrificed to the gods. Tributary peoples seethed with revolt. When the Spaniards appeared, the Totonacs greeted them as liberators, and other subject groups joined them in battle against the Aztecs.

Montezuma refrained from attacking the Spaniards as they advanced toward his capital and welcomed Cortés and his men into Tenochtitlán. Historians have often condemned the Aztec ruler for vacillation and weakness. Is this a fair assessment? Montezuma relied on the advice of his state council, itself divided, and on the dubious loyalty of tributary communities. When Cortés—with incredible boldness—took Montezuma hostage, the emperor's influence over his people crumbled.

But the major explanation for the collapse of the Aztec Empire to six hundred Spaniards lies in the Aztec's notion of warfare and level of technology. Forced to leave Tenochtitlán to settle a conflict elsewhere, Cortés placed his lieutenant, Alvarado, in charge. Alvarado's harsh rule drove the Aztecs to revolt, and they almost succeeded in destroying the Spanish garrison. When Cortés returned just in time, the Aztecs allowed his reinforcements to join Alvarado's besieged force. No threatened European or Asian state would have conceived of doing such a thing: dividing an enemy's army and destroying the separate parts was basic to European and Asian military tactics. But for the Aztecs warfare was a ceremonial act, in which "divide and conquer" had no place.

Having allowed the Spanish forces to reunite, the entire population of Tenochtitlán attacked the invaders. The Aztecs killed many Spaniards, who in retaliation executed Montezuma. The Spaniards escaped from the city and inflicted a crushing defeat on the Aztec army at Otumba near Lake Texcoco on July 7, 1520. The Spaniards won because "the simple Indian methods of mass warfare were of little avail against the manoeuvring of a well-drilled force."[8] Aztec weapons proved no match for the terrifyingly noisy and lethal Spanish cannon, muskets, crossbows, and steel swords. European technology decided the battle. Cortés began the systematic conquest of Mexico.

In 1527 the Inca ruled as a benevolent despot. His power was limited only by custom. His millions of subjects looked on him as a god, firm but just to his people, merciless to his enemies. ("Looked on" is figurative. Only a few of the Inca's closest relatives dared look at his divine face: nobles approached him on their knees, and the masses kissed the dirt as he rode by in his litter.) The borders of his vast empire were well fortified, threatened by no foreign invaders. No sedition or civil disobedience disturbed the domestic tranquillity. Grain was plentiful, and apart from an outbreak of smallpox in a distant province—introduced by the Spaniards—no natural disaster upset the general peace. An army of 50,000 loyal troops stood at the Inca's instant disposal. Why, then, did this powerful empire fall so easily to Francisco Pizarro and his band of 175 men armed with one small ineffective cannon? This question has troubled students for centuries. There can be no definitive answers, but several explanations have been offered.

First, the Incas were totally isolated. They had no contact with other Amerindian cultures and knew nothing at all of Aztec civilization or its collapse to the Spaniards in 1521. Since about the year 1500, Inca scouts had reported "floating houses" on the seas, manned by white men with beards. Tradesmen told of strange large animals with feet of silver (as horseshoes appeared in the brilliant sunshine). Having observed a border skirmish between Indians and white men, intelligence sources advised the Inca that the Europeans' swords were as harmless as women's weaving battens. A coastal chieftain had poured chicha, the native beer, down the barrel of a gun to appease the god of thunder. These incidents suggest that Inca culture provided no basis for understanding the Spaniards and the significance of their arrival. Moreover, if the strange pale men planned war, there were very few of them, and the Incas believed that they could not be reinforced from the sea.[9]

At first the Incas did not think that the strangers intended trouble. They believed the old Inca legend that the creator-god Virocha—who had brought civilization to them, become displeased, and sailed away promising to return someday—

had indeed returned. Belief in a legend prevented the Incas, like the Aztecs, from taking prompt action.

A political situation may also have lain at the root of their difficulty. The Incas apparently had no definite principle for the succession of the emperor. The reigning emperor, with the advice of his council, chose his successor—usually the most capable son of his chief wife. In 1527, however, the Inca Huayna Capac died without naming his heir. The council chose Huascar, son of Huayna's chief wife, who was accordingly crowned at Cuzco with the imperial *borla,* the fringed headband symbolizing the imperial office. The people and the generals, however, supported Atahualpa, son of a secondary wife and clearly Huayna's favorite son. A bitter civil war ensued. Atahualpa emerged victorious, but the five-year struggle may have exhausted him and damaged his judgment.

Soon after Pizarro landed at Tumbes on May 13, 1532—the very day Atahualpa won the decisive battle against his brother—he learned of all these events. As Pizarro advanced across the steep Andes toward the capital at Cuzco, Atahualpa—simultaneously proceeding to the capital for his coronation—stopped at the provincial town of Cajamarca. He, like Montezuma, was kept fully informed of the Spaniards' movements. The Inca's strategy was to lure the Spaniards into a trap, seize their horses and ablest men for his army, and execute the rest. What had the Inca, surrounded by his thousands of troops, to fear? Atahualpa thus accepted Pizarro's invitation to come with his bodyguards "unarmed so as not to give offense" into the central plaza of Cajamarca. He rode right into the Spaniard's trap. Pizarro knew that if he could capture that Inca, from whom all power devolved, he would have the "Kingdom of Gold" for which he had come to the New World.

The Inca's litter arrived in the ominously quiet town square. One cannon blast terrified the Indians. The Spaniards rushed out from hiding and ruthlessly slaughtered the Indians. Atahualpa's headband was instantly torn from his head. He offered to purchase his freedom with a roomful of gold. Pizarro agreed to this ransom, and an appropriate document was drawn up and signed. After the gold had been gathered from all parts of the empire to fill the room—17 feet by 22 feet by 9 feet—the Spaniards trumped up charges against the Inca and strangled him. The Inca Empire lay at Pizarro's feet.

The South American Holocaust

In the sixteenth century, about 200,000 Spaniards immigrated to the New World. Soldiers demobilized from the Spanish and Italian campaigns, adventurers and drifters unable to find work in Spain, they did not intend to work in the New World either. After having assisted in the conquest of the Aztecs and the subjugation of the Incas, these drifters wanted to settle down and become a ruling class. In temperate grazing areas they carved out vast estates and imported Spanish sheep, cattle, and horses for the kinds of ranching with which they were familiar. In the coastal tropics, unsuited for grazing, the Spanish erected huge sugar plantations. Columbus had introduced sugar into the West Indies; Cortés, into Mexico. Sugar was a great luxury in Europe, and demand for it was high. Around 1550 the discovery of silver at Zacatecas and Guanajuato in Mexico and Potosí in present-day Bolivia stimulated silver rushes. How were the cattle ranches, sugar plantations, and silver mines to be worked? Obviously, by the Indians.

The Spanish quickly established the *encomiendas* system, whereby the Crown granted the conquerors the right to employ groups of Indians in a town or area as agricultural or mining laborers or as tribute-payers. Theoretically, the Spanish were forbidden to enslave the Indian natives; in actuality, the encomiendas were a legalized form of slavery. The European demand for sugar, tobacco, and silver prompted the colonists to exploit the Indians mercilessly. Unaccustomed to forced labor, especially in the blistering heat of tropical cane fields or the dark, dank, and dangerous mines, Indians died like flies. Recently scholars have tried to reckon the death rate of the Amerindians in the sixteenth century. Some historians maintain that when Columbus landed at Hispaniola in 1492, the island's population stood at 100,000; in 1570, 300 people survived. The Indian population of Peru is estimated to have fallen from 1.3 million in 1570 to 600,000 in 1620; central Mexico had 25.3 million Indians in 1519 and 1 million in 1605.[10] Some demographers dispute these figures, but all agree that the decline of the native Indian population in all of Spanish-occupied America amounted to a catastrophe greater in scale than any that has occurred even in the twentieth century.

What were the causes of this devastating slump in population? Students of the history of medicine have suggested the best explanation: disease. The major cause of widespread epidemics is migration, and those peoples isolated longest from other societies suffer most. Contact with disease builds up bodily resistance. At the beginning of the sixteenth century, American Indians probably had the unfortunate distinction of longer isolation from the rest of humankind than any other people on earth. Crowded concentrations of laborers in the mining camps bred infection, which was then carried by the miners back to their home villages. With little or no resistance to diseases brought from the Old World, the inhabitants of the highlands of Mexico and Peru, especially, fell victim to smallpox. According to one expert, smallpox caused "in all likelihood the most severe single loss of aboriginal population that ever occurred."[11]

Disease was the prime cause of the Indian holocaust, but the Spaniards contributed heavily to the Indians' death rate.[12] According to the Franciscan missionary Bartolomé de Las Casas (1474–1566), the Spanish maliciously murdered thousands:

This infinite multitude of people [the Indians] was . . . without fraud, without subtilty or malice . . . toward the Spaniards *whom they serve, patient, meek and peaceful. . . .*

To these quiet Lambs . . . came the Spaniards *like most c(r)uel Tygres, Wolves and Lions, enrag'd with a sharp and tedious hunger; for these forty years past, minding nothing else but the slaughter of these unfortunate wretches, whom with divers kinds of torments neither seen nor heard of before, they have so cruelly and inhumanely butchered, that of three millions of people which* Hispaniola *it self did contain, there are left remaining alive scarce three hundred persons. And for the Island of* Cuba *. . . it lies wholly desert, until'd and ruin'd. The Islands of St. John and Jamaica lie waste and desolate. The Lucayan Islands . . . are now totally unpeopled and destroyed; the inhabitants thereof amounting to above 5,000,000 souls, partly killed, and partly forced away to work in other places.*[13]

Las Casas's remarks concentrate on the tropical lowlands, but the death rate in the highlands was also staggering.

The Christian missionaries who accompanied the conquistadors and settlers—Franciscans, Dominicans, and Jesuits—played an important role in converting the Indians to Christianity, teaching them European methods of agriculture, and inculcating loyalty to the Spanish crown. In terms of numbers of people baptized, missionaries enjoyed phenomenal success, though the depth of the Indians' understanding of Christianity remains debatable. Missionaries, especially Las Casas, asserted that the Indians had human rights, and through Las Casas's persistent pressure the emperor Charles V abolished the worst abuses of the encomiendas system.

Some scholars offer a psychological explanation for the colossal death rate of the Indians: they simply lost the will to survive. Their gods appeared to have abandoned them to a world over which they had no control. Hopelessness, combined with abusive treatment and overwork, pushed many men to suicide, many women to abortion or infanticide. Whatever its precise causes, the astronomically high death rate created a severe labor shortage in Spanish America. As early as 1511, King Ferdinand of Spain observed that the Indians seemed to be "very frail" and that "one black could do the work of four Indians."[14] Thus was born an absurd myth and the massive importation of black slaves from Africa (see pages 595–598).

Colonial Administration

Having seized the great Indian ceremonial centers in Mexico and Peru, the Spanish conquistadors proceeded to subdue the main areas of native American civilization in the New World. Columbus, Cortés, and Pizarro claimed the lands they had "discovered" for the crown of Spain. How were these lands to be governed?

According to the Spanish theory of absolutism, the Crown was entitled to exercise full authority over all imperial lands. In the sixteenth century the Crown divided Spain's New World territories into four *viceroyalties*, or administrative divisions: New Spain, with its capital at Mexico City, consisted of Mexico, Central America, and present-day California, Arizona, New Mexico, and Texas. Peru, with its viceregal seat at Lima, originally consisted of all the lands in continental South America but later was reduced to the territory of modern Peru, Chile, Bolivia, and Ecuador. New Granada, with Bogotá as its administrative center, included present-day Venezuela, Colombia, Panama, and after 1739 Ecuador. La Plata, with Buenos Aires as its capital, consisted of Argentina, Uruguay, and Paraguay. Within each territory a *viceroy* or imperial governor, had broad military and civil authority as the Spanish sovereign's direct representative. The viceroy presided over the *audiencia,* twelve to fifteen judges who served as advisory council and as the highest judicial body.

From the early sixteenth century to the beginning of the nineteenth, the Spanish monarchy acted on the mercantilist principle that the colonies existed for the financial benefit of the mother country. The mining of gold and silver was always the most important industry in the colonies. The Crown claimed the *quinto,* one-fifth of all precious metals mined in the Americas. Gold and silver yielded the Spanish monarchy 25 percent of its total income. In return, Spain shipped manufactured goods to the New World and discouraged the development of native industries.

The Portuguese governed their colony of Brazil in a similar manner. After the union of the crowns of Portugal and Spain in 1580, Spanish administrative forms were introduced. Local officials called *corregidores* held judicial and military powers. Mercantilist policies placed severe restrictions on Brazilian industries that might compete with those of Portugal. In the seventeenth century the use of black slave labor made possible the cultivation of coffee, cotton, and sugar; and in the eighteenth century Brazil led the world in the production of sugar. The unique feature of colonial Brazil's culture and society was its thoroughgoing mixture of Indians, whites, and blacks.

The Economic Effects of Spain's Discoveries in the New World

The sixteenth century has often been called the "Golden Century" of Spain. The influence of Spanish armies, Spanish Catholicism, and Spanish wealth was felt all over Europe. This greatness rested largely on the influx of precious metals from the New World.

The mines at Zacatecas and Guanajuato in Mexico and Potosí in Peru poured out huge quantities of precious metals. To protect this treasure from French and English pirates, armed convoys transported it each year to Spain. Between 1503 and 1650, 16 million kilograms of silver and 185,000 kilograms of gold entered Seville's port. Spanish predominance, however, proved temporary.

In the sixteenth century, Spain experienced a steady population increase, creating a sharp rise in the demand for food and goods. Spanish colonies in the Americas also represented a demand for products. Since Spain had expelled some of the best farmers and businessmen, the Muslims and the conversos, in the fifteenth century, the Spanish economy was suffering and could not meet the new demands. Prices rose. Because the cost of manufacturing cloth and other goods increased, Spanish products could not compete in the international market with cheaper products made elsewhere. The textile industry was badly hurt. Prices spiraled upward, faster than the government could levy taxes to dampen the economy. (Higher taxes would have cut the public's buying power; with fewer goods sold, prices would have come down.)

Did the flood of American silver bullion cause the inflation? Prices rose most steeply before 1565, but bullion imports reached their peak between 1580 and 1620. Thus there is no direct correlation between silver imports and the inflation rate. Did the substantial population growth accelerate the inflation rate? Perhaps, since when the population pressure declined after 1600, prices gradually stabilized. One fact is certain: the price revolution severely strained government budgets. Several times between 1557 and 1647, Philip II and his successors repudiated the state debt, in turn undermining confidence in the government and leading the economy into shambles.

As Philip II paid his armies and foreign debts with silver bullion, the Spanish inflation was transmitted to the rest of Europe. Between 1560 and 1600, much of Europe experienced large price increases. Prices doubled and in some cases quadrupled. Spain suffered most severely, but all European countries were affected. People who lived on fixed incomes, such as the continental nobles, were badly hurt because their money bought less. Those who owed fixed sums of money, such as the middle class, prospered: in a time of rising prices, debts had less value each year. Food costs rose most sharply, and the poor fared worst of all.

Seaborne Trading Empires

By 1550, European overseas reconnaissance had led to the first global seaborne trade. For centuries the Muslims had conducted sophisticated commercial activities that spanned continents. Although they controlled the rich spice trade of the Indian Ocean, most Muslim expeditions had been

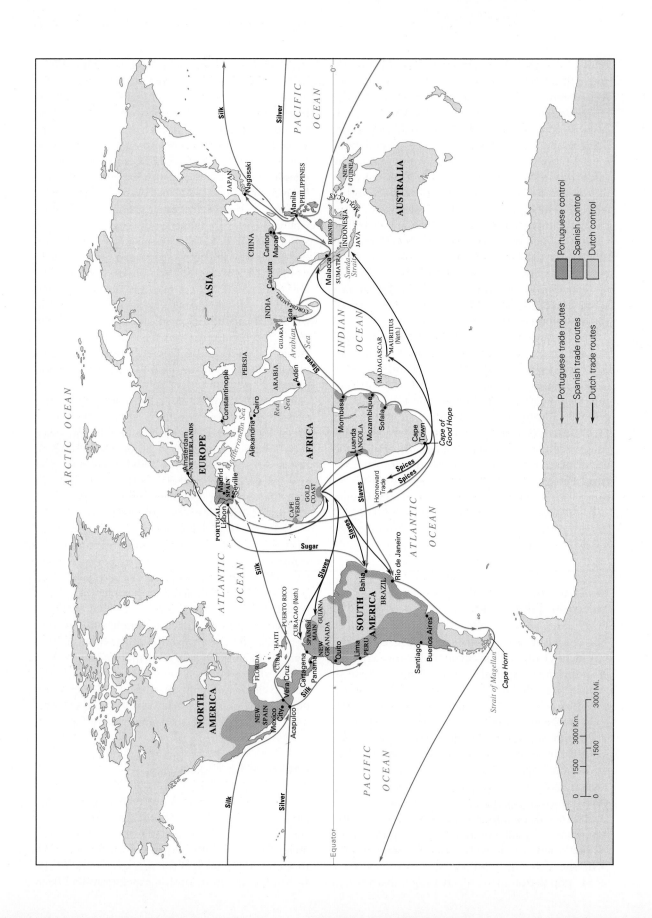

across Asian and African land routes. The Europeans' discovery of the Americas and their exploration of the Pacific for the first time linked the entire world by intercontinental seaborne trade. That trade brought into being three successive commercial empires: the Portuguese, the Spanish, and the Dutch.

In the sixteenth century, naval power and ship-borne artillery gave the Portuguese hegemony over the sea route to India. Their fleet brought spices to Lisbon, which the Portuguese paid for with textiles produced at Gujarat and Coromandel in India and with gold and ivory from East Africa. From their fortified bases at Goa on the Arabian Sea and at Malacca in the Malay Peninsula, ships of Malabar teak carried goods to the Portuguese settlement at Macao on the South China Sea. From Macao, loaded with Chinese silks and porcelains, Portuguese ships sailed to the Japanese port of Nagasaki and to the Philippine port of Manila, where Chinese goods were exchanged for Spanish (that is, Latin American) silver. Throughout Asia, the Portuguese traded in slaves—blacks from Africa, Chinese, and Japanese. The Portuguese imported to India horses from Mesopotamia and copper from Arabia; they exported from India hawks and peacocks for the Chinese and Japanese markets. Across the Atlantic, Portuguese Brazil provided most of the sugar consumed in Europe in the sixteenth and early seventeenth centuries. African slave labor produced the sugar on the plantations of Brazil, and Portuguese merchants, many of them Jewish, controlled both the slave trade between West Africa and Brazil (see pages 734–740) and the commerce in sugar between Brazil and Portugal. The Portuguese were the first worldwide traders, and Portuguese was the language of the Asian maritime trade (Map 18.2).

Spanish possessions in the New World constituted basically a land empire and, as already described, in the sixteenth century the Spaniards devised a method of governing that empire. But across the Pacific the Spaniards also built a sea-

MAP 18.2 Seaborne Trading Empires in the Sixteenth and Seventeenth Centuries   In the sixteenth century, for the first time the entire globe was linked by seaborne trade. In the seventeenth century American silver paid for Asian silks and spices; African slaves in Latin America produced sugar for the tables of Europe.

borne empire, centered at Manila in the Philippines, which had been discovered by Magellan in 1563. Between 1564 and 1571, the Spanish navigator Miguel Lopez de Legazpi sailed from Mexico and through a swift and almost bloodless conquest took over the Philippine Islands. Legazpi founded Manila, which served as the trans-Pacific bridge between Spanish America and the extreme Eastern trade. Chinese silk, sold by the Portuguese in Manila for American silver, was transported to Acapulco in Mexico, from which it was carried overland to Vera Cruz for re-export to Spain. Because hostile Pacific winds prohibited direct passage from the Philippines to Peru, large shipments also went south from Acapulco to Peru (see Map 18.2). Spanish merchants could never satisfy the European demand for silk, which meant that huge amounts of bullion went from Acapulco to Manila. For example, in 1597, 12 million pesos of silver, almost the total value of the transatlantic trade, crossed the Pacific. After about 1640, the Spanish silk trade declined because it could not compete with Dutch imports.

In the latter half of the seventeenth century, the worldwide Dutch seaborne trade predominated. The Dutch Empire was built on spices. In 1599 a Dutch fleet returned to Amsterdam carrying 600,000 pounds of pepper and 250,000 pounds of cloves and nutmeg. Those who had invested in the expedition received a 100 percent profit. The voyage led to the establishment in 1602 of the Dutch East India Company, founded with the stated intention of capturing the spice trade from the Portuguese. The Dutch fleet, sailing from the Cape of Good Hope and avoiding the Portuguese forts in India, steered directly for the Sunda Strait in Indonesia. The Dutch wanted direct access to and control of the Indonesian sources of spices. In return for assisting Indonesian princes in local squabbles and disputes with the Portuguese, the Dutch won broad commercial concessions. Through agreements, seizures, and outright war, they gained control of the western access to the Indonesian archipelago. Gradually, they acquired political domination over the archipelago itself. Exchanging European manufactured goods—armor, firearms, linens, and toys—the Dutch soon had a monopoly on the very lucrative spice trade.[15]

The seaborne empires profited from the geographical reconnaissance and technological developments of the sixteenth century. The empires of

Portugal, Spain, and Holland had strong commercial ambitions. They also paved the way for the eighteenth-century mercantilist empires of France and Great Britain (see page 832).

The Chinese and Japanese Discovery of the West

The desire to Christianize pagan peoples was a major motive in Europeans' overseas expansion. The Indians of Central and South America, the Muslims and polytheistic peoples of the Pacific, and the Confucian, Buddhist, and Shinto peoples of China and Japan became objects of Christianizing efforts. In this missionary activity the new Jesuit Order was dominant and energetic.

In 1582 the Jesuit Matteo Ricci (1552–1610) settled at Macao on the mouth of the Canton River. Like the Christian monks who had converted the Germanic tribes of early medieval Europe (see page 236), Ricci sought first to convert the emperor and elite groups and then, through gradual assimilation, to win the throngs of Chinese. Ricci tried to present Christianity to the Chinese in Chinese terms. He understood the Chinese respect for learning and worked to win converts among the scholarly class. When Ricci was admitted to the Imperial City at Peking, he addressed the emperor Wan-li:

Li Ma-tou [Ricci's name transliterated into Chinese], your Majesty's servant, comes from the Far West, addresses himself to Your Majesty with respect, in order to offer gifts from his country. Your Majesty's servant comes from a far distant land which has never exchanged presents with the Middle Kingdom [the Chinese name for China, based on the belief that the Chinese empire occupied the middle of the earth and was surrounded by barbarians]. Despite the distance, fame told me of the remarkable teaching and fine institutions with which the imperial court has endowed all its peoples. I desired to share these advantages and live out my life as one of Your Majesty's subjects, hoping in return to be of some small use.[16]

Ricci presented the emperor with two clocks, one of them decorated with dragons and eagles in the Chinese style. The emperor's growing fascination with clocks gave Ricci the opportunity to display other examples of Western technology. He instructed court scholars about astronomical equipment and the manufacture of cannons and drew for them a map of the world—with China at its center. These inventions greatly impressed the Chinese intelligentsia. Over a century later a Jesuit wrote, "The Imperial Palace is stuffed with clocks . . . watches, carillons, repeaters, organs, spheres, and astronomical clocks of all kinds—there are more than four thousand pieces from the best masters of Paris and London."[17] The Chinese first learned about Europe from the Jesuits.

But the Christians and the Chinese did not understand one another. Because the Jesuits served the imperial court as mathematicians, astronomers, and cartographers, the Chinese emperors allowed them to remain in Peking. For the Jesuits, however, their service was only a means for converting the Chinese to Christianity. The missionaries thought that by showing the pre-eminence of Western science, they were demonstrating the superiority of Western religion. This was a relationship that the Chinese did not acknowledge. They could not accept a religion that required total commitment and taught the existence of an absolute. Only a small number of the highly educated, convinced of a link between ancient Chinese tradition and Christianity, became Christians. Most Chinese were hostile to the Western faith. They accused Christians of corrupting Chinese morals because they forbade people to honor their ancestors—and corruption of morals translated into disturbing the public order—of destroying Chinese sanctuaries, of revering a man (Christ) who had been executed as a public criminal, and of spying on behalf of the Japanese.

The "Rites Controversy," a dispute over ritual between the Jesuits and other Roman Catholic religious orders, sparked a crisis. The Jesuits supported the celebration of the Mass in Chinese and the performance of other ceremonies in terms understandable by the Chinese. The Franciscans and other missionaries felt that the Jesuits had sold out the essentials of the Christian faith in order to win converts. One burning issue was whether Chinese reverence for ancestors was homage to the good that the dead had done during their lives or an act of worship. The Franciscans secured the support of Roman authorities who considered themselves authorities on Chinese culture and decided against the Jesuits. In 1704 and again in 1742 Rome decreed that Roman ceremonial practice (that is, in Latin) was to be the law for Chinese missions. (This decision continued to govern Roman Catholic missionary activity until the Second Vatican Council in 1962.) Papal letters also forbade Chinese Christians from participating in the rites of ancestor worship. The emperor in turn banned Christianity in China, and the missionaries were forced to flee.

The Christian West and the Chinese world learned a great deal from each other. The Jesuits probably were "responsible for the rebirth of Chinese mathematics in the seventeenth and eighteenth centuries," and Western contributions stimulated the Chinese development of other sciences.[18] From the Chinese, Europeans got the idea of building bridges suspended by chains. The first Western experiments in electrostatics and magnetism in the seventeenth century derived from Chinese models. Travel accounts about Chinese society and customs had a profound impact on Europeans, making them more sensitive to the beautiful diversity of peoples and manners, as the essays of Montaigne (see pages 598–599) and other Western thinkers reveal.

Initial Japanese contacts with Europeans paralleled those of the Chinese. In 1542, Portuguese merchants arrived in Japan and quickly won large profits carrying goods between China and Japan. Dutch and English ships followed, also enjoying the rewards of the East Asian trade. The Portuguese merchants vigorously supported Christian missionary activity, and in 1547 the Jesuit missionary Saint Francis Xavier landed at Kagoshima, preached widely, and in two short years won many converts. From the beginning, however, the Japanese government feared that native converts might have conflicting political loyalties. Divided allegiance could encourage European invasion of the islands—the Japanese authorities had the example of the Philippines, where Spanish conquest followed missionary activity.

Convinced that European merchants and missionaries had contributed to the general civil disorder, which the regime was trying to eradicate, the Japanese government decided to expel the Spanish and Portuguese, to destroy every trace of Christianity, and to close Japan to all foreign influence. A decree of 1635 was directed at the commissioners of the port of Nagasaki, a center of Japanese Christianity:

If there is any place where the teachings of the padres (Catholic priests) is practiced, the two of you must order a thorough investigation. . . .

If there are any Southern Barbarians (Westerners) who propagate the teachings of the padres, or otherwise commit crimes, they may be incarcerated in the prison. . . .[19]

In 1639, an imperial memorandum decreed: "hereafter entry by the Portuguese galeota (galleon or large ocean going warship) is forbidden. If they insist on coming (to Japan), the ships must be destroyed and anyone aboard those ships must be beheaded. . . ."[20]

When tens of thousands of Japanese Christians made a stand on the peninsula of Shimabara, the Dutch lent the Japanese government cannon. As Protestants, the Dutch hated Catholicism, and as businessmen they hated Portuguese, their great commercial rivals. Thus convinced that the Dutch had come only for trade and did not want to proselytize, the imperial government allowed the Dutch to remain. But Japanese authorities ordered them to remove their factory-station from Hirado on the western tip of Kyushu to the tiny island of Deshima, which covered just 2,100 square feet. The government limited Dutch trade to one ship a year, watched the Dutch very closely, and required Dutch officials to pay an annual visit to the capital to renew their loyalty. The Japanese also compelled the Dutch merchants to perform servile acts that other Europeans considered humiliating.

Long after Christianity ceased to be a potential threat to the Japanese government, the fear of Christianity sustained a policy of banning all Western books on science or religion. Until well into the eighteenth century, Japanese intellectuals were effectively cut off from Western developments. The Japanese view of Westerners was not high. What little the Japanese knew derived from the few Dutch businessmen at Deshima. Very few Japanese people ever saw Europeans. If they did, they considered them "a special variety of goblin that bore only a superficial resemblance to a normal human being." The widespread rumor was that when Dutchmen urinated they raised one leg like dogs.[21]

POLITICS, RELIGION, AND WAR

In 1559 France and Spain signed the Treaty of Cateau-Cambrésis, which ended the Habsburg-Valois Wars. This event marks a watershed in early modern European history. Spain was the victor. France, exhausted by the struggle, had to acknowledge Spanish dominance in Italy, where much of the war had been fought. Spanish governors ruled in Sicily, Naples, and Milan, and Spanish influence was strong in the Papal States and Tuscany.

Emperor Charles V had divided his attention between the Holy Roman Empire and Spain. Under his son Philip II (r. 1556–1598), however, the center of the Habsburg Empire and the political center of gravity for all of Europe shifted westward to Spain. Before 1559, Spain and France had fought bitterly for control of Italy; after 1559, the two Catholic powers aimed their guns at Protestantism. The Treaty of Cateau-Cambrésis ended an era of strictly dynastic wars and initiated a period of conflicts in which politics and religion played the dominant roles.

Because a variety of issues were stewing, it is not easy to generalize about the wars of the late sixteenth century. Some were continuations of struggles between the centralizing goals of monarchies and the feudal reactions of nobilities. Some were crusading battles between Catholics and Protestants. Some were struggles for national independence or for international expansion.

These wars differed considerably from earlier wars. Sixteenth- and seventeenth-century armies were bigger than medieval ones; some forces numbered as many as fifty thousand men. Because large armies were expensive, governments had to reorganize their administrations to finance them. The use of gunpowder altered both the nature of war and popular attitudes toward it. Guns and cannon killed and wounded from a distance, indiscriminately. Gunpowder weakened the notion, common during the Hundred Years' War, that warfare was an ennobling experience. Governments had to utilize propaganda, pulpits, and the printing press to arouse public opinion to support war.[22]

Late-sixteenth-century conflicts fundamentally tested the medieval ideal of a unified Christian society governed by one political ruler, the emperor, to whom all rulers were theoretically subordinate, and one church, to which all people belonged. The Protestant Reformation had killed this ideal, but few people recognized it as dead. Catholics continued to believe that Calvinists and Lutherans could be reconverted. Protestants persisted in thinking that the Roman church should be destroyed. Most people believed that a state could survive only if its members shared the same faith. Catholics and Protestants alike feared people of the other faith living in their midst. The settlement finally achieved in 1648, known as the "Peace of Westphalia," signaled acknowledgment of the end of the medieval ideal.

The Origins of Difficulties in France (1515–1559)

In the first half of the sixteenth century, France continued the recovery begun under Louis XI (see page 529). The population losses caused by the plague and the disorders accompanying the Hundred Years' War had created such a labor shortage that serfdom virtually disappeared. Cash rents replaced feudal rents and servile obligations. This development clearly benefited the peasantry. Meanwhile, the declining buying power of money hurt the nobility. The steadily increasing French population brought new lands under cultivation, but the division of property among sons meant that most peasant holdings were very small. Domestic and foreign trade picked up; mercantile centers such as Rouen and Lyon expanded; and in 1517 a new port city was founded at Le Havre.

The charming and cultivated Francis I (r. 1515–1547) and his athletic, emotional son Henry II (r. 1547–1559) governed through a small, efficient council. Great nobles held titular authority in the provinces as governors, but Paris-appointed baillis and seneschals continued to exercise actual fiscal and judicial responsibility (see page 407). In 1539 Francis issued an ordinance that placed the whole of France under the jurisdiction of the royal law courts and made French the language of those courts. This act had a powerful centralizing impact. The taille land tax provided what strength the monarchy had and supported a strong standing army. Unfortunately, the tax base was too narrow for France's extravagant promotion of the arts and ambitious foreign policy.

Deliberately imitating the Italian Renaissance princes, the Valois monarchs lavished money on a magnificent court, a vast building program, and Italian artists. Francis I commissioned the Paris architect Pierre Lescot to rebuild the palace of the Louvre. Francis secured the services of Michelangelo's star pupil, Il Rosso, who decorated the wing of the Fontainebleau chateau, subsequently called

Rossi and Primaticcio: The Gallery of Francis I Flat paintings alternating with rich sculpture provide a rhythm that directs the eye down the long gallery at Fontainebleau, constructed between 1530 and 1540. Francis I sought to re-create in France the elegant Renaissance lifestyle found in Italy. *(Source: Art Resource)*

the "Gallery Francis I," with rich scenes of classical and mythological literature. After acquiring Leonardo da Vinci's *Mona Lisa,* Francis brought Leonardo himself to France, where he soon died. Henry II built a castle at Dreux for his mistress, Diana de Poitiers, and a palace in Paris, the Tuileries, for his wife, Catherine de' Medici. Art historians credit Francis I and Henry II with importing Italian Renaissance art and architecture to France. Whatever praise these monarchs deserve for their cultural achievement, they spent far more than they could afford.

The Habsburg-Valois Wars, waged intermittently through the first half of the sixteenth century, also cost more than the government could afford. Financing the war posed problems. In addition to the time-honored practices of increasing taxes and heavy borrowing, Francis I tried two new devices to raise revenue: the sale of public

offices and a treaty with the papacy. The former proved to be only a temporary source of money. The offices sold tended to become hereditary within a family, and once a man bought an office he and his heirs were exempt from taxes. The sale of public offices thus created a tax-exempt class called the "nobility of the robe," whose members were beyond the jurisdiction of the Crown.

The treaty with the papacy was the Concordat of Bologna (1516), which in effect rescinded the Pragmatic Sanction of Bourges (see page 529). In it Francis agreed to recognize the supremacy of the papacy over a universal council. In return, the French crown gained the right to appoint all French bishops and abbots. This understanding gave the monarchy a rich supplement of money and offices and power over the church that lasted until the Revolution of 1789. The Concordat of Bologna helps to explain why France did not later

Triple Profile Portrait This portrait from the late sixteenth century exemplifies the very high finish and mannered sophistication of the School of Fontainebleau. These courtiers served Henry III, one of the weak sons of Henry II. *(Source: Milwaukee Art Museum, Gift of Women's Exchange)*

become Protestant: in effect, the concordat established Catholicism as the state religion. Because French rulers possessed control over appointments and had a vested financial interest in Catholicism, they had no need to revolt from Rome.

However, the Concordat of Bologna perpetuated disorders within the French church. Ecclesiastical offices were used primarily to pay and reward civil servants. Churchmen in France, as elsewhere, were promoted to the hierarchy not because of any special spiritual qualifications but because of their services to the state. Such bishops were unlikely to work to elevate the intellectual and moral standards of the parish clergy. Few of the many priests in France devoted scrupulous attention to the needs of their parishioners. The teachings of Luther and Calvin found a receptive audience.

Luther's tracts first appeared in France in 1518, and his ideas attracted some attention. After the publication of Calvin's *Institutes* in 1536, sizable numbers of French people were attracted to the "reformed religion," as Calvinism was called. Be-

cause Calvin wrote in French rather than Latin, his ideas gained wide circulation. Initially, Calvinism drew converts from among reform-minded members of the Catholic clergy, the industrious middle classes, and artisan groups. Most Calvinists lived in major cities, such as Paris, Lyon, Meaux, and Grenoble.

In spite of condemnation by the universities, government bans, and massive burnings at the stake, the numbers of Protestants grew steadily. When Henry II died in 1559, there were 40 well-organized churches and 2,150 mission churches in France. Perhaps one-tenth of the population had become Calvinist (see Map 17.4).

Religious Riots and Civil War in France (1559–1589)

For thirty years, from 1559 to 1589, violence and civil war divided and shattered France. The feebleness of the monarchy was the seed from which the weeds of civil violence germinated. The three weak sons of Henry II who occupied the throne could not provide the necessary leadership. Francis II (r. 1559–1560) died after seventeen months. Charles IX (r. 1560–1574) succeeded at the age of ten and was thoroughly dominated by his opportunistic mother, Catherine de' Medici, who would support any party or position to maintain her influence. The intelligent and cultivated Henry III (r. 1574–1589) divided his attention between debaucheries with his male lovers and frantic acts of repentance.

The French nobility took advantage of this monarchial weakness. In the second half of the sixteenth century, between two-fifths and one-half of the nobility at one time or another became Calvinist. Just as German princes in the Holy Roman Empire had adopted Lutheranism as a means of opposition to the emperor Charles V, so French nobles frequently adopted the "reformed religion" as a religious cloak for their independence. No one believed that peoples of different faiths could coexist peacefully within the same territory. The Reformation thus led to a resurgence of feudal disorder. Armed clashes between Calvinist antimonarchial lords and Catholic royalist lords occurred in many parts of France.

Among the upper classes the Calvinist-Catholic conflict was the surface issue, but the fundamental object of the struggle was power. Working-class

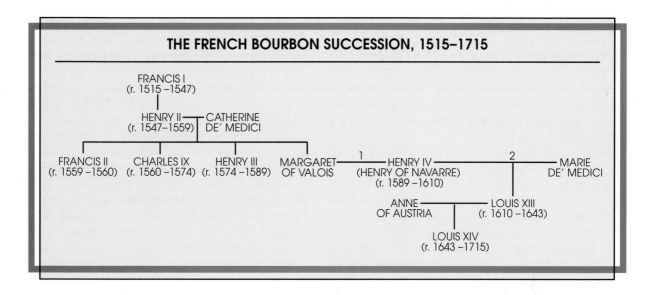

THE FRENCH BOURBON SUCCESSION, 1515–1715

crowds composed of skilled craftsmen and the poor wreaked terrible violence on people and property. Both Calvinists and Catholics believed that the others' books, services, and ministers polluted the community. Preachers incited violence, and ceremonies (baptisms, marriages, funerals) triggered it. Protestant pastors encouraged their followers to destroy statues and liturgical objects in Catholic churches. Catholic priests urged their flocks to shed the blood of the Calvinist heretics.

In 1561 in the Paris church of Saint-Médard, a Protestant crowd cornered a baker guarding a box containing the consecrated Eucharistic bread. Taunting "Does your God of paste protect you now from the pains of death?" the mob proceeded to kill the poor man.[23] Calvinists believed that the Catholics' emphasis on symbols in their ritual desecrated what was truly sacred and promoted the worship of images. In scores of attacks on Catholic churches, religious statues were knocked down, stained-glass windows smashed, and sacred vestments, vessels, and Eucharistic elements defiled. In 1561 a Catholic crowd charged a group of just-released Protestant prisoners, killed them, and burned their bodies in the street. Hundreds of Huguenots, as French Calvinists were called, were tortured, had their tongues or throats slit, were maimed or murdered.

In the fourteenth and fifteenth centuries, crowd action—attacks on great nobles and rich prelates—had expressed economic grievances. Religious rioters of the sixteenth century believed that they could assume the power of public magistrates and

rid the community of corruption. Municipal officials criticized the crowds' actions, but the participation of pastors and priests in these riots lent them some legitimacy.[24]

A savage Catholic attack on Calvinists in Paris on August 24, 1572 (Saint Bartholomew's Day), followed the usual pattern. The occasion was a religious ceremony, the marriage of the king's sister Margaret of Valois to the Protestant Henry of Navarre, which was intended to help reconcile Catholics and Huguenots. Among the many Calvinists present for the wedding festivities was the admiral of Coligny, head of one of the great noble families of France and leader of the Huguenot party. Coligny had recently replaced Catherine de' Medici in influence over the young king Charles IX. The night before the wedding, Henry of Guise, the leader of the Catholic aristocracy, had Coligny murdered. Rioting and slaughter then followed. Huguenot gentry in Paris were massacred, and religious violence spread to the provinces. Between August 25 and October 3, perhaps twelve thousand Huguenots perished at Meaux, Lyon, Orléans, and Paris. The contradictory orders of the unstable Charles IX worsened the situation.

The Saint Bartholomew's Day Massacre led to fighting that launched the "War of the Three Henrys," a civil conflict among factions led by the Catholic Henry of Guise, the Protestant Henry of Navarre, and King Henry III, who succeeded the tubercular Charles IX. Though he remained Catholic, King Henry realized that the Catholic Guise group represented his greatest danger. The Guises wanted, through an alliance of Catholic nobles called the "Holy League," not only to destroy Calvinism but to replace Henry III with a member of the Guise family. France suffered fifteen more years of religious rioting and domestic anarchy. Agriculture in many areas was destroyed; commercial life declined severely; starvation and death haunted the land.

What ultimately saved France was a small group of Catholic moderates called *politiques,* who believed that only the restoration of strong monarchy could reverse the trend toward collapse. Believing that no religious creed was worth the incessant disorder and destruction, the politiques supported religious toleration. The death of Catherine de' Medici, followed by the assassinations of Henry of Guise and King Henry III, paved the way for the accession of Henry of Navarre, a politique who became Henry IV (r. 1589–1610).

MAP 18.3 The Netherlands, 1578–1609 Though small in geographical size, the Netherlands held a strategic position in the religious struggles of the sixteenth century.

This glamorous prince, "who knew how to fight, to make love, and to drink," as a contemporary remarked, wanted above all a strong and united France. He knew, too, that the majority of the French were Roman Catholics. Declaring "Paris is worth a Mass," Henry knelt before the archbishop of Bourges and was received into the Roman Catholic church. Henry's willingness to sacrifice religious principles to political necessity saved France. The Edict of Nantes, which Henry published in 1598, granted to Huguenots liberty of conscience and liberty of public worship in two hundred fortified towns, such as La Rochelle. The reign of Henry IV and the Edict of Nantes prepared the way for French absolutism in the seventeenth century by helping restore internal peace.

The Netherlands Under Charles V

In the last quarter of the sixteenth century, the political stability of England, the international prestige of Spain, and the moral influence of the Roman papacy all became mixed up with the religious crisis in the Low Countries. The Netherlands was the pivot around which European money, diplomacy, and war revolved. What began as a movement for church reformation developed into a struggle for Dutch independence.

The emperor Charles V (r. 1519–1556) had inherited the seventeen provinces that compose present-day Belgium and Holland (Map 18.3). Ideally situated for commerce between the Rhine and Scheldt rivers, the great towns of Bruges, Ghent, Brussels, Arras, and Amsterdam made their living by trade and industry. The French-speaking southern towns produced fine linens and woolens; the wealth of the Dutch-speaking northern cities rested on fishing, shipping, and international banking. The city of Antwerp was the largest port and the greatest money market in Europe. In the cities of the Low Countries, trade and commerce had produced a vibrant cosmopolitan atmosphere, which was well personified by the urbane Erasmus of Rotterdam (see page 525).

Each of the seventeen provinces of the Netherlands possessed historical liberties: each was self-governing and enjoyed the right to make its own laws and collect its own taxes. Only the recognition of a common ruler in the person of the emperor Charles V united the provinces. Delegates from each province met together in the Estates

General, but important decisions had to be referred back to each province for approval. In the middle of the sixteenth century, the provinces of the Netherlands had a limited sense of federation.

In the Low Countries, as elsewhere, corruption in the Roman church and the critical spirit of the Renaissance provoked pressure for reform. Lutheran tracts and Dutch translations of the Bible flooded the seventeen provinces in the 1520s and 1530s, attracting many people to Protestantism. Charles V's government responded with condemnation and mild repression. This policy was not particularly effective, however, because ideas circulated freely in the cosmopolitan atmosphere of the commercial centers. But Charles's Flemish loyalty checked the spread of Lutheranism. Charles had been born in Ghent and raised in the Netherlands; he was Flemish in language and culture. He identified with the Flemish and they with him.

In 1556, however, Charles V abdicated, dividing his territories between his brother Ferdinand, who received Austria and the Holy Roman Empire, and his son Philip, who inherited Spain, the Low Countries, Milan and the kingdom of Sicily, and the Spanish possessions in America. Charles delivered his abdication speech before the Estates General at Brussels. The emperor was then fifty-five years old, white haired, and so crippled in the legs that he had to lean for support on the young Prince William of Orange. According to one contemporary account of the emperor's appearance:

His under lip, a Burgundian inheritance, as faithfully transmitted as the duchy and county, was heavy and hanging, the lower jaw protruding so far beyond the upper that it was impossible for him to bring together the few fragments of teeth which still remained, or to speak a whole sentence in an intelligible voice.[25]

Charles spoke in Flemish. His small, shy, and sepulchral son Philip responded in Spanish; he could speak neither French nor Flemish. The Netherlanders had always felt Charles one of themselves. They were never to forget that Philip was a Spaniard.

The Revolt of the Netherlands (1566–1587)

By the 1560s, there was a strong, militant minority of Calvinists in most of the cities of the Netherlands. The seventeen provinces possessed a large middle-class population, and the "reformed religion," as a contemporary remarked, had a powerful appeal "to those who had grown rich by trade and were therefore ready for revolution."[26] Calvinism appealed to the middle classes because of its intellectual seriousness, moral gravity, and emphasis on any form of labor well done. It took deep root among the merchants and financiers in Amsterdam and the northern provinces. Working-class people were also converted, partly because their employers would hire only fellow Calvinists. Well organized and with the backing of wealthy merchants, Calvinists quickly gained a wide following. Lutherans taught respect for the powers that be. The reformed religion, however, tended to encourage opposition to "illegal" civil authorities.

In 1559 Philip II appointed his half-sister Margaret as regent of the Netherlands (1559–1567). A proud, energetic, and strong-willed woman, who once had Ignatius Loyola as her confessor, Margaret pushed Philip's orders to wipe out Protestantism. She introduced the Inquisition. Her more immediate problem, however, was revenue to finance the government of the provinces. Charles V had steadily increased taxes in the Low Countries. When Margaret appealed to the Estates General, they claimed that the Low Countries were more heavily taxed than Spain. Nevertheless, Margaret raised taxes. In so doing, she quickly succeeded in uniting opposition to the government's fiscal policy with opposition to official repression of Calvinism.

In August 1566, a year of very high grain prices, fanatical Calvinists, primarily of the poorest classes, embarked on a rampage of frightful destruction. As in France, Calvinist destruction in the Low Countries was incited by popular preaching, and attacks were aimed at religious images as symbols of false doctrines, not at people. The cathedral of Notre Dame at Antwerp was the first target. Begun in 1124 and finished only in 1518, this church stood as a monument to the commercial prosperity of Flanders, the piety of the business classes, and the artistic genius of centuries. On six successive summer evenings, crowds swept through the nave. While the town harlots held tapers to the greatest concentration of art works in northern Europe, people armed with axes and sledgehammers smashed altars, statues, paintings, books, tombs, ecclesiastical vestments, missals, manuscripts, ornaments, stained-glass windows,

To Purify the Church   The destruction of pictures and statues representing biblical events, Christian doctrine, or sacred figures was a central feature of the Protestant Reformation. Here Dutch Protestant soldiers destroy what they consider idols in the belief that they are purifying the church. *(Source: Fotomas Index)*

and sculptures. Before the havoc was over, thirty more churches had been sacked and irreplaceable libraries burned. From Antwerp the destruction spread to Brussels and Ghent and north to the provinces of Holland and Zeeland.

From Madrid, Philip II sent twenty thousand Spanish troops under the duke of Alva to pacify the Low Countries. To Alva, "pacification" meant the ruthless extermination of religious and political dissidents. On top of the Inquisition he opened his own tribunal, soon called the "Council of Blood." On March 3, 1568, fifteen hundred men were executed. Alva resolved the financial crisis by levying a 10 percent sales tax on every transaction. In the commercial Dutch society, this tax caused widespread hardship and confusion.

For ten years, between 1568 and 1578, civil war raged in the Netherlands between Catholics and Protestants and between the seventeen provinces

and Spain. A series of Spanish generals could not halt the fighting. In 1576 the seventeen provinces united under the leadership of Prince William of Orange, called "the Silent" because of his remarkable discretion. In 1578 Philip II sent his nephew Alexander Farnese, duke of Parma, to crush the revolt once and for all. A general with a superb sense of timing, an excellent knowledge of the geography of the Low Countries, and a perfect plan, Farnese arrived with an army of German mercenaries. Avoiding pitched battles, he fought by patient sieges. One by one the cities of the south fell—Maastricht, Tournai, Bruges, Ghent, and finally the financial capital of northern Europe, Antwerp. Calvinism was forbidden in these territories, and Protestants were compelled to convert or leave. The collapse of Antwerp marked the farthest extent of Spanish jurisdiction and ultimately the religious division of the Netherlands.

The ten southern provinces, the Spanish Netherlands (the future Belgium), remained under the control of the Spanish Habsburgs. The seven northern provinces, led by Holland, formed the Union of Utrecht and in 1581 declared their independence from Spain. Thus was born the United Provinces of the Netherlands (see Map 18.3).

Geography and sociopolitical structure differentiated the two countries. The northern provinces were ribboned with sluices and canals and therefore were highly defensible. Several times the Dutch had broken the dikes and flooded the countryside to halt the advancing Farnese. In the southern provinces the Ardennes Mountains interrupt the otherwise flat terrain. In the north the commercial aristocracy possessed the predominant power; in the south the landed nobility had the greater influence. The north was Protestant; the south remained Catholic.

Philip II and Alexander Farnese did not accept this geographical division, and the struggle continued after 1581. The United Provinces repeatedly begged the Protestant queen Elizabeth of England for assistance.

The crown on the head of Elizabeth I (r. 1558–1603) did not rest easily. She had steered a moderately Protestant course between the Puritans, who sought the total elimination of Roman Catholic elements in the English church, and the Roman Catholics, who wanted full restoration of the old religion (see page 553). Elizabeth survived a massive uprising by the Catholic north in 1569 to 1570. She survived two serious plots against her life. In the 1570s the presence in England of Mary, Queen of Scots, a Roman Catholic and the legal heir to the English throne, produced a very embarrassing situation. Mary was the rallying point of all opposition to Elizabeth, yet the English sovereign hesitated to set the terrible example of regicide by ordering Mary executed.

Elizabeth faced a grave dilemma. If she responded favorably to Dutch pleas for military support against the Spanish, she would antagonize Philip II. The Spanish king had the steady flow of silver from the Americas at his disposal, and Elizabeth, lacking such treasure, wanted to avoid war. But if she did not help the Protestant Netherlands and they were crushed by Farnese, the likelihood was that the Spanish would invade England.

Three developments forced Elizabeth's hand. First, the wars in the Low Countries—the chief market for English woolens—badly hurt the English economy. When wool was not exported, the Crown lost valuable customs revenues. Second, the murder of William the Silent in July 1584 eliminated not only a great Protestant leader but the chief military check on the Farnese advance. Third, the collapse of Antwerp appeared to signal a Catholic sweep through the Netherlands. The next step, the English feared, would be a Spanish invasion of their island. For these reasons, Elizabeth pumped £250,000 and two thousand troops into the Protestant cause in the Low Countries between 1585 and 1587. Increasingly fearful of the plots of Mary, Queen of Scots, Elizabeth finally signed her death warrant. Mary was beheaded on February 18, 1587. Sometime between March 24 and 30, the news of her death reached Philip II.

Philip II and the Spanish Armada

Philip pondered the Dutch and English developments at the Escorial northwest of Madrid. Begun in 1563 and completed under the king's personal supervision in 1584, the monastery of Saint Lawrence of the Escorial served as a monastery for Jeromite monks, a tomb for the king's Habsburg ancestors, and a royal palace for Philip and his family. The vast buildings resemble a gridiron, the instrument on which Saint Lawrence (d. 258) had supposedly been roasted alive. The royal apartments were in the center of the Italian Renaissance building complex. King Philip's tiny bedchamber possessed a concealed sliding window that opened directly onto the high altar of the monastery church so he could watch the services and pray along with the monks. In this somber atmosphere, surrounded by a community of monks and close to the bones of his ancestors, the Catholic ruler of Spain and much of the globe passed his days.

Philip of Spain considered himself the international defender of Catholicism and the heir to the medieval imperial power. Hoping to keep England within the Catholic church when his wife Mary Tudor died, Philip had asked Elizabeth to marry him. She had emphatically refused. Several popes had urged him to move against England. When Pope Sixtus V (r. 1585–1590) heard of the death of the queen of Scots, he promised to pay Philip one million gold ducats the moment Spanish troops landed in England. Alexander Farnese had repeatedly warned that to subdue the Dutch, he would have to conquer England and cut off the source of Dutch support. Philip worried that the vast amounts of South American silver that he was pouring into the conquest of the Netherlands seemed to be going into a bottomless pit. Two plans for an expedition were considered. Philip's naval adviser recommended that a fleet of 150 ships sail from Lisbon, attack the English navy in the Channel, and invade England. Another proposal was to assemble a collection of barges and troops in Flanders to stage a cross-Channel assault. With the expected support of English Catholics, Spain would achieve a great victory. Farnese opposed the latter plan as militarily unsound.

Philip compromised. He prepared a vast armada to sail from Lisbon to Flanders, fight off Elizabeth's navy if it attacked, rendezvous with Farnese, and escort his barges across the English Channel. The expedition's purpose was to transport the Flemish army to England.

On May 9, 1588, *la felicissima armada*—"the most fortunate fleet," as it was called in official documents—sailed from Lisbon harbor on the last

medieval crusade. The Spanish fleet of 130 vessels carried 123,790 cannon balls and perhaps 30,000 men, every one of whom had confessed his sins and received the Eucharist. An English fleet of about 150 ships met the Spanish in the Channel. It was composed of smaller, faster, more maneuverable ships, many of which had greater firing power. A combination of storms and squalls, spoiled food and rank water, inadequate Spanish ammunition, and, to a lesser extent, English fire ships that caused the Spanish to panic and scatter gave England the victory. Many Spanish ships went to the bottom of the ocean; perhaps 65 managed to crawl home by way of the North Sea.

The battle in the Channel has frequently been described as one of the decisive battles in world history. In fact, it had mixed consequences. Spain soon rebuilt its navy, and the quality of the Spanish fleet improved. The destruction of the armada did not halt the flow of silver from the New World. More silver reached Spain between 1588 and 1603 than in any other fifteen-year period.

Defeat of the Spanish Armada The crescent-shaped Spanish formation was designed to force the English to fight at close quarters—by ramming and boarding. When the English sent burning ships against the Spaniards, the crescent broke up, the English pounced on individual ships, and an Atlantic gale swept the Spaniards into the North Sea, finishing the work of destruction. *(Source: National Maritime Museum, London)*

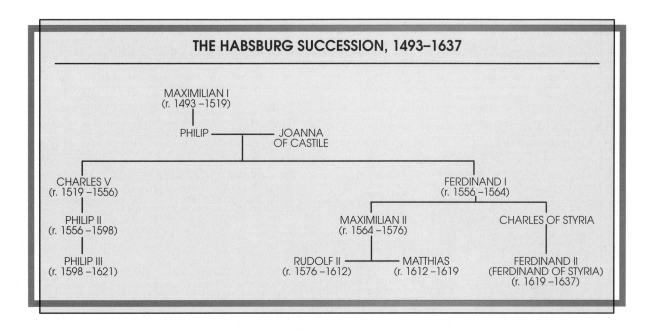

THE HABSBURG SUCCESSION, 1493–1637

MAXIMILIAN I
(r. 1493–1519)

PHILIP ——— JOANNA
OF CASTILE

CHARLES V
(r. 1519–1556)

FERDINAND I
(r. 1556–1564)

PHILIP II
(r. 1556–1598)

MAXIMILIAN II
(r. 1564–1576)

CHARLES OF STYRIA

PHILIP III
(r. 1598–1621)

RUDOLF II ——— MATTHIAS
(r. 1576–1612)   (r. 1612–1619)

FERDINAND II
(FERDINAND OF STYRIA)
(r. 1619–1637)

The war between England and Spain dragged on for years.

The defeat of the Spanish Armada was decisive, however, in the sense that it prevented Philip II from reimposing unity on western Europe by force. He did not conquer England, and Elizabeth continued her financial and military support of the Dutch. In the Netherlands, however, neither side gained significant territory. The borders of 1581 tended to become permanent. In 1609 Philip III of Spain (r. 1598–1621) agreed to a truce, in effect recognizing the independence of the United Provinces. In seventeenth-century Spain memory of the defeat of the armada contributed to a spirit of defeatism.

The Thirty Years' War (1618–1648)

While Philip II dreamed of building a second armada and Henry IV began the reconstruction of France, the political-religious situation in central Europe deteriorated. An uneasy truce had prevailed in the Holy Roman Empire since the Peace of Augsburg of 1555 (see page 545). The Augsburg settlement, in recognizing the independent power of the German princes, had destroyed the authority of the central government. The Habsburg ruler in Vienna enjoyed the title "emperor" but had no power.

According to the Augsburg settlement, the faith of the prince determined the religion of his subjects. Later in the century, though, Catholics grew alarmed because Lutherans, in violation of the Peace of Augsburg, were steadily acquiring north German bishoprics. The spread of Calvinism further confused the issue. The Augsburg settlement had pertained only to Lutheranism and Catholicism, but Calvinists ignored it and converted several princes. Lutherans feared that the Augsburg principles would be totally undermined by Catholic and Calvinist gains. Also, the militantly active Jesuits had reconverted several Lutheran princes to Catholicism. In an increasingly tense situation, Lutheran princes formed the Protestant Union (1608), and Catholics retaliated with the Catholic League (1609). Each alliance was determined that the other should make no religious (that is, territorial) advance. The empire was composed of two armed camps.

Dynastic interests were also involved in the German situation. When Charles V abdicated in 1556, he had divided his possessions between his son Philip II and his brother Ferdinand I. This partition began the Austrian and Spanish branches of the Habsburg family. Ferdinand inherited the imperial title and the Habsburg lands in central Europe, including Austria. Ferdinand's grandson Matthias had no direct heirs and promoted the candidacy of his fiercely Catholic cousin,

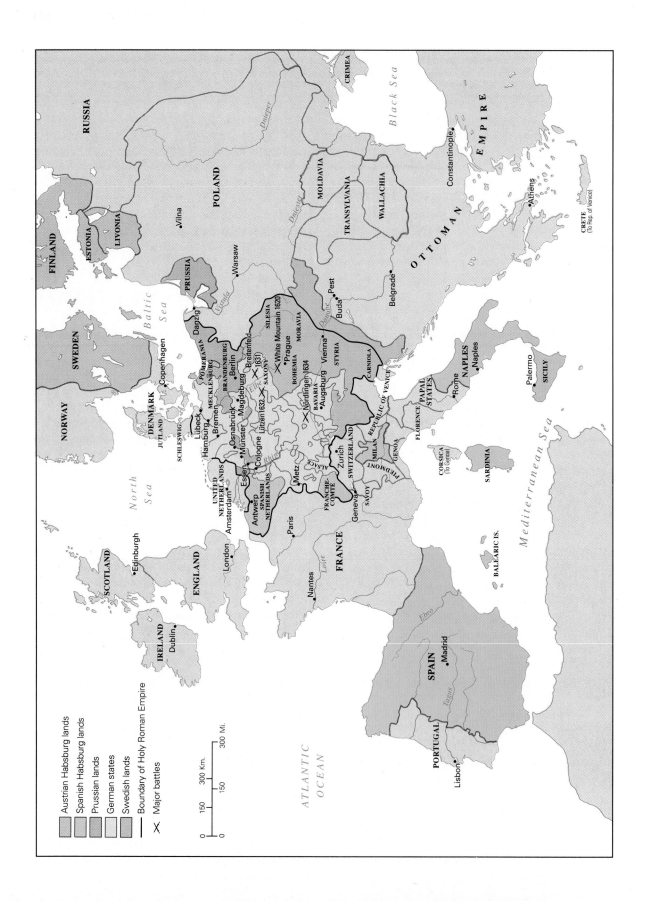

Austrian Habsburg lands

Spanish Habsburg lands

Prussian lands

German states

Swedish lands

—— Boundary of Holy Roman Empire

✕ Major battles

| 0 | | 150 | | 300 Km. |
| 0 | | 150 | | 300 Mi. |

ATLANTIC OCEAN

IRELAND
•Dublin

SCOTLAND
•Edinburgh

ENGLAND
•London

North Sea

•Nantes

FRANCE

Loire

Paris•

NORWAY

SWEDEN

FINLAND

Baltic Sea

DENMARK
•Copenhagen

JUTLAND

SCHLESWIG

Lübeck•
Hamburg•
•Bremen

MECKLENBURG

POMERANIA

•Berlin
BRANDENBURG

•Danzig
PRUSSIA

Vistula

•Warsaw

POLAND

•Vilna

RUSSIA

Dnieper

ESTONIA

LIVONIA

SILESIA
White Mountain 1620 ✕
•Prague
BOHEMIA
Breitenfeld ✕ 1631
SAXONY
Elbe
Lützen 1632 ✕
Nördlingen 1634 ✕
•Augsburg
BAVARIA

MORAVIA

Buda•
Pest•

Danube

•Vienna
STYRIA

CARNIOLA

MOLDAVIA

TRANSYLVANIA

WALLACHIA

Dniester

CRIMEA

Black Sea

•Belgrade

OTTOMAN EMPIRE

•Constantinople

•Athens

CRETE
(To Rep. of Venice)

Osnabrück•
Münster•
•Essen
Cologne•
Rhine
Metz•
ALSACE

UNITED NETHERLANDS
•Amsterdam
Antwerp•
SPANISH NETHERLANDS

FRANCHE-COMTÉ

Geneva•
SAVOY
SWITZERLAND
•Zurich

PIEDMONT
•Milan
•Genoa

REPUBLIC OF VENICE

FLORENCE
PAPAL STATES
Rome•

NAPLES
•Naples

CORSICA
(To Genoa)

SARDINIA

Palermo•
SICILY

Mediterranean Sea

BALEARIC IS.

SPAIN
Madrid•

Tagus

Ebro

PORTUGAL
•Lisbon

Ferdinand of Styria for the imperial crown. The Spanish Habsburgs strongly supported the goals of their Austrian relatives: the unity of the empire and the preservation of Catholicism within it.

In 1617 Ferdinand of Styria secured election as king of Bohemia, a title that gave him jurisdiction over Silesia and Moravia as well as Bohemia. The Bohemians were Czech and German in nationality and Lutheran, Calvinist, Catholic, and Hussite in religion; all these faiths enjoyed a fair degree of religious freedom. When Ferdinand proceeded to close some Protestant churches, the heavily Protestant Estates of Bohemia protested. On May 23, 1618, Protestants hurled two of Ferdinand's officials from a castle window in Prague. They fell seventy feet but survived. Catholics claimed that angels had caught them; Protestants said the officials fell on a heap of soft horse manure. Called the "defenestration of Prague," this event marked the beginning of the Thirty Years' War (1618–1648).

Historians traditionally divide the war into four phases. The first, or Bohemian, phase (1618–1625) was characterized by civil war in Bohemia between the Catholic League, led by Ferdinand, and the Protestant Union, headed by Prince Frederick of the Palatinate. The Bohemians fought for religious liberty and independence from Habsburg rule. In 1618 the Bohemian Estates deposed Ferdinand and gave the crown of Bohemia to Frederick, thus uniting the interests of German Protestants with those of the international enemies of the Habsburgs. Frederick wore his crown only a few months. In 1620 he was totally defeated by Catholic forces at the Battle of the White Mountain (Map 18.4). Ferdinand, who had recently been elected Holy Roman emperor as Ferdinand II, followed up his victories by wiping out Protestantism in Bohemia through forcible conversions and the activities of militant Jesuit missionaries. Within ten years, Bohemia was completely Catholic.

The second, or Danish, phase of the war (1625–1629)—so called because of the participation of King Christian IV of Denmark (r. 1588–1648), the ineffective leader of the Protes-

MAP 18.4 Europe in 1648 Which country emerged from the Thirty Years' War as the strongest European power? What dynastic house was that country's major rival in the early modern period?

tant cause—witnessed additional Catholic victories. The Catholic imperial army led by Albert of Wallenstein scored smashing victories. It swept through Silesia, north through Schleswig and Jutland to the Baltic Sea, and east into Pomerania. Wallenstein had made himself indispensable to the emperor Ferdinand, but he was an unscrupulous opportunist who used his vast riches to build an army loyal only to himself. The general seemed interested more in carving out an empire for himself than in aiding the Catholic cause. He quarreled with the league, and soon the Catholic forces were divided. Religion was eclipsed as a basic issue of the war.

The year 1629 marked the peak of Habsburg power. The Jesuits persuaded the emperor to issue the Edict of Restitution, whereby all Catholic properties lost to Protestantism since 1552 were to be restored and only Catholics and Lutherans (not Calvinists, Hussites, or other sects) were to be allowed to practice their faiths. Ferdinand appeared to be embarked on a policy to unify the empire. When Wallenstein began ruthless enforcement of the edict, Protestants throughout Europe feared collapse of the balance of power in the north central region.

The third, or Swedish, phase of the war (1630–1635) began with the arrival in Germany of the Swedish king Gustavus Adolphus (r. 1594–1632). The ablest administrator of his day and a devout Lutheran, Gustavus Adolphus intervened to support the oppressed Protestants within the empire and to assist his relatives, the exiled dukes of Mecklenburg. Cardinal Richelieu, the chief minister of King Louis XIII of France (r. 1610–1643), subsidized the Swedes, hoping to weaken Habsburg power in Europe. In 1631, with a small but well-disciplined army equipped with superior muskets and warm uniforms, Gustavus Adolphus won a brilliant victory at Breitenfeld. In 1632 he was victorious again, at Lützen, though he was fatally wounded in the battle.

The participation of the Swedes in the Thirty Years' War proved decisive for the future of Protestantism and later German history. When Gustavus Adolphus landed on German soil, he had already brought Denmark, Poland, Finland, and the smaller Baltic States under Swedish influence. The Swedish victories ended the Habsburg ambition of uniting all the German states under imperial authority.

The death of Gustavus Adolphus, followed by the defeat of the Swedes at the Battle of Nördlingen in 1634, prompted the French to enter the war on the side of the Protestants. Thus began the French, or international, phase (1635–1648) of the Thirty Years' War. For almost a century, French foreign policy had been based on opposition to the Habsburgs, because a weak empire divided into scores of independent principalities enhanced France's international stature. In 1622, when the Dutch had resumed the war against Spain, the French had supported Holland. Now, in 1635, Cardinal Richelieu declared war on Spain and again sent financial and military assistance to the Swedes and the German Protestant princes. The war dragged on. French, Dutch, and Swedes, supported by Scots, Finns, and German mercenaries, burned, looted, and destroyed German agriculture and commerce. The Thirty Years' War lasted so long because neither side had the resources to win a quick, decisive victory. Finally, in October 1648, peace was achieved.

The treaties signed at Münster and Osnabrück, commonly called the "Peace of Westphalia," mark a turning point in European political, religious, and social history. The treaties recognized the sovereign, independent authority of the German princes. Each ruler could govern his particular territory and make war and peace as well. With power in the hands of more than three hundred princes, and no central government or courts to control them, the Holy Roman Empire as a real state was effectively destroyed (see Map 18.4).

The independence of the United Provinces of the Netherlands was acknowledged. The international stature of France and Sweden was also greatly improved. The political divisions within the empire, the weak German frontiers, and the acquisition of the province of Alsace increased France's size and prestige. The treaties allowed France to intervene at will in German affairs. Sweden received a large cash indemnity and jurisdiction over German territories along the Baltic Sea. The powerful Swedish presence in northeastern Germany subsequently posed a major threat to the future kingdom of Brandenburg-Prussia. The treaties also denied the papacy the right to participate in German religious affairs—a restriction symbolizing the reduced role of the church in European politics.

In religion, the Westphalian treaties stipulated that the Augsburg agreement of 1555 should stand permanently. The sole modification was that Calvinism, along with Catholicism and Lutheranism, would become a legally permissible creed. In practice, the north German states remained Protestant, the south German states Catholic. The war settled little. Both sides had wanted peace, and with remarkable illogic they fought for thirty years to get it.

Germany After the Thirty Years' War

The Thirty Years' War was a disaster for the German economy and society, probably the most destructive event in German history before the twentieth century. Population losses were frightful. Perhaps one-third of the urban residents and two-fifths of the inhabitants of rural areas died. Entire areas of Germany were depopulated, partly by military actions, partly by disease—typhus, dysentery, bubonic plague, and syphilis accompanied the movements of armies—and partly by the flight of thousands of refugees to safer areas.

In the late sixteenth and early seventeenth centuries, all Europe experienced an economic crisis caused primarily by the influx of silver from the Americas. Because the Thirty Years' War was fought on German soil, these economic difficulties were badly aggravated in the empire. Scholars still cannot estimate the value of losses in agricultural land and livestock, in trade and commerce. The trade of southern cities like Augsburg, already hard hit by the shift in transportation routes from the Mediterranean to the Atlantic, was virtually destroyed by the fighting in the south. Meanwhile, towns like Lübeck, Hamburg, and Bremen in the north and Essen in the Ruhr area actually prospered because of the many refugees they attracted. The destruction of land and foodstuffs, compounded by the flood of Spanish silver, brought on severe price increases. During and after the war, inflation was worse in Germany than anywhere else in Europe.

Agricultural areas suffered catastrophically. The population decline caused a rise in the value of labor, so owners of great estates had to pay more for agricultural workers. Farmers who needed only small amounts of capital to restore their lands started over again. Many small farmers, however, lacked the revenue to rework their holdings and had to become day laborers. Nobles and landlords bought up many small holdings and acquired great estates. In some parts of Germany, especially east of the Elbe River in areas like Mecklenburg and Pomerania, peasants' loss of land led to a new serfdom.[27] Thus the war contributed to the legal and economic decline of the largest segment of German society.

CHANGING ATTITUDES

The age of religious wars revealed extreme and violent contrasts. While some Europeans indulged in gross sensuality, the social status of women declined. The exploration of new continents reflected deep curiosity and broad intelligence, yet Europeans believed in witches and burned thousands at the stake. Europeans explored new continents, partly with the missionary aim of Christianizing native peoples. Yet the Spanish, Portuguese, Dutch, and English proceeded to enslave the Indians and blacks they encountered. It was a deeply religious period in which men fought passionately for their beliefs, and 70 percent of the books printed dealt with religious subjects. Yet the times saw the stirring of religious skepticism, and sexism, racism, and skepticism, all present since antiquity, began to take on their familiar modern forms.

The Status of Women

Did new ideas about women appear in this period? Theological and popular literature on marriage in Reformation Europe helps to answer this question. Manuals emphasized the qualities expected of each partner. A husband was obliged to provide for the material welfare of his wife and children, to protect his family while remaining steady and self-controlled. He was to rule his household firmly but justly; he was not to behave like a tyrant, a guideline counselors repeated frequently. A wife was to be mature, a good household manager, and subservient and faithful to her spouse. The husband also owed fidelity. Both Protestant and Catholic moralists rejected the double standard of sexual morality, viewing it as a threat to family unity. Counselors believed that marriage should be based on mutual respect and trust. Although they discouraged impersonal unions arranged by parents, they did not think romantic attachments—based on physical attraction and emotional love—a sound basis for an enduring relationship.

Moralists held that the household was a woman's first priority. She might assist in her own or her husband's business and do charitable work. Involvement in social or public activities, however, was inappropriate because it distracted the wife from her primary responsibility: her household. If women suffered under their husbands' yoke, writers explained, that submission was their punishment inherited from Eve; it included the pain of childbearing. Moreover, they said, a woman's lot was no worse than a man's: he must earn the family's bread by the sweat of his brow.[28]

Catholics viewed marriage as a sacramental union, which, validly entered into, could not be dissolved. Protestants stressed a contractual form of marriage, whereby each partner promised the other support, companionship, and the sharing of mutual goods. Protestants recognized a mutual right to divorce and remarry for various reasons, including adultery and irreparable breakdown.[29] Society in the early modern period was patriarchal. Women neither lost their identity nor lacked meaningful work, but the all-pervasive assumption was that men ruled. Leading students of the Lutherans, Catholics, French Calvinists, and English Puritans tend to concur that there was no improvement of women's definitely subordinate status.

There are some remarkable success stories, however. Elizabeth Hardwick, the orphaned daughter of an obscure English country squire, made four careful marriages. Each of them brought her more property and carried her higher up the social ladder. She managed her estates, amounting to more than a hundred thousand acres, with a degree of business sense rare in any age. The two great mansions she built, Chatsworth and Hardwick, stand today as monuments to her acumen. As countess of Shrewsbury, "Bess of Hardwick" so thoroughly enjoyed the trust of Queen Elizabeth that Elizabeth appointed her jailer of Mary, Queen of Scots. Having established several aristocratic dynasties, the countess of Shrewsbury died in 1608, past her eightieth year, one of the richest people in England.[30]

Artists' drawings of plump, voluptuous women and massive, muscular men reveal the contemporary standards of physical beauty. It was a sensual age that gloried in the delights of the flesh. Some people found sexual satisfaction with both sexes.

Reformers and public officials simultaneously condemned and condoned sexual "sins." The oldest profession had many practitioners, and, when in 1566 Pope Pius IV expelled all the prostitutes from Rome, so many people left and the city suffered such a loss of revenue that in less than a month the pope was forced to rescind the order. Scholars debated Saint Augustine's notion that whores serve a useful social function by preventing worse sins.

Prostitution was common because desperate poverty forced women and young men into it. The general public took it for granted. Consequently, civil authorities in both Catholic and Protestant countries licensed houses of public prostitution. These establishments were intended for the convenience of single men, and some Protestant cities, such as Geneva and Zurich, installed officials in the brothels with the express purpose of preventing married men from patronizing them. Moralists naturally railed against prostitution. For example, Melchior Ambach, the Lutheran editor of many tracts against adultery and whoring, wrote in 1543 that if "houses of women" for single and married men were allowed, why not provide a "house of boys" for women folk who lack a husband to service them? "Would whoring be any worse for the poor, needy female sex?"[31] Ambach, of course, was not being serious: by treating infidelity from the perspective of female rather than male customers, he was still insisting that prostitution destroyed the family and society.

What became of the thousands of women who left their convents and nunneries during the Reformation? The question concerns primarily women of the upper classes, who formed the dominant social group in the religious houses of late medieval Europe. (Single women of the middle and working classes in the sixteenth and seventeenth centuries worked in many occupations and professions—as butchers, shopkeepers, nurses, goldsmiths, and midwives and in the weaving and printing industries. Those who were married normally assisted in their husbands' businesses.) Luther and the Protestant reformers believed that the monastic cloister symbolized antifeminism, that young girls were forced by their parents into convents and once there were bullied by men into staying. Thus reformers favored the suppression of women's religious houses and encouraged former nuns to marry. Marriage, the reformers maintained, not only gave women emotional and sexual

satisfaction but freed them from clerical domination, cultural deprivation, and sexual repression.[32] It would appear, consequently, that women passed from clerical domination to subservience to husbands.

If some nuns in the Middle Ages lacked a genuine religious vocation and if some religious houses witnessed financial mismanagement and moral laxness, convents nevertheless provided women of the upper classes with scope for their literary, artistic, medical, or administrative talents if they could not or would not marry. Marriage became virtually the only occupation for Protestant women. This helps explain why Anglicans, Calvinists, and Lutherans established communities of religious women, such as the Lutheran one at Kaiserwerth in the Rhineland, in the eighteenth and nineteenth centuries.[33]

The Great European Witch Hunt

The period of the religious wars witnessed a startling increase in the phenomenon of witch-hunting, whose prior history was long but sporadic. "A witch," according to Chief Justice Edward Coke of England (1552–1634), "was a person who hath conference with the Devil to consult with him or to do some act." This definition by the highest legal authority in England demonstrates that educated people, as well as the ignorant, believed in *witches*—individuals who could mysteriously injure other people by, for instance, causing them to become blind or impotent and who could harm animals by, for example, preventing cows from giving milk.

Belief in witches dates back to the dawn of time. For centuries, tales had circulated about old women who made nocturnal travels on greased broomsticks to assemblies of witches, where they participated in sexual orgies and feasted on the flesh of infants. In the popular imagination witches had definite characteristics. The vast majority were married women or widows between fifty and seventy years old, crippled or bent with age, with pockmarked skin. They often practiced midwifery or folk medicine, and most had sharp tongues.

In the sixteenth century, religious reformers' extreme notions of the Devil's powers and the insecurity created by the religious wars contributed to the growth of belief in witches. The idea developed that witches made pacts with the Devil in return for the power to work mischief on their enemies. Since pacts with the Devil meant the renunciation of God, witchcraft was considered heresy, and all religions persecuted it.

Fear of witches took a terrible toll of innocent lives in parts of Europe. In southwestern Germany, 3,229 witches were executed between 1561 and 1670, most by burning. The communities of the Swiss Confederation tried 8,888 persons between 1470 and 1700 and executed 5,417 of them as witches. In all the centuries before 1500, witches in England had been suspected of causing perhaps "three deaths, a broken leg, several destructive storms and some bewitched genitals." Yet between 1559 and 1736, witches were thought to have caused thousands of deaths, and almost 1,000 witches were executed in England.[34]

Historians and anthropologists have offered a variety of explanations for the great European witch hunt. Some scholars maintain that charges of witchcraft were a means of accounting for inexplicable misfortunes. Just as the English in the fifteenth century had blamed their military failures in France on Joan of Arc's sorcery, so in the seventeenth century the English Royal College of Physicians attributed undiagnosable illnesses to witchcraft. Some scholars hold that in small communities, which typically insisted on strict social conformity, charges of witchcraft were a means of attacking and eliminating nonconformists. Witches, in other words, served the collective need for scapegoats. Some writers suggest that the evidence of witches' trials shows that women were accused not because they harmed or threatened their neighbors but because their communities believed that they worshiped the Devil, engaged in wild sexual activities with him, and ate infants. Other scholars argue the exact opposite: that women were tried and executed as witches because their neighbors feared their evil powers. Finally, there is a theory that the unbridled sexuality attributed to women accused of witchcraft was a psychological projection made by the women's accusers, and resulting from Christianity's repression of sexuality.

The reasons for the persecution of women as witches probably varied from place to place. Though several hypotheses exist, scholars still cannot fully understand the phenomenon. Nevertheless, given the broad strand of *misogyny* (hatred of women) in Western religion, the ancient belief in the susceptibility of women (so-called weaker vessels) to the Devil's allurements, and the pervasive seventeenth-century belief about women's multiple and demanding orgasms and thus their sexual insatiability, it is not difficult to understand why women were accused of all sorts of mischief and witchcraft. Charges of witchcraft provided a legal basis for the execution of tens of thousands of women. As the most important capital crime for women in early modern times, witchcraft has significance for the history and status of women.[35]

European Slavery and the Origins of American Racism

Almost all peoples in the world have enslaved other human beings at some time in their histo-

Witches Worshiping the Devil In medieval Christian art, a goat symbolizes the damned at the Last Judgment, following Christ's statement that the Son of Man would separate believers from nonbelievers, as a shepherd separates the sheep from the goats (Matthew 25: 31–32). In this illustration, a witch arrives at a sabbat and prepares to venerate the devil in the shape of a goat by kissing its anus. *(Source: Bodleian Library, Oxford)*

ries. Since ancient times, victors in battle have enslaved conquered peoples. In the later Middle Ages slavery was deeply entrenched in southern Italy, Sicily, Crete, and Mediterranean Spain. The bubonic plague, famines, and other epidemics created severe shortages of agricultural and domestic workers in parts of northern Europe, encouraging Italian merchants to buy slaves from the Balkans, Thrace, southern Russia, and central Anatolia for sale in the West. In 1364 the Florentine government allowed the unlimited importation of slaves, so long as they were not Roman Catholics. Between 1414 and 1423, at least ten thousand slaves were sold in Venice alone. Where profits were lucrative, papal threats of excommunication completely failed to stop Genoese slave traders. The Genoese set up colonial stations in the Crimea and along the Black Sea. According to an international authority on slavery, these outposts were "virtual laboratories" for the development of slave plantation agriculture in the New World.[36] This form of slavery had nothing to do with race; almost all slaves were white. How, then, did black African slavery enter the European picture and take root in the New World?

In 1453 the Ottoman capture of Constantinople halted the flow of white slaves from the Black Sea region and the Balkans. Mediterranean Europe, cut off from its traditional source of slaves, had no alternative source for slave labor but sub-Saharan Africa. The centuries-old trans-Saharan trade was greatly stimulated by a ready market in the vineyards and sugar plantations of Sicily and Majorca. By the later fifteenth century, the Mediterranean had developed an "American" form of slavery before the discovery of America.

Meanwhile, the Genoese and other Italians had colonized the Canary Islands off the western coast of Africa. Prince Henry the Navigator's sailors discovered the Madeira Islands and made settlements there. In this stage of European expansion, "the history of slavery became inextricably tied up with the history of sugar." Although sugar was an expensive luxury that only the affluent could afford, population increases and monetary expansion in the fifteenth century led to a growing demand for it. Resourceful Italians provided the capital, cane, and technology for sugar cultivation on plantations in southern Portugal, Madeira, and the Canary Islands. In Portugal between 1490 and 1530, between 300 and 2,000 black slaves were annually imported into the port of Lisbon (Map 18.5). From Lisbon, where African slaves performed most of the manual labor and constituted about 10 percent of the city's population, slaves were transported to the sugar plantations of Madeira, the Azores, the Cape Verdes, and then Brazil. Sugar and the small Atlantic islands gave New World slavery its distinctive shape.[37]

As already discussed, European expansion across the Atlantic led to the economic exploitation of the Americas. In the New World the major problem faced by settlers was a shortage of labor. As early as 1495 the Spanish solved the problem by enslaving the native Indians. In the next two centuries, the Portuguese, Dutch, and English followed suit.

Unaccustomed to any form of forced labor, certainly not to panning gold for more than twelve hours a day in the broiling sun, the Amerindians died "like fish in a bucket."[38] In 1517 Las Casas urged King Charles V to end Indian slavery in his American dominions (see page 574). Las Casas recommended the importation of blacks from Africa, both because church law did not strictly forbid black slavery and because blacks could better survive under South American conditions. The king agreed, and in 1518 the African slave trade began. Columbus's introduction of sugar plants into Santo Domingo, moreover, stimulated the need for black slaves; and the experience and model of plantation slavery in Portugal and the Atlantic islands encouraged a similar agricultural pattern in the New World.

Several European nations participated in the African slave trade. Portugal brought the first slaves to Brazil; by 1600, about 4,000 were being imported annually. After its founding in 1621, the Dutch West India Company, with the full support of the government of the United Provinces, transported thousands of Africans to Brazil and the Caribbean. Only in the late seventeenth century, with the chartering of the Royal African Company, did the English get involved. Thereafter, large numbers of African blacks poured into the West Indies and North America (see Map 18.5). In 1790 there were 757,181 blacks in a total U.S. population of 3,929,625. When the first census was taken in Brazil in 1798, blacks numbered about 2 million among 3.25 million people.

Settlers brought to the Americas the racial attitudes they had absorbed in Europe. Their beliefs about and attitudes toward blacks derived from two basic sources: Christian theological specula-

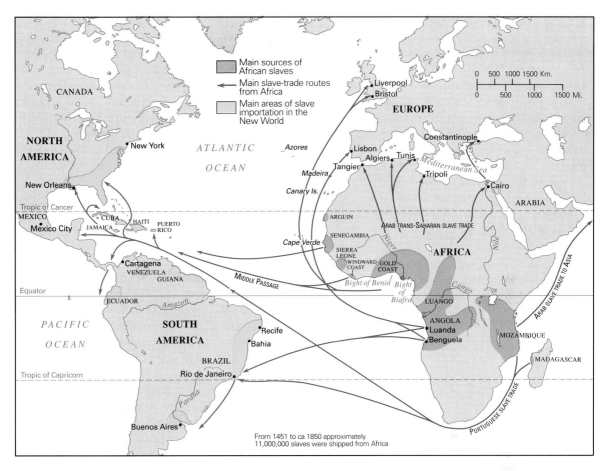

MAP 18.5 The African Slave Trade   Decades before the discovery of America, Greek, Russian, Bulgarian, Armenian, and then black slaves worked the plantation economies of southern Italy, Sicily, Portugal, and Mediterranean Spain—thereby serving as models for the American form of slavery.

tion (see page 524) and Muslim ideas. In the sixteenth and seventeenth centuries, the English, for example, were extremely curious about Africans' lives and customs, and slavers' accounts were extraordinarily popular. Travel literature depicted Africans as savages because of their eating habits, morals, clothing, and social customs; as barbarians because of their language and methods of war; and as heathens because they were not Christian. English people saw similarities between apes and Africans; thus the terms *bestial* and *beastly* were frequently applied to Africans. Africans were believed to possess a potent sexuality. One seventeenth-century observer considered African men "very lustful and impudent . . . their members' extraordinary greatness . . . is a token of their lust." African women were considered sexually aggressive with a "temper hot and lascivious."[39]

"At the time when Columbus sailed to the New World, Islam was the largest world religion, and the only world religion that showed itself capable of expanding rapidly in areas as far apart and as different from each other as Senegal in northwest Africa, Bosnia in the Balkans, Java, and the Philippines."[40] Medieval Arabic literature characterized blacks as physically repulsive, mentally inferior, and primitive. In contrast to civilized peoples from the Mediterranean to China, Muslim writers claimed, sub-Saharan blacks were the only peoples who had produced no sciences or stable states. The fourteenth-century Arab historian Ibn Khaldun wrote that the "only people who accept slavery are the Negroes, owing to their low degree of humanity and their proximity to the animal stage." Though black kings, Ibn Khaldun alleged, sold their subjects without even a pretext of crime or war, the victims bore no resentment because they gave no thought to the future and have "by nature few cares and worries; dancing and rhythm are for them inborn."[41] It is easy to see how such absurd images would develop into the classic stereotypes used to justify black slavery in South and North America in the seventeenth, eighteenth, and nineteenth centuries. Medieval Christians and Muslims had similar notions of blacks as inferior and primitive people ideally suited to enslavement.

African Slave and Indian Woman A black slave approaches an Indian prostitute. Unable to explain what he wants, he points with his finger; she eagerly grasps for the coin. The Spanish caption above moralizes on the black man using stolen money—yet the Spaniards ruthlessly expropriated all South American mineral wealth. *(Source: New York Public Library)*

Perhaps centuries of commercial contacts between Muslim and Mediterranean peoples had familiarized the latter with Muslim racial attitudes.

The biased racial attitudes of fourteenth- and fifteenth-century European and Muslim intellectuals, however, did not automatically become the views of the general populace in eighteenth-century America. It was the institutionalization of slavery, as manifested by slave plantation society in the Americas, that served as the laboratory of modern racism.[42]

The Origin of Modern Skepticism: Michel de Montaigne

Decades of religious fanaticism, bringing in their wake death, famine, and civil anarchy, caused both Catholics and Protestants to doubt that any one faith contained absolute truth. The late sixteenth and early seventeenth centuries witnessed the beginnings of modern skepticism. *Skepticism* is an attitude of thought based on doubt that total certainty or definitive knowledge is ever attainable. A skeptic is cautious and critical and suspends judgment. Perhaps the finest representative of early modern skepticism is the Frenchman Michel de Montaigne (1533–1592).

Montaigne came from a bourgeois family that had made a fortune selling salted herring and in 1477 had purchased the title and property of Montaigne in Gascony. Montaigne received a classical education before studying law and securing a judicial appointment in 1554. Though a member of the nobility, in embarking on a judicial career, he identified with the new nobility of the robe. He condemned the ancient nobility of the sword for being concerned more with war and sports than with the cultivation of the mind.

At the age of thirty-eight, Montaigne resigned his judicial post, retired to his estate, and devoted the rest of his life to study, contemplation, and the effort to understand himself. Like the Greeks, he believed that the object of life was to "know thyself," for self-knowledge teaches men and women how to live in accordance with nature and God. Montaigne developed a new literary genre, the essay—from the French *essayer,* meaning "to test" or "to try"—to express his thoughts and ideas.

Montaigne's *Essays* provide insight into the mind of a remarkably humane, tolerant, and civilized man. He was a humanist; he loved the Greek and Roman writers and was always eager to learn from them. In his essay "On Solitude," he quoted the Roman poet Horace:

Reason and sense remove anxiety,
Not villas that look out upon the sea

Some said to Socrates that a certain man had grown no better by his travels. "I should think not," he said; "he took himself along with him. . . ."
    We should have wife, children, goods, and above all health, if we can; but we must not bind ourselves to them so strongly that our happiness depends on them. We must reserve a back shop all our own, entirely free, in which to establish our real liberty and our principal retreat and solitude.[43]

From the ancient authors, especially the Roman Stoics, Montaigne acquired a sense of calm, inner peace, and patience. The ancient authors also inculcated in him tolerance and broad-mindedness.
    Montaigne came of age during the French civil wars, perhaps the worst kind of war. He wrote:

In this controversy . . . France is at present agitated by civil wars, the best and soundest side is undoubtedly that which maintains both the old religion and the old government of the country. However, among the good men who follow that side . . . we see many whom passion drives outside the bounds of reason, and makes them sometimes adopt unjust, violent, and even reckless courses.[44]

Though he remained a Catholic, Montaigne possessed a detachment, an independence, and a willingness to look at all sides of a question: "I listen with attention to the judgment of all men; but so far as I can remember, I have followed none but my own. Though I set little value upon my own opinion, I set no more on the opinions of others."
    In the book-lined tower where Montaigne passed his days, he became a deeply learned man. Yet he was not ignorant of world affairs, and he criticized scholars and bookworms who ignored the life around them. Montaigne's essay "On Cannibals" reflects the impact of overseas discoveries on Europeans' consciousness. His tolerant mind rejected the notion that one culture is superior to another:

I long had a man in my house that lived ten or twelve years in the New World . . . in . . . Brazil. . . .

I find that there is nothing barbarous and savage in that nation, by anything that I can gather, excepting, that every one gives the title of barbarism to everything that is not in use in his own country. As, indeed, we have no other level of truth and reason, than the example and idea of the opinions and customs of the place wherein we live.[45]

In his belief in the nobility of human beings in the state of nature, uncorrupted by organized society, and in his cosmopolitan attitude toward different civilizations, Montaigne anticipated many eighteenth-century thinkers.
    The thought of Michel de Montaigne marks a sharp break with the past. Faith and religious certainty had characterized the intellectual attitudes of Western society for a millennium. Montaigne's rejection of any kind of dogmatism, his secularism, and his skepticism represented a basic change. In his own time and throughout the seventeenth century, few would have agreed with him. The publication of his ideas, however, anticipated a basic shift in attitudes. Montaigne inaugurated an era of doubt. "Wonder," he said, "is the foundation of all philosophy, research is the means of all learning, and ignorance is the end."[46]

ELIZABETHAN AND JACOBEAN LITERATURE

The age of the religious wars and European expansion also experienced an extraordinary degree of intellectual ferment. In addition to the development of the essay as a distinct literary genre, the late sixteenth and early seventeenth centuries fostered remarkable creativity in other branches of literature. England, especially in the latter part of Elizabeth's reign and the first years of the reign of her successor, James I (r. 1603–1625), witnessed unparalleled brilliance. The terms *Elizabethan* and *Jacobean* (referring to the reign of James) are used to designate the English music, poetry, prose, and drama of this period. The poems of Sir Philip Sidney (1554–1586), such as *Astrophel and Stella,* strongly influenced later poetic writing. *The Faerie Queene* of Edmund Spenser (1552–1599) endures as one of the greatest moral epics in any language. The rare poetic beauty of the plays of Christopher Marlowe (1564–1593), such as *Tamburlaine* and *The Jew of Malta,* paved the way for

A Royal Hunt In the sixteenth and seventeenth centuries, hunting remained an aristocratic pastime. Here a courtier, having slain a deer, presents the dagger to Queen Elizabeth I. *(Source: By permission of the Folger Shakespeare Library)*

the work of Shakespeare. Above all, the immortal dramas of Shakespeare and stately prose of the Authorized or King James Bible mark the Elizabethan and Jacobean periods as the golden age of English literature.

William Shakespeare (1564–1616), the son of a successful glove manufacturer who rose to the highest municipal office in the Warwickshire town of Stratford-on-Avon, chose a career on the London stage. By 1592 he had gained recognition as an actor and playwright. Between 1599 and 1603, Shakespeare performed in the Lord Chamberlain's Company and became co-owner of the Globe Theatre, which after 1603 presented his plays.

Shakespeare's genius lies in the originality of his characterizations, the diversity of his plots, his understanding of human psychology, and his unexcelled gift for language. Shakespeare was a Renaissance man in his deep appreciation for classical culture, individualism, and humanism. Such plays as *Julius Caesar, Pericles,* and *Antony and Cleopatra* deal with classical subjects and figures. Several of his comedies have Italian Renaissance settings. The nine history plays, including *Richard II, Richard III,* and *Henry IV,* enjoyed the greatest popularity among Shakespeare's contemporaries. Written during the decade after the defeat of the Spanish Armada, the history plays express English national consciousness. Lines such as these from *Richard II* reflect this sense of national greatness with unparalleled eloquence:

This royal Throne of Kings, this sceptre'd Isle,
This earth of Majesty, this seat of Mars,
This other Eden, demi-paradise,
This fortress built by Nature for herself,
Against infection and the hand of war:
This happy breed of men, this little world,
This precious stone, set in the silver sea,
Which serves it in the office of a wall,
Or as a moat defensive to a house,
Against the envy of less happier Lands,
This blessed plot, this earth, this Realm,
  this England.

Shakespeare's later plays, above all the tragedies *Othello, Macbeth,* and *Hamlet,* explore an enormous range of human problems and are open to an almost infinite variety of interpretations. *Othello,* which the nineteenth-century historian Thomas Macaulay called "perhaps the greatest work in the world," portrays an honorable man destroyed by a flaw in his own character and the satanic evil of his supposed friend. The central theme of *Macbeth* is exorbitant ambition. Shakespeare analyzes the psychology of sin in the figures of Macbeth and Lady Macbeth, whose mutual love under the pressure of ambition leads to their destruction. The central figure in *Hamlet,* a play suffused with individuality, wrestles with moral problems connected with revenge and with man's relationship to life and death. The soliloquy in which Hamlet debates suicide is perhaps the most widely quoted passage in English literature:

To be, or not to be: that is the question:
Whether 'tis nobler in the mind to suffer
The slings and arrows of outrageous fortune,
Or to take arms against a sea of troubles,
And by opposing end them? . . .

Hamlet's sad cry, "There is nothing either good or bad but thinking makes it so," expresses the anguish and uncertainty of modern man. *Hamlet* has always enjoyed great popularity because in Hamlet's many-faceted personality people have seen an aspect of themselves.

Shakespeare's dynamic language bespeaks his extreme sensitivity to the sounds and meanings of words. Perhaps no phrase better summarizes the reason for his immortality than these lines, slightly modified, from *Antony and Cleopatra:* "Age cannot wither [him], nor custom stale/[his] infinite variety."

The other great masterpiece of the Jacobean period was the Authorized Bible. At a theological conference in 1604, a group of Puritans urged James I to support a new translation of the Bible. The king assigned the task to a committee of scholars, who published their efforts in 1611. Based on the best scriptural research of the time and divided into chapters and verses, the "Authorized Version," so called because it was produced under royal sponsorship—it had no official ecclesiastical endorsement—is actually a revision of earlier Bibles more than an original work. Yet it provides a superb expression of the mature English vernacular in the early seventeenth century. Thus Psalm 37:

Fret not thy selfe because of evill doers, neither bee
    thou envious against the workers of iniquitie.
For they shall soone be cut downe like the grasse;
    and wither as the greene herbe.
Trust in the Lord, and do good, so shalt thou dwell in
    the land, and verely thou shalt be fed.
Delight thy selfe also in the Lord; and he shall give
    thee the desires of thine heart.
Commit thy way unto the Lord: trust also in him, and
    he shall bring it to passe.
And he shall bring forth thy righteousness as the
    light, and thy judgement as the noone day.

The Authorized Version represented the Anglican and Puritan desire to encourage laypeople to read the Scriptures. It quickly achieved great popularity and displaced all earlier versions. British settlers carried this Bible to the North American colonies, where it became known as the "King James Bible." For centuries the King James Bible has had a profound influence on the language and lives of English-speaking peoples.

BAROQUE ART AND MUSIC

Throughout European history, the cultural tastes of one age have often seemed quite unsatisfactory to the next. So it was with the baroque. The term *baroque* itself may have come from the Portuguese word for an "odd-shaped, imperfect pearl" and was commonly used by late-eighteenth-century art critics as an expression of scorn for what they considered an overblown, unbalanced style. The hostility of these critics, who also scorned the Gothic style of medieval cathedrals in favor of a classicism inspired by antiquity and the Renaissance, has long since passed. Specialists agree that the

Veronese: Mars and Venus United by Love (ca 1580) Taking a theme from classical mythology, the Venetian painter Veronese celebrates in clothing, architecture, and landscape the luxurious wealth of the aristocracy. The lush and curvaceous Venus and the muscular and powerfully built Mars suggest the anticipated pleasures of sexual activity and the frank sensuality of the age. *(Source: The Metropolitan Museum of Art, New York, John Stewart Kennedy Fund, 1910)*

triumphs of the baroque marked one of the high points in the history of Western culture.

The early development of the baroque is complex, but most scholars stress the influence of Rome and the revitalized Catholic church of the later sixteenth century. The papacy and the Jesuits encouraged the growth of an intensely emotional, exuberant art. These patrons wanted artists to go beyond the Renaissance focus on pleasing a small, wealthy cultural elite. They wanted artists to appeal to the senses and thereby touch the souls and kindle the faith of ordinary churchgoers, while proclaiming the power and confidence of the reformed Catholic church. In addition to this underlying religious emotionalism, the baroque drew its sense of drama, motion, and ceaseless striving from the Catholic Reformation. The interior of the famous Jesuit Church of Jesus in Rome—the Gesù—combined all these characteristics in its lavish, shimmering decorations and frescoes.

Velázquez: Juan de Pareja This portrait (1650) of the Spanish painter Velázquez's one-time assistant, a black man of obvious intellectual and sensual power and himself a renowned religious painter, suggests the integration of some blacks in seventeenth-century society. The elegant lace collar attests to his middle-class status. *(Source: The Metropolitan Museum of Art)*

Taking definite shape in Italy after 1600, the baroque style in the visual arts developed with exceptional vigor in Catholic countries—in Spain and Latin America, Austria, southern Germany, and Poland. Yet baroque art was more than just "Catholic art" in the seventeenth century and the first half of the eighteenth. True, neither Protestant England nor the Netherlands ever came fully under the spell of the baroque, but neither did Catholic France. And Protestants accounted for some of the finest examples of baroque style, especially in music. The baroque style spread partly because its tension and bombast spoke to an agitated age, which was experiencing great violence and controversy in politics and religion.

In painting, the baroque reached maturity early with Peter Paul Rubens (1577–1640), the most outstanding and representative of baroque painters. Studying in his native Flanders and in Italy, where he was influenced by masters of the High Renaissance, such as Michelangelo, Rubens developed his own rich, sensuous, colorful style, which was characterized by animated figures, melodramatic contrasts, and monumental size. Although Rubens excelled in glorifying monarchs such as Queen Mother Marie de' Medici of France, he was also a devout Catholic. Nearly half of his pictures treat Christian subjects. Yet one of Rubens's trademarks was fleshy, sensual nudes, who populate his canvases as Roman goddesses, water nymphs, and remarkably voluptuous saints and angels.

Rubens was enormously successful. To meet the demand for his work, he established a large studio and hired many assistants to execute his rough sketches and gigantic murals. Sometimes the master artist added only the finishing touches. Rubens's wealth and position—on occasion he was given special diplomatic assignments by the Habsburgs—attest that distinguished artists continued to enjoy the high social status they had won in the Renaissance.

In music, the baroque style reached its culmination almost a century later in the dynamic, soaring lines of the endlessly inventive Johann Sebastian Bach (1685–1750), one of the greatest composers the Western world has ever produced. Organist and choir master of several Lutheran churches across Germany, Bach was equally at home writing secular concertos and sublime religious cantatas. Bach's organ music, the greatest ever written, combined the baroque spirit of invention, tension, and emotion in an unforgettable striving toward the infinite. Bach was not fully appreciated in his lifetime, but since the early 1800s his reputation has grown steadily.

SUMMARY

In the sixteenth and seventeenth centuries, Europeans for the first time gained access to large parts of the globe. European peoples had the intellectual curiosity, driving ambition, and scientific technology to attempt feats that were as difficult and expensive then as going to the moon is today. Exploration and exploitation contributed to a more sophisticated standard of living in the form of spices and Asian luxury goods and to a terrible international inflation resulting from the influx of South American silver and gold. Governments, the upper classes, and especially the peasantry were badly hurt by the inflation. Meanwhile the middle class of bankers, shippers, financiers, and manufacturers prospered for much of the seventeenth century.

Europeans' technological development contributed to their conquest of Aztec Mexico and Inca Peru. Along with technology, Europeans brought disease to the New World, which caused a terrible holocaust among the Indians. Overseas reconnaissance led to the first global seaborne commercial empires of the Portuguese, the Spanish, and the Dutch.

European expansion and colonization took place against a background of religious conflict and rising national consciousness. The sixteenth and seventeenth centuries were by no means a secular period. Although the medieval religious framework had broken down, people still thought largely in religious terms. Europeans explained what they did politically and economically in terms of religious doctrine. Religious ideology served as a justification for a variety of conflicts: the French nobles' opposition to the Crown, the Dutch struggle for political and economic independence from Spain. In Germany, religious pluralism and foreign ambitions added to political difficulties. After 1648 the divisions between Protestant and Catholic tended to become permanent. Sexism, racism, and religious skepticism were harbingers of developments to come.

NOTES

1. Quoted in C. M. Cipolla, *Guns, Sails, and Empires: Technological Innovation and the Early Phases of European Expansion, 1400–1700* (New York: Minerva Press, 1965), pp. 115–116.
2. Quoted in S. E. Morison, *Admiral of the Ocean Sea: A Life of Christopher Columbus* (Boston: Little, Brown, 1946), p. 154.
3. See C. R. Phillips, *Ciudad Real, 1500–1750: Growth, Crisis, and Readjustment in the Spanish Economy* (Cambridge, Mass.: Harvard University Press, 1979), pp. 103–104, 115.
4. Quoted in Cipolla, p. 132.
5. Quoted in F. H. Littell, *The Macmillan Atlas History of Christianity* (New York: Macmillan, 1976), p. 75.
6. Quoted in Cipolla, p. 133.
7. J. H. Parry, *The Age of Reconnaissance: Discovery, Exploration and Settlement, 1450–1650* (Berkeley: University of California Press, 1981), chaps. 3, 5.
8. G. C. Vaillant, *Aztecs of Mexico* (New York: Penguin Books, 1979), p. 241. Chapter 15, on which this section leans, is fascinating.
9. V. W. Von Hagen, *Realm of the Incas* (New York: New American Library, 1961), pp. 204–207.
10. N. Sanchez-Albornoz, *The Population of Latin America: A History*, trans. W. A. R. Richardson (Berkeley: University of California Press, 1974), p. 41.
11. Quoted in A. W. Crosby, *The Columbian Exchange: Biological and Cultural Consequences of 1492* (Westport, Conn.: Greenwood Publishing, 1972), p. 39.
12. Ibid., chap. 2, pp. 35–59.
13. Quoted in C. Gibson, ed., *The Black Legend: Anti-Spanish Attitudes in the Old World and the New* (New York: Knopf, 1971), pp. 74–75.
14. Quoted in L. B. Rout, Jr., *The African Experience in Spanish America* (New York: Cambridge University Press, 1976), p. 23.
15. See Parry, chaps. 12, 14, 15.
16. Quoted in S. Neill, *A History of Christian Missions* (New York: Penguin Books, 1977), p. 163.
17. Quoted in C. M. Cipolla, *Clocks and Culture: 1300–1700* (New York: Norton, 1978), p. 86.
18. J. Gernet, *A History of Chinese Civilization* (New York: Cambridge University Press, 1982), p. 458.
19. Quoted in A. J. Andrea and J. H. Overfield, *The Human Record*, vol. 1, Boston: Houghton Mifflin, 1990), pp. 406–407.
20. Ibid., p. 408.
21. See Donald Keene, *The Japanese Discovery of Europe*, rev. ed. (Stanford, Calif.: Stanford University Press, 1969), pp. 1–17. The quotation is on page 16.
22. See J. Hale, "War and Public Opinion in the Fifteenth and Sixteenth Centuries," *Past and Present* 22 (July 1962): 18–32.

23. Quoted in N. Z. Davis, "The Rites of Violence: Religious Riots in Sixteenth Century France," *Past and Present* 59 (May 1973): 59.

24. See ibid., pp. 51–91.

25. Quoted in J. L. Motley, *The Rise of the Dutch Republic,* vol. 1 (Philadelphia: David McKay, 1898), p. 109.

26. Quoted in P. Smith, *The Age of the Reformation* (New York: Henry Holt, 1951), p. 248.

27. H. Kamen, "The Economic and Social Consequences of the Thirty Years' War," *Past and Present* 39 (April 1968): 44–61.

28. Based heavily on S. Ozment, *When Fathers Ruled: Family Life in Reformation Europe* (Cambridge, Mass.: Harvard University Press, 1983), pp. 50–99.

29. Ibid., pp. 85–92.

30. See D. Durant, *Bess of Hardwick: Portrait of an Elizabethan Dynasty* (London: Weidenfeld & Nicolson, 1977).

31. Quoted in Ozment, p. 56.

32. Ibid., pp. 9–14.

33. See F. Biot, *The Rise of Protestant Monasticism* (Baltimore: Helicon Press, 1968), pp. 74–78.

34. N. Cohn, *Europe's Inner Demons: An Enquiry Inspired by the Great Witch-Hunt* (New York: Basic Books, 1975), pp. 253–254; K. Thomas, *Religion and the Decline of Magic* (New York: Scribner's, 1971), pp. 450–455.

35. See E. W. Monter, "The Pedestal and the Stake: Courtly Love and Witchcraft," in *Becoming Visible: Women in European History,* ed. R. Bridenthal and C. Koonz (Boston: Houghton Mifflin, 1977), pp. 132–135, and A. Fraser, *The Weaker Vessel* (New York: Random House, 1985), pp. 100–103.

36. See C. Verlinden, *The Beginnings of Modern Colonization,* trans. Y. Freccero (Ithaca, N.Y.: Cornell University Press, 1970), pp. 5–6, 80–97.

37. This section leans heavily on D. B. Davis, *Slavery and Human Progress* (New York: Oxford University Press, 1984), pp. 54–62.

38. Quoted in D. P. Mannix with M. Cordley, *Black Cargoes: A History of the Atlantic Slave Trade* (New York: Viking, 1968), p. 5.

39. Ibid., p. 19.

40. Quoted in Davis, p. 40.

41. Ibid., pp. 43–44.

42. W. Rodney, "Africa, Europe and the Americas," in R. Gray, ed., *Cambridge History of Africa,* vol. 4 (Cambridge, England: Cambridge University Press, 1975), pp. 580–581, 590.

43. Quoted in D. M. Frame, trans., *The Complete Works of Montaigne* (Stanford, Calif.: Stanford University Press, 1958), pp. 175–176.

44. Ibid., p. 177.

45. Quoted in C. Cotton, trans., *The Essays of Michel de Montaigne* (New York: A. L. Burt, 1893), pp. 207, 210.

46. Ibid., p. 523.

SUGGESTED READING

Perhaps the best starting point for the study of European society in the age of exploration is Parry's *Age of Reconnaissance,* cited in the Notes, which treats the causes and consequences of the voyages of discovery. Parry's splendidly illustrated *The Discovery of South America* (1979) examines Europeans' reactions to the maritime discoveries and treats the entire concept of new discoveries. For the earliest British reaction to the Japanese, see *A World Elsewhere: Europe's Encounter with Japan in the Sixteenth and Seventeenth Centuries* (1990). The urbane studies of C. M. Cipolla present fascinating material on technological and sociological developments written in a lucid style: In addition to the titles cited in the Notes, see *Cristofano and the Plague: A Study in the History of Public Health in the Age of Galileo* (1973) and *Public Health and the Medical Profession in the Renaissance* (1976). Morison's *Admiral of the Ocean Sea,* also listed in the Notes, is the standard biography of Columbus. The advanced student should consult F. Braudel, *Civilization and Capitalism, 15th–18th Century,* trans. S. Reynolds, vol. 1, *The Structures of Everyday Life* (1981); vol. 2, *The Wheels of Commerce* (1982); and vol. 3, *The Perspective of the World* (1984). These three fat volumes combine vast erudition, a global perspective, and remarkable illustrations. For the political ideas that formed the background of the first Spanish overseas empire, see A. Pagden, *Spanish Imperialism and the Political Imagination* (1990).

For the religious wars, in addition to the references in the Suggested Reading for Chapter 17 and the Notes to this chapter, see J. H. M. Salmon, *Society in Crisis: France in the Sixteenth Century* (1975), which traces the fate of French institutions during the civil wars. A. N. Galpern, *The Religions of the People in Sixteenth-Century Champagne* (1976), is a useful case study in religious anthropology, and W. A. Christian, Jr., *Local Religion in Sixteenth Century Spain* (1981), traces the attitudes and practices of ordinary people.

A cleverly illustrated introduction to the Low Countries is K. H. D. Kaley, *The Dutch in the Seventeenth Century* (1972). The old study of J. L. Motley cited in the Notes still provides a good comprehensive treatment and makes fascinating reading. For Spanish military operations in the Low Countries, see G. Parker, *The Army of Flanders and the Spanish Road, 1567–1659: The Logistics of Spanish Victory and Defeat in the Low Countries' Wars* (1972). The same author's *Spain and the Nether-*

lands, 1559–1659: Ten Studies (1979) contains useful essays, of which students may especially want to consult "Why Did the Dutch Revolt Last So Long?" For the later phases of the Dutch-Spanish conflict, see J. I. Israel, *The Dutch Republic and the Hispanic World, 1606–1661* (1982), which treats the struggle in global perspective.

Of the many biographies of Elizabeth of England, W. T. MacCaffrey, *Queen Elizabeth and the Making of Policy, 1572–1588* (1981), examines the problems posed by the Reformation and how Elizabeth solved them. J. E. Neale, *Queen Elizabeth I* (1957), remains valuable, and L. B. Smith, *The Elizabethan Epic* (1966), is a splendid evocation of the age of Shakespeare with Elizabeth at the center. The best recent biography is C. Erickson, *The First Elizabeth* (1983), a fine, psychologically resonant portrait.

Nineteenth- and early twentieth-century historians described the defeat of the Spanish Armada as a great victory for Protestantism, democracy, and capitalism, which those scholars tended to link together. Recent historians have treated the event in terms of its contemporary significance. For a sympathetic but judicious portrait of the man who launched the armada, see G. Parker, *Philip II* (1978). The best recent study of the leader of the armada is P. Pierson, *Commander of the Armada: The Seventh Duke of Medina Sidonia* (1989). D. Howarth, *The Voyage of the Armada* (1982), discusses the expedition largely in terms of the individuals involved, and G. Mattingly, *The Armada* (1959), gives the diplomatic and political background; both Howarth and Mattingly tell very exciting tales. M. Lewis, *The Spanish Armada* (1972), also tells a good story, but strictly from the English perspective. Significant aspects of Portuguese culture are treated in A. Hower and R. Preto-Rodas, eds., *Empire in Transition: The Portuguese World in the Time of Camões* (1985).

C. V. Wedgwood, *The Thirty Years' War* (1961), must be qualified in light of recent research on the social and economic effects of the war, but it is still a good (if detailed) starting point on a difficult period. Various opinions on the causes and results of the war are given in T. K. Rabb's anthology, *The Thirty Years' War* (1981). In addition to the articles by Hale and Kamen cited in the Notes, the following articles, both of which appear in the scholarly journal *Past and Present,* provide some of the latest important findings: J. V. Polisensky, "The Thirty Years' War and the Crises and Revolutions of Sixteenth Century Europe," 39 (1968), and M. Roberts, "Queen Christina and the General Crisis of the Seventeenth Century," 22 (1962).

As background to the intellectual changes instigated by the Reformation, D. C. Wilcox, *In Search of God and Self: Renaissance and Reformation Thought* (1975), contains a perceptive analysis, and T. Ashton, ed., *Crisis in Europe, 1560–1660* (1967), is fundamental. For women, marriage, and the family, see L. Stone, *The Family, Sex, and Marriage in England, 1500–1800* (1977), an important but controversial work; D. Underdown, "The Taming of the Scold," and S. Amussen, "Gender, Family, and the Social Order," in A. Fletcher and J. Stevenson, eds., *Order and Disorder in Early Modern England* (1985); A. Macfarlane, *Marriage and Love in England: Modes of Reproduction, 1300–1848* (1986); C. R. Boxer, *Women in Iberian Expansion Overseas, 1415–1815* (1975), an invaluable study of women's role in overseas immigration; and S. M. Wyntjes, "Women in the Reformation Era," in Bridenthal and Koonz's *Becoming Visible* (see the Notes), a quick survey of conditions in different countries. Ozment's *When Fathers Ruled,* cited in the Notes, is a seminal study concentrating on Germany and Switzerland.

On witches and witchcraft see, in addition to the titles by Cohn and Thomas in the Notes, J. B. Russell, *Witchcraft in the Middle Ages* (1976) and *Lucifer: The Devil in the Middle Ages* (1984); M. Summers, *The History of Witchcraft and Demonology* (1973); and H. R. Trevor-Roper, *The European Witch-Craze of the Sixteenth and Seventeenth Centuries* (1967), an important collection of essays.

As background to slavery and racism in North and South America, students should see J. L. Watson, ed., *Asian and African Systems of Slavery* (1980), a valuable collection of essays. Davis's *Slavery and Human Progress,* cited in the Notes, shows how slavery was viewed as a progressive force in the expansion of the Western world. For North American conditions, interested students should consult W. D. Jordan, *The White Man's Burden: Historical Origins of Racism in the United States* (1974), and the title by Mannix listed in the Notes, a hideously fascinating account. For Caribbean and South American developments, see F. P. Bowser, *The African Slave in Colonial Peru* (1974); J. S. Handler and F. W. Lange, *Plantation Slavery in Barbados: An Archeological and Historical Investigation* (1978); and R. E. Conrad, *Children of God's Fire: A Documentary History of Black Slavery in Brazil* (1983).

The leading authority on Montaigne is D. M. Frame. In addition to his translation of Montaigne's works cited in the Notes, see his *Montaigne's Discovery of Man* (1955).

19

Absolutism and Constitutionalism in Europe, ca 1589–1725

Peter the Great's Summer Palace at Peterhof

The seventeenth century in Europe was an age of intense conflict and crisis. The crisis had many causes, but the era's almost continuous savage warfare—which led governments to build enormous armies and levy ever higher taxes on an already hard-pressed, predominately peasant population—was probably the most important factor. Deteriorating economic conditions also played a major role, although economic depression was not universal and it struck different regions at different times and in varying degrees. An unusually cold and wet climate over many years resulted in smaller harvests, periodic food shortages, and even starvation. Not least, the combination of war, increased taxation, and economic suffering triggered social unrest and widespread peasant revolts, which were both a cause and an effect of profound dislocation.

The many-sided crisis of the seventeenth century posed a grave challenge to European governments: how were they to maintain order? Although there were significant variations in timing and tactics, the most basic response of monarchical governments was to seek more power to deal with the problems and the threats that they perceived. Indeed, European rulers in this period generally sought to attain complete or "absolute" power and build absolutist states. Thus monarchs fought to free themselves from the restrictions of custom, competing institutions, and powerful social groups. Above all, monarchs sought freedom from the nobility and from traditional representative bodies—most commonly known as Estates or Parliament—that were usually dominated by the nobility. The monarchical demand for freedom of action upset the status quo and it led to furious political battles; but in most countries the monarch was largely successful.

Not surprisingly, there were important national variations in the development of absolutism. The most spectacular example occurred in western Europe, where Louis XIV built upon the heritage of a well-developed monarchy and a strong royal bureaucracy. Moreover, when Louis XIV came to the throne, the powers of the nobility were already somewhat limited, the French middle class was relatively strong, and the peasants were generally free from serfdom. In eastern Europe and Russia, absolutism emerged out of a very different social reality: a powerful nobility, a weak middle class, and an oppressed peasantry composed of serfs. Thus eastern monarchs generally had to compromise with their nobilities as they fashioned absolutist states. Finally, royal absolutism did not triumph in Holland and England. In England especially the opponents of unrestrained monarchical authority succeeded in firmly establishing a constitutional state, which guaranteed that henceforth Parliament and the monarch would share power.

Thus in the period between roughly 1589 and 1725, two basic patterns of government emerged in Europe: absolute monarchy and the constitutional state. Almost all subsequent governments in the West have been modeled on one of these patterns, which have also influenced greatly the rest of the world in the last three centuries.

- How did absolute monarchy and the constitutional state differ from the feudal and dynastic monarchies of earlier centuries?
- How and why did Louis XIV of France lead the way in forging the absolute state?
- Why did the basic structure of society in eastern Europe move away from that of western Europe in the early modern period?
- How did Austrian, Prussian, and Russian rulers build powerful absolute monarchies more durable than the monarchy of Louis XIV?
- How did the absolute monarchs' interaction with artists, architects, and writers contribute to the splendid cultural achievements of both western and eastern Europe in this period?
- What were the characteristics of the constitutional state, and why did it rather than absolutism triumph in Holland and England?

This chapter explores these questions.

ABSOLUTISM: AN OVERVIEW

In an *absolutist* state, the ultimate political power—what legal theorists call sovereignty—is embodied in the person of the ruler. Whether or not Louis XIV actually said, "L'état, c'est moi!" ("I am the state!"), the remark expresses his belief that he personified the French nation. Absolute kings claim to rule by *divine right:* they believe that they are responsible to God alone.

Claiming that they alone possessed sovereignty, absolute rulers tried to control competing jurisdictions, institutions, or interest groups in their territories. They regulated religious sects. They abolished the liberties long held by certain areas, groups, or provinces. They also curtailed or eliminated the traditional representative bodies that had frequently consulted and sometimes even legislated with the monarchs. Absolute kings also secured the cooperation of the one class that had posed the greatest threat to monarchy: the nobility. Medieval governments, restrained by the church, the feudal nobility, and their own financial limitations, had been able to exert none of these controls.

In some respects, the key to the power and success of absolute monarchs lay in how they solved their financial problems. Medieval kings frequently had found temporary financial support through bargains with the nobility: the nobility would agree to an ad hoc grant in return for freedom from future taxation. In contrast, the absolutist solution was the creation of new state bureaucracies, which directed the economic life of the country in the interests of the king, either forcing taxes ever higher or devising alternative methods of raising revenue.

Bureaucracies were composed of career officials appointed by and solely accountable to the king. The backgrounds of these civil servants varied. Absolute monarchs sometimes drew on the middle class, as in France, or they utilized members of the nobility, as in Spain and eastern Europe. Where there was no middle class or an insignificant one, as in Austria, Prussia, Spain, and Russia, the government of the absolutist state consisted of an interlocking elite of monarchy, aristocracy, and bureaucracy.

Royal agents in medieval and Renaissance kingdoms had used their public offices and positions to benefit themselves and their families. Seventeenth-century civil servants, however, served the state as represented by the king. Bureaucrats recognized that the offices they held were public, or state, positions. The state paid them salaries to handle revenues that belonged to the Crown, and they were not supposed to use their positions for private gain. Bureaucrats gradually came to distinguish between public duties and private property.

Absolute monarchs also won the right to maintain permanent standing armies. Medieval armies had been raised by feudal lords for particular wars or campaigns, after which the troops were disbanded. In the seventeenth century, monarchs alone recruited and maintained armies—in peacetime as well as during war. Kings deployed their troops both inside and outside the country in the interests of the monarchy. Absolute rulers also invented new methods of compulsion. They concerned themselves with the private lives of potentially troublesome subjects, often through the use of secret police.

The rule of absolute monarchs was not all-embracing because they lacked the financial and military resources and the technology to make it so. Thus the absolutist state was not the same as a totalitarian state. *Totalitarianism* is a twentieth-century phenomenon; it seeks to direct all facets of a state's culture—art, education, religion, the economy, and politics—in the interests of the state. By definition totalitarian rule strives for *total* regulation. By twentieth-century standards, the ambitions of absolute monarchs were quite limited. Yet the absolutist state did foreshadow recent totalitarian regimes in two fundamental respects: in the glorification of the state over all other aspects of the culture and in the use of war and an expansionist foreign policy to divert attention from domestic ills.

All of this is well illustrated by the experience of France, aptly known as the model of absolute monarchy.

FRANCE: THE MODEL OF ABSOLUTE MONARCHY

France had a long history of unifying and centralizing monarchy, although the actual power and effectiveness of the French kings had varied enormously over time. Passing through a time of troubles and civil war after the death of Henry II in 1559, both France and the monarchy recovered under Henry IV and Cardinal Richelieu in the early seventeenth century. They laid the foundations for fully developed French absolutism under the "Great Monarch," Louis XIV. Having provided inspiration for rulers all across Europe, Louis XIV and the mighty machine he fashioned deserve special attention.

The Foundations of French Absolutism: Henry IV and Richelieu

Henry IV, the ingenious Huguenot-turned-Catholic, ended the French religious wars with the Edict of Nantes (1598). The first of the Bourbon dynasty, and probably the first French ruler since Louis IX in the thirteenth century genuinely to care about the French people, Henry IV and his great minister Maximilian de Béthune, duke of Sully (1560–1641), laid the foundations of later French absolutism. Henry denied influence on the royal council to the nobility, which had harassed the countryside for half a century. Maintaining that "if we are without compassion for the people, they must succumb and we all perish with them," Henry also lowered taxes paid by the overburdened peasantry.

Sully reduced the crushing royal debt accumulated during the era of religious conflict and began to build up the treasury. One of the first French officials to appreciate the significance of overseas trade, Sully subsidized the Company for Trade with the Indies. He started a countrywide highway system and even dreamed of an international organization for the maintenance of peace.

In twelve years, Henry IV and Sully restored public order in France and laid the foundation for economic prosperity. By the standards of the time, Henry IV's government was progressive and promising. His murder in 1610 by a crazed fanatic led to a severe crisis.

After the death of Henry IV, the queen-regent Marie de' Medici led the government for the child-king Louis XIII (r. 1610–1643), but feudal nobles and princes of the blood dominated the political scene. In 1624 Marie de' Medici secured the appointment of Armand Jean du Plessis—Cardinal Richelieu (1585–1642)—to the council of ministers. It was a remarkable appointment. The next year Richelieu became president of the council, and after 1628 he was first minister of the French crown. Richelieu used his strong influence over King Louis XIII to exalt the French monarchy as the embodiment of the French state. One of the greatest servants of the French state, Richelieu set in place the cornerstone of French absolutism, and his work served as the basis for France's cultural domination of Europe in the later seventeenth century.

Richelieu's policy was the total subordination of all groups and institutions to the French monarchy. The French nobility, with its selfish and independent interests, had long constituted the foremost threat to the centralizing goals of the Crown and to a strong national state. Therefore, Richelieu tried to break the power of the nobility. He leveled castles, long the symbol of feudal independence. He crushed aristocratic conspiracies with quick executions, and he never called a session of the Estates General—the ancient representative body of the medieval orders that was primarily a representative of the nobility.

The constructive genius of Cardinal Richelieu is best reflected in the administrative system he established. He extended the use of the royal commissioners called *intendants,* each of whom held authority in one of France's thirty-two *généralités* ("districts"). The intendants were authorized "to decide, order and execute all that they see good to do." Usually members of the upper middle class or minor nobility, the intendants were appointed directly by the monarch, to whom they were solely responsible. The intendants recruited men for the army, supervised the collection of taxes, presided over the administration of local law, checked up on the local nobility, and regulated economic activities—commerce, trade, the guilds, marketplaces—in their districts. They were to use their power for two related purposes: to enforce royal orders in the généralités of their jurisdiction and to weaken the power and influence of the regional nobility. As the intendants' power grew during Richelieu's administration, so did the power of the centralized state.

The cardinal perceived that Protestantism often served as a cloak for the political intrigues of ambitious lords. When the Huguenots revolted in 1625, under the duke of Rohan, Richelieu personally supervised the siege of their walled city, La Rochelle, and forced it to surrender. Thereafter, fortified cities were abolished. Huguenots were allowed to practice their faith, but they no longer possessed armed strongholds or the means to be an independent party in the state.

French foreign policy under Richelieu was aimed at the destruction of the fence of Habsburg territories that surrounded France. Consequently, Richelieu supported the Habsburgs' enemies. In 1631 he signed a treaty with the Lutheran king Gustavus Adolphus, promising French support against the Catholic Habsburgs in what has been called the Swedish phase of the Thirty Years' War (see page 591). French influence became an important factor in the political future of the German Empire.

These new policies, especially war, cost money. Richelieu fully realized that revenues determine a government's ability to inaugurate and enforce policies and programs. A state secures its revenues through taxation. But seventeenth-century France remained "a collection of local economies and local societies dominated by local elites." The government's power to tax was limited by the rights of assemblies in some provinces (such as Brittany) to vote their own taxes, the hereditary exemption from taxation of many wealthy members of the nobility and the middle class, and the royal pension system. Richelieu—and later Louis XIV—temporarily solved their financial problems by securing the cooperation of local elites. But because the French monarchy could not tax at will, it never completely controlled the financial system. Thus French absolutism was restrained by its need to compromise with the financial interests of well-entrenched groups.[1]

In building the French state, Richelieu believed that he had to take drastic measures against persons and groups within France and conduct a tough anti-Habsburg foreign policy. He knew that his approach sometimes seemed to contradict traditional Christian teaching. As a priest and bishop, how did he justify his policies? He developed his own *raison d'état* ("reason of state"): "What is done for the state is done for God, who is the basis and foundation of it." Richelieu had no doubt that "the French state was a Christian state . . . governed by a Christian monarch with the valuable aid of an enlightened Cardinal Minister." "Where the interests of the state are concerned," the cardinal himself wrote, "God absolves actions which, if privately committed, would be a crime."[2]

Richelieu persuaded Louis XIII to appoint his protégé Jules Mazarin (1602–1661) as his successor. When Louis XIII followed Richelieu to the grave in 1643 and a regency headed by Queen Anne of Austria governed for the child-king Louis XIV, Mazarin became the dominant power in the government. He continued the centralizing policies of Richelieu, but his attempts to increase royal revenues led to the civil wars known as the "Fronde." The word *fronde* means "slingshot" or "catapult," and a *frondeur* was originally a street urchin who threw mud at the passing carriages of the rich. The term came to be used for anyone who opposed the policies of the government.

Philippe de Champaigne: Cardinal Richelieu This portrait, with its penetrating eyes, expression of haughty and imperturbable cynicism, and dramatic sweep of red robes, suggests the authority, grandeur, and power that Richelieu wished to convey as first minister of France. *(Source: Reproduced by courtesy of the Trustees, The National Gallery, London)*

By 1660 the state bureaucracy included about sixty thousand officeholders, who represented a great expansion of the royal presence. These officeholders and state bureaucrats extracted the wealth of the working people and were the bitter targets of the exploited peasants and artisans. But these officials, who considered their positions the path to economic and social advancement, felt that they were being manipulated by the Crown and their interests ignored.[3] When in 1648 Mazarin proposed new methods of raising state income, bitter civil war ensued between the monarchy and the frondeurs (the nobility and middle class). Riots and turmoil wracked Paris and the nation. Violence continued intermittently for the next twelve years.

The conflicts of the Fronde had three significant results for the future. First, it became apparent that the government would have to compromise with the bureaucrats and social elites who controlled local institutions and constituted the state bureaucracy. These groups were already largely exempt from taxation, and Louis XIV confirmed their privileged social status. Second, the French economy was badly disrupted and would take years to rebuild. Finally, the Fronde had a traumatic effect on the young Louis XIV. The king and his mother were frequently threatened and sometimes treated as prisoners by aristocratic factions. This period formed the cornerstone of Louis's political education and of his conviction that the sole alternative to anarchy was to concentrate as much power as possible in his hands.

The Absolute Monarchy of Louis XIV

In the reign of Louis XIV (r. 1643–1715), the longest in European history, the French monarchy reached the peak of its absolutist development. In the magnificence of his court, in his absolute power, in the brilliance of the culture over which he presided and which permeated all of Europe, and in his remarkably long life, the "Sun King" dominated his age. It was said that when Louis sneezed, all Europe caught cold.

Born in 1638, king at the age of five, Louis entered into personal, or independent, rule in 1661. He imbibed the devout Catholicism of his mother, Anne of Austria, and throughout his life scrupulously performed his religious duties. Religion, Anne, and Mazarin all taught Louis that God had established kings as his rulers on earth. The royal coronation consecrated Louis to God's service, and he was certain that although kings were a race apart, they had to obey God's laws and rule for the good of the people.

Louis's education was more practical than formal. Under Mazarin's instruction, he conscientiously studied state papers as they arrived, and he attended council meetings. He learned by direct experience, and the misery he suffered during the Fronde gave Louis an eternal distrust of the nobility and a profound sense of his own isolation. Accordingly, silence, caution, and secrecy became political tools for the achievement of his goals. His characteristic answer to requests of all kinds became the enigmatic "Je verrai" ("I shall see").

Louis grew up with a strong sense of his royal dignity. Contemporaries considered him tall and distinguished in appearance but inclined to heavi-

Coysevox: Louis XIV (1687–1689) The French court envisioned a new classical age with the Sun King as emperor and his court as a new Rome. This statue depicts Louis in a classical pose, clothed (except for the wig) as for a Roman military triumph. *(Source: Caisse Nationale des Monuments Historiques et des Sites, Paris. Copyright 1990 ARS N.Y./SPADEM)*

ness because of the gargantuan meals in which he indulged. A highly sensual man easily aroused by an attractive female face and figure, Louis nonetheless ruled without the political influence of either his wife, Queen Maria Theresa, or his mistresses. A consummate actor, he worked extremely hard and succeeded in being "every moment and every inch a king."

Historians have often said that Louis XIV was able to control completely the nobility, which historically had opposed the centralizing goals of the French monarchy. Recent research, however, has demonstrated that Louis XIV actually secured the cooperation or collaboration of the nobility. The nobility agreed to participate in projects that both exalted the monarchy and reinforced the aristocrats' ancient prestige. Through collaboration, the nobility and the king achieved goals that neither could have won alone. Thus French government in the seventeenth century rested on a social and political structure in which the nobility exercised great influence. In this respect, French absolutism was not so much modern as the last phase of a feudal society.[4]

Louis XIV installed his royal court at Versailles, a small town 10 miles from Paris. Louis XIII began Versailles as a hunting lodge, a retreat from a queen he did not like. His son's architects, Le Nôtre and Le Vau, turned what the duke of Saint-Simon called "the most dismal and thankless of sights" into a veritable paradise. Louis XIV required all the great nobility of France—at the peril of social, political, and sometimes economic disaster—to live at Versailles for at least part of the year. Today Versailles stands as the best surviving museum of a vanished society. In the seventeenth century, it became a model of rational order, the center of France and thus the center of Western civilization, the perfect symbol of the king's power. In the gigantic Hall of Mirrors, later to reflect so much of German as well as French history, hundreds of candles illuminated the domed ceiling, where allegorical paintings celebrated the king's victories. Thus Louis skillfully used the art and architecture of Versailles to overawe his subjects and foreign visitors and reinforce his power. Many monarchs subsequently imitated Louis XIV's example.

As in architecture, so too in language. Beginning in the reign of Louis XIV, French became the language of polite society and the vehicle of diplomatic exchange. French gradually replaced Latin as the language of international scholarship and learning. The wish of other kings to ape the courtly style of Louis XIV spread the language all over Europe. The royal courts of Sweden, Russia, Poland, and Germany all spoke French. France inspired a cosmopolitan European culture in the late seventeenth century, and that culture was inspired by the king.

Against this background of magnificent splendor, as Saint-Simon describes him, Louis XIV

> . . . reduced everyone to subjection, and brought to his court those very persons he cared least about. Whoever was old enough to serve did not dare demur. It was still another device to ruin the nobles by accustoming them to equality and forcing them to mingle with everyone indiscriminately. . . .
>
> Upon rising, at bedtime, during meals, in his apartments, in the gardens of Versailles, everywhere the courtiers had a right to follow, he would glance right and left to see who was there; he saw and noted everyone; he missed no one, even those who were hoping they would not be seen. . . .
>
> Louis XIV took great pains to inform himself on what was happening everywhere, in public places, private homes, and even on the international scene. . . . Spies and informers of all kinds were numberless. . . .
>
> But the King's most vicious method of securing information was opening letters.[5]

Although this passage was written by one of Louis's severest critics, all agree that the king used court ceremonial to curb the great nobility. By excluding the highest nobles from his councils, he weakened their ancient right to advise the king and to participate in government; they became mere instruments of royal policy. Operas, fêtes, balls, gossip, and trivia occupied the nobles' time and attention. Thus Louis XIV separated power from status and grandeur: he secured the nobles' cooperation, and the nobility enjoyed the status and grandeur in which they lived.

In government Louis utilized several councils of state, which he personally attended, and the intendants, who acted for the councils throughout France. A stream of questions and instructions flowed between local districts and Versailles, and under Louis XIV a uniform and centralized administration was imposed on the country. The councilors of state came from the upper middle class or from the recently ennobled, who were popularly known as the "nobility of the robe" (because of the long judicial robes many of them wore). These ambitious professional bureaucrats served the state in the person of the king, but they clearly did not share power with the monarch, as great nobles had in the past.

Throughout Louis's long reign and despite increasing financial problems, he never called a meeting of the Estates General. Thus the nobility had no means of united expression or action. Nor did Louis have a first minister; he kept himself free from worry about the inordinate power of a Richelieu. Louis's use of spying and terror—a secret police force, a system of informers, and the practice of opening private letters—foreshadowed some of the devices of the modern state. French government remained highly structured, bureaucratic, centered at Versailles, and responsible to Louis XIV.

Financial and Economic Management Under Louis XIV: Colbert

Louis XIV's bureaucracy, court, and army cost a great amount of money, and the French method of collecting taxes consistently failed to produce the necessary revenue. Tax collectors pocketed a good portion of what they raked in. In addition, an old agreement between the Crown and the nobility permitted the king to tax the common people if he did not tax the nobles. That agreement weakened the nobility's role in government: since they did not pay taxes, they could not legitimately claim a say in how tax money was spent. Louis, however, lost enormous potential revenue. The middle classes, moreover, secured many tax exemptions. With the rich and prosperous classes exempt, the tax burden fell heavily on those least able to pay: the poor peasants.

The king named Jean-Baptiste Colbert (1619–1683), the son of a wealthy merchant-financier of Reims, as controller-general of finances. Colbert came to manage the entire royal administration and proved himself a financial genius. Colbert's central principle was that the wealth and the economy of France should serve the state. He did not invent the system called "mercantilism," but he rigorously applied it to France.

Mercantilism is a collection of government policies for the regulation of economic activities, especially commercial activities, by and for the state. In seventeenth- and eighteenth-century economic theory, a nation's international power was thought to be based on its wealth, and specifically the gold so necessary for fighting wars. To accumulate gold, a country should always sell more goods abroad than it bought. Colbert, however, insisted that France should be self-sufficient, able to produce within its borders everything needed by the subjects of the French king. Consequently, the outflow of gold would be halted; debtor states would pay in bullion; and, with the wealth of the nation increased, its power and prestige would be enhanced.

Colbert attempted to accomplish self-sufficiency through state support for both old industries and newly created ones. He subsidized the established cloth industries at Abbeville, Saint-Quentin, and Carcassonne. New factories at Saint-Antoine in Paris manufactured mirrors to replace Venetian imports, and foundries at Saint-Étienne made steel and firearms that reduced Swedish imports. To ensure a high-quality finished product, Colbert set up a system of state inspection and regulation. He compelled all craftsmen to organize into guilds, and within every guild he gave the masters absolute power over their workers. Colbert encouraged skilled foreign craftsmen and manufacturers to immigrate to France, and he gave them special privileges. To improve communications, he built roads and canals, the most famous linking the Mediterranean and the Bay of Biscay. To protect French goods, he abolished many domestic tariffs and enacted high foreign tariffs, which prevented foreign products from competing with French ones.

Colbert's most important work was the creation of a powerful merchant marine to transport French goods. He gave bonuses to French shipowners and shipbuilders and established maritime conscription, arsenals, and academies for the training of sailors. In 1661 France possessed 18 unseaworthy vessels; by 1681 it had 276 frigates, galleys, and ships of the line. Colbert tried to organize and regulate the entire French economy for the glory of the French state as embodied in the king.

Colbert's achievement in the development of manufacturing was prodigious. The textile industry, especially in woolens, expanded enormously, and "France . . . had become in 1683 the leading nation of the world in industrial productivity."[6] The commercial classes prospered, and between 1660 and 1700 their position steadily improved.

The national economy, however, rested on agriculture. Although French peasants were not serfs, as were the peasants of eastern Europe, they were mercilessly taxed. After 1685 other hardships afflicted them: poor harvests, continuing deflation of the currency, and fluctuation in the price of grain. Many peasants emigrated. With the decline in population and thus in the number of taxable people, the state's resources fell. A totally inadequate tax base and heavy expenditure for war in the later years of Louis's reign made Colbert's goals unattainable.

Revocation of the Edict of Nantes

In 1685, Louis XIV revoked the Edict of Nantes. The new law ordered the destruction of churches, the closing of schools, the Catholic baptism of Huguenots, and the exile of Huguenot pastors who refused to renounce their faith. Why? During previous years there had been so many mass conversions (many of them forced) that Madame de Maintenon, Louis's second wife, could say that "nearly all the Huguenots were converted." Some Huguenots had emigrated. Richelieu had already deprived French Calvinists of political rights. Why, then, did Louis, by revoking the edict, persecute some of his most loyal and industrially skilled subjects, force others to flee abroad, and provoke the outrage of Protestant Europe?

Recent scholarship has convincingly shown that Louis XIV was basically tolerant. He insisted on religious unity not for religious but for political reasons. His goal was "one king, one law, one faith." He hated division within the realm and insisted that religious unity was essential to his royal dignity and to the security of the state. The seventeenth century, moreover, was not a tolerant one. France in the early years of Louis's reign permitted religious liberty, but it was not a popular policy. In fact, aristocrats had petitioned Louis to crack down on Protestants. The revocation, however, was solely the king's decision, and it won him enormous praise: "If the flood of congratulation means anything, it . . . was probably the one act of his reign that, at the time, was popular with the majority of his subjects."[7]

Although contemporaries applauded Louis XIV, writers in the eighteenth century and later damned him for intolerance and for the adverse impact that revocation had on the economy and foreign af-

The Spider and the Fly   In reference to the insect symbolism (upper left), the caption on the lower left side of this illustration states, "The noble is the spider, the peasant the fly." The other caption (upper right) notes, "The more people have, the more they want. The poor man brings everything—wheat, fruit, money, vegetables. The greedy lord sitting there ready to take everything will not even give him the favor of a glance." This satirical print summarizes peasant grievances. *(Source: New York Public Library)*

fairs. They claimed that tens of thousands of Huguenot craftsmen, soldiers, and business people emigrated, depriving France of their skills and tax revenues and carrying their bitterness to Holland, England, and Prussia. Modern scholarship has greatly modified this picture. Huguenot settlers in northern Europe did aggravate Protestant hatred for Louis, but the revocation of the Edict of Nantes had only minor and scattered effects on French economic development.[8]

French Classicism

Scholars characterize French art and literature during the age of Louis XIV as "French classicism." French artists and writers of the late seventeenth century deliberately imitated the subject matter and style of classical antiquity; their work resembled that of Renaissance Italy. French art possessed the classical qualities of discipline, balance, and restraint. Classicism was the official style of Louis's court.

After Louis's accession to power, the principles of absolutism molded the ideals of French classicism. Individualism was not allowed, and artists glorified the state as personified by the king. Precise rules governed all aspects of culture. Formal and restrained perfection was the goal.

Contemporaries said that Louis XIV never ceased playing the role of grand monarch on the stage of his court, and he used music and theater as a backdrop for court ceremonial. Louis favored

Jean-Baptiste Lully (1632–1687), whose orchestral works combine lively animation with the restrained austerity typical of French classicism. Lully also composed court ballets, and his operatic productions were a powerful influence throughout Europe. Louis also supported François Couperin (1668–1733), whose harpsichord and organ works possess the grandeur the king loved, and Marc-Antoine Charpentier (1634–1704), whose solemn religious music entertained him at meals.

Louis XIV loved the stage, and in the plays of Molière and Racine his court witnessed the finest achievements of the French theater. When Jean-Baptiste Poquelin (1622–1673), the son of a pros-

Poussin: The Rape of the Sabine Women   (ca 1636) Considered the greatest French painter of the seventeenth century, Poussin in this dramatic work shows his complete devotion to the ideals of classicism. The heroic figures are superb physical specimens, but hardly lifelike. *(Source: The Metropolitan Museum of Art, New York, Harris Brisbane Dick Fund, 1946 (46.160)).*

perous tapestry maker, refused to join his father's business and entered the theater, he took the stage name "Molière." As playwright, stage manager, director, and actor, Molière produced comedies that exposed the hypocrisies and follies of society through brilliant caricature. *Tartuffe* satirized the religious hypocrite; *Les Femmes Savantes (The Learned Women)* mocked the fashionable pseudo-intellectuals of the day. In structure Molière's plays followed classical models, but they were based on careful social observation. Molière made the bourgeoisie the butt of his ridicule; he stopped short of criticizing the nobility, thus reflecting the policy of his royal patron.

While Molière dissected social mores, his contemporary Jean Racine (1639–1699) analyzed the power of love. Racine based his tragic dramas on Greek and Roman legends, and his persistent theme is the conflict of good and evil. Several of his plays—*Andromaque, Bérénice, Iphigénie,* and *Phèdre*—bear the names of women and deal with the power of passion in women. For simplicity of language, symmetrical structure, and calm restraint, the plays of Racine represent the finest examples of French classicism. His tragedies and Molière's comedies are still produced today.

Louis XIV's Wars

Visualizing himself as a great military hero, Louis XIV used almost endless war to exalt himself above the other rulers of Europe. "The character of a conqueror," he remarked, "is regarded as the noblest and highest of titles." Military glory was his aim. In 1666 Louis appointed François le Tellier (later marquis of Louvois) secretary of war. Louvois created a professional army, which was modern in the sense that the French state, rather than private nobles, employed the soldiers. The king himself took personal command of the army and directly supervised all aspects and details of military affairs.

A commissariat was established to feed the troops, taking the place of the usual practice of living off the countryside. An ambulance corps was formed to look after the wounded. Uniforms and weapons were standardized. A rational system of recruitment, training, discipline, and promotion was imposed. With this new military machine, one national state, France, was able to dominate the politics of Europe for the first time.

Louis continued on a broader scale the expansionist policy begun by Cardinal Richelieu. In 1667, using a dynastic excuse, he invaded Flanders, part of the Spanish Netherlands, and Franche-Comté. He thus acquired twelve towns, including the important commercial centers of Lille and Tournai (Map 19.1). Five years later, Louis personally led an army of over 100,000 men into Holland, and the Dutch ultimately saved themselves only by opening the dikes and flooding the countryside. This war, which lasted six years and eventually involved the Holy Roman Empire and Spain, was concluded by the Treaty of Nijmegen (1678). Louis gained additional Flemish towns and all of Franche-Comté.

Encouraged by his successes, by the weakness of the German Empire, and by divisions among the other European powers, Louis continued his aggression. In 1681 he seized the city of Strasbourg and three years later sent his armies into the province of Lorraine. At that moment the king seemed invincible. In fact, Louis had reached the limit of his expansion at Nijmegen. The wars of the 1680s and 1690s brought him no additional territories. In 1689 the Dutch prince William of Orange, a bitter foe, became king of England. William joined the League of Augsburg—which included the Habsburg emperor, the kings of Spain and Sweden, and the electors of Bavaria, Saxony, and the Palatinate—adding British resources and men to the alliance. Neither the French nor the league won any decisive victories. France lacked the means to win; it was financially exhausted.

Louis was attempting to support an army of 200,000 men, in several different theaters of war. The weight of taxation fell on the already overburdened peasants. The frustrated workers revolted all over France late in the century.

A series of bad harvests between 1688 and 1694 brought catastrophe. Cold, wet summers reduced the harvests by an estimated one-third to two-thirds. The price of wheat skyrocketed. The result was widespread starvation, and in many provinces the death rate rose to several times the normal figure. Rising grain prices, new taxes for war on top of old ones, a slump in manufacturing and thus in exports, and the constant nuisance of pillaging troops—all these meant great suffering for the French people. France wanted peace at any price. Louis XIV granted a respite for five years while he prepared for the conflict later known as the "War of the Spanish Succession."

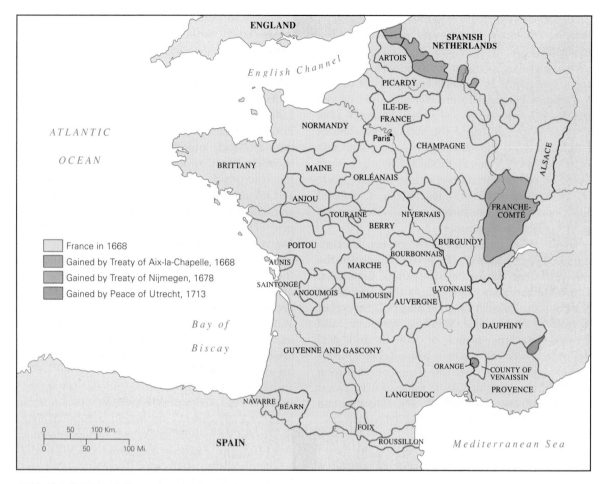

MAP 19.1 The Acquisitions of Louis XIV, 1668–1713   The desire for glory and the weakness of his German neighbors encouraged Louis's expansionist policy. But he paid a high price for his acquisitions.

This struggle (1701–1713), provoked by the territorial disputes of the past century, also involved the dynastic question of the succession to the Spanish throne. It was an open secret in Europe that the king of Spain, Charles II (r. 1665–1700), was mentally defective and sexually impotent. In 1698 the European powers, including France, agreed by treaty to partition, or divide, the vast Spanish possessions between the king of France and the Holy Roman emperor, who were Charles II's brothers-in-law. When Charles died in 1700, however, his will left the Spanish crown and the worldwide Spanish Empire to Philip of Anjou, Louis XIV's grandson. Louis, who obviously would gain power in Spain, reneged on the treaty and accepted the will.

The Dutch and the English would not accept French acquisition of the Spanish Netherlands and

of the rich trade with the Spanish colonies. The union of the Spanish and French crowns, moreover, would have totally upset the European balance of power. The Versailles declaration that "the Pyrenees no longer exist" provoked the long-anticipated crisis.

In 1701 the English, Dutch, Austrians, and Prussians formed the Grand Alliance against Louis XIV. They claimed that they were fighting to prevent France from becoming too strong in Europe, but the allied powers also wanted to check France's expanding commercial power in North America, Asia, and Africa. In the ensuing series of conflicts, Louis suffered major defeats at Blenheim in Bavaria and at Ramillies near Namur in Brabant.

The war was finally concluded at Utrecht in 1713, where the principle of partition was applied.

Louis's grandson Philip remained the first Bourbon king of Spain on the understanding that the French and Spanish crowns would never be united. France surrendered Newfoundland, Nova Scotia, and the Hudson Bay territory to England, which also acquired Gibraltar, Minorca, and control of the African slave trade from Spain. The Dutch gained little because Austria received the former Spanish Netherlands (Map 19.2).

The Peace of Utrecht had important international consequences. It represented the balance-of-power principle in operation, setting limits on the extent to which any one power, in this case France, could expand. The treaty completed the decline of Spain as a great power. It vastly expanded the British Empire. Finally, Utrecht gave European powers experience in international cooperation, thus preparing them for the alliances against France at the end of the century.

The Peace of Utrecht marked the end of French expansionist policy. In Louis's thirty-five-year quest for military glory, his main territorial acquisition was Strasbourg. Even revisionist historians, who portray the aging monarch as responsible in negotiation and moderate in his demands, acknowledge "that the widespread misery in France during the period was in part due to royal policies, especially the incessant wars."[9]

THE DECLINE OF ABSOLUTIST SPAIN IN THE SEVENTEENTH CENTURY

Spanish absolutism and greatness had preceded that of the French. In the sixteenth century, Spain (or, more precisely, the kingdom of Castile) had developed the standard features of absolute monarchy: a permanent bureaucracy staffed by professionals employed in the various councils of state, a standing army, and national taxes, the *servicios,* which fell most heavily on the poor.

France depended on financial and administrative unification within its borders; Spain had developed an international absolutism on the basis of silver bullion from Peru. Spanish gold and silver, armies, and glory had dominated Europe for most of the sixteenth century, but by the 1590s the seeds of disaster were sprouting. While France in the seventeenth century represented the classic model of the modern absolute state, Spain was experiencing steady decline. The lack of a strong middle class (largely the result of the expulsion of the Jews and Moors), agricultural crisis and population decline, failure to invest in productive enterprises, intellectual isolation and psychological malaise—by 1715 all combined to reduce Spain to a second-rate power.

The fabulous and seemingly inexhaustible flow of silver from Mexico and Peru had led Philip II (see page 587) to assume the role of defender of Roman Catholicism in Europe. In order to humble the Dutch and to regain control of all the Low Countries, Philip believed that England, the Netherlands' greatest supporter, had to be crushed. He poured millions of Spanish ducats and all of Spanish hopes into the vast fleet that sailed in 1588. When the "Invincible Armada" went down, a century of Spanish pride and power went with it. After 1590 a spirit of defeatism and disillusionment crippled most reform efforts.

Philip II's Catholic crusade had been financed by the revenues of the Spanish-Atlantic economy. These included, in addition to silver and gold bullion, money from the sale of cloth, grain, oil, and wine to the colonies. In the early seventeenth century, the Dutch and English began to trade with the Spanish colonies, cutting into the revenues that had gone to Spain. Mexico and Peru themselves developed local industries, further lessening their need to buy from Spain. Between 1610 and 1650, Spanish trade with the colonies fell 60 percent.

At the same time, the native Indians and African slaves, who worked the South American silver mines under conditions that would have shamed the ancient Egyptian pharaohs, suffered frightful epidemics of disease. Moreover, the lodes started to run dry. Consequently, the quantity of metal produced for Spain steadily declined. Nevertheless, in Madrid royal expenditures constantly exceeded income. The remedies applied in the face of a mountainous state debt and declining revenues were devaluation of the coinage and declarations of bankruptcy. In 1596, 1607, 1627, 1647, and 1680, Spanish kings found no solution to the problem of an empty treasury other than to cancel the national debt. Given the frequency of cancellation, public confidence in the state deteriorated.

Spain, in contrast to the other countries of western Europe, had only a tiny middle class. The Spanish disdain for money, in a century of increasing commercialism and bourgeois attitudes, reveals a significant facet of the Spanish national

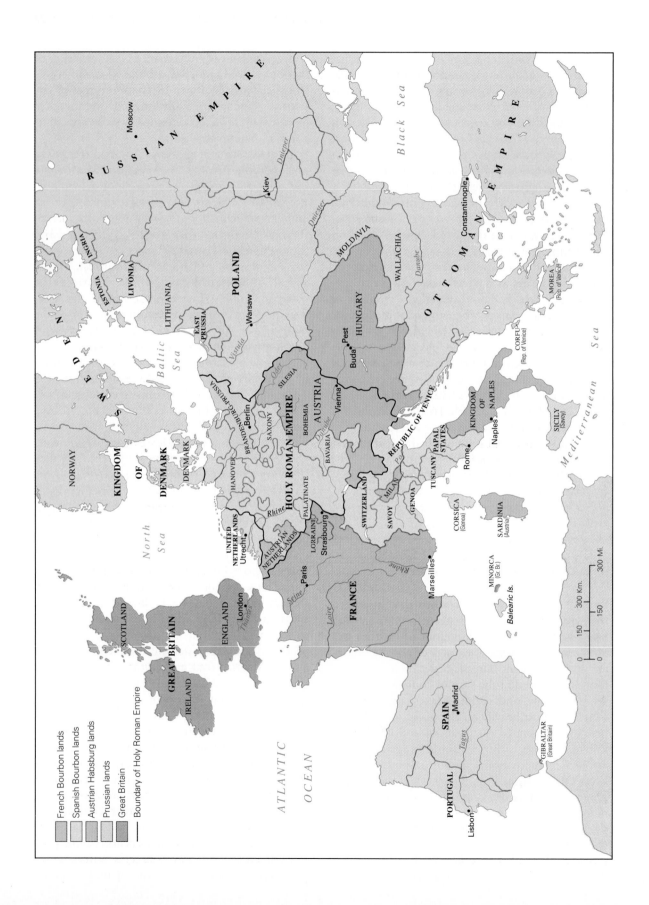

RUSSIAN EMPIRE

Moscow

Dnieper

Kiev

Dniester

Black Sea

OTTOMAN EMPIRE

Constantinople

MOLDAVIA

WALLACHIA

Danube

POLAND

Warsaw

LIVONIA

ESTONIA

INGRIA

LITHUANIA

EAST PRUSSIA

Vistula

BRANDENBURG-PRUSSIA

Oder

SILESIA

SAXONY

Berlin

HUNGARY

Pest
Buda

AUSTRIA

Vienna

BOHEMIA

Danube

HOLY ROMAN EMPIRE

BAVARIA

REPUBLIC OF VENICE

Po

MOREA
(Rep. of Venice)

CORFU
(Rep. of Venice)

KINGDOM OF NAPLES

Naples

SICILY
(Savoy)

Mediterranean Sea

SWEDEN

NORWAY

Baltic Sea

KINGDOM OF DENMARK

DENMARK

HANOVER

North Sea

Rhine

UNITED NETHERLANDS

Utrecht

AUSTRIAN NETHERLANDS

LORRAINE

PALATINATE

Strasbourg

SWITZERLAND

SAVOY

MILAN

GENOA

TUSCANY

PAPAL STATES

Rome

CORSICA
(Genoa)

SARDINIA
(Austria)

GREAT BRITAIN

SCOTLAND

ENGLAND

London

Thames

IRELAND

ATLANTIC OCEAN

FRANCE

Paris

Seine

Loire

Rhône

Marseilles

MINORCA
(Gr. Br.)

Balearic Is.

SPAIN

Madrid

Tagus

PORTUGAL

Lisbon

GIBRALTAR
(Great Britain)

300 Mi.

300 Km.

150

150

0

0

French Bourbon lands
Spanish Bourbon lands
Austrian Habsburg lands
Prussian lands
Great Britain
Boundary of Holy Roman Empire

character. Public opinion, taking its cue from the aristocracy, condemned moneymaking as vulgar and undignified. Those with influence or connections sought titles of nobility and social prestige or became priests, monks, and nuns. The flood of gold and silver had produced severe inflation, pushing the costs of production in the textile industry higher and higher, to the point that Castilian cloth could not compete in colonial and international markets. Many businessmen found so many obstacles in the way of profitable enterprise that they simply gave up.[10]

Spanish aristocrats, attempting to maintain an extravagant lifestyle that they could no longer afford, increased the rents on their estates. High rents and heavy taxes in turn drove the peasants from the land. Agricultural production suffered, and the peasants departed for the large cities, where they swelled the ranks of beggars.

Their most Catholic majesties, the kings of Spain, had no solutions to these dire problems. If one can discern personality from pictures, the portraits of Philip III (r. 1598–1622), Philip IV (r. 1622–1665), and Charles II hanging in the Prado (the Spanish national museum in Madrid) reflect the increasing weakness of the dynasty. Their faces—the small, beady eyes, the long noses, the jutting Habsburg jaws, the pathetically stupid expressions—tell a story of excessive inbreeding and decaying monarchy.

Philip IV left the management of his several kingdoms to Count Olivares. An able administrator, the count did not lack energy and ideas. He devised new sources of revenue, but he clung to the grandiose belief that the solution to Spain's difficulties rested in a return to the imperial tradition. Unfortunately, the imperial tradition demanded the revival of war with the Dutch, at the expiration of a twelve-year truce in 1622, and a long war with France over Mantua (1628–1659). Spain thus became embroiled in the Thirty Years' War. These conflicts, on top of an empty treasury, brought disaster.

In 1640 Spain faced serious revolts in Catalonia and Portugal; in 1643 the French inflicted a crushing defeat on a Spanish army in Belgium. By the Treaty of the Pyrenees of 1659, which ended the French-Spanish wars, Spain was compelled to surrender extensive territories to France. This treaty marked the end of Spain as a great power.

Seventeenth-century Spain was the victim of its past. It could not forget the grandeur of the sixteenth century and look to the future. The most cherished Spanish ideals were military glory and strong Roman Catholic faith. In the seventeenth century, Spain lacked the finances and the manpower to fight the expensive wars in which it foolishly got involved. Spain also ignored the new mercantile ideas and scientific methods because they came from heretical nations, Holland and England.

In the brilliant novel *Don Quixote,* the Spanish writer Miguel de Cervantes (1547–1616) produced one of the masterpieces of world literature. *Don Quixote*—on which the modern play *Man of La Mancha* is based—delineates the whole fabric of sixteenth-century Spanish society. The main character, Don Quixote, lives in a dream world, traveling about the countryside seeking military glory. A leading scholar wrote, "The Spaniard convinced himself that reality was what he felt, believed, imagined. He filled the world with heroic reverberations. Don Quixote was born and grew."[11]

MAP 19.2 Europe in 1715 The series of treaties commonly called the Peace of Utrecht (April 1713–November 1715) ended the War of the Spanish Succession and redrew the map of Europe. A French Bourbon king succeeded to the Spanish throne on the understanding that the French not attempt to unite the French and Spanish crowns. France surrendered to Austria the Spanish Netherlands (later Belgium), then in French hands; and France recognized the Hohenzollern rulers of Prussia. Spain ceded Gibraltar to Great Britain, for which it has been a strategic naval station ever since. Spain also granted to Britain the *asiento,* the contract for supplying African slaves to America.

LORDS AND PEASANTS IN EASTERN EUROPE (CA 1050–1650)

The rulers of eastern Europe also struggled to build strong absolutist states in the seventeenth century. But they built on different social and economic foundations, which were laid between 1400 and 1650. In those years, the princes and the landed nobility of eastern Europe rolled back the gains made by the peasantry during the High Middle Ages and reimposed serfdom on the rural masses. The nobility also reduced the importance of the towns and the middle classes. This process—another manifestation of the shattered unity of medieval Latin Christendom—differed profoundly from developments in western Europe at the same time. In the West, peasants were winning greater freedom and the rise of the urban capitalistic middle class was continuing.

The Medieval Background

Between roughly 1400 and 1650, nobles and rulers re-established serfdom in Bohemia, Silesia, Hungary, eastern Germany, Poland, Lithuania, and Russia. The east—the land east of the Elbe River in Germany, which historians often call "East Elbia"—gained a certain social and economic unity in the process. But eastern peasants lost their rights and freedoms. They became bound first to the land they worked and then, by degrading obligations, to the lords they served.

This development was a tragic reversal of trends in the High Middle Ages. The period from roughly 1050 to 1300 had been a time of general economic expansion characterized by the growth of trade, towns, and population. Expansion had also meant clearing the forests and colonizing the frontier beyond the Elbe River. Eager to attract German settlers to their sparsely populated lands, the rulers and nobles of eastern Europe had offered potential newcomers economic and legal incentives. Large numbers of incoming settlers had obtained land on excellent terms and gained much personal freedom. These benefits were gradually extended to the local Slavic populations, even those of central Russia. Thus by 1300 peasant conditions in eastern Europe had improved. Serfdom had all but disappeared. Peasants were able to bargain freely with their landlords and move about as they pleased. Opportunities and improvements east of the Elbe had a positive impact on western Europe, where the weight of serfdom was also reduced between 1100 and 1300.

After about 1300, however, as Europe's population and economy declined grievously, mainly because of the Black Death, eastern and western Europe went in different directions. In both east and west landlords sought to solve their tough economic problems by more heavily exploiting the peasantry. In the west this attempt generally failed. In many western areas by 1500, almost all of the peasants were completely free, and in the rest of western Europe the obligations of serfs had declined greatly. East of the Elbe, however, the landlords were successful. By 1500 eastern peasants were on their way to becoming serfs again.

Throughout eastern Europe, as in western Europe, the drop in population and prices in the fourteenth and fifteenth centuries caused severe labor shortages and hard times for the nobles. Yet rather than offer better economic and legal terms to keep old peasants and attract new ones, eastern landlords used political and police power to turn the tables on peasants. They did this in two ways.

First, the lords made their kings and princes issue laws that restricted or eliminated the peasants' right of free movement. As a result, a peasant could no longer move to take advantage of better opportunities elsewhere without the lord's permission, and the lord had no reason to make such a concession. In Prussian territories by 1500, the law required that runaway peasants be hunted down and returned to their lords, and a runaway servant was to be nailed to a post by one ear and given a knife to cut himself loose. Until the middle of the fifteenth century, medieval Russian peasants had been free to move wherever they wished and seek the best landlord. This freedom was gradually curtailed, and by 1497 a Russian peasant had the right to move only during a two-week period after the fall harvest. Eastern peasants were losing their status as free and independent men and women.

Second, lords steadily took more and more of their peasants' land and imposed heavier and heavier labor obligations. Instead of being independent farmers paying reasonable, freely negotiated rents, peasants tended to become forced laborers on the lords' estates. By the early 1500s, lords in many territories could command their peasants to work for them without pay as many as six days a week.

The gradual erosion of the peasantry's economic position was bound up with manipulation of the legal system. The local lord was also the local prosecutor, judge, and jailer. He generally ruled in his own favor in disputes with his peasants. There were no independent royal officials to provide justice or uphold the common law.

The Consolidation of Serfdom

Between 1500 and 1650, the social, legal, and economic conditions of peasants in eastern Europe

Punishing Serfs This seventeenth-century illustration from Olearius's famous *Travels to Moscovy* suggests what eastern serfdom really meant. The scene is set in eastern Poland. There, according to Olearius, a common command of the lord was, "Beat him till the skin falls from the flesh." *(Source: University of Illinois, Champaign)*

continued to decline. In Poland, for example, nobles gained complete control over their peasants in 1574. They could legally inflict the death penalty on their serfs whenever they wished. In Prussia a series of oppressive measures reached a culmination in 1653. All the old privileges of the lords were reaffirmed, and peasants were assumed to be in "hereditary subjugation" to their lords unless they could prove the contrary in the lords' courts (doing so was practically impossible). Prussian peasants were serfs tied to their lords as well as to the land.

In Russia the right of peasants to move from a given estate was "temporarily" suspended in the 1590s and permanently abolished in 1603. In 1649 a new law code completed the legal reestablishment of permanent hereditary serfdom. Henceforth runaway peasants were to be returned to their lords whenever they were caught, as long as they lived. The new law code set no limits on the lords' authority over their peasants, so control of serfs was strictly the lords' own business. Although the political development of the various eastern states differed, the common fate of

peasants in eastern Europe and Russia by the middle of the seventeenth century was serfdom.

The consolidation of serfdom between 1500 and 1650 was accompanied by the growth of estate agriculture, particularly in Poland and eastern Germany. In the sixteenth century, European economic expansion and population growth resumed after the great declines of the late Middle Ages. Prices for agricultural commodities also rose sharply as gold and silver flowed in from the New World. Thus Polish and German lords had powerful economic incentives to increase the production of their estates, and they did so.

Lords seized more and more peasant land for themselves and then demanded ever more unpaid serf labor on their enlarged estates. Generally, the estates were inefficient and technically backward. Nevertheless, the great Polish nobles and middle-rank German lords squeezed sizable, cheap, and profitable surpluses out of their impoverished peasants. These surpluses in wheat and timber were sold to foreign merchants, who exported them to the growing western cities. The poor east helped feed the much wealthier west.

The re-emergence of serfdom in eastern Europe in the early modern period was a momentous human development, and historians have advanced a variety of explanations for it. Some scholars have stressed an economic interpretation. According to this view, agricultural depression and population decline in the fourteenth and fifteenth centuries led to a severe labor shortage, and thus eastern landlords naturally tied their peasants to the land. In the sixteenth century, when prosperity returned, they grabbed the peasants' land and made them work as unpaid serfs on the enlarged estates. This explanation by itself is not very convincing, for almost identical economic developments "caused" the opposite result in western Europe.

It seems fairly clear that political rather than economic factors were crucial in the simultaneous rise of serfdom in the east and decline of serfdom in the west. Specifically, eastern lords enjoyed much greater political power than their western counterparts. In the late Middle Ages, when much of eastern Europe was experiencing innumerable wars and general political chaos, the noble landlord class greatly increased its political power at the expense of the ruling monarchs. Because many royal successions were disputed, weak eastern kings were forced to grant political favors to win the support of the nobility, and such weak kings could not resist the lords' demands for their peasants. Moreover, most eastern monarchs did not want to resist. The typical king was only first among equals in the noble class. He, too, thought mainly in private rather than public terms. He, too, wanted to squeeze as much as he could out of his peasants and enlarge his estates. The western concept and reality of sovereignty, as embodied in a king who protected the interests of all his people, was not well developed in eastern Europe before 1650.

The political power of the peasants was also weaker in eastern Europe and declined steadily after about 1400. Although there were occasional bloody peasant uprisings against the oppression of the landlords, they never succeeded. Nor did eastern peasants effectively resist their landlords' day-by-day infringements on their liberties. One reason for their predicament was that the lords, rather than the kings, ran the courts, control of the legal system being one of the important concessions that nobles extorted from weak monarchs.

Finally, with the approval of weak kings, the landlords systematically undermined the medieval privileges of the towns and the power of the urban classes. Instead of selling their products to local merchants in the towns, as required in the Middle Ages, the landlords sold directly to foreign capitalists. For example, Dutch ships sailed up the rivers of Poland and eastern Germany to the loading docks of the great estates, completely by-passing the local towns. Moreover, "town air" no longer "made people free," for the eastern towns had lost their medieval right of refuge and were compelled to return runaways to their lords. The population of the towns and the importance of the urban middle classes declined greatly. This development both reflected and promoted the supremacy of noble landlords in most of eastern Europe in the sixteenth century.

THE RISE OF AUSTRIA AND PRUSSIA

Despite the strength of the nobility and the weakness of many monarchs before 1600, strong kings did begin to emerge in many eastern European lands in the course of the seventeenth century. War and the threat of war aided rulers greatly in their attempts to build absolute monarchies. There was an endless struggle for power, as eastern rulers not only fought each other but also battled with hordes of Asiatic invaders. In this atmosphere of continuous wartime emergency, monarchs reduced the political power of the landlord nobility. Cautiously leaving the nobles the unchallenged masters of their peasants, the absolutist monarchs of eastern Europe gradually gained and monopolized political power in three key areas. They imposed and collected permanent taxes without consent. They maintained permanent standing armies, which policed their subjects in addition to fighting abroad. And they conducted relations with other states as they pleased.

There were important variations on the absolutist theme in eastern Europe. The royal absolutism created in Prussia was stronger and more effective than that established in Austria. This advantage gave Prussia a thin edge over Austria in the struggle for power in east-central Europe in the eighteenth century. That edge had enormous long-term political significance, for it was a rising Prussia that unified the German people in the nineteenth century and imposed on them a fateful Prussian stamp.

Austria and the Ottoman Turks

Like all the other peoples and rulers of central Europe, the Habsburgs of Austria emerged from the Thirty Years' War (see pages 589–592) impoverished and exhausted. The effort to root out Protestantism in the German lands had failed utterly, and the authority of the Holy Roman Empire and its Habsburg emperors had declined almost to the vanishing point. Yet defeat in central Europe also opened new vistas. The Habsburg monarchs were forced to turn inward and eastward to try to fuse their diverse holdings into a strong unified state.

An important step in this direction had actually been taken in Bohemia during the Thirty Years' War. Protestantism had been strong among the Czechs, a Slavic people concentrated in Bohemia. In 1618 the Czech nobles who controlled the Bohemian Estates—the semiparliamentary body of Bohemia—had risen up against their Habsburg king. Not only was this revolt crushed, but the old Czech nobility was wiped out as well. Those Czech nobles who did not die in 1620 at the Battle of the White Mountain (see page 591), a momentous turning point in Czech history, had their landholdings confiscated. The Habsburg king, Ferdinand II (r. 1619–1637), then redistributed the Czech lands to a motley band of aristocratic soldiers of fortune who had nothing in common with the Czech-speaking peasants.

With the help of this new nobility, the Habsburgs established strong direct rule over reconquered Bohemia. The condition of the enserfed peasantry worsened: three days per week of unpaid labor—the *robot*—became the norm, and a quarter of the serfs worked for their lords every day but Sundays and religious holidays. Serfs also paid the taxes, which further strengthened the alliance between the Habsburg monarch and the Bohemian nobility. Protestantism was also stamped out, and religious unity began to emerge. The reorganization of Bohemia was a giant step toward absolutism.

After the Thirty Years' War, Ferdinand III centralized the government in the hereditary German-speaking provinces, most notably Austria, Styria, and the Tyrol. For the first time, Ferdinand III's reign saw the creation of a permanent standing army ready to put down any internal opposition. The Habsburg monarchy was then ready to turn toward the vast plains of Hungary, in opposition to the Ottoman Turks.

The Ottomans had come out of Anatolia, in present-day Turkey, to create one of history's greatest military empires. At their peak in the middle of the sixteenth century under Suleiman the Magnificent (r. 1520–1566), their possessions stretched from western Persia across North Africa and up into the heart of central Europe (Map 23.2, page 751). Apostles of Islam, the Ottoman Turks were old and determined foes of the Catholic Habsburgs. Their armies had almost captured Vienna in 1529, and for more than 150 years thereafter the Ottomans ruled all of the Balkan territories, almost all of Hungary, and part of southern Russia.

In the late seventeenth century, under vigorous reforming leadership, the Ottoman Empire succeeded in marshaling its forces for one last mighty blow at Christian Europe. After wresting territory from Poland, fighting a long inconclusive war with Russia, and establishing an alliance with Louis XIV of France, the Turks turned again on Austria. A huge Turkish army surrounded Vienna and laid siege to it in 1683. After holding out against great odds for two months, the city was relieved at the last minute by a mixed force of Habsburg, Saxon, Bavarian, and Polish troops. The Ottomans were forced to retreat, and the retreat soon became a rout. As their Russian and Venetian allies attacked on other fronts, the Habsburgs conquered all of Hungary and Transylvania (part of present-day Romania) by 1699 (Map 19.3).

The Turkish wars and this great expansion strengthened the Habsburg army and promoted some sense of unity in the Habsburg lands. The Habsburgs moved to centralize their power and make it as absolute as possible. These efforts to create a fully developed, highly centralized, absolutist state were only partly successful.

The Habsburg state was composed of three separate and distinct territories: the old "hereditary provinces" of Austria, the kingdom of Bohemia, and the kingdom of Hungary. These three parts were tied together primarily by their common ruler, the Habsburg monarch. Each part had its own laws and political life, for the three noble-dominated Estates continued to exist, though with reduced powers. The Habsburgs themselves were well aware of the fragility of the union they had forged.

The Hungarian nobility, despite its reduced strength, effectively thwarted the full development of Habsburg absolutism. Time and again

The Siege of Vienna, 1683   Seeking to tunnel under the city walls and blow them up with mines, a huge Turkish army besieged the Habsburg capital and penetrated the outer fortifications on September 2, 1683. As the Turks launched the final assault on the city ten days later, a relief army led by John Sobieski, the King of Poland (shown in foreground), arrived and delivered a successful surprise attack. This painting shows the battle at its height. *(Source: Heeresgeschichtliches Museum, Vienna)*

throughout the seventeenth century, Hungarian nobles—the most numerous in Europe, making up 5 to 7 percent of the Hungarian population—rose in revolt against the attempts of Vienna to impose absolute rule. They never triumphed decisively, but neither were they ever crushed and replaced, as the Czech nobility had been in 1620.

Hungarians resisted because many of them were Protestants, especially in the area long ruled by the more tolerant Turks, and they hated the heavy-handed attempts of the conquering Habsburgs to re-Catholicize everyone. Moreover, the lords of Hungary often found a powerful military ally in Turkey. Finally, the Hungarian nobility, and even part of the Hungarian peasantry, had become attached to a national ideal long before most of the other peoples of eastern Europe. They were determined to maintain as much independence and local control as possible. Thus when the Habs-

burgs were bogged down in the War of the Spanish Succession (see page 617), the Hungarians rose in one last patriotic rebellion under Prince Francis Rákóczy in 1703. Rákóczy and his forces were eventually defeated, but this time the Habsburgs had to accept a definitive compromise. Charles VI restored many of the traditional privileges of the Hungarian aristocracy in return for Hungarian acceptance of hereditary Habsburg rule. Thus Hungary, unlike Austria or Bohemia, never came close to being fully integrated into a centralized, absolute Habsburg state.

Prussia in the Seventeenth Century

After 1400 the status of east German peasants declined steadily; their serfdom was formally spelled out in the early seventeenth century. While the local princes lost political power and influence, a revitalized landed nobility became the undisputed ruling class. The Hohenzollern family, which ruled through its senior and junior branches as the electors of Brandenburg and the dukes of Prussia, had little real princely power. The Hohenzollern rulers were nothing more than the first among equals, the largest landowners in a landlord society.

Nothing suggested that the Hohenzollerns and their territories would ever play an important role in European or even German affairs. The right of the elector of Brandenburg to help choose the Holy Roman emperor with six other electors was of little practical value, and the elector had no military strength whatsoever. The territory of his cousin, the duke of Prussia, was actually part of the kingdom of Poland. Moreover, geography

conspired against the Hohenzollerns. Brandenburg, their power base, was completely cut off from the sea (see Map 19.3), lacked natural frontiers, and lay open to attack from all directions. The land was poor, a combination of sand and swamp. Contemporaries contemptuously called Brandenburg the "sand-box of the Holy Roman Empire."[12]

Brandenburg was a helpless spectator in the Thirty Years' War, its territory alternately ravaged by Swedish and Habsburg armies. Population fell drastically, and many villages disappeared. The power of the Hohenzollerns reached its lowest point. Yet the country's devastation made the way for Hohenzollern absolutism, because foreign armies dramatically weakened the political power of the Estates—the representative assemblies of

MAP 19.3 The Growth of Austria and Brandenburg-Prussia to 1748 Austria expanded to the southwest into Hungary and Transylvania at the expense of the Ottoman Empire. It was unable to hold the rich German province of Silesia, however, which was conquered by Brandenburg-Prussia.

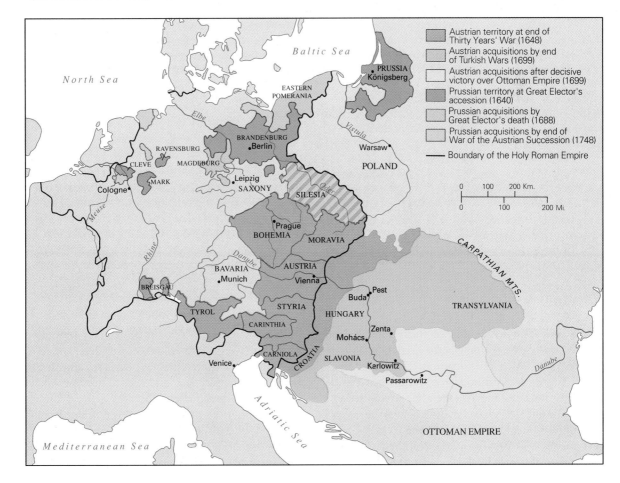

THE RISE OF WESTERN ABSOLUTISM AND CONSTITUTIONALISM

1581	Formation of the United Provinces of the Netherlands
1588	Defeat of the Spanish Armada
1589–1610	Reign of Henry IV of France; economic reforms help to restore public order, lay foundation for absolutist rule
1598	Edict of Nantes: Henry IV ends the French wars of religion
1608	France establishes its first Canadian settlement, at Quebec
1609	Philip III of Spain recognizes Dutch independence
1610–1650	Spanish trade with the New World falls by 60 percent
1618–1648	Thirty Years' War
1624–1643	Richelieu dominates French government
1625	Huguenot revolt in France; siege of La Rochelle
1629–1640	Eleven Years' Tyranny: Charles I attempts to rule England without the aid of Parliament
1640–1660	Long Parliament in England
1642–1646	English civil war
1643–1661	Mazarin dominates France's regency government during Louis XIV's minority
1643–1715	Reign of Louis XIV
1648–1660	The Fronde: French nobility opposes centralizing efforts of monarchy
1648	Peace of Westphalia confirms Dutch independence from Spain
1649	Execution of Charles I; beginning of the Interregnum in England
1653–1658	The Protectorate: Cromwell heads military rule of England
1659	Treaty of the Pyrenees forces Spain to cede extensive territories to France, marks end of Spain as a great power
1660	Restoration of the English monarchy: Charles II returns from exile
1661	Louis XIV enters into independent rule
ca 1663–1683	Colbert directs Louis XIV's mercantilist economic policy
1670	Treaty of Dover: Charles II secretly agrees with Louis XIV to re-Catholicize England
1673	Test Act excludes Roman Catholics from public office in England
	France invades Holland
1678	Treaty of Nijmegen: Louis XIV acquires Franche-Comté
1681	France acquires Strasbourg
1685	Louis XIV revokes the Edict of Nantes
1685–1688	James II rules England, attempts to restore Roman Catholicism as state religion
1688	The Glorious Revolution establishes a constitutional monarchy in England under Mary and William III
1689	Enactment of the Bill of Rights
1701–1713	War of the Spanish Succession
1713	Peace of Utrecht ends French territorial acquisitions, expands the British Empire

the realm. The weakening of the Estates helped the very talented young elector Frederick William (r. 1640–1688), later known as the "Great Elector," to ride roughshod over traditional parliamentary liberties and to take a giant step toward royal absolutism. This constitutional struggle, often unjustly neglected by historians, was the most crucial in Prussian history for hundreds of years, until that of the 1860s.

When Frederick William came to power in 1640, the twenty-year-old ruler was determined to unify his three quite separate provinces and to add to them by diplomacy and war. These provinces were Brandenburg itself, the area around Berlin; Prussia, inherited in 1618 when the junior branch of the Hohenzollern family died out; and completely separate, scattered holdings along the Rhine in western Germany, inherited in 1614 (see

THE RISE OF ABSOLUTISM IN EASTERN EUROPE

1050–1300	Increasing economic development in eastern Europe encourages decline in serfdom
1054	Death of Great Prince Iaroslav the Wise, under whom the Kievan principality reached its height of unity
1054–1237	Kiev is divided into numerous territories ruled by competing princes
1237–1242	Mongol invasion of Russia
1252	Alexander Nevsky, prince of Moscow, recognizes Mongol overlordship
1327–1328	Suppression of the Tver revolt; Mongol khan recognizes Ivan I as great prince
1400–1650	The nobility reimposes serfdom in eastern Europe
ca 1480	Ivan III rejects Mongol overlordship and begins to use the title of tsar
1520–1566	Rule of Suleiman the Magnificent: Ottoman Empire reaches its height
1533–1584	Rule of Tsar Ivan IV (the Terrible): defeat of the khanates of Kazan and Astrakhan; subjugation of the boyar aristocracy
1574	Polish nobles receive the right to inflict the death penalty on their serfs
1598–1613	Time of Troubles in Russia
1613	Election of Michael Romanov as tsar: re-establishment of autocracy
1620	Battle of the White Mountain in Bohemia: Ferdinand II initiates Habsburg confiscation of Czech estates
1640–1688	Rule of Frederick William, the Great Elector, who unites Brandenburg, Prussia, and western German holdings into one state, Brandenburg-Prussia
1649	Tsar Alexis lifts the nine-year limit on the recovery of runaway serfs
1652	Patriarch Nikon's reforms split the Russian Orthodox church
1653	Principle of peasants' hereditary subjugation to their lords affirmed in Prussia
1670–1671	Cossack revolt of Stenka Razin in Russia
1683	Siege of Vienna by the Ottoman Turks
1683–1699	Habsburg conquest of Hungary and Transylvania
1689–1725	Rule of Tsar Peter the Great
1700–1721	Great Northern War between Russia and Sweden, resulting in Russian victory and territorial expansion
1701	Elector Frederick III crowned king of Prussia
1703	Founding of St. Petersburg
	Rebellion of Prince Francis Rakoczy in Hungary
1713	Pragmatic Sanction: Charles VII guarantees Maria Theresa's succession to the Austrian empire
1713–1740	Rule of King Frederick William I in Prussia

Map 19.3). Each of the three provinces was inhabited by Germans; but each had its own Estates, whose power had increased until about 1600 as the power of the rulers declined. Although the Estates had not met regularly during the chaotic Thirty Years' War, they still had the power of the purse in their respective provinces. The Estates of Brandenburg and Prussia were dominated by the nobility and the landowning classes, known as the "Junkers."

The struggle between the Great Elector and the provincial Estates was long, complicated, and intense. After the Thirty Years' War, the representatives of the nobility zealously reasserted the right of the Estates to vote taxes, a right the Swedish armies of occupation had simply ignored. Yet first in Brandenburg in 1653 and then in Prussia between 1661 and 1663, the Great Elector eventually had his way.

To pay for the permanent standing army that he first established in 1660, Frederick William forced the Estates to accept the introduction of permanent taxation without consent. The soldiers doubled as tax collectors and policemen, becoming the core of the expanding state bureaucracy. The power of the Estates declined rapidly thereafter, for the Great Elector had both financial independence and superior force. He turned the screws of taxation: the state's total revenue tripled during his reign. The size of the army leaped about tenfold.

In accounting for the Great Elector's fateful triumph, two factors appear central. First, as in the formation of every absolutist state, war was a decisive factor. The ongoing struggle between Sweden and Poland for control of the Baltic after 1648 and the wars of Louis XIV in western Europe created an atmosphere of permanent crisis. The Tartars of southern Russia swept through Prussia in the winter of 1656 to 1657, killing and carrying off as slaves more than fifty thousand people, according to an old estimate. This invasion softened up the Estates and strengthened the urgency of the elector's demands for more money for more soldiers. It was no accident that, except in commercially minded Holland, constitutionalism won out only in England, the only major country to escape devastating foreign invasions in the seventeenth century.

Second, the nobility had long dominated the government through the Estates but only for its own narrow self-interest. The nobility was all too concerned with its own rights and privileges, especially its freedom from taxation and its unlimited control over the peasants. When, therefore, the Great Elector reconfirmed these privileges in 1653 and after, even while reducing the political power of the Estates, the nobility accepted a compromise whereby the bulk of the new taxes fell on towns, and royal authority stopped at the landlords' gates. The elector could and did use naked force to break the liberties of the towns. The main leader of the urban opposition in the key city of Königsberg, for example, was simply arrested and imprisoned for life without trial.

The Consolidation of Prussian Absolutism

By the time of his death in 1688, the Great Elector had created a single state out of scattered principalities. But his new creation was still small and

Molding the Prussian Spirit Discipline was strict and punishment brutal in the Prussian army. This scene, from an eighteenth-century book used to teach school children, shows one soldier being flogged while another is being beaten with canes as he walks between rows of troops. The officer on horseback proudly commands. *(Source: University of Illinois, Champaign)*

fragile. Moreover, the Great Elector's successor, Elector Frederick III, "the Ostentatious" (r. 1688–1713), was weak of body and mind. His only real political accomplishment was to gain the title of king from the Holy Roman emperor, a Habsburg, in return for military aid in the War of the Spanish Succession, and in 1701 he was crowned King Frederick I.

The tendency toward luxury-loving, happy, and harmless petty tyranny was completely reversed by Frederick William I, "the Soldiers' King" (r. 1713–1740). A crude, dangerous psychoneurotic, Frederick William I was nevertheless the most talented reformer ever produced by the Hohenzollern family. It was he who truly established Prussian absolutism and gave it its unique character. It was he who created the best army in Europe, for its size, and who infused military values into a whole society.

Frederick William's attachment to the army and military life was intensely emotional. He had, for example, a bizarre, almost pathological love for tall soldiers, whom he credited with superior strength and endurance. Austere and always faithful to his wife, he confided to the French ambassador: "The most beautiful girl or woman in the world would be a matter of indifference to me, but tall soldiers—they are my weakness." Like some fanatical modern-day basketball coach in search of a championship team, he sent his agents throughout both Prussia and all of Europe, tricking, buying, and kidnapping top recruits. Neighboring princes sent him their giants as gifts to win his gratitude. Prussian mothers told their sons: "Stop growing or the recruiting agents will get you."[13]

Frederick William's love of the army was also based on a hardheaded conception of the struggle for power and a dog-eat-dog view of international politics. Even before ascending the throne, he bitterly criticized his father's ministers: "They say that they will obtain land and power for the king with the pen; but I say it can be done only with the sword."[14] Throughout his long reign he never wavered in his conviction that the welfare of king and state depended above all else on the army.

As in France, the cult of military power provided the rationale for a great expansion of royal absolutism. As the ruthless king himself put it: "I must be served with life and limb, with house and wealth, with honour and conscience, everything must be committed except eternal salvation—that belongs to God, but all else is mine."[15] To make good these extraordinary demands, Frederick William created a strong centralized bureaucracy. More commoners probably rose to top positions in the civil government than at any other time in Prussia's history. The last traces of the parliamentary Estates and local self-government vanished.

The king's grab for power brought him into considerable conflict with the noble landowners, the Junkers. In his early years, he even threatened to destroy them; yet in the end the Prussian nobility was not destroyed but enlisted—into the army. Responding to a combination of threats and opportunities, the Junkers became the officer caste. By 1739 all but 5 of 245 officers with the rank of major or above were aristocrats, and most of them were native Prussians. A new compromise had been worked out: the nobility imperiously commanded the peasantry in the army as well as on its estates.

Coarse and crude, penny-pinching and hard working, Frederick William achieved results. Above all, he built a first-rate army on the basis of third-rate resources. The standing army increased from 38,000 to 83,000 during his reign. Prussia, twelfth in Europe in population, had the fourth largest army by 1740, behind France, Russia, and Austria. Moreover, soldier for soldier, the Prussian army became the best in Europe, astonishing foreign observers with its precision, skill, and discipline. For the next two hundred years, Prussia and then Prussianized Germany almost always won the crucial military battles.

Frederick William and his ministers also built an exceptionally honest and conscientious bureaucracy, which not only administered the country but tried with some success to develop it economically. Finally, like the miser he was, living very frugally off the income of his own landholdings, the king loved his "blue boys" so much that he hated to "spend" them. This most militaristic of kings was, paradoxically, almost always at peace.

Nevertheless, the Prussian people paid a heavy and lasting price for the obsessions of the royal drillmaster. Civil society became rigid and highly disciplined. Prussia became the "Sparta of the North"; unquestioning obedience was the highest virtue. As a Prussian minister later summed up, "To keep quiet is the first civic duty."[16] Thus the absolutism of Frederick William I combined with harsh peasant bondage and Junker tyranny to lay the foundations for probably the most militaristic country of modern times.

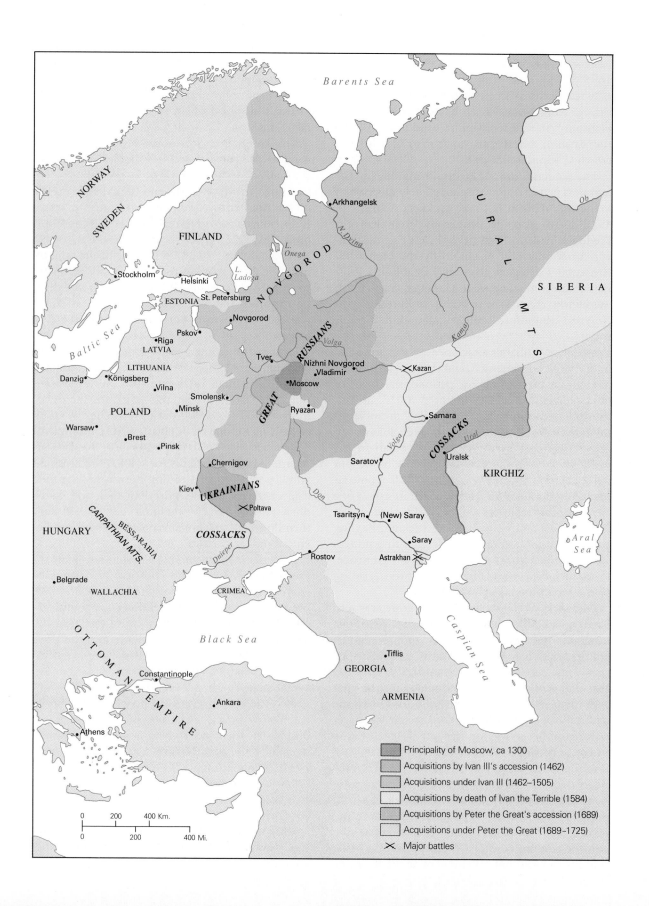

Barents Sea

NORWAY

SWEDEN

FINLAND

Stockholm

Helsinki

ESTONIA

St. Petersburg

Riga
LATVIA

Pskov

LITHUANIA

Danzig   Königsberg

Vilna

POLAND

Warsaw

Brest

Pinsk

Chernigov

Kiev

UKRAINIANS

Poltava

HUNGARY

BESSARABIA

CARPATHIAN MTS.

COSSACKS

Belgrade

WALLACHIA

CRIMEA

OTTOMAN EMPIRE

Constantinople

Ankara

Athens

Black Sea

Baltic Sea

L. Ladoga

L. Onega

NOVGOROD

Novgorod

Tver

Arkhangelsk

N. Dvina

RUSSIANS

GREAT

Nizhni Novgorod
Vladimir
Moscow

Smolensk

Minsk

Ryazan

Volga

Kazan

Kama

Samara

COSSACKS

Uralsk

Ural

KIRGHIZ

Saratov

Volga

Tsaritsyn   (New) Saray

Don

Saray

Rostov   Astrakhan

Dnieper

Tiflis

GEORGIA

ARMENIA

Caspian Sea

Aral Sea

URAL MTS.

SIBERIA

Ob

Principality of Moscow, ca 1300

Acquisitions by Ivan III's accession (1462)

Acquisitions under Ivan III (1462–1505)

Acquisitions by death of Ivan the Terrible (1584)

Acquisitions by Peter the Great's accession (1689)

Acquisitions under Peter the Great (1689–1725)

X   Major battles

0   200   400 Km.

0   200   400 Mi.

THE DEVELOPMENT OF RUSSIA

One of the favorite parlor games of nine-teenth-century Russian (and non-Russian) intellectuals was debating whether Russia was a Western and European or a non-Western Asiatic society. This question was particularly fascinating because it was unanswerable. To this day Russia differs fundamentally from the West in some basic ways, though Russian history has paralleled that of the West in other ways: thus the hypnotic attraction of Russian history.

The differences between Russia and Western Europe were particularly striking before 1700, when Russia's overall development began to draw progressively closer to that of its western neighbors. These early differences and Russia's long isolation from Europe explain why little has so far been said here about Russia. Yet it is impossible to understand how Russia has increasingly influenced and been influenced by western European civilization since roughly the late seventeenth century without looking at the course of early Russian history. Such a brief survey will also help explain how, when absolute monarchy finally and decisively triumphed under the rough guidance of Peter the Great in the early eighteenth century, it was a type of absolute monarchy quite different from that of France or even Prussia.

The Vikings and the Kievan Principality

In antiquity the Slavs lived as a single people in central Europe. With the start of the mass migrations of the late Roman Empire, the Slavs moved in different directions and split into three groups. Between the fifth and ninth centuries, the eastern Slavs, from whom the Ukrainians, the Russians, and the White Russians descend, moved into the vast and practically uninhabited area of present-day European Russia and the Ukraine (Map 19.4).

This enormous area consisted of an immense virgin forest to the north, where most of the east-

MAP 19.4 The Expansion of Russia to 1725 After the disintegration of the Kievan state and the Mongol conquest, the princes of Moscow and their descendants gradually extended their rule over an enormous territory.

ern Slavs settled, and an endless prairie grassland to the south. Probably organized as tribal communities, the eastern Slavs, like many North American pioneers much later, lived off the great abundance of wild game and a crude "slash and burn" agriculture. After clearing a piece of the forest to build log cabins, they burned the stumps and brush. The ashes left a rich deposit of potash and lime, and the land gave several good crops before it was exhausted. The people then moved on to another untouched area and repeated the process.

In the ninth century, the Vikings, those fearless warriors from Scandinavia, appeared in the lands of the eastern Slavs. Called "Varangians" in the old Russian chronicles, the Vikings were interested primarily in international trade, and the opportunities were good because the Muslim conquests of the eighth century had greatly reduced Christian trade in the Mediterranean. Moving up and down the rivers, the Vikings soon linked Scandinavia and northern Europe to the Black Sea and to the Byzantine Empire with its capital at Constantinople. Along the rivers they built a few strategic forts, from which they raided the neighboring Slavic tribes and collected tribute. Slaves were the most important article of tribute, and *Slav* even became the word for "slave" in a number of European languages.

In order to increase and protect their international commerce, the Vikings declared themselves the rulers of the eastern Slavs. The Varangian ruler Oleg (r. 878–912) established his residence at Kiev. He and his successors ruled over a loosely united confederation of Slavic territories—the Kievan state—until 1054. The Viking prince and his clansmen quickly became assimilated into the Slavic population, taking local wives and emerging as the noble class.

Assimilation and loss of Scandinavian ethnic identity was speeded up by the conversion of the Vikings and local Slavs to Eastern Orthodox Christianity by missionaries from the Byzantine Empire. Thus the rapidly Slavified Vikings left two important legacies for the future. They created a loose unification of Slavic territories under a single ruling prince and a single ruling dynasty. And they imposed a basic religious unity by accepting Orthodox Christianity (as opposed to Roman Catholicism) for themselves and the eastern Slavs.

Even at its height under Great Prince Iaroslav the Wise (r. 1019–1054), the unity of the Kievan principality was extremely tenuous. Trade, not government, was the main concern of the rulers. Moreover, the Slavified Vikings failed to find a way of peacefully transferring power from one generation to the next. In medieval western Europe this fundamental problem of government was increasingly resolved by resort to the principle of *primogeniture:* the king's eldest son received the crown as his rightful inheritance when his father died. In early Kiev, however, there were apparently no fixed rules, and much strife accompanied each succession.

After Iaroslav's death in 1054, Kiev disintegrated into more and more competing units, each ruled by a prince. Even when only one prince was claiming to be the great prince, the whole situation was very unsettled.

The princes divided their land like private property because they thought of it as private property. A given prince owned a certain number of farms or landed estates and had them worked directly by his people, mainly slaves, called *kholops* in Russian. Outside of these estates, which constituted the princely domain, the prince exercised limited authority in his principality. Excluding the clergy, two kinds of people lived there: the noble *boyars* and the commoner peasants.

The boyars were the descendants of the original Viking warriors, and they also held their lands as free and clear private property. Although the boyars normally fought in princely armies, the customary law declared that they could serve any prince they wished. The ordinary peasants were also truly free; they could move at will wherever opportunities were greatest. In the touching phrase of the times, theirs was "a clean road, without boundaries."[17] In short, fragmented princely power, private property, and personal freedom all went together.

The Mongol Yoke and the Rise of Moscow

The eastern Slavs, like the Germans and the Italians, might have emerged from the Middle Ages weak and politically divided had it not been for the Mongol conquest of the Kievan state. Wild nomadic tribes from present-day Mongolia, the Mongols were temporarily unified in the thirteenth century by Jenghiz Khan (1162–1227), one of history's greatest conquerors. In five years

his armies subdued all of China. His successors then wheeled westward, smashing everything in their path and reaching the plains of Hungary victorious before they pulled back in 1242. The Mongol army—the Golden Horde—was savage in the extreme, often slaughtering the entire populations of cities before burning them to the ground. A chronicler passing in 1245 through Kiev, which the Mongols had sacked in 1242, wrote,

When we passed through that land, we found lying in the field countless heads and bones of dead people; for this city had been extremely large and very populous, whereas now it has been reduced to nothing: barely two hundred houses stand there, and those people are held in the harshest slavery.[18]

Having devastated and conquered, the Mongols ruled the eastern Slavs for more than two hundred years. They forced all the bickering Slavic princes to submit to their rule and to give them tribute and slaves. If the conquered peoples rebelled, the Mongols were quick to punish with death and destruction. Thus the Mongols unified the eastern Slavs, for the Mongol khan was acknowledged by all as the supreme ruler.

Beginning with Alexander Nevsky in 1252, the previously insignificant princes of Moscow became particularly adept at serving the Mongols. They loyally put down popular uprisings and collected the khan's harsh taxes. By way of reward, the princes of Moscow emerged as hereditary great princes. Eventually the Muscovite princes were able to destroy their princely rivals and even to replace the khan as supreme ruler. In this complex process, two princes of Moscow after Alexander Nevsky—Ivan I and Ivan III—were especially noteworthy.

Ivan I (r. 1328–1341) was popularly known as "Ivan the Moneybag." A bit like Frederick William of Prussia, he was extremely stingy and built up a large personal fortune. This enabled him to buy more property and to increase his influence by loaning money to less frugal princes to pay their Mongol taxes. Ivan's most serious rival was the prince of Tver, whom the Mongols at one point appointed as great prince.

In 1327 the population of Tver revolted against Mongol oppression, and the prince of Tver joined his people. Ivan immediately went to the Mongol capital of Saray, where he was appointed commander of a large Russian-Mongol army, which then laid waste to Tver and its lands. For this proof of devotion, the Mongols made Ivan the general tax collector for all the Slavic lands they had subjugated and named him great prince. Ivan also convinced the metropolitan of Kiev, the leading churchman of all eastern Slavs, to settle in Moscow. Ivan I thus gained greater prestige. The church gained a powerful advocate before the khan.

In the next hundred-odd years, in the course of innumerable wars and intrigues, the great princes of Moscow significantly increased their holdings. Then, in the reign of Ivan III (r. 1462–1505), the process of gathering the territories around Moscow was largely completed. After purchasing Rostov, Ivan conquered and annexed other principalities, of which Novgorod with its lands extending almost to the Baltic Sea was most crucial (see Map 19.4). Thus, more than four hundred years after Iaroslav the Wise had divided the embryonic Kievan state, the princes of Moscow defeated all rivals to win complete princely authority.

Another dimension to princely power developed. Not only was the prince of Moscow the *unique* ruler, he was the *absolute* ruler, the autocrat, the *tsar*—the Slavic contraction for "caesar," with all its connotations. This imperious conception of absolute power is expressed in a famous letter from the aging Ivan III to Holy Roman Emperor Frederick III (r. 1440–1493). Frederick had offered Ivan the title of king in conjunction with the marriage of his daughter to Ivan's nephew. Ivan proudly refused:

We by the grace of God have been sovereigns over our domains from the beginning, from our first forebears, and our right we hold from God, as did our forebears. . . . As in the past we have never needed appointment from anyone, so now do we not desire it.[19]

The Muscovite idea of absolute authority was powerfully reinforced by two developments. First, about 1480 Ivan III stopped acknowledging the khan as his supreme ruler. There is good evidence to suggest that Ivan and his successors saw themselves as khans. Certainly they assimilated the Mongol concept of kingship as the exercise of unrestrained and unpredictable power.

Second, after the fall of Constantinople to the Turks in 1453, the tsars saw themselves as the heirs of both the caesars and Orthodox Christianity, the one true faith. All the other kings of Europe were heretics: only the tsars were rightful and holy rulers. This idea was promoted by Orthodox churchmen, who spoke of "holy Russia" as the "Third Rome." Ivan's marriage to the daughter of the last Byzantine emperor further enhanced the aura of an imperial inheritance for Moscow. Worthy successor to the mighty khan and the true Christian emperor, the Muscovite tsar was a king above all others.

Tsar and People to 1689

By 1505 the great prince of Moscow, the tsar, had emerged as the single hereditary ruler of "all the Russias"—all the lands of the eastern Slavs—and he was claiming unrestricted power as his God-given right. In effect, the tsar was demanding the same kind of total authority over all his subjects that the princes had long exercised over their slaves on their own landed estates.

As peasants had begun losing their freedom of movement in the fifteenth century, so had the noble boyars begun losing power and influence. Ivan III pioneered in this regard, as in so many others. When Ivan conquered the principality of Novgorod in the 1480s, he confiscated fully 80 percent of the land, executing the previous owners or resettling them nearer Moscow. He then kept more than half of the confiscated land for himself and distributed the remainder to members of a newly emerging service nobility, who held the tsar's land on the explicit condition that they serve in the tsar's army. Moreover, Ivan III began to require boyars outside of Novgorod to serve him if they wished to retain their lands. Since there were no competing princes left to turn to, the boyars had to yield.

The rise of the new service nobility accelerated under Ivan IV (r. 1533–1584), the famous Ivan the Terrible. Having ascended the throne at age three, Ivan suffered insults and neglect at the hands of the haughty boyars after his mother mysteriously died, possibly poisoned, when he was just eight. At age sixteen he suddenly pushed aside his hated boyar advisers, crowned himself, and officially took the august title of tsar for the first time.

Selecting the beautiful and kind Anastasia of the popular Romanov family for his wife and queen, the young tsar soon declared war on the remnants of Mongol power. He defeated the faltering khanates of Kazan and Astrakhan between 1552 and

1556, adding vast new territories to Russia. In the course of these wars, Ivan virtually abolished the old distinction between hereditary boyar private property and land granted temporarily for service. All nobles, old and new, had to serve the tsar in order to hold any land.

The transformation of the entire nobility into a service nobility was completed in the second part of Ivan the Terrible's reign. In 1557 Ivan turned westward, and for the next twenty-five years Muscovy waged an exhausting, unsuccessful war primarily with the large Polish-Lithuanian state, which controlled not only Poland but much of the Ukraine in the sixteenth century. Quarreling with the boyars over the war and blaming them for the sudden death of his beloved Anastasia in 1560, the increasingly cruel and demented Ivan turned to strike down all who stood in his way.

Above all, he reduced the ancient Muscovite boyar families with a reign of terror. Leading boyars, their relatives, and even their peasants and servants were executed en masse by a special corps of unquestioning servants. Dressed in black and riding black horses, they were forerunners of the modern dictator's secret police. Large estates were confiscated, broken up, and reapportioned to the lower service nobility. The service nobility, still less than half a percent of the total population, was totally dependent on the autocrat.

Ivan also took giant strides toward making all commoners servants of the tsar. His endless wars and demonic purges left much of central Russia depopulated. It grew increasingly difficult for the lower service nobility to squeeze a living for themselves out of the peasants left on their landholdings. As the service nobles demanded more from the remaining peasants, more and more peasants fled toward the wild, recently conquered territories to the east and south. There they formed free groups and outlaw armies known as "Cossacks." The Cossacks maintained a precarious independence beyond the reach of the oppressive landholders and the tsar's hated officials. The solution to this problem was to complete the tying of the peasants to the land, making them serfs perpetually bound to serve the noble landholders, who were bound in turn to serve the tsar.

In the time of Ivan the Terrible, urban traders and artisans were also bound to their towns and jobs so that the tsar could tax them more heavily. The urban classes had no security in their work or property, and even the wealthiest merchants were basically dependent agents of the tsar. The royal monopolization of many of the best commercial activities was in sharp contrast to developments in western Europe, where the capitalist middle classes were gaining strength and security in their private property. The Russian urban classes remained weak and divided.

Ivan the Terrible's system of autocracy and compulsory service struck foreign observers forcibly. Jean Bodin, the French thinker who did so much to develop the modern concept of sovereignty, concluded that Russia's political system was fundamentally different from the systems of all other European monarchies and comparable only to that of the Turkish empire. In both Turkey and Russia, as in other parts of Asia and in Africa, "the prince is become lord of the goods and persons of his subjects . . . governing them as a master of a family does his slaves."[20] The Mongol inheritance weighed heavily on Russia.

As has so often occurred in Russia, the death of an iron-fisted tyrant—in this case, Ivan the Terrible in 1584—ushered in an era of confusion and violent struggles for power. Events were particularly chaotic after Ivan's son Theodore died in 1598 without an heir. The years 1598 to 1613 are aptly called the "Time of Troubles."

Close relatives of the deceased tsar intrigued against and murdered each other, alternately fighting and welcoming the invading Swedes and Poles, who even occupied Moscow. Most serious for the cause of autocracy, there was a great social upheaval as Cossacks marched northward, rallying peasants and slaughtering nobles and officials.

This social explosion from below, which combined with a belated surge of patriotic opposition to Polish invaders, brought the nobles to their senses. In 1613 they elected Ivan's sixteen-year-old grandnephew, Michael Romanov, the new hereditary tsar and rallied around him in the face of common internal and external threats. Michael's election was a real restoration, and his reign saw the gradual re-establishment of tsarist autocracy. Michael was understandably more kindly disposed toward the supportive nobility than toward the sullen peasants. Thus, while the peasants were further ground down, Ivan's heavy military obligations on the nobility were relaxed considerably, a trend that continued in the long reign of Michael's successor, the pious Alexis (r. 1645–1676).

The result was a second round of mass upheaval and protest. In the later seventeenth century, the

St. Basil's Cathedral in Moscow, with its sloping roofs and colorful onion-shaped domes, is a striking example of powerful Byzantine influences on Russian culture. According to tradition, an enchanted Ivan the Terrible blinded the cathedral's architects to ensure that they would never duplicate their fantastic achievement, which still dazzles the beholder in today's Red Square. *(Source: George Holton/Photo Researchers)*

unity of the Russian Orthodox church was torn apart by a great split. The surface question was the religious reforms introduced in 1652 by the patriarch Nikon, a dogmatic purist who wished to bring "corrupted" Russian practices of worship into line with the Greek Orthodox model. The self-serving church hierarchy quickly went along, but the intensely religious common people resisted. They saw Nikon as the anti-Christ, who was stripping them of the only thing they had—the true religion of "holy Russia." Great numbers left the church and formed illegal communities of "Old Believers," who were hunted down and persecuted. After the great split, the Russian masses were alienated from the established church, which became totally dependent on the state for its authority.

Again the Cossacks revolted against the state, which was doggedly trying to catch up with them on the frontiers and reduce them to serfdom. Under Stenka Razin they moved up the Volga River in 1670 and 1671, attracting a great undisciplined army of peasants, murdering landlords and high church officials, and proclaiming freedom from oppression. In response to this rebellion, finally defeated by the government, the thoroughly scared upper classes tightened the screws of serfdom even further. Holding down the peasants and thereby maintaining the tsar became almost the principal obligation of the nobility until 1689.

The Reforms of Peter the Great

It is now possible to understand the reforms of Peter the Great (r. 1682–1725) and his kind of monarchial absolutism. Contrary to some historians' assertions, Peter was interested primarily in

"The Bronze Horseman"   This equestrian masterpiece of Peter the Great, finished for Catherine the Great in 1783, dominates the center of St. Petersburg (modern Leningrad). The French sculptor Falconnet has captured the tsar's enormous energy, power, and determination. *(Source: Courtesy of The Conway Library, Courtauld Institute of Art)*

military power and not in some grandiose westernization plan. A giant for his time, at six feet seven inches, and possessing enormous energy and will power, Peter was determined to redress the defeats that the tsar's armies had occasionally suffered in their wars with Poland and Sweden since the time of Ivan the Terrible. And although Russia had gained a large mass of the Ukraine in 1667 and completed the conquest of Siberia in the seventeenth century, the tsar's vast kingdom had been built on a fierce drive for territorial expansion. Thus it was natural that the seventeen-year-old Peter would seek further gains when he overturned the regency in 1689 and assumed personal rule. The thirty-six years of that rule knew only one year of peace.

When Peter took control in 1689, the heart of his part-time army still consisted of cavalry made up of boyars and service nobility. The Russian army was lagging behind the professional standing armies being formed in Europe in the seventeenth

century. The core of such armies was a highly disciplined infantry—an infantry that fired and refired rifles as it fearlessly advanced, until it charged with bayonets fixed. Such a large, permanent army was enormously expensive and could be created only at the cost of great sacrifice. Given the desire to conquer more territory, Peter's military problem was serious.

Peter's solution was, in essence, to tighten up Muscovy's old service system and really make it work. He put the nobility back in harness with a vengeance. Every nobleman, great or small, was once again required to serve in the army or in the civil administration—for life. Since a more modern army and government required skilled technicians and experts, Peter created schools and even universities. One of his most hated reforms required five years of compulsory education away from home for every young nobleman. Peter established a merit-based military-civilian bureaucracy in which some people of non-noble origin rose to high positions. He also searched out talented foreigners—twice in his reign he went abroad to study and observe—and placed them in his service. These measures combined to make the army and government more powerful and efficient.

Peter also greatly increased the service requirements of the commoners. He established a regular standing army of more than 200,000 soldiers, made up mainly of peasants commanded by officers from the nobility. In addition, special forces of Cossacks and foreigners numbered more than 100,000. The departure of a drafted peasant boy was regarded by his family and village as almost like a funeral, as indeed it was, since the recruit was drafted for life. The peasantry also served with its taxes, which increased threefold during Peter's reign, as people—"souls"—replaced land as the primary unit of taxation. Serfs were also arbitrarily assigned to work in the growing number of factories and mines.

The constant warfare of Peter's reign consumed 80 to 85 percent of all revenues but brought only modest territorial expansion. Yet after initial losses in the Great Northern War with Sweden, which lasted from 1700 to 1721, Peter's new war machine crushed the smaller army of Sweden's Charles XII in the Ukraine at Poltava in 1709, one of the most significant battles in Russian history. Sweden never really regained the offensive, and Russia eventually annexed Estonia and much of present-day Latvia (see Map 19.4), lands that had never before been under Russian rule. Russia became the dominant power on the Baltic Sea and very much a European Great Power. If victory or defeat is the ultimate historical criterion, Peter's reforms were a success.

There were other important consequences of Peter's reign. Because of his feverish desire to use modern technology to strengthen the army, many Westerners and Western ideas flowed into Russia for the first time. A new class of educated Russians began to emerge. At the same time, vast numbers of Russians, especially among the poor and weak, hated Peter's massive changes. The split between the enserfed peasantry and the educated nobility thus widened, even though all were caught up in the endless demands of the sovereign.

A new idea of state interest, distinct from the tsar's personal interests, began to take hold. Peter himself fostered this conception of the public interest by claiming time and again to be serving the common good. For the first time, a Russian tsar attached explanations to his decrees in an attempt to gain the confidence and enthusiastic support of the populace. Yet, as before, the tsar alone decided what the common good was. Here was a source of future tension between tsar and people.

In sum, Peter built on the service obligations of old Muscovy. His monarchial absolutism was truly the culmination of the long development of a unique Russian civilization. Yet the creation of a more modern army and state introduced much that was new and Western to that civilization. This development paved the way for Russia to move much closer to the European mainstream in its thought and institutions during the Enlightenment, especially under that famous administrative and sexual lioness, Catherine the Great.

ABSOLUTISM AND THE BAROQUE IN EASTERN EUROPE

The rise of royal absolutism in eastern Europe had many consequences. Nobles served their powerful rulers in new ways while the great inferiority of the urban middle classes and the peasants was reconfirmed. Armies became larger and more professional; taxes rose. Royal absolutism also interacted with baroque culture and art. Inspired in part by Louis XIV of France, the great and not-so-great rulers called on the artistic talent of the age to glo-

rify their power and magnificence. This exaltation of despotic rule was particularly striking in the lavish masterpieces of architecture.

Palaces and Power

As soaring Gothic cathedrals expressed the idealized spirit of the High Middle Ages, so dramatic baroque palaces symbolized the age of absolutist power. By 1700 palace building had become a veritable obsession for the rulers of central and eastern Europe. Their baroque palaces were clearly intended to overawe the people with the monarch's strength. The great palaces were also visual declarations of equality with Louis XIV and were therefore modeled after Versailles to a greater or lesser extent. One such palace was Schönbrunn, an enormous Viennese Versailles begun in 1695 by Emperor Leopold to celebrate Austrian military victories and Habsburg might.

Petty princes also contributed mightily to the mania of palace-building. The not-very-important elector-archbishop of Mainz, the ruling prince of that city, confessed apologetically that "building is a craze which costs much, but every fool likes his own hat."[21] The archbishop of Mainz's own "hat" was an architectural gem, like that of another churchly ruler, the prince-bishop of Würzburg.

In central and eastern Europe, the favorite noble servants of royalty became extremely rich and powerful, and they, too, built grandiose palaces in the capital cities. These palaces were in part an extension of the monarch, for they surpassed the buildings of less favored nobles. Take, for example, the palaces of Prince Eugene of Savoy. A French nobleman by birth and education, Prince Eugene entered the service of Emperor Leopold I with the relief of the besieged Vienna in 1683, and he became Austria's most famous military hero. It was he who smashed the Turks and fought Louis XIV to a standstill. Rewarded with great wealth by his grateful royal employer, Eugene called on the leading architects of the day, J. B. Fischer von Erlach and Johann Lukas von Hildebrandt, to consecrate his glory in stone and fresco. Fischer built Eugene's Winter (or Town) Palace in Vienna, and he and Hildebrandt collaborated on the prince's Summer Palace on the city's outskirts.

The Summer Palace was actually two enormous buildings, the Lower Belvedere and the Upper Belvedere, completed in 1713 and 1722 respectively and joined by one of the most exquisite gardens in Europe. The Upper Belvedere, Hildebrandt's masterpiece, stood gracefully, even playfully, behind a great sheet of water. One entered through magnificent iron gates into a hall where sculptured giants crouched as pillars; then one moved on to a great staircase of dazzling whiteness and ornamentation. Even today, the emotional impact of this building is great: here art and beauty create a sense of immense power and wealth.

Palaces like the Upper Belvedere were magnificent examples of the baroque style. They expressed the baroque delight in bold, sweeping statements intended to provide a dramatic emotional experience. To create this experience, baroque masters dissolved the traditional artistic frontiers: the architect permitted the painter and the artisan to cover the undulating surfaces with wildly colorful paintings, graceful sculptures, and fanciful carvings. Space was used in a highly original way, to blend everything together in a total environment. These techniques shone in all their glory in the churches and palaces of southern Germany. Artistic achievement and political statement reinforced each other.

Royal Cities

Not content with fashioning ostentatious palaces, absolute monarchs and baroque architects remodeled existing capital cities or built new ones to reflect royal magnificence and the centralization of political power. Karlsruhe, founded in 1715 as the capital city of a small German principality, is one extreme example. There, broad, straight avenues radiated out from the palace, so that all roads—like all power—were focused on the ruler. More typically, the monarch's architects added new urban areas alongside the old city, and these areas became the real heart of the expanding capital.

The distinctive features of the new additions were their broad avenues, their imposing government buildings, and their rigorous mathematical layout. Along major thoroughfares the nobles built elaborate townhouses; stables and servants' quarters were built on the alleys behind. Wide avenues facilitated the rapid movement of soldiers through the city to quell any disturbance (the king's planners had the needs of the military constantly in mind). Under arcades along the avenues

appeared smart and expensive shops, the first department stores, with plate-glass windows and fancy displays.

The new avenues brought reckless speed to the European city. Whereas everyone had walked through the narrow, twisting streets of the medieval town, the high and mighty raced down the broad boulevards in elegant carriages. A social gap opened between the wealthy riders and the gaping, dodging pedestrians. "Mind the carriages!" wrote one eighteenth-century observer in Paris:

Here comes the black-coated physician in his chariot, the dancing master in his coach, the fencing master in his surrey—and the Prince behind six horses at the gallop as if he were in the open country. . . . The threatening wheels of the overbearing rich drive as rapidly as ever over stones stained with the blood of their unhappy victims.[22]

Speeding carriages on broad avenues, an endless parade of power and position: here were the symbol and substance of the baroque city.

The Growth of St. Petersburg

No city illustrates better than St. Petersburg the close ties among politics, architecture, and urban development in this period. In 1702 Peter the Great's armies seized a desolate Swedish fortress on one of the water-logged islands at the mouth of the Neva River on the Baltic Sea. Within a year the tsar had decided to build a new city there and to make it, rather than ancient Moscow, his capital.

Since the first step was to secure the Baltic coast, military construction was the main concern for the next eight years. The land was swampy and uninhabited, the climate damp and unpleasant. But Peter cared not at all. For him, the inhospitable northern marshland was a future metropolis gloriously bearing his name.

After the decisive Russian victory at Poltava in 1709 greatly reduced the threat of Swedish armies, Peter moved into high gear. In one imperious decree after another, he ordered his people to build a city that would equal any in the world. Such a city had to be Western and baroque, just as Peter's army had to be Western and permanent. From such a new city, his "window on Europe," Peter believed that it would be easier to reform the country militarily and administratively.

These general political goals matched Peter's architectural ideas, which had been influenced by his travels in western Europe. First, Peter wanted a comfortable, "modern" city. Modernity meant broad, straight, stone-paved avenues, houses built in a uniform line and not haphazardly set back from the street, large parks, canals for drainage, stone bridges, and street lighting. Second, all building had to conform strictly to detailed architectural regulations set down by the government. Finally, each social group—the nobility, the merchants, the artisans, and so on—was to live in a certain section of town. In short, the city and its population were to conform to a carefully defined urban plan of the baroque type.

Peter used the traditional but reinforced methods of Russian autocracy to build his modern capital. The creation of St. Petersburg was just one of the heavy obligations he dictatorially imposed on all social groups in Russia. The peasants bore the heaviest burdens. Just as the government drafted peasants for the army, it also drafted from 25,000 to 40,000 men each summer to labor in St. Petersburg for three months, without pay. Every ten to fifteen peasant households had to furnish one such worker each summer and then pay a special tax in order to feed that worker in St. Petersburg.

Peasants hated forced labor in the capital, and each year one-fourth to one-third of those sent risked brutal punishment and ran away. Many

Würzburg, the Prince-Bishop's Palace   The baroque style brought architects, painters, and sculptors together in harmonious, even playful partnership. This magnificent monumental staircase, designed by Johann Balthasar Neumann in 1735, merges into the vibrant ceiling frescos by Giovanni Battista Tiepolo. A man is stepping out of the picture, and a painted dog resembles a marble statue. *(Source: Erich Lessing Culture and Fine Arts Archive)*

peasant construction workers died each summer from hunger, sickness, and accidents. Many also died because peasant villages tended to elect old men or young boys to labor in St. Petersburg, since strong and able-bodied men were desperately needed on the farm in the busy summer months. Thus beautiful St. Petersburg was built on the shoveling, carting, and paving of a mass of conscripted serfs.

Peter also drafted more privileged groups to his city, but on a permanent basis. Nobles were summarily ordered to build costly stone houses and palaces in St. Petersburg and to live in them most of the year. Merchants and artisans were also commanded to settle and build in St. Petersburg. These nobles and merchants were then required to pay for the city's avenues, parks, canals, embankments, pilings, and bridges, all of which were very costly in terms of both money and lives because they were built on a swamp. The building of St. Petersburg was, in truth, an enormous direct tax levied on the wealthy, who in turn forced the peasantry to do most of the work. The only immediate beneficiaries were the foreign architects and urban

planners. No wonder so many Russians hated Peter's new city.

Yet the tsar had his way. By the time of his death in 1725, there were at least six thousand houses and numerous impressive government buildings in St. Petersburg. Under the remarkable women who ruled Russia throughout most of the eighteenth century, St. Petersburg blossomed completely as a majestic and well-organized city, at least in its wealthy showpiece sections. Peter's youngest daughter, the quick-witted, sensual beauty Elizabeth (r. 1741–1762), named as her chief architect Bartolomeo Rastrelli, who had come to Russia from Italy as a boy of fifteen in 1715. Combining Italian and Russian traditions into a unique, wildly colorful St. Petersburg style, Rastrelli built many palaces for the nobility and all the larger government buildings erected during Elizabeth's reign. He also rebuilt the Winter Palace as an enormous, aqua-colored royal residence, now the Hermitage Museum. There Elizabeth established a flashy, luxury-loving, and slightly crude court, which Catherine the Great in turn made truly imperial. All the while St. Petersburg grew rapidly, and its

St. Petersburg, ca 1760 Rastrelli's remodeled Winter Palace, which housed the royal family until the Russian Revolution of 1917, stands on the left along the Neva River. The Navy Office with its famous golden spire and other government office buildings are nearby and across the river. Russia became a naval power and St. Petersburg a great port. *(Source: Michael Holford)*

almost 300,000 inhabitants in 1782 made it one of the world's largest cities. Peter and his successors had created out of nothing a magnificent and harmonious royal city, which unmistakably proclaimed the power of Russia's rulers and the creative potential of the absolutist state.

CONSTITUTIONALISM: AN OVERVIEW

The march toward absolutism seemed almost irresistible in seventeenth-century Europe. Yet while France, Austria, Prussia, and Russia responded to the challenge of war and social unrest by forging the absolutist state, England and Holland evolved toward limited monarchial power and the constitutional state.

Constitutionalism is the limitation of government by law. Constitutionalism implies a balance between (1) the authority and power of the government and (2) the rights and liberties of the subjects. The balance is often very delicate.

A nation's constitution may be written or unwritten. It may be embodied in one basic document, occasionally revised by amendment or judicial decision, like the Constitution of the United States. Or it may be partly written and partly unwritten and include parliamentary statutes, judicial decisions, and a body of traditional procedures and practices, like the English and Canadian constitutions. Whether written or unwritten, a constitution gets its binding force from the government's acknowledgment that it must respect that constitution—that is, that the state must be governed according to the laws. Men and women living in a constitutional state look on the law and the constitution as the protectors of their rights, liberties, and property.

Modern constitutional governments may take either a republican or a monarchial form. In a constitutional republic, sovereign power resides in the electorate and is exercised by the electorate's representatives. In a constitutional monarchy, a king or queen serves as the head of state and may possess considerable political authority but sovereign power rests in the electorate.

A constitutional government is not necessarily a democratic government. In a complete democracy, *all* the people have the right to participate in the government of the state. Their participation is either indirect, through their elected representatives, or direct. Thus democratic government is intimately tied up with the *franchise* (the vote). Most European men could not vote until the later nineteenth century. Women gained the right to vote only in the twentieth century. Consequently, although constitutional government developed in the seventeenth century, full democracy was achieved only in recent times.

ENGLAND: THE TRIUMPH OF CONSTITUTIONAL MONARCHY

In 1588 Queen Elizabeth I of England exercised great personal power, but by 1689 the power of the English monarchy was severely limited. Change in England was anything but orderly. Seventeenth-century England displayed little political stability. It executed one king, experienced a bloody civil war, experimented with military dictatorship, then restored the son of the murdered king, and finally, after a bloodless revolution, established constitutional monarchy. Political stability came only in the 1690s. How do we account for the fact that out of this violent and tumultuous century England built the foundations for a strong and enduring constitutional monarchy?

The Decline of Royal Absolutism in England (1603–1649)

Elizabeth I's extraordinary success was the result of her political shrewdness and flexibility, her careful management of finances, her wise selection of ministers, her clever manipulation of Parliament, and her sense of royal dignity and devotion to hard work. After her Scottish cousin James Stuart succeeded her as James I (r. 1603–1625), Elizabeth's strengths seemed even greater.

King James was well educated, learned, and, with thirty-five years' experience as king of Scotland, politically shrewd. But he was not as interested in displaying the majesty and mystique of monarchy as Elizabeth had been. He also lacked the common touch. Urged to wave at the crowds who waited to greet their new ruler, James complained that he was tired and threatened to drop his breeches "so they can cheer at my arse." The new king failed to live up to the role expected of him in England.

James was devoted to the theory of divine right of kings. He expressed his ideas about divine right in his essay "The Trew Law of Free Monarchy." According to James I, a monarch has a divine (or God-given) right to authority and is responsible only to God. Rebellion is the worst of political crimes. If a king orders something evil, the subject should respond with passive disobedience but should be prepared to accept any penalty for noncompliance. "There are no privileges and immunities," said James, "which can stand against a divinely appointed King." This typically absolutist notion implied total royal jurisdiction over the liberties, persons, and properties of English men and women. Such a view ran directly counter to many long-standing English ideas, including the belief that a person's property could not be taken away without due process of law. And in the House of Commons the English had a strong representative body to question these absolutist pretensions.

The House of Commons guarded the state's pocketbook, and James and later Stuart kings badly needed to open that pocketbook. Elizabeth had bequeathed to James a sizable royal debt, but James I looked on all revenues as a windfall to be squandered on a lavish court and favorite courtiers. The extravagance displayed in James's court, as well as the public flaunting of his male lovers, weakened respect for the monarchy. These actions also stimulated the knights and burgesses who sat in the House of Commons at Westminster to press for a thorough discussion of royal expenditures, religious reform, and foreign affairs. In short, the Commons aspired to sovereignty—the ultimate political power in the realm.

During the reigns of James I and his son Charles I (r. 1625–1649) the English House of Commons was very different from the assembly that Henry VIII had manipulated into passing his Reformation legislation. The class that dominated the Commons during the Stuarts' reign wanted political power corresponding to its economic strength. A social revolution had brought about the change.

Agricultural techniques like the draining of wasteland and the application of fertilizer had improved the land and increased its yield. In the seventeenth century old manorial common land was enclosed and profitably turned into sheep runs. The dissolution of the monasteries and the sale of monastic land had enriched many people. Many invested in commercial ventures at home, such as the expanding cloth industry, and through part-nerships and joint stock companies engaged in foreign enterprises. Many also made prudent marriages. These developments increased social mobility. The typical pattern was for the commercially successful to set themselves up as country gentry. This elite group possessed a far greater proportion of the land and of the nation's wealth in 1640 than in 1540. Increased wealth resulted in a better-educated and more articulate House of Commons.

In England, unlike France, no social stigma was attached to paying taxes. Members of the House of Commons were willing to tax themselves provided they had some say in the expenditure of those taxes and in the formulation of state policies. The Stuart kings, however, considered such ambitions intolerable presumption and a threat to their divine-right prerogative. Consequently, at every Parliament between 1603 and 1640, bitter squabbles erupted between Crown and Commons. Like the Great Elector in Prussia, Charles I tried to govern without Parliament (1629–1640) and to finance his government by arbitrary levies. And as in Prussia these absolutist measures brought intense political conflict.

An issue graver than royal extravagance and Parliament's desire to make law was religion. In the early seventeenth century, increasing numbers of English people felt dissatisfied with the Church of England established by Henry VIII and reformed by Elizabeth. Many Puritans (see page 553) believed that Reformation had not gone far enough. They wanted to "purify" the Anglican church of Roman Catholic elements—elaborate vestments and ceremonial, the position of the altar in the church, even the giving and wearing of wedding rings.

It is very difficult to establish what proportion of the English population was Puritan. But it seems clear that many English men and women were attracted by the socioeconomic implications of John Calvin's theology. Calvinism emphasized hard work, sobriety, thrift, competition, and postponement of pleasure, and it tended to link sin and poverty with weakness and moral corruption. These attitudes, which have frequently been called the "Protestant ethic," "middle-class ethic," or "capitalist ethic," fit in precisely with the economic approaches and practices of many (successful) business people and farmers. Although it is hazardous to identify capitalism and progress with Protestantism—there were many successful Catholic capitalists—the "Protestant virtues" represented the prevailing values of members of the House of Commons.

James I and Charles I both gave the impression of being highly sympathetic to Roman Catholicism. Charles supported the policies of Archbishop of Canterbury William Laud (1573–1645), who tried to impose elaborate ritual and rich ceremonial on all churches. Laud insisted on complete uniformity of church services and enforced that uniformity through an ecclesiastical court called the "Court of High Commission." People believed that the country was being led back to Roman Catholicism. In 1637 Laud attempted to impose two new elements on the church organization in Scotland: a new prayer book, modeled on the Anglican Book of Common Prayer, and bishoprics, which the Presbyterian Scots firmly rejected. The Scots revolted. To finance an army to put down the Scots, King Charles was compelled to summon Parliament in November 1640. It was a fatal decision.

For eleven years Charles I had ruled without Parliament, financing his government through extraordinary stopgap levies considered illegal by most English people. For example, the king had revived a medieval law requiring coastal districts to help pay the cost of ships for defense, and he levied the tax, called "ship money," on both inland and coastal counties. Most members of Parliament believed that such taxation without consent amounted to absolute despotism. Thus they were not willing to trust the king with an army. Accordingly, the Parliament summoned in November 1640 (commonly called the "Long Parliament" because it sat from 1640 to 1660) enacted legislation that limited the power of the monarch and made arbitrary government impossible.

In 1641 the Commons passed the Triennial Act, which compelled the king to summon Parliament every three years. The Commons impeached Archbishop Laud and abolished the House of Lords and the Court of High Commission. King Charles, fearful of a Scottish invasion—the original reason for summoning Parliament—accepted these measures. Understanding and peace were not achieved, however, partly because radical members of the Commons pushed increasingly revolutionary propositions, partly because Charles maneuvered to rescind those he had already approved. An uprising in Ireland precipitated civil war.

Ever since Henry II had conquered Ireland in 1171, English governors had mercilessly ruled the land, and English landlords had ruthlessly exploited the Irish people. The English Reformation had made a bad situation worse: because the Irish remained Catholic, religious differences united with economic and political oppression. Without an army, Charles I could neither come to terms with the Scots nor put down the Irish rebellion, and the Long Parliament remained unwilling to place an army under a king it did not trust. Charles thus instigated military action against parliamentary forces. He recruited an army drawn from the nobility and the nobility's cavalry staff, the rural gentry, and mercenaries. The parliamentary army was composed of the militia of the city of London, country squires with business connections, and men with a firm belief that serving was their spiritual duty.

The English civil war (1642–1649) tested whether ultimate political power in England was to reside in the king or in Parliament. The civil war did not resolve that problem, although it ended in 1649 with the execution of King Charles on the charge of high treason and thus dealt a severe blow to the theory of divine-right, absolute monarchy in England. The years from 1649 to 1660, called the "Interregnum" because it separated two monarchial periods, was a transitional period of military dictatorship.

Puritanical Absolutism in England: Cromwell and the Protectorate

In the middle years of the seventeenth century, the problem of sovereignty was vigorously debated. In *Leviathan,* the English philosopher and political theorist Thomas Hobbes (1588–1679) maintained that sovereignty is ultimately derived from the people, who transfer it to the monarchy by implicit contract. The power of the ruler is absolute, but kings do not hold their power by divine right. This abstract theory pleased no one in the seventeenth century.

When Charles I was beheaded on January 30, 1649, the kingship was abolished in England. A *commonwealth,* or republican form of government, was proclaimed. In fact, the army that had defeated the royal forces controlled the government, and Oliver Cromwell controlled the army. Though called the "Protectorate," the rule of

Cromwell Dismisses the Rump Parliament In 1648 the army disposed of its enemies in Parliament; those who remained were known as the Rump Parliament. After the execution of Charles I and the establishment of the Commonwealth, legislative power in England theoretically rested in Parliament. But in 1653, concluding that he could not work with this body, Cromwell turned out the Rump. In this satirical Dutch print, Cromwell ordered members to go home. The sign on the wall reads, "This house is to let." *(Source: The British Library/Pat Hodgson Library)*

Cromwell (1653–1658) constituted military dictatorship.

Oliver Cromwell (1599–1658) came from the country gentry, the class that dominated the House of Commons in the early seventeenth century. He had sat in the Long Parliament. Cromwell rose in the parliamentary army and achieved nationwide fame by infusing the army with his Puritan convictions and molding it into the highly effective military machine, called the "New Model Army," that defeated the royalist forces.

Parliament had written a constitution, the Instrument of Government (1653), that invested executive power in a lord protector (Cromwell) and a council of state. The instrument provided for triennial parliaments and gave Parliament the sole power to raise taxes. But after repeated disputes, Cromwell tore up the document and proclaimed quasi-martial law.

On the issue of religion, Cromwell favored broad toleration, and the Instrument of Government gave all Christians, except Roman Catholics, the right to practice their faith. Toleration, however, meant state protection of many different Protestant sects, and most English people had no enthusiasm for such a notion; the idea was far ahead of its time. As for Irish Catholicism, Cromwell identified it with sedition. In 1649 he crushed rebellion in Ireland with merciless savagery, leaving a legacy of Irish hatred for England. He also rigorously censored the press, forbade sports, and kept the theaters closed in England.

Cromwell pursued mercantilist economic policies, similar to those that Colbert established in France. Cromwell enforced a navigation act requiring that English goods be transported on English ships. The navigation act was a great boost to the development of an English merchant marine and brought about a short but successful war with the commercially threatened Dutch. Cromwell also welcomed the immigration of Jews, because of their skills, and they began to return to England after four centuries of absence.

Military government collapsed when Cromwell died in 1658. Fed up with military rule, the English longed for a return to civilian government, restoration of the common law, and social stability. Moreover, the strain of creating a community of puritanical saints proved too psychologically exhausting. Government by military dictatorship was an unfortunate experiment that the English never forgot or repeated. By 1660 they were ready to try a restoration of monarchy.

The Restoration of the English Monarchy

The Restoration of 1660 re-established the monarchy in the person of Charles II (r. 1660–1685), eldest son of Charles I. At the same time both houses of Parliament were also restored, together with the established Anglican church. The Restoration failed to resolve two serious problems. What was to be the attitude of the state toward Puritans, Catholics, and dissenters from the established church? And what was to be the constitutional position of the king—that is, what was to be the relationship between the king and Parliament?

About the first of these issues, Charles II, a relaxed, easygoing, and sensual man, was basically indifferent. He was not interested in doctrinal issues. But the new members of Parliament were, and they proceeded to enact a body of laws that sought to compel religious uniformity. Those who refused to receive the sacrament of the Church of England could not vote, hold public office, preach, teach, attend the universities, or even assemble for meetings, according to the Test Act of 1673. These restrictions could not be enforced. When the Quaker William Penn held a meeting of his Friends and was arrested, the jury refused to convict him.

In politics, Charles II was determined to get along with Parliament and share power with it.

His method for doing so had profound importance for later constitutional development. The king appointed a council of five men who served both as his major advisers and as members of Parliament, thus acting as liaison agents between the executive and the legislature. This body was an ancestor of the cabinet system (see page 649). It gradually came to be accepted that the council of five was answerable in Parliament for the decisions of the king. This development gave rise to the concept of ministerial responsibility: royal ministers must answer to the Commons.

Harmony between the Crown and Parliament rested on the understanding that Charles would summon Parliament frequently and Parliament would vote him sufficient revenues. However, although Parliament believed that Charles should have large powers, it did not grant him an adequate income. Accordingly, in 1670 Charles entered into a secret agreement with Louis XIV. The French king would give Charles £200,000 annually. In return Charles would relax the laws against Catholics, gradually re-Catholicize England, support French policy against the Dutch, and convert to Catholicism himself.

When the details of this secret treaty leaked out, a wave of anti-Catholic fear swept England. This fear was compounded by a crucial fact: although Charles had produced several bastards, he had no legitimate children. It therefore appeared that his brother and heir, James, duke of York, who had publicly acknowledged his Catholicism, would inaugurate a Catholic dynasty. The combination of hatred for the French absolutism embodied in Louis XIV, hostility to Roman Catholicism, and fear of a permanent Catholic dynasty produced virtual hysteria. The Commons passed an exclusion bill denying the succession to a Roman Catholic, but Charles quickly dissolved Parliament and the bill never became law.

James II (r. 1685–1688) indeed succeeded his brother. Almost at once the worst English anti-Catholic fears, already aroused by Louis XIV's revocation of the Edict of Nantes, were realized. In direct violation of the Test Act, James appointed Roman Catholics to positions in the army, the universities, and local government. When these actions were tested in the courts, the judges, whom James had appointed, decided for the king. The king was suspending the law at will and appeared to be reviving the absolutism of his father (Charles I) and grandfather (James I). He went further. Attempting to broaden his base of support with Protestant dissenters and nonconformists, James issued a declaration of indulgence granting religious freedom to all.

Two events gave the signals for revolution. First, seven bishops of the Church of England petitioned the king that they not be forced to read the declaration of indulgence because of their belief that it was an illegal act. They were imprisoned in the Tower of London but subsequently acquitted amid great public enthusiasm. Second, in June 1688 James's second wife produced a male heir. A Catholic dynasty seemed assured. The fear of a Roman Catholic monarchy, supported by France and ruling outside the law, prompted a group of eminent persons to offer the English throne to James's Protestant daughter, Mary, and her Dutch husband, Prince William of Orange. In December 1688 James II, his queen, and their infant son fled to France and became pensioners of Louis XIV. Early in 1689, William and Mary were crowned king and queen of England.

Constitutional Monarchy and Cabinet Government

The English call the events of 1688 to 1689 the "Glorious Revolution." The revolution was indeed glorious in the sense that it replaced one king with another with a minimum of bloodshed. It also represented the destruction, once and for all, of the idea of divine-right absolutism in England. William and Mary accepted the English throne from Parliament and in so doing explicitly recognized the supremacy of Parliament. The revolution of 1688 established the principle that sovereignty, the ultimate power in the state, was divided between king and Parliament and that the king ruled with the consent of the governed.

The men who brought about the revolution quickly framed their intentions in the Bill of Rights, the cornerstone of the modern British constitution. The basic principles of the Bill of Rights were formulated in direct response to Stuart absolutism. Law was to be made in Parliament; once made, it could not be suspended by the Crown. Parliament had to be called at least every three years. Both elections to and debate in Parliament were to be free, in the sense that the Crown was not to interfere in them (this aspect of the bill was widely disregarded in the eighteenth century).

Judges would hold their offices "during good behavior," a provision that assured judicial independence. No longer could the Crown get the judicial decisions it wanted by threats of removal.

In striking contrast to continental states, there was to be no standing army that could be used against the English population in peacetime. The Bill of Rights granted "that the subjects which are Protestants may have arms for their defense suitable to their conditions and as allowed by law,"[23] meaning that Catholics could not possess firearms because the Protestant majority feared them. Additional legislation granted freedom of worship to Protestant dissenters and nonconformists and required that the English monarch always be Protestant.

The Glorious Revolution found its best defense in John Locke's *Second Treatise of Civil Government* (1690). The political philosopher Locke (1632–1704) maintained that people set up civil governments in order to protect life, liberty, and property. A government that oversteps its proper function—protecting the natural rights of life, liberty, and property—becomes a tyranny. (By "natural" rights, Locke meant rights basic to all men because all have the ability to reason.) Under a tyrannical government, the people have the natural right to rebellion. Rebellion can be avoided if the government carefully respects the rights of citizens and if the people zealously defend their liberty. Recognizing the close relationship between economic and political freedom, Locke linked economic liberty and private property with political freedom.

Locke served as the great spokesman for the liberal English revolution of 1688 to 1689 and for representative government. His idea, inherited from ancient Greece and Rome, that there are natural or universal rights equally valid for all peoples and societies, played a powerful role in eighteenth-century Enlightenment thought. His ideas on liberty and tyranny were especially popular in colonial America.

The events of 1688 to 1689 did not constitute a *democratic* revolution. The revolution formalized Parliament's great power, and Parliament represented the upper classes. The great majority of English people had little say in their government. The English revolution established a constitutional monarchy; it also inaugurated an age of aristocratic government, which lasted at least until 1832 and in many ways until 1914.

In the course of the eighteenth century, the cabinet system of government evolved. The term *cabinet* derives from the small private room in which English rulers consulted their chief ministers. In a cabinet system, the leading ministers, who must have seats in and the support of a majority of the House of Commons, formulate common policy and conduct the business of the country. During the administration of one royal minister, Sir Robert Walpole, who led the cabinet from 1721 to 1742, the idea developed that the cabinet was responsible to the House of Commons. Walpole enjoyed the favor of the monarchy and of the House of Commons and came to be called the king's first, or "prime," minister. In the English cabinet system, both legislative and executive power are held by the leading ministers, who form the government.

THE DUTCH REPUBLIC IN THE SEVENTEENTH CENTURY

In the late sixteenth century, the seven northern provinces of the Netherlands, of which Holland and Zeeland were the most prosperous, had thrown off Spanish domination. This success was based on their geographical lines of defense, the wealth of their cities, the military strategy of William the Silent, the preoccupation of Philip II of Spain with so many additional concerns, and the northern provinces' vigorous Calvinism. In 1581 the seven provinces of the Union of Utrecht had formed the United Provinces (see page 587). The Peace of Westphalia in 1648 confirmed the Dutch republic's independence. The seventeenth century witnessed an unparalleled flowering of Dutch scientific, artistic, and literary achievement. In this period, often called the "golden age of the Netherlands," Dutch ideas and attitudes played a profound role in shaping a new and modern world view.

The Republic of the United Provinces of the Netherlands represents a variation in the development of the modern constitutional state. Within each province an oligarchy of wealthy merchants called "regents" handled domestic affairs in the local Estates. The provincial Estates held virtually all the power. A federal assembly, or States General, handled matters of foreign affairs, such as war. But the States General did not possess sovereign authority, since all issues had to be referred back to the local Estates for approval. The regents in each province jealously guarded local independence and resisted efforts at centralization. Nevertheless, Holland, which had the largest navy and the most wealth, dominated the republic and the States General. Significantly, the Estates assembled at Holland's capital, The Hague.

The government of the United Provinces conforms to none of the standard categories of seventeenth-century political organization. The Dutch were not monarchial but fiercely republican. The government was controlled by wealthy merchants and financiers. Though rich, their values were not aristocratic but strongly middle class, emphasizing thrift, hard work, and simplicity in living. The Dutch republic was not a strong federation but a confederation—that is, a weak union of strong provinces. The provinces were a temptation to powerful neighbors, yet the Dutch resisted the Spanish effort at reconquest and withstood both French and English attacks in the second half of the century. Louis XIV's hatred of the Dutch was proverbial. They represented all that he despised—middle-class values, religious toleration, and independent political institutions.

The political success of the Dutch rested on the phenomenal commercial prosperity of the Netherlands. The moral and ethical bases of that commercial wealth were thrift, frugality, and religious toleration. John Calvin had written, "From where do the merchant's profits come except from his own diligence and industry." This attitude undoubtedly encouraged a sturdy people who had waged a centuries-old struggle against the sea.

Alone of all European peoples in the seventeenth century, the Dutch practiced religious toleration. Peoples of all faiths were welcome within their borders. Although there is scattered evidence of anti-Semitism, Jews enjoyed a level of acceptance and absorption in Dutch business and general culture unique in early modern Europe. It is a testimony to the urbanity of Dutch society that in a century when patriotism was closely identified with religious uniformity, the Calvinist province of Holland allowed its highest official, Jan van Oldenbarneveldt, to continue to practice his Roman Catholic faith. As long as business people conducted their religion in private, the government did not interfere with them.

Toleration paid off. It attracted a great amount of foreign capital and investment. The Bank of

Amsterdam became Europe's best source of cheap credit and commercial intelligence and the main clearinghouse for bills of exchange. People of all races and creeds traded in Amsterdam, at whose docks on the Amstel River five thousand ships were berthed. Joost van den Vondel, the poet of Dutch imperialism, exulted:

God, God, the Lord of Amstel cried, hold every
  conscience free;

And Liberty ride, on Holland's tide, with billowing
  sails to sea,
And run our Amstel out and in; let freedom gird the
  bold,
And merchant in his counting house stand elbow
  deep in gold.[24]

The fishing industry was the cornerstone of the Dutch economy. For half the year, from June to December, fishing fleets combed the dangerous

Vermeer: A Woman Weighing Gold (ca 1657) Vermeer painted pictures of middle-class women involved in ordinary activities in the quiet interiors of their homes. Unrivaled among Dutch masters for his superb control of light, in this painting Vermeer illuminates a pregnant woman weighing gold on her scales, as Christ in the painting on the wall weighs the saved and the damned. *(Source: National Gallery of Art, Washington; Widener Collection)*

Job Berckheyde: The Amsterdam Stock Exchange   Small shareholders (through brokers) as well as rich capitalists could buy and sell and, by various combinations, speculate without having any money at all in the Amsterdam stock market. Shares in the Dutch East India Company were major objects of speculation. The volume, fluidity, and publicity of the Exchange were its new and distinctly modern features. *(Source: Museum Boymans-van Beuningen, Rotterdam)*

English coast and the North Sea, raking in tiny herring. Profits from herring stimulated ship-building, and even before 1600 the Dutch were offering the lowest shipping rates in Europe. The merchant marine was the largest in Europe. In 1650 contemporaries estimated that the Dutch had sixteen thousand merchant ships, half the European total. All the wood for these ships had to be imported: the Dutch bought whole forests from Norway. They also bought entire vineyards from French growers before the grapes were harvested. They controlled the Baltic grain trade,

buying entire wheat and rye crops in Poland, east Prussia, and Swedish Pomerania. Because they dealt in bulk, nobody could undersell the Dutch. Foreign merchants coming to Amsterdam could buy anything from precision lenses for the newly invented microscope to muskets for an army of five thousand. Although Dutch cities became famous for their exports—diamonds and linens from Haarlem, pottery from Delft—Dutch wealth depended less on exports than on transport.

In 1602 a group of the regents of Holland formed the Dutch East India Company, a joint

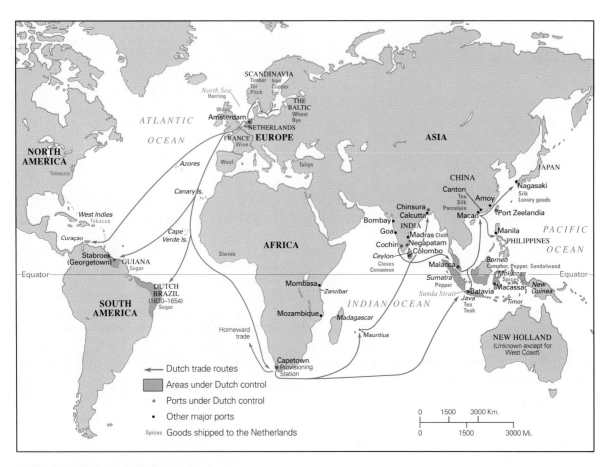

MAP 19.5 Seventeenth-Century Dutch Commerce   Dutch wealth rested on commerce, and commerce depended on the huge Dutch merchant marine, manned by perhaps 48,000 sailors. The fleet carried goods from all parts of the globe to Amsterdam.

stock company. Each investor received a percentage of the profits proportional to the amount of money he had put in. Within half a century, the Dutch East India Company had cut heavily into Portuguese trading in East Asia. The Dutch seized the Cape of Good Hope, Ceylon, and Malacca and established trading posts in each place. In the 1630s the Dutch East India Company was paying its investors about a 35 percent annual return on their investments. The Dutch West India Company, founded in 1621, traded extensively with Latin America and Africa (Map 19.5).

Trade and commerce brought the Dutch prodigious wealth. In the seventeenth century, the Dutch enjoyed the highest standard of living in Europe, perhaps in the world. Amsterdam and Rotterdam built massive granaries where the surplus of one year could be stored against possible shortages the next. Thus food prices fluctuated

very little, except during the 1650s when bad harvests reduced supplies. By the standards of Cologne, Paris, or London, salaries were high for all workers, except women. All classes of society, including unskilled laborers, ate well. The low price of bread meant that, compared with other places in Europe, a higher percentage of the worker's income could be spent on fish, cheese, butter, vegetables, even meat. A scholar recently described the Netherlands as "an island of plenty in a sea of want."[25]

Although the initial purpose of the Dutch East and West India companies was commercial—the import of spices and silks to Europe—the Dutch found themselves involved in the imperialist exploitation of parts of East Asia and Latin America, with great success. In 1652 the Dutch founded Cape Town on the southern tip of Africa as a fueling station for ships planning to cross the Pacific.

But war with France and England in the 1670s hurt the United Provinces. The long War of the Spanish Succession, in which the Dutch supported England against France, was a costly drain on Dutch manpower and financial resources. The peace signed in 1713 to end the war marked the beginning of Dutch economic decline.

SUMMARY

War, religious strife, economic depression, and peasant revolts were all aspects of a deep crisis in seventeenth-century Europe. Rulers responded by aggressively seeking to expand their power, which they claimed was essential to meet emergencies and quell disorders. Claiming also that they ruled by divine right, monarchs sought the freedom to wage war, levy taxes, and generally make law as they saw fit. Although they were limited by technology and inadequate financial resources, monarchial governments on the continent succeeded to a large extent, overpowering organized opposition and curbing the power of the nobility and the traditional representative institutions.

The France of Louis XIV led the way to royal absolutism. France developed a centralized bureaucracy, a professional army, a state-directed economy, all of which Louis personally supervised. The king saw himself as the representative of God on earth and accountable to no one here below. His majestic bearing and sumptuous court dazzled contemporaries. Yet behind the grand façade of unchallenged personal rule and obedient bureaucrats working his will there stood major limitations on Louis XIV's power, most notably the financial independence of some provinces and the nobility's traditional freedom from taxation, which Louis himself was compelled to reaffirm.

Within a framework of resurgent serfdom and entrenched nobility, Austrian and Prussian monarchs also fashioned absolutist states in the seventeenth and early eighteenth centuries. These monarchs won absolutist control over standing armies, permanent taxes, and legislative bodies. But they

Pieter Claesz: Still Life The term "still life" became popular after 1650 as a reference to paintings of inanimate objects—flowers, fruit, all kinds of food, tableware, musical instruments—and the term was usually applied to Dutch paintings. As this scene suggests, the enormously successful Dutch commercial society took great pleasure in sensuous materialism. Yet the tortoise, a symbol of long life, and the watch, a reminder of the passage of time, imply that all is vanity. *(Source: Louvre/Cliché des Musées Nationaux, Paris)*

did not question the underlying social and economic relationships. Indeed, they enhanced the privileges of the nobility, which furnished the leading servitors for enlarged armies and growing government bureaucracies.

In Russia, social and economic trends were similar to those in Austria and Prussia. Unlike those two states, however, Russia had a long history of powerful princes. Tsar Peter the Great succeeded in tightening up Russia's traditional absolutism and modernizing it by reforming the army, the bureaucracy, and the defense industry. In Russia and throughout eastern Europe, war and the needs of the state in time of war weighed heavily in the triumph of absolutism.

Holland and England defied the general trend toward absolute monarchy. While Holland prospered under a unique republican confederation that placed most power in the hands of the different provinces, England—fortunately shielded from continental armies and military emergencies by its navy and the English Channel—evolved into the first modern constitutional state. The bitter conflicts between Parliament and the first two Stuart rulers, James I and Charles I, tested where sovereign power would rest in the state. The resulting civil war deposed the king, but it did not settle the question. A revival of absolutist tendencies under James II brought on the Glorious Revolution of 1688 to 1689, and the people who made that revolution settled three basic issues. Sovereign power was divided between king and Parliament, with Parliament enjoying the greater share. Government was to be based on the rule of law. And the liberties of English people were to be made explicit in written form, in the Bill of Rights. This constitutional settlement marked an important milestone in world history, although the framers left to later generations the task of making constitutional government work.

Triumphant absolution interacted spectacularly with the arts. It molded the ideals of French classicism, which glorified the state as personified by Louis XIV. Baroque art, which had grown out of the Catholic Reformation's desire to move the faithful and exalt the faith, admirably suited the secular aspirations of eastern European rulers. Thus baroque art attained magnificent heights in eastern Europe, symbolizing the ideal and harmonizing with the reality of imperious royal absolutism.

NOTES

1. J. B. Collins, *Fiscal Limits of Absolutism: Direct Taxation in Early Seventeenth Century France* (Berkeley: University of California Press, 1988), pp. 1, 3–4, 215–222.
2. Quoted in J. H. Elliot, *Richelieu and Olivares* (Cambridge: Cambridge University Press, 1984), p. 135; and in W. F. Church, *Richelieu and Reason of State* (Princeton, N.J.: Princeton University Press, 1972), p. 507.
3. D. Parker, *The Making of French Absolutism* (New York: St. Martin's Press, 1983), pp. 146–148.
4. See W. Beik, *Absolutism and Society in Seventeenth Century France: State Power and Provincial Aristocracy in Languedoc* (Cambridge: Cambridge University Press, 1985), pp. 279–302.
5. S. de Gramont, ed., *The Age of Magnificence: Memoirs of the Court of Louis XIV by the Duc de Saint Simon* (New York: Capricorn Books, 1964), pp. 141–145.
6. Quoted in A. Trout, *Jean-Baptiste Colbert* (Boston: Twayne, 1978), p. 128.
7. Ibid.
8. See W. C. Scoville, *The Persecution of the Huguenots and French Economic Development: 1680–1720* (Berkeley: University of California Press, 1960).
9. W. F. Church, *Louis XIV in Historical Thought: From Voltaire to the Annales School* (New York: Norton, 1976), p. 92.
10. J. H. Elliott, *Imperial Spain, 1469–1716* (New York: Mentor Books, 1963), pp. 306–308.
11. B. Bennassar, *The Spanish Character: Attitudes and Mentalities from the Sixteenth to the Nineteenth Century,* trans. B. Keen (Berkeley: University of California Press, 1979), p. 125.
12. F. L. Carsten, *The Origins of Prussia* (Oxford: Clarendon Press, 1954), p. 175.
13. Quoted in R. Ergang, *The Potsdam Fuhrer: Frederick William I, Father of Prussian Militarism* (New York: Octagon Books, 1972), pp. 85, 87.
14. Ibid., pp. 6–7, 43.
15. Quoted in R. A. Dorwart, *The Administrative Reforms of Frederick William I of Prussia* (Cambridge, Mass.: Harvard University Press, 1953), p. 226.
16. Quoted in H. Rosenberg, *Bureaucracy, Aristocracy, and Autocracy: The Prussian Experience, 1660–1815* (Boston: Beacon Press, 1966), p. 38.
17. Quoted in R. Pipes, *Russia Under the Old Regime* (New York: Scribner, 1974), p. 48.
18. Quoted in N. V. Riasanovsky, *A History of Russia* (New York: Oxford University Press, 1963), p. 79.
19. Quoted in I. Grey, *Ivan III and the Unification of Russia* (New York: Collier Books, 1967), p. 39.

20. Quoted in Pipes, p. 85.
21. Quoted in J. Summerson, in *The Eighteenth Century: Europe in the Age of Enlightenment,* ed. A. Cobban (New York: McGraw-Hill, 1969), p. 80.
22. Quoted in L. Mumford, *The Culture of Cities* (New York: Harcourt Brace Jovanovich, 1938), p. 97.
23. C. Stephenson and G. F. Marcham, *Sources of English Constitutional History* (New York: Harper & Row, 1937), p. 601.
24. Quoted in D. Maland, *Europe in the Seventeenth Century* (New York: Macmillan, 1967), pp. 198–199.
25. S. Schama, *The Embarrassment of Riches: An Interpretation of Dutch Culture in the Golden Age* (New York: Knopf, 1987), pp. 165–170.

SUGGESTED READING

Students who wish to explore the problems presented in this chapter will find a rich and exciting literature with many works available in paperback editions. The following surveys provide good background material. G. Parker, *Europe in Crisis, 1598–1618* (1980), provides a sound introduction to the social, economic, and religious tensions of the period. R. S. Dunn, *The Age of Religious Wars, 1559–1715,* 2d ed. (1979), examines the period from the perspective of the confessional strife between Protestants and Catholics, but there is also stimulating material on absolutism and constitutionalism. T. Aston, ed., *Crisis in Europe, 1560–1660* (1967), contains essays by leading historians. P. Anderson, *Lineages of the Absolutist State* (1974), is a Marxist interpretation of absolutism in western and eastern Europe. M. Beloff, *The Age of Absolutism* (1967), concentrates on the social forces that underlay administrative change. H. Rosenberg, "Absolute Monarchy and Its Legacy," in N. F. Cantor and S. Werthman, eds., *Early Modern Europe, 1450–1650* (1967), is a seminal study. The classic treatment of constitutionalism remains that of C. H. McIlwain, *Constitutionalism: Ancient and Modern* (1940), written by a great scholar during the rise of German fascism. S. B. Crimes, *English Constitutional History* (1967), is an excellent survey with useful chapters on the sixteenth and seventeenth centuries.

Louis XIV and his age have attracted the attention of many scholars. J. Wolf, *Louis XIV,* cited in the Notes, remains the best available biography. Two works of W. H. Lewis, *The Splendid Century* (1957) and *The Sunset of the Splendid Century* (1963), make delightful light reading, especially for the beginning student. The advanced student will want to consult the excellent historiographical analysis by W. F. Church mentioned in the Notes, *Louis XIV in Historical Thought.* Perhaps the best works of the Annales school on the period are P. Goubert, *Louis XIV and Twenty Million Frenchmen* (1972), and Goubert's heavily detailed *The Ancien Régime: French Society, 1600–1750,* 2 vols. (1969–1973), which contains invaluable material on the lives and work of ordinary people. For the French economy and financial conditions, the old study of C. W. Cole, *Colbert and a Century of French Mercantilism,* 2 vols. (1939), is still valuable but should be supplemented by R. Bonney, *The King's Debts: Finance and Politics in France, 1589–1661* (1981), and by the works of Trout and Scoville listed in the Notes. R. Hatton, *Europe in the Age of Louis XIV* (1979), is a splendidly illustrated survey of many aspects of seventeenth-century European culture. O. Ranum, *Paris in the Age of Absolutism* (1968), describes the geographical, political, economic, and architectural significance of the cultural capital of Europe. V. L. Tapie, *The Age of Grandeur: Baroque Art and Architecture* (1960), also emphasizes the relationship between art and politics with excellent illustrations.

For Spain, in addition to the works in the Notes, see M. Defourneaux, *Daily Life in Spain in the Golden Age* (1976), highly useful for an understanding of ordinary people and of Spanish society. See also C. R. Phillips, *Ciudad Real, 1500–1750: Growth, Crisis, and Readjustment in the Spanish Economy* (1979), a significant case study

The following works offer solid material on English political and social issues of the seventeenth century: M. Ashley, *England in the Seventeenth Century,* rev. ed. (1980), and *The House of Stuart: Its Rise and Fall* (1980); C. Hill, *A Century of Revolution* (1961); J. P. Kenyon, *Stuart England* (1978); and K. Wrightson, *English Society, 1580–1680* (1982). Perhaps the most comprehensive treatments of Parliament are C. Russell, *Crisis of Parliaments, 1509–1660* (1971), and Russell, *Parliaments and English Politics, 1621–1629* (1979). On the background of the English civil war, L. Stone, *The Crisis of the Aristocracy* (1965), and Stone, *The Causes of the English Revolution* (1972), are standard works. Both B. Manning, *The English People and the English Revolution* (1976), and D. Underdown, *Revel, Riot, and Rebellion* (1985), discuss the extent of popular involvement. For English intellectual currents, see J. O. Appleby, *Economic Thought and Ideology in Seventeenth Century England* (1978), and C. Hill, *Intellectual Origins of the English Revolution* (1966).

For the several shades of Protestant sentiment in the early seventeenth century, see P. Collinson, *The Religion of Protestants* (1982). C. M. Hibbard, *Charles I and the Popish Plot* (1983), treats Roman Catholic influence and may be compared with W. Haller, *The Rise of Puritanism* (1957). For women, see R. Thompson, *Women in Stuart England and America* (1974), and A. Fraser, *The Weaker Vessel* (1985). For Cromwell and the Interregnum, C. Firth, *Oliver Cromwell and the Rule of the Puritans in England* (1956), and A. Fraser, *Cromwell, the Lord Protector* (1973), are both valuable. J. Morrill, *The Revolt of the Provinces,* 2d ed. (1980), is the best study of religious neutralism. C. Hill, *The World Turned Upside Down* (1972), discusses radical thought during the period.

For the Restoration and the Glorious Revolution, see R. Hutton, *Charles II: King of England, Scotland and Ireland* (1989), and A. Fraser, *Royal Charles: Charles II and the Restoration* (1979), two highly readable biographies; R. Ollard, *The Image of the King: Charles I and Charles II* (1980), which examines the nature of monarchy; J. Miller, *James II: A Study in Kingship* (1977); J. Childs, *The Army, James II, and the Glorious Revolution* (1980); J. R. Jones, *The Revolution of 1688 in England* (1972); and L. G. Schwoerer, *The Declaration of Rights, 1689* (1981), a fine assessment of that fundamental document. The ideas of John Locke are analyzed by J. P. Kenyon, *Revolution Principles: The Politics of Party, 1689–1720* (1977).

On Holland, K. H. D. Haley, *The Dutch Republic in the Seventeenth Century* (1972), is a splendidly illustrated appreciation of Dutch commercial and artistic achievements, and J. L. Price, *Culture and Society in the Dutch Republic During the Seventeenth Century* (1974), is a sound scholarly work. R. Boxer, *The Dutch Seaborne Empire* (1980), and the appropriate chapters of D. Maland, *Europe in the Seventeenth Century,* cited in the Notes, are useful for Dutch overseas expansion and the reasons for Dutch prosperity. The following works focus on the economic and cultural life of the leading Dutch city: V. Barbour, *Capitalism in Amsterdam in the Seventeenth Century* (1950), and D. Regin, *Traders, Artists, Burghers: A Cultural History of Amsterdam in the Seventeenth Century* (1977). The leading statesmen of the period may be studied in these biographies: H. H. Rowen, *John de Witt, Grand Pensionary of Holland, 1625–1672* (1978); S. B. Baxter, *William the III and the Defense of European Liberty, 1650–1702* (1966); and J. den Tex, *Oldenbarnevelt,* 2 vols. (1973).

The best study on early Prussian history is Carsten, *The Origin of Prussia* (see the Notes). Rosenberg, *Bureaucracy, Aristocracy, and Autocracy* is a masterful analysis of the social context of Prussian absolutism. In addition to Ergang, *The Potsdam Fuhrer,* an exciting and critical biography of ramrod Frederick William I, there is G. Ritter, *Frederick the Great* (1968), a more sympathetic study of the talented son by one of Germany's leading conservative historians. G. Craig, *The Politics of the Prussian Army, 1640–1945* (1964), expertly traces the great influence of the military on the Prussian state over three hundred years. R. J. Evans, *The Making of the Habsburg Empire, 1550–1770* (1979), and R. A. Kann,

A History of the Habsburg Empire, 1526–1918 (1974), analyze the development of absolutism in Austria, as does A. Wandruszka, *The House of Habsburg* (1964). J. Stoye, *The Siege of Vienna* (1964), is a fascinating account of the last great Ottoman offensive, which is also treated in the interesting study by P. Coles, *The Ottoman Impact on Europe, 1350–1699* (1968). The Austro-Ottoman conflict is also a theme of L. S. Stavrianos, *The Balkans Since 1453* (1958), and D. McKay, *Prince Eugene of Savoy* (1978), a fine biography. A good general account is provided in D. McKay and H. Scott, *The Rise of the Great Powers, 1648–1815* (1983), and R. Vierhaus, *Germany in the Age of Absolutism* (1988), offers a good survey of the different German states.

On eastern European peasants and serfdom, D. Chirot, ed., *The Origins of Backwardness in Eastern Europe: Economics and Politics from the Middle Ages Until the Twentieth Century* (1989), is a wide-ranging introduction that may be compared with J. Blum, "The Rise of Serfdom in Eastern Europe," *American Historical Review* 62 (July 1957): 807–836. E. Levin, *Sex and Society in the World of the Orthodox Slavs, 900–1700* (1989), carries family history to eastern Europe. R. Mousnier, *Peasant Uprisings in Seventeenth-Century France, Russia, and China* (1970), is a fine comparative study. J. Blum, *Lord and Peasant in Russia from the Ninth to the Nineteenth Century* (1961), provides a good look at conditions in rural Russia, and P. Avrich, *Russian Rebels, 1600–1800* (1972), treats some of the violent peasant upheavals those conditions produced. R. Hellie, *Enserfment and Military Change in Muscovy* (1971), is outstanding, as is A. Yanov, *Origins of Autocracy: Ivan the Terrible in Russian History* (1981). In addition to the fine surveys by Pipes and Riasanovsky cited in the Notes, J. Billington, *The Icon and the Axe* (1970), is a stimulating history of early Russian intellectual and cultural developments, such as the great split in the church. M. Raeff, *Origins of the Russian Intelligentsia* (1966), skillfully probes the mind of the Russian nobility in the eighteenth century. B. H. Sumner, *Peter the Great and the Emergence of Russia* (1962), is a fine brief introduction, which may be compared with the brilliant biography by Russia's greatest prerevolutionary historian, V. Klyuchevsky, *Peter the Great* (English trans., 1958), and with N. Riasanovsky, *The Image of Peter the Great in Russian History and Thought* (1985). G. Vernadsky and R. Fisher, eds., *A Source Book of Russian History from Early Times to 1917,* 3 vols. (1972), is an invaluable, highly recommended collection of documents and contemporary writings.

Three good books on art and architecture are E. Hempel, *Baroque Art and Architecture in Central Europe* (1965); G. Hamilton, *The Art and Architecture of Russia* (1954); and N. Pevsner, *An Outline of European Architecture,* 6th ed. (1960).

Chapter Opener Credits

Chapter 1: *Courtesy of the Trustees of the British Museum.* The Royal Standard of Ur, peace panel.

Chapter 2: *Ronny Jaques/Photo Researchers.* Audience hall of King Darius, Persepolis.

Chapter 3: *Courtesy of the Freer Gallery of Art, Smithsonian Institution, Washington, D.C.* King Vidudabha visiting the Buddha.

Chapter 4: *J. C. Francolon/Gama-Liaison.* Clay warriors from the tomb of the First Emperor.

Chapter 5: *John Veltri/Photo Researchers.* The Erechtheum, Parthenon.

Chapter 6: *Robert Harding Picture Library.* (Detail) Panel from Alexander Sarcophagus.

Chapter 7: *Michael Holford.* The Pont du Gard, a Roman aqueduct at Nîmes in southern France.

Chapter 8: *TSW/CLICK/Chicago Ltd.* Hadrian's Wall Cuddy's Crag, Northumberland.

Chapter 9: *Scala/Art Resource.* Apse mosaic of S. Apollinare in Classe, Ravenna.

Chapter 10: © *Ric Ergenbright.* Alhambra Palace, Granada.

Chapter 11: *The Museum Yamato Bunkakan.* Portrait of the poet Kodai-no-Kimi, or Koogimi.

Chapter 12: *Giraudon/Art Resource.* St. Bernard, Abbot of Clairvaux, preaching to his fellow Cistercians.

Chapter 13: *The Pierpont Morgan Library.* "April," from *Hours of the Virgin.*

Chapter 14: *Jonathan Blair/Woodfin Camp & Associates.* Carcassonne, southern France.

Chapter 15: *Robert Aberman/Barbara Heller Photo Library.* Ruins of Great Zimbabwe.

Chapter 16: *Photo Jean Mazenod. From L'ART PRECOLOMBIEN, Editions Citadelles, Paris.* Toltec statuary.

Chapter 17: *Scala/Art Resource.* The family and court of Lodovico II Gonzaga, of Mantua.

Chapter 18: *Reproduced by courtesy of the Trustees, The National Gallery, London.* Jean de Dinteville and Bishop Georges de Selve, the French ambassadors, 1533.

Chapter 19: *Robert Harding Picture Library.* Peter the Great's Summer Palace at Peterhof.

Notes on the Illustrations

Pages 2–3: Peace panel of the Royal Standard of Ur, mosaic, ca 2500 B.C. The "standard," a rectangular wooden box 18 inches long, was probably a sounding board of a musical instrument used on ceremonial occasions.

Page 7: Paintings by Stone Age hunters, from Lascaux caves in southern France, 15,000–10,000 B.C.

Page 19: Commemorative stele from Susa of the victory of Naramsin, after the Babylonian conquest of Sippar and other cities, ca 2389–2353 B.C. Pink sandstone; 78⅘ × 41⅓ in.

Page 23: Detail from an inlaid panel from a harp found in the Royal Cemetery at Ur, ca 2500 B.C.

Page 24: The judgments of Hammurabi were inscribed in 3600 lines of cuneiform writing on the 8 ft. high black basalt pillar. Late Larsa period, 1930–1888 B.C.

Page 27: The Narmer Palette was found in the ruins of a temple at Nekhen, ca 3100 B.C. Made of carved schist, h. 29¼ in., it is the earliest example of the Egyptians' hieroglyphic writing. From the Egyptian Museum, Cairo.

Page 30: Detail from a wall painting from an Old Kingdom tomb, ca 2300 B.C.

Page 32: This statue of the Goddess Selket is of gilded and painted wood, h. 90 cm., from the tomb of Tutankhamen, Valley of the Kings, Thebes. New Kingdom, 18th dynasty, 1347–1337 B.C.

Page 35: These four seated figures of Ramses II, h. 67 ft., each weighing 1,200 tons, are part of the façade fronting Ramses' Great Temple at Abu Simbel, 3200 B.C.

Pages 38–39: At Persepolis, Persians and delegations of subject peoples mounted the wide apadana steps with tributes for King Darius I, climbing past the figures of royal guards.

Page 43: A stone relief from Sargon II's palace at Dur-Sharrukin (modern Khorsabad), 8th century B.C.

Page 44: Fresco from a tomb at Beni-Hassan in Upper Egypt, ca 1890 B.C. From the Kunsthistorisches Museum, Vienna.

Page 45: This silver calf and its ceramic byre (ca 1600–1550 B.C.) were found during the Ashkelon excavations by the Leon Levy Expedition.

Pages 49 and 51: Alabaster reliefs from the center palace, Nimrud, ca 745–727 B.C.

Page 54: From the Teheran Bastan Museum, Iran.

Page 55: Cyrus the Great's tomb at Pasargadae, Iran, is of limestone; from the achaemenid Period, ca 530 B.C. From the Iranian Expedition of The Oriental Institute of The University of Chicago, 1932.

Page 56: Attributed to the "painter of Myson," ca 500 B.C.

Page 58: Closeup of relief on the southern wall, Persepolis, B.C., from Achaemenid Period.

Pages 62–63: King Vidudabha visiting the Buddha, from the Bharhut stupa, Shunga, 2nd c. B.C. Red sandstone, h. 18⅞″.

Page 66: Statue of a god or priest-king ca 2100 B.C., from the Indus city of Mohenjo-daro.

Page 67: The great bath (39′ × 23′) at Mohenjo-daro, ca 2600–1800 B.C.

Page 70: Bronze sword with forked antennae from North India, ca 1000 B.C.

Page 74: Siva (on a bull) destroys the demon Andhakari. From the MS. of Harivamsa (Mughal, ca 1590), Victoria and Albert Museum, London.

Page 75: The mother goddess Kali Ma from Orissa, India, 9th century A.D. The British Museum. Kali Ma, the fiercest wife of Siva, brings in her train bloodshed, terror, and death. She is frequently depicted wearing a necklace of human skulls.

Page 77: The Great Buddha, cave 10, Jung Kang, China, 5th century A.D.

Page 80: The Sarnath lion-capital with its four lions was carved for the Mauryan Emperer Ashoka in the third century B.C. It was adopted as India's national emblem.

Page 82: North gate to the largest memorial mound in Sanchi, India, the oldest building in India, believed to have been erected by Ashoka in the 3rd century B.C. The carving illustrates Buddhist writings. There are four 18-foot gateways to this mound, or *tope,* which is built like a big compass; the mound is 42 feet high and 103 feet in diameter.

Pages 86–87 and 103: Terracotta figurines of warriors and horses buried in 250 B.C. to guard the tomb of Qin Shih Huang Ti, China's first emperor. Unearthed in 1974 in Lintong County, Shaanxi Province. The tomb itself has not yet been excavated.

Page 94: Bronze ritual vessel in the shape of an animal, excavated in 1959 at Shu-Ch'eng, Anhui. Height 27.5 cm. 7th or early 6th century B.C.

Page 105: Detail of simulated Chinese village with earthenware tomb figures, Han dynasty. The custom of placing pottery models of buildings in tombs began in the 1st century A.D. The village can be seen at the St. Louis Art Museum.

Pages 114–115: The Erechtheum, built during the reconstruction of the Acropolis by Pericles after its devastation by the Persians, is unique among Greek buildings; it has porches on three sides, each quite different in size and rising from different levels. It was constructed as a shrine enclosing the site where the city of Athens had its beginnings.

Page 119: One of the best-preserved of the lavish wall paintings that were covered by a thick layer of ash and pumice when a volcanic explosion tore apart half of the island of Santorini, or Thera, ca 1500 B.C.

Page 120: Funeral games of Patrochus: A fragment of an Athenian bowl from Pharsalus (Thessaly), 6th century B.C., signed by the painter Sophilus.

Page 125: This painting from the "Chigi" vase is the earliest surviving picture of the new style of close-order, heavily-armed infantry adopted by the Greeks, ca end of 8th century B.C. Found at Formello, near Rome; h. 10 ¼ in.

Page 135: This 5th century B.C. bronze, dredged from the sea near Cape Artemisium, in Attica, is thought to represent Poseidon or Zeus.

Page 138: Black-figured amphora, *Women working wool,* from Lekythos, ca 560 B.C., h. 6 ¾ in.

Page 146–147: Detail from the Alexander Sarcophagus, ca 325–300 B.C.; h. of Frieze 69 cm; found in the royal cemetery at Sidon, Phoenicia, late 4th century B.C. Alexander, wearing the heroic lion's-scalp helmet, is on horseback at the left. From the Archaeological Museum, Istanbul.

Page 150: This mosaic, found at Pompeii, is thought to be a copy of an original painting of ca 330 B.C.

Page 160: The Tyche (or Fortune) of Antioch; the original probably executed by Eutychides of Sikyon, ca 300 B.C. Marble; h. 37¾ in. Vatican, Galleria Candelabri: Scomparto IV, 48 inv. 2672.

Page 162: Life-size marble genre statue, probably created as a garden sculpture, ca 180 B.C. From the Palazzo dei Conservatori, Rome.

Pages 170–171: The Pont du Gard, at Nîmes in southern France, is the finest example of Roman practical engineering. This great aqueduct, 885 ft. long and made of unadorned stone blocks, was built ca A.D. 14 to bring water to Nîmes from higher ground to the north.

Page 175: This terracotta statue of the Sun god Aplu—known as Apollo to the Greeks—stood on a temple ridgepole in Veii. It was probably made by the sculptor Vulca, or his school, ca 500 B.C.

Page 183: Roman bronze decoration forming part of a horse harness, 3rd century B.C.

Page 190: Stone bas-relief, found in Saint Remy, Provence; 59 × 83 cm. From the Musée de la Civilisation Gallo-Romaine, Lyon.

Pages 194–195: A section of Hadrian's Wall at Cuddy's Crag, Northumberland. Hadrian's Wall was the formidable barrier that wound across northern Britain, 2nd century A.D.

Page 197: From the Museo della Terme, Rome.

Page 198: Detail, the onyx Chalcedony gem (cameo) of Augustus and Roma, early 1st century A.D. From the Kunsthistorisches Museum, Vienna.

Page 201: In this mosaic Virgil is seated between the muses of Epic and Tragedy, and reading from his *Aeneid.* From the Bardo Museum, Tunis.

Page 202: The reliefs adorning the Ara Pacis Augustae, the altar of Augustan peace, are among the greatest works of art of the early Roman empire. The Roman senate had the altar erected on the Campus Martius to commemorate Augustus' return from Gaul, where he had been living for three years.

Page 205: Mosaic from the Sant'Apollinare Nuovo, Ravenna, 6th century A.D.

Page 208: Bas-relief of spoils being carried from the temple in Jerusalem. From the Arch of Titus, Rome, 80–85 A.D.

Page 211: The port of Ostia had been pillaged by pirates in 68 B.C. Augustus made it one of his many rebuilding projects. By A.D. 150 this large cosmopolitan city boasted new harbors, fine public buildings, airy apartments, and had become the largest receiving port in Italy.

Page 218: This 4th century porphyry group shows Diocletian and Maximian with their respective caesars, their sons-in-law. From the Basilica of San Marco, Venice.

Page 220: Roman mosaic of a North African villa, from the Bardo Museum, Tunis, 3rd or 4th century A.D.

Pages 228–229: Apse mosaic, S. Apollinare in Classe, Ravenna; ca A.D. 533–549.

Page 231: This uncolored pen and ink drawing is from the *Utrecht Psalter,* an outstanding example of a new mode of Carolingian illustration developed from a fusion of Anglo-Saxon, Irish, and Frankish techniques, 9th century. MS 32, fol. 90v.

Page 243: Miniature of St. Benedict, founder of the Abbey of Monte Cassino, blessing the Abbot Desiderius, who rebuilt the Abbey and founded a school of Byzantine-influenced mosaicists and painters.

Page 250: Mosaic from Carthage, ca 500 A.D.

Page 253: Emperor Justinian and his court, A.D. 546–548, in mosaic at San Vitale, Ravenna, Italy.

Pages 262–263: Alhambra Palace in Granada, from which the Nasrid sultans ruled southern Spain until Christian armies expelled them in 1492.

Page 266: Arabic manuscript (Persia): 9th-century page from the *Qur'an,* Kufic script. 6½ by 4⁹⁄₁₆ inches.

Page 268: From the Edinburgh Rashid al-Din, Or MS 20, f. 23v.

Page 269: From the Turkish version of the *Siyar-i-Nabi,* 16th c., folio 309 recto.

Page 278: From the Edinburgh Rashid al-Din, Or MS 20, f. 52R.

Page 280: Detail of an ivory casket of Al Mughira, son of the caliph Abd-el-Rahman III, who was assassinated in A.D. 176.

Page 281: The slave market in Zabid, in the Yemen, 13th century. From an illustration of the Makamats 635/1237 of Al-Hariri. Bibliothèque Nationale, MS. Ar. 5847.

Page 283: Persian pottery: Seljuk, late 12th–early 13th century bowl. 3¼ by 9¹⁄₁₆ inches.

Page 285: Miniature, Iran, Tabriz, 16th c. Sultan-Muhammad, Allegory of Worldly and other Wordly Drunkenness: illustration from *Divan of Hafiz.* Opaque watercolor on paper, 21.5 × 15 cm. (1988.460)

Page 286: A trading boat on the Euphrates: Arab manuscript, Baghdad school, 13th century.

Page 289: The most important monument of Islamic Cordoba is the Great Mosque, or Mezquita Grande, which was converted to a church in later centuries.

Begun by Abd al-Rahman (756–768), it was enlarged three times: in A.D. 848, 961–965, and 987.

Page 290: Miniature from the Makamat of Al-Hariri, a 12th-century historical work showing everyday life. Depicted here is the public library of Hulwan, near Baghdad.

Page 291: Iraqi painting: *Abdallah ibn al-Fadl.* A.D. 1224 (Rajab 621 H.), Baghdad school; 13¹⁄₁₆ by 9¹³⁄₁₆ inches. Outdoor scene with mad dog biting man, onlooker with sword on left.

Pages 296–297: Portrait of the poet Kodai-no-kimi, or Koogimi, attributed to Fujiwara-no-Nobuzane (1176–?). Kamakura period, 13th c.; color on paper.

Page 311: Scroll of the Diamond Sutra, the Sanskrit Buddhist work *Vajraccedikā prajña pāramitā* in Chinese translation found at Tunhuang. The earliest specimen of block printing, A.D. 868. Buddha is addressing Subhiti, and aged disciple.

Page 317: (detail #8) Chinese, Ming Dynasty. After Ch'iu Ying (flourished 1622–1660), "Ch'ing Ming (Spring Festival) on the River." (47.18.1)

Page 324: "Creation of Japan: Izanagi and Izanami Standing in Clouds and Creating Island out of Sea Water," Kobayashi, Eitaku (1843–1890). Japanese, Ukiyoe, late 19th-century hanging scroll. Ink on silk, 1.257 by 0.546 m.

Page 325: Shōtoku Taishi in prince regent form. Late Kamakura period, 14th century. Colors on silk, mounted as a panel; 109.5 by 82.0 cm. The full ceremonial court dress, scepter, and sword depicted here identify Shōtoku Taishi as prince regent. His actual regency lasted 29 years, A.D. 592–622.

Page 327: Five-story pagoda, Daigo. Heian period, A.D. 951.

Pages 332–333: Miniature from Jean Fouquet, *Les Heures d'Etienne Chevalier,* ca 1460. From Musée Conde, Chantilly.

Page 337: This bronze statue of the Emperor Charlemagne shows him carrying an orb to symbolize wordly peace. He was the first Chirstian monarch to be sculpted in an equestrian statue. 9th–10th century A.D.; h. 24 cm. (Louvre)

Page 345: Wellcome Institute Western MS 290, ps.-Galen, *Anatomy,* 15th century, fol. 53v.

Page 349: Cod. Pal. Germ. 164, fol. 6v (Heidelberger Sachsenspiegel)

Page 353: The invasion of Danes under Hinguar (Ingrar) and Bubba: Seven shiploads of men in three tiers. From *Life, Passion and Miracles of St. Edmunds, King and Martyr* in Latin, Bury St. Edmund's, ca 1130. Ms. 736, f. 9v.

Page 354: This plaque is one from a series of nineteen, known as the Magdeberg ivories (German or Northern Italian), 10th century; 5 × 4 ½ in. (41.100.157)

Page 356: Benedictine Abbey of Mont-Saint-Michel, founded in 708 in the Department of the Manche in northwestern France, a mile off the French coast in the English Channel and formerly an island at high tide. Heavily fortified.

Page 357: The third and greatest of the abbey churches of Cluny was begun by St. Hugh in 1088.

By 1095 the east end was finished, and was consecrated by Pope Urban II, himself a former Cluniac monk. LAT 177 16, f. 91. Bibliothèque Nationale.

Page 358: Rievaulx Abbey was founded in Yorkshire, England, as a Cistercian house in 1130. By 1175 all of its monastic buildings were complete. The nave of Rievaulx Abbey, dating to 1135–1140, is today the oldest remaining Cistercian structure in the world.

Page 365: Crusaders fighting the Saracens, *Roman de Godefroi,* fol. 19r. Paris, 1337. Bibliothèque Nationale.

Page 366: FR 352, f. 62. Bibliothèque Nationale.

Pages 372–373: "April" miniature from the *Hours of the Virgin,* MS 399 fol. 5v. Flanders, ca 1515.

Page 375: From MS Sloane 2435, fol. 85, British Library.

Page 379: From *Piers Plowman,* MS. R.3, fol. 3v.

Page 381: From Rene I, d'Anjoy, *Le Mortifiement de vaine plaisance.* MS 705, f. 38v. French, 15th century.

Page 384: Miniature from the *Winchester Psalter;* English, painted at Winchester for the Bishop, Henry of Bois, ca 1150–1160. Cott. Ner. CIV, fol. 39r, British Library.

Page 387: From MS Bodley 270b, fol. 176, Bodleian Library, Oxford.

Page 390: This is one of the most famous of a group of finely carved Parisian Caskets for jewels or other precious objects, probably all made in the same workshop. French, first half of the 14th century. L. 9¾ in.

Page 393: Miniature from Jean de Wavrin's *Chronique d'Angleterre,* siege of the castle of Mortagne. Flemish, late fifteenth century. MS Roy. 14. E.IV, fol. 23r. British Library.

Page 394: From MS 13 321, Wiesbaden, Codex B, f lr. Museum of the City of Cologne.

Page 397: From the Exultet Roll (Burberini lat. 592), ca A.D. 1075; w. 11⅜ in.

Page 398: From Kenneth John Conant, *Cluny: Les églises et la maison du chef d'ordre.* The Mediaeval Academy of America Publication No. 77. Cambridge, Mass., 1968.

Pages 402–403: Carcassonne, in south-western France, is the most complete example today of a medieval fortified town. Parts of the walls go back to the Visigothic period, but most of the inner wall, with the citadel, dates from the 11th and 12th centuries, and the outer from the end of the 13th century. Extensive restoration was carried out in the 19th century.

Page 405: Presumed to be the work of Matilda, queen of William the Conqueror, the original tapestry (ca 1100) can be seen in the city of Bayeux, France. A replica is in the Victoria and Albert Museum, London.

Page 412: From Petro d'Eboli, *De Rebus siclis carmen,* Italian, ca 1200. Codex 120, f. 101.

Page 414: Carrow Psalter MS., fol. 15v. Thirteenth century.

Page 419: From Jacques de Guisis, *Chroniques de Hainaut,* Flemish, 1448. Ms 9242, fol. 48 verso.

Pages 421 and 425: Miniatures from the town laws of Hamburg, 1497.

Page 433: Detail, fresco by Domenico di Michelino, *Allegory of the Divine Comedy,* of Dante with *La Divina Commedia* 1465. Florence Cathedral.

Page 435: Pedro Berruguete (Spanish, 1477–1504), *St. Dominick presiding over an Auto da Fé.* Tempera on panel; 5′ ½″ × 3′ ¼″. From the sacristy of Santo Tomás of Avila, where there was a companion panel now believed to be in a private collection in London.

Page 438: *St. Sebastian Interceding for the Plague-Stricken* by Josse Lieferinxe.

Page 445: This is the only known contemporary picture of Joan of Arc. AE^{II} 447, f. 27.

Page 449: From MS Bodley 264, fol. 245v, Bodleian Library, Oxford.

Page 451: Misericord from Henry VII's Chapel, Westminster Abbey.

Page 453: During the French peasant rebellion of the 14th century, the most famous uprising was the *Jacquerie,* which began in the Beqauvais region in 1358, when men were killed if they didn't have worker's hands. From Sir Jean Froissart's *Chronicles,* MS Fr. 2643, fol. 226v. Bibliothèque Nationale.

Page 455: *The Four Horsemen of the Apocalypse,* woodcut ca 1498, by Albrecht Dürer, German painter and engraver (1471–1528) regarded as leader of the German Renaissance school of painting.

Page 464: Rock painting from the "Shelter of Horses," Tassili n'Ajjer Range, Algeria, ca 3500–3000 B.C.

Page 467: Brass casting of an armed warrior made for weighing gold dust. It shows a typical Akan warrior holding a shield and a now-broken sword. H. 108 cm.

Page 469: The travelers Abu Zayd and Al Harith arrive in a village. From the Bibliothèque Nationale, Ar. 5847 fol. 138r.

Page 472: Djenneh, Mali. Horse and rider, 14th century. Terracotta, 66.0 × 38.0 cm.

Page 487: Primitive. Mexican, Olmec, 10th–6th c. Stone. Figure on bench with baby. H. 11.3 cm. The Metropolitan Museum of Art, The Michael C. Rockefeller Memorial Collection of Primitive Art, Bequest of Nelson A. Rockefeller, 1979. (1979.206.940)

Page 492: Quetzalcoatl, "Feathered Serpent" (left), and Tezcatlipoca, "Smoking Mirror" (right). Codex Borbonicus, p. 22 (detail). Screenfold manuscript, panel 39 × 39.5 cm.

Page 503: Inca tunic, cotton and wool. Peru, ca A.D. 1500.

Page 506–507: Andrea Mantegna (Italian, 1431–1506), *The Court of the Gonzaga Family,* 1473–1474. Fresco, w. ca 19′ 8″. From the Palazzo Ducale, Mantua. The Gonzaga family, who reigned over Mantua from 1328 to 1627, invited Mantegna to their court in 1460. He continued to paint there until his death. In this fresco, from the walls of the Camera degli Sposi, Mantegna shows an intimate family festivity, the visit paid by Cardinal Francesco Gonzaga to his parents in Mantua.

Page 509: Woodcut, Italian (Florence), probably late 15th century.

Page 512: The Palazzo Vecchio (1298–1314) is attributed to Arnolfo di Cambio and was built as the seat of the Signoria, the government of the Florentine republic. This fortified palace is also known as the Palazzo della Signoria.

Page 514: Filippo Brunelleschi (1377–1440), *Sacrifice of Isaac,* from the competition to design the north doors of the Baptistry of S. Giovanni, Florence, 1401–1402. Gilded bronze relief, 21 × 17½ in. (inside molding). From the Museo Nazionale del Bargello, Florence. Brunelleschi, trained as a sculptor, was the founder of the Renaissance style in architecture.

Page 517: Benozzo Gozzolli (Italian), *Journey of the Magi,* ca 1459. From the Medici Riccardi Palace, Florence. Nominally of the journey of the Magi, this painting in fact shows the magnificence of the Florentine Renaissance Court, with Lorenzo de' Medici on a hunting expedition in the foreground.

Page 521: Engraving by Johannes Stradanus (J. van der Straet), Belgian painter (1523–1605).

Page 523: Sofonisba Anguissola (Italian, 1532/35–1625), *Portrait of the Artist's Sister,* ca 1559. Oil on canvas; 33½ × 26 in. This prolific artist was the first of Renaissance women artists to establish an international reputation, and the first for whom a substantial body of work exists. In this portrait, her sister Minerva wears a medallion that depicts another Minerva, the ancient Roman goddess of wisdom and the arts.

Page 525: *The Adoration,* 1507, by Hans Baldung (also called Hans Grien or Grün), German painter, engraver, and designer of woodcuts and glass painting (1476?–1545).

Page 527: Jan van Eyck (Flemish, 1422–1441), *Madonna of Chancellor Rodin,* ca 1435.

Page 528: Hieronymus Bosch (Hieronymus van Aeken), Dutch painter (ca 1450–1516), *Death and the Miser.*

Page 530: From *Ethique d'Aristotle,* French, 15th century. MS I.2 (927), fol. 145r. Bibliothèque de la Ville, Rouen.

Page 536: Lucas Cranach the Elder (1472–1553), *Passional Christi und Antichristi,* Wittenberg, 1521.

Page 539: Lucas Cranach the Younger (German, 1515–1586), *Martin Luther and the Wittenberg Reformers,* ca 1543. Oil on panel; 27⅝ × 15⅝ in.

Page 540: *The Small Crucifixion,* ca 1510, by Matthias Grünewald, German painter (ca 1465–1528). Wood; 24¼ × 18⅛ in. (1961.9.19)

Page 542: Detail from the 1528 escutcheon of the town of Überlingen town hall.

Page 543: Titian (Tiziano Vecellio, 1487–1577), *Charles V on Horseback,* 1548. Oil on canvas; 10′ 10½″ × 9′ 2″. The colors of this portrait are dark, perhaps emphasized by restorations that followed damage incurred in a fire in the eighteenth century.

Page 547: Attributed to Jean Perrissin (ca 1530–1611), *Temple de Lyon, nommé Paradis,* 1565.

Page 551: Woodcut from Foxe, 1569 edition, British Library.

Page 552: *Sir Thomas More* (1478–1535), painted in 1527 by Hans Holbein the Younger, German painter (1497?–1543) and court painter to Henry VIII.

Page 555: Council of Trent by an unknown artist; detached fresco, Secretariat of State, Vatican.

Pages 562–563: Hans Holbein the Younger (1497?–1543), *Jean de Dinteville and Georges de Seluc (The Ambassadors),* 1533. 81¼ × 82½ in.

Page 564: *Cantino Planisphere,* Portuguese, color on parchment, ca 1502.

Page 581: Long the site of a royal residence and hunting lodge, Fontainebleau was expanded and transformed by Francis I in 1530–1540. Il Rosso (Giovanni Battista de'Rossi, 1494–1540), Florentine painter; Francesco Primaticcio, Italian painter and architect (1504–1570); and Sebastiano Serlio, Italian architect and writer on art (1475–1554) were called by Francis I from Italy to build and decorate the palace. The gallery of Francis I set a fashion in decoration imitated throughout Europe.

Page 582: School of Fontainebleau (French, 16th century), *Triple Profile Portrait;* oil on slate, ca 1560–1580; 22½ × 22½ in. (Acc. no. M1965.55)

Page 595: MS Rawl. D 410, fol. 1, Bodleian Library, Oxford.

Page 601: Paulo Veronese (Paulo Caliari: 1528?–1588), *Mars and Venus United by Love.* Oil on canvas; 81 × 63⅜ in.

Page 602: Diego Rodriguez de Silva y Velázquez (1599–1660), *Juan de Pareja,* ca 1610–1670. Oil on canvas; h. 32 in.; w. 27½ in. The Metropolitan Museum of Art, Fletcher Fund, Rogers Fund, and Bequest of Miss Adelaide Milton de Groot (1876–1967), by exchange, supplemented by gifts from friends of the Museum, 1971.

Pages 606–607: Peter the Great brought architects and artists from the West to design and build his Summer Palace at Peterhof.

Page 611: Philippe de Champaigne (French, 1602–1674), *Cardinal Richelieu Swearing the Order of the Holy Ghost.*

Page 612: Antoine Coysevox (French, 1640–1730), *Louis XIV,* statue for the Town Hall of Paris, 1687–1689.

Page 615: "The Noble Is the Spider," from Jacques Lagnier, *Receuil des Proverbes,* 1657–1663.

Page 616: Nicholas Poussin (French, 1594–1665), *The Rape of the Sabine Women,* ca 1636–1637. Oil on canvas; 60⅞ × 82⅝ in. (46.160)

Page 637: The Church of St. Basil (formerly the Cathedral of the Intercession), Moscow, 1555–1560, with 17th century additions.

Page 638: Etienne Falconnet (1716–1791), *The Bronze Horseman, St. Petersburg* (Leningrad), completed in 1783.

Page 641: The grand stairway of the Residenz at Würzburg (built by the powerful Schönborn family) was intended by its architect Balthasar Neumann (1678–1753) to allow a slow ascent to be able to take in gradually the ceiling paintings by Giovanni Battista Tiepolo glorifying Bishop Schönborn, 1750–1753.

Page 650: Johannes Vermeer, known as Jan Vermeer van Delft (Dutch, 1632–1675), *Woman Holding a Balance,* ca 1664. Canvas; 16¾ × 15 in.

Page 651: Hiob Adriaensz Berckheyde, *The Old Stock Exchange, Amsterdam.* Canvas; 85 × 105 cm. (Inv. no. 1043)

Page 653: Pieter Claesz (Dutch, 1597–1660), *Still Life with Musical Instruments.*

Index